Praise for ... ne Design, Prote... oment

"*Introduction to Game Design, Prototyping, and Development* has truly helped me in my game development journey and has opened my mind to many helpful techniques and practices. This book not only contains a full introduction to the C# language, but also includes information about playtesting, game frameworks, and the game industry itself. Jeremy is able to explain complex concepts in a way that is very informative and straightforward. I have also found the prototype tutorials to be useful and effective for developing good programming practices. I would highly recommend this book to anyone looking to learn game development from scratch, or simply brush up on their skills. I look forward to using it as a guide and reference for future projects."

—**Logan Sandberg,** Pinwheel Games & Animation

"Jeremy Gibson Bond's breadth of knowledge and incisively analytical perspective on game design infuse each page of this highly engaging primer on game development. His coupling of industry and academic experience provides readers the tools for a running start in creating games—offering an incredibly valuable and rare synthesis of the conceptual and the practical. Newcomers to game development will walk away from this book with an enhanced analytical toolkit and internalized understanding of the value of iteration, as well as several playable games under their belt. Perfect for the new student yet teeming with wisdom and enrichment for experienced developers."

—**Eileen Hollinger,** Game Producer, Instructor, Independent Developer, and Activist. Former Lead Producer at Funomena

"One of the greatest challenges in learning (and teaching) game development is that only a few concepts and techniques are truly applicable to all kinds of games—a space shooter shares very little with a card game, which in turn has little in common with a dungeon crawler. It's a common experience for an aspiring game developer to complete a dozen tutorials and still not know how to start the game they want to make.

"Jeremy's approach in this book reflects his long experience as both a game developer and an educator. He provides a structured introduction to that small set of core ideas and skills, and then provides tutorials for, literally, a space shooter, a card game, a dungeon crawler, and several more besides, showing the coding tools and techniques needed for each.

"No other Unity book covers such a broad variety of games, and I've seen very few tutorials that were so well-made. Each step is explained; each game is self-contained and carefully designed to demonstrate specific concepts, from basic ideas like GameObjects all the way to powerful object-oriented techniques like *Boids*.

"I've both used this book in my introductory Unity class and recommended it to many students for self-study. They appreciate the clear and thorough explanation of the C# language and the Unity engine, and they are invariably surprised at how much they learn by completing the prototypes. I use the book myself as a primary reference for good code architecture in Unity.

"The second edition promises to be even more valuable, with updates to every chapter and a brand-new tutorial, based on *The Legend of Zelda*, that includes advanced techniques like tile-based movement and even a simple level editor. Like the previous edition, it will be a vital part of both my classroom instruction and my personal Unity library."

—Margaret Moser, Assistant Professor, University of Southern California Interactive Media & Games Division

"If you want to take your game development to the next level, this book is a must! Not only does it give you a lot of game examples from beginning to end, it also—and this is the most important part—makes you think like a game designer. What makes a game fun and engaging? What makes a player come back to your game over and over again? The answers are all here. This book gives you a lot more than a couple of online tutorials can give you. It gives you the whole picture!"

—David Lindskog, Founder, Monster Grog Games

"Prototyping and play-testing are often the most misunderstood and/or underutilized steps in the game design and development process. Iterative cycles of testing and refining are key to the early stages of making a good game. Novices often believe that they need to know everything about a language or build every asset of the game before they can really get started. Jeremy's second edition of his already terrific book builds on the design aspects of his first, and even better, prepares readers to go ahead and dive in to the actual design and prototyping process right away. The changes and additions to the paper prototyping chapter alone make it well worth the price of admission; for both new readers and fans of the first addition."

—Stephen Jacobs, Professor, School of Interactive Games and Media and FOSS@MAGIC Faculty Lead, RIT. Visiting Scholar, The Strong National Museum of Play

"I used Professor Bond's book to teach myself how to code in C# and familiarize myself with Unity. Since then I have used the book as the backbone for my high school Digital Game Design class. The programming lessons are top-notch, the prototypes clearly demonstrate the myriad facets of programming and how those are used to create recognizable game mechanics, and the prototypes are easily adapted for student personalization. I can't wait to get hold of the second edition and begin using it in my classroom."

—Wesley Jeffries, Game Design Teacher, Riverside Unified School District

"With the latest edition of *Introduction to Game Design, Prototyping, and Development*, Bond builds on the solid foundation of the first. The new edition adds new content throughout the book, with updated examples and topics across all the chapters. This is a thorough and thoughtful exploration of the process of making games."

—**Drew Davidson,** Director, Entertainment Technology Center at Carnegie Mellon University

"*Introduction to Game Design, Prototyping, and Development* combines a solid grounding in evolving game design theory with a wealth of detailed examples of prototypes for digital games. Together, these provide an excellent introduction to game design and development that culminates in making working games with Unity. This book is useful for both introductory courses and as a reference for expert designers. I use this book in my game design classes, and it is among those few to which I often refer."

—**Michael Sellers,** Professor of Practice and Director of Game Design Program at Indiana University. Former Creative Director at Rumble Entertainment and General Manager at Kabam

"When teaching about game design and development, you often get asked the dreaded question: 'Where can I learn all this?' *Introduction to Game Design, Prototyping, and Development* has been my deliverance, as it provides a one-stop solution and answer. This book is quite unique in covering both game design and development in depth because it embraces and exemplifies the idea that design, prototyping, development, and balancing combine in an iterative process. By sending the message that creating games is both complex and feasible, I believe this to be a great learning tool, and the new edition with even more detailed examples seems even better."

—**Pietro Polsinelli,** Applied Game Designer at Open Lab

"Jeremy's approach to game design shows the importance of prototyping game rules and prepares readers to be able to test their own ideas. Being able to create your own prototypes allows for rapid iteration and experimentation, and makes better Game Designers."

—**Juan Gril,** Executive Producer, Flowplay. Former President of Joju Games

"*Introduction to Game Design, Prototyping, and Development* combines the necessary philosophical and practical concepts for anyone looking to become a Game Designer. This book will take you on a journey from high-level design theories, through game development concepts and programming foundations. I regularly recommend this book to any aspiring game designers who are looking to learn new skills or strengthen their design chops. Jeremy uses his years of experience as a professor to teach you how to think with vital game design mindsets so that you can create a game with all the right tools at hand. Regardless of how long you've been in the games industry, you're bound to find inspirational ideas that will help you improve your design process. I'm personally excited to dive into the updates in this latest edition and get a refresher course on some of the best practices for creating amazing games!"

—**Michelle Pun,** Game Producer at Osmo. Former Lead Game Designer at Disney and Zynga

"One of the most popular practice targets for new developers is a 1980's-era '*Zelda*'-like action adventure dungeon game. In the last chapter of his newly updated edition of *Introduction to Game Design, Prototyping, and Development*, Jeremy thoroughly explains exactly what a new game programmer needs to know in order to use Unity's capabilities to faithfully re-create this type of game. His approach includes a healthy mix of leveraging Unity's built-in structures and frameworks while extending it through well-organized custom functionality. He covers technical and design concepts in a totally natural way, right when and how they have practical application to the example at hand. This pragmatic, just-in-time approach can help new developers retain and apply the information for their own future projects."

—**Chris DeLeon,** Founder of Gamkedo Game Development Training, IndieCade Workshops Co-Chair, Forbes 30 Under 30 in Entertainment

"Whether you're just curious about making games or are on your way to becoming a professional, this book provides an accessible introduction to game design. Jeremy's experience as a game developer and professor are evident in the iterative structure he uses to explain the core fundamentals of game development. Each chapter and lesson combine a basic technical approach with game theory fundamentals that also challenge your own creativity to grow as a developer. As a former student of his, I can tell you that this book is the next best thing to actually being in his class."

—**Juan Vaca,** Associate Designer, Telltale Games

"Jeremy Gibson Bond's *Introduction to Game Design, Prototyping, and Development* is a crucial text that introduces students to critical game design theory and the process of rapid, iterative prototyping within Unity. Jeremy's sample games demonstrate how various game genres can be developed in the engine and introduce the student to useful software patterns that leverage the power of the core Unity objects and other libraries available to C# to move the reader from an introductory to intermediate level of coding expertise."

—**Bill Crosbie,** Assistant professor of computer science, Raritan Valley Community College

Introduction to Game Design, Prototyping, and Development

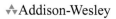

Introduction to Game Design, Prototyping, and Development

From Concept to Playable Game with Unity and C#

Jeremy Gibson Bond

✦Addison-Wesley

Upper Saddle River, NJ • Boston • Indianapolis • San Francisco
New York • Toronto • Montreal • London • Munich • Paris • Madrid
Capetown • Sydney • Tokyo • Singapore • Mexico City

Library of Congress Control Number: 2017935715

ISBN-13: 978-0-13-465986-2
ISBN-10: 0-13-465986-4

2   18

Editor-in-Chief
Greg Wiegand

Senior Acquisitions Editor
Laura Lewin

Development Editor
Chris Zahn

Managing Editor
Sandra Schroeder

Senior Project Editor
Lori Lyons

Production Manager
Dhayanidhi Karunanidhi

Copy Editor
Paula Lowell

Indexer
Erika Millen

Proofreader
H S Rupa

Technical Editors
Stephen Beeman
Reed Coke
Grace Kendall

Publishing Coordinator
Olivia Basegio

Cover Designer
Chuti Prasersith

Compositor
codeMantra

This book is dedicated to:

My wife Melanie, the love of my life,
for her love, intellect, and support

My parents and sisters

My many professors, colleagues, and students
who inspired me to write this book

And everyone who read the first edition
and sent me comments and feedback;
all of you helped to make this
second edition even better.

Contents at a Glance

Contents

FOREWORD

I have a theory about game designers and teachers. I think that, beneath the possible differences of our outer appearances, we're secretly the same; that many of the skills possessed by a good game designer are the same skills held by a great teacher. Have you ever had a teacher who held a class spellbound with puzzles and stories? Who showed you simple demonstrations of skills that were easy for you to understand and copy, but were difficult for you to master? Who gradually, cleverly, helped you put together pieces of information in your mind, maybe without your even realizing it, until one day your teacher was able to step aside and watch you do something amazing, something that you never would have thought was possible?

We video game designers spend a lot of our time finding ways to teach people the skills they need to play our games, while keeping them entertained at the same time. We sometimes don't want people to be aware that we're teaching them, though—the best tutorial levels that video games open with are usually the ones that seem like the beginning of a thrilling adventure. I was lucky to work at the award-winning game studio Naughty Dog for eight amazing years, where I was the Lead or Co-Lead Game Designer on all three PlayStation 3 games in the *Uncharted* series. Everyone at the studio was very happy with the sequence that opened our game *Uncharted 2: Among Thieves*. It effectively taught each player all the basic moves they would need to play the game, while keeping them on the edge of their seat because of the gripping predicament our hero Nathan Drake found himself in, dangling over the edge of a cliff in a ruined train carriage.

Video game designers do this kind of thing over and over again as they create digital adventures for us to play. Working on a sequence of player experiences like those found in the *Uncharted* games, I have to stay very focused on what the player has recently learned. I have to present my audience with interesting situations that use their new skills and are easy enough that they won't get frustrated, but challenging enough to hold their interest. To do this with complete strangers, through the channels of communication that a game provides—the graphics of the environments and the characters and objects within them, the sounds that the game makes, and the interactivity of the game's controls—is tremendously challenging. At the same time, it is one of the most rewarding things I know how to do.

Now that I've become a professor, teaching game design in a university setting, I've discovered firsthand just how many of the skills I developed as a game designer are useful in my teaching. I'm also discovering that teaching is just as rewarding as game design. So it came to me as no surprise when I discovered that Jeremy Gibson Bond, the author of this book, is equally talented as a game designer and a teacher, as you're about to find out.

I first met Jeremy around 15 years ago, at the annual Game Developers Conference in Northern California, and we immediately hit it off. He already had a successful career as a game developer, and his enthusiasm for game design struck a chord with me. As you'll see when you begin to read this book, he loves to talk about game design as a craft, a design practice, and an emerging art form. Jeremy and I stayed in touch over the years, as he went back to graduate school at Carnegie Mellon University's excellent Entertainment Technology Center to study under visionaries like Doctor Randy Pausch and Jesse Schell. Eventually, I came to know Jeremy as a professor and a colleague in the Interactive Media & Games Division of the School of Cinematic Arts at the University of Southern California—part of USC Games, the program in which I now teach.

In fact, I got to know Jeremy even better during his time at USC—and I did it by becoming his student! In order to acquire the skills that I needed to develop experimental research games as part of USC's Game Innovation Lab, I took one of Jeremy's classes, and his teaching transformed me from a Unity n00b with some basic programming experience into an experienced C# programmer with a strong set of skills in Unity—one of the world's most powerful, usable, adaptable game engines. Every single one of Jeremy's classes was not only packed with information about Unity and C#, but was also peppered with inspirational words of wisdom about game design and practical pieces of advice related to game development—everything from his thoughts about good "lerping," to great tips for time management and task prioritization, to the ways that game designers can use spreadsheets to make their games better. I graduated from Jeremy's class wishing that I could take it again, knowing that there was a huge amount more I could learn from him.

So I was very happy when I heard that Jeremy was writing a book—and I became even happier when I read the volume that you now hold in your hands. The good news for both you and me is that Jeremy has loaded this book with everything that I wanted more of. I learned a lot in the game industry about best practices in game design, production, and development, and I'm happy to tell you that in this book, Jeremy does a wonderful job of summarizing those ways of making games that I've found work best. Within these pages, you'll find step-by-step tutorials and code examples that will make you a better game designer and developer in innumerable ways. While the exercises in this book might get complex, Jeremy won't ask you to do anything complicated without guiding you through it in clear, easy-to-follow language.

You'll also find history and theory in this book. Jeremy has been thinking deeply about game design for a long time and is very well-read on the subject. In the first part of this volume, you'll find an extraordinarily wide and deep survey of the state-of-the-art in game design theory, along with Jeremy's unique and strongly developed synthesis of the very best ideas he's encountered. Jeremy supports his discussion with interesting historical anecdotes and fascinating glimpses of the long traditions of play in human culture, all of which help to frame his conversation in valuable and progressive ways. He continually pushes you to question your assumptions about games, and to think beyond the console, the controller, the screen, and the speakers, in ways that might just spur a whole new generation of game innovators.

Game design is an iterative process, where we test what we've made, receive feedback about it, revise our designs, and make a new, improved version. If an author is lucky enough to be able to publish a new edition of their book, they get to iterate on it too, and that's exactly what Jeremy has done. He spent more than a year writing this second edition, which you now hold in your hands, and in the process he has reviewed and revised every single chapter. He has updated some of the game design theory, all the code is now in color to improve readability, and he has made significant improvements to all of the in-depth game tutorials in Part III. Each tutorial now has step-by-step, numbered instructions, and everything has been updated to the latest version of Unity. The Space SHMUP chapter—one of the most useful but also longest in the first edition—has been split into two separate, easier-to-understand chapters, and the outdated final two tutorials have been replaced by *Dungeon Delver*, a *Legend of Zelda*-inspired game that neatly illustrates the power of component-based design in game prototyping. As someone who loves the first edition and has recommended it widely to students, teachers, and developers alike, I am very excited about these new changes and am very happy to see this wonderful book evolve.

In 2013, Jeremy Gibson Bond moved on from USC, and he now teaches at the fantastic gamedev.msu.edu program at Michigan State University. I'm very happy for the generations of MSU students that he'll lead to new understandings of the craft of game design in the coming years. The first spring after he left USC, when Jeremy walked into the restaurant at the annual Game Developers Conference alumni dinner hosted by the USC Games program, the room full of our current and former students came alive with whoops and cheers, and moments later broke out into applause. That tells you a lot about what Jeremy is like as a teacher. You're lucky that, thanks to this book, he can now be your teacher, too.

The world of game design and development is changing at a rapid pace. You can be part of this wonderful world—a world unlike any other I know, and which I love with all my heart. You can use the skills you learn through reading this book to develop new prototypes for new kinds of games and other types of interactive media as well; and in doing so, you might eventually create whole new genres, in expressive new styles, which appeal to new markets. You might help people relax and unwind by entertaining them, you might touch peoples' lives in the way that great art does, and you might even make something that helps solve some of the thorny problems that our world faces by educating, illuminating, and explaining the universe as you see it. Some of tomorrow's stars of game design are currently learning to design and program in homes, schools, and offices all around the world, and many of them are using this book. If you follow the advice and do the exercises you find in here, it might just help your chances of creating a modern game design classic.

Good luck, and have fun!

Richard Lemarchand
Associate Professor, USC Games
Associate Chair, Interactive Media & Games Division

PREFACE

Welcome to the second edition of *Introduction to Game Design, Prototyping, and Development*. This book is based on my work over many years as both a professional game designer and a professor of game design at several universities, including the Media and Information Department at Michigan State University and the Interactive Media and Games Division at the University of Southern California.

This preface introduces you to the purpose, scope, and approach of this book.

The Purpose of This Book

My goal in this book is simple: I want to give you all the tools and knowledge you need to get started down the path to being a successful game designer and prototyper. This book is the distillation of as much knowledge as I can cram into it to help you toward that goal. Unlike most books out there, this book combines both the disciplines of game design and digital development (i.e., computer programming) and wraps them both in the essential practice of iterative prototyping. The emergence of advanced, yet approachable, game development engines such as Unity has made it easier than ever before to create playable prototypes that express your game design concepts to others, and the ability to do so will make you a much more skilled (and employable) game designer.

The book is divided into four parts:

Part I: Game Design and Paper Prototyping

The first part of the book starts by exploring various theories of game design and the analytical frameworks for game design that have been proposed by several earlier books. This section then describes the *Layered Tetrad* as a way of combining and expanding on many of the best features of these earlier theories. The Layered Tetrad is explored in depth as it relates to various decisions that you must make as a designer of interactive experiences. This part also covers information about the interesting challenges of different game design disciplines; describes the process of paper prototyping, testing, and iteration; gives you concrete information to help you become a better designer; and presents you with effective project and time management strategies to help keep your projects on track.

Part II: Digital Prototyping

The second part of the book teaches you how to program. This part draws upon my many years of experience as a professor teaching nontechnical students how to express their game design ideas through digital code. If you have no prior knowledge or experience with programming or development, this part is designed for you. However, even if you do have some programming experience, you might want to take a look at this part to learn a few new tricks or get a refresher on some approaches. Part II covers C#—our programming language—from the basics through class inheritance and object-oriented programming.

Part III: Game Prototype Examples and Tutorials

The third part of the book encompasses several different tutorials, each of which guides you through the development of a prototype for a specific style of game. The purpose of this part is twofold: It reveals some best practices for rapid game prototyping by showing you how I personally approach prototypes for various kinds of games, and it provides you with a basic foundation on which to build your own games in the future. Many other books on the market that attempt to teach Unity (our game development environment) do so by taking the reader through a single, monolithic tutorial that is hundreds of pages long. In contrast, this book takes you through several much smaller tutorials. The final products of these tutorials are necessarily less robust than those found in some other books, but my belief is that the variety of projects in this book will better prepare you for creating your own projects in the future.

Part IV: Appendices

This book has several important appendices that merit mention here. Rather than repeat information throughout the book or require you to go hunting through various chapters for it, any piece of information that is referenced several times in the book or that I think you would be likely to want to reference later (after you've finished reading the book once) is placed in the appendices. Appendix A is just a quick step-by-step introduction to the initial creation process for a game project in Unity. The longest appendix is Appendix B, "Useful Concepts." Though it has a rather lackluster name, this is the portion of the book that I believe you will return to most often in the years following your initial read through the book. "Useful Concepts" is a collection of several go-to technologies and strategies that I use constantly in my personal game prototyping process, and I think you'll find a great deal of it to be very useful. The third and final appendix is a list of very useful online references where you can find answers to questions not covered in this book. It is often difficult to know the right places to look for help online; this appendix lists those that I personally turn to most often.

There Are Other Books Out There

As a designer or creator of any kind, I think that it's absolutely essential to acknowledge those on whose shoulders you stand. Many books have been written on games and game design, and the few that I list here are those that have had the most profound effect on either my process or my thinking about game design. You will see these books referenced many times throughout this text, and I encourage you to read as many of them as possible.

Game Design Workshop by Tracy Fullerton

Initially penned by Tracy Fullerton, Chris Swain, and Steven S. Hoffman, *Game Design Workshop* is now in its third edition. More than any other text, this is the book that I turn to for advice on game design. This book was initially based on the Game Design Workshop class that Tracy and Chris taught at the University of Southern California, a class that formed the foundation for the entire games program at USC (and a class that I myself taught there from 2009–2013). The USC Interactive Media and Games graduate program has been named the number one school for game design in North America by *Princeton Review* nearly every year that they have been ranking game programs, and the *Game Design Workshop* book and class were the foundation for that success.

Unlike many other books that speak volumes of theory about games, Tracy's book maintains a laser focus on information that helps budding designers improve their craft. I taught from this book for many years (even before I started working at USC), and I believe that if you actually attempt all the exercises listed in the book, you can't help but have a pretty good paper game at the end.

> Fullerton, Tracy, Christopher Swain, and Steven Hoffman, *Game Design Workshop: A Playcentric Approach to Creating Innovative Games,* 2nd ed. (Boca Raton, FL: Elsevier Morgan Kaufmann, 2008)

The Art of Game Design by Jesse Schell

Jesse Schell was one of my professors at Carnegie Mellon University and is a fantastic game designer with a background in theme park design gained from years working for Walt Disney Imagineering. Jesse's book is a favorite of many working designers because it approaches game design as a discipline to be examined through 100 different lenses that are revealed throughout the book. Jesse's book is a very entertaining read and broaches several topics not covered in this book.

> Jesse Schell, *The Art of Game Design: A Book of Lenses* (Boca Raton, FL: CRC Press, 2008)

The Grasshopper by Bernard Suits

While not actually a book on game design at all, *The Grasshopper* is an excellent exploration of the definition of the word *game*. Presented in a style reminiscent of the Socratic method, the book presents its definition of game very early in the text as the Grasshopper (from Aesop's fable *The Ant and the Grasshopper*) gives his definition on his deathbed, and his disciples spend the remainder of the book attempting to critique and understand this definition. This book also explores the question of the place of games and play in society.

> Bernard Suits, *The Grasshopper: Games, Life and Utopia* (Peterborough, Ontario: Broadview Press, 2005)

Level Up! by Scott Rogers

Rogers distills his knowledge from many years in the trenches of game development into a book that is fun, approachable, and very practical. When he and I co-taught a level design class, we used this textbook. Rogers is also a comic book artist, and his book is full of humorous and helpful illustrations that drive home the design concepts.

> Scott Rogers, *Level Up!: The Guide to Great Video Game Design* (Chichester, UK: Wiley, 2010)

Imaginary Games by Chris Bateman

Bateman uses this book to argue that games are a legitimate medium for scholarly study. He pulls from several scholarly, practical, and philosophical sources; and his discussions of books like *Homo Ludens* by Johan Huizinga; *Man, Play, and Games* by Roger Caillois; and the paper "The Game" by Mary Midgley are both smart and accessible.

> Chris Bateman, *Imaginary Games* (Washington, USA: Zero Books, 2011)

Game Programming Patterns by Robert Nystrom

This book is an excellent resource for intermediate-level game programmers. In it, Nystrom explores the software development patterns (initially cataloged in the book *Design Patterns: Elements of Reusable Object-Oriented Software*[1]) that he believes are most useful for game development. It's a truly excellent book that you should check out if you already have some experience with game programming. All of his examples are in a pseudocode that is similar to C++, but it's not too difficult to understand if you know C#. Also, although it can be bought in paperback or electronic versions, the entire text of the book is available for free at:

> http://gameprogrammingpatterns.com

---

1. Erich Gamma, Richard Help, Ralph Johnson, and John Vlissides, *Design Patterns: Elements of Reusable Object-Oriented Software* (Upper Saddle River, NJ: Addison-Wesley, 1995)

Game Design Theory by Keith Burgun

In this book, Burgun explores what he believes are faults in the current state of game design and development and proposes a much narrower definition of *game* than does Suits. Burgun's goal in writing this text was to be provocative and to push the discussion of game design theory forward. While largely negative in tone, Burgun's text raises a number of interesting points, and helped me to refine my personal understanding of game design.

> Keith Burgun, *Game Design Theory: A New Philosophy for Understanding Games* (Boca Raton, FL: A K Peters/CRC Press, 2013)

Our Digital Prototyping Environment: Unity and C#

All the digital game examples in this book are based on the Unity Game Engine and the C# programming language. I have taught students to develop digital games and interactive experiences for more than a decade, and in my experience, Unity is—by far—the best environment for learning to develop games. I have also found that C# is the best initial language for game prototypers to learn. Some other tools out there are easier to learn and require no real programming (Game Maker and Construct 2 are two examples), but Unity allows you much more flexibility and performance in a package that is basically free (the free version of Unity includes nearly all the capabilities of the paid version, and it is the version used throughout this book). Unreal is another game engine that is used by many studios, but in Unreal, there is very little middle ground between the simplified graphical programming of the Blueprint system and the very complex C++ code on which the engine is built. If you want to actually learn to program games and have success doing it, Unity is the engine you want to use.

Similarly, some programming languages are initially a little more approachable than C#. In the past, I have taught my students both ActionScript and JavaScript. However, C# is the one language I have used that continually impresses me with its flexibility and feature set. Learning C# means learning not only programming but also good programming practices. Languages such as JavaScript allow a lot of sloppy behaviors that I have found actually lead to slower development. C# keeps you honest (via things like strongly typed variables), and that honesty will not only make you a better programmer but will also result in your being able to code more quickly (e.g., strong variable typing enables very robust code hinting and auto-completion, which makes coding faster and more accurate).

Who This Book Is For

There are many books about game design, and there are many books about programming. This book seeks to fill the gap between the two. As game development technologies like Unity become more ubiquitous, it is increasingly important that game designers have the ability to sketch their design ideas not only on paper but also through working digital prototypes. This book exists to help you learn to do just that:

- **If you're interested in game design but have never programmed**, this book is perfect for you. **Part I** introduces you to several practical theories for game design and presents you with the practices that can help you develop and refine your design ideas. **Part II** teaches you how to program from nothing to understanding object-oriented class hierarchies. Since I became a college professor, the majority of my classes have focused on teaching nonprogrammers how to program games. I have distilled all of my experience doing so into Part II of this book. **Part III** takes you through the process of developing several different game prototypes across several different game genres. Each demonstrates fast methods to get from concept to working digital prototype. Lastly, the appendices explain specific game development and programming concepts in-depth and guide you to resources to learn more after you've finished the book. This in depth content was moved largely to Appendix B, "Useful Concepts," so that you could continue to use that section of the book as a reference in the years to come.

- **If you're a programmer who is interested in game design**, Parts I and III of this book will be of most interest to you. **Part I** introduces you to several practical theories for game design and presents you with the practices that can help you develop and refine your design ideas. You can skim **Part II**, which introduces C# and how it is used in Unity. If you are familiar with other programming languages, C# looks like C++ but has the advanced features of Java. **Part III** takes you through the process of developing several different game prototypes across several different game genres. Game development in Unity is very different from what you might be used to from other game engines. Many elements of development are managed outside of the code. Each prototype will demonstrate the style of development that works best in Unity to get from concept to working digital prototype quickly. You will also want to look carefully at Appendix B, "Useful Concepts," which is full of detailed information about various Unity development concepts and is arranged as a reference that you can return to later.

Conventions

This book maintains several writing conventions to help make the text more easily understandable.

Any place that specific button names, menu commands, other multi-word nouns, or new key terms appear in the text, they will be listed in *italics*. This includes terms like the *Main Camera* GameObject. An example menu command is *Edit > Project Settings > Physics*, which would instruct you to select the *Edit* menu from the menu bar, choose the *Project Settings* submenu, and then select *Physics*.

Book Elements

The book includes several different types of asides that feature useful or important information that does not fit in the flow of the regular body text.

note

Callouts in this format are for information that is useful but not critical. Information in notes will often be an interesting aside to the main text that provides a little bit more info about the topic.

tip

This element provides additional information that is related to the book content and can help you as you explore the concepts in the book.

warning

BE CAREFUL   Warnings cover information about things that you need to be aware of to avoid mistakes or other pitfalls.

SIDEBAR

The sidebar is for discussions of longer topics that are important to the text but should be considered separately from it.

Code

Several conventions apply to the code samples in this book. When specific elements from the code listing are placed in regular paragraph text, they appear in a `monospaced` font. The variable `variableOnExistingLine` from the following code listing is an example of this.

Code listings also utilize a monospaced font and appear as follows:

```
1 public class SampleClass {
2     public GameObject    variableOnExistingLine;                    // a
3     public GameObject    variableOnNewLine;                         // b
      …                                                               // c
7     void Update() { … }                                            // d
8 }
```

   a. Code listings are often annotated; in this case, additional information about the line marked with // a would appear in this first annotation.

   b. Many code listings will be expansions on code that you've already written or that already exists in the C# script file for another reason. In this case, the old lines will be at `normal weight`, and the new lines will be at **`bold weight`**. In all of these cases, I endeavor to include enough other existing lines that you can understand where to put the new bolded lines.

   c. Anywhere that code has been omitted (to save printing space), I include ellipses (…). In this code listing, I've skipped lines 4 through 6.

   d. In places where I've omitted the entire text of a pre-existing function or method, you will often see ellipses between braces ({ … }) to denote this.

Most of the code listings in the first two parts of the book include line numbers (as shown in the preceding listing). You do not need to type the line numbers when entering the code into MonoDevelop (it automatically numbers all lines). In the final part of the book, there are no line numbers due to the size and complexity of the code listings.

Finally, if a line of code is too long to fit within the width of the page, you will see a continuation character (➥) at the start of the next line on the printed page. This indicates that as you type these lines into the computer, they should be entered as a single line. You should not type the continuation character.

Book Website

The website for this book includes all the files referenced in the chapters, lecturer notes, starter packages, playable examples of some of the games, updates, and much more! It is available at

   http://book.prototools.net

ACKNOWLEDGMENTS

A tremendous number of people deserve to be thanked here. First and foremost, I want to thank my wife, Melanie, whose help and feedback on my chapters throughout the entire process improved the book tremendously. I also want to thank my family for their many years of support, with special thanks to my father for teaching me how to program as a child.

On this second time into the breach, several people at Pearson provided support to me and once more shepherded me through the process. Chief among them were Chris Zahn, Laura Lewin, Paula Lowell, Lori Lyons, Olivia Basegio, and Dhayanidhi Karunanidhi, who each demonstrated laudable patience in working with me. I also had the support of some fantastic technical reviewers: Marc Destefano, Charles Duba, and Margaret Moser on the first edition and Grace Kendall, Stephen Beeman, and Reed Coke for the second edition. Their keen eyes and minds found many places in the original text that could be clarified or improved.

I would also like to thank all the educators who have taught me and worked as my colleagues. Special thanks go to Dr. Randy Pausch and Jesse Schell. Though I had worked as a professor and game designer before meeting them, they each had a profound effect on my understanding of design and education. I also owe tremendous thanks to Tracy Fullerton, Mark Bolas, and Scott Fisher, who were friends and mentors to me in the years I taught at the University of Southern California's Interactive Media and Games Division. My new work family at Michigan State University has also been tremendous to work with, including Andrew Dennis (who did the art for Chapter 35), Brian Winn, Elizabeth LaPensée, Ricardo Guimaraes, and many others. Many other brilliant faculty and friends at USC and University of Michigan also helped me to flesh out the ideas in this book, including Adam Liszkiewicz, William Huber, Richard Lemarchand, Scott Rogers, Vincent Diamante, Sam Roberts, Logan Ver Hoef, and Marcus Darden.

Many of my friends in the industry have also helped me by giving me suggestions for the book and feedback on the ideas presented therein. These included Michael Sellers, Nicholas Fortugno, Jenova Chen, Zac Pavlov, Joseph Stevens, and many others.

Thanks as well to all the fantastic students whom I have taught over the past nearly two decades. It is you who inspired me to want to write this book and who convinced me that there was something important and different about the way that I was teaching game development. Every day that I teach, I find myself inspired and invigorated by your creativity, intelligence, and passion.

Finally, I would like to thank you. Thank you for purchasing this book and for your interest in developing games. I hope that this book helps you get started, and I would love to see what you make with the knowledge you gain here.

ABOUT THE AUTHOR

Jeremy Gibson Bond is a Professor of Practice, teaching game design and development in the Media and Information Department at Michigan State University (http://gamedev.msu.edu), which has been ranked a top-ten game design program for the last several years. Since 2013, he has served the IndieCade independent game festival and conference as the Chair of Education and Advancement, where he co-chairs the IndieXchange summit each year. In 2013, Jeremy founded the company ExNinja Interactive, through which he develops his independent game projects. Jeremy has also spoken several times at the Game Developers Conference.

Prior to joining the faculty at Michigan State, Jeremy taught for three years as a Lecturer in the Electrical Engineering and Computer Science department at the University of Michigan Ann Arbor, where he taught game design and software development. From 2009 to 2013, Jeremy was an Assistant Professor of Practice teaching game design for the Interactive Media and Games Division of the University of Southern California's School of Cinematic Arts, which was named the number one game design school in North America throughout his tenure there.

Jeremy earned a Master of Entertainment Technology degree from Carnegie Mellon University's Entertainment Technology Center in 2007 and a Bachelor of Science degree in Radio, Television, and Film from the University of Texas at Austin in 1999. He started his career as a programmer and prototyper for companies such as Human Code and frog design; has also taught classes for Great Northern Way Campus (in Vancouver, BC), Texas State University, the Art Institute of Pittsburgh, Austin Community College, and the University of Texas at Austin; and has worked for Walt Disney Imagineering, Maxis, and Electronic Arts/Pogo.com, among others. While in graduate school, his team created the online game *Skyrates*, which won the Silver Gleemax Award for Strategic Gaming at the 2008 Independent Games Festival. Jeremy also apparently has the distinction of being the first person to ever teach game design in Costa Rica.

CHAPTER 1

THINKING LIKE A DESIGNER

Our journey starts here. This chapter presents the basic theories of design upon which the rest of the book is built. In this chapter, you also encounter your first game design exercise and learn more about the underlying philosophy of this book.

You Are a Game Designer

As of this moment, you are a game designer, and I want you to say it out loud:[1]

"I am a game designer."

It's okay. You can say it out loud, even if other people can hear you. In fact, according to psychologist Robert Cialdini's book *Influence: The Psychology of Persuasion*,[2] if other people hear you commit to something, you're more likely to follow through. So, go ahead and post it to Facebook, tell your friends, tell your family:

"I am a game designer."

But, what does it mean to be a game designer? This book will help you answer that question and will give you the tools to start making your own games. Let's start with a design exercise.

Bartok: A Game Exercise

I first saw this exercise used by game designer Malcolm Ryan as part of a Game Design Workshop session at the Foundations of Digital Gaming conference. The goal of this exercise is to demonstrate how even a simple change to the rules of a game can have a massive effect on the experience of playing the game.

Bartok is a simple game played with a single deck of cards that is very similar to the commercial game *Uno*. In the best case scenario, you would play this game with three friends who are also interested in game design; however, I've also made a digital version of the game for you to play solo. Either the paper or digital version will work fine for our purposes.[3]

GETTING THE DIGITAL VERSION OF *BARTOK*

The digital version of Bartok is available in the Chapter 1 section of the website for this book:

http://book.prototools.net

---

1. I thank my former professor Jesse Schell for asking me to make this statement publicly in a class full of people. He also includes this request in his book *The Art of Game Design: A Book of Lenses* (Boca Raton, FL: CRC Press, 2008), 1.
2. Robert B. Cialdini. *Influence: The Psychology of Persuasion* (New York: Morrow, 1993).
3. The card images in this book and in the digital card games presented in the book are based on Vectorized Playing Cards 1.3, Copyright 2011, Chris Aguilar. Licensed under LGPL 3—http://www.gnu.org/copyleft/lesser.html, http://sourceforge.net/projects/vector-cards/.

Objective

Be the first player to get rid of all the cards in your hand.

Getting Started

Here are the basic rules for *Bartok*:

1. Start with a regular deck of playing cards. Remove the Jokers, leaving you with 52 cards (13 of each suit ranked Ace–King).

2. Shuffle the deck and deal seven cards to each player.

3. Place the rest of the cards face-down in a draw pile.

4. Pick the top card from the draw pile and place it on the table face-up to start the discard pile.

5. Starting with the player to the left of the dealer and proceeding clockwise, each player must play a card onto the discard pile if possible, and if she cannot play a card, the player must draw a single card from the draw pile (see Figure 1.1).

6. A player may play a card onto the discard pile if the card is either:

   a. The same suit as the top card of the discard pile. (For example, if the top card of the discard pile is a 2 of Clubs (2C), any other Club may be played onto the discard pile.)

   b. The same rank as the top card of the discard pile. (For example, if the top card of the discard pile is a 2C, any other 2 may be played onto the discard pile.)

7. The first player to successfully get rid of all of her cards wins.

Figure 1.1 The initial layout of *Bartok*. In the situation shown, the player can choose to play any one of the cards highlighted with blue borders (7C, JC, 2H, 2S)

Playtesting

Try playing the game a couple of times to get a feel for it. Be sure to thoroughly shuffle the cards between each playthrough. Games will often result in a somewhat sorted discard pile, and without a good shuffle, subsequent games may have results weighted by the nonrandom card distribution.

> ### tip
>
> **DEBLOCKING**   This is the term for strategies used to break up blocks of cards (that is, groups of similar cards). In *Bartok*, each successful game ends with all the cards sorted into blocks of the same suit and blocks of the same rank. If you don't deblock those groups, the subsequent game will end much faster because players are more likely to be dealt cards that match each other.
>
> According to mathematician and magician Persi Diaconis, seven good riffle shuffles should be sufficient for nearly all games;[4] if you run into issues, though, some of these de-blocking strategies can help.
>
> Here are some standard strategies for deblocking a deck of cards if standard shuffling doesn't work:
>
> - Deal the cards into several different piles. Then shuffle these piles together.
>
> - Deal the cards out face-down into a large, spread-out pool. Then use both hands to move the cards around almost like mixing water. This is how dominoes are usually shuffled, and it can help break up your card blocks. Then gather all the cards into a single stack.
>
> - Play *52 Pickup*: Throw all the cards on the floor and pick them up.
>
> ---
>
> 4. Persi Diaconis, "Mathematical Developments from the Analysis of Riffle Shuffling," *Groups, Combinatorics and Geometry,* edited by Ivanov, Liebeck, and Saxl. *World Scientific* (2003): 73–97. Also available online at http://statweb.stanford.edu/~cgates/PERSI/papers/Riffle.pdf.

Analysis: Asking the Right Questions

After each playtest, it's important to ask the right questions. Of course, each game will require slightly different questions, though you can base many of them on these general guidelines:

- Is the game of the appropriate difficulty for the intended audience? Is it too difficult, too easy, or just right?

- Is the outcome of the game based more on strategy or chance? Does randomness play too strong a role in the game, or, alternatively, is the game too deterministic so that after one player has taken the lead, the other players are unable to catch up?

- Does the game have meaningful, interesting decisions? When it's your turn, do you have several choices, and is the decision between those choices an interesting one?

- Is the game interesting when it's not your turn? Do you have any effect on the other players' turns, or do their turns have any immediate effect on you?

We could ask many other questions, but these are some of the most common.

Take a moment to think about your answers to these questions relative to the games of *Bartok* you just played and write them down. If you're playing the paper version of this game with other human players, it's worthwhile to ask them to write down their own answers to the questions individually and then discuss the questions as a group afterward. This keeps the responses from being influenced by other players.

Modifying the Rules

As you'll see throughout this book, game design is primarily a process:

1. Incrementally modify the rules, changing very few things between each playtest.

2. Playtest the game with the new rules.

3. Analyze how the feel of the game is altered by the new rules.

4. Design new rules that you think may move the feel of the game in the direction you want.

5. Repeat this process until you're happy with the game.

Iterative design is the term for this repetitive process of deciding on a small change to the game design, implementing that change, playtesting the game, analyzing how the change affected the gameplay, and then starting the process over again by deciding on another small change. Chapter 7, "Acting Like a Designer," covers iterative design in detail.

For the *Bartok* example, why don't you start by picking one of the following three rule changes and playtesting it:

- **Rule 1:** If a player plays a 2, the person to her left must draw two cards instead of playing.

- **Rule 2:** If any player has a card that matches the number and color (red or black) of the top card, she may announce "Match card!" and play it out of turn. Play then continues with the player to the left of the one who just played the out-of-turn card. This can lead to players having their turns skipped.

    For example: The first player plays a 3C (three of Clubs). The third player has the 3S, so she calls "Match card!" and plays the 3S on top of the 3C out-of-turn, skipping the second player's turn. Play then continues with the fourth player.

- **Rule 3:** A player must announce "Last card" when she has only one card left. If someone else calls it first, she must draw two cards (bringing her total number of cards to three).

Choose only one of the rule changes from the previous listing and play the game through a couple of times with the new rule. Then have each player write their answers to the four playtest questions. You should also try playing with another one of the rules (although I would recommend still only using one of them at a time when trying a new rule for the first time).

If you're playing the digital version of the game, you can use the check boxes on the menu screen to choose various game options.

> ### warning
>
> **WATCH OUT FOR PLAYTESTING FLUKES**   A weird shuffle or other external factor can sometimes cause a single play through the game to feel really different from the others. This is known as a *fluke*, and you want to be careful not to make game design decisions based on flukes. If something you do seems to affect the game feel in a very unexpected way, be sure to play through the game multiple times with that rule change to make sure you're not experiencing a fluke.

Analysis: Comparing the Rounds

Now that you've played through the game with some different rule options, it's time to analyze the results from the different rounds. Look back over your notes and see how each different rule set felt to play. As you experienced, even a simple rule change can greatly change the feel of the game. Here are some common reactions to the previously listed rules:

- **The original rules**

  Many players find the original version of the game to be pretty boring. There are no interesting choices to make, and as the players remove cards from their hands, the number of possible choices dwindles, as well, often leaving the player with only one valid choice for most of the later turns of the game. The game is largely based on chance, and players have no real reason to pay attention to other players' turns because they don't really have any way of affecting each other.

- **Rule 1:** *If a player plays a 2, the person to her left must draw two cards instead of playing.*

  This rule allows players to directly affect each other, which generally increases interest in the game. However, whether a player has 2s is based entirely on luck, and each player only really has the ability to affect the player on her left, which often seems unfair. However, this does make other players' turns a bit more interesting because other players (or at least the player to your right) have the ability to affect you.

- **Rule 2:** *If any player has a card that matches the number and color (red or black) of the top card, she may announce "Match card!" and play it out of turn. Play then continues with the player to the left of the one who just played the out-of-turn card.*

This rule often has the greatest effect on player attention. Because any player has the opportunity to interrupt another player's turn, all players tend to pay a lot more attention to each other's turns. Games played with this rule often feel more dramatic and exciting than those played with the other rules.

- **Rule 3:** *A player must announce "Last card!" when she has only one card left. If someone else calls it first, she must draw two cards.*

    This rule only comes into play near the end of the game, so it doesn't have any effect on the majority of gameplay, however, it does change how players behave at the end. This can lead to some interesting tension as players try to jump in and say "last card" before the player who is down to only one card. This is a common rule in both domino and card games where the players are trying to empty everything from their hands because it gives other players a chance to catch up to the lead player if the leader forgets about the rule.

Designing for the Game Feel That You Want

Now that you've seen the effects of a few different rules on *Bartok*, it's time to do your job as a designer and make the game better. First, decide on the feel that you want the game to have: do you want it to be exciting and cutthroat, do you want it to be leisurely and slow, or do you want it to be based more on strategy than chance?

Once you have a general idea of how you want the game to feel, think about the rules that we tried out and try to come up with additional rules that can push the feel of the game in the direction that you want. Here are some tips to keep in mind as you design new rules for the game:

- Change only one thing in between each playtest. If you change (or even tweak) a number of rules between each play through the game, it can be difficult to determine which rule is affecting the game in what way. Keep your changes incremental, and you'll be better able to understand the effect that each is having.

- The bigger change you make, the more playtests it will take to understand how it changes the game feel. If you only make a subtle change to the game, one or two plays can tell you a lot about how that change affects the feel. However, if it's a major rule change, you will need to test it more times to avoid being tricked by a fluke game.

- Change a number and you change the experience. Even a seemingly small change can have a huge effect on gameplay. For instance, think about how much faster this game would be if there were two discard piles to choose from or if the players started with five cards instead of seven.

Of course, adding new rules is a lot easier to do when playing the card game in person with friends than when working with the digital prototype. That's one of the reasons that paper prototypes can be so important, even when you're designing digital games. The first part of this book discusses both paper and digital design, but most of the examples and design exercises are done with paper games because they can be so much faster to develop and test than digital games.

The Definition of *Game*

Before moving too much further into design and iteration, we should probably clarify what we're talking about when we use terms such as *game* and *game design*. Many very smart people have tried to accurately define the word *game*. Here are a few of them in chronological order:

- In his 1978 book *The Grasshopper*, Bernard Suits (who was a professor of philosophy at the University of Waterloo) declares that "a game is the voluntary attempt to overcome unnecessary obstacles."[5]

- Game design legend Sid Meier says that "a game is a series of interesting decisions."

- In *Game Design Workshop*, Tracy Fullerton defines a game as "a closed, formal system that engages players in a structured conflict and resolves its uncertainty in an unequal outcome."[6]

- In *The Art of Game Design*, Jesse Schell playfully examines several definitions for game and eventually decides on "a game is a problem-solving activity, approached with a playful attitude."[7]

- In the book *Game Design Theory*, Keith Burgun presents a much more limited definition of game: "a system of rules in which agents compete by making ambiguous, endogenously meaningful decisions."[8, 9]

As you can see, all of these are compelling and correct in their own way. Perhaps even more important than each individual definition is the insight that it gives us into the author's intent when crafting that definition.

Bernard Suits' Definition

In addition to the short definition "a game is the voluntary attempt to overcome unnecessary obstacles," Suits also offers a longer, more robust version:

> To play a game is to attempt to achieve a specific state of affairs, using only means permitted by rules, where the rules prohibit use of more efficient in favor of less efficient means, and where the rules are accepted just because they make possible such activity.

---

5. Bernard Suits, *The Grasshopper* (Toronto: Toronto University Press, 1978), 56.
6. Tracy Fullerton, Christopher Swain, and Steven Hoffman. *Game Design Workshop: A Playcentric Approach to Creating Innovative Games*, 2nd ed. (Boca Raton, FL: Elsevier Morgan Kaufmann, 2008), 43.
7. Jesse Schell, *Art of Game Design: A Book of Lenses* (Boca Raton, FL: CRC Press, 2008), 37.
8. Keith Burgun. *Game Design Theory: A New Philosophy for Understanding Games* (Boca Raton, FL: A K Peters/CRC Press, 2013), 10, 19.
9. *Endogenous* means inherent to or arising from the internal systems of a thing, so "endogenously meaningful decisions" are those decisions that actually affect the game state and change the outcome. Choosing the color of your avatar's clothing in *Farmville* is not endogenously meaningful, whereas choosing the color of your clothing in *Metal Gear Solid 4* is, because the color of your clothing affects whether your avatar is visible to enemies.

Throughout his book, Suits proposes and refutes various attacks on this definition; and having read the book, I am certainly willing to say that he has found the definition of "game" that most accurately matches the way that the word is used in day-to-day life.

However, it's also important to realize that this definition was crafted in 1978, and even though digital games and role-playing games existed at this time, Suits was either unaware of them or intentionally ignored them. In fact, in Chapter 9 of *The Grasshopper*, Suits laments that there is no kind of game with rules for dramatic play through which players could burn off dramatic energy (much like children can burn off excess athletic energy via play of any number of different sports), even though that is exactly the kind of play that was enabled by role-playing games like *Dungeons & Dragons*.[10]

Although this is a small point, it gets at exactly what is missing from this definition: Whereas Suits' definition of game is an accurate definition of the word, it offers nothing to designers seeking to craft good games for others.

For an example of what I mean, take a moment to play Jason Rohrer's fantastic game *Passage*: http://hcsoftware.sourceforge.net/passage/ (see Figure 1.2).[11] The game only takes 5 minutes to play, and it does a fantastic job of demonstrating the power that even short games can have. Try playing through it a couple of times.

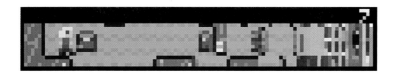

Figure 1.2 *Passage* by Jason Rohrer (released December 13, 2007)

Suits' definition will tell you that yes, this is a game. In fact, it is specifically an "open game," which he defines as a game that has as its sole goal the continuance of the game.[12] In *Passage*, the goal is to continue to play for as long as possible…or is it? *Passage* has several potential goals, and it's up to the player to choose which of these she wants to achieve. These goals could include the following:

- Moving as far to the right as possible before dying (exploration)
- Earning as many points as possible by finding treasure chests (achievement)
- Finding a wife (socialization)

---

10. Suits, *Grasshopper*, 95.
11. At this time, *Passage* is about a decade old, and Rohrer is sometimes not able to keep it running on newer systems. However, in the past, I've written him about it, and he's updated the build.
12. Suits contrasts these with closed games, which have a specific goal (for example, crossing a finish line in a race or ridding yourself of all your cards in *Bartok*). Suits' example of an open game is the games of make-believe that children play.

The point of *Passage* as an artistic statement is that each of these can be a goal in life, and to some extent, these goals are mutually exclusive. If you find a wife early in the game, getting treasure chests is subsequently more difficult because the two of you together are unable to enter areas that could be entered singly (however, moving a step to the right now gains you two points instead of one). If you choose to seek treasure, you will spend your time exploring the vertical space of the world and won't be able to explore as much of the scenery to the right. If you choose to move as far to the right as possible, you won't rack up nearly as much treasure.

In this incredibly simple game, Rohrer exposes a few of the fundamental decisions that every one of us must make in life and demonstrates how even early decisions can have a major effect on the rest of our lives. The important thing here is that he is giving players choice and demonstrating to them that their choices matter.

This is an example of one of a number of designer's goals that I will introduce in this book: *experiential understanding*. Whereas a linear story like a book can encourage empathy with a character by exposing the reader to the character's life and the decisions that she has made, games can allow players to not only understand the outcome of decisions but also to be complicit in that outcome by giving the player the power and the responsibility of making decisions and then showing her the outcome wrought by her decisions. Chapter 8, "Design Goals," explores experiential understanding and other designer's goals in greater depth.

Sid Meier's Definition

By stating that "a game is a series of interesting decisions," Meier is saying very little about the definition of the word *game* (there are many, many things that could be categorized as a series of interesting decisions and yet are not games) and quite a bit about what he personally believes makes for a good game. As the designer of games such as *Pirates*, *Civilization*, *Alpha Centauri*, and many more, Sid Meier is one of the most successful game designers alive, and he has consistently produced games that present players with interesting decisions. This, of course, raises the question of what makes a decision *interesting*. An interesting decision is generally one where

- The player has multiple valid options from which to choose.
- Each option has both positive and negative potential consequences.
- The outcome of each option is predictable but not guaranteed.

This brings up the second of our designer's goals: to *create interesting decisions*. If a player is presented with a number of choices, but one choice is obviously superior to the others, the experience of deciding which to choose doesn't actually exist. If a game is designed well, players will often have multiple choices from which to choose, and those decisions will be tricky ones.

Tracy Fullerton's Definition

As she states in her book, Tracy is much more concerned with giving designers tools to make better games than she is with the philosophical definition of *game*. Accordingly, her definition of a game as "a closed, formal system that engages players in a structured conflict and resolves its uncertainty in an unequal outcome" is not only a good definition of game but also a list of elements that designers can modify in their games:

- **Formal elements:** The elements that differentiate a game from other types of media: rules, procedures, players, resources, objectives, boundaries, conflict, and outcome.
- **(Dynamic) systems:** Methods of interaction that evolve as the game is played.
- **Conflict structure:** The ways in which players interact with each other.
- **Uncertainty:** The interaction between randomness, determinism, and player strategy.
- **Unequal outcome:** How does the game end? Do players win, lose, or something else?

Another critical element in Fullerton's book is her continual insistence on *actually making games*. The only way to become a better game designer is to make games. Some of the games you'll design will probably be pretty awful—some of mine certainly have been—but even designing a terrible game is a learning process, and every game you create improves your design skills and helps you better understand how to make great games.

Jesse Schell's Definition

Schell defines a game as "a problem-solving activity, approached with a playful attitude." This is similar in many ways to Suits' definition, and like that definition, it approaches the definition of game from the point of view of the player. According to both, it is the playful attitude of the player that makes something a game. In fact, Suits argues in his book that two people could both be involved in the same activity, and to one, it would be a game, whereas to the other, it would not be. Suits example is a foot race where one runner is just running because he wants to take part in the race, but the other runner knows that at the finish line there is a bomb she must defuse before it explodes. According to Suits, although the two runners would both be running in the same foot race, the one who is simply racing would follow the rules of the race because of what Suits calls his *lusory attitude*. On the other hand, the bomb-defusing runner would break the rules of the game the first chance she got because she has a *serious attitude* (as is required to defuse a bomb) and is not engaged in the game.

Ludus is the Latin word for play, so Suits proposes the term *lusory attitude* to describe the attitude of one who willingly takes part in playing a game. It is because of their lusory attitude that players will happily follow the rules of a game even though there might be an easier way to achieve the stated goal of the game (what Suits would call the *pre-lusory goal*). For example, the pre-lusory goal of golf is to get the golf ball into the cup, but there are many easier ways to do so than to stand hundreds of yards away and hit the ball with a bent stick. When people have a lusory attitude, they set challenges for themselves just for the joy of overcoming them.

So, another design goal is to *encourage a lusory attitude*. Your games should be designed to encourage players to enjoy the limitations placed on them by the rules. Think about why each rule is there and how it changes the player experience. If a game is balanced well and has the proper rules, players will enjoy the limitations of the rules rather than feel exasperated by them.

Keith Burgun's Definition

Burgun's definition of a game as "a system of rules in which agents compete by making ambiguous, endogenously meaningful decisions" is his attempt to push the discourse on games forward from a rut that he feels it has fallen into by narrowing the meaning of game down to something that can be better examined and understood. The core of this definition is that the player is making choices and that those choices are both ambiguous (the player doesn't know exactly what the outcome of the choice will be) and endogenously meaningful (the choice is meaningful because it has a noticeable effect upon the game system).

Burgun's definition is intentionally limited and purposefully excludes several of the things that many people think of as games (including foot races and other competitions based on physical skill) as well as reflective games like *The Graveyard*, by Tale of Tales, in which the player experiences wandering through a graveyard as an old woman. Both of these are excluded because the decisions in them lack ambiguity and endogenous meaning.

Burgun chooses such a limited definition because he wants to get down to the essence of games and what makes them unique. In doing so, he makes several good points, including his statement that whether an experience is fun or not has little to do with the question of whether it is a game. Even a terribly boring game is still a game; it's just a bad game.

In my discussions with other designers, I have found that a lot of contention can exist about this question of what types of things should fall under the term *game*. Games are a medium that has experienced a tremendous amount of growth, expansion, and maturation over the last couple of decades, and the current explosion of independent game development has only hastened the pace. Today, more people with disparate voices and backgrounds are contributing work to the field of games than ever before, and as a result, the definition of the medium is expanding, which is understandably bothersome to some people because it can be seen as blurring the lines of what is considered a game. Burgun's response to this is his concern that rigorously advancing a medium is difficult if we lack a good definition of the boundaries of what that medium comprises.

Why Care About the Definition of Game?

In his 1953 book *Philosophical Investigations*, Ludwig Wittgenstein proposed that the term *game*, as it is used colloquially, had come at that time to refer to several very different things that shared some traits (which he likened to a family resemblance) but couldn't be encapsulated in a single definition. In 1978, Bernard Suits attacked this idea by using his book, *The Grasshopper*, to argue very stringently for the specific definition of *game* that you read earlier in this chapter. However, as

Chris Bateman points out in his book, *Imaginary Games*, though Wittgenstein used the word *game* as his example, he was really trying to make a larger point: that words are created to define things rather than things being created to meet the definition of words.

In 1974 (between the publications of *Philosophical Investigations* and *The Grasshopper*), the philosopher Mary Midgley published a paper titled "The Game Game" in which she explored and refuted the "family resemblance" claim by Wittgenstein not by arguing for a specific definition of *game* herself but instead by exploring why the word *game* existed. In her paper, she agrees with Wittgenstein that the word *game* came into being long after games existed, but she makes the statement that words like *game* are not defined by the *things* that they encompass but instead by the *needs* that they meet. As she states:

> Something can be accepted as a chair provided it is properly made for sitting on, whether it consists of a plastic balloon, a large blob of foam, or a basket slung from the ceiling. Provided you understand the need you can see whether it has the right characteristics, and aptness for that need *is* what chairs have in common.[13]

In her paper, Midgley seeks to understand some of the needs that games fulfill. She completely rejects the idea that games are closed systems by both citing many examples of game outcomes that have effects beyond the game and pointing out that games cannot be closed because humans have a reason for entering into them. To her, that reason is paramount. The following are just a few reasons for playing games:

- **Humans desire structured conflict:** As Midgley points out, "The Chess Player's desire is not for general abstract intellectual activity, curbed and frustrated by a particular set of rules. It is a desire for a particular kind of intellectual activity, whose channel is the rules of chess." As Suits pointed out in his definition, the rules that limit behavior are there precisely because the challenge of those limitations is appealing to players.

- **Humans desire the experience of being someone else:** We are all acutely aware that we have but one life to live (or at least one at a time), and play can allow us to experience another life. Just as a game of *Call of Duty* allows a player to pretend to experience the life of a soldier, so too does *The Graveyard* allow the player to pretend to experience the life of an old woman, and playing the role of Hamlet allows an actor to pretend to experience the life of a troubled Danish prince.

- **Humans desire excitement:** Much popular media is devoted to this desire for excitement, be it action films, courtroom dramas, or romance novels. The thing that makes games different in this regard is that the player is actively taking part in the excitement rather than vicariously absorbing it, as is the case for the majority of linear media. As a player, you aren't watching someone else be chased by zombies, you're being chased yourself.

Midgley found it critical to consider the needs that are fulfilled by games in order to understand both their importance in society and the positive and negative effects that games can have

---

13. Mary Midgley. "The Game Game," *Philosophy 49,* no. 189 (1974): 231–53.

on the people who play them. Both Suits and Midgley spoke about the potentially addictive qualities of games in the 1970s, long before video games became ubiquitous and public concern emerged about players becoming addicted. As game designers, understanding these needs and respecting their power can be incredibly useful.

The Nebulous Nature of Definitions

As Midgley pointed out, thinking of the word *game* as being defined by the need that it fills is worthwhile. However, she also stated that a chess player doesn't want to play just any kind of game; he specifically wants to play chess. Not only is coming up with an all-encompassing definition for *game* difficult, it's also true that the same word will mean different things to different people at different times. When I say that I'm going to play a game, I usually mean a console or video game; when my wife says the same thing, though, she usually means *Scrabble* or another word game. When my parents say they want to play a game, it means something like Alan R. Moon's *Ticket to Ride* (a board game that is interesting but doesn't require players to be overly competitive with each other), and my in-laws usually mean a game of cards or dominoes when they use the word. Even within our family, the word has great breadth.

The meaning of the word *game* is also constantly evolving. When the first computer games were created, no one could have possibly imagined the multibillion-dollar industry that we now have or the rise of the fantastic indie renaissance that we've seen over the past several years. All that they knew was that these things people were doing on computers were kind of like tabletop war board games (I'm thinking of *Space War* here), and they were called "computer games" to differentiate them from the preexisting meanings of *game*.

The evolution of digital games was a gradual process with each new genre building in some way on the ones that had come before, and along the way, the term *game* expanded further and further to encompass all of them.

Now, as the art form matures, many designers are entering the field from various other disciplines and bringing with them their own concepts about what can be created with the technologies and design methodologies that have been developed to make digital games. (You might even be one of them.) As these new artists and designers enter the space, some of them are making things that are very different from what we think of as a stereotypical game. That's okay; in fact, I think it's fantastic! And, this isn't just my opinion. IndieCade, the international festival of independent games, seeks every year to find games that push the envelope of what is meant by *game*. According to Festival Chair Celia Pearce and Festival Director Sam Roberts, if an independent developer wants to call the interactive piece that she has created a game, IndieCade will accept it as one.[14]

---

14. This was stated during the Festival Submission Workshop given by Celia Pearce and Sam Roberts at IndieCade East 2014 and is paraphrased on the IndieCade submissions website at http://www.indiecade.com/submissions/faq/.

Summary

After all these interwoven and sometimes contradictory definitions, you might be wondering why this book has spent so much time exploring the definition of the word *game*. I have to admit that in my day-to-day work as an educator and game designer, I don't spend a lot of time wrestling with the definitions of words. As Shakespeare points out, were a rose to be named something else, it would still smell as sweet, still have thorns, and still be a thing of fragile beauty. However, I believe that an understanding of these definitions can be critical to you as a designer in the following three ways:

- Definitions help you understand what people expect from your games. This proves especially true if you're working in a specific genre or for a specific audience. Understanding how your audience defines the term can help you to craft better games for them.

- Definitions can lead you to understand not only the core of the defined concept but also the periphery. As you read through this chapter, you encountered several different definitions by different people, and each had both a core and a periphery (i.e., games that fit the definition perfectly [the core] and games that just barely fit the definition [the periphery]). The places where these peripheries don't mesh can be hints at some of the interesting areas to explore with a new game. For example, the area of disagreement between Fullerton and Midgley about whether a game is a closed system highlights the previously untracked ground that in the 2000s grew into alternate reality games (ARGs), a genre centered on perforating the closed magic circle of play.[15]

- Definitions can help you speak eloquently with others in the field. This chapter has more references and footnotes than any other in the book because I want you to be able to explore the philosophical understanding of games in ways that are beyond the scope of this one book (especially since this book focuses on the practicalities of actually making digital games). Following these footnotes and reading the source material can help improve your critical thinking about games.

The Core Lessons of This Book

This book teaches you how to design a lot more than just games. In fact, it teaches you how to craft any kind of interactive experience. As I define it:

> An interactive experience is any experience created by a designer; inscribed into rules, media, or technology; and decoded by people through play.

---

15. The first large-scale ARG was *Majestic* (Electronic Arts, 2001), a game that would phone players in the middle of the night and send them faxes and emails. Smaller-scale ARGs include the game *Assassin*, which is played on many college campuses, where players can "assassinate" each other (usually with Nerf or water guns, or by snapping a photo) any time that they are outside of classes. One of the fun aspects of these games is that they are always happening and can interfere with normal life.

That makes *interactive experience* an intentionally expansive term. In fact, any time that you attempt to craft an experience for people—whether you're designing a game, planning a surprise birthday party, or even planning a wedding—you're using the same tools that you will learn as a game designer. The processes described in this book are more than just the proper way to approach game design. They are a meaningful way to approach any design problem, and the *iterative process of design* that is introduced in Chapter 7, "Acting Like a Designer," is *the* essential method for improving the quality of any design.

No one bursts forth from the womb as a brilliant game designer. My friend Chris Swain[16] is fond of saying that "Game design is 1% inspiration and 99% iteration," a play on the famous quote by Thomas Edison. He is absolutely correct, and one of the great things about game design (unlike the previously mentioned examples of the surprise party and the wedding) is that you get the chance to iterate on your designs, playtest the game, make subtle tweaks, and play it again. With each prototype you make—and with every iteration of each prototype—your skills as a designer improve. Similarly, after you reach the parts of this book that teach digital development, be sure to keep experimenting and iterating. The code samples and tutorials are designed to show you how to make a playable game prototype, but every tutorial in this book ends where your work as a designer should begin. Each one of these prototypes could be built into a larger, more robust, better balanced game, and I encourage you to do so.

Moving Forward

Now that you've experienced a bit of game design and explored various definitions of *game,* it's time to move on to a more in-depth exploration of a few different analytical frameworks that game designers use to understand games and game design. The next chapter explores various frameworks that have been used over the past several years, and the chapter that follows synthesizes those into the *Layered Tetrad* framework used throughout the remainder of this book.

---

16. Chris Swain co-wrote the first edition of *Game Design Workshop* with Tracy Fullerton and taught the class of the same name at the University of Southern California for many years. He is now an entrepreneur and independent game designer.

CHAPTER 2

GAME ANALYSIS FRAMEWORKS

Ludology is the fancy name for the study of games and game design. Over the past decade, ludologists have proposed various analytical frameworks for games to help them understand and discuss the structure and fundamental elements of games and the impact of games on players and society.

This chapter presents a few of the most commonly used frameworks that you should know as a designer. The next chapter, Chapter 3, "The Layered Tetrad," synthesizes ideas from these common frameworks into the Layered Tetrad framework used throughout this book.

Common Frameworks for Ludology

The frameworks presented in this chapter include the following:

- **MDA:** First presented by Robin Hunicke, Marc LeBlanc, and Robert Zubek, *MDA* stands for mechanics, dynamics, and aesthetics. It is the framework that is most familiar to professional game designers, and it provides important points to consider about the difference between how designers and players approach games.

- **Formal, Dramatic, and Dynamic Elements:** Presented by Tracy Fullerton and Chris Swain in the book *Game Design Workshop*, the FDD framework focuses on concrete analytical tools to help designers make better games and push their ideas further. It owes a lot to the history of film studies.

- **Elemental Tetrad:** Presented by Jesse Schell in his book *The Art of Game Design*, the elemental tetrad splits games into four core elements: mechanics, aesthetics, story, and technology.

Each of these frameworks has benefits and drawbacks, and each has contributed to the Layered Tetrad presented in this book. They are covered here in the order that they were published.

MDA: Mechanics, Dynamics, and Aesthetics

First proposed at the Game Developers Conference in 2001 and formalized in the 2004 paper "MDA: A Formal Approach to Game Design and Game Research,"[1] MDA is the most commonly referenced analytical framework for ludology. The key elements of MDA are its definitions of mechanics, dynamics, and aesthetics; its understanding of the different perspectives from which the designer and player view a game; and its proposal that designers should first approach a game through the lens of aesthetics and then work back toward the dynamics and mechanics that will generate those aesthetics.

Definitions of Mechanics, Dynamics, and Aesthetics

One of the things that can be confusing about the three frameworks presented in this chapter is that they each reuse some of the same words, and each framework defines them slightly differently. MDA defines these terms as follows:[2]

---

1. Robin Hunicke, Marc LeBlanc, and Robert Zubek, "MDA: A Formal Approach to Game Design and Game Research," in *Proceedings of the AAAI workshop on Challenges in Game AI Workshop* (San Jose, CA: AAAI Press, 2004), http://www.cs.northwestern.edu/~hunicke/MDA.pdf.

2. Ibid. p. 2.

- **Mechanics:** The particular components of the game at the level of data representation and algorithms
- **Dynamics:** The runtime behavior of the mechanics acting on player inputs and each other's outputs over time
- **Aesthetics:** The desirable emotional responses evoked in the player when she interacts with the game system[3]

Designer and Player Views of a Game

According to MDA, designers should consider games first in terms of the *aesthetics*, the emotions that the designer wants players to feel while playing the game. After a designer has decided on the aesthetics, she will work backward to the kinds of dynamic play that would prompt those feelings, and finally to the gameplay mechanics that will create those dynamics. Players tend to view the game in the opposite way: first experiencing the mechanics (often by reading the written rules for the game), then experiencing the dynamics by playing the game, and finally (hopefully) experiencing the aesthetics that were initially envisioned by the designer (see Figure 2.1).

Figure 2.1 According to MDA, designers and players view a game from different directions[4]

Design from Aesthetics to Dynamics to Mechanics

Based on these differing views, MDA proposes that designers should first approach a game by deciding on the emotional response (aesthetics) that they want to engender in the player and then work backward from that to create dynamics and mechanics that fit this chosen aesthetic.

For example, children's games are often designed to make each player feel like they're doing well and have a chance to win up until the very end. To have this feeling, players must feel that the end of the game is not inevitable and must be able to hope for good luck throughout the game. Keep this in mind when looking at the layout of a *Snakes and Ladders* game.

---

3. Note that this is a very singular definition of *aesthetics*. No other framework defines aesthetics this way. Aesthetics usually refers to the branch of philosophy having to do with notions of beauty, ugliness, etc. And, more colloquially, a design aesthetic is the cohesive intent of a design.

4. Adapted from: Hunicke, LeBlanc, and Zubek, "MDA: A Formal Approach to Game Design and Game Research," 2.

Snakes and Ladders

Snakes and Ladders is a board game for children that originated in ancient India where it was known as *Moksha Patamu*.[5] The game requires no skill and is entirely based on chance. Each turn, a player rolls one die and moves her counter the number of spaces shown. Counters are not placed on the board initially, so if a player rolls a 1 on her first turn, she lands on the first space of the board. The goal is to be the first player to reach the end of the board (space 100). If a player ends her move on a space at the start of a green arrow (a ladder), she must move to the space at the end of the arrow (for example, a player ending her move on the 1 space must move her piece to the 38). If a player ends her move on the start of a red arrow (a snake), she must move her piece to the space at the end of the arrow (for example, a player ending her move on space 87 must move her piece all the way down to 24).

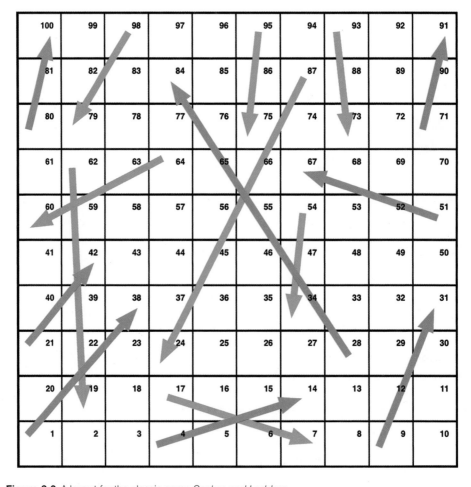

Figure 2.2 A layout for the classic game *Snakes and Ladders*

5. Jack Botermans, *The Book of Games: Strategy, Tactics, & History* (New York / London: Sterling, 2008), 19.

In the board layout depicted in Figure 2.2, the positioning of the snakes and ladders is very important. Here are just a few examples of how:

- There is a ladder from 1 to 38. This enables a player who rolls a 1 on her first turn (which would normally feel unlucky) to move immediately to 38 and gain a strong lead.

- There are three snakes in the final row of the game (93 to 73, 95 to 75, and 98 to 79). These serve to slow any player who is nearing the end of the game.

- The snake 87 to 24 and the ladder 28 to 84 form an interesting pair. If a player lands on 28 and moves to 84, her opponents can hope that she will subsequently land on 87 and be forced back to 24. Contrastingly, if a player lands on 87 and moves to 24, she can then hope to land on 28 and be moved back up to 84.

Each of these examples of snake and ladder placement are based on building hope in players and helping them to believe that dramatic changes in position are possible in the game. If the snakes and ladders were absent from the board, a player who was significantly behind the others would have little hope of catching up.

In this original version of the game, the desired aesthetic is for the players to experience hope, reversal of fortune, and excitement in a game in which the players never make any choices. The *mechanic* is the inclusion of the snakes and the ladders, and the *dynamic* is the intersection of the two where the act of the players encountering the mechanics leads to the *aesthetic* feelings of hope and excitement.

Modifying Snakes and Ladders for More Strategic Play

Young adult and adult players often look for more challenge in games and want to feel that they have won a game not by chance but by making strategic choices along the way. Given that we as designers want the game to feel more strategic and intentional, it is possible to modify the rules (an element of the mechanics) without changing the board to achieve this aesthetic change. One example of this would be accomplished by adding the following rules:

1. Players each control two pieces instead of one.

2. On her turn, each player rolls two dice.

3. She may either use both dice for one piece or one die for each piece.

4. She may alternatively sacrifice one die and use the other to move one opponent's piece backward the number of spaces shown on the die.

5. If a player's piece lands on the same space as any opponent's piece, the opponent's piece is knocked down one row. (For example, a piece knocked off of 48 would fall to 33, and a piece knocked off 33 would fall to 28 and then take the ladder up to 84!)

6. If a player's piece lands on the same space as her own other piece, the other piece is knocked up one row. (For example, a piece knocked off of 61 could be knocked up to 80 and then follow the ladder to 100!)

These changes allow for a lot more strategic decision making on the part of the players (a change to the dynamic play of the game). With rules 4 and 5 in particular, it is possible to directly hurt or help other players,[6] which can lead to players forming alliances or grudges. Rules 1 through 3 also allow for more strategic decisions and make the game much less susceptible to chance. With the choice of which die to use for either piece, and the option for a player to choose to not move her own pieces, a smart player will never be forced to move her own piece onto a snake.

This is but one of many demonstrations of how designers can modify mechanics to change dynamic play and achieve aesthetic goals.

Formal, Dramatic, and Dynamic Elements

Where MDA seeks to help both designers and game critics better understand and discuss games, the framework of formal, dramatic, and dynamic elements[7] was created by Tracy Fullerton and Chris Swain to help students in their Game Design Workshop class at the University of Southern California more effectively design games.

This framework breaks games down into three types of elements:

- **Formal elements:** The elements that make games different from other forms of media or interaction and provide the structure of a game. Formal elements include things like rules, resources, and boundaries.

- **Dramatic elements:** The story and narrative of the game, including the premise. Dramatic elements tie the game together, help players understand the rules, and encourage the player to become emotionally invested in the outcome of the game.

- **Dynamic elements:** The game in motion. After players turn the rules into actual gameplay, the game has moved into dynamic elements. Dynamic elements include things like strategy, behavior, and relationships between game entities. It is important to note that this is related to the use of the term *dynamics* in MDA but is broader because it includes more than just the runtime behavior of the mechanics.

---

6. An example of how this could be used to help another player would be a situation in which knocking another player's piece down a row would land the piece on the beginning of a ladder.

7. Tracy Fullerton, Christopher Swain, and Steven Hoffman. *Game Design Workshop: A Playcentric Approach to Creating Innovative Games, 2nd ed.* (Boca Raton, FL: Elsevier Morgan Kaufmann, 2008).

Formal Elements

Game Design Workshop proposes seven formal elements of games that differentiate them from other forms of media:

- **Player interaction pattern:** How do the players interact? Is the game single-player, one-on-one, team versus team, multilateral (multiple players versus each other, as is the case in most board games), unilateral (one player versus all the other players like some *Mario Party* minigames or the board game *Scotland Yard*), cooperative play, or even multiple individual players each working against the same system?

- **Objectives:** What are the players trying to achieve in the game? When has someone won the game?

- **Rules:** Rules limit the players' actions by telling them what they may and may not do in the game. Many rules are explicitly written and included in the game, but others are implicitly understood by all players. (For example, no rule says so, but it's implicitly understood that you can't steal money from the bank in *Monopoly*.)

- **Procedures:** The types of actions taken by the players in the game. A rule in *Snakes and Ladders* tells you to roll the die and move the number of spaces shown. The procedure dictated by that rule is the actual action of rolling the die and moving the piece. Procedures are often defined by the interaction of a number of rules. Some are also outside of the rules; though it is not explicitly dictated in the rules of poker, bluffing is an important procedure in the game.

- **Resources:** Resources are elements that have value in the game. These include things like money, health, items, and property.

- **Boundaries:** Where does the game end and reality begin? In his book *Homo Ludens,* Johan Huizinga describes how games create a temporary world where the rules of the game apply rather than the rules of the ordinary world, something that has come to be known as the "magic circle." In a sport like football or ice hockey, the magic circle is defined by the boundaries of the playing field; but in an alternative reality game like *I Love Bees* (the ARG for *Halo 2*), the boundaries are more vague.

- **Outcome:** How did the game end? There are both final and incremental outcomes in games. In a zero-sum game like chess, the final outcome is that one player wins and the other loses. In a pen-and-paper roleplaying game like *Dungeons & Dragons*, there are incremental outcomes when a player defeats an enemy or gains a level, and even death is often not a final outcome because it is possible to resurrect players.

According to Fullerton, another way to look at formal elements is that the game ceases to exist when they are removed. If one removes the rules, outcome, and so on from a game, it ceases to be a game.

Dramatic Elements

Dramatic elements help make the rules and resources more understandable to players and can give players greater emotional investment in the game.

Fullerton presents three types of dramatic elements:

- **Premise:** The basic story of the game world. In *Monopoly*, the premise is that each of the players is a real-estate developer trying to get a monopoly on corporate real estate in Atlantic City, New Jersey. In *Donkey Kong*, the player is trying to single-handedly save Pauline from a gorilla that has kidnapped her. The premise forms the basis around which the rest of the game's narrative is built.

- **Character:** Characters are the individuals around whom the story revolves, be it the nameless and largely undefined silent first-person protagonist of games like *Quake* or a character like Nathan Drake, from the *Uncharted* series of games, who is as deep and multidimensional as the lead characters in most movies. Unlike movies, where the goal of the director is to encourage the audience to have empathy for the film's protagonist, in games, the player actually *is* the protagonist character, and designers must choose whether the protagonist will act as an *avatar* for the player (conveying the emotions, desires, and intentions of the player into the world of the game and following the wishes of the player) or as a *role* that the player must take on (so that instead the player acts out the wishes of the game character). The latter is the most common of the two and is much simpler to implement.

- **Story:** The plot of the game. Story encompasses the actual narrative that takes place through the course of the game. The premise sets the stage on which the story takes place.

One of the central purposes of dramatic elements that is not specifically covered in the preceding three types is that of helping the player to better understand the rules. In the board game *Snakes and Ladders*, the fact that the green arrows in our diagram are called "ladders" in the game implies that players are meant to move up them. In 1943, when Milton Bradley began publishing the game in the United States, they changed the name to *Chutes and Ladders*.[8] Presumably, this helped American children to better grasp the rules of the game because the chutes (which look like playground slides) were a more obvious path downward than the original snakes, just as the ladders were an obvious path upward.

In addition to this, many versions of the game have included images of a child doing a good deed at the bottom of a ladder and an image of her being rewarded for doing so at the top

---

8. About.com entry on *Chutes and Ladders* versus *Snakes and Ladders*: http://boardgames.about.com/od/gamehistories/p/chutes_ladders.htm. Last accessed March 1, 2014.

of the ladder. Conversely, the top of chutes depicted a child misbehaving, and the bottom of the chute showed her being punished for doing so. In this way, the narrative embedded in the board also sought to encourage the moral standards of 1940s America. Dramatic elements cover both the ability of the embedded narrative to help players remember rules (as in the case of the snakes being replaced by chutes) and the ability of the game narrative to convey meaning to the players that persists outside of the game (as was intended by the images of good and bad deeds and their consequences).

Dynamic Elements

Dynamic elements are those that occur only when the game is being played. The core concepts of Fullerton's dynamic game elements are:

- **Emergence:** Collisions of seemingly simple rules can lead to unpredictable outcomes. Even an incredibly simplistic game like *Snakes and Ladders* can lead to unexpected dynamic experiences. If one player of the game happened to exclusively land on ladders throughout the game while another exclusively landed on snakes, each would have a very different experience of the game. If you consider the six "more strategic" rules proposed earlier in this chapter, you can easily imagine that the range of gameplay experienced by players would expand due to the new rules. (For example, now, instead of just fate being against player A, perhaps player B would choose to attack A at every possible opportunity, leading to a very negative play experience for A.) Simple rules lead to complex and unpredictable behavior. One of a game designer's most important jobs is to attempt to understand the emergent implications of the rules in a game.

- **Emergent narrative:** In addition to the dynamic behavior of mechanics covered in the MDA model, Fullerton's model also recognizes that narrative can also be dynamic, with a fantastic breadth of narratives emerging from the gameplay itself. Games, by their nature, put players in extra-normal situations, and as a result, they can lead to interesting stories. This is one of the central appeals of pen-and-paper roleplaying games like *Dungeons & Dragons*, in which a single player acts as the Dungeon Master and crafts a scenario for the other players to experience and characters for them to interact with. This is different from the embedded narrative covered by Fullerton's dramatic elements and is one of the entertainment possibilities that is unique to interactive experiences.

- **Playtesting is the only way to understand dynamics:** Experienced game designers can often make better predictions about dynamic behavior and emergence than novice designers, but no one understands exactly how the dynamics of a game will play out without playtesting them. The six additional rules proposed for *Snakes and Ladders* seem like they would increase strategic play, but it is only through several rounds of playtests that one could determine the real effect the rules changes would have on the game. Repeated playtesting reveals information about the various dynamic behaviors that a game could have and helps designers understand the range of experiences that could be generated by their game.

The Elemental Tetrad

In *The Art of Game Design: a Book of Lenses,*[9] Jesse Schell describes the elemental tetrad, through which he presents his four basic elements of games:

- **Mechanics:** The rules for interaction between the player and the game. Mechanics are the elements in the tetrad that differentiate games from all noninteractive forms of media (like film or books). Mechanics contain things like rules, objectives, and the other formal elements described by Fullerton. This is different from the *mechanics* presented by MDA because Schell's use of the term differentiates between game mechanics and the underlying technology that enables them.

- **Aesthetics:** Aesthetics describe how the game is perceived by the five senses: vision, sound, smell, taste, and touch. Aesthetics cover everything from the soundtrack of the game to the character models, packaging, and cover art. This is different from MDA's use of the word "*aesthetics*" because MDA uses the word to refer to the emotional response engendered by the game, whereas Schell uses the word to refer to assets that are crafted by the game developers like actual game art and sound.

- **Technology:** This element covers all the underlying technology that makes the game work. Although this most obviously refers to things such as console hardware, computer software, rendering pipelines, and such, it also covers technological elements in board games. Technology in board games can include things like the type and number of dice that are chosen, whether dice or a deck of cards are used as a randomizer, and various stats and tables used to determine the outcome of actions. In fact, the Technology Award at the IndieCade game conference in 2012 went to Zac S. for *Vornheim*, a collection of tools—in the form of a printed book—to be used by game masters when running tabletop roleplaying games set in a city.[10]

- **Story:** Schell uses the term *story* to convey everything covered by Fullerton's dramatic elements, not just what she terms "*story*." Story is the narrative that occurs in your game and includes both premise and characters as well.

Schell arranges these elements into the tetrad shown in Figure 2.3.

---

9. Jesse Schell, *The Art of Game Design: a Book of Lenses* (Boca Raton, FL: CRC Press, 2008).

10. http://www.indiecade.com/2012/award_winners/.

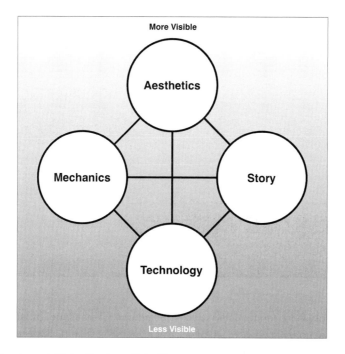

Figure 2.3 The elemental tetrad by Jesse Schell[11]

The tetrad shows how the four elements all interrelate with each other. In addition, Schell points out that the aesthetics of the game are always very visible to the player (again, this is different from the aesthetic feelings described in MDA), and the technology of the game is the least visible with players generally having a better understanding of the game mechanics (e.g., the way that snakes and ladders affect the position of the player) than game technology (e.g., the probability distribution of a pair of six-sided dice). Schell's tetrad does not touch on dynamic play of the game and is more about the static elements of the game as it comes in a box (in the case of a board game) or on disk. Schell's elemental tetrad is discussed and expanded considerably in the next chapter as it forms the elemental aspect of the Layered Tetrad.

Summary

Each of these frameworks for understanding games and interactive art approaches the understanding of games from a different perspective:

- MDA seeks to demonstrate and concretize the idea that players and designers approach games from different directions and proposes that designers can be more effective by learning to see their games from the perspective of their players.

---

11. Adapted from Schell, *The Art of Game Design*, 42.

- The Formal, Dramatic, and Dynamic elements framework breaks game design into specific components that can each be considered and improved. It is meant to be a designer's toolkit and to enable designers to isolate and examine all the parts of their games that could be improved. FDD also asserts the primacy of narrative in player experience.

- The Elemental Tetrad is more of a game developer's view on games. It separates the basic elements of a game into the sections that are generally assigned to various teams: game designers handle mechanics, artists handle aesthetics, writers handle story, and programmers handle technology.

The following chapter presents the Layered Tetrad as a combination of and expansion on the ideas presented in all of these frameworks. It is important to understand these frameworks as the underlying body of theory that led to the Layered Tetrad, and I strongly recommend reading the original paper and books in which they were presented.

CHAPTER 3

THE LAYERED TETRAD

The previous chapter presented you with various analytical frameworks for understanding games and game design. This chapter presents the Layered Tetrad, a combination and extension of many of the best aspects of those frameworks. Each layer of the Layered Tetrad is further expanded in one of the following chapters.

The Layered Tetrad tool helps you understand and create the various aspects of a game. It helps you analyze games you love and look at your game holistically, leading to an understanding of not only the game's mechanics but also their implications in terms of play, socialization, meaning, and culture.

The Layered Tetrad is an expansion and combination of the ideas expressed by the three game analysis frameworks presented in the previous chapter. The Layered Tetrad does not define what a game is. Rather, it is a tool to help you understand all the different elements that need to be designed to create a game and what happens to those elements both during play and beyond as the game becomes part of culture.

The Layered Tetrad is composed of four elements—as was Schell's elemental tetrad—but those four elements are experienced through three layers. The first two layers—*inscribed and dynamic*—are based on the division between Fullerton's formal and dynamic elements. In addition, a third *cultural* layer is added that covers the game's life and effects outside of play, providing a link between game and culture that is critical to understand for us to be responsible game designers and creators of meaningful art.

Each of the layers is described briefly in this chapter, and each layer has a chapter devoted to it later in the book.

The Inscribed Layer

The *inscribed* layer of the tetrad (see Figure 3.1) is very similar to Schell's elemental tetrad. The definitions of the four elements are similar to Schell's, but they are limited to the aspects of the game that exist when the game is not being played.

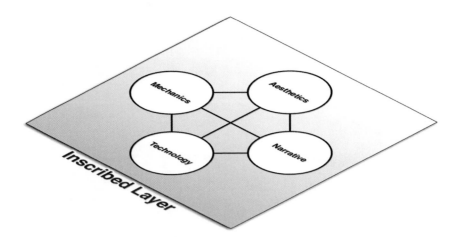

Figure 3.1 The inscribed layer of the Layered Tetrad[1]

- **Mechanics:** The systems that define how the player and the game will interact. This includes the rules of the game and the following additional formal elements from Fullerton's book: player interaction patterns, objectives, resources, and boundaries.

---

1. Adapted from: Jesse Schell, *The Art of Game Design: A Book of Lenses* (Boca Raton, FL: CRC Press, 2008), 42.

- **Aesthetics:** Aesthetics describe how the game looks, sounds, smells, tastes, and feels. Aesthetics cover everything from the soundtrack of the game to the character models, packaging, and cover art. This definition differs from the use of the word "*aesthetics*" in the MDA (Mechanics, Dynamics, Aesthetics) framework because the MDA used the word to refer to the emotional response engendered by the game, whereas Schell and I use the word to refer to game elements that are sensed by the player such as art and sound assets.

- **Technology:** Just as with Schell's technology element, this element covers all the underlying technology that makes the game work for both paper and electronic games. For digital games, the technology element is primarily developed by programmers, but it is vital for designers to understand this element because the technology written by programmers forms the possibility space of decisions that can be made by game designers. This understanding is also critical because a seemingly simple design decision (for example, let's move this level from solid ground onto a rocking ship in a massive storm) can require thousands of hours of development time to implement.

- **Narrative:** Schell uses the term "*story*" in his elemental tetrad, but I've chosen to use the broader term "*narrative*" to encompass the premise and characters in addition to the plot and to be more in line with Fullerton's use of these terms. The inscribed narrative includes all pre-scripted story and pre-generated characters that are in the game.

The Dynamic Layer

As in Fullerton's book *Game Design Workshop,* the *dynamic layer* (see Figure 3.2) emerges when the game is played.

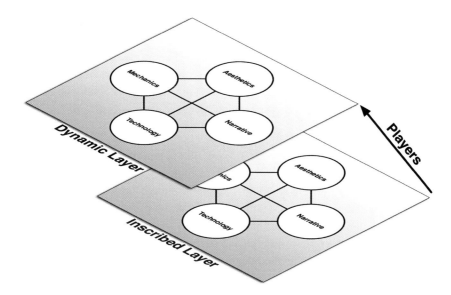

Figure 3.2 The dynamic layer positioned relative to the inscribed layer

As you can see in the figure, it is players who take the static inscribed layer of the game and from it construct the dynamic layer. Everything in the dynamic layer arises from the game during play, and the dynamic layer is composed of both elements in the players' direct control and of the results of their interaction with the inscribed elements. The dynamic layer is the realm of *emergence*, the phenomenon of complex behavior arising from seemingly simple rules. The emergent behavior of a game is often difficult to predict, but one of the great skills of game design that you will build over time is the ability to do so, or at least make pretty good guesses. The four dynamic elements are:

- **Mechanics:** Whereas inscribed mechanics covers rules, objectives, and so on, the dynamic mechanics cover how the players interact with those inscribed elements. Dynamic mechanics include procedures, strategies, emergent game behavior, and eventually the outcome of the game.

- **Aesthetics:** Dynamic aesthetics cover the way that aesthetic elements are generated for the player during play. This includes everything from procedural art (digital game art or music generated on the fly by computer code) to the physical strain that can result from having to mash a button repeatedly over a long period of time.

- **Technology:** Dynamic technology describes the behavior of the technological components of a game during play. This covers how a pair of dice never actually seems to generate the smooth bell curve of results predicted by mathematical probability. It also covers nearly everything that is done by computer code in digital games. One specific example of this could be the performance of the game's artificial intelligence code for enemies, but in its broadest sense, dynamic technology covers absolutely everything that a digital game's code does after the game has been launched.

- **Narrative:** Dynamic narrative refers to stories that emerge procedurally out of game systems. This can mean an individual player's path through a branching scripted narrative such as *L.A. Noire* or *Heavy Rain*, the family story created by a play through *The Sims*, or the stories generated by team play with other human players. In 2013, the Boston Red Sox baseball team went from worst to first in a story that mirrored the city of Boston's recovery from the bombing at the 2013 Boston Marathon. That kind of story, enabled by the rules of professional baseball, also fits under dynamic narrative.

The Cultural Layer

The third and final layer of the Layered Tetrad is cultural, and it describes the game beyond play (see Figure 3.3). The cultural layer covers both the impact of culture upon the game and the impact of the game upon culture. The community of players around the game moves it into the cultural layer, and at this point players actually have more control and ownership over the game than the designers, and it is through this layer that our societal responsibility as designers becomes clear.

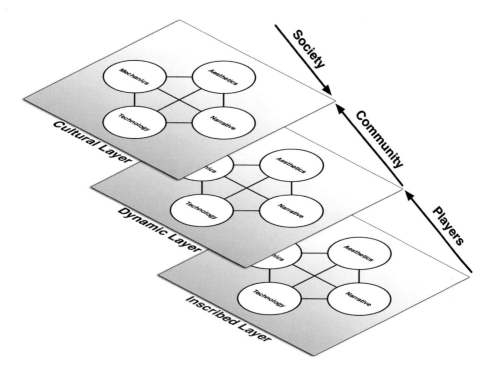

Figure 3.3 The cultural layer exists at the collision of the game and society

The delineations between the four elements are much blurrier in the cultural layer, but it is still worthwhile to approach this layer through the lens of the four elements:

- **Mechanics:** The simplest form of cultural mechanics is represented by things like *game mods* (modifications to a game that are created by players to affect the inscribed mechanics of the game). This also covers things as complex as the impact that the emergent play of a game can have on society. For instance, the much-maligned ability for the player character in *Grand Theft Auto 3* to sleep with a prostitute and then kill her to get his money back was a result of emergent dynamic mechanics in the game, but it had a massive impact on the perception of the game by the general public (which is part of the cultural layer).

- **Aesthetics:** As with the mechanics, cultural aesthetics can cover things like fan art, remixes of the music for the game or other aesthetic fan activities like *cosplay* (short for costume play, when fans of the game dress in costume to resemble game characters). One key point here is that *authorized* transmedia properties (i.e., a conversion of the game's intellectual property [IP] to another medium by the owners of that IP, such as the movie version of *Tomb Raider*, a *Pokémon* lunchbox, etc.) are not part of the cultural layer. This is because authorized transmedia properties are controlled by the original owners of the game's intellectual property, whereas cultural aesthetics are controlled and created by the community of the game's players.

- **Technology:** Cultural technology covers both the use of game technologies for non-game purposes (e.g., flocking algorithms for game characters could also be used in robotics) and the ability of technology to affect the game experience. Back in the days of the NES (Nintendo Entertainment System), having an Advantage or Max controller gave the player the ability to press turbo buttons (which was an automated method of pressing the regular A or B controller buttons very rapidly). This was a massive advantage in some games and had an effect on the game experience. Cultural technology also covers the expansion of possibilities of what the word "*game*" can mean by continually expanding the possibility space of gaming and the technological aspects of mods made by players to alter the inscribed elements of a game.

- **Narrative:** Cultural narrative encompasses the narrative aspects of fan-made transmedia properties created from the game (e.g., fan fiction, the narratives of fan-made tribute movies, and the fan-made characters and premises that are part of some game mods). It also covers the stories told about the game in culture and society, including both the stories that vilify games like *Grand Theft Auto* and the stories that extol the virtues and artistic merit of games like *Journey* and *Ico*.

The Responsibility of the Designer

All designers are aware of their responsibility for the inscribed layer of the game. It's obvious that the developers of the game must include clear rules, interesting art, and so on to enable and encourage players to play a game.

At the dynamic layer, some designers get a little muddier about their responsibility. Some designers are surprised by the behavior that emerges out of their games and want to pass responsibility for that behavior on to the players. For example, a few years ago, Valve decided to give hats to players of their game *Team Fortress 2*. The mechanic they chose was to randomly reward hats to players who were logged in at randomly selected times. Because the distribution of hats was based exclusively on whether the player was logged in to a game at the right time, servers sprouted up that had players camping in them—not actually playing the game—just waiting for hat drops. Valve discovered this behavior and chose to punish the players for it by taking hats back from any player that they suspected of having camped on a server rather than actually playing the game.

One way of interpreting this is to see the players as trying to cheat the game. However, another is to realize that the players were just engaging in the most efficient method for obtaining hats as defined by the rules for hat drops that Valve had created. Because the system was designed to give players hats any time they were online regardless of whether they were actually doing anything, the players settled on the easiest path to get the hats. The players may not have honored the intent of the designers of the hat drop system, but they didn't cheat the system itself. Their dynamic behavior was exactly what was implied by the rules of the system that

Valve set in place. As you can see from this example, the designer is also responsible for the experience at the dynamic layer through the implications of the systems she designs. In fact, one of the most important aspects of game design is the anticipation and crafting of the dynamic player experience. Of course, doing so is a very difficult task, but that's part of what makes it interesting.

So, what is the designer's responsibility at the cultural layer? As a result of most game designers rarely if ever considering the cultural layer, video games are generally regarded in society as puerile and vulgar—selling violence and misogyny to teenage boys. You and I know that this doesn't have to be the case and that it isn't actually true of many or even most games, but this is the ubiquitous perception among the general public. Games can teach, games can empower, and games can heal. Games can promote pro-social behavior and help players learn new skills. A ludic attitude and some quickly devised rules can make even the dullest task enjoyable. As a designer, you are responsible for what your game says to society about gaming and for the impact that it has on players. We have become so good at making games compelling that some players are addicted to them to their detriment. Some designers have even made games that attempted to scam children into spending hundreds or thousands of dollars (eventually leading to a massive class-action lawsuit in at least one case). This kind of behavior by designers damages the reputation of games in society and prevents many people from considering games worthy of either their time or of being regarded as art, and that's truly sad.

I believe that it is our responsibility as designers to promote pro-social, thoughtful behavior through our games and to respect our players and the time that they dedicate to experiencing what we create.

Summary

As demonstrated in this chapter, it's important to explicitly realize that the three layers of the Layered Tetrad represent a transition of ownership from the developers of the game to the players of the game. Everything in the inscribed layer is owned, developed, and implemented by the game designers and developers. The inscribed layer is completely within the developers' control.

The dynamic layer is the point at which the game is actually experienced, so game designers require that players take action and make decisions for the games inscribed by the designers to actually be experienced. Through players' decisions and their effect on game systems, players take some ownership of the experience, yet that experience is still subject to the inscribed decisions of the developers. Thus, the ownership over the dynamic layer is shared between the developers and the players.

At the cultural layer, the game is no longer under the developers' control. This is why things like game mods fit in the cultural layer; through a game mod, a player takes control of and changes inscribed aspects of the game. Of course, most of the original inscribed game still remains, but the player (as mod developer) determines which inscribed elements she chooses to leave and which she chooses to replace; the player is in control. This is also why I have excluded authorized transmedia from the cultural layer. The developers and owners of the inscribed game maintain ownership over the authorized transmedia, and the cultural layer is defined by the shift of ownership to the players and the communities that surround the game. Additionally, the aspect of the cultural layer that covers the perception of the game by non-players in society is also largely controlled by the player community's representation of their gameplay experience. People who don't play a game have their opinion of that game shaped by the media they read, which was (hopefully) written by people who did actually play the game. However, even though the cultural layer is largely controlled by players, the developers and designers of a game still have an important influence over and responsibility for the game and its effect on society.

The next three chapters each cover one layer of the Layered Tetrad and reveal it in more detail.

CHAPTER 4

THE INSCRIBED LAYER

This is the first of three chapters that explore the layers of the Layered Tetrad in greater depth.

As you learned in Chapter 3, "The Layered Tetrad," the inscribed layer covers all elements that are directly designed and encoded by game developers.

In this chapter, we look at the inscribed aspects of all four elements: mechanics, aesthetics, narrative, and technology.

Inscribed Mechanics

The inscribed mechanics are most of what one would think of as the traditional job of the game designer. In board games, this includes designing the board layout, the rules, the various cards that might be used, and any tables that could be consulted. Much of the inscribed mechanics are described very well by Tracy Fullerton's book *Game Design Workshop* in her chapter on formal elements of games, and for the sake of lexical solidarity (and my distaste for every game design book using different terminology), I reuse her terminology throughout this section of the chapter as much as the Layered Tetrad framework allows.

In Chapter 2, "Game Analysis Frameworks," I listed seven formal elements of games that were presented in *Game Design Workshop*: player interaction patterns, objectives, rules, procedures, resources, boundaries, and outcomes. In the formal, dramatic, and dynamic elements framework, these seven elements constitute the aspects that make games different from other media.

Inscribed mechanics are a bit different from this, though there is a lot of overlap because mechanics is the element of the tetrad that is unique to games. However, the core of the inscribed layer is that everything in it is intentionally designed by a game developer, and the mechanics are no exception. As a result of this, inscribed mechanics does not include procedures or outcomes (although they are part of Fullerton's formal elements) because both are controlled by the player and therefore part of the dynamic layer. We'll also add a couple of new elements to give us the following list of inscribed mechanical elements:

- **Objectives:** Objectives cover the goals of the players in the game. What are the players trying to accomplish?
- **Player relationships:** Player relationships define the ways that players combat and collaborate with each other and the game. How do the players' objectives intersect, and does this cause them to collaborate or compete?
- **Rules:** Rules specify and limit player actions. What can and can't the players do to achieve their objective?
- **Boundaries:** Boundaries define the limits of the game and relate directly to the magic circle. Where are the edges of the game? Where does the magic circle exist?
- **Resources:** Resources include assets or values that are relevant within the boundaries of the game. What does the player own in-game that enables her in-game actions?
- **Spaces:** Spaces define the shape of the game space and the possibilities for interaction therein. This is most obvious in board games, where the board itself is the space of the game.
- **Tables:** Tables define the statistical shape of the game. How do players level up as they grow in power? What moves are available to a player at a given time?

All of these inscribed mechanical elements interact with each other, and overlap certainly exists between them (e.g., the tech tree in *Civilization* is a table that is navigated like a space). The purpose of dividing them into these seven categories for this book is to help you as a designer think about the various possibilities for design in your game. Not all games have all elements, but as with the "lenses" in Jesse Schell's book *The Art of Game Design: A Book of Lenses,* these inscribed mechanical elements are seven different ways to look at the various things that you can design for a game.

Objectives

Although many games have an apparently simple objective—to win the game—in truth, every player constantly weighs several objectives every moment of your game. These can be categorized based on their immediacy and their import to the player, and some objectives may be considered very important to one player while being less important to another.

Immediacy of Objectives

As shown in the image in Figure 4.1 from the beautiful game *Journey* by thatgamecompany (TGC), nearly every screen of a modern game presents the player with short-, mid-, and long-term objectives.

Figure 4.1 Short-, mid-, and long-term objectives in the first level of *Journey* with objectives highlighted in green, blue, and purple respectively

- **Short-term objectives:** The player wants to charge her scarf (which enables flying in *Journey*), so she is singing (the white sphere around her) to draw the highlighted scarf pieces to her. She also is drawn to explore the nearby building.
- **Mid-term objectives:** Three additional structures can be seen near the horizon. Because the rest of the desert is largely barren, the player is attracted to these ruins and is very likely to head toward one of them (this *indirect guidance* strategy is used several times throughout *Journey* and is analyzed in Chapter 13, "Guiding the Player").

■ **Long-term objectives:** In the first few minutes of the game, the player is shown the mountain with the shaft of light (shown in the top-left corner of Figure 4.1), and her long-term goal throughout the game is to reach the top of this mountain.

Importance of Objectives

Just as objectives vary in immediacy, they also vary in importance to the player. An open-world game like *Skyrim* by Bethesda Game Studios has both primary and optional objectives. Some players may choose to exclusively seek the primary objectives and can play through *Skyrim* in as little as 10 to 20 hours, whereas others who want to explore various side quests and optional objectives can spend more than 400 hours in the game without exhausting the content (and even without finishing the primary objectives). Optional objectives are often tied to specific types of gameplay; in *Skyrim*, a whole series of missions exists for players who want to join the Thieves Guild and specialize in stealth and theft. Other series of missions are also available for those who want to focus on archery or melee[1] combat. This ensures that the game can adapt to the varying gameplay styles of different players.

Conflicting Objectives

As a player, the objectives that you have will often conflict with each other or compete for the same resources. In a game like *Monopoly*, the overall objective of the game is to finish the game with the most money, but you must give up money to purchase assets like property, houses, and hotels that will eventually make you more money later. Looking at the design goal of presenting the player with interesting choices, a lot of the most interesting choices that a player can make are those that are *double-edged*, benefitting one objective while hurting another.

Approaching it from a more pragmatic perspective, each objective in the game takes time to complete, and a player may only have a certain amount of time that she is willing to devote to the game. Returning to the *Skyrim* example, many people (myself included) never finished the main quest of *Skyrim* because they spent all of their time playing the side quests and lost track of the urgency of the main story. Presumably, the goal of *Skyrim's* designers was to allow each player to form her own story as she played through the game—and it's possible that the designers wouldn't care that I hadn't finished the main quest as long as I enjoyed playing the game—but as a player, I felt that the game ended not with a bang but a whimper as the layers upon layers of quests I was given had seemingly smaller and smaller returns. If, as a designer, it's important to you that your players complete the main quest of the game, you need to make sure that the player is constantly reminded of the urgency of the task and (unlike many open world games) you might need to have consequences for the player if she does not complete the main quest in a timely manner. As an example, in the classic game *Star Control*, if the player did not save a certain alien species within a given amount of time from the start of the game, the species' planet actually disappeared from the universe.

---

1. This is a word that is often mispronounced by gamers. The French word *melee* is pronounced "may-lay." The word *mealy* (pronounced "mee-lee") means either pale or in some other way like grain meal (e.g., cornmeal).

Player Relationships

Just as an individual player has several objectives in mind at any given time, the objectives that players have also determine relationships between them.

Player Interaction Patterns

In *Game Design Workshop*, Fullerton lists seven different player interaction patterns:

- **Single player versus game:** The player has the objective of beating the game.
- **Multiple individual players versus game:** Several co-located players each have the objective of beating the game, but they have little or no interaction with each other. This can often be seen in MMOs (massively multiplayer online roleplaying games [also seen as "MMORPGs"]) such as *World of Warcraft* when players each seek to succeed at their missions in the same game world but are not required to interact with each other.
- **Cooperative play:** Multiple players share the common objective of beating the game together.
- **Player versus player:** Each of two players has the objective of defeating the other.
- **Multilateral competition:** The same as player versus player, except that there are more than two players, and each player is trying to defeat all the others.
- **Unilateral competition:** One player versus a team of other players. An example is the board game *Scotland Yard* (also called *Mr. X*), where one player plays a criminal trying to evade the police and the other 2 to 4 players of the game are police officers trying to collaborate to catch the criminal.
- **Team competition:** Two teams of players, each with the objective of beating the other.

Some games, such as BioWare's *Mass Effect*, provide computer-controlled allies for the player. In terms of designing player interaction patterns, you can think of these computer-controlled allies either as an element of the single player's abilities in the game or as proxies for other players that could play the game, so a designer could approach a single-player game with computer-controlled allies either as single player versus game or as cooperative play.

Objectives Define Player Relationships and Roles

In addition to the interaction patterns listed in the preceding section, various combinations of them also exist, and in several games, one player might be another player's ally at one point and their competitor at another. For example, when trading money for property in a game such as *Monopoly*, two players make a brief alliance with each other, even though the game is primarily multilateral competition.

At any time, the relationship of each player to the game and to other players is defined by the combination of all the players' layered objectives. These relationships lead each player to play one of several different roles:

- **Protagonist:** The protagonist role is that of the player trying to conquer the game.
- **Competitor:** The player trying to conquer other players. This is usually done solely to win the game, but in rare cases can be done on behalf of the game (e.g., in the 2004 board

game *Betrayal at House on the Hill*, partway through the game, one of the players is turned evil and then must try to kill the other players).

- **Collaborator:** The player working to aid other players.

- **Citizen:** The player in the same world as other players but not really collaborating or competing with them.

In many multiplayer games, all players will play each of these roles at different times, and as you'll see when we look into the dynamic layer, different types of players prefer different roles.

Rules

Rules limit the players' actions. Rules are also the most direct inscription of the designer's concept of how the game should be played. In the written rules of a board game, the designer attempts to inscribe and encode the experience that she wants for the players to have when they play the game. Later, the players decode these rules through play and hopefully experience something like what the designer intended.

Unlike paper games, digital games usually have very few inscribed rules that are read directly by the player; however, the programming code written by game developers is another way of encoding rules that will be decoded through play. Because rules are the most direct method through which the game designer communicates with the player, rules act to define many of the other elements. The money in *Monopoly* only has value because the rules declare that players can use it to buy assets and other resources.

Explicitly written rules are the most obvious form of rules, but implicit rules also exist. For example, when you play poker, an implicit rule is that you shouldn't hide cards up your sleeve. This is not explicitly stated in the rules of poker, but every player understands that doing so would be cheating.[2]

Boundaries

Boundaries define the edges of the space and time in which the game takes place. Within the boundaries, the rules and other aspects of the game apply: poker chips are worth something, it is okay to slam into other hockey players on the ice, and which car crosses an arbitrary line on the ground first matters. Sometimes, boundaries are physical, like the wall around a hockey rink. Other times, boundaries are less obvious. When someone plays an ARG (Alternate Reality Game),

---

2. This is a good example of one of the differences between single-player and multiplayer game design. In a multiplayer poker game, concealing a card would be cheating and could ruin the game. However, in the game *Red Dead Redemption* by Rockstar Studios, the in-game poker tournaments become much more interesting and entertaining once the player acquires the suit of clothes that allows her character to conceal and swap poker cards at will, with a risk of being discovered by NPCs (Non-Player Characters).

the point of playing the game is that it surrounds and permeates the player's normal life. In one of the first ARGs, *Majestic* (a 2001 game by Electronic Arts), players of the game gave EA their phone number, fax number, email address, and home address and then would receive phone calls, faxes, and so on at all times of the day from characters in the game. The intent of the game was to blur the boundaries between gaming and everyday life.

Resources

Resources are things of value in a game. These can be either *assets* (in-game objects) or non-material *attributes*. Assets in games include things such as the equipment that Link has collected in a *Legend of Zelda* game; the resource cards that players earn in the board game *Settlers of Catan*; and the houses, hotels, and property deeds that players purchase in *Monopoly*. Attributes often include things such as health, the amount of air left when swimming under water, and experience points. Because money is so versatile and ubiquitous, it is somewhere between the two. A game can have physical money assets (like the cash in *Monopoly*), or it can have a nonphysical money attribute (like the amount of money that a player has in *Grand Theft Auto*).

Spaces

Designers are often tasked with creating navigable spaces. This includes both designing the board for a board game and designing virtual levels in a digital game. In both cases, you want to think about both flow through the space and making the areas of the space unique and interesting. Things to keep in mind when designing spaces include the following:

- **The purpose of the space:** Architect Christopher Alexander spent years researching why some spaces were particularly well suited to their use and why others weren't. He distilled this knowledge into the concept of *design patterns* in his book *A Pattern Language*,[3] which explored various patterns for good architectural spaces. The purpose of that book was to put forward a series of patterns that others could use to make a space that correctly matched the use for which it was intended.

- **Flow**: Does your space allow the player to move through it easily, or if it does restrict movement, is there a good reason? In the board game *Clue*, players roll a single die each turn to determine how far they can move. This can make it very slow to move about the game board. (The board is 24 x 25 spaces, so with an average roll of 3.5, it could take 7 turns to cross the board.) Realizing this, the designers added secret passages that allow players to teleport from each corner of the board to the opposite corner, which helped flow through the mansion quite a bit.

- **Landmarks:** It is more difficult for players to create a mental map of 3D virtual spaces than actual spaces through which they have walked in real life. Because of this, it is important

---

3. Christopher Alexander, Sara Ishikawa, and Murray Silverstein, *A Pattern Language: Towns, Buildings, Construction* (New York: Oxford University Press, 1977).

that you create landmarks in your virtual spaces that players can use to more easily orient themselves. In Honolulu, Hawaii, people don't give directions in terms of compass directions (north, south, east, and west) because these are not terribly obvious unless it's sunrise or sunset. Instead, the people of Honolulu navigate by obvious landmarks: *mauka* (the mountains to the northeast), *makai* (the ocean to the southwest), Diamond Head (the landmark mountain to the southeast), and Ewa (the area to the northwest). On other parts of the Hawaiian Islands, *mauka* means inland and *makai* means toward the ocean, regardless of compass direction (islands being circular). Making landmarks that players can easily see limits the number of times your players need to consult the map to figure out where they are.

- **Experiences:** The game as a whole is an experience, but the map or space of the game also needs to be sprinkled with interesting experiences for your players. In *Assassin's Creed 4: Black Flag*, the world map is a vastly shrunken version of the Caribbean Sea. Even though the actual Caribbean has many miles of empty ocean between islands that would take a sailing vessel hours or days to cross, the Caribbean of *AC4* has events sprinkled throughout it that ensure that the player will encounter a chance to have an experience several times each minute. These could be small experiences such as finding a single treasure chest on a tiny atoll, or large experiences such as coming across a fleet of enemy ships.

- **Short-, mid-, and long-term objectives:** As demonstrated in the screen shot from *Journey* shown in Figure 4.1, your space can contain multiple levels of goals. In open-world games, a player is often shown a high-level enemy early on so that she has something to aspire to defeat later in the game. Many games also clearly mark areas of the map as easy, medium, or high difficulty.

Tables

Tables are a critical part of game balance, particularly when designing modern digital games. Put simply, tables are grids of data that are often synonymous with spreadsheets, but tables can be used to design and illustrate many different things:

- **Probability:** Tables can be used to determine probability in very specific situations. In the board game *Tales of the Arabian Nights*, the player selects the proper table for the individual creature she has encountered, and it gives her a list of possible reactions that she can have to that encounter and the various results of each of her possible reactions.

- **Progression:** In paper role-playing games (RPGs) such as *Dungeons & Dragons*, tables show how a player's abilities increase and change as her player character's level increases.

- **Playtest Data:** In addition to tables that players use during the game, you as a designer will also create tables to hold playtest data and information about player experiences. You can find more info on this in Chapter 10, "Game Testing."

Of course, tables are also a form of technology in games, so they cross the line between mechanics and technology. Tables as technology include the storage of information and any transformation of information that can happen in the table (e.g., formulae in spreadsheets). Tables as mechanics include the design decisions that game designers make and inscribe into the table.

Inscribed Aesthetics

Inscribed aesthetics are those aesthetic elements that are crafted by the developers of the game. These cover all five senses, and as a designer, you should be aware that throughout the time that your player is playing the game, she will be sensing with all five of her senses.

The Five Aesthetic Senses

Designers must consider all five human senses when inscribing games. These five senses are:

- **Vision:** Of the five senses, vision is the one that gets the most attention from most game development teams. As a result, the fidelity of the visual experience that we can deliver to players has seen more obvious improvement over the past decades than that of any other sense. When thinking about the visible elements of your game, be sure to think beyond the 3D art in the game or the art of the board or cards in a paper game. Realize that everything that players (or potential players) see that has anything to do with your game affects both their impression and their enjoyment of it. Some game developers in the past have put tremendous time into making their in-game art beautiful only to have the game packaged in (and hidden behind) awful box art.

- **Hearing:** Audio in games is second only to video in the amazing level of fidelity that can be delivered to players. All modern consoles can output 5.1-channel sound, and some can do even better than that. Game audio is composed of sound effects, music, and dialogue. Each takes a different amount of time to be interpreted by the player, and each has a different best use. In addition, on a medium-to-large development team, a different artist usually handles each of the three audio types.

Audio Type	Immediacy	Best For
Sound effects	Immediate	Alerting the player; conveying simple information
Music	Medium	Setting the mood
Dialogue	Medium / Long	Conveying complex information

Another aspect of audio to consider is background noise. For mobile games, you can almost always expect that the player is going to be in a non-optimal audio situation when playing your game. Though audio can always add to a game, it's just not prudent to make audio a vital aspect of a mobile game unless it's the core feature of the game (e.g., games such as *Papa Sangre* by Somethin' Else or *Freeq* by Psychic Bunny). You must also consider background noise in computer and console games. Some cooling fans are very loud, which you must take into account when developing quiet audio for digital games.

- **Touch:** Touch is very different between board games and digital games, but in both cases, it's the most direct contact that you have with the player. In a board game, touch comes down to the feel of the playing pieces, cards, board, and so on. Do the pieces for your game feel high quality or do they feel cheap? Often you want them to be the former, but the latter isn't terrible. James Ernst—possibly the most prolific board game designer in the world for several years—ran a company called Cheap Ass Games, the mission of which was to get great games to players at as low a cost to them as possible. To cut costs, playing pieces were made of cheap materials, but this was fine with players because the games from his company cost less than $10 each instead of the $40–$50 that many board games cost. All design decisions are choices; just make sure that you're aware of the options.

  One of the most exciting recent technological advancements for board game prototyping is 3D printing, and many board game designers are starting to print pieces for their game prototypes. There are also several online companies now that can print your game board, cards, or pieces.

  Digital games also have aspects of touch. The way that the controller feels in a player's hands and the amount of fatigue that it causes are definitely aspects that a designer needs to consider. When the fantastic PlayStation 2 game *Okami* was ported to the Nintendo Wii, the designers chose to change the attack command from a button press (the X on the PlayStation controller) to a waggle of the Wiimote (which mimicked the attack gesture from *The Legend of Zelda: Twilight Princess* that had done very well on the Wii). However, while attacks in the heat of battle in *Twilight Princess* happen about once every couple of seconds, attacks in *Okami* happen several times per second, so the attack gesture that worked well in *Twilight Princess* instead caused player fatigue in *Okami*. With the rise of tablet and smartphone gaming, touch and gesture are elements that every digital game designer must consider carefully.

  Another aspect of touch in digital games is rumble-style player feedback. As a designer, you can choose the intensity and style of rumble feedback in most modern console controllers, and some controllers—such as those for the Nintendo Switch—offer tremendous control over rumble feedback.

- **Smell:** Smell is not often a designed aspect of inscribed aesthetics, but it is there. Just as different book printing processes have different smells, so too do different board and card game printing processes. Make sure that you get a sample from your manufacturer before committing to printing 1,000 copies of something that might smell strange.

- **Taste**: Taste factors into even fewer games than smell, yet it is still a factor in some games, including drinking games and some kissing games.

Aesthetic Goals

Humankind has been making art and music since long before the dawn of written history. Therefore, when designing and developing the inscribed aesthetic elements of a game, we as game developers are taking advantage of hundreds of years of cultural understanding of other forms of art. Interactive experiences have the advantages of being able to pull from all of that experience and of allowing us as designers to incorporate all the techniques and knowledge of aesthetic art into the games that we create. However, when we do so, it must be done with a reason, and it must mesh cohesively with the other elements of the game. Two important goals that aesthetic elements can serve well in our games are *mood* and *information*.

- **Mood:** Aesthetics do a fantastic job of helping to set the emotional mood of a game. Though mood can definitely be conveyed through game mechanics, both visual art and music can do a fantastic job of influencing a player's mood much faster than mechanics are able to.

- **Information:** Several informational colors are built in to our psyche as mammals. For example, many species in the animal kingdom perceive the color red or patterns of alternating yellow and black as indicators of danger.[4] In contrast, cool colors like blue and green are usually seen as peaceful.

  In addition, designers can train players to understand various aesthetics as having specific meaning. The LucasArts game *X-Wing* was one of the first to have a soundtrack that was procedurally generated by the in-game situation.[5] The music would rise in intensity to warn the player that enemies were attacking. Similarly, as described in Chapter 13, "Guiding the Player," the Naughty Dog game *Uncharted 3* uses the colors bright blue and yellow throughout the game to help the player identify handholds and footholds for climbing.

Inscribed Narrative

As with all forms of experience, dramatics and narrative are an important part of many interactive experiences. However, game narratives face challenges that are not present in any form of linear media, and as such, writers are still learning how to craft and present interactive narratives. This section explores the components of inscribed dramatics, purposes for which they are used, methods for storytelling in games, and differences between game narrative and linear narrative.

---

4. Warning coloration like this is called *aposematism*, another name for the idea of "warning colors" proposed in 1867 by Alfred Russel Wallace and then published in 1877. Wallace, Alfred Russel (1877). "The Colours of Animals and Plants. I.—The Colours of Animals." Macmillan's Magazine. 36 (215): 384–408.

5. Other very early games with a procedurally generated soundtrack include *Wing Commander* (1990) by Origin Systems and *Monkey Island 2: Le Chuck's Revenge* (1991) by LucasArts.

Components of Inscribed Narrative

In both linear and interactive narrative, the components of the dramatics are the same: premise, setting, character, and plot.

- **Premise:** The premise is the narrative basis from which the story emerges:[6]

  A long time ago in a galaxy far, far away, an intergalactic war is brought to the doorstep of a young moisture farmer who doesn't yet realize the importance of his ancestry or himself.

  Gordon Freeman has no idea about the surprises that are in store for him on his first day of work at the top-secret Black Mesa research facility.

  Edward Kenway must fight and pirate his way to fortune on the high seas of the Caribbean while discovering the secret of the mysterious Observatory, sought by Templars and Assassins alike.

- **Setting:** The setting expands upon the skeleton of the premise to provide a detailed world in which the narrative can take place. The setting can be something as large as a galaxy far, far away or as small as a tiny room beneath the stairs, but it's important that it is believable within the bounds of the premise and that it is internally consistent; if your characters will choose to fight with swords in a world full of guns, you need to have a good reason for it.

  In *Star Wars*, when Obi Wan Kenobi gives the lightsaber to Luke, he explains to Luke and the audience why someone would use a sword in the *Star Wars* universe by stating that it is "not as clumsy or random as a blaster; an elegant weapon for a more civilized age."

- **Character:** Stories are about characters, and the best stories are about characters we care about. Narratively, characters are composed of a backstory and one or more objectives. These combine to give the character a role in the story: protagonist, antagonist, companion, lackey, mentor, and so on.

- **Plot:** Plot is the sequence of events that take place in your narrative. Usually, this takes the form of the protagonist wanting something but having difficulty achieving it because of either an antagonist or an antagonistic situation getting in the way. The plot then becomes the story of how the protagonist attempts to overcome this difficulty or obstruction.

Traditional Dramatics

Though interactive narrative offers many new possibilities to writers and developers, it still generally follows traditional dramatic structures.

Five-Act Structure

German writer Gustav Freytag wrote about five-act structure in his 1863 book *Die Technik des Dramas* (The Technique of Dramas). It described the purpose of the five acts often used by Shakespeare and many of his contemporaries (as well as Roman playwrights) and proposed

---

6. These are the premises of *Star Wars: A New Hope*, *Half-Life*, and *Assassin's Creed 4: Black Flag*.

what has come to be known as Freytag's pyramid (see Figure 4.2). The vertical axes in Figures 4.2 and 4.3 represent the level of audience excitement at that point in the story.

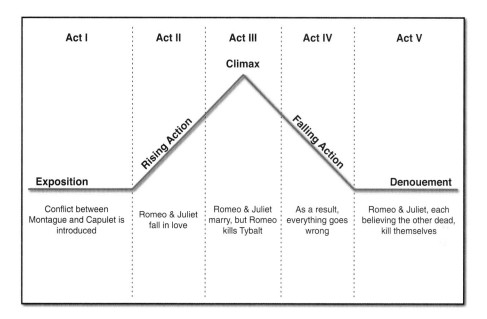

Figure 4.2 Freytag's pyramid of five-act structure showing examples from *Romeo and Juliet* by William Shakespeare

According to Freytag, the acts work as follows:

- **Act I: Exposition:** Introduces the narrative premise, the setting, and the important characters. Act I of William Shakespeare's *Romeo and Juliet* introduces us to Verona, Italy and the feud between the powerful Montague and Capulet families. Romeo is introduced as the son of the Montague family and is infatuated with Rosaline.

- **Act II: Rising action:** Something happens that causes new tension for the important characters, and the dramatic tension rises. Romeo sneaks into the Capulet's ball and is instantly smitten with Juliet, the daughter of the Capulet family.

- **Act III: Climax:** Everything comes to a head, and the outcome of the play is decided. Romeo and Juliet are secretly married, and the local friar hopes that this may lead to peace between their families. However, the next morning, Romeo is accosted by Juliet's cousin Tybalt. Romeo refuses to fight, so his friend Mercutio fights in his stead, and Tybalt accidentally kills Mercutio (because Romeo got in the way). Romeo is furious and chases Tybalt, eventually killing him. Romeo's decision to kill Tybalt is the moment of climax of the play because before that moment, it seemed like everything might work out for the two lovers, and after that moment, the audience knows that things will end horribly.

- **Act IV: Falling action:** The play continues toward its inevitable conclusion. If it's a comedy, things get better; if it's a tragedy, things might appear to be getting better, but inevitably just get worse. The results of the climax are played out for the audience. Romeo is banished from Verona. The friar concocts a plan to allow Romeo and Juliet to escape together. He has Juliet fake her death and sends a message to Romeo to let him know, but the messenger never makes it to Romeo.

- **Act V: Denouement (pronounced "day-new-maw"):** The play resolves. Romeo enters the tomb believing Juliet to be truly dead and kills himself. She immediately awakens to find him dead and then kills herself as well. The families become aware of this tragedy, and everyone weeps, promising to end the feud.

Three-Act Structure

In his books and lectures, American screenwriter Syd Field has proposed another way of understanding traditional narrative in terms of three acts.[7] Between each act, a plot point changes the direction of the story and forces the characters' actions. Figure 4.3 provides an example that is further explained in the following list.

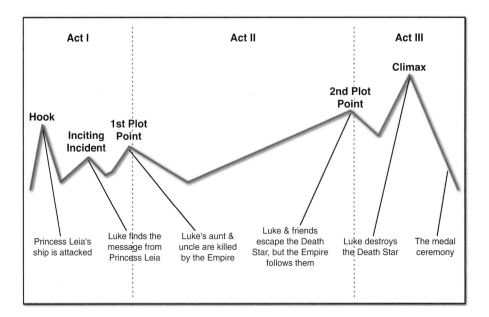

Figure 4.3 Syd Field's three-act structure, with examples from *Star Wars: A New Hope*

---

7. Syd Field, *Screenplay: The Foundations of Screenwriting* (New York: Delta Trade Paperbacks, 2005).

The core elements of Field's three-act structure are:

- **Act I: Exposition:** Introduces the audience to the world of the narrative and presents the premise, setting, and main characters. In Act I of *Star Wars*, Luke is a young, idealistic kid who works on his uncle's moisture farm. Out in the galaxy, a rebellion is happening against a fascist Empire, but he's just a simple farm boy dreaming of flying starfighters.

    - **Hook:** Gets the audience's attention quickly. According to Field, an audience decides in the first few minutes whether they're going to watch a film, so the first few minutes should be really exciting, even if the action in them has nothing to do with the rest of the film
    (e.g., the beginning of any James Bond film). In *Star Wars,* the opening scene of Princess Leia's ship being attacked by a Star Destroyer had some of the best special visual effects that 1977 audiences had ever seen and a fantastic score by John Williams, both of which helped make it an exciting hook.

    - **Inciting Incident:** Something new enters the life of the main character, causing her to start the adventure. Luke is leading a pretty normal life until he finds Leia's secret message stored inside of R2-D2. This discovery causes him to seek out "Old Ben" Kenobi, who changes his life.

    - **First Plot Point:** The first plot point ends the first act and pushes the protagonist down the path toward the second. Luke has decided to stay home and not help Obi-Wan Kenobi, but when he finds that the Empire has killed his aunt and uncle, he changes his mind and decides to join Obi-Wan and train to become a Jedi.

- **Act II: Antagonism:** The protagonist starts her journey, but a series of obstacles get in her way. Luke and Obi-Wan hire Han Solo and Chewbacca to help them deliver the secret plans carried by R2-D2 to Alderaan; however, when they arrive Alderaan has been destroyed, and their ship is captured by the Death Star.

    - **Second Plot Point:** The second plot point ends the second act and pushes the protagonist into her decision of what she will attempt in the third act. After much struggle, Luke and his friends escape from the Death Star with both the princess and the plans, but his mentor, Obi-Wan Kenobi, is killed in the process. The Death Star follows them to the rebel's secret base, and Luke must choose whether to aid in the attack on the Death Star or to leave with Han Solo.

- **Act III: Resolution:** The story concludes, and the protagonist either succeeds or fails. Either way, she emerges from the story with a new understanding of who she is. Luke chooses to help attack the Death Star and ends up saving the day.

    - **Climax:** The moment when everything comes to a head and the main question of the plot is answered. Luke is alone in the Death Star trench having lost both his wingmen and R2-D2. Just as he is about to be shot down by Darth Vader, Han and Chewbacca appear to save him, allowing him a clean shot. Luke chooses to trust the Force rather than technology and shoots with his eyes closed, successfully making an extremely difficult shot and destroying the Death Star.

In most modern movies and in nearly all video games, the climax is very close to the end of the narrative with almost no time for falling action or denouement. One marked example of this not being the case is *Red Dead Redemption* by Rockstar Games. After the big climax where the main character, John Marston, finally defeats the man the government hired him to kill, he is allowed to go home to his family, with the game playing its only sung musical track as John rides home slowly in the snow. The player is then subjected to a series of rather dull missions where John clears crows out of the family grain silo, teaches his petulant son to wrangle cattle, and does other chores around the house. The player feels the boredom of these missions much like John does. Then, the same government agents that initially hired John come to his farm to kill him, eventually succeeding in their task. After John dies, the game fades to black and fades back in on the player in the role of Jack (John's son) three years after his father's death. The game returns to more action-based missions as Jack attempts to track down the agents who killed his father. This kind of falling action is rare and refreshing to see in games, and it made the narrative of *Red Dead Redemption* one of the most memorable that I've played.

Differences Between Interactive and Linear Narrative

At their core, interactive, and linear narratives are quite different because of the difference in the role of the audience versus the player. Though an audience member of course brings her own background and interpretations to any media that she consumes, she is still unable to change the actual media itself, only her perception thereof. However, a player is constantly affecting the media in which she is taking part, and therefore a player has actual agency in the interactive narratives that she experiences. This means that authors of interactive narrative must be aware of some core differences in how they can craft their narratives.

Plot Versus Free Will

One of the most difficult things to give up when crafting interactive narratives is control over the plot. Both authors and readers/viewers are accustomed to plots with elements such as foreshadowing, fate, irony, and other ways in which the intended outcome of the plot actually influences earlier parts of the story. In a truly interactive experience, this would be impossible because of the free will of the player. Without knowing what choices the player will make, it is very difficult to intentionally foreshadow the results of those choices. However, several possibilities exist for dealing with this dichotomy, some of which are already used often in digital games and others of which can be used in pen-and-paper RPGs but have not yet been implemented in many digital games:

- **Limited possibilities:** Limited possibilities are an important part of nearly all interactive narrative experiences. In fact, most games, at their inscribed level, are not actually interactive narratives. All the most popular series of games over the past decade (*Prince of Persia*, *Call of Duty*, *Halo*, *Uncharted*, and so on) have exclusively linear stories at their core. No matter what you do in the game, your choices are to either continue with the narrative or quit the game. *Spec Ops: The Line* by Yager Development explored this issue beautifully, placing the player and the main character of the story in the same position of having only two real choices: continue to perform increasingly horrific acts or just stop playing the game. In *Prince of Persia: The Sands of Time*, this is handled by having the narrator (the prince of the title and the protagonist) say "No, no, no; that's not the way it happened. Shall I start again?" whenever the player dies and the game has to back up to the most recent checkpoint. In the *Assassin's Creed* series, this is handled by stating that you have become "desynchronized" from your ancestor's story if (through lack of player skill) the ancestor is allowed to die.

Several examples also exist of games that limit choices to only a few possibilities and base those on the player's actions throughout the game. Both *Fable*, by Lionhead Studios, and *Star Wars: Knights of the Old Republic*, by BioWare, claimed to be watching the player throughout the game to determine the final game outcome, but though each did track the player on a good versus evil scale throughout the game, in both cases (as in many other games), a single choice made at the end of the game could override an entire game of good or evil behavior.

Other games such as the Japanese RPGs *Final Fantasy VII* and *Chrono Trigger* have more subtle and varied possibilities. In *Final Fantasy VII*, there is a point when the main character, Cloud, goes on a date with one of the other major characters at the Golden Saucer amusement park. The default is for Cloud to go out with Aeris; however, if the player has ignored Aeris throughout the game and kept her out of the battle party, Cloud will instead go out with Tifa. The possibilities for the date are the characters Aeris, Tifa, Yuffie, and Barrett, although having the date with Barrett takes resolute effort. The game never explains that this math is happening in the background but it is always there, and the Final Fantasy team used a similar strategy in *Final Fantasy X* to determine with whom the protagonist, Tidus, would share a romantic snowmobile ride. *Chrono Trigger* uses several metrics to determine which of the game's thirteen endings to choose (and some of those endings have multiple possibilities within them). Again, the calculations for this are largely invisible to the player.

- **Allow the player to choose from several linear side quests:** Many of Bethesda Softworks' open-world games use this strategy, including *Fallout 3* and *Skyrim*. Although the main quest is generally pretty linear for these games, it is only a small fraction of the game's total content. In *Skyrim*, for instance, the main quest takes about 12 to 16 hours to complete, but the game has more than 400 hours of additional side quests. A player's reputation and history in the game lead to some side quests being unlocked and exclude her from playing others. This means that each individual who plays the game has the potential to have a different combination of linear experiences that add up to a different overall game experience from other players.

- **Foreshadowing multiple things:** If you foreshadow several different things that might happen, some of them probably will happen. Players generally ignore the foreshadowing that does not eventually pay off while noticing that which does. This happens often in serial television shows where several possibilities for future plots are put in place but only a few are ever actually executed (e.g., the Nebari plot to take over the universe that is revealed in the *Farscape* episode "A Clockwork Nebari" but is never mentioned again and the titular character from the *Doctor Who* episode "The Doctor's Daughter" who never returns to the show).

- **Develop minor non-player characters (NPCs) into major ones:** Game masters (GMs) of pen-and-paper RPGs often use this tactic. An example of this would be if the players were attacked by a group of ten bandits, and the players defeated the bandits, but one got away. The GM could then choose to have that bandit return at some point with a vendetta against the players for killing his friends. This differs significantly from games like *Final Fantasy VI* (originally titled *Final Fantasy III* in the U.S.), where it is rather obvious from early in the game that Kefka will be a recurring, annoying, and eventually wholly evil nemesis character. Though the characters in the player's party don't realize this, just the fact that the developers chose to give Kefka a special sound effect for his laugh makes it apparent to the player.

---

tip

Pen-and-paper RPGs still offer players a unique interactive gaming experience, and I highly recommend them. In fact, when I taught at the University of Southern California, I required all of my students to run an RPG and play in a couple run by their peers. Roughly 40% of the students each semester listed it as their favorite assignment.

Because pen-and-paper RPGs are run by a person, that game master (GM) can craft the narrative in real time for the players in a way that computers have yet to match. GMs use all the strategies listed earlier to guide their players and make their experiences seem fated, foreshadowed, or ironic in ways that are usually reserved for linear narrative.

The perennial RPG *Dungeons & Dragons*, by Wizards of the Coast, is a good place to get started, and a tremendous number of source books are available for it. However, I have found that *D&D* campaigns tend to be rather combat-focused, and the combat can take a very long time. For an experience that allows you to most easily create and experience interactive stories, I recommended the *FATE Accelerated* system by Evil Hat Productions.[8]

---

8. http://www.evilhat.com/home/fae/, accessed April 1, 2017.

Empathetic Character Versus Avatar

In linear narratives, the protagonist is often a character with whom the audience is expected to empathize. When the audience watches Romeo and Juliet make stupid decisions, they remember being young themselves and empathize with the feelings that lead the two lovers down their fatal path. In contrast, the protagonist in an interactive narrative is not a character separate from the player but instead the player's *avatar* in the world. (*Avatar* is a word from Sanskrit that refers to the physical embodiment of a god on Earth; in games, it is the virtual embodiment of the player in the game world.) This can lead to a dissonance between the actions and personality that the player would like to have in the world and the personality of the player-character (PC). For me, this was driven home by my experience with Cloud Strife as the protagonist of *Final Fantasy VII*. Throughout the game, Cloud was a little more petulant than I would have liked, but in general, his silence allowed me to project my own character on to him. However, after a pivotal scene where Cloud loses someone close to him, he chose to sit, unresponsive in a wheelchair instead of fighting to save the world from Sephiroth, as I wanted to. This dichotomy between the PC's choice and the choice that I as the player wanted to make was extremely frustrating for me.

An excellent example of this dichotomy being used to great effect happens in the fantastic game *Okami* (2006), by Clover Studio. In *Okami*, the player character is Amaterasu, a reincarnation of the female god of the sun in the form of a white wolf. However, Amaterasu's powers have diminished over the past 100 years, and the player must work to reclaim them. About a quarter of the way through the narrative, the main antagonist, the demon Orochi, chooses a maiden to be sacrificed to him. Both the player and Amaterasu's companion, Issun, know that Amaterasu has only regained a few of her powers at this point, and the player feels wary of facing Orochi in such a weakened state. However, despite Issun's protests, Amaterasu runs directly to the fight. As the music swells in support of her decision, my feelings as a player changed from trepidation to temerity, and I, as the player, actually felt like a hero because I knew that the odds were against me, but I was still doing what needed to be done.

Designers of games and interactive narratives have approached this character versus avatar dichotomy in several ways:

- **Role fulfillment:** By far, the most common approach in games is to have the player roleplay the game character. When playing character-driven games like the *Tomb Raider* or *Uncharted* series, players do not play themselves but instead play Lara Croft or Nathan Drake. The player sets aside her own personality to fulfill the inscribed personality of the game's protagonist.

- **The silent protagonist:** In a tradition reaching at least as far back as the first *Legend of Zelda* game, many protagonists are largely silent. Other characters talk to them and react as if they've said things, but the player never sees the statements made by the player character. This was done with the idea that the player could then impress her own personality on the protagonist rather than being forced into a personality inscribed by the game developers. However, regardless of what Link says or doesn't say, his personality is demonstrated rather clearly by his actions, and even without Cloud saying a word, players can still experience a dissonance between their wishes and his actions as described in the preceding example.

- **Multiple dialogue choices:** Many games offer the player multiple dialogue choices for her character, which can certainly help the player to feel more control over the character's personality. However, a couple of important requirements are:

  - **The player must understand the implications of her statement:** Sometimes, a line that might seem entirely clear to the game's writers does not seem to have the same connotations to the player. If the player chooses dialogue that seems to her to be complimentary, but the writer meant for it to be antagonistic, the NPC's reaction can seem very strange to the player.

  - **The choice of statement must matter:** Some games offer the player a fake choice, anticipating that she will make the choice that the game desires. If, for instance, she's asked to save the world, and she just says "No," the game responds with something like "Oh, you can't mean that," and refuses to actually accept her choice.

  One fantastic example of this being done well is the dialog wheel in the *Mass Effect* series by BioWare. These games present the player with a wheel of dialog choices, and the sections of the wheel are coded with meaning. A choice on the left side of the wheel usually extends the conversation, whereas one on the right side shortens it. A choice on the top of the wheel is friendly, whereas one on the bottom is surly or antagonistic. By positioning the dialog options in this way, the player is granted important information about the connotations of her possible choices and is not surprised by the outcome.

  Another very different but equally compelling example is *Blade Runner* by Westwood Studios (1997). The designers felt that choosing dialog options would interrupt the flow of the player experience, so instead of offering the player a choice between dialogue options at every statement, the player was able to choose a mood for her character (friendly, neutral, surly, or random). The protagonist would act and speak as dictated by his mood without any interruption in the narrative flow, and the player could change the mood at any time to alter her character's response to the situation.

- **Track player actions and react accordingly:** Some games now track the player's relationships with various factions and have the faction members react to the player accordingly. Do a favor for the Orcs, and they might let you sell goods at their trading post. Arrest a member of the Thieves Guild, and you might find yourself mugged by them in the future. This is a common feature of open-world western roleplaying games like those by Bethesda Softworks and is in some ways based on the morality system of eight virtues and three principles that was introduced in *Ultima IV*, by Origin Systems, one of the first examples of complex morality systems in a digital game.

Purposes for Inscribed Narrative

Inscribed narrative can serve several purposes in game design:

- **Evoking emotion:** Over the past several centuries, writers have gained skill in manipulating the emotions of their audiences through dramatics. This holds true in games and interactive narrative as well, and even purely linear narrative inscribed over a game can focus and shape the player's feelings.

- **Providing motivation and justification:** Just as dramatics can shape emotions, they can also be used to encourage the player to take certain actions or to justify actions if those actions seem distasteful. This is very true of the fantastic retelling of Joseph Conrad's *Heart of Darkness* in the game *Spec Ops: The Line*. A more positive example comes from *The Legend of Zelda: The Wind Waker*. At the beginning of the game, Link's sister Aryll lets him borrow her telescope for one day because it's his birthday. On the same day, she is kidnapped by a giant bird, and the first part of the game is driven narratively by Link's desire to rescue her. The inscribed storytelling of her giving something to the player before being kidnapped increases the player's personal desire to rescue her.

- **Providing progression and reward:** Many games use cut scenes and other inscribed narrative to help the player know where she is in the story and to reward her for progression. If the narrative of a game is largely linear, the player's understanding of traditional narrative structure can help her to understand where in the three-act structure the game narrative currently is, and thereby, she can tell how far she has progressed in the overall plot of the game. Narrative cut scenes are also often used as rewards for players to mark the end of a level or other section of the game. This is true in the single-player modes of nearly all top-selling games with linear narratives (e.g., the *Modern Warefare*, *Halo*, and *Uncharted* series).

- **Reinforcing mechanics:** One of the most critical purposes of inscribed dramatics is the reinforcement of game mechanics. The German board game *Up the River* by Ravensburger is a fantastic example of this. In the game, players are trying to move their three boats forward along a board that is constantly moving backward. Calling the board a "river" reinforces the backward movement game mechanic. A board space that stops forward progress is called a "sandbar" (as boats often get hung up on sandbars). Similarly, the space that pushes the player forward is called a "high tide." Because each of these elements has narrative meaning associated with it, it is much easier to remember than, for instance, if the player were asked to remember that space #3 stopped the boat and #7 moved the boat forward.

Inscribed Technology

Much like inscribed mechanics, inscribed technology is largely understood only through its dynamic behavior. This is true whether considering paper or digital technology. The choice of how many dice of how many sides each to be thrown by the player only really matters when those dice are in play just as the code written by a programmer is only really understood by the player when she sees the game in action. This is one of the reasons that—as pointed out in Jesse Schell's Elemental Tetrad[9]—technology is the least visible of the inscribed elements.

In addition, a large overlap exists between inscribed mechanics and inscribed technology. Technology enables mechanics, and mechanical design decisions can lead to a choice of which technologies to use.

---

9. Schell's Elemental Tetrad is covered in Chapter 2, "Game Analysis Frameworks."

Inscribed Paper Game Technology

Inscribed technologies in paper games are often used for randomization, state tracking, and progression.

- **Randomization:** Randomization is the most common form of technology in paper games. This ranges from dice, to cards, to dominoes, to spinners, and so on. As a designer, you have a lot of control over which of these you choose and how the randomization works. You can also combine randomization with tables to do things such as generate random encounters or characters for a game. In Chapter 11, "Math and Game Balance," you can read about the various types of randomizers and when you might want to use them.

- **State tracking:** State tracking can be everything from keeping track of the scores of the different players of the game (like a cribbage board) or tables like the complex character sheets used in some roleplaying games.

- **Progression:** Progression is often inscribed via charts and tables. This includes things such as player progression of abilities when the player levels up, the progression of various technologies and units in the technology tree of a game like *Civilization*, progression of resource renewal in the board game *Power Grid*, and so on.

Inscribed Digital Game Technology

The latter sections of this book extensively cover digital game technology in the form of programming games using Unity and the C# programming language. Just as with inscribed paper game technology, the art of game programming is that of encoding the experience you want the player to have into inscribed rules (in the form of programming code) that the player then decodes as she plays the game.

Summary

The four elements of the inscribed layer make up everything that players receive when they purchase or download your game, and therefore the inscribed layer is the only one over which the game developers have complete control. In the next chapter, we allow players to move our games from the static form of the inscribed layer up to the emergence of the dynamic layer.

In a final note on the inscribed layer—as Jesse Schell pointed out in his discussion of the Elemental Tetrad—each of the elements of the inscribed layer align well with a job within a small game studio: Game Designers create the mechanics, Artists create the aesthetics, Writers craft the narrative, and Programmers develop the technology.

CHAPTER 5

THE DYNAMIC LAYER

When players start playing a game, it moves from the inscribed layer into the dynamic layer of the Layered Tetrad. Play, strategy, and meaningful player choices all emerge in this layer.

This chapter explores the dynamic layer, various qualities of emergence, and how designers can anticipate the dynamic play that emerges from their inscribed design decisions.

The Role of the Player

A fellow designer once told me that a game isn't a game unless someone is playing it. Although this might sound initially like a rehash of "if a tree falls in the woods, and there's no one to hear it, does it make a sound?" this definition is actually much more important for interactive media than any other medium. A film can still exist and show in a theater if there's no one to watch it.[1] Television can be sent out over the airwaves and still be television, even if no one is tuned to that station. Games, however, just don't exist without players, for it is through the actions of players that games transform from a collection of inscribed elements into a dynamic experience (see Figure 5.1).

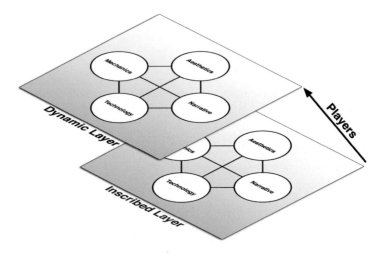

Figure 5.1 Players move the game from the inscribed layer into the dynamic layer

There are, of course, some edge cases to this, as there are to all things. The game *Core War* is a hacking game where players each try to write a computer virus that will propagate and take over a fake computer core from the viruses of their competitors. Players submit their viruses and wait for them to fight each other for memory and survival. In the yearly *RoboCup* tournament, various teams of robots compete against each other in soccer without any interference by the programmers during the game. In the classic card game *War*, players make no decision beyond the choice of which of the two decks to take at the beginning of the game, and the game plays out entirely based on the luck of the initial shuffle. Though in each of these cases, the player has no input and makes no choices during the actual play of the game, the play is still influenced by player decisions made before the official start of the match, and the players certainly have

---

1. Some films, like *The Rocky Horror Picture Show,* owe a lot of their cult fandom to presentations in which the audience takes part, and the audience reactions in those films do alter the viewing experience of the other audience members. However, the film itself is completely unaffected by the audience. The dynamism in games comes from the ability of the medium to react to the player.

interest in and are waiting for the outcome of the game. Additionally, all of these cases also require players to set up the game and to make the choices that determine its outcome.

Though players have a tremendous effect on the game and gameplay (including influences on the tetrad elements), players sit outside of the tetrad as the engine that makes it work. Players cause games to come into being and allow them to become the experience that game developers have encoded into the inscribed layer of the game. As designers, we rely on players to aid us in helping the game become what we intend. Several aspects of gameplay in the dynamic layer are completely beyond our control as designers, including: whether the player is actually trying to follow the rules, whether the player cares about winning or not, the physical environment in which the game is played, the emotional state of the players, and so on. Because players are so important, we as developers need to treat them with respect and take care to ensure that the inscribed elements of the game—especially the rules—are clear enough to the players that they can decode them into the game experience that we intend.

Emergence

The most important concept in this chapter is *emergence*, the core of which is that even very simple rules can beget complex dynamic behaviors. Consider the game of *Bartok* that you played and experimented with in Chapter 1, "Thinking Like a Designer." Though *Bartok* had very few rules, complex play emerged from them. When you started changing rules and adding your own, you were also able to see that even simple, seemingly innocuous rule changes had the potential to lead to large changes in both the feel and the play of the game.

The dynamic layer of the Layered Tetrad encompasses the results of the intersection of player and game across all four elements of the tetrad: mechanics, aesthetics, dramatics, and technology.

Unexpected Mechanical Emergence

My friend Scott Rogers, author of two great books on game design,[2] once told me that he "didn't believe in emergence." After discussing it with him for a while, we came to the conclusion that he did believe in emergence, but he didn't believe that it was legitimate for game designers to use emergence as an excuse for irresponsible design. We agree that as the designer of the systems within a game, you are responsible for the play that emerges from those systems. Of course, it's extremely difficult to know what possibilities will emerge from the rules that you put in place, which is why playtesting is so critically important. As you develop your games, playtest early and often, and take special care to note unusual things that happen in only one playtest. After your game gets out in the wild, the sheer number of people playing

---

2. Scott Rogers, *Level up!: The Guide to Great Video Game Design* (Chichester, UK: Wiley, 2010) and Scott Rogers, *Swipe this! The Guide to Great Tablet Game Design* (Hoboken, NJ: John Wiley & Sons, 2012).

will cause those unusual flukes to happen a lot more often than you would expect. Of course, this happens to all designers—look at some of the cards that have been declared illegal in *Magic: The Gathering*—but as Scott says, it's important that designers take responsibility for these issues and for resolving them.

Dynamic Mechanics

Dynamic *mechanics* are the dynamic layer of the elements that separate games and interactive media from other media; the elements that make them games. Dynamic mechanics include procedures, meaningful play, strategy, house rules, player intent, and outcome. As with the inscribed mechanics, many of these are an expansion of elements described in Tracy Fullerton's book *Game Design Workshop*.[3] The dynamic mechanics we will cover are:

- **Procedures:** Actions that players take
- **Meaningful Play:** Giving weight to player decisions
- **Strategy:** Plans devised by players
- **House Rules:** Simple game modifications made by players
- **Player Intent:** The motivations and goals of players
- **Outcome:** The result(s) of playing the game

Procedures

Mechanics in the inscribed layer included *rules*, the instructions from the designer to the players about how to play the game. *Procedures* are the dynamic actions taken by the players in response to those rules. Another way to say this is that procedures emerge from rules. Consider this optional rule from the Bartok game in Chapter 1:

- **Rule 3:** A player must announce "Last card" when she has only one card left. If someone else calls it first, she must draw two cards (bringing her total number of cards to three).

This rule directly instructs the active player to follow the procedure of announcing when she has only one card remaining. However, the rule also indirectly implies another procedure: that of other players watching the hand of the active player so that they can catch her if she forgets to announce it. Prior to this rule, there was no real reason for a player to pay attention to the game during another person's turn, but this simple rule change altered the procedures of playing the game for both the active and inactive players.

---

3. Tracy Fullerton, Christopher Swain, and Steven Hoffman, *Game Design Workshop: A Playcentric Approach to Creating Innovative Games* (Burlington, MA: Morgan Kaufmann Publishers, 2008), Chapters 3 and 5.

Meaningful Play

In *Rules of Play*, Katie Salen and Eric Zimmerman define *meaningful play* as play that is both *discernable* to the player and *integrated* into the larger game.[4]

- **Discernable:** An action is discernable to the player if the player can tell that the action has been taken. For example, when you press the call button for an elevator, the action is discernable because the call button lights up. If you've ever tried to call an elevator when the light inside the button was burned out, you know how frustrating it can be to attempt an action and yet not be able to discern whether the game interpreted your action.

- **Integrated:** An action is integrated if the player can tell that it is tied to the outcome of the game. For example, when you press the call button for the elevator, that action is integrated because you know that doing so will cause the elevator to stop on your floor. In *Super Mario Bros.*, the decision of whether to stomp an individual enemy or just avoid it is generally not very meaningful because that individual action is not integrated into the overall outcome of the game. *Super Mario Bros.* never gives you a tally of the number of enemies defeated; it only requires that you finish each level before the time runs out and finish the game without running out of lives. In HAL Laboratories' series of *Kirby* games, however, the player character Kirby gains special abilities by defeating enemies, so the decision of which enemy to defeat is directly integrated into the acquisition of abilities, making the decision more meaningful.

If a player's actions in the game are not meaningful, she can quickly lose interest. Salen and Zimmerman's concept of meaningful play reminds designers to constantly think about the mindset of the player and whether the interactions of their games are transparent or opaque from the player's perspective.

Strategy

When a game allows meaningful actions, players will usually create strategies to try to win the game. A *strategy* is a calculated set of actions to help the player achieve a goal. However, that goal can be anything of the player's choosing and does not necessarily need to be the goal of winning the game. For instance, when playing with a young child or with someone of a lower skill level in a game, the player's goal might be to make sure that the other person enjoys playing the game and learns something, sometimes at the expense of the player winning the game.

Optimal Strategy

When a game is very simple and has few possible actions, it is possible for a player to devise an *optimal strategy* for the game. If both players of a game are playing rationally with the goal of winning, an optimal strategy is the possible strategy with the highest likelihood of winning.

---

4. Katie Salen and Eric Zimmerman, *Rules of Play: Game Design Fundamentals* (Cambridge, MA: MIT Press, 2003), 34.

Most games are too complex to really have an optimal strategy, but some games like Tic-Tac-Toe are simple enough to allow one. In fact, Tic-Tac-Toe is so simple that chickens have (possibly) been trained to play it and force a draw or a win almost every time.[5]

An optimal strategy is more often a fuzzy idea of the kind of thing that would likely improve a player's chance of winning. For instance, in the board game *Up the River* by Manfred Ludwig, players are trying to move three boats up a river to dock at the top of the game board, and arriving at the dock is worth 12 points to the first boat to arrive, then 11 points for the second boat, and down to only 1 point for the twelfth boat. Every round (that is, every time that all players have taken one turn), the river moves backward 1 space, and any boat that falls off the end of the river (the waterfall) is lost. Each turn, the player rolls 1d6 (a single six-sided die) and chooses which boat to move. Because the average roll of a six-sided die is 3.5, and the player must choose from among her three boats to move every turn, each boat will move an average of 3.5 spaces every three of her turns. However, the board will move backward 3 spaces every three turns, so each boat only makes an average forward progression of 0.5 spaces every three turns (or 0.1666 [or 1/6] spaces every turn).[6]

In this game, the optimal strategy is for the player to never move one of her boats and just let it fall off the waterfall. Then each boat would move forward an average of 3.5 spaces every two turns instead of three. With the board moving backward 2 spaces in two turns, this would give each of her boats an average movement forward of 1.5 spaces every two turns (or 0.75 spaces each turn), which is much better than the 0.1666 afforded to the player if she tries to keep all of her boats. Then this player would have a better chance of getting to the dock in first and second place, giving her 23 total points (12 + 11). In a two-player game, this strategy wouldn't work because the second player would tie up at 10, 9, and 8 for 27 points, but in a three- or four-player game, it's the closest thing to an optimal strategy for *Up the River*. However, the other players' choices, randomized outcomes of the dice, and additional factors mean that the strategy won't always ensure a win; it just makes a win more likely.

Designing for Strategy

As a designer, you can do several things to make strategy more important in your game. For now, the main thing to keep in mind is that presenting the player with multiple possible ways to win will require her to make more difficult strategic decisions during play. In addition, having some of these goals conflict with each other while others are complementary (i.e., some of the requirements for the two goals are the same) can actually cause individual players to move into certain roles as the game progresses. When a player can see that she is starting to fulfill one of the goals, she will pick its complementary goals to pursue as well, and this will lead her to make tactical decisions that fulfill the role for which those goals were designed. If these goals cause her to take a specific type of action in the game, it can alter her in-game relationship with other players.

---

5. Kia Gregory, "Chinatown Fair Is Back, Without Chickens Playing Tick-Tack-Toe," *New York Times*, June 10, 2012.

6. In this example, I am omitting additional rules of the game for the sake of simplicity.

An example of this comes from the game *Settlers of Catan*, designed by Klaus Teuber. In this game, players acquire resources through random die rolls or trade, and some of the five game resources are useful in the early game, while others are useful at the end. Three that are less useful at the beginning are sheep, wheat, and ore; however, together, the three can be traded for a development card. The most common development card is the soldier card, which can move the robber token onto any space, allowing the player moving it to steal from another player. Therefore, a player with an excess of ore, wheat, and sheep at the beginning of the game will often purchase development cards, and because having played the largest number of soldier cards can earn the player victory points, the combination of those resources and that potential goal can influence the player to rob the other players more often and strongly encourage her play the role of a bully in the game.

House Rules

House rules occur when the players themselves intentionally modify the rules. As you saw in the *Bartok* game example, even a simple rule change can have drastic effects on the game. For instance, most players of *Monopoly* have house rules that omit the auction of properties (which would normally happen if a player landed on an unowned property and chose not to buy it) and add collection of all fines to the Free Parking space to be picked up by any player who lands on that space. The omission of the auction rule removes nearly all potential strategy from the beginning of *Monopoly* (converting it into an extremely slow random property distribution system), and the second rule removes some determinism from the game (because it could benefit any player, either the one in the lead or in last place). Though the first house rule in this example makes the game a bit worse, most house rules are intended to make games considerably more fun.[7] In all cases, house rules are an example of the players beginning to take some ownership of the game, making it a little more theirs and a little less the designer's. The fantastic thing about house rules is that they are many people's first experimentation with game design.

Player Intent: Bartle's Types, Cheaters, and Spoilsports

One thing that you have little or no control over is the intent of your players. Though most players will play your game rationally to win, you might also have to contend with cheaters and spoilsports. Even within legitimate players of games, we find four distinct personality types as defined by Richard Bartle, one of the designers of the first MUD (Multi-User Dungeon, a text-based online ancestor of modern massively multiplayer online role-playing games).

---

7. If you're ever playing the game *Lunch Money* by Atlas Games, try allowing players to attack another player, heal themselves, *and* discard any cards they don't want each turn (rather than having to choose one of the three). It makes the game a lot more frantic!

The four types of players that he defined have existed since his early MUD and carry through all multiplayer online games today. His 1996 article "Hearts, Clubs, Diamonds, Spades: Players Who Suit MUDs"[8] contains fantastic information on how these types of players interact with each other and the game as well as information about how to grow your community of players in positive ways.

Bartle's four types (which he identified with the four suits of a deck of cards) are as follows:

- **Achiever (♦ Diamond):** Seeks to get the highest score in the game. Wants to dominate the game.
- **Explorer (♠ Spade):** Seeks to find all the hidden places in the game. Wants to understand the game.
- **Socializer (♥ Heart):** Wants to play the game with friends. Wants to understand the other players.
- **Killer (♣ Club):** Wants to provoke other players of the game. Wants to dominate the other players.

These can be understood as belonging to a 2x2 continuum (also from Bartle's article). Figure 5.2 represents this graphically.

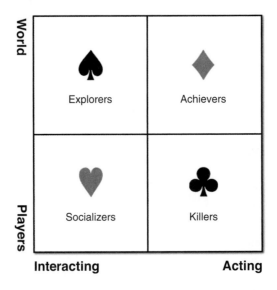

Figure 5.2 Richard Bartle's four players who suit MUDs

---

8. Richard Bartle, "Hearts, Clubs, Diamonds, Spades: Players Who Suit Muds," http://www.mud.co.uk/richard/hcds.htm, accessed January 12, 2017.

Certainly other theories of player motivation and player types exist,[9] but Bartle's are the most widely recognized and understood in the game industry.

Two other player types that you might encounter are *cheaters* and *spoilsports*:

- **Cheaters:** Care about winning but don't care about the integrity of the game. Cheaters bend or break the rules to win.

- **Spoilsports:** Don't care about winning or about the game. Spoilsports often break the game to ruin the other players' experiences.

Neither of these are players that you want in your game, but you need to understand their motivations. For instance, if a cheater feels that she has a chance of winning legitimately, she might not feel as driven to cheat. Spoilsports are much more difficult to deal with because they don't care about the game or winning, but you rarely have to deal with spoilsports in digital single-player games, as they would have no reason to play the game if they weren't interested in it in the first place. However, even great players can sometimes become spoilsports when they encounter terrible game mechanics…often right before they choose to turn the game off.

Outcome

Outcome is the result of playing the game. All games have an outcome. Many traditional games are *zero-sum,* meaning that one player wins and the other loses. However, this is not the only kind of outcome that a game can have. In fact, every individual moment in a game has its own outcome. Most games have several different levels of outcome:

- **Immediate outcome:** Each individual action has an outcome. When a player attacks an enemy, the outcome of that attack is either a miss or a hit and the resultant damage to the enemy. When a player purchases property in *Monopoly*, the outcome is that the player has less money available but now owns the potential to earn more money.

- **Quest outcome:** Many games send the player on missions or quests and offer some sort of reward for completing that quest. Missions and quests often have narratives constructed around them (e.g., a little girl has lost her balloon in *Spider-Man 2* [Treyarch, 2004], so Spider-Man must retrieve it for her), and the outcome of the quest also marks the end of the tiny narrative surrounding it.

- **Cumulative outcome:** This occurs when the player has been working toward a goal over time and finally achieves it. One of the most common examples is leveling up in a game with experience points (XP). Everything that the player does accrues a few experience points, and when the total number of XP reaches a threshold, the player's in-game character gains a new level, which grants the character a boost in stats or abilities. The main difference

---

9. See Nick Yee's "Motivations of Play in MMORPGs: Results from a Factor Analytic Approach," http://www.nickyee.com/daedalus/motivations.pdf, accessed April 1, 2017.

   Another excellent resource is Scott Rigby and Richard Ryan's paper "The Player Experience of Need Satisfaction (PENS)," http://immersyve.com/white-paper-the-player-experience-of-need-satisfaction-pens-2007/, accessed April 1, 2017.

between this and a quest outcome is that the cumulative outcome usually doesn't have a narrative wrapped around it, and the player often reaches the cumulative outcome passively while actively doing something else (e.g., a player of *Dungeons & Dragons 4th Edition* actively takes part in a game session and then, while adding up earned XP at the end of the evening, notices that she has exceeded 10,000 XP and achieved level 7.)[10]

- **Final outcome:** Most games have an outcome that ends the game: A player wins chess (and the other loses), a player finishes *Final Fantasy VII* and saves the world from Sephiroth, and so on. In some games the final outcome doesn't end the game (e.g., in *Skyrim*, even when the player has finished the main quest, she can still continue to play in the world and experience other quests).[11] Interestingly, the death of the player character is very rarely a final outcome in games.

  In the few games where death is a final outcome (e.g., the game *Rogue* [A.I. Design, 1980], where a single loss causes the player to lose all progress in the game), the individual game session is usually relatively short so that the player doesn't feel a tremendous loss at the death of the player character. In most games, however, death is just a temporary setback and in-game checkpoints usually ensure that the player never loses more than five minutes of progress in the game.

Dynamic Aesthetics

Just as with dynamic mechanics, dynamic *aesthetics* are those that emerge during gameplay. The two different primary categories are:

- **Procedural aesthetics:** Aesthetics that are programmatically generated by digital game code (or via the application of mechanics in a paper game). These include procedural music and art that emerge directly from inscribed aesthetics and technology.
- **Environmental aesthetics:** These are the aesthetics of the environment in which the game is played, and they are largely beyond the control of the game developers.

Procedural Aesthetics

Procedural aesthetics, as we generally think of them in digital games, are created programmatically by combining technology and inscribed aesthetics.[12] They are called *procedural* because they arise from procedures (also known as functions) that have been

---

10. Rob Heinsoo, Andy Collins, and James Wyatt, *Dungeons & Dragons Player's Handbook: Arcane, Divine, and Martial Heroes: Roleplaying Game Core Rules* (Renton, WA: Wizards of the Coast, 2008).

11. *Fallout 3* initially ended the game when the player reached the final outcome of completing the main story but then released DLC (downloadable content) that allowed players to continue playing after this point.

12. Examples of procedural art in board games include things like the map created by the progressive laying of tiles in *Carcassonne* (Klaus-Jürgen Wrede, 2000), but digital procedural game art is much more common.

written as programming code. The cascading waterfall of objects that you create in Chapter 18, "Hello World: Your First Program," could be considered procedural art because it is an interesting visual that emerges from C# programming code. In professional games, two of the most common forms of procedural aesthetics are music and visual art.

Procedural Music

Procedural music has become very common in modern videogames, and it is currently created through three different techniques:

- **Horizontal Re-Sequencing (HRS):** HRS rearranges the order of several precomposed sections of music according to the emotional impact that the designers want for the current moment in the game. An example of this is LucasArts' iMUSE (Interactive MUsic Streaming Engine), which was used in the *X-Wing* game series as well as many of LucasArts adventure games. In *X-Wing*, the pre-composed music is sections of John William's score for the *Star Wars* films. Using iMUSE, designers can play peaceful music when the player is just flying through space, ominous music when enemy forces are about to attack, victory music whenever a player destroys an enemy craft or achieves an objective, and so on. There are also longer sections of music that are meant to loop and provide a single mood as well as very short *stings* (sections of music one or two measures in length) that are used to mask the transition from one mood to the next. This is currently the most common type of procedural music technology and harkens at least as far back as *Super Mario Bros.* (Nintendo, 1985), which played a transitional musical sting and then switched to a faster version of the background music when the player had less than 99 seconds left to complete the current level.

- **Vertical Re-Orchestration (VRO):** VRO includes recordings of various tracks of a single song that can be individually enabled or disabled. This is used very commonly in rhythm games like *PaRappa the Rapper* and *Frequency*. In *PaRappa*, four different tracks of music represent four different levels of success for the player. The player's success is ranked every few measures, and if she either drops or increases in rank, the background music switches to a worse- or better-sounding track to reflect this. In *Frequency* and its sequel *Amplitude*, the player controls a craft traveling down a tunnel, the walls of which represent various tracks in a studio recording of a song. When the player succeeds at the rhythm game on a certain wall, that track of the recording is enabled.[13] VRO like this is nearly ubiquitous in rhythm games— with the fantastic Japanese rhythm game *Osu Tatake Ouendan!* and its Western successor *Elite Beat Agents* as marked exceptions—and has also become common in other games to give the player musical feedback on the health of their character, speed of their vehicle, and so on.

- **Procedural Composition (PCO):** PCO is the rarest form of procedural music because it takes the most time and skill to execute. In PCO, rather than rearrange various precomposed tracks of music or enable and disable precomposed tracks, the computer program actually composes music from individual notes based on programmed rules of composition, pacing, and so on. One of the earliest commercial experiments in this realm

---

13. *Amplitude* also includes a mode where players can choose which tracks to enable at any point in the song to use VRO to create their own remix of the tracks included with the game.

was *C.P.U. Bach* by Sid Meier and Jeff Brigs (1994), a title for the 3DO console. In *C.P.U. Bach*, the listener/player was able to select various instruments and parameters, and the game would craft a Bach-like musical composition based on procedural rules.

Another fantastic example of procedural composition is the music created by composer and game designer Vincent Diamante for the game *Flower* by thatgamecompany (2009). For the game, Diamante created both precomposed sections of music and rules for procedural composition. During gameplay, background music is usually playing (some of which is rearranged based on the situation using HRS) as the player flies over flowers in a field and opens them by passing near. Each flower that is opened creates a single note as it blooms, and Diamante's PCO engine chooses a note for that flower that blends harmoniously with the precomposed music and creates a melody along with other flower notes. Regardless of when the player passes over a flower, the system chooses a note that fits well with the current audio soundscape, and passing over several flowers in sequence procedurally generates pleasing melodies.

Procedural Visual Art

Procedural visual art is created when programming code acts dynamically to create in-game visuals. You are probably already familiar with a few forms of procedural visuals:

- **Particle systems:** As the most common form of procedural visuals, particle systems exist in most games developed in the last decade. The dust cloud that rises when Mario lands a jump in *Super Mario Galaxy*, the fire effects in *Uncharted 3*, and the sparks that appear when cars crash into each other in *Burnout* are all various versions of particle effects. Unity has a very fast and robust particle effects engine (see Figure 5.3).

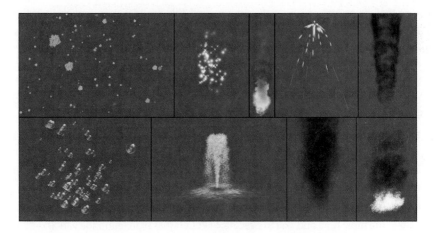

Figure 5.3 Various particle effects created with Unity

- **Procedural animation:** Procedural animation covers everything from flocking behavior for groups of creatures to the brilliant procedural character animation engine in Will Wright's *Spore* that created walk, run, attack, and other animations for any creature that

Player Considerations

Another critical thing to consider about the environment in which your game will be played is the player herself. Not all players have the same level of sensitivity in their five senses. A player who is deaf should really be able to play your game with little trouble, especially if you follow the advice in the last few paragraphs. However, there are two other considerations in particular that many designers miss:

- **Color blindness:** In the United States, up to 8% of men and 0.5% of women with Northern European ancestry have some form of color deficiency.[14] Several different forms of deficiency in color perception exist, the most common of which causes a person to be unable to differentiate between similar shades of red and green. Because color blindness is so common, you should be able to find a colorblind friend whom you can ask to playtest your game and make sure that there isn't key information being transmitted by color in a way that they can't see. Another fantastic way to check for your game is to download a smartphone app that can modify what you see through the camera to simulate various kinds of color blindness.[15]

- **Epilepsy and migraine:** Both migraines and epileptic seizures can be caused by rapidly flashing lights, and children with epilepsy are particularly prone to having seizures triggered by light. In 1997, an episode of the *Pokémon* television show in Japan triggered simultaneous seizures in hundreds of viewers because of flickering images in one scene.[16] Nearly all games now ship with a warning that they may cause epileptic seizures, but the occurrence of that is now very rare because developers have accepted the responsibility to think about the effect their games might have on their players and have largely removed rapidly flashing lights from their games.

Dynamic Narrative

There are several ways of looking at narrative from a dynamic perspective. The epitome of the form is the experience of players and their game master throughout a traditional pen-and-paper role-playing campaign. Although there have certainly been experiments into crafting truly interactive digital narratives, after more than 30 years, they still haven't reached the level of interaction in a well-run game of *Dungeons & Dragons* (*D&D*). The reason that *D&D* can create such fantastic dynamic narratives is that the dungeon master (DM: the game master in D&D) constantly considers the desires, fears, and evolving skills of her players' characters and crafts a story around them. As mentioned earlier in this book, if the players run into a low-level enemy that (due to random die rolls working in its favor) is very difficult to fight, the DM can

---

14. Color blindness is much more common in males than females. https://nei.nih.gov/health/color_blindness/facts_about, accessed April 2, 2017.

15. Two examples of this kind of app are *Chromatic Vision Simulator* by Kazunori Asada for iOS and Android and *Color DeBlind* for iOS by electron software.

16. Sheryl WuDunn, "TV Cartoon's Flashes Send 700 Japanese Into Seizures," *New York Times*, December 18, 1997.

choose to have that enemy escape at the last minute and then return as a nemesis for the players to fight later. A human DM can adapt the game and the game narrative to the players in a way that is very difficult for a computer to replicate.

Interactive Narrative Incunabula

In 1997, Janet Murray, a professor at the Georgia Institute of Technology, published the book *Hamlet on the Holodeck*[17] in which she examined the early history of interactive narrative in relation to the early history of other forms of narrative media. In her book, Murray explores the incunabular stage of other media, which is the stage when that medium was between its initial creation and its mature form. For instance, in the incunabular stage of film, directors were attempting to shoot 10-minute versions of *Hamlet* and *King Lear* (due to the 10-minute length of a single reel of 16mm film), and incunabular television was largely just televised versions of popular radio programs. Through comparisons to many examples from various media, Murray proceeds to talk about the growth of interactive digital fiction and where it is currently in its incunabular stage. She covers early Infocom text adventure games like the *Zork* series and *Planetfall* and points out two very compelling aspects that make interactive fiction unique.

Interactive Fiction Happens to the Player

Unlike nearly every other form of narrative, interactive fiction happens directly to the player. The following happens near the beginning of the Infocom game *Zork*. [18] (The lines preceded by a right angle bracket [e.g., > open trap door] are the commands entered by the player.)

```
...With the rug moved, the dusty cover of a closed trap door appears.

> open trap door

The door reluctantly opens to reveal a rickety staircase
descending into darkness.

> down

It is pitch dark. You are likely to be eaten by a grue.

> light lamp

The lamp is now on.
You are in a dark and damp cellar with a narrow passageway leading
east and a crawlway to the south. To the west is the bottom of a
steep metal ramp which is unclimbable.
The door crashes shut, and you hear someone barring it.
```

17. Janet Horowitz Murray, *Hamlet on the Holodeck* (New York: Free Press, 1997).

18. *Zork* was created at the Massachusetts Institute of Technology in 1977–79 by Tim Anderson, Marc Blank, Bruce Daniels, and Dave Lebling. They formed Infocom in 1979 and released *Zork* as a commercial product.

The key element here is that *you* hear someone barring it. *You* are now trapped. Interactive fiction is the only narrative medium where the player/reader is the character taking actions and suffering consequences in the narrative.

Relationships Are Developed Through Shared Experiences

Another compelling aspect of interactive fiction is that it allows the player to develop a relationship with other characters through their shared experiences. Murray cites *Planetfall*,[19] another Infocom text adventure, as a fantastic example of this. Following the destruction of the spaceship on which she was a janitor, the player is largely alone for the first section of *Planetfall*. Eventually, she comes across a machine to make warrior robots, but when she engages it, it malfunctions and produces a child-like, mostly useless robot named Floyd. Floyd follows the player around for the remainder of the game and does little more than provide comic relief. Much later in the game, the player must retrieve a device from a bio-lab, but the lab is full of both radiation and vicious aliens. Immediately, Floyd simply says, "Floyd go get!" and enters the lab to retrieve the item. Floyd soon returns, but he is leaking oil and barely able to move. He dies in the player's arms as she sings *The Ballad of the Starcrossed Miner* to him. Many players reported to the designer of *Planetfall*, Steven Meretzky, that they cried when Floyd died, and Murray cites this as one of the first examples of a tangible emotional connection between a player and an in-game character.

Emergent Narrative

True dynamic narrative emerges when the players and game mechanics contribute to the story. Several years ago, I was playing in a *Dungeons & Dragons 3.5 edition* game with some friends. The game master had us in a pretty tight spot. We had just retrieved an artifact from some forces of evil in another dimension and were being chased by a large balrog[20] as we fled down a narrow cave on our flying carpet toward the portal back to our dimension. It was gaining on us quickly, and our weapons were having little effect. However, I remembered a little-used property of the Rod of Splendor that I possessed. Once per week, I could use the Rod of Splendor to create a "huge pavilion of silk, 60 feet across, inside of which were the furnishings and food for a party to entertain 100 people."[21] Often, we would use this capability of the rod to throw a party when we'd finished a mission, but this time I cast the tent directly behind us in the tunnel. Because the tunnel was only 30 feet wide, the balrog crashed into the tent and became entangled, allowing us to escape without anyone dying.

This kind of unexpected story emerges from a combination of the situation created by the game master, the game's rules, and the creativity of individual players. I have encountered

---

19. *Planetfall* was designed by Steve Meretzky and published by Infocom in 1983.

20. A balrog is the giant winged demon of fire and smoke that faced Gandalf in the "you shall not pass" scene of *The Fellowship of the Ring* by J. R. R. Tolkien.

21. The *Dungeons & Dragons 3.5e System Reference Document* entry for the Rod of Splendor is at http://www.d20srd.org/srd/magicItems/rods.htm#splendor, accessed April 2, 2017.

many similar stories through the role-playing campaigns that I have been part of (as both a player and game master), and you can do several things to encourage this kind of collaborative storytelling in roleplaying campaigns that you run. For more information about role-playing games and how to run a good campaign, see the *Role-Playing Games* section of Appendix B, "Useful Concepts."

Dynamic Technology

As with the previous chapter, because other large sections of this book are devoted to both digital and physical game technologies, they are covered very little in this chapter. The core concept for you to know at this point is that the game code you author (your inscribed technology) will be a system that runs as the player experiences the game. As with all dynamic systems, emergence will occur, and this means that many opportunities exist for unexpected things to happen, both wonderful and horrible. Dynamic technology covers all the runtime behavior of your code and the ways in which it affects the player. This could be anything from a system to simulate physics to artificial intelligence to anything else that is implemented in your code.

To find information on the dynamic behavior of paper game technologies such as dice, spinners, cards, and other randomizers, look to Chapter 11, "Math and Game Balance." For information on digital game technologies, you can look to the latter two parts of the book as well as Appendix B, "Useful Concepts."

Summary

Dynamic mechanics, aesthetics, narrative, and technology all emerge from the act of players playing a game. Though the elements that emerge can be challenging to predict, designers have a responsibility to playtest and understand the envelope of that emergence.

The next chapter explores the cultural layer of the Layered Tetrad, the layer beyond gameplay. In the cultural layer players gain more control over the game than the original game developers, and the cultural layer is the only layer of the tetrad that is experienced by members of society who do not ever play the game.

CHAPTER 6

THE CULTURAL LAYER

As the final layer in the Layered Tetrad, the cultural layer is the furthest from the designer's hand, yet it is still critical to a holistic understanding of game design and the implications of game development.

This chapter explores the cultural layer, the space where the player and society take control of the game and make it their own.

Beyond Play

The inscribed and dynamic layers are obvious to all game designers, because they are both integral to the concept of interactive experiences. The cultural layer, however, is a little less obvious. The cultural layer exists at the intersection of the game and society. Players of a game become a community united by their shared experience of play, and that community takes the concepts and intellectual property of the game out into the world. The cultural layer of the game is seen from one side by the community of players who have intimate knowledge of the game and from the other by the members of general society, who have no knowledge of the game at all and first encounter it not through play but through the artifacts created by this community of players (see Figure 6.1).

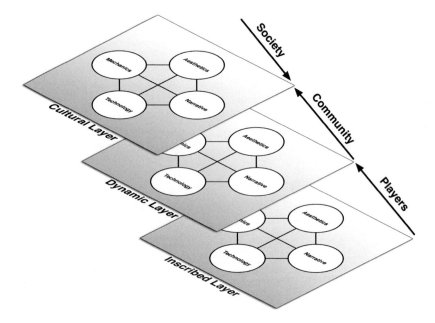

Figure 6.1 The cultural layer, created by the community of game players and witnessed by society

As Constance Steinkuehler points out in her paper "The Mangle of Play,"[1] the dynamic play of a game—particularly a massively multiplayer game—is an "interactively stabilized mangle of practice." In saying so, she points out that, as discussed in the preceding chapter, the dynamic layer of a game is composed not only of the intents of the game developers but also of the intents of the players, and the overall responsibility for and control over the experience is shared between players and developers. Extending this concept, in the cultural layer the players (and society in general) have more control and agency than the original developers. The cultural layer is where player communities actually change the inscribed game through game mods (that is, modifications to the game through software that changes the inscribed

---

1. Constance Steinkuehler. "The Mangle of Play." *Games and Culture 1*, no. 3 (2006): 199–213.

game elements), it is where player communities seize ownership of the game narrative by writing their own fan fiction, and it is where players create their own game-related aesthetics through fan art and music.

Unlike the inscribed layer, where the four elements (mechanics, aesthetics, narrative, and technology) are distinctly assigned to different members of the development team, there is much more overlap and fuzziness of borders between elements when they are examined through the lens of the cultural layer. Fan-made game mods—which feature prominently in the cultural layer—are often combinations of all four elements with the responsibility for each element within the mod often shared by the players and communities who make them.[2]

In the sections that follow, the four elemental divisions are maintained to provide consistency with the preceding chapters and to encourage you to look at the examples listed through the lens of that particular element. However, many of the examples under one cultural element could also have been listed under another.

Cultural Mechanics

Cultural mechanics occur when players take the mechanics of the game into their own hands, sometimes even crafting a new experience out of the game. The most common examples of this include the following:

- **Game mods:** Players repurpose the game to accommodate their own mechanics. This is most extensive in games for Windows-based personal computers. Players modded *Quake 2* by Id to make dozens if not hundreds of new games that all used the technology of *Quake 2* but replaced the mechanics with gameplay and levels of their own (often also replacing the aesthetics and dramatics).

   Several fantastic game mods have become commercial products in their own right. *Counter Strike* started as a mod for *Half-Life* and was subsequently purchased by Valve, the *Half-Life* developers.[3] Similarly, *Defense of the Ancients* (*DotA*) started as a fan mod for Blizzard's game *Warcraft III* and eventually popularized the entire genre of multi-user online battle arenas (MOBAs).[4]

---

2. I definitely do not mean to disparage the developers of game mods by continuing to refer to them throughout this chapter as *players*. By doing so, I am only attempting to be clear so that there is no confusion between the *developers* (i.e., developers of the inscribed content) and *players* (i.e., those who played the game and who might develop game mods). Many fantastic game designers and developers have started by making game mods, and doing so is a fantastic way to practice the craft.

3. http://www.ign.com/articles/2000/11/23/counter-strike-2 and http://en.wikipedia.org/wiki/Counter-Strike

4. According to http://en.wikipedia.org/wiki/Multiplayer_online_battle_arena and http://themittani.com/features/dota-2-history-lesson, *DotA* was actually a *Warcraft III* remake of a mod for *Starcraft* known as *Aeon of Strife*.

In addition, many companies have released editors for their games that encourage and allow players to create custom content for the game. For example, Bethesda Softworks has released Creation Kit™ for its game *The Elder Scrolls V: Skyrim*. Creation Kit allows players to create their own levels, quests, NPCs (nonplayer characters), and so forth. Bethesda has also done this before for other games, including *Fallout 3* and earlier games in the *Elder Scrolls* series.

- **Custom game levels:** Even without changing the other mechanics, some games accommodate player-made levels. In fact, some games rely on players to make levels for the game. *Little Big Planet* by Media Molecule and *Sound Shapes* by Queasy Games both included simple level-editor tools and expected some of their players to create levels for the game. Both games also had systems for players to distribute the levels they had created and to rate levels created by other players. The game editors and mod creation kits like those released for *Skyrim* and *Fallout 3* also include level editors, and the level editing community for Epic's first-person shooter *Unreal* is one of the broadest and most mature in modern gaming.

The major aspect that differentiates cultural mechanics like game mods from house rules (a dynamic mechanic) is how drastically the inscribed mechanics of the game are actually changed. If the inscribed mechanics largely remain the same but players choose to apply their own goals to the game (e.g., players choosing to do a "speed run" and finish the game as quickly as possible or attempting to play through a usually violent game like *Skyrim* without directly killing any enemies), that behavior still fits within the realm of dynamic mechanics. It is only when players take control from the designers by modifying the inscribed elements of the game that the behavior moves into the cultural layer.

Cultural Aesthetics

Cultural aesthetics occur when the community of players creates their own aesthetics that relate to the game. This is often in the form of their own versions of the character art, music, or other aesthetics of the game but can also take the form of the community using the game engine to achieve their own aesthetic purposes:

- **Fan art:** Many artists take games and game characters as inspiration for their work and create new art that depicts those characters.
- **Cosplay:** Similar to fan art, cosplay (a portmanteau of costume and play) is the practice of a fan of a game (or comic, anime, manga, or film) dressing up as one of the characters from the game. The cosplayer takes on the role and personality of the game character in the real world, just as she did in the virtual world of the game. Cosplay is most commonly seen at game, anime, and comic fan conventions.
- **Gameplay as art:** In Keith Burgun's book *Game Design Theory*, he proposes that some game developers should be seen in much the same way as those who make musical instruments: artisans who craft tools that performers can use to make art. According to him, there is an art not only to crafting games but also to gameplay itself, and the elegance

with which some highly skilled players can play a game should be regarded as an aesthetic in and of itself. Games with broad vocabularies of movement or player actions can evoke this kind of artistic play. Examples include complex fighting games like *Street Fighter* and creative traversal games like *Tony Hawk's Pro Skater*.

Cultural Narrative

Sometimes, the community of players of a game will use the game or the world of the game to tell their own stories and create their own narratives. With pen-and-paper roleplaying games such as *Dungeons & Dragons*, this is a necessary part of the dynamics of play. However, there are also examples of players doing this far outside of the standard or expected dynamics of gameplay:

- **Fan fiction:** Just as with film, television, or any other form of narrative media, some fans of games write their own stories about the game's characters or world.

- **Narrative game mods:** Some games like *Skyrim* and *Neverwinter Nights* allow the players to use authorized tools to create their own interactive narratives within the game world. This allows players to tell their own stories with the game's characters, and because they are built with tools similar to those used by the game developers, these stories can have the same depth and branching as the narratives originally inscribed in the game.

  One particularly inspiring narrative game mod was a simple change made by Mike Hoye, a father and fan of *The Legend of Zelda: The Windwaker*. Hoye had been playing the game with his daughter, Maya, and she absolutely loved it, but he was bothered by the game constantly referring to Link (as played by Maya) as a boy. Mike hacked the game to create a version that referred to Link as a girl. In Hoye's words, "As you might imagine, I'm not having my daughter growing up thinking girls don't get to be the hero and rescue their little brothers." This small change by a player of the game allowed his daughter to feel empowered as the hero of the story in a way she couldn't have playing the original, boy-focused game. [5]

- **Machinima:** Another interesting example of dramatics in the cultural layers is machinima, which are linear videos made by capturing in-game footage. One of the most famous of these is the *Red vs. Blue (RvB)*, a comedy series by Rooster Teeth Productions that takes place entirely within the world of Bungie's first-person shooter, *Halo*. In its original incarnation, the videos were all asymmetrically letterboxed with a thin bar at the top and a thick black bar at the bottom. The bottom bar was there to cover the gun that would have been in the scene because the creators of *Red vs. Blue* originally used footage exactly as seen by players in the game. In those early videos, you can still see the aiming reticle of the gun.

  Red vs. Blue began in April 2003 and has become much more successful and polished over the years, eventually even receiving direct support from the Bungie team. A bug in the original version of *Halo* caused a character's head to pop back up to looking

---

5. You can read Mike Hoye's original blog post about this and download the custom patch that he made at http://exple.tive.org/blarg/2012/11/07/flip-all-the-pronouns/.

straight forward when the character's gun was aimed all the way down. This was used by Rooster Teeth to make it look like the characters were nodding their heads while talking (without their guns pointing at each other). In *Halo 2*, Bungie fixed this bug but enabled a non-aiming posture for characters to make machinima like *RvB* easier to make.

Other game engines have also embraced machinima. *Quake* was one of the earliest heavily used machinima engines. *Uncharted 2: Drake's Deception* by Naughty Dog had a multiplayer online Machinima Mode that encouraged players to make machinima with the game engine and enabled several changes to camera angles, animation, and more.

Cultural Technology

As mentioned earlier in this chapter, a lot of fuzziness exists between the four elements in the cultural layer, and therefore, most of the examples of cultural technology have already been listed under the other three elements (e.g., game mods, which are listed under cultural mechanics but also require technology for their implementation). As with the other three elements, the core of cultural technology is twofold; it covers both the effect that the technology of the game has on the lives of players outside of the time that they are playing and the technology that player communities develop to alter the inscribed elements of the game or the dynamic game experience:

- **Game technology beyond games:** Over the past few decades, game technology has expanded by leaps and bounds. The increasing resolution of displays (e.g., the transition of television from 480i to 1080p and 4K) and the appetite of players for progressively better-looking games have driven developers to constantly improve their techniques for rendering high-quality graphics quickly. These real-time techniques, developed for games, have found their way into everything from medical imaging to previsualization of films (the practice of using game-like animations and real-time graphics to carefully plan complicated shots).

- **Player-made external tools:** External tools, created by players, that can change a player's game experience but don't count as game mods because they don't alter any of the inscribed mechanics of the game are part of the technical layer. Examples include the following:

  - Map applications for *Minecraft* that enable players to see a large-area map of their game, giving them the capability to search for specific geographic features or minerals

  - Damage per second (DPS) calculators for massively multiplayer online games (MMOGs) like *World of Warcraft* that can help players determine the best ways to level their characters and the best equipment to obtain to do the most average damage per second of combat

  - Any of several tools for the MMOG *Eve Online* that are available on mobile devices, including tools to manage skill training, assets, in-game mail, and so on[6]

---

6. In *Eve Online*, skills are trained in real time regardless of whether the player is currently logged in; so, having an alarm to tell the player that a skill is done and she can now select a new one to train is very useful (information from http://pozniak.pl/wp/?p=4882 and https://itunes.apple.com/us/app/neocom/id418895101).

- Fan-made game guides like those available at http://gamefaqs.com that help players understand the game better and can improve a player's ability to play a game well but don't actually modify the inscribed game

Authorized Transmedia Are Not Part of the Cultural Layer

The word *transmedia* refers to narrative or intellectual property that exists across more than one medium. An excellent example of this is *Pokémon*, which since its creation in 1996 has been extremely successful as a television show, a card game, a series of handheld games for portable Nintendo consoles and mobile phones, and a manga series. Many other examples of transmedia exist, including the video games made to accompany the release of nearly every new Disney film and the movies that have been made from famous games like *Resident Evil* and *Tomb Raider*.

Transmedia can be an important part of the brand of a game and can be a strategy to increase market penetration and duration of that brand. However, it is important to draw a distinction between authorized transmedia (like the *Pokémon* example) and unauthorized fan-made transmedia. The latter belongs in the cultural layer, but the former does not (see Figure 6.2).

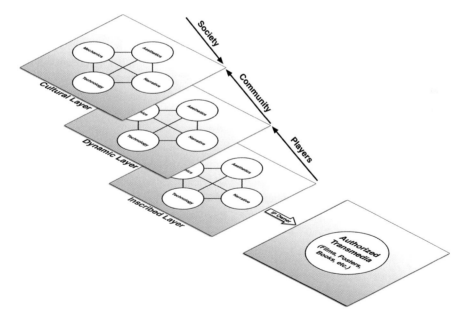

Figure 6.2 The location of authorized transmedia relative to the Layered Tetrad

The inscribed, dynamic, and cultural layers of the Layered Tetrad are separated based on the progression from the elements inscribed by the game's creators through the dynamic play of the game by players and out to the cultural impact that playing the game has on the players and society. In contrast, authorized transmedia are the re-inscribing of the game's brand into something else by the owners of that brand and intellectual property. This places authorized transmedia firmly on the inscribed layer, just as a new game in the same series would be. Each individual transmedia property is another product on the inscribed layer that has the possibility of its own dynamic and cultural layers. The important distinction is one of who has control. In both the inscribed layer of a game and an authorized transmedia companion product to a game, the control is held by the company that develops the game. When the game moves into the dynamic layer, the control is shared between technologies and mechanics put in place by the developers and the actual actions, procedures, strategies, and such executed by the players. In the cultural layer, the control has shifted completely from the developers of the game to the community of players of the game. For this reason, fan fiction, cosplay, game mods, and fan-made transmedia all belong in the cultural layer, but authorized transmedia products do not.

To learn more about transmedia, I recommend reading Professor Henry Jenkins' books and papers on the topic.

The Cultural Impact of a Game

So far, we've looked at the cultural layer as the way in which players take ownership of a game and move it out into the culture at large. Another very different way of looking at this is to consider the impact that gameplay has on players. Disappointingly, the game industry over the past several decades has been quick to acknowledge and promote psychological studies that found evidence of the positive effects of game playing (e.g., improved multitasking skills, improved situational awareness), while simultaneously denying studies that found evidence of the negative impact of gaming (e.g., addiction to games and the negative effects of violence in video games).[7] In the case of violent video games in particular, it's probable that this was largely defensive. Nearly every company that belongs to the Entertainment Software Association (the lobbying group for video game companies) has made games where the core mechanic is some type of violence, and it seems that "violent video games" are a common culprit that journalists tend to blame when people commit horrible acts.[8] However, in 2011, the landscape for this discussion changed in a critical way when the Supreme Court of the United States decided in *Edmund G. Brown, Jr., Governor of California, et al., Petitioners v. Entertainment Merchants Association et al.,* 564 U.S. (2011), that games are art and are therefore protected by

---

7. Even a cursory perusal of the Entertainment Software Association's (ESA's) archive of noteworthy news (at http://www.theesa.com/category/around-the-industry/, accessed January 19, 2017) reveals a plethora of articles about the positive benefits of gameplay and almost none about the potential negative effects.

8. Dave Moore and Bill Manville. "What role might video game addiction have played in the Columbine shootings?" *New York Daily News,* April 23, 2009.

   Kevin Simpson and Jason Blevins. "Did Harris preview massacre on *Doom*?" *Denver Post*, May 4, 1999.

the First Amendment to the United States Constitution. Up to this point, members of the ESA and other game developers had good reason to fear government action to ban violent games. Now, just like most other forms of media, games are protected as art, and developers can make games about whatever they want without fear of government bans.

Examples of Negative Cultural Impact

Of course, with this liberty also comes a responsibility to acknowledge the effects that the games we make have upon society, and this isn't limited exclusively to the violence in games. In the 2011 class-action suit *Meguerian v. Apple Inc.,*[9] Apple paid more than $100 million in settlement because games developed by third-party companies and approved by Apple had been designed with mechanics that encouraged children to pay hundreds of dollars for in-app purchases as part of gameplay. Though Apple settled the suit and thereby avoided a judgment, the complaint was that the games had been designed to prey on children's underdeveloped understanding of real money, and some children had charged over $1,000 in less than a month without their parents' knowledge or approval. It has also been shown that the peak time that people play casual social network games (e.g., Facebook games) is during work hours, and many of these games are designed with "energy" and "spoilage" mechanics that encourage players to return to the game every fifteen minutes, which one could assume has a negative effect on workplace productivity.

Messages that Our Games—and Fans—Send

The first time that anything video game related made the front page of the *New York Times* was an article on October 15, 2014 titled "Feminist Critics of Video Games Facing Threats in 'Gamer-Gate' Campaign."[10] GamerGate was a small, very vocal, misogynistic movement that purported concern for ethics in video game journalism but in practice was a gathering place for men who feared that games were falling under the control of women, liberals, and other "social justice warriors."

The article was written in response to the cancellation of an appearance by feminist cultural critic, Anita Sarkeesian, at Utah State University. Leading up to the cancellation, Sarkeesian had been receiving death and rape threats for months in response to her *Feminist Frequency* YouTube series of insightful analyses of the latent misogyny that has pervaded many games over the past decades. However, in this instance, someone threatened a mass shooting at her talk, and USU refused to ban weapons at the talk, so she canceled.

---

9. Meguerian v. Apple Inc., case number 5:11-cv-01758, in the U.S. District Court for the Northern District of California.

10. You can find the article at http://nyti.ms/1wHspJH, accessed January 19, 2017.

Let me be very clear: GamerGate was the wolf of misogyny dressed in the sheep's clothing of complaints about ethics in video game journalism. I spoke with many game developers about GamerGate, and the overwhelming majority of them were deeply disturbed by the hatred that GamerGate stood for. However, as the game development community, I believe that we must own the fact that through our actions, we created GamerGate. By objectifying women in games and in game advertisements, by presenting straight, white men as heroes and women as objects to be rescued and trophies to be won, we created an audience who believed that this was true and felt threatened when people like Sarkeesian pointed this out. In the latest Mario game, *Super Mario Odyssey*, Mario walks around a realistic New York City and converses with talking forks, but after over 30 years, the plot is still that of him fighting Bowser to save an entirely passive Princess Peach whose only role in the entire series has been to be kidnapped and serve as a prize for Mario to win.[11] Of course, misogyny is not the only issue we face in terms of representation of women in games; the vast majority of main characters in games are still cis white males. This has been slowly improving in commercial games, but it is still a real problem.

Additionally, I believe that we need to be careful of the messages embedded in the mechanics of our games. *Minecraft*—a truly excellent game that encourages creativity and exploration— also includes the embedded concept that the entire world is simply a mine of resources to be consumed by the players. 2b2t.org is one of the oldest existing continually running *Minecraft* servers, and entering into the world for the first time, players find themselves in a barren hellscape completely devoid of any resources. All the resources in the world have been consumed for kilometers in any direction, and what is left is an empty husk of stone bridges left behind, floating in the air, on which players can walk for hours to reach parts of the game where resources remain. One seasoned player stated "The million [brick] mark...that's where all the cool stuff is."[12] At standard walking speed of about 5m/s, it would take a player over 2.3 days of real-time walking (about 166 *Minecraft* days) to travel the 1,000 kilometers necessary to reach that million brick mark (and that's assuming there were no obstacles, gaps, traps, or other players trying to kill you along the way). Though this is certainly an unusual experience in *Minecraft*, it is also an ultimate expression of the core mechanic of the game: that of mining the earth to take what you want and create what you desire with little regard for what you leave behind.

---

11. Princess Peach was an active player character in the U.S. release of *Super Mario Bros. 2* for the NES; however, that game was just a reskinned and improved version of the Japanese game *Yume Kōjō: Doki Doki Panic* (*Dream Factory: Heart-Pounding Panic*, also designed by Shigeru Miyamoto), and not a true *Super Mario* game. Peach has also been an active player character in many of the Mario offshoot games (e.g., *Mario Kart*, *Mario Party*, *Mario Tennis*), but she is still treated as an object in the core Mario games. Reference: http://www.ign.com/articles/2010/09/14/ign-presents-the-history-of-super-mario-bros—accessed January 19, 2017.

12. http://www.newsweek.com/2016/09/23/minecraft-anarchy-server-2b2t-will-kill-you-498946.html – accessed January 19, 2017.

Like all forms of media, games have impact, and they contribute to the actions and world views of those who play them. Games absolutely aren't going to cause someone to choose to perpetrate a mass shooting, but games and many police procedural shows do normalize violence by showing police officers using their guns on a nearly daily basis. To contrast that with reality, only 1/850 officers in New York City fired a weapon at a suspect in 2013; that's an average of a 0.00032% chance of an individual officer firing a weapon at a suspect on any given day (or 1/310,250). I believe that we as designers and media creators have a responsibility for the games that we make and the messages that they send into the world.

Just as game mechanics can normalize consumption or violence, by the same token, they can also promote pro-social or pro-ecological behavior. A version of *Minecraft* could be made with a much smaller world size that required things like crop rotation and responsible use of limited water resources to sustain the world and feed the players on a server. A social network game could be created where the resources a player owned would spoil over time and she would gain points for giving those resources to others in need, perhaps in trade for other resources that she couldn't acquire on her own. If pervasive in games and other media, mechanics like these could normalize sustainable practices and altruism.

Summary

The inscribed and dynamic layers of the Layered Tetrad have been discussed in several books prior to this one, but the cultural layer has received far less attention. In fact, even in my personal practice as a game designer and game design professor, though I think very concretely about the inscribed and dynamic layers on a daily basis, I spend much less time than I should considering the cultural impact of my work and the changes that players might make to my games.

Covering game design ethics in meaningful detail is largely beyond the scope of this book, but it is important that designers think about the consequences of the games they create, particularly because after a player finishes playing a game and sets it aside, the cultural layer is all that remains.

CHAPTER 7

ACTING LIKE A DESIGNER

Now that you've learned something about how to take a designer's approach to thinking about and analyzing games, it's time to look at how game designers go about crafting interactive experiences.

As mentioned in previous chapters, game design is a practice, and therefore, the more design you do, the better you will get at it. However, you also need to make sure that you're starting with the kinds of effective practices that will yield you the greatest gains over time. That is the purpose of this chapter.

Iterative Design

"Game design is 1% inspiration and 99% iteration." —Chris Swain

Remember this saying from the first chapter? In this section, we explore it further.

The number one key to good design—in fact, the most important thing that you can learn from this book—is the process of iterative design shown in Figure 7.1. I have seen iterative design take some games that were initially terrible and make them great, and I've seen it at work across all forms of design from furniture to illustration to game design.

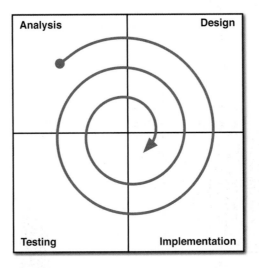

Figure 7.1 The iterative process of design[1]

The four phases of the iterative process of design are:

- **Analysis:** The analysis phase is all about understanding where you are and what you want to accomplish. You must clearly understand the problem that you're trying to solve (or opportunity that you're trying to take advantage of) with your design. You must also understand the resources that you can bring to bear on the project and the amount of time you have in which to implement your design.

- **Design:** Now that you have a clear idea where you are and what you're trying to accomplish with your design, create a design that will solve the problem/opportunity with the resources you have available to you. This phase starts with brainstorming and ends with a concrete plan for implementation.

---

1. Based on Tracy Fullerton, Christopher Swain, and Steven Hoffman, *Game Design Workshop: A Playcentric Approach to Creating Innovative Games* (Burlington, MA: Morgan Kaufmann Publishers, 2008), 36.

- **Implementation:** You have the design in hand; now execute it. There's an old adage: "A game is not a game until people are playing it." The implementation phase is about getting from game design idea to playable prototype as quickly as possible. As you'll see in the digital game tutorials later in this book, the earliest implementations are sometimes just moving a character around the screen—with no enemies or objectives—and seeing whether the movement feels responsive and natural. Implementing just a small part of the game before testing is perfectly fine; a test of just a portion of the game can often be more focused than a large-scale implementation could be. At the end of implementation, you're ready to run a playtest.

- **Testing:** Put people in front of your game and get their reactions. As your experience as a designer grows, you will get better at knowing how the various game mechanics you design will play out when the game is being tested, but even with years of experience, you will never know for sure. Testing will tell you. You always need to test early, when it is still possible to make changes to the game and get it on the right track. You must test frequently so that you can best understand the causes of the changes in player feedback that you witness. If you've changed too many things between two test cycles, it can be difficult to know which one caused a change in player feedback.

Let's look at each phase in more detail.

Analysis

Every design seeks to solve a problem or take advantage of an opportunity, and before you can start to design, you need to have a clear idea of what that problem or opportunity is. You might be saying to yourself "I just want to make a great game," which is true of most of us, but even with that as your initial statement, you can dig deeper and analyze your problem further.

To start, try asking yourself these questions:

1. **For whom am I designing the game?** Knowledge of your target audience can dictate many other elements of design. If you're creating a game for children, it is more likely that their parents would let them use a mobile device than a computer connected to the Internet. If you're designing a game for people who like strategy games, they will most likely be used to playing on a PC. If you're designing a game for men, be aware that nearly 10% of white men are colorblind.

   One thing to always be aware of is the danger of designing a game for yourself. If you just make a game for you, a legitimate possibility exists that *only* you will want to play it. Researching your intended audience and understanding what makes them tick can tell you a tremendous amount about where your game design should go and help you to make your game better.

   It's also important to realize that what players think they want and what they will actually enjoy are sometimes two different things. In your research, it is important to differentiate between your audience's stated desires and the things that actually motivate and engage them.

2. **What are my resources?** Most of us don't have a budget of tens of millions of dollars with which to employ a studio of 200 people to make a game over the span of two years. But you probably do have some time and talent and maybe even a group of talented friends as well. Being honest with yourself about your resources, strengths, and weaknesses can help shape your design. As an independent developer, your primary resources are talent and time. Money can help you purchase either of these through hiring contractors or purchasing assets, but especially if you're working on a small indie game team, you want to make sure that the game you're developing makes the best use of the resources on your team. When working on a game, treat your time and that of your team members as a precious resource; be sure not to waste it.

3. **What prior art exists?** This is the single question that is most often ignored by my students (often to their detriment). *Prior art* is the term used to describe existing games and other media that are related to yours in some way. No game comes from a vacuum, and as a designer, it is up to you to know not only the other games that have inspired you (which, of course, you know), but also what other games exist in the same space that came before or after your primary inspirations.

   For instance, if you were to design a first-person shooter for console, of course you would look at *Destiny*, *Titanfall*, and the *Call of Duty* series, but you would also need to be familiar with *Halo* (the earliest first-person shooter [FPS] that worked well on a console when conventional wisdom held that it was impossible to do so), *Marathon* (Bungie's game prior to *Halo*, which forms the basis for a lot of the design decisions and mythology in *Halo*), and the other FPSs that were precursors for *Marathon*.

   Prior art research is necessary because you must understand everything you can about the ways that other people have tried to approach the design problem that you're tackling. Even if others had the exact same idea as you, they almost certainly approached it in a different way, and understanding both their successes and failures will better equip you to make your game better.

4. **What is the fastest path to a playable game that demonstrates what I want to test?** Though often overlooked, this question is critical for obvious reasons. You only have 24 hours available to you each day, and if you're at all like me, only a small fraction of them can be devoted to game development. Knowing this, it is critical that your time is used as efficiently as possible if you want to get your game made. Think about the *core mechanic* of the game you want to create—the thing that the player does most throughout the game (for example, in *Super Mario Bros.*, the core mechanic is jumping)—and make sure that you design and test that first. By developing and playtesting that, you'll know whether making more of the game is worth it. Art, music, and all other aesthetic elements are certainly important to your final game, but at this point, you must focus on the mechanics—on gameplay—and get that working first. That is your goal as a game designer.

Of course, you'll have many more questions of your own to add to these, but regardless of the game you're making, these four are critical to keep in mind during the analysis phase.

Design

A large portion of this book is about design, but in this section, I focus on the attitude of a professional designer. (Chapter 15, "The Digital Game Industry," covers the industry itself in more detail.)

Design isn't about getting your way, it's not about being a great genius or auteur who is followed by everyone else on the team, and it's not even about doing a great job of communicating your vision to the rest of the team. Design isn't about you—it is about the project. Working as a game designer is about collaborating with the rest of the team, compromising, and above all, listening.

In the first few pages of his book *The Art of Game Design,* Jesse Schell states that listening is the most important skill that a game designer can have, and I emphatically agree. Schell lists five kinds of listening that you need to develop:[2]

- **Listen to your audience:** Whom do you want to play your game? Whom do you want to buy your game? As mentioned earlier, these are critical questions that you must answer, and after you have answered them, you need to listen to the kinds of experiences that your audience wants to have. The whole purpose of the iterative process of design is to make something, throw it out to playtesters, and get their feedback. Make sure you listen to that feedback when they give it, even (especially!) if it's not what you expected or wanted to hear.

- **Listen to your team:** On most game projects, you'll work with a team of other talented people. Your job as the designer is to listen to all of their thoughts and ideas and work with them to unearth the ideas that will create the best game for your audience. Surrounding yourself with people who are willing to speak up when they disagree with you will result in a better game. Your team should not be contentious; rather, it should be a team of creative individuals who all care passionately about both the game and each other.

- **Listen to your client:** A lot of the time, as a professional game designer, you'll be working for a client (boss, committee, etc.), and you must listen to their input. They aren't usually going to be expert game designers—that's why they hired you—but they will have specific needs that you must meet. At the end of the day, your job is to listen to them at several levels: what they tell you they want, what they think they want but don't say out loud, and even what they really want deep down but might not even admit to themselves. With clients, listening carefully can help you leave them with not only an excellent game but also an excellent impression of working with you.

- **Listen to your game:** Sometimes certain elements of a game design fit together like a hand in a glove, and sometimes, it's more like a wolverine in a paper bag (p.s.: *bad idea*). As the designer, you'll be the team member closest to the gameplay, and understanding the game from a *gestalt* (i.e., holistic) perspective is up to you. Even if a certain aspect of

---

2. Jesse Schell, *The Art of Game Design: A Book of Lenses* (Boca Raton, FL: CRC Press, 2008), 4–6.

a game is brilliant design, it might not fit well with the rest. Don't worry; if it is a great bit of design, there is a good chance that you can find a place for it in another game. You'll have numerous chances across the many games you'll make in your career.

- **Listen to yourself:** Important aspects of listening to yourself include the following:

  - **Listen to your gut:** Sometimes you'll get a gut feeling about something, and sometimes these will be wrong, but other times they'll be very right. When your gut tells you something about a design, give it a try. It might be that some part of your mind figured out the answer before your conscious mind had a chance to.

  - **Listen to your health:** Take care of yourself and stay healthy. Seriously. A tremendous amount of research out there shows that pulling all-nighters, being stressed, and not exercising have a real and tremendously negative effect on your ability to do creative work. To be the best designer you can be, you need to be healthy and well rested. Don't let yourself get caught in a cycle of one crisis after another that you try to solve by working crazy hours into the night.

  - **Listen to how you sound to other people:** When you say things to your colleagues, peers, friends, family, and acquaintances, take a moment every once in a while to really listen to how you sound. I don't want you to get a complex about it or anything, but I do want you to listen to yourself and ask these questions:

    Do I sound respectful?

    Do I sound like I care about the other person?

    Do I sound like I care about the project?

    All other things being equal, the people who do best in life are those who consistently demonstrate respect and care for others. I've known some really talented people who didn't get this; they did all right initially, but without fail, their careers sputtered and failed as fewer and fewer people wanted to work with them. Game design is a community of shared respect.

There are, of course, many more aspects to acting like a professional designer than just listening, but Schell and I agree that it is one of the most important. The rest of this book covers more nuts-and-bolts aspects of being a designer, but you must approach all of it with a humble, healthy, collaborative, and creative attitude.

Implementation

The latter two-thirds of this book are about digital implementation, but it's important to realize that the key to effective implementation in the process of iterative design is to get from design to playtest in the *most efficient* way possible. If you're testing the jump of a character in a platform game like *Super Mario Bros.* or *Mega Man*, you must make a digital prototype. However, if you're testing a graphical user interface (GUI) menu system, you don't need to build a fully working digital version; printing out images of the various states of the menu and asking testers to navigate through them with you acting as the computer (and swapping the printed images by hand) is perfectly fine (see the "Paper Prototyping for Interfaces" section in Chapter 9, "Paper Prototyping").

A paper prototype can enable you to quickly test ideas and generate feedback. They usually take drastically less time to implement than digital prototypes and can give you the unique ability to change the game rules in the middle of a play session if the initial rules aren't working. Chapter 9, "Paper Prototyping," includes in-depth information about paper prototyping techniques and both good and bad uses for paper prototypes.

Another important way that you can shorten your implementation time is to realize that you don't have to do everything yourself. Many of my new students approach game development with a desire to learn it all: they want to design the game; write all the code; model, texture, rig, and animate game characters; build environments; write the story; create game code; and sometimes even want to write their own game engine. If you were a multimillion-dollar studio with years of time, this might be an okay idea, but as an independent designer, it's ludicrous. Even indie developers like Notch (the creator of *Minecraft*), who are often seen as solitary geniuses, have stood on the shoulders of *many* giants. *Minecraft* was initially based on an open-source project created by many other people. If you wanted to make a computer game, you could start by building a computer from individual transistors, but that would be ludicrous. It's nearly as ridiculous to think that you would want to write your own game engine. I chose *Unity* as the game engine for this book because hundreds of people are working at Unity Technologies every day to make our job as game developers easier. By trusting them to do their job well, I enable myself to focus on the interesting work of game design and development that I would much rather do than write my own game engine.[3]

Similarly, the *Unity Asset Store* is a fantastic place to trade money for time. The Asset Store enables you to purchase thousands of time-saving assets, including models, animations, and code libraries for everything from controller input to better text rendering, to gorgeous physically based rendering libraries.[4] It also includes several free assets that you can easily use as placeholders in your prototypes. Any time you're thinking about taking the time to write a robust, reusable piece of code for one of your prototypes, I recommend checking on the Asset Store to see whether someone else has already done it for you. Kicking that person a few bucks could save you dozens of hours of development time.

Testing

After you have the barest minimum of a prototype working, it's time to test it. The key thing to keep in mind now is that regardless of what you think about your game, you won't really know anything until a player *who is not you* has tested it and given you feedback. The more people who play your game, the more accurate that feedback will be.

---

3. If you do really want to write your own game engine, my friend Jason Gregory has written a fantastic book on the subject: Jason Gregory, *Game Engine Architecture, 2nd Edition* (Boca Raton, FL: CRC Press 2014).

4. For these three things, I recommend Controller Input—*InControl* by Gallant Games, Better Text Rendering—*TextMeshPro* by Digital Native Studios, Physically Based Rendering—*Alloy* by RUST, LTD.

In my Game Design Workshop class at the University of Southern California, each of our board game projects took place over four weeks of labs. In the first lab, the students were placed in teams and given time to brainstorm their game ideas. Every subsequent lab was devoted entirely to playtesting the latest prototypes of their games. By the end of a four-week project, each student team had completed nearly six hours of in-class playtesting and had drastically improved their designs as a result. The best thing you can do for your designs is to have people playing them and giving you feedback as often as possible. And, for the sake of all that is good, please write down what your playtesters tell you. If you forget what they said, the playtest is a waste.

Making sure that your playtesters are giving you honest feedback is also important. Playtesters sometimes will give you overly positive feedback because they don't want to hurt your feelings. In *The Art of Game Design,* Jesse Schell recommends telling your testers something like the following to encourage them to be honest with you about flaws they see in the game:

> "I need your help. This game has some real problems, but we're not sure what they are. Please, if there is anything at all you don't like about this game, it will be a great help to me if you let me know"[5]

Chapter 10, "Game Testing," covers several different aspects of testing in much more detail.

Iterate, Iterate, Iterate, Iterate, Iterate!

After you have run your playtest, you should have a lot of feedback written down from your testers. Now it's time to analyze again. What did the players like? What didn't they like? Were there places in the game that were overly easy or difficult? Was it interesting and engaging?

From all of these questions, you will be able to determine a new problem to solve with your design. Try to take time to interpret and synthesize player feedback (see the sidebar in Chapter 10 about this). After doing so, try to pick a specific, achievable design goal for your next iteration. For instance, you might decide that you need to make the second half of the first level more exciting or instead decide to reduce the amount of randomness in the game.

Each subsequent iteration of your game should include some changes, but don't try to change too many things or solve too many problems all at the same time. The most important thing is to get to the next playtest quickly and determine whether the solutions that you *have* implemented solved the problems they were meant to solve.

Innovation

In his book *The Medici Effect,*[6] author Frans Johansson writes about two kinds of innovation: *incremental* and *intersectional*.

---

5. Jesse Schell, *The Art of Game Design: A Book of Lenses* (Boca Raton, FL: CRC Press, 2008), 401.

6. Frans Johansson, *The Medici Effect: What Elephants and Epidemics Can Teach Us about Innovation* (Boston, MA: Harvard Business School Press, 2006).

- **Incremental innovation** is making something a little better in a predictable way. The progressive improvement of Pentium processors by Intel throughout the 1990s was incremental innovation; each year, a new Pentium processor was released that was larger and had more transistors than the previous generation. Incremental innovation is reliable and predictable, and if you're looking for investment capital, it's easy to convince investors that it will work. However, as its name suggests, incremental innovation can never make great leaps forward precisely because it is exactly what everyone expects.

- **Intersectional innovation** occurs at the collision of two disparate ideas, and it is where a lot of the greatest ideas can come from. However, because the results of intersectional innovation are novel and often unpredictable, it is often more difficult to convince others of the merit of these ideas.

In 1991, Richard Garfield was trying to find a publisher for his game *RoboRally*. One of the people he approached was Peter Adkison, founder and CEO of Wizards of the Coast. Though Adkison liked the game, he didn't feel that Wizards had enough resources to publish a game like *RoboRally* that had so many different pieces, but he mentioned to Richard that they had been looking for a new game that could be played with very little equipment and resolve in 15 minutes.

Richard intersected this idea of a fast-play, low-equipment card game with another idea that had been kicking around in his head for a while—that of playing a card game with cards that were collected like baseball cards—and in 1993, Wizards of the Coast released *Magic: The Gathering*, which started the entire genre of collectible card games (CCGs).

Though Garfield had been thinking about a card game that was collectible for a little while before his meeting with Adkison, it was the intersection of that idea with Adkison's specific needs for a fast-play game that gave birth to the collectible card game genre, and nearly all CCGs that have come since have the same basic formula: a basic rule set, cards that have printed rules on them that override the basic rules, deck construction, and fast play.

The brainstorming procedure described next takes advantage of both kinds of innovation to help you create better ideas.

Brainstorming and Ideation

"The best way to have a good idea is to have a lot of ideas and throw out all the bad ones." — Linus Pauling, solo winner of both the Nobel Prize in Chemistry and the Nobel Peace Prize

Just like anyone else, not all of your ideas are going to be great ones, so the best you can do is to generate a lot of ideas and then sift through them later to find the good ones. This is the whole concept behind brainstorming. This section covers a specific brainstorming process that I have seen work very well for many people, especially in groups of creative individuals.

For this process, you need a whiteboard, a stack of 3x5 note cards (or just a bunch of slips of paper), a notebook for jotting down ideas, and various whiteboard markers, pens, pencils, and so on. The process works best with five to ten people, but you can alter it to work for fewer people by repeating tasks, and I've modified it in the past to work for a classroom of 65 students. (For instance, if you're by yourself, and it says that each person should do something once, just do it yourself multiple times until you're satisfied.)

Step 1: Expansion Phase

Let's say that you are just starting a 48-hour game jam with a few friends. The theme of the game jam is uroboros (the snake eating its own tail symbol that was the theme of the Global Game Jam in 2012). Not much to go on, right? So, you start with the kind of brainstorming that you learned in grade school. Draw an uroboros in the middle of a whiteboard, draw a circle around it, and start free-associating. Don't worry about what you're writing at this point—don't censor anything—just write whatever comes to mind as you go. Figure 7.2 shows an example.

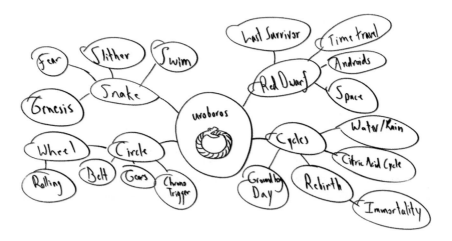

Figure 7.2 The expansion phase of brainstorming a game for uroboros

> ### warning
>
> **BEWARE THE TYRANNY OF THE MARKER**   If you have more people taking part in the brainstorm than you have whiteboard markers, always be careful to make sure that everyone is being heard. Creative people come in all types, and the most introverted person on your team might have some of the best ideas. If you're managing a creative team, try to make sure that the more introverted members of your team are the ones holding the whiteboard markers. They might be willing to write something on the board that they aren't willing to say out loud.

When you're done, take a picture of the whiteboard. I have hundreds of pictures of whiteboards in my phone, and I've never regretted taking one. After capturing it, email it out to everyone in the group.

Step 2: Collection Phase

Collect all the nodes of the brainstorming expansion phase and write them each down on one 3 x 5 note card. These are called *idea cards* (see Figure 7.3), and they'll be used in the next phase.

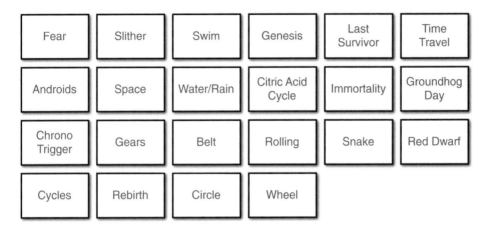

Figure 7.3 Uroboros idea cards

A QUICK ASIDE AND A BAD JOKE OR TWO

Let's start with a bad joke:

> There are two lithium atoms walking along, and one says to the other, "Phil, I think I lost an electron back there." So Phil says, "Really Jason, are you sure?" And Jason replies, "Yeah, I'm positive!"

Here's another:

> Did you hear about the fire at the circus?
>
> It was intense!

Sorry, I know. They're terrible.

You may be wondering why I'm subjecting you to these bad jokes. I'm doing so because jokes like these work on the same principle as intersectional innovation. Humans are creatures who love to think and combine weird ideas. Jokes are funny because they lead our minds down one track and then throw a completely different concept into the mix. Your mind makes the link between the two disparate, seemingly unrelated concepts, and the joy that causes comes across as humor.

The same thing happens when you intersect two ideas, and this is why getting the eureka moment of intersecting two common ideas into a new uncommon one is so pleasurable for us.

Step 3: Collision Phase

Here's where the fun begins. Shuffle together all the idea cards and deal two to each person in the group. Each person takes their two cards up to the whiteboard and reveals them to everyone. Then the group collectively comes up with three different game ideas inspired by the collision of the two cards. (If the two cards either are too closely paired or just don't work together at all, it's okay to skip them.) Figure 7.4 presents a couple of examples.

1. Gardener building crazy contraptions to trap a groundhog that's been eating her garden.
2. Gears of War-style shooter where soldiers must relive a battle until they get it perfect (like in the movie *Groundhog Day*).
3. A time-management game (e.g., *Diner Dash* by Nick Fortugno) where the player must manage the weather so that each season accomplishes its goals and transitions to the next on time.

1. Classic game of *Snake* (snake eats apples and grows but must avoid running into itself), but on a moving conveyor belt.
2. A snake must move across a room camouflaged as people's belts by jumping from waist to waist.
3. A snake hypnotizes a person but can only control them to do very simple things. As the person's belt, the snake must swing and platform them through a dangerous level to escape the zoo.

Figure 7.4 Uroboros idea collisions

Now, the examples in Figure 7.4 are just the first ideas that came to me, as they should be for you. We're still not doing a lot of filtering in this phase. Write down all the different ideas that you come up with in this phase.

Step 4: Rating Phase

Now that you have a lot of ideas, it's time to start culling them. Each person should write on the whiteboard the two ideas from Step 3 that she thinks have the most merit.

After everyone does this, then everyone should simultaneously put a mark next to the three ideas written on the board that they like the most. You should end up with some ideas with lots of marks and some with very few.

Step 5: Discussion

Continue the culling process by modifying and combining several of the ideas with the highest rating. With dozens of different crazy ideas to choose from, you should be able to find a couple that sound really good and to combine them into a great starting point for your design.

Changing Your Mind

Changing your mind is a key part of the iterative design process. As you work through the different iterations of your game, you will inevitably make changes to your design.

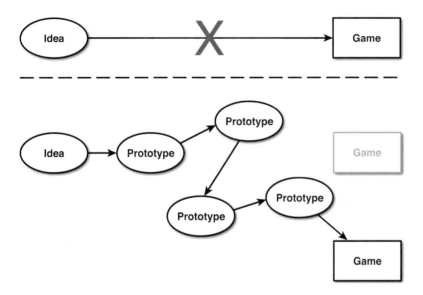

Figure 7.5 The reality of game design

As shown in Figure 7.5, no one ever has an idea and turns it directly into a game with no changes at all (as shown in the top part of the figure), or if anyone ever does, it's almost certain to be a terrible game. In reality, what happens is a lot more like the bottom part of the figure. You have an idea and make an initial prototype. The results of that prototype give you some ideas, and you make another prototype. Maybe that one didn't work out so well, so you backtrack and make another. You continue this process until you've forged your idea over time into a great game, and if you stick to the process and engage in listening and creative collaboration, it'll be a much better game than the original one you set out to make.

As the Project Progresses, You're More Locked In

The process just described is fantastic for small projects or the preproduction phase of any project, but after you have a lot of people who have put a lot of time into something, changing your mind becomes much more difficult and expensive. A standard professional game is developed in several distinct phases:

- **Preproduction:** This is the phase covered by most of this book. In the preproduction phase, you experiment with different prototypes and try to find something that is demonstrably enjoyable and engaging. During preproduction, changing your mind about things is perfectly fine. On a large industry project, there would be between 4 and 16 people on the project during preproduction, and at the end of this phase, you typically would want to have created a *vertical slice*, which is a short, five-minute section of your game at the same level of quality as the final game. This is like a demo level for the executives and other decision-makers to play and decide whether or not to move the game into production. Other sections of your game should be designed at this point, but for the most part, they won't be implemented.

- **Production:** In the industry, when you enter the production phase of a game, your team will grow considerably in size. On a large game title, there could be well over 100 people working on the game at this point, many of whom might not be in the same city or even country as you. During production, all the *systems design* (i.e., the game mechanics) must be locked down very early, and other design aspects (like level design, tuning character abilities, and such) will be progressively locked down throughout production as the team finalizes them. From an aesthetics side, the production phase is when all the modeling, texturing, animation, and other implementation of aesthetic elements take place. The production phase expands the high quality of the vertical slice out across the rest of the project.

- **Alpha:** When you reach the alpha phase of your game, all the functionality and game mechanics should be 100% locked down. At this point, there are no more changes to the systems design of the game, and the only changes you should make to things like level design will be in response to specific problems discovered through playtesting. This phase is where the playtesting transitions to quality assurance (QA) testing in an effort to find problems and bugs (see Chapter 10 for more information). When you start alpha, the game might still have some bugs (i.e., errors in programming), but you should have identified all of them and know how to reproduce them.

- **Beta:** When you reach beta, the game should be effectively done. At beta, you should have fixed any bugs that had the potential to crash your game, and the only remaining bugs should be minor. The purpose of the beta period is to find and fix the last of the bugs in your game. From the art side, this means making sure that every texture is mapped properly, that every bit of text is spelled properly, etc. You do not make any new changes in the beta phase, just fix any last problems that you can find.

- **Gold:** When your project goes gold, it is ready to ship. This name is a holdover from the days of CD-ROM production when the master for all the CDs was actually a disc made of gold that the foil layer of each CD was physically pressed onto. Now that even disc-based console games have updates delivered online, the gold phase has lost some of its finality, but gold is still the name for the game being ship-ready.

- **Post-release:** With the ubiquity of the Internet today, all games that aren't on cartridges (e.g., Nintendo DS games and some 3DS games are delivered on cartridges) can be *tuned*[7]

---

7. *Tuning* is the term for the final stages of adjustments to game mechanics where only tiny changes are made. Even though many Nintendo Switch games ship on cartridges, they can still be tuned via downloadable updates.

after they're released. The post-release period can also be used for development of downloadable content (DLC). Because DLC is often composed of new missions and levels, each DLC release goes through the same phases of development as the larger game (though on a much smaller scale): preproduction, production, alpha, beta, and gold.

Even though your initial projects will usually be much smaller than the professional ones just described, it is still imperative that you lock into design decisions as early as is reasonable. On a professional team, a major design change in the production phase can cost millions of dollars, but on an indie team, it can easily push the release of the game back months, years, or forever. As you move forward in your career, no one will care about your half-finished games or unimplemented game ideas, but everyone *will* care about the games you have finished and shipped. Shipping games builds a reputation for effectiveness, and that's what people are looking for in a game developer.

Scoping

One critical concept you must understand to act like a game designer is how to scope your work. *Scoping* is the process of limiting the design to what can reasonably be accomplished with the time and resources that you have available. *Overscoping* is the number one killer of amateur game projects.

I'll say that again: ***Overscoping is the number one killer of game projects.***

Most of the games you see and play took dozens of people months and months of full-time work to create. Some large console games cost nearly $500 million to develop. The teams on these projects are all composed of fantastic people who have been doing their jobs well for years.

I'm not trying to discourage you, but I am trying to convince you to think small. For your own sake, don't try to make the next *Titanfall* or *World of Warcraft* or any other large, famous game you can think of. Instead find a small, really cool core mechanic and explore it deeply in a small game.

If you want some fantastic inspiration, check out the games that are nominated each year at the IndieCade Game Festival. IndieCade is the premier festival for independent games of various sizes, and I think it represents the vanguard of where independent games are going.[8] If you take a look at their website (http://indiecade.com), you can see tons of fantastic games, each of which pushes the boundaries of gaming in a cool new way. Each of these was someone's passion project, and many of them took hundreds or thousands of hours of effort for a small team or an individual to create.

---

8. For purposes of full disclosure, since 2013, I have served as IndieCade's Chair for Education and Advancement, and I am very proud to belong to such a great organization.

As you look at them, you might be surprised by how small in scale some of them are. That's okay. Even though the scope of these games is pretty small, they are still fantastic enough to be considered for an IndieCade award.

As you progress in your career, you might go on to make massive games like *Starcraft* or *Grand Theft Auto*, but remember that everyone got their start somewhere. Before George Lucas made *Star Wars,* he was just a talented kid in the film program at the University of Southern California. In fact, even when he made *Star Wars,* he scoped it down so perfectly that he was able to make one of the highest-grossing movies of all time for only $11 million. (It went on to make over $775 million at the box office and many, many times that in toy sales, home movie sales, and so on.)

So for now, think small. Come up with something that you know you can make in a short amount of time, work on it efficiently, and above all, **finish it**. If you make something great, you can always add on to it later.

Summary

The tools and theories you've read in this chapter are the kinds of things that I teach to my students and use in my personal design. I have seen the brainstorming strategies that I listed work in both big and small groups to create interesting, off-the-wall, yet implementable ideas, and every experience that I have had in the industry and academia has led me to feel that iterative design, rapid prototyping, and proper scoping are the key processes that you can implement to improve your designs. I cannot more highly recommend them to you.

CHAPTER 8

DESIGN GOALS

This chapter explores several important goals that you might have for your games. We cover everything from the deceptively complex goal of *fun* to the goal of *experiential understanding*, which might be unique to interactive experiences.

As you read this chapter, think about which of these goals matter to you. The relative importance of these goals to each other will shift as you move from project to project and often even shift as you move through the various phases of development. However, always be aware of all of them, and even if one is not important to you, that should be due to deliberate choice rather than unintentional omission.

Design Goals: An Incomplete List

You could have any number of goals in mind when designing a game or interactive experience, and I'm sure that each of you has one that won't be covered in this chapter. However, I try to cover most of the goals that I see in my personal work as a designer and in the design work of my students and friends.

Designer-Centric Goals

Designer-centric goals focus on you as the designer. What do you personally want to get out of designing this game?

- **Fortune:** You want to make money.
- **Fame:** You want people to know who you are.
- **Community:** You want to be part of something.
- **Personal expression:** You want to communicate with others through games.
- **Greater good:** You want to make the world better in some way.
- **Becoming a better designer:** You simply want to make games and improve your craft.

Player-Centric Goals

Player-centric goals focus on what you want for the players of your game:

- **Fun:** You want players to enjoy your game.
- **Lusory attitude:** You want players to take part in the fantasy of your game.
- **Flow:** You want players to be optimally challenged.
- **Structured conflict:** You want to give players a way to combat others or challenge your game systems.
- **Empowerment:** You want players to feel powerful both in the game and in the metagame.
- **Interest / attention / involvement:** You want players to be engaged by your game.
- **Meaningful decisions:** You want players' choices to have meaning to them and the game.
- **Experiential understanding:** You want players to gain understanding through play.

Now let's explore each in detail.

Designer-Centric Goals

As a game designer and developer, you have some goals for your life that you hope the games you make might help you achieve.

Fortune

My friend John "Chow" Chowanec has been in the game industry for years. The first time I met him, he gave me some advice about making money in the game industry. He said:

> "You can literally make hundreds of…
>
> dollars in the game industry."

As he hinted through this joke, there are *many* faster, better ways to make money than the game industry. I tell my programming students that if they want to make money, they should go work for a bank; banks have lots of money and are very interested in paying someone to help them keep it. However, the game industry is just like every other entertainment industry job: Fewer jobs are available than people who want them, and people generally enjoy doing the work; so, game companies can pay less than other companies for the same kind of employees. There are certainly people in the game industry who make a lot of money, but they are few and far between.

It is absolutely possible—particularly if you're a single person without kids—to make a decent living working in the game industry. This is especially true if you're working for a larger game company where they tend to have good salaries and benefits. Working for a smaller company (or starting your own small company) is generally a lot riskier and usually pays worse, but you might have a chance to earn a percentage ownership in the company, which could have a small chance of eventually paying out very nicely.

Fame

I'll be honest: Very, very few people become famous for game design. Becoming a game designer because you want to be famous is a little like becoming a special effects artist in film because you want to be famous. Usually with games, even if millions of people see your work, very few will know who you are.

Of course, there are some famous names like Sid Meier, Will Wright, and John Romero, but all of those people have been making games for years and have been famous for it for equally long. There are also some newer people whom you might know, like Jenova Chen, Jonathan Blow, and Markus "Notch" Persson; but even then, many more people are familiar with their games (*Flow/Flower/Journey*, *Braid/The Witness*, and *Minecraft,* respectively) than with them.

However, what I personally find to be far better than fame is community, and the game industry has that in spades. The game industry is smaller than anyone on the outside would ever expect, and it's a great community. In particular, I have always been impressed by the acceptance and openness of the independent game community and the IndieCade game conference.

Community

There are, of course, many different communities within the game industry, but on the whole, I have found it to be a pretty fantastic place filled with great people. Many of my closest friends are people whom I met through working in the game industry or in games education. Though a sad number of high-budget, AAA games appear sexist and violent, in my experience, most of the people working on games are genuinely good people. There is also a large and vibrant community of developers, designers, and artists who work to make games that are more progressive and created from more varied perspectives. Over the past several years of the IndieCade independent game conference, there have been very well-attended panels on diversity in both the games we make and the development teams who are making those games. The independent game community in particular is a meritocracy; if you make great work, the indie community will welcome and respect you regardless of your race, gender, sexual orientation, religion, or any other ridiculous thing people might use to discriminate against someone. Certainly room still exists to improve the openness of the game development community—and some jerks always appear in any group—but the game development community is full of people who want to make it a welcoming place for everyone.

Personal Expression and Communication

This goal is the flip side of the player-centric goal of *experiential understanding* that you'll find later in this chapter. However, personal expression and communication can take many more forms than experiential understanding (which is the exclusive domain of interactive media). Designers and artists have been expressing themselves in all forms of media for thousands of years. If you have something that you want to express, you must ask yourself two important questions:

What form of media could best express this concept?

What forms of media am I adept at using?

Somewhere between these two questions you'll find the answer of whether an interactive piece is the best way for you to express yourself. The good news is that there is a very eager audience seeking new personal expressions in the interactive realm. Very personal interactive pieces like *Papo y Yo, Mainichi,* and *That Dragon, Cancer* have received a lot of attention and critical acclaim recently, signaling the growing maturity of interactive experiences as a conduit for personal expression.[1]

---

1. *That Dragon, Cancer* (2014, by Ryan Green and Josh Larson) relates the experience of a couple learning that their young son has terminal cancer and helped Ryan deal with his own son's cancer. *Mainichi* (2013, by Mattie Brice) was designed to express to a friend of hers what it was like to be a transgender woman living in San Francisco. *Papo y Yo* (2014, by Minority Media) places the player in the dream world of a boy trying to protect himself and his sister from a sometimes-helpful, sometimes-violent monster that represents his alcoholic father.

Greater Good

A number of people make games because they want to make the world a better place. These games are often called *serious games* or *games for change* and are the subject of several developer's conferences, including the Meaningful Play conference at Michigan State University. This genre of games can also be a great way for a small studio to get off the ground and do some good in the world; a number of government agencies, companies, and nonprofit organizations offer grants and contracts for developers interested in making serious games.

Many names are used to describe games for the greater good. Three of the biggest are:

- **Serious games:** This is one of the oldest and most general names for games of this type. These games can of course still be fun; the "serious" moniker is just to note that there is a purpose behind the game that is more than just playful. One common example of this category is educational games.

- **Games for social change:** This category of games for good is typically used to encompass games that are meant to influence people or change their minds about a topic. Games about things like global warming, government budget deficits, or the virtues or vices of various political candidates fall into this category.

- **Games for behavioral change:** The intent of these games is not to change the mind or opinion of the player (as in games for social change) but instead to change a player's behavior outside of the game. For example, many games have been created in the medical field to discourage childhood obesity, improve attention spans, combat depression, and detect things such as childhood amblyopia. A large and growing body of research demonstrates that games and game play can have significant effects (both positive and negative) on mental and physical health.

Becoming a Better Designer

The number one thing you can do to become a great game designer is make games…or more accurately, make *a lot* of games. The purpose of this book is to help you get started doing this, and it's one of the reasons that the tutorials at the end of the book cover several different games rather than having just one monolithic tutorial that meanders through various game development topics. Each tutorial focuses on making a prototype for a specific kind of game, and each covers a few specific topics. The prototypes you make in these chapters are meant to serve not only as learning tools but also as foundations upon which you can build your own games in the future.

Player-Centric Goals

As a game designer and developer, some goals for your game center on the effects that you want the game to have on your player.

Fun

Many people regard fun as the only goal of games, although as a reader of this book, you should know by now that this is not true. As discussed later in this chapter, players are willing to play something that isn't fun as long as it grabs and holds their attention in some way. This is true with all forms of art; I am glad to have watched the movies *Schindler's List, Life is Beautiful,* and *What Dreams May Come,* but none of them were at all "fun" to watch. Even though it is not the only goal of games, the elusive concept of fun is still critically important to game designers.

In his book *Game Design Theory,* Keith Burgun proposes three aspects that make a game fun. According to him, it must be enjoyable, engaging, and fulfilling:

- **Enjoyable:** Something can be enjoyable in many ways, and enjoyment in one form or another is what most players are seeking when they approach a game. In his 1958 book *Les Jeux et Les Hommes,*[2] Roger Caillois identified four different kinds of play:
  - **Agon:** Competitive play (e.g., chess, baseball, the *Uncharted* series)
  - **Alea:** Chance-based play (e.g., gambling and rock, paper, scissors)
  - **Ilinx:** Vertiginous play (e.g., roller coasters, children spinning around until they're dizzy, and other play that makes the player feel vertigo)
  - **Mimicry:** Play centered on make-believe and simulation (e.g., playing house, playing with action figures, role-playing games)

  Each of these kinds of play is enjoyable in its own way, though in all of them, that fun depends on having a *lusory attitude* (i.e., an attitude of play, as discussed in the next section). As Chris Bateman points out in his book *Imaginary Games,* a fine line exists between excitement and fear in games of ilinx, the only difference being the lusory attitude of the player.[3] The *Tower of Terror* attraction at Disney theme parks is a fun simulation of an out-of-control elevator, but actually being in an out-of-control elevator is not fun at all.
- **Engaging:** The game must grab and hold the player's attention. In his 2012 talk, "Attention, Not Immersion," at the Game Developers Conference in San Francisco, Richard Lemarchand, co-lead game designer of the first three *Uncharted* games, referred to this as "attention," and it's a very important aspect of game design. I discuss his talk in greater detail later in this chapter.
- **Fulfilling:** Playing the game must fill some need or desire of the player. As humans, we have many needs that can be met through play in both real and virtual ways. The need for socialization and community, for instance, can be met both through playing a board game with friends or experiencing the day-to-day life of *Animal Crossing* with the virtual friends who live in your town. The feeling of *fiero* (the Italian word for personal triumph over

---

2. Roger Caillois, *Le Jeux et Les Hommes (Man, Play, & Games)* (Paris: Gallimard, 1958).

3. Chris Bateman, *Imaginary Games* (Washington, USA: Zero Books, 2011), 26–28.

adversity)[4] can be achieved by helping your team win a soccer match, defeating a friend in a fighting game such as *Tekken*,[5] or by eventually defeating the final level in a difficult rhythm game such as *Osu! Tatake! Ouendan*. Different players have different needs, and the same player can have drastically different needs from day to day.

Lusory Attitude

In *The Grasshopper,* Bernard Suits talks at length about the *lusory attitude*: the attitude one must have to take part in a game. When in the lusory attitude, players happily follow the rules of the game for the joy of eventually winning via the rules (and not by avoiding them). As Suits points out, neither cheaters nor spoilsports have a lusory attitude; cheaters want to win but not to follow the rules, while spoilsports have no interest in winning the game and might or might not follow the rules (they mostly want to stop other players from having fun).

As a designer, you should work toward games that encourage players to maintain this lusory attitude. In large part, I believe that this means you must show respect for your players and not take advantage of them. In 2008, my colleague Bryan Cash and I gave two talks at the Game Developers Conference about what we termed *sporadic-play* games,[6] games that the player plays sporadically throughout her day. Both talks were based on our experience designing *Skyrates*[7] (rhymes with *pirates*), a graduate school project for which our team won some design awards in 2008. In designing *Skyrates* we sought to make a persistent online game (like the massively multiplayer online games [MMOs] of the time; e.g., Blizzard's *World of Warcraft*) that could easily be played by busy people. *Skyrates* set players in the role of privateers of the skies, flying from skyland (floating island) to skyland trading goods and battling pirates. The sporadic aspect of the game was that each player was able to check in for a few minutes at a time throughout her day, set orders for her skyrate character, fight a few pirate battles, upgrade her ship or character, and then let her skyrate play out the orders while the player herself went about her day. At various times during the day, she might receive a text message on her phone letting her know that her skyrate was under attack, but it was her choice whether to jump into combat or to let her skyrate handle it on their own.

---

4. Nicole Lazzaro discusses *fiero* often in her talks at GDC about emotions that drive players.

5. Thanks to my good friends Donald McCaskill and Mike Wabschall for introducing me to the beautiful intricacies of *Tekken 3* and for the thousands of matches we've played together.

6. Cash, Bryan and Gibson, Jeremy. "Sporadic Games: The History and Future of Games for Busy People" (presented as part of the Social Games Summit at the Game Developers Conference, San Francisco, CA, 2010). Cash, Bryan and Gibson, Jeremy "Sporadic Play Update: The Latest Developments in Games for Busy People" (presented at the Game Developers Conference Online, Austin, TX, 2010).

7. *Skyrates* was developed over the course of two semesters in 2006 while we were all graduate students at Carnegie Mellon University's Entertainment Technology Center. The developers were Howard Braham, Bryan Cash, Jeremy Gibson (Bond), Chuck Hoover, Henry Clay Reister, Seth Shain, and Sam Spiro, with character art by Chris Daniel. Our faculty advisors were Jesse Schell and Dr. Drew Davidson. After *Skyrates* was released, we added the developers Phil Light and Jason Buckner. You can still play the game at http://skyrates.net.

As designers in the industry at the time, we were witnessing the rise of social media games like *FarmVille* and the like that seemed to have little or no respect for their players' time. It was commonplace for games on social networks to demand (through their mechanics) that players log in to the game continually throughout the day, and players were punished for not returning to the game on time. This was accomplished through a few nefarious mechanics, the chief of which were *energy* and *spoilage*.

In social network games with energy as a resource, the player's energy level built slowly over time regardless of whether she was playing or not, but there was a cap on the energy that could be earned by waiting, and that cap was often considerably less than the amount that could be accrued in a day and less than the amount needed to accomplish the optimal player actions each day. The result was that players were required to log in several times throughout the day to spend the energy that had accrued and not waste potential accrual time on capped-out energy. Of course, players were also able to purchase additional energy that was not capped and did not expire, and this drove a large amount of the sales in these games.

The spoilage mechanic is best explained through *FarmVille*, in which players could plant crops and were required to harvest them later. However, if a crop was left unharvested for too long, it would spoil, and the player would lose her investment in both the seeds and the time spent to grow and nurture the crop. For higher-value crops, the delay before spoilage was drastically less than that of low-value, beginner-level crops, so habitual players found themselves required to return to the game within increasingly small windows of time to get the most out of their investments.

Bryan and I hoped through our GDC talks to counter these trends or at least offer some alternatives. The idea of a sporadic-play game is to give the player the most agency (ability to make choices) in the least amount of time. Our professor, Jesse Schell, once commented that *Skyrates* was like a friend who reminded him to take a break from work every once in a while, but after several minutes of play also reminded him to get back to work. This kind of respect caused our game to have a conversion rate of more than 90%, meaning that in 2007, more than 90% of the players who initially tried the game became regular players.

Respecting your players helps keep them in the lusory attitude, and a lusory attitude is what allows the *magic circle* to exist.

The Magic Circle

As was mentioned briefly in Chapter 2, "Game Analysis Frameworks," in his 1938 book *Homo Ludens*, Johan Huizinga proposed an idea that has come to be known as the *magic circle*. The magic circle is the space in which a game takes place, and it can be mental, physical, or some combination of the two. Within the magic circle, the rules hold sway over the players, and the amount that certain actions are encouraged or discouraged is different from the world of everyday life.

For example, when two friends are playing poker against each other, they will often bluff (or lie) about the cards that they have and how certain they are that they will win the pot. However, outside of the game, these same friends would consider lying to each other to be a violation of their friendship. Similarly, on the ice in the game of hockey, players routinely shove and slam into each other (within specific rules, of course); however, these players will still shake hands and sometimes be close friends outside of the boundaries of the game.

As Ian Bogost and many other game theorists have pointed out, the magic circle is a porous and temporary thing. Even children recognize this and will sometimes call "time out" during make-believe play. Time out in this sense denotes a suspension of the rules and a temporary cessation of the magic circle, which is often done so that the players can discuss how the rules should be shaped for the remainder of the game. When the discussion is complete, "time in" is called, and both play and the magic circle continue where they left off.

Though pausing and resuming the magic circle is possible, maintaining the integrity of the magic circle through those pauses is sometimes difficult. During long delays of football games (for example, if the game is delayed 30 minutes for weather in the middle of the second quarter), commentators will often discuss how difficult it is for players to either maintain the game mindset through the delay or get back into the game mindset after play resumes.

Flow

As described by psychologist Mihaly Csíkszentmihályi (pronounced chick-sent-me-high), *flow* is the state of optimal challenge, and it has been discussed frequently at the Game Developers Conference because it relates so closely to what many game designers are trying to create within their games. In a flow state, a player is focused intently on the challenge before her and often loses awareness of things that are outside of the flow experience. You have probably felt this at times when you have played or worked so intently on something that time seems distorted, seeming to pass either more quickly or more slowly than normal.

Flow in this sense was the subject of Jenova Chen's MFA thesis paper at the University of Southern California as well as the subject of his thesis game, appropriately titled *Flow*.[8] Jenova also spoke about this concept in a couple of talks at GDC.

As you can see in Figure 8.1, the flow state exists between boredom and frustration. If the game is too challenging for the player's skill level, she will feel frustrated; conversely, if the player is too skilled for the game, she will feel bored.

---

8. You can play the original Flash-based version of *Flow* at http://interactive.usc.edu/projects/cloud/flowing/. An updated and expanded PlayStation 3 (and PS4) version is available from the PlayStation Store.

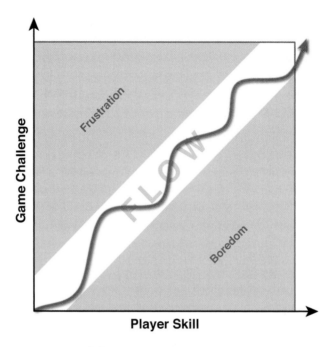

Figure 8.1 Flow as described by Csíkszentmihályi

According to the 2002 article, "The Concept of Flow," by Jeanne Nakamura and Mihaly Csíkszentmihályi, the experience of flow is the same across cultures, genders, ages, and various kinds of activity, and it relies on two conditions:[9]

- Perceived challenges, or opportunities for action, that stretch (neither overmatching nor underutilizing) existing skills; a sense that one is engaging challenges at a level appropriate to one's capacities

- Clear proximal goals and immediate feedback about the progress that is being made

This is what much of the discussion of flow has centered on in the realm of game design. Both of these conditions are concrete enough for designers to understand how to implement them in their games, and through careful testing and player interviews, measuring whether your game is doing so is easy.

Since 1990, when Csíkszentmihályi published his book *Flow: The Psychology of Optimal Experience*, additional research has expanded our understanding of flow as it relates to games in one very important way: Designers now realize that flow is exhausting for players to maintain. While players enjoy flow—and moments of flow are some of the most memorable of your

---

9. Jeanne Nakamura and Mihaly Csíkszentmihályi, "The Concept of Flow." *Handbook of Positive Psychology* (2002): 89–105, 90.

games—maintaining flow for more than 15 or 20 minutes is tiring. In addition, if the player is always kept in a perfect state of flow, she might never have an opportunity to realize that her skill is improving. So, for many players, you actually want a flow diagram like the one shown in Figure 8.2.

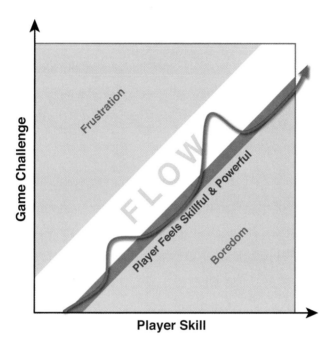

Figure 8.2 Updated flow

A border exists between flow and boredom where players feel powerful and skillful (i.e., they feel awesome!), and players actually need that. Although the flow state is often fun for players, letting your players out of the flow state so that they can reflect on what they accomplished while experiencing flow is also important. Think about the best boss fight you've ever had in a game. When in a flow state, by definition, you lose track of everything outside of the moment because flow requires total attention. If you are like me, it wasn't until you had actually defeated the boss that you had a moment to breathe and realize how amazing the fight had been. Players need not only flow moments but also moments to revel in their increased skill.

Like many other games, the original *God of War* game did this very well. It consistently introduced the player to a single opponent of a new type, and this often felt like a mini boss fight because the player hadn't yet figured out the strategies for defeating that type of enemy. The player eventually learned the strategy for that particular enemy and over several encounters with single enemies of this type perfected her skill. Then, several minutes later, the player was required to fight more than one of this enemy type simultaneously, though because she had increased in skill, this was actually less of a challenge than the single opponent had been originally. Her ability to easily dispatch several copies of the enemy that had earlier given her trouble singly demonstrated to her that she had increased in skill and made her feel awesome.

As you design your games, remember that great game design is not just about giving the player an optimal challenge, it's also about giving her the understanding that she is getting better and granting her time to be awesome. After a difficult fight, give the player some time to just be powerful. This encourages feelings of empowerment.

Structured Conflict

As you saw in Chapter 1, "Thinking Like a Designer," structured conflict is one of the human needs that games can fulfill. One of the primary differences between *play* and *game* is that a game always involves struggle or conflict, which can be conflict against other players or conflict against the systems of the game (see the section *Player Relationships* section in Chapter 4, "The Inscribed Layer"). This conflict gives players a chance to test their skill (or that of their team) against others, systems, chance, or themselves.

This desire for structured conflict is also evident in the play of animals. As Chris Bateman points out in *Imaginary Games:*

> When our puppy plays with other dogs, there are clear limits as to what is acceptable behavior. When play fighting with another puppy, there is much gentle biting, climbing upon one another and general rolling around in frenzied mock violence; there are rules of a kind here.[10]

Even some actual wars have had game-like rules. In the memoir of his life, Chief Plenty Coups (Alaxchiiaahush) of the Crow tribe in North America relates some of the rules of counting coup in battle. Coup was counted for getting away with dangerous actions on the battlefield. Striking an armed and able enemy warrior with a coup-stick, quirt (short riding whip), or bow before otherwise harming him; stealing an enemy's weapons while he was still alive; stealing horses or weapons from an enemy camp; and striking the first enemy to fall in battle (before he was killed) all counted for coup. Doing so while avoiding injury to oneself counted more. Plenty Coups also spoke of rules regarding the two symbolic sticks of tribal communities.

> One of these sticks in each society was straight and bore one eagle's feather on its smaller end. If in battle its carrier stuck this stick into the ground, he must not retreat or leave the stick. He must drop his robe [die] there unless relieved by a brother member of his society riding between him and the enemy. He might then move the stick with honor, but while it was sticking in the ground it represented the Crow country. The bearers of the crooked sticks, each having two feathers, might at their discretion move them to better stands after sticking them to mark a position. But they must die in losing them to the enemy. By striking coup with any of these society coup-sticks, the bearers counted double, two for one, since their lives were in greater danger while carrying them.[11]

---

10. Christ Bateman, *Imaginary Games* (Washington, USA: Zero Books, 2011), 24.

11. Frank Bird Linderman, *Plenty-Coups, Chief of the Crows*, New ed. (Lincoln, NE: University of Nebraska Press, 2002), 31–32.

After the battle, coup was counted, as each warrior related the tales of his exploits during the battle. For successfully performing a coup and escaping without being harmed, the warrior would receive an eagle feather that could be worn in the hair or attached to a coup-stick. If he had been injured, the feather was painted red.

The activity of counting coup among the Plains tribes of the Americas lent additional meaning to the wars between nations and provided a structured way for acts of bravery on the battlefield to translate into increased respect after the battle was complete.

Many of today's most popular games provide for structured conflict between teams of players, including all traditional team sports (soccer, cricket, and basketball being some of the most popular worldwide) as well as online team competitions like *League of Legends*, *Team Fortress 2*, and *Overwatch*. But even without teams, games as a whole provide ways for players to engage in conflict and triumph over adversity.

Empowerment

The earlier section on flow covered one kind of empowerment (giving the player the feeling that she is powerful in the game world). This section covers another kind of empowerment: giving the player power over what she chooses to do in the game. I mean this in two senses: autotelic and performative.

Autotelic

The term *autotelic* comes from the Latin words for self (auto) and goal (telos). A person is autotelic when she is determining her own goals for herself. When Csíkszentmihályi initially started developing his theory of flow, he knew that autotelisis would have a major role in it. According to his research, autotelic individuals get the most pleasure out of flow situations, whereas nonautotelic individuals (that is, those who don't enjoy setting their own goals) tend to get more pleasure out of easy situations where they perceive their skill level to be much higher than the difficulty level of the challenge.[12] Csíkszentmihályi believes that an autotelic personality is what enables a person to find happiness in life regardless of situation.[13]

So, what kinds of games encourage autotelic behavior? One fantastic example is *Minecraft*. In this game, the player is dropped into a randomly generated world where her only real goal is survival. (Zombies and other monsters will attack the player at night.) However, she is also given the ability to mine the environment for resources and then use those resources to make both tools and structures. Players of *Minecraft* have not only built castles, bridges, and a full-scale model of the *Star Trek Enterprise NCC-1701D* but also roller coasters that run for many kilometers

---

12. Nakamura and Csíkszentmihályi, "The Concept of Flow," 98.

13. Mihaly Csíkszentmihályi, *Flow: The Psychology of Optimal Experience* (New York: Harper & Row, 1990), 69.

and even simple working computers with RAM.[14] This is the true genius of *Minecraft*: it gives players the opportunity to choose their own path as players and provides them with flexible game systems that enable that choice.

Although most games are less flexible than *Minecraft*, allowing the player multiple ways to approach a problem is still possible. One of the reasons for the loss in popularity of both text-based adventures (e.g., *Zork*, *Planetfall*, and *The Hitchhiker's Guide to the Galaxy* by Infocom) and the point-and-click adventure games that followed them (e.g., the early *King's Quest* and *Space Quest* series by Sierra OnLine) is that they often only allowed a single (often obtuse) approach to most problems. In *Space Quest II*, if you didn't grab a jockstrap from a random locker at the very beginning of the game, you couldn't use it as a sling much later in the game, and you would have to restart the game from the beginning. In Infocom's game version of *The Hitchhiker's Guide to the Galaxy* when a bulldozer approached your house, you had to lie down in the mud in front of it and then "wait" three times. If you didn't do this *exactly,* you would die and have to restart the game.[15] Contrast this with more modern games like *Dishonored*, where nearly every problem has at least one violent and one nonviolent solution. Giving the player choice over how she will accomplish her goals builds player interest in the game and player ownership over successes.[16]

Performative

The other kind of empowerment that is important to games is performative empowerment. In *Game Design Theory,* Keith Burgun states that not only are game designers creating art, they're creating the ability for players to make art. The creators of passive media can be thought of as composers; they create something to be consumed by the audience. However, as a game designer, you're actually somewhere between a composer and an instrument maker. Instead of just creating the notes that others will play, you're also creating the instrument that they can use to make art. One excellent example of this kind of game is *Tony Hawk's Pro Skater*, where the player has a large vocabulary of moves to draw from and must choose how to string them together in harmony with the environment to get a high score. Just as the cellist Yo-Yo Ma is an artist, a game player can be an artist when empowered by a game designer who crafts a game for her that she can play artistically. We can also see this in other games with large vocabularies of moves or strategies such as fighting and real-time strategy games.

---

14. http://www.escapistmagazine.com/news/view/109385-Computer-Built-in-Minecraft-Has-RAM-Performs-Division.

15. One of the major reasons that this was done was because of the multiplicative explosions of content that would occur if the player were allowed to do anything in the game narrative. The closest thing that I have seen to a truly open, branching narrative is the interactive drama *Façade* by Michael Mateas and Andrew Stern.

16. However, you must also keep development cost and time in perspective. If you're not careful, every option that you give your player could increase the cost of development, both in terms of monetary cost and in terms of time. It's a careful balance that you must maintain as a designer and developer.

Attention and Involvement

As mentioned earlier in this chapter, the fantastic game designer Richard Lemarchand spoke about attention in his GDC 2012 talk, "Attention, Not Immersion: Making Your Games Better with Psychology and Playtesting, the Uncharted Way." The purpose of his talk was to expose confusion about the use of the word *immersion* in game design and to demonstrate that talking about getting and holding an audience's *attention* was a much clearer way of describing what game designers usually seek to do.

Prior to Lemarchand's talk, many designers sought to increase immersion in their games. This led to things like the reduction or removal of the HUD (the onscreen Heads-Up Display) and the minimization of elements that could pull the player out of the experience of the game. But as Lemarchand pointed out in his talk, gamers never truly achieve immersion, nor would they want to. If a gamer actually believed that he was in Nathan Drake's position halfway through *Uncharted 3*, being shot at while clinging to a cargo net that was hanging out of the open door of a transport plane thousands of feet above a desert, the player would be absolutely terrified! One of the critical aspects of the magic circle is that both entry into the circle and remaining in the circle are choices made by the player, and she is always aware that the game is voluntary. (As Suits points out, once participation is no longer voluntary, the experience is no longer a game.)

Instead of immersion, Lemarchand seeks to initially gain the player's attention and then to maintain hold upon it. For the sake of clarity, I use *attention* to describe immediate interest that can be grabbed and *involvement* to describe long-term interest that needs to be held (a distinction that Lemarchand now uses as well). Lemarchand also differentiates between *reflexive attention* (the involuntary response that we have to stimuli around us) and *executive attention* (which occurs when we choose to pay attention to something).

According to his talk, the elements of beauty, aesthetics, and contrast are great at grabbing attention. James Bond films always open with an action scene for this very reason. They begin *in medias res* (in the middle of things) because doing so creates a marked contrast between the boredom of sitting in the theater waiting for the film to start and the excitement of the beginning of the film. This kind of attention grab exploits reflexive attention, the attention shift that is evolutionarily hard-wired into you. When you see something moving out of the corner of your eye, it will grab your attention regardless of whether you want it to. Then, after the Bond movie has your attention, it switches to the rather tedious exposition required to set up the rest of the film. Because the viewer is already hooked by the film, she will make the choice to use her executive attention to listen to this exposition.

In *The Art of Game Design,* Jesse Schell presents his theory of the *interest curve*. The interest curve is also about grabbing attention, and according to Schell, a good interest curve looks like Figure 8.3.

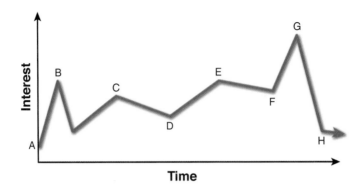

Figure 8.3 Interest curve from Jesse Schell's book

According to Schell, in a good interest curve, the audience will enter with a little interest (A), and then you want to grab them with a "hook" that piques their interest (B). After you have them interested, you can drop it back down and steadily build interest with little peaks and valleys (C, E and D, F, respectively) that should slowly build to the highest point of interest: the climax (G). After the climax, the audience's interest is let back down to (H) in a denouement as the experience comes to a close. This is actually very similar to Syd Field's standard three-act dramatic curve diagram (described in Chapter 4, "The Inscribed Layer"), and it has been shown to work well for time spans between a few minutes and a couple of hours. Schell tells us that this interest curve can be repeated in fractal fashion to cover longer periods of time. One way this could be accomplished is by having a mission structure within a larger game and making sure that each mission has its own good interest curve within the larger interest curve of the entire game. However, it's more complex than that because the interest that Schell discusses is what I'm calling *attention*, and we still need to account for involvement if we want to hold player interest over long periods of time.

Taking a closer look at attention and involvement, attention is directly paired with reflexive attention (the involuntary response), whereas involvement is almost exclusively voluntary/ executive attention. The diagram in Figure 8.4 depicts a synthesis of Lemarchand's concepts and my personal experience as both a designer and player.

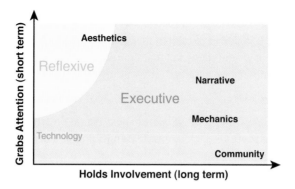

Figure 8.4 The four elements of the Layered Tetrad plus Community in relation to attention and involvement (because technology is largely invisible to the player, it doesn't register much on this graph)

As you can see in the diagram, aesthetics (in terms of the aesthetic element in the tetrad) are best at grabbing our attention, and in the case of aesthetics, that attention is largely reflexive. This is because aesthetics deal directly with our senses and call for attention.

Narrative and mechanics both require executive attention. As pointed out by Lemarchand, narrative has a greater ability to grab our attention, but I disagree with Lemarchand and Jason Rohrer when they state that mechanics have a greater ability to sustain involvement than narrative. Although a single movie tends to last only a couple of hours, the same is also relatively true of the mechanics in a single session of play. Also, in my personal experience, I have found that just as great mechanics can hold my involvement for over 100 hours, so can a series of narratives hold my attention through more than 100 episodes of a serial television show. The major difference between mechanics and narrative here is that narrative must be ever evolving whereas gameplay mechanics can exist unchanged for years and still hold interest due to the different circumstances of play (for example, consider a player's lifelong devotion to chess or go).

The one thing that I have seen outlast both narrative and mechanics in terms of long-term involvement is community. When people find that a community exists around a game, movie, or activity, and they feel part of that community, they will continue to take part long after the hold of narrative or mechanics have lost their sway. Community is what kept many guilds together in *Ultima Online* long after most people had moved on to other games. Also, when the members of the community did eventually move on, they more often than not chose as a community which new game to play together and all switched to the new game at the same time, thus continuing the same community through multiple different online games.

Interesting Decisions

As you read in Chapter 1, Sid Meier has stated that games are (or should be) a series of interesting decisions, but we questioned at that time what exactly was meant by *interesting*. Throughout the book thus far, we have seen several concepts presented that can help illuminate this.

Katie Salen and Eric Zimmerman's concept of *meaningful play* as presented in Chapter 5, "The Dynamic Layer," gives us some insight into this. To be meaningful, a decision must be both *discernible* and *integrated*:[17]

- **Discernible:** The player must be able to tell that the game received and understood her decision (i.e., immediate feedback).
- **Integrated:** The player must believe that her decision will have some effect on the long-term outcome of the game (i.e., long-term impact).

In his definition of game, Keith Burgun points out the importance of decisions being *ambiguous*:

- **Ambiguous:** A decision is ambiguous for the player if she can guess at how it might affect the system but can never be sure. The decision to wager money in the stock market is ambiguous. As a savvy investor, you should have a pretty decent guess about whether the value of the stock will go up or down, but the market is so volatile that you can never know for sure.

Almost all interesting decisions are also *double-edged* (as in the saying "a double-edged sword"):

- **Double-edged**: A decision is double-edged when it has both an upside and a downside. In the previous stock purchase example, the upside is the longer-term potential to make money, and the downside is the immediate loss of the resource (money) used to purchase the stock as well as the potential for the stock to lose value.

Another aspect involved in making a decision interesting is the *novelty* of the decision.

- **Novel**: A decision is novel if it is sufficiently different from other decisions that the player has made recently. In the classic Japanese roleplaying game (JRPG) *Final Fantasy VII*, combat with a specific enemy changes little throughout each battle, meaning that few novel decisions exist for the player to make. If the enemy is weak to fire, and the player has enough mana and fire magic, she will generally attack every round with fire magic until the enemy is defeated. In contrast, the excellent combat in the JRPG *Grandia III* makes positioning and location important for most special attacks, but the player's characters move around the field autonomously (independent of player input). Whenever the player is

---

17. Katie Salen and Eric Zimmerman, *Rules of Play* (Cambridge, MA: MIT Press, 2003), 34.

able to make a decision, time freezes for her, and she must reevaluate the positions of allies and enemies before making her decision. This autonomous movement of her characters and the importance of position make every combat decision novel.

The final requirement for interesting decisions is that they must be *clear*.

- **Clear**: Although it is important for the outcomes of a choice to have some ambiguity, the choice itself must be clear. Choices can lack clarity in many ways:
  - A choice can be unclear if there are too many options to choose from at a given time; the player can have difficulty discerning the differences between them. This leads to *choice paralysis*, the inability to choose because there are too many options.
  - A choice can be unclear if the player can't intuit the likely outcome of the choice. This was often a problem in the dialog trees in some older games, which for years just listed the possible statements that a player could make without any information about the implied meaning of those statements. In contrast, the dialog tree decision wheel in *Mass Effect* included information about both whether a statement would be said in a friendly or antagonistic way and whether it would extend or shorten the conversation. This allowed the player to choose an attitude rather than specific wording of a statement and removed the ambiguity in the dialog tree.
  - A choice can also be unclear if the player doesn't understand the significance of the choice. One of the great advances in the combat system of *Grandia III* over *Grandia II* allowed threatened characters to automatically call for help during another character's turn. If Character A is about to be hit by an attack, and Character B can prevent it by acting on this turn, Character A will cry for help during Character B's turn. The player might still choose to have Character B do something other than prevent the attack, but the game has made it clear to her that this is her last chance to prevent the attack on A.

We can combine these six aspects together into a decent understanding of the things that make a decision interesting. An interesting decision is discernible, integrated, ambiguous, double-edged, novel, and clear. By making your decisions more interesting, you can increase the appeal of your mechanics and thereby the player's long-term involvement in your game.

Experiential Understanding

The final goal for players that we'll discuss in this chapter is *experiential understanding*, a design goal that is far more accessible to game designers than designers of any other kind of media.

In 2013, game critic and theorist Mattie Brice released *Mainichi*,[18] the first game that she had designed and developed (see Figure 8.5).

---

18. You can download and play *Mainichi* at http://www.mattiebrice.com/mainichi/.

Figure 8.5 *Mainichi* by Mattie Brice (2013)

As described by Brice, *Mainichi* is a personal letter from her to a friend to help her friend understand what her daily life is like. In her real life, Brice is a transgender woman who at the time lived in the Castro district of San Francisco. In *Mainichi*, the player takes on the role of Mattie Brice and must choose what to do to prepare to go out for coffee with a friend: does she dress nicely, put on makeup, eat a bite? Each of these decisions change how some (but not all) of the people around town react to her as she walks to the coffee shop and orders her drink. Even a simple decision like whether to pay with a credit card or cash has meaning in the game. (Paying with a credit card will cause the barista to refer to you as "Ms… er… Mr. Brice" because he reads Brice's old, male name on the credit card.)

The game is very short, and as a player, you are compelled to try again and see what happens differently based on the seemingly small choices that you make throughout the game. Because the player's decisions change how the character of Mattie is perceived, you feel *complicit* in her being treated well or poorly by the people around her. Though some kind of branching chart or a story structured like the movie *Groundhog Day* (in which Bill Murray's character must relive the same day hundreds of times until he finally gets it right) could convey the same information about the large implications of the tiny choices that Brice makes every day, neither would convey a sense of responsibility to the audience. At this time, it is only through a game (be it a video game, make-believe, or roleplaying) that a person can actually walk in the shoes of another and gain insight into what it must be like to make the decisions that they make. This experiential understanding is one of the most interesting goals that we can seek to achieve as game designers.

Summary

Everyone making games has different feelings about each of the design goals presented in this chapter. Some people just want to make fun experiences, some people want to give players interesting puzzles, some people want to encourage players to think deeply about a specific topic, and some people want to give players an arena in which to be empowered. Regardless of what your reasons are for wanting to make a game, it is time now to start making them.

The next two chapters are about paper prototyping and playtesting. Together, prototyping and playtesting form the core of the real work of game design. In almost any game—especially a digital game—there are hundreds of small variables that you can tweak to modify the experience. However, in digital games, even seemingly small changes can take considerable development time to implement. The paper prototyping strategies presented in the next chapter can help you get from concept to playable (paper) prototype very quickly and then get you from one prototype to the next even more rapidly. For many games, this paper prototyping phase can save you a lot of time in digital development because you will have already run several paper playtests to find the fun before writing a single line of code.

CHAPTER 9

PAPER PROTOTYPING

In this chapter, you learn about paper prototyping, one of the best tools available to game designers to rapidly test and iterate on game ideas. Although simple to implement, paper prototypes can teach you a tremendous amount about various aspects of your game, even if that game will eventually be digital.

By the end of the chapter, you will know the best practices for implementing paper prototypes and understand the parts of a digital game that can best be understood and tested through paper.

The Benefits of Paper Prototypes

Although digital technologies have enabled a whole new world of possibilities for game development, many designers still find themselves exploring their initial ideas using traditional paper methods. With computers able to calculate and display information much faster than a person could draw or calculate by hand, you might be wondering why this is. It largely comes down to two factors: speed and ease of implementation. These two factors lead to several benefits, including the following:

- **Initial development speed:** For quickly throwing together a game, nothing beats paper. You can combine some dice, 3 x 5 note cards, and other simple elements to make a game in very little time. Even when you have a lot of experience as a game designer, starting on a new digital game project can take quite a bit of time if it's significantly different from anything you've done before.

- **Iteration speed:** Making changes to paper games is also very fast; in fact, you can even make changes to the games while you're playing. Because of the ease of changes, paper prototypes are a great fit for game brainstorming at the beginning of preproduction on a project (when large changes to the project can happen frequently). If a paper prototype isn't working, making a change can take as little as a few minutes.

- **Low technical barrier to entry:** Because very little technical knowledge or artistic talent is required to make a paper prototype, anyone on the game development team can take part in the process. This is a way to get great ideas from people on your team who would not be able to effectively contribute to a digital prototype.

- **Collaborative prototyping:** Because of the low barrier to entry and the rapid iteration, you can collaboratively create and modify a paper prototype in a way that is not yet possible for digital prototypes. A group of people from across your team can work together on a paper prototype and share ideas quickly. As an added benefit, bringing people from across your game development team into the design process in this way can help to increase their buy-in for the entirety of the project and can serve as a fantastic team-building activity.

- **Focused prototyping and testing:** It is obvious to even a complete novice that a paper prototype of a digital game is going to be very different from the final digital product. This allows you to test specific elements of your game without your testers getting hung up on details. In the 1980s, an internal document to user interface designers at Apple Computer recommended that they make rough sketches of the buttons for their interfaces on paper, scan the paper, and then make their UI prototypes from the scanned images. Because the sketched and scanned images of UI elements like buttons and menus were so obviously not the final look that Apple would choose for the UI, testers didn't get hung up on the look of the buttons and instead focused on the usability of the interface, which is what Apple was interested in testing. A paper prototype can help direct the attention of your testers in the same way so that they don't get hung up on the look of the prototype but instead focus on the specific aspect of gameplay that you intend to test.

Paper Prototyping Tools

There are several tools for paper prototyping that you might want to have handy. You can make a paper prototype from almost anything, but some tools can help make the process go faster:

- **Large sheets of paper:** At most office supply stores, you can get easel-sized sheets of paper (something like 24" wide by 36" tall). These often come in a pad of several sheets, and some have a mild adhesive on the back of each sheet to stick them to walls and such. You can also often find large sheets of paper inscribed with a square or hexagonal grid. See the "Movement on Different Grid Types" sidebar for information about why you would choose a hexagonal or square grid and how to handle free movement on an open grid game board.

- **Dice:** Most people have some d6 dice (normal six-sided dice) sitting around. As a game designer, it's also really good to own some of the other dice varieties. Your local game store should have sets for sale that include all the dice normally used for d20 roleplaying games including 2d6 (2 six-sided dice), 1d8, 1d12, 1d20, and percentile dice (2d10 with one marked 0–9 and the other marked 00–90; rolled together, they give you a number between 00 and 99). Chapter 11, "Math and Game Balance," includes a lot of information about different kinds of dice and what the probability space of their randomness looks like. For example, with 1d6, you have an even chance of any number from 1 to 6, but with 2d6 there are 6 different ways to roll a 7 (a 6/36 chance) but only one way to roll a 12 (a 1/36 chance).

- **Cards:** Cards are a fantastic prototyping tool because they are so malleable. Create cards numbered 1–6, and you have a 1d6 deck. If you shuffle before every draw, it acts just like a 1d6, but if you draw all the cards before reshuffling, then you're guaranteed to get one each of 1, 2, 3, 4, 5, and 6 before seeing any number for a second time.

- **Card sleeves:** Most gaming stores sell several different styles of card sleeves. Card sleeves were initially developed to protect baseball cards, and they were extended to the gaming industry with the rise of collectible card games like *Magic: The Gathering* in the '90s. Each card sleeve is a protective plastic cover for an individual card, and there's enough room inside of them for both a regular card and a slip of paper. This is great for prototyping because it means that you can print the cards for your prototype on regular printer paper and then put them into a sleeve in front of a regular playing card. The regular card will give the card enough stiffness to be shuffled without the time and expense of writing or printing on card stock. The card sleeves can also ensure that all the card backs look uniform, or alternatively, several sets of card sleeves can be used to keep different decks of designed cards separate.

MOVEMENT ON DIFFERENT GRID TYPES

As shown in Figure 9.1, if your game includes player movement, you must make choices about how players can move across the board. As depicted in image A, on a square grid diagonal movement moves the player almost 50% further than orthogonal movement. (According to the Pythagorean theorem, the diagonal distance is $\sqrt{2}$ or roughly 1.414.) However, movement to any adjacent hex in a hexagonal grid is the same, regardless of which hex you choose (image B).

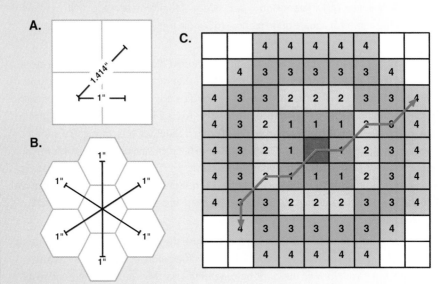

Figure 9.1 Movement systems

Image C shows a simple alternative movement system across a square grid that can be used in board games to still allow diagonal movement yet prevent abuse thereof. Players are allowed to move diagonally with every other movement. This evens out the distances somewhat and makes possible movement within a specific number of moves roughly circular. The purple lines on diagram C show two different possible paths of four moves each. This movement system is used in *Dungeons & Dragons* by Wizards of the Coast.

Hexagonal grids are often used for military simulation board games where an accurate representation of distances and movement is critical. However, most buildings in the real world are rectangular, so they don't fit as well on a hexagonal board. The choice of which type of grid to use is up to you as a designer.

- **3 x 5 note cards:** Cut in half, 3 x 5 note cards are a great size for a deck of cards. At their regular size, they're fantastic for brainstorming. Some stores now sell 3 x 5 cards that have already been cut in half (to 3 x 2.5).

- **Post-It® notes:** These simple little sticky notes are fantastic for quickly arranging and sorting ideas.

- **Whiteboard:** Nothing says brainstorming like a whiteboard. Be sure to have lots of colors of markers available. Whiteboards tend to get erased often, so be sure to snap a digital photo of anything you write on one that is at all worth keeping. If you have a whiteboard tabletop or a vertical whiteboard that is magnetic, you can also draw a game board on it, but I tend to prefer large sheets of paper for game boards because they won't be erased.

- **Pipe cleaners / LEGO blocks:** Both of these can be used for the same purpose: quickly building little things. These could be playing pieces, set pieces, or really anything you can think of. LEGO blocks are a lot sturdier, but pipe cleaners are much cheaper and more flexible.

- **A notebook:** As a designer, you should always have a notebook handy. I like the pocket-size Moleskine with unlined paper, but several types are available. The key element of your notebook is that it needs to be small enough to carry with you and large enough that you won't be filling it up and replacing it every few weeks. Any time someone plays your game prototype, you should be taking notes. Although during a playtest, you might think you'll remember important things that happen or were said by players, even a few hours later—that is often not the case.

Paper Prototyping for Interfaces

One example of a great place to use a paper prototype is when making interface decisions. For instance, the diagram in Figure 9.2 shows some different screens from a Graphical User Interface (GUI) mockup of an options menu for a touchscreen mobile game. Each playtester would only be shown one screen at a time, starting with #1, the *Options Menu*. While shown screen #1, the playtester would be instructed to "Press the selections you would make to turn the subtitles on." (You would encourage the playtesters to actually touch the paper as if they were touching a touchscreen.)

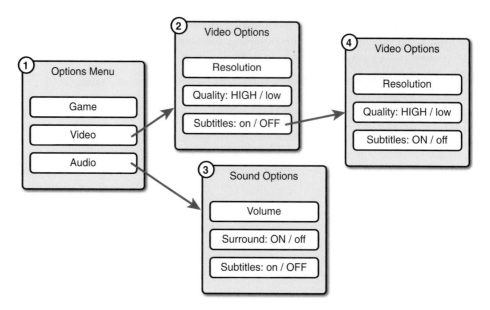

Figure 9.2 A simple paper GUI prototype

Some playtesters might press the *Video* button, whereas others might press *Audio* (and a few might press *Game*). After the user makes a selection, you would replace the #1 sheet of paper with the menu of her selection (for example, #2 *Video Options*). Then, presumably, the playtester would press the *Subtitles: on / OFF* button to switch the subtitles on, when you would replace #2 with #4 *Video Options*.

One important thing to note here is that subtitles are available to be changed on both the video and sound options screens. For testing this works well because regardless of which of the two options the player chooses (Video or Audio), you can then subsequently test whether the *on / OFF* capitalization clearly conveys that the subtitles are currently turned off.

An Example Paper Prototype

In this section of the chapter, I take you through the process of designing a paper prototype for a level that you will implement in Chapter 35, "Dungeon Delver." You'll see it from the initial phase of ideation through to the creation of a clear, limited paper prototype that can teach us something useful for the final digital version of the game.

Game Concept—A 2D Adventure Game Level

In the last chapter of this book, I'll lead you through developing a top-down 2D adventure game based on the original *Legend of Zelda* for the Nintendo Entertainment System (NES). In games like this, one of the most important level design questions has to do with locks and keys.

As a designer, you place locks on doors and keys to those locks in rooms with the expectation that your players will approach the dungeon in a specific way; however, players are often unpredictable. Take a look at the two identical versions of the first dungeon from *The Legend of Zelda* shown in Figure 9.3. The green line in the top map shows a completionist player's path through the dungeon. Here, she has collected and used every key and every item in the dungeon (including the collection of the bow in B1 and the boomerang in D3). This is generally how new players experience the level, but it's not the only way to reach the goal at the end.

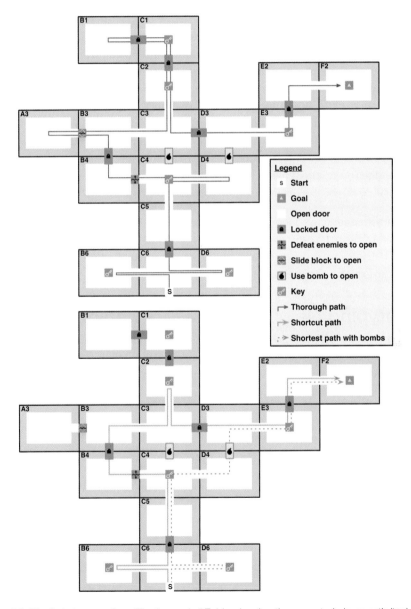

Figure 9.3 The first dungeon from *The Legend of Zelda*, showing the expected player path (top) and two possible shortcut paths (bottom)

The bottom map of Figure 9.3 shows two shortcut paths through the dungeon. Following either of these paths, the player will not collect the bow from room B1, though she will still get the boomerang in room D3. The purple shortcut path shows one that a player can take without any special items. The dashed red shortcut path shows the fastest way that a player can get to the boss battle if she has the bomb item. This red path only requires the use of 2 out of 6 keys and only visits 9 of the 17 rooms. The bow obtained in room B1 is a strong impetus for the player to go all the way up to that room, but she has the option not to if she chooses to forego the bow in exchange for extra keys that she can use in other dungeons.

If the player wanted to get the bow but use bombs to walk the shortest path possible, what path could she take? You should make a paper prototype to find out! Try drawing the map of this dungeon on a piece of paper. Put a marker in each room that has a key (something like a coin or a small bit of paper with a key drawn on it). Place paper clips (or something else rectangular) over each of the locked doors that you haven't yet opened. Find another rectangular marker and place it over the bombable walls.[1] Then, place a marker for yourself in the starting room. Move into rooms and pick up keys when you encounter them, then discard 1 key and 1 paper clip whenever you unlock a door. Use bombs whenever you want. How few rooms can you visit and still make it to B1 before finishing at F2?[2] If you had bombs and wanted to get the bow from B1, could you exit the dungeon without using all the keys?[3]

This is a very-well designed dungeon, and all of these behaviors are intentional, but you can see how players can exploit even a great dungeon design. Try designing your own *Legend of Zelda* dungeon with just keys and locked doors (and no bombable walls) and see whether players you give it to can exploit it in some way.

Prototyping New Traversal Mechanics

In later games in the *Legend of Zelda* series, several items increased the main character Link's ability to move through dungeons. One classic example of this is the *hookshot*, a grappling hook that allows Link to connect to a wall on the other side of a gap and pull himself across. A hookshot-like item is another thing that you can easily explore using a paper prototype.

Figure 9.4 shows a dungeon that I designed using this concept. You can see the dungeon layout on top with the full traversal path in green.

---

1. In *The Legend of Zelda* the bombable walls in the first dungeon look just like normal walls, but we don't need to worry about that for this prototype.

2. The shortest path I found visited 12 rooms, picked up 5 keys, and only used 4 of them. There is also a path that visits 13 rooms, picks up 5 keys, and only uses 3 of them.

3. Yes, this is possible, and you can exit the dungeon with extra keys that you can use in any dungeon in the game.

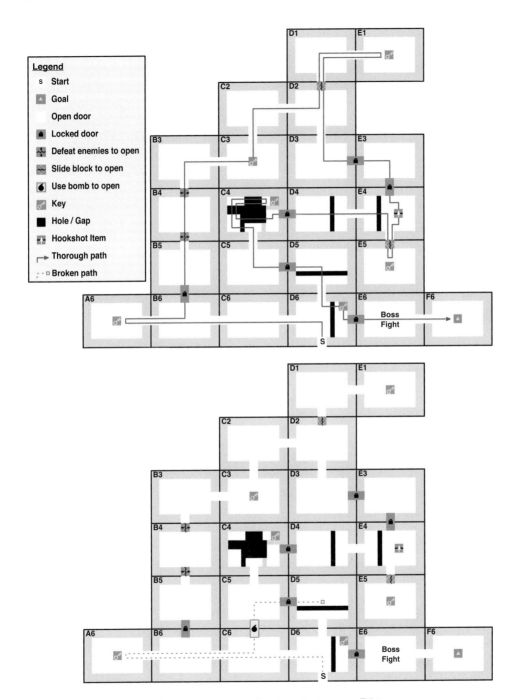

Figure 9.4 A new dungeon that uses a hookshot item (acquired in room E4) to cross gaps

> **warning**
>
> **THE DANGER OF ALLOWING SHORTCUTS**   There are no bombable walls in the Figure 9.4 level because allowing shortcuts can also allow players to get into unwinnable situations. For example, in the bottom diagram of Figure 9.4, a single bombable wall between C6 and C5 would allow the player to follow the broken red path and get stuck, having used the one key she could acquire on the wrong door. This is another big thing that a paper prototype can help you solve.

Playtesting

Play the prototype a few times yourself and then get a few different friends to play it as well. They might find some paths through the dungeon that you had missed.

One thing that this prototype doesn't handle well in its current state is the surprise of each new room in a *Legend of Zelda* dungeon. What I mean by this is that players are able to plan their moves ahead of time by seeing the whole dungeon at once instead of seeing each room one at a time. The best way to implement this discovery would be to draw (or print out) your dungeon with each room on a separate piece of paper. In this case, putting each room on a separate 3 x 5" notecard (or on the blank back of business cards) would allow you to place them on the playing surface one by one as they're discovered. Players will almost certainly follow different paths if they don't have an understanding of the whole map (which is why the map and compass items in *The Legend of Zelda* are so important[4]).

Every time you play, be sure to keep these questions in mind:

- Is the player following a path that surprises you?
- Is it possible for her to get herself stuck in any way?
- Is the player having fun?

The third question might seem a little strange for a prototype that doesn't even have a single enemy in it, but the levels for a game like this are puzzles in and of themselves, and puzzles should be fun.

Be sure to write down notes on what the player does and what she thinks of the prototype every time you play it. As you modify the prototype, you might find that your opinions change over time. Taking notes is critical because it allows you to understand how your game changed throughout the course of development and gives you more awareness of trends over time.

---

4. In the original NES version, the map shows you a grid with blue blocks representing every room in the dungeon, and the compass places a red dot on the map showing you where the boss fight room is.

Chapter 10, "Game Testing," includes a lot of information about how to run playtests, and Chapter 13, "Puzzle Design," covers several aspects of the puzzle design process and why it is so important for single-player games.

Best Uses for Paper Prototyping

Paper prototyping for digital games has both strengths and weaknesses. Here are some things that paper prototypes are particularly good at:

- **Understanding player movement through space:** This is the core purpose of the example prototype in this chapter. Keep track of which directions players tend to go through your dungeon. Do they usually turn left or right when given two equal options? Understanding player flow through space helps you in all aspects of level design.

- **Balancing simple systems:** Even with just a few variables, balancing the strength of similar items in a game can be very complex. For example, consider the balancing of two weapons—a shotgun and a machine gun—each having three simple variables: accuracy over distance, number of shots, and damage per shot. Although there are only three variables, balancing each weapon against the others is more complex than it might originally seem. For example, consider the shotgun and the machine gun relative to each other:

  - **Shotgun:** The shotgun would do lots of damage up close, but its accuracy would decrease very quickly as distance increased. Additionally, it has only one shot, so if that shot misses, the enemy will take no damage at all.

  - **Machine Gun:** The machine gun would only do a little damage per shot, but could fire a number of bullets in a single turn and it would lose less accuracy over distance. The randomness aspect of accuracy could also be calculated on a per-bullet basis.

  If accuracy in the game includes some randomness in the calculation, the multiple per-bullet random chances offered by the machine gun in a single turn will make it much more likely to do a reliable amount of damage when fired, whereas the shotgun's single shot is an all-or-nothing thing. With these stats, the shotgun is risky but powerful, whereas the machine gun is reliable but a little less powerful. We'll explore the math behind this much more in Chapter 11, "Math and Game Balance."

- **Graphical user interface:** As shown earlier in Figure 9.2, you can easily print several mock-ups of a GUI (i.e., buttons, menus, input fields) and then ask testers which on-screen button they would press to accomplish a certain task (e.g., pausing the game, picking a character).

- **Trying wild ideas:** Because of the rapid iteration and development speed of paper prototypes, trying a crazy rule every once in a while to see how it changes gameplay is also easy.

Poor Uses for Paper Prototyping

Although it has many great uses, paper prototyping is pretty awful at some things:

- **Tracking lots of information:** Many digital games constantly keep track of hundreds of variables. In a stealth combat game, these could include visibility calculations, health tracking, the distance of a ranged attacker from their target, and so on. In paper prototypes, you want to focus on the simple systems in a game and get a good idea of things like the layout of a level or the general feel of various weapons (e.g., the "risky" shotgun and the "reliable" machine gun could be prototyped with a single d20 die roll for the shotgun versus 4d4 for the machine gun). You'll then fine tune this information with the digital prototype.

- **Game rhythm for fast or slow games:** Paper prototypes can also give you a false impression of game rhythm and feel if the game will be played much more quickly or more slowly than the paper prototype. For example, I once saw a team put too much stock in a paper prototype for a game that would be played by players around the world over the span of a month. The paper prototype had a number of interesting revenge mechanics where players could directly taunt and compete with each other. These worked really well with all players in the same room and the paper prototype lasting only an hour or so. However, with players distributed around the world and the actual game lasting weeks or months, the revenge mechanics were less immediate and didn't work very well.

- **Physical interface:** Although paper prototypes can work well for GUIs, they have very little to tell us about physical interfaces (e.g., gamepad controllers, touchscreens, keyboard, and mouse). Until you have a digital prototype working with the actual physical interface that the player will use, you really won't know anything about how well the physical control scheme maps to your game. This is a tough issue, as can be evidenced by the subtle changes to controls for many long-running game series (for example, all the changes over the years to the controls of the various *Assassin's Creed* games).

Summary

I hope that this chapter has demonstrated to you the power and ease of paper prototyping. At some of the best university game design programs, students spend their first game design class working primarily on board games and card games to build their skills in paper prototyping, game balance, and tuning. Not only can paper prototypes help you rapidly explore concepts for your digital games, they can also help you build skills in iterative design and decision making that will be invaluable to you when you start making digital games.

Each time you start designing a new game (or a new system for a game you're already developing), ask yourself the question of whether that game or system could benefit from a paper prototype. For example, the new dungeon level that is shown in Figure 9.4 took me less than an hour to design, implement, and test several times; yet it took me several days to develop all the different logic, camera moves, artificial intelligence, controls, and so on for the digital version in Chapter 35, "Dungeon Delver." Adding something like the hookshot would take just minutes on paper and hours or days in Unity and C#.

Another thing that you can learn from paper prototypes is to not be discouraged when a design decision you make backfires. We all make bad design decisions throughout our careers as designers, and doing so is okay. The benefit of a bad decision in a paper prototype is that you can quickly discover that it is a bad decision, toss it out, and move on to the next idea.

In the next chapter, you will learn about various forms of playtesting and usability testing. This knowledge can help you get more valid and specific information from your playtests. Then, in Chapter 11, "Math and Game Balance," you'll explore some of the math behind game design and look at how to use a spreadsheet program to help you balance your games.

GAME TESTING

Inherent in the concepts of prototyping and iteration is an understanding that high-quality testing is absolutely necessary for good game design. But the question becomes: How exactly should this testing be performed?

In this chapter, you learn about various methods of playtesting for games, how to implement them properly, and at what stage in development each method is appropriate.

Why Playtest?

After you've analyzed your goals, designed a solution, and implemented a prototype, it's time to test that prototype and get some feedback on your design. I understand that this can be a frightening proposition. Games are difficult to design, and you'll need a lot of experience to get good at it. Even when you become a great designer, you'll still probably have some trepidation when you think about people playing your game for the first time. That's okay. The number one thing to keep in mind is that every person who plays your game is making it better; every comment you get, whether positive or negative, can help steer you in a direction that can improve player experience and hone your design.

Refining the design is what it's all about, and you absolutely must have external feedback to do so. I've served as a judge for several game design festivals over the years, and it always amazes me how easy it is to tell whether a dev team has done sufficient playtesting. For example, without enough playtesting, the goals of the game are often not clearly specified, and the difficulty of the game often ramps up very erratically. These are both common indications that the game was most often played by people who already knew how to play and knew how to get through the difficult parts, so they couldn't see the ambiguity of the goals or the variations in difficulty the way that a naïve tester would have.

This chapter gives you the knowledge and skills to run meaningful playtests and get the information from them that you need to make your games better.

> ### note
>
> **INVESTIGATORS VERSUS PLAYTESTERS**   In the game industry, we often refer to both the people running the playtests and the participants in those tests as *playtesters*. For clarity, in this book, I use these terms as follows:
>
> - **Investigator:** A person administering a playtest, usually someone on your team
> - **Playtester:** A person taking part in the playtest by playing games and giving feedback

Being a Great Playtester Yourself

Before getting into how to run various types of playtests for your games or what to look for in playtesters, let's examine how you can be a great playtester for other people.

- **Think out loud:** One of the best things you can do as a playtester is to describe your internal thought processes out loud while playing. Doing so helps the investigator running the test to correctly interpret the thoughts behind your actions. This can be especially helpful if it's the first time that you've ever encountered the game.

- **Reveal your biases:** We are all biased by our experiences and tastes, but investigators often have difficulty knowing where their playtesters are coming from. As you're playing, talk about other games, films, books, experiences, and so on that the game reminds you of. This helps the investigators understand the background and biases that you bring with you to the playtest.

- **Self-analyze:** Try to help the investigators understand why you're experiencing the reactions that you're having to the game. Instead of just saying something like "I feel happy," say something more specific like "I feel happy because the jumping mechanic makes me feel powerful and joyful."

- **Separate elements:** As a playtester, after you've given overall feedback on the game experience, try to see each element separately; analyze art, game mechanics, game feel, sound, music, and so on as individual elements. This can be very helpful to investigators and is akin to saying, "The cellos sounded out of tune" rather than "I didn't like that symphony." As a designer, your insight into games can allow you to give more specific feedback than most players, so take advantage of it.

- **Don't worry if they don't like your ideas:** As a designer, you should tell the investigators any ideas you have to make their game better, but you also shouldn't be at all offended if they don't use them. A lot of game design is about checking your ego at the door; it turns out that playtesting has an element of that, too.

The Circles of Playtesters

The game testing you do will go through several expanding circles of playtesters, starting with you and expanding outward through your friends and acquaintances to eventually encompass many people you have never met. Each circle of people can help with different aspects of your playtesting.

The First Circle—You

As a game designer, the first and last playtester of the games you design will most likely be you. You will be the first person to try out each of your ideas, and you'll be the first person to decide whether the game mechanics and interface feel right.

A central theme of this book is that you always want to get a prototype of your game working as soon as possible. Until you have a working prototype, all you have is a jumble of ideas, but after you have a prototype, you have something concrete for others to react to.

Later in this book, you'll be making digital game prototypes in Unity. Every time you click the Play button in Unity to run your game, you are acting as a playtester. Even if you're working in a team and are not the primary engineer on the project, as a designer, your job is to determine whether the game is heading toward the kind of experience your team wants to create. Your skills as a playtester are most useful in the very early stages of prototyping when you are working toward an early internal prototype to help other team members understand the design or when you are still trying to discover the core mechanic or core experience of the game.

However, you can never get a first impression of your own game; you know too much about it. At some point you must show your game to other people. After you feel that your game is anything better than terrible, it's honestly time to find a few other people and show it to them.

TISSUE PLAYTESTERS

Tissue playtester is an industry term to describe playtesters who are brought in to play the game and give their feedback once and are then discarded. They are one-use, like facial tissues. This kind of tester is important because they can give you a naïve reaction to your game. After anyone has played your game even a single time, they know something about it, and that knowledge biases subsequent playtest sessions. This kind of naïve perspective is critically important when testing:

- The tutorial system
- The first few levels
- The emotional impact of any plot twists or other surprises
- The emotional impact of the end of the game

Everyone Is a Tissue Playtester Only Once

Your game never gets a second chance to make a first impression. When Jenova Chen was working on his most famous game, *Journey*, he and I were housemates. However, he asked me to wait until more than a year into the development of the game before I playtested it. Later, he expressed to me that he specifically wanted my feedback on the level of polish of the game and whether it was achieving its intended emotional arc. As such, playing it in the early stages of development before any of that polish existed would have ruined the experience for me. Keep this in mind when playtesting with close friends. Think about the most valuable kinds of feedback that each person can give and make sure to show them the game at the best time for each individual.

That being said, never use that point as an excuse for hiding your game from everyone "until it's ready." Hundreds of people playtested *Journey* before I saw it. You will find that in the initial stages of playtesting, most people tell you the same things in slightly different ways. You need that feedback, and even very early in the development process, you need tissue playtesters to tell you which of your game mechanics are confusing or need work for a variety of reasons. Just save a couple of trusted people for later when you know that their specific feedback will be most useful.

The Second Circle—Trusted Friends

After you've playtested your game, iterated, made improvements, and actually crafted something that approximates the experience that you want, it's time to show it to others. The first people should be trusted friends and family members, preferably those either in your target audience or in the game development community. Members of your target audience give you good feedback from the point of view of your future players, and game developers can help by sharing their considerable insight and experience. Game developers also often have the ability to overlook aspects of the game that are obviously unfinished, which can be very useful for relatively early prototypes.

The Third Circle—Acquaintances and Others

After you've been iterating on your game for a while and you have something that seems pretty solid, it's time to take it out into the wild. This isn't yet the time to post a beta to the Internet and expose your game to the rest of the world, but this is when feedback from others with whom you don't normally associate can be helpful. The people who make up your friends and family often share your background and experiences, meaning that they will also often share some of your tastes and biases. If you only test with them, you will get a biased understanding of your game.

A corollary to this would be someone in Austin, Texas, being surprised that the state of Texas voted for a Republican presidential candidate. Most people in Austin are liberal, whereas the rest of the state is primarily conservative. If you only polled people in Austin and didn't break out of that left-leaning bubble, you would never know the opinion of the state as a whole. Similarly, you must get out of your normal social circles to find more playtesters for your game and to understand a larger audience's reaction to your game.

So, where do you look for more people to playtest your game? Here are some possibilities:

- **Local universities:** Many college students love playing games. You could try setting up your game in the student center or quad and showing it to groups of people. Of course, you'll want to check with the campus security before doing so.

  You could also look into whether your local university has a game development club or a group that meets for weekly game nights and ask whether they would mind your bringing a game for them to playtest.

- **Local game stores / malls:** People head to these places to buy games, so they could be a fantastic place to get some playtest feedback. Each of these places has different corporate policies on these kinds of things, so you need to talk with them first.

■ **Farmers markets / community events / parties:** These kinds of public gatherings of people can have incredibly diverse audiences. I've gotten some great feedback on games from people I met at parties.

The Fourth Circle—The Internet

The Internet can be a scary place. Anonymity ensures that little or no accountability exists for actions or statements, and some people online are mean just for kicks. However, the Internet also contains the largest circle of playtesters that you can possibly get. If you're developing an online game, you're eventually going to have to reach out to the Internet and see what happens. However, before you do so, you need to have considerable data and user tracking in place, which you can read about in the later section *Online Playtesting*.

Methods of Playtesting

Several different methods of playtesting exist, each of which is most appropriate for different phases of your game. The following pages explore various methods of playtesting that I have found to be useful in my design process.

Informal Individual Testing

As an independent developer this is how I tend to do most of my testing. I've been focusing on mobile games lately, so carrying my device around with me and showing my games to people is easy to do. More often than not, during a break in conversation I'll ask whether the person I'm speaking with would mind taking a look at my game. This is, of course, most useful in the early stages of development or when you have a specific new feature that you want to test. Things to keep in mind during this kind of testing include the following:

■ **Don't tell the player too much:** Even in the early stages, learning whether your interface is intuitive and the goals of your game are clear is important. Try giving your game to players and watching what they do before they've had any instruction. This can tell you a lot about what interactions your game implies on its own. Eventually, you'll learn the specific short sentences you need to say to people to help them understand your game, and these can form the basis of your in-game tutorial.

■ **Don't lead the playtester:** Be sure you don't ask leading questions that might inadvertently bias your player. Even a simple question like "Did you notice the health items?" informs your playtester that health items exist and implies that it is important for her to collect them. After you release your game, players won't have you there to explain the game to them, and letting your playtesters struggle a bit to help you learn which aspects of your game are unintuitive is important.

■ **Don't argue or make excuses:** As with everything in design, your ego has no place in a playtest. Listen to the feedback that playtesters are giving you, even (or possibly especially) if you disagree with it. This isn't the time to defend your game; it's the time to learn what you can from the person who is taking time out of her day to help the design improve.

■ **Take notes:** Keep a small notebook with you and take notes on the feedback you get, especially if it's not what you expected or wanted to hear. Later, you can collate these notes and look for statements that you heard multiple times. You shouldn't really put too much stock in what is said by a single playtester, but you should definitely pay attention if you hear the same feedback from many different people.

TAKING PLAYTEST NOTES

Playtest notes can be one of your most valuable tools for understanding and improving your games, however, you need to make sure that you're taking notes in an effective way. Just writing down a bunch of notes randomly or writing notes and never reviewing them aren't going to help you much. Figure 10.1 shows the grid of information that I typically use when writing down playtest notes.

Player	Where	Feedback	Underlying Issue	Severity	Proposed Solution
(Name and Contact Info)	Boss1	"I didn't know what to do after the first boss. Where do I go?"	Players are not sure what the next step is after the first boss fight. The play has been really directed prior to this.	High	The mentor character could return after the boss is defeated and give the player her 2nd mission.

Figure 10.1 A single example row of playtest notes.

As mentioned in Chapter 7, it is critical to gather as much usable information from each playtest as possible, and this form can help you to do so. Record the first three columns (with black headers) during the playtest. You should add a new row for each different comment that is made by the playtester.

After the playtest has finished, meet with your team and fill out the three columns with *green* headers. As you do this, you will see that some issues were only experienced by a few playtesters, while others issues were experienced by nearly everyone. In this phase, you can also combine several rows into one if you think a single solution can fix several issues.

Formal Group Testing

For many years, formal group testing was the only form of playtesting done at large studios, and when I worked at Electronic Arts, I took part in many playtests for other teams. In formal group testing, several people are brought into a room full of individual stations at which they can play the game. They are given little or no instruction and allowed to play the game for a specific amount of time (usually about 30 minutes). After this time, the playtesters are given a written survey to fill out, and investigators sometimes interview them individually. This is a great way to get feedback from a high volume of people, and it can get you a large number of answers to some important questions.

Some example post-playtest survey questions include:

- "What were your three favorite parts of the game?"
- "What were your three least favorite parts of the game?"
- Provide the playtesters with a sequential list of various points in the game (or even better a series of images) and ask them, "How would you describe the way you felt at each of these points in the game?"
- "How do you feel about the main character (or other characters) in the game? Did your feelings about the main character change over the course of the game?"
- "How much would you pay for this game?" or "How much would you charge for this game?"[1]
- "What were the three most confusing things about the game?"

Investigators outside of the core development team often administer formal group testing, and there are companies that provide testing services like this.

All Formal Testing Requires a Script

You need to write a script for your investigators any time you do formal testing, regardless of whether or not the investigators are members of your team. A script helps ensure that every playtester has the same setup for their game experience, which minimizes the number of external factors that could cause flukes in your testing. The script should include the following information:

- What should investigators say to the playtesters to set up the game? What instructions should they give?
- How should investigators react during the playtest? Should they ask questions if they see a playtester do something interesting or unusual? Should they provide any hints to playtesters during the test?

---

1. These are two great questions to A/B test on your playtesters (i.e., give the first question to some playtesters and the second question to others). When asked how much they would pay, people usually pick a lower price. When asked how much they would charge, people choose a higher one. A fair price is usually in between.

- What should the environment be like for the playtest? How long should the playtester be allowed to play?

- What specific survey questions should be asked of the playtester after the playtest is complete?

- What kinds of notes should the investigator take during the playtests?

Formal Individual Testing

Where formal group testing seeks to gather small bits of information from many different people and grant investigators a gestalt understanding of how playtesters react to a game, formal individual testing seeks to understand the fine details of a single playtester's experience. To accomplish this goal, investigators carefully record the details of a single individual's experience with the game and then review the recordings later to make sure that they haven't missed anything. You should record several different data streams when doing formal individual testing:

- **Record the game screen:** You want to see what the player is seeing.

- **Record the playtester's actions:** You want to see the input attempted by the player. If the game is controlled with mouse and keyboard, place a camera above them. If the game is tested on a touchscreen tablet, you should have a shot of the player's hands touching the screen.

- **Record the playtester's face:** You want to see the player's face so that you can read her emotions.

- **Record audio of what the playtester says:** Even if the player doesn't vocalize her stream of consciousness, hearing utterances she makes can give you more information about her internal thought process.

- **Log game data:** Your game should also be logging time-stamped data about its internal state. This can include input from the player (e.g., button presses on the controller), the player's success or failure at various tasks, the location of the player, time spent in each area of the game, and so on. See the "Automated Data Logging" sidebar later in this chapter for more information.

All of these data streams are later synched to each other so that designers can clearly see the relationships between them. This allows you to see the elation or frustration in a player's face while simultaneously viewing exactly what the player was seeing on-screen at the time and the input their hands were attempting on the controls. Though this is a considerable amount of data, modern technology has actually made it relatively cheap to create a reasonably good lab for individual testing. See the "Setting Up a Lab…" sidebar for more information.

SETTING UP A LAB FOR FORMAL INDIVIDUAL PLAYTESTING

You can easily spend tens of thousands of dollars setting up a lab for formal individual testing—and many game studios have—but you can also mock up a pretty decent one for not a lot of money.

For any computer platform, you should be able to capture all the data streams listed in the chapter with a powerful gaming laptop and just one additional camera: Modern graphics cards can record the screen as the game is played, the laptop's webcam can record the player's face, and the one separate camera should be set up to show the player's hands. Recording audio on all streams can help you to synchronize them later. The game data log should also be time stamped to allow for synchronization.

Synchronizing Data

Many software packages out there enable you to synch several video streams, but often the oldest methods are the easiest, and in this case, you can use a digital version of the *slate* from the early days of sound in film, when the image and sound were recorded by separate machines. In a film, the slate is the little clapboard that is shown at the beginning of a take. A member of the crew holds the slate, which shows the name of the film, the scene number, and the take number. She reads these three things out loud and then claps the slate together. This later enables the editor to match the visual film frame where the clapper closed with the moment in the audio tape that the sound was made, synching the separate video and audio tracks.

You can do the same thing by making a digital slate part of your game. At the beginning of a playtest session, the game screen can show a digital slate containing a unique ID number for the session. An investigator can read the ID number out loud and then press a button on the controller. Simultaneously, the software can show a digital clapper closing, make a clapper sound, and log game data with the time stamp according to the internal clock on your playtest machine. You can use all of these to synch the various video streams later (with the clapper sound used to synch streams that cannot see the screen), and you can even synch the game data log. Most even half-decent video editing programs allow you to put each of these videos into one quarter of the screen and fill the fourth quarter with the date, time, and unique ID of the playtest session. Then you can see all of this data synchronized in a single video.

Privacy Concerns

Many people are understandably concerned about their personal privacy. You must be upfront with your playtesters and let them know that they will be recorded. However, you should also promise them that the video will only be used for internal purposes and will never be shared with anyone outside of the company.

Running a Formal Individual Playtest

Investigators should seek to make the individual playtest as similar as possible to the experience a player who had bought the game would have at home. The player should be comfortable and at ease. You might want to provide snacks or drinks, and if the game is designed for tablet or console, you might want to give the player a couch or other comfortable seat to sit on. (For computer games, a desk and office chair are often more appropriate.)

Start the playtest by telling the playtester how much you appreciate the time she has set aside to test your game and how useful getting her feedback will be for you. You should also request that she please speak out loud while playing. Few playtesters will actually do so, but asking can't hurt.

After the playtester finishes the section of the game that you want her to play, an investigator should sit with her and discuss her experience with the game. The questions the investigator asks should be similar to those that are asked at the end of formal group testing, but the one-on-one format allows the investigator to frame meaningful follow-up questions and get better information. Also record the post-playtest question-and-answer sessions, though audio recording is more important than video for the post-play interview.

As with all formal playtesting, it is best if the investigator is not part of the game development team. This helps the investigator's questions and perceptions to not be biased by personal investment in the game. However, after you have found a good investigator, working with the same investigator throughout the development process is very useful so that she can provide you information about the progression of playtesters' reactions to the game.

Online Playtesting

As mentioned previously, the largest circle of playtesters is composed of online playtest communities. Your game must be in the beta phase before you attempt this, so these are colloquially known as *beta tests,* and they come in a few forms:

- **Closed:** An invite-only test with a limited number of people. This is where your online tests should start. Initially, you should have only a few trusted people serve as online playtesters. This gives you a chance to find any bugs with your server architecture or any aspects of your game that are unclear before a larger audience sees it.

For my graduate school project, *Skyrates*,[2] our first closed online beta started eight weeks into the project and was composed of the four members of the dev team and only 12 other people, all of whom had offices in the same building as the development team. After two weeks of fixing both game and server issues and adding a few more features, we expanded the playtest group to 25 people, all of whom were still in the same building. Two weeks later, we expanded to 50. Up until this point, a member of the dev team had individually sat down with each player and taught her how to play the game.

Over the next two weeks, we developed an online game tutorial document and entered the limited beta phase.

- **Limited:** A limited beta is generally open to anyone who signs up, though a few specific limitations are often in place. The most common limitation is the number of players.

  When *Skyrates* first entered the limited beta phase, we capped the number of players at 125 and told our players that they could invite one friend or family member to join the game. This was a much larger number of concurrent players than we had managed in prior rounds, and we wanted to make sure that the server could handle it. After that, we limited the next round to 250 before moving on to our first open beta.

- **Open:** Open betas allow anyone online to play. This can be fantastic because you can watch your game gain popularity halfway around the globe, but it can also be terrifying because a spike in players can threaten to overload your server. Generally, you want to make sure that your game is near completion before you do an online, open beta.

Skyrates entered open beta at the end of the first semester of development. We didn't expect to work on the game for a second semester, so we left our game server running over the summer. To our surprise, even though *Skyrates* was initially developed as a two-week game experience, several people played the game throughout the summer, and our total numbers for the summer were somewhere between 500 and 1000 players. However, this all happened in 2006 before Facebook became a game platform and before the ubiquity of gaming on smartphones and tablets. Although 99% of all games on these platforms don't gain much popularity at all, be aware that a game released on any of them has the potential to go from only a few players to millions in just a few days. Be wary of open betas on social platforms, but know that you will need to open up the game eventually.

---

2. *Skyrates* (Airship Studios, 2006) is a game that was introduced in Chapter 8, "Design Goals." It made extensive use of the concept of *sporadic play*, where players interacted with the game for only a few minutes at a time throughout their day. Though this is now common behavior for Facebook games, at the time we were developing it, this was an unusual concept, and it required many rounds of playtesting to refine it.

AUTOMATED DATA LOGGING

You should include automated data logging (ADL) in your game as early as possible. ADL occurs when your game automatically records information about player performance and events any time someone plays your game. This is often recorded to a server online, but can just as easily be stored as local files and then output by your game later.

At Electronic Arts in 2007, I designed and produced the game *Crazy Cakes* for Pogo.com. *Crazy Cakes* was the first Pogo game to ever use ADL, but afterward it became a standard part of production. The ADL for *Crazy Cakes* was really pretty simple. For each level of the game that was played, we recorded several pieces of data:

- Timestamp: The date and time that the round started.

- Player username: This allowed us to talk to players with very high scores and ask them what strategies they employed or contact them if something unusual happened during gameplay.

- Difficulty level and round number: We had a total of five difficulty levels, each of which contained four progressively more challenging rounds.

- Score.

- Number and type of power-up items used during the round.

- Number of tokens earned.

- Number of patrons served.

- Number of desserts served to patrons: Some patrons requested multiple desserts, which this helped us track.

At the time, Pogo.com had hundreds of beta testers, so three days after releasing *Crazy Cakes*, we had recorded data from more than 25,000 playtest sessions! I culled this data to a more manageable 4,000 randomly selected rows and brought it into a spreadsheet application that I used to balance the game based on real data rather than conjecture. When I thought that the game was well-balanced relative to the data, I selected another 4,000 random rows and confirmed the balance with them.

Other Important Types of Testing

In addition to playtesting, you can do several other important types of testing on a game.

Focus Testing

Focus testing involves gathering a group of people in your game's core demographic (a *focus group*) and getting their reaction to the look, premise, music, or other aesthetic and narrative elements of your game. Studios sometimes use focus testing to determine whether developing a certain game is a good business decision.

Interest Polling

You can now use social networks like Facebook or crowdfunding sites like Kickstarter to poll the level of interest that your game could generate in the online public. On these websites, you can post a pitch video for a game and receive feedback, either in the form of likes on a social media site or pledges on a crowdfunding site. If you are an independent developer with limited resources, interest polling might be a way to secure some funding for your game, but of course, the results are incredibly varied.

Usability Testing

Many of the techniques now used in formal individual testing grew out of the field of usability testing. At its core, usability testing is about understanding how well testers can understand and use the interface for a piece of software. Because understanding is so important to usability, data gathering of the screen, interaction, and face of the tester are common practices. In addition to the playtesting of your game, engaging in some individual usability testing that investigates how easily the playtester can interact with and gain critical information from your game is also important. This can include testing of various layouts for on-screen information, several different control configurations, etc.

Quality Assurance (QA) Testing

Quality assurance testing focuses specifically on finding bugs in your game and ways to reliably reproduce them. An entire industry is devoted to this kind of testing. QA testing is largely outside the scope of this book, but the core elements are as follows:

1. Find a bug in the game (a place where it breaks or doesn't react properly).
2. Discover and write down the steps required to reliably reproduce the bug.
3. Prioritize the bug. Does it crash the game? How likely is it to occur for a normal player? How noticeable is it?
4. If the bug is high enough priority, tell the engineering team so that they can fix it.

QA is most often done simultaneously by both the development team and a group of game testers hired for the final phase of a project. Setting up ways for players to submit bugs that they find is also possible, although most players don't have the training to generate good bug reports that include clear steps for reproducing the bug. Many free bug tracking tools are available that can deploy on your project website, including *Bugzilla*, *Mantis Bug Tracker*, and *Trac*.

Automated Testing

Automated testing (AT) occurs when a piece of software attempts to find bugs in your game or game server without requiring human input. For a game, AT could simulate rapid user input (like hundreds of clicks per second all over the screen). For a game server, AT could inundate the server with thousands of requests per second to determine the level of server load that could cause the server to fail. Although AT is complex to implement, it can effectively test your game in ways that are very difficult for human QA testers to accomplish. As with other forms of testing, several companies provide automated testing services.

Summary

The intent of this chapter was to give you a broad understanding of various forms of testing for your games. As a new game designer, you should find the ones that seem most useful to you and try to implement them. I have had success with several different forms of testing, and I believe that all the forms covered in this chapter can provide you with important information that can improve your game.

The next chapter covers some of the math that lies beneath the surface of the fun in games. You'll also learn about how to use a spreadsheet application to aid you in game balancing.

CHAPTER 11

MATH AND GAME BALANCE

This chapter explores various systems of probability and randomness and how they relate to paper game technologies. You also learn a little about the online Google Sheets spreadsheet application that can help you explore these possibilities.

Following the mathematical explorations (which I promise are as clear and easy to understand as possible), I cover how to use these systems in both paper and digital games to balance and improve gameplay.

The Meaning of Game Balance

Now that you've made your initial game prototype and experimented with it a few times through playtests, you will probably need to *balance* it as part of your iteration process. Balance is a term that you will often hear when working on games, but it means different things depending on the context.

In a multiplayer game, balance most often means *fairness*: each player should have an equal chance of winning the game. This is most easily accomplished in *symmetric* games where each player has the same starting point and abilities. Balancing an *asymmetric* game is considerably more difficult because player abilities or start positions that might seem balanced could, in practice, demonstrate a bias toward one set of player abilities over the others. This is one of the many reasons why playtesting is critically important.

In a single-player game, balance usually means that the game is at an *appropriate level of difficulty* for the player and the *difficulty changes gradually*. If a game has a large jump in difficulty at any point, that point becomes a place where the game tends to lose players. This relates to the discussion of flow as a player-centric design goal in Chapter 8, "Design Goals."

In this chapter, you learn about several disparate aspects of math that are all part of game design and balance. This includes understanding probability, an exploration of different randomizers for paper games, and the concepts of weighted distribution, permutations, and positive and negative feedback. Throughout this exploration, you use Google Sheets, a free online spreadsheet program, to better explore and understand the concepts presented.

The Importance of Spreadsheets

For some of the things that you'll be doing in this chapter, a spreadsheet program like Sheets isn't strictly necessary—you could get the same results with a piece of scratch paper and a calculator—however, I feel that introducing spreadsheets as an aspect of game balance is important for a few reasons:

- A spreadsheet can help you quickly grasp gestalt information from numerical data. In Chapter 9, I presented you with two weapons—a shotgun and a machine gun—that each had different stats. At the end of this chapter, I will take you through the process that I went through to balance those weapons to each other as well as three others, contrasting the weapon stats that I initially created based on gut feeling with those that I refined through use of a spreadsheet.

- Charts and spreadsheet data can be used to convince non-designers of the validity of a game design decision that you have made. To develop a game, you often work with many different people, some of whom prefer to see numbers behind decisions rather than instinct. That doesn't mean that you should always make decisions with numbers; I just want you to be able to do so if necessary.

- Many professional game designers work with spreadsheets on a daily basis, but I have seen very few game design programs that teach students anything about how to use them. In addition, the classes at universities that do cover spreadsheet use tend to be more interested in business or accounting than game balance, and therefore focus on different spreadsheet capabilities than those I have found useful in my work.

As with all aspects of game development, the process of building a spreadsheet is an iterative and somewhat messy process. Rather than show you perfect examples of making spreadsheets from start to finish with every little thing planned ahead of time, the tutorials in this chapter are designed to demonstrate not only the steps to make a spreadsheet but also a realistic iterative process of both building and planning the spreadsheet.

The Choice of Google Sheets for This Book

For this book, I have chosen to use Google Sheets because it is free, cross-platform, and easily available. Most other spreadsheet programs have many of the same capabilities as Sheets (e.g., Microsoft Excel, Open Office Calc, and LibreOffice Calc Spreadsheet), but each program is subtly different from the others, so attempting to follow the directions in this chapter in an application other than Google Sheets may lead to frustration.

See the sidebar "Not All Spreadsheet Programs Are Created Equal" for more information on the various programs.

NOT ALL SPREADSHEET PROGRAMS ARE CREATED EQUAL

Spreadsheet programs are most commonly used to manage and analyze large amounts of numerical data. Some popular spreadsheet programs in use today are Microsoft Excel, Apache OpenOffice Calc, LibreOffice Calc, Google Sheets, and Apple Numbers.

- **Google Sheets** (http://sheets.google.com) is part of the free, online suite of Google Drive tools. Because it is written in HTML5, it is compatible with most modern web browsers, though you should have a good Internet connection to use it effectively. Google Sheets has improved dramatically since the first edition of this book and is now my spreadsheet of choice. One other advantage that it offers is the ability to work synchronously with several team members online. Free app versions exist for iOS and Android that can be used offline.

- **Microsoft Excel** (http://office.microsoft.com) was once the most commonly used spreadsheet program, though it was also the most expensive. Some differences also exist between the PC and macOS platforms because they are on different release schedules. Excel uses the same syntax for formulae as Google Sheets and is still considered the industry standard for most businesses, though in practice, I have found it slower and less elegant than Google Sheets.

- **Apache OpenOffice Calc** (http://openoffice.org) is a free, open source program intended to offer the same functionality as Excel at no cost to the user. It is compatible with PC, macOS, and Linux platforms. Excel and OpenOffice spreadsheets differ from each other in some subtle ways, including the user interface, but they largely share the same functionality. One major difference is that OpenOffice uses semicolons (;) to separate the arguments of a formula, whereas Excel and Google Sheets use commas (,). OpenOffice Calc was the spreadsheet program that I used in the first edition of the book, but Google Sheets has now improved enough to where I no longer use Calc.

- **Apple Numbers** (http://www.apple.com/numbers/) is included with new Mac computers, but it is also downloadable for about $20. Numbers works only on macOS computers and includes some nice-looking features not available in the other programs, though I find some of them get in the way. The core functionality is very comparable to the rest, but I believe that better options are available.

- **LibreOffice Calc** (http://libreoffice.org) is a free, open source program intended to offer the same functionality as Excel at no cost to the user. LibreOffice was originally spun off of the OpenOffice source code, so they share many similarities. One small advantage that LibreOffice has over OpenOffice if you come from an Excel background is that commas are used to separate parameters in LibreOffice formulae (like Excel) instead of the semicolons used in OpenOffice.

Any of these programs can open and export Microsoft Excel files, though each also has its own native format. Even if you already own or are familiar with one of the others, I would like for you to give Google Sheets a chance in this chapter.

Examining Dice Probability with Sheets

A large portion of game math comes down to probability, so understanding a little about how probability and chance work is critical. You'll start by using Google Sheets to help you understand the probability distribution of rolling various numbers using 2d6 (two six-sided dice).

On a single roll of 1d6 (a single six-sided die), you have an even chance of getting a 1, 2, 3, 4, 5, or 6. That's pretty obvious. However, things get much more interesting when you consider adding the results of two dice together. If you roll 2d6, then there are 36 different possibilities for the outcome, all of which are shown here:

Die A: 1 2 3 4 5 6 1 2 3 4 5 6 1 2 3 4 5 6 1 2 3 4 5 6 1 2 3 4 5 6 1 2 3 4 5 6

Die B: 1 1 1 1 1 1 2 2 2 2 2 2 3 3 3 3 3 3 4 4 4 4 4 4 5 5 5 5 5 5 6 6 6 6 6 6

Writing all of these by hand is certainly possible, but I would like you to learn how to use Sheets to do it as an introduction to using a spreadsheet to aid in game balance. You can look ahead to Figure 11.5 to see what you'll be making.

Getting Started in Google Sheets

You need to be online to use Google Sheets. This is a bit of a negative for it, but it is quickly becoming the standard spreadsheet program that most designers I know use, so you should be familiar with it. To start your exploration into game math, please do the following:

1. In a web browser, go to: **http://sheets.google.com**.

    This redirects you to the main Sheets page, where you can get started. I strongly recommend either Google Chrome or Mozilla Firefox as your browser for this work. Chrome has the advantage of allowing some offline editing of Google Sheets spreadsheets, though it is limited and sometimes confusing. Even when using Chrome, being online is much better.

Figure 11.1 Creating a new spreadsheet at http://sheets.google.com

2. Under the *Start a new spreadsheet* heading, click the *Blank* button as shown in Figure 11.1. This creates an *Untitled spreadsheet* like the one shown in Figure 11.2.

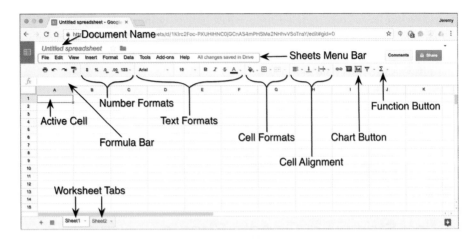

Figure 11.2 A new Google Sheets spreadsheet with important parts of the interface labeled

Getting Started with Sheets

The cells in a spreadsheet are each named with a column letter and a row number. The top-left cell in the spreadsheet is A1. In Figure 11.2, cell A1 is highlighted with a blue border and a small blue box in its bottom-right corner, showing that it is the *Active Cell*. Follow these steps to get started using Sheets:

1. Click cell *A1* to select it and ensure that it is the Active Cell.

2. Type the number 1 on your keyboard and press Return. A1 now holds the value 1.

3. Click cell *B1,* type =A1+1, and press Return. This creates a formula in B2 that will constantly calculate its value based on A1. All formulas start with an =. You'll see that the value of B1 is now 2 (the number you get when you add 1 to the value in A1). If you change the value in A1, B1 will automatically update.

4. Click *B1* and copy the cell (choose *Edit > Copy* or press Command-C on macOS or Ctrl+C on PC).

5. Shift-click cell *K1* (by holding Shift on the keyboard and clicking cell K1). This highlights the cells B1:K1 (i.e., all cells from B1 to K1; the colon is used to define a range between the two listed cells). You might need to use the scroll bar at the bottom of the Sheets window to scroll to the right and bring K1 into view.

6. Paste the formula from B1 into the highlighted cells (choose *Edit > Paste* or press Command-V on macOS or Ctrl+V on PC). This pastes the formula that you copied from B1 into the cells B1:K1 (i.e., the formula =A1+1). Because the cell reference A1 in the formula is a *relative reference,* it will update based on the position of the new cell into which it has been pasted. In other words, the formula in K1 will be =J1+1 because J1 is one cell to the left of K1 just as A1 was one to the left of B1.

For more information on relative and absolute references, please read the *Relative and Absolute References* sidebar.

RELATIVE AND ABSOLUTE REFERENCES

As part of the formula =A1+1 in cell B1, the A1 is storing a *relative reference*, meaning that the formula stores the *location* of the referenced cell *relative to* cell B1 rather than an absolute reference to cell A1. In other words, the A1 in this formula refers to the cell one to the left of the cell the formula is in (B1) and will change if the formula is copied to another cell. This is critical to making spreadsheets easy to use, as you saw in step 6 of the "Getting Started with Sheets" heading.

In Sheets, it is also possible to create *absolute reference* to a cell; that is, a reference to a cell that will not change if the formula is moved or copied. To make a cell reference absolute, add a $ (dollar sign) before both the column and row. For example, to make the A1 reference absolute, convert it to A1. You can also make just the column or just the row absolute by adding the $ to only the column letter or row number.

In Figure 11.3, you can see an example of partial absolute references. Here, I've written a function to subtract various numbers of days from people's birthdays so that I know when to start looking for presents for them. You can see that the formula in B5 is =B$3-$A5, and this same formula was copied and pasted across B5:O7. The partial absolute reference B$3 indicates that the column should change, but not the row, and the partial absolute reference $A5 indicates that the row should change, but not the column.

	A	B	C	D	E	F	G	H	I	J	K	L	M	N	O
		Angus	Gromit	Zoe	Thomas	Jim	Shep	Coop	Jin	Marty	Henry	Jean-Luc	Scott	James	—
3	Birthday	1/23	2/12	2/15	3/11	3/22	4/11	4/19	4/23	6/12	7/1	7/13	9/27	11/11	12/31
4	Days before														
5	7	1/16	2/5	2/8	3/4	3/15	4/4	4/12	4/16	6/5	6/24	7/6	9/20	11/4	12/24
6	14	1/9	1/29	2/1	2/26	3/8	3/28	4/5	4/9	5/29	6/17	6/29	9/13	10/28	12/17
7	30	12/24	1/13	1/16	2/10	2/21	3/12	3/20	3/24	5/13	6/1	6/13	8/28	10/12	12/1

fx =B$3-$A5

Figure 11.3 An example of partially absolute references

In Figure 11.3, the formula changed as I copied it across the other cells as follows:

B5: =B$3-$A5   O5: =O$3-$A5

H6: =H$3-$A6

B7: =B$3-$A7   O7: =O$3-$A7

Naming the Document

To name the document, do the following:

1. Click the words *Untitled spreadsheet* in the Document Name area shown in Figure 11.2.

2. Change the name of this spreadsheet to *2d6 Dice Probability* and press Return.

Creating a Row of Numbers from 1 to 36

The preceding instructions should leave you with the numbers 1 through 11 in the cells A1:K1. Next, you will extend the numbers to count all the way from 1 to 36 (for the 36 possible die rolls).

Adding More Columns

First, you must make enough columns to hold all the cells. Right now, all the columns are quite wide, and if you scroll to the right, you can see that the columns stop at Z. First, you will narrow the columns and then add sufficient columns to hold 36 different numbers.

1. Click directly on the *column A header* (i.e., the *A* at the top of column A).

2. Scroll to the right (using the scroll bar at the bottom of the Sheets window) and Shift-click the *column Z header*. This selects all columns A:Z.

3. When you hover your mouse cursor over the Z column header, a box with a downward-pointing arrow appears. Click that downward arrow box, and select *Insert 26 Right* from the pop-up menu as shown in the left side of Figure 11.4A. This creates 26 additional columns lettered AA:AZ.

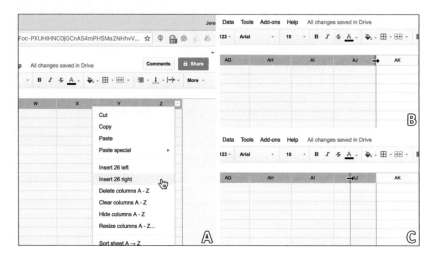

Figure 11.4 Adding 26 columns to the right of column Z

Setting Column Widths

You want to be able to see 36 columns (A:AJ) on screen at once. To make the columns narrower do the following:

1. Click the *column A header*.

2. Scroll to the right and Shift-click the *column AJ header*. This selects all 36 columns A:AJ.

3. Hover the mouse over the right edge of the column AJ header; and you will see the edge thicken and turn blue (as shown in Figure 11.4B).

4. Click and hold the mouse button to grab the thick blue border like a handle and make column AJ about 1/3 its original width (as shown in Figure 11.4C). This resizes all columns A:AJ. If these columns are still too wide to fit on your screen, feel free to make them narrower.

Filling Row 1 with the Numbers 1 to 36

Fill row 1 by doing the following:

1. Click *B1* to select it. Another way that you can copy the contents of a single cell over a large range is to use the blue square in the lower-right corner of a selected cell (which you can see at the lower-right corner of cell A1 in Figure 11.2).

2. Click and drag the blue square from the corner of B1 to the right until you have selected cells B1:AJ1. When you release the mouse button, cells A1:AJ1 will be filled with the series of numbers from 1 to 36.

3. If your columns are too narrow to show the numbers, select columns A:AJ again and resize them to a comfortable width. Instead of dragging the edge between columns, you can also double-click the thickened edge between any two columns to set all columns to their optimal width; however, if you do so here, the columns with a single digit will be narrower than those with two digits.

Making the Row for Die A

Now, you have a series of the numbers 1 to 36, but what you really want is two rows like those for Die A and Die B that were listed earlier in this chapter. You can achieve this with some simple formulae:

1. Click the *Function* button (labeled in Figure 11.2) and choose *More Functions…* .

2. In the *Filter with a few keywords…* text field, replace the text with MOD, which will filter the long list of functions down to less than a dozen. Look for the function named *MOD*, which is listed under the *Math* type.

3. On the right side of the row for MOD, click the *Learn more* link. A new browser tab will open showing a description of MOD. According to it, the MOD function divides one number by another and returns the remainder. For example, the two formulae =MOD(1,6) and =MOD(7,6) would both return a 1 because 1/6 and 7/6 both have a remainder of 1.

4. Return to the spreadsheet by clicking the *2d6 Dice Probability* tab at the top of your browser window.

5. Click cell *A2* to select it.

6. Type =MOD(A1,6) and press Return. As you type, text will appear in both cell A2 and the Formula Bar (labeled in Figure 11.2). After you're finished, 1 is shown in the cell A2.

7. Click cell *A2* and Shift-click cell *AJ2* (to select cells A2:AJ2).

8. Press Command-R on your keyboard (Ctrl+R on PC). This fills cells to the right, copying the contents of the leftmost cell (A2) over everything to the right (B2:AJ2).

Now you can see that the MOD function is working properly for all 36 cells; however, you wanted the numbers 1 through 6, not 0 through 5, so you need to iterate a bit.

Iterating on the Row for Die A

You need to fix two issues: First, the lowest number should be in columns A, F, L, and so on; and second, the numbers should range from 1 to 6, not 0 to 5. You can fix both of these with simple adjustments:

1. Select cell A1, change its value from 1 to 0, and press Return (Enter on PC). This change cascades through the formulae in B1:AJ1 and gives you a series of numbers on row 1 from 0 to 35. Now, the formula in A2 returns 0 (the remainder when 0 is divided by 6), and the numbers in A2:AJ2 are six series of 0 1 2 3 4 5, which fixes the first issue.

2. To fix the second issue, select A2 and change the formula in A2 to =MOD(A1,6)+1. This simply adds 1 to the result of the previous formula, which increases the formula result in A2 from 0 to 1. This might seem like you've gone in a circle, but after you complete step 3, you'll see the reason for doing so.

3. Select A2, hold Shift-Command (Shift+Ctrl on PC) and press the right arrow on your keyboard. This highlights all the filled cells to the right of A2, which should be A2:AJ2. Press Command-R on macOS (Ctrl+R on PC) to *fill right* again.

Now, the row for Die A is complete and you have six series of the numbers 1 2 3 4 5 6. The mod values still range from 0 to 5, but now they are in the correct order, and adding +1 to them has generated the numbers that you wanted for Die A.

Making the Row for Die B

The row for Die B includes six repetitions of each number on the die. To accomplish this, you will use the division and floor functions in Sheets. Division works as you would expect it to (for example, =3/2 returns the result 1.5); however, floor might be a function that you have not encountered before.

1. Select cell *A3*.

2. Type =**FLOOR** into A3, and as you do so a pop-up appears below cell A3 containing the text "FLOOR Rounds number down to nearest multiple of a factor." (The "factor" is 1 by default.)

   FLOOR is used to round decimal numbers to integers, but FLOOR *always rounds down*. For example, =FLOOR(5.1) returns 5 and =FLOOR(5.999) also returns 5.

3. Enter =**FLOOR(A1/6)** into cell *A3*. The pop-up result field updates to show a result of 0.

4. As was needed with the Die A row, you must add 1 to the result of the formula. Change the formula in A3 to =**FLOOR(A1/6)+1**; the result is now 1.

5. Copy the contents of A3. Highlight cells *A3:AJ3*, and paste (Command-V on macOS, Ctrl+V on PC, or choose *Edit > Paste* on either). This copies the formula from A3 and pastes it into A3:AJ3.

Your spreadsheet should now look like top image in Figure 11.5. However, it would be much easier to understand if it were labeled as is shown in the bottom image of Figure 11.5.

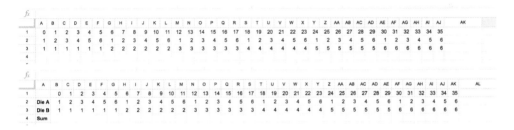

Figure 11.5 Adding clarity with labels

Adding Clarity with Labels

To add the labels shown in the second image of Figure 11.5, you need to insert a new column to the left of column A:

1. Right-click the *column A header* and choose *Insert 1 left*. This inserts one new column to the left of the current column A. The new column becomes A, and the old column A now becomes column B. If you're on macOS and don't have a right-click button, you can Ctrl-click. See the section *Right-Click on macOS* in Appendix B, "Useful Concepts," for a more permanent way to enable right-click on macOS.

2. Click on the new, empty cell *A2* to select it and enter the text Die A.

3. To make the column wide enough to see the entire label, either double-click on the edge to the right of the *column A header* or click and drag the column A header edge to the right.

4. Enter the text Die B into *A3*.

5. Enter the text Sum into *A4*.

6. To make all the text in column A bold, click the *column A header* (to select all of column A) and then press Command-B (Ctrl+B on PC) or click the **B** *formatting button* in the *Text Formats* area shown in Figure 11.2.

7. To make the background of column A slightly gray, make sure that all of column A is still highlighted, and click the *paint bucket* above the Formula Bar (on the left side of *Cell Formats* in Figure 11.2). From the paint bucket pop-up menu, choose one of the lighter gray colors. This sets the background color of all highlighted cells.

8. To make the background of row 1 also gray, click the *row 1 header* (the 1 to the left of row 1) to select the whole row, and then choose the same gray background from the *paint bucket* pop-up menu.

Now your spreadsheet should look like the bottom half of Figure 11.5.

---

tip

THERE'S NO NEED TO SAVE IN GOOGLE SHEETS!   Throughout this book— and especially in the tutorials at the end—I constantly remind you to save your files. I've lost a ton of work in many programs due to crashes and other computer errors. However, I've never lost work in Google Sheets because it constantly saves the work I'm doing online to the cloud. The one caveat to this is: if you're working offline in a Google Sheets window in the Chrome browser and close the window before you go online again, your changes might not be saved, although in experiments I've run, they have been auto-saved even in that case.

Summing the Results of the Two Dice

Another formula will enable you to sum the results of the two dice.

1. Click *B4* and enter the formula =SUM(B2,B3), which sums the values in cells B2 and B3 (the formula =B2+B3 would also work equally well). This puts the value 2 into B4.

2. Copy B4 and paste it into *B4:AK4*. Now, row 4 shows the results of all 36 possible rolls of 2d6.

3. To make this visually stand out, click the *row 4 header* and make all of row 4 bold.

Counting the Sums of Die Rolls

Row 4 now shows all the results of the 36 possible rolls of 2d6. However, although the data is there, interpreting it is still not as easy as it could be. This is where you can really use the strength of a spreadsheet. To start the data interpretation, let's create formulae to count the occurrences of each sum (that is, count how many different ways a 7 can be rolled with 2d6). First, you create a vertical series of the possible sums, 2 to 12:

1. Enter 2 into *A7*.

2. Enter 3 into *A8*.

3. Select cells *A7 and A8*.

4. Drag the little blue box at the bottom-right of A8 down until you've selected cells *A7:A17*, and release the mouse button.

Cells A7:A17 fill with the numbers from 2 to 12. Google Sheets recognizes that you're starting a series of numbers with the 2 and 3 in adjacent cells, and when you drag that series over other cells, it continues it.

Next, you create a formula to count how many times the 2 occurs in row 4:

5. Select cell *B7* and type `=COUNTIF (` but don't press the Return or Enter key.

6. Use your mouse to click and drag from *B4 to AK4*. This draws a box around B4:AK4 and enters `B4:AK4` into your in-progress formula.

7. Type `,` (a comma).

8. Click *A7*. This enters A7 into the formula. At this point, the entire formula should be
   `=COUNTIF(B4:AK4,A7.`

9. Type `)` and press Return (or in Windows, Enter). Now, the formula in B7 will be
   `=COUNTIF(B4:AK4,A7).`

The COUNTIF function counts the number of times within a series of cells that a certain criterion is met. The first parameter of COUNTIF is the range of cells to search within (B4:AK4 in this case), and the second parameter (the entry after the comma) is the entry to search for (the value of A7, which is 2). In cell B7, the COUNTIF function looks at all the cells B4:AK4 and counts the number of times that the number 2 occurs (which is once).

Counting All Possible Rolls

Next, you want to extend this from just counting the number of 2s to counting the number of rolls of all numbers from 2 to 12 in the A:A17 vertical series:

1. Copy the formula from B7 and paste it into *B7:B17*.

You will notice that this doesn't work properly. The counts for all the numbers other than 2 are 0. Let's explore why this is happening.

2. Select cell *B7* and then click once in the Formula Bar. This highlights all the cells that are used in the calculation of the formula in cell B7.

3. Press the Esc (escape) key. This is a critical step because it returns you from the cell-editing mode. If you were to click another cell without first pressing Esc, this would enter the clicked cell's reference into the formula. See the following warning for more information.

> **warning**
>
> **EXITING FORMULA EDITING**   When working in Sheets, you need to press either Return, Tab, or Esc (Enter, Tab, or Esc on PC) to exit from editing a formula. Use Return or Tab to accept the changes that you have made or Escape to cancel them. If you don't properly exit from formula editing, any cell you click will be added to the formula (which you don't want to do accidentally). If this does happen to you, you can press Esc to exit editing without changing the actual formula.

4. Select cell *B8* and click once in the Formula Bar.

Now, you should see the problem with the formula in B8. Instead of counting the occurrence of 3s in B4:AK4, it is looking for 3s in B5:AK5. This is a result of the automatic updating of relative references that was covered earlier in this chapter. Because B8 is one cell lower than B7, all the references in B8 were updated to be one cell lower as well. This is correct for the second argument in the formula (i.e., B8 should be looking for the number in A8 and not A7), but it you need to make the row reference in the first argument absolute to force the function to look at row 4 regardless of where it is pasted.

5. Press Esc to exit from editing B8.

6. Select *B7* and change the formula to `=COUNTIF(B$4:AK$4,A7)`. The $ in the formula creates an absolute reference to row 4 in the first parameter of the COUNTIF function.

7. Copy the formula from B7 and paste it into *B7:B17*. You can see that the numbers update correctly, and each formula in B7:B17 properly searches the cells B$4:AK$4.

Charting the Results

Now, the cells B7:B17 show you the data you wanted. Across the 36 possible rolls of 2d6, there are six possible ways to roll a 7 but only one way to roll a 2 or a 12. This information can be read in the numbers in the cells, but a chart can make this much easier to understand. Follow these steps to create a chart for the die rolls. As you do so, refer to the several images of the *Chart editor* shown in Figure 11.6 with circled letters like (A) for each step of the process. The bottom section of Figure 11.6 shows the chart at each step of the process.

1. Select cells *A7:B17*.

2. Click the *chart button* shown in Figure 11.2. (If you don't see the chart button on your screen, your window might be too narrow; in this case, click the *More* button at the right of the button bar, and the *chart button* will be in the pop-up menu that appears.) This opens the *Chart editor* pane shown in Figure 11.6.

3. Click the *Chart type* dropdown menu (which currently displays "Scatter chart") (A) and choose the first *Column* chart type (B).

4. Near the bottom of the Chart editor DATA pane, check the box next to the *Use column A as labels* option (C). This converts column A from data shown in the chart to labels shown at the bottom.

5. Click the *CUSTOMIZE* tab (D) and click the *Chart & axis titles* heading (E) to expand that area of the pane. Set the *Title text* of the chart to *2d6 Dice Roll Probability* (F).

6. Click the *Horizontal axis* heading (G) further down in the same pane. Within the Horizontal axis section, check the *Treat labels as text* option (H). This ensures that a number label is shown at the bottom of every column.

7. Click the close button of the Chart editor (I). Move and resize the chart if you want.

Figure 11.6 A probability distribution chart for 2d6

I know that this was a pretty exhausting way to get this data, but I wanted to introduce you to spreadsheets because they can be an extremely important tool to use when balancing your games.

The Math of Probability

At this point, you are probably thinking that there must be an easier way to learn about the probability of rolling dice than just enumerating all the possibilities. Happily, an entire branch of mathematics deals with probability, and this section of the chapter covers several of the rules that it has taught us.

First, let's try to determine how many possible different combinations there can be if you roll 2d6. Because there are two dice, and each has 6 possibilities, there are 6 x 6 = 36 different possible rolls of the two dice. For 3d6, there are 6 x 6 x 6 = 216, or 6^3 different combinations. For 8d6, there are 6^8 = 1,679,616 possibilities! This means that you would require a ridiculously large spreadsheet to calculate the distribution of results from 8d6 if you used the enumeration method that was employed earlier in the chapter for 2d6.

In *The Art of Game Design,* Jesse Schell presents "Ten Rules of Probability Every Game Designer Should Know,"[1] which I have paraphrased here:

- **Rule 1: Fractions are decimals are percents:** Fractions, decimals, and percents are interchangeable, and you'll often find yourself switching between them when dealing with probability. For instance, the chance of rolling a 1 on 1d20 is 1/20 or 0.05 or 5%. To convert from one to the other, follow these guidelines:
    - **Fraction to Decimal**: Type the fraction into a calculator. (Typing `1 ÷ 20 =` gives you the result `0.05`.) Note that decimals are not able to accurately represent many numbers (e.g., 2/3 is accurate, whereas 0.666666667 is just an approximation).
    - **Percent to Decimal**: Divide by 100 (e.g., 5% = 5 ÷ 100 = 0.05).
    - **Decimal to Percent**: Multiply by 100 (e.g., 0.05 = (0.05 * 100)% = 5%).
    - **Anything to Fraction**: This is pretty difficult, because there is often no easy way to convert a decimal or percent to a fraction except for the few equivalencies that most people know (e.g., 0.5 = 50% = 1/2, 0.25 = 1/4).
- **Rule 2: Probabilities range from 0 to 1 (which is equivalent to 0% to 100% and 0/1 to 1/1):** There can never be less than a 0% chance or higher than a 100% chance of something happening.
- **Rule 3: Probability is "sought outcomes" divided by "possible outcomes":** If you roll 1d6 and want to get a 6, that means that there is 1 sought outcome (the 6) and 6 possible

---

1. Schell, *The Art of Game Design,* 155–163.

outcomes (1, 2, 3, 4, 5, or 6). The probability of rolling a 6 is 1/6 (which is roughly equal to 0.16666 or about 17%). A regular deck of 52 playing cards has 13 spades, so if you pick one random card, the chance of it being a spade is 13/52 (which is equal to 1/4 or 0.25 or 25%).

- **Rule 4: Enumeration can solve difficult mathematical problems:** If you have a low number of possible outcomes, enumerating all of them can work fine, as you saw in the earlier 2d6 spreadsheet example. If you have a larger number (something like 10d6, which has 60,466,176 possible rolls), you could write a computer program to enumerate them. After you have some programming under your belt, you should check out the program to do so that is in the *Dice Probability* section of Appendix B, "Useful Concepts."

- **Rule 5: When sought outcomes are mutually exclusive, add their probabilities:** Schell's example of this is figuring the chance of drawing either a face card **OR** an ace from the deck. There are 12 face cards (3 per suit) and 4 aces in the deck. Aces and face cards are mutually exclusive, meaning that there is no card that is both an ace and a face card. The question for this is "What is the probability of drawing a face card **OR** an ace from the deck?" The answer: 12/52 + 4/52 = 16/52 (0.3077 ≈ 31%).

What is the probability of rolling a 1, 2, **OR** 3 on 1d6? 1/6 + 1/6 + 1/6 = 3/6 (0.5 = 50%). Any time you use an **OR** to combine mutually exclusive sought outcomes, you can *add* their probabilities.

- **Rule 6: When sought outcomes are not mutually exclusive, multiply their probabilities:** If you want to know the probability of choosing a card that is both a face card **AND** a spade, you can multiply the two probabilities together. Because probabilities are less than or equal to 1, multiplying them usually makes it less likely that the thing will happen. A deck has 13 spades (13/52) and 12 face cards (12/52). Multiplied together, you get the following:

$$13/52 \times 12/52 = (13 \times 12) / (52 \times 52)$$

$$= 156/2704 \qquad \textit{Both numerator and denominator are divisible by 52.}$$

$$= 3/52 \ (0.0577 \approx 6\%)$$

You know this is correct because there are actually 3 spades in the deck that are also face cards (which is 3 out of 52).

Another example would be the probability of rolling a 1 on 1d6 **AND** a 1 on another 1d6. This would be 1/6 × 1/6 = 1/36 (0.0278 ≈ 3%), and as you saw in the enumerated example in Sheets, there is exactly a 1/36 chance of getting a 1 on both dice when you roll 2d6.

Remember, if you use an **AND** to combine non-mutually exclusive sought outcomes, you can *multiply* their probabilities.

Corollary: When sought outcomes are independent, multiply their probabilities: If two actions are completely independent of each other (which is a subset of them not being mutually exclusive), the probability of them both happening is the multiplication of their individual probabilities.

The probability of getting a six on 1d6 (1/6) **AND** getting heads on a coin toss (1/2) **AND** drawing an Ace from a deck of cards (4/52) is 1/156 ($1/6 \times 1/2 \times 4/52 = 6/624 = 1/156$).

- ■ **Rule 7: One minus "does" = "doesn't":** The probability of something happening is 1 minus the probability of it not happening. For instance, the chance of rolling a 1 on 1d6 is 1/6, as you know. This means that the chance of *not* rolling a 1 on 1d6 is $1 - 1/6 = 5/6$ (0.8333 ≈ 83%). This is useful because it is sometimes easier to figure out the chance of something not happening than the chance of it happening.

For example, what if you wanted to calculate the odds of rolling a 6 on at least one die when you roll 2d6? If you enumerate, you'll find that the answer is 11/36 (the sought outcomes being 6_x, x_6, and 6_6 where the x could be any number other than six). You can also count the number of columns with at least one 6 in them in the Sheets chart you made. However, you can also use probability rules 5, 6, and 7 to figure this out.

The possibility of rolling a 6 on 1d6 is 1/6. The possibility of rolling a non-6 on 1d6 is 5/6, so the possibility of rolling 6 on one die **AND** a non-6 on the other (i.e., 6_x) is $1/6 \times 5/6 = 5/36$. (Remember from Rule 6 that **AND** means multiply.) Because this can be accomplished by either rolling 6_x **OR** x_6, you add those two possibilities together: $5/36 + 5/36 = 10/36$. (Rule 5: **OR** means add.)

The possibility of rolling a 6 on one die **AND** a 6 on the other (6_6) is $1/6 \times 1/6 = 1/36$.

Because all three cases (6_x, x_6, **OR** 6_6) are mutually exclusive, you can add all of them together: $5/36 + 5/36 + 1/36 = 11/36$ (0.3055 ≈ 31%).

This got complicated pretty quickly, but you can actually use Rule 7 to simplify it. If you reverse the problem and look for the chance of *not* getting a 6 in two rolls, that can be restated "What is the chance of getting a non-6 on the first die **AND** a non-6 on the second die (i.e., x_x)?" These two sought possibilities are not mutually exclusive, so you can multiply them! So, the chance of getting a non-6 on both rolls is just $5/6 \times 5/6 = 25/36$. Using Rule 7, $1 - 25/36 = 11/36$, which is pretty awesome and a lot easier to figure out!

Now, what if you were to roll 4d6 and sought at least one 6? This is now simply:

$$1 - (5/6 \times 5/6 \times 5/6 \times 5/6)$$
$$= 1 - (5^4 / 6^4)$$
$$= 1 - (625 / 1{,}296)$$
$$= (1{,}296 / 1{,}296) - (625 / 1{,}296) \qquad \textit{1,296/1,296 is equal to 1.}$$
$$= (1{,}296 - 625) / 1{,}296 \qquad\qquad \textit{Both are divisible by 1,296.}$$
$$= 671 / 1{,}296 \quad (0.5177 \approx 52\%)$$

There is about a 52% chance of rolling at least one 6 on 4d6.

■ **Rule 8: The sum of multiple dice is not a linear distribution:** As you saw in the enumerated Sheets example of 2d6, though each of the individual dice has a linear distribution—that is, each number 1–6 has an equal chance of happening on 1d6—when you sum multiple dice together, you get a weighted distribution of probability. It gets even more complex with more than two dice, as shown in Figure 11.7.

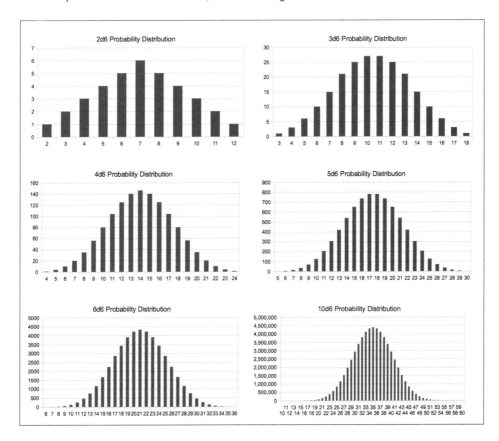

Figure 11.7 Probability distribution for 2d6, 3d6, 4d6, 5d6, and 10d6

As you can see in the figure, the more dice you add, the more severe the bias is toward the average sum of the dice. In fact, with 10d6, you have a 1/60,466,176 chance of rolling all 6s, but a 4,395,456/60,466,176 (0.0727 ≈ 7%) chance of rolling exactly 35 or a 41,539,796/60,466,176 (0.6869922781 ≈ 69%) chance of rolling a number from 30 to 40. There are some complex math papers about how to calculate these values with a formula, but I instead chose to follow Rule 4 and wrote a program to do so (see Appendix B).

As a game designer, it is not important to understand the exact numbers of these probability distributions. The thing that it *is* very important to remember is this: *The more dice you have the player roll, the more likely they are to get a number near the average.*

- **Rule 9: Theoretical versus practical probability:** In addition to the theoretical probabilities that we've been talking about, it is sometimes easier to approach probability from a more practical perspective. There are both digital and analog ways to do so.

  Digitally, you could write a simple computer program to do millions of trials and determine the outcome. This is often called the *Monte Carlo* method, and it is actually used by some of the best artificial intelligences that have been devised to play chess and go. Go is so complex that until recently, the best a computer could do was to calculate the results of millions of random plays by both the computer and its human opponent and determine the play that statistically led to the best outcome for it. This can also be used to determine the answers to what would be very challenging theoretical problems. Schell's example of this is a computer program that could rapidly simulate millions of rolls of the dice in *Monopoly* and let the programmer know which spaces on the board players were most likely to land on.

  Another aspect of this rule is that not all dice are created equal. For instance, if you wanted to publish a board game and were looking for a manufacturer for your dice, it would be very worthwhile to get a couple of dice from each potential manufacturer and roll each of them a couple hundred times, recording the result each time. This might take an hour or more to accomplish, but it would tell you whether the dice from the manufacturer were properly weighted or if they would instead roll a certain number more often than the others.

- **Rule 10: Phone a friend:** Nearly all college students who major in computer science or math must take a probability class or two as part of their studies. If you run into a difficult probability problem that you can't figure out on your own, try asking one of them. In fact, according to Schell, the study of probability began in 1654 when the Chevalier de Méré couldn't figure out why he seemed to have a better than even chance of rolling at least one 6 on four rolls of 1d6 but seemed to have a less than even chance of rolling at least one 12 on 24 rolls of 2d6. The Chevalier asked his friend Blaise Pascal for help. Pascal wrote to his father's friend Pierre de Fermat, and their conversation became the basis for probability studies.[2]

In Appendix B, "Useful Concepts," I have included a Unity program that calculates the distribution of rolls for any number of dice with any number of sides (as long as you have enough time to wait for it to calculate).

Randomizer Technologies in Paper Games

Some of the most common randomizers used in paper games include dice, spinners, and decks of cards.

---

2. Schell, *The Art of Game Design*, 154.

Dice

This chapter has already covered a lot of information about dice. The important elements are as follows:

- A single die generates randomness with a linear probability distribution.

- The more dice you add together, the more the result is biased toward the average (and away from a linear distribution), and the more extreme the bell curve becomes.

- Standard die sizes include d4, d6, d8, d10, d12, and d20. Commonly available packs of dice for gaming usually include 1d4, 2d6, 1d8, 2d10, 1d12, and 1d20.

- The 2d10 in a standard dice pack are sometimes called *percentile dice* because one will be used for the 1s place (marked with the numbers from 0–9) and the other for the 10s place (marked with the multiples of 10 from 00–90), giving an even distribution of the numbers from 00 to 99 (where a roll of 0 and 00 is usually counted as 100%).

Spinners

Multiple kinds of spinners are available, but all have a rotating element and a still element. In most board games, the spinner is composed of a cardboard base that is divided into sections with a plastic spinning arrow mounted above it (see Figure 11.8A). Larger spinners (e.g., the wheel from the television show *Wheel of Fortune*) often have the sections on the spinning wheel and the arrow on the base (Figure 11.8B). As long as players spin the spinner with enough force, a spinner is effectively the same as a die from a probability standpoint.

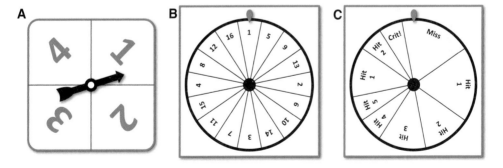

Figure 11.8 Various spinners. In all diagrams, the green elements are static, and the black element rotates.

Spinners are often used in children's games for two major reasons:

- Young children lack the motor control to throw a die within a small area, so they will often accidentally throw dice in a way that they roll off of the gaming table.

- Spinners are a lot more difficult for young children to swallow.

Though they are less common in games for adults, spinners provide interesting possibilities that are not feasible with dice:

- Spinners can be made with any number of slots, whereas it is difficult—though not impossible—to construct a die with 3, 7, 13, or 200 sides.[3]

- Spinners can be weighted very easily so that not all possibilities have the same chance of happening. Figure 11.8C shows a hypothetical spinner to be used by a player when attacking. On this spinner, the player would have the following chances on a spin:

    - 3/16 chance of Miss

    - 1/16 chance of Hit 4

    - 5/16 chance of Hit 1

    - 1/16 chance of Hit 5

    - 3/16 chance of Hit 2

    - 1/16 chance of Crit!

    - 2/16 chance of Hit 3

Decks of Cards

A standard deck of playing cards includes 13 cards of 4 different suits and sometimes two jokers (see Figure 11.9). This includes the ranks 1 (also called the Ace) through 10, Jack, Queen, and King in each of the four suits: Clubs, Diamonds, Hearts, and Spades.

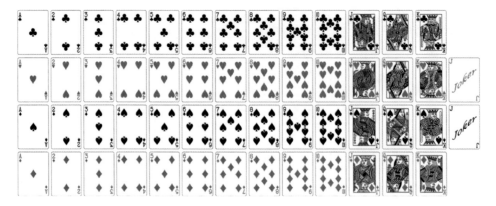

Figure 11.9 A standard deck of playing cards with two jokers[4]

---

3. This is most often done by creating a die shaped like an American football with flat sides for whatever number is desired. Search for "oblong dice," "crystal dice," or "d7 dice" online to see examples.

4. Vectorized Playing Cards 1.3 (http://sourceforge.net/projects/vector-cards/ —Accessed January 28, 2017) ©2011, Chris Aguilar, Licensed under LGPLv3. www.gnu.org/copyleft/lesser.html

Playing cards are very popular because of both their compactness and the many different ways in which they can be divided.

In a draw of a single card from a deck without Jokers, you have the following probabilities:

- Chance of drawing a particular single card: 1/52 (0.0192 ≈ 2%)
- Chance of drawing a specific suit: 13/52 = 1/4 (0.25 = 25%)
- Chance of drawing a face card (J, Q, or K): 12/52 = 3/13 (0.2308 ≈ 23%)

Custom Card Decks

A deck of cards is one of the easiest and most configurable randomizers that you can make for a paper game. You can very easily add or remove copies of a specific card to change the probability of that card appearing in a single draw from the deck. See the section on weighted distributions later in this chapter for more information.

TIPS FOR MAKING CUSTOM CARD DECKS

One of the difficulties in making custom cards is getting material for them that you can easily shuffle. 3x5 note cards don't work particularly well for this, but there are a couple of better options:

- Use marker or stickers to modify an existing set of cards. Sharpies work well for this and don't add thickness to the card like stickers do.

- Buy a deck of card sleeves and insert a slip of paper along with a regular card into each, as described in Chapter 9, "Paper Prototyping."

The key thing you want to avoid when making a deck (or any element of a paper prototype) is putting too much time into any one piece. After you've devoted time to making a lot of nice cards (for instance) you might be less willing to remove any of those cards from the prototype or to scrap them and start over.

Digital Deck Construction

I have recently started using digital deck construction tools like *nanDECK* in my game prototyping (http://www.nand.it/nandeck/). *nanDECK* is Windows software that builds a deck of cards from a simple markup language (somewhat like HTML). My favorite *nanDECK* feature is its ability to pull card data from an online Google Sheets file and turn it into a full deck of cards. There isn't room in this book to describe how this works, but I recommend checking out *nanDECK* if you're interested. In addition to the PDF reference file on the website, you can also find several useful video tutorials by searching YouTube for "nanDECK."

When to Shuffle a Deck

Shuffling the entire deck of cards before every draw gives you an equal likelihood of drawing any of the cards (just like when you roll a die or use a spinner). However, this isn't how most people use decks of cards. In general, people draw until the deck is completely exhausted and then shuffle all the cards. This leads to very different behavior from a deck than from an equivalent die. If you had a deck of six cards numbered 1–6, and you drew every card before reshuffling, you would be guaranteed to see each of the numbers 1–6 once for every six times you drew from the deck. Rolling a die six times will not give you this same consistency. An additional difference is that players could count cards and know which have and have not been drawn thus far, giving them insight into the probability of a certain card being drawn next. For example, if the cards 1, 3, 4, and 5 have been drawn from the six-card deck, there is a 50% chance that the next card will be a 2 and a 50% chance that it will be a 6.

This difference between decks and dice came up in the board game *Settlers of Catan* where some players got so frustrated at the difference between the theoretical probability of the 2d6 rolls in the game versus the actual numbers that came up in play that the publisher of the game now sells a deck of 36 cards (marked with each of the possible outcomes of 2d6) as an option to replace the dice in play, ensuring that the practical probability experienced in the game is the same as the theoretical probability.

Weighted Distributions

A weighted distribution is one in which some options are more likely to come up than others. Most of the randomizer examples that you've looked at so far involve equal distributions of random possibilities, but it is common for designers to want to weight one option more heavily than another. For example, in the board game *Small World*, the designers wanted an attacker to get a random bonus on her final attack of each turn about half of the time, and they wanted that bonus to range from +1 to +3. To do this, they created a die with the six sides shown in Figure 11.10.

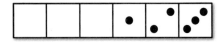

Figure 11.10 The attack bonus die from *Small World* with weighted bonus distribution

With this die, the chance of getting zero bonus is 3/6 = 1/2 (0.5 = 50%), and the chance of getting a bonus of 2 is 1/6 (0.1666 ≈ 17%), so the chance of zero bonus is weighted much more heavily than the other three choices.

What if instead, you still wanted the player to get a bonus only half of the time, but you wanted for the bonus of 1 to be three times more likely than the 3, and the 2 to be twice as likely as the 3? This would provide the weighted distribution shown in Figure 11.11.

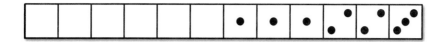

Figure 11.11 Die with 1/2 chance of 0, 1/4 chance of 1, 1/6 chance of 2, and 1/12 chance of 3

Luckily, this adds up to 12 total possible sides for a die (a common die size). However, if it didn't add up to a common size, you could always create a spinner or a deck of cards with the same probabilities (though the card deck would need to be shuffled each time before drawing a card). Modeling weighted distributions with randomized outcomes is also possible in Sheets. The process is very similar to how you will deal with random numbers later in Unity and C#.

Weighted Probability in Sheets

Weighted probability is commonplace in digital games. For instance, if you wanted an enemy who encounters the player to attack her 40% of the time, adopt a defensive posture 40% of the time, and run away 20% of the time, you could create an array of values [Attack, Attack, Defend, Defend, Run][5] and have the enemy's artificial intelligence code pull a random value from it when the player was first detected.

Take the following steps to make a Sheets worksheet that you can use to randomly select from a series of values. Initially, it picks a random number between 1 and 12. When you have completed the worksheet, you can replace choices in column A with any that you wish.

	A	B	C
1		# Choices:	12
2		Random:	0.4843701814
3		Index:	6
4		Result:	6
5			
6			
7			
8			
9			
10			
11			
12			

Figure 11.12 Google Sheets table for weighted random number selection

---

5. Square brackets (i.e., [ ]) are used in C# to define arrays (a group of values), so I use them here to group the five possible action values.

1. Add a new Worksheet to your existing Sheets document by clicking the plus symbol to the left of the existing *Sheet 1* worksheet tab at the bottom of the window (refer to Figure 11.2, earlier this chapter).

2. In this new worksheet, fill in the text and numbers shown in *columns A and B* of Figure 11.12 but leave column C empty for now. To right-align the text in column B, select cells *B1:B4* and choose *Format > Align > Right* from the Sheets menu bar (inside the browser window, as shown highlighted in a blue rectangle in Figure 11.2).

3. Select cell *C1* and enter the formula =`COUNTIF(A1:A100,"<>")`. This counts the number of cells in the range A1:A100 that are not empty (in a Sheets formula, `<>` means "different from," and not following it with a specified value means "different from nothing"). This results in the number of valid choices that are listed in column A (you currently have 12).

4. In cell *C2* enter the formula =`RAND()`, which generates a number from 0 (*inclusive*) to 1 (*exclusive*).[6]

5. Select cell *C3* and enter the formula =`FLOOR(C2*C1)+1`. The number you're flooring is the random number between 0 and ≈0.9999 multiplied by the number of possible choices, which is 12 in this case. This means that you're flooring numbers between 0 and ≈11.9999 to give you the integers from 0 to 11. You then add 1 to the result to give you the integers 1 to 12.

6. In cell *C4*, enter the formula =`INDEX(A1:A100,C3)`. `INDEX()` takes a range of values (e.g., A1:A100) and chooses from them based on an index (C3 in this case, which can range from 1 to 12). Now, C4 will choose a random value from the list in column A.

To get a different random value, copy cell C2 and paste it back into C2. This forces a recalculation of the RAND function. You can also make any change to the spreadsheet to cause it to recalculate the RAND (for instance, you could type 1 into E1 and press Return to force a recalculation). Any time you change any cell in the spreadsheet, RAND will recalculate.

You can put either numbers or text into the cells in column A as long as you don't skip any rows. Try replacing the numbers in cells A1:A12 with the weighted values from Figure 11.11 (that is, [0, 0, 0, 0, 0, 0, 1, 1, 1, 2, 2, 3]). If you do so and try recalculating the random value in C2 several times, you will see that zero comes up in cell C4 about half of the time. You can also fill the values A1:A5 with [Attack, Attack, Defend, Defend, Run] and see the weighted enemy AI choice that was used as an example at the beginning of this section.

Permutations

There is a traditional game called *Bulls and Cows* (see Figure 11.13) that served as the basis for the popular board game *Master Mind* (1970 by Mordecai Meirowitz). In this game, each player writes down a secret four-digit code (where each of the digits is different). Players take turns

---

6. "0 (*inclusive*)" means that the random number returned could be 0, while "1 (exclusive)" means that the random number returned will never be 1 (though it can be 0.99999999).

trying to guess their opponent's code, and the first person to guess correctly wins. When a player guesses, her opponent responds with a number of *bulls* and a number of *cows*. The guesser gets a bull for each number she guessed that is in the correct position and a cow for each number that is part of the code but not in the right position. In Figure 11.13 green represents a bull, and white represents a cow.

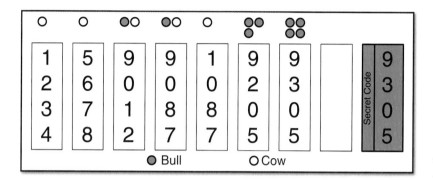

Figure 11.13 An example game of *Bulls and Cows*

From the perspective of the guesser, the secret code is effectively a series of random choices. Mathematicians call series like these *permutations*. In *Bulls and Cows*, the secret code is a permutation of the ten digits 0–9, where four are chosen with no repeating elements. In the game *Master Mind*, there are eight possible colors, of which four are chosen with no repetition. In both cases, the code is a permutation and not a *combination* because the positions of the elements matter (9305 is not the same as 3905). A combination is a selection of choices where the position doesn't matter. For example, 1234, 2341, 3421, 2431, and so on are all the same thing in a combination. A good example of a combination is the combination of three flavors of ice cream you want in your sundae; it doesn't matter what order they're added in, as long as they're all there.

Permutations with Repeating Elements

The math is a little easier for permutations that allow repetition, so we'll start there. If there were four digits with repetition allowed, there would be 10,000 possible combinations (the numbers 0000 through 9999). This is easy to see with numbers, but you need a more general way of thinking about it (for cases where there are not exactly 10 choices per slot). Because each digit is independent of the others and each has 10 possible choices, according to probability Rule 6, the probability of getting any one number is $1/10 \times 1/10 \times 1/10 \times 1/10 = 1/10{,}000$. This also tells you that there are 10,000 possible choices for the code (if repetition is allowed).

The general calculation for permutations with repetition allowed is to multiply the number of choices for each slot by each other. With four slots and ten choices each, this is

$10 \times 10 \times 10 \times 10 = 10,000$. If you were to make the code from six-sided dice instead of digits, then there would be six choices per slot, making $6 \times 6 \times 6 \times 6 = 1296$ possible choices.

Permutations with No Repeating Elements

But what about the actual case for *Bulls and Cows* where you're not allowed to repeat any digits? It's actually simpler than you might imagine. After you've used a digit, it's no longer available. So, for the first slot, you can pick any number from 0–9, but after a number (e.g., 9) has been chosen for the first slot, only 9 choices remain for the second slot (0–8). This continues for the rest of the slots, so the calculation of possible codes for *Bulls and Cows* is $10 \times 9 \times 8 \times 7 = 5040$. Not allowing repeating digits eliminates almost half of the possible choices.

Using Sheets to Balance Weapons

Another use of math and programs like Google Sheets in game design is the balance of various weapons or abilities. In this section, you'll look at an example weapon balancing process for a game similar to *Valkyria Chronicles* by Sega. In this example game, each weapon has three important values:

- The number of shots fired at a time
- The damage done by each shot
- The chance that each shot will hit at a given distance

As you balance these weapons, you want them to feel roughly equal to each other in power, though you also want each weapon to have a distinct personality. For each weapon, these personalities are the following:

- **Pistol:** A basic weapon; pretty decent in most situations but doesn't excel in any
- **Rifle:** A good choice for mid and long range
- **Shotgun:** Deadly up close but its power falls off quickly; only one shot, so a miss really matters
- **Sniper Rifle:** Terrible at close range but fantastic at long range
- **Machine Gun:** Fires many shots, so even if some miss, the others will usually hit; this should feel like the most reliable gun, though not the most powerful

Figure 11.14 shows the values for the weapons as I initially imagined they might work. The ToHit value is the minimum roll on 1d6 that would hit at that range. For example, in cell K3, you can see that the ToHit for the pistol at a range of 7 is 4, so if the player is shooting a target 7 spaces away, a roll of 4 or higher would be a hit. This is a 50% chance of hitting on 1d6 (because it would hit on a roll of 4, 5, or 6).

	A	B	C	D E F	G	H	I	J	K	L	M	N O	P	Q	R	S	T	U	V	W	X	Y	Z
1	**Weapon**	**Shots**	**D/Shot**	**ToHit**									**Percent Chance**										
2	Original			1	2	3	4	5	6	7	8	9 10	1	2	3	4	5	6	7	8	9	10	
3	Pistol	4	2	2	2	2	3	3	4	4	5	5 6											
4	Rifle	3	3	4	3	2	2	2	3	3	3	4 4											
5	Shotgun	1	10	2	2	3	3	4	5	6													
6	Sniper Rifle	1	8	6	5	4	4	3	3	2	2	3 4											
7	Machine Gun	6	1	3	3	4	4	5	5	6	6												

Figure 11.14 Initial values for the weapons balance spreadsheet

Determining the Percent Chance for Each Bullet

In the cells under the heading Percent Chance, you want to calculate the chance that each shot of a weapon will hit at a certain distance. To do so, follow these steps.

1. Create a new spreadsheet document in Sheets and enter all the data shown in Figure 11.14. To change the background color of a cell, you can use the *Cell Color* button shown in Figure 11.2.

In cell E3, you can see that each shot from a pistol will hit at a distance of 1 if the player rolls a 2 or better on 1d6. This means that it will miss on a 1 and hit on 2, 3, 4, 5, or 6. This is a 5/6 chance (or ≈83%), and you need a formula to calculate this. Looking at probability Rule 7, you know that there is a 1/6 chance of it missing (which is the same as the ToHit number minus one).

2. Select cell *P3* and enter the formula `= (E3-1) /6`. This causes P3 to display the chance of the pistol *missing* at a range of one. Order of operations does work in Sheets, so divide operations happen before minus operations, necessitating the parentheses around `E3-1`.

3. Using Rule 7 again, you know that 1 – miss = hit, so change the formula in *P3* to `=1- ((E3-1) /6)`. After you've done this, P3 will hold the value 0.8333333.

4. To convert P3 from showing decimal numbers to showing a percentage, select *P3* and click the button labeled **%** in the *Number Formats* area shown in Figure 11.2. You will also probably want to click the button just to the right of **%** a couple of times (this button looks like a **.0** with a left arrow). This removes decimal places from the cell view to show 83% instead of the more accurate but messier %83.33. This only changes the view—not the underlying data—so the cell still maintains accuracy for further calculations.

5. Copy the formula in P3 and paste it into all the cells in the range *P3:Y7*. You'll see that everything works perfectly except for the blank ToHit cells, which now have a percent chance of %117! You need to alter the formula to ignore blank cells.

6. Select *P3* again and change the formula to `=IF(E3="", "", 1-((E3-1)/6))`. The IF function in Sheets has three parts, which are divided by commas.

   - `E3="":` Part 1 is a question: is E3 equal to ""? (i.e., is E3 equal to an empty cell?)
   - `"":` Part 2 is what to put in the cell if the question in part 1 evaluates to true. That is, if E3 is empty, make cell P3 empty as well.

- **1-((E3-1)/6): Part 3** is what to put in the cell if the question in part 1 evaluates to false. That is, if E3 is not empty, then use the same formula you had before.

7. Copy the new formula from P3 and paste it into *P3:Y7*. The empty cells in the ToHit area now result in empty cells in the Percent Chance area. (E.g., L5:N5 are empty, so W5:Y5 are empty as well.)

8. Next, you'll add some color to this chart. Select cells *P3:Y7*. From the Sheets menu bar choose *Format > Conditional formatting*. A new *Conditional format rules* pane opens on the right side of your window. Conditional formatting is formatting that adjusts based on the contents of a cell.

9. Click *Color scale* near the top of the *Conditional format rules* pane.

10. Under the *Preview* heading in the *Color scale* section, you can see the word *Default* over a gradient of green color swatches. Click *Default* and choose the bottom, middle option: *Green to yellow to red*.

11. Click *Done*, and your spreadsheet will look like the *Percent Chance* section in Figure 11.15.

	O	P	Q	R	S	T	U	V	W	X	Y	Z	AA	AB	AC	AD	AE	AF	AG	AH	AI	AJ	AK
1		Percent Chance											Average Damage										
2		1	2	3	4	5	6	7	8	9	10		1	2	3	4	5	6	7	8	9	10	
3		83%	83%	83%	67%	67%	50%	50%	33%	33%	17%		6.67	6.67	6.67	5.33	5.33	4.00	4.00	2.67	2.67	1.33	
4		50%	67%	83%	83%	83%	67%	67%	67%	50%	50%		4.50	6.00	7.50	7.50	7.50	6.00	6.00	6.00	4.50	4.50	
5		83%	83%	67%	67%	50%	33%	17%					8.33	8.33	6.67	6.67	5.00	3.33	1.67				
6		17%	33%	50%	50%	67%	67%	83%	83%	67%	50%		1.33	2.67	4.00	4.00	5.33	5.33	6.67	6.67	5.33	4.00	
7		67%	67%	50%	50%	33%	33%	17%	17%				4.00	4.00	3.00	3.00	2.00	2.00	1.00	1.00			

Figure 11.15 The Percent Chance and Average Damage sections of the weapons spreadsheet. You will make the Average Damage section next. (Note that I've scrolled the spreadsheet to the right so you can also see Average Damage.)

Calculating Average Damage

The next step in the balancing process is to determine how much average damage each gun inflicts at a certain distance. Because some guns fire multiple shots, and each shot causes a certain amount of damage, the average damage will be equal to the number of shots fired * the amount of damage per shot * the chance that each shot will hit:

1. Highlight columns *O:Z* and copy them (press Command-C, or Ctrl+C on PC, or choose *Edit > Copy*).

2. Select cell *Z1* and paste (Command-V, Ctrl+V on PC, or choose *Edit > Paste*). This expands your worksheet out to column AK and fills it with a duplicate of the columns you copied.

3. Enter `Average Damage` into cell AA1.

4. Select cell *AA3* and enter the formula `=IF(P3="", "", $B3*$C3*P3)`. Just as in the formula for P3, the `IF` function here ensures that only non-empty cells are calculated. The formula includes absolute column references to columns $B and $C because column B holds the number of shots, and C holds the damage per shot regardless of the distance to

the enemy. You don't want those references moving to other columns (though you do want them able to move to other rows, so only the column reference is absolute).

5. Select cell *AA3* and click the rightmost button in the *Number Formats* area of the button bar (the button looks like **123 ▼**). Select *Number* from the pop-up menu.

6. Copy cell AA3 and paste it into *AA3:AJ7*. Now the numbers are accurate, but the conditional formatting is still tied to that for the Percent Chance section, causing the numbers above 1 to cause the percentages between 0 and 100% in the Percent Chance section to all turn green.

7. Select cells *AA3:AJ7*. If the Conditional format rules pane is no longer showing, choose *Format > Conditional formatting* from the Sheets menu bar to open it again.

8. With AA3:AJ7 selected, you should see a rule in the Conditional format rules pane that reads *Color scale* with the cell references P3 : Y7 , AA3 : AJ7 under it. Click this rule.

9. This expands the rule and allows you to edit it, allowing you to change the *Apply to range* to just P3 : Y7 and click *Done*. This causes the previous format to only apply to the Percent Chance section.

10. Select *AA3:AJ7* once more. In the *Conditional format rules* pane, click *Add new rule*.

11. Choose *Color scale* and *Green to yellow to red* as you did before. Then click *Done*.

This results in two separate conditional formatting rules, one for the Percent Chance section and another for the Average Damage section. Keeping these rules separate causes the colors to be determined for each separately, which is important because the ranges of the numbers in each section are so different from each other. Now your Average Damage section should look like the one shown in Figure 11.15.

Charting the Average Damage

The next important step is to chart the average damage. Although you can look carefully at the numbers and interpret them, having Sheets do the job of charting information is much easier and allows you to visually assess what is going on. Follow these steps to do so:

1. Select cells *A2:A7*.

2. Scroll over to where you can see the Average Damage section. With A2:A7 still selected, hold Command (or Ctrl on PC), click on *AA2*, and drag to select *AA2:AJ7*. You should now have A2:A7,AA2:AJ7 selected.

3. Click the *Chart* button (refer to Figure 11.2) to open the Chart Editor.

4. Click the *Chart type* pop-up menu (which currently shows "Column chart") (Figure 11.6.A) and click the leftmost chart type under the *Line* heading (it is the top-left image showing blue and red lines with sharp angles).

5. Near the bottom of the DATA tab, check the box for *Switch rows / columns*.

6. Check the box for *Use column A as headers*. Also make sure that the box next to the *Use row 2 as labels* option is checked.

7. Click the close box in the *Chart editor* to complete the chart.

You can see the results of the chart in Figure 11.16. As you can see, there are some problems with the weapons. Some, like the sniper rifle and shotgun have personalities as we had hoped (the shotgun is deadly at close range, and the sniper rifle is better at long range), but there are a lot of other problems:

- The machine gun is ridiculously weak.
- The pistol might be too strong.
- The rifle is also overly strong compared to the other weapons.

In short, the weapons are not balanced well to each other.

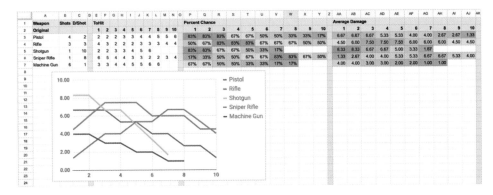

Weapon	Shots	D/Shot	ToHit										Percent Chance										Average Damage									
Original			1	2	3	4	5	6	7	8	9	10	1	2	3	4	5	6	7	8	9	10	1	2	3	4	5	6	7	8	9	10
Pistol	4	2	2	2	2	3	4	4	5	5	6		83%	83%	83%	67%	67%	50%	50%	33%	33%	17%	6.67	6.67	6.67	5.33	5.33	4.00	4.00	2.67	2.67	1.33
Rifle	3	3	4	3	2	2	2	3	3	3	4	4	50%	67%	83%	83%	83%	67%	67%	67%	50%	50%	4.50	6.00	7.50	7.50	7.50	6.00	6.00	6.00	4.50	4.50
Shotgun	1	10	2	2	3	4	5	6					83%	83%	67%	67%	50%	33%	17%				8.33	8.33	6.67	6.67	5.00	3.33	1.67			
Sniper Rifle	1	8	6	5	4	4	3	3	2	2	3	4	17%	33%	50%	50%	67%	67%	83%	83%	67%	50%	1.33	2.67	4.00	4.00	5.33	5.33	6.67	6.67	5.33	4.00
Machine Gun	6	1	3	3	4	4	5	5	6	6			67%	67%	50%	50%	33%	33%	17%	17%			4.00	4.00	3.00	3.00	2.00	2.00	1.00	1.00		

Figure 11.16 The weapon balance at the halfway point showing the chart of initial weapon stats. (I did some tweaking to the CUSTOMIZE tab of the chart to make the text more legible in the book figure.)

Duplicating the Weapon Data

To rebalance the weapons, having the original and rebalanced information next to each other is very helpful:

1. Start by moving the chart further down the worksheet. It should be somewhere below row 16.

2. Double-click anywhere in the chart, which reopens the Chart editor. Select the CUSTOMIZE tab at the top of the Chart editor (Figure 11.6.D). Click the *Chart axis & titles* header (Figure 11.6.E) and set the *Title text* of the chart to `Original` (Figure 11.6.F).

3. You need to make a copy of the data and formulas that you've already worked out. Select the cells *A1:AK8* and copy them.

4. Click cell *A9* and paste. This should create a full copy of all the data you just created in cells A9:AK16.

5. Change the text in *A10* to `Rebalanced`.

   This set of rebalanced data will be where you make the changes and try out new numbers.

6. Now, to make a chart for the new data that is identical to the one for the original weapon stats, select *A10:A15,AA10:AJ15* just as you selected A2:A7,AA2:AJ7 in steps 1 and 2 of "Charting the Average Damage." Follow the rest of the instructions in that section to create a second chart showing the rebalanced values.

7. Position the new chart to the right of the original one so that you can see both charts and the data above them.

8. Change the title of the new chart to `Rebalanced`.

Showing Overall Damage

One final stat that you might want to track is overall damage. This sums the average damage that a weapon can do at all ranges to give you an idea of the overall power of the weapon. To do this, you can take advantage of a trick I use frequently to make a simple bar chart within the cells of the spreadsheet (i.e., not inside a chart). The results are shown in Figure 11.17.

1. Right-click the *AK* column header and choose *Insert 1 right*.

2. Right-click the *B* column header and choose *Copy*. This will copy the entire B column.

3. Right-click the *AL* column header and choose *Paste*. This pastes everything from column B into AL, including the background color and font style.

4. Right-click the *AL* column header and choose *Insert 1 right*.

5. Enter `Overall Damage` into cells *AL1* and *AL9*.

6. Select cell *AL3* and enter the formula `=SUM(AA3:AJ3)`. This adds up the average damage done by the pistol at all ranges (it should equal `45.33`).

7. For the bar chart trick, you must convert this decimal value to an integer, so the SUM needs to be rounded. Change the formula in AL3 to `=ROUND( SUM(AA3:AJ3) )`. The result will now be `45.00`. To remove the extra zeroes, highlight cell *AL3* and click the button to remove decimal places as you did earlier (the third button in the *Number Formats* group).

8. Select cell *AM3* and enter the formula `=REPT("|", AL3)`. The REPT function repeats text a certain number of times. The text in this case is the pipe character (you type a pipe by holding Shift and pressing the backslash (\) key, which is above the Return/Enter key on most U.S. keyboards), and it is repeated 45 times because the value in AL3 is 45. A little bar of pipe characters appears, extending to the right in cell AM3. Double-click the right edge of the AM column heading to expand the AM column to show this.

9. Select cells *AL3:AM3* and copy them. Paste them into cells *AL3:AM7* and *AL11:AM15*. This gives you a text-based total damage bar chart for all weapons, both original and balanced. Finally, adjust the width of column AM again to make sure you can see all the repeated characters.

Rebalancing the Weapons

Now that you have two sets of data and two charts, you can try rebalancing the weapons. How will you make the machine gun more powerful? Will you increase its number of shots, its chance to hit, or its damage per shot? Some additional game rules to keep in mind as you balance include:

- In this example game, units have only 6 health, so they will fall unconscious if 6 or more damage is dealt to them.

- In *Valkyria Chronicles*, if an enemy is not downed by an attacking soldier, the enemy automatically counterattacks. This makes dealing 6 damage in an attack much more powerful than dealing 5 damage because it also protects the attacker from counterattack.

- Weapons with many shots (e.g., the machine gun) have a much higher chance of dealing the average amount of damage in a single turn, whereas guns with a single shot will feel much less reliable (e.g., the shotgun and sniper rifle). Figure 11.7 shows how the probability distribution shifts toward the average when you start rolling dice for multiple shots instead of a single one.

- Even with all this information, this chart does not show some aspects of weapon balance. This includes things like the point made earlier about multishot weapons having a much higher chance of dealing the average amount of damage as well as the benefit of the sniper rifle to deal damage to enemies who are too far away to effectively counterattack.

Try your hand at balancing the stats for these weapons. You should only change the values in the range B11:N15. Leave the original stats alone, and don't touch the Percent Chance and Average Damage sections; both they and the Rebalanced chart will update to reflect the changes you make to the Shots, D/Shot, and ToHit cells. After you've played with this for a while, continue reading.

One Example of Balanced Values

In Figure 11.17, you can see the weapon stats that I chose when I did this exercise for a prototype that I designed.[7] This is absolutely not the only way to balance these weapons or even the best way to balance them, but it does achieve many of the design goals.

---

7. I used the game described here and these balanced values as the example paper prototype for Chapter 9, "Paper Prototyping," in the first edition of the book.

Weapon	Shots	D/Shot	ToHit									
Rebalanced			1	2	3	4	5	6	7	8	9	10
Pistol	3	2	2	2	2	3	3	4	4	5	6	6
Rifle	2	4	5	4	4	4	3	3	3	4	5	5
Shotgun	1	6	2	2	2	2	3	4	5	6		
Sniper Rifle	1	6	6	6	5	5	4	3	3	2	2	3
Machine Gun	10	1	4	4	4	4	5	5	6	6		

	Overall Damage
Pistol	33 ||||||||||||||||||||||||||||||||
Rifle	40 |||||||||||||||||||||||||||||||||||||||
Shotgun	30 |||||||||||||||||||||||||||
Sniper Rifle	31 ||||||||||||||||||||||||||||
Machine Gun	30 |||||||||||||||||||||||||||

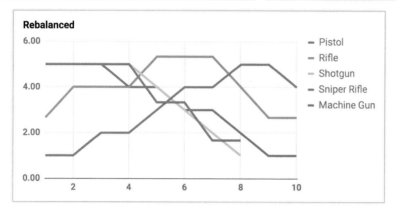

Figure 11.17 The weapon balance chosen for Chapter 9

- The weapons each have a personality of their own, and none is too overpowered or underpowered.

- Though the shotgun might look a little too similar to the machine gun in this chart, the two guns will feel very different due to two factors: 1) A hit with the 6-damage shotgun is an instant knockout; and 2) The machine gun fires many bullets, so it will deal average damage much more often.

- The pistol is pretty decent at close range and is more versatile than the shotgun or machine gun with its ability to attempt to hit enemies at longer range.

- The rifle really shines at mid-range.

- The sniper rifle is terrible at close range, but it dominates long-distance. A hit with the sniper rifle is 6 points of damage like the shotgun, so it can also take down an enemy in one shot.

Even though this kind of spreadsheet-based balancing doesn't cover all possible implications of the design of the weapons, it's still an important tool to have in your game design arsenal because it can help you understand large amounts of data quickly. Several designers of free-to-play games spend most of their day modifying spreadsheets to make slight tweaks in game balance, so if you're interested in a job in that field, spreadsheets and data-driven design (like you just did) are very important skills.

Positive and Negative Feedback

One final critical element of game balance to discuss is the concept of positive and negative feedback. In a game with positive feedback, a player who takes an early lead gains an advantage over the other players and is more likely to win the game. In a game with negative feedback, the players who are losing have an advantage.

Poker is an excellent example of a game with positive feedback. If a player wins a big pot and has more money than the other players, individual bets matter less to her, and she has more freedom to do things like bluff (because she can afford to lose). However, a player who loses money early in the game and has little left can't afford to take risks and has less freedom when playing. *Monopoly* has a strong positive feedback mechanism where the player with the best properties consistently gets more money and is able to force other players to sell her their properties if they can't afford the rent when they land on her spaces. Positive feedback is generally frowned upon in most games, but it can be very good if you want the game to end quickly (though *Monopoly* does not take advantage of this because its designer wished to demonstrate the pain of the poor in capitalist societies). Single-player games also often have positive feedback mechanisms to make the player feel increasingly powerful throughout the game.

Mario Kart is a great example of a game with negative feedback in the form of the random items that it awards to players when they drive through item boxes. The player in the lead usually only gets a banana (a largely defensive weapon), a set of three bananas, or a green shell (one of the weakest attacks). A player in last place often gets much more powerful items such as the lightning bolt that slows down every other player in the race. Negative feedback makes games feel fairer to the players who are not in the lead and generally leads to both longer games and to all players feeling that they have still have a chance of winning even if they're pretty far behind.

Summary

This chapter had a lot of math, but I hope you saw that learning a little about math will be very useful for you as a game designer. Most of the topics covered in this chapter could merit their own book or course, so I encourage you to look into them further if your interest has been piqued.

CHAPTER 12

GUIDING THE PLAYER

As you've read in earlier chapters, your primary job as a designer is to craft an experience for players to enjoy. However, the further you get into your project and your design, the more obvious and intuitive your game appears to you. This comes from your familiarity with the game and is entirely natural.

However, this means that you need to keep a wary eye on your game, making sure that players who have never seen your game before also intuitively understanding what they need to do to experience the game as you intended. This requires careful, sometimes invisible, guidance.

This chapter covers two styles of player guidance: *direct*, where the player knows that she is being guided; and *indirect*, where the guidance is so subtle that players often don't even realize that the guidance is there. The chapter concludes with information about *sequencing*, a style of progressive instruction to teach players new concepts or introduce them to new game mechanics.

Direct Guidance

Direct guidance methods are those that the player is explicitly aware of. Direct guidance takes many forms, but in all of them, quality is determined by immediacy, scarcity, brevity, and clarity:

- **Immediacy:** The message must be given to the player when it is immediately relevant. Some games try to tell the player all the possible controls for the game at the very beginning (sometimes showing a diagram of the controller with all of the buttons labeled), but it is ridiculous to think that a player will be able to remember all of these controls when the time comes that she actually needs to use them. Direct information about controls should be provided immediately the first time that the player needs it. In the PlayStation 2 game *Kya: Dark Lineage*, a tree falls into the path of the player character that she must jump over, and as it is falling, the game shows the player the message "Press X to jump" at exactly the time she needs to know that information.

- **Scarcity:** Many modern games have lots of controls and lots of simultaneous goals. Not flooding the player with too much information all at one time is important. Making instructions and other direct controls scarcer makes them more valuable to the player and more likely to be heeded. This is also the case with missions. A player can only really concentrate on a single mission at once, and some otherwise fantastic open world games like *Skyrim* inundate the player with various missions to the point that after several hours of gameplay, the player could potentially be in the middle of dozens of different missions, many of which will just be ignored.

- **Brevity:** Never use more verbiage than is necessary, and don't give the player too much information at one time. In the tactical combat game *Valkyria Chronicles*, if you wanted to teach the player to press O to take cover behind some sandbags, the least you would need to say is "When near sandbags, press O to take cover and reduce damage from enemy attacks."

- **Clarity:** Be very clear about what you're trying to convey. In the previous example, you might be tempted to just tell the player "When standing near sandbags, press O to take cover," because you might assume that players should know that cover will shield them from incoming bullets. However, in *Valkyria Chronicles*, cover not only shields you but also drastically reduces the amount of damage you take from bullets that do hit (even if the cover is not between the attacker and the target). For the player to understand everything she needs to know about cover, she must also be told about the damage reduction.

Four Methods of Direct Guidance

There are a number of direct guidance methods that you will find in games.

Instructions

The game explicitly tells the player what to do. These can take the form of text, dialogue with an authoritative non-player character (NPC), or visual diagrams and often incorporate combinations of the three. Instructions are one of the clearest forms of direct guidance, but they also have the greatest likelihood of either overwhelming the player with too much information or annoying her by pedantically telling her information she already knows.

Call to Action

The game explicitly gives the player an action to perform and a reason to do so. This often takes the form of missions that are given to the player by NPCs. A good strategy is to present the player with a clear long-term goal and then give her progressively smaller medium- and short-term goals that must be accomplished on the way to the long-term goal.

The *Legend of Zelda: Ocarina of Time* begins with the fairy Navi waking Link to tell him that he has been summoned by the Great Deku Tree. This message is then reinforced by the first person Link encounters upon leaving his home, who tells him that it is a great honor to be summoned and that he should hurry. This gives Link a clear long-term goal of seeking the Great Deku Tree (and the Great Deku Tree's conversation with Navi before Link is awoken hints to the player that she will be assigned a much longer-term goal when she arrives). Link's path to the Great Deku Tree is blocked by Mido, who tells him that he will need a sword and shield before venturing into the forest. The player now has two medium-term goals she must achieve before she can reach her long-term goal. Along the way to obtaining both, Link must navigate a small maze, converse with several people, and earn at least 40 rupees. These are all small-term, clear goals that are directly tied to the long-term goal of reaching the Great Deku Tree.

Map or Guidance System

Many games include a map or other GPS-style guidance system that directs the player toward her goals or toward the next step in her mission. For example, *Grand Theft Auto V* has a radar/mini-map in the corner of the screen with a highlighted route for the player to follow to the next objective. The world of *GTA V* is so vast that missions often take the player into an unfamiliar part of the map, where the player relies heavily on the GPS. However, be aware that this kind of guidance can lead to players spending most of their time just following the directions of the virtual GPS rather than actually thinking about a destination and choosing a path of their own, which can increase the time it takes for the player to learn the layout of the game world.

Pop-Ups

Some games have contextual controls that change based on the objects near the player. In *Assassin's Creed IV: Black Flag,* the same button controls such diverse actions as opening doors, lighting barrels of gunpowder on fire, and taking control of mounted weapons. To help the player understand all the possibilities, pop-ups with the icon for the button and a very short description of the action appear whenever an action is possible.

Indirect Guidance

Indirect guidance is the art of influencing and guiding the player without her actually knowing that she is being controlled. Several different methods of indirect guidance can be useful to you as a designer. The quality of indirect guidance can be judged using the same criteria as direct guidance (immediacy, scarcity, brevity, and clarity) with the addition of invisibility and reliability:

- **Invisibility:** How aware is the player that she is being guided? Will her awareness negatively impact her experience of the game? Once you've answered the second question, you can set a goal for how invisible the guidance should be. Sometimes, you'll want the guidance to be completely invisible; other times, it will be fine if the player recognizes it. In all cases, the quality of the indirect guidance is based on how the player's awareness will affect the way she experiences game.

- **Reliability:** How often does the indirect guidance influence the player to do what you want? Indirect guidance is subtle, and as a result, it is somewhat unreliable. While most players in a dark area of the game will head toward a lit doorway, some other players will not. When you employ indirect guidance in your games, be sure to test it thoroughly to ensure that a high enough percentage of players are following the guidance. If not, your guidance may be too subtle.

Seven Methods of Indirect Guidance

I was first introduced to the idea of indirect guidance by Jesse Schell, who presents it as "indirect control" in Chapter 16 of his book *The Art of Game Design: A Book of Lenses.* This list is an expansion of his six methods of indirect control.[1]

Constraints

If you give the player limited choices, she will choose one of them. This seems elementary, but think about the difference between a question that asks you to fill in the blank and one that gives you four choices to pick from. Without constraint, players run the risk of choice paralysis, which occurs when a person is presented with so many choices that she can't weigh them all

---

1. Jesse Schell, *The Art of Game Design: A Book of Lenses* (Boca Raton, FL: CRC Press, 2008), pp. 283–298.

against each other and instead just doesn't make a choice. This is the same reason that a restaurant menu might have 100 different items on it but only feature images of 20. The restaurant owners want to make it easier for you to make a decision about dinner.

Goals

As Schell points out, if the player has a goal to collect bananas and has two possible doors to go through, placing clearly visible bananas behind one of the doors encourages the player to head toward the door with bananas.

Players are also often willing to create their own goals, to which you can guide them by giving them the materials to achieve those goals. In the game *Minecraft* (the name of which includes the two direct instructions "mine" and "craft"), the designers defined which items the players are able to craft from which materials, and these design choices in turn imply the goals that players are able to create for themselves. Because most of the simplest recipes allow the player to make building materials, simple tools, and weapons, these recipes start the player down the path toward building a defensible fort to make her home. That goal then causes her to explore for materials. For example, the knowledge that diamond makes the best tools will lead a player to explore deeper and deeper tunnels to find diamond (which is rare and only occurs at depths of about 50–55 meters) and encourage her to expand the amount of world that she has seen.

Physical Interface

Schell's book covers information about how designers can use the shape of a physical interface to indirectly guide the player: If you give a player of *Guitar Hero* or *Rock Band* a guitar-shaped controller, she will generally expect to use it to play music. Giving a *Guitar Hero* player a regular game controller might lead her to think that she could control her character's movement around the stage (because a standard game controller usually directs character movement), but with a guitar controller, her thoughts focus on making music.

The physical sense of touch can also be used for indirect guidance. One example is the rumble feature on many game controllers, which enables the controller to vibrate in the players' hands at various intensities. Actual automobile racetracks include red and white *rumble strips* on the inside of turns. The rumble strips alternate height along with color, allowing the driver to feel rumbling in the steering wheel if her wheel goes too far to the inside of the turn and makes contact with the rumble strip. This is helpful because racers are often trying to be as close to the inside of a turn as possible to be on the perfect racing line, and seeing exactly where the wheels are touching the road from inside the car is usually impossible. This same method— rumbling the controller when the player is at the extreme inside edge of a turn—is used in many racing games. Expanding on this, you could imagine keeping the controller still when the player is on the track but causing it to rumble erratically if the player goes off the track into some grass. The tactile sensation would help the player understand that she should return to the track.

Visual Design

You can use visuals in several different ways to indirectly guide the player:

- **Light:** Humans are naturally drawn to light. If you place a player in a dark room with a pool of light at one end, she will usually move toward that light before exploring anything else.

- **Similarity:** After a player has seen that something in the world is good in some way (helpful, healing, valuable, etc.), she will seek out similar things.

- **Trails:** Similarity can lead to a "breadcrumb trail" effect where the player picks up a certain item and then follows a trail of similar items to a location that the designer wants her to explore.

- **Landmarks:** Visually interesting and distinct objects can be used as landmarks. At the beginning of *Journey* by thatgamecompany, the player starts in the middle of a desert next to a sand dune. Everything around her looks like sand and dunes except for a few dark stone markers atop the tallest nearby dune (see Figure 12.1, left). Because this group of markers is the only thing in the landscape that stands out, the player is driven to move up the dune toward it. When she reaches the top, the camera rises above her, revealing a towering mountain with light bursting from the top (see Figure 12.1, right). The camera move causes the mountain to emerge from directly behind the stone markers, signifying to the player that the mountain is her new goal. The camera move directly transfers the goal state from the markers to the mountain.

Figure 12.1 Landmarks in *Journey*

When initially designing Disneyland, Walt Disney Imagineering (which at the time was named WED Enterprises) designed various landmarks to guide guests around the park and keep them from bunching up in the main hub. When guests first enter the park, they are located in Main Street USA, which looks like an idealized small American town from the early twentieth century. However, very soon into their journey down Main Street, they notice Sleeping Beauty's Castle at the end of the street and are immediately drawn to it. Upon finally reaching the castle, guests notice that it is much smaller than it initially appeared and that there's really nothing to do there. Now that they are in the main hub of Disneyland, they can see the mountain of the Matterhorn rising in front of them, the space-age statue at the entrance to Tomorrowland to their right, and the fort of Frontierland to their left. From their position in the hub, these new landmarks look much more interesting than the small castle, and guests soon leave the castle area to disperse through the park toward them.[2]

Landmarks also appear throughout the *Assassin's Creed* series. When the player first enters a new part of the map, she should notice a few structures that are taller than the others in the area. In addition to the natural attraction of these landmarks, each is also a *view point* in the game from which the player can *synchronize*, which updates her in-game map with detailed information about the area. Because the designers have given the player both a landmark and a goal (filling in her map), they can guess that players will often seek a view point as their first activity in a new part of the world.

- **Arrows:** The annotated image in Figure 12.2 shows examples of subtle arrows used to direct the player in the game *Uncharted 3: Drake's Deception* by Naughty Dog. In these images, the player (as Drake) is chasing an enemy named Talbot.

Figure 12.2 Arrows created by line and contrast in *Uncharted 3* direct the player where to run.

A. As the player vaults up to the roof of a building, numerous lines are formed by physical edges and contrasting light that direct the player's attention to the left. These lines include the ledge she is vaulting, the short half-wall in front of her, the boards on the left, and even the facing of the gray plastic chair.

B. As soon as the player is on top of the roof, the camera angle rotates, and now the ledge, the wall, and the wooden planks all point directly at the next location where the player must jump (the roof of the building at the top of the frame). The cinderblock next to the wall in shot B even forms the head of an arrow made by the wall.

2. This was first pointed out to me by Scott Rogers, who covers it in more detail in Level 9 (i.e., Chapter 9) of his book *Level Up!: The Guide to Great Video Game Design* (Chichester, UK: Wiley, 2010).

This is particularly important in this moment of the chase because the landing area will collapse when the player hits it, which could cause the player to doubt whether jumping on that roof was the correct direction for her to have gone. The arrows in the environment minimize this doubt.

The *Uncharted 3* dev team referred to wooden planks like those shown in this image as *diving boards*, and they were used throughout the game to guide players to make leaps in a specific direction. You can see another diving board in image A of Figure 12.3.

C. In this part of the same chase, Talbot has run through a gate and slams it in the player's face. The blue fabric on the short wall draws the player's eye to the left, and the left corner of the fabric forms an arrow to the left as well.

D. The camera has now panned to the left, and from this perspective, the blue fabric forms an arrow pointing directly at the yellow window frame (the player's next goal). Bright blue and yellow colors like those seen in this image are used throughout the game to show the correct path to the player, so their presence here confirms the player's decision to head through the yellow window.

■ **Camera:** Many games that involve traversal puzzles use the camera to guide the player. By showing the player the next objective or next jump, the camera guides her in areas where she might otherwise be confused. This is demonstrated in the shots from *Uncharted 3* that are shown in Figure 12.3.

In shot A, the camera is directly behind the player; however, when the player jumps to the handholds in front of her, the camera pans to the left, directing her to move left (shot B). The camera continues to face left (shot C) until the player reaches the far left ladder, at which point the camera straightens out and pans down to reveal the yellow rungs going forward (shot D).

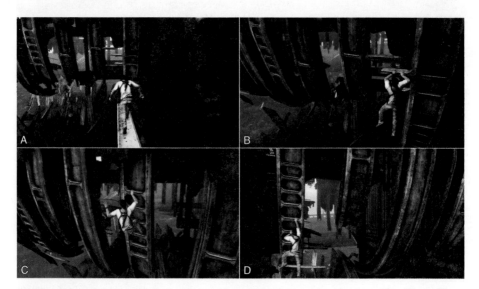

Figure 12.3 Camera-based guidance in *Uncharted 3*

- **Contrast:** The shots in Figures 12.2 and 12.3 each also demonstrate the use of contrast to guide player attention. There are several forms of contrast demonstrated in Figures 12.2 and 12.3 that contribute to player guidance:

  - **Brightness:** In shots A and B of Figure 12.2, the ledge and the wall that form the arrows have the highest range of brightness contrast in the image. The dark areas alongside light areas cause the lines stand out visually.

  - **Texture:** In shots A and B of Figure 12.2, the wooden planks are smooth whereas the surrounding stone textures are rough. In shots C and D of Figure 12.2, the soft texture of the blue fabric contrasts with the hard stone on which it rests. By laying over the stone edge, the fabric also serves to soften the edge, making the player more aware that she can leap over it.

  - **Color:** In shots C and D of Figure 12.2, the blue fabric, yellow window frame, and yellow bars contrast with the dullness of the other colors in the scene. In shot D of Figure 12.3, the yellow rung at the bottom stands out because the rest of the scene is mostly blue and gray.

  - **Directionality:** Though it is not as commonly used as the other three, you can also use contrast in directionality to draw the eye. In shot A of Figure 12.3, the horizontal rungs stand out because every other line in that part of the screen is vertical.

Audio Design

Schell states that music can be used to influence the player's mood and thereby her behavior.[3] Certain types of music have become linked to various types of activity: Slow, quiet, somewhat jazzy music is often linked to activities like sneaking or searching for clues (as seen in the *Scooby Doo* cartoon series), whereas loud, fast, powerful music (like that in an action movie) is better suited to scenes where the player is expected to brazenly fight through enemies and feel invincible.

Sound effects can also be used to influence player behavior by drawing attention to possible actions that the player can take. In the *Assassin's Creed* series, a shimmering, ringing sound effect plays whenever the player is near a treasure chest. This informs the player that she could choose to take the action of looking for the chest and, because it only happens when a chest is nearby, it tells her that it wouldn't be too far out of her way to do so. With a guaranteed reward in close proximity, the player is usually guided to search for the chest unless she is already engaged in another more important activity.

Player Avatar

The model of the player's avatar (that is, player character) can have a strong effect on player behavior. If the player character looks like a rock star and is holding a guitar, the player might

---

3. Schell, *Art of Game Design*, 292–293.

expect for her character to be able to play music. If the player character has a sword, the player would expect to be able to hit things and run into combat. If the player character walks around in a wizard hat and long robe while holding a book instead of a weapon, the player would be encouraged to stay back from direct combat and focus on spells.

Non-Player Characters

Non-player characters (NPCs) in games are one of the most complex and flexible forms of indirect player guidance, and that guidance can take many forms.

Modeling Behavior

NPC characters can model several different types of behavior. In games, behavior modeling is the act of demonstrating a specific behavior and allowing the player to see the consequences of that behavior. Figure 12.4 shows various examples of behavior modeling in the game *Kya: Dark Lineage* by Atari. Types of modeling include:

- **Negative behavior:** In modeling negative behavior, the NPC does something that the player should avoid doing and demonstrates the consequences. In image A of Figure 12.4, circled in red, one of the Nativs has stepped onto one of the circular traps on the ground and has been caught (it then lifted the Nativ up and flew him back to the enemies pursuing both the Nativs and the player).

- **Positive behavior:** The other Nativ in image A (circled in green) jumped over a trap, showing how to avoid it. This models positive behavior, showing the player how to act properly in the game world. Image B shows another example—the Nativ has stopped immediately before a place in the level where air currents blow swiftly from left to right in timed pulses, even though the air isn't blowing yet. The Nativ waits for the air current to blow, and when it stops, he continues running. This models for the player that she should stop before these air current areas, get the timing right, and then continue.

- **Safety:** In images C and D, the Nativ is jumping onto or into something that looks quite dangerous. However, because of his willingness to jump, the player knows that it is safe to follow.

Figure 12.4 NPC Nativs modeling behavior in *Kya: Dark Lineage*

Using Emotional Connections

Another way in which NPCs influence player behavior is through the emotional connections that the player develops with them.

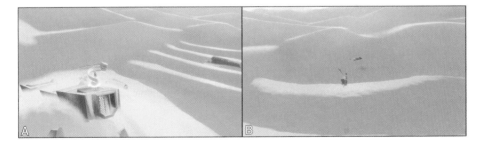

Figure 12.5 Emotional connections in *Journey*

In the *Journey* images shown in Figure 12.5, the player is following the NPC because of an emotional connection. The beginning of *Journey* is very lonely, and the NPC in these images is the first emotive creature that the player has encountered on her journey through the desert.

When she encounters the creature, it flies around her joyfully (shot A) and then takes off (shot B). In this situation, a player will almost always follow the NPC.

You can also cause the player to follow an NPC because of a negative emotional connection. For example, the NPC could steal something from the player and run, causing the player to chase him in order to retrieve her property. In either case, the reaction of the player is to follow the NPC, and this is an excellent way to guide the player to another location.

Teaching New Skills and Concepts

Although direct and indirect guidance usually focus on moving the player through the virtual locations of the game, this final section is devoted to methods to guide the player to a better understanding of how to play the game.

When games were simpler, designers could present the player with a simple diagram of the controls or even just let them experiment. In *Super Mario Bros.* for the Nintendo Entertainment System (NES), one button caused Mario to jump, and the other button caused him to run (and to shoot fireballs after he picked up a fire flower). Through just a small amount of experimentation, the player could easily understand the functions of the A and B buttons on the NES controller. Modern controllers, however, typically have two analog sticks (that can also be clicked like buttons), one 8-direction D-Pad, six face buttons, two shoulder buttons, and two triggers. Even with all of these possible controls, many modern games have so many possible interactions allowed to the player that individual controller buttons have various uses based on the current context, as was mentioned during the *Pop-Ups* point of the *Direct Guidance* section.

With so much complexity in some modern games, teaching players how to play the game as they go along becomes critical. An instruction booklet won't cut it anymore; now designers must guide the player through experiences that are properly *sequenced*.

Sequencing

Sequencing is the art of gently presenting new information to the player, and most examples follow the basic style shown in Figure 12.6. The figure shows several steps in the sequence from *Kya: Dark Lineage* that first introduces the player to a hovering mechanic that is used many times throughout the game:

- **Isolated introduction:** The player is introduced to a new mechanic that she must use to continue in the game. In image A of Figure 12.6, air is constantly blowing upward, and the player must press and hold X to drop down far enough to go under the upcoming wall. Nothing progresses until she holds X and passes under the wall, so there is no time pressure while she learns the new skill.

- **Expansion:** Image B of Figure 12.6 shows the next step of this sequence. Here, the player is presented with walls blocking both the top and the bottom of the tunnel, so she must learn to hover in the middle of the tunnel by "pumping" (i.e., tapping) the X button. However, there is still no penalty for failing to do so correctly.

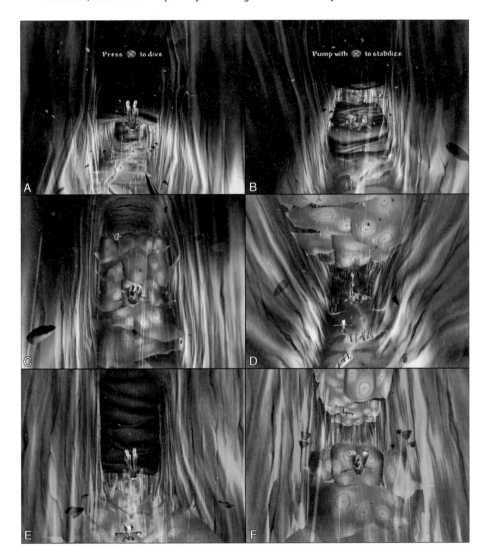

Figure 12.6 The sequence teaching hovering in *Kya: Dark Lineage*

- **Adding danger:** In image C of Figure 12.6, some danger has been added. The red surface of the floor will harm the player if she gets too close; however, the roof is still completely safe, so not pressing X will keep the player safe. Next, in image D, the ceiling is dangerous, and the floor is completely safe, so if the player is still building her skills, she can simply hold the X button and glide forward along the floor.

- **Increased difficulty:** Images E and F of Figure 12.6 show the final stages of this introduction sequence. In image E, the ceiling is still safe, but the player must navigate through the narrow channel ahead. Image F also requires navigation through a narrow channel, but now the danger has been expanded to both ceiling and floor. The player must demonstrate mastery of the X tapping mechanic to hover safely through the tunnel. [4]

I've used several images from *Kya: Dark Lineage* throughout this chapter because it is one of the best examples I have ever seen of this kind of sequencing. In the first 6 minutes of gameplay, the player learns about moving, jumping, avoiding traps, avoiding thorns, dribbling and kicking ball-like animals to defuse traps, avoiding horizontal air gusts, base jumping, hovering (Figure 12.6), being stealthy, and about a dozen other mechanics. All of them are taught using sequencing, and at the end of playing through the introduction for the first time, I remembered all of them.

Many different games use sequencing. In the *God of War* series, every time Kratos receives a new weapon or spell, he is told how to use it through pop-up text messages, but then he is immediately shown through sequencing as well. For a spell such as a lightning strike that the player could use either to power devices or electrocute enemies, she is first asked to use it for the non-combat purpose (e.g., the player would receive the lightning spell in a room with locked doors and must use the lightning to activate devices to open the doors). The player is then presented with a combat that she easily wins using the new spell. This technique not only gives the player experience using the spell in combat but also demonstrates how powerful the spell is, making the player feel powerful as well.

Integration

After the player understands how to use the new game mechanic in isolation (as described in the previous examples), it's time to teach her how to combine it with other mechanics. You can do this explicitly (e.g., you could tell the player that casting the lightning spell in water will expand its range from a 6 feet radius when used outside the water to the entire pool when used in the water) or implicitly (e.g., you could place the player in combat in a pool of water and she can notice for herself that when she uses the lightning spell, everything in the water is electrocuted, not just those enemies within 6 feet). When later in the game the player attains a spell that allows her to drench her enemies and cause a temporary pool of water, she would immediately realize that this mechanic also allows her to expand the reach of her lightning spell.

---

4. Figure 12.6 also shows the use of color contrast to convey information about safety. The color of the tunnel shifts from green to red to show increasing danger, and in image F, the purple light at the end of the tunnel signifies to the player that this trial will be ending soon.

Summary

There are many more methods of player guidance than could fit in this chapter, but I hope that it gave you a good introduction not only to some specific methods but also to the reasons why you might want to use them. As you design your games, remember to keep player guidance in mind at all times. Doing this can be one of your toughest tasks, because to you (as the designer), every game mechanic will seem obvious. Breaking out of your own perspective is so difficult that most game companies seek dozens or hundreds of one-time testers to play their game throughout the development process. Always finding new people to test your game and give you feedback on the quality of the guidance from the perspective of someone who has never seen the game before is critically important. Games developed in isolation without the benefit of naïve testers are often either too difficult for new players or have uneven, staggered rises in difficulty that cause frustration. As described in Chapter 10, "Game Testing," you must test early, often, and with new people whenever you can.

CHAPTER 13

PUZZLE DESIGN

Puzzles are an important part of many digital games as well as an interesting design challenge in their own right. This chapter starts by exploring puzzle design through the eyes of one of the greatest living puzzle designers, Scott Kim.

The latter part of the chapter explores various types of puzzles that are common in modern games, some of which might not be what you would expect.

As you'll learn through this chapter, most single-player games have some sort of puzzle in them, though multiplayer games often do not. The primary reason for this is that both single-player games and puzzles rely on the game system to provide challenge to the player, whereas multiplayer digital games (that are not cooperative) more often rely on other human players to provide the challenge. Because of this parallel between single-player games and puzzles, learning about how to design puzzles can help you with the design of any game in which you intend to have a single-player or cooperative mode.

Scott Kim on Puzzle Design

Scott Kim is one of today's leading puzzle designers. Since 1990, he has written puzzles for magazines such as *Discover, Scientific American,* and *Games*, and he has designed the puzzle modes of several games including *Bejeweled 2*. He has lectured about puzzle design at both the TED conference and the Game Developers Conference. His influential full-day workshop, "The Art of Puzzle Design"[1]—which he delivered with Alexey Pajitnov (the creator of *Tetris*) at the 1999 and 2000 Game Developers Conferences—has shaped many game designers' ideas about puzzles for more than a decade. This chapter explores some of the content of that workshop.

Defining *Puzzle*

Kim states that his favorite definition of puzzle is also one of the simplest:

> "A puzzle is fun, and it has a right answer."[2]

This differentiates puzzles from toys—which are fun but don't have a right answer—and from games—which are fun but have a goal rather than a specific correct answer. Kim sees puzzles as separate from games, although I personally see them as more of a highly developed subset of games. Even though this definition of puzzles is very simple, some important subtleties lie hidden therein.

A Puzzle Is Fun...

Kim states that puzzles have three elements of fun:

- **Novelty:** Many puzzles rely on a certain specific insight to solve them, and after the player has gained that insight, finding the puzzle's solution is rather simple. A large part of the fun of solving a puzzle is that flash of insight, the joy of creating a new solution. If a puzzle lacks

---

1. Scott Kim and Alexey Pajitnov, "The Art of Puzzle Game Design" (presented at the Game Developers Conference, San Jose, CA, March 15, 1999). Accessed January 21, 2017. https://web.archive.org/web/20030219140548/http://scottkim.com/thinkinggames/GDC99/gdc1999.ppt

2. Scott Kim, "What Is a Puzzle?" Accessed January 21, 2017. https://web.archive.org/web/20070820000322/http://www.scottkim.com/thinkinggames/whatisapuzzle/.

novelty, the player will often already have the insight required to solve it before even starting the puzzle, and thus that element of the puzzle's fun is lost.

- **Appropriate difficulty:** Just as games must seek to give the player an adequate challenge, puzzles must also be matched to the player's skill, experience, and type of creativity. Each player approaching a puzzle has a unique level of experience with puzzles of that type and a certain level of frustration that she is willing to experience before giving up. Some of the best puzzles in this regard have both an adequate solution that is of medium difficulty and an expert solution that requires advanced skill to discover. Another great strategy for puzzle design is to create a puzzle that appears to be simple although it is actually quite difficult. If the player perceives the puzzle to be simple, she'll be less likely to give up.

- **Trickiness:** Many great puzzles cause the player to shift her perspective or thinking to solve them. However, even after having that perspective shift, the player should still feel that executing her plan to solve the puzzle requires skill and cunning. The puzzle-based stealth combat of Klei Entertainment's *Mark of the Ninja*, in which the player must use insight to solve the puzzle of how to approach a room full of enemies and then, after she has a plan, must physically execute that plan with precision,[3] exemplifies this characteristic.

...and It Has a Right Answer

Every puzzle needs to have a right answer, although many puzzles have several right answers. One of the key elements of a great puzzle is that after the player has found the right answer, it is clearly obvious to her that she is right. If the correctness of the answer isn't easily evident, the puzzle can seem muddled and unsatisfying.

Genres of Puzzles

Kim identifies four genres of puzzle (see Figure 13.1),[4] each of which causes the player to take a different approach and use different skills. These genres are at the point of intersection between puzzles and other activities. For example, a story puzzle is the mixture of a narrative and a series of puzzles.

---

3. Nels Anderson, "Of Choice and Breaking New Ground: Designing *Mark of the Ninja*" (presented at the Game Developers Conference, San Francisco, CA, March 29, 2013). Nels Anderson, the lead designer of *Mark of the Ninja*, spoke in this talk about narrowing the gulf between intent and execution. The team found that making it easier for a player to execute her plans in the game shifted the skill of the game from physical execution to mental planning, making the game more puzzle-like and more interesting to players. He has posted a link to his slides and his script for the talk on his blog at http://www.above49.ca/2013/04/gdc-13-slides-text.html, accessed March 6, 2014. His talk is also available for free on the GDC Vault at http://gdcvault.com.

4. Scott Kim and Alexey Pajitnov, "The Art of Puzzle Game Design," slide 7.

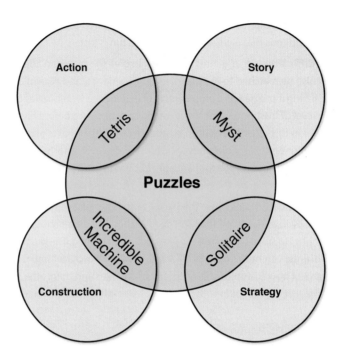

Figure 13.1 Kim's four genres of puzzles[5]

- **Action:** Action puzzles like *Tetris* have time pressure and allow players a chance to fix their mistakes. They are the combination of an action game with a puzzle mindset.

- **Story:** Story puzzles like *Myst*, the *Professor Layton* series, and most hidden-object games[6] have puzzles that players must solve to progress through the plot and explore the environment. They combine narrative and puzzles.

- **Construction:** Construction games invite the player to build an object from parts to solve a certain problem. One of the most successful of these was *The Incredible Machine*, in which players built Rube Goldberg–like contraptions to cause the cats in each scene to run away. Some construction games even include a construction set that allows the player to devise and distribute her own puzzles. They are the intersection of construction, engineering, and spatial reasoning with puzzles.

---

5. Scott Kim and Alexey Pajitnov, "The Art of Puzzle Game Design," slide 7.

6. *Myst* was one of the first CD-ROM adventure games, and was the number one best-selling CD-ROM game until *The Sims* took that title. The *Professor Layton* series of games is an ongoing series for Nintendo's handheld platforms that wraps many individual puzzles inside an overarching mystery story. Hidden-object games are a popular genre of game where a player must find a list of hidden objects in a complicated scene. These games often have mystery plots that the player is attempting to solve by finding the objects.

- **Strategy:** Many strategy puzzle games are the solitaire versions of the kinds of puzzles that players encounter in games that are traditionally multiplayer. These include things like bridge puzzles (which present players with various hands in a bridge game and ask how play should proceed) and chess puzzles (which give players a few chess pieces positioned on a board and ask how the player could achieve checkmate in a certain number of moves). These combine the thinking required for the multiplayer version of the game with the skill building of a puzzle to help players train to be better at the multiplayer version.

Kim also holds that some pure puzzles don't fit in any of the other four genres. These include games like *Sudoku* or crossword puzzles.

The Four Major Reasons that People Play Puzzles

Kim's research and experience have led him to believe that people primarily play puzzles for the following reasons: [7]

- **Challenge:** People like to feel challenged and to feel the joy of overcoming those challenges. Puzzles are an easy way for players to feel a sense of achievement, accomplishment, and progress.

- **Mindless distraction:** Some people seek big challenges, but others are more interested in having something interesting to do to pass the time. Several puzzles like *Bejeweled* and *Angry Birds* don't provide the player with a big challenge but rather a low-stress interesting distraction. Puzzle games of this type should be relatively simple and repetitive rather than relying on a specific insight (as is common in puzzles played for challenge).

- **Character and environment:** People like great stories and characters, beautiful images, and interesting environments. Puzzle games like *Myst*, *The Journeyman Project*, the *Professor Layton* series, and *The Room* series rely on their stories and art to propel the player through the game.

- **Spiritual journey:** Finally, some puzzles mimic spiritual journeys in a couple of different ways. Some famous puzzles like *Rubik's Cube* can be seen as a rite of passage—either you've solved one in your life or you haven't. Many mazes work on this same principle. Additionally, puzzles can mimic the archetypical hero's journey: The player starts in regular life, encounters a puzzle that sends her into a realm of struggle, fights against the puzzle for a while, gains an epiphany of insight, and then can easily defeat the puzzle that had stymied her just moments earlier.

Modes of Thought Required by Puzzles

Puzzles require players to think in different ways to solve them, and most players have a particular mode of thought that they prefer to engage in (and therefore a favorite class of puzzle). Figure 13.2 illustrates these concepts.

---

7. Scott Kim and Alexey Pajitnov, "The Art of Puzzle Game Design," slide 8.

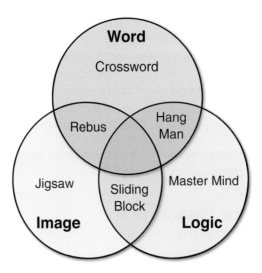

Figure 13.2 A Venn diagram showing the three modes of thought often used in puzzles (Word, Image, and Logic), including examples of puzzles that use each mode and some that use two modes simultaneously[8]

Single-Mode Puzzle Types

The following list describes the single-mode puzzle types shown in Figure 13.2:

- **Word:** There are many different kinds of word puzzles, most of which rely on the player having a large and varied vocabulary. Word puzzles are often particularly good if you're designing games for older adults, because most people's vocabularies peak later in life.

- **Image:** Image puzzle types include jigsaw, hidden-object, and 2D/3D spatial puzzles. Image puzzles tend to exercise the parts of the brain connected to visual/spatial processing and pattern recognition.

- **Logic:** Logic puzzles like *Bulls & Cows* (described in Chapter 11, "Math and Game Balance"), riddles, and deduction puzzles cause players to exercise their logical reasoning. Many games are based on *deductive* reasoning: the top-down elimination of several false possibilities, leaving only one that is true (e.g., a player reasoning "I know that all the other suspects are innocent, so Colonel Mustard must have killed Mr. Boddy"). These include *Clue*, *Bulls & Cows*, and *Logic Grid* puzzles. Far fewer games use *inductive* reasoning: the bottom-up extrapolation from a specific certainty to a general probability (e.g., a player reasoning "The last five times that John bluffed in poker, he habitually scratched his nose; John is scratching his nose now, so he's probably bluffing"). Deductive logic leads to certainty, whereas inductive logic makes an educated guess based on reasonable probability. The certainty of the answers has traditionally made deductive logic more attractive to puzzle designers.

---

8. Scott Kim and Alexey Pajitnov, "The Art of Puzzle Game Design," slide 9.

Mixed-Mode Puzzle Types

The following list refers to the mixed-mode puzzle types shown in the overlapping areas of Figure 13.2. Figure 13.3 includes examples of each of these mixed-mode puzzles.

- **Word / Image:** Many games like *Scrabble*, rebuses (like the one in Figure 13.3), and word searches incorporate both the word and image modes of thought to solve. *Scrabble* is a mixed-mode puzzle, but crossword puzzles are not, because in *Scrabble* the player is determining where to place the word and attempting to arrange it relative to score multipliers on the board. A crossword puzzle does not require either of these two acts of visual/spatial reasoning and decision-making.[9]

- **Image / Logic:** Sliding block puzzles, laser mazes, and puzzles like those shown in the second category of Figure 13.3 require players to use logic to solve image-based problems.

- **Logic / Word:** Most riddles fall into the Logic / Word category, including the classic "Riddle of the Sphinx," which is the first riddle in Figure 13.3. It was given by the sphinx to Oedipus in the classic Greek tragedy *Oedipus Rex* by Sophocles.

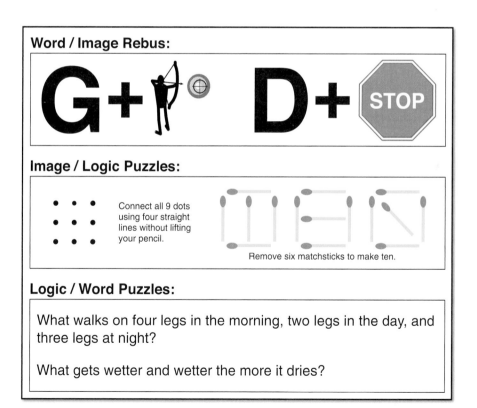

Figure 13.3 Various mixed-mode puzzles (solutions are at the end of the chapter)

---

9. While writing the second edition of this book, I've been working on a Word / Image puzzle game for mobile devices named *Ledbetter*. You can check it out at http://exninja.com/ledbetter.

Kim's Eight Steps of Digital Puzzle Design

Scott Kim describes eight steps that he typically goes through when designing a puzzle:[10]

1. **Inspiration:** Just like a game, inspiration for a puzzle can come from anywhere. Alexey Pajitnov has stated that his inspiration for *Tetris* was the mathematician Solomon Golomb's concept of pentominoes (12 different shapes, each made of five blocks, which could be fit together into an optimal space-filling puzzle) and the desire to use them in an action game. However, there were too many different five-block pentomino shapes, so he reduced it to the seven four-block tetrominoes found in Tetris.

2. **Simplification:** Usually you need to go through some form of simplification to get from your original inspiration to a playable puzzle.

    a. Identify the core puzzle mechanic: the essential tricky skill required.

    b. Eliminate any irrelevant details, and narrow the focus.

    c. Make pieces uniform. For example, if you're dealing with a construction puzzle, move the pieces onto a uniform grid to make it easier for the player to manipulate.

    d. Simplify the controls. Make sure that the controls for the puzzle are appropriate to the interface. Kim talks about how great a *Rubik's Cube* feels in real life but how terrible it would be to manipulate a digital version with a mouse and keyboard.

3. **Construction set:** Build a tool that makes construction of puzzles quick and easy. Many puzzles can be built and tested as paper prototypes, but if that isn't the case for your puzzle, this is the first place that you will need to do some programming. Regardless of whether it is paper or digital, an effective construction set can make the creation of additional levels much easier for you. Discover which tasks are repetitive time-wasters in the puzzle construction process and see whether you can make reusable parts or automated processes for them.

4. **Rules:** Define and clarify the rules. This includes defining the board, the pieces, the ways that they can move, and the ultimate goal of the puzzle or level.

5. **Puzzles:** Create some levels of the puzzle. Make sure that you design different levels that explore various elements of your design and game mechanics.

6. **Testing:** Just like a game, you don't know how players will react to a puzzle until you place it in front of them. Even with his many years of experience, Kim still finds that some puzzles he expects to be simple are surprisingly difficult, whereas some he expects to be difficult are easily solved. Playtesting is a key step in all forms of design. Usually, step 6 leads the designer to iteratively return to steps 4 and 5 and refine previous decisions.

7. **Sequence:** After you have refined the rules of the puzzle and have several levels designed, it's time to put them in a meaningful sequence. Every time you introduce a new concept, do it in isolation to require the player to use just that concept in the most elementary way.

---

10. Scott Kim and Alexey Pajitnov, "The Art of Puzzle Game Design," slide 97.

You can then progressively increase the difficulty of the puzzle that must be solved using that concept. Finally, you can create puzzles that mix that concept with other concepts that the player already understands. This is very similar to the sequencing in Chapter 12, "Guiding the Player," that is recommended for teaching any new game concept to a player.

8. **Presentation:** With the levels, rules, and sequence all created, it's now time to refine the look of the puzzle. Presentation also includes refinements to the interface and to the way you display that information to the player.

Seven Goals of Effective Puzzle Design

You need to keep several things in mind when designing a puzzle. Generally, the more of these goals that you can meet, the better puzzle you will create:

- **User friendly:** Puzzles should be familiar and rewarding to their players. Puzzles can rely on tricks, but they shouldn't take advantage of the player or make the player feel stupid.

- **Ease of entry:** Within one minute, the player must understand how to play the puzzle. Within a few minutes, the player should be immersed in the experience.

- **Instant feedback:** The puzzle should be "juicy" in the way that Kyle Gabler (co-creator of *World of Goo* and *Little Inferno*) uses the word: The puzzle should react to player input in a way that feels physical, active, and energetic.

- **Perpetual motion:** The game should constantly prod the player to take the next step, and there should be no clear stopping point. When I worked at Pogo.com, all of our games ended with a *Play Again* button instead of a game over screen. Even a simple thing like that can keep players playing for longer.

- **Crystal-clear goals:** The player should always clearly understand the primary goal of the puzzle. However, having advanced goals for players to discover over time is also useful. The puzzle games *Hexic* and *Bookworm* are examples of puzzles that have very clear initial goals and also include advanced expert goals that veteran players can discover and enjoy over time.

- **Difficulty levels:** The player should be able to engage the puzzle at a level of difficulty that is appropriate to her skill. As with all games, appropriate puzzle difficulty is critical to making the experience fun for players.

- **Something special:** Most great puzzle games include something that makes them unique and interesting. Alexey Pajitnov's game *Tetris* combines apparent simplicity with the chance for deep strategy and steadily increasing intensity. Both *World of Goo* and *Angry Birds* have incredibly juicy, reactive gameplay.

Puzzle Examples in Action Games

Modern AAA game titles frequently include a number of puzzles. Most of these fall into one of the following categories.

Sliding Blocks / Position Puzzles

Sliding block or position puzzles usually take place in third-person action games and require the player to move large blocks around a gridded floor to create a specific pattern. An alternative version of this involves positioning mirrors that are used to bounce light or laser beams from a source to a target. One common variation is a slippery floor that causes the blocks to move continuously until they hit a wall or other obstacle.

- **Game examples:** *Soul Reaver, Uncharted, Prince of Persia: The Sands of Time, Tomb Raider,* several games in *The Legend of Zelda* series

Physics Puzzles

Physics puzzles all involve using the physics simulation built in to the game to move objects around the scene or hit various targets with either the player character or other objects. This is the core mechanic in the *Portal* series and has become increasingly popular as reliable physics engines like Havok and the Nvidia PhysX system (built in to Unity) have become ubiquitous in the industry.

- **Game examples:** *Portal, Half-Life 2, Super Mario Galaxy, Rochard, Angry Birds*

Traversal

Traversal puzzles show you a place in the level that you need to reach but often make it less than obvious how to get there. The player must frequently take detours to unlock gates or open bridges that will allow her to reach the objective. Racing games like *Gran Turismo* are also traversal puzzles; the player must discover the perfect racing line that will enable her to complete each lap as efficiently and quickly as possible. This is critically important in the "Burning Lap" puzzles of the *Burnout* series, which require players to avoid making a single mistake while traversing a racecourse that includes sections of oncoming traffic, cross traffic, and hairpin turns.

- **Game examples:** *Uncharted, Tomb Raider, Assassin's Creed, Oddworld: Abe's Oddysee, Gran Turismo, Burnout, Portal*

Stealth

An extension of traversal puzzles that became important enough to merit its own genre, stealth puzzles ask the player to traverse a level while also avoiding detection by enemy characters, who are generally patrolling a predetermined path or following a specific schedule. Players usually have a way to disable the enemy characters, though this can also lead to detection if performed poorly.

- **Game examples:** *Metal Gear Solid, Uncharted, Oddworld: Abe's Oddysee, Mark of the Ninja, Beyond Good and Evil, The Elder Scrolls V: Skyrim, Assassin's Creed*

Chain Reaction

Chain reaction games include physics systems in which various components can interact, often to create explosions or other mayhem. Players use their tools to set traps or other series of events to either solve a puzzle or gain them an advantage over attacking enemies. The *Burnout* series of racing games include a Crash Mode that is a puzzle game where the player must drive her car into a specific traffic situation and cause the greatest amount of monetary damage through a fantastic multicar collision.

- **Game examples:** *Pixel Junk Shooter*, *Tomb Raider (2013)*, *Half-Life 2*, *The Incredible Machine*, *Magicka*, *Red Faction: Guerilla*, *Just Cause 3*, *Bioshock*, *Burnout*

Boss Fights

Many boss fights, especially in classic games, involve some sort of puzzle where the player is required to learn the pattern of reactions and attacks used by a boss and determine a series of actions that would exploit this pattern and defeat the boss. This is especially common in third-person action games by Nintendo like those in the *Zelda*, *Metroid*, and *Super Mario* series. One element that is very common in this kind of puzzle is the *rule of three:*[11]

1. The first time the player performs the correct action to damage the boss, it is often a surprise to her.

2. The second time is an experiment to see whether she now has the insight to defeat the puzzle/boss.

3. The third time, she demonstrates her mastery over the puzzle and defeats the boss.

Players can defeat most bosses throughout the *Legend of Zelda* series since *The Ocarina of Time* in three attacks, as long as the player understands the solution to the puzzle of that boss.

- **Game examples:** *The Legend of Zelda*, *God of War*, *Metal Gear Solid*, *Metroid*, *Super Mario 64/Sunshine/Galaxy*, *Guacamelee*, *Shadow of the Colossus*, multiplayer cooperative raids in *World of Warcraft*

Summary

As you've seen in this chapter, puzzles are an important aspect of many games that have single-player or multiplayer co-op modes. Puzzle design is not a large departure from the skills you've already learned as a game designer, but there are some subtle differences. When you design a game, the most important aspect is the moment-to-moment gameplay, whereas in puzzle design, the solution and the moment of insight are of primary importance. (In an action puzzle like *Tetris*, however, insight and solution happen with the drop and placement of every piece.) In addition, when the player solves a puzzle, being able to tell with certainty that she has found

---

11. I believe that this "rule of three" was first pointed out to me by Jesse Schell.

the right answers is important; but in games, interesting decisions rely on uncertainty in the player's mind about the outcome or correctness of decisions.

Regardless of the differences between designing puzzles and games, the iterative design process is as critical for puzzles as it is for all other kinds of interactive experiences. As a puzzle designer, you want to make prototypes and playtest just as you would for a game; however, with puzzles, ensuring that your playtesters have not seen the puzzle before is even more important (because they will have already had the moment of insight).

To close, Figure 13.4 shows the solutions to the puzzles in Figure 13.3. I didn't want to give away the answer by saying so, but the insight of the matchstick puzzle is that it actually requires all three modes of thought: logic, image, and word.

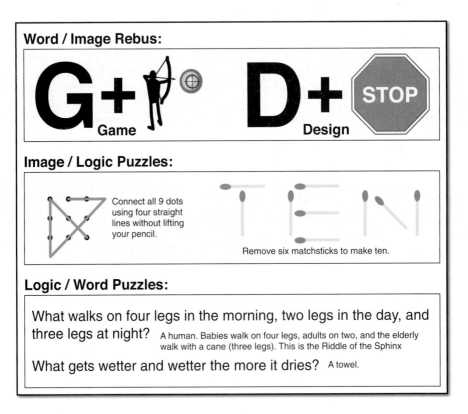

Figure 13.4 Mixed-mode puzzle solutions for the puzzles shown in Figure 13.4

CHAPTER 14

THE AGILE MENTALITY

In this chapter, you learn how to think about projects as an agile prototyper and how to weigh your options when beginning to tackle a project. The chapter introduces you to the Agile development mindset and Scrum methodology. It also extensively covers burndown charts, which I recommend using on all your game projects.

After this chapter, you'll have a better understanding of how to approach game projects, how to break them down into sprints that you can tackle in a specific amount of time, and how to prioritize tasks within those sprints.

The Manifesto for Agile Software Development

For many years, a large number of software titles, including games, tended to be developed using what is commonly known as the *waterfall* method of development. Using the waterfall method, a small preproduction team would define the entire project via a massive game design document that the production team was expected to follow to the letter as they developed the game. Sticking to waterfall too strictly often led to games that were not tested until they neared completion, and members of these production teams could feel more like cogs in a massive machine than actual game developers.

With the experience you've now gained through paper and digital prototyping in this book, I'm sure you can immediately see some issues with this approach. In 2001, the developers who formed the Agile Alliance saw these issues as well, leading to their Manifesto for Agile Software Development,[1] which reads as follows:

> We are uncovering better ways of developing software by doing it and helping others do it. Through this work we have come to value:
>
> - **Individuals and interactions**   over processes and tools
> - **Working software**   over comprehensive documentation
> - **Customer collaboration**   over contract negotiation
> - **Responding to change**   over following a plan
>
> That is, while there is value in the items on the right, we value the items on the left more.

Embedded in these four core values, you can see many of the principles that I've tried to impress upon you throughout this book:

- Following your individual design sense, continually asking questions, and developing an understanding of procedural thinking are more important than following predefined rules or using a specific development framework.

- Making a simple prototype that works and iterating on it until it's fun is more successful than waiting for months until you have the perfect game idea or solution to your problem.

- Bouncing your ideas off of other creative people in a positive, collaborative environment is more important than worrying about who owns specific intellectual property.[2]

- Listening to and reacting to playtesters' feedback about your game is much more important than following your original design vision. You must let your game evolve.

---

1. Kent Beck, et al. "Manifesto for Agile Software Development," Agile Alliance (2001).

2. You do, of course, want to respect other people's ownership of their IP. My point here is that making something is more important than arguing over who should own what percentage of it.

Prior to my introduction of Agile development methodologies into my classes, students often got drastically behind schedule when developing their games. In fact, they even had trouble understanding how behind they were because they lacked the tools to manage their development process. This also meant that playtesting student work was difficult until very late in the project.

After my introduction of Agile and its associated tools and methodologies to my classes, I found that several things occurred:

- Students had a much better understanding of their progress on projects and were better able to stick to their schedule.

- The games being produced by students showed a marked improvement, largely because the students' focus on constantly having a playable build allowed them to playtest the games earlier and more frequently.

- Student understanding of both C# and Unity increased as did their confidence in their technical skills.

Of those three points, the first two were expected. The third initially took me by surprise, but I have found it to be the case in every class that I have taught using Agile methodologies. As a result, I have continued to use Agile in all of my classes, in my own personal game development practice, and even while writing this book. I hope that you will, too.[3]

Scrum Methodology

In the years since 2001, many people have developed tools and methodologies to help teams easily adapt to the Agile mentality. One of my favorites is Scrum.

Scrum actually started several years before the Agile Manifesto and was developed by various people, but its relationship to Agile was solidified in the 2002 book *Agile Software Development with Scrum* by Ken Schwaber and Mike Beedle.[4] In it, they describe many of the common elements of the Scrum methodology that are still popular.

The goal of Scrum, like most Agile methodologies, is to get to a working product or game as quickly as possible while allowing for the design to flexibly adapt to feedback from playtesters and members of the design team. The remainder of this chapter introduces you to some of the terminology and practices used in the Scrum methodology and shows you how to use a spreadsheet-based burndown chart that I have developed for this book.

---

3. Thank you to my friend and colleague, Tom Frisina, who first introduced me to Scrum and Agile.

4. Ken Schwaber and Mike Beedle, *Agile Software Development with Scrum* (Upper Saddle River, NJ: Prentice Hall, 2002).

The Scrum Team

A Scrum team for game prototyping is composed of one *product owner,* one *Scrum master,* and an interdisciplinary *development team* consisting of up to ten other people who are skilled in various fields, including programming, game design, modeling, texturing, audio, etc.

- **Product Owner:** The voice of the client or the voice of the future players of your game.[5] The product owner wants to make sure that all the cool features make it into the game, and she is responsible for understanding the gestalt vision of the game.

- **Scrum Master:** The voice of reason. The Scrum Master runs the daily Scrum meeting and wants to make sure that everyone is on-task without being overworked. The Scrum master acts as a foil for the product owner by keeping a realistic eye on how much work remains on the project and how quickly the members of the development team are completing the tasks assigned to them. If the project is behind schedule or certain features need to be cut, the Scrum master is responsible for getting the schedule back on track and ensuring any required changes happen.

- **Development team:** The people in the trenches. The development team is composed of everyone working on the project and can include the product owner and Scrum master, who often work as standard members of the team outside of the Scrum meeting. Members of the development team are assigned tasks at the daily Scrum meeting and are relied on to accomplish those tasks by the next meeting. In Scrum, individual team members are given far more agency than in other development methods, but that agency comes with accountability of daily check-ins with the rest of the team.

Product Backlog / Feature List

A Scrum project starts with a *product backlog* (also known as a *feature list*), which is a list of all the features, mechanics, art, and so on that the team expects to implement for the final game. Some of these start out pretty vague and are broken down into more specific sub-features as development progresses.

Releases and Sprints

A product is broken down into *releases* and *sprints*. You can think of a release as a known time when you will show the game to others (for example, a meeting with investors, a public beta, or a formal playtest round) whereas a sprint is a step along the way to a release. At the beginning of a sprint, a *sprint backlog* list is created that contains all the features to complete by the end of the sprint. A sprint usually takes between 1 and 4 weeks, and regardless of what you choose to work on during the sprint, it is important that you have a playable game (or playable part of a game) by the end of the sprint. In fact, in the best case, from the moment when you have your first

---

5. Though on rare occasions, the Product Owner is the actual client, more often it is someone internal to the company who acts as an advocate for the client.

playable prototype, you should strive to never have a day that ends with the game in an unplayable state (though ensuring that is sometimes a difficult task).

Scrum Meetings

A *Scrum meeting* is a daily 15-minute stand-up meeting (literally, everyone stands throughout the meeting) that keeps the whole team on track. The Scrum Master runs the meeting, during which each person answers three questions:

1. What did you accomplish since yesterday?
2. What do you plan to accomplish today?
3. What obstacles might get in your way?

That's it. The Scrum meeting is meant to get everyone on the same page quickly. Questions 1 and 2 are checked against the *burndown chart* (BDC) to see how the project is progressing. You want to keep the Scrum meeting as short as possible so that the creative people on your team are wasting as little time as possible in full-group meetings. For example, any issues that arise as part of question 3 are not discussed during the meeting. Instead, the Scrum master asks for a volunteer to help the person with the potential obstacle and then moves on. Then, after the meeting is over, the person with the issue and the volunteer discuss the obstacle without the rest of the team.

As a result of Scrum meetings, everyone on the team knows their responsibilities, what everyone else is working on, and whom they can ask for help if they need it. Because Scrum meetings happen every day, problems are addressed as soon as they arise and not left to fester.

The Burndown Chart

I have found the burndown chart to be one of the most useful tools in my game development process and my classes. A burndown chart starts with a list of tasks to be performed during a sprint (the sprint backlog) and estimates of the amount of time required to complete each task (in hours, days, weeks, and so on). Throughout the project, the burndown chart tracks each team member's progress on the goals that have been assigned to her and converts it into a chart that not only tracks the total number of hours of work remaining on the project but also shows whether the team is on track to finish the project on time.

The beauty of the burndown chart is that it converts a tremendous amount of data into a simple chart that answers three critical questions:

1. Is the team on track to finish the sprint on time?
2. What tasks are assigned to each person?
3. Is everyone on the team being utilized well? (Is everyone pulling their weight?)

These three questions are often difficult to answer when you're working on any team, but the burndown chart answers all of them very efficiently. Burndown charts are so important that the rest of this chapter is devoted to helping you understand how to use the burndown chart template that I've provided for you.

Burndown Chart Example

I have created a burndown chart (BDC) template that is available online as a Google Sheets document. Google Sheets is the free online competitor to the Microsoft Excel that was featured in Chapter 11, "Math and Game Balance." Explaining the spreadsheet formulae used in this burndown chart is beyond the scope of this book, but you can learn the basics of spreadsheets and how to use them to balance games in Chapter 11.

The link for this example burndown chart spreadsheet is:

- At the link: **http://bit.ly/IGDPD_BDC_Example**

  Or

- The website for this book: **http://book.prototools.net** under Chapter 14

This chart is referenced several times on the following pages, so please follow the link to it now. If you want to make any edits to the sheet, you should make your own copy. To do so choose *File > Make a copy…* from the Sheets menu bar (in the browser window), as shown on the left side of Figure 14.1.

After making your own copy of the example burndown chart, please open it in Google Sheets and continue this chapter.

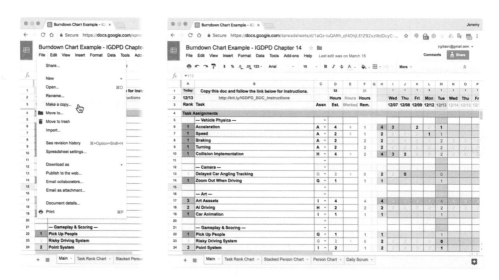

Figure 14.1 The menu to make your own copy of a Google Sheet and the Main example worksheet

Burndown Chart Example: Worksheets

Modern spreadsheets are broken into several worksheets, which you can select by choosing from among the tabs at the bottom of the window (labeled *Main, Task Rank Chart,* and so on in Figure 14.1). As you look at the descriptions of each worksheet that follow, click the tab at the bottom of the spreadsheet to view that worksheet.

Each worksheet in this spreadsheet has a specific purpose:

- **Main:** The worksheet where you track tasks and hours remaining. This is where you input most of the data.
- **Task Rank Chart:** This chart shows current progress toward the project deadline, sorted by the rank (or importance) of the tasks.
- **Stacked Person Chart:** This chart shows current progress toward the project deadline, sorted by the person to whom the task is assigned.
- **Person Chart:** This chart shows each individual's assigned tasks and progress toward the deadline.
- **Daily Scrum:** This worksheet allows team members to have a daily virtual Scrum meeting with each other, even if they can't meet in person.

Next, you'll explore each worksheet in more detail.

> ## warning
>
> **ONLY CHANGE VALUES IN CELLS WITH A DARK GRAY BORDER!**   In both the Burndown Chart Example and the Burndown Chart Template spreadsheets, you should only edit cells that have a dark gray border. All other cells either have unchanging data or (more likely) data that is calculated using a formula. For example, the dates shown in cells I3:Z3 on the chart are calculated by formulae that use the start date (F102), end date (F103), and workday data (J102:J108) entered into dark gray bordered cells in the Sprint Settings area. You should never directly edit I3:Z3.

Worksheet—Main

The Main worksheet is where you make most of your burndown chart edits. The top section of this worksheet includes nearly 100 lines for tracking tasks, to whom they're assigned, and how much work is left. The bottom half includes cells for entering team member names, the start and end date of the project, and workdays. It also has an area at the bottom of the worksheet that is entirely for calculation of data to be displayed in the charts on other tabs.

Sprint Settings

Scroll down to line 101 to look at the Sprint Settings shown in Figure 14.2. As mentioned earlier in this chapter, a *sprint* is usually a couple of weeks long and has specific tasks that must be completed (the *sprint backlog*). This section of the Main worksheet includes information that you must set as you create the BDC spreadsheet for each sprint.

	A	B	C	D	E	F	G	H	I	J	K	L	M	N
1	Today	Copy this doc and follow the link below for instructions.		32		21			1	1	1	3	1	1
2	12/13	http://bit.ly/IGDPD_BDC_Instructions		Hours	Hours	Hours			Wed	Thu	Fri	Mon	Tue	Wed
3	Rank	Task	Assn	Est.	Worked	Rem.			12/07	12/08	12/09	12/12	12/13	12/14
100														
101	Sprint Settings – Only change cells with dark gray borders								Workdays					
102		Archon	A		Start Date	12/07			Sun	0	0			
103		Henri	H		End Date	12/21			Mon	1	1			
104		Icarus	I						Tue	1	4			
105		Gilbert	G		Total Days	14			Wed	1	1			
106					Work Days	10			Thu	1	1			
107									Fri	1	3			
108		All	ALL						Sat	0	0			
109		Unassigned												
110		Days to Look Back for Burndown Velocity	2											

Figure 14.2 The Sprint Settings section of the Main worksheet

- **Team Members:** A list of up to six team members working on this sprint (B102:B107) as well as one- or two-letter identifying initials for them (C102:C107), which will be used to assign them tasks in the section above.

- **Sprint Dates:** Set the start date of your sprint in F102, and put the end date in F103.

- **Workdays:** In cells J102:J107, enter a 1 on days of the weeks that are typically workdays for your team and a 0 on days of the week that you don't plan to work. This information factors into the number of Work Days shown in F106.

The rest of the spreadsheet uses the information from this section to populate itself. This information is below all the rest on the Main worksheet because it you will set it only once at the beginning of the sprint.

> ### tip
>
> **ESTIMATING HOURS**   In this example burndown chart, today (cell A2) is always Tuesday, December 13. However, in the Burndown Chart Template, today (A2) reflects the actual current date.

Task Assignments and Time Estimation

Scroll back up to the top of the Main worksheet (see Figure 14.3).

The spreadsheet Task Assignments section contains the following:

Rank	Task	Assn	Est. (Hours)	Worked (Hours)	Rem. (Hours)	Wed 12/07	Thu 12/08	Fri 12/09	Mon 12/12	Tue 12/13	Wed 12/14	Thu 12/15	Fri 12/16	Mon 12/19	Tue 12/20	Wed 12/21
Today	Copy this doc and follow the link below for instructions.		32		21	1	1	1	3	1	1	1	1	3	1	1
12/13	http://bit.ly/IGDPD_BDC_Instructions															
Task Assignments																
	— Vehicle Physics —															
1	Acceleration	A	4	8	1	4	3		2	1						
1	Speed	A	2	2	1	2		1	1							
1	Braking	A	2		2	2			2							
1	Turning	A	2		2	2			2							
1	Collision Implementation	H	4	3	2	4	3	2	2							
	— Camera —															
	Delayed Car Angling Tracking	G	2	3	0	2			0							
1	Zoom Out When Driving	G	1		1	1			1							
	— Art —															
3	Art Asssets	I	4		4	4	4	4	4	4	4	4	4	4	4	4
2	AI Driving	H	2		2	2			2							
1	Car Animation	I	1		1	1			1							
	— Gameplay & Scoring —															
1	Pick Up People	G	1		1	1			1							
	Risky Driving System	G	2	1	0	2			0							
2	Point System	I	2		1	2			1							
2	Time Limit	I	1		1	1			1							
	— AI Behavior —															
4	AI Driving	H	2		2	2			2							

Figure 14.3 The Task Assignments section of the Main worksheet

In columns A:D of each row, you must also set some important information before the sprint can begin. Each row has the following columns:

A Rank: The importance of this task from 1 (Critical) to 5 (Low Priority)

B Task: A short description of the task

C Assignment: The initials of the team member to whom this task is assigned

D Hours Estimate: The estimated number of hours to complete this task

The estimated number of hours for each task is key to the concept of a BDC. Throughout the project you will refer to this number, so estimating as accurately and honestly as you can is important. See the tip "Estimating Hours."

tip

ESTIMATING HOURS   One of the toughest tasks for programmers, artists, and other creative workers is estimating the number of hours required to finish a task. Things almost always take longer than you expect, except for the one thing that you think will take 20 hours but is then somehow completed in only 2. For now, you need to just make the best guess that you can while following some simple estimation rules, all based on the fact that as the size of a task increases, the accuracy of your estimate necessarily decreases.

- If you're estimating in hours, stick to values of 1, 2, 4, or 8 hours.

- In days: 1, 2, 3, or 5 days.

- In weeks: 1, 2, 4, or 8 weeks.

However, if you're estimating anything in weeks for a sprint, you need to break it down into much smaller tasks!

Sprint Progress

The right half of the Main worksheet is where all the tracking of progress toward the sprint deadline occurs. Column H reflects the initial estimated hours for each task, and all the columns to the right of that show the team's progress toward completing them. Today's date is highlighted by a blue column with red numbers (column M in this example).

As team members work on various tasks, they report the number of *estimated hours* remaining on that task in columns I:Z. At the very least, you should fill out the BDC at the end of every workday, and you should only ever enter numbers for hours remaining into the column for today (the blue column). On both today and the days leading up to it, you can see bold, black numbers where a team member has done work on a task and reduced the number of estimated hours remaining.

Estimated Hours Versus Real Hours

One of the most important concepts in a burndown chart is the difference between estimated hours and real hours. After you have estimated the number of hours for a task, the time you spend working on that task is counted not in actual hours worked but instead *in terms of the percent of the task that is still incomplete*. For an example, take a look at the Acceleration task on row 6 of the example spreadsheet (see Figure 14.4).

	A	B	C	D	E	F	G	H	I	J	K	L	M
1	Today	Copy this doc and follow the link below for instructions.		32		21			1	1	1	3	1
2	12/13	http://bit.ly/IGDPD_BDC_Instructions		Hours	Hours	Hours			Wed	Thu	Fri	Mon	Tue	W
3	Rank	Task	Assn	Est.	Worked	Rem.			12/07	12/08	12/09	12/12	12/13	1
4	Task Assignments												
5		— Vehicle Physics —											
6	1	Acceleration	A	4	6	1		4	3		2		1
7	1	Speed	A	2	2	1		2				1	1
8	1	Braking	A	2		2		2					2

Figure 14.4 Close up of the Acceleration task work for the first 5 days of the project

The initial estimate of hours for the Acceleration task was 4.

- **12/07 (December 7):** Archon (A) worked on Acceleration for 2 hours but only accomplished about 25% of the task. This left 75% of the work remaining on the task, so he entered a 3 into the spreadsheet (cell I6) for 12/07 because 3 is 75% of the original 4-hour estimate. He also placed a 2 into the *Hours Worked* column (E) to track his actual hours worked.

- **12/09:** He worked another 3 hours, bringing the task to 50% complete and leaving 2 hours of the original 4-hour estimate remaining. So, he entered a 2 into the column for 12/09 (K6) and added the 3 hours he actually worked to the Hours Worked column, resulting in a value of 5 total hours worked.

- **12/13 (Today):** One hour of work burned down another 25% of the task (he's working a bit faster now), and now, as of today, he has 25%—or 1 estimated hour—remaining of the Acceleration task. He places a 1 in the 12/13 column (L6) and increases the Hours Worked in cell E6 to 6.

As you can see, the most important data is the *percent of the task remaining* as represented in the number of hours left of the original estimate. However, Archon has also recorded the 6 hours he has put in on the Acceleration task in the *Hours Worked* column (E) to help him improve his task estimation in the future (right now, it looks like it's taking about twice as long as his initial estimate).

The data from the Main worksheet is compiled into three charts that can help you better understand your team's progress toward the deadline and each teammate's contribution.

Worksheet—Task Rank Chart

The Task Rank Chart (see Figure 14.5) shows the progress toward the goal stacked by task rank. Here, you can see in two different ways that the team is behind schedule:

- The black *On-Track* line shows the average amount of work that must be completed each workday for the team to finish on time. If the total of all the ranks is above this line, then the team is not on track for completion; if the total of all ranks is below this line, the team is ahead of schedule. This gives the team a good gestalt idea of their progress toward the deadline.

■ The red *Burndown Velocity* line uses the team's recent burndown velocity to predict what the team will accomplish in coming days. If this line touches the baseline (i.e., 0 Estimated Work Hours) before the final date, then the team is doing well based on their current rate of task completion. On the other hand, if it never touches the baseline, the team is projected to not finish the project on time.

Burndown Velocity (BDV) is the current rate of progress in terms of estimated hours of work completed per day. Cell C110 of the Main worksheet determines how many days will be considered to determine the recent BDV (see Figure 14.2). In this case, it's two, which is why the red line only extends backwards 2 workdays from today (back from 12/13 to 12/9 without counting the weekend days of the 10th and 11th).

Another thing that you want to see in the Task Rank Chart is the team taking care of Rank 1 (red/bottom) tasks first and leaving lower-priority tasks (Ranks 4 and 5) for later. That is something that this team is doing well. The Rank 1 (red) area is tapering while the Rank 4 (purple) area is the same.

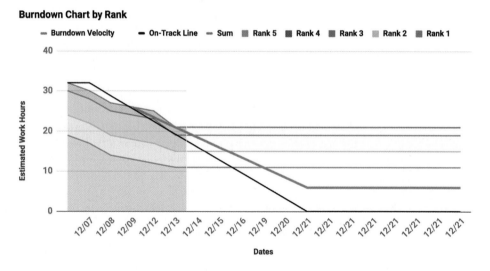

Figure 14.5 Burndown Chart by Task Rank

Worksheet—Stacked Person Chart

The Stacked Person Chart (see Figure 14.6) shows the progress toward the goal stacked by individual team member. This chart can help you see how each member is contributing to the overall deadline. On this chart, you want each team member's contribution to the whole to be tapering in similar ways. You also want each team member's section to be roughly the same width as the others on any given day. Here, you can tell that Archon (red) has more assigned to him than other members of the team, and you can see that Icarus (green) has not been completing tasks as much as other team members, because the green band of the chart has only narrowed slightly.

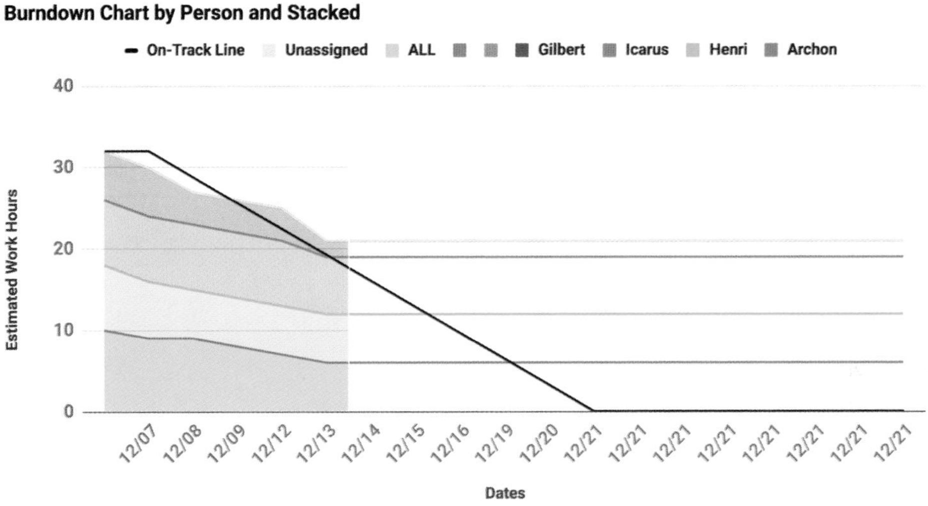

Burndown Chart by Person and Stacked

Figure 14.6 Burndown Chart by Person and Stacked

Worksheet—Person Chart

In the (unstacked) Person Chart, shown in Figure 14.7, you can see the tasks of team members relative to each other. The filled gray area in the background shows the average amount of work that would be assigned to each team member if the workloads were exactly equal. The black On-Track line shows how much each team member needs to accomplish every day to be on track (if they were assigned equal amounts of work). The various colored lines show the burndown of work for each team member.

From this, you can see that Archon is doing really well, even though he has been assigned more work than anyone else. Henri and Icarus have not been accomplishing enough, and Gilbert has been working sporadically but has gotten a lot done each time he worked on the project.

This chart is an excellent way to see what's really going on in your project and understand who is contributing the most and who needs to push harder.

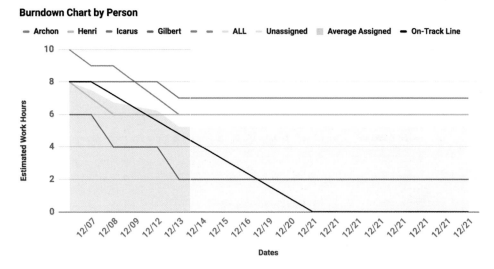

Figure 14.7 Burndown Chart by Person

Worksheet—Daily Scrum

Having your team members meet for an in-person Scrum each day is always best, but if they can't, this worksheet (see Figure 14.8) can help the team stay connected. As with any Scrum, each team member is responsible for reporting three things every day:

- **Yesterday (Y):** Each team member reports what she accomplished yesterday (or since the last Scrum).

- **Today (T):** Each team member reports what she plans to work on today (or before the next Scrum).

- **Help (H):** Each team member asks for help if she needs it.

The entire team should complete the Scrum report by a certain time of day each day. This team has chosen to report by 10 a.m. each morning. If a team chose to report by 6 p.m. at the end of each day, then their terms would instead be Today (T), Next (N), and Help (H).

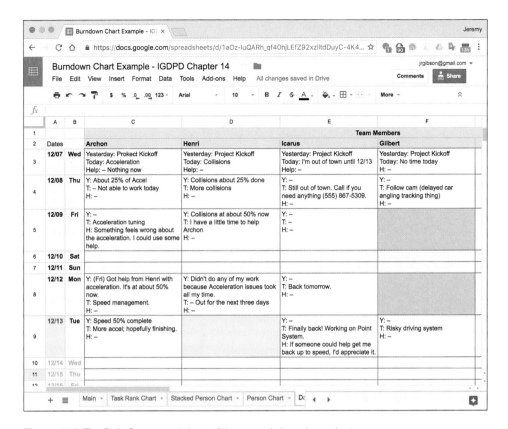

Figure 14.8 The Daily Scrum worksheet of the example burndown chart

The daily Scrum can provide a different kind of insight into the team than the other worksheets of the burndown chart. For example, according to the Person chart, it looked like Icarus hadn't done any work; however, looking at the Daily Scrum worksheet, you can see that he has been out of town since the sprint began and just got back today. Regardless of his being out of town, he reported in each day, and he has offered his contact info in case anyone needs his help.

On the other hand, even though Gilbert has completed several tasks, he doesn't check in at all on days that he's not working, and he doesn't tell us much when he does. Even though he's doing a lot of work, he's not communicating well with the team, which is something that should be addressed soon.

Looking at today's row (12/13) on the chart, you can see that Henri has yet to fill in the Scrum today (which might be because he's out). The Daily Scrum worksheet highlights today's row in green if it has not yet been filled out and highlights empty entries for past days in red.

When working with teams, good communication is critical, and this worksheet can help you achieve this. I have had several students approach me concerned because they didn't know where their team members were or what they were working on. After implementing this worksheet in my classes, the students who used it found that they were far less stressed about their projects. Even if someone is unable to work for a day or two, it can be managed as long as the rest of the team knows to expect it.

Creating Your Own Burndown Charts

Now that you're familiar with the features of the Burndown Chart Example, you can create your own charts from the template I used to build this example chart. As with the example chart, you can get this in two places:

- At the link: **http://bit.ly/IGDPD_BDC_Template**

  Or

- The website for this book: **http://book.prototools.net**, under Chapter 14

Summary

As you move on to designing and developing your own games, keeping your development process on track can be difficult. In my years as a developer and professor, I have found that the Agile mindset and Scrum methodology are two of the best tools for doing so. Of course, I can't tell you for sure whether these tools work as well for you as they have for my students and me, but I strongly encourage you to give them a try. In the end, it is not important whether Scrum and Agile are the perfect tools for you. The important thing is that you find tools that do work for you and that you use them to help you stay motivated and productive when working on your games.

In the next chapter, I'll examine the digital game industry and discuss ways in which you can get involved. I'll also look at how to meet people at game development conferences and what to look for in a university game program.[6]

---

6. You may wonder why I used male pronouns for Archon, Henri, Icarus, and Gilbert when I've used female pronouns throughout the rest of the book. These were the player character names that three of my teammates and I used when we worked together on the *Skyrates* game during grad school, and I put them into the burndown chart as a bit of an homage. Regardless of what the fictional chart here might say, they were three of the best people whom I have ever had the pleasure of working with, and I would be honored to work with any of them again.

CHAPTER 15

THE DIGITAL GAME INDUSTRY

If you're taking the time to read this book and learn about prototyping games, it's probably safe to assume that you might have some interest in joining the game industry.

In this chapter, I present a little information about the current state of the industry and then talk a bit about university games education programs. I give you some tips on meeting people, networking, and looking for work. Finally, I tell you about how to prepare for your own projects.

About the Game Industry

The most definitive thing that I can tell you about the game industry right now is that it is changing. A lot of big names like Electronic Arts and Activision are still around, as they have been for the last three decades, but we've also seen the rise of new startups like Riot Games—the developer of *League of Legends*—which went from just a few employees in 2008 to having one of the world's most played online games today. It wasn't too long ago that no one would have believed a cell phone could be one of the most successful game platforms, but sales of games for Apple's iOS devices alone are now worth billions of dollars. Because everything is changing so quickly, I'm not going to give you specific numbers for most things. Instead, I'll point you to resources that can (and that will be updated yearly).

Entertainment Software Association Essential Facts

The ESA (http://theesa.com) is the trade association and lobbying organization for most large game development companies, and it was the ESA who argued before the United States Supreme Court for games to be protected by the first amendment. The ESA releases a yearly report on the state of the game industry called the Essential Facts that you can find by searching for "ESA essential facts" on Google. Certainly the reports have some bias issues (the ESA's job is to see the game industry through rose-colored glasses), but the reports are still a good way to get an idea of what the overall industry looks like. Here are ten facts from the Essential Facts 2016 report:[1]

1. **63% of U.S. households** have at least one person who plays games at least 3 hours/week, with an average of **1.7 gamers per household**. With the current number of households in the U.S., this comes to about **125 million total gamers** in the United States.[2]

2. Consumers spent **$23.5 billion** on video games, hardware, and accessories in 2015.

3. Purchases of digital content, including games, add-on content, mobile apps, subscriptions, and social networking games accounted for **56% of game sales** in 2015 (up from 40% in 2012).

4. The average male game player is 35 years old and has been playing games for 13 years. The average female game player is 44.

5. **26% of game players are over age 50**. Based on our earlier number this means there are more than **32 million gamers over the age of 50** in the U.S.! That's a **huge** untapped market!

6. **41% of all game players are women** (though, unfortunately, this is down from a peak of 48% in 2014). Women over the age of 18 still represent a larger portion of the game-playing population (31%) than boys age 17 or younger (17%).

---

1. http://essentialfacts.theesa.com/Essential-Facts-2016.pdf. Emphasis mine.

2. Additional information from the U.S. Census Bureau: https://www.census.gov/quickfacts/. 116,926,305 households in the U.S. * 63% * 1.7 gamers/household ≈ 125 million.

7. The most frequent device on which people play games is a personal computer (56%). Other common platforms include dedicated game consoles (53%), smartphone (36%), wireless devices like iPads (31%), and dedicated handheld systems (17%).

8. Puzzle games dominate the market on wireless and mobile devices. The most common types of games for wireless and mobile devices are puzzle/board/card games (38%), action games (6%), and strategy games (6%).

9. In all, 89% of games rated by the ESRB (Entertainment Software Ratings Board) in 2012 received a rating of "E" for Everyone, "E10+" for Everyone 10+, or "T" for Teen. (See www.esrb.org or www.pegi.info for more information on game ratings.)

10. Of the most frequent gamers, 55% are familiar with Virtual Reality (VR), and 22% expect to purchase VR hardware within the next year.

Things That Are Changing

The things that are changing in the industry have to do with working conditions, the costs of producing games, freemium games, and independent developers.

Working Conditions at Game Companies

If you know nothing about the game industry, you might think that working at a game company is fun and easy. If you know a little about it, you might have heard that game company employees routinely work 60-hour weeks with mandatory overtime for no additional pay. Though the real story now for most companies is better than that, the stories you might have heard were based on fact, and I do have friends in the industry who still sometimes have mandatory 70-hour workweeks (10 hours/day, no weekends) during "crunch time" on their projects, but luckily that trend has diminished greatly over the past decade. Most companies, especially larger companies, will still ask you to work overtime sometimes, but the stories of game developers who haven't seen their partners or kids for a week have become rarer (though sadly, they do still exist). However, when interviewing with any game company, you should definitely ask about their overtime policy and history of crunch time on projects.

Rising Costs of AAA Development

Each generation of gaming consoles has seen a rise in the cost of developing a top title (also known as a "AAA" game, pronounced "triple-a"). This was especially true with the PlayStation 3 and Xbox 360 versus the PlayStation 2 and Xbox, and the trend has continued for the Xbox One and PlayStation 4 as well. Teams for AAA titles are now routinely more than 100 or 200 people, and even some apparently small teams actually have outsourced several aspects of the game's development to other studios, each having hundreds of their own employees. It is still unusual—but no longer unheard of—for a AAA game budget to exceed $100 million and have a combined total team of more than 1,000 people spread across several studios.

The effect of all of this on the game industry has been the same as the effect that budget inflation had on the film industry: The more money that a company spends on a project, the less willing it is to take risks. This is why in Figure 15.1 of the ESA's list of the top 20 best-selling console games of 2015, only one game (*Dying Light*) isn't a sequel (this version of *Minecraft* is a console remake of the PC version).

1	CALL OF DUTY: BLACK OPS III (M)	11	BATMAN: ARKHAM KNIGHT (M)
2	MADDEN NFL 16 (E)	12	LEGO: JURASSIC WORLD (E)
3	FALLOUT 4 (M)	13	BATTLEFIELD HARDLINE (M)
4	STAR WARS BATTLEFRONT 2015 (T)	14	HALO 5: GUARDIANS (T)
5	NBA 2K16 (E)	15	SUPER SMASH BROS. (E)
6	GRAND THEFT AUTO V (M)	16	THE WITCHER 3: WILD HUNT (M)
7	MINECRAFT (E 10+)	17	DYING LIGHT (M)
8	MORTAL KOMBAT X (M)	18	DESTINY: THE TAKEN KING (T)
9	FIFA 16 (E)	19	NBA 2K15 (E)
10	CALL OF DUTY: ADVANCED WARFARE (M)	20	METAL GEAR SOLID V: THE PHANTOM PAIN (M)

Figure 15.1 The 20 top-selling video games in 2015 by units sold (according to "ESA Essential Facts 2016")

The Rise (and Fall) of Freemium Games

According to Flurry Analytics, during a six-month period between January and June of 2011, free-to-play games rapidly overtook paid games in terms of iOS revenue.[3] In January of 2011, premium games (which are purchased upfront) accounted for 61% of the game revenue on the iOS App Store. By June, that number had crashed down to 35%, with 65% of revenue then coming from *freemium* games. The freemium model—where the player gets the game for free but is asked to pay small amounts to gain gameplay advantages or customization—catapulted Zynga from a two-person start-up to more than 2,000 employees in just a few years. However, this model has been shown to work much better for casual games than more traditional genres, and some developers of more traditional genres who are now creating mobile games have chosen to return to the premium model because they believe that their market is averse to the freemium model.

A few freemium games have done well with a more core (that is, less casual) audience of gamers. The primary differentiating factor between these and the casual freemium games is that many of the casual games allow and encourage players to purchase a competitive edge in the game (i.e., pay more to win more), whereas core games like *Team Fortress 2* (TF2) only allow players to purchase aesthetic items (e.g., hats) or items that change game mechanics without making them imbalanced (e.g., the Black Box rocket launcher for Soldiers that has –25% clip size yet grants the Soldier +15 health whenever it hits an enemy). In addition, nearly every item that is purchasable in TF2 can alternatively be crafted by players from items gained through gameplay. The critical element in this is that core players don't want to feel that someone else has bought a gameplay advantage over them.

---

3. "Free-to-play Revenue Overtakes Premium Revenue in the App Store" by Jeferson Valadares (Jul 07, 2011), http://web.archive.org/web/20140108025130/http://blog.flurry.com/bid/65656/Free-to-play-Revenue-Overtakes-Premium-Revenue-in-the-App-Store. Accessed January 29, 2017.

Whether you choose to go for freemium or premium relies largely on the genre of game you want to develop and the market and type of players that you are seeking. Look at other games in the market and see what the standards are, then decide whether you want to go along with them or buck the trend.

The Rise of the Indie Scene

While AAA games have become much more expensive to create, the ubiquity of free or cheap game development tools like *Unity, GameMaker,* and *Unreal Engine* has led to the rise of a worldwide independent development community to an extent that has never been seen before. As you'll see when you read the rest of this book, almost anyone can learn to program, and dozens of developers have now proven that all you need to make a game is a great idea, some talent, and a lot of time. Many of the most famous independent game projects started as the passion project of a single person, including *Minecraft, Spelunky,* and *The Stanley Parable.* IndieCade is a game conference that started in 2005 and is dedicated exclusively to independent games. Beyond that, dozens of other conferences either focus on independent development or have a track or contest for indie developers.[4] Making video games is now easier than it has ever been, and the rest of this book can teach you how.

Game Education

Over the past decade, game design and development education at the university level has gone from a curiosity to a legitimate field of study. The *Princeton Review* now ranks the top graduate and undergraduate game programs yearly, and some programs even offer Ph.D. degrees in games and game studies.

People generally have two core questions about these programs:

- Should I enroll in a game education program?
- Which game education programs should I apply to?

Should I Enroll in a Game Education Program?

As a professor who has spent the last several years of my life teaching in these programs, I can say that my answer to this question is a qualified yes. Game education programs offer several clear benefits:

- You have a concentrated space and time in which to build your design and development skills in a structured way.

---

4. Full disclosure: Since IndieCade 2013, I have been the IndieCade Chair of Education and Advancement and have programmed the IndieXchange and Game U (2013–15) conference tracks. I'm honored to be part of such a fantastic organization and conference.

- You'll be surrounded by faculty who can give you honest, meaningful feedback on your work and peers who can become great collaborators. In addition, many of the faculty in these programs have worked in the game industry and have connections to several game companies.

- Many game companies actively recruit from the top schools. Being at one of them means that you could have the chance to interview for an internship with one of your favorite studios.

- When new employees are hired out of university game programs—especially master-level programs—they usually enter the company at a higher level than others. Traditionally, people got into game companies by working in QA (quality assurance) and testing games. If they excelled at QA, they could get noticed and move up into one of the other positions. Although this is still a very valid way to enter the industry, I have seen new people coming out of university programs often get hired above talented people with several years of seniority who came up through QA.

- Higher education in general will push you to grow and become a better person.

However, you should be aware of some definite caveats. School takes both time and money. If you don't have a bachelor's degree, I personally think that you should absolutely get one. Throughout your life, it will open more doors and grant you more opportunities than not having one. A master's degree is much less necessary in the industry, but programs at the master level are able to offer much more focused education and can be truly transformative. Master's programs generally take between 2 and 3 years and can cost $60,000 or more. However, as my professor Dr. Randy Pausch was fond of saying, your time should be more of a consideration for you than the cost of education. Long-term debt and predatory lending practices are real concerns and have raised the potential price of an advanced degree. But even with that being the case, the most important question you should ask yourself is whether getting an advanced degree is worth two to six years of your life when you could potentially have been out in the industry already. When I chose to go to Carnegie Mellon, it was because I wanted to change the trajectory of my career. I chose to spend two years of my life paying money instead of earning it, and for me, that decision absolutely paid off. You must do what you feel is right, of course.

Which Game Education Programs Should I Apply To?

Hundreds of universities now offer game education programs, and new ones are being added every year. The *Princeton Review's* list of the top schools is generally well respected, but picking a school that is right for you and what you want to do in the industry is much more important. Take time to research the program and learn about the classes and faculty. Investigate how much emphasis the program puts on the different aspects of game development: design, art, programming, management, and so on. Do the program's faculty currently work in the game industry, or do they focus entirely on teaching? Each school will have certain aspects that are their strengths.

As a student, I attended Carnegie Mellon University's Entertainment Technology Center (ETC) for my Master of Entertainment Technology degree. At its core, the ETC is based around team-work and client work. In the first semester (which was for me the best educational semester I have ever experienced), each incoming student works on five collaborative two-week assign-ments with a randomly selected team of peers in a class called Building Virtual Worlds (BVW). The incoming class size is generally more than 60 students, and this helps them experience working with new people continuously throughout the semester. In that semester, each person works about 80 hours each week on her team assignment in addition to taking two or three other classes that supplement BVW. Then, for the remaining three semesters, each student is assigned to a single project team for the full semester and takes only one additional class. Most of these semester-long projects have a real client for whom they are being produced, so ETC students learn firsthand how to manage client expectations, work with peers, and handle internal disputes. These projects are designed to give students several years' worth of industry experience in only two years of grad school. The goal of the ETC is to prep game designers, producers, programmers, and technical artists for work on industry teams.

In contrast, the Master of Fine Arts program in the Interactive Media & Games Division (IMGD) at the University of Southern California (where I taught for four years) is structured very dif-ferently. The size of the incoming cohort each year is generally 15 or less, and all students take several classes together in the first year. Though there are group projects, the students do several independent assignments as well. In the second year, students are encouraged to branch out and explore their personal interests. Students take roughly half of the classes in the second year with their cohort, but they can select the other half of the classes from across the university. The third year in the IMGD is devoted almost entirely to each student's work on her individual thesis project. Though each student leads a thesis project, students very rarely work alone. Most thesis teams are 6 to 10 people in size, and the other team members are pulled from interested students across the university. Each thesis project also has a thesis committee composed of mentors from the industry and academia who are interested in the project and led by a thesis chair from the IMGD faculty. The goal of the IMGD is to "create thought leaders." It is more important to this program that the individual students grow and produce something innovative than that they are prepared for industry jobs.

In my current job, I teach students in the Game Design and Development minor of the Media and Information Department at Michigan State University, the highest-ranked game minor program in the world. Our minor focuses on prepping students to go directly into professional jobs in the industry. One of the major advantages of the program being a minor is that every student in the program gets major-level experience in Media & Information, Computer Science, or Studio Art (the three most common majors in the game development minor) as well as the best possible game design and development education available at our university. This is very different from most other universities where the minor students get a second-class version of games education.

As you can imagine, each of these programs benefit students in very different ways. I have chosen these three to illustrate the point because they are the three with which I am most familiar, but every single school is different, and you owe it to yourself to learn the goals that each school has for its students and how it hopes to achieve them through the classes it teaches.

Getting Into the Industry

I have condensed the content in this section from the "Networking with the Pros" talk that I gave at the 2010 Game Developers Conference Online. If you would like to see the expanded version, you can find the slides on the website for this book.[5]

Meeting People in the Industry

The best way to meet people in the game industry is to go where they are. If you're interested in board games, this means Gen Con; if you are interested in AAA development, this means the Game Developers Conference in San Francisco; and if you're interested in independent game development, this means IndieCade. Many other conferences out there are quite good, but those are the three that have the biggest draw from each of those groups.[6]

However, being at a dev conference only means that you are *co-located* with game developers. To meet them, you must find a way to go up and say hello. Some good times to do so include parties, after a talk that they've given, and when they're working the Expo floor. However, in each of these cases, you need to be courteous, concise, and respectful both to the developer and especially to the other people who want to talk to her. Game developers are busy people, and they each have a reason to be at the conference. They, too, want to meet people, expand their networks, and talk shop with other developers. So don't take too much of their time, don't ever make them feel trapped in a conversation with you, and always have something to bring to the table. That is, make sure that you have something to say that will be interesting to them before you start the conversation.

When meeting people for the first time, don't act like a fawning fan. Every game designer from Will Wright to Jenova Chen is a regular person, and very few of them have any interest in being idolized. Along these lines, avoid saying things like "I love you! I'm your biggest fan!" Frankly, that's pretty damn creepy. Instead, saying things like "I really enjoyed playing *Journey*" is much better. That way, you're complimenting the game—a game that several people worked on—rather than complimenting the individual person, about whom you actually know very little.

Of course, the very best time to meet someone new is when you're introduced. This gives you an in as well as something to talk about (your mutual friend). However, when this happens, you

---

5. The complete slides from the talk are available at http://book.prototools.net.
6. E3 and PAX are also famous game conferences, but you're less likely to meet actual game developers there.

have a critical responsibility to the friend who introduced you—the responsibility to not make her look bad. Whenever someone introduces you, she is vouching for you, and if you do something embarrassing, it reflects badly on her.

Also, don't just focus on meeting famous game developers. Everyone at these conferences loves games, and students and volunteers at the conference are some of the most passionate and creative people you can talk to. Plus, who knows—anyone you meet at a dev conference could be the next great designer everyone is talking about, and later they'll be a great friend to have take a look at your games as you develop them.

Things to Take to the Game Conference

If you're going to meet people, you should always have business cards on you. You can put whatever you want on the front, as long as you make sure it's legible. I usually recommend leaving the back largely blank so that the person to whom you give the card can write notes on it that will remind her later of what you talked about.

Other things I tend to take with me include the following:

- **Breath mints and toothpicks.** Seriously.
- **A pocket tool like a small Leatherman.** Being the person in the room who can fix little things that break is nice.
- **A resume.** I don't carry these with me anymore—because I'm very happy with my current job—but if you're seeking a job, you really want to have a few copies with you.

Following Up

So, you've met someone at the conference and gotten her business card. What's the next step?

About two weeks after the conference, write the person an email. You generally want to wait a couple of weeks because everyone is completely flooded with emails and work when they get back from a dev conference. Your email should generally follow a format similar to that shown in Figure 15.2.

Send the letter and wait a couple of weeks. If you don't hear anything back, write one more time with a lead in like "I'm willing to bet that you were pretty busy after the conference, so I wanted to write again and make sure that you got my email." If she doesn't respond after the second email, do not email again. You'll meet a lot of people in the game industry, and you don't want to bother anyone or creep them out.

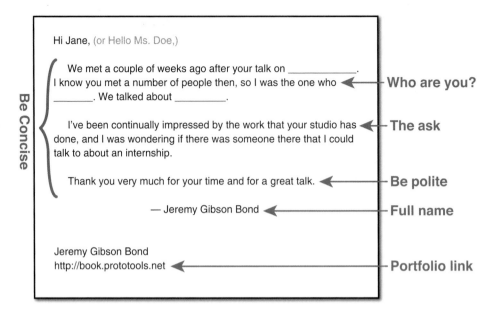

Figure 15.2 An example letter

Interviewing

If everything goes well, you might have a chance to interview at the studio. Now, how do you prepare?

Questions to Ask Before the Day of the Interview

When you interview, you'll be talking to people who are actually on game development teams. Before the interview, the person you talk to will usually be a recruiter. Part of the recruiter's job is to make sure that candidates are properly prepared for the interview, and her evaluation at the end of the year will be partially based on the quality of candidates she brings in. This means that it is in her best interest for you to be perfect for the job, and she is more than willing to answer any questions that can help you better prepare for the interview.

Questions to ask include:

- **What would my job be?** You want to know the answer to this as specifically as possible so that you can prepare.

- **On which project would I be working?** This also answers whether the company is interviewing you for a specific position or is interested in hiring good people regardless of what project they will work on.

- **What is the company culture like?** Each company culture is different, particularly in the game industry. A question like this can also lead to a discussion of things like overtime and crunch time. You don't really need to know the answer to questions about company culture before interviewing, but you definitely need to know them before you sign a contract.

- **What would be appropriate for me to wear to the interview?** Many, many people skip this simple but important question. In general, I tend to dress more formally than I would on a normal workday, but for most game companies, that doesn't mean wearing a suit (and it almost never means wearing a tie). Remember, you're not going to a nice dinner, a party, a date, or a religious ceremony. My wife, a professional costume designer and professor, recommends this: You want to look nice, but you want to make sure that the focus is on your skills and mind, not on how you look.

  Another thing to consider is: Though you definitely want to wear something that makes you feel comfortable, you also want to wear something that makes the interviewers feel comfortable. Every studio talks at some point to investors, the press, publishers, and other people who tend to work in more formal cultures than a game development studio. One of the things that the studio needs to know about you is whether you can be part of those discussions or whether they would have to hide you in a back room so you don't embarrass them when guests visit. Be sure that they place you in the former category.

  A lot of different opinions are out there on the web about what is appropriate to wear, so the best thing you can do is ask the recruiter. The recruiter will have seen every candidate who comes in, and she'll know what works and what doesn't.

  In addition to clothing, you should also think about making sure your hair (including any facial hair) looks deliberate instead of accidental.

- **Are there any games by other studios that I should play before the interview?** You absolutely must play games made by the studio where you're interviewing before you go in, and if you're interviewing to work on a specific game, not having played it or its prequels is unforgivable. This question helps you understand which other games they think you should have played to be knowledgeable about the state of the art in their genre.

- **Can you tell me who will be interviewing me?** If you know this ahead of time, you can do some research into their background. Knowing other projects that your interviewers worked on before coming to the current studio or other studios where they worked previously can give you more insight into their background and more things to talk about.

Some questions you should definitely *not* ask include the following:

- **What games has the studio made? / How long has the studio been around?** The answers to these questions are easily available online. Asking something like this makes it seem like you haven't done your research before coming to the interview (and consequently like you don't really care much about the interview or job).

- **How much will I get paid?** Though this will eventually be a very important question, asking this of an interviewer or recruiter is inappropriate. Instead, it will be part of your negotiations after you have been offered the job. For information on industry averages, you can look to the Game Developer Salary Survey at GameCareerGuide.com[7] or sites like glassdoor.com.

After the Interview

After the interview, sending handwritten thank you notes to the people with whom you spoke is best. Try to take notes throughout the day so that you can comment on something specific to each individual. "Thank you very much for walking me through the studio and especially for introducing me to Team X" is much better than "It was great to meet you, and I'm glad we talked about generic things." Just like items in games, handwritten letters are valuable because they are rare. Every month, I get thousands of emails, more than 100 printed letters through postal mail, and less than 1 handwritten thank you note. Handwritten notes are never spam.

Don't Wait to Start Making Games!

Just because you're not yet a game company employee doesn't mean that you can't make games. After you've finished this book and gotten some experience programming and developing prototypes, you'll probably be looking for a game to work on. Here are some tips for that time.

Join a Project

I'm sure you have a ton of great ideas for games bouncing around in your head, but the best thing you can do if you're new to development is to join a team that already has some experience developing a game. Working with a team of other developers—even if they're still learning like you are—is one of the best ways to quickly grow your skills.

Start Your Own Project

After you've either gotten some experience on a team or if you just can't find a team to work with, it's time to start creating your own games. To do so, you need five critical elements: the right *idea*, the right *scope*, the right *team*, the right *schedule*, and the *will to finish*.

The Right Idea

Millions of different game ideas are out there. You need to pick one that will actually work. It must be something that you know you won't lose interest in, something that doesn't just copy a

---

7. The salary surveys were traditionally a yearly article in *Game Developer Magazine,* which had the same owners as GameCareerGuide.com. However, the magazine ceased publication in 2013. You can still see the salary survey that was published in 2013 at http://gamecareerguide.com/features/1279/game_developer_salary_survey_.php.

game you love, something that other people find interesting, and most importantly, something that you know you can make. This leads us to…

The Right Scope

The number one thing that stops teams from finishing games is *overscoping*—in other words, biting off more than you can chew. Most new developers don't understand how long making a game can take, so their game concepts are drastically overscoped. Scoping-down is the process of getting the game down to its bare essentials and eliminating fluff. For a game to have good scope, you must have a true and realistic understanding of the amount of effort needed to implement the game, and you must make sure—you must be absolutely certain—that you have the team and the time to finish it.

Making a tiny game and expanding on it is drastically better than starting by trying to make something huge. Remember that most games you have played took a large team of professionals about two years and millions of dollars to make. Even indie games often take years of work by an experienced and talented team. When you're just starting out, think small. You can always add more to the game later.

The Right Team

Working on a game with someone is a long-term relationship, and you need to treat it that way. It's also sadly true that the things that make you great friends with someone might not be the same things that are required to make you great team members. When you're thinking about working with people, make sure that they have similar work habits to yours, and it's best if they tend to work at similar times of day as well. Even if you're part of a remote team, texting or video chatting with your teammates while you work can really help.

While creating your team, you also need to have a conversation about ownership of the intellectual property (IP) of the game. If no agreement is in place, the default is that everyone who had anything to do with the project owns an equal share.[8] IP issues are sticky, and they might seem kind of ridiculous to talk about before any game exists, but it is a critical conversation to have. However, the flip side of this is that I have actually seen game teams never get started because people were bickering about the IP ownership of a game that didn't exist. You definitely don't want to get stuck in that trap.

---

8. I am not a lawyer, and I am not trying to give legal advice. I'm just sharing my personal understanding of the situation. If you have a friend who is a lawyer, I recommend asking her about it or looking for information online.

ROYALTY POINTS

At my company, I've been using *royalty points* as what I believe to be a fair way of distributing royalties for work done on the independent games we make. The core idea of royalty points is that everyone earns royalties for time that they dedicate to the project throughout the entire development of the project. Here's how it works for my teams:

- 50% of any income for a project goes directly to the company. This helps us build up cash so that we can pay people in the future (right now, people are working exclusively for future royalties).

- The other 50% is distributed to people who worked on the project based on their percentage of the total royalty points.

- For every 10 hours of work that someone puts in to the project, they earn 1 royalty point.

- These points accrue throughout both the development and support of the project.

- The points are tracked in a spreadsheet that any member of the team can view at any time (though only I can edit it).

With this royalty point system, team members directly earn royalties as they work on the project, and the more good work they do, the larger percentage of the royalties they will earn. If someone on the team isn't doing good work, you remove them from the team, and they still earn royalties for the work they did do, but they earn a smaller and smaller percentage relative to the other team members who are continuing to contribute.

This also means that members of the support team could eventually have a greater percentage of the royalty points than the original development team; this is by design. Most small, independent projects in the past have granted a specific percentage of royalties to each person at the beginning of the project, which makes it very difficult to alter things in the future and adapt to a changing work situation. I believe that royalty points allow you flexibility as a studio while still being clear and fair to everyone involved.

The Right Schedule

In Chapter 14, "The Agile Mentality," I cover agile development practices and burndown charts. Make sure that you read it before you start a project. Though your mileage may vary, I have found that for my teams and the vast majority of my student teams, burndown charts are a fantastic tool to keep them on track and aware of where each person is in her individual development tasks. In addition, burndown charts do a fantastic job of helping you to understand the difference between how long you estimate a task will take and how long it actually takes you to accomplish it. By looking at the difference between the two in the chart up to the point where you are currently, you can get a more realistic estimate of how long completing the remaining tasks will take.

The Will to Finish

As you make progress on your project, you will come to a point where you clearly see all the things that you could have done better. You'll see that your code is a mess, your art could be better, and the design has some holes in it. A lot of teams get to this point surprisingly close to the end of the project. If you are near the end, you need to push on through. *You must have the will to finish your game.* If the number one killer of games is bad scoping, the number two killer is that the last 10% of the project is always the hardest climb. Keep pushing, because even if the game isn't perfect—and trust me, no game ever is—even if the game isn't all you hoped, even if it is far less than what you hoped, it will be done. You will be a game developer with a finished title, and that means a tremendous amount to everyone you hope to work with in the future.

Summary

There is much more to be learned about the game industry than was able to fit in this single chapter. Luckily, many websites and publications cover the game industry, and talks at conferences often address both what it takes to join the industry and the process of starting a company. A simple web search should surface several of them, and the GDC Vault (http://gdcvault.com) is a great place to find videos of many talks.

If you do choose to start a company, be sure that you find a lawyer and an accountant that you can trust to help you before you actually run into any bumps in the process. Lawyers and accountants have years of training in how to build and protect companies, and having them available to consult can make your path to incorporation much easier.

PART II

DIGITAL PROTOTYPING

CHAPTER 16

THINKING IN DIGITAL SYSTEMS

If you've never programmed before, this chapter will be your introduction to a new world: one where you have the ability and skills to make digital prototypes of the games you imagine.

This chapter describes the mindset you need to have when approaching programming projects. It gives you exercises to explore that mindset and helps you think about the world in terms of systems of interconnected relationships and meaning. At the conclusion of this chapter, you will be in the right mindset to explore the challenges of the "Digital Prototyping" part of this book.

Systems Thinking in Board Games

In the first part of the book, you learned that games are created from interconnected systems. In games, these systems are encoded into the rules of the game and into the players themselves, meaning that all players bring certain expectations, abilities, knowledge, and social norms to the games that they play. For example, when you see a standard pair of six-sided dice included in the box with a new board game, you immediately start to make assumptions about how the dice will be used in the game:

- **Common assumed behaviors of 2d6 (two six-sided dice) in board games**
    1. Each die is rolled to generate a random number between 1 and 6 (inclusive).
    2. The dice are often rolled together, especially if they are the same color and size.
    3. When rolled together, the dice are usually summed. For example, a 3 on one die and a 4 on the other would sum to a total of 7.
    4. If "doubles" are rolled (that is, both dice show the same value), sometimes the player receives a special benefit.

You also probably make assumptions about several things that will not be done with the dice:

- **Common assumed restrictions on 2d6 usage in board games**
    1. A player will not just place the dice on the values that she would prefer to have.
    2. The dice must stay on the table and must land completely flat on a side to be considered a valid roll.
    3. When rolled, the dice are generally not touched for the rest of that player's turn.
    4. Dice are generally not thrown at other players (or eaten).

Although exploring such simple, often unwritten, rules in detail might seem somewhat pedantic, it serves to show how many of the rules of board games are not actually present in the rule book; rather they are based on the shared understanding of *fair play* among the players. This idea is incumbent in the concept of the magic circle, and it's a large part of what makes it so easy for a group of children to spontaneously create a game that they all intuitively understand how to play. Most human players carry within them massive preconceptions about how games are played.

Computer games, however, rely on specific instructions to do absolutely everything. At their core—regardless of how powerful they have become over the past several decades—computers are mindless machines that follow very specific instructions billions of times per second. Providing the computer with a semblance of intelligence by encoding your ideas into very simple instructions for it to follow is up to you, the programmer.

An Exercise in Simple Instructions

One classic exercise for budding computer science students to help them understand how to think in terms of very simple instructions involves telling another person how to stand up from a prone position. You'll need a friend for this.

Ask your friend to lie on his back on the floor, and ask him to only follow your exact instructions to the letter. Your goal is to give your friend instructions that will move him into a standing position; however, you cannot use any complex commands like "stand up." Instead, you must only use the kind of simple commands that you might imagine giving to a robot. Examples of the level of detail you could offer him are:

- Bend your left elbow closed 90 degrees.
- Extend your right leg toward the doorway.
- Place your left hand on the ground with your palm facing downward.
- Point your right arm at the television.

In reality, even these simple instructions are drastically more complex than anything that could be sent to most robots, and they're pretty open to interpretation. However, for the sake of this exercise, this level of simplicity will suffice.

Give it a try.

How long did it take you to give your friend the right instructions to stand up? If you and your friend try to follow both the rules and the spirit of the exercise, it will take quite a while. If you try it with different people, you'll find that it takes much, much longer if your friend doesn't know ahead of time that you have the end goal of getting him into a standing position.

How old were you the first time you were asked by a member of your family to set the table for a meal? I think I was only about four when my parents decided that I could handle that complex task with my only instruction being "Please set the table for dinner." Based on the exercise that you just completed, imagine how many simple instructions you would have to give to a person to recreate the complex task of setting the table; yet children are often able to do this before they start elementary school.

What This Means to Digital Programming

Now, of course, I didn't give you that exercise to discourage you. In fact, the following two chapters are meant to be really inspirational! Rather, I gave it to help you understand the mentality of computers and to set up several metaphors for aspects of computer programming. Let's take a look.

Computer Language

When I gave you the list of four example commands that you could give, I was outlining the parameters of the language that you could use to talk to your friend. Obviously, this was a pretty loose language definition. Throughout this book, you will use the programming language C# (pronounced "see sharp"), and thankfully, its language definition is far more specific. You will explore C# throughout the chapters in this part of the book, but suffice to say that I have taught thousands of students several different programming languages over more than a decade, and my experience has shown me that C# is one of the best languages for people to learn as their first programming language. Though learning it requires slightly more diligence than learning simpler languages like Processing or JavaScript, it gives learners a far better understanding of core development concepts that will help them throughout their game prototyping and development careers, and it enforces good coding practices that will eventually make their code development faster and easier.

Code Libraries

In the previous exercise, you can see that being able to tell your friend to "stand up" would have been much easier than going through the trouble of having to give so many low-level commands. In that case, "stand up" would have been a multipurpose high-level instruction that you could have used to tell your friend what you wanted regardless of the starting position that he was in. Similarly, "please set the table" is a common, high-level instruction that generates the desired outcome regardless of what meal is being prepared, how many people will be eating, or even what household you are in. In C#, collections of high-level instructions for common behaviors are called *code libraries*, and hundreds of them are available to you as a C# and Unity developer.

The most common code library that you will use is the collection of code that tailors C# to work properly with the Unity development environment. In your code, this extremely powerful library will be imported under the name `UnityEngine`. The `UnityEngine` library includes code for the following:

- Awesome lighting effects like fog and reflections
- Physics simulations that cover gravity, collisions, and even cloth simulation
- Input from mouse, keyboard, gamepad, and touch-based tablets
- Hundreds of other things

In addition, there are thousands of free (and paid) code libraries out there to help make your coding easier. If the thing you want to do is pretty common (e.g., moving an object across the screen smoothly over the course of one second), there's a good chance that someone has already written a great code library to do so (in this case, the free library iTween by Bob Berkebile, http://itween.pixelplacement.com/ is pretty good).

The prevalence of great code libraries for Unity and C# means that *you* can concentrate on writing code for the new, unique aspects of your games rather than reinventing the wheel every time you start a new game project. In time, you will also start collecting commonly used bits of your own code into libraries that you will use across multiple projects. In this book, you will start doing so through a code library called `ProtoTools` that will grow in capability across several projects.

Development Environment

The Unity game development environment is an essential part of your development experience. You can best think of the Unity application as an environment in which to collect and compose all the *assets* that you create for a game. In Unity, you will bring together 3D models, music and audio clips, 2D graphics and textures, and finally the C# scripts that you author. None of these assets are created directly within Unity; rather, Unity is where they are all composed together into a cohesive computer game. You will also use Unity to position game objects in three-dimensional space, handle user input, set up a virtual camera in your scene, and finally compile all of these assets together into a working, executable game. Chapter 17, "Introducing the Unity Development Environment" discusses the capabilities of Unity extensively.

Breaking Down Complex Problems into Simpler Ones

One of the key things you must have noticed in the exercise is that the exclusion from giving complex commands like "stand up" meant that you needed to think about breaking complex commands down into smaller, more discrete commands. Although this activity was difficult in the exercise, in your programming, you will find the skill of breaking complex tasks into simpler ones to be one of the greatest tools that you have for tackling the challenges that you face and helping you make the games you want one small piece at a time. I use this skill every day in the development of my games, and I promise that it will serve you well. As an example, let's break down the Apple Picker game that you will make in Chapter 28, "Prototype 1: Apple Picker" into simple commands.

Game Analysis: *Apple Picker*

Apple Picker is the first prototype that you will make in this book. It is based on the game play of the classic Activision game *Kaboom!*, which Larry Kaplan designed and Activision published in 1981.[1] Many clones of *Kaboom!* have been made through the years, and ours is a somewhat less violent version. In the original game, the player moved buckets back and forth in an attempt to catch bombs being dropped by a "Mad Bomber." In this version, the player uses a basket to collect apples that are falling from a tree (see Figure 16.1).

In this analysis, you will look at each of the *GameObjects*[2] in Apple Picker, analyze each of their behaviors, and break down those behaviors to simple commands in flowchart form. This demonstrates how simple commands can lead to complex behavior and fun gameplay.

---

1. http://en.wikipedia.org/wiki/Kaboom!_(video_game)
2. A GameObject is Unity's name for an object that is active in a game. Each GameObject can contain many components like a 3D model, texture information, collision information, C# code, and so on.

I recommend searching for "play Kaboom!" online to see whether you can find an online version of the game to play before digging into this analysis, but the game is simple enough that doing so is not necessary. You can also find a version of the Apple Picker game prototype on the http://book.prototools.net website under Chapter 16, although the Apple Picker game is only a single endless level, whereas *Kaboom!* had eight distinct difficulty levels.

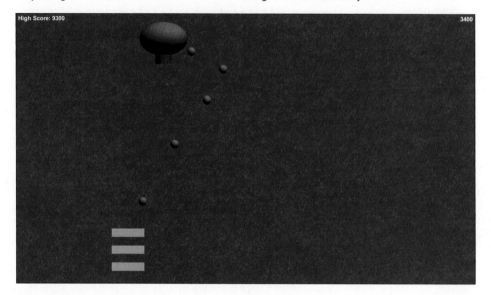

Figure 16.1 The Apple Picker game you will make in Chapter 28

Apple Picker Basic Gameplay

The player controls the three baskets at the bottom of the screen and can move them left and right using the mouse. The apple tree moves back and forth randomly while dropping apples, and the player must use her baskets to catch the apples before they hit the ground. For each apple that the player catches, she earns points, but if even a single apple hits the ground, it and all other remaining apples disappear, and the player loses a basket. When the player loses all three baskets, the game is over. (The original *Kaboom!* game had a few other rules about the number of points earned per bomb [apple] and the progression of the various levels, but those are unimportant for this analysis.)

Apple Picker GameObjects

In Unity terminology, any object in the game—usually meaning anything that you see on screen—is a *GameObject*. We can also use this term in discussing the elements shown in the screenshot in Figure 16.2. For consistency with later Unity projects, I capitalize the name of all GameObjects (e.g., Apples, Baskets, and AppleTree) in the following list.

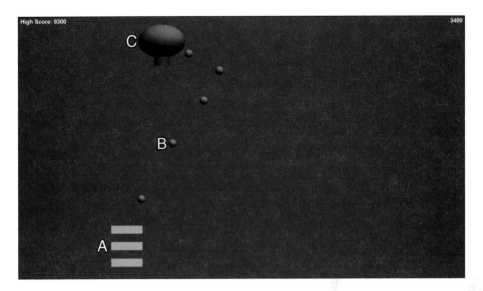

Figure 16.2 Apple Picker with GameObjects labeled

A. **Baskets:** Controlled by the player, the Baskets move left and right following the player's mouse movements. When a Basket collides with an Apple, the Apple is caught, and the player gains points.

B. **Apples:** The Apples are dropped by the AppleTree and fall straight down. If an Apple collides with any of the three Baskets, the Apple is caught and disappears from the screen (granting the player some points). If an Apple passes off the bottom of the screen, it disappears, and it causes all other Apples on screen to disappear as well. This destroys one of the Baskets (starting with the top Basket). When this is resolved, the AppleTree starts dropping Apples again.

C. **AppleTree:** The AppleTree moves left and right randomly while dropping Apples. The Apples are dropped at a regular interval, so the only randomness in the behavior is the left and right movement.

Apple Picker GameObject Action Lists

This analysis does not consider the increasing difficulty levels that are present in the original *Kaboom!* game. Instead the focus is on the moment-to-moment actions taken by each GameObject.

Basket Actions

Basket actions include the following:

- Move left and right following the player's mouse.
- If any Basket collides with an Apple, catch the Apple.[3]

That's it! The Baskets are very simple.

Apple Actions

Apple actions include the following:

- Fall down.
- If an Apple hits the bottom of the screen, the end of the round is triggered.[4]

The Apples are also very simple.

AppleTree Actions

AppleTree actions include the following:

- Move left and right randomly.
- Drop an Apple every 0.5 seconds.

The AppleTree is pretty simple, too.

Apple Picker GameObject Flowcharts

A flowchart is often a good way to think about how the flow of actions and decisions works in your game. Let's look at some for Apple Picker. Though the following flowcharts refer to things like adding points and ending the round, right now, just look at the actions that take place in a single round and don't worry about how those kinds of scoring and round actions actually work.

Basket Flowchart

In Figure 16.3 shows the behavior of the Basket outlined in a flowchart. The game loops through this flowchart every *frame* (which is at least 30 times every second). This is shown by the oval that is at the top left of the chart. Boxes in the flowchart contain actions (e.g., *Match Left/Right Mouse Movement*), and diamonds contain decisions. See the sidebar "Frames in Computer Games" to learn more about what constitutes a frame.

---

3. Making this collision and reaction part of the Apple actions would also be possible, but I have chosen to make it part of Basket.

4. The end of a round causes all the Apples on screen to disappear and deletes one of the Baskets before starting the next round, but that does not need to be part of the Apple action list. It will be handled instead by an ApplePicker script that will manage overall game elements.

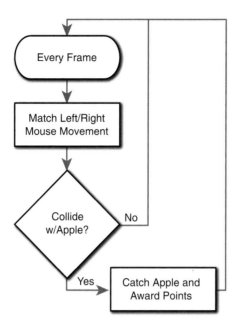

Figure 16.3 Basket flowchart

FRAMES IN COMPUTER GAMES

The term *frame* comes from the world of film. Historically, films were composed of strips of celluloid containing thousands of individual pictures (known as frames). When those pictures were shown in quick succession (at either 16 or 24 frames per second [*fps*]), it produced the illusion of movement. Later, on televisions, the movement was constructed from a series of electronic images projected onto the screen, which were also called frames (and operated at about 30 fps in the United States).

When computer graphics became fast enough to show animation and other moving images, each individual image shown on the computer screen was also called a frame. In addition, all the computation that takes place leading up to showing that image on screen is also part of that frame. When Unity runs a game at 60 fps, it is not only creating and displaying a new image on screen 60 times per second. In that time, it is also calculating the tremendous amount of math required to properly move objects between one frame to the next.

Figure 16.3 shows a flowchart representation of the computation that is involved in moving the Basket from one frame to the next.

Apple Flowchart

The Apple has a pretty simple flowchart as well (see Figure 16.4). Remember that the collision between the Apple and the Basket is part of the Basket behavior, so it does not need to be handled in the Apple flowchart.

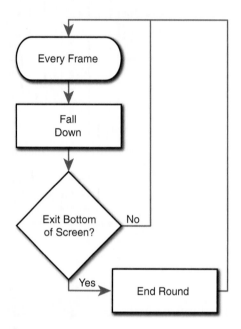

Figure 16.4 Apple flowchart

AppleTree Flowchart

The AppleTree flowchart is slightly more complex (see Figure 16.5) because the AppleTree has two decisions to make each frame:

- Does it change direction?
- Does it drop an Apple?

The decision of whether to change direction could just as easily come before or after the actual movement. For the purposes of this chapter, either would have worked.

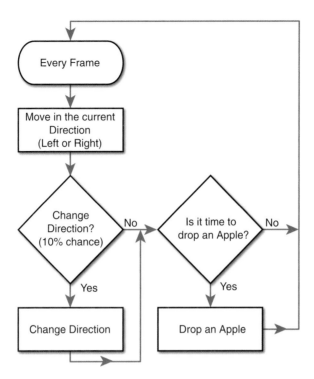

Figure 16.5 AppleTree flowchart

Summary

As you've now seen, digital games can be broken down into a set of very simple decisions and commands. This task is implicit in how I approached creating the prototypes for this book, and it is something that you will do yourself when you approach your own game design and development projects.

Chapter 28, "Prototype 1: Apple Picker," expands on this analysis and shows how to convert these action lists into lines of code that make your Baskets move, your Apples fall, and your AppleTrees run around like a Mad Bomber dropping Apples.

CHAPTER 17

INTRODUCING THE UNITY DEVELOPMENT ENVIRONMENT

This is the start of your programming adventure.

In this chapter, you download Unity, the game development environment that you will use throughout the rest of this book. The chapter covers why Unity is a fantastic game development tool for any budding game designer or developer and addresses why I've chosen C# as the language for you to learn.

You also take a look at the sample project that ships with Unity, learn about the various window panes in the Unity interface, and move these panes into a logical arrangement that will match the examples you see in the rest of the book.

Downloading Unity

First things first—let's start downloading Unity. The installation size of Unity is more than 1 GB, so depending on your Internet speed, this could take anywhere from a few minutes to a couple of hours. After you've gotten this process started, we can move on to talking about Unity.

As of this writing, the latest major version of Unity is Unity 2017. Under the current Unity release plan, a new version is released every 90 days. Regardless of version, Unity is always available for free from Unity's store:

> http://store.unity.com

This should take you to a page that with links to several different versions of Unity (see Figure 17.1). Unity is available for both Windows and macOS, and it is nearly identical on both platforms. The free Personal version can handle everything that is covered in this book. Click the green *Try Personal* button in the *Personal* column to start the process. Then click the *Download Installer* button on page that appears. Unity makes relatively frequent changes to their store, but this process should stay largely the same.

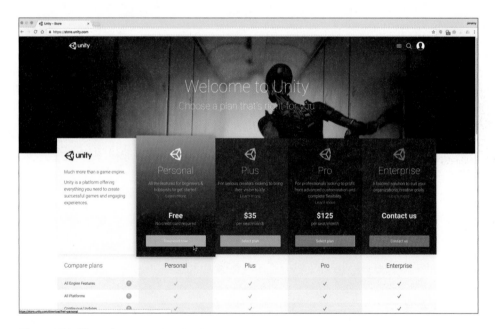

Figure 17.1 The web page to download Unity

This causes your computer to download the *Unity Download Assistant*, a small program (less than 1MB) that will download the rest of Unity when you run it. You can find the Unity Download Assistant in your Downloads folder.

On macOS

To install Unity on macOS, follow these steps:

1. Open the UnityDownloadAssistant-x.x.x.dmg file that was downloaded (where the x.x.x represents the Unity version to be installed). A folder opens.

2. Double-click the *Unity Download Assistant.app* inside this folder to launch it (see Figure 17.2A).

3. macOS asks whether you're sure you want to launch this application, because it was downloaded from the Internet. Click *Open* to confirm (see Figure 17.2B).

4. On the *Install, activate and get creating with Unity* screen that appears, click *Continue*.

5. To install Unity, you must agree to the terms of service by clicking *Agree*.

6. On the screen shown in Figure 17.2C, be sure to check the following options:

   - **Unity x.x.x**—The current Unity version

   - **Documentation**—Trust me, you'll definitely need this!

   - **Standard Assets**—A number of useful assets that ship with Unity. Includes some nice particle effects, terrain stuff, etc.

   - **Example Project**—We will look at this later in the chapter.

   - **WebGL Build Support**—This is now the only way to get your Unity projects online, and you will use it later in the book.

   You might need to enter the account password for your macOS or Windows PC to install.

7. The Download Assistant asks you where to install Unity. I recommend your main hard drive because you want Unity to be quickly accessible. Click *Continue*.

The Download Assistant will start its long process of downloading. With the options I recommended, my download size was about 3GB, so this might take a while.

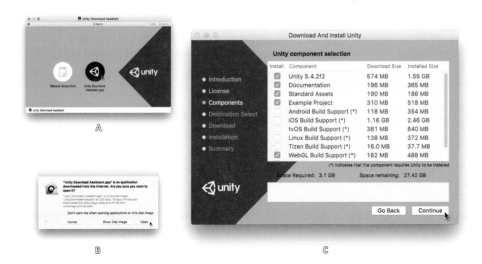

Figure 17.2 Installation steps for macOS

On Windows

To install Unity on Windows, follow these steps:

1. Open the UnityDownloadAssistant-x.x.x.exe app that was downloaded (where the x.x.x represents the Unity version to be installed).

2. Windows asks whether you want to allow this app to make changes to your PC. Click *Yes* to confirm (see Figure 17.3A).

3. On the first screen of the installer, click *Next >*.

4. To install Unity, you must check the box next to *I accept the terms of the License Agreement,* and then click *Next >*.

5. You should probably be running a 64-bit version of Windows by now, so select *64-bit* on the next screen. However, if you are still running 32-bit Windows, choose 32-bit. To make sure, open Windows Settings and choose the *System* icon (which looks like a computer). Then click *About* in the listing on the left. Beside the heading *System type*, you should see either 64-bit or 32-bit (see Figure 17.3B). After selecting a version, click *Next >*.

6. On the screen shown in Figure 17.3C, be sure to check the following options:[1]

   ▪ **Unity x.x.x**—The current Unity version

   ▪ **Documentation**—Trust me, you'll definitely need this!

   ▪ **Standard Assets**—A number of useful assets that ship with Unity. Includes some nice particle effects, terrain stuff, etc.

   ▪ **Example Project**—We look at this in this chapter.

   ▪ **WebGL Build Support**—This is now the only way to get your Unity projects online, and you use it later in the book.

7. The Download Assistant asks you where to install Unity. I recommend the default location of *C:\Program Files\Unity*. Click *Next >*.

The Download Assistant will start its long process of downloading. With the options I recommended, you might be downloading about 3GB of data, so it could take a long time. While you wait, you should read the next section *Introducing Our Development Environment*.

---

1. You may be tempted to also install Microsoft Visual Studio Community, but I recommend against this for now. Visual Studio is a more robust code editor than MonoDevelop (which is included with Unity), and it is now available to install along with Unity. But I do not recommend it because this entire book uses MonoDevelop examples. However, if you have a lot of experience using Visual Studio already, you might want to give it a try.

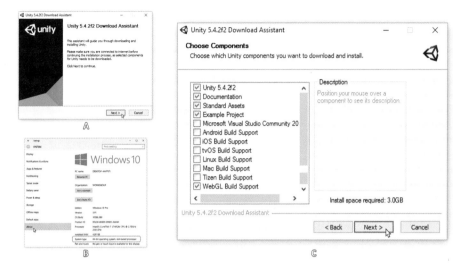

Figure 17.3 Installation steps for Windows

Introducing Our Development Environment

Before you can begin prototyping in earnest, you must first become familiar with Unity, our chosen development environment. You can think of Unity itself as a synthesis program; although you will bring all the elements of your game prototypes together in Unity, production of the actual assets is usually done in other programs. You program in MonoDevelop; model and texture in a 3D modeling program like Maya, Autodesk 3ds Max, or Blender; edit images in a photo editor such as Affinity Photo, Photoshop, or GIMP; and edit sound in an audio program such as Pro Tools or Audacity. Throughout the tutorials in this book, you'll be spending most of your time writing C# (pronounced "see-sharp") code in MonoDevelop and managing your project and scene in Unity. Because Unity will be so important to your process, please carefully follow the *Setting Up the Unity Window Layout* instructions later in this chapter.

Why Choose Unity?

There are many game development engines out there, but I focus on Unity for several reasons:

- **Unity is free:** With the free Personal version of Unity, you can create and sell games that run on a multitude of platforms. As of the writing of this edition of the book, there are very few features of Unity Plus or Unity Pro that are not included for free in Unity Personal. The one caveat is that if you work for a company or organization that made more than $100,000 last year, you must purchase Unity Plus ($35/month), and if your organization made more than $200,000 last year, you must purchase Unity Pro ($125/month). The Plus and Pro versions do allow you slightly better analytics, the ability to set the splash screen when your app launches, more concurrent players in multiplayer games, and a dark editor skin, but that's about it. For a game designer learning to prototype, the free version is really all that you need.

> ## tip
>
> **UNITY PRICING** Unity has made several changes to its licensing and pricing structure since the first edition of the book was written, so I recommend exploring the current pricing structure at http://store.unity.com.

- **Write once, deploy anywhere:** The free version of Unity can build applications for macOS, PC, the Internet via WebGL, Linux, iOS, Apple tvOS, Android, Samsung TV, Tizen, Windows Store, and more—all from the same code and files. This kind of flexibility is at the core of Unity; in fact, it's what the product and company are named for. Professionals can even use Unity to create games for the PlayStation 4, Xbox One, and several other game consoles.

- **Great support:** In addition to excellent documentation, Unity has an incredibly active and supportive development community. Millions of developers use Unity, and many of them contribute to the discussions on Unity forums across the web. The official Unity forum is at https://forum.unity3d.com/.

- **It's awesome!:** My students and I have joked that Unity has a "make awesome" button. Although this is not strictly true, there are several phenomenal features built in to Unity that will make your games both play and look better by simply checking an option box. Unity engineers have already handled a lot of the difficult game programming tasks for you. Collision detection, physics simulation, pathfinding, particle systems, draw call batching, shaders, the game loop, and many other tough coding issues are already solved. All you need to do is make a game that takes advantage of them!

Why Choose C#?

Within Unity, you have the choice to use one of two programming languages: JavaScript or C#.

JavaScript

JavaScript is often seen as a language for beginners; it's easy to learn, the syntax is forgiving and flexible, and it's also used for scripting web pages. JavaScript was initially developed in the mid-1990s by Netscape as a "lite" version of the Java programming language. It was used as a scripting language for web pages, although that often meant that various JavaScript functions worked fine in one web browser but didn't work at all in another. The syntax of JavaScript was the basis for HTML5 and is very similar to Adobe Flash's ActionScript 3. Despite all of this, JavaScript's flexibility and forgiving nature is actually the thing that makes it an inferior language for this book. As one example, JavaScript uses *weak typing*, which means that if you were to create a variable (or container) named *bob*, you could put anything you wanted into that variable: a number, a word, an entire novel, or even the main character of your game. Because the JavaScript variable bob wouldn't have a variable type, Unity would never really know what kind of thing bob was, and bob could change at any time. Flexibilities like this in JavaScript make scripting more tedious and prevent programmers from taking advantage of some of the most powerful and interesting features of modern languages.

C#

C# was developed in 2000 as Microsoft's response to Java. It took a lot of the modern coding features of Java and put them into a syntax that was much more familiar to and comfortable for traditional C++ developers. This means that C# has all the capabilities of a modern language. For you experienced programmers, these features include function virtualization and delegates, dynamic binding, operator overloading, lambda expressions, and the powerful LINQ query language among many others. For those of you new to programming, all you really need to know is that working in C# from the beginning will make you a better programmer and prototyper in the long run. In my prototyping class at the University of Southern California, I taught using both JavaScript and C#, and I found that students who were taught C# consistently produced better game prototypes, exhibited stronger coding practices, and felt more confident about their programming abilities than their peers who had been taught JavaScript in prior semesters of the class.

RUNTIME SPEED OF EACH LANGUAGE

If you've had some experience programming, you might assume that C# code in Unity would execute faster than code written in JavaScript. This assumption would come from the understanding that C# code is usually *compiled* whereas JavaScript is *interpreted* (meaning that compiled code is converted into a computer's machine language by a compiler as part of the coding process, whereas interpreted code is translated on-the-fly as the player is playing the game, making interpreted code generally slower; this is discussed more in Chapter 18, "Introducing Our Language: C#"). However, in Unity, every time you save a file of either C# or JavaScript code, Unity imports it, converts either of the two languages to the same *Common Intermediate Language* (CIL), and then compiles that CIL into machine language. So, regardless of the language you use, your Unity game prototypes will execute at the same speed.

On the Daunting Nature of Learning a Language

There's no way around it: Learning a new language is tough. I'm sure that's one of the reasons that you bought this book rather than just trying to tackle things on your own. Just like Spanish, Japanese, Mandarin, French, or any other human language, some things in C# won't make any sense at first, and there are places that I'm going to tell you to write something that you don't immediately understand. There will also probably be a point where you are just starting to understand some things about the language but feel utterly confused by the language as a whole (which is the exact same feeling you would have if you took one semester of Spanish class and then tried to watch soap operas on Telemundo). This feeling comes for almost all of my students about halfway through the semester, and by the end of the semester, every one of them feels much more confident and comfortable with both C# and game prototyping.

Rest assured, this book is here for you, and if you read it in its entirety, you will emerge with not only a working understanding of C# but also several simple game prototypes that you can use as foundations on which to build your own projects. The approach that I take in this book comes from many semesters of experience teaching "nonprogrammers" how to find the hidden coder within themselves and, more broadly, how to convert their game ideas into working prototypes. As you'll see throughout this book, that approach is composed of three steps:

1. **Concept introduction:** Before asking you to code anything for each project, I'll tell you what we're doing and why. This general concept of what you're working toward in each tutorial gives you a framework on which to hang the various coding elements that I introduce in the chapter.

2. **Guided tutorial:** I guide you step by step through a tutorial that demonstrates these concepts in the form of a playable game. Unlike some other tutorials you may have seen, I have you compile and test the game throughout the process so that you can identify and repair bugs (problems in the code) as you go, rather than trying to fix all of them at the end. Additionally, I'll even guide you to create some bugs so that you can see the errors they cause and become familiar with them; this will make it easier to deal with encountering your own bugs later.

3. **Lather, rinse, repeat:** In many tutorials, I ask you to repeat something. For instance, in Chapter 30, "Prototype 3: Space SHMUP"—a top-down shooter game like *Galaga*—the tutorial guides you through the process of making one single enemy type, and then in Chapter 31, "Prototype 3.5: Space SHMUP Plus," it leads you to create three others. Don't skip this part! This repetition can really drive the concept home and help your understanding solidify later.

pro tip

90% OF BUGS ARE JUST TYPOS. I've spent so much time helping students fix bugs that now I can very quickly spot a typo in code. The most common include the following:

- **Misspellings:** If you type even one letter wrong, the computer won't have any idea what you're talking about.

- **Capitalization:** To your C# compiler, `A` and `a` are two completely different letters, so `variable`, `Variable`, and `variAble` are all completely different words.

- **Missing semicolons:** Just like almost every sentence in English should end in a period, nearly every statement in C# should end in a semicolon (`;`). Leaving the semicolon out often causes an error on the next line. FYI: It's a semicolon because the period was needed for decimal numbers and what's called *dot syntax* in variable referencing (e.g., `varName.x`).

Earlier, I mentioned that most of my students feel confused and daunted by C# at about the midway point of the semester, and it's at exactly that time that I assign them the Classic Games Project. They are asked to faithfully recreate the mechanics and game feel of a classic game over the course of four weeks. Some great examples have included *Super Mario Bros.*, *Metroid*, *Castlevania*, *Pokemon*, and even *Crazy Taxi*.[2] By being forced to work things out on their own, to schedule their own time, and to dig deeply into the inner workings of these seemingly simple games, the students come to realize that they understand much more C# than they thought, and this is when everything really falls into place. The key component here is that the thought process changes from "I'm following this tutorial" to "I want to do this—now how do I make it happen?" At the end of this book, you will be prepared to tackle your own game projects (or your own Classic Game Project, if you want). The tutorials in this book can be a fantastic starting point on which to build your own games.

Launching Unity for the First Time

When you first launch Unity, you must set up some things.[3]

1. On Windows, you might be asked to allow Unity to communicate through the firewall to the Internet. You should allow this.

---

2. One of my favorite classic games to recreate is *The Legend of Zelda*, and that is what you'll do in Chapter 35, "Prototype 7: Dungeon Delver."

3. Of course, with Unity releasing new versions every 90 days, these steps could change. If anything is drastically different, you can always find the latest information on the website for this book: http://book.prototools.net.

2. You will be asked to sign into your Unity Account. If you don't have one, create it now.

3. In the next screen, choose *Unity Personal* and click *Next*. A License agreement screen appears.

4. You will not be allowed to install Unity Personal if the company or organization you represent earned more than $100,000 in gross revenue in the previous fiscal year. As a reader of this book, you should probably choose "I don't use Unity in a professional capacity" and click *Next*.

5. Click the *Getting started* tab at the top of the Unity screen and check out the video there. It gives you a little information about getting started. Don't worry if this is all a little fast. We'll be going over it.

The Example Project

To access the example project, do the following:[4]

1. Click the *Projects* tab in the Unity launch window, and you should see a Standard Assets Example Project listed. Click the name of this example project; it should open.

2. When the project opens, you should see something like Figure 17.4. Click the *Play* button to play this scene (highlighted by a light blue rectangle in Figure 17.4).

While playing, you can press Esc at any time to open the menu of various scenes. When I played, there was a bug with the *Characters > First Person Character* scene where the mouse cursor would disappear during playback of that scene (probably intentional) but then not reappear upon switching to another scene (probably a bug), so I recommend playing the First Person Character scene last. You can then press Esc to get your mouse cursor back and click the *Play* button again to stop.

To be honest, I think that the Unity 4 example project, *Angry Bots*, did a much better job of showing off the engine, but this project does show you some of the breadth of what Unity can do.

To see video of more exciting games made with Unity, I recommend going to Unity's YouTube channel either by searching online for "YouTube Unity" or by going directly to https://www.youtube.com/user/Unity3D and looking for the "Made with Unity" group of videos.

Setting Up the Unity Window Layout

The last thing you need to do before you start actually making things in Unity is to get your environment laid out properly. Unity is very flexible, and one of those flexibilities is that it allows you to arrange its window panes however you like. You can see several window layouts by choosing various options from the *Layout* pop-up menu in the top-right corner of the Unity window (see Figure 17.5).

---

4. These instructions are for the Unity 5.6 Example Project. Hopefully Unity will release a better one soon.

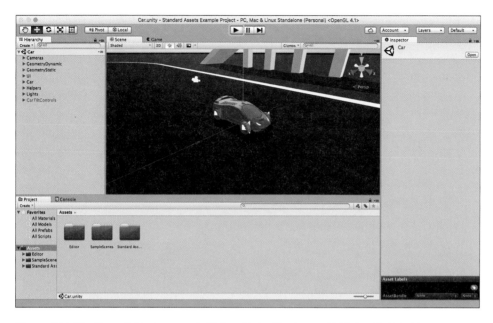

Figure 17.4 The Example Project open in Unity with the Play button highlighted in light blue

Figure 17.5 Position of the Layout pop-up menu and selection of the *2 by 3* layout

1. Choose *2 by 3* from the Layout pop-up menu shown in Figure 17.5. This is the starting point for making your custom layout.

2. Before doing anything else, make the Project pane look a little cleaner. Click on the options pop-up for the Project pane (shown in the blue rectangle in Figure 17.6) and choose *One Column Layout*. This converts the Project pane to the hierarchical list view used throughout this book.

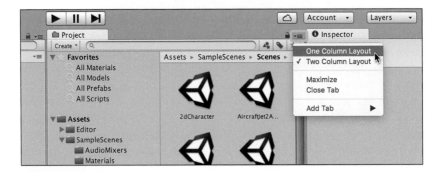

Figure 17.6   Choosing the *One Column Layout* for the Project pane

Unity enables you to both move window panes around and adjust the borders between them. As shown in Figure 17.7, you can move a pane by dragging its tab (the arrow cursor) or adjust a border between panes by dragging the border between them (the left-right resize arrow).

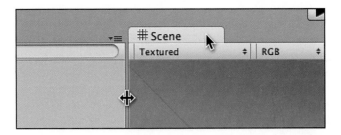

Figure 17.7   Two types of cursors for moving and resizing Unity's window panes

When you drag a pane by its tab, a small ghosted version appears (see Figure 17.8). Some locations cause the pane to snap into place. When this happens, the ghosted version of the tab jumps to the snapped location.

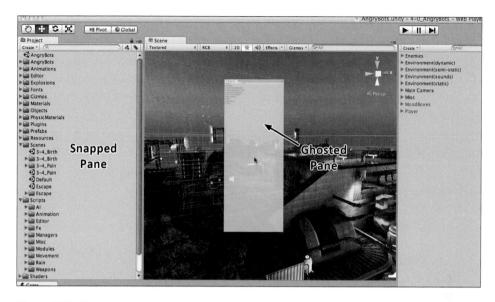

Figure 17.8 Ghosted and snapped panes when moving them around the Unity window

3. Play around with moving the window panes—using dragging and resizing—until your window looks like Figure 17.9.

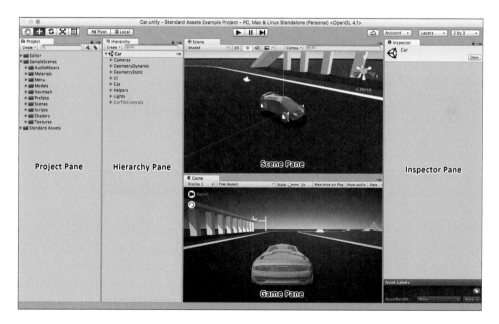

Figure 17.9 Proper layout for the Unity window—but it's still missing something

4. The last thing to add is the *Console* pane. From the menu bar, choose *Window > Console*, and drag the Console pane below the Hierarchy pane. This puts the Console pane below the Hierarchy pane but not below the Project pane.

5. Click the tab at the top of the Project pane and drag it to the right. You should see it snap into position over the left half of the Hierarchy pane. Release the mouse button, and you should see something similar to the final layout shown in Figure 17.10.

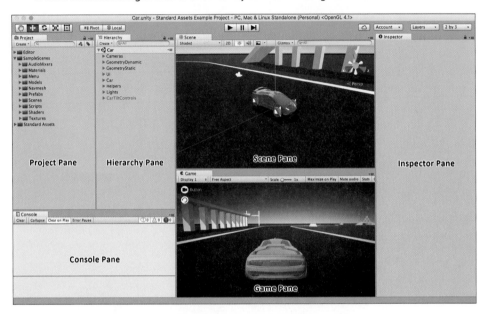

Figure 17.10   Final layout of the Unity window, including the Console pane

6. Now you just need to save this layout in the Layout pop-up menu so that you don't have to go through all that again. Click the *Layout* pop-up menu and choose *Save Layout…*, as shown in Figure 17.11.

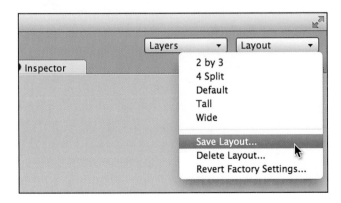

Figure 17.11   Saving the layout

7. Save this layout with the name *Game Dev*, using the technique on your platform that pushes the layout name to the top of the menu. On macOS, that would be putting a space before the *G*. On a Windows machine, that would be putting an underscore before the *G*. By putting a space or an underscore at the beginning of the name, you make sure that this layout is sorted to the top of the menu. Now, any time you need to return to this layout, you can simply choose it from this pop-up menu.

Learning Your Way Around Unity

Before you can really get into coding things, you need to get to know the various window panes that you've just arranged. Refer to Figure 17.10 as you read about each pane:

- **Scene pane**: The Scene pane allows you to navigate around your scene in 3D and to select, move, rotate, and scale objects.

- **Game pane**: The Game pane is where you preview your actual gameplay; it's the window in which you played the Example Project. This pane also shows you the view from the Main Camera in your scene.

- **Hierarchy pane**: The Hierarchy pane shows you every GameObject that is included in your current scene. For now, you can think of each scene as a level of your game. Everything that exists in your scene, from the camera to your player-character, is a GameObject.

- **Project pane**: The Project pane contains all the assets that are part of your project. An asset is any kind of file that is part of your project, including images, 3D models, C# code, text files, sounds, and fonts among many others. The Project pane is a reflection of the contents of the Assets folder within your Unity project folder on your computer hard drive. These assets are not necessarily in your current scene.

- **Inspector pane**: When you click on an asset in the Project pane or a GameObject in the Scene or Hierarchy panes you can see and edit information about it in the Inspector pane.

- **Console pane**: The Console pane enables you to see messages from Unity about errors or bugs in your code as well as messages from yourself that will help you understand the inner workings of your own code.[5] You will use the Console pane extensively in Chapter 19, "Hello World: Your First Program," and Chapter 20, "Variables and Components."

Summary

That's it for setup. Now, let's move on to actually developing! As you've seen in this chapter, Unity can create some pretty stunning visuals and compelling gameplay. In the next chapter, you'll write your first Unity program.

---

5. Unity's `print()` and `Debug.Log()` functions allow you to print messages to the Console pane.

CHAPTER 18

INTRODUCING OUR LANGUAGE: C#

This chapter introduces you to the key features of C# and describes some important reasons why I chose it as the language for this book. It also examines the basic syntax of C#, explaining what is meant by the structure of some simple C# statements.

By the end of this chapter, you will better understand C# and be ready to tackle the more in-depth chapters that follow.

Understanding the Features of C#

As covered in Chapter 16, "Thinking in Digital Systems," programming consists of giving the computer a series of simple commands, and C# is the language through which we will do so. However, many different programming languages exist out there, each of which has benefits and drawbacks. Some of the features of C# are that it is:

- A compiled language
- Managed code
- Strongly typed
- Function based
- Object oriented

Each of these features is described further in the following sections, and each will help you in various ways.

C# Is a Compiled Language

When most people write computer programs, they are not actually writing in a language that the computer itself understands. In fact, each computer chip on the market has a slightly different set of very simple commands that it understands, known as *machine language*. This language is very, very fast for the chip to execute, but it is incredibly difficult for a person to read. For example, the machine language line

```
000000 00001 00010 00110 00000 100000
```

would certainly mean something to the right computer chip, but it means next to nothing to human readers. You might have noticed, however, that every character of that machine code is either a 0 or 1. That's because all the more complex types of data—numbers, letters, and so on—have been converted down to individual *bits* of data (i.e., ones or zeros). If you've ever heard of people programming computers using punch cards, this is exactly what they were doing: For most formats of binary punch cards, physically punching a hole in card stock represented a one, and an unpunched hole represented a zero.

For people to be able to write code more easily, human-readable programming languages—sometimes called *authoring languages*—were created. You can think of an authoring language as an intermediate language meant to act as a go-between from you to the computer. Authoring languages like C# are logical and simple enough for a computer to interpret while also being close enough to written human languages to allow programmers to easily read and understand them.

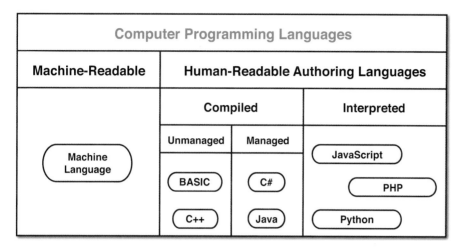

Figure 18.1 A simple taxonomy of programming languages

There is also a major division in authoring languages between *compiled* languages such as BASIC, C++, C#, and Java, and *interpreted* languages such as JavaScript, Perl, PHP, and Python (see Figure 18.1).

In an *interpreted* language, authoring and executing code is a two-step process:

- The programmer writes the code.
- Then, each time any player plays the game, the code is converted from the authoring language to machine language in real time on the player's machine.

The good thing about this is that it enables code portability, because the authoring code can be interpreted specifically for the type of computer on which it is running. For example, the JavaScript of a given web page will run on almost any modern computer regardless of whether the computer is running macOS, Windows, Linux, or one of many mobile operating systems like iOS, Android, Windows Phone, and so on. However, this flexibility also causes the code to execute more slowly due to the time required to interpret the code on the player's computer, the authoring language not being well optimized for the device on which it will run, and a host of other reasons. Because the same interpreted code is run on all devices, optimizing for the specific device on which it happens to be running is impossible. This is the reason why 3D games created in an interpreted language like JavaScript generally run much more slowly than those created in a compiled language, even when running on the same computer.

In a *compiled* language, such as C#, the programming process comprises three separate steps:

- The programmer writes the code in an authoring language like C#.
- A compiler converts the code from the authoring language to a compiled application in machine language for a specific kind of machine.
- The computer executes the compiled application.

This added middle process of *compilation* converts the code from the authoring language into an executable (that is, an application or app) that a computer can run directly without needing an interpreter. Because the compiler has both a complete understanding of the program and a complete understanding of the execution platform on which the program will run, it is able to incorporate many optimizations into the process. In games, these optimizations translate directly into higher frame rates, more detailed graphics, and more responsive interactions. Most high-budget games are authored in a compiled language because of this optimization and speed advantage, but this means that a different executable must be compiled for each execution platform.

In many cases, compiled authoring languages are only suited for specific execution platforms. For instance, *Objective-C* is Apple Computer's proprietary authoring language for making applications for both macOS and iOS. This language is based on C (a predecessor of C++), but it includes a number of features that are unique to macOS or iOS development. Similarly, XNA was a flavor of C# developed by Microsoft specifically to enable students to author games for both Windows-based personal computers and the Xbox 360.

As mentioned in Chapter 17, "Introducing the Unity Development Environment," Unity uses either C# or a JavaScript flavor named UnityScript to create games. Either of these languages are compiled into a Common Intermediate Language (CIL) in an additional compilation step, and that CIL is then compiled to target any number of platforms, from iOS to Android to macOS, Windows PC, game consoles such as the PlayStation and Xbox, and even interpreted languages such as WebGL (a specific form of JavaScript used in web pages). This additional CIL step ensures that Unity programs can be compiled across many platforms regardless of whether they are written in C# or UnityScript.

The ability to write once and compile anywhere is not unique to Unity, but it is one of Unity Technologies' core goals for the Unity game engine, and it is better integrated into Unity than any other game development software I have seen. However, as a game designer, you will still need to think seriously about the design differences between a game meant for a handheld phone controlled by touch, a game meant to run on a personal computer controlled by mouse and keyboard, or a game built for virtual or augmented reality, so you will usually have slightly different code for the different platforms.

C# Is Managed Code

More traditional compiled languages such as BASIC, C++, and Objective-C require programmers to directly manage computer memory, obliging a programmer to manually allocate and de-allocate memory any time she creates or destroys a variable.[1] If a programmer doesn't

---

1. Memory allocation is the process of setting aside a certain amount of Random-Access Memory (RAM) in the computer to enable it to hold a chunk of data. While computers now often have hundreds of gigabytes (GB) of hard drive space, they still usually have less than 20GB of RAM. RAM is *much* faster than hard drive memory, so all applications pull assets like images and sounds from the hard drive, allocate some space for them in RAM, and then store them in RAM for fast access.

manually de-allocate RAM in these languages, her programs will have a "memory leak" and eventually allocate more than the maximum amount of the computer's RAM, causing it to crash.

Luckily for us, C# is *managed code*, which means that the allocation and de-allocation of memory is handled automatically.[2] You can still cause memory leaks in managed code, but it is more difficult to do so accidentally.

C# Is Strongly Typed

Later chapters cover variables in more detail, but there are a couple of things that you should know about them now. First, a *variable* is just a named container for a value. For instance, in algebra, you might have seen an expression like this:

```
x = 5
```

In this one line, you have created a variable, named it x, and assigned it the value 5. Later, if I asked you the value of $x+2$, I'm sure you could tell me that the answer is 7 because you remember that x was holding the value 5 and know to add 2 to that value. That is exactly what variables do for you in programming.

In most interpreted languages, like JavaScript, a single variable can hold any kind of data. The variable x could hold the number 5 one minute, an image the next, and a sound file thereafter. This capability for a single variable to hold any type of value is what is meant when we say that a programming language is *weakly typed*.

C#, in contrast, is *strongly typed*. This means that when you initially create a variable, you must tell it at that moment what kind of value it can hold:

```
int x = 5;
```

In the preceding statement, you have created a variable named x that it is exclusively allowed to hold `int` values (that is, positive or negative numbers without a decimal point), and assigned it the integer value 5. Although it might seem like strong typing would make programming more difficult, the use of strong typing enables the compiler to make several optimizations and makes it possible for the authoring environment, MonoDevelop, to perform real-time syntax checking on the code you write (much like the grammar checking that is performed by Microsoft Word). This also enables and enhances code-completion, a technology in MonoDevelop that enables it to predict the words you're typing and provide you with valid completion options based on the other code that you've written. With code-completion, if you're typing and see MonoDevelop suggest the correct completion of the word, you simply press Tab to accept the suggestion. When you've become used to this, it can save you hundreds of keystrokes every minute.

---

2. One disadvantage of managed code is that it makes controlling exactly when memory is deallocated and reclaimed very difficult. Instead, memory is automatically reclaimed in a process called *garbage collection*. This can sometimes lead to a hitch in the frame rate of a game on less powerful devices such as cell phones, but it's usually not noticeable.

C# Is Function-Based

In the early days of programming, a program was composed of a single series of commands. These programs were run directly from beginning to end much like the directions you would give to a friend who was trying to drive to your house:

1. From school, head north on Vermont.
2. Head west on I-10 for about 7.5 miles.
3. At the intersection with I-405, take the 405 south for 2 miles.
4. Take the exit for Venice Blvd.
5. Turn right onto Sawtelle Blvd.
6. My place is just north of Venice on Sawtelle.

As authoring languages improved, repeatable sections were added to programming in the form of things like *loops* (a section of code that repeats itself) and *subroutines* (an otherwise inaccessible section of code that is jumped to, executed, and then returned from).

The development of *procedural languages* (i.e., those that make use of functions)[3] allowed programmers to name chunks of code and thereby encapsulate functionality (that is, group a series of actions under a single function name). For example, if in addition to giving someone detailed directions to your house as described in the preceding list, you also asked him to pick up some milk for you on the way, he would know that if he saw a grocery store on the way, he should stop the car, get out, walk to find milk, pay for it, return to his car, and continue on his way to your house. Because your friend already knows how to buy milk, you just need to request that he do so rather than giving him explicit instructions for every tiny step. This could look something like this:

"If you see a store on the way, could you please `BuySomeMilk()`?"

This statement encapsulates all the instructions to buy milk into the single function named `BuySomeMilk()`. You can do the same thing in any procedural language. When the computer is processing C# and encounters a function name followed by parentheses, it will *call* that function (that is, it will execute all the actions encapsulated in the function). You will learn much more about functions in Chapter 24, "Functions and Parameters."

The other fantastic thing about functions is that after you have written the code for the function `BuySomeMilk()` one time, you should never have to write it again. Even if you're working on a completely different program, you can often copy and paste functions like `BuySomeMilk()` and reuse them without having to write the whole thing again from scratch. The C# script named `Utils.cs` that you will see in several of the tutorials in this book includes several reusable functions.

---

3. There are also *functional languages* like Lisp, Scheme, Mathematica (Wolfram Language), and Haskell, but for these functional languages, "functional" means something different than the capabilities we have to write functions in C#.

C# Is Object-Oriented

Many years after functions were invented, the idea of *Object-Oriented Programming* (OOP) was created. In OOP, not only functionality but also data are encapsulated together into something called an *object*, or more correctly a *class*. This is covered extensively in Chapter 26, "Classes," but here's a metaphor for now.

Consider a group of various animals. Each animal has specific information that it knows about itself. Some examples of this data could be its species, age, size, emotional state, level of hunger, current location, and so on. Each animal also has certain things that it can do: eat, move, breath, etc. The data about each animal are analogous to variables in code, and the actions that the animal can perform are analogous to functions.

Before OOP, an animal represented in code could hold information (i.e., variables) but could not perform any actions. Those actions were performed by functions that were not directly connected to the animal. A programmer could write a function named Move() that could move any kind of animal, but she would have to write several lines of code in that function that determined what kind of animal it was and what type of movement was appropriate for it. For example, dogs walk, fish swim, and birds fly. Any time the programmer added a new animal, she was required to change Move() to accommodate the new type of locomotion, and Move() would thereby grow larger and more complex with the addition of each new animal.

Object orientation changed all of this by introducing the ideas of *classes* and *class inheritance*. A *class* combines both variables and functions into one whole object. In OOP, instead of having a huge Move() function that can handle any animal, a much smaller and more specific Move() function is attached to each animal. This eliminates the need for you to expand Move() every time you add a new type of animal, and it eliminates the need for all the type-checking of animal types in the non-OOP version of Move(). Instead, each new animal class is given its own small Move() function when it is created.

Object orientation also includes the concept of *class inheritance*. This enables classes to have *subclasses* that are more specific, and it allows the subclasses to either inherit or override functions in their *superclasses*. Through inheritance, a single Animal class could be created that included declarations of all the data types that are shared by all animals. This class would also have a Move() function, but it would be nonspecific. In subclasses of Animal, like Dog or Fish, the function Move() could be overridden to cause specific behavior like walking or swimming. This is a key element of modern game programming, and it will serve you well when you want to create something like a basic Enemy class that is then further specified into various subclasses for each individual enemy type that you want to create.

Reading and Understanding C# Syntax

Just like any other language, C# has a specific syntax that you must follow. Take a look at these example statements in English:

- The dog barked at the squirrel.
- At the squirrel the dog barked.
- The dog at the squirrel. barked
- barked The dog at the squirrel.

Each of these English statements has the same words and punctuation, but they are in a different order, and the punctuation and capitalization is changed. Because you are familiar with the English language, you can easily tell that the first is correct and the others are just wrong. Another way of examining this is to look at it more abstractly as just the parts of speech:

- [Subject] [verb] [object].
- [Object] [subject] [verb].
- [Subject] [object]. [verb]
- [verb] [Subject] [object].

When parts of speech are rearranged like this, doing so alters the *syntax* of the sentence, and the latter three sentences are incorrect because they have *syntax errors*.

Just like any language, C# has specific syntax rules for how statements must be written. Let's examine this simple statement in detail:

```
int x = 5;
```

As explained earlier, this statement does several things:

- Declares a variable named x of the type int

    Any time a statement starts with a variable type, the second word of the statement becomes the name of a new variable of that type (see Chapter 20, "Variables and Components"). This is called *declaring* a variable.

- Assigns x the value 5

    The = symbol is used to *assign* values to variables (which is also called *initializing* a variable if it is the first time that any value has been assigned to the variable). When you do this, the variable name is on the left, and the value assigned is on the right.

- Ends with a semicolon (;)

    Every simple statement in C# must end with a semicolon (;). This is similar in use to the period at the end of sentences in the English language.

> **note**
>
> Why not end C# statements with a period? Computer programming languages are meant to be very clear. The period is not used at the end of statements in C# because it is already in use in numbers as a decimal point (for example, the period in 3.14159). For clarity, the only use of the semicolon in C# is to end statements.

Now, let's add a second simple statement:

```
int x = 5;
int y = x * ( 3 + x );
```

The second line does the following:

- Declares a variable named `y` of the type `int`
- Adds `3 + x` (which is 3 + 5, for a result of 8)

  Just like in algebra, *order of operations* follows parentheses first, meaning that `3+x` is evaluated first because it is surrounded by parentheses. The sum is 8 because the value of `x` was set to `5` in the previous statement. In Appendix B, "Useful Concepts," you can read the section *Operator Precedence and Order of Operations,* to learn more about order of operations in C#, but the main thing to remember for your programs is that if you have *any* doubt about the order in which things will occur, you should use parentheses to remove that doubt (and increase the readability of your code).

- Multiplies `x * 8` (x is 5, so the result is 40)

  If there had been no parentheses, the order of operations would have handled multiplication and division *before* addition and subtraction. This would have resulted in `x * 3 + 5`, which would become `5 * 3 + 5`, then `15 + 5`, and finally `20`.

- Assigns the value `40` to `y`
- Ends with a semicolon (`;`)

This chapter finishes with a breakdown of one final couplet of C# statements. In this example, the statements are now numbered. Line numbers can make referencing a specific line in code much simpler, and my hope is that they will make it easier for you to read and understand the code in this book when you're typing it into your computer. The important thing to remember is that **you do not need to type the line numbers** into MonoDevelop. MonoDevelop automatically numbers (and renumbers) your lines as you work:

```
1    string greeting = "Hello World!";
2    print( greeting );
```

These two statements deal with *strings* (a series of characters like a word or sentence) rather than integers. The first statement (numbered 1):

- Declares a variable named `greeting` of the type `string`

  `string` is another type of variable just like `int`.

- Assigns the string value `"Hello World!"` to `greeting`

  The double quotes around `"Hello World!"` tell C# that the characters in between them are to be treated as a *string literal* and not interpreted by the compiler to have any additional meaning. Putting the string literal `"x = 10"` in your code will **not** assign the value `10` to `x` because the compiler knows to ignore all string literals between quotes and does not try to interpret them as C# code.

- Ends with a semicolon (`;`)

The second statement (numbered 2):

- Calls the function `print()`

  As discussed earlier, functions are named collections of actions. When a function is *called*, the function executes the actions it contains. As you might expect, `print()` contains actions that will output a string to the Console pane. Any time you see a word in code followed by parentheses, it is either calling or defining a function. Writing the name of a function followed by parentheses calls the function, causing that functionality to execute. You'll see an example of defining a function in the next chapter.

- Passes `greeting` to `print()`

  Some functions just do things and don't require parameters, but many require that you *pass* something in. Any variable placed between the parentheses of a function call is *passed* into that function as an *argument*. In this case, the string `greeting` is passed into the function `print()`, and the characters `Hello World!` are output to the Console pane.

- Ends with a semicolon (`;`)

  Every simple statement ends with a semicolon.

Summary

Now that you understand a little about C# and about Unity, it's time to put the two together into your first program. The next chapter takes you through the process of creating a new Unity project, making a few C# scripts, adding some simple code to those scripts, and manipulating 3D GameObjects.

CHAPTER 19

HELLO WORLD: YOUR FIRST PROGRAM

Welcome to coding.

By the end of this chapter, you'll have created your own new project and written your first bits of code. We start with the classic "Hello World" project that has been a traditional first program to write in a new language since long before I started coding, and then we move on to something with more of a Unity flair to it.

Creating a New Project

Now that you have the Unity window set up properly (from the previous chapter), it's time to start writing your own code. Not surprisingly, you start this by creating a new project.

Appendix A, "Standard Project Setup Procedure," contains detailed instructions that show you how to set up Unity projects for the chapters in this book. At the start of each project, you will see a sidebar like the one here. Please follow the directions in the sidebar to create the project for this chapter.

SET UP THE PROJECT FOR THIS CHAPTER

Following the standard project setup procedure in Appendix A, create a new project in Unity.

- **Project name:** Hello World

- **Scene name:** (none yet)

- **C# Script names:** (none yet)

You should read the whole procedure in Appendix A; but for now, you only need to create the project. You learn to create the scene and C# scripts as part of this chapter.

When you create a project in Unity, you're actually making a folder that will hold all the files that make up your project. When Unity has finished creating the project, the new project comes with an open scene containing only a *Main Camera* and a *Directional Light* in the Project pane. Before doing anything else, save your scene by choosing *File > Save Scene* from the menu bar. Unity automatically chooses the correct place to save the scene, so just name it *_Scene_0* and click *Save*.[1] Now your saved scene appears in the Project pane.

Right-click on the background of the Project pane and choose *Reveal in Finder* (or *Show in Explorer* for Windows) as shown in Figure 19.1.

---

1. The underscore (_) at the beginning of the scene name *_Scene_0* causes the scene to be sorted to the top of the Project pane (on macOS).

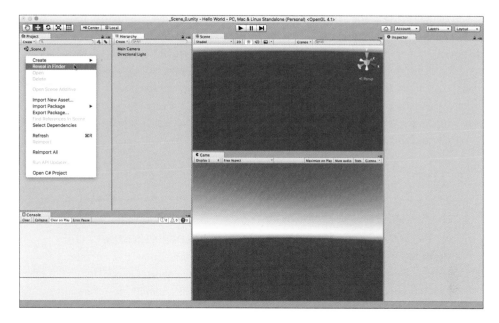

Figure 19.1 The blank canvas of a new Unity project (showing Reveal in Finder in the Project pane pop-up menu)

> **tip**
>
> Performing a right-click on a mouse or trackpad in macOS is not as straightforward as it is on a Windows PC. For information on how to do so, check out the *Right-Click on Macintosh* section of Appendix B, "Useful Concepts."

Selecting *Reveal in Finder* opens a Finder window (or Explorer window) showing you the contents of your Project folder (see Figure 19.2).

Figure 19.2 The project folder for Hello World as it appears in the macOS Finder

As you can see in the image in Figure 19.2, the *Assets* folder holds everything that appears in the Project pane inside of Unity. In theory, you can use the Assets folder and the Project pane interchangeably (for example, if you drop an image into the Assets folder, it appears in the Project pane and vice versa), but I highly recommend working exclusively with the Project pane rather than the Assets folder. Making changes in the Assets folder directly can occasionally lead to problems, and the Project pane is generally safer. In addition, it is very important that you not touch the *Library*, *ProjectSettings*, or *Temp* folders. Doing so could cause unexpected behavior from Unity and could possibly damage your project.

Switch back to Unity now.

> ## warning
>
> **NEVER CHANGE THE NAME OF YOUR PROJECT FOLDER WHILE UNITY IS RUNNING**   If you change the name of the project folder or move it to another location while Unity is running, Unity will crash in a very ungraceful way. Unity does a lot of file management in the background while it's running, and changing a folder name on it will almost always cause a crash. If you want to change your project folder name, quit Unity, change the folder name, and launch Unity again.

Making a New C# Script

It is time. Now you're going to write your first chunk of code (later chapters cover a lot more about C#, but for now, just copy what you see here):

1. Click the *Create* button in the Project pane and choose *Create > C# Script* (as shown in Figure 19.3). This adds a new script to the Project pane, and its name will automatically be highlighted for you to change.

2. Name this script *HelloWorld* (make sure there's no space between the two words) and press Return to set the name.

3. Double-click the name or the icon of the HelloWorld script (in the Project pane) to launch MonoDevelop, our C# editor. When you first open it, your script should already look exactly like the one in Figure 19.3 except for line 8.

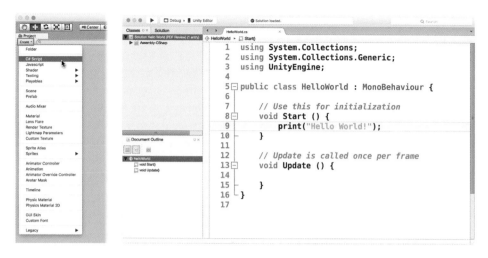

Figure 19.3 Creating a new C# script and viewing that script in MonoDevelop

4. On line 9 of this script, press Tab twice, and enter the code `print ("Hello World");`
    as shown in the code listing that follows. Make sure to spell and capitalize everything cor-
    rectly and to put a semicolon (;) at the end of the line.

Your HelloWorld script should now look exactly like the following code listing. In code listings
throughout the book, anything new that you need to type or modify is in **bold weight**, and
code that is already there is in normal weight.

Each line in the code listing also has a line number preceding it. As you can see in Figure 19.3,
MonoDevelop automatically shows you line numbers for your code, so you do not need to type
them yourself. The line numbers are just here in the book to help make the code listings easier
to read.

```
 1 using System.Collections;
 2 using System.Collections.Generic;
 3 using UnityEngine;
 4
 5 public class HelloWorld : MonoBehaviour {
 6
 7     // Use this for initialization
 8     void Start () {
 9         print("Hello World!");
10     }
11
12     // Update is called once per frame
13     void Update () {
14
15     }
16 }
```

> **note**
>
> Your version of MonoDevelop might automatically add extra spaces in some parts of the code. For example, it might have added a space between `print` and `(` in line 9 of the `Start()` function. This is okay, and you shouldn't be too concerned about it. In general, though capitalization matters tremendously to programming, spaces are more flexible. A series of several spaces (or several line breaks/returns) is interpreted by the C# compiler as just one space, so you can add extra spaces and returns if it makes your code more readable (though extra returns might make your line numbers different from those in the code listings).
>
> You should also not be too upset if your line numbers differ from the ones in the examples. As long as the code is the same, the line numbers don't matter.

5. Now, save this script by choosing *File > Save* from the MonoDevelop menu bar and switch back to Unity.

This next part's a bit tricky, but you'll soon be used to it because you will do it so often in Unity.

6. Click and hold on the name of the *HelloWorld* script in the Project pane, drag it over on top of the *Main Camera* in the scene Hierarchy pane, and release the mouse button as shown in Figure 19.4. When you drag the script, the words *HelloWorld (Monoscript)* will follow the mouse, and when you release the mouse button over *Main Camera*, the *HelloWorld (Monoscript)* words will disappear.

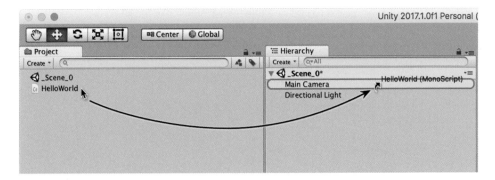

Figure 19.4 Attaching the HelloWorld C# script to the Main Camera in the Hierarchy pane

Dragging the HelloWorld script onto Main Camera *attaches* the script to Main Camera as a *component*. All objects that appear in the scene Hierarchy pane (for example, Main Camera) are known as *GameObjects*, and GameObjects are made up of *components*. If you now click Main Camera in the Hierarchy pane, you should see *HelloWorld (Script)* listed as one of Main Camera's components in the Inspector pane. As you can see in Figure 19.5, the Inspector pane shows several components of the Main Camera, including its Transform, Camera, GUILayer, Flare Layer,

Audio Listener, and HelloWorld (Script). Later chapters cover GameObjects and components in much more detail.[2]

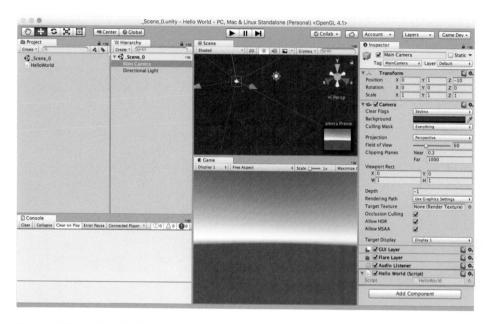

Figure 19.5 The HelloWorld script now appears in the Inspector pane for Main Camera (highlighted in red)

7. Now, click the *Play* button (the triangle facing to the right at the top of the Unity window) and watch the magic!

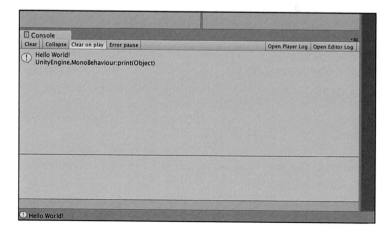

Figure 19.6 Hello World! printed to the Console pane

---

2. If you accidentally attached more than one *HelloWorld (Script)* component to Main Camera, you can always remove any extras by clicking the small gear-shaped icon to the right of the "HelloWorld (Script)" name and choosing Remove Component from the pop-up menu.

The script printed *Hello World!* to the Console pane, as shown in Figure 19.6. Notice that it also printed *Hello World!* to the small gray bar at the bottom-left corner of the screen. This probably isn't the most magical thing that's ever happened in your life, but you have to start somewhere. As a wise old man once said, you've taken your first step into a larger world.

`Start()` Versus `Update()`

Now try moving the `print()` function call from the `Start()` method to the `Update()` method.

1. Go back to MonoDevelop and edit your code as shown in the following code listing.

```
1 using System.Collections;
2 using System.Collections.Generic;
3 using UnityEngine;
4
5 public class HelloWorld : MonoBehaviour {
6
7    // Use this for initialization
8    void Start () {
9        // print("Hello World!"); // This line is now ignored.
10    }
11
12    // Update is called once per frame
13    void Update () {
14        print("Hello World!");
15    }
16 }
```

Adding the two forward slashes (//) to the beginning of line 9 converts everything on line 9 that follows the slashes to a *comment*. Comments are completely ignored by the computer and are used to either disable code (as you are now doing to line 9) or to leave messages for other humans reading the code (as you can see on lines 7 and 12). Adding two slashes before a line (as you've done to line 9) is referred to as *commenting out* the line. Be sure to type the statement `print("Hello World!");` into line 14 to make it part of the `Update()` function.

2. Save the script (replacing the original version) and try clicking the Unity *Play* button again.

You'll see that *Hello World!* is now printed many, many times in rapid succession (see Figure 19.7). You can click the *Play* button again to stop execution now, and you'll see that Unity stops generating *Hello World!* messages.

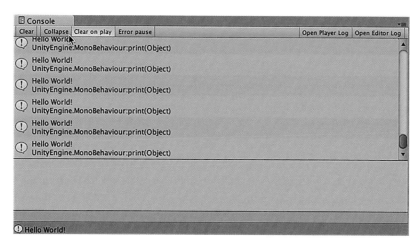

Figure 19.7 `Update()` causes *Hello World!* to be printed once every frame

`Start()` and `Update()` are both special functions in Unity's version of C#. `Start()` is called once on the first frame that an object exists, whereas `Update()` is called every frame,[3] hence the single message of Figure 19.6 versus the multiple messages of Figure 19.7. Unity has a whole list of these special functions that are called at various times. I cover many of them later in the book.

> ### tip
>
> In Figure 19.7, you can see that the same *Hello World!* message is repeated many times. If you select the *Collapse* button of the Console pane (indicated by the mouse arrow in Figure 19.7) all of these *Hello World!* messages will be collapsed to a single line with a count of how many times that same message has been sent to the Console pane. This might make it easier for you to pick out any unique messages that post.

Making Things More Interesting

Now, it is time to add more Unity style to your first program. In this example, you're going to create many, many copies of a cube. Each of these cube copies will independently bounce around and react to physics. This exercise demonstrates both the speed at which Unity runs and the ease with which it enables you to create content.

---

3. As discussed earlier in the book (particularly in Chapter 16, "Thinking in Digital Systems"), a frame occurs every time that Unity redraws the screen, which typically happens anywhere from 30 to 200 times per second.

Start by creating a new scene:

1. Choose *File > New Scene* from the menu bar. You won't notice much of a difference because you didn't really have much in _Scene_0 other than the script on the camera, but if you click the Main Camera, you can see that it no longer has a script attached, and the Unity window's title bar has changed from _Scene_0.unity - to *Untitled -*.

2. As always, the first thing you should do is save this new scene. Choose *File > Save Scene* from the menu bar and name this _Scene_1.

3. Choose *GameObject > 3D Object > Cube* from the menu bar to place a GameObject named *Cube* in the Scene pane (and in the Hierarchy pane). If it's difficult to see Cube in the Scene pane, try double-clicking its name in the Hierarchy pane, which should focus the scene on Cube. For more information, read the "Changing the Scene View" sidebar later in this chapter that covers how to manipulate the view of the Scene pane.

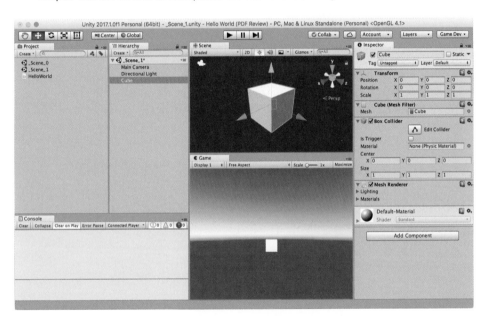

Figure 19.8 The new Cube GameObject visible in the Scene and Hierarchy panes

4. Click Cube in the Hierarchy pane, and you should see it selected in the Scene pane and see its components appear in the Inspector pane (see Figure 19.8). The primary purpose of the Inspector pane is to enable you to view and edit the components that make up any GameObject. This Cube GameObject has Transform, Mesh Filter, Box Collider, and Mesh Renderer components:

   ■ **Transform:** The *Transform* component sets the position, rotation, and scale of the GameObject. This is the only component that is required for every GameObject.

While looking at this, make sure that the Cube's Position X, Y, and Z values are set to 0.

- **Cube (Mesh Filter):** The *Mesh Filter* component gives the GameObject its three-dimensional shape, which is modeled as a mesh composed of triangles. 3D models in games are generally a surface that is hollow inside. Unlike a real egg (which is filled with a yolk and albumen), a 3D model of an egg would just be a mesh simulating an empty eggshell. The Mesh Filter component attaches a 3D model to the GameObject. In the case of Cube, the Mesh Filter is using a simple 3D cube model that is built into Unity, but you can also import complex 3D model assets into the Project pane to bring more complex meshes into your game.

- **Box Collider:** *Collider* components enable a GameObject to interact with other objects in the physics simulation that Unity runs. The PhysX physics engine in Unity uses several different kinds of colliders, including Sphere, Capsule, Box, and Mesh (in increasing order of computational complexity; i.e., a *Mesh Collider* is much more difficult for the computer to calculate than a *Box Collider*). A GameObject with a collider component (and no *Rigidbody* component) acts as an immovable object in space that other GameObjects can run into.

- **Mesh Renderer:** Whereas the Mesh Filter provides the actual geometry of the GameObject, the *Mesh Renderer* component makes that geometry visible. Without a renderer, nothing in Unity will appear on screen. Renderers work with the Main Camera to convert the 3D geometry of the Mesh Filter into the pixels you actually see on screen.

5. Now you're going to add one more component to this GameObject: a *Rigidbody*. With the Cube still selected in the hierarchy, choose *Component > Physics > Rigidbody* from the menu bar, and you'll see a Rigidbody component added to the Inspector:

   - **Rigidbody:** The *Rigidbody* component tells Unity that you want physics to be simulated for this GameObject. This includes physical forces like gravity, friction, collisions, and drag. A Rigidbody enables a GameObject with a Collider component to move through space. Without a Rigidbody, even if the GameObject is moved by adjusting its transform, the Collider component of the GameObject will not move reliably. You should attach a Rigidbody component to any GameObject that you want to both move and properly collide with other colliders.

6. Click the *Play* button; the box falls due to gravity.

All the physical simulations in Unity are based on the metric system. This means that:

- 1 unit of distance = 1 meter (for example, the units for the position of a transform).
- 1 unit of mass = 1 kilogram (for example, the units of mass of a Rigidbody).
- The default gravity of $-9.8 = 9.8$ m/s^2 in the downward (negative y) direction.
- An average human character is about 2 units (2 meters) tall.

7. Click the *Play* button again to stop the simulation.

Your scene came with a Directional Light already included. This is why the box is lit so brightly. For now, this is all you need, you'll learn more about lights in later chapters.

Making a Prefab

It's time to make Cube into a *prefab*. A prefab is a reusable element in a project that can be instantiated (cloned into existence) any number of times. You can think of a prefab as a mold for a GameObject, and each GameObject made from that prefab is called an *instance* of the prefab (hence the word *instantiate*). To make the prefab, click *Cube* in the Hierarchy pane, drag it over to the Project pane, and release the mouse button (see Figure 19.9).

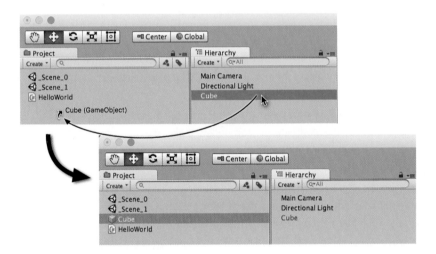

Figure 19.9 Making Cube into a prefab

You'll see that a couple of things have just happened:

- A prefab named *Cube* has been created in the Project pane. You can tell it's a prefab by the blue cube icon next to it. (The prefab icon is always a cube regardless of the shape of the prefab itself.)
- The name of the Cube GameObject in the Hierarchy has turned blue. If a GameObject has a blue name in the Hierarchy it means that that GameObject is an instance of a prefab (which is like a copy made from the prefab mold).

Just for the sake of clarity, rename the Cube prefab in the Project pane to *Cube Prefab*.

1. Click once on the *Cube* prefab to select it, and then click a second time to rename it (you can also try pressing Return (or F2 on PC) after it's selected to rename it) and then change the name to *Cube Prefab*. You'll see that because the instance in the Hierarchy panel had

the default name *Cube*, its name changes as well. If you had renamed the instance in the Hierarchy to be different from the name of the prefab, the instance name would not have been affected.

2. Now that the prefab is set up, you don't actually need the instance of Cube in the scene any more. Click *Cube Prefab* in the Hierarchy pane (not the Project pane!). Choose *Edit > Delete* from the menu bar; the cube disappears from your scene.

It's time to get your hands dirty with some more code:

3. Choose *Assets > Create > C# Script* from the menu bar and rename the newly created script *CubeSpawner* (making sure that it has two capital letters and no spaces in the name).

4. Double-click the *CubeSpawner* script to open MonoDevelop, add the bolded code shown here, and save it:

```
1 using System.Collections;
2 using System.Collections.Generic;
3 using UnityEngine;
4
5 public class CubeSpawner : MonoBehaviour {
6     public GameObject       cubePrefabVar;
7
8     // Use this for initialization
9     void Start () {
10         Instantiate( cubePrefabVar );
11     }
12
13     // Update is called once per frame
14     void Update () {
15
16     }
17 }
```

note

In addition to adding spaces—as was mentioned in an earlier note—some versions of MonoDevelop also remove extra spaces when you add the semicolon to the end of a line or when you press Return/Enter after doing so. That's okay as well. In my code listings, you'll often see lines—like line 6 in the preceding code listing—where I have added tabs before the name of a variable/field (e.g., `cubePrefabVar`). I do this because I think lining up all the field names makes it easier to read, but sometimes as you're typing it, MonoDevelop will remove those extra spaces or tabs that cause the alignment. Don't worry about this; the presence or lack of those extra spaces won't affect the code at all.

5. As with the previous script, you must attach this script to a GameObject in the scene for the code of this script to be executed. In Unity, drag the *CubeSpawner* script over to *Main Camera* as shown in Figure 19.4.

6. Click *Main Camera* in the Hierarchy pane. You'll see that a *Cube Spawner (Script)* component has been added to the Main Camera GameObject (see Figure 19.10).

Figure 19.10 The CubeSpawner script component in the Inspector pane for Main Camera

You can also see a variable called *Cube Prefab Var* in this component (though it really should be cubePrefabVar, as explained in the nearby warning). That comes from the `public GameObject cubePrefabVar;` statement you typed on line 6. In general, if a variable of a script is labeled `"public"`, it will appear in the Inspector pane.

> ## warning
>
> **VARIABLE NAMES LOOK DIFFERENT IN THE INSPECTOR**   Someone at Unity thought it would look nice to change the capitalization and spacing of variable names in the Inspector pane. I have no idea why this has lasted into the current version, but it means that your variable names like `cubePrefabVar` will incorrectly appear in the Inspector as *Cube Prefab Var*. Be careful to always refer to your variable names properly in your programming and please ignore the strange capitalization and spacing that you see in the Inspector. Throughout the book, I refer to variables by their proper name in code rather than the names that appear in the Inspector.

7. As you can see in the Inspector, `cubePrefabVar` currently has no value assigned. Click the circular target to the right of the `cubePrefabVar` value (as shown by the arrow cursor in Figure 19.10) to open the *Select GameObject* dialog box from which you can select a prefab to assign to this variable. Make sure that the *Assets* tab is selected. (The Assets tab shows GameObjects in your Project pane, whereas the Scene tab shows GameObjects in your Hierarchy.) Double-click *Cube Prefab* to select it (see Figure 19.11).

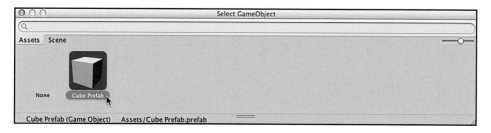

Figure 19.11 Selecting *Cube Prefab* for the `cubePrefabVar` variable of the CubeSpawner script

8. Now you can see in the Inspector that the value of cubePrefabVar is *Cube Prefab* from the Project pane. To double-check this, click the value *Cube Prefab* in the Inspector, and you will see that *Cube Prefab* is highlighted yellow in the Project pane.

9. Click the *Play* button. You'll see that a single *Cube Prefab(Clone)* GameObject is instantiated in the Hierarchy. Just like you saw in the Hello World script, the `Start()` function is called once, and it creates a single instance (or clone) of the Cube Prefab.

10. Now switch to MonoDevelop, comment out the `Instantiate( cubePrefabVar )` call on line 10 in the `Start()` function, and add an `Instantiate( cubePrefabVar );` statement to line 15 in the `Update()` function, as shown in the following code.

```
1 using System.Collections;
2 using System.Collections.Generic;
3 using UnityEngine;
4
5 public class CubeSpawner : MonoBehaviour {
6     public GameObject        cubePrefabVar;
7
8     // Use this for initialization
9     void Start () {
10         // Instantiate( cubePrefabVar );
11     }
12
13     // Update is called once per frame
14     void Update () {
15         Instantiate( cubePrefabVar );
16     }
17 }
```

11. Save the CubeSpawner script, switch back to Unity, and click *Play* again. As shown in Figure 19.12, this gives you cubes galore.[4]

---

4. You might be wondering why these cubes are flying all over the place rather than falling straight down. If so, good question! This is happening because the cubes spawn right on top of each other, and the PhysX physics system decides that it needs to move them away from each other (because Unity Colliders should not be able to occupy the same space), so it gives them a velocity that causes them to move away from each other quickly.

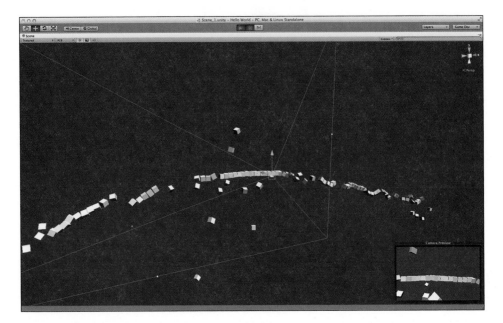

Figure 19.12 Creating a new instance of the CubePrefab every `Update()` quickly adds up to a lot of cubes!

This is an example of the power of Unity. Very quickly, you were able to get up to speed and make something cool and interesting. Now, add some more objects to the scene for the cubes to interact with:

1. Click *Play* again to stop playback.

2. In the Hierarchy, click the *Create* pop-up menu and choose *3D Object > Cube*. Rename this cube *Ground*.

3. With the Ground object selected in the Scene pane or Hierarchy pane, press the W, E, or R to translate (move), rotate, or scale the GameObject. This shows *gizmos* (the arrows, circles, and such shown around the cube in Figure 19.13) around Ground.

In translation (W) mode, clicking and dragging on one of the arrows moves the cube exclusively along the axis of that arrow (X, Y, or Z). The colored elements of the rotation and scale gizmos lock the transformation to a specific axis in similar ways. See the "Changing the Scene View" sidebar for information about how to use the hand tool shown in Figure 19.13.

4. Try moving Ground to a Y position of –4 and setting its scale in the X and Z dimensions to 10. Throughout the book, I suggest positions, rotations, and scales using this format.

    Ground (Cube)   P:[0, –4, 0]   R:[0, 0, 0]   S:[10, 1, 10]

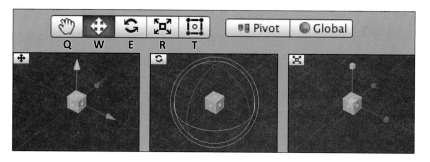

Figure 19.13 The translate (position), rotate, and scale gizmos. Q, W, E, R, and T are the keys that select each tool. The T tool is used for positioning 2D and GUI GameObjects.

Ground here is the name of the GameObject, and *(Cube)* is the type of the GameObject. *P:[0, –4, 0]* means to set the X position to 0, the Y position to –4, and the Z position to 0. Similarly, *R:[0, 0, 0]* means to keep the X, Y, and Z rotations all set to 0. *S:[10, 1, 10]* means to set the X scale to 10, the Y scale to 1, and the Z scale to 10. You can either use the tools and gizmos to make these changes or just type them into the Transform component of the GameObject's Inspector.

Feel free to play around with this and add more objects. The instances of Cube Prefab will bounce off of the *static* objects that you put into the scene (see Figure 19.14). As long as you don't add a Rigidbody to any of the new shapes, they should be static (i.e., solid and immovable). When you're done, be sure to save your scene!

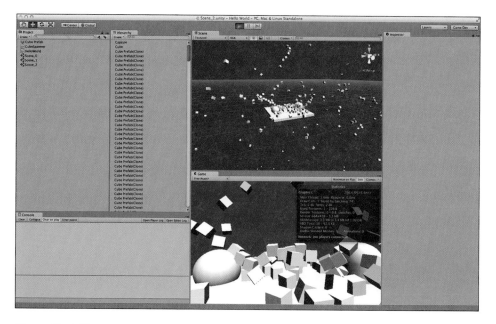

Figure 19.14 The scene with static shapes added

CHANGING THE SCENE VIEW

The first tool on the toolbar shown in Figure 19.13—known as the *hand tool*—is used to manipulate the view shown in the Scene pane. The Scene pane has its own invisible *scene camera* that is different from the Main Camera in the Hierarchy. The hand tool has several different abilities. Select the hand tool (by either clicking it or pressing Q on your keyboard) and try the following:

- Left-dragging (that is, clicking and dragging using the left mouse button) in the Scene pane moves the position of the scene camera without changing the position of any of the objects in the scene. To be technical, the scene camera is moved in a plane perpendicular to the direction that the camera is facing (that is, perpendicular to the camera's forward vector).

- Right-dragging in the Scene pane rotates the scene camera to look in the direction of your drag. The scene camera stays in the same position when right-dragging.

- Holding the Option key (or Alt key on a PC) changes the cursor over the Scene pane from a hand to an eye, and left-dragging with the Option key held causes the Scene view to rotate around objects in the Scene pane (this is known as orbiting the camera around the scene). When Option+left-dragging, the position of the scene camera changes, but the location that the scene camera is looking at does not.

- Scrolling with the scroll wheel on your mouse causes the scene camera to zoom in and out of the scene. You can also zoom by Option+right-dragging in the Scene pane.

The best way to get a feel for the hand tool is to try moving around the scene using the different methods described in this sidebar. After you have played with it a little, it should become second nature to you.

Summary

In about 20 pages, you've gone from nothing to having a working Unity project with a little programming in it. Admittedly, this project was pretty small, but I hope that it has served to show you the raw speed at which Unity can operate as well as the speed at which you can get something running in Unity.

The next chapter will continue your introduction to C# and Unity by introducing you to variables and increasing your knowledge of the most common components that can be added to a GameObject.

CHAPTER 20

VARIABLES AND COMPONENTS

This chapter introduces you to many of the variable and component types used throughout Unity C# programming. By the end of the chapter, you will understand several common types of C# variables and some important variable types that are unique to Unity.

This chapter also introduces you to Unity's GameObjects and components. Any object in a Unity scene is a GameObject, and the components that a GameObject contains enable everything from the positioning of a GameObject to physics simulation, special effects, displaying a 3D model on screen, character animation, and more.

Introducing Variables

To recap a bit of Chapter 18, "Introducing Our Language: C#," a *variable* is just a name that can be defined to be equal to a specific value. This concept comes from the study of algebra. In algebra, for instance, you can be given the definition:

```
x = 5
```

This *defines* the *variable* x to be equal to the *value* 5. In other words, it assigns the value 5 to the name x. If you later encounter the definition:

```
y = x + 2
```

Then you know that the value of the variable y is 7 (because $x = 5$ and $5 + 2 = 7$). x and y are called *variables* because their value can be redefined at any time, and the order in which these definitions occur matters. Take a look at these definitions. (I include *comments* after double slashes [//] in the following lines to help explain what each statement is doing.)

```
x = 10      // x is now equal to the value 10
y = x - 4   // y is now 6 because 10-4 = 6
x = 12      // x is now equal to the value 12, but y is still 6
z = x + 3   // z is now 15 because 12+3 = 15
```

After this sequence of definitions, the values assigned to x, y, and z are 12, 6, and 15, respectively. As you can see, even though x changed value, y was not affected because y is defined as the value 6 before x is assigned the new value 12, and y is not retroactively affected.

Strongly Typed Variables in C#

Instead of being able to be assign any kind of value to any variable, C# variables are *strongly typed*, meaning that they can only accept a specific type of value. This is necessary because the computer needs to know how much space in memory to allocate to each variable. A large image can take up many megabytes or even gigabytes of space, whereas a Boolean value (which can only hold either a 1 or a 0) only really requires a single bit. Even just a single megabyte is equivalent to 8,388,608 bits!

Declaring and Assigning Variables in C#

In C#, you must both declare and assign a value to a variable for it to have a usable value.

Declaring a variable creates it and gives it a name and type. However, this does not give the variable a value (though some simple variable types do have default values).

```
bool    bravo;   // Declares a variable named bravo   of the bool (Boolean) type
int     india;   // Declares a variable named india   of the int (integer) type
float   foxtrot; // Declares a variable named foxtrot of the float (number) type
char    charlie; // Declares a variable named charlie of the char (character) type
```

Assigning a variable gives that variable a value. Here are some examples of how to use these declared variables:

```
bravo = true;
india = 8;
foxtrot = 3.14f; // The f makes this numeric literal a float, as described later
charlie = 'c';
```

Whenever you write a specific value in your code (e.g., `true`, `8`, or `'c'`), that specific value is called a *literal*. In the preceding code listing, `true` is a bool literal, `8` is an int (integer) literal, `3.14f` is a float literal, and `'c'` is a char literal. By default, MonoDevelop shows these literals in a bright orange color (though `true` is colored teal on some computers for esoteric reasons), and each variable type has certain rules about how its literals are represented. Check out each of the variable types in the following sections for more information on this.

Declaration Before Assignment

You must first declare a variable before you can assign a value to it, although this is often done on the same line:

```
string   sierra = "Mountain";
```

Initializing C# Variables Before Accessing Them

The first time you ever assign a value to a new variable is called *initializing* the variable. Some simple variable types (like the bool, int, float, etc. in the example lines above) come with a default value when they are declared (respectively `false`, `0`, and `0f`). More complex variable types (e.g., GameObject, List, etc.) default to `null`, a non-initialized state, and are not fully usable until they have been initialized.

In general, even if a simple variable comes with a default value, Unity complains and throws a compiler error[1] if you try to access (i.e., read) a variable that has been declared but has not yet been initialized.

---

1. In Chapter 18, "Introducing Our Language: C#," you read that C# is a compiled language. A compiler error is one that is found during the compilation process when Unity is trying to interpret the C# code that you've written. Chapter 25, "Debugging," covers errors and error types in more detail.

Important C# Variable Types

Several different types of variables are available to you in C#. The following are a few important ones that you'll encounter frequently. All of these basic C# variable types begin with a lower-case letter, whereas most Unity data types begin with an uppercase letter. For each, I've listed information about the variable type and an example of how to declare and define the variable.

bool: A 1-Bit True or False Value

The term *bool* is short for Boolean. At their heart, all variables are composed of bits that you can set to either true or false. A bool is 1 bit in length, making it the smallest possible variable.[2] Bools are extremely useful for logic operations like `if` statements and other conditionals, which the next two chapters cover. In C#, bool literals are limited to the lowercase keywords `true` and `false`:

```
bool verified = true;
```

int: A 32-Bit Integer

Short for integer, an *int* can store a single integer number (integers are numbers without any fractional value like 5, 2, and –90). Integer math is very accurate and *very* fast. An int in Unity can store a number between –2,147,483,648 and 2,147,483,647 with 1 bit used for the positive or negative sign of the number and 31 bits used for the numerical value. An int can hold any integer value between these two numbers (*inclusive*, meaning that an int could also hold either number, not just those in between):

```
int nonFractionalNumber = 12345;
```

float: A 32-Bit Decimal Number

A floating-point number,[3] or *float*, is the most common form of decimal number used in Unity. It is called "floating point" because it is stored using a system similar to *scientific notation*. Scientific notation is the representation of numbers in the form $a \times 10^b$ (for example, 300 would be written 3×10^2, and 12,345 would be written 1.2345×10^4). Floating-point numbers are stored in a similar format as $a \times 2^b$. When a computer stores a number as a float in memory, 1 bit represents whether the number is positive or negative, 23 bits are allocated to the significand (the *a* part of the number), and 8 are allocated to the exponent to which the number is raised or lowered (the *b* part). This storage method compromises the precision of very large numbers

---

2. Because of the way that modern computers and C# handle memory, a single bool now actually uses 32 to 64 bits of memory, but the actual true/false value of the bool could potentially be stored in a single bit.

3. http://en.wikipedia.org/wiki/Floating_point

and any number between 1 and –1 that is difficult to represent as a power of 2. For instance, there is no way to accurately represent 1/3 using a float.[4]

Most of the time, the imprecise nature of floats doesn't matter much in your games, but it can cause small errors in things like collision detection; so in general, keeping objects in your game larger than 1 unit and smaller than several thousand units in size will make collisions a little more accurate. Float literals must be either a whole number or a decimal number followed by an f. This is because C# assumes that any decimal literal without a trailing f is a *double* (which is a float data type with double the precision) instead of the single-precision floats that Unity uses. Floats are used in all built-in Unity functions instead of doubles to enable the fastest possible calculation, though this comes at the expense of accuracy:

```
float notPreciselyOneThird = 1.0f/3.0f;
```

One way to handle this float inaccuracy is to use the `Mathf.Approximately()` comparison function described in the *Mathf: A Library of Mathematical Functions* section later in this chapter. This function returns `true` if two float values are very close to each other.

> **tip**
>
> If you see the following compile-time error in your code
>
> ```
> error CS0664: Literal of type double cannot be implicitly converted to
> type 'float'. Add suffix 'f' to create a literal of this type
> ```
>
> it means that somewhere you have forgotten to add the f after a float literal.

char: A 16-Bit Single Character

A *char* is a single character represented by 16 bits of information. Chars in Unity's C# use Unicode[5] values for storing characters, enabling the representation of more than 110,000 different characters from more than 100 different character sets and languages (including, for instance, all the characters in Simplified Chinese). A char literal is surrounded by single-quote marks (apostrophes):

```
char theLetterA = 'A';
```

string: A Series of 16-Bit Characters

A *string* is used to represent everything from a single character to the text of an entire book. The theoretical maximum length of a string in C# is more than 2 billion characters, but most

---

4. This floating point precision issue is also the reason that positions and rotations in the Unity Transform component that should be zero sometimes appear as a very complex number that is not exactly zero.

5. http://en.wikipedia.org/wiki/Unicode

computers will encounter memory allocation issues long before that limit is reached. To give some context, the full version of Shakespeare's play *Hamlet* comprises a little more than 175,000 characters,[6] including stage directions, line breaks, and so on. This means that *Hamlet* could be repeated more than 12,000 times in a single string. A string literal is surrounded by double-quote marks:

```
string theFirstLineOfHamlet = "Who's there?";
```

Bracket Access and Strings

Bracket access can be used to read the individual chars of a string:

```
char theCharW = theFirstLineOfHamlet[0]; // W is the 0th char in the string
char theChart = theFirstLineOfHamlet[6]; // t is the 6th char in the string
```

Placing a number in brackets after the variable name retrieves the character in that position of the string (without affecting the original string). When you use bracket access, counting starts with the number 0; so in the preceding example, W is the 0th character of the first line of *Hamlet*, and t is the 6th character. You will encounter bracket access much more in Chapter 23, "Collections in C#."

> **tip**
>
> If you see any of the following compile-time errors in your code
>
> ```
> error CS0029: Cannot implicitly convert type 'string' to 'char'
> error CS0029: Cannot implicitly convert type 'char' to 'string'
> error CS1012: Too many characters in character literal
> error CS1525: Unexpected symbol '<internal>'
> ```
>
> it usually means that somewhere you have accidentally used double quotes (" ") for a char literal or single quotes (' ') for a string literal. String literals always require double quotes, and char literals always require single quotes.

class: The Definition of a New Variable Type

A *class* defines a new type of variable that you can best think of as a collection of both variables and functionality. All the Unity variable types and components listed in the "Important Unity Variable Types" section later in this chapter are examples of classes. Chapter 26, "Classes," covers classes in much greater detail.

---

6. http://shakespeare.mit.edu/hamlet/full.html

The Scope of Variables

In addition to variable type, another important concept for variables is *scope*. The scope of a variable refers to the range of code in which the variable exists and is understood. If you declare a variable in one part of your code, it might not have meaning in another part. I cover this complex issue throughout this book. If you want to learn about it progressively, just read the book in order. If you want to get a lot more information about variable scope right now, you can read the section *Variable Scope* in Appendix B, "Useful Concepts."

Naming Conventions

The code in this book follows a number of rules governing the naming of variables, functions, classes, and so on. Although none of these rules are mandatory, following them makes your code more readable not only to others who try to decipher it but also to yourself if you ever need to return to it months later and hope to understand what you wrote. Every coder follows slightly different rules—my personal rules have even changed over the years—but the rules I present here have worked well for both me and my students, and they are consistent with most C# code that I've encountered in Unity:

CAMEL CASE

camelCase is a common way of writing variable names in programming. It allows the programmer or someone reading her code to easily parse long variable names. Here are some examples:

- aVeryLongNameThatIsEasierToReadBecauseOfCamelCase

- variableNamesStartWithALowerCaseLetter

- ClassNamesStartWithACapitalLetter

The key feature of camelCase is that it allows multiple words to be combined into one with a medial capital letter at the beginning of each original word. It is named camelCase because it looks a bit like the humps on a camel's back.

- Use *camelCase* for pretty much everything (see the camelCase sidebar).
- Variable names should start with a lowercase letter (e.g., someVariableName).
- Function names should start with an uppercase letter (e.g., Start(), Update()).
- Class names should start with an uppercase letter (e.g., GameObject, ScopeExample).

- Private variable names often start with an underscore (e.g., `_hiddenVariable`).

- Static variable names are often all caps with snake_case (e.g., `NUM_INSTANCES`). As you can see, snake_case combines multiple words with an underscore in between them.

For your later reference, I repeat and expand on this information in the *Naming Conventions* section of Appendix B.

Important Unity Variable Types

Unity has a number of variable types that you will encounter in nearly every project. All of these variable types are actually classes and follow Unity's naming convention that all class types start with an uppercase letter.[7] For each of the Unity variable types, you will see information about how to create a new *instance* of that class (see the nearby sidebar on class instances) followed by listings of important variables and functions for that data type. For most of the Unity classes listed in this section, the variables and functions are split into two groups:

- **Instance variables and functions:** These variables and functions are tied directly to a single instance of the variable type. If you look at the *Vector3* information that follows, you will see that `x`, `y`, `z`, and `magnitude` are all instance variables of Vector3, and each one is accessed by using the name of a Vector3 variable, a period, and then the name of the instance variable (for example, `position.x`). Each Vector3 instance can have different values for these variables. Similarly, the `Normalize()` function acts on a single instance of Vector3 and sets the `magnitude` of that instance to one. Instance variables are often referred to as *fields*, and instance functions are referred to as *methods*.

- **Static class variables and functions:** *Static* variables are tied to the class definition itself rather than being tied to an individual instance. These are often used to store information that is the same across all instances of the class (for example, `Color.red` is always the same red color) or to act on multiple instances of the class without affecting any of those instances (for example, `Vector3.Cross( v3a, v3b )` is used to calculate the cross product of two Vector3s and return that value as a new Vector3 without changing either `v3a` or `v3b`).

For more information on any of these Unity types, check out the Unity documentation links referenced in the footnotes.

---

7. To be more correct, some of these Unity variable types are classes, and others are *structs*. A struct is similar to a class in most respects, and you won't be writing them in this book, so I've chosen to refer to everything as classes.

CLASS INSTANCES AND STATIC FUNCTIONS

Just like the prefabs that you saw in Chapter 19, "Hello World: Your First Program," classes can also have *instances*. An instance of any class (also known as a *member* of the class) is a data object that is of the type defined by the class.

For example, you could define a class Human, and everyone you know would be an instance of that class. Several functions are defined for all humans (for example, Eat(), Sleep(), Breathe()).

Just as you differ from all other humans around you, each instance of a class differs from the other instances. Even if two instances have perfectly identical values, they are stored in different locations in computer memory and seen as two distinct objects.
(To continue the human analogy, you could think of them as identical twins.) Class instances are referred to by *reference*, not value. This means that if you are comparing two class instances to see whether they are the same, the thing that is compared is their *location in memory*, not their values (just as two identical twins are different people, even though they have the same DNA).

Referencing the same class instance using different variables is possible, of course. Just as the person I might call "daughter" would also be called "granddaughter" by my parents, a class instance can be assigned to any number of variable names yet still be the same data object, as is shown in the following code:

```
 1 using System.Collections;
 2 using System.Collections.Generic;
 3 using UnityEngine;
 4
 5 // Defining the class Human
 6 public class Human {
 7     public string     name;
 8     public Human      partner;
 9 }
10
11 public class Family : MonoBehaviour {
12     // public variable declaration
13     public Human husband;
14     public Human wife;
15
16     void Start() {
17         // Initial state
18         husband = new Human();
19         husband.name = "Jeremy Gibson";
20         wife = new Human();
21         wife.name = "Melanie Schuessler";
22
```

```
23          // My wife and I get married
24          husband.partner = wife;
25          wife.partner = husband;
26
27          // We change our names
28          husband.name = "Jeremy Gibson Bond";
29          wife.name = "Melanie Schuessler Bond";
30
31          // Because wife.partner refers to the same instance as husband,
32          //   the name of wife.partner has also changed
33          print(wife.partner.name);
34          // prints "Jeremy Gibson Bond"
35      }
36 }
```

Creating *static functions* on the class Human that are able to act on one or more instances of the class is also possible. The static function Marry() allows you to set any two humans to be each other's partner with a single function, as shown in the following code.

```
33          print(wife.partner.name);
34          // prints "Jeremy Gibson Bond"
35      }
36      // This code goes between lines 35 and 36 in the previous code listing
37      // In the process, line 36 becomes line 42
38      static public void Marry(Human h0, Human h1) {
39          h0.partner = h1;
40          h1.partner = h0;
41      }
42 }
```

With this function, replacing lines 23 and 24 from the initial code listing with the single line Human.Marry(wife, husband); would now be possible. Because Marry() is a static function, you can use it almost anywhere in your code. You will learn more about static functions and variables later in the book.

Vector3: A Collection of Three Floats

Vector3[8] is a very common data type for working in 3D. It is used most often to store the three-dimensional position of objects in Unity. Follow the URL in the footnote for more detailed information about Vector3s.

```
Vector3 position = new Vector3( 0.0f, 3.0f, 4.0f ); // Sets the x, y, & z values
```

---

8. http://docs.unity3d.com/Documentation/ScriptReference/Vector3.html

Vector3 Instance Variables and Functions

As a class, each Vector3 instance also contains a number of useful built-in values and functions:

```
print( position.x );  // 0.0, The x value of the Vector3
print( position.y );  // 3.0, The y value of the Vector3
print( position.z );  // 4.0, The z value of the Vector3
print( position.magnitude );  // 5.0, The distance of the Vector3 from 0,0,0
                              //  Magnitude is another word for "length".
position.Normalize();  // Sets the magnitude of position to 1, meaning that the
                       //  x, y, & z values of position are now [0.0, 0.6, 0.8]
```

Vector3 Static Class Variables and Functions

In addition, several static class variables and functions are associated with the Vector3 class itself:

```
print( Vector3.zero );    // (0,0,0), Shorthand for: new Vector3( 0, 0, 0 )
print( Vector3.one );     // (1,1,1), Shorthand for: new Vector3( 1, 1, 1 )
print( Vector3.right );   // (1,0,0), Shorthand for: new Vector3( 1, 0, 0 )
print( Vector3.up );      // (0,1,0), Shorthand for: new Vector3( 0, 1, 0 )
print( Vector3.forward ); // (0,0,1), Shorthand for: new Vector3( 0, 0, 1 )
Vector3.Cross( v3a, v3b );// Computes the cross product of the two Vector3s
Vector3.Dot( v3a, v3b );  // Computes the dot product of the two Vector3s
```

This is only a sampling of the fields and methods affiliated with Vector3. To find out more, check out the Unity documentation referenced in the footnote.

Color: A Color with Transparency Information

The *Color*[9] variable type can store information about a color and its transparency (alpha value). Colors on computers are mixtures of the three primary colors of light: red, green, and blue. These are different from the primary colors of paint you might have learned as a child (red, yellow, and blue) because color on a computer screen is *additive*, rather than *subtractive*. In a subtractive color system like paint, mixing more and more different colors together moves the mixed color toward black (or a really dark, muddy brown). By contrast, in an additive color system (like a computer screen, theatrical lighting design, or HTML colors on the Internet), adding more and more colors together results in a brighter and brighter colors until the final mixed color is eventually white. The red, green, and blue components of a color in C# are stored as floats that range from `0.0f` to `1.0f` with `0.0f` representing none of that color channel and `1.0f` representing as much of that color channel as possible. A fourth float named *alpha* sets the transparency of the Color. A color with an alpha of `0.0f` is fully transparent, and a color with an alpha of `1.0f` is fully opaque:

```
// Colors are defined by floats for the Red, Green, Blue, and Alpha channels
Color darkGreen = new Color( 0f, 0.25f, 0f ); // If no alpha info is passed in,
                                              // the alpha value is assumed to
                                              // be 1 (fully opaque)
Color darkRedTranslucent = new Color( 0.25f, 0f, 0f, 0.5f );
```

---

9. http://docs.unity3d.com/Documentation/ScriptReference/Color.html

As you can see, there are two different ways to define a color: one with three parameters (red, green, and blue) and one with four parameters (red, green, blue, and alpha).[10]

Color Instance Variables and Functions

You can reference each channel of a color through instance variables:

```
print( Color.yellow.r ); // 1, The red value of the yellow Color
print( Color.yellow.g ); // 0.92f, The green value of the yellow Color
print( Color.yellow.b ); // 0.016f, The blue value of the yellow Color
print( Color.yellow.a ); // 1, The alpha value of the yellow Color
```

Color Static Class Variables and Functions

Several common colors are predefined in Unity as static class variables:

```
// Primary Colors: Red, Green, and Blue
Color.red      = new Color(1, 0, 0, 1); // Solid red
Color.green    = new Color(0, 1, 0, 1); // Solid green
Color.blue     = new Color(0, 0, 1, 1); // Solid blue

// Secondary Colors: Cyan, Magenta, and Yellow
Color.cyan     = new Color(0, 1, 1, 1); // Cyan, a bright greenish blue
Color.magenta  = new Color(1, 0, 1, 1); // Magenta, a pinkish purple
Color.yellow   = new Color(1, 0.92f, 0.016f, 1); // A nice-looking yellow
// As you can imagine, a standard yellow would be new Color(1,1,0,1), but in
//   Unity's opinion, this yellow looks better.

// Black, White, and Clear
Color.black    = new Color(0, 0, 0, 1); // Solid black
Color.white    = new Color(1, 1, 1, 1); // Solid white
Color.gray     = new Color(0.5f, 0.5f, 0.5f, 1) // Gray
Color.grey     = new Color(0.5f, 0.5f, 0.5f, 1) // British spelling of gray
Color.clear    = new Color(0, 0, 0, 0); // Completely transparent
```

Quaternion: Rotation Information

Explaining the inner workings of the *Quaternion*[11] class is far beyond the scope of this book, but you will use them often to set and adjust the rotation of objects through the Quaternion `GameObject.transform.rotation`, which is part of every GameObject. Quaternions define rotations in a way that avoids gimbal lock, a problem with standard X, Y, Z (or Euler, pronounced "oiler") rotations where one axis can align with another and limit rotation possibilities. Most of the time, you will define a Quaternion by passing in Euler rotations and allowing Unity to convert them into the equivalent Quaternion:

```
Quaternion lookUp45Deg = Quaternion.Euler( -45f, 0f, 0f );
```

---

10. The ability of the new `Color()` function to accept either three or four different arguments is called *function overloading*, and you can read more about it in Chapter 24, "Functions and Parameters."

11. http://docs.unity3d.com/Documentation/ScriptReference/Quaternion.html

In cases like this, the three floats passed into `Quaternion.Euler()` are the number of degrees to rotate around the X, Y, and Z axes (respectively colored red, green, and blue in Unity). GameObjects, including the Main Camera in a scene, are initially oriented to be looking down the positive Z axis. The rotation in the preceding code would rotate the camera –45 degrees around the red X axis, causing it to then be looking up at a 45° angle relative to the positive Z axis. If that last sentence was confusing, don't worry about it too much right now. Later, you can try going into Unity and changing the X, Y, and Z rotation values in the Transform Inspector for a GameObject and see how it alters the object's orientation.

Quaternion Instance Variables and Functions

You can also use the instance variable `eulerAngles` to cause a Quaternion to return its rotation information to you in Euler angles as a Vector3:

```
print( lookUp45Deg.eulerAngles ); // ( -45, 0, 0 ), the Euler rotation
```

Mathf: A Library of Mathematical Functions

Mathf[12] isn't really a variable type as much as a fantastically useful library of math functions. All the variables and functions attached to Mathf are static; you cannot create an instance of Mathf. Far too many useful functions are available in the Mathf library to list here, but a few include the following:

```
Mathf.Sin(x);          // Computes the sine of x
Mathf.Cos(x);          // .Tan(), .Asin(), .Acos(), & .Atan() are also available
Mathf.Atan2( y, x );   // Gives you the angle to rotate around the z-axis to
                       //  change something facing along the x-axis to face
                       //  instead toward the point x, y.13
print(Mathf.PI);       // 3.141593; the ratio of circumference to diameter
Mathf.Min( 2, 3, 1 );  // 1, the smallest of the three numbers (float or int)
Mathf.Max( 2, 3, 1 );  // 3, the largest of the three numbers (float or int)
Mathf.Round( 1.75f );  // 2, rounds up or down to the nearest number
Mathf.Ceil( 1.75f );   // 2, rounds up to the next highest integer number
Mathf.Floor( 1.75f );  // 1, rounds down to the next lowest integer number
Mathf.Abs( -25 );      // 25, the absolute value of -25

Mathf.Approximately( a, b ); // Compares approximate equality of two floats
```

`Mathf.Approximately()` is a great tool to help you deal with float inaccuracy because (unlike ==) it returns `true` if two floats are so close to each other that float inaccuracy could cause them to appear to be unequal. This method is not used in this book because we don't compare two floats using == in any code examples, but in your work, if you're ever comparing two floats for equality, use `Mathf.Approximately()` instead of ==.

---

12. http://docs.unity3d.com/Documentation/ScriptReference/Mathf.html

13. http://docs.unity3d.com/Documentation/ScriptReference/Mathf.Atan2.html

Screen: Information about the Display

Screen[14] is another library like Mathf that can give you information about the specific computer screen that your Unity game is using. This works regardless of device, so Screen provides you accurate info whether you're on a PC, macOS, an iOS device, an Android device, or WebGL:

```
print( Screen.width );    // Prints the width of the screen in pixels
print( Screen.height );   // Prints the height of the screen in pixels
```

SystemInfo: Information about the Device

SystemInfo[15] provides specific information about the device on which the game is running. It includes information about operating system, number of processors, graphics hardware, and more. I recommend following the link in the footnote to learn more.

```
print( SystemInfo.operatingSystem ); // Mac OS X 10.8.5, for example
```

GameObject: The Type of Any Object in the Scene

GameObject[16] is the base class for all entities in Unity scenes. Anything you see on screen in a Unity game is a subclass of the GameObject class. GameObjects can contain any number of different *components*, including all of those referenced in the next section: *Unity GameObjects and Components*. However, GameObjects also have a few important variables beyond what is covered there:

```
GameObject gObj = new GameObject("MyGO"); // Creates a new GameObject named MyGO
print( gObj.name );    // MyGO, the name of the GameObject gObj
Transform trans = gObj.GetComponent<Transform>(); // Defines trans to be a
                                                   //  reference to the Transform
                                                   //  Component of gObj
Transform trans2 = gObj.transform; // A shortcut to access the same Transform
gObj.SetActive(false);    // Makes gObj inactive, rendering it invisible and
                          //  preventing it from running code.
```

The *method*[17] gObj.GetComponent<Transform>() shown here is of particular importance because it can enable you to access any of the components attached to a GameObject. You will sometimes see methods with angle brackets <> like GetComponent<>(). These are called *generic methods* because they are a single method designed to be used with many different data types. In the case of GetComponent<Transform>(), the data type is Transform, which

---

14. http://docs.unity3d.com/Documentation/ScriptReference/Screen.html

15. http://docs.unity3d.com/Documentation/ScriptReference/SystemInfo.html

16. http://docs.unity3d.com/Documentation/ScriptReference/GameObject.html

17. *Function* and *method* have the same basic meaning. The only difference is that *function* is the word for a standalone function whereas *method* refers to a function that is part of a class.

tells `GetComponent<>()` to find the Transform component of the GameObject and return it to you. You can also use it to get any other component of the GameObject by typing that component type inside the angle brackets instead of Transform. Examples include the following:

```
Renderer rend = gObj.GetComponent<Renderer>(); // Gets the Renderer component
Collider coll = gObj.GetComponent<Collider>(); // Gets the Collider component
HelloWorld hwInstance = gObj.GetComponent<HelloWorld>();
```

As shown in the third line of the preceding code listing, you can also use `GetComponent<>()` to return the instance of any C# class that you've attached to the GameObject. If there were an instance of the HelloWorld C# script class attached to gObj, then `gObj.GetComponent <HelloWorld>()` would return it. This technique is used several times throughout this book.

Unity GameObjects and Components

As mentioned in the previous section, all on-screen elements in Unity are *GameObjects*, and all GameObjects contain one or more components (a Transform component is *always* included). When you select a GameObject in either the Hierarchy pane or the Scene pane of Unity, the components of that GameObject display in the Inspector pane, as shown in Figure 20.1.

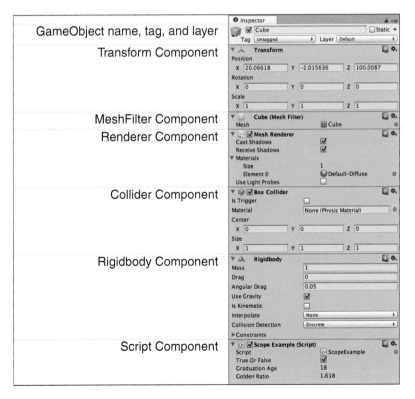

Figure 20.1 The Inspector pane showing various important components

Transform: Position, Rotation, and Scale

Transform[18] is a mandatory component that is present on all GameObjects. Transform handles critical GameObject information like *position* (the location of the GameObject), *rotation* (the orientation of the GameObject), and *scale* (the size of the GameObject). Though the information is not displayed in the Inspector pane, Transform is also responsible for the parent/child relationships in the Hierarchy pane. When one object is the child of another, it moves with that parent object as if attached to it.

MeshFilter: The Model You See

A *MeshFilter*[19] component attaches a 3D mesh in your Project pane to a GameObject. To see a model on screen, the GameObject must have both a MeshFilter that handles the actual 3D mesh information and a MeshRenderer that combines that mesh with a shader or material and displays the image on screen. The MeshFilter creates a skin or surface for a GameObject, and the MeshRenderer determines the shape, color, and texture of that surface.

Renderer: Allows You to See the GameObject

A *Renderer*[20] component—in most cases, a MeshRenderer—allows you to see the GameObject in the Scene and Game panes. The MeshRenderer requires a MeshFilter to provide 3D mesh data as well as at least one Material if you want it to look like anything other than an ugly magenta blob (Materials apply textures to objects, and when no Material is present, Unity defaults to solid magenta to alert you to the problem). Renderers bring the MeshFilter, the Material(s), and lighting together to show the GameObject on screen.

Collider: The Physical Presence of the GameObject

A *Collider*[21] component enables a GameObject to have a physical presence in the game world and collide with other objects. Unity has four different kinds of Collider components, which I've arranged below in order of their speed. Calculating whether another object has collided with a Sphere Collider is extremely fast, but calculating whether an object has collided with a Mesh Collider is much slower:

- **Sphere Collider:**[22] The fastest collision shape to calculate. A ball or sphere.
- **Capsule Collider:**[23] A pipe with spheres at each end. The second fastest type.

---

18. http://docs.unity3d.com/Documentation/Components/class-Transform.html

19. http://docs.unity3d.com/Documentation/Components/class-MeshFilter.html

20. http://docs.unity3d.com/Documentation/Components/class-MeshRenderer.html

21. http://docs.unity3d.com/Documentation/Components/comp-DynamicsGroup.html

22. http://docs.unity3d.com/Documentation/Components/class-SphereCollider.html

23. http://docs.unity3d.com/Documentation/Components/class-CapsuleCollider.html

- **Box Collider:**[24] A rectangular solid. Useful for crates and other boxy things.
- **Mesh Collider:**[25] A collider formed from a 3D mesh. Although useful and accurate, mesh colliders are much, much slower than any of the other three. Also, only Mesh Colliders with Convex set to `true` can collide with other Mesh Colliders.

Physics and collision are handled in Unity via the NVIDIA PhysX engine. Although this does usually provide very fast and accurate collisions, be aware that all physics engines have limitations, and even PhysX sometimes has issues with fast-moving objects or thin walls.

Later chapters of this book cover Colliders in much more depth. You can also learn more about them from the Unity documentation.

Rigidbody: The Physics Simulation

The *Rigidbody*[26] component controls the physics simulation of your GameObject. The Rigidbody component simulates acceleration and velocity every *FixedUpdate*[27] (generally every 50th of a second) to update the position and rotation of the Transform component over time. It also uses the Collider component to handle collisions with other GameObjects. The Rigidbody component can also model things like gravity, drag, and various forces like wind and explosions. Set `isKinematic` to `true` if you want to directly set the position of your GameObject without using the physics provided by Rigidbody.

> **warning**
>
> For the position of a Collider component to move with its GameObject, the GameObject must have a Rigidbody. Otherwise—as far as Unity's PhysX physics simulation is concerned—the collider will not move. In other words, if a Rigidbody is not attached, the GameObject will appear to move across the screen, but in PhysX, the location of the Collider component will not be updated, and therefore the physical presence of the GameObject will remain in the original location.

Script: The C# Scripts That You Write

All C# scripts are also GameObject components. One of the benefits of scripts being components is that you can attach more than one script to each GameObject, a capability that you will take advantage of in some of the tutorials in Part III of this book. Later in the book, you will read much more about Script components and how to access them.

---

24. http://docs.unity3d.com/Documentation/Components/class-BoxCollider.html

25. http://docs.unity3d.com/Documentation/Components/class-MeshCollider.html

26. http://docs.unity3d.com/Documentation/Components/class-Rigidbody.html

27. In Unity, an Update happens every visual frame (often ranging between 30-300 times/second depending on the speed of your computer), whereas a FixedUpdate happens on a regular, fixed schedule (at a default of 50 times/second regardless of the platform). Physics engines work better with a fixed update schedule, hence the difference between the two.

warning

VARIABLE NAMES WILL CHAGE IN THE INSPECTOR   In Figure 20.1, you can see that the name of the script is *Scope Example (Script)*, but that breaks the naming rules for classes, because class names cannot have spaces in them.

The actual script name in my code is a single word in camelCase: `ScopeExample`. I'm not sure why exactly, but in the Inspector, the spelling of class and variable names is changed from their actual spelling in the C# scripts you write by the following rules:

- The class name `ScopeExample` becomes *Scope Example (Script)*.

- The variable `trueOrFalse` becomes *True Or False*.

- The variable `graduationAge` becomes *Graduation Age*.

- The variable `goldenRatio` becomes *Golden Ratio*.

This is an important distinction, and it has confused some of my students in the past. Even though the names appear differently in the Inspector, the variable names in your code have not been changed. Throughout the book, I refer to variables by their names as they are written in code, regardless of how they appear in the Inspector.

Summary

This was a long chapter with a lot of information in it, and you might need to read it again or refer to it later after you've had some more experience with code. However, all of this information will prove invaluable to you as you continue through this book and as you start writing your own code. After you understand the GameObject/Component structure of Unity and how to take advantage of the Unity Inspector to set and modify variables, you'll find that your Unity coding moves a lot faster and more smoothly.

CHAPTER 21

BOOLEAN OPERATIONS AND CONDITIONALS

Most people have heard that computer data is, at its base level, composed entirely of 1s and 0s—bits that are either true or false. However, only programmers really understand how much of programming is about boiling a problem down to a true or false value and then responding to it.

In this chapter, you learn about Boolean operations like AND, OR, and NOT; you learn about comparison statements like >, <, ==, and !=; and you come to understand conditionals like `if` and `switch`. These all lie at the heart of programming.

Booleans

As you learned in the previous chapter, a bool is a variable that can hold a value of either `true` or `false`. Booleans were named after George Boole, a mathematician who worked with true and false values and logical operations (now known as "Boolean operations"). Though computers did not exist at the time of his research, computer logic was fundamentally based on it.

In C# programming, bools are used to store simple information about the state of the game (e.g., `bool gameOver = false;`) and to control the flow of the program through the `if` and `switch` statements covered later in this chapter.

Boolean Operations

Boolean operations allow programmers to modify or combine bool variables in meaningful ways.

! (The NOT Operator)

The `!` (either pronounced "not" or "bang") operator reverses the value of a bool. False becomes true, and true becomes false:

```
print( !true );      // Outputs: false
print( !false );     // Outputs: true
print( !(!true) );   // Outputs: true      (the double negative of true is true)
```

`!` is also sometimes referred to as the *logical negation operator* to differentiate it from ~ (the bitwise not operator), which is explained in the "Bitwise Boolean Operators and Layer Masks" section of Appendix B, "Useful Concepts."

&& (The AND Operator)

The `&&` operator returns true only if both operands are true:[1]

```
print( false && false );    // false
print( false && true  );    // false
print( true  && false );    // false
print( true  && true  );    // true
```

|| (The OR Operator)

The `||` operator returns true if either operand is true as well as if both are true:

```
print( false || false );    // false
print( false || true  );    // true
print( true  || false );    // true
print( true  || true  );    // true
```

---

1. I have inserted additional spaces in several of these code listings to help make them more readable. Remember that any number of spaces are interpreted by C# as a single space.

Shorting Versus Non-Shorting Boolean Operators

The standard forms of AND and OR (&& and ||) are *shorting* operators, which means that after the operator has determined the return value, it returns that value without executing the rest of the code. For example, the code `false && SomeFunction()` would never call `SomeFunction()` because once the `false` was evaluated, the `&&` would know that its return value would be false and would short before evaluating `SomeFunction()`. There are also *non-shorting* versions of AND and OR (& and |) that will evaluate both sides of the operator regardless of the value of the first. The following code listing includes several examples of how this works.

> **tip**
>
> In the following code listing, a double slash followed by a lowercase letter (e.g., // a) to the right of a line indicates that there is an explanation of that line following the code listing. Throughout the book, the explanations usually appear at the end of the code listing, though in this example, they are included in the middle of the code to ease you into it.

```
1  // This function prints "--true" and returns a true value.
2  bool printAndReturnTrue() {
3      print( "--true" );
4      return( true );
5  }
6
7  // This function prints "--false" and returns a false value.
8  bool printAndReturnFalse() {
9      print( "--false" );
10     return( false );
11 }
12
13 void ShortingOperatorTest() {
14     // Lines 15, 17, 19, & 21 make use of the shorting && and || operators
15     bool andTF = ( printAndReturnTrue() && printAndReturnFalse() );    // a
16     print( "andTF: "+andTF ); //  Output: "--true --false andTF: false"
```

a. This line prints --true and --false before setting andTF to false. Because the first argument that the shorting && operator evaluates is true, it must also evaluate the second argument to determine that the result is false.

```
17     bool andFT = ( printAndReturnFalse() && printAndReturnTrue() );    // b
18     print( "andFT: "+andFT ); // Output: " --false andFT: false"
```

b. This line only prints --false before setting andFT to false. Because the first argument that the shorting && operator evaluates is false, it returns false without evaluating the second argument at all. On this line, printAndReturnTrue() is *not* executed.

```
19     bool orTF = ( printAndReturnTrue() || printAndReturnFalse() );    // c
20     print( "orTF: "+orTF ); // Output: "--true orTF: true"
```

    c. This line only prints `--true` before setting `orTF` to `true`. Because the first argument that the shorting `||` operator evaluates is true, it returns `true` without evaluating the second.

```
21      bool orFT = ( printAndReturnFalse() || printAndReturnTrue() );    // d
22      print( "orFT: "+orFT ); // Output: "--false --true orTF: true"
```

    d. This line prints `--false` and `--true` before setting `orFT` to `true`. Because the first argument that the shorting `||` operator evaluates is false, it must evaluate the second argument to determine which value to return.

```
23      // Lines 24 and 26 use the non-shorting & and | operators
24      bool nsAndFT = ( printAndReturnFalse() & printAndReturnTrue() );    // e
25      print( "nsAndFT: "+nsAndFT ); // Output: "--false --true nsAndFT: false"
```

    e. The non-shorting `&` operator evaluates both arguments regardless of the value of the first argument. This line prints `--false` and `--true` before setting `nsAndFT` to `false`.

```
26      bool nsOrTF = (printAndReturnTrue() | printAndReturnFalse() );    // f
27      print( "nsOrTF: "+nsOrTF ); // Output: "--true --false nsOrTF: false"
28 }
```

    f. The non-shorting `|` operator evaluates both arguments regardless of the value of the first argument. This line prints `--true` and `--false` before setting `nsOrTF` to `true`.

Knowing about both shorting and non-shorting operators is useful when writing your code. Shorting operators (`&&` and `||`) are much more commonly used, but `&` and `|` can be used when you want to ensure that you evaluate all the arguments of a Boolean operator.

If you want, I recommend entering this code into Unity and running the debugger to step through the behavior and really understand what is happening. To learn about the fantastic debugger in MonoDevelop and Unity, read Chapter 25, "Debugging."

Bitwise Boolean Operators

`|` and `&` are sometimes referred to as *bitwise OR* and *bitwise AND* because they can also be used to perform bitwise operations on integers. These are useful for a few esoteric things having to do with collision detection in Unity that you can learn more about in the *Bitwise Boolean Operators and Layer Masks* section of Appendix B, "Useful Concepts."

Combination of Boolean Operations

Combining various Boolean operations in a single line is often useful:

```
bool tf = true || false && false;
```

However, you must take care when doing so because order of operations extends to Boolean operations as well. In C#, the order of operations for Boolean operations is as follows:

!   NOT

&   Non-shorting AND / Bitwise AND

| Non-shorting OR / Bitwise OR

&&   AND

|| OR

This means that the previous line would be interpreted by the compiler as

```
bool tf = true || ( false && false );
```

The `&&` comparison is executed before the `||` comparison every time. Had you ignored order of operations and interpreted this line left-to-right, you might have expected the result to be false (e.g., `(true || false) && false` is false), but without any parentheses, the line actually evaluates to true!

> **tip**
>
> Regardless of the order of operations, you should use parentheses for clarity in your code as often as possible. Good readability is essential in your code if you ever plan to work with someone else (or even if you want to read the same code yourself weeks or months later). I code by a simple rule: If there's any chance *at all* that something might be misunderstood later, I use parentheses and add comments to clarify what I am doing in the code and how it will be interpreted by the computer.

Logical Equivalence of Boolean Operations

The depths of Boolean logic are beyond the scope of this book, but suffice it to say, you can accomplish some very interesting things by combining Boolean operations. In the examples of logic rules that follow, `a` and `b` are bool variables. These rules hold true regardless of whether `a` and `b` are true or false and regardless of whether the shorting or non-shorting operators are used:

- Associativity: `( a & b ) & c` is the same as `a & ( b & c )`
- Commutativity: `( a & b )` is the same as `( b & a )`
- Distributivity of AND over OR: `a & ( b | c )` is the same as `( a & b ) | ( a & c )`
- Distributivity of OR over AND: `a | ( b & c )` is the same as `( a | b ) & ( a | c )`
- `( a & b )` is the same as `!( !a | !b )`
- `( a | b )` is the same as `!( !a & !b )`

If you're interested in more of these equivalencies and how they could be used, you can find many resources about Boolean logic online.

Comparison Operators

In addition to comparing Boolean values to each other, you can also create a Boolean value by using comparison operators on any other values.

== (Is Equal To)

The equality comparison operator checks to see whether the values of any two variables or literals are equivalent to each other. The result of this operator is a Boolean value of either true or false.

> ### warning
>
> **DON'T CONFUSE = AND ==**   New coders are often confused by the difference between the assignment operator (=) and the equality operator (==). The assignment operator (=) is used to set the value of a variable whereas the equality operator (==) is used to compare two values. Consider the following code listing:
>
> ```
> 1 bool f = false;
> 2 bool t = true;
> 3 print( f == t ); // prints: False
> 4 print( f = t );  // prints: True
> ```
>
> On line 3, f is compared to t, and because they are not equal, `false` is returned and printed. However, on line 4, f is assigned the value of t, causing the value of f to now be true, and `true` is printed.
>
> Confusion is also sometimes an issue when talking about the two operators. To avoid confusion, I usually pronounce i=5; as "i equals 5," and I pronounce i==5; as "i is equal to 5."

```
 1 int i0 = 10;
 2 int i1 = 10;
 3 int i2 = 20;
 4 float f0 = 1.23f;
 5 float f1 = 3.14f;
 6 float f2 = Mathf.PI;
 7
 8 print( i0 == i1 );    // Outputs: True
 9 print( i1 == i2 );    // Outputs: False
10 print( i2 == 20 );    // Outputs: True
11 print( f0 == f1 );    // Outputs: False
12 print( f0 == 1.23f ); // Outputs: True
13 print( f1 == f2 );    // Outputs: False              // a
```

a.   The comparison in line 13 is false because Math.PI is far more accurate than 3.14f, and == requires that the values be exactly equivalent.

See the "Testing Equality by Value or Reference" sidebar for more detailed information about how equality is handled for several different variable types.

TESTING EQUALITY BY VALUE OR REFERENCE

Unity's version of C# compares most simple data types *by value*. This means that as long as the values of the two variables are the same, they will be seen as equivalent. This works for all of the following data types:

- bool
- int
- float
- char

- string
- Vector3
- Color
- Quaternion

However, with more complex variable types like GameObject, Material, Renderer, and so on, C# instead checks equality *by reference*. When comparing equality by reference, it does not compare whether the values of the two variables are equal but instead checks to see whether the *references* of the two variables are equal. In other words, it checks to see whether the two variables are referencing (or pointing to) the same single object in the computer's memory. In the following example of comparison by reference, boxPrefab is a pre-existing variable that references a GameObject prefab.

```
1 GameObject go0 = Instantiate<GameObject>( boxPrefab );
2 GameObject go1 = Instantiate<GameObject>( boxPrefab );
3 GameObject go2 = go0;
4 print( go0 == go1 ); // Output: false
5 print( go0 == go2 ); // Output: true
```

Even though the two instantiated boxPrefabs assigned to the variables go0 and go1 have the same values (they have the exact same default position, rotation, and so on) the == operator sees them as different because they are actually two different objects, and therefore reside in two different places in memory. go0 and go2 are seen as equal by == because they both refer to the exact same object. Let's continue the previous code:

```
6 go0.transform.position = new Vector3( 10, 20, 30);
7 print( go0.transform.position); // Output: (10.0, 20.0, 30.0)
8 print( go1.transform.position); // Output: ( 0.0,  0.0,  0.0)
9 print( go2.transform.position); // Output: (10.0, 20.0, 30.0)
```

Here, the position of go0 is changed. Because go1 is a different GameObject instance, its position remains the same. However, because go2 and go0 reference the same GameObject instance, go2.transform.position reflects the change as well.

> Next, we'll change the position of go1 to match that of go0 (which is the same GameObject as that referenced by go2).
>
> ```
> 10 go1.transform.position = new Vector3( 10, 20, 30);
> 11 print( go0.transform == go1.transform);                    // Output: false
> 12 print( go0.transform.position == go1.transform.position); // Output: true
> ```
>
> The transforms of the go0 and go1 are not equal, but their positions are equivalent because the Vector3 positions are being compared by value.

!= (Not Equal To)

The inequality operator returns true if two values are not equal and false if they are equal. It is the opposite of ==. When comparing objects by reference, != returns true when the two objects point to different locations in memory. (For the remaining comparisons, literal values will be used in the place of variables for the sake of clarity and space.)

```
print( 10 != 10 );          // Outputs: False
print( 10 != 20 );          // Outputs: True
print( 1.23f != 3.14f );    // Outputs: True
print( 1.23f != 1.23f );    // Outputs: False
print( 3.14f != Mathf.PI ); // Outputs: True
```

> (Greater Than) and < (Less Than)

> returns true if the value on the left side of the operator is greater than the value on the right:

```
print( 10 > 10 );          // Outputs: False
print( 20 > 10 );          // Outputs: True
print( 1.23f > 3.14f );    // Outputs: False
print( 1.23f > 1.23f );    // Outputs: False
print( 3.14f > 1.23f );    // Outputs: True
```

< returns true if the value on the left side of the operator is less than the value on the right:

```
print( 10 < 10 );          // Outputs: False
print( 20 < 10 );          // Outputs: False
print( 1.23f < 3.14f );    // Outputs: True
print( 1.23f < 1.23f );    // Outputs: False
print( 3.14f < 1.23f );    // Outputs: False
```

The characters < and > are also sometimes referred to as *angle brackets,* especially when they are used as tags in languages like HTML and XML or in generic functions in C#. However, when they are used as comparison operators, they are always called *greater than* and *less than.* Comparing objects by reference using >, <, >=, or <= is not possible.

>= (Greater Than or Equal To) and <= (Less Than or Equal To)

>= returns true if the value on the left side is greater than or equivalent to the value on the right:

```
print ( 10 >= 10 );          // Outputs: True
print ( 10 >= 20 );          // Outputs: False
print ( 1.23f >= 3.14f );    // Outputs: False
print ( 1.23f >= 1.23f );    // Outputs: True
print ( 3.14f >= 1.23f );    // Outputs: True
```

<= returns true if the value on the left side is less than or equal to the value on the right:

```
print ( 10 <= 10 );          // Outputs: True
print ( 10 <= 20 );          // Outputs: True
print ( 1.23f <= 3.14f );    // Outputs: True
print ( 1.23f <= 1.23f );    // Outputs: True
print ( 3.14f <= 1.23f );    // Outputs: False
```

Conditional Statements

Conditional statements can be combined with Boolean values and comparison operators to control the *flow* of your programs. This means that a true value can cause the code to follow one path while a false value can cause it to follow another. The two most common forms of conditional statements are if and switch.

if Statements

An if statement only executes the code inside its braces { } if the value inside its parentheses () evaluates to true:

```
if (true) {
    print ( "The code in the first if statement executed." );
}
if (false) {
    print ( "The code in the second if statement executed." );
}

// The output of this code will be:
//     The code in the first if statement executed.
```

The code inside the braces { } of the first if statement executes, yet the code inside the braces of the second if statement does not.

> ### note
>
> Statements enclosed in braces do not require a semicolon after the closing brace. Other statements that have been covered all require a semicolon at the end:
>
> ```
> float approxPi = 3.14159f; // There's the standard semicolon
> ```
>
> Compound statements (that is, those surrounded by braces) do not require a semicolon after the closing brace:
>
> ```
> if (true) {
>     print( "Hello" );      // This line needs a semicolon.
>     print( "World" );      // This line needs a semicolon.
> }                          // No semicolon required after the
>                            //     closing brace!
> ```
>
> The same is true for *any* compound statement surrounded by braces.[2]
>
> ---
>
> 2. I can only think of a single common instance when this is not the case: a special form of array initialization.

Combining `if` Statements with Comparison and Boolean Operations

You can combine Boolean operators with `if` statements to react to various situations in your game:

```
bool night = true;
bool fullMoon = false;

if (night) {
    print( "It's night." );
}
if (!fullMoon) {
    print( "The moon is not full." );
}
if (night && fullMoon) {
    print( "Beware werewolves!!!" );
}
if (night && !fullMoon) {
    print( "No werewolves tonight. (Whew!)" );
}

// The output of this code will be:
//     It's night.
//     The moon is not full.
//     No werewolves tonight. (Whew!)
```

And, of course, you can also combine `if` statements with comparison operators:

```
if (10 == 10 ) {
    print( "10 is equal to 10." );
}
if ( 10 > 20 ) {
    print( "10 is greater than 20." );
}
if ( 1.23f <= 3.14f ) {
    print( "1.23 is less than or equal to 3.14." );
}
if ( 1.23f >= 1.23f ) {
    print( "1.23 is greater than or equal to 1.23." );
}
if ( 3.14f != Mathf.PI ) {
    print( "3.14 is not equal to "+Mathf.PI+"." );
    // + can be used to concatenate strings with other data types.
    // When this happens, the other data type is converted to a string.
}

// The output of this code will be:
//     10 is equal to 10.
//     1.23 is less than or equal to 3.14.
//     1.23 is greater than or equal to 1.23.
//     3.14 is not equal to 3.141593.
```

warning

AVOID USING = IN AN `if` STATEMENT   As I mentioned in the previous warning, `==` is a comparison operator that determines whether two values are equivalent. `=` is an assignment operator that assigns a value to a variable. If you accidentally use `=` in an `if` statement, the result will actually be an assignment instead of a comparison.

Sometimes Unity catches this by giving you an error about not being able to implicitly convert a value to a Boolean. You get that error from this code:

```
float f0 = 10f;
if ( f0 = 10 ) {
    print( "f0 is equal to 10.");
}
```

Other times, Unity gives you a very polite warning stating that it found an `=` in an `if` statement and asking whether you really meant to type `==`. Sometimes, however, Unity might not give you any warning, so you need to be careful and watch out for this yourself.

if...else Statements

Many times, you will want to do one thing if a value is true and another if it is false. At these times, you add an `else` clause to the `if` statement:

```
bool night = false;

if (night) {
    print( "It's night." );
} else {
    print( "It's daytime. What are you worried about?" );
}

// The output of this code will be:
//    It's daytime. What are you worried about?
```

In this case, because `night` is false, the code in the `else` clause is executed.

if...else if...else Chains

Having a chain of `else` clauses is also possible:

```
bool night = true;
bool fullMoon = true;

if (!night) {                 // Condition 1 (evaluates to false)
    print( "It's daytime. What are you worried about?" );
} else if (fullMoon) {        // Condition 2 (evaluates to true)
    print( "Beware werewolves!!!" );
} else {                      // Condition 3 (not evaluated)
    print( "It's night, but the moon is not full." );
}

// The output of this code will be:
//    Beware werewolves!!!
```

Once any condition in the `if...else if...else` chain evaluates to true, all subsequent conditions are no longer evaluated (the rest of the chain is shorted). In the previous listing, Condition 1 is false, so Condition 2 is checked. Because Condition 2 is true, the computer will completely skip Condition 3 and not evaluate it.

Nesting if Statements

Nesting `if` statements inside of each other for more complex behavior is also possible:

```
bool night = true;
bool fullMoon = false;

if (!night) {
    print( "It's daytime. What are you worried about?" );
} else {
```

```
    if (fullMoon) {
        print( "Beware werewolves!!!" );
    } else {
        print( "It's night, but the moon is not full." );
    }
}

// The output of this code will be:
//     It's night, but the moon is not full.
```

`switch` Statements

A `switch` statement can take the place of several `if...else` statements, but it has some strict limitations:

- Switch statements can only compare for equality.
- Switch statements can only compare a single variable.
- Switch statements can only compare that variable against literals (not other variables).

Here is an example:

```
int num = 3;

switch (num) {  // The variable in parentheses (num) is the one being compared
    case (0):  // Each case is a literal number that is compared against num
        print( "The number is zero." );
        break;  // Each case must end with a break statement.
    case (1):
        print( "The number is one." );
        break;
    case (2):
        print( "The number is two." );
        break;
    default:  // If none of the other cases are true, default will happen
        print( "The number is more than a couple." );
        break;
}  // The switch statement ends with a closing brace.

// The output of this code is:
//     The number is more than a couple.
```

If one of the cases holds a literal with the same value as the variable being checked, the code in that case is executed until the `break` is reached. When the computer hits the `break`, it exits the switch and does not evaluate any other cases.

Having one case "fall through" to the next is also possible, but only if no lines of code exist between the case lines (e.g., cases 3, 4, and 5 in the following code listing):

```
int num = 4;

switch (num) {
    case (0):
        print( "The number is zero." );
        break;
    case (1):
        print( "The number is one." );
        break;
    case (2):
        print( "The number is a couple." );
        break;
    case (3):
    case (4):
    case (5):
        print( "The number is a few." );
        break;
    default:
        print( "The number is more than a few." );
        break;
}


// The output of this code is:
//     The number is a few.
```

In the previous code, if num is equal to 3, 4, or 5, the output will be The number is a few.

Knowing what you know about combining conditionals and if statements, you might question when switch statements are used, because they have so many limitations. They are used quite often to deal with the different possible states of a GameObject. For instance, if you made a game where the player could transform into a person, bird, fish, or wolverine, you might have a chunk of code that looked like this:

```
string species = "fish";
bool   onLand = false;

// Each different species type will move differently
public function Move() {
    switch (species) {
        case ("person"):
            Run(); // Calls a function named Run()
            break;
        case ("bird"):
            Fly();
            break;
        case ("fish"):
```

```
            if (!onLand) {
                Swim();
            } else {
                FlopAroundPainfully();
            }
            break;
        case ("wolverine"):
            Scurry();
            break;
        default:
            print( "Unknown species type: "+species );
            break;
    }
}
```

In the preceding code, the player (as a fish in water) would `Swim()`. It's important to note that the `default` case here is used to catch any species that the `switch` statement isn't ready for and that it will output information about any unexpected species it comes across. For instance, if `species` were somehow set to `"lion"`, the output would be:

```
Unknown species type: lion
```

In the preceding code syntax, you also see the names of several functions that are not yet defined (e.g., `Run()`, `Fly()`, `Swim()`). The next chapter covers the creation of your own functions.[3]

Summary

Though Boolean operations might seem a bit dry, they form a big part of the core of programming. Computer programs are full of hundreds, even thousands, of branch points where the computer can do either one thing or another, and these all boil down in some way to Booleans and comparisons. As you continue through the book, you might want to return to this section from time to time if you're ever confused by any comparisons in the code you see.

---

3. For some pretty esoteric reasons, having a different named function for each kind of movement like this is not great code style. However, the reasons for this are beyond the scope of this book. After you've read this book, check out Robert Nystrom's website and book, *Game Programming Patterns* (http://gameprogrammingpatterns.com) for some great information on good programming strategies.

CHAPTER 22

LOOPS

Computer programs are usually designed to do the same thing repeatedly. In a standard game loop, the game draws a frame to the screen, takes input from the player, considers that input, and then draws the next frame, repeating this behavior at least 30 times every second.

A loop in C# code causes the computer to repeat a certain behavior several times. This could be anything from looping over every enemy in the scene and considering the AI of each to looping over all the physics objects in a scene and checking for collisions. By the end of this chapter, you'll understand all you need to know about loops, and in the next chapter, you'll learn how to use them with various C# collections.

Types of Loops

C# has only four kinds of loops: `while`, `do...while`, `for`, and `foreach`. Of those, you'll be using `for` and `foreach` much more often than the others because they are generally safer and more adaptable to the challenges you'll encounter while making games:

- `while` loop: The most basic type of loop. Checks a condition before each loop to determine whether to continue looping.

- `do...while` loop: Similar to the `while` loop, but checks a condition *after* each loop to determine whether to continue looping.

- `for` loop: A loop statement that includes an initial statement, a variable that increments with each iteration, and an end condition. The most commonly used loop structure.

- `foreach` loop: A loop statement that automatically iterates over every element of an enumerable object or collection. This chapter contains some discussion of `foreach`, and I cover it more extensively in the next chapter as part of the discussion of C# collections, such as List and array.

Set Up a Project

In Appendix A, "Standard Project Setup Procedure," detailed instructions show you how to set up Unity projects for the chapters in this book. At the start of each project chapter, you will also see a sidebar like the one here. Please follow the directions in the sidebar to create the project for this chapter.

SET UP THE PROJECT FOR THIS CHAPTER

Following the standard project setup procedure, create a new project in Unity. For information on the standard project setup procedure, see Appendix A.

- **Project name:** Loop Examples

- **Scene name:** _Scene_Loops

- **C# Script names:** Loops

Attach the script Loops to the Main Camera in the scene.

`while` Loops

The `while` loop is the most basic loop structure. However, this also means that it lacks the safety of using a more modern form of loop. In my coding, I almost never use `while` loops because of the danger that using one could create an *infinite loop*.

The Danger of Infinite Loops

An infinite loop occurs when a program enters a loop and is unable to escape it. Let's write one to see what happens. Open the Loops C# script in MonoDevelop (by double-clicking it in the Project pane), add the following bolded code (lines 7–9), and delete any extra lines from the default script.

```
 1 using System.Collections;
 2 using System.Collections.Generic;
 3 using UnityEngine;
 4
 5 public class Loops : MonoBehaviour {
 6     void Start () {
 7         while (true) {
 8             print( "Loop" );
 9         }
10     }
11 }
```

Save this script by choosing *File > Save* from the MonoDevelop menu bar. Switch back to Unity and click the triangular Play button at the top of the Unity window. See how nothing happens… see how nothing happens *forever?* In fact, you're probably going to have to *force quit* Unity now (see the sidebar for instructions). What you have just encountered is an *infinite loop*, and as you can see, an infinite loop will completely freeze Unity. It is lucky that we all run multithreaded computer operating systems now, because in the old days of single-threaded systems, infinite loops wouldn't just freeze a single application, they would freeze the entire computer and require a restart.

So, what happened there that caused the infinite loop? To discover that, take a look at the while loop.

```
7         while (true) {
8             print( "Loop" );
9         }
```

Everything within the braces of a while loop will be executed repeatedly as long as the *condition clause* within the parentheses is true. On line 7, the condition is always true, so the line print("Loop"); will repeat infinitely.

But, you might wonder, if this line was repeating infinitely, why did you never see "Loop" printed in the Console pane? Though the print() function was called many times (probably hundreds of thousands or even millions of times before you decided to force quit Unity), you were never able to see the output in the Console pane because Unity was trapped in the infinite while loop and was unable to redraw the Unity window (which would have needed to happen for you to see the changes to the Console pane).

HOW TO FORCE QUIT AN APPLICATION

On macOS

Implement a force quit by doing the following:

1. Press *Command-Option-Esc* on the keyboard. The *Force Quit* window appears.

2. Find the application that is misbehaving. Its name is often followed by "(not responding)" in the applications list.

3. Click that application name in the list, and then click *Force Quit*. You might need to wait a few seconds for the force quit to happen.

On Windows

Implement a force quit by doing the following:

1. Press *Shift+Ctrl+Esc* on the keyboard. The *Windows Task Manager* appears.

2. Find the application that is misbehaving.

3. Click that application and then click *End Task*. You might need to wait a few seconds for the force quit to happen.

If you force quit Unity while it is running, you will lose any work that you've done since your last save. Because you must constantly save C# scripts, they shouldn't be an issue, but you might have to redo unsaved changes made to your scene. For example, in _Scene_Loops, if you did not save the scene after adding the Loops C# script to the Main Camera, you will need to attach it to the Main Camera again.

A More Useful `while` Loop

Open the Loops C# script in MonoDevelop and modify it to read as follows:

```
1 using System.Collections;
2 using System.Collections.Generic;
3 using UnityEngine;
4
5 public class Loops : MonoBehaviour {
6     void Start () {
7         int i=0;
8         while ( i<3 ) {
9             print( "Loop: "+i );
10            i++;    // See the sidebar on Increment and Decrement Operators
11        }
12    }
13 }
```

Save your code, switch back to Unity and click *Play*. This time, Unity does not get stuck in an infinite loop because the `while` condition clause (`i<3`) eventually becomes false. The output from this program to the console (minus all the extra stuff Unity throws in) is as follows:

```
Loop: 0
Loop: 1
Loop: 2
```

That is because it calls `print ( i )` every time the `while` loop iterates. It's important to note that the condition clause is checked *before* each iteration of the loop.

> ### tip
>
> In most of the examples in this chapter, the *iteration variable* used will be named `i`. The variable names `i`, `j`, and `k` are often used by programmers as iteration variables (i.e., the variable that increments in a loop), and as a result, they are rarely used in any other code situations. Because these variables are created and destroyed so often in various loop structures, you should generally avoid using the variable names `i`, `j`, or `k` for anything else.

INCREMENT AND DECREMENT OPERATORS

Line 10 of the code listing for the "more useful" `while` loop is the first instance in this book of the *increment operator* (++), which increases the value of the variable adjacent to it by 1. So, if `i=5`, then the `i++;` statement would set the value of `i` to 6.

There is also a *decrement operator* (--), which decreases the value of the variable by 1.

The increment and decrement operators can be placed either before or after the variable name, and doing so causes the statement to be treated differently (i.e., `++i` and `i++` act slightly differently). The difference is in whether the initial value is returned (`i++`) or whether the incremented value is returned (`++i`). Here's an example to clarify.

```
 6    void Start () {
 7        int i = 1;
 8        print ( i );     // Output: 1
 9        print ( i++ );   // Output: 1
10        print ( i );     // Output: 2
11        print ( ++i );   // Output: 3
12    }
```

As you can see, line 8 prints the current value of `i`, which is 1. Then, on line 9, the post-increment operator `i++` first returns the current value of `i`, which is printed (resulting in the 1), and then increments the `i`, setting its value to 2.

Line 10 prints the current value of `i`, which is 2. Then, on line 10, the pre-increment operator `++i` first increments the value of `i` from 2 to 3 and then returns it to the print function, which prints a 3.

do...while Loops

A do...while loop works in the same manner as a while loop, except that the condition clause is checked *after* each iteration. This guarantees that the loop will run at least once. Modify the code to read as follows:

```
1 using System.Collections;
2 using System.Collections.Generic;
3 using UnityEngine;
4
5 public class Loops : MonoBehaviour {
6     void Start () {
7         int i=10;
8         do {
9             print( "Loop: "+i );
10            i++;
11        } while ( i<3 );
12     }
13 }
```

Make sure that you change line 7 of the Start() function to int i=10;. Even though the while condition is not ever true (10 is never less than 3), the loop still goes through a single iteration before testing the condition clause on line 11. Had i been initialized to 0 here as it was in the while loop example, the console output would have looked the same, so we set i=10 in line 7 to demonstrate that a do...while loop will always run at least once regardless of the value of i. You must always place a trailing semicolon (;) after the condition clause in a do...while loop.

Save this script and try it out in Unity to see the result.

for Loops

In both the while and do...while examples, you needed to declare and define a variable i, increment the variable i, and then check the condition clause on the variable i; and each of these actions was performed by a separate statement. The for loop handles all of these actions in a single line. Write the following code in the Loops C# script, and then save and run it in Unity.

```
1 using System.Collections;
2 using System.Collections.Generic;
3 using UnityEngine;
4
5 public class Loops : MonoBehaviour {
6     void Start() {
7         for ( int i=0; i<3; i++ ) {
```

```
 8                print( "Loop: "+i );
 9            }
10      }
11 }
```

The `for` loop in this example sends the same output to the Console pane as was sent by the preceding "more useful" `while` loop, yet it does so in fewer lines of code. The structure of a `for` loop requires an *initialization* clause, a *condition* clause, and an *iteration* clause to be valid. In the preceding example, the three clauses are shown in bold here:

Initialization clause:	`for ( int i=0; i<3; i++ ) {`
Condition clause:	`for ( int i=0; i<3; i++ ) {`
Iteration clause:	`for ( int i=0; i<3; i++ ) {`

The *initialization clause* (`int i=0;`) is executed before the `for` loop begins. It declares and defines a variable that is scoped locally to the `for` loop. This means that, the earlier `int i` will cease to exist when the for loop is complete. For more information on variable scoping, see the *Variable Scope* section of Appendix B, "Useful Concepts."

The *condition clause* (`i<3`) is checked before the first iteration of the `for` loop (just as the condition clause is checked before the first iteration of a `while` loop). If the condition clause is true, the code between the braces of the `for` loop is executed.

After an iteration of the code between the braces of the for loop has completed, the *iteration clause* (`i++`) is executed (i.e., after `print( "Loop: "+i );` has executed once, `i++` is executed). Then the condition clause is checked again, and if the condition clause is still true, the code in the braces is executed again, and the iteration clause is executed again. This continues until the condition clause evaluates to false, and then the `for` loop ends.

Because `for` loops mandate that each of these three clauses be included and that they all be on the same line, avoiding writing infinite loops is easier when working with `for` loops.

warning

DON'T FORGET THE SEMICOLONS BETWEEN EACH CLAUSE OF THE `for` STATEMENT   Separating the initialization, condition, and iteration clauses with semicolons is critical. This is because each is an independent clause that must be terminated by a semicolon like any independent clause in C#. Just as most lines in C# must be terminated by a semicolon, so must the independent clauses in a `for` loop.

The Iteration Clause Doesn't Have to Be ++

Though the iteration clause is commonly an increment statement like `i++`, it doesn't have to be. Any operation can be used in the iteration clause.

Decrement

One of the most common alternate iteration clauses is counting down rather than counting up. You do this by using a decrement operator in a `for` loop.

```
 6    void Start() {
 7        for ( int i=5; i>2; i-- ) {
 8            print( "Loop: "+i );
 9        }
10    }
```

The output to the Console pane would be as follows:

```
Loop: 5
Loop: 4
Loop: 3
```

foreach Loops

A `foreach` loop is kind of like an automatic `for` loop to use on anything that is enumerable. In C#, most collections of data are enumerable, including strings (which are a collection of chars) and the Lists and arrays covered in the next chapter. Try this example in Unity.

```
 1 using System.Collections;
 2 using System.Collections.Generic;
 3 using UnityEngine;
 4
 5 public class Loops : MonoBehaviour {
 6     void Start() {
 7         string str = "Hello";
 8         foreach( char chr in str ) {
 9             print( chr );
10         }
11     }
12 }
```

The Console output prints a single char from the string `str` on each iteration, resulting in:

```
H
e
l
l
o
```

The `foreach` loop guarantees that it will iterate over all the elements of the enumerable object. In this case, it iterates over each character in the string "Hello." I cover `foreach` loops further in the next chapter as part of the discussion of Lists and arrays.[1]

Jump Statements within Loops

A *jump statement* is any statement that causes code execution to jump to another location in the code. One example that has already been covered is the `break` statement at the end of each case in a `switch` statement.

The `break` Statement

`break` statements can also be used to prematurely break out of any kind of loop structure. To see an example, change your `Start()` function to read as follows:

```
6     void Start() {
7         for ( int i=0; i<10; i++ ) {
8             print( i );
9             if ( i==3 ) {
10                break;
11            }
12        }
13    }
```

Note that in this code listing, I have omitted lines 1-5, and the final line containing only a closing brace } (which was line 12 in prior listings), because they should not be changed from the lines in previous code listings. Those lines should still be there, and you should just replace the `foreach` loop from lines 7–10 of the preceding `foreach` code listing with lines 7–12 of this code listing.

Run this in Unity, and you get this output:

```
0
1
2
3
```

---

1. Though this shouldn't be a concern for you now, you should be aware that `foreach` loops are less performant than other kinds, meaning that they run slightly more slowly and that they generate more allocated memory garbage that will need to be automatically collected and managed by the computer. If you're working on a speed- or memory-critical game on a weaker computer like a mobile phone, you might want to avoid `foreach` loops. Additionally, `foreach` loops do not guarantee that they will iterate over a collection (i.e., array, List, etc.) in the expected order, though usually they do.

The `break` statement exits the `for` loop prematurely. You can also use `break` to break out of `while`, `do...while`, and `foreach` statements.

Code examples: Console output from that code:

```
for ( int i=0; i<10; i++ ) {                     0
    print ( i );                                 1
    if ( i==3 ) {                                2
        break;                                   3
    }
}
```

```
int i = 0;                                       0
while (true) {                                    1
    print ( i );                                 2
    if ( i > 2 ) break;        // a               3
    i++;
}
```

```
int i = 3;                                        3
do {                                              2
    print ( i );
    i--;
    if ( i==1 ) break;          // b
} while ( i > 0 );
```

```
foreach (char c in "Hello") {                     H
    if (c == 'l') {                               e
        break;
    }
    print ( c );
}
```

The following lettered paragraphs refer to lines in the preceding code that are marked with `// a` and `// b` to the right of the line (these have been bolded in the code listing for emphasis).

a. This line shows the single-line version of an `if` statement. If there is only one line, the braces are not necessary.

b. This code only outputs 3 and 2 because on the second iteration of the loop, the `i--` decrement reduces i to 1. Then the condition clause of the `if` statement is true, and the `break` statement is executed, breaking out of the do...while loop.

Take the time to look at each of the preceding code examples, and make sure you understand why each generates the output shown in the column on the right. If any look confusing, type the code into Unity and then run through it with the debugger. (See Chapter 25, "Debugging.")

The `continue` Statement

`continue` is used to force the program to skip the remainder of the current iteration and continue to the next.

Code: Output:

```
for (int i=0; i<=360; i++) {                          0
    if (i % 90 != 0) {                                90
        continue;                                     180
    }                                                 270
    print( i );                                       360
}
```

In the preceding code, any time that `i%90 != 0` (i.e., any time that `i/90` has a remainder other than 0), the `continue` statement will cause the `for` loop to move on to the next iteration, skipping the `print( i );` line. You can also use the `continue` statement to skip to the next iteration of `while`, `do...while`, and `foreach` loops.

% – MODULUS OPERATOR

The line `if  (i % 90 != 0)  {` in the code listing for the `continue` jump statement is the first instance in this book of the C# *modulus* operator (`%`). Modulus (or mod) *returns the remainder* of dividing one number by another. For example, `12 % 10` would return a value of 2 because the remainder of 12/10 is 2.

You can also use mod with floats, so `12.4f % 1f` would return `0.4f`, the remainder when 12.4 is divided by 1. However, when you use mod with floats, it is susceptible to standard float inaccuracy, so `12.4f % 1f` might give you a result of `0.3999996f` or something similar.

Summary

Understanding loops is one of the key elements of becoming a good programmer. However, it's fine if not all of this makes perfect sense now. After you start using loops in the development of some actual game prototypes, they will become clearer to you. Just make sure that you are actually typing each code example into Unity and running it to help with your understanding of the material.

Also remember that in my coding, I commonly used `for` and `foreach` but rarely or never use `while` and `do...while` because of the danger of infinite loops.

In the next chapter, you will learn about arrays, Lists, and other forms of ordered collections of similar items, and you will see how loops are used to iterate over these collections.

CHAPTER 23

COLLECTIONS IN C#

C# collections enable you to act on several similar things as a group. For example, you could store all the enemy GameObjects in a List and loop over that List each frame to update all of their positions and states.

This chapter covers three important types of these collections in detail: Lists, arrays, and Dictionaries. By the end of this chapter, you will understand how these collection types work and which to use in various situations.

C# Collections

A collection is a group of objects that are referenced by a single variable. In regular life, collections would be things like a group of people, a pride of lions, a parliament of rooks, or a murder of crows. Just like these animal grouping terms, the collections you'll use in C# can only hold a single type of data (e.g., you couldn't include a tiger in a pride of lions), though some rarely used collections do allow multiple data types. The array type is built in to C# at a low level, whereas the other collection types in this chapter rely on the System.Collections.Generic code library to work, as described later in the chapter.

Commonly Used Collections

The following is a brief overview of some of the most commonly used collections. If a collection is described in more depth later in this chapter, an asterisk (*) appears after the name of the collection type.

- **array*:** An array is an indexed, ordered list of objects. You must set the length of an array when defining it, and it cannot be altered, which differentiates it from the more flexible List type. I capitalize the word *array* only when referring to the C# class Array, which is different from the primitive arrays of data described in this chapter. As the most basic type of collection, arrays have few special class functions. However, arrays do have numeric bracket access, meaning that objects can be added to and read from the array using the array name and `[]` like:

```
stringArray[0] = "Hello";
stringArray[1] = "World";
print( stringArray[0]+" "+stringArray[1] ); // Output: Hello World
```

- **List*:** Lists are similar to arrays, except they are flexible in length and very slightly slower for performance. In this book, I capitalize List when referring to the C# type to help distinguish it from the common usage of the word "list." The List is the most commonly used collection in this book. Lists can use numeric bracket access like arrays. Lists also include the following methods:

  - `new List<T>()`—Declares a new List of the type T[1]

  - `Add(X)` —Adds an object X of the type T to the end of the List

  - `Clear()`—Removes all objects from the List

---

[1]. A List is a kind of *generic collection*. In C#, the word *generic* refers to the ability to be used on a variety of types. The <T> denotes that when creating a List, you must declare the type that it will be used for (e.g., `new List<GameObject>()` or `new List<Vector3>()`). You also see the generic <T> used for some methods like the `GetComponent<T>()` method used on GameObjects, where the type of the desired component is passed between the angle brackets (e.g., `gameObject.GetComponent<Rigidbody>()`).

- Contains(X)—Returns true if the object X (of the type T) is in the List
- Count—Property[2] that returns the number of objects in the List
- IndexOf(X)—Returns the numeric index of where the object X exists in the List. If the object X is not in the List, -1 is returned.
- Remove(X)—Removes the object X from the List
- RemoveAt(#)—Removes the object that is at the index # from the List

- **Dictionary*:** Dictionaries enable you to associate key/value pairs, where an object is stored based on a particular key. A real-world example of this is a library, where the *key* of the Dewey Decimal system allows readers to access the *value* of the individual books. Unlike all other collections in this chapter, Dictionaries are declared with two types (the key type and value type).[3] Values can be added to and read from the Dictionary using bracket access (e.g., dict["key"]). Dictionaries include the following methods:
  - new Dictionary<Tkey, Tvalue>()—Declares a new Dictionary with key and value types
  - Add(TKey, TValue)—Adds the object TValue to the Dictionary with the key TKey
  - Clear()—Removes all objects from the Dictionary
  - ContainsKey(TKey)—Returns true if the key TKey is in the Dictionary
  - ContainsValue(TValue)—Returns true if the value TValue is in the Dictionary
  - Count—Property that returns the number of key/value pairs in the Dictionary
  - Remove(TKey)—Removes the value at key TKey from the Dictionary.

- **Queue:** As a first-in, first-out (FIFO) ordered collection, a Queue is similar to a line you might stand in at an amusement park. Objects are added to the end of the Queue with Enqueue() and removed from the beginning of the Queue with Dequeue(). Queues include the following methods:
  - Clear()—Removes all objects from the Queue
  - Contains(X)—Returns true if X is in the Queue
  - Count—Property that returns the number of objects in the Queue
  - Dequeue()—Removes and returns the object at the beginning of the Queue
  - Enqueue(X)—Adds the object X to the end of the Queue
  - Peek()—Returns the object at the beginning of the Queue without removing it

---

2. As a property, Count looks like a field but is actually a function under the hood (see Chapter 26, "Classes").

3. The new Dictionary<Tkey, Tvalue>() function includes two generic designations allowing a Dictionary to be created with any key type and any value type. There is more information about this later in the chapter.

- **Stack:** As a first-in, last-out (FILO) ordered collection, a Stack is similar to a stack of cards. Objects are added to the top of the Stack with `Push()` and removed from the top of the Stack with `Pop()`. Stacks include the following methods:
  - `Clear()`—Removes all objects from the Stack
  - `Contains(X)`—Returns true if X is in the Stack
  - `Count`—Property that returns the number of objects in the Stack
  - `Peek()`—Returns the object at the top of the Stack without removing it
  - `Pop()`—Removes and returns the object at the top of the Stack
  - `Push(X)`—Adds the object X to the top of the Stack

Because Lists are the most used collection in this book, I'll start with them and then cover both Dictionaries and arrays in detail.

SET UP A PROJECT FOR THIS CHAPTER

Following the standard project setup procedure, create a new project in Unity. If you need a refresher on the standard project setup procedure, see Appendix A, "Standard Project Setup Procedure."

- **Project name:** Collections Project
- **Scene name:** _Scene_Collections
- **C# script names:** ArrayEx, DictionaryEx, ListEx

Attach all three C# scripts to *Main Camera* in _Scene_Collections.

Using Generic Collections

The beginning of all Unity C# scripts automatically includes three lines that start with the word `using`:[4]

```
using UnityEngine;
using System.Collections;
using System.Collections.Generic;
```

Each of these `using` lines loads a library of code and gives the script the ability to use code within those libraries. The first line is the most important in Unity coding, as it gives this C#

---

4. Prior to Unity 5.5, `using System.Collections.Generic;` was not added to the top of scripts by default, and developers had to add it manually. Also, this isn't the order that you'll see in Unity 5.5 and later, but the order doesn't really matter, and it is easier to describe them in this order.

script knowledge of all the standard Unity objects, including things like MonoBehaviour, GameObject, Rigidbody, Transform, and so on.

The second line allows the script to use several *un-typed* collections like ArrayList (which you see in some Unity tutorials). As un-typed collections, these can hold any kind of data in each element (e.g., a string in one element and an image or song in another). This flexibility can lead to sloppiness that can make things a lot more difficult to debug and code, so I strongly recommend against using un-typed collections.

The third line is critical for this chapter, because it enables several *generic collections*, including List and Dictionary. A generic collection is one that is *strongly typed*, meaning that it can only hold a single specific data type that is specified using angle brackets.[5] Example declarations of generic collections (i.e., initial creations of generic collections) include:

- `public List<string> sList;`—This declares a List of strings.
- `public List<GameObject> goList;`—This declares a List of GameObjects.
- `public Dictionary<char,string> acronymDict;`—This declares a Dictionary of string values that have chars as keys (e.g., you could use the char `'o'` to access the string `"Okami"`).

`System.Collections.Generic` also defines several other generic data types that are beyond the scope of this chapter. These include the generic versions of Queue and Stack mentioned earlier. Unlike arrays, which are locked to a specified length, all generic collection types can adjust their length dynamically.

List

Double-click the ListEx C# script in the Project pane to open it in MonoDevelop and add the following bolded code. The `//` a-style comments on the far-right side of the code listing are references to explanations listed after the code. Lines that you must add appear in bold type.

```
1 using System.Collections;                              // a
2 using System.Collections.Generic;                      // b
3 using UnityEngine;                                      // c
4
5 public class ListEx : MonoBehaviour {
6     public List<string>        sList;                   // d
7
8     void Start () {
```

---

5. It may seem strange for a "generic" collection to only be able to hold one type of data. The word generic is used here to refer to the ability (via the `<T>`) to allow a data type like List to be created in a generic way that can be strongly typed for any data type. Writing generic classes like List is outside the scope of this book, but you can search online for "C# generic" to learn more.

```
9        sList = new List<string>();                                    // e
10       sList.Add( "Experience" );                                      // f
11       sList.Add( "is" );
12       sList.Add( "what" );
13       sList.Add( "you" );
14       sList.Add( "get" );
15       sList.Add( "when" );
16       sList.Add( "you" );
17       sList.Add( "don't" );
18       sList.Add( "get" );
19       sList.Add( "what" );
20       sList.Add( "you" );
21       sList.Add( "wanted." );
22       // This quote is from my professor, Dr. Randy Pausch (1960-2008)
23
24       print( "sList Count = "+sList.Count );                          // g
25       print( "The 0th element is: "+sList[0] );                       // h
26       print( "The 1st element is: "+sList[1] );
27       print( "The 3rd element is: "+sList[3] );
28       print( "The 8th element is: "+sList[8] );
29
30       string str = "";
31       foreach (string sTemp in sList) {                               // i
32           str += sTemp+" ";
33       }
34       print( str );
35   }
36 }
```

a. The System.Collections library that is at the beginning of all C# scripts enables the ArrayList type (among others). ArrayList is another type of C# collection that is similar to List except that ArrayLists are not limited to a single type of data. This enables more flexibility, but I have found it to have more detriments than benefits when compared to Lists (including a significant performance penalty).

b. The List collection type is part of the System.Collections.Generic C# library, so that library must be imported to enable the use of Lists. Unity 5.5 and later do this automatically, but you must do it manually in earlier versions. As mentioned earlier, this library enables a whole slew of generic collection types beyond just List. You can learn more about them online by searching "C# System.Collections.Generic" if you're curious.

c. The UnityEngine library enables all the classes and types that are specific to Unity (e.g., GameObject, Renderer, Mesh). Including it in any MonoBehaviour script is mandatory.

d. This declares the `List<string>` sList. All generic collection data types have their name followed by angle brackets `<>` surrounding a specified data type. In this case, the List is a List of strings. However, the strength of generics is that you can use them for any data type. You could just as easily create a `List<int>`, `List<GameObject>`, `List<Transform>`, `List<Vector3>`, and so on. You must assign the type of the List at the time of declaration.

e. The declaration of `sList` on line 6 makes `sList` a variable name that can hold a List of strings, but the value of `sList` is `null` (i.e., it has no value) until you initialize `sList` on line 9. Before this initialization, any attempt to add elements to `sList` would have caused an error. The List initialization must repeat the type of the List in the `new` statement. A newly initialized List contains no elements and has a `Count` of zero.

f. A List's `Add()` function adds an element to the List. This inserts the string literal `"Experience"` into the 0th (pronounced "zeroth") element of the List. See the "Lists and Arrays Are Zero-Indexed" sidebar for information about zero-indexed Lists.

g. A List's `Count` property returns an int representing the number of elements in the List. Output:

```
sList Count = 12
```

h. Lines 25–28 demonstrate the use of *bracket access* (e.g., `sList[0]`). Bracket access uses brackets `[]` and an integer to reference a specific element in a List or array. The integer between the brackets is known as the "index." Output:

```
The 0th element is: Experience
The 1st element is: is
The 3rd element is: you
The 8th element is: get
```

i. `foreach` (introduced in the previous chapter) is often used with Lists and other collections. Just as a string is a collection of chars, `List<string> sList` is a collection of strings. The string `sTemp` variable is scoped to the `foreach` statement, so it will cease to exist after the `foreach` loop completes. Because Lists are strongly typed (i.e., C# knows that `sList` is a `List<string>`) the elements of `sList` can be assigned to string `sTemp` without requiring any kind of conversion. This is one of the major advantages of the List type over the nontyped ArrayList type. Output:

```
Experience is what you get when you don't get what you wanted.
```

As always, remember to save your script in MonoDevelop when you're done editing. Then, switch back to Unity and select *Main Camera* in the Hierarchy pane. You can see that `List<string> sList` appears in the *ListEx (Script)* component of the Inspector pane. If you play the Unity scene, you can click the disclosure triangle next to `sList` in the Inspector and actually see the values that populate it. Arrays and Lists appear in the Inspector, but Dictionaries do not.

LISTS AND ARRAYS ARE ZERO-INDEXED

List and array collection types are *zero indexed*, meaning that what you might think of as the "first" element is actually element [0]. Throughout the book, I refer to this element as the 0th or "zeroth" element.

For these examples, we'll consider the *pseudocode* collection `coll`. Pseudocode is code that is not from any specific programming language but is used to illustrate a conceptual point more easily.

```
coll = [ "A", "B", "C", "D", "E" ]
```

The *count* or *length* of `coll` is 5, and the valid indices for the elements would be from 0 to `coll.Count-1` (i.e., 0, 1, 2, 3, and 4).

```
print( coll.Count );   // 5

print( coll[0] );      // A
print( coll[1] );      // B
print( coll[2] );      // C
print( coll[3] );      // D
print( coll[4] );      // E

print( coll[5] );      // Index Out of Range Exception!!!
```

If you try to use bracket access to access an index that is not in range, the following runtime error appears:

```
IndexOutOfRangeException: Array index is out of range.
```

Keeping this in mind as you work with any collection in C# is important.

IMPORTANT LIST PROPERTIES AND METHODS

Many properties and methods are available for Lists, but the following ones are the most often used. All of these method examples refer to the following `List<string>` `sL` and are noncumulative. In other words, each example starts with the List `sL` as it is defined in the following three lines, unmodified by the other examples.

```
List<string> sL = new List<string>();
sL.Add( "A" ); sL.Add( "B" ); sL.Add( "C" ); sL.Add( "D" );
// Resulting in the List: [ "A", "B", "C", "D" ]
```

Properties

Properties allow you access to information about the List.

- `sL[2]` (Bracket access): Returns the element of the List at the index specified by the parameter (2). Because C is the second element, `sL[2]` returns C.

- `sL.Count`: Returns the number of elements currently in the List. Because the length of a List can vary over time, `Count` is very important. The last valid index in a List is always `Count-1`. The value of `sL.Count` is 4, so the last valid index is 3.

Methods

Methods are functions that allow you to alter the list.

- `sL.Add("Hello")`: Adds the parameter `"Hello"` to the end of `sL`. In this case, `sL` becomes: `[ "A", "B", "C", "D", "Hello" ]`.

- `sL.Clear()`: Removes all existing elements from `sL` returning it to an empty state. `sL` becomes empty: `[   ]`.

- `sL.IndexOf("A")`: Finds the first instance in the `sL` of the parameter `"A"` and returns the index of that element. Because `"A"` is the 0th element of `sL`, this call returns 0.

  If the variable does not exist in the List, a `-1` is returned. This is a safe and fast method to determine whether a List contains an element.

- `sL.Insert(2, "B.5")`: Inserts the second parameter (`"B.5"`) into `sL` at the index specified by the first parameter (2). This shifts the subsequent elements of the List backward. In this case, this would cause `sL` to become `[ "A", "B", "B.5", "C", "D" ]`. Valid index values for the first parameter are 0 through `sL.Count`. Any value outside this range causes a runtime error.

- `sL.Remove("C")`: Removes the specified element from the List. If there happened to be two `"C"`s in the List, only the first would be removed. `sL` becomes `[ "A", "B", "D" ]`.

- `sL.RemoveAt(0)`: Removes the element at the specified index from the List. Because `"A"` is the 0th element of the List, `sL` becomes `[ "B", "C", "D" ]`.

Converting a list to an array

It is possible to convert a List to a simple array (described later in this chapter). This is useful because some Unity functions expect an array of objects instead of a List.

- `sL.ToArray()`: Generates an array that has all the elements of `sL`. The new array will be of the same type as the List and returns a new string array with the elements `[ "A", "B", "C", "D" ]`.

To move on to learning about Dictionaries, make sure that Unity playback is stopped and then uncheck the check box next to the name of the *ListEx (Script)* component in the Inspector pane to make the ListEx script inactive (as is shown in Figure 23.1).

Figure 23.1 Clicking the check box to deactivate the ListEx Script component

Dictionary

You can't view Dictionaries in the Inspector, yet they can be a fantastic way to store information. One of the major benefits of a Dictionary is its *constant access time*. This means that no matter how many items you insert into a Dictionary, it will take the same amount of time to find an item. Contrast this with a List or array, where you must iterate over each of the items in the linear collection one by one; as the size of the List or array grows, the amount of time needed to find a specific element grows as well, especially if the element you're searching for happens to be the last one in the collection.

Dictionaries pair a *key* and *value*. The key can then be used to access the value. Open the DictionaryEx C# script and enter the following code to see how this works.

```
1 using System.Collections;
2 using System.Collections.Generic;                                  // a
3 using UnityEngine;
4
5 public class DictionaryEx : MonoBehaviour {
6     public Dictionary<string,string>    statesDict;                 // b
7
8     void Start () {
9         statesDict = new Dictionary<string, string>();              // c
10
11         statesDict.Add( "MD", "Maryland" );                        // d
12         statesDict.Add( "TX", "Texas" );
13         statesDict.Add( "PA", "Pennsylvania" );
14         statesDict.Add( "CA", "California" );
15         statesDict.Add( "MI", "Michigan" );
16
17         print("There are "+statesDict.Count+" elements in statesDict.");  // e
18
19         foreach (KeyValuePair<string,string> kvp in statesDict) {  // f
20             print( kvp.Key + ": " + kvp.Value );
21         }
22
23         print( "MI is " + statesDict["MI"] );                      // g
24
25         statesDict["BC"] = "British Columbia";                     // h
26
```

```
27            foreach (string k in statesDict.Keys)  {                    // i
28                print( k + " is " + statesDict[k] );
29            }
30      }
31
32 }
```

a. You must include the System.Collections.Generic library to enable Dictionary use.

b. A Dictionary is declared with both a key and value type in a statement like this. For this Dictionary, both the key and value are strings, but you can use any data type for either.

c. Like a List, a Dictionary is not ready to be used until it is initialized in a statement like this.

d. When you add elements to the Dictionary, you must pass in both a key and a value for each element. These five `Add` statements add postal codes and state names to the Dictionary for the states where I've lived in my life.

e. As with other C# collections, you can use `Count` to determine how many elements are in a Dictionary. Output:

```
There are 5 elements in the Dictionary.
```

f. You can use `foreach` on Dictionaries, but the type of the value that is iterated is a KeyValuePair<,>. The two types of the KeyValuePair<,> must match those of the Dictionary (e.g., <string, string> here). Output:

```
MD: Maryland
TX: Texas
PA: Pennsylvania
CA: California
MI: Michigan
```

g. If you know the key, you can use it to access the value in the Dictionary via bracket access. Output:

```
MI: Michigan
```

h. Another way to add values to a Dictionary is to use bracket access as shown here. I also lived in BC for a brief time.

i. The Keys of the Dictionary can also be iterated over using a `foreach` loop. Output:

```
MD is Maryland
TX is Texas
PA is Pennsylvania
CA is California
MI is Michigan
BC is British Columbia
```

Save the DictionaryEx script, switch back to Unity, and click *Play*. You should see the output described. Remember that Dictionaries do not appear in the Unity inspector, so even though `statesDict` is a public variable, you will not see it in the Inspector.

IMPORTANT DICTIONARY PROPERTIES AND METHODS

Many properties and methods are also available for Dictionaries, but the ones listed in this sidebar are the most often used. All of these examples refer to the following `Dictionary<int, string>` `dIS` and are noncumulative. In other words, each example starts with the Dictionary `dIS` as it is defined in the following lines, unmodified by the other examples.

```
Dictionary<int,string> dIS;
dIS = new Dictionary<int, string>();
dIS[0] = "Zero";
dIS[1] = "One";
dIS[10] = "Ten";
dIS[1234567890] = "A lot!";
```

Another way of writing this same Dictionary declaration and definition would be:

```
dIS = new Dictionary<int, string>() {
    { 0, "Zero" },
    { 1, "One" },
    { 10, "Ten" },
    { 1234567890, "A lot!" }
};
```

This kind of combined declaration and definition of a Dictionary is one of the rare cases where you will see a semicolon at the end of a pair of braces.

Properties

- `dIS[10]` (Bracket access): Returns the element of the Dictionary array at the index specified by the parameter (`10`). Because `"Ten"` is the element at the key `10`, `dIS[10]` returns: `"Ten"`. If you try to access an element with a key that doesn't exist, you will receive a `KeyNotFoundException` runtime error that will crash your code.

- `dIS.Count`: Returns the number of key/value pairs currently in the Dictionary. Because the length of a Dictionary can vary over time, `Count` is very important.

Methods

- `dIS.Add(12, "Dozen")`: Adds the value `"Dozen"` to the Dictionary at the key `12`.

- `dIS[13]` = `"Baker's Dozen"`: Adds the value `"Baker's Dozen"` to the Dictionary at the key `13`. If you use bracket access to set an already-existing, key, it will replace the value. For example `dIS[0]` = `"None"` would replace the value at key `0` with `"None"`.

- `dIS.Clear()`: Removes all existing key/value pairs from `dIS`, leaving it empty.

- `dIS.ContainsKey(1)` : Returns true if the key 1 is in the Dictionary. This is a very fast call because the Dictionary is designed to find things quickly by key. Keys in the Dictionary are exclusive, so you can only have one value for each key.

- `dIS.ContainsValue("A lot!")`: Returns true if the value `"A lot!"` is in the Dictionary. This is a slow call because a Dictionary is optimized to find things by key, not value. Values are also non-exclusive, meaning that several keys could hold the same value.

- `dIS.Remove(10)`: Removes the key/value pair at the key 10 from the Dictionary.

Setting the equivalent of something like a Dictionary in the Inspector is sometimes desirable. In that case, I often create a List of a simple class that includes both a key and a value. You can see an example of this in Chapter 31, "Space SHMUP Plus."

Before moving on to looking at arrays, make sure that Unity playback is stopped and then uncheck the check box next to the name of the *DictionaryEx (Script)* component in the Inspector pane to make the DictionaryEx script inactive.

Array

An array is the simplest collection type, which also makes it the fastest. Arrays do not require any libraries to be imported (via the `using` command) to work because they are built into core C#. In addition, arrays have multidimensional and jagged forms that can be very useful.

Arrays are of a fixed length that must be assigned when the array is initialized. Double-click the ArrayEx C# script in the Project pane to open it in MonoDevelop and enter the following code:

```
1 using System.Collections;                              // a
2 using UnityEngine;
3
4 public class ArrayEx : MonoBehaviour {
5     public string[]        sArray;                      // b
6
7     void Start () {
8         sArray = new string[10];                        // c
9
10        sArray[0] = "These";                            // d
11        sArray[1] = "are";
12        sArray[2] = "some";
13        sArray[3] = "words";
14
15        print( "The length of sArray is: "+sArray.Length );  // e
16
```

```
17          string str = "";
18          foreach (string sTemp in sArray)  {                          // f
19              str += "|"+sTemp;
20          }
21          print( str );
22      }
23 }
```

a. Unlike a List or Dictionary, arrays do not require `System.Collections.Generic` in order to work.

b. Also unlike a List or Dictionary, an array in C# isn't actually a separate data type (which is why it's not capitalized here); rather it's a collection formed from any existing data type by adding brackets after the type name. The type of `sArray` is not declared as `string`; it is `string[]`, a collection of multiple `strings`. Note: Although `sArray` is declared to be an array here, its length is not yet set.

c. Here, `sArray` is initialized as a `string[]` with a length of 10. When an array is initialized, its length is filled with elements of the default value for that data type. For `int[]` or `float[]`, the default would be `0`. For `string[]` and other complex data types like `GameObject[]`, each element of the array is filled with `null` (which indicates that no value has been assigned).

d. Rather than using the `Add()` method like Lists, standard arrays use bracket access for assignment of value as well as retrieval of value from the array.

e. Rather than using `Count` like the generic C# collections, arrays use the property `Length`. It is important to note (as you can see from the preceding code output) that `Length` returns the entire length of the array, including both defined elements (e.g., `sArray[0]` through `sArray[3]` in the previous code) and elements that are empty (i.e., still their default, undefined value as are `sArray[4]` through `sArray[9]` in the previous code). Output:

   ```
   The length of sArray is 10.
   ```

f. `foreach` works for arrays just as it does for other C# collections. The only difference is that the array might have empty or null elements, and `foreach` will iterate over them. As in the List<string> example earlier, here `sTemp` is a string that will temporarily be assigned the value of each element of `sArray` by the `foreach` loop. Output:

   ```
   |These|are|some|words||||||
   ```

When you run the code, be sure to have Main Camera selected in the Hierarchy pane. This enables you to open the disclosure triangle next to `sArray` in the *ArrayEx (Script)* component of the Inspector pane and see the elements of `sArray`.

The code output looks like this:

```
The length of sArray is: 10
|These|are|some|words||||||
```

Empty Elements in the Middle of an Array

One thing allowed by arrays that is not possible in Lists[6] is an empty element in the middle of an array. This would be useful in a game if you had something like a scoring track where each player had a marker on the track but it was possible to have empty spaces in between the markers.

Modify lines 12 and 13 of the previous code as follows:

```
10          sArray[0]  =  "These";
11          sArray[1]  =  "are";
12          sArray[3]  =  "some";
13          sArray[6]  =  "words";
```

The code output would look like this: |These|are||some|||words|||

As you can see from the output, sArray now has empty elements at indices 2, 4, 5, 7, 8, and 9. As long as the index (e.g., 0, 1, 3, and 6 here) of the assignment is within the valid range for the array, you can use bracket access to place a value anywhere in the array, and the foreach loop will handle it gracefully.

Attempting to assign a value to an index that is outside of the defined range for the array (e.g., sArray[10] = "oops!"; or sArray[99] = "error!";) will lead to the following runtime error: IndexOutOfRangeException: Array index is out of range.

Attempting to access a non-existent array index will also give you the same runtime error. For example, print(sArray[20]); would also give you an IndexOutOfRangeException.

Return the code back to its original state:

```
10          sArray[0]  =  "These";
11          sArray[1]  =  "are";
12          sArray[2]  =  "some";
13          sArray[3]  =  "words";
```

Empty Array Elements and `foreach`

Play the project again and look at the output, which has returned to its previous state:

|These|are|some|words||||||

The str += " | "+sTemp; statement on line 19 concatenates (i.e., adds) a pipe (|) to the end of str before each element of the array. Even though sArray[4] through sArray[9] are still the default value of null, they are counted by foreach and iterated over. This is a good

---

6. Adding a null element to a list, resulting in an empty element in the middle, is technically possible, but I've never used that myself.

opportunity to use a `break` jump statement to escape the `foreach` loop early. Modify the code as follows:

```
18          foreach (string sTemp in sArray) {
19              str += "|"+sTemp;
20              if (sTemp == null) break;
21          }
```

The new code output is as follows: `|These|are|some|words|`

When C# iterates over `sArray[4]`, it still concatenates `"|"+null` onto the end of `str` but then checks `sArray[4]`, sees that it is `null`, and breaks out of the `foreach` loop, preventing it from iterating over `sArray[5]` through `sArray[9]`.

IMPORTANT ARRAY PROPERTIES AND METHODS

Of the properties and methods available for arrays, the ones listed in this sidebar are the most often used. All of these refer to the following array and are noncumulative.

```
string[] sA = new string[] { "A", "B", "C", "D" };
// Resulting in the Array: [ "A", "B", "C", "D" ]
```

Here you see the array definition expression that allows the declaration, initialization, and population of an array in a single line (as opposed to the array initialization statement shown on line 8 of the previous code listing. Note that when using this form of the array initialization expression, the `Length` of the array is implied by the number of elements between the braces and does not need to be specified; in fact, if you use braces to define an array, you cannot use the brackets in the array declaration to specify a length that is different from the number of elements between the braces.

Properties

- `sA[2]` (bracket access): Returns the element of the array at the index specified by the parameter (2). Because `"C"` is the second element of `sA`, this returns: `"C"`.

  If the index parameter is outside of the valid range of the array (which for `sA` is 0 to 3), it will generate an `IndexOutOfRangeException` runtime error.

- `sA[1] = "Bravo"` (bracket access used for assignment): Assigns the value on the right side of the = assignment operator to the specified position in the array, replacing the previous value. `sA` would become `[ "A", "Bravo", "C", "D" ]`.

  If the index parameter is outside of the valid range of the array, it will generate an `IndexOutOfRangeException` runtime error.

- `sA.Length`: Returns the total capacity of the array. Elements will be counted regardless of whether they have been assigned or are still default values. Returns 4.

Static Methods

The static methods here are part of the System.Array class (i.e., defined by the System. Collections library) and can act on arrays to give them some of the abilities of Lists.

- `System.Array.IndexOf( sA, "C" )`: Finds the first instance in the array `sA` of the element `"C"` and returns the index of that element. Because `"C"` is the second element of `sA`, this returns 2.

  If the variable does not exist in the array, a `-1` is returned. This is often used to determine whether an array contains a specific element.

- `System.Array.Resize( ref sA, 6 )`: This is a C# method that adjusts the length of an array. The first parameter is a reference to the array instance (which is why the `ref` keyword is required), and the second parameter is the new length. `sA` would then become `[ "A", "B", "C", "D", null, null ]`.

  If the second parameter specifies a Length that is shorter than the original array, the extra elements will be culled. `System.Array.Resize( ref sA, 2 )` would cause `sA` to become `[ "A", "B" ]`. `System.Array.Resize()` does not work for the multidimensional arrays described later in this chapter.

Converting an Array to a List

As mentioned in the List section, it's possible to convert a List to an array. It is also possible to go the other direction and convert an array to a List.

- `List<string> sL = new List<string>( sA )`: This line creates a List `sL` that duplicates all the elements of `sA`.

You can also use the array initialization expression to declare, define, and populate a List in one line, but it's a little convoluted:

- `List<string> sL = new List<string>( new string[] { "A", "B", "C" } );`

This declares, defines, and populates an anonymous new `string[]` array that is immediately passed into the `new List<string>()` function.

To prepare for the next example, deactivate the ArrayEx script by clicking the check box next to its name in the Inspector pane for Main Camera.

Multidimensional Arrays

Creating multidimensional arrays that have two or more indices is possible—and often useful. This means that instead of just one index number in the brackets, the array could use two or more. This would be useful for creating a two-dimensional grid that could hold one item in each grid square.

Create a new C# script named *Array2dEx* and attach it to Main Camera. Open Array2dEx in MonoDevelop and enter the following code:

```
1 using System.Collections;
2 using System.Collections.Generic;
3 using UnityEngine;
4
5 public class Array2dEx : MonoBehaviour {
6
7     public string[,]                sArray2d;
8
9     void Start () {
10        sArray2d = new string[4,4];
11
12        sArray2d[0,0] = "A";
13        sArray2d[0,3] = "B";
14        sArray2d[1,2] = "C";
15        sArray2d[3,1] = "D";
16
17        print( "The Length of sArray2d is: "+sArray2d.Length );
18    }
19 }
```

The code yields the following output: `The Length of sArray2d is: 16`

As you can see, `Length` is still only a single int, even though this is a multidimensional array. `Length` here is now just the total number of elements in the array, so it is the coder's responsibility to keep track of each separate dimension of the array.

Now, let's create a nicely formatted output of the values in sArray2d array. When you're done, it should look something like this:

```
|A| | |B|
| | |C| |
| | | | |
| |D| | |
```

As you can see, the A is in the 0th row, 0th column ([0,0]), the B is in the 0th row, 3rd column ([0,3]), and so on. To implement this, add the following bolded lines to the code:

```
17          print( "The Length of sArray2d is: "+sArray2d.Length );
18          string str = "";
19          for ( int i=0; i<4; i++ ) {                              // a
20              for ( int j=0; j<4; j++ ) {
21                  if (sArray2d[i,j] != null) {                     // b
22                      str  +=  "|"+sArray2d[i,j];
23                  } else {
24                      str += "|_";
25                  }
26              }
27              str += "|"+"\n";                                     // c
28          }
29          print( str );
30      }
31 }
```

a. Lines 19 and 20 demonstrate the use of two nested `for` loops to iterate over a
   multidimensional array. When nested in this manner, the code:

   1. Starts with `i=0` (line 19)

   2. Iterates over all `j` values from 0 to 3 (lines 20 to 26)

   `str` is now `"|A|  |B|\n"` (line 27)

   3. Increments to `i=1` (line 19)

   4. Iterates over all `j` values from 0 to 3 (lines 20 to 26)

   `str` is now `"|A|  |B|\n|  |C|  |\n"` (line 27)

   5. Increments to `i=2` (line 19)

   6. Iterates over all `j` values from 0 to 3 (lines 20 to 26)

   `str` is now `"|A|  |B|\n|  |C|  |\n|  |  |\n"` (line 27)

   7. Increments to `i=3` (line 19)

   8. Iterates over all `j` values from 0 to 3 (lines 20 to 26)

   `str` is now `"|A|  |B|\n|  |C|  |\n|  |  |\n|D|  |\n"` (line 27)

This guarantees that the code moves through the multidimensional array in an orderly manner.
Keeping the grid example, it moves through all the elements in a row (by incrementing `j` from 0
to 3) and then advances to the next row by incrementing `i` to the next value.

b. Lines 21–25 check to see whether the string at `sArray[i,j]` has a value other than `null`.
   If so, it concatenates a pipe and `sArray2d[i,j]` onto `str`. If the value is `null`, a pipe and
   one space are concatenated onto `str`. You can find the pipe character on the keyboard
   above the Return (or Enter) key. It is usually Shift+backslash (\).

c. This line occurs after all the iterations of the `j` for loop but before the next iteration of the `i`
   for loop. The effect of it is to concatenate a trailing pipe and carriage return (i.e., line break)
   onto `str`, giving the output the nice formatting of a line for each iteration of the `i` for loop.[7]

---

7. The `"\n"` character here is seen by C# as a single character that indicates a new line. It causes a line
   break in the final output.

The code produces the following output:

```
The Length of sArray2d is: 16

|A| | |B|
| | |C| |
| | | | |
| |D| | |
```

If you just look at the output in the Console pane of Unity, you only see the top two lines of the sArray2d grid array listed in the output. However, clicking that line in the Console pane reveals more data in the bottom half of the Console pane (see Figure 23.2).

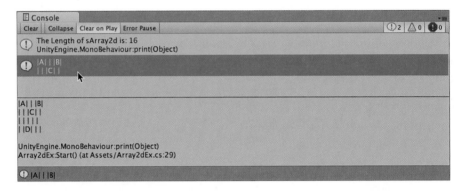

Figure 23.2 Clicking an output message in the Console causes an expanded view to appear below. Note that the first line of the most recent Console message is also shown in the lower-left corner of the Unity window.

As you can see in the figure, the fancy text formatting doesn't line up as well in the Console pane because it uses a *non-monospaced* font (i.e., a font where an *i* and *m* have different widths; in monospaced fonts, i and m have the same width). You can click any line in the Console pane and choose *Edit > Copy* from the menu bar to copy that data and then paste it into another program. This is something that I do often, and I most commonly paste into a text editor. (I prefer *BBEdit*[8] on macOS or *EditPad Pro*[9] on Windows, both of which are quite powerful.)

You also should be aware that the Unity Inspector pane does not display multidimensional arrays. In fact, similar to Dictionaries, if the Inspector does not know how to properly display a variable, it completely ignores it, so not even the name of a public multidimensional array will appear in the Inspector pane.

---

8. *BBEdit* has a free evaluation version available from BareBones Software: http://www.barebones.com.

9. *EditPad Pro* has a free trial available from Just Great Software: http://editpadpro.com.

Stop Unity's execution by clicking the *Play* button again (so that it is not blue) and then use the Main Camera Inspector to disable the *Array2dEx (Script)* component.

Jagged Arrays

A jagged array is an array of arrays. This is similar to the multidimensional array, but it allows the subarrays to be different lengths. You'll create a jagged array that holds the following data:

```
| A | B | C | D |
| E | F | G |
| H | I |
| J |   |   | K |
```

As you can see, the 0th and 3rd rows each contain four elements, whereas rows 1 and 2 contain three and two elements, respectively. Note that null elements are allowed as is shown in the 3rd row. In fact, as far as C# is concerned, an entire row could be null (though in the code listing that follows, this would cause an error on line 33).

Create a new C# script named *JaggedArrayEx* and attach it to Main Camera. Open JaggedAr-rayEx in MonoDevelop and enter the following code:

```
 1 using System.Collections;
 2 using System.Collections.Generic;
 3 using UnityEngine;
 4
 5 public class JaggedArrayEx : MonoBehaviour {
 6     public string[][]          jArray;                              // a
 7
 8     void Start () {
 9         jArray = new string[4][];                                   // b
10
11         jArray[0] = new string[4];                                  // c
12         jArray[0][0] = "A";
13         jArray[0][1] = "B";
14         jArray[0][2] = "C";
15         jArray[0][3] = "D";
16
17         // The following lines use single-line Array initialization    // d
18         jArray[1] = new string[] { "E", "F", "G" };
19         jArray[2] = new string[] { "H", "I" };
20
21         jArray[3] = new string[4];                                  // e
22         jArray[3][0] = "J";
23         jArray[3][3] = "K";
24
25         print( "The Length of jArray is: "+jArray.Length );          // f
26         // Outputs: The Length of jArray is: 4
```

```
27
28          print( "The Length of jArray[1] is: "+jArray[1].Length );       // g
29          // Outputs: The Length of jArray[1] is: 3
30
31          string str = "";
32          foreach (string[] sArray in jArray) {                            // h
33              foreach( string sTemp in sArray ) {
34                  if (sTemp != null) {
35                      str += " | "+sTemp;                                   // i
36                  } else {
37                      str += " | ";                                        // j
38                  }
39              }
40              str += " | \n";
41          }
42
43          print( str );
44      }
45 }
```

a. Line 6 declares `jArray` as a jagged array (i.e., an array of arrays). Where a `string[]` is a collection of strings, a `string[][]` is a collection of string arrays (or `string[]`s).

b. Line 8 defines `jArray` as a jagged array with a length of 4. Note that the second set of brackets is still empty, denoting that the subarrays can still be of any length—although after their length is set, it is fixed and difficult to alter.

c. Line 11 defines the 0th element of `jArray` to be an array of strings with a length of 4. Lines 12–15 insert elements into that subarray, using the first set of brackets (`[0]`) to access the 0th subarray of `jArray` and the second set of brackets to insert a string into each of the four elements of that subarray.

d. Lines 18 and 19 use the single-line form of array definition. Because the elements of the array are defined between the braces, the length of the array does not need to be explicitly stated (hence the empty brackets in `new string[]`).

e. Lines 21–23 define the 3rd element of `jArray` to be a `string[]` with a length of 4 and then fill only the 0th and 3rd elements of that `string[]`, leaving elements 1 and 2 null.

f. Line 25 outputs `"The Length of jArray is: 4"`. Because `jArray` is an array of arrays (rather than a multidimensional array), `jArray.Length` counts only the number of elements that can be accessed via the first set of brackets (i.e., the four subarrays).

g. Line 28 outputs `"The Length of jArray[1] is: 3"`. Because `jArray` is an array of arrays, subarray `Length` can be easily determined.

h. In jagged arrays, `foreach` works separately on the array and sub-arrays. `foreach` on `jArray` iterates through the four `string[]` (string array) elements of `jArray`, and `foreach` on any of those `string[]` subarrays iterates over the strings within. Note that `sArray` is a `string[]` (string array) and that `sTemp` is a string.

As I mentioned previously, line 33 would throw a `NullReferenceException` error if one of the rows of `jArray` were `null`. In that case, `sArray` would be `null`, and trying to run the `foreach` statement in line 33 on a null variable would lead to a `NullReference-Exception` error (the attempt to reference an element of something that is `null`). The `foreach` statement would be attempting to access data of `sArray` like `sArray.Length` and `sArray[0]`. Because `null` data have no elements or value, accessing things like `null.Length` throws this error.

i. On a keyboard, you type the string literal in line 35 as space pipe space.

j. On a keyboard, you type the string literal in line 37 as space pipe space space.

The code outputs the following to the Console pane:

```
The Length of jArray is: 4
The Length of jArray[1] is: 3
 | A | B | C | D |
 | E | F | G |
 | H | I |
 | J |   | K |
```

Using for Loops Instead of `foreach` for Jagged Arrays

You can also use for loops based on the `Length` of the array and subarrays. You could replace the `foreach` loop on lines 32–41 in the preceding code listing with this code:

```
31          string str = "";
32          for (int i=0; i<jArray.Length; i++) {
33              for (int j=0; j<jArray[i].Length; j++) {
34                  if (jArray[i][j] != null) {
35                      str += " | "+jArray[i][j];
36                  } else {
37                      str += " | ";
38                  }
39              }
40              str += " | \n";
41          }
```

This code produces the exact same output as the `foreach` loops shown earlier. Whether you choose to use `for` or `foreach` will depend on the situation.

Jagged Lists

As a final note on jagged collections, creating jagged Lists is also possible. A jagged two-dimensional list of strings would be declared `List<List<string>> jaggedStringList`. Just as with jagged arrays, the subLists would initially be null, so you would have to initialize them as you added them as shown in the following code. Just like all Lists, jagged Lists do *not* allow empty elements. Create a new C# script named *JaggedListTest*, attach it to Main Camera, and enter this code:

```
1 using System.Collections;                                              // a
2 using System.Collections.Generic;
3 using UnityEngine;
4
5 public class JaggedListTest : MonoBehaviour {
6     public List<List<string>> jaggedList;
7
8     // Use this for initialization
9     void Start () {
10         jaggedList = new List<List<string>>();
11
12         // Add two List<string>s to jaggedList
13         jaggedList.Add( new List<string>() );
14         jaggedList.Add( new List<string>() );
15
16         // Add two strings to jaggedList[0]
17         jaggedList[0].Add ("Hello");
18         jaggedList[0].Add ("World");
19
20         // Add a third List<string> to jaggedList, including data
21         jaggedList.Add ( new List<string>( new string[] {"complex",
            ➥"initialization"})  );                                     // b
22
23         string str = "";
24         foreach (List<string> sL in jaggedList) {
25             foreach (string sTemp in sL) {
26                 if (sTemp != null) {
27                     str += " | "+sTemp;
28                 } else {
29                     str += " | ";
30                 }
31             }
32             str += " | \n";
33         }
34         print( str );
35     }
36 }
```

 a. Although `using System.Collections;` is included in all Unity C# scripts by default, it's not actually necessary for Lists (though System.Collections.Generic is required for Lists).

 b. This is one of the first instances in this book of the ➥ code continuation character. This is used throughout the book when a single line is longer than can fit the width of the page.

You should **not** type the ➡ character; rather, it is there to let you know to continue typing the single line as if there were no line break. With no leading tabs, line 21 would appear as follows:

```
jaggedList.Add ( new List<string>( new string[] {"complex","initialization"} ) );
```

The code outputs the following to the Console pane:

```
| Hello | World |
|
| complex | initialization |
```

Whether to Use Array or List

Arrays and Lists are very similar, so people are often unsure which one to use in any given situation. The primary differences between the array and List collections types are as follows:

- List has flexible length, whereas array length is more difficult to change.
- Array is very slightly faster.
- Array allows multidimensional indices.
- Array allows empty elements in the middle of the collection.

Because they are simpler to implement and take less forethought (due to their flexible length), I personally tend to use Lists much more often than arrays. This is especially true when prototyping games, because prototyping requires a lot of flexibility.

Summary

Now that you have a handle on Lists, Dictionaries, and arrays, you can work easily with large numbers of objects in your games. For example, you could return to the Hello World project from Chapter 19, "Hello World: Your First Program," and add a `List<GameObject>` to the CubeSpawner code that had every new cube added to it at the time the cube was instantiated. This would give you a reference to each cube, allowing you to manipulate the cube after it was created. The following exercise shows you how to do so.

Summary Exercise

In this exercise, you return to the Hello World project from Chapter 19 and write a script that will add each new cube created to a `List<GameObject>` named `gameObjectList`. Every frame that a cube exists, it will be scaled down to 95% of its size in the previous frame. After a cube shrinks to a scale of 0.1 or less, it will be deleted from the scene and `gameObjectList`.

However, deleting an element from `gameObjectList` while the `foreach` loop is iterating over it will cause an error. To avoid this, the cubes that need to be deleted will be temporarily stored in another list named `removeList`, and then the list will be iterated over to remove them from `gameObjectList`. (You'll see what I mean in the code.)

Open your Hello World project and create a new scene (*File > Scene* from the menu bar). Save the scene as *_Scene_3*. Create a new script named *CubeSpawner3* and attach it to the Main Camera in the scene. Then, open CubeSpawner3 in MonoDevelop and enter the following code:

```
1  using System.Collections;
2  using System.Collections.Generic;
3  using UnityEngine;
4
5  public class CubeSpawner3 : MonoBehaviour {
6      public GameObject          cubePrefabVar;
7      public List<GameObject>  gameObjectList; // Will hold all the Cubes
8      public float              scalingFactor = 0.95f;
9      // ^ Amount that each cube will shrink each frame
10     public int                numCubes = 0; // Total # of Cubes instantiated
11
12     // Use this for initialization
13     void Start() {
14         // This initializes the List<GameObject>
15         gameObjectList = new List<GameObject>();
16     }
17
18     // Update is called once per frame
19     void Update () {
20         numCubes++; // Add to the number of Cubes                       // a
21
22         GameObject gObj = Instantiate<GameObject>( cubePrefabVar );     // b
23
24         //  These lines set some values on the new Cube
25         gObj.name = "Cube "+numCubes;                                   // c
26         Color c = new Color(Random.value, Random.value, Random.value); // d
27         gObj.GetComponent<Renderer>().material.color  =  c;
28         // ^ Gets the Renderer component of gObj & gives gObj a random color
29         gObj.transform.position = Random.insideUnitSphere;             // e
30
31         gameObjectList.Add (gObj); // Add gObj to the List of Cubes
32
33         List<GameObject> removeList = new List<GameObject>();          // f
34         // ^ This removeList will store information on Cubes that should be
35         //     removed from gameObjectList
36
37         //     Iterate through each Cube in gameObjectList
38         foreach (GameObject goTemp in gameObjectList) {                // g
39
```

```
40                  // Get the scale of the Cube
41                  float scale = goTemp.transform.localScale.x;              // h
42                  scale *= scalingFactor; // Shrink it by the scalingFactor
43                  goTemp.transform.localScale = Vector3.one * scale;
44
45                  if (scale <= 0.1f) { // If the scale is less than 0.1f...   // i
46                      removeList.Add (goTemp); // ...then add it to the removeList
47                  }
48              }
49
50          foreach (GameObject goTemp in removeList) {                       // g
51              gameObjectList.Remove (goTemp);                              // j
52              // ^ Remove the Cube from gameObjectList
53              Destroy (goTemp);  // Destroy the Cube's GameObject
54          }
55      }
56 }
```

a. The increment operator (++) is used to increase the field that tracks the total number of cubes that have been created.

b. An instance of `cubePrefabVar` is instantiated. The generic type declaration here "`<GameObject>`" is necessary because you can use `Instantiate()` on any kind of object (meaning that without the generic type declaration, C# has no way of knowing what kind of data `Instantiate()` will return). The "`<GameObject>`" tells C# that a GameObject will be returned by the `Instantiate()` function.

c. The `numCubes` variable is used to give unique names to each cube. The first cube will be named *Cube 1*, the second *Cube 2*, and so on.

d. Lines 26 and 27 assign a random color to each cube. Colors are accessed through the material attached to the GameObject's Renderer component, as demonstrated on line 27.

e. `Random.insideUnitSphere` returns a random location that is inside a sphere with a radius of 1 (centered on the point [0,0,0]). This code makes the cubes spawn at a random location near [0,0,0] rather than all at exactly the same point.

f. As is stated in the code comments, `removeList` will be used to store cubes that will need to be removed from `gameObjectList`. This is necessary because C# does not allow you to remove elements from a list in the middle of a `foreach` loop that is iterating over the list. (i.e., you can't call `gameObjectList.Remove()` anywhere within the `foreach` loop on lines 38–48 that iterates over `gameObjectList`.)

g. This `foreach` loop iterates over all the cubes in `gameObjectList`. Note that the temporary variable created for the `foreach` is `goTemp`. `goTemp` is also used in the `foreach` loop on line 50, so `goTemp` is declared on both lines 38 and 50. Because `goTemp` is locally scoped to the `foreach` loop in each case, there is no conflict caused by declaring the variable twice in the same `Update()` function. See *Variable Scope* in Appendix B, "Useful Concepts," for more information.

h. Lines 41–43 get the current scale of a cube (by getting the X dimension of its `transform.localScale`), multiply that scale by 95%, and then set the `transform.localScale` to this new value. Multiplying a Vector3 by a float (as is done on line 43) multiplies each individual dimension by that same number, so [2, 4, 6] * 0.5f would yield [1, 2, 3].

i. As mentioned in the code comments, if the newly reduced scale is less than 0.1f, the cube will be added to `removeList`.

j. The `foreach` loop from lines 50–54 iterates over `removeList` and removes any cube that is in `removeList` from `gameObjectList`. Because the `foreach` is iterating over `removeList`, removing elements from `gameObjectList` is perfectly fine. The removed cube GameObject still exists on screen until the `Destroy()` command is used to destroy it. Even then, it still exists in the computer's memory because it is still an element of `removeList`. However, because `removeList` is a local variable scoped to the `Update()` function, when the `Update()` function completes, `removeList` ceases to exist, and then any objects that are exclusively stored in `removeList` will also be deleted from memory.

Save your script and then switch back to Unity. You must assign *Cube Prefab* from the Project pane to the cubePrefabVar variable in the *Main Camera:CubeSpawner3 (Script)* component of the Main Camera Inspector if you want to actually instantiate any cubes.

After you do this, click *Play* in Unity, and you should see that a number of cubes spawn in as they did in previous versions of Hello World. However, they spawn in different colors, they shrink over time, and they are eventually destroyed (instead of existing indefinitely as they did in earlier versions).

Because the CubeSpawner3 code keeps track of each cube through the `gameObjectList`, it is able to modify each cube's scale every frame and then destroy each cube after it's smaller than a scale of 0.1f. At a `scalingFactor` of 0.95f, it takes each cube 45 frames to shrink to a scale <= 0.1f, so what would be the 0th cube in `gameObjectList` is always removed and destroyed for being too small, and the `Count` of `gameObjectList` stays at 45.

Moving Forward

In the next chapter, you learn how to create and name functions other than `Start()` and `Update()`.

CHAPTER 24

FUNCTIONS AND PARAMETERS

In this chapter, you learn to take advantage of the immense power of functions. You write your own custom functions that can take various kinds of variables as input arguments and can return a single variable as the function's result. I also cover some special cases of parameters for function input like function overloading, optional parameters, and the `params` keyword modifier, all of which will help you to write more effective, modular, reusable, and flexible code.

Setting Up the Function Examples Project

In Appendix A, "Standard Project Setup Procedure," detailed instructions show you how to set up Unity projects for the chapters in this book. At the start of each project, you will also see a sidebar like the one here. Please follow the directions in the sidebar to create the project for this chapter.

SET UP THE PROJECT FOR THIS CHAPTER

Following the standard project setup procedure, create a new project in Unity. For information on the standard project setup procedure, see Appendix A.

- **Project name:** Function Examples

- **Scene name:** _Scene_Functions

- **C# Script names:** CodeExample

Attach the script CodeExample to the Main Camera in the scene _Scene_Functions.

Definition of a Function

You've actually been writing functions since your first Hello World program, but prior to now, you've been adding content to built-in Unity MonoBehaviour functions like `Start()` and `Update()`. From now on, you'll also be writing custom functions.

The best way to think about a function is as a chunk of code that does something. For instance, to count the number of times that `Update()` has been called, you can create a new C# script with the following code (you will need to add the bold lines):

```
1  using UnityEngine;
2  using System.Collections;
3
4  public class CodeExample : MonoBehaviour {
5
6      public int        numTimesCalled = 0;                              // a
7
8      void Update() {
9          numTimesCalled++;                                             // b
10         PrintUpdates();                                              // c
11     }
12
13     void PrintUpdates() {                                            // d
14         string outputMessage = "Updates: "+numTimesCalled;          // e
15         print( outputMessage ); // Output example: "Updates: 1"     // f
16     }
17
18 }
```

a. Declares the public variable `numTimesCalled` and assigns 0 as its initial value. Because `numTimesCalled` is declared as a public variable inside the class `CodeExample` but outside of any function, it is available to be accessed by any of the functions within the CodeExample class.

b. `numTimesCalled` is incremented (1 is added to it).

c. Line 10 *calls* the function `PrintUpdates()`. When your code calls a function, it causes the function to be executed. I describe this in more detail soon.

d. Line 13 *declares* the function `PrintUpdates()`. Declaring a function is similar to declaring a variable. `void` is the return type of the function, meaning that the function is not expected to return a value (as I cover in more detail soon). Lines 13–16 collectively *define* the function. All lines of code between the opening brace { on line 13 and the closing brace } on line 16 are part of the definition of `PrintUpdates()`.

Note that the order in which your functions are declared in the class does not matter. Whether `PrintUpdates()` or `Update()` is declared first is irrelevant as long as they are both within the braces of the class CodeExample. C# will look through all the declarations in a class before running any code. It's perfectly fine for `PrintUpdates()` to be called on line 10 and declared on line 13 because both `PrintUpdates()` and `Update()` are functions declared in the class CodeExample.

e. Line 14 defines a *local* string variable named `outputMessage`. Because `outputMessage` is defined within the function `PrintUpdates()` its *scope* is limited to `PrintUpdates()`, meaning that the variable name `outputMessage` has no value outside of the function `PrintUpdates()`. For more information about variable scope, see the *Variable Scope* section of Appendix B, "Useful Concepts."

Line 14 also defines `outputMessage` to be the concatenation of `"Updates: "` and the public integer `numTimesCalled`.

f. The Unity function `print()` is called with the single *argument* `outputMessage`. This prints the value of `outputMessage` to the Unity Console. I cover function arguments later in this chapter.

In an actual game, `PrintUpdates()` would not be a terribly useful function, but it does showcase two of the important concepts covered in this chapter:

- **Functions encapsulate actions:** You can think of a function as a named collection of several lines of code. Every time the function is called, those lines of code are executed. This was demonstrated by both `PrintUpdates()` and the `BuySomeMilk()` example from Chapter 18, "Introducing Our Language: C#."

- **Functions contain their own scope:** As you can read in the *Variable Scope* section of Appendix B, "Useful Concepts," variables declared within a function have their scope limited to that function. Therefore, the variable `outputMessage` (declared on line 14) has a scope limited to just the function `PrintUpdates()`. This can either be stated as "outputMessage is scoped to the function `PrintUpdates()`" or "outputMessage is *local to* the function `PrintUpdates()`."

Contrast the scope of the local variable `outputMessage` with that of the public variable `numTimesCalled`, which has a scope of the entire CodeExample class and can be used by any function in CodeExample.

If you run this code in Unity, you will see that `numTimesCalled` is incremented every frame and `PrintUpdates()` is called every frame (which outputs the value of `numTimesCalled` to the Console pane). Calling a function causes it to execute, and when the function is done, execution then returns to the point from where it was called. So, in the class CodeExample, the following happens every frame:

1. Every frame, the Unity engine calls the `Update()` function (line 8).

2. Line 9 increments `numTimesCalled`.

3. Line 10 calls `PrintUpdates()`.

4. Execution then jumps to the beginning of the `PrintUpdates()` function on line 13.

5. Lines 14 and 15 are executed.

6. When Unity reaches the closing brace of `PrintUpdates()` on line 16, execution returns to line 10 (the line from which it was called).

7. Execution continues to line 11, which ends the `Update()` function.

The remainder of this chapter covers both simple and complex uses of functions, and it's an introduction to some rather complicated concepts. As you continue into the tutorials later in this book, you'll get a much better understanding of how functions work and get more ideas for your own functions, so if there's anything that doesn't make sense the first time through this chapter, that's okay. You can return to it after you've read a bit more of the book.

USING CODE FROM THIS CHAPTER IN UNITY

Though the first code listing in this chapter includes all the lines of the CodeExample class, later code examples do not. If you want to actually run the rest of the code from this chapter in Unity, you must wrap it inside of a class. Chapter 26, "Classes," covers classes in detail, but for now, you can accomplish this by adding the bolded lines that follow around any of the code listed in this chapter:

```
1  using UnityEngine;
2  using System.Collections;
3
4  public class CodeExample : MonoBehaviour {
5
       // The code listing would replace this comment
16
17 }
```

For example, without the immediately preceding bold lines, the first code listing in this chapter would have looked like this:

```
6    public int         numTimesCalled = 0;
7
8    void Update() {
9        PrintUpdates();
10   }
11
12   void PrintUpdates() {
13       numTimesCalled++;
14       print( "Updates: "+numTimesCalled );   // Example: "Updates: 5"
15   }
```

If you wanted to enter this listing of lines 6–15 into a C# script in MonoDevelop, you would need to add the bold lines from the previous listing around them and indent each of these lines (6–15) one tab. The final version of code in MonoDevelop would be the code listing on the first page of this chapter.

The remainder of the code listings in this chapter have numbering that starts on line 6 to indicate that other lines would need to precede and follow them. I've omitted the tab at the beginning of each line to allow more space for the code on each line.

Function Parameters and Arguments

Some functions are called with empty parentheses following them (for example, PrintUpdates() in the first code listing). Other functions can be passed information in between the parentheses (for example, Say("Hello") in the following listing). When a function is designed to receive outside information via the parentheses like this, the type of information is specified by one or more *parameters* that create a local function variable (with a specific type) to hold the information. In line 10 of the following code listing, void Say (string sayThis) declares a parameter named sayThis that is of the string type. sayThis can then be used as a local variable within the Say() function.

When information is sent to a function via its parameters, it is referred to as *passing* information to the function. Each variable passed into a parameter is called an *argument*. In line 7 of the following listing, the function Say() is called with the argument "Hello". Another way to say this is that "Hello" is passed to the function Say(). The argument passed to a function must match the parameters of the function, or it will cause an error.

```
6    void Awake() {
7        Say("Hello");                          // a
8    }
9
10   void Say( string sayThis ) {               // b
11       print(sayThis);
12   }
```

a. When Say() is called by line 7, the string literal "Hello" is passed into the function Say() as an argument, and line 10 then sets the value of sayThis to "Hello".

b. The string sayThis is declared as a parameter variable of the function Say(). This makes sayThis a local variable that is scoped to the function Say(), in other words, the variable sayThis does not exist outside of the function Say().

UNDERSTANDING AWAKE(), START(), AND UPDATE()

As you experienced in Chapter 19, "Hello World: Your First Program," Update() is called on every GameObject once every frame, and Start() is called once, right before the first Update() is called on a GameObject. Just like Start() and Update(), Awake() is a key method of many Unity scripts. Awake() is called once, just like Start(), but Awake() is called immediately at the moment that a GameObject is created. This means that on any single GameObject, Awake() will always happen before Start().

In the following script, an Awake() method on a script attached to testPrefab would be called before "After instantiation" is printed, while a Start() method on testPrefab would be called several milliseconds later, after the entire Test() function is finished, just before the first Update() is called on the testPrefab GameObject instance.

```
void Test() {
    print( "Before instantiation" );
    Instantiate<GameObject>( testPrefab );
    print( "After instantiation" );
}
```

In the function Say() in the previous listing, we've added a single parameter named sayThis. Just as with any other variable declaration, the first word, string, is the variable type and the second word, sayThis, is the name of the variable.

Just like other local function variables, the parameter variables of a function disappear from memory as soon as the function is complete; if the parameter sayThis were used anywhere in the Awake() function, it would cause a compiler error due to sayThis being exclusively limited in scope to the function Say().

In line 7 of the preceding code listing, the argument passed into the function is the string literal "Hello", but any type of variable or literal can be specified as the parameter type for a function, and any variable or literal that matches the specified type can be passed into that function as an argument (e.g., line 7 of the following code listing passes this. gameObject as an argument to the function PrintGameObjectName()). If a function has multiple parameters, arguments passed to it must be separated by commas (see line 8 in the following code listing).

```
6     void Awake() {
7         PrintGameObjectName( this.gameObject );
8         SetColor( Color.red, this.gameObject );
9     }
10
11    void PrintGameObjectName( GameObject go ) {
12        print( go.name );
13    }
14
15    void SetColor( Color c, GameObject go ) {
16        Renderer r = go.GetComponent<Renderer>();
17        r.material.color = c;
18    }
```

> **tip**
>
> **C# FUNCTIONS CAN BE DEFINED IN ANY ORDER**   You probably noticed in the previous code listing that both `PrintGameObject()` and `SetColor()` are called by the `Awake()` function on lines 7 and 8, yet they aren't defined until lines 11–18. This is absolutely fine in C#. C# searches your entire script for function names before executing any of the script, so it doesn't matter where in your script the functions are defined.

Returning Values

In addition to receiving values as parameters, functions can also return a single value, known as the *result* of the function as shown on line 13 of the following code listing.

```
6     void Awake() {
7         int num = Add( 2, 5 );
8         print( num ); // Prints the number 7 to the Console
9     }
10
11    int Add( int numA, int numB ) {
12        int sum = numA + numB;
13        return( sum );
14    }
```

In this example, the function `Add()` has two parameters, the integers `numA` and `numB`. When called, it will sum the two integers that were passed in and then return the result. The `int` at the beginning of the function definition on line 11 declares that `Add()` will be returning an integer as its result. Just as you must declare the type of any variable for it to be useful, you must also declare the return type of a function for it to be used elsewhere in code.

Returning `void`

Most of the functions that we've written so far have had a return type of `void`, which means that no value can be returned by the function. Though these functions don't return a specific value, there are still times that you might want to call `return` within them.

Any time `return` is used within a function, it stops execution of the function and returns execution back to the line from which the function was called. (For example, the `return` on line 16 of the following code listing returns execution back to line 9.)

Returning from a function to avoid the remainder of the function is sometimes useful. For example, if you had a list of more than 100,000 GameObjects (e.g., `reallyLongList` in the following code listing), and you wanted to move the GameObject named "Phil" to the origin (Vector3.zero), but didn't care about doing anything else, you could write this function:

```
 6    public List<GameObject> reallyLongList; // Defined in the Inspector    // a
 7
 8    void Awake() {
 9        MoveToOrigin("Phil");                                               // b
10    }
11
12    void MoveToOrigin(string theName) {
13        foreach (GameObject go in reallyLongList) {                         // c
14            if (go.name == theName) {                                       // d
15                go.transform.position = Vector3.zero;                       // e
16                return;                                                     // f
17            }
18        }
19    }
```

a. `List<GameObject> reallyLongList` is a very long list of GameObjects that we are imagining has been predefined in the Unity Inspector. Because this predefined List doesn't really exist, entering this code into Unity would not work unless you defined `really-LongList` yourself.

b. The function `MoveToOrigin()` is called with the string literal `"Phil"` as its argument.

c. The `foreach` statement iterates over `reallyLongList`.

d. If a GameObject with the name `"Phil"` (i.e., `theName`) is found...

e. ...then it is moved to the position [0, 0, 0].

f. Line 16 returns execution to line 9. This avoids iterating over the rest of the List.

In `MoveToOrigin()`, you really don't care about checking the other GameObjects after you've found the one named Phil, so it is better to short circuit the function and return before wasting computing power on checking the rest of the list. If Phil is the last GameObject in the list, you haven't saved any time; however, if Phil is the first GameObject, you have saved a lot.

Note that when `return` is used in a function with the `void` return type, it does not use parentheses (and even when returning a value, the parentheses are optional).

Proper Function Names

As you'll recall, variable names should be sufficiently descriptive, start with a lowercase letter, and use camelCase (uppercase letters at each word break). For example:

```
int       numEnemies;
float     radiusOfPlanet;
Color     colorAlert;
string    playerName;
```

Function names are similar; however, function names should all start with a capital letter so that they are easier to differentiate from the variables in your code. Here are some good function names:

```
void ColorAGameObject( GameObject go, Color c ) {…}
void AlignX( GameObject go0, GameObject go1, GameObject go2 ) {…}
void AlignXList( List<GameObject> goList ) {…}
void SetX( GameObject go, float eX ) {…}
```

Why Use Functions?

Functions are a perfect method for encapsulating code and functionality in a reusable form. Generally, any time that you would write the same lines of code more than a couple of times, it's good style to define a function to do so instead. Let's start with a code listing that has some repeated code in it.

The function `AlignX()` in the following code listing takes three GameObjects as parameters, averages their position in the X direction, and sets them all to that average X position:

```
6    void AlignX( GameObject go0, GameObject go1, GameObject go2 ) {
7        float avgX = go0.transform.position.x;
8        avgX += go1.transform.position.x;
9        avgX += go2.transform.position.x;
10       avgX = avgX/3.0f;
11
12       Vector3 tempPos;
13       tempPos = go0.transform.position;                          // a
14       tempPos.x = avgX;                                          // a
15       go0.transform.position = tempPos;                         // a
16
17       tempPos = go1.transform.position;
18       tempPos.x = avgX;
19       go1.transform.position = tempPos;
```

```
20
21          tempPos = go2.transform.position;
22          tempPos.x = avgX;
23          go2.transform.position = tempPos;
24      }
```

a. In lines 13–15, you can see how to handle the Unity restriction that does not allow you to directly set the position.x of a transform. Instead, you must first copy the current position to another variable (e.g., `Vector3 tempPos`), then change the x value, and finally copy the whole Vector3 back onto `transform.position`. This is very tedious to write repeatedly, which led to the `SetX()` function shown in the next code listing. The `SetX()` function in that listing enables you to set the x position of a transform in a single step (e.g., `SetX( this.gameObject, 25.0f )`).

Because of the limitations on directly setting an x, y, or z value of the `transform.position`, the `AlignX()` function has a lot of repeated code on lines 13 through 23. Typing that code can be very tedious, and if you needed to change anything later, it would necessitate changing the same thing three times in this `AlignX()` function. This is one of the main reasons for writing functions. In the following code listing, lines 11–23 from the previous code listing have been replaced by calls to a new function, `SetX()`. The bold lines in the following code listing have been altered from the previous listing.

```
6    void AlignX( GameObject go0, GameObject go1, GameObject go2 ) {
7        float avgX = go0.transform.position.x;
8        avgX += go1.transform.position.x;
9        avgX += go2.transform.position.x;
10       avgX = avgX/3.0f;
11
12       SetX ( go0, avgX );
13       SetX ( go1, avgX );
14       SetX ( go2, avgX );
15   }
16
17   void SetX( GameObject go, float eX ) {
18       Vector3 tempPos = go.transform.position;
19       tempPos.x = eX;
20       go.transform.position = tempPos;
21   }
```

In this improved code listing, the removed lines from the previous code have been replaced by the definition of a new function `SetX()` (lines 17–21) and three calls to it (lines 12–14). If anything needed to change about how you were setting the x value, it would only require making a change once to `SetX()` rather than making the change three times in the prior code listing. Although this is a simple example, I hope it serves to demonstrate the power that functions allow us as programmers.

The remainder of this chapter covers some more complex and interesting ways to write functions in C#.

Function Overloading

Function overloading is a fancy term for the capability of functions in C# to act differently based on the type and number of parameters that are passed into them. The **bold** sections of the following code demonstrate function overloading.

```
6    void Awake() {
7        print( Add( 1.0f, 2.5f ) );
8        // ^ Prints: "3.5"
9        print( Add( new Vector3(1, 0, 0), new Vector3(0, 1, 0) ) );
10       // ^ Prints "(1.0, 1.0, 0.0)"
11       Color colorA = new Color( 0.5f,  1,     0, 1);
12       Color colorB = new Color( 0.25f, 0.33f, 0, 1);
13       print( Add( colorA, colorB ) );
14       // ^ Prints "RGBA(0.750, 1.000, 0.000, 1.000)"
15   }
16
17   float Add( float f0, float f1 ) {                        // a
18       return( f0 + f1 );
19   }
20
21   Vector3 Add( Vector3 v0, Vector3 v1 ) {                  // a
22       return( v0 + v1 );
23   }
24
25   Color Add( Color c0, Color c1 ) {                        // a
26       float r, g, b, a;
27       r = Mathf.Min( c0.r + c1.r, 1.0f );                  // b
28       g = Mathf.Min( c0.g + c1.g, 1.0f );                  // b
29       b = Mathf.Min( c0.b + c1.b, 1.0f );                  // b
30       a = Mathf.Min( c0.a + c1.a, 1.0f );                  // b
31       return( new Color( r, g, b, a ) );
32   }
```

a. Three different `Add()` functions are declared and defined in the previous listing, and each is called based on the parameters passed in by various lines of the `Awake()` function. When two floating-point numbers are passed in, the float version of `Add()` is used; when two Vector3s are passed in, the Vector3 version is used; and when two Colors are passed in, the Color version is used.

b. In the Color version of `Add()`, care is taken to not allow `r`, `g`, `b`, or `a` to exceed 1 because the red, green, blue, and alpha channels of a color are limited to values between 0 and 1. This is done through the use of the `Mathf.Min()` function. `Mathf.Min()` takes any number of arguments as parameters and returns the one with the minimum value. In the previous listing, if the summed reds are equal to 0.75f, then 0.75f will be returned in the red channel; however, if the greens were to sum to any number greater than 1.0f, a green value of 1.0f will be returned instead.

Optional Parameters

Sometimes you want a function to have *optional parameters* that may either be passed in or omitted. In the following code, the float eX parameter of SetX() is optional. If you give a parameter a default value in the definition of the function, the compiler will interpret that parameter as optional (e.g., line 13 in the following code listing, where the float eX is given a default value of 0.0f). The **bold** code demonstrates optional parameters.

```
 6    void Awake() {
 7        SetX( this.gameObject, 25 );                                         // b
 8        print( this.gameObject.transform.position.x ); // Outputs: "25"
 9        SetX( this.gameObject );                                             // c
10        print( this.gameObject.transform.position.x ); // Outputs: "0"
11    }
12
13    void SetX( GameObject go, float eX=0.0f ) {                              // a
14        Vector3 tempPos = go.transform.position;
15        tempPos.x = eX;
16        go.transform.position = tempPos;
17    }
```

a. The float eX is defined as an optional parameter with a default value of 0.0f. Giving eX a default value in the function declaration (the =0.0f part) is what makes eX an optional parameter. If no argument is passed in for the eX parameter, it will have a value of 0.0f.

b. Because a float can hold any integer value,[1] passing an int into a float is perfectly fine. (For example, the integer literal 25 on line 7 is passed as an argument into the float eX parameter on line 13.)

c. On line 9, no eX argument is passed to the SetX() method (though an argument is passed for the required go parameter). When no argument is passed for an optional parameter, the default value is used. In this case, the default value for eX was defined as 0.0f on line 13.

The first time it's called from Awake(), the eX parameter is set to 25.0f, which overrides the default of 0.0f. However, the second time it's called, the eX parameter is omitted, leaving SetX() to default to a value of 0.0f.

Optional parameters must come after any required parameters in the function definition.

---

1. To be more precise, a float can hold *most* int values. As described in Chapter 19, "Variables and Components," floats get somewhat inaccurate for very big and very small numbers, so a very large int might be rounded to the nearest number that a float can represent. Based on an experiment I ran in Unity, a float seems to be able to represent every whole number up to 16,777,217, after which it will lose accuracy.

The `params` Keyword

As shown on line 13 of the following code listing, the `params` keyword can be used to allow a function to accept any number of parameters of the same type. These parameters are converted into an array of that type. The **bold** code demonstrates the `params` keyword.

```
6    void Awake() {
7        print( Add( 1 ) );          // Outputs: "1"
8        print( Add( 1, 2 ) );       // Outputs: "3"
9        print( Add( 1, 2, 3 ) );    // Outputs: "6"
10       print( Add( 1, 2, 3, 4 ) ); // Outputs: "10"
11   }
12
13   int Add( params int[] ints ) {
14       int sum = 0;
15       foreach (int i in ints) {
16           sum += i;
17       }
18       return( sum );
19   }
```

`Add()` can now accept any number of integers and return their sum. As with optional parameters, the `params` list needs to come after any other parameters in your function definition (meaning that you can have other required parameters before the `params` list).

This also allows you to rewrite the `AlignX()` function from before to take any number of possible GameObjects, as demonstrated in the following code listing.

```
6    void AlignX( params GameObject[] goArray ) {          // a
7        float sumX = 0;
8        foreach (GameObject go in goArray) {              // b
9            sumX += go.transform.position.x;              // c
10       }
11       float avgX = sumX / goArray.Length;               // d
12
13       foreach (GameObject go in goArray) {              // e
14           SetX ( go, avgX );
15       }
16   }
17
18   void SetX( GameObject go, float eX ) {
19       Vector3 tempPos = go.transform.position;
20       tempPos.x = eX;
21       go.transform.position = tempPos;
22   }
```

a. The `params` keyword creates an array of GameObjects from any GameObjects passed in.

b. `foreach` can iterate over every GameObject in `goArray`. The `GameObject go` variable is scoped to the `foreach` loop on lines 8–10, so it does not conflict with the `GameObject go` variable in the `foreach` loop on lines 13–15.

    c. The X position of the current GameObject is added to `sumX`.

    d. The average X position is found by dividing the sum of all X positions by the number of GameObjects. Note that if zero GameObjects are passed in, this line will generate an error when it tries to divide by zero.

    e. Another `foreach` loop iterates over all the GameObjects in `goArray` and calls `SetX()` with each GameObject as a parameter.

Recursive Functions

Sometimes a function is designed to call itself repeatedly; this is known as a *recursive function*. One simple example of this is calculating the factorial of a number.

In math, 5! (5 factorial) is the multiplication of that number and every other natural number below it. (Natural numbers are the integers greater than 0.)

    $5! = 5 * 4 * 3 * 2 * 1 = 120$

It is a special case in math that 0! is equal to 1.

    $0! = 1$

For our purposes, let's return a 0 any time a negative number is passed into the factorial function:

    $-5! = 0$

You can write a recursive function `Fac()` to calculate the factorial of any integer:

```
6    void Awake() {
7        print( Fac(5)  );     // Outputs: "120"              // a
8        print( Fac(0)  );     // Outputs: "1"
9        print( Fac(-5) );     // Outputs: "0"
10   }
11
12   int Fac( int n ) {                                        // b, d
13       if (n < 0) {      // This handles the case if n<0
14           return( 0 );
15       }
16       if (n == 0) {     // This is the "terminal case"      // e
17           return( 1 );
18       }
19       int result = n * Fac( n-1 );                          // c, f
20       return( result );                                     // g
21   }
```

a. When `Fac()` is called with the integer parameter 5.

b. This enters the first iteration of `Fac()` with n = 5.

c. On line 19, n (as 5) is then multiplied by the result of calling `Fac()` with a value of 4. This process of a function calling itself is called *recursion*.

d. Which enters the second iteration of `Fac()` with n = 4. The process continues until the sixth iteration of `Fac()`, where n = 0.

e. Because n is 0, a 1 is returned back up to the fifth iteration.

f. …which then multiplies 1 * 1

g. …and passes a 1 back up to the fourth iteration and so on until all the recursions of `Fac()` have completed, and the first iteration of `Fac()` returns a value of 120 to line 7.

The chain of all these recursive `Fac()` calls works something like this:

```
Fac(5)                          // 1st Iteration
5 * Fac(4)                       // 2nd Iteration
5 * 4 * Fac(3)                    // 3rd Iteration
5 * 4 * 3 * Fac(2)                 // 4th Iteration
5 * 4 * 3 * 2 * Fac(1)              // 5th Iteration
5 * 4 * 3 * 2 * 1 * Fac(0)           // 6th Iteration
5 * 4 * 3 * 2 * 1 * 1               // 5th Iteration
5 * 4 * 3 * 2 * 1                  // 4th Iteration
5 * 4 * 3 * 2                     // 3rd Iteration
5 * 4 * 6                       // 2nd Iteration
5 * 24                         // 1st Iteration
120                           // Final Return Value
```

The best way to really understand what's happening in this recursive function is to explore it using the debugger, a feature in MonoDevelop that enables you to watch each step of the execution of your programs and see how different variables are affected by your code. The process of debugging is the topic of the next chapter.

Summary

In this chapter, you have seen the power of functions and many different ways that you can use them. Functions are a cornerstone of most modern programming languages, and the more programming you do, the more you will see how powerful and necessary they are.

The upcoming Chapter 25, "Debugging," shows you how to use the debugging tools in Unity. These tools are meant to help you find problems with your code, but they are also very useful for understanding how your code works. After you have learned about debugging from the next chapter, I recommend returning to this chapter and examining the `Fac()` function in more detail. Of course, also feel free to explore any of the functions in this chapter or others using the debugger to better understand them.

CHAPTER 25

DEBUGGING

To the uninitiated, debugging can seem somewhat like a black art. On the contrary, it's actually one of the best skills you can have as a developer—though it's rarely taught to novice coders, which I think is a tragic missed opportunity. All beginning coders make mistakes, and knowing about debugging enables you to find and correct those mistakes much faster than just staring at the code and hoping the bug will reveal itself.

By the end of this chapter, you'll understand the difference between a compile-time error and a runtime error, you'll know how to set breakpoints in your code, and you'll know how to step through the lines of your program one at a time to help you root out hard-to-find bugs.

Getting Started with Debugging

Before you can start finding bugs, you need to make some. For this chapter, you'll start from the project you created for Chapter 19, "Hello World: Your First Program." If you don't have that project on hand, you can always download it from this book's website:

> http://book.prototools.net/

On the website, find Chapter 25, "Debugging," and click to download the project for the beginning of the chapter.

Throughout this chapter, I instruct you to make a number of bugs on purpose. This might seem like a strange way to do things, but my goal in doing so is to give you some experience with tracking down and fixing several different kinds of bugs and other errors you will almost certainly encounter while working with Unity. Each of these example bugs will introduce you to a different kind of potential future problem and help you understand how to go about finding and fixing bugs when you encounter them.

> **note**
>
> Throughout this chapter, I refer to errors occurring on specific line numbers. Sometimes this will be the exact same line number that you get for the error, and sometimes it might be shifted up or down by a couple of lines. Don't worry if you don't have exactly the same line numbers as I do, just look for the content that I'm discussing *near* the line numbers that I reference.

As mentioned earlier, in this chapter, you'll make modifications to the CubeSpawner script from Chapter 19. In case you made any of your own changes to that script, here is the CubeSpawner script that this chapter expects, complete with line numbers:

```
 1 using System.Collections;
 2 using System.Collections.Generic;
 3 using UnityEngine;
 4
 5 public class CubeSpawner : MonoBehaviour {
 6     public GameObject      cubePrefabVar;
 7
 8     // Use this for initialization
 9     void Start () {
10         // Instantiate( cubePrefabVar );
11     }
12
13     // Update is called once per frame
14     void Update () {
15         Instantiate( cubePrefabVar );
16     }
17 }
```

---

pro tip

90% OF BUGS ARE JUST TYPOS   I've spent so much time helping students fix bugs that now I can very quickly spot a typo in code.[1] The most common include the following:

- **Misspellings:** If you type even one letter wrong, the computer won't have any idea what you're talking about.

- **Capitalization:** To your C# compiler, A and a are two completely different letters, so `variable`, `Variable`, and `variAble` are all completely different words.

- **Missing semicolons:** Just like almost every sentence in English should end in a period, nearly every statement in C# should end in a semicolon (;). If you leave the semicolon out, it often causes an error on the next line. FYI: A semicolon is used because the period was needed for decimal numbers and what's called *dot syntax* in variable names and subnames (e.g., varName.subVarName.subSubVarName).

---

1. If you're reading carefully, you might have noticed that this is a repeat of a tip in Chapter 17, "Introducing the Unity Development Environment." Yes, it's important enough to print it twice!

Compile-Time Bugs

A *compile-time bug* (or error) is a problem that Unity discovers when it is compiling C# code (i.e., attempting to interpret the C# code and turn it into the Common Intermediate Language that is later converted by Unity to machine language that can run on your computer). After you have opened the Hello World project in Unity, follow these instructions to intentionally cause a compile-time error and explore how they work:

1. Duplicate the existing _Scene_1. To do so, click *_Scene_1* in the Project pane to select it and choose *Edit > Duplicate* from the menu bar. Unity is pretty good at counting things, so it will automatically increment the name of the scene and call this new scene _Scene_2.

2. Double-click *_Scene_2* to open it in the Hierarchy and Scene panes. After it's open, the title of your Unity window should be *_Scene_2.unity - Hello World - PC, Mac, & Linux Standalone*. If you click Play, you should see everything behaving just as it did in _Scene_1.

3. Now you should make a second version of the CubeSpawner class so that you don't end up damaging the one from _Scene_1. Click the *CubeSpawner* script in the Project pane to select it and then choose *Edit > Duplicate* from the menu bar. This creates a script named CubeSpawner1, and an error immediately appears in the Console pane (see Figure 25.1). Click the error to see more information in the lower half of the Console pane.

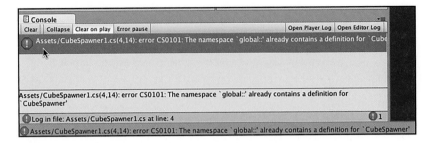

Figure 25.1 Your first intentional error: a compile-time error caught by Unity

This error message holds a lot of useful information, so let's go through it bit by bit.

Assets/CubeSpawner1.cs(4,14):

Every error that appears includes information about where Unity encountered it. This tells you that the error was in the CubeSpawner1.cs script inside the Assets folder of your project and that it happened on line 4, character 14.

error CS0101:

The second chunk of the message tells you what kind of error you've encountered. If you encounter an error that you don't understand, you can do a web search for the words "Unity error" and the error code. (In this example, your web search would be for "Unity error CS0101".) A search like this will almost always find a forum post or something similar that describes the problem you're having. In my experience, you will generally get good results from http://forum.unity3d.com and http://answers.unity3d.com, and some of the best answers to issues come from http://stackoverflow.com.

The namespace 'global::' already contains a definition for 'CubeSpawner'

The final chunk of the error message attempts to put the error into plain English. In this case, it's telling you that the term *CubeSpawner* is already defined somewhere else in your code, which it is. At this time, the scripts CubeSpawner and CubeSpawner1 are both attempting to define the class CubeSpawner.

Let's get to work fixing this:

1. Double-click CubeSpawner1 to open MonoDevelop. (Alternatively, you can double-click the error message in the Console pane, which on a Mac opens the script to the line that produced the error; the Windows version sometimes does this.)

2. Within the CubeSpawner1 script, change line 4 (the line that declares CubeSpawner) to read:

```
5 public class CubeSpawner2 : MonoBehaviour {
```

> (The CubeSpawner2 class name is intentionally different from the name of the script so that you can see another error in a moment.)

3. Save your file and return to Unity, where you can see that the error message disappears from the Console pane.

Whenever you save a script in MonoDevelop, Unity detects the save and recompiles the script to make sure that there are no errors. If it does run into a bug, you'll get a compile-time error message like the one you just fixed. These are the easiest bugs to fix because Unity knows exactly where the problem took place and passes this information on to you. Now that the CubeSpawner script is defining the class CubeSpawner and the CubeSpawner1 script is defining the class CubeSpawner2, the compile-time error is gone.

Compile-Time Errors Caused by a Missing Semicolon

Now create another kind of compile-time error by deleting a semicolon:

1. Delete the semicolon (;) at the end of line 14, which is the line that reads:

```
15        Instantiate( cubePrefabVar );
```

2. Save the script and return to Unity. Two new compile-time error messages appear:

    Assets/CubeSpawner1.cs(15,9): error CS1525: Unexpected symbol '}'

    Assets/CubeSpawner1.cs(17,1): error CS8025: Parsing error

The first thing to know here is that you should **always fix error messages top-to-bottom**, so start with the first line: Assets/CubeSpawner1.cs(15,9): error CS1525: Unexpected symbol '}'

This error message doesn't say "Hey, you forgot a semicolon," but it does tell you where it ran into trouble compiling the script (line 15, character 9). It also tells you that it encountered the closing brace (}) in an unexpected place. Given this information, you should be able to look around that area of the code and discover the missing semicolon.

3. Add the semicolon back on to the end of line 14 and save. When you return to Unity, you can see that **both** errors have disappeared.

A compile-time error will almost always be discovered either on the line that has the problem or on a later line. In this example, the missing semicolon was on line 14, but the problem was discovered on line 15. Additionally, many compile-time errors cause cascading problems further down the code. If you always fix issues in code from top-to-bottom, fixing one error often also corrects many of the errors that followed it.

Attaching and Removing Scripts

In Unity, try dragging the CubeSpawner1 script onto *Main Camera* in the hierarchy. This time, the error shown in Figure 25.2 appears.

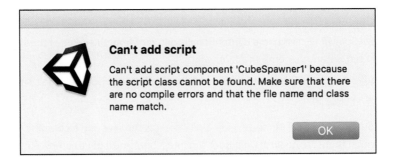

Figure 25.2 Some errors are only caught when you try to attach a script to a GameObject

Unity is complaining because the name of the script CubeSpawner1 doesn't match the name of the class that you're defining in the script: CubeSpawner2. In Unity, when you create a class that extends MonoBehaviour (for example, `CubeSpawner2 : Monobehaviour`), the name of the class must match the name of the file in which it is defined. To fix this, just make sure that the two names match.

1. Click once on CubeSpawner1 in the Project pane to select it and then click a second time on the name to rename it. (You can also press the Return key on macOS or the F2 key on Windows to rename the script.)

2. Change the name to *CubeSpawner2* and try dragging it onto the *Main Camera* again. This time, it should go with no problems.

3. Click *Main Camera* in the hierarchy. In the Inspector, you should now see that Main Camera has both a CubeSpawner and a CubeSpawner2 script attached.

4. You don't want both scripts, so click the small gear icon to the right of the name *Cube Spawner (Script)* in the Inspector and choose *Remove Component* from the drop-down menu, as shown in Figure 25.3. (You can also right-click the name *Cube Spawner (Script)* to get the same menu.)

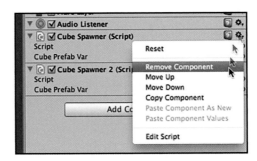

Figure 25.3 Removing the extra CubeSpawner Script component

This way, you won't have two different scripts trying to spawn cubes at the same time. For the next several chapters, you'll only attach a single script component to each GameObject.

Runtime Errors

Follow these steps to explore another type of error:

1. Click *Play* to encounter another kind of error (see Figure 25.4).

2. Click the *Pause* button to pause playback (the button with two vertical bars next to the Play button) to take a look at this error.

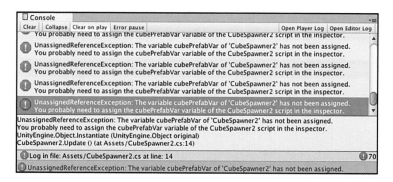

Figure 25.4 Many repetitions of the same runtime error

This is a *runtime error*, which means it's an error that only occurs when Unity is actually trying to play the project. Runtime errors occur when—as far as the compiler can determine—you've typed everything correctly yet something is not right when the code actually runs.

This error looks a little different from the others you've seen so far. For one thing, the beginning of the error message doesn't include information about where the error occurred; however, if you click one of the error messages, additional information pops up in the bottom half of the Console. With runtime errors, the last line tells you the point at which Unity realized that an error had occurred. This sometimes happens on the line with the bug, and it sometimes happens on the next line. The error message here indicates to look at or near line 14 of CubeSpawner2.cs for the error.

CubeSpawner2.Update () (at Assets/**CubeSpawner2.cs:14**)

Looking at line 14 of CubeSpawner2, you can see that it's the line where you instantiate an instance of `cubePrefabVar`. (Note that your line number might be slightly different; if so, that's okay.)

```
14        Instantiate( cubePrefabVar );
```

Just as the compiler thought, this line looks fine. Let's delve into the error message further:

UnassignedReferenceException: The variable cubePrefabVar of 'CubeSpawner2' has not been assigned. You probably need to assign the cubePrefabVar variable of the Cube-Spawner2 script in the inspector. UnityEngine.Object.Instantiate (UnityEngine.Object original) CubeSpawner2.Update () (at Assets/CubeSpawner2.cs:14)

This indicates that the variable `cubePrefabVar` has not been assigned, and if you look at the *CubeSpawner2 (Script)* component of Main Camera in the Inspector (click *Main Camera* in the Hierarchy to do so), you'll see that this is correct.

3. As you did in Chapter 19, click the circular target next to `cubePrefabVar` in the Inspector and choose *Cube Prefab* from the list of assets. You should now see it assigned to `cubePrefabVar` in the Inspector.

4. Click the *Pause* button again to resume simulation; the cubes start spawning happily.

5. Click the *Play* button to stop the simulation. Click *Play* once more to start it up again.

What happened?!? You got the same error again!

6. Click the *Play* button once more to stop the simulation again.

> ### warning
>
> **CHANGES MADE WHILE PLAYING DON'T STICK!**   This is an issue that you will encounter many times. There are good reasons for making Unity work this way, but it's sometimes confusing to new users. Any changes you make while Unity is playing or paused (like the change you just made to `cubePrefabVar`) are reset back to their previous values when playback is stopped. If you want a change to stick, make sure that Unity is not playing when you make the change.

7. Now that Unity is stopped again, use the Main Camera Inspector to assign Cube Prefab to the field `cubePrefabVar` again, and this time—because Unity was stopped when you set it—it should stick.

8. Click *Play*, and everything should work out fine.

Stepping Through Code with the Debugger

In addition to the automatic code-checking tools that you've already explored in this chapter, Unity and MonoDevelop also enable you to step through code one line at a time, which can be very helpful for understanding what's happening in your code.

Open the *CubeSpawner2* script in MonoDevelop and add the bolded lines in the following code listing (that is, add lines 14 and 18–27). If you need to make room in the script, just press Return (Enter on Windows keyboards). The code is also shown in Figure 25.5.

```
 1 using UnityEngine;                                              // a
 2 using System.Collections;
 3
 4 public class CubeSpawner2 : MonoBehaviour {
 5     public GameObject          cubePrefabVar;
 6
 7     // Use this for initialization
 8     void Start () {
 9         // Instantiate( cubePrefabVar );
10     }
11
12     // Update is called once per frame
13     void Update () {
14         SpellItOut();                                            // b
15         Instantiate( cubePrefabVar );
16     }
17
18     public void SpellItOut () {                                  // c
19         string sA = "Hello World!";
20         string sB = "";
21
22         for (int i=0; i<sA.Length; i++) {                        // d
23             sB += sA[i];                                         // e
24         }
25
26         print(sB);
27     }
28 }
```

a. Note that this code listing does not include the `System.Collections.Generic` library; it's not needed here, though as of Unity 5.5+, it is included by default in all C# scripts.

b. Line 14 calls the `SpellItOut()` function.

c. Lines 18–27 declare and define the function `SpellItOut()`. This function copies the contents of string `sA` to string `sB` one character at a time.

d. This `for` loop iterates over the length of `sA`. Because `"Hello World"` consists of 11 chars, the loop will iterate 11 times.

e. Line 23 pulls the ith character from `sA` and concatenates it onto the end of `sB`. This is a horribly inefficient way to copy a string, but it will work very well to demonstrate how the debugger works.

Figure 25.5 The `SpellItOut()` function showing a breakpoint on line 14

After you've typed in all the code and double-checked it, click in the gutter to the left of line 14 (as shown in Figure 25.5). This creates a breakpoint on line 14, which appears as a red circle. When you set a breakpoint and MonoDevelop is debugging Unity, Unity will pause execution every time it hits that breakpoint. Let's check it out.

HOW TO FORCE QUIT AN APPLICATION

Before getting too far into debugging, knowing how to force quit an application (that is, quit an application that won't respond to any user input) is useful. Sometimes, either Unity or MonoDevelop will just stop responding, and you might need to do this to quit them.

On a macOS Computer

Implement a force quit by doing the following:

1. Press *Command+Option+Esc* on the keyboard. The Force Quit window appears.

2. Find the application that is misbehaving. Its name is often followed by "(not responding)" in the applications list.

3. Click that application, and then click *Force Quit*.

On a Windows Computer

Implement a force quit by doing the following:

1. Press *Shift+Ctrl+Esc* on the keyboard. The Windows Task Manager opens.

2. Find the application that is misbehaving.

3. Click that application, and then click *End Task*.

If you have to force quit Unity while it's running, you will lose any work that you've done since your last save. Because you must constantly save C# scripts, they shouldn't be an issue, but you might have to redo unsaved changes made to your scene. This is one of the reasons that I encourage you to save your scenes as often as possible.

Attaching the Debugger to Unity

For MonoDevelop to be able to debug what's happening in Unity when it plays, you need to attach it to the Unity process. After the MonoDevelop debugger is attached to Unity, it will be able to peer into the depths of what's happening in your C# code and can pause execution of the code at breakpoints (like the one you set on line 14).

1. In MonoDevelop, click the Play button. These appear differently on macOS and Windows, as shown in the top (macOS) and bottom (Windows) sections of Figure 25.6. In either case, the Play button is the one shown under the mouse pointer.

Figure 25.6 Click this button to attach the debugger to the Unity Editor process

This automatically searches for the Unity process and attaches the MonoDevelop debugger to it. If this is the first time you've ever done this, you might be asked whether you grant MonoDevelop permission to do so. Please do grant it permission.

When the process is finished, you'll notice that the MonoDevelop window has changed (see Figure 25.7). The Play button in the top left has become a Stop button, a couple panes have appeared at the bottom of the MonoDevelop window, and a number of buttons to control the debugger have appeared (see Figure 25.8).

> note
>
> **MY MONODEVELOP MIGHT LOOK A BIT DIFFERENT**   In MonoDevelop, you can
> move window panes (or panels) around just as you can in Unity. I've moved mine to
> make it easier for you to see what I'm doing in these book examples, but that will
> probably mean that it looks a little different from what you're seeing on your screen.
> You should have all the same panes; they will just be arranged slightly differently.

Using the Debugger to Examine code

Now that you have the debugger ready and attached, it's time to see how it works.

1. Switch to Unity and click the *Play* button to start the scene. Almost immediately, Unity will
    freeze, and MonoDevelop should pop up. Sometimes, on Windows, MonoDevelop won't
    automatically pop up, but Unity will look frozen. Just switch to the MonoDevelop task
    manually, and you should see what is shown in Figure 25.7.

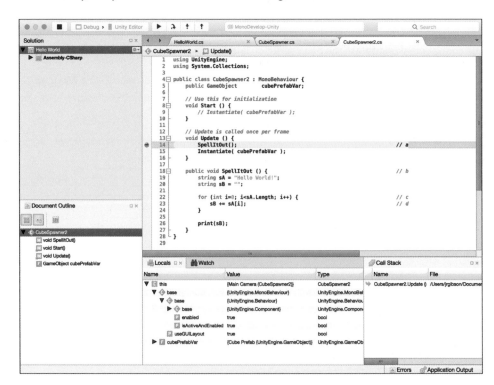

Figure 25.7 Execution stopped at line 14 in the debugger

Execution of the `Update()` function has paused on line 14 where you placed the breakpoint. The gray arrow in the gutter and the yellow line next to it show the current line of execution. While execution is stopped in the debugger, the Unity process is completely frozen. That means that you can't switch to it through any normal means until it is running again.

In debug mode, some of the buttons at the top of the toolbar have changed (see Figure 25.8).

Figure 25.8 The debugger control buttons

The following steps show you how the various debugger control buttons work. Before following these steps, I recommend reading the "Watching Variables in the Debugger" sidebar near the end of the chapter.

  2. Click the debugger's *Run* button in MonoDevelop (shown in Figure 25.8). This causes Unity to continue the execution of the script. When Unity is stopped at a breakpoint like the one on line 14, everything about Unity is frozen until you tell it to continue.

When you click the Run button, Unity starts running again and does so until it hits another breakpoint. When you clicked Run, Unity passed through the game loop, started a new frame, and then stopped on line 14 again (when `Update()` was called), so you might not even notice that it happened other than a blink or flicker of the MonoDevelop window.

> ### note
>
> Depending on the type of computer you have, you might need to switch back to the Unity process (that is, application) for Unity to actually move on to the next frame. On some machines, Unity will continue on to the next frame while you are using MonoDevelop, and on some it won't. If the yellow arrow doesn't return to the breakpoint in the debugger after you've clicked run, switch to the Unity process, and it should start the next frame and then stop on the breakpoint again.
>
> As mentioned previously, while the code is stopped in the debugger (that is, when you can see the yellow arrow shown in Figure 25.7), you cannot switch to the Unity process. This is normal and occurs because Unity is completely frozen while it is waiting for you to look at code in the debugger. Unity will resume normal function after you're no longer debugging.

3. When the yellow execution arrow has stopped on the line 14 breakpoint again, click the *Step Over* button. The yellow arrow moves on to line 15 without stepping into the function `SpellItOut()`. The `SpellItOut()` function is still called and still runs, but the debugger passes over it. Step Over is useful if you don't want to see the inner working of a function that is called.

4. Click *Run* again. Unity advances to the next frame, and the yellow execution arrow again stops on the line 14 breakpoint.

5. This third time around, click *Step Into*. The yellow arrow jumps from line 14 into line 19 of the function `SpellItOut()`. Any time you click Step Into, the debugger enters into any functions called, whereas *Step Over* jumps over them.

6. Now that you are inside the `SpellItOut()` function, click *Step Over* several times to walk through the execution of the `SpellItOut()` function.

7. As you continue to click Step Over, you can watch `sA` and `sB` change through the course of this function (see the sidebar "Watching Variables in the Debugger"). Each pass through the `for` loop on lines 22–24 adds a character from `sA` to the string `sB`. You can see the values of the variables change in the *Locals* debugger panel (which you can open by choosing *View > Debug Windows > Locals* from the MonoDevelop menu bar).

8. If the yellow execution arrow is still within `SpellItOut()`, continue to step 9, but if you clicked Step Over enough times to exit the function `SpellItOut()`, click *Run*, and then click *Step Into* to return execution to the inside of `SpellItOut()`.

9. While still inside the `SpellItOut()` function, click *Step Out*. This causes the debugger to exit the `SpellItOut()` function and then continue to line 15 (the line immediately after `SpellItOut()` was called). The rest of the `SpellItOut()` function is still executed; you just don't witness it in the debugger. This is useful when you want to skip past the current function yet don't want to completely return to full-speed execution by clicking Run.

10. Press the *Stop Debug* button shown in Figure 25.8 to detach the MonoDevelop debugger from the Unity process, stop debugging, and return Unity to normal execution.

I highly recommend using the debugger to examine the execution of the recursive `Fac()` function that is featured at the end of Chapter 24, "Functions and Parameters." That function is an excellent example of how the debugger can help you better understand code.

WATCHING VARIABLES IN THE DEBUGGER

One of the great strengths of any debugger is the capability to look at the value of an individual variable at almost any time. MonoDevelop's debugger gives you three different ways to do this. Before trying any of these, be sure that you've followed the directions in this chapter and started the debugging process.

The first and simplest method is to just hover your mouse pointer over any variable in the MonoDevelop code pane. If you position the mouse pointer over a variable name and keep it still for about one second, a tool tip will appear telling you the value of that variable. However, it is very important to note that the value shown is the current value of the variable based on the position of the yellow arrow, not the position of that variable in the code. For example, the variable `sB` of the function `SpellItOut()` is repeated several times throughout the code, and holding the mouse over any of them will show the same value.

The second method is to find the variable in the Locals pane of the debugger. To view this pane, choose *View > Debug Windows > Locals* from the MonoDevelop menu bar. This brings the Locals variable watching pane to the front. Here, you can see a list of all local variables that are available to the debugger at the current time. If you step into the `SpellItOut()` function as instructed in this chapter and are on line 19, you will see three local variables listed: `this`, `sA`, and `sB`. The variables `sA` and `sB` are initially set to null, but their values appear in the Locals pane after they have been defined on lines 19 and 20, respectively. When you have used *Step Over* a few times and reached line 22 in the debugger, you will see that the integer `i` is both declared and defined on that line. The variable `this` refers to the current instance of the CubeSpawner2 script. Click the disclosure triangle next to `this` to reveal the public field `cubePrefabVar` inside `this` as well as a variable named `base`. Opening the disclosure triangle next to `base` reveals all the variables associated with the base class of CubeSpawner2, which is MonoBehaviour. Base classes like MonoBehaviour (a.k.a. superclasses or parent classes) are covered in Chapter 26, "Classes."

The third way that you can view a variable is to enter it explicitly into the Watch pane. To bring the pane to the front, choose *View > Debug Windows > Watch* from the menu bar. In the Watch pane, click a blank line to add a watched variable. (Click in the field with the text "Click here to add a new watch.") In this field, type the name of a variable, and MonoDevelop will try to show you its value. For example, enter the variable `this.gameObject.name` and press Return, and "Main Camera," the name of the GameObject to which this script is attached, appears. If the value is ever too large to fit in the Watch pane, you can click the magnifying glass next to the value to read the whole thing; this sometimes happens when you're working with large strings of text.

It's worth noting here that sometimes a bug in the debugging process (ironic) causes `this` to be undefined in the Locals pane. If that is the case, you can always just add `this` as a watched variable in the Watch pane, which usually works even when `this` isn't working in the Locals pane.

Summary

That's it for your introduction to debugging. Although in this case you did not use the debugger to root out an unknown bug, you can see how it can help you better understand code. Remember this: Whenever something is confusing in your code, you can always step through it using the debugger.

Though it might have seemed a bit frustrating for me to instruct you to generate so many bugs, my sincere hope is that helping you to experience and understand these bugs and how to investigate and fix them will give you a leg up later when you encounter real bugs on your own. Remember that you can always search the Internet for the text of the bug (or at least the error number) to find clues for fixing it. As I wrote at the beginning of the chapter, good debugging skills are one of the major things that can help you to become both a competent and confident programmer.

CHAPTER 26

CLASSES

By the end of this chapter, you will understand how to create and use classes. A class is a collection of both variables and functions in a single C# object. Classes are an essential building block in modern games and, more widely, in object-oriented programming.

Understanding Classes

Classes combine functionality and data. Another way to put this is that classes are composed of both functions and variables, which when used within a class are called *methods* and *fields*, respectively. Classes are often used to represent objects in the world of your game project. For example, consider a character in a standard roleplaying game. There are several fields (or variables) that she might have:

```
string      name;       // The character's name
float       health;     // The current amount of health she has
float       healthMax;  // The maximum amount of health she could have
List<Item>  inventory;  // A List of all Items in her inventory
List<Item>  equipped;   // A List of Items that she currently has equipped
```

All of these fields are applicable to any character in a roleplaying game (RPG), because all characters have health, equipment, and a name. Also, several methods (functions) could be used by or on that character. (The ellipses [...] in the following code listing show where you would need to add code to make the functions work.)

```
void Move(Vector3 newLocation) {...}       // Allows the character to move
void Attack(Character target) {...}         // Attacks target Character with the
                                            //   currently equipped weapon or spell
void TakeDamage(float damageAmt) {...}      // Causes this character to lose health
void Equip(Item newItem) {...}              // Adds an Item to the equipped List
```

Obviously, you would want a character in an actual game to have many more fields and methods than are described here, but the core idea is that all characters in your RPG would need to have these functions and variables on them.

> **tip**
>
> You're already using classes! In fact, though it wasn't explicitly stated until now, every bit of code you've written so far in this book has been part of a class, and in general, you can think of each C# file that you create as being its own class.

The Anatomy of a Class (and of a C# Script)

Several important elements of many classes are illustrated in Figure 26.1. Not all of them are necessary in every class, but they are extremely common.

- **Includes** make it possible for your C# scripts to make use of various classes that have been created by others. Includes are enabled by `using` statements, and the includes shown here enable all the standard elements of Unity as well as collections like Lists. These must be the first part of your script.

- The **class declaration** names your class and determines what other classes it extends (see the *Class Inheritance* section later in this chapter). In this case, the class Enemy *extends* the class MonoBehaviour (making MonoBehaviour the *superclass* of Enemy).

- **Fields** are variables that are local to your class, meaning that any function inside the class can access them by name. In addition, variables labeled `public` can be accessed by any other entity that can see the class (see the *Variable Scope* section of Appendix B, "Useful Concepts").

- **Methods** are functions contained within a class. They can access any of the fields in the class, and they can also have local variables (for example, the Vector3 `tempPos` in `Move()`) that only exist within each function. Methods are what enable classes to do things. `virtual` methods are a special type of function that is covered in the *Class Inheritance* section later in this chapter.

- **Properties** can be thought of as functions masquerading as fields through use of the `get` and `set` accessors. See the *Properties* section later in this chapter for details.

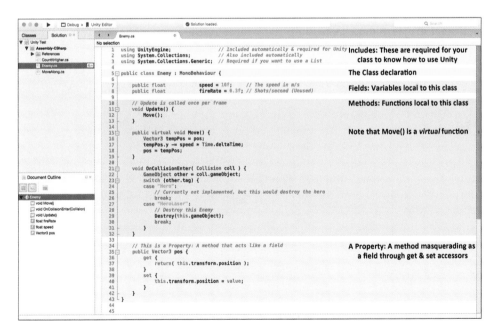

Figure 26.1 Diagram showing some important elements of a class

Before getting into this too much more, set up a project in which you can use this code.

Set Up the Enemy Class Sample Project

Appendix A, "Standard Project Setup Procedure," contains information about how to create a new Unity project for the examples in this chapter. Please follow the instructions in the appendix using the information contained in the sidebar.

SET UP THE PROJECT FOR THIS CHAPTER

Following the standard project setup procedure, create a new project in Unity. Appendix A provides information on the standard project setup procedure.

- **Project name:** Enemy Class Sample Project

- **Scene name:** _Scene_0 (The underscore at the beginning of the scene name should keep it sorted at the top of the Project pane.)

- **C# script names:** None at this time

You do not need to follow the instructions in Appendix A to attach a script to the Main Camera. There is not yet a Main Camera script in this project.

---

1. After following the Appendix A instructions to create a new project and saving your new scene as _Scene_0, use the Create menu in the Hierarchy pane to create a new sphere by selecting *Create > 3D Object > Sphere*, as shown in Figure 26.2.

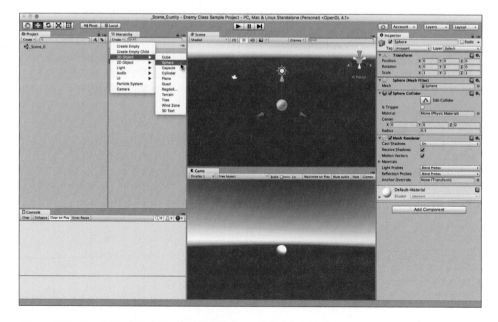

Figure 26.2 Creating a sphere in _Scene_0

2. Select *Sphere* by clicking its name in the Hierarchy pane. Then set the position of the sphere to the origin [0, 0, 0] (i.e., x=0, y=0, z=0) using the Transform component (highlighted with a red box in Figure 26.2).

3. In the Project pane, choose *Create > C# Script* and name the script *Enemy*. Double-click the script to open it in MonoDevelop, and enter the following code (identical to that in Figure 26.1). Lines that you need to add are bolded in the code listing.

```
1 using System.Collections;
2 using System.Collections.Generic;
3 using UnityEngine;
4
5 public class Enemy : MonoBehaviour {
6
7     public float        speed = 10f;     // The speed in m/s
8     public float        fireRate = 0.3f; // Shots/second (Unused)
9
10    // Update is called once per frame
11    void Update() {
12        Move();
13    }
14
15    public virtual void Move() {
16        Vector3 tempPos = pos;
17        tempPos.y -= speed * Time.deltaTime;
18        pos = tempPos;
19    }
20
21    void OnCollisionEnter( Collision coll ) {
22        GameObject other = coll.gameObject;
23        switch (other.tag) {
24            case "Hero":
25                // Currently not implemented, but this would destroy the hero
26                break;
27            case "HeroLaser":
28                // Destroy this Enemy
29                Destroy(this.gameObject);
30                break;
31        }
32    }
33
```

```
34     // This is a Property: A method that acts like a field
35     public Vector3 pos {
36         get {
37             return( this.transform.position );
38         }
39         set {
40             this.transform.position = value;
41         }
42     }
43
44 }
```

Most of this should look pretty straightforward and familiar to you except for the property and the virtual function, both of which I will cover in this chapter.

Properties: Methods That Work Like Fields

You can see in the previous code listing that the property pos is treated as if it were a field in both lines 16 and 18 of Move(). This is accomplished through the use of the get{} and set{} *accessor* clauses on lines 36–41 that enable this class to run code each time you read or set the pos property. Every time the pos property is read, the code within the get{} accessor is run, and the get{} accessor must return a value of the same type as the property (i.e., Vector3). Code within set{} is run every time the pos property is assigned a value, and the value keyword is used as an *implicit variable* that holds the value assigned. In other words, in line 18, pos is assigned the value of tempPos, which calls the set accessor of pos on line 39; then on line 40, the value of tempPos is held by the variable value and assigned to this.transform.position. An implicit variable is one that exists without you, the programmer, explicitly declaring it. All set{} clauses in properties have the implicit variable value. You can create a property with only a get{} accessor to make the property read-only (or with only a set{} accessor to make the property write-only).

In the pos property example of the preceding Enemy class, pos is used simply to access the field this.transform.position with less typing. However, the following code listing holds a more interesting example.

1. Create a new C# script named *CountItHigher*.

2. Attach the CountItHigher script to Sphere in the scene.

3. Double-click the *CountItHigher* script in the Project pane to open it in MonoDevelop, and enter the following code:

```
1 using System.Collections;
2 using System.Collections.Generic;
3 using UnityEngine;
4
```

```
 5 class CountItHigher : MonoBehaviour {                              // a
 6     private int        _num = 0;
 7
 8     void Update() {
 9         print( nextNum );
10     }
11
12     public int nextNum {                                          // b
13         get {
14             _num++;              // Increase the value of _num by 1
15             return( _num );  // Return the new value of _num
16         }
17     }
18
19     public int currentNum {                                       // c
20         get { return( _num ); }                                   // d
21         set { _num = value;    }                                  // d
22     }
23 }
```

a. The integer field `_num` is `private`, so it can only be accessed by this instance of the CountItHigher class. Other classes and other CountItHigher class instances are not able to see the private variables of this class instance (and other CountItHigher class instances would have their own `_num` field that this instance could not see).

b. `nextNum` is a property that is read-only. Because there is no `set{}` clause, it can only be read (e.g., `int x = nextNum;`) and cannot be set (e.g., `nextNum = 5;` would cause an error).

c. `currentNum` is a property that can either be read or set. Both `int x = current-Num;` and `currentNum = 5;` would work.

d. The `get{}` and `set{}` clauses can alternatively each be written on a single line. Note that when in the single-line format, the semicolon ending the statement (`;`) comes before the closing brace (`}`) as shown on lines 20 and 21.

4. Return to Unity and click *Play*. As the `Update()` function is called by Unity each frame, the output of the `print( nextNum );` statement increments every frame. The output from the first five frames is as follows:

```
1
2
3
4
5
```

Each time that the property `nextNum` is read (by `print( nextNum );`), it increments the private field `_num` and then returns the new value (lines 14 and 15 of the code listing). Though this is a small example, a `get` or `set` accessor can do anything that a regular method can do, even call another method or function.

Similarly, `currentNum` is a public property that enables you to either read or set the value of `_num`. Because `_num` is a private field, having the property `currentNum` publicly available is helpful.

Class Instances Are GameObject Components

As you've seen in previous chapters, when you drag a C# script onto a GameObject, it becomes a component of that GameObject just as Transform, Rigidbody, and other elements that you see in the Unity Inspector are GameObject components. This means that you can get a reference to any class that is attached to a GameObject via `GameObject.GetComponent<>()` with the type of the class placed between the angle brackets (see line 7 of the following code listing).

1. Create a new C# script named *MoveAlong*.

2. Attach the *MoveAlong* script to the same Sphere GameObject as CountItHigher.

3. Open the *MoveAlong* script in MonoDevelop and enter the following bolded code:

```
1 using System.Collections;
2 using System.Collections.Generic;
3 using UnityEngine;
4
5 class MoveAlong : MonoBehaviour {
6
7     void LateUpdate() {                                               // a
8         CountItHigher cih=this.gameObject.GetComponent<CountItHigher>();  // b
9         if ( cih != null ) {                                          // c
10            float tX = cih.currentNum/10f;                            // d
11            Vector3 tempLoc = pos;                                    // e
12            tempLoc.x = tX;
13            pos = tempLoc;
14        }
15    }
16
17    public Vector3 pos {                                             // f
18        get { return( this.transform.position ); }
19        set { this.transform.position = value;   }
20    }
21
22 }
```

a. `LateUpdate()` is another built-in function call that Unity makes every frame. Each frame, Unity first calls `Update()` on all classes that are attached to GameObjects and then, when all the `Update()`s are complete, Unity calls `LateUpdate()` on all objects. Using `LateUpdate()` here ensures that `Update()` in the CountItHigher class is called before `LateUpdate()` in the MoveAlong class. This avoids what is known as a *race condition* (see the warning that follows for more information).

b. `cih` is a local variable of the type CountItHigher, meaning that it can hold a reference to the instance of CountItHigher that is a component attached to the Sphere GameObject. The `GetComponent<CountItHigher>()` call finds the *CountItHigher (Script)* component attached to the same Sphere GameObject as this *MoveAlong (Script)* component.[1]

c. If you use the `GetComponent<>()` method, and the type of component you ask for is *not* attached to the GameObject, `GetComponent<>()` will return `null` (a value that means nothing is there). Checking whether `cih` is `null` before trying to use it will help you a avoid Null Reference Exception errors.

d. Although `cih.currentNum` is an int, when it is used in a mathematical operation with a float (e.g., `cih.currentNum/10f`) or assigned to a float (both of which occur in line 9), it is automatically treated as a float.

e. Lines 11 and 13 use the `pos` property that is defined in lines 17–20.

f. This is effectively the same as the `pos` property of the `Enemy` class, but it uses a single line to define each of the `get{}` and `set{}` accessor clauses.

Every `LateUpdate`, this code will find the *CountItHigher (Script)* component of this GameObject and then pull the `currentNum` from it. The script then divides `currentNum` by 10 and sets the X position of the GameObject to the resultant value (using the `pos` property). As `CountItHigher._num` increases every frame, the GameObject will also move along the X axis.

4. Be sure that you save both this script and CountItHigher. From the MonoDevelop menu bar choose *File > Save All*. If *Save All* is grayed out, then you have already saved everything.

5. Click *Play* in Unity to see this happen.

6. Be sure to save your scene (from the Unity menu bar, choose *File > Save Scene*).

---

1. Making a call to `GetComponent()` every frame is rather inefficient, so you would normally make something like `cih` a class field and set its value as part of an `Awake()` or `Start()` method. However, at this point in the book, code efficiency is less important than simplicity and clarity, so `GetComponent()` is called every frame.

> ### warning
>
> **WATCH OUT FOR RACE CONDITIONS!**   A race condition occurs any time two things rely on each other, but you're not certain which one will happen first. This is why `LateUpdate()` is used in the preceding example. Had `Update()` been used in MoveAlong, it would be uncertain whether the `Update()` in CountItHigher or MoveAlong would be called by Unity first, so the GameObject could be moved either before or after _num was incremented, depending on which was called first. Using `LateUpdate()` provides assurance that all `Update()`s in the scene will be called first, followed by all `LateUpdate()`s.
>
> Chapter 31, "Prototype 3.5: Space SHMUP Plus" covers more on race conditions.

Class Inheritance

Classes usually extend the contents of other classes (i.e, they are based on other classes). In the first code listing of the chapter, Enemy extends MonoBehaviour, as do all the classes you've seen so far in this book. Implement the following instructions to get Enemy working in your game, and then we'll discuss this further.

Implementing the Enemy Class Sample Project

Complete the following steps:

1. Create a new scene (*File > New Scene* from the menu bar). Immediately save it as _Scene_1.

2. Create a new sphere in the scene (*GameObject > 3D Object > Sphere*).

   a. Rename the Sphere to *EnemyGO* (the GO stands for GameObject). This new sphere is not connected in any way to the Sphere in _Scene_0. (i.e., it doesn't have the two script components attached.)

   b. Set the transform.position of EnemyGO to [*0, 4, 0*] using the Transform component in the Inspector.

   c. Drag the *Enemy* script you wrote earlier from the Project pane onto *EnemyGO* in the Hierarchy pane of _Scene_1.

   d. Select *EnemyGO* in the Hierarchy; *Enemy (Script)* now appears as a component of the EnemyGO GameObject.

3. Drag EnemyGO from the Hierarchy pane into the Project pane to create a prefab named EnemyGO. As described in previous chapters, you'll know that the prefab was created successfully because an item named EnemyGO with a blue box icon will appear in the

Project pane, and the name of the EnemyGO GameObject in the Hierarchy pane will turn blue, indicating that it's an instance of the EnemyGO prefab.

4. Select the Main Camera in the Hierarchy and set its position and camera settings to those highlighted by green boxes in Figure 26.3:

   a. Set the transform position to *[0, -15, -10]*.

   b. Set the camera *Clear Flags* to *Solid Color.*

   c. Change the camera *Projection* from *Perspective* to *Orthographic.*

   d. Set the camera *Size* to *20.*

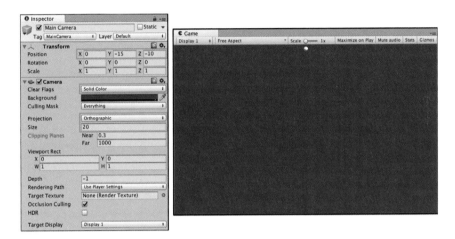

Figure 26.3 Camera settings for _Scene_1 and the resultant Game pane

The Game pane shown at the right of Figure 26.3 should approximate what you now see through the camera.

4. Click *Play*. You should see the Enemy instance move down the screen at a constant rate.

5. Save your scene! Always save your scene.

Understanding Superclasses and Subclasses

Superclass and *subclass* describe the relationship between two classes where the subclass *inherits* from the superclass. For example, the Enemy class inherits from MonoBehaviour, which means that the Enemy class is composed of not only the fields and methods of the Enemy C# script but also of all the fields and methods of its superclass, MonoBehaviour, and all the classes from which MonoBehaviour inherits. This is why any C# script that we write in Unity already knows about fields such as `gameObject` and `transform` and methods such as `GetComponent<>()`.

Creating subclasses that extend Enemy is also possible:

1. Create a new C# script in the Project pane and name it *EnemyZig*.

2. Open the EnemyZig script in MonoDevelop, change the superclass from MonoBehaviour to Enemy, and delete the `Start()` and `Update()` methods, leaving you with the following code.

```
1 using System.Collections;
2 using System.Collections.Generic;
3 using UnityEngine;
4
5 public class EnemyZig : Enemy {
6     // Delete all the default code that Unity puts here in the EnemyZig class
7 }
```

3. Choose *Create > 3D Object > Cube* in the Hierarchy pane.

   a. Rename it to *EnemyZigGO*.

   b. Set EnemyZigGO's position to *[-4, 4, 0]*.

   c. Drag the EnemyZig Script onto the EnemyZigGO GameObject in the Hierarchy.

   d. Drag EnemyZigGO from the Hierarchy pane to the Project pane, creating a prefab of EnemyZigGO.

4. Click *Play*. See how the EnemyZigGO box falls at exactly the same rate as the EnemyGO sphere? That's because the EnemyZig class has inherited all the behaviors of Enemy!

5. Now try adding a new `Move()` method to EnemyZig (new lines are bolded):

```
1 using System.Collections;
2 using System.Collections.Generic;
3 using UnityEngine;
4
5 public class EnemyZig : Enemy {
6
7     public override void Move () {
8         Vector3 tempPos = pos;
9         tempPos.x = Mathf.Sin(Time.time * Mathf.PI*2) * 4;
10        pos = tempPos;      // Uses the pos property of the superclass
11        base.Move();        // Calls Move() on the superclass
12    }
13
14 }
```

In this code, you've *overridden* the *virtual function* `Move()` from the superclass Enemy and replaced it with a new one in `EnemyZig`. The `Enemy.Move()` method must be declared as `virtual` in the superclass (as it is on line 15 of the Enemy class script) for C# to allow it to be overridden in a subclass.

This new `Move()` function causes the box to zigzag right and left following a sine wave (sine and cosine are often useful for cyclical behavior like this). In this code, the x component of the position of the GameObject is set to the sine of the current time (the number of seconds since the Play button was clicked) times 2π, which causes a full cycle of the sine wave to occur every second. This value is then multiplied by 4 to cause the x position to range from −4 to 4.

The `base.Move()` call on line 11 tells EnemyZig to call the version of `Move()` on the superclass (or "base" class). As a result, `EnemyZig.Move()` handles the left and right motion, while `Enemy.Move()` causes the EnemyZigGO to fall at the same rate as EnemyGO.

The GameObjects in this example are called *Enemies* because you will use a similar class hierarchy system for the various Enemy subclasses in Chapter 31.

Summary

A class's ability to combine data with functionality enables developers to use the object-oriented approach that is presented in the next chapter. Object-oriented programming enables programmers to think of their classes as objects that can move and think on their own, and this approach combines very well with the GameObject-based structure of Unity and will help you make games more easily and rapidly.

CHAPTER 27

OBJECT-ORIENTED THINKING

This chapter covers how to think in terms of object-oriented programming (OOP), the logical extension of the classes discussed in the preceding chapter.

By the end of this chapter, you'll understand not only how to think in terms of OOP but also how to specifically structure projects in the manner that is best for the Unity development environment.

The Object-Oriented Metaphor

The easiest way to describe object orientation is through a metaphor. Think about all the birds in a flock. Flocks can consist of hundreds or even thousands of individual birds, each of which must avoid obstacles and other birds while still moving along with the flock. Flocks of birds exhibit brilliantly coordinated behaviors that for many years defied simulation.

Simulating a Flock of Birds in a Monolithic Way

Before the advent of object-oriented programming (OOP), a program was basically a single large function that did everything.[1] That single function controlled all data, moved sprites on screen, and handled everything from keyboard input to game logic, music, and graphic display. This is now referred to as *monolithic programming,* the attempt to do everything with a single, gigantic function.

To attempt to simulate a flock of birds in a monolithic way, it would make sense to store a large array of the birds and create a program that would consider every bird in the flock and attempt to generate swarming-style behavior for them. This program would individually move each bird from its position in one frame to its position in the next, and it would maintain all data about the birds in the array.

A monolithic program like this would be very large, unwieldy, and difficult to debug. For example, if the Enemy and EnemyZig classes from the previous chapter were combined into a single monolithic class that controlled all enemies, the code would have looked like this:

```
 1 using System.Collections;
 2 using System.Collections.Generic;
 3 using UnityEngine;
 4
 5 public class MonolithicEnemyController : MonoBehaviour {
 6     // The List of all enemies. This is populated in the Unity inspector
 7     public List<GameObject>        enemies;                          // a
 8     public float                   speed = 10f;
 9
10     void Update () {
11         Vector3 tempPos;
12
13         foreach ( GameObject enemy in enemies ) {                    // b
14             tempPos = enemy.transform.position;
15
16             switch ( enemy.name ) {                                  // c
17                 case "EnemyGO":
18                     tempPos.y -= speed * Time.deltaTime;
19                     break;
```

---

1. This is, of course, a drastic simplification, but it serves to make the point.

```
20                  case "EnemyZigGO":
21                      tempPos.x = 4 * Mathf.Sin(Time.time * Mathf.PI*2);
22                      tempPos.y -= speed * Time.deltaTime;
23                      break;
24              }
25
26              enemy.transform.position = tempPos;
27          }
28      }
29 }
```

   a. This list of GameObjects holds all the enemies. None of the enemies have any code
   attached to them.

   b. The `foreach` loop on line 13 iterates over each GameObject in the list enemies.

   c. Because the enemies don't have any code on them, this `switch` statement is required to
   store all information about all kinds of movement available to the enemies.

In this simple example, this code is rather short and isn't really very "monolithic," but it does lack
the elegance and extensibility of the code from Chapter 26, "Classes." If one were to create a
game with 20 different enemy types using this monolithic class, the single `Update()` function
would easily grow to several hundred lines as cases were added for each type. Thankfully, there
is a better way. Adding 20 additional enemies using the object-oriented subclassing method
from Chapter 26 would instead generate 20 small classes (like EnemyZig), each of which would
be short and easy to both understand and debug.

When OOP attempts to simulate a flock of birds, rather than a single monolithic function, OOP
takes a different approach by simulating each individual bird and its perceptions and actions
(all local to itself).

Simulating a Flock of Birds Using OOP and Boids

Prior to 1987, several attempts had been made at simulating the flocking behavior of birds and
the schooling behavior of fish via monolithic programming practices. It was generally thought
that to generate the complex coordinated behavior of a swarm, a single function would need to
manage all the data in the simulation.

This preconception was shattered with the publication of the paper "Flocks, Herds, and
Schools: A Distributed Behavioral Model" by Craig W. Reynolds in 1987.[2] In this paper, Reynolds
described an incredibly simple, object-oriented approach to simulating swarm-like behavior,
which he called *Boids*. At its most basic level, Boids uses only three simple rules:

---

2. C. W. Reynolds, "Flocks, Herds, and Schools: A Distributed Behavioral Model," *Computer Graphics, 21*(4),
   July 1987 (acm SIGGRAPH '87 Proceedings), 25–34.

1. **Collision Avoidance:** Avoid collisions with nearby flockmates

2. **Velocity Matching:** Attempt to match velocity with nearby flockmates

3. **Flock Centering:** Attempt to stay near the average location of nearby flockmates

An Object-Oriented Boids Implementation

In this tutorial, you'll build a simple implementation of Reynold's Boids that shows the power of simple object-oriented code to create complex, emergent behavior. First, create a new project following the instructions in the sidebar. As you're going through the steps of this tutorial, I recommend using a pencil to check off each step as you complete it.

SET UP THE BOIDS PROJECT

Create a new project in Unity, following the standard project setup procedure described in Appendix A, "Standard Project Setup Procedure."

- **Project Name:** Boids

- **Scene Name:** _Scene_0

You will create everything else through the course of the chapter.

Making a Simple Boid Model

To make a model for each Boid, we'll build something from a combination of stretched cubes. When it's finished, the Boid GameObject prefab will be similar to that shown in Figure 27.1.

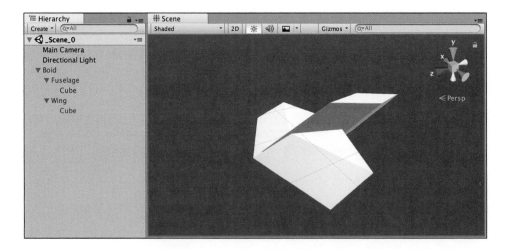

Figure 27.1 The finished Boid model

Follow these steps:

1. Select *GameObject > Create Empty* from the Unity menu bar.

   a. Rename the new GameObject to *Boid*.

   b. Click on the background of the Hierarchy pane to deselect Boid.

2. Select *GameObject > Create Empty* from the Unity menu bar again.

   a. Rename this GameObject *Fuselage.*

   b. Press the mouse down on Fuselage (Figure 27.2A) and drag Fuselage onto Boid in the Hierarchy pane (Figure 27.2B).

This makes Fuselage a child of Boid. A new disclosure triangle appears next to Boid that you can click to show Boid's children (at the pointer tip in Figure 27.2C). With the disclosure triangle open, your Hierarchy should look like Figure 27.2C.

Figure 27.2 Nesting GameObjects in the hierarchy (i.e., making one a child of another)

3. Right-click on *Fuselage* and choose *3D Object > Cube* from the pop-up menu that appears. This creates a new Cube as a child of Fuselage (if it doesn't appear under Fuselage, then you should drag Cube under Fuselage manually).

4. Set the transforms of the Fuselage and Cube to match those shown in Figure 27.3. The combination of scaling and rotation of the parent Fuselage will cause the child Cube to skew into a sleek, pointed shape.

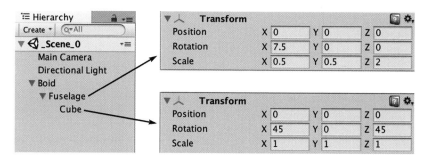

Figure 27.3 Transform settings for Fuselage and its child Cube

5. Select the *Cube* under Fuselage. Right-click the *Box Collider* component name in the Inspector pane and choose *Remove Component* from the pop-up menu. This removes the Box Collider from Cube, which will allow other objects to move through it. Another reason for removing the collider is that colliders don't stretch the same way that cubes do, so the physical boundaries of the collider would not match the visual dimensions of the cube.

6. Select *Fuselage* and select *Edit > Duplicate* from the menu bar. A second Fuselage named *Fuselage (1)* should appear under Boid in the Hierarchy.

    a. Rename the GameObject *Fuselage (1)* to *Wing*.

    b. Set the transform for Wing to match that shown in Figure 27.4.

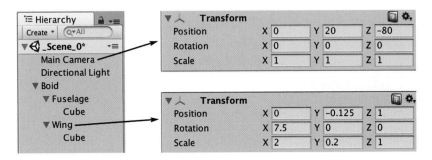

Figure 27.4 Transform settings for Wing and Main Camera (steps 6 and 13)

7. Now create a Material to form a trail behind each Boid as it moves through space:

    a. From the Unity menu bar, choose *Assets > Create > Material*, and name the new material *TrailMaterial*.

    b. Select *TrailMaterial* in the Project pane, and at the top of the Inspector pane, choose *Particles > Additive* from the Shader pop-up menu.

    c. To the right of the *Particle Texture* section of the Inspector that appears is an empty box for a texture that currently reads *None (Texture)*. Click the *Select* button in this box, and choose the *Default-Particle* texture from the window that appears. Now a white, blurred circle should appear in the texture box.

8. Click *Boid* in the Hierarchy pane to highlight it. Select *Component > Effects > Trail Renderer* from the menu bar. This adds a *Trail Renderer* component to the Boid. In the Trail Renderer component of the Inspector pane:

    a. Click the disclosure triangle next to *Materials* to open it.

    b. Click the small circle to the right of *Element 0   None (Material)*.

    c. Choose the *TrailMaterial* we just made from the list of materials that appears.

    d. Set the *Time* of the Trail Renderer to 1.

    e. Set the *Width* of the Trail Renderer to 0.25. Now, if you use the Move tool to move the Boid in the Scene window, it should leave a trail.

9. With Boid still highlighted in the Hierarchy, from the Unity menu bar, choose *Component > Physics > Sphere Collider*. This adds a Sphere Collider component to Boid. In the Sphere Collider component of the Inspector:

    a. Set *Is Trigger* to true (checked).

    b. Set *Center* to [0, 0, 0].

    c. Set *Radius* to 4 (this will be adjusted with code later).

10. With Boid still highlighted in the Hierarchy, from the Unity menu bar, choose *Component > Physics > Rigidbody*. Be sure to then set *Use Gravity* to false (unchecked) in the Rigidbody component of the Inspector.

11. Drag Boid from the Hierarchy pane to the Project pane, which will make a prefab named Boid. Your finished Boid model should look like the one in Figure 27.1.

12. Delete the blue Boid instance from the Hierarchy pane. Now that you have a Boid prefab in the Project pane, the Boid in the Hierarchy is no longer necessary.

13. Select the *Main Camera* in the Hierarchy and set its transform to match that shown in Figure 27.4. This gives the Main Camera a distant view that will enable us to see many boids at the same time.

14. Select *GameObject > Create Empty* from the menu bar. Rename this new GameObject to *BoidAnchor*. This empty BoidAnchor GameObject will act as a parent for all the Boid instances that are added to the scene, keeping the Hierarchy pane as clean as possible.

15. Save your scene. You've changed a lot, and I would hate for you to lose all of that work.

The C# Scripts

This program will use five different C# scripts, each of which has an important job.

- **Boid**—This script will be attached to the Boid prefab, and its job is to handle the movement of each individual Boid. Because this is an object-oriented program, each Boid will think for itself and react to its own individual understanding of the world.

- **Neighborhood**— This script will also be attached to the Boid prefab, and it keeps track of which other Boids are nearby. Key to each Boid's individual understanding of the world is its knowledge of which other Boids are close enough to worry about.

- **Attractor**—The Boids need something to flock around, and this simple script will be attached to a GameObject used for that purpose.

- **Spawner**—This script will be attached to Main Camera. Spawner stores the fields (variables) that are shared by all Boids and instantiates all the instances of the Boid prefab.

- **LookAtAttractor**—Also attached to the Main Camera, this script causes the camera to turn and look at the Attractor each frame.

Of course, we could certainly do this with fewer scripts, but each one would be much larger than is necessary. This example follows an expansion of Object-Oriented Programming known as *Component-Oriented Design*. See the sidebar for more info.

COMPONENT-ORIENTED DESIGN

The Component Pattern was formalized in the 1994 book *Design Patterns: Elements of Reusable Object-Oriented Software*[3] by the "Gang of Four." The core idea of the Component Pattern is to group closely related functions and data into a single class while at the same time keeping each class as small and focused as possible.[4]

As you might have guessed from the name, you've been working with components the whole time you've been using Unity. Each GameObject in Unity is a very small class that can act as a container for several components that each do a specific—and isolated—job. For example:

- Transform handles position, rotation, scale, and hierarchy.

- Rigidbody handles motion and physics.

- Colliders handle actual collision and the shape of the collision volume.

Although each of these is related, they are separate enough to each warrant a separate component. Making each a component also enables easy expansion in the future: separating Colliders from the Rigidbody means that we could easily add a new kind of Collider—a ConeCollider for instance—and Rigidbody would not need to change at all to accommodate the new Collider type.

This is certainly important for game engine developers, but what does it mean to us as game designers and prototypers? The most important thing that thinking in a component-oriented way gives us is smaller, shorter classes. When your scripts are shorter, they are easier to code, share with other people, reuse, and debug, all of which are very noble goals.

The only real negative of component-oriented design is that implementing it well takes a decent amount of forethought, which somewhat flies in the face of our prototyping philosophy of getting things working as quickly as possible. As a result of this dilemma, in Part III of this book, you will encounter both a more traditional prototyping style of just writing what works in the first several chapters and a much more component-oriented approach in Chapters 35, "Prototype 6: Dungeon Delver."

For more information about various software design patterns, please check out the *Software Design Patterns* section of Appendix B, "Useful Concepts."

---

3. Erich Gamma, Richard Helm, Ralph Johnson, and John Vissides, *Design Patterns: Elements of Reusable Object-Oriented Software* (Reading, MA: Addison-Wesley, 1994). *Design Patterns* was also the book that formalized the Singleton pattern and others used throughout my book.

4. The full description of the Component pattern is far more complex, but this will serve our needs.

Attractor Script

We'll start with the Attractor script. The Attractor is the object that all the Boids flock to. Without it, they would flock with each other, but the flock as a whole would fly off screen.

1. From the Unity menu bar, choose *GameObject > 3D Object > Sphere* to create a new Sphere and then rename this Sphere to *Attractor*.

2. Select *Attractor*. In the Inspector for Attractor, right-click the name of the *Sphere Collider* component and choose *Remove Component* from the pop-up menu to remove the Sphere Collider component from Attractor.

3. Set the scale of the transform of Attractor to S:[4, 0.1, 4] (i.e., X=4, Y=0.1, and Z=4).

4. From the Unity menu bar, choose *Component > Effects > Trail Renderer*. In the *Trail Renderer* component of the Attractor Inspector, do the following:

   a. Click the disclosure triangle next to *Materials* to open it.

   b. Click the small circle to the right of *Element 0   None (Material)*.

   c. Choose *Sprites-Default* from the list of materials that appears.

   d. Set the *Time* of the Trail Renderer to 4.

   e. Set the *Width* of the Trail Renderer to 0.25.

5. At the bottom of the Inspector for Attractor, click the *Add Component* button and choose *New Script* from the pop-up menu that appears. Name the new script *Attractor* and click *Create and Add* to create the script and add it to Attractor in one step.

6. Open the Attractor script in MonoDevelop and enter the code in the following listing. Lines that you need to type appear in bold.

```
1 using System.Collections;
2 using System.Collections.Generic;
3 using UnityEngine;
4
5 public class Attractor : MonoBehaviour {
6     static public Vector3    POS = Vector3.zero;                    // a
7
8     [Header("Set in Inspector")]
9     public float        radius = 10;
10     public float        xPhase = 0.5f;
11     public float        yPhase = 0.4f;
12     public float        zPhase = 0.1f;
13
14     // FixedUpdate is called once per physics update (i.e., 50x/second)
15     void FixedUpdate () {                                          // b
16         Vector3 tPos = Vector3.zero;
17         Vector3 scale = transform.localScale;
18         tPos.x = Mathf.Sin(xPhase * Time.time) * radius * scale.x;  // c
19         tPos.y = Mathf.Sin(yPhase * Time.time) * radius * scale.y;
```

```
20          tPos.z = Mathf.Sin(zPhase * Time.time) * radius * scale.z;
21          transform.position = tPos;
22          POS = tPos;
23      }
24 }
```

a. As a `static` variable, POS is shared by all instances of Attractor (though in this case, there will be only ever one instance of Attractor). When a field is *static*, it is scoped to the class itself rather than any instance of the class. This makes POS a *class variable* rather than an *instance field*. This means that as long as both POS and the class Attractor are `public`, any instance of any other class can access POS via `Attractor.POS`. This will be used by all the Boid instances to easily access the location of the Attractor.

b. `FixedUpdate()` is similar to `Update()`, but it is called once per physics frame as opposed to once per visual frame. See the sidebar for more information.

c. As was mentioned in the previous chapter, sine waves are often used for cyclical movement. Here, the various phase fields (e.g., `xPhase`) cause the Attractor to move around the scene with each axis (X, Y, and Z) slightly out of phase with the others.

7. Save the Attractor script, return to Unity, and click Play. You should see the Attractor moving due to the sine equations within a volume that is defined by `radius` * the `transform.localScale` of the Attractor.

FIXED UPDATES AND THE PHYSICS ENGINE

Because Unity is trying to run as quickly as possible, it displays a new frame whenever possible. This means that the `Time.deltaTime` between each `Update()` can range anywhere from less than 1/400 of a second on a fast computer to 1 second or more on a slow mobile device. Additionally, the frequency of `Update()`s changes drastically from one frame to the next on the same computer based on a number of factors, so the `Time.deltaTime` between each `Update()` is always different.

Physics engines—like the NVIDIA PhysX engine used by Unity—rely on predictability and stability, something that `Update()` cannot offer. As a result, Unity has a physics update that always runs at the same rate, regardless of the computer on which it is running. The frequency of this `FixedUpdate()` is set by setting the static field `Time.fixedDeltaTime`. By default, `Time.fixedDeltaTime` is 0.02f (i.e., 1/50), meaning that 50 times per second `FixedUpdate()` will be called and the PhysX engine will update.

As a result, `FixedUpdate()` is best used for tasks that deal with anything moving due to a Rigidbody (which is why we use it for both the Attractor and Boid updates), and it is also very useful for things that you want to be consistent regardless of the computer on which they are running.

`FixedUpdate()` is called immediately before the update to the PhysX engine.

Also be aware that the Input methods `GetKeyDown()`, `GetKeyUp()`, `GetButton-Down()`, and `GetButtonUp()` should never be called as part of `FixedUpdate()` because they only work on the single `Update()` call when the event happened. For example, `GetKeyDown()` is only true on the single `Update()` when a key was pressed down, so if multiple `Update()`s happen between two `FixedUpdates()`, a call to `Input.GetKeyDown()` inside of `FixedUpdate()` would only be true if the key happened to be pressed on the final `Update()` before `FixedUpdate()` was called. Regardless of whether that makes complete sense right now, just remember: Never use `Input.GetKeyDown()` or any other Input method that ends in ...`Down()` or ...`Up()` inside of `FixedUpdate()`. Other Input methods like `GetAxis()`, `GetKey()`, and `GetButton()` work fine inside either `FixedUpdate()` or `Update()`. You will use Input methods like these throughout Part III of the book.

LookAtAttractor Script

Next, you want to make the Main Camera follow the Attractor's movements.

1. Select *Main Camera* in the Hierarchy.

2. Create a C# script named *LookAtAttractor* and attach it to the Main Camera (using any of the methods that you've seen for doing so).

3. Open the *LookAtAttractor* script in MonoDevelop and enter the following code:

```
5 public class LookAtAttractor : MonoBehaviour {
6
7     void Update () {
8         transform.LookAt(Attractor.POS); // Yep, just add this one line!
9     }
10
11 }
```

4. Save the script, return to Unity and click Play.

Now, the Main Camera will constantly look at the Attractor.

Boid Script—Part 1

Because so many other scripts will reference the Boid class, you will create it now, though you won't yet add any additional code to it. This allows other C# scripts to reference a Boid class and compile without causing errors (and without having the word Boid appear red in MonoDevelop).

1. Select the *Boid* prefab in the Project pane.

2. At the bottom of the Inspector, click the *Add Component* button and choose *New Script* from the pop-up menu that appears. Name the script *Boid* and click *Create and Add*.

For now, that's all we need from Boid. Let's move on.

Spawner Script—Part 1

The Spawner script will be attached to the Main Camera, and as such, you will be able to edit the public fields of Spawner in the Unity Inspector. This will give you a central place to tweak all the numbers that influence the Boids' movement.

1. Select *Main Camera* in the Hierarchy.

2. Use any of the methods you've seen to create a C# script named *Spawner* and attach it to the Main Camera.

3. Open the *Spawner* script in MonoDevelop and enter the following code:

```
1  using System.Collections;
2  using System.Collections.Generic;
3  using UnityEngine;
4
5  public class Spawner : MonoBehaviour {
6      // This is a Singleton of the BoidSpawner. There is only one instance
7      //   of BoidSpawner, so we can store it in a static variable named S.
8      static public Spawner      S;                                          // a
9      static public List<Boid>     boids;                                    // b
10
11     // These fields allow you to adjust the spawning behavior of the Boids
12     [Header("Set in Inspector: Spawning")]
13     public GameObject        boidPrefab;                                   // c
14     public Transform         boidAnchor;
15     public int               numBoids = 100;
16     public float             spawnRadius = 100f;
17     public float             spawnDelay = 0.1f;
18
19     // These fields allow you to adjust the flocking behavior of the Boids
20     [Header("Set in Inspector: Boids")]
21     public float             velocity = 30f;
22     public float             neighborDist = 30f;
23     public float             collDist = 4f;
24     public float             velMatching = 0.25f;
25     public float             flockCentering = 0.2f;
26     public float             collAvoid = 2f;
27     public float             attractPull = 2f;
28     public float             attractPush = 2f;
29     public float             attractPushDist = 5f;
30
31     void Awake () {
32         // Set the Singleton S to be this instance of BoidSpawner
33         S = this;                                                          // d
34         // Start instantiation of the Boids
35         boids = new List<Boid>();
36         InstantiateBoid();
37     }
38
```

```
39    public void InstantiateBoid() {
40        GameObject go = Instantiate(boidPrefab);
41        Boid b = go.GetComponent<Boid>();
42        b.transform.SetParent(boidAnchor);                      // e
43        boids.Add( b );
44        if (boids.Count < numBoids) {
45            Invoke( "InstantiateBoid", spawnDelay );            // f
46        }
47    }
48 }
```

a. The field S is a *singleton*, which is one of the Software Design Patterns covered in Appendix B, "Useful Concepts." A singleton is sometimes used when there will only ever be one instance of a particular class. Because there will only ever be one instance of the class Spawner, it can be stored in the *static* field S. Therefore—just as with the public static POS field of Attractor—anywhere in code, you can use Spawner.S to refer to this singleton Spawner instance.

b. The List<Boid> boids will hold a reference to all the Boids instantiated by Spawner.

c. You must use the Unity Inspector to set the values of the fields boidPrefab and boidAnchor for this script to work (in steps 5 and 6 that follow).

d. Here, this instance of Spawner is assigned to the singleton S. In the code for a class, this refers to the current instance of the class. For the Spawner script, this refers to the instance of Spawner that is attached to Main Camera, which is the only instance of Spawner in _Scene_0.

e. Making all the Boids children of the same GameObject helps keep the Hierarchy pane organized. This line places them all underneath a single parent Transform boidAnchor (in step 6, you will assign the BoidAnchor GameObject to the boidAnchor field of the Spawner inspector). If you want to see all the Boids listed in the hierarchy, you just need to click the disclosure triangle next to the parent GameObject BoidAnchor.

f. InstantiateBoid() is initially called once by Awake(), and then InstantiateBoid() uses the Invoke() function to call itself again until the number of Boids instantiated is equal to numBoids. The two arguments that Invoke takes are the name of the method to be called (as a string: "InstantiateBoid") and the amount of time to wait before calling it (spawnDelay, or 0.1 seconds).

4. Save the Spawner script, return to Unity, and select *Main Camera* in the Hierarchy pane.

5. Assign the *Boid* prefab from the Project pane to the boidPrefab field in the Main Camera *Spawner (Script)* component Inspector.

6. Assign the *BoidAnchor* GameObject in the Hierarchy pane to the boidAnchor field in the Main Camera *Spawner (Script)* component Inspector.

Try clicking Play in Unity. You'll see that Spawner instantiates a new instance of Boid as a child of BoidAnchor every tenth of a second for ten seconds, but the Boids are all stacked under the BoidAnchor in the middle of the scene doing nothing. It's time to return to the Boid script.

Boid Script—Part 2

Returning to the Boid script, follow these steps:

1. Open the *Boid* script in MonoDevelop and enter the bolded code that follows.

```
 1 using System.Collections;
 2 using System.Collections.Generic;
 3 using UnityEngine;
 4
 5 public class Boid : MonoBehaviour {
 6
 7     [Header("Set Dynamically")]
 8     public Rigidbody        rigid;                                      // a
 9
10     // Use this for initialization
11     void Awake () {
12         rigid = GetComponent<Rigidbody>();                              // a
13
14         // Set a random initial position
15         pos = Random.insideUnitSphere * Spawner.S.spawnRadius;          // b
16
17         // Set a random initial velocity
18         Vector3 vel = Random.onUnitSphere * Spawner.S.velocity;         // c
19         rigid.velocity = vel;
20
21         LookAhead();                                                    // d
22
23         // Give the Boid a random color, but make sure it's not too dark // e
24         Color randColor = Color.black;
25         while ( randColor.r + randColor.g + randColor.b < 1.0f ) {
26             randColor = new Color(Random.value, Random.value, Random.value);
27         }
28         Renderer[] rends = gameObject.GetComponentsInChildren<Renderer>();// f
29         foreach ( Renderer r in rends ) {
30             r.material.color = randColor;
31         }
32         TrailRenderer tRend = GetComponent<TrailRenderer>();
33         tRend.material.SetColor("_TintColor", randColor);
34     }
35
36     void LookAhead() {                                                  // d
37         // Orients the Boid to look at the direction it's flying
38         transform.LookAt(pos + rigid.velocity);
39     }
40
```

```
41        public Vector3 pos {                                    // b
42            get { return transform.position; }
43            set { transform.position = value; }
44        }
45
46  }
```

a. The `GetComponent<>()` call is a bit time consuming, so for performance, it's important to cache a reference to (i.e., store a way to quickly access) the Rigidbody component. The `rigid` field then allows us to avoid a call to `GetComponent<>()` every frame.

b. The `insideUnitSphere` static property of the `Random` class is a read-only property that generates a random Vector3 located somewhere within a sphere with a radius of 1 unit. We then multiply this by the `spawnRadius` public field of the Spawner single-ton to give this Boid instance a random location somewhere within `spawnRadius` distance from the origin (position [0, 0, 0]). This resultant Vector3 is assigned to the `pos` property that is defined at the end of this code listing.

c. The `Random.onUnitSphere` static property generates a Vector3 somewhere on the surface of a sphere with a radius of 1. In other words, it makes a Vector3 that is 1 unit long, pointing in a random direction. We multiply this by the `velocity` field set on the Spawner singleton and then assign it to the velocity of the Boid's Rigidbody component.

d. `LookAhead()` orients the Boid to face in the direction of its `rigid.velocity`.

e. Lines 24–33 are not strictly necessary, but they makes the scene look nicer. These lines set the color of this Boid to something random (but sufficiently bright to be seen).

f. The `gameObject.GetComponentsInChildren<Renderer>()` call returns an array of all the Renderer components attached to this Boid GameObject *and* any of its children. This returns the Renderer components of the Cubes under both Fuselage and Wing.

2. Save the script, return to Unity, and click Play.

Now the Boids are created in different positions, fly in various directions, and are sundry colors, but they still don't react to anything in the world.

3. Return to MonoDevelop and add the following bolded lines to the Boid script. Note that several lines are skipped in the following code listing. Throughout the book, I use ellipses (...) to denote anywhere that lines are skipped. Don't delete any of the lines skipped by ellipses.

```
5  public class Boid : MonoBehaviour {
   ...                                                            // a
41        public Vector3 pos {
```

```
42          get { return transform.position; }
43          set { transform.position = value; }
44      }
45
46      // FixedUpdate is called once per physics update (i.e., 50x/second)
47      void FixedUpdate () {
48          Vector3 vel = rigid.velocity;                              // b
49          Spawner spn = Spawner.S;                                   // c
50
51          // ATTRACTION - Move towards the Attractor
52          Vector3 delta = Attractor.POS - pos;                       // d
53          // Check whether we're attracted or avoiding the Attractor
54          bool attracted = (delta.magnitude > spn.attractPushDist);
55          Vector3 velAttract = delta.normalized * spn.velocity;      // e
56
57          // Apply all the velocities
58          float fdt = Time.fixedDeltaTime;
59
60          if (attracted) {                                           // f
61              vel = Vector3.Lerp(vel, velAttract, spn.attractPull*fdt);
62          } else {
63              vel = Vector3.Lerp(vel, -velAttract, spn.attractPush*fdt);
64          }
65
66          // Set vel to the velocity set on the Spawner singleton
67          vel = vel.normalized * spn.velocity;                       // g
68          // Finally assign this to the Rigidbody
69          rigid.velocity = vel;
70          // Look in the direction of the new velocity
71          LookAhead();
72      }
73  }
```

a. The ellipses (...) here mark several lines that we've skipped in this listing because they have not changed since the previous Boid code listing.

b. This Vector3 vel is a different variable than the Vector3 vel in Awake() because each is a local variable scoped only to the method in which it is declared.

c. I've created the local variable spn to cache Spawner.S because the width of the page made it difficult to fit long lines that used Spawner.S.

d. Here, we get the position of the Attractor by reading the static public Attractor. POS field. By subtracting pos (this Boid's position) from the position of the Attractor, we get a Vector3 that points from the Boid to the Attractor. Then, based on how close this Boid is to the Attractor, it will either be pulled or pushed. On line 54, you see an example of assigning the bool result of a comparison to a variable (rather than using the comparison result as part of an if statement).

e. The `delta` vector to the Attractor is *normalized* to unit length (i.e., a length of 1) and multiplied by `spn.velocity` to give `velAttract` the same length as `vel`.

f. If the Boid is far enough from the Attractor to be attracted to it, a `Lerp()` is called on `vel` to *linearly interpolate* it toward the `velAttract` direction. Because `vel` and `velAttract` have the same magnitude (length), the interpolation is weighted evenly. If the Boid is too close to `Attractor.POS`, then `vel` will linearly interpolate toward the opposite direction of `velAttract`.

Linear interpolation takes two Vector3s as input and creates a new Vector3 that is a weighted mixture of the two. The amount of each original Vector3 that is used is based on the third argument. If the third argument is 0, `vel` will equal the original `vel`; if the third argument is 1, `vel` will equal `velAttract`. Because we multiply `spn.attractPull` by `fdt`, (which is our shortened variable name version of multiplying `Spawner.S.attractPull` by `Time.fixedDeltaTime`) the third parameter here is equal to `Spawner.S.attractPull/50`. You can find much more information about linear interpolation in the *Interpolation* section of Appendix B, "Useful Concepts."

g. By working with vectors of equal magnitude this whole time, we've been setting the direction of `vel` at a certain velocity. Now, `vel` is normalized and multiplied by the `velocity` field set on the Spawner singleton to get the final velocity for this Boid.

4. Save the script, return to Unity, and click Play.

Now you can see that the Boids are all attracted to the Attractor. As the Attractor changes directions, the Boids overshoot and have to turn to fly toward the Attractor once more. This is pretty nice already, but we can do better. To do so, we'll need to know something about the other nearby Boids.

Neighborhood Script

The *Neighborhood* script is a component that will track which other Boids are near this one and to give us information about them, including the average position and average velocity of all nearby Boids as well as information about which Boids are too close.

1. Create a new C# script named *Neighborhood* and attach it to the Boid prefab in the Project pane.

2. Open the *Neighborhood* script in MonoDevelop and enter the following code:

```
1  using System.Collections;
2  using System.Collections.Generic;
3  using UnityEngine;
4
5  public class Neighborhood : MonoBehaviour {
6      [Header("Set Dynamically")]
7      public List<Boid>      neighbors;
8      private SphereCollider  coll;
9
```

```
10      void Start() {                                              // a
11          neighbors = new List<Boid>();
12          coll = GetComponent<SphereCollider>();
13          coll.radius = Spawner.S.neighborDist/2;
14      }
15
16      void FixedUpdate() {                                        // b
17          if (coll.radius != Spawner.S.neighborDist/2) {
18              coll.radius = Spawner.S.neighborDist/2;
19          }
20      }
21
22      void OnTriggerEnter(Collider other) {                       // c
23          Boid b = other.GetComponent<Boid>();
24          if (b != null) {
25              if (neighbors.IndexOf(b) == -1) {
26                  neighbors.Add(b);
27              }
28          }
29      }
30
31      void OnTriggerExit(Collider other) {                        // d
32          Boid b = other.GetComponent<Boid>();
33          if (b != null) {
34              if (neighbors.IndexOf(b) != -1) {
35                  neighbors.Remove(b);
36              }
37          }
38      }
39
40      public Vector3 avgPos {                                     // e
41          get {
42              Vector3 avg = Vector3.zero;
43              if (neighbors.Count == 0) return avg;
44
45              for (int i=0; i<neighbors.Count; i++) {
46                  avg += neighbors[i].pos;
47              }
48              avg /= neighbors.Count;
49
50              return avg;
51          }
52      }
53
54      public Vector3 avgVel {                                     // f
55          get {
56              Vector3 avg = Vector3.zero;
57              if (neighbors.Count == 0) return avg;
58
```

```
59              for (int i=0; i<neighbors.Count; i++) {
60                  avg += neighbors[i].rigid.velocity;
61              }
62              avg /= neighbors.Count;
63
64              return avg;
65          }
66      }
67
68      public Vector3 avgClosePos {                                        // g
69          get {
70              Vector3 avg = Vector3.zero;
71              Vector3 delta;
72              int nearCount = 0;
73              for (int i=0; i<neighbors.Count; i++) {
74                  delta = neighbors[i].pos - transform.position;
75                  if (delta.magnitude <= Spawner.S.collDist) {
76                      avg += neighbors[i].pos;
77                      nearCount++;
78                  }
79              }
80              // If there were no neighbors too close, return Vector3.zero
81              if (nearCount == 0) return avg;
82
83              // Otherwise, average their locations
84              avg /= nearCount;
85              return avg;
86          }
87      }
88
89  }
```

a. This `Start()` method instantiates the `neighbors` List, gets a reference to this GameObject's SphereCollider (remember, this is a Boid GameObject, which also has a SphereCollider attached), and sets the radius of the SphereCollider to be half of the Spawner singleton's `neighborDist`. It is half because the `neighborDist` is the distance at which we want these GameObjects to see each other, and if each has a radius of half this distance, they will just barely touch at exactly the `neighborDist`.

b. Every `FixedUpdate()` Neighborhood checks to see whether the `neighborDist` has changed, and if so, it changes the radius of the SphereCollider. Setting the radius of the SphereCollider could cause a lot of PhysX recalculation, so we only set it if necessary.

c. `OnTriggerEnter()` is called when something else enters this SphereCollider trigger (a *trigger* is a collider that allows other things to pass through it). Other Boids should be the only things that have colliders on them, but to be sure, we `GetComponent<Boid>()` on the `other` Collider and only continue if the result is not `null`. At that point, if the Boid that moved within the neighborhood is not yet in our `neighbors` List, we add it.

    d. Similarly, when another Boid is no longer touching this Boid's trigger, `OnTrigger-Exit()` is called, and we remove the Boid from our `neighbors` List.

    e. The `avgPos` read-only property looks at all Boids in the `neighbors` List and averages their position. Note how it takes advantage of the public `pos` property on each Boid. If there are no neighbors, this returns Vector3.zero.

    f. Similarly, the `avgVel` property returns the average velocity of all neighbor Boids.

    g. The `avgClosePos` read-only property looks for neighbors that are within the `collisionDist` (from the Spawner singleton) and averages their position.

3. Be sure to save the Neighborhood script and switch back to Unity to give it a chance to recompile and present you with any errors it might have.

Boid Script—Part 3

Now that the Neighborhood component exists and is attached to the Boid GameObject, it's time to finalize the Boid class.

1. Open the Boid script in MonoDevelop and enter the new lines that are bolded in the following code listing. When you enter the code that follows, your line numbers might not match mine exactly. That's okay as long as the code is the same otherwise. C# treats all *whitespace* (spaces, returns, tabs, and so on) as the same thing, so an extra return here or there doesn't matter. I've included the entire Boid script for clarity.

```
1  using System.Collections;
2  using System.Collections.Generic;
3  using UnityEngine;
4
5  public class Boid : MonoBehaviour {
6
7      [Header("Set Dynamically")]
8      public Rigidbody        rigid;
9
10     private Neighborhood    neighborhood;
11
12     // Use this for initialization
13     void Awake () {
14         neighborhood = GetComponent<Neighborhood>();
15         rigid = GetComponent<Rigidbody>();
16
17         // Set a random initial position
18         pos = Random.insideUnitSphere * Spawner.S.spawnRadius;
19
20         // Set a random initial velocity
21         Vector3 vel = Random.onUnitSphere * Spawner.S.velocity;
22         rigid.velocity = vel;
23
24         LookAhead();
25
```

```
26          // Give the Boid a random color, but make sure it's not too dark
27          Color randColor = Color.black;
28          while ( randColor.r + randColor.g + randColor.b < 1.0f ) {
29              randColor = new Color(Random.value, Random.value, Random.value);
30          }
31          Renderer[] rends = gameObject.GetComponentsInChildren<Renderer>();
32          foreach ( Renderer r in rends ) {
33              r.material.color = randColor;
34          }
35          TrailRenderer trend = GetComponent<TrailRenderer>();
36          trend.material.SetColor("_TintColor", randColor);
37      }
38
39      void LookAhead() {
40          // Orients the Boid to look at the direction its flying
41          transform.LookAt(pos + rigid.velocity);
42      }
43
44      public Vector3 pos {
45          get { return transform.position; }
46          set { transform.position = value; }
47      }
48
49      // FixedUpdate is called once per physics update (i.e., 50x/second)
50      void FixedUpdate () {
51          Vector3 vel = rigid.velocity;
52          Spawner spn = Spawner.S;
53
54          // COLLISION AVOIDANCE - Avoid neighbors who are too close
55          Vector3 velAvoid = Vector3.zero;
56          Vector3 tooClosePos = neighborhood.avgClosePos;
57          // If the response is Vector3.zero, then no need to react
58          if (tooClosePos != Vector3.zero) {
59              velAvoid = pos - tooClosePos;
60              velAvoid.Normalize();
61              velAvoid *= spn.velocity;
62          }
63
64          // VELOCITY MATCHING - Try to match velocity with neighbors
65          Vector3 velAlign = neighborhood.avgVel;
66          // Only do more if the velAlign is not Vector3.zero
67          if (velAlign != Vector3.zero) {
68              // We're really interested in direction, so normalize the velocity
69              velAlign.Normalize();
70              // and then set it to the speed we chose
71              velAlign *= spn.velocity;
72          }
73
74          // FLOCK CENTERING - Move towards the center of local neighbors
```

```
75          Vector3 velCenter = neighborhood.avgPos;
76          if (velCenter != Vector3.zero) {
77              velCenter -= transform.position;
78              velCenter.Normalize();
79              velCenter *= spn.velocity;
80          }
81
82          // ATTRACTION - Move towards the Attractor
83          Vector3 delta = Attractor.POS - pos;
84          // Check whether we're attracted or avoiding the Attractor
85          bool attracted = (delta.magnitude > spn.attractPushDist);
86          Vector3 velAttract = delta.normalized * spn.velocity;
87
88          // Apply all the velocities
89          float fdt = Time.fixedDeltaTime;
90          if (velAvoid != Vector3.zero) {
91              vel = Vector3.Lerp(vel, velAvoid, spn.collAvoid*fdt);
92          } else {
93              if (velAlign != Vector3.zero) {
94                  vel = Vector3.Lerp(vel, velAlign, spn.velMatching*fdt);
95              }
96              if (velCenter != Vector3.zero) {
97                  vel = Vector3.Lerp(vel, velAlign, spn.flockCentering*fdt);
98              }
99              if (velAttract != Vector3.zero) {
100                 if (attracted) {
101                     vel = Vector3.Lerp(vel, velAttract, spn.attractPull*fdt);
102                 } else {
103                     vel = Vector3.Lerp(vel, -velAttract, spn.attractPush*fdt);
104                 }
105             }
106         }
107
108         // Set vel to the velocity set on the Spawner singleton
109         vel = vel.normalized * spn.velocity;
110         // Finally assign this to the Rigidbody
111         rigid.velocity = vel;
112         // Look in the direction of the new velocity
113         LookAhead();
114     }
115 }
```

2. Make sure that all of your scripts are saved, return to Unity, and click Play.

Now the Boids should exhibit more flock-like behavior. You can select Main Camera in the Hierarchy to play with the various values for Boids on the Spawner singleton. Table 27.1 lists some interesting versions of the values to try.

Table 27.1 Boids values

	Default	Sparse Follow	Small Groups	Formation
velocity	30	30	30	30
neighborDist	30	30	8	30
collDist	4	10	2	10
velMatching	0.25	0.25	0.25	10
flockCentering	0.2	0.2	8	0.2
collAvoid	2	4	10	4
attractPull	2	1	1	3
attractPush	2	2	20	2
attractPushDist	5	20	20	1

Summary

In this chapter, you learned about object-orientation, a concept that is exhibited throughout the rest of the book. Because of its structure of GameObjects with components, Unity is perfectly designed for an OOP mindset. You also learned about component-oriented design, a programming design pattern that works very well with Unity and—while a bit more complicated conceptually—can make your code simpler and more manageable.

Along with the idea of component-oriented OOP comes the concept of *modularity*. In many ways, modular code is the opposite of monolithic code. Modular coding focuses on making small, reusable functions and classes that do one thing really well. Because modular classes and functions are small (usually fewer than 500 lines), they are easier to debug and understand. Modular code is also designed to be reusable.

Next, you'll start Part III of the book, a series of focused tutorials that will help you learn how to make prototypes for various kinds of games. I hope you enjoy what you find there and can use them to start your journey as a designer, prototyper, and developer.

GAME PROTOTYPE EXAMPLES AND TUTORIALS

CHAPTER 28

PROTOTYPE 1: *APPLE PICKER*

Here it is. Today, you make your first digital game prototype.

Because this is your first prototype, it is rather simple. As you continue through the prototyping chapters, the projects get more complex and use more of the features of Unity.

By the end of this chapter, you will have a working prototype of a simple arcade game.

The Purpose of a Digital Prototype

Before we start making the prototype of Apple Picker, now is probably a good time to think again about the purpose of a digital prototype. The first part of the book provided considerable discussion of paper prototypes and why they are useful. Paper game prototypes help you do the following:

- Test, reject, and/or refine game mechanics and rules quickly
- Explore the dynamic behavior of your game and understand the emergent possibilities created by the rules
- Ascertain whether rules and gameplay elements are easily understood by players
- Understand the emotional response that players have to your game

Digital prototypes also add the fantastic ability to see how the game *feels*; in fact, that is their primary purpose. Although you could spend hours describing game mechanics to someone in detail, having them just play the game and see how it feels is much more efficient (and more interesting). This is discussed at length in the book *Game Feel* by Steve Swink.[1]

In this chapter, you create a working game, and the end result will be something that you can show to friends and colleagues. After letting them play it for a while, you can ask whether the difficulty feels too easy, too difficult, or just right. Use that information to tweak the variables in the game and custom craft a specific difficulty for each of them.

Let's get started making Apple Picker.

SET UP THE PROJECT FOR THIS CHAPTER

Following the standard project setup procedure, create a new project in Unity. If you need a refresher on the standard project setup procedure, see Appendix A, "Standard Project Setup Procedure."

- **Project name:** Apple Picker Prototype
- **Scene name:** _Scene_0
- **C# script names:** ApplePicker, Apple, AppleTree, and Basket

Do not attach the C# scripts to anything.

---

1. Steve Swink, *Game Feel: A Game Designer's Guide to Virtual Sensation* (Boston: Elsevier, 2009).

Preparing

Happily, you've already done a lot of the preparation for this prototype in Chapter 16, "Thinking in Digital Systems," when we analyzed Apple Picker and the classic game *Kaboom!*. As mentioned in that chapter, Apple Picker will have the same basic game mechanics as *Kaboom!*. Take a moment to look back at Chapter 16 and make sure that you understand the flow charts for each element: the AppleTree, the Apple, and the Basket.

As you work through these tutorials, I recommend using a pencil to check off each step as you complete them.

Getting Started: Art Assets

As a prototype, this game doesn't need fantastic art; it needs to work. The kind of art that you'll create throughout this book is known as *programmer art,* which is the placeholder art made by programmers that will eventually be replaced by the actual game art created by artists. As with nearly everything in a prototype, the purpose of this art is to get you from a concept to a working prototype as quickly as possible. If your programmer art doesn't look terrible, that's nice, but it's certainly not necessary.

AppleTree

Let's start with the tree.

1. From the Unity menu bar, choose *GameObject > 3D Object > Cylinder*. This will be the trunk of the tree. Set the name of the Cylinder to *Trunk* by selecting it in the Hierarchy and clicking its name at the top of the Inspector. Set the Transform component of Cylinder to match the settings of the Transform component shown in Figure 28.1.

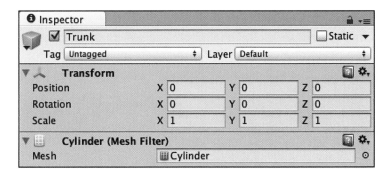

Figure 28.1 The Transform component for the Cylinder named Trunk

Throughout the tutorials in this book, I use the following format to give you settings for GameObject transform components:

Trunk (Cylinder)   P:[0, 0, 0]   R:[0, 0, 0]   S:[1, 1, 1]

The preceding line instructs you to set the transform of the GameObject named Trunk to a Position of X=0, Y=0, and Z=0; a Rotation of X=0, Y=0, and Z=0; and a Scale of X=1, Y=1, and Z=1. The word *Cylinder* in parentheses tells you the type of GameObject that it is. You will also sometimes see this format listed in the middle of a paragraph as P:[0, 0, 0] R:[0, 0, 0] S:[1, 1, 1].

2. Now choose *GameObject > 3D Object > Sphere*. Rename Sphere to *Leaves* and set its transform as follows:

    Leaves (Sphere)   P:[0, 0.5, 0]   R:[0, 0, 0]   S:[3, 2, 3]

The Leaves and the Trunk together should look (a bit) like a tree, but they are currently two separate objects. You need to create an empty GameObject to act as their *parent* and encapsulate the two of them under a single object.

3. From the menu bar, choose *GameObject > Create Empty*. This should create an empty GameObject. Make sure that its transform is set to the following:

    GameObject (Empty)   P:[0, 0, 0]   R:[0, 0, 0]   S:[1, 1, 1]

An empty GameObject only includes a Transform component, and it is therefore a simple, useful container for other GameObjects.

4. In the Hierarchy pane, first change the name of GameObject to *AppleTree*. Another way to do this is by clicking the name *GameObject* to highlight it, waiting for a second, and either pressing Return on the keyboard (F2 on Windows) or clicking it a second time.

5. Individually drag the Trunk and Leaves GameObjects onto AppleTree (you will get the same curved arrow icon as you do when you attach a C# script to a GameObject [Figure 19.4]), and they will be placed under AppleTree in the Hierarchy. You can click the new disclosure triangle next to the word *AppleTree* to see them. Your Hierarchy pane and AppleTree should now look like those shown in Figure 28.2.

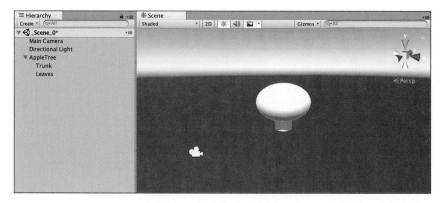

Figure 28.2 AppleTree shown in the Hierarchy and Scene panes with Leaves and Trunk as its children. The asterisk (*) next to **_Scene_0** at the top of the Hierarchy pane indicates that I have unsaved changes in my scene. I should save!

Now that the Trunk and Leaves GameObjects are parented to AppleTree, if you move, scale, or rotate AppleTree, both Trunk and Leaves will move, rotate, and scale alongside it. Give it a try by manipulating the Transform component of AppleTree.

6. After you're done playing with this, set the transform of AppleTree to the following:

   AppleTree   P:[0, 0, 0]   R:[0, 0, 0]   S:[2, 2, 2]

These settings center the AppleTree and scale it to twice as large as it was initially.

7. Add a Rigidbody component to AppleTree by selecting it in the Hierarchy and choosing *Component > Physics > Rigidbody* from the Unity menu.

8. In the Rigidbody component Inspector of AppleTree, uncheck *Use Gravity*. If you left it checked, the tree would fall out of the sky when you played the scene.

As covered in Chapter 20, "Variables and Components," the Rigidbody component ensures that the colliders of the Trunk and Sphere are properly updated in the physics simulation when you move the AppleTree across the stage.

Simple Materials for AppleTree

Though this is all *programmer art*, that doesn't mean that it has to be all basic white objects. Let's add a little color to the scene.

1. From the menu bar, choose *Assets > Create > Material*. This makes a new material in the Project pane.

   a. Rename this material to *Mat_Wood*.

   b. Drag the *Mat_Wood* material onto Trunk in your scene or Hierarchy pane.

   c. Select *Mat_Wood* in the Project pane again.

   d. Set the *Albedo* color under *Main Maps* in the Inspector for Mat_Wood to a brown of your liking.[2] You can also adjust the Metallic and Smoothness sliders to your liking.[3]

2. Do the same to create a material named *Mat_Leaves*.

   a. Drag *Mat_Leaves* onto Leaves in either the Hierarchy or Scene pane.

   b. Set the *Albedo* color of Mat_Leaves to a leafy-looking green.

---

2. When you work with the Unity Standard Shader, Albedo is the main color of the shader. To learn more about the Standard Shader, search for "Standard Shader" in the Unity Manual (http://docs.unity.com). This is a pretty deep topic with several subsections in the table of contents at the left side of the Unity documentation. If you want to learn about Albedo directly, you can search for "Albedo Color and Transparency."

3. I chose Metallic=0 and Smoothness=0.25. As you adjust these, you can see the effect on the Trunk in the Scene pane. You can also look at the material preview sphere at the bottom of the Inspector. If you don't see the preview, click the dark gray Mat_Wood bar at the bottom of the Inspector.

3. Drag *AppleTree* from the Hierarchy pane over to the Project pane to make a prefab from it. As you saw in previous chapters, this creates an AppleTree prefab in the Project pane and turns the name of AppleTree in the Hierarchy blue.

4. By default, Unity scenes come with a *Directional Light* already included. Set the position, rotation, and scale of Directional Light in the Hierarchy to the following:

    Directional Light   P:[0, 20, 0]   R:[50, -30, 0]   S:[1, 1, 1]

This should put a nice diagonal light across the scene. It's worth noting here that the position of a directional light is unimportant—directional lights shine in the same direction regardless of position—but I've given you the position of [0, 20, 0] to move it out of the middle of the scene view because its *gizmo* (that is, icon) would be in the middle of the Scene pane otherwise. If you play with the rotation of Directional Light, you will see that the first directional light in the scene is tied to the sun in Unity's default skybox. This isn't used in Apple Picker, but it can be a great effect in 3D games.

5. To move AppleTree up and out of the way a bit, select *AppleTree* in the Hierarchy and change its position to P:[0, 10, 0]. This might move it out of the view of the Scene pane, but you can zoom out to see it by scrolling your mouse wheel.

Apple

Now that you have the AppleTree, you need to make the *Apple* GameObject prefab that it will drop.

1. From the menu bar, choose *GameObject > 3D Object > Sphere*. Rename this sphere to *Apple*, and set its transform as follows:

    Apple (Sphere)   P:[0, 0, 0]   R:[0, 0, 0]   S:[1, 1, 1]

2. Create a new material named *Mat_Apple* and set its albedo color to red (or light green, if you prefer green apples).

3. Drag *Mat_Apple* onto Apple in the Hierarchy.

Adding Physics to the Apple

As you might remember from Chapter 17, "Introducing the Unity Development Environment," the *Rigidbody* component enables an object to react to physics (for example, falling or colliding with other objects).

1. Select *Apple* in the Hierarchy pane. From the Unity menu bar, choose *Component > Physics > Rigidbody*.

2. Click the Unity *Play* button, and the Apple will fall off screen due to gravity.

3. Click the *Play* button again to stop playback, and the Apple will return to its start location.

Giving Apples the Tag "Apple"

Eventually you will want to query the scene for an array of all the Apple GameObjects on screen, and giving the Apples a specific tag can help with this.

1. With Apple selected in the Hierarchy, click the pop-up menu button in the Inspector next to *Tag* (that currently displays "Untagged") and choose *Add Tag* from the pop-up menu, as shown in section A of Figure 28.3. This will open Unity's *Tags & Layers Manager*.

2. You might need to click the disclosure triangle next to *Tags* to see the view shown in section B of Figure 28.3. Click the + symbol to add a new tag.

3. Type *Apple* into the *New Tag Name* field (C) and click *Save*. Apple is now in the Tags list (D).

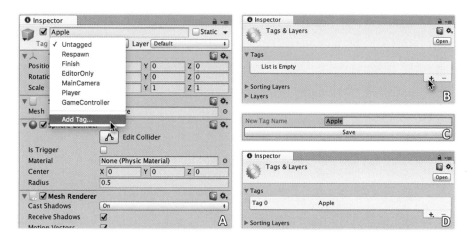

Figure 28.3 Steps 1, 2, and 3 of adding the Apple tag to the list of tags

4. Click *Apple* in the Hierarchy again to return to the Inspector for Apple.

5. Clicking the *Tag* pop-up menu once more now gives you *Apple* as a tag option. Choose *Apple* from the list of tags. Apple GameObjects will now have the tag *Apple*, which makes them easier to identify and select.

Making the Apple into a Prefab

To make the Apple into a prefab, follow these steps:

1. Drag *Apple* from the Hierarchy pane to the Project pane to make it a prefab.[4]

2. After you're sure an Apple prefab is in the Project pane, click the *Apple* instance in the Hierarchy pane and delete it (by choosing Delete from the right-click menu or by pressing Command-Delete [just Delete for Windows] on your keyboard). Because the apples in the game will be instantiated from the Apple prefab in the Project pane, you don't need to start with one in the scene.

---

4. See Chapter 19, "Hello World: Your First Program," for a discussion of prefabs.

Basket

Like the other art assets, the programmer art for the basket is very simple.

1. Choose *GameObject > 3D Object > Cube* from the Unity menu bar. Rename Cube to *Basket* and set its transform to the following:

   Basket (Cube)   P:[0, 0, 0]   R:[0, 0, 0]   S:[4, 1, 4]

This should give you a flat, wide rectangular solid.

2. Create a new material named *Mat_Basket*, color it a light, desaturated yellow (like straw), and apply it to the basket.

3. Add a Rigidbody component to Basket. Select *Basket* in the Hierarchy and choose *Component > Physics > Rigidbody* from the Unity menu.

   a. Set *Use Gravity* to false (unchecked) in Basket's Rigidbody Inspector.

   b. Set *Is Kinematic* to true (checked) in Basket's Rigidbody Inspector.

4. Drag *Basket* from the Hierarchy pane to the Project pane to make it into a prefab and delete the remaining instance of Basket from the Hierarchy (just as you did for Apple).

5. Be sure to save your scene.

Your Project and Hierarchy panes should now look like Figure 28.4.

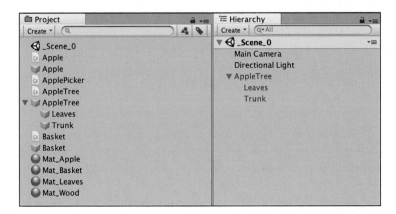

Figure 28.4 The Project and Hierarchy panes at this point in the prototype. You should have created the Apple, ApplePicker, AppleTree, and Basket scripts as part of the project setup at the beginning of this chapter.

Camera Setup

One of the most important things to get right in your games is the position of the camera. For Apple Picker, you want a camera that shows a decent-sized play area. Because the gameplay in this game is entirely two dimensional, you also want an orthographic camera instead of a perspective one.

ORTHOGRAPHIC VERSUS PERSPECTIVE CAMERAS

Orthographic and *perspective* are two types of virtual 3D cameras in games; see Figure 28.5.

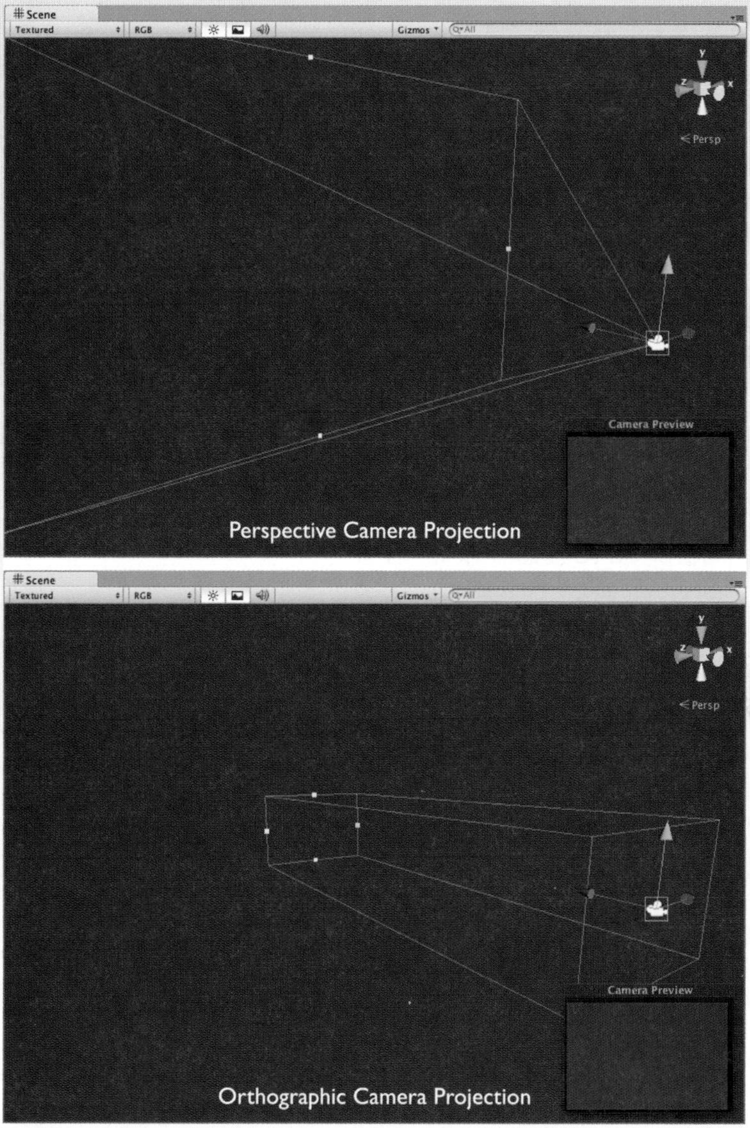

Figure 28.5 Comparison of perspective and orthographic camera projections

A *perspective* camera works like the human eye; because light comes in through a lens, objects that are close to the camera appear large, and objects that are far away appear smaller. This gives a perspective camera a *field of view* (a.k.a. projection) shaped like a square frustum (or more simply, a square pyramid). To see this, click *Main Camera* in your hierarchy, and then zoom out in the Scene pane. The pyramidal wireframe shape extending out from the camera is the *view frustum* and shows everything that the camera will see.

Through an *orthogonal* camera, an object will appear to be the same size regardless of how far it is from the camera. The projection for an orthogonal camera is rectangular rather than frustum shaped. To see this, select *Main Camera* in the Hierarchy pane. Find the Camera component in the Inspector and change the projection from Perspective to *Orthogonal*. Now, the gray view frustum represents a 3D rectangle rather than a pyramid.

Setting the Scene pane to be orthogonal rather than perspective is also sometimes useful. To do this, click the word *<Persp* under the axes gizmo in the upper-right corner of the Scene pane (see each of the images in Figure 28.5). Click the *<Persp* under the axes gizmo to switch between perspective and *isometric* (abbreviated *=Iso*) scene views (isometric being another word for orthographic).

Camera Settings for Apple Picker

Now, establish the camera settings for Apple Picker:

1. Select *Main Camera* in the Hierarchy pane and set its transform as follows:

    Main Camera (Camera)   P:[0, 0, -10]   R:[0, 0, 0]   S:[1, 1, 1]

This position moves the camera viewpoint down 1 meter (a unit in Unity is the equivalent of 1m in length) to be at a height of exactly 0. Because Unity units are equivalent to meters, I sometimes abbreviate "1 Unity unit" as 1m in this book.

2. In the Camera component of the Inspector, set the following (as shown in Figure 28.6):

    a. Set the Projection to *Orthographic*.

    b. Set the Size to *16*.

This makes the AppleTree a good size in the Game pane and leaves room for the apples to fall and be caught by the player. Often, you can make a good first guess at things like camera settings and then refine them after you've had a chance to play the game. Just like everything else in game development, finding the right settings for the camera is an iterative process. Your final Main Camera Inspector should now look like what is shown in Figure 28.6.

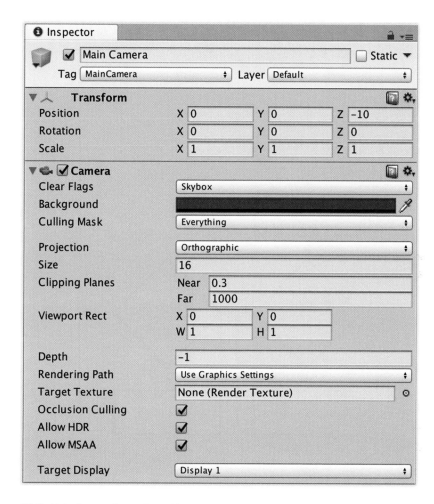

Figure 28.6 Main Camera Inspector settings

Game Panel Settings

Another contributing factor to your game view is the aspect ratio of the Game pane.

1. At the top of the Game pane is a pop-up menu that currently displays *Free Aspect*. This is the aspect ratio pop-up menu.

2. Click the aspect ratio pop-up menu and choose *16:9*. This is the standard format for widescreen televisions and computer monitors, so it will look nice when you play the game full-screen. You also should uncheck the *Low Resolution Aspect Ratios* option if you're on macOS.

Coding the Apple Picker Prototype

Now it's time to make the code of this game prototype actually work. Figure 28.7 presents the flow chart of the AppleTree's actions from Chapter 16, "Thinking in Digital Systems."

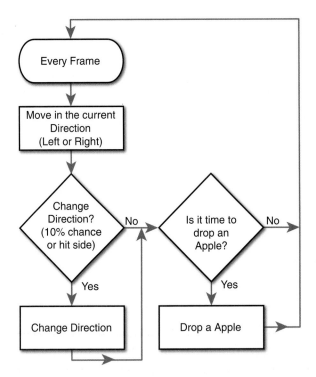

Figure 28.7 AppleTree flow chart

The actions you need to code for the AppleTree are as follows:

- Move at a certain speed every frame.
- Change directions upon hitting the edge of the play area.
- Change directions based on random chance.
- Drop an apple every second.

That's it! Let's start coding. Double-click the AppleTree C# script in the Project pane to open it.

1. You need some configuration variables, so open the AppleTree class in MonoDevelop and enter code to match the following. The code you need to change is bolded.

```
using System.Collections;
using System.Collections.Generic;
using UnityEngine;
```

```
public class AppleTree : MonoBehaviour {
    [Header("Set in Inspector")]
    // Prefab for instantiating apples
    public GameObject    applePrefab;

    // Speed at which the AppleTree moves
    public float         speed = 1f;

    // Distance where AppleTree turns around
    public float         leftAndRightEdge = 10f;

    // Chance that the AppleTree will change directions
    public float         chanceToChangeDirections = 0.1f;

    // Rate at which Apples will be instantiated
    public float         secondsBetweenAppleDrops = 1f;

    void Start () {
        // Dropping apples every second
    }

    void Update () {
        // Basic Movement
        // Changing Direction
    }
}
```

You might have noticed that the preceding code does not include the line numbers that were shown at the beginnings of lines in some prior chapters. The code listings in this part of the book will generally not have line numbers because there will likely be variance between your line numbers and mine due to differences in carriage returns over the course of many lines of code.[5] Save the AppleTree script in MonoDevelop and return to Unity.

2. To see this code actually do something, you need to attach it to the AppleTree GameObject.

    a. Drag the *AppleTree* C# script from the Project pane onto the AppleTree prefab that is also in the Project pane.

    b. Click the AppleTree instance in the Hierarchy pane; the script has been added not only to the AppleTree prefab but also to all of its instances.

    c. With the AppleTree selected in the Hierarchy, you should see all the variables you just declared appear in the Inspector under the *AppleTree (Script)* component.

3. Try moving the AppleTree around in the scene by adjusting the X and Y coordinates in the Transform Inspector to find a good height (position.y) for the AppleTree and a good limit

---

5. Another reason for omitting line numbers is that I needed every single character I could get to fit some long lines of code on a single line of the printed page.

for left and right movement. On my machine, 12 looks like a good position.y, and it looks like the tree can move from -20 to 20 in position.x and still be seen well in the Game pane.

   a.   Set the position of AppleTree to P:[0, *12*, 0]

   b.   Set the leftAndRightEdge float in the *AppleTree (Script)* component Inspector to *20*.

THE UNITY ENGINE SCRIPTING REFERENCE

Before you get too far into this project, it's extremely important that you remember to look at the Unity Scripting Reference if you have any questions at all about the code you see here. There are two ways to get into the Script Reference:

1. Choose *Help > Scripting Reference* from the menu bar in Unity. This opens your web browser and brings up the Scripting Reference that is saved *locally* on your machine, meaning that it will work even without a connection to the Internet. You can type any function or class name into the search field on the left to find out more about it.

    Enter *MonoBehaviour* into the search field on the Scripting Reference web page and press Return. Click the top result to see all the methods built in to every MonoBehaviour script (and by extension, built in to every class script you will write and attach to a GameObject in Unity). For readers from the United States, note the European spelling of *Behaviour.*

2. When working in MonoDevelop, select any text you want to learn more about and then choose *Help > Unity API Reference* from the menu bar. This launches an Internet version of the Unity Scripting Reference, so it won't work properly without Internet access, but it has the exact same information as the local reference that you can reach through the first method.

The first time you visit the Scripting Reference, you might be asked to choose between C# and JS from a couple of rectangular buttons near the top-right of the window. Make sure that you click the *C#* button in the top-right of the page to select C# as your preferred language. Most Unity code examples are available in both C# and JavaScript, though some very old examples might still only exist in JavaScript.

Basic Movement

Now make the following changes to add movement:

1. Make the following bolded changes to the `Update()` method in the AppleTree script. Note the ellipses in the code listing (...). These indicate where I've skipped over lines in this listing to conserve space. Please do not delete those lines!

```
public class AppleTree : MonoBehaviour {
    ...                                                      // a
    void Update () {
        // Basic Movement
        Vector3 pos = transform.position;                    // b
        pos.x += speed * Time.deltaTime;                     // c
        transform.position = pos;                            // d

        // Changing Direction
    }
}
```

The // indicators at the right side of lines reference the following additional info.

a. Throughout the tutorial chapters of this book, I use ellipses (...) to indicate parts of the code that I am skipping in the code listing. Without these, the code listings would be ridiculously long in some of the later chapters. When you see ellipses like these, you shouldn't change anything about the code where they are; just leave it alone and focus on the new code (which is bolded for clarity). This code listing requires no changes to any lines of code between the AppleTree class declaration and the Update() method, so I have used ellipses to skip those unchanged lines.

b. This line defines the Vector3 pos to be the current position of the AppleTree.

c. The x component of pos is increased by the speed times Time.deltaTime (which is a measure of the number of seconds since the last frame). This makes the movement of the AppleTree *time based*, which is a very important concept in game programming (see the "Making Your Games Time Based" sidebar).

d. Assigns this modified pos back to transform.position (which moves AppleTree to a new position). If you don't set transform.position to pos, AppleTree will not move.

You might be wondering why the preceding code changes were three lines instead of just one. Why couldn't the code just be this?

```
transform.position.x += speed * Time.deltaTime;
```

The answer is that transform.position is a *property*, a method that is masquerading as a field (i.e., a function masquerading as a variable) through the use of get{} and set{} accessors (see Chapter 26, "Classes"). Although reading the value of a property's subcomponent is possible, setting a subcomponent of a property is not. In other words, transform.position.x can be read, but it cannot be set directly. This necessitates the creation of the intermediate Vector3 pos that can be modified and then assigned back to transform.position.

2. Save the script, return to Unity, and press the *Play* button. You'll notice that the AppleTree is moving very slowly. Try some different values for speed in the Inspector and see what feels good to you. I personally set speed to 10, which makes it move at 10m/s (10 meters per second or 10 Unity units per second). Stop Unity playback and set speed to 10 in the Inspector.

MAKING YOUR GAMES TIME BASED

When movement in a game is *time based*, it happens at the same rate regardless of the framerate at which the game is running. `Time.deltaTime` enables this because it tells us the number of seconds that have passed since the last frame. `Time.deltaTime` is usually very small. For a game running at 25 fps (frames per second), `Time.deltaTime` is 0.04f, meaning that each frame takes 4/100 of a second to display. If the `// b` line of code were run at 25 fps, the result would resolve like this:

```
pos.x += speed * Time.deltaTime;
pos.x += 1.0f * 0.04f;
pos.x += 0.04f;
```

So, in 1/25 of a second, `pos.x` would increase by 0.04m per frame. Over the course of a full second, `pos.x` would increase by 0.04m per frame * 25 frames, for a total of 1 meter in 1 second.

If instead the game were running at 100 fps, it would resolve as follows:

```
pos.x += speed * Time.deltaTime;
pos.x += 1.0f * 0.01f;
pos.x += 0.01f;
```

So, in 1/100 of a second, `pos.x` would increase by 0.01m per frame. Over the course of a full second, `pos.x` would increase by 0.01m per frame * 100 frames, for a total of 1 meter in 1 second.

Time-based movement ensures that regardless of framerate, the elements in your game will move at a consistent speed, and this consistency enables you to make games that are enjoyable for both players using the latest hardware and those using older machines. Time-based coding is also very important to consider when programming for mobile devices because the speed and power of mobile devices vary broadly.

Changing Direction

Now that the AppleTree is moving at a decent rate, it will run off of the screen pretty quickly. Let's make it change directions when it hits the `leftAndRightEdge` value. Modify the Apple-Tree script as follows:

```
public class AppleTree : MonoBehaviour {
    …
    void Update () {
        // Basic Movement
        …
        // Changing Direction
```

```
        if ( pos.x < -leftAndRightEdge ) {                          // a
            speed = Mathf.Abs(speed);  // Move right                 // b
        } else if ( pos.x > leftAndRightEdge ) {                     // c
            speed = -Mathf.Abs(speed); // Move left                  // c
        }
    }
}
```

a. Test whether the new pos.x that was just set in the previous lines is less than the negative side-to-side limit that is set by leftAndRightEdge.

b. If pos.x is too small, speed is set to Mathf.Abs(speed), which takes the absolute value of speed, guaranteeing that the resulting value will be positive, which translates into movement to the right.

c. If pos.x is greater than leftAndRightEdge, then speed is set to the negative of Mathf.Abs(speed), ensuring that the AppleTree will move to the left.

Save the script, return to Unity, and click *Play* to see what happens.

Changing Direction Randomly

To introduce random changes in direction, follow these steps:

1. Add the bolded lines shown here:

```
public class AppleTree : MonoBehaviour {
    …
    void Update () {
        // Basic Movement
        …
        // Changing Direction
        if ( pos.x < -leftAndRightEdge ) {
            speed = Mathf.Abs(speed);  // Move right
        } else if ( pos.x > leftAndRightEdge ) {
            speed = -Mathf.Abs(speed); // Move left
        } else if ( Random.value < chanceToChangeDirections ) {      // a
            speed *= -1;  // Change direction                        // b
        }
    }
}
```

a. Random.value returns a random float value between 0 and 1 (including 0 and 1 as possible values). If this random number is less than chanceToChangeDirections, …

b. …the AppleTree will change directions by setting speed to the negative of itself.

2. If you click Play, you'll see that the default chanceToChangeDirections of 0.1 changes direction far too often. In the Inspector, change the value of chanceToChangeDirections to 0.02, and it should feel a lot better.

To continue the discussion of time based games from the "Making Your Games Time Based" sidebar, this chance to change directions is actually *not* time based. Every frame, a 2% chance exists that the AppleTree will change directions. On a very fast computer, that chance could happen 400 times per second (yielding an average of 8 directions changes per second), whereas on a slow computer, it could happen as few as 30 times per second (for an average of 0.6 direction changes per second).

3. To fix this, move the direction change code out of `Update()` (which is called as fast as the computer can render frames) into `FixedUpdate()` (which is called exactly 50 times per second, regardless of the computer on which it's running).

```
public class AppleTree : MonoBehaviour {
    ...
    void Update () {
        // Basic Movement
        ...
        // Changing Direction
        if ( pos.x < -leftAndRightEdge ) {
            speed = Mathf.Abs(speed);   // Move right
        } else if ( pos.x > leftAndRightEdge ) {
            speed = -Mathf.Abs(speed); // Move left
        }                                                          // a
    }

    void FixedUpdate() {
        // Changing Direction Randomly is now time-based because of FixedUpdate()
        if ( Random.value < chanceToChangeDirections ) {           // b
            speed *= -1;   // Change direction
        }
    }
}
```

a. Cut the two lines that were marked `//` a and `//` b in the code listing for step 1, replace them with the closing brace, …

b. …and paste them here.

This causes the AppleTree to randomly change directions an average of 1 time every second (50 `FixedUpdates` per second * a random chance of 0.02 = an average of 1 time per second).

Dropping Apples

Next comes dropping apples:

1. Select *AppleTree* in the Hierarchy and look at the *Apple Tree (Script)* component in its Inspector. Currently, the value of the field `applePrefab` is *None (Game Object)*, meaning that it has not yet been set (the *GameObject* in parentheses is there to let you know that

the type of the `applePrefab` field is GameObject). This value needs to be set to the Apple GameObject prefab in the Project pane. You can do this in either of two ways:

- Click the tiny target to the right of *Apple Prefab None (Game Object)* in the Inspector and select *Apple* from the Assets tab in the window that appears.

  or

- Drag the *Apple* GameObject prefab from the Project pane onto the *ApplePrefab* value in the Inspector pane. This process is shown graphically in Figure 19.4 of Chapter 19, "Hello World: Your First Program."

2. Return to MonoDevelop and add the following bolded code to the AppleTree class:

```
public class AppleTree : MonoBehaviour {
    ...

    void Start () {
        // Dropping apples every second
        Invoke( "DropApple", 2f );                              // a
    }

    void DropApple() {                                          // b
        GameObject apple = Instantiate<GameObject>( applePrefab );   // c
        apple.transform.position = transform.position;         // d
        Invoke( "DropApple", secondsBetweenAppleDrops );       // e
    }

    void Update () { ... }                                      // f
    ...

}
```

a. The `Invoke()` function calls a named function in a certain number of seconds. In this case, it is calling the new function `DropApple()`. The second parameter, `2f`, tells `Invoke()` to wait 2 seconds before it calls `DropApple()`.

b. `DropApple()` is a custom function to instantiate an Apple at the AppleTree's location.

c. `DropApple()` creates an instance of `applePrefab` and assigns it to the GameObject variable `apple`.

d. The position of this new `apple` GameObject is set to the position of the AppleTree.

e. `Invoke()` is called again. This time, it will call the `DropApple()` function in `secondsBetweenAppleDrops` seconds (in this case, in 1 second based on the default settings in the Inspector). Because `DropApple()` invokes itself every time it is called, the effect will be for an Apple to be dropped every second that the game runs.

f. The `{ ... }` on this line indicates that I've omitted the content of the `Update()` method in this code listing. You do not need to change anything about the `Update()` method when you see ellipses like this.

3. Save the AppleTree script, return to Unity, click *Play*, and see what happens.

Did you expect the Apples and the AppleTree to go flying off? The same thing occurs here as did in the Chapter 19, "Hello World" example with the cubes flying all over the place. I did this on purpose here to show you how to fix this issue if you encounter it in your games. The first thing to do is to set the AppleTree's Rigidbody to be *kinematic*, meaning that we can move it via code, but it will not react to collisions with other objects.

4. In the Rigidbody component Inspector for AppleTree, check *Is Kinematic*.

5. Click *Play* again, and you can see that you still have an issue with the Apples.

Though this fixes the AppleTree, the Apples are still colliding with the AppleTree, causing them to fly off to the left, right or down faster than they would normally due to gravity. To fix this, you need to put them in a *physics layer* that doesn't collide with the AppleTree. Physics layers are groups of objects that can either collide with or ignore each other. If the AppleTree and Apple GameObjects are placed in two different physics layers, and those physics layers are set to ignore each other, then the AppleTree and Apples will cease colliding with each other.

Setting Physics Layers

First, you need to make some new physics layers. These steps are shown in Figure 28.8.

1. Click the *AppleTree* in the Hierarchy and in the Inspector choose *Add Layer…* from the pop-up menu next to *Layer*. This opens the *Tags & Layers Manager* in the Inspector, which allows you to set the names of physics layers under the *Layers* label (make sure you're not editing *Tags* or *Sorting Layers*). You can see that *Builtin Layers* 0 through 7 are grayed out, but you are able to edit Layers 8 through 31.

2. Name layer 8 *AppleTree*, layer 9 *Apple*, and layer 10 *Basket*.

Figure 28.8 The steps required to make new physics layers (steps 1 and 2) and assign them (step 5)

3. From the Unity menu bar, choose *Edit > Project Settings > Physics*. This sets the Inspector to the *Physics Manager* (see Figure 28.9). The *Layer Collision Matrix* grid of check boxes at the bottom of the Physics Manager sets which physics layers will collide with each other (and whether GameObjects in the same Physics Layer will collide with each other as well).

4. You want the Apple to collide with the Basket and to not collide with either the AppleTree or other Apples. To do this, your Layer Collision Matrix grid should look like what is shown in Figure 28.9.

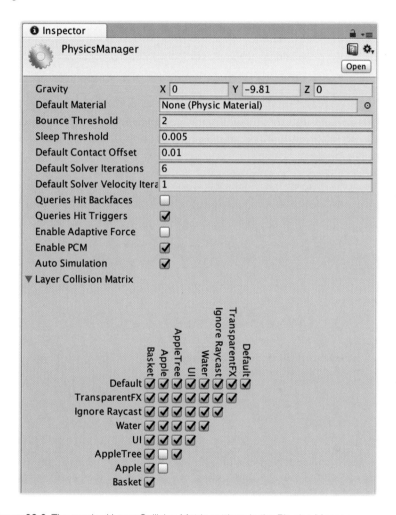

Figure 28.9 The required Layer Collision Matrix settings in the Physics Manager

5. Now that the Layer Collision Matrix is set properly, it's time to assign physics layers to the important GameObjects in the game.

   a. Click *Apple* in the Project pane, and then select *Apple* from the *Layer* pop-up menu at the top of the Inspector pane.

   b. Select the *Basket* in the Project pane and set its Layer to *Basket*.

   c. Select the *AppleTree* in the Project pane and set its Layer to *AppleTree* (refer to Figure 28.8).

When you choose the physics layer for AppleTree, Unity asks whether you want to change the layer for just AppleTree or for both AppleTree and its children. You definitely want to choose *Yes, change children* because you need the Trunk and Sphere child objects of AppleTree to also be in the AppleTree physics layer. This change will also trickle forward to the AppleTree instance in the scene. You can click AppleTree in the Hierarchy pane to confirm this.

Now if you click Play, you should see the apples dropping properly from the tree.

Stopping Apples If They Fall Too Far

If you leave the current version of the game running for a while, you'll notice that there are *a lot* of apples in the Hierarchy. That's because the code is creating a new apple every second but never deleting the apples.

1. Open the Apple C# script and add the following code to kill the apples when they reach a depth of `transform.position.y == -20` (which is comfortably off screen). Here's the code:

```
using System.Collections;
using System.Collections.Generic;
using UnityEngine;

public class Apple : MonoBehaviour {
    public static float     bottomY = -20f;                           // a

    void Update () {
        if ( transform.position.y < bottomY ) {
            Destroy( this.gameObject );                               // b
        }
    }
}
```

a. The bolded `public static float` line declares and defines a *static variable* named `bottomY`. As was mentioned in Chapter 26, "Classes," static variables are shared by all instances of a class, so every instance of Apple will have the same value for `bottomY`. If `bottomY` is ever changed for one instance, it will simultaneously change for all instances. However, it's also important to point out that static fields like `bottomY` do not appear in the Inspector.

b. The `Destroy()` function removes things that are passed into it from the game, and it can be used to destroy both components and GameObjects. You must use `Destroy(this.gameObject)` in this case because `Destroy(this)` would just remove the *Apple (Script)* component from the Apple GameObject instance. In any script, `this` references the current instance of the C# class in which it is called (in this code listing, `this` references the *Apple (Script)* component instance), not the entire GameObject. Any time you want to destroy an entire GameObject from within an attached component class, you must call `Destroy( this.gameObject )`.

2. Save the Apple script.

3. You must attach the Apple C# script to the Apple GameObject prefab in the Project window for this code to function in the game. You already know about dragging a script onto a GameObject to attach the script, so here's another way to do this:

    a. Select *Apple* in the Project pane.

    b. Scroll to the bottom of the Inspector, and click the *Add Component* button.

    c. From the pop-up menu that appears, select *Scripts > Apple*.

Now, if you click Play in Unity and zoom out in the scene, you can see that apples drop for a ways and then disappear when they reach a Y position of -20.

This is all you need to do for the apples.

Instantiating the Baskets

To make the Baskets work, I am going to introduce a concept that will recur throughout these prototype tutorials. Although object-oriented thinking encourages designers to create an independent class for each GameObject (as we have just done for AppleTree and Apple), it is often very useful to also have a script that runs the game as a whole.

1. Attach the *AplePicker* script to *Main Camera* in the Hierarchy. I often attach these game management scripts to Main Camera because I am guaranteed that there is a Main Camera in every scene.

2. Open the ApplePicker script in MonoDevelop, type the following code, and then save:

```csharp
using System.Collections;
using System.Collections.Generic;
using UnityEngine;

public class ApplePicker : MonoBehaviour {
    [Header("Set in Inspector")]                               // a
    public GameObject      basketPrefab;
    public int            numBaskets = 3;
    public float          basketBottomY = -14f;
    public float          basketSpacingY = 2f;

    void Start () {
        for (int i=0; i<numBaskets; i++) {
            GameObject tBasketGO = Instantiate<GameObject>( basketPrefab );
            Vector3 pos = Vector3.zero;
            pos.y = basketBottomY + ( basketSpacingY * i );
            tBasketGO.transform.position = pos;
        }
    }
}
```

a. This line adds a header to the Inspector in Unity so that you can see which variables should be set in the Inspector. In later code listings, it will be accompanied by a "Set Dynamically" header for variables that are calculated while the game is running.

This code instantiates three copies of the Basket prefab that are spaced out vertically.

3. In Unity, click *Main Camera* in the Hierarchy pane and set the basketPrefab in the Inspector to be the Basket GameObject prefab from the Project pane. Click Play, and you'll see that this code creates three baskets at the bottom of the screen.

Moving the Baskets with the Mouse

Next, you need to write some code to get each Basket moving along with the mouse.

1. Attach the *Basket* script to the *Basket* prefab in the Project pane.

2. Open the Basket C# script in MonoDevelop, enter this code, and save:

```
using System.Collections;
using System.Collections.Generic;
using UnityEngine;

public class Basket : MonoBehaviour {

    void Update () {
        // Get the current screen position of the mouse from Input
        Vector3 mousePos2D = Input.mousePosition;                      // a

        // The Camera's z position sets how far to push the mouse into 3D
        mousePos2D.z = -Camera.main.transform.position.z;              // b

        // Convert the point from 2D screen space into 3D game world space
        Vector3 mousePos3D = Camera.main.ScreenToWorldPoint( mousePos2D );   // c

        // Move the x position of this Basket to the x position of the Mouse
        Vector3 pos = this.transform.position;
        pos.x = mousePos3D.x;
        this.transform.position = pos;
    }
}
```

a. Input.mousePosition is assigned to mousePos2D. This value is in screen coordinates, meaning that it measures how many pixels the mouse is from the top-left corner of the screen. The z position of Input.mousePositon is always 0 because it is essentially a two-dimensional measurement.

b. This line sets the z coordinate of mousePos2D to the negative of the Main Camera's Z position. In the game, the Main Camera is at a Z of -10, so mousePos2D.z is set to 10. This tells the upcoming ScreenToWorldPoint() function how far to push the mousePos3D into the 3D space, placing the final world point on the Z=0 plane.

c. `ScreenToWorldPoint()` converts `mousePoint2D` into a point in 3D space inside the scene. If `mousePos2D.z` were 0, the resulting `mousePos3D` point would be at a Z of -10 (the same as the Main Camera). By setting `mousePos2D.z` to 10, `mousePos3D` is pushed into the 3D space 10 meters away from the Main Camera position, resulting in a `mousePos3D.z` of 0. This matters little in Apple Picker, but it will become much more important in future games. If this is at all confusing, I recommend looking at `Camera.ScreenToWorldPoint()` in the Unity Scripting Reference.[6]

Now the Baskets will move when you press *Play* in Unity, and you can use them to collide with apples, though the Apples aren't really being caught yet.

Catching Apples

Next up—catching apples:

1. Add the following bold lines to the Basket C# script:

```
public class Basket : MonoBehaviour {

    void Update () { … }

    void OnCollisionEnter( Collision coll ) {                    // a
        // Find out what hit this basket
        GameObject collidedWith = coll.gameObject;              // b
        if ( collidedWith.tag == "Apple" ) {                    // c
            Destroy( collidedWith );
        }
    }
}
```

a. The `OnCollisionEnter` method is called whenever another GameObject collides with this basket, and a Collision argument is passed in with information about the collision, including a reference to the GameObject that hit this basket's Collider.

b. This line assigns this colliding GameObject to the local variable `collidedWith`.

c. Check to see whether `collidedWith` is an apple by looking for the `"Apple"` tag that was assigned to all Apple GameObjects. If `collidedWith` is an apple, it is destroyed. Now, if an apple hits this basket, it will be destroyed.

2. Save the Basket script, return to Unity, and click *Play*.

---

6. The reference is located at https://docs.unity3d.com/ScriptReference/. Be sure to click the C# button there so that you're looking C# documentation (as opposed to JavaScript).

At this point, the game functions very similarly to the classic game *Kaboom!* However, it doesn't yet have any *graphical user interface* (GUI) elements like a score or a representation of how many lives the player has remaining. However, even without these elements, Apple Picker would be a successful prototype in its current state. As is, this prototype will allow you to tweak several aspects of the game to give it the right level of difficulty.

3. Save your scene.

4. Make a duplicate of the current scene to use for testing game balance tweaks.

    a. Click the *_Scene_0* in the Project pane to select it.

    b. Press *Command-D* on the keyboard (*Ctrl+D* on Windows) to duplicate the scene or choose *Edit > Duplicate* from the menu bar. This creates a new scene named *_Scene_1*.

    c. Double-click *_Scene_1* to open it.

As an exact duplicate of _Scene_0, the game in this new scene will work without any changes.

Click *AppleTree* in the Hierarchy to tweak variables in _Scene_1 while leaving the variables in _Scene_0 unchanged (any changes made to GameObjects in the Project pane apply to both scenes). Try making the game more difficult. After you have the game balanced for a harder difficulty level in _Scene_1, save it and reopen _Scene_0. If you're ever concerned about which scene you have opened, just look at the title at the top of the Unity window or the top of the Hierarchy pane. Each will always include the scene name.

GUI and Game Management

The final things to add to our game are the GUI and *game management* that will make it feel like more of a real game. The GUI element we'll add is a score counter, and the game management elements we'll add are levels and lives.

Score Counter

The score counter helps players get a sense of their level of achievement in the game.

1. Open _Scene_0 by double-clicking it in the Project pane.

2. From the Unity menu bar choose *GameObject > UI > Text*.[7]

Because this is the first *uGUI* (Unity Graphical User Interface) element to be added to this scene, it will add several things to the Hierarchy pane. The first you'll see is a *Canvas*. The Canvas is

---

7. Once, when I was testing this section of the tutorial, the *GameObject > UI > Text* option of the Unity menu was grayed out for some reason. If that happens for you, right-click in the empty part of the Hierarchy pane and choose *UI > Text* from the right-click menu.

the two-dimensional board on which the GUI will be arranged. Looking in the Scene pane, you should also see a *very* large 2D box extending from the origin out very far in the x and y directions.

3. Double-click on *Canvas* in the Hierarchy to zoom out and see the whole thing. This will be scaled to match your Game pane, so if you have the Game pane set to a 16:9 aspect ratio, the Canvas will follow suit. You might also want to click the *2D* button atop the Scene pane to switch to a two-dimensional view that can make working with the Canvas easier.

The other GameObject added at the top level of the Hierarchy is the *EventSystem*. The EventSystem is what allows buttons, sliders, and other interactive GUI elements that you build in uGUI to work; however, you will not be making use of it in this prototype.

As a child of the Canvas, you will see a *Text* GameObject. If you don't see it there, click the disclosure triangle in the Hierarchy next to Canvas to show its child objects. Double-click on the *Text* GameObject in the Hierarchy pane to zoom in on it. It is very likely that the text color defaulted to black, which might be difficult to see over the background of the Scene pane.

4. Select the *Text* GameObject in the Hierarchy and use the Inspector pane to change its name to *HighScore*.

5. Follow these directions to make the HighScore Inspector match that shown in Figure 28.10:

   a. In the *RectTransform* component of the HighScore Inspector:

   ▪ Set *Anchors* Min X=0, Min Y=1, Max X=0, and Max Y=1.

   ▪ Set *Pivot* X=0 and Y=1.

   ▪ Set Pos X=10, Pos Y = −6, and Pos Z = 0.

   ▪ Set Width=256 and Height=32.

   After doing this, you should double-click HighScore in the Hierarchy again to re-center the view of it in the Scene pane.

   b. In the *Text (Script)* component of the HighScore Inspector:

   ▪ Set the *Text* section to "High Score: 1000" (without the quotes around it).

   ▪ Set the *Font Style* to Bold.

   ▪ Set the *Font Size* to 28.

   ▪ Set the *Color* to white, which will make it much more visible in the Game pane.

6. Right-click on HighScore in the Hierarchy and choose *Duplicate*.[8]

7. Select the new *HighScore (1)* GameObject and change its name to *ScoreCounter*.

8. Alter the RectTransform and Text values of ScoreCounter in the Inspector to match those shown in Figure 28.10. Don't forget to set the *Anchors* and *Pivot* in the RectTransform component and the *Alignment* in the Text component. Notice that when you change the

---

8. You might need to click once in the Hierarchy pane to see the *HighScore (1)* duplicate appear.

Anchors or Pivot in the RectTransform, Unity automatically changes the *Pos X* to keep the ScoreCounter in the same place within the Canvas. To prevent Unity from doing this, click the *R* button in the RectTransform that is shown under the mouse cursor in the ScoreCounter Inspector in Figure 28.10.

As you've seen here, the coordinates for uGUI GameObjects differ completely from those for regular GameObjects and use a RectTransform instead of a regular Transform. The coordinates for a RectTransform are all relative to the Canvas parent of the uGUI GameObject. Clicking the help icon for the RectTransform component (circled in Figure 28.10) can give you more information about how this works. Be sure to save your scene before moving on.

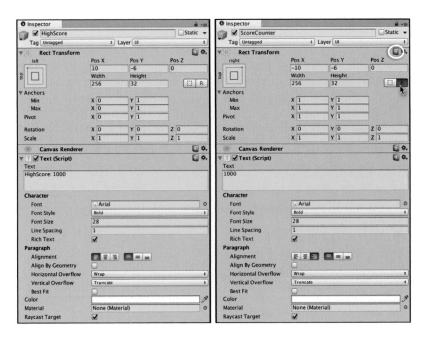

Figure 28.10 RectTransform and Text component settings for HighScore and ScoreCounter

Add Points for Each Caught Apple

When a collision occurs between an apple and a basket, two scripts are notified: the Apple and Basket scripts. In this game, there is already an `OnCollisionEnter()` method on the Basket C# script, so in the following steps you modify the Basket script to give the player points for each Apple that is caught. One hundred points per apple seems like a reasonable number (though I've personally always thought it was a little ridiculous to have those extra zeroes at the end of scores).

1. Open the Basket script in MonoDevelop and add the bolded lines shown here:

```csharp
using System.Collections;
using System.Collections.Generic;
using UnityEngine;
using UnityEngine.UI;      // This line enables use of uGUI features.          // a

public class Basket : MonoBehaviour {
    [Header("Set Dynamically")]
    public Text            scoreGT;                                            // a

    void Start() {
        // Find a reference to the ScoreCounter GameObject
        GameObject scoreGO = GameObject.Find("ScoreCounter");                 // b
        // Get the Text Component of that GameObject
        scoreGT = scoreGO.GetComponent<Text>();                               // c
        // Set the starting number of points to 0
        scoreGT.text = "0";
    }

    void Update () { … }

    void OnCollisionEnter( Collision coll ) {
        // Find out what hit this basket
        GameObject collidedWith = coll.gameObject;
        if ( collidedWith.tag == "Apple" ) {
            Destroy( collidedWith );

            // Parse the text of the scoreGT into an int
            int score = int.Parse( scoreGT.text );                            // d
            // Add points for catching the apple
            score += 100;
            // Convert the score back to a string and display it
            scoreGT.text = score.ToString();
        }
    }
}
```

a. Be sure you don't neglect to enter these lines. They are separated from the others.

b. GameObject.Find("ScoreCounter") searches through all the GameObjects in the scene for one named "ScoreCounter" and assigns it to the local variable scoreGO. Make sure "ScoreCounter" does not contain a space in code or in the Hierarchy.

c. scoreGO.Getcomponent<Text>() searches for a Text component on the scoreGO GameObject, and this is assigned to the public field scoreGT. The starting score is then set to zero on the next line. Without the earlier using UnityEngine.UI; line, the Text component would not be defined for C# within Unity. As Unity Technology's coding practices get stronger, they are moving to more of a model like this where you must include the code libraries for their new features manually.

d. `int.Parse( scoreGT.text )` takes the text shown in ScoreCounter and converts it to an integer. 100 points are added to the int `score`, and it is then assigned back to the text of `scoreGT` after being parsed from an int to a string by `score.ToString()`.

Notifying Apple Picker That an Apple Was Dropped

Another aspect of making Apple Picker feel more like a game is ending the round and deleting a basket if an apple is dropped. At this point, apples manage their own destruction, which is fine, but the apple needs to somehow notify the ApplePicker script of this event so that it can end the round and destroy the rest of the apples. This involves one script calling a function on another.

1. Start by making these modifications to the Apple C# script in MonoDevelop:

```
public class Apple : MonoBehaviour {
    [Header("Set in Inspector")]
    public static float     bottomY = -20f;

    void Update () {
        if ( transform.position.y < bottomY ) {                              // a
            Destroy( this.gameObject );

            // Get a reference to the ApplePicker component of Main Camera
            ApplePicker apScript = Camera.main.GetComponent<ApplePicker>();  // b
            // Call the public AppleDestroyed() method of apScript
            apScript.AppleDestroyed();                                       // c
        }
    }
}
```

a. Note that all of these added lines are within this `if` statement.

b. This grabs a reference to the *ApplePicker (Script)* component on the Main Camera. Because the Camera class has a built-in static variable `Camera.main` that references the Main Camera, using `GameObject.Find("Main Camera")` to obtain a reference to Main Camera is not necessary. `GetComponent<ApplePicker>()` is then used to grab a reference to the *ApplePicker (Script)* component on Main Camera and assign it to `apScript`. After this is done, accessing public variables and methods of the ApplePicker class instance attached to Main Camera becomes possible.

c. This calls a non-existent `AppleDestroyed()` method of the ApplePicker class. Because it doesn't exist yet, MonoDevelop will color it red, and you will not be able to play the game in Unity until `AppleDestroyed()` is defined.

2. A public `AppleDestroyed()` method does not yet exist in the ApplePicker script, so open the ApplePicker C# script in MonoDevelop and make the following bolded changes:

```
public class ApplePicker : MonoBehaviour {
    …
```

```
void Start () { … }

public void AppleDestroyed() {                                          // a
    // Destroy all of the falling apples
    GameObject[] tAppleArray=GameObject.FindGameObjectsWithTag("Apple"); // b
    foreach ( GameObject tGO in tAppleArray ) {
        Destroy( tGO );
    }
}
}
```

a. The `AppleDestroyed()` method must be declared `public` for other classes (like Apple) to be able to call it. By default, methods are all private and unable to be called (or even seen) by other classes.

b. `GameObject.FindGameObjectsWithTag("Apple")` will return an array of all existing Apple GameObjects.[9] The subsequent `foreach` loop iterates through each of these and destroys them.

Save All scripts in MonoDevelop. With `AppleDestroyed()` now defined, the game is once again playable in Unity.

Destroying a Basket When an Apple Is Dropped

The final bit of code for this scene will manage the deletion of one of the baskets each time an apple is dropped and stop the game when all the baskets have been destroyed. Make the following changes to the ApplePicker C# script (this time, the entire code is listed, just in case):

```
using System.Collections;
using System.Collections.Generic;                                      // a
using UnityEngine;
using UnityEngine.SceneManagement;                                     // b

public class ApplePicker : MonoBehaviour {
    [Header("Set in Inspector")]
    public GameObject       basketPrefab;
    public int              numBaskets = 3;
    public float            basketBottomY = -14f;
    public float            basketSpacingY = 2f;
    public List<GameObject> basketList;

    void Start () {
        basketList = new List<GameObject>();                           // c
        for (int i=0; i<numBaskets; i++) {
            GameObject tBasketGO = Instantiate<GameObject>( basketPrefab );
            Vector3 pos = Vector3.zero;
```

9. `GameObject.FindGameObjectsWithTag()` is actually a rather processor-intensive function, so I wouldn't recommend using it inside an `Update()` or `FixedUpdate()`. However, because this is only happening when the player loses a Basket (and the gameplay is already slowed here), in this case, it's fine to use.

```
                    pos.y = basketBottomY + ( basketSpacingY * i );
                    tBasketGO.transform.position = pos;
                    basketList.Add( tBasketGO );                              // d
            }
    }

    public void AppleDestroyed() {
            // Destroy all of the falling apples
            GameObject[] tAppleArray=GameObject.FindGameObjectsWithTag("Apple");
            foreach ( GameObject tGO in tAppleArray ) {
                    Destroy( tGO );
            }

            // Destroy one of the baskets                                     // e
            // Get the index of the last Basket in basketList
            int basketIndex = basketList.Count-1;
            // Get a reference to that Basket GameObject
            GameObject tBasketGO = basketList[basketIndex];
            // Remove the Basket from the list and destroy the GameObject
            basketList.RemoveAt( basketIndex );
            Destroy( tBasketGO );
    }
}
```

a. You will be storing the Basket GameObjects in a List, so it is necessary to use the System.Collections.Generic code library, which as of Unity 5.5 is included in all new scripts. (For more information about lists, see Chapter 23, "Collections in C#.") The public List<GameObject> basketList is declared at the beginning of the class, and it is defined and initialized in the first line of Start().

b. This will be used in step 3 of *Adding a High Score* later in the chapter.

c. This line defines basketList as a new List<GameObject>. Though this was already declared by the line at // b, the value of basketList after declaration is null. The initialization on this line makes it an actual List that can be used.

d. A new line is added to the end of the for loop that Adds the baskets to basketList. The baskets are added in the order they are created, which means that they are added bottom to top.

e. In the method AppleDestroyed() a new section has been added to destroy one of the baskets. Because the baskets are added from bottom to top, it's important that the last basket in the list is destroyed first (to destroy the baskets top to bottom).

If you play the game now and run out of baskets, Unity will throw an IndexOutOfRange exception.

Adding a High Score

Now you'll make use of the *HighScore* Text GameObject that you created earlier:

1. Create a new C# script named *HighScore*, and attach it to the HighScore GameObject in the Hierarchy pane.

2. Open the HighScore script in MonoDevelop and give it the following code:

```
using System.Collections;
using System.Collections.Generic;
using UnityEngine;
using UnityEngine.UI;      // Remember, we need this line for uGUI to work.

public class HighScore : MonoBehaviour {
    static public int    score = 1000;                                     // a

    void Update () {                                                       // b
        Text gt = this.GetComponent<Text>();
        gt.text = "High Score: "+score;
    }
}
```

    a. Making the int `score` not only `public` but also `static` gives you the ability to access it from any other script by simply typing `HighScore.score`. This is one of the powers of static variables that you will use throughout the prototypes in this book.

    b. The lines in `Update()` simply display the value of `score` in the Text component. Calling `ToString()` on the `score` is not necessary in this instance because when the + operator is used to concatenate a string with another data type (the `"High Score: "` string literal is concatenated with the int `score` in this case), `ToString()` is called implicitly (that is, automatically).

3. Open the Basket C# script and add the following bolded lines to see how this is used:

```
public class Basket : MonoBehaviour {
    …
    void OnCollisionEnter( Collision coll ) {
        …
        if ( collidedWith.tag == "Apple" ) {
            …
            // Convert the score back to a string and display it
            scoreGT.text = score.ToString();

            // Track the high score
            if (score > HighScore.score) {
                HighScore.score = score;
            }
        }
    }
}
```

Now `HighScore.score` will be set any time the current score exceeds it.

4. Open the ApplePicker C# script and add the following lines to reset the game whenever a player runs out of baskets. This code avoids the IndexOutOfRange exception mentioned earlier.

```
public class ApplePicker : MonoBehaviour {
    ...
    public void AppleDestroyed() {
        ...
        // Remove the Basket from the list and destroy the GameObject
        basketList.RemoveAt( basketIndex );
        Destroy( tBasketGO );

        // If there are no Baskets left, restart the game
        if ( basketList.Count == 0 ) {
            SceneManager.LoadScene( "_Scene_0" );                       // a
        }
    }
}
```

a. `SceneManager.LoadScene( "_Scene_0" )` will reload _Scene_0. It will not work unless you added the line `using UnityEngine.SceneManagement;` under the *Destroying a Basket When an Apple Is Dropped* heading earlier. Reloading the scene effectively resets the game to its beginning state.[10]

5. You've changed a number of scripts now. Did you remember to save after changing each one? If not—or if you're not sure, as I often am—you can choose *File > Save All* from the MonoDevelop menu bar to save all modified but unsaved scripts. If *Save All* is grayed out, then congratulations—all your scripts are already saved.

Preserving the High Score in PlayerPrefs

Because `HighScore.score` is a static variable, it is *not* reset along with the rest of the game. This means that high scores will remain from one round to the next. However, whenever you stop the game (by clicking the Play button again), `HighScore.score` *will* reset. You can fix this through the use of Unity's *PlayerPrefs*. PlayerPrefs variables store information from Unity scripts on the computer so that the information can be recalled later and isn't destroyed when playback stops. PlayerPrefs also work across the Unity editor, compiled builds, and WebGL builds, so the high score you get in one will carry over to the others, as long as they're run on the same machine.

---

10. In all recent versions of Unity up to at least Unity 2017, a known bug often occurs when reloading a level. If you see the scene get much darker when it reloads using the SceneManager, then you're encountering this issue. Until Unity fixes the bug, one interim fix for this is to disable automatic light baking (which pre-computes some of the lighting for the scene). To do so, open the Lighting pane by selecting *Window > Lighting > Settings* from the Unity menu bar. Uncheck *Auto Generate* at the bottom of the Lighting pane (next to the *Generate Lighting* button). Then click the *Generate Lighting* button once to manually rebuild lighting, wait for it to complete, and close the Lighting window. This bug should only occur inside the Unity editor and shouldn't affect any WebGL or standalone application builds that you make.

1. Open the HighScore C# script and add the following bolded changes:

```csharp
using System.Collections;
using System.Collections.Generic;
using UnityEngine;
using UnityEngine.UI;     // Remember, we need this line for uGUI to work.

public class HighScore : MonoBehaviour {
    static public int    score = 1000;

    void Awake() {                                                   // a
        // If the PlayerPrefs HighScore already exists, read it
        if (PlayerPrefs.HasKey("HighScore")) {                       // b
            score = PlayerPrefs.GetInt("HighScore");
        }
        // Assign the high score to HighScore
        PlayerPrefs.SetInt("HighScore", score);                      // c
    }

    void Update () {
        Text gt = this.GetComponent<Text>();
        gt.text = "High Score: "+score;
        // Update the PlayerPrefs HighScore if necessary
        if (score > PlayerPrefs.GetInt("HighScore")) {               // d
            PlayerPrefs.SetInt("HighScore", score);
        }
    }
}
```

a. `Awake()` is a built-in Unity MonoBehaviour method (like `Start()` or `Update()`) that happens when this instance of the HighScore class is first created (so `Awake()` always occurs before `Start()`).

b. PlayerPrefs is a dictionary of values that are referenced through keys (that is, unique strings). In this case, you're referencing the key *HighScore*. This line checks to see whether a HighScore int already exists in PlayerPrefs and reads it in if it does exist.

    PlayerPrefs are stored separately for each project/application, so naming this HighScore is okay; it won't conflict with a HighScore stored in PlayerPrefs by a different project.

c. The last line of `Awake()` assigns the current value of `score` to the HighScore Player-Prefs key. If a HighScore int already exists, this will rewrite the value back to PlayerPrefs; if the key does not already exist, however, this ensures that an HighScore key is created.

d. With the added lines, `Update()` now checks every frame to see whether the current `HighScore.score` is higher than the one stored in PlayerPrefs and updates Player-Prefs if that is the case.

This usage of PlayerPrefs enables the Apple Picker high score to be remembered on this machine, and the high score will survive stopping playback, quitting Unity, and even restarting your computer.

2. *Save All* in MonoDevelop again, just to be sure. Switch back to Unity and click Play.

Now, you should be able to play the game complete with score and high score. If you attain a new high score, try stopping the game and restarting it, and you'll see that your high score is saved.

Summary

Now you have a game prototype that plays very similarly to the classic Activision game *Kaboom!*. Although this game still lacks elements like steadily increasing difficulty and an opening and closing screen, you can add these things yourself after you gain more experience.

Next Steps

Here are some ideas for additional elements that you could add to the prototype in the future. One of the best ways to learn coding is to follow a tutorial like this chapter and then try to add your own modifications to it.

- **Start screen:** You could build a start screen in its own scene and give it a splash image and a Start button. The Start button could then call `SceneManager.LoadScene ( "_Scene_0" );` to start the game. Remember that you need to enable SceneManager by adding the line `using UnityEngine.SceneManagement;` to the top of your script.

- **Game Over screen:** You could also create a Game Over screen. The Game Over screen could display the final score that the player achieved and could let the player know if she exceeded the previous high score. It should have a button labeled *Play Again* that calls `SceneManager.LoadScene( "_Scene_0" );`.

- **Increasing difficulty:** Varying difficulty levels are discussed in later prototypes, but if you wanted to add them here, it would make sense to store an array or list for each of the values on AppleTree, such as speed, chanceToChangeDirections, and secondsBetween-AppleDrops. Each element in the list could be a different level of difficulty, with the 0th element being the easiest and the last element being the most difficult. As the player played the game, a level counter could increase over time and be used as the index for these lists; so at level=0, the 0th element of each variable would be used.

If you choose to add either a Start screen or Game Over scene to the game, you will need to add every scene in your game to the Build Settings scene list one at a a time. To do so, open each scene in Unity and then choose *File > Build Settings…* from the Unity menu. In the Build Settings window that opens, click *Add Open Scenes*, and the name of the currently open scene will be added to the *Scenes in Build* list. If you do create a build of this game, the scene numbered zero will be the one that loads when the game first runs.

CHAPTER 29

PROTOTYPE 2: *MISSION DEMOLITION*

Physics games are some of the most popular around, making games like *Angry Birds* household names. In this chapter, you make your own physics game that is inspired by *Angry Birds* and all the other physics games that came before it, such as *Crossbows and Catapults, Worms, Scorched Earth*, and so on.

This chapter covers the following: physics, collision, mouse interaction, levels, and game state management.

Getting Started: Prototype 2

Because this is the second prototype, and you now have some experience under your belt, this chapter is going to move a bit faster than the last on things that you already know. Of course, I still cover new topics in detail. I recommend using a pencil to check off each step in this tutorial as you complete them.

SET UP THE PROJECT FOR THIS CHAPTER

Following the standard project setup procedure, create a new project in Unity. If you need a refresher on the procedure, see Appendix A, "Standard Project Setup Procedure."

- **Project name:** Mission Demolition Prototype
- **Scene name:** _Scene_0
- **C# script names:** None yet

Game Prototype Concept

In this game, the player uses a slingshot to fire projectiles at a castle, hoping to demolish it. Each castle has a goal area that the projectile must touch for the player to continue to the next level.

This is the desired sequence of events:

1. When the player's mouse pointer is in range of the slingshot, the slingshot should glow.
2. If the player presses the left mouse button (*mouse button 0* in Unity) down while the slingshot is glowing, a projectile will instantiate at the location of the mouse pointer.
3. As the player moves and drags the mouse around with the button held down, the projectile follows it, yet remains within the limits of the Sphere Collider on the slingshot.
4. A white line stretches from each arm of the slingshot around the projectile to make it look more like an actual slingshot.
5. When the player releases mouse button 0, the projectile fires from the slingshot.
6. The player's goal is to knock down a castle that is several meters away and hit a target area inside.
7. The player has a total of three shots to hit the goal. The most recent shot will leave a trail so that the player can better judge her next shot.

Many of the preceding events relate to mechanics, but one is exclusively aesthetics: step 4. All the other elements that mention art use that art for the purpose of game mechanics, but step 4 is just to make the game look nicer, so it's less critical to the prototype. When you're writing down your concepts for games, this is an important thing to keep in mind. That isn't to say that you shouldn't implement things that are entirely aesthetic in a prototype; you just need to be aware of and prioritize the elements that will have the most direct impact on the game mechanics. For the sake of time and space, this prototype focuses on the other elements, and I leave the implementation of step 4 for you to tackle later.

Art Assets

You should create several art assets now to prepare the project for coding.

Ground

To create the ground, follow these steps:

1. Open _Scene_0. Make sure that you can see the contents of _Scene_0 in the Hierarchy pane, which should be Main Camera and Directional Light (if you can't see them, click the disclosure triangle next to _Scene_0 in the Hierarchy pane).

2. Create a cube (select *GameObject > 3D Object > Cube* from the menu bar). Rename the cube to *Ground*. To make Ground a rectangular solid that is very wide in the X direction, set its transform to the following:

    Ground (Cube)   P:[0, -10, 0]   R:[0, 0, 0]   S:[100, 1, 4]

3. Create a new material (*Assets > Create > Material*) and name it *Mat_Ground*.

    a. Give *Mat_Ground* a brown *Albedo* color.

    b. Also set the *Smoothness* of the material to *0* (the ground is not very shiny).

    c. Attach *Mat_Ground* to the *Ground* GameObject in the Hierarchy. (The previous chapter describes how to do this.)

4. Save your scene.

Directional Light

In the most recent versions of Unity, a Directional Light exists in a new scene by default, but you still need to give it the right settings for your project.

1. Select *Directional Light* in the Hierarchy pane. One of the features of directional lights is that their position doesn't matter to the scene; only the rotation of a directional light is taken into consideration. That being the case, move it out of the way by setting its transform to the following:

    Directional Light   P:[-10, 0, 0]   R:[50, -30, 0]   S:[1, 1, 1].

2. Save your scene.

Camera Settings

Camera settings are next:

1. Select the *Main Camera* in the Hierarchy and rename it to *_MainCamera*.

2. Give *_MainCamera* the following Transform settings (be sure that you set the Y position to 0):

    _MainCamera   P:[0, 0, -10]   R:[0, 0, 0]   S:[1, 1, 1].

3. Give the _MainCamera *Camera* component these settings:

   a. Set *Clear Flags* to *Solid Color*.

   b. Choose a brighter *Background* color to look more like a sky blue.

   c. Set *Projection* to *Orthographic*.

   d. Set *Size* to *10*.

The final settings should look like Figure 29.1. Note in particular that the bar at the bottom of the *Background* color should be white, not black. If it is black, that means that the Alpha (or transparency) value of the color is set to 0 (or fully transparent/invisible). To fix this, click on the color and set the A value of the color to 255.[1]

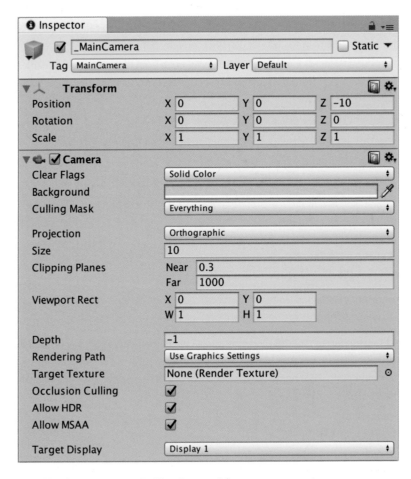

Figure 29.1 _MainCamera settings for Transform and Camera components

---

1. Setting the Alpha of the Background color doesn't really matter that much, but Unity commonly defaults to an Alpha of 0 for colors—and I've had it cause problems in the past—so I want to get you in the habit of checking the Alpha of any colors set in the Inspector.

Though you have used orthographic cameras before, I did not previously clarify the meaning of the *Size* setting. In an orthographic projection, Size sets the distance from the center to the bottom of the camera view, so Size is half the height of what the camera is able to see. You can see that illustrated in the Game pane shown in Figure 29.2. Ground is at a Y position of -10, and it is perfectly bisected by the bottom of the Game window.[2] Try changing the aspect ratio of the Game pane via the pop-up menu highlighted under the mouse pointer in Figure 29.2. You will see that no matter what aspect ratio you select, the center of the Ground cube is still positioned perfectly at the bottom of the Game pane.

4. After you've explored this for a while, choose an aspect ratio of 16:9, as shown in the figure.

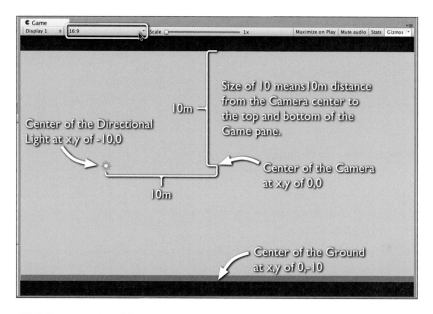

Figure 29.2 Demonstration of the meaning of an orthographic camera size of 10

5. Save your scene. Always save your scene.

The Slingshot

Now make a simple slingshot out of three cylinders:

1. Create an empty GameObject (*GameObject > Create Empty*). Change the GameObject's name to *Slingshot* and set its transform to the following:

   Slingshot (Empty)   P:[0, 0, 0]   R:[0, 0, 0]   S:[1, 1, 1].

---

2. If you don't see Ground at the bottom of your Game pane, double-check that the Y position of _Main-Camera is 0 and the Y position of Ground is -10. If you don't see the Directional Light in the Game pane, you can click the Gizmos button to make it visible.

2. Create a new cylinder (*GameObject > 3D Object > Cylinder*) and change its name to *Base*. In the Hierarchy, drag *Base* onto *Slingshot*, making Slingshot its parent. Click the disclosure triangle next to Slingshot and select *Base* again. Set Base's transform to the following:

   Base (Cylinder)   P:[0, 1, 0]   R:[0, 0, 0]   S:[0.5, 1, 0.5]

3. With Base selected, click the gear icon next to the *Capsule Collider* component in the Inspector and select *Remove Component* (see Figure 29.3). This removes the Collider component from Base.

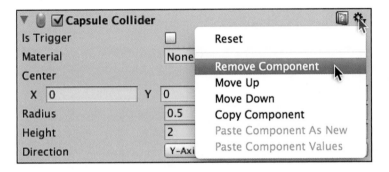

Figure 29.3 Removing the Collider Component

4. Create a new Material named *Mat_Slingshot*, color its Albedo a light yellow (or whatever color you want), and set its smoothness to *0*. Drag *Mat_Slingshot* onto *Base* to apply the material to the GameObject.

5. Select *Base* in the Hierarchy pane and duplicate it by pressing Command-D on your keyboard (Ctrl+D on Windows machines; or by selecting *Edit > Duplicate* from the menu bar). By duplicating, you ensure that the new duplicate is also a child of Slingshot, that it retains the Mat_Slingshot material, and that it won't have a Collider.

6. Change the name of the new duplicate from *Base (1)* to *LeftArm*. Set the transform of LeftArm to the following:

   LeftArm (Cylinder)   P:[0, 3, 1]   R:[45, 0, 0]   S:[0.5, 1.414, 0.5]

This makes one of the arms of the slingshot.

7. Select *LeftArm* in the Hierarchy and duplicate it (Command-D or Ctrl+D). Rename this instance *RightArm*. Set the transform of RightArm to the following:

   RightArm (Cylinder)   P:[0, 3, -1]   R:[-45, 0, 0]   S:[0.5, 1.414, 0.5].

8. Select the *Slingshot* in the Hierarchy. Add a Sphere Collider component to Slingshot (*Component > Physics > Sphere Collider*). Set the Sphere Collider component to the settings shown in Figure 29.4 (*Is Trigger* = true, *Center* = [0, 4, 0], *Radius* = 3).

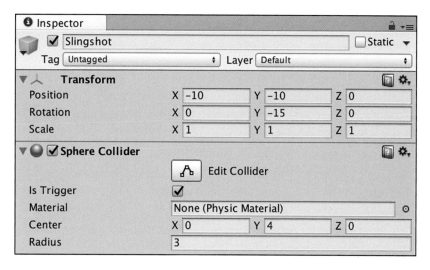

Figure 29.4 Settings for the Sphere Collider component of Slingshot

As you might expect, a collider with *Is Trigger = true* is known as a *trigger*. Triggers are part of the physics simulation in Unity and send notifications when other colliders or triggers pass through them. However, other objects don't bounce off of triggers as they do normal colliders. You'll use this large spherical trigger to handle the mouse interaction with Slingshot.

9. Set the transform of Slingshot to the following:

    Slingshot (Empty)   P:[-10, -10, 0]   R:[0, -15, 0]   S:[1, 1, 1]

This grounds it on the left side of the screen, and the -15° Y rotation gives it a bit of dimensionality, even through an orthographic camera.

10. Add a launch point to the slingshot to give it a specific location from which to shoot the projectiles. Right-click *Slingshot* in the Hierarchy and choose *Create Empty* from the pop-up menu to make a new empty child GameObject of Slingshot. Rename this GameObject *LaunchPoint*. Set the transform of LaunchPoint to the following:

    LaunchPoint (Empty)   P:[0, 4, 0]   R:[0, 15, 0]   S:[1, 1, 1]

The 15° Y rotation causes LaunchPoint to align with the XYZ axes in world coordinates. (That is, it removes the -15° rotation that was added to Slingshot.) If you choose the Move tool (press W on your keyboard), you can see the location and orientation of LaunchPoint in the Scene pane.[3]

11. Save your scene.

---

3. At the top-left of the Unity window are two buttons: one that toggles between Pivot and Center, and the other that toggles between Local and Global. The Local/Global button sets whether the move gizmo shows local or global coordinates. Try choosing the Move tool (W), selecting a rotated object (e.g., Slingshot), and toggling each of these buttons to see the effect they have on the positioning of the gizmo.

Projectile

Next comes the projectile.

1. Create a sphere in the scene (*GameObject > 3D Object > Sphere*) and name it *Projectile*.

2. Select *Projectile* in the Hierarchy and attach a Rigidbody component (*Component > Physics > Rigidbody*). This Rigidbody component enables the projectile to be physically simulated, similar to the apples in Apple Picker.

   a. Set *Mass* to *5* in the Projectile Rigidbody Inspector.

3. Create a new material and name it *Mat_Projectile*. Make Mat_Projectile's *Albedo* a dark gray color. Set *Metallic* to *0.5* and *Smoothness* to *0.65* to make it look more like a metal ball. Apply Mat_Projectile to the Projectile in the Hierarchy.

4. Drag *Projectile* from the Hierarchy pane to the Project pane to make it a prefab. Delete the Projectile instance that remains in the Hierarchy pane.

Your Project and Hierarchy panes should now look like those shown in Figure 29.5.

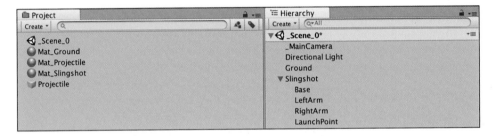

Figure 29.5 Project and Hierarchy panes at this point. The asterisk next to _Scene_0 means I should save.

5. Save your scene.

Coding the Prototype

With the art assets in place, it's time to start adding code to this project. The first script to add is one for Slingshot that will cause it to react to mouse input, instantiate a projectile, and fire that projectile. You will write this script an iterative manner by adding only small sections of code at a time, testing the code, and then adding a little more. When you start creating your own scripts, this is a fantastic way to approach them: Implement something small and easy to code, test it, implement another small thing, repeat.

Creating the Slingshot Class

Follow these steps to create the Slingshot class:

1. Create a new C# script and name it *Slingshot* (*Assets > Create > C# Script*). Attach it to the Slingshot in the Hierarchy and open the Slingshot C# script in MonoDevelop. Enter the following code and delete any extra lines that were placed there by default:

```csharp
using UnityEngine;
using System.Collections;

public class Slingshot : MonoBehaviour {

    void OnMouseEnter() {
        print("Slingshot:OnMouseEnter()");
    }

    void OnMouseExit() {
        print("Slingshot:OnMouseExit()");
    }

}
```

2. Save the Slingshot script in MonoDevelop and return to Unity.

3. Click Play and move the mouse within the Sphere Collider of Slingshot in the Game pane. Doing so outputs `"Slingshot:OnMouseEnter()"` to the Console pane. Moving the mouse out of the Slingshot Sphere Collider causes `"Slingshot:OnMouseExit()"` to output. The `OnMouseEnter()` and `OnMouseExit()` functions in this script work automatically on any collider or trigger.

This is just the first step of the script you'll write to launch projectiles, but it's important to start with small steps and build progressively.

Showing When the Slingshot Is Active

Next, add a highlight to show the player that the slingshot is active:

1. Select *LaunchPoint* in the Hierarchy. Add a *Halo* component to LaunchPoint (*Component > Effects > Halo*), which will create a glowing sphere effect at the Launch Point location. Set the *Size* of the halo to *3* and make the *Color* a light gray to make sure that it's visible (my settings are [r:191, g:191, b:191, a:255]).

2. Now add the following code to the Slingshot C# script. As you can see, this is also a good time to comment out the `print()` statements from the last test:

```csharp
public class Slingshot : MonoBehaviour {
    public GameObject          launchPoint;
```

```
void Awake() {
    Transform launchPointTrans = transform.Find("LaunchPoint");          // a
    launchPoint = launchPointTrans.gameObject;
    launchPoint.SetActive( false );                                       // b
}


void OnMouseEnter() {
    //print("Slingshot:OnMouseEnter()");
    launchPoint.SetActive( true );                                        // b
}


void OnMouseExit() {
    //print("Slingshot:OnMouseExit()");
    launchPoint.SetActive( false );                                       // b
}


}
```

a. `transform.Find("LaunchPoint")` searches for a child of Slingshot named LaunchPoint and returns its Transform. The next line gets the GameObject associated with that Transform and assigns it to the GameObject field launchPoint.

b. The `SetActive()` method on GameObjects like launchPoint tells the game whether or not to ignore them. More on this soon.

3. Save the Slingshot script, return to Unity, and click Play. You can see that as your mouse enters and leaves the sphere collider trigger of Slingshot, the halo turns on and off, indicating the range at which the player can interact with the slingshot.

As mentioned in `// b`, the `SetActive()` method on GameObjects like launchPoint tells the game whether or not to ignore them. If a GameObject has `active` set to false, it will not render on screen, and it will not receive any calls to functions like `Update()` or `OnCollisionEnter()`. This does not destroy the GameObject, but just removes it from being an active part of the game. In the Inspector for a GameObject, the check box at the top of the Inspector just to the left of the GameObject's name indicates whether the GameObject is active (see Figure 29.6).

Components have a similar check box. This sets whether a component is enabled. For most components (e.g., Renderer and Colliders) this can also be set in code (e.g., `Renderer.enabled = false`), but for some reason, Halo is not an accessible component in Unity, meaning that we can't affect a Halo component from C#. Every once in a while, you will encounter an inconsistency like this, and you need to find a workaround. In this case, we can't disable the Halo, so instead let's deactivate the GameObject that contains it.

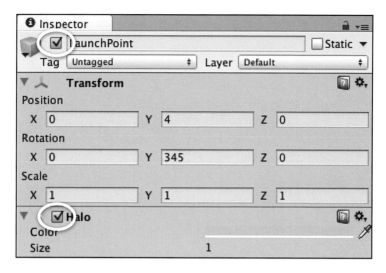

Figure 29.6 The GameObject active check box and the component enabled check box.

4. Save your scene.

Instantiating a Projectile

The next step is to instantiate the projectile when the player presses mouse button 0.

> ### warning
>
> **DON'T CHANGE THE** `OnMouseEnter()` **OR** `OnMouseExit()` **CLAUSES IN THE FOLLOWING CODE LISTING!**   This was mentioned in previous chapters, but I repeat it here just in case.
>
> In the `OnMouseEnter()` and `OnMouseExit()` clauses of the code listing for Slingshot, you will see the symbol { … } (braces around ellipses). As we write more and more complicated games, the scripts are going to get longer and longer. Whenever you see the name of a preexisting function followed by { … }, this indicates that all the code from the previous listing is to remain unchanged between those braces. In this example, `OnMouseEnter()` and `OnMouseExit()` should still remain:
>
> ```
> void OnMouseEnter() {
>     //print("Slingshot:OnMouseEnter()");
>     launchPoint.SetActive( true );
> }
> ```

```
    void OnMouseExit() {
        //print("Slingshot:OnMouseExit()");
        launchPoint.SetActive( false );
    }
```

Be sure to watch for these. Anywhere that you see ellipses in code, it means that I've used them to help shorten the code listings in this book and eliminate things you've already typed. { … } is **not** actual C# code.

1. Add the following bolded code to Slingshot:

```
public class Slingshot : MonoBehaviour {
    // fields set in the Unity Inspector pane
    [Header("Set in  Inspector")]                                    // a
    public GameObject        prefabProjectile;

    // fields set dynamically
    [Header("Set Dynamically")]                                      // a
    public GameObject        launchPoint;
    public Vector3           launchPos;                              // b
    public GameObject        projectile;                             // b
    public bool              aimingMode;                             // b

    void Awake() {
        Transform launchPointTrans = transform.FindChild("LaunchPoint");
        launchPoint = launchPointTrans.gameObject;
        launchPoint.SetActive( false );
        launchPos = launchPointTrans.position;                       // c
    }

    void OnMouseEnter() { … }    // Do not change OnMouseEnter()

    void OnMouseExit() { … }     // Do not change OnMouseExit()

    void OnMouseDown() {                                             // d
        // The player has pressed the mouse button while over Slingshot
        aimingMode = true;
        // Instantiate a Projectile
        projectile = Instantiate( prefabProjectile ) as GameObject;
        // Start it at the launchPoint
        projectile.transform.position = launchPos;
        // Set it to isKinematic for now
        projectile.GetComponent<Rigidbody>().isKinematic = true;
    }
}
```

a. Code between brackets like this is called a *compiler attribute*, and it gives specific instructions to either Unity or the compiler. In this case, the *Header* attribute tells Unity to create a header in the Inspector view of this script. After you have saved this code, select *Slingshot* in the Hierarchy pane and look at the *Slingshot (Script)* component. You will see headers separating the public fields into two sections: one that you are meant to set within the Inspector, and a second section that will be set dynamically when your game is running.

   In this example, you must set `prefabProjectile` (a reference to the prefab for all the projectiles) in the Unity Inspector before running the game, whereas all the other variables are meant to be set dynamically. The headers allow you to easily see the difference between these in the Inspector.

b. Looking now at the other new fields:

   ▪ `launchPos` stores the 3D world position of `launchPoint`.

   ▪ `projectile` is a reference to the new Projectile instance that is created.

   ▪ `aimingMode` is normally false, but is set to true when the player presses mouse button 0 down over Slingshot. This state variable lets the rest of the code know how to behave. In the next section, we'll write code for Slingshot's `Update()` that only runs when `aimingMode == true`.

c. In `Awake()`, we've added a single line to set `launchPos`.

d. The `OnMouseDown()` method contains the bulk of changes for this listing.

`OnMouseDown()` will only be called on the frame that the player presses the mouse button down over the Collider component of the Slingshot GameObject, so this method can only be called if the mouse is in a valid start position. An instance of `prefabProjectile` is created and assigned to `projectile`. Then `projectile` is placed at the `launchPos` location. Finally, `isKinematic` on the projectile's Rigidbody is set to true. When a Rigidbody is kinematic, it is not moved automatically by physics but is still part of the simulation (meaning that a kinematic Rigidbody will not move as a result of a collision or gravity but can still cause other nonkinematic Rigidbodies to move).

2. Save and return to Unity. Select *Slingshot* in the Hierarchy pane and set *prefabProjectile* to be the Projectile prefab in the Project pane (either by clicking the target to the right of prefabProjectile in the Inspector or by dragging the Projectile prefab from the Project pane onto the prefabProjectile in the Inspector).

3. Click *Play*, move your mouse pointer inside the active area for the slingshot, and click. The Projectile instance appears.

4. Let's make it do more. Add the following field and `Update()` method to the Slingshot class:

```
public class Slingshot : MonoBehaviour {
    // fields set in the Unity Inspector pane
    [Header("Set in  Inspector")]
    public GameObject          prefabProjectile;
    public float               velocityMult = 8f;                              // a

    // fields set dynamically
    [Header("Set Dynamically")]
    ...
    public bool                aimingMode;

    private Rigidbody          projectileRigidbody;                            // a

    void Awake() { ... }
    ...

    void OnMouseDown() {
        ...
        // Set it to isKinematic for now
        projectileRigidbody = projectile.GetComponent<Rigidbody>();            // a
        projectileRigidbody.isKinematic = true;                               // a
    }

    void Update() {
        // If Slingshot is not in aimingMode, don't run this code
        if (!aimingMode) return;                                              // b

        // Get the current mouse position in 2D screen coordinates
        Vector3 mousePos2D = Input.mousePosition;                            // c
        mousePos2D.z = -Camera.main.transform.position.z;
        Vector3 mousePos3D = Camera.main.ScreenToWorldPoint( mousePos2D );

        // Find the delta from the launchPos to the mousePos3D
        Vector3 mouseDelta = mousePos3D-launchPos;
        // Limit mouseDelta to the radius of the Slingshot SphereCollider    // d
        float maxMagnitude = this.GetComponent<SphereCollider>().radius;
        if (mouseDelta.magnitude > maxMagnitude) {
            mouseDelta.Normalize();
            mouseDelta *= maxMagnitude;
        }
```

```
    // Move the projectile to this new position
    Vector3 projPos = launchPos + mouseDelta;
    projectile.transform.position = projPos;

    if ( Input.GetMouseButtonUp(0) ) {                        // e
        // The mouse has been released
        aimingMode = false;
        projectileRigidbody.isKinematic = false;
        projectileRigidbody.velocity = -mouseDelta * velocityMult;
        projectile = null;
    }
}
}
```

a. Be sure that you make all three of these changes. These new last two lines of OnMouseDown() replace the line you typed in the previous code listing.

b. If Slingshot is not in aimingMode, then return and don't run the rest of this code.

c. Convert the mouse position from screen coordinates to world coordinates. The previous chapter provides a discussion of how this works.

d. This code limits the movement of the projectile to keep the center of the projectile within the radius of the Sphere Collider on Slingshot. More on this soon.

e. Input.GetMouseButtonUp(0) is another way to read the state of the mouse buttons.

Most of this is explained in the in-line comments; however, the vector math involved bears a closer examination.

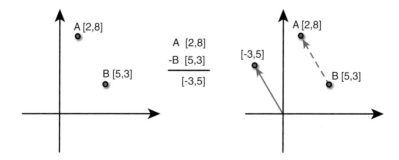

Figure 29.7 Two-dimensional vector subtraction: *A minus B looks at A.*

As you can see in Figure 29.7, vectors are added and subtracted one component at a time. The figure is two dimensional, but the same methods work for 3D. The X components of the vectors

A and B are subtracted as are the Y components, making a new Vector2 defined as Vector2(2-5, 8-3), which becomes Vector2(-3, 5). The figure illustrates that A-B gives us the vector distance between A and B, which is also the distance and direction that one must move to get from point B to point A. A mnemonic to remember which one the vector will point at is "A minus B looks at A."

This is important in the `Update()` method because `projectile` needs to be positioned along the vector from `launchPos` to the current `mousePos3D`, and this vector is named `mouseDelta`. However, the distance that the projectile can move along `mouseDelta` is limited to `maxMagnitude`, which is the radius of the SphereCollider on Slingshot (currently set to 3m in the Inspector for the Collider component).

If `mouseDelta` is longer than `maxMagnitude`, its magnitude is clamped to `maxMagnitude`. This is accomplished by first calling `mouseDelta.Normalize()` (which sets the length of `mouseDelta` to 1 but keeps it pointing in the same direction) and then multiplying `mouseDelta` by `maxMagnitude`.

`projectile` is moved to this new position, and if you play the game, you will see that the projectile moves with the mouse but is limited to a specific radius.

`Input.GetMouseButtonUp(0)` returns true only on the first frame that the left mouse button (the 0th button) has been released.[4] That means that the `if` statement at the end of `Update()` is executed on the frame that the mouse button is released. On this frame:

- `aimingMode` is set to false.
- `projectile`'s Rigidbody is set to non-kinematic , allowing it to once again move due to velocity and gravity.
- The Rigidbody of `projectile` is given a velocity that is proportional to the distance that it is from `launchPos`.
- Finally, `projectile` is set back to `null`. This doesn't delete the Projectile instance that was created; it just opens the field `projectile` to be filled by another instance when the slingshot is fired again.

---

4. This is why `Input.GetMouseButtonUp()`, `Input.GetKeyDown()`, and other similar Input methods ending in Up or Down, can't be used reliably inside of `FixedUpdate()`. A FixedUpdate occurs exactly 50 times per second, while an Update (or visual frame) could happen up to 400 times per second. If that occurs, multiple Updates could occur between two FixedUpdates; and if `Input.GetKeyDown()` was true on anything other than the very last of those multiple Updates, it would be false within the `FixedUpdate()`. When this happens, the result is that it feels like the keyboard or mouse button is broken because it doesn't work most of the time when you press it. Move the Input ...Up or ...Down code into `Update()`, and all will be well.

5. Click *Play* and see how the Slingshot feels. Is the `Projectile` instance launching at a good velocity? Try adjusting `velocityMult` in the Inspector to see what value feels right to you. I ended up with a value of 10. Remember to stop Unity playback to make settings that stay.

6. Save your scene.

As it is now, the `Projectile` instance flies off screen very quickly. Let's make a follow camera to chase after the projectile as it flies.

Making a Follow Camera

You need _MainCamera to follow the projectile when it is launched, but the behavior is a little more complicated than that. The eventual full behavior should be as follows:

A. The camera sits at an initial position and doesn't move during Slingshot's aimingMode.

B. After the projectile is launched, the camera follows it (with a little easing to make it feel smoother).

C. As the camera moves up into the air, increase the Camera.orthographicSize to keep the ground in view.

D. When the projectile comes to rest, the camera stops following it and returns to the initial position.

Follow these steps:

1. Start by creating a new C# script (*Assets > Create > C# Script*) and name it *FollowCam*.

2. Drag the *FollowCam* Script onto _MainCamera in the Hierarchy pane to make it a component of _MainCamera.

3. Double-click the FollowCam script to open it and input the following code:

```
using UnityEngine;
using System.Collections;

public class FollowCam : MonoBehaviour {
    static public GameObject POI; // The static point of interest          // a

    [Header("Set Dynamically")]
    public float            camZ; // The desired Z pos of the camera

    void Awake() {
        camZ = this.transform.position.z;
    }
```

```
void FixedUpdate () {
    // if there's only one line following an if, it doesn't need braces
    if (POI == null) return; // return if there is no poi                    // b

    // Get the position of the poi
    Vector3 destination = POI.transform.position;
    // Force destination.z to be camZ to keep the camera far enough away
    destination.z = camZ;
    // Set the camera to the destination
    transform.position = destination;
    }
}
```

   a. POI is the point of interest that the camera should follow (e.g., a Projectile). As a static public field, the same value for POI is shared by all instances of the Follow-Cam class, and POI can be accessed anywhere in code as FollowCam.POI. This makes it easy for the Slingshot code to tell _MainCamera which Projectile to follow.

   b. If POI is set to null (the default), the FixedUpdate() method returns, and none of the rest of the code in this method is executed.

The camZ field holds the initial z position of the camera. In FixedUpdate(), the camera is moved to the position of POI, except for the z coordinate, which is set to camZ every frame. (This prevents the camera from being so close to POI that POI fills the frame or becomes invisible.) We chose FixedUpdate() here instead of Update() because we're following a projectile that is moved by the PhysX physics engine, and that engine updates in sync with FixedUpdate().

   4. Open the *Slingshot* C# script and add the single bold line near the end of Update():

```
public class Slingshot : MonoBehaviour {
    ...
    void Update() {
        ...
        if ( Input.GetMouseButtonUp(0) ) {
            ...
            projectileRigidbody.velocity = -mouseDelta * velocityMult;
            FollowCam.POI = projectile;
            projectile = null;
        }
    }
}
```

This new line sets the static public field FollowCam.POI to be the newly fired projectile. Save All scripts in MonoDevelop, return to Unity, and try clicking *Play* to see how it looks.

You should notice a few issues:

A. If you zoom out the Scene pane view enough, you can see that the projectile actually flies past the end of the ground.

B. If you fire at the ground, the projectile neither bounces nor stops after it has hit the ground. If you pause right after firing, select the projectile in the Hierarchy (to highlight it and center the Scene pane gizmos around it), and then unpause, you'll see that it rolls upon hitting the ground and never stops rolling.

C. When the projectile is first launched, the camera immediately jumps to the position of the projectile, which is visually jarring.

D. After the projectile is at a certain height—or if it's gone past the end of the ground—all you see is sky, so it's difficult to tell how high up the projectile is.

Use the following steps (which are generally ordered from the easiest fix to the most difficult) to fix each of these issues in order.

First, fix issue **A** by setting the transform of the Ground to P:[100, -10, 0] R:[0, 0, 0] S:[400, 1, 4]. This makes the ground extend much farther to the right.

To fix issue **B**, you must add both *Rigidbody constraints* and a *Physic Material* to Projectile:

1. Select the *Projectile* prefab in the Project pane.

2. In the Rigidbody component, set the pop-up menu for *Collision Detection* to *Continuous*. For information about the types of collision detection, click the help icon in the top-right corner of the Rigidbody component. In short, *continuous* collision detection takes more processor power than *discrete*, but it is more accurate for fast-moving objects like the projectile.

3. Also in the Projectile Rigidbody component:

    a. Open the disclosure triangle next to Constraints.

    b. Check *Freeze Position* Z

    c. Check *Freeze Rotation* X, Y, and Z.

Freeze Position Z keeps the projectile from moving toward or away from the camera (basically keeping it in the same Z depth as both the ground and the castle that will be added later). Freeze Rotation X, Y, and Z keep it from rolling around.

4. Save the scene, click *Play*, and try launching the projectile again.

These Rigidbody settings keep the projectile from rolling endlessly, but it still doesn't feel right. You've spent your whole life experiencing physics, and that gives you an intuitive feel for the kinds of behaviors that feel like natural, real-world physics. This is true for your players as well, which means that even though physics is a complex system that requires a lot of math to model, if you make your game physics feel like the physics that players are used to, you won't have to explain that math to them. Adding a *Physic Material* can make your physically simulated objects feel a lot more realistic.

5. From the Unity menu bar, choose *Assets > Create > Physic Material*.

6. Name this Physic material *PMat_Projectile*.

7. Click *PMat_Projectile* and set the *bounciness* to 1 in the Inspector.

8. Drag *PMat_Projectile* in the Project pane onto the Projectile prefab (also in the Project pane) to apply it to Projectile.SphereCollider.

9. Save the scene, click Play, and try launching the projectile again.

Selecting Projectile should reveal that PMat_Projectile has been assigned as the material of the Sphere Collider in the Inspector. Now when you launch a projectile, you'll see that it bounces to a stop instead of just gliding on the ground.

You will fix issue **C** via two means: easing through interpolation and adding limits on the camera's location. Let's do that:

1. To start with easing, add the following bolded lines to FollowCam:

```
public class FollowCam : MonoBehaviour {
    static public GameObject POI; // The static point of interest

    [Header("Set in Inspector")]
    public float              easing = 0.05f;

    [Header("Set Dynamically")]
    ...
    void FixedUpdate () {
        // if there's only one line following an if, it doesn't need braces
        if (POI == null) return; // return if there is no poi

        // Get the position of the poi
        Vector3 destination = POI.transform.position;
        // Interpolate from the current Camera position toward destination
        destination = Vector3.Lerp(transform.position, destination, easing);
        // Force destination.z to be camZ to keep the camera far enough away
        destination.z = camZ;
        // Set the camera to the destination
        transform.position = destination;
    }
}
```

The Vector3.Lerp() method interpolates between two points, returning a weighted average of the two. If easing is 0, Lerp() returns the first point (transform.position); if easing is 1, Lerp() returns the second point (destination). If easing is any value in between 0 and 1, Lerp() returns a point between the two (with an easing of 0.5 returning the midpoint halfway between the two). Setting easing = 0.05f tells Unity to move the camera about 5% of the way from its current location to the location of the POI every FixedUpdate (i.e., each update of the physics engine, which occur 50 times per second). Because the POI is constantly moving, this gives you a nice smooth camera follow movement. Try playing with the value of easing to see how it affects the camera movement. This kind of use of Lerp() is a very simplistic form of *linear interpolation*. For more information on linear interpolation, you can read about it in Appendix B, "Useful Concepts."

2. Add some limits to the FollowCam position by adding the bolded lines to FollowCam:

```
public class FollowCam : MonoBehaviour {

    ...

    [Header("Set in Inspector")]
    public float                easing = 0.05f;
    public Vector2          minXY = Vector2.zero;

    [Header("Set Dynamically")]
    ...

    void FixedUpdate () {
        // if there's only one line following an if, it doesn't need braces
        if (POI == null) return; // return if there is no poi                    // b

        // Get the position of the poi
        Vector3 destination = POI.transform.position;
        // Limit the X & Y to minimum values
        destination.x = Mathf.Max( minXY.x, destination.x );
        destination.y = Mathf.Max( minXY.y, destination.y );
        // Interpolate from the current Camera position toward destination
        ...
    }
}
```

The default value of Vector2 minXY is [0, 0], which works perfectly for your needs. The Mathf.Max() function chooses the maximum value of the two floats passed in. When the projectile is initially launched, its X coordinate is negative, so the Mathf.Max() ensures that the camera never moves left of the X = 0 plane into negative territory. Similarly, the second Mathf.Max() line keeps the camera from dipping below the Y = 0 plane when the projectile's Y coordinate is less than 0. (Remember that the Y position of Ground is -10.)

To fix issue **D** you must dynamically adjust the `orthographicSize` of the camera.

1. Add the following bolded lines to the FollowCam script:

```
public class FollowCam : MonoBehaviour {

    ...

    void FixedUpdate () {

        ...

        // Set the camera to the destination
        transform.position = destination;
        // Set the orthographicSize of the Camera to keep Ground in view
        Camera.main.orthographicSize = destination.y + 10;

    }

}
```

This works because you know that due the `Mathf.Max()` lines you just added, the `destination.y` will never be allowed to be less than 0. So, the minimum `orthographic-Size` is 10, and the camera's `orthographicSize` will expand as needed to always keep the ground in view.

2. Double-click *Ground* in the Hierarchy to zoom out and show the entire Ground GameObject in the Scene pane.

3. Select *_MainCamera*, click *Play*, and launch a projectile straight up. In the Scene pane, you can see the field of view of the camera expand smoothly as the projectile flies.

4. Save your scene.

Providing Vection and a Sense of Speed

The FollowCam moves pretty well now, but it's still difficult to tell how fast the projectile is moving, especially when it's high in the air. To fix this issue, let's take advantage of the concept of *vection*. Vection is the sensation of movement that you get from seeing other things passing by quickly, and it is the concept that led to *parallax scrolling* in 2D video games. Parallax scrolling causes foreground objects to pass by quickly while background objects move more slowly relative to the movement of the main camera in a 2D game. While a full parallax system is beyond the scope of this tutorial, you can at least get a simple feeling of vection by creating a lot of clouds and distributing them randomly through the sky. As the projectile passes by them, the player will get more of a feeling of movement.

Making Cloud Art

To make this work, you must make some simple clouds:

1. Create a new sphere (*GameObject > 3D Object > Sphere*).

   a. Hover your mouse over the name of the *Sphere Collider* component in the Inspector for the sphere. Right-click and choose *Remove Component* from the pop-up menu.

    b. Set the Transform.Position of the Sphere to P:[0, 0, 0] so that it is visible in the Game pane as well as the Scene pane.

    c. Rename Sphere to *CloudSphere*.

2. Create a new material and name it *Mat_Cloud* (*Assets > Create > Material*).

    a. Drag *Mat_Cloud* onto CloudSphere and then select *Mat_Cloud* in the Project pane.

    b. From the pop-up menu next to *Shader* in the Mat_Cloud Inspector, choose *Legacy Shaders > Self-Illumin > Diffuse*. This shader is self-illuminating (it generates its own light), and it also responds to the directional light in the scene.

    c. Click the color swatch next to *Main Color* in the Inspector for Mat_Cloud and set it to a 50% gray (or RGBA of [128, 128, 128, 255] in the Unity color picker). This should give CloudSphere just a little gray on the bottom-left side in the Game pane, which looks a bit like a cloud in the sun.

    d. Drag CloudSphere to the Project pane to make it a prefab.

    e. Delete the instance of CloudSphere from the Hierarchy.

3. Create an Empty GameObject in the Scene (GameObject > Create Empty) named *Cloud*.

    a. Select *Cloud* in the Hierarchy and set its Transform to P:[0, 0, 0].

    b. In the Cloud Inspector, click the *Add Component* button and choose *New Script*.

    c. Name the new script *Cloud*, make sure the *Language* is *C Sharp*, and click *Create and Add*. This creates a new script and automatically attaches it to Cloud.

Rather than make a bunch of clouds ourselves, let's generate them *procedurally* (i.e., through randomization and code). This is how games like *Minecraft* create their worlds. The code for creating these clouds will be very simplistic relative to things like *Minecraft*, but it will give you a little experience with randomization and tweaking procedural generation.

4. Open the Cloud script in MonoDevelop and enter this code:

```
using System.Collections;
using System.Collections.Generic;
using UnityEngine;

public class Cloud : MonoBehaviour {
    [Header("Set in Inspector")]                                        // a
    public GameObject        cloudSphere;
    public int               numSpheresMin = 6;
    public int               numSpheresMax = 10;
    public Vector3           sphereOffsetScale = new Vector3(5,2,1);
    public Vector2           sphereScaleRangeX = new Vector2(4,8);
    public Vector2           sphereScaleRangeY = new Vector2(3,4);
```

```
public Vector2          sphereScaleRangeZ = new Vector2(2,4);
public float            scaleYMin = 2f;

private List<GameObject>  spheres;                                      // b

void Start () {
    spheres = new List<GameObject>();

    int num = Random.Range(numSpheresMin, numSpheresMax);              // c
    for (int i=0; i<num; i++) {
        GameObject sp = Instantiate<GameObject>( cloudSphere );        // d
        spheres.Add( sp );
        Transform spTrans = sp.transform;
        spTrans.SetParent( this.transform );

        // Randomly assign a position
        Vector3 offset = Random.insideUnitSphere;                      // e
        offset.x *= sphereOffsetScale.x;
        offset.y *= sphereOffsetScale.y;
        offset.z *= sphereOffsetScale.z;
        spTrans.localPosition = offset;                                // f

        // Randomly assign scale
        Vector3 scale = Vector3.one;                                   // g
        scale.x = Random.Range(sphereScaleRangeX.x, sphereScaleRangeX.y);
        scale.y = Random.Range(sphereScaleRangeY.x, sphereScaleRangeY.y);
        scale.z = Random.Range(sphereScaleRangeZ.x, sphereScaleRangeZ.y);

        // Adjust y scale by x distance from core
        scale.y *= 1 - (Mathf.Abs(offset.x) / sphereOffsetScale.x);    // h
        scale.y = Mathf.Max( scale.y, scaleYMin );

        spTrans.localScale = scale;                                    // i

    }
}
```

```
// Update is called once per frame
void Update () {
    if (Input.GetKeyDown(KeyCode.Space)) {                          // j
        Restart();
    }
}


void Restart() {                                                    // k
    // Clear out old spheres
    foreach (GameObject sp in spheres) {
        Destroy(sp);
    }

    Start();
}
}
```

a. All of these fields are used to set the parameters of the random generation of clouds.

- numSpheresMin / numSpheresMax—The min and max (actually 1 more than the actual max) number of CloudSpheres that could be instantiated.

- sphereOffsetScale—The maximum distance (positive or negative) that a CloudSphere could be from the center of the Cloud in each dimension.

- sphereScaleRangeX / Y / Z—The range in scales in each dimension. The default settings create CloudSpheres that are usually wider than they are tall.

- scaleYMin—At the end of the Start() function, each CloudSphere is scaled down in the Y dimension based on how far it is from the center in the X dimension. This makes clouds taper at their left and right extents. scaleYMin is the lowest Y scale that you will allow (otherwise, you would get some super skinny clouds).

b. The List<GameObject> spheres holds a reference to all the CloudSpheres that are instantiated by this Cloud.

c. Randomly choose how many CloudSpheres to attach to this Cloud.

d. Each CloudSphere is instantiated and added to spheres. The CloudSphere's transform is then assigned to spTrans, and the parent of each CloudSphere is set to the transform of this Cloud. this.transform is identical to transform; the this is optional.

e. A random point inside a unit sphere is chosen (that is a point anywhere within 1 unit of the origin: [0, 0, 0]). Each dimension (X, Y, Z) of that point is then multiplied by the corresponding sphereOffsetScale.

f. The offset is assigned to the localPosition of the CloudSphere. transform. position is always in world coordinates, whereas transform.localPosition is relative to the center of the parent (which is this Cloud in this case).

g. Randomization of scales is handled differently. For each of the `sphereScaleRange` Vector2s, the X dimension stores the minimum value, and the Y dimension holds the maximum value.

h. After the randomized scale is chosen, the Y dimension is altered based on how far the CloudSphere is offset from Cloud in the X direction. The further out in X, the smaller the scale in Y.

i. `scale` is assigned to the `localScale` of the CloudSphere. Because scale is always relative to the parent transform, there is no `transform.scale` field. Just `localScale` and `lossyScale`. The read-only property `lossyScale` attempts to return the scale in world coordinates, with the understanding that it is just an estimate.

j. This section of the code is just for testing. Pressing the space bar in Unity will call `Restart()` (see `// k`).

k. When `Restart()` is called, it destroys all the child CloudSpheres and calls `Start()` again to generate new ones.

5. Save the Cloud script and return to Unity.

6. Select *Cloud* in the Hierarchy and assign the *CloudSphere* prefab to the *cloudSphere* field in the *Cloud (Script)* Inspector.

Click *Play*, and you will see that a randomized cloud is generated. Every time you press the space bar, `Restart()` is called, destroying the current cloud and creating a new one. This ability allows you to repeatedly press the space bar to test different settings in the *Cloud (Script)* Inspector. Try it out for a little while and adjust the settings to fine ones you like.

Avoid Losing Inspector Values Set During Play

As you've experienced in previous chapters, the moment you stop the game (by clicking the Play button again), any values you changed in the *Cloud (Script)* Inspector return to their initial values before you started the game. Here's a way to get around this.

1. While the game is still playing, click the little gear to the right of the *Cloud (Script)* component name. Choose *Copy Component* from the pop-up menu.

2. Stop playback (by clicking *Play* again).

3. Click the gear next to *Cloud (Script)* again, and this time choose *Paste Component Values*.

This replaces the values in the Inspector with the ones that you had chosen while the game was running.

Commenting Out Test Code

The ability to press the space bar and generate new clouds was really only needed for testing, so after you have *Cloud (Script)* Inspector values that you're happy with, it's time to get rid of the testing code. You might want to use this test code again later, so instead of deleting the code, just comment it out.

1. Open the Cloud script in MonoDevelop.

2. Comment out all the lines in the `Update()` method.

```
public class Cloud : MonoBehaviour {

    ...

    void Update () {
//        if (Input.GetKeyDown(KeyCode.Space)) {
//            Restart();
//        }
    }

    ...

}
```

Because `Restart()` will now no longer be called, there's no reason to comment out the `Restart()` method.

Crafting Many Clouds

Now that you have one cloud, let's make several.

1. Make a Cloud prefab by dragging the *Cloud* GameObject from the Hierarchy to the Project pane. Delete the Cloud instance from Hierarchy.

2. Create a new empty GameObject named *CloudAnchor* (*GameObject > Create Empty*). This gives you a GameObject to act as the parent for all Cloud instances, which will keep the Hierarchy tidy while the game is running. Set the CloudAnchor transform to P:[0, 0, 0].

3. Create a new C# script titled *CloudCrafter* and attach it to _MainCamera. This adds a second Script component to _MainCamera, which is perfectly fine in Unity as long as the two scripts don't conflict with each other (e.g., as long as they don't both try to set the position of the GameObject each frame). Because FollowCam is moving the camera, and Cloud-Crafter will just be placing Cloud_#s in the air, they shouldn't conflict at all.

4. Open CloudCrafter in MonoDevelop and enter the following code:

```
using UnityEngine;
using System.Collections;

public class CloudCrafter : MonoBehaviour {
    [Header("Set in Inspector")]
    public int          numClouds = 40;         // The # of clouds to make
    public GameObject   cloudPrefab;            // The prefab for the clouds
    public Vector3      cloudPosMin = new Vector3(-50,-5,10);
    public Vector3      cloudPosMax = new Vector3(150,100,10);
    public float        cloudScaleMin = 1;      // Min scale of each cloud
    public float        cloudScaleMax = 3;      // Max scale of each cloud
    public float        cloudSpeedMult = 0.5f; // Adjusts speed of clouds
```

```
private GameObject[]    cloudInstances;

void Awake() {
    // Make an array large enough to hold all the Cloud_ instances
    cloudInstances = new GameObject[numClouds];
    // Find the CloudAnchor parent GameObject
    GameObject anchor = GameObject.Find("CloudAnchor");
    // Iterate through and make Cloud_s
    GameObject cloud;
    for (int i=0; i<numClouds; i++) {
        // Make an instance of cloudPrefab
        cloud = Instantiate<GameObject>( cloudPrefab );
        // Position cloud
        Vector3 cPos = Vector3.zero;
        cPos.x = Random.Range( cloudPosMin.x, cloudPosMax.x );
        cPos.y = Random.Range( cloudPosMin.y, cloudPosMax.y );
        // Scale cloud
        float scaleU = Random.value;
        float scaleVal = Mathf.Lerp( cloudScaleMin, cloudScaleMax, scaleU );
        // Smaller clouds (with smaller scaleU) should be nearer the ground
        cPos.y = Mathf.Lerp( cloudPosMin.y, cPos.y, scaleU );
        // Smaller clouds should be further away
        cPos.z = 100 - 90*scaleU;
        // Apply these transforms to the cloud
        cloud.transform.position = cPos;
        cloud.transform.localScale = Vector3.one * scaleVal;
        // Make cloud a child of the anchor
        cloud.transform.SetParent( anchor.transform );
        // Add the cloud to cloudInstances
        cloudInstances[i] = cloud;
    }
}

void Update() {
    // Iterate over each cloud that was created
    foreach (GameObject cloud in cloudInstances) {
        // Get the cloud scale and position
        float scaleVal = cloud.transform.localScale.x;
        Vector3 cPos = cloud.transform.position;
        // Move larger clouds faster
        cPos.x -= scaleVal * Time.deltaTime * cloudSpeedMult;
```

```
                // If a cloud has moved too far to the left...
                if (cPos.x <= cloudPosMin.x) {
                    // Move it to the far right
                    cPos.x = cloudPosMax.x;
                }
                // Apply the new position to cloud
                cloud.transform.position = cPos;
            }
        }
}
```

5. Save the CloudCrafter script and return to Unity.

6. Assign the *Cloud* prefab from the Project pane to the `cloudPrefab` field of the *CloudCrafter (Script)* Inspector of _MainCamera. All the other values should be fine at their default settings.

7. Save your scene.

In the CloudCrafter class, the `Awake()` method creates all the clouds and positions them. The `Update()` method moves each cloud a little to the left of every frame. When a cloud moves to the left past cloudPosMin.x, it is moved to cloudPosMax.x on the far right.

8. Click *Play*, and you can see several clouds are instantiated and moves across the screen.

Zoom out in the Scene pane and watch the clouds blow by. Now when you launch the projectile, the vection of the clouds passing by should make it feel much more like the projectile is actually moving.

Organizing the Project Pane

Now that you've created many different assets, it's time to talk about organizing the Project pane. The mess you have now should look like the image on the left side of Figure 29.8.

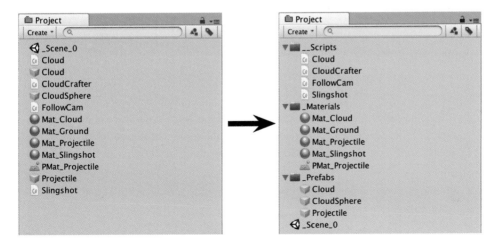

Figure 29.8 Disorganized (left) and organized (right) Project panes

On the right side of Figure 29.8, you can see that I've added folders to organize my Project pane. I usually do this at the very beginning of a project but have waited until now on this project so that you can experience how much better the project feels when it's organized.

1. Create three folders (*Assets > Create > Folder*) named __Scripts, _Materials, and _Prefabs. The underscores in their names help sort them above any non-folder assets, and the double-underscore of the __Scripts folder ensures that it is the top folder in the Project pane. This simultaneously creates folders on your hard drive inside the Assets folder for your project, so not only your Project pane but also your Assets folder will be organized.

2. Drag the proper assets into each folder in the Project pane. Both the physic material and regular materials go into the _Materials folder.

Unity's Two-Column Project pane layout does attempt to do some of this organizing for you, but I've always hated the way that the Two-Column view defaults to an icon view of all the assets, and using the Two-Column view does not have the same benefit of organizing the Assets folder on your hard drive that making folders does.

Building the Castle

Mission Demolition needs something to demolish, so let's build a castle to serve that purpose. Figure 29.10 shows how the final castle will look.

1. Adjust the Scene pane so that you are viewing the scene from the back in isometric view by clicking the arrow on the axes gizmo opposite the z-axis (see the left side of Figure 29.9). If you have a wedge (<) next to the word *Back* under the axes gizmo, click the wedge, and it will become three parallel lines, signifying that you've switched from a perspective to an isometric (i.e., orthographic) view.

Figure 29.9 Selecting the Back view

2. This would also be a good time to get rid of the Skybox view in the Scene pane. To do so, click the mountain-looking button to the right of the speaker button at the top of the Scene pane (under the mouse cursor shown on the right side of Figure 29.9) until the background turns gray.

3. Double click _MainCamera in the Hierarchy to zoom the Scene pane to a good view from which to build the castle.

Making Walls and Slabs

Start by making the GameObject prefabs for the castle bits:

1. Create a duplicate of the Mat_Cloud material and name it Mat_Stone.[5]

   a. Select *Mat_Cloud* in the Project pane.

   b. Choose *Edit > Duplicate* from the Unity menu bar.

   c. Change the name from *Mat_Cloud 1* to *Mat_Stone*.

   d. Select *Mat_Stone* and set the Main Color to *25% gray* (RGBA: [64, 64, 64, 255]).

2. Create a new cube (*GameObject > 3D Object > Cube*) and rename it *Wall*.

   a. Set the Wall Transform to P:[0, 0, 0] R:[0, 0, 0] S:[1, 4, 4].

   b. Add a Rigidbody component to Wall (*Component > Physics > Rigidbody*).

   c. Constrain the Z position of the Wall by setting the Rigidbody FreezePosition Z to *true*.

   d. Constrain rotation by setting the Rigidbody FreezeRotation X and Y to *true*.

   e. Set the Rigidbody.mass to *4*.

   f. Drag the *Mat_Stone* material onto Wall to color it *gray*.

3. Create a new script in the __Scripts folder named *RigidbodySleep* and enter this code:

```
using UnityEngine;

public class RigidbodySleep : MonoBehaviour {
    void Start () {
        Rigidbody rb = GetComponent<Rigidbody>();
        if (rb != null) rb.Sleep();
    }
}
```

This will cause the Wall's Rigidbody to initially assume that it should not be moving, which will help castles to initially be stable (there were issues in some versions of Unity with castles falling down before the projectile hit them).

4. Attach the *RigidbodySleep* script to *Wall*.

5. Drag *Wall* to the Project pane to make it a prefab (be sure to put it in the _Prefabs folder), and after doing so, delete the Wall instance from the Hierarchy pane.

6. Select the *Wall* prefab in the _Prefabs folder of the Project pane and duplicate it.

   a. Rename Wall 1 to *Slab*.

   b. Select *Slab* in the _Prefabs folder and set its transform scale to S:[4, 0.5, 4].

---

5. When I taught at the University of Michigan, I had a great TA named Matt Stone. If you see him at a game conference, tell him "Jeremy says hi."

Making a Castle from Walls and Slabs

Now make a castle from the walls and slabs:

1. Create an empty GameObject to be the root node of the castle (*GameObject > Create Empty*).

    a. Name it *Castle*.

    b. Set its transform to P:[0, -9.5, 0] R:[0, 0, 0] S:[1, 1, 1]. This positions it well for construction and puts its base resting exactly on top of the Ground.

2. Drag *Wall* from the _Prefabs folder to the Hierarchy under Castle, making it a child of Castle.

3. Make three duplicates of Wall and set their positions to:

    Wall P:[-6, 2, 0]   *Wall (1)* P:[-2, 2, 0]   *Wall (2)* P:[2, 2, 0]   *Wall (3)* P:[6, 2, 0]

4. Drag *Slab* from the _Prefabs folder of the Project pane to the Hierarchy under Castle, making it a child as well.

5. Make two duplicates of Slab and set their positions to:

    Slab P:[-4, 4.25, 0]   *Slab (1)* P:[0, 4.25, 0]   *Slab (2)* P:[4, 4.25, 0]

6. To make the second floor of the castle, use your mouse to select three adjacent Walls and the two Slabs above them. Duplicate them (Command-D or Ctrl+D) and hold Command (Ctrl on PC) while moving them to be resting above the others.[6] You will need to tweak their positions, and the final positions for the new Walls should be as follows:

    Wall (4) P:[-4, 6.5, 0]   *Wall (5)* P:[0, 6.5, 0]   *Wall (6)* P:[4, 6.5, 0]

    Slab (3) P:[-2, 8.75, 0]   *Slab (4)* P:[2, 8.75, 0]

7. Continue the duplication trick to make the third and fourth levels by adding three more vertical walls and one more horizontal wall:

    Wall (7) P:[-2, 11, 0]   *Wall (8)* P:[2, 11, 0]   *Slab (5)* P:[0, 13.25, 0]
    Wall (9) P:[0, 15.5, 0]

One of the major advantages of building a castle out of prefabs like this is that you can easily change every Slab simultaneously by changing the Slab prefab.

8. Select the *Slab* prefab in the Project pane and set its transform.scale.x to *3.5*. Every Slab in your castle should reflect this change. Your castle should now look like Figure 29.10, though it doesn't yet have the green goal area.

---

6. Holding Command (Ctrl on PC) while moving objects in Unity will snap them to a grid, which may obviate the need for tweaking their positions.

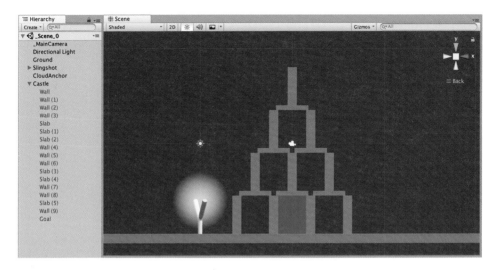

Figure 29.10 The finished castle

Making a Goal

The final GameObject to add to Castle is a goal for the player to hit with the projectile.

1. Create a cube named *Goal* and:
   a. Make it a child of Castle.
   b. Set the transform of Goal to P:[0, 2, 0] R:[0, 0, 0] S:[3, 4, 4].
   c. In the Goal Inspector, set BoxCollider.isTrigger to *true*.
   d. Drag *Goal* into the _Prefabs folder in the Project pane to make it a prefab.
2. Create a new material in the *_Materials* folder named Mat*Goal*.
   a. Drag *Mat_Goal* onto the Goal prefab in the _Prefabs folder of the Project to apply it.
   b. Select *Mat_Goal* in the Project pane and choose the *Legacy Shaders > Transparent > Diffuse* shader.
   c. Set the Main Color of Mat_Goal to a *bright green* with an opacity of *25%* (an RGBA in the Unity color picker of [0, 255, 0, 64]).

Testing the Castle

To test the castle, do the following:

1. Set the *Castle* position to P:[50, -9.5, 0], and then click *Play*. You might have to try and restart a couple of times, but you should be able to hit the castle with the projectile.
2. Save your scene.

Returning for Another Shot

Now that there's a castle to knock down, it's time to add a little more game logic. After the projectile has settled, the camera should move back to focus on the slingshot again:

1. Before doing anything else, you should add a tag of *Projectile* to the projectile.

   a. Select the *Projectile* prefab in the Project pane.

   b. In the Inspector, click the pop-up menu next to *Tag* and choose *Add Tag*. This opens the Tags & Layers Inspector.

   c. Click the + button at the bottom-right of the empty Tags list.

   d. Set *New Tag Name* to *Projectile* and click *Save*.

   e. Select *Projectile* in the Project pane again.

   f. Give it the Projectile tag by selecting *Projectile* from the *Tag* pop-up menu in the Inspector.

2. Open the FollowCam C# script in MonoDevelop and modify the following lines:

```
public class FollowCam : MonoBehaviour {

    …

    void FixedUpdate () {
//--      // if there's only one line following an if, it doesn't need braces      // a
//--      if (POI == null) return; // return if there is no poi
//--
//--      // Get the position of the poi
//--      Vector3 destination = POI.transform.position;

        Vector3 destination;
        // If there is no poi, return to P:[ 0, 0, 0 ]
        if (POI == null) {
            destination = Vector3.zero;
        } else {
            // Get the position of the poi
            destination = POI.transform.position;
            // If poi is a Projectile, check to see if it's at rest
            if (POI.tag == "Projectile") {
                // if it is sleeping (that is, not moving)
                if ( POI.GetComponent<Rigidbody>().IsSleeping() ) {
                    // return to default view
                    POI = null;
                    // in the next update
                    return;
                }
            }
        }
    }
```

```
        // Limit the X & Y to minimum values
        destination.x = Mathf.Max( minXY.x, destination.x );
        …
    }
}
```

    a. All of the lines preceded by //-- should be deleted or commented out.

Now, after the projectile has stopped moving (which makes `Rigidbody.IsSleeping()` true), the FollowCam will nullify its POI, resetting the camera back to its default position. However, it sure does take a long time for the projectile to come to rest. Let's make the physics engine "sleep a little easier," meaning that we will cause it to stop simulating physics on an object earlier than it otherwise would.

  3. Adjust the *Sleep Threshold* of the PhysicsManager:

    a. Open the PhysicsManager (*Edit > Project Settings > Physics*).

    b. Change *Sleep Threshold* from 0.005 to *0.02*. The Sleep Threshold is the amount of movement in a single physics engine frame that will cause a Rigidbody to continue to be simulated in the following frame. If an object moves less than this amount (now 2cm) in a single frame, PhysX will *sleep* that Rigidbody object and cease simulating it (i.e., cease moving the GameObject) until something happens to make it move again.

  4. Save your scene. Now when you play the game, the camera will reset, and you can fire again.

Adding a Projectile Trail

While Unity does have a built-in Trail Renderer effect, it won't really serve our purpose because we need more control over the trail than it allows. Instead, we'll make use of the *Line Renderer* upon which the Trail Renderer is built:

  1. Start by creating an empty GameObject (*GameObject > Create Empty*) and naming it *ProjectileLine.*

    a. Add a Line Renderer component (*Components > Effects > Line Renderer*).

    b. In the Inspector for ProjectileLine, expand the disclosure triangle for *Materials*. Set all Line Renderer component settings to those shown in Figure 29.11.

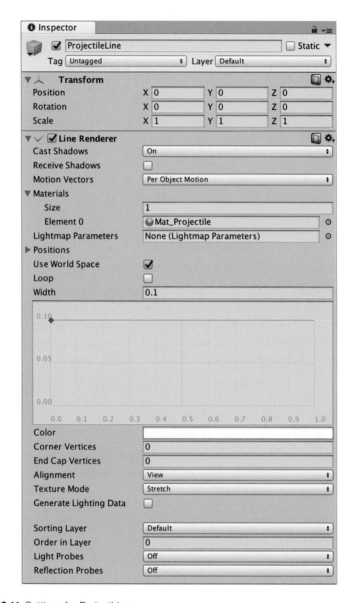

Figure 29.11 Settings for ProjectLine

2. Create a C# script (*Asset > Create > C# Script*) in the __Scripts folder. Name it *ProjectileLine* and attach it to the ProjectileLine GameObject. Open the *ProjectileLine* script in MonoDevelop and write the following code:

```
using System.Collections;
using System.Collections.Generic;
using UnityEngine;
```

```
public class ProjectileLine : MonoBehaviour {
    static public ProjectileLine S; // Singleton


    [Header("Set in Inspector")]
    public float                minDist = 0.1f;


    private LineRenderer        line;
    private GameObject          _poi;
    private List<Vector3>       points;


    void Awake() {
        S = this; // Set the singleton
        // Get a reference to the LineRenderer
        line = GetComponent<LineRenderer>();
        // Disable the LineRenderer until it's needed
        line.enabled = false;
        // Initialize the points List
        points = new List<Vector3>();
    }


    // This is a property (that is, a method masquerading as a field)
    public GameObject poi {
        get {
            return( _poi );
        }
        set {
            _poi = value;
            if ( _poi != null ) {
                // When _poi is set to something new, it resets everything
                line.enabled = false;
                points = new List<Vector3>();
                AddPoint();
            }
        }
    }


    // This can be used to clear the line directly
    public void Clear() {
        _poi = null;
        line.enabled = false;
        points = new List<Vector3>();
    }
```

```
public void AddPoint() {
    // This is called to add a point to the line
    Vector3 pt = _poi.transform.position;
    if ( points.Count > 0 && (pt - lastPoint).magnitude < minDist ) {
        // If the point isn't far enough from the last point, it returns
        return;
    }
    if ( points.Count == 0 ) {  // If this is the launch point...
        Vector3 launchPosDiff = pt - Slingshot.LAUNCH_POS; // To be defined
        // ...it adds an extra bit of line to aid aiming later
        points.Add( pt + launchPosDiff );
        points.Add(pt);
        line.positionCount = 2;
        // Sets the first two points
        line.SetPosition(0, points[0] );
        line.SetPosition(1, points[1] );
        // Enables the LineRenderer
        line.enabled = true;
    } else {
        // Normal behavior of adding a point
        points.Add( pt );
        line.positionCount = points.Count;
        line.SetPosition( points.Count-1, lastPoint );
        line.enabled = true;
    }
}


// Returns the location of the most recently added point
public Vector3 lastPoint {
    get {
        if (points == null) {
            // If there are no points, returns Vector3.zero
            return( Vector3.zero );
        }
        return( points[points.Count-1] );
    }
}


void FixedUpdate () {
    if ( poi == null ) {
        // If there is no poi, search for one
        if (FollowCam.POI != null) {
```

```
            if (FollowCam.POI.tag == "Projectile") {
                poi = FollowCam.POI;
            } else {
                return; // Return if we didn't find a poi
            }
        } else {
            return; // Return if we didn't find a poi
        }
    }
    // If there is a poi, it's loc is added every FixedUpdate
    AddPoint();
    if ( FollowCam.POI == null ) {
        // Once FollowCam.POI is null, make the local poi nulll too
        poi = null;
    }
}
}
```

3. You must also add a static LAUNCH_POS property to the Slingshot C# script to allow AddPoint() to reference the location of Slingshot's launchPoint:

```
public class Slingshot : MonoBehaviour {
    static private Slingshot S;                                          // a
    // fields set in the Unity Inspector pane
    [Header("Set in  Inspector")]
    …
    private Rigidbody          projectileRigidbody;

    static public Vector3 LAUNCH_POS {                                   // b
        get {
            if (S == null) return Vector3.zero;
            return S.launchPos;
        }
    }

    void Awake() {
        S = this;                                                       // c
        Transform launchPointTrans = transform.FindChild("LaunchPoint");
        …
    }
    …
}
```

a. This is a private static instance of Slingshot that will act like a Singleton, except it will be private, so only instances of the Slingshot class can access it.

b. This static public property uses the static private Slingshot instance S to allow public access to read the value of the Slingshot's launchPos. If somehow S is null, [0, 0, 0] returns.

c. Here, this instance of Slingshot is assigned to S. Because `Awake()` is the first thing that runs on any instance of a MonoBehaviour subclass, S should be set before LAUNCH_POS is ever requested.

Now when you play the game, you should get a nice gray line that traces the path of the projectile as it moves. The line is replaced with each subsequent shot.

4. Save your scene.

Hitting the Goal

The goal of the castle needs to react when hit by the projectile:

1. Create a new C# script named *Goal* and attach it to the Goal prefab in the _Prefabs folder of the Project pane. Then, enter the following code into the Goal script.

```csharp
using UnityEngine;
using System.Collections;

public class Goal : MonoBehaviour {
    // A static field accessible by code anywhere
    static public bool       goalMet = false;

    void OnTriggerEnter( Collider other ) {
        // When the trigger is hit by something
        // Check to see if it's a Projectile
        if ( other.gameObject.tag == "Projectile" ) {
            // If so, set goalMet to true
            Goal.goalMet = true;
            // Also set the alpha of the color to higher opacity
            Material mat = GetComponent<Renderer>().material;
            Color c = mat.color;
            c.a = 1;
            mat.color = c;
        }
    }
}
```

Now, if you can hit the goal with a projectile, the goal will turn bright green. It might take several shots to actually get through this castle. To make this easier, you can select a lot of the walls of the castle and deactivate them by unchecking the check box directly beneath the word *Inspector* at the top of the Inspector pane. Just be sure to reactivate them after you've tested the Goal.

2. Save your scene.

Adding More Castles

The single castle as served well so far, but let's add a few more.

1. Rename Castle to *Castle_0*.

2. Make Castle_0 a prefab by dragging it into the _Prefabs folder of the Project pane. When you're sure there is a Castle_0 prefab, delete the Castle_0 instance in the Hierarchy.[7]

3. Make a duplicate of the Castle_0 prefab in the Project pane (which will name itself *Castle_1*).

4. Drop Castle_1 into the Scene pane, and change its layout. You will likely "Break Prefab Instance" if you delete one of the walls. That is completely fine. Just structure Castle_1 however you like.[8]

5. When you have finished designing your Castle_1, select Castle_1 in the Hierarchy and click the *Prefab Apply* button near the top of the Castle_1 Inspector (it's in a row with the Select and Revert buttons). Clicking Apply assigns changes to this instance back to the Castle_1 prefab.

6. Now you can delete the Castle_1 instance in the Hierarchy.

Repeat this process to make a few different castles. Figure 29.12 shows a few that I made.

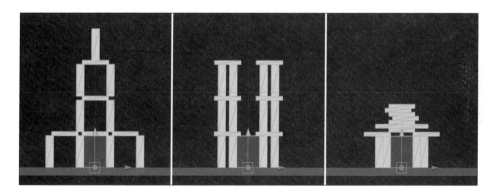

Figure 29.12 More castles

7. After you've created all the castles, make sure that none are left in the Hierarchy, and save your scene.

---

7. When you make Castle_0 a prefab, all the Slab and Wall instances lose their links to the Slab and Wall prefabs. Unity is in the middle of changing this and allowing *nested* prefabs, but this was not yet complete in Unity 2017. See http://book.prototools.net for more information if your prefabs seem to work strangely, and I'll have an update there.

8. If you hold down the Command key on macOS (or the Ctrl key on Windows), it should snap your movement of Walls and Slabs to every 0.5m, which can make it easier to arrange a castle. Also, you want to avoid having any castle blocks actually intersect each other, or they could push apart like the blocks did in the Chapter 19, "Hello World" example. Because the RigidbodySleep function forces the blocks to sleep initially, this pushing-apart effect won't happen until the projectile hits the castle, so it could make a nice exploding castle effect, if that's what you want.

Adding UI to the Scene

Follow these steps to add UI to the scene:

1. Add a UI Text to your scene (*GameObject > UI > Text*) and name it *UIText_Level*.

2. Create a second UI Text and name it *UIText_Shots*.

3. Give each the settings shown in Figure 29.13.

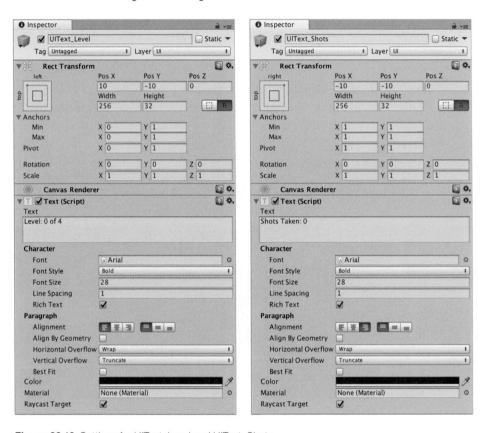

Figure 29.13 Settings for UIText_Level and UIText_Shots

4. Create a UI Button (*GameObject > UI > Button*). Name this button *UIButton_View*.

5. Set the *Rect Transform* of UIButton_View to the settings shown in Figure 29.14, but ignore the settings outside of Rect Transform for now.

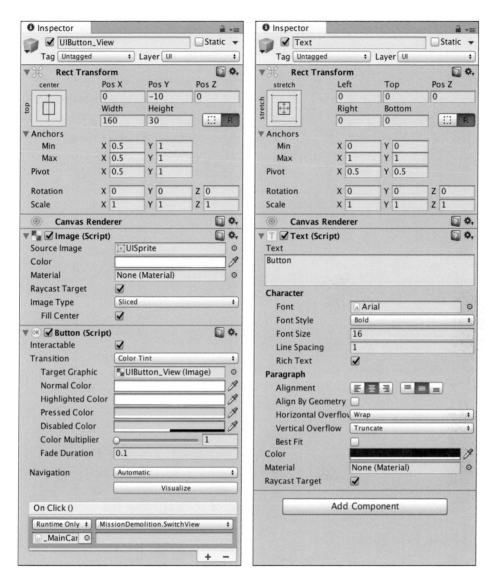

Figure 29.14 Settings for UIButton_View and its Text child

6. Open the disclosure triangle next to UIButton_View in the Hierarchy and give the *Text* child of UIButton_View the *Text (Script)* settings shown in Figure 29.14. You shouldn't need to change anything outside the *Character* section. Save your scene when you're done.

Adding More Game Management

First, you need a camera location from which you can view both the slingshot and castle.

1. Create a new empty GameObject (*GameObject > Create Empty*) and name it *ViewBoth*. Set the transform of ViewBoth to P:[25, 25, 0] R:[0, 0, 0] S:[1, 1, 1]. This serves as the POI for the camera when you want to view both the castle and the slingshot.

2. Create a new C# script in the __Scripts folder named *MissionDemolition*, and attach it to _MainCamera. This serves as the game state manager for the game. Open the MissionDemolition script and write the following code:

```csharp
using UnityEngine;
using System.Collections;
using UnityEngine.UI;                                              // a

public enum GameMode {                                            // b
    idle,
    playing,
    levelEnd
}

public class MissionDemolition : MonoBehaviour {
    static private MissionDemolition S; // a private Singleton

    [Header("Set in Inspector")]
    public Text             uitLevel;  // The UIText_Level Text
    public Text             uitShots;  // The UIText_Shots Text
    public Text             uitButton; // The Text on UIButton_View
    public Vector3          castlePos; // The place to put castles
    public GameObject[]     castles;   // An array of the castles

    [Header("Set Dynamically")]
    public int          level;     // The current level
    public int          levelMax;  // The number of levels
    public int          shotsTaken;
    public GameObject   castle;    // The current castle
    public GameMode     mode = GameMode.idle;
    public string       showing = "Show Slingshot"; // FollowCam mode
```

```
void Start() {
    S = this; // Define the Singleton

    level = 0;
    levelMax = castles.Length;
    StartLevel();
}

void StartLevel() {
    // Get rid of the old castle if one exists
    if (castle != null) {
        Destroy( castle );
    }

    // Destroy old projectiles if they exist
    GameObject[] gos = GameObject.FindGameObjectsWithTag("Projectile");
    foreach (GameObject pTemp in gos) {
        Destroy( pTemp );
    }

    // Instantiate the new castle
    castle = Instantiate<GameObject>( castles[level] );
    castle.transform.position = castlePos;
    shotsTaken = 0;

    // Reset the camera
    SwitchView("Show Both");
    ProjectileLine.S.Clear();

    // Reset the goal
    Goal.goalMet = false;

    UpdateGUI();

    mode = GameMode.playing;
}

void UpdateGUI() {
    // Show the data in the GUITexts
    uitLevel.text = "Level: "+(level+1)+" of "+levelMax;
    uitShots.text = "Shots Taken: "+shotsTaken;
}
```

```
void Update() {
    UpdateGUI();

    // Check for level end
    if ( (mode == GameMode.playing) && Goal.goalMet ) {
        // Change mode to stop checking for level end
        mode = GameMode.levelEnd;
        // Zoom out
        SwitchView("Show Both");
        // Start the next level in 2 seconds
        Invoke("NextLevel", 2f);
    }
}

void NextLevel() {
    level++;
    if (level == levelMax) {
        level = 0;
    }
    StartLevel();
}

public void SwitchView( string eView = "" ) {                    // c
    if (eView == "") {
        eView = uitButton.text;
    }
    showing = eView;
    switch (showing) {
        case "Show Slingshot":
            FollowCam.POI = null;
            uitButton.text = "Show Castle";
            break;

        case "Show Castle":
            FollowCam.POI = S.castle;
            uitButton.text = "Show Both";
            break;

        case "Show Both":
            FollowCam.POI = GameObject.Find("ViewBoth");
            uitButton.text = "Show Slingshot";
            break;
```

```
        }
    }


    // Static method that allows code anywhere to increment shotsTaken
    public static void ShotFired() {                                    // d
        S.shotsTaken++;
    }


}
```

a. You must add this `using UnityEngine.UI;` statement to use any of the uGUI classes like Text and Button.

b. This is the first instance of an enum in this part of the book. See the "Enum" sidebar for more info.

c. The `public SwitchView()` method will be called both by this instance of MissionDemolition and by the Button in the GUI (that you'll implement soon). The `string eView = ""` default parameter gives `eView` a default value of `""`, meaning that you don't need to pass in a string. This allows `SwitchView()` to be called either as `SwitchView("Show Both")` or as `SwitchView()`. If no string is passed in, the first `if` statement of the method sets `eView` to the current text on the Button at the top of the GUI.

d. `ShotFired()` is a `static public` method that Slingshot calls to let MissionDemolition know when a shot was fired.

ENUM

An *enum* (or enumeration) is a way of defining specific, named numbers in C#. The enum definition at the top of the MissionDemolition C# script declares an enum type `GameMode` with three potential values: `idle`, `playing`, and `levelEnd`. After you define an enum, you can then declare a variable that uses the defined enum as its type.

```
public GameMode mode = GameMode.idle;
```

The preceding line creates a new variable named `mode` that is of the type `GameMode` and has the value `GameMode.idle`.

You often use enums in code when only a few specific options exist for a variable and you want those options to be easily readable by humans. Alternatively, passing the type of game mode as a string (e.g., "idle," "playing," or "levelEnd") would be possible, but the enum is a much cleaner way of doing this that isn't as susceptible to misspelling and that allows for autocomplete while typing.

For more information about enums, see Appendix B, "Useful Concepts."

3. Now that a static `ShotFired()` method exists in the MissionDemolition class, calling it from the Slingshot class is possible. Add the following bold line to the Slingshot C# script:

```
public class Slingshot : MonoBehaviour {

    ...

    void Update() {

        ...

        if ( Input.GetMouseButtonUp(0) ) {
            // The mouse has been released

            ...

            FollowCam.POI = projectile;
            projectile = null;
            MissionDemolition.ShotFired();                          // a
            ProjectileLine.S.poi = projectile;                      // b
        }

    }

}
```

a. Because the `ShotFired()` method on MissionDemolition is static, you can access it through the MissionDemolition class itself rather than being required to access it via a specific instance of MissionDemolition. When Slingshot calls `MissionDemolition.ShotFired()`, it causes `MissionDemolition.S.shotsTaken` to increment.

b. This line causes the ProjectileLine to follow the new Projectile when it's fired.

4. Save all of your scripts and switch back to Unity.

5. Select *UIButton_View* in the Hierarchy, and look at the bottom of the *Button (Script)* Inspector. Click the + button in the *On Click()* section of that Inspector.

a. Underneath the *Runtime Only* button is a field that currently displays *None (Object)*.

b. Click the tiny circular target to the right of this *None (Object)* field and choose *_Main-Camera* from the window that pops up (double-click *_MainCamera*). This chooses *_MainCamera* as the GameObject that will receive the call from UIButton_View.

c. Click the pop-up menu button that currently displays *No Function* and choose *Mission-Demolition > SwitchView(String)*.[9]

As a result of this, whenever UIButton_View is clicked, it calls the public `SwitchView()` method of the MissionDemolition instance attached to _MainCamera. Your *Button (Script)* inspector should now look like the one shown in Figure 29.14.

6. Select *_MainCamera* in the Hierarchy. In the *MissionDemolition (Script)* component Inspector, you must set a few variables.

---

9. The gray field that appears below the *MissionDemolition.SwitchView* button allows you to enter a string to be passed into the SwitchView method. Leaving this blank passes the empty string " " into SwitchView, which is the same as the default value for the optional eView parameter, so you do not need to change this field.

a. Set `castlePos` to [50, -9.5, 0], placing the castles a nice distance from your slingshot.

b. To set `uitLevel`, click the target in the Inspector to the right of uitLevel and select *UIText_Level* from the Scene tab in the pop-up dialog box.

c. Click the target next to `uitShots` in the Inspector and choose *UIText_Shots* from the Scene tab.

d. Click the target next to `uitButton` and choose *Text* from the Scene tab (this is the only other uGUI Text in the scene, and it's the Text label on UIButton_View).

e. Click the disclosure triangle next to `castles` and set *Size* to the number of castles you made previously. (In the example in Figure 29.15, I made four castles.)

f. Drag each of the numbered Castle prefabs you made into an element of the `castles` array to set the levels for your game. Try to order them from easiest to most difficult.

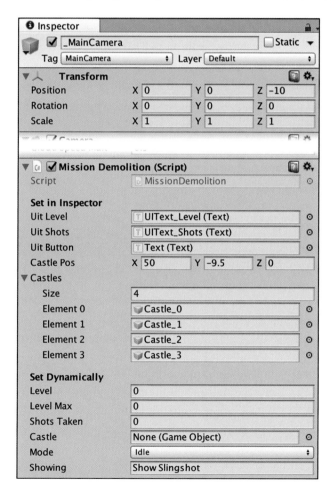

Figure 29.15 Final settings (with Castles array) for _MainCamera:MissionDemolition

7. Save your scene!

Now the game can play through various levels and keep track of how many shots you've fired. You can also click the button at the top of the screen to switch views.

Summary

That's it for the *Mission Demolition* prototype. In just one chapter, you've made a physics-based game like *Angry Birds* that you can continue to improve and expand on your own. This and all the following tutorials are really meant to be frameworks on top of which you can build whatever game you want.

Next Steps

You could add a ton of additional features, some of which include the following:

- Use PlayerPrefs to store the best score on each level as you did in Apple Picker.
- Make the castle parts out of various materials, some of which would have more or less mass. Some materials could even break if struck hard enough.
- Show lines for multiple previous paths rather than just the most recent one.
- Use a Line Renderer to draw the rubber band of the slingshot.
- Implement actual parallax scrolling on the background clouds, and add more background elements like mountains or buildings.
- Anything else you want!

After you've worked your way through the other prototypes in this book, come back to this one and think about what you could add to it. Create your own designs, show them to people, and iterate to make the game better. Remember that design is always an iterative process. If you make a change you don't like, don't let it discourage you; just chalk it up to experience and try something else.

CHAPTER 30

PROTOTYPE 3: *SPACE SHMUP*

The SHMUP (or shoot 'em up) game genre includes such classic games as *Galaga* and *Galaxian* from the 1980s and the modern masterpiece *Ikaruga*.

In this chapter, you create a SHMUP using several programming techniques that will serve you well throughout your programming and prototyping careers. These include class inheritance, static fields and methods, and the singleton pattern. Though you've seen many of these techniques before, you will use them more extensively in this prototype.

Getting Started: Prototype 3

In this project, you make a prototype for a classic space-based SHMUP. This chapter will get you to the same basic prototype level as the previous two chapters, and the next chapter will show you how to implement several additional features. Figure 30.1 shows an image of what the finished prototype will look like after both chapters. These images show the player ship at the bottom surrounded by a green shield as well as several enemy types and upgrades (the power-up cubes marked B, O, and S).

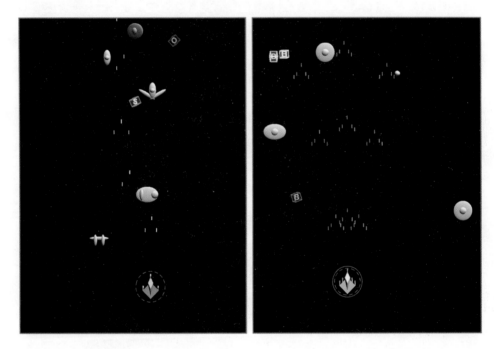

Figure 30.1 Two views of the *Space SHMUP* game prototype. The player is using the blaster weapon in the left image and the spread weapon in the right.

Importing a Unity Asset Package

One new thing in the setup for this prototype is that you must download and import a custom Unity asset package. The creation of complex art and imagery for games is beyond the scope of this book, but I've created a package of some simple assets for you that will allow you to create all the visual effects required for this game. Of course, as mentioned several times throughout this book, when you're making a prototype, how it plays and feels are much more important than how it looks, but having an understanding of how to work with art assets is still important.

To download and install the package mentioned in the sidebar "Set Up the Project for This Chapter," first follow the URL listed (http://book.prototools.net) and search for this chapter. Download C30_Space_SHMUP_Starter.unitypackage to your machine, which will usually place it in your *Downloads* folder. Open your project in Unity and select *Assets > Import Package > Custom Package* from the menu bar. Navigate to and select *C30_Space_SHMUP_Starter.unitypackage* from your Downloads folder. The import dialog box opens, as shown in Figure 30.2.

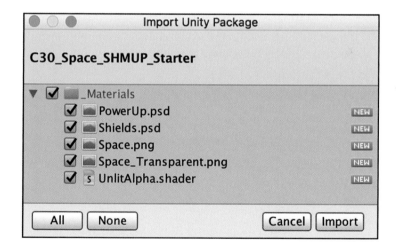

Figure 30.2 The .unitypackage import dialog box

Select all the files as shown in Figure 30.2 (by clicking the *All* button), and click *Import*. This places four new *textures* and one new *shader* into the *_Materials* folder. Textures are usually just image files. The creation of textures is beyond the scope of this book, but many books and online tutorials cover texture creation. *Adobe Photoshop* is probably the most commonly used image editing tool, but it is very expensive. A common open source alternative is *Gimp* (http://www.gimp.org), and a very good, surprisingly cheap commercial competitor is *Affinity Photo* (https://affinity.serif.com/photo).

The creation of *shaders* is also far beyond the scope of this book. Shaders are programs that tell your computer how to render a texture on a GameObject. They can make a scene look realistic, cartoony, or however else you like, and they are an important part of the graphics of any modern game. Unity uses its own unique shader language called ShaderLab. If you want to learn more about it, a good place to start is the Unity Shader Reference documentation (http://docs.unity3d.com/Documentation/Components/SL-Reference.html).

The included shader is a simple one that bypasses most of the things a shader can do to simply render a colored, non-lit shape on the screen. For on-screen elements that you want to be a specific bright color, this custom UnlitAlpha.shader is perfect. UnlitAlpha also allows for alpha blending and transparency, which will be very useful for the power-up cubes in this game.

Setting the Scene

Follow these steps to set the scene (use a pencil to check them off as you go):

1. Select *Directional Light* in the Hierarchy and set its transform to:

   P:[0, 20, 0]   R:[50, –30, 0]   S:[1, 1, 1]

2. Make sure that you renamed *Main Camera* to *_MainCamera* (as you were instructed in the project setup sidebar). Select *_MainCamera* and set its transform to:

   P:[0, 0, -10]   R:[0, 0, 0]   S:[1, 1, 1]

3. In the Camera component of *_MainCamera*, set the following. Then save your scene.

   - *Clear Flags* to Solid Color
   - *Background* to black (with 255 alpha; RGBA:[0, 0, 0, 255])
   - *Projection* to Orthographic
   - *Size* to 40 (after setting Projection)
   - *Near Clipping Plane* to 0.3
   - *Far Clipping Plane* to 100

4. Because this game will be a vertical, top-down shooter, you need to set an aspect ratio for the Game pane that is in portrait orientation. In the Game pane, click the pop-up menu list of aspect ratios that should currently show *Free Aspect* (see Figure 30.3). At the bottom of the list is a + symbol. Click it to add a new aspect ratio preset. Set the values to those shown in Figure 30.3, and then click *Add*. Set the Game pane to this new *Portrait (3:4)* aspect ratio.

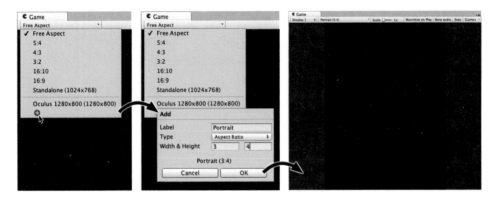

Figure 30.3 Adding a new aspect ratio preset to the Game pane

Making the Hero Ship

In this chapter, you will interleave the construction of artwork and code rather than building all the art first. To make the player's spaceship, complete these steps:

1. Create an empty GameObject and name it _Hero (*GameObject > Create Empty*). Set its transform to P:[0, 0, 0] R:[0, 0, 0] S:[1, 1, 1].

2. Create a cube (*GameObject > 3D Object > Cube*) and drag it onto _Hero, making it a child thereof. Name the cube *Wing* and set its transform to P:[0, -1, 0] R:[0, 0, 45] S:[3, 3, 0.5].

3. Create an empty GameObject, name it *Cockpit*, and make it a child of _Hero.

4. Create a cube and make it a child of Cockpit (you can do this by right-clicking on Cockpit and choosing *3D Object > Cube*). Set the Cube's transform to P:[0, 0, 0] R:[315, 0, 45] S:[1, 1, 1].

5. Select Cockpit again and set its transform to P:[0, 0, 0] R:[0, 0, 180] S:[1, 3, 1]. This uses the same trick you learned in Chapter 27, "Object-Oriented Thinking," to make a quick, angular ship.

6. Select _Hero in the Hierarchy and click the *Add Component* button in the Inspector. Choose *New Script* from the pop-up menu. Name the script *Hero*, double-check that *Language* is C Sharp, and click *Create and Add*. This is another way to make a new script and attach it to a GameObject. In the Project pane, move the Hero script into the __Scripts folder.

7. Add a Rigidbody component to _Hero by selecting _Hero in the Hierarchy and then choosing *Add Component > Physics > Rigidbody* from the *Add Component* button in the Inspector. Set the following on the Rigidbody component of _Hero:

   ▪ *Use Gravity* to false (unchecked)

   ▪ *isKinematic* to true (checked)

   ▪ *Constraints*: freeze Z position and X, Y, and Z rotation (by checking them)

You'll add more to _Hero later, but this will suffice for now.

8. Save your scene! Remember that you should be saving your scene every time you make a change to it. I'll quiz you later.

The Hero `Update()` Method

In the code listing that follows, the `Update()` method first reads the horizontal and vertical axes from the InputManager (see the "`Input.GetAxis()` and The InputManager" sidebar), placing values between –1 and 1 into the floats `xAxis` and `yAxis`. The second chunk of `Update()` code moves the ship in a time-based way, taking into account the `speed` setting.

The last line (marked `//  c`) rotates the ship based on the input. Although you earlier froze the rotation in _Hero's Rigidbody component, you can still manually set the rotation on a Rigidbody with isKinematic set to true. (As discussed in the previous chapter, isKinematic = true means that the Rigidbody will be tracked by the physics system but that it will not move automatically due to Rigidbody.velocity.) This rotation makes the movement of the ship feel more dynamic and expressive, or "juicy."[1]

Open the Hero C# script in MonoDevelop and enter the following code:

```
using System.Collections;
using System.Collections.Generic;
using UnityEngine;

public class Hero : MonoBehaviour {
    static public Hero        S; // Singleton                                    // a

    [Header("Set in Inspector")]
    // These fields control the movement of the ship
    public float            speed = 30;
    public float            rollMult = -45;
    public float            pitchMult = 30;

    [Header("Set Dynamically")]
    public float            shieldLevel = 1;

    void Awake() {
        if (S == null) {
```

---

1. *Juiciness,* as a term that relates to gameplay, was coined in 2005 by Kyle Gabler and the other members of the Experimental Gameplay Project at Carnegie Mellon University's Entertainment Technology Center. To them, a juicy element had "constant and bountiful user feedback." You can read about it more in their Gamasutra article by searching online for "Gamasutra How to Prototype a Game in Under 7 Days."

```
            S = this; // Set the Singleton                              // a
        } else {
            Debug.LogError("Hero.Awake() - Attempted to assign second Hero.S!");
        }
    }

    void Update () {
        // Pull in information from the Input class
        float xAxis = Input.GetAxis("Horizontal");                      // b
        float yAxis = Input.GetAxis("Vertical");                        // b

        // Change transform.position based on the axes
        Vector3 pos = transform.position;
        pos.x += xAxis * speed * Time.deltaTime;
        pos.y += yAxis * speed * Time.deltaTime;
        transform.position = pos;

        // Rotate the ship to make it feel more dynamic                 // c
        transform.rotation = Quaternion.Euler(yAxis*pitchMult,xAxis*rollMult,0);
    }
}
```

a. The singleton for the Hero class (see *Software Design Patterns* in Appendix B). The code in `Awake()` shows an error in the Console pane if you try to set Hero.S after it has already been set (which would happen if somehow there were two GameObjects in the same scene that both had Hero scripts attached or two Hero components attached to a single GameObject).

b. These two lines use Unity's Input class to pull information from the Unity InputManager. See the sidebar for more information.

c. The `transform.rotation`... line below this comment is used to give the ship a bit of rotation based on the speed at which it is moving, which can make the ship feel more reactive and juicy.

Try playing the game and moving the ship with the WASD or arrow keys to see how it feels. The settings for `speed`, `rollMult`, and `pitchMult` work for me, but this is your game, and you should have settings that feel right to you. Make changes as necessary in the Unity Inspector for _Hero.

Part of what makes this feel nice is the apparent inertia that the ship carries. When you release the movement key, the ship takes a little while to slow down. Similarly, upon pressing a movement key, the ship takes a little while to get up to speed. This apparent movement inertia is caused by the *sensitivity* and *gravity* axis settings that are described in the sidebar. Changing these settings in the InputManager will affect the movement and maneuverability of _Hero.

INPUT.GETAXIS() AND THE INPUTMANAGER

Much of the code in the `Hero.Update()` code listing should look familiar to you, though this is the first time in the book that you've seen the `Input.GetAxis()` method. Unity's InputManager allows you to configure various input axes, and those axes can be read through `Input.GetAxis()`. To view the default Input axes, choose *Edit > Project Settings > Input* from the menu bar.

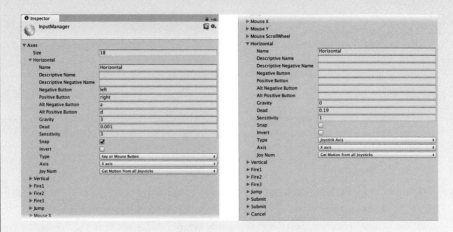

Figure 30.4 Unity's InputManager showing some of the default settings (split in two halves)

One thing to note about the settings in Figure 30.4 is that several axis names are listed twice (e.g., Horizontal, Vertical, and Jump). As you can see in the expanded view of the two Horizontal axes in the figure, this allows the Horizontal axis to be controlled by either presses on the keyboard (shown in the left image of Figure 30.4) or a joystick axis (shown in the right image). This is one of the great strengths of the input axes; several different types of input can control a single axis. As a result, your games only need one line to read the value of an axis rather than a line to handle joystick input, a line for each arrow key, and a line each for the A and D keys to handle horizontal input.

Every call to `Input.GetAxis()` returns a float between –1 and 1 in value (with a default of 0). Each axis in the InputManager also includes values for *Sensitivity* and *Gravity*, though these are only used for *Key or Mouse Button* input (see the left image of Figure 30.4). Sensitivity and gravity cause the axis value to *interpolate* smoothly when a key is pressed or released (i.e., instead of immediately jumping to the final value, the axis value will blend from the original value to the final value over time). In the Horizontal axis shown, a sensitivity of 3 means that when the right-arrow key is pressed, it takes 1/3 of a second for the value to interpolate from 0 to 1. A gravity of 3 means that when the right-arrow key is released, it takes 1/3 of a second for the axis value to interpolate back to 0. The higher the sensitivity or gravity, the faster the interpolation takes place.

As with many things in Unity, you can find out a lot more about the InputManager by clicking the Help button (that looks like a blue book with a question mark and is between the name InputManager and the gear at the top of the Inspector).

The Hero Shield

The shield for _Hero is a combination of a transparent, textured quad (to provide the visuals) and a Sphere Collider (for collision handling):

1. Create a new quad (*GameObject > 3D Object > Quad*). Rename the quad *Shield* and make it a child of _Hero. Set the transform of Shield to P:[0, 0, 0], R:[0, 0, 0], S:[8, 8, 8].

2. Select *Shield* in the Hierarchy and delete the existing Mesh Collider component by clicking the tiny gear to the right of the Mesh Collider name in the Inspector and choosing *Remove Component* from the pop-up menu. Add a *Sphere Collider* component (*Component > Physics > Sphere Collider*).

3. Create a new material (*Assets > Create > Material*), name it *Mat_Shield*, and place it in the _Materials folder in the Project pane. Drag *Mat_Shield* onto the *Shield* under _Hero in the Hierarchy to assign it to the Shield quad.

4. Select *Shield* in the Hierarchy, and you can now see Mat_Shield in the Inspector for Shield. Set the Shader of Mat_Shield to *ProtoTools > UnlitAlpha*. Below the shader selection pop-up for Mat_Shield, you should see an area that allows you to choose the main color for the material as well as the texture. (If you don't see the shader properties, click once on the name *Mat_Shield* in the Inspector, and it should appear.)

5. Click *Select* in the bottom-right corner of the texture square and select the texture named *Shields*. Click the color swatch next to *Main Color* and choose a bright green (RGBA:[0, 255, 0, 255]). Then set:
   - *Tiling.x* to 0.2
   - *Offset.x* to 0.4
   - *Tiling.y* should remain 1.0
   - *Offset.y* should remain 0

The Shield texture was designed to be split into five sections horizontally. The X Tiling of 0.2 causes Mat_Shield to only use 1/5 of the total Shield texture in the X direction, and the X Offset chooses which fifth. Try X Offsets of 0, 0.2, 0.4, 0.6, and 0.8 to see the different levels of shield strength.

6. Create a new C# script named *Shield* (*Asset > Create > C# Script*). Drop it into the __Scripts folder in the Project pane and then drag it onto Shield in the Hierarchy to assign it as a component of the Shield GameObject.

7. Open the Shield script in MonoDevelop and enter the following code:

```csharp
using System.Collections;
using System.Collections.Generic;
using UnityEngine;

public class Shield : MonoBehaviour {
    [Header("Set in Inspector")]
    public float    rotationsPerSecond = 0.1f;

    [Header("Set Dynamically")]
    public int      levelShown = 0;

    // This non-public variable will not appear in the Inspector
    Material        mat;                                            // a

    void Start() {
        mat = GetComponent<Renderer>().material;                   // b
    }

    void Update () {
        // Read the current shield level from the Hero Singleton
        int currLevel = Mathf.FloorToInt( Hero.S.shieldLevel );    // c
        // If this is different from levelShown...
        if (levelShown != currLevel) {
            levelShown = currLevel;
            // Adjust the texture offset to show different shield level
            mat.mainTextureOffset = new Vector2( 0.2f*levelShown, 0 );  // d
        }
        // Rotate the shield a bit every frame in a time-based way
        float rZ = -(rotationsPerSecond*Time.time*360) % 360f;     // e
        transform.rotation = Quaternion.Euler( 0, 0, rZ );
    }
}
```

a. The Material field `mat` is *not* declared public, so it will not be visible in the Inspector, and it will not be able to be accessed outside of this Shield class.

b. In `Start()`, `mat` is defined as the material of the Renderer component on this GameObject (Shield in the Hierarchy). This allows you to quickly set the texture offset in the line marked // d.

c. `currLevel` is set to the *floor* of the current `Hero.S.shieldLevel` float. Flooring the `shieldLevel` ensures that the shield jumps to the new X Offset rather than show an Offset between two shield icons.

d. This line adjusts the X Offset of Mat_Shield to show the proper shield level.

e. This line and the next cause the Shield GameObject to rotate slowly about the z axis.

Keeping _Hero on Screen

The motion of your _Hero ship should feel pretty good now, and the rotating shield looks pretty nice, but at this point, you can easily drive the ship off the screen. To resolve this, you're going to make a reusable *component* script.[2] You can read more about the component software design pattern in Chapter 27, "Object-Oriented Thinking" and under *Software Design Patterns* in Appendix B, "Useful Concepts." In brief, a component is a small piece of code that is meant to work alongside others to add functionality to a GameObject without conflicting with other code on that object. Unity's components that you've worked with in the Inspector (e.g., Renderer, Transform, and so on) all follow this pattern. Now, you'll do the same with a small script to keep _Hero on screen. Note that this script only works with orthographic cameras.

1. Select _Hero in the Hierarchy and using the *Add Component* button in the Inspector, choose *Add Component > New Script*. Name the script *BoundsCheck* and click *Create and Add*. Drag the BoundsCheck script in the Project pane into the __Scripts folder.

2. Open the BoundsCheck script and add the following code:

```
using System.Collections;
using System.Collections.Generic;
using UnityEngine;

// To type the next 4 lines, start by typing /// and then Tab.
/// <summary>
/// Keeps a GameObject on screen.
/// Note that this ONLY works for an orthographic Main Camera at [ 0, 0, 0 ].
/// </summary>
public class BoundsCheck : MonoBehaviour {                           // a
    [Header("Set in Inspector")]
    public float    radius = 1f;

    [Header("Set Dynamically")]
    public float    camWidth;
    public float    camHeight;

    void Awake() {
        camHeight = Camera.main.orthographicSize;                    // b
        camWidth = camHeight * Camera.main.aspect;                   // c
    }

    void LateUpdate () {                                             // d
        Vector3 pos = transform.position;

        if (pos.x > camWidth - radius) {
            pos.x  = camWidth - radius;
        }
```

---

2. The first edition of this book had a much more complex system for keeping GameObjects on screen that was more than was needed for this chapter and somewhat confusing. I've replaced it with this version in the second edition to both streamline the chapter and to reinforce the concept of components.

```
    if (pos.x < -camWidth + radius) {
        pos.x  = -camWidth + radius;
    }

    if (pos.y > camHeight - radius) {
        pos.y  = camHeight - radius;
    }
    if (pos.y < -camHeight + radius) {
        pos.y  = -camHeight + radius;
    }

    transform.position = pos;
}

// Draw the bounds in the Scene pane using OnDrawGizmos()
void OnDrawGizmos () {                                                   // e
    if (!Application.isPlaying) return;
    Vector3 boundSize = new Vector3(camWidth*2, camHeight*2, 0.1f);
    Gizmos.DrawWireCube(Vector3.zero, boundSize);
}
}
```

a. Because this is intended to be a reusable piece of code, adding some internal documentation to it is useful. The lines above the class declaration that all begin with `///` are part of C#'s built-in documentation system.[3] After you've typed this, it interprets the text between the `<summary>` tags as a summary of what the class is used for. After typing it, hover your mouse over the name BoundsCheck on the line marked `// a`, and you should see a pop-up with this class summary.

b. `Camera.main` gives you access to the first camera with the tag *MainCamera* in your scene. Then, if the camera is orthographic, `.orthographicSize` gives you the Size number from the Camera Inspector (which is 40 in this case). This makes `camHeight` the distance from the origin of the world (position [0, 0, 0]) to the top or bottom edge of the screen in world coordinates.

c. `Camera.main.aspect` is the aspect ratio of the camera in width/height as defined by the aspect ratio of the Game pane (currently set to *Portrait (3:4)*). By multiplying `camHeight` by `.aspect`, you can get the distance from the origin to the left or right edge of the screen.

d. `LateUpdate()` is called every frame after `Update()` has been called on all GameObjects. If this code were in the `Update()` function, it might happen either before or after the `Update()` call on the Hero script. Putting this code in `LateUpdate()` avoids causing a *race condition* between the two `Update()` functions and ensures that `Hero.Update()` moves the _Hero GameObject to the new position each frame before this function is called and bounds _Hero to the screen.

---

3. Search online for "C# XML documentation" to learn more.

    e. `OnDrawGizmos()` is a built-in MonoBehaviour method that can draw to the Scene pane.

A *race condition* is an instance where the order in which two pieces of code execute (i.e., A before B or B before A) matters, but you don't have control over that order. For example, in this code, if `BoundsCheck.LateUpdate()` were to execute before `Hero.Update()`, the _Hero GameObject would potentially be moved out of bounds (because it would first limit the ship to the bounds and *then* move the ship). Using `LateUpdate()` in BoundsCheck enforces the execution order of the two scripts.

3. Click *Play* and try flying your ship around. Based on the default setting for `radius`, you should see that the ship stops while it is still 1m on screen. If you set `BoundsCheck.radius` to 4 in the _Hero Inspector, the ship stays entirely on screen. If you set `radius` to -4, the ship can exit the edge of the screen but will be locked there, ready to come right back on. Stop playback and set `radius` to 4.

Adding Some Enemies

Chapter 26, "Classes," covered a bit about the Enemy class and subclasses for a game like this. There you learned about setting up a superclass for all enemies that can be extended by subclasses. For this game, will you extend that further in the next chapter, but first, let's create the artwork.

Enemy Artwork

Because the hero ship has such an angular aesthetic, all the enemies will be constructed of spheres as shown in Figure 30.5.

Figure 30.5 Each of the five enemy ship types (lighting will differ slightly in Unity)

To create the artwork for Enemy_0 do the following:

1. Create an empty GameObject, name it *Enemy_0*, and set its transform to P:[-20, 10, 0], R:[0, 0, 0], S:[1, 1, 1]. This position is to make sure it doesn't overlap with _Hero as you build it.

2. Create a sphere named *Cockpit*, make it a child of Enemy_0, and set its transform to P:[0, 0, 0], R:[0, 0, 0], S:[2, 2, 1].

3. Create a second sphere named *Wing*, make it a child of Enemy_0, and set its transform to P:[0, 0, 0], R:[0, 0, 0], S:[5, 5, 0.5].

Another way of writing the preceding three steps for Enemy_0 would be:

Enemy_0 (Empty)	P:[-20, 10, 0]	R:[0, 0, 0]	S:[1, 1, 1]
Cockpit (Sphere)	P:[0, 0, 0]	R:[0, 0, 0]	S:[2, 2, 1]
Wing (Sphere)	P:[0, 0, 0]	R:[0, 0, 0]	S:[5, 5, 0.5]

4. Follow this formatting to make the remaining four enemies. When finished, they should look like the enemies shown in Figure 30.5.

   Enemy_1

Enemy_1 (Empty)	P:[-10, 10, 0]	R:[0, 0, 0]	S:[1, 1, 1]
Cockpit (Sphere)	P:[0, 0, 0]	R:[0, 0, 0]	S:[2, 2, 1]
Wing (Sphere)	P:[0, 0, 0]	R:[0, 0, 0]	S:[6, 4, 0.5]

   Enemy_2

Enemy_2 (Empty)	P:[0, 10, 0]	R:[0, 0, 0]	S:[1, 1, 1]
Cockpit (Sphere)	P:[-1.5, 0, 0]	R:[0, 0, 0]	S:[1, 3, 1]
Reactor (Sphere)	P:[2, 0, 0]	R:[0, 0, 0]	S:[2, 2, 1]
Wing (Sphere)	P:[0, 0, 0]	R:[0, 0, 0]	S:[6, 4, 0.5]

   Enemy_3

Enemy_3 (Empty)	P:[10, 10, 0]	R:[0, 0, 0]	S:[1, 1, 1]
CockpitL (Sphere)	P:[-1, 0, 0]	R:[0, 0, 0]	S:[1, 3, 1]
CockpitR (Sphere)	P:[1, 0, 0]	R:[0, 0, 0]	S:[1, 3, 1]
Wing (Sphere)	P:[0, 0.5, 0]	R:[0, 0, 0]	S:[5, 1, 0.5]

   Enemy_4

Enemy_4 (Empty)	P:[20, 10, 0]	R:[0, 0, 0]	S:[1, 1, 1]
Cockpit (Sphere)	P:[0, 1, 0]	R:[0, 0, 0]	S:[1.5, 1.5, 1.5]
Fuselage (Sphere)	P:[0, 1, 0]	R:[0, 0, 0]	S:[2, 4, 1]
WingL (Sphere)	P:[-1.5, 0, 0]	R:[0, 0, -30]	S:[5, 1, 0.5]
WingR (Sphere)	P:[1.5, 0, 0]	R:[0, 0, 30]	S:[5, 1, 0.5]

5. You must add a Rigidbody component to each of the enemy GameObjects (i.e., Enemy_0, Enemy_1, Enemy_2, Enemy_3, and Enemy_4). To add a Rigidbody, complete these steps:

   a. Select *Enemy_0* in the Hierarchy and choose *Component > Physics > Rigidbody* from the menu bar to add the Rigidbody component.

   b. In the Rigidbody component for the enemy, set *Use Gravity* to false.

   c. Set *isKinematic* to true.

   d. Open the disclosure triangle for *Constraints* and freeze Z position and X, Y, and Z rotation.

6. Now copy the Rigidbody component from Enemy_0 to all four other enemies. Do the following steps for each of the four other enemies:

a. Select *Enemy_0* in the Hierarchy and click the little *gear button* in the top-right corner of the Enemy_0 *Rigidbody* component.

b. From the pop-up menu, choose *Copy Component*.

c. Select the enemy that you want to add a Rigidbody to (e.g., Enemy_1).

d. Click the gear button in the top-right of the Transform component on the enemy.

e. Choose *Paste Component As New* from the pop-up menu.

This attaches a Rigidbody component to the enemy with the same settings as the Rigidbody that you copied from Enemy_0. Be sure to do this for all enemies. If a moving GameObject doesn't have a Rigidbody component, the GameObject's collider location will not move with the GameObject, but if a moving GameObject does have a Rigidbody, the colliders of both it and all of its children are updated every frame (which is why you don't need to add a Rigidbody component to any of the children of the enemy GameObjects).

7. Drag each of these enemies to the _Prefabs folder of the Project pane to create a prefab for each.

8. Delete all the enemy instances from the Hierarchy except for Enemy_0.

The Enemy C# Script

To create the Enemy script, follow these steps:

1. Create a new C# script named *Enemy* and place it into the __Scripts folder.

2. Select *Enemy_0* in the Project pane (not in the Hierarchy). In the Inspector for Enemy_0, click the *Add Component* button and choose *Scripts > Enemy* from the pop-up menu. After doing this, when you click on Enemy_0 in either the Project or Hierarchy panes, you should see an *Enemy (Script)* component attached.

3. Open the *Enemy* script in MonoDevelop and enter the following code:

```csharp
using System.Collections;          // Required for Arrays & other Collections
using System.Collections.Generic;  // Required for Lists and Dictionaries
using UnityEngine;                 // Required for Unity

public class Enemy : MonoBehaviour {
    [Header("Set in Inspector: Enemy")]
    public float      speed = 10f;      // The speed in m/s
    public float      fireRate = 0.3f;  // Seconds/shot (Unused)
    public float      health = 10;
    public int        score = 100;      // Points earned for destroying this

    // This is a Property: A method that acts like a field
    public Vector3 pos {                                        // a
```

```
        get {
            return( this.transform.position );
        }
        set {
            this.transform.position = value;
        }
    }

    void Update() {
        Move();
    }

    public virtual void Move() {                                    // b
        Vector3 tempPos = pos;
        tempPos.y -= speed * Time.deltaTime;
        pos = tempPos;
    }
}
```

   a. As was discussed in Chapter 26, "Classes," a *property* is a function masquerading as a field. This means that you can get and set the value of `pos` as if it were a class variable of Enemy.

   b. The `Move()` method gets the current position of this Enemy_0, moves it in the downward Y direction, and assigns it back to `pos` (setting the position of the GameObject).

4. In Unity, click *Play*, and the instance of Enemy_0 in the scene should move toward the bottom of the screen. However, with the current code, this instance will continue off screen and exist until you stop your game. You need to have the enemy destroy itself after it has moved entirely off screen. This is a great place to reuse the BoundsCheck component.

5. To attach the BoundsCheck script to the Enemy_0 prefab, select the *Enemy_0* prefab in the Hierarchy (not the Project pane this time). In the Inspector, click *Add Component* and choose *Add Component > Scripts > BoundsCheck*. This attaches the script to the instance of Enemy_0 in the Hierarchy, but it has not yet attached it to the Enemy_0 prefab in the Project pane. You can tell this because all the text in the *BoundsCheck (Script)* component is bold.

6. To apply this change made to the Enemy_0 instance back to its prefab, click *Apply* at the top of the Inspector for the Enemy_0 instance in the Hierarchy. Now check the Enemy_0 prefab in the Project pane to see that the script is attached.

7. Select the *Enemy_0* instance in the Hierarchy and set the `radius` value in the Bounds-Check Inspector to -2.5. Note that this value is bolded because it is different from the value on the prefab. Click *Apply* at the top of the Inspector again, and the radius value will no longer be bolded, showing you that it is the same value as the one on the prefab.

8. Click *Play*, and you'll see that the Enemy_0 instance stops right after it has gone off screen. However, instead of forcing Enemy_0 to remain on screen, you really want to be able to check whether it has gone off screen and then destroy it when it has.

9. To do so, make the following bolded modifications to the BoundsCheck script.

```
/// <summary>
/// Checks whether a GameObject is on screen and can force it to stay on screen.
/// Note that this ONLY works for an orthographic Main Camera.
/// </summary>
public class BoundsCheck : MonoBehaviour {
    [Header("Set in Inspector")]
    public float    radius = 1f;
    public bool     keepOnScreen = true;                            // a

    [Header("Set Dynamically")]
    public bool     isOnScreen = true;                              // b
    public float    camWidth;
    public float    camHeight;

    void Awake() { … }       // Remember, ellipses mean to not alter this method.

    void LateUpdate () {
        Vector3 pos = transform.position;                          // c
        isOnScreen = true;                                         // d

        if ( pos.x > camWidth - radius ) {
            pos.x  = camWidth - radius;
            isOnScreen = false;                                    // e
        }
        if ( pos.x < -camWidth + radius ) {
            pos.x  = -camWidth + radius;
            isOnScreen = false;                                    // e
        }

        if ( pos.y > camHeight - radius ) {
            pos.y  = camHeight - radius;
            isOnScreen = false;                                    // e
        }
        if ( pos.y < -camHeight + radius ) {
            pos.y  = -camHeight + radius;
            isOnScreen = false;                                    // e
        }

        if ( keepOnScreen && !isOnScreen ) {                       // f
            transform.position = pos;                              // g
            isOnScreen = true;
        }
    }

    …

}
```

a. `keepOnScreen` allows you to choose whether BoundsCheck forces a GameObject to stay on screen (`true`) or allows it to exit the screen and notifies you that it has done so (`false`).

b. `isOnScreen` turns false if the GameObject exits the screen. More accurately, it turns false if the GameObject goes past the edge of the screen minus the value of `radius`. This is why `radius` is set to –2.5 for Enemy_0, so that it is completely off screen before `isOnScreen` is set to `false`.

c. Remember that ellipses in code mean you should *not* modify the `Start()` method.

d. `isOnScreen` is set to true until proven false. This allows the value of `isOnScreen` to return to true if the GameObject was off screen in the last frame but has come back on in this frame.

e. If any of these four `if` statements are true, then the GameObject is outside of the area it is supposed to be in. `isOnScreen` is set to `false`, and `pos` is adjusted to a position that would bring the GameObject back "on screen."

f. If `keepOnScreen` is `true`, then you are trying to force the GameObject to stay on screen. If `keepOnScreen` is `true` and `isOnScreen` is `false`, then the GameObject has gone out of bounds and needs to be brought back in. In this case, `transform. position` is set to the updated `pos` that is on screen, and `isOnScreen` is set to `true` because this position assignment has now moved the GameObject back on screen.

   If `keepOnScreen` is `false`, then `pos` is *not* assigned back to `transform.position`, the GameObject is allowed to go off screen, and `isOnScreen` is allowed to remain `false`. The other possibility is that the GameObject was on screen the whole time, in which case, `isOnScreen` would still be `true` from when it was set on line `// d`.

g. Note that this line is now indented and inside the `if` statement on line `// f`.

Happily, all of these modifications to the code do not negatively impact the way it was used for _Hero, and everything there still works fine. You've created a reusable component that you can apply to both _Hero and the Enemy GameObjects.

Deleting the Enemy When It Goes Off Screen

Now that BoundsCheck can tell you when Enemy_0 goes off screen, you need to set it to properly do so.

1. Set `keepOnScreen` to `false` in the *BoundsCheck (Script)* component of the Enemy_0 prefab in the _Prefabs folder of the Project pane.

2. To ensure that this propagates to the Enemy_0 instance in the Hierarchy, select the instance in the Hierarchy and click the gear to the right of the *BoundsCheck (Script)* component heading in the Inspector. From the gear pop-up menu, choose *Revert to Prefab* to set the values of the instance in the Hierarchy to those on the prefab.

When you've done this, the *BoundsCheck (Script)* component on both the Enemy_0 prefab in the Project pane and the Enemy_0 instance in the Hierarchy should look like Figure 30.6.

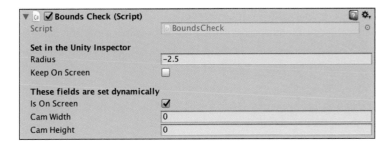

Figure 30.6 The *BoundsCheck (Script)* component settings for both the prefab and instance of Enemy_0

3. Add the following bold code to the Enemy script:

```
public class Enemy : MonoBehaviour {
    ...
    public int        score = 100; // Points earned for destroying this

    private BoundsCheck bndCheck;                                           // a

    void Awake() {                                                          // b
        bndCheck = GetComponent<BoundsCheck>();
    }

    ...

    void Update() {
        Move();

        if ( bndCheck != null && !bndCheck.isOnScreen ) {                   // c
            // Check to make sure it's gone off the bottom of the screen
            if ( pos.y < bndCheck.camHeight - bndCheck.radius ) {           // d
                // We're off the bottom, so destroy this GameObject
                Destroy( gameObject );
            }
        }
    }

    ...
}
```

a. This private variable allows this Enemy script to store a reference to the *BoundsCheck (Script)* component attached to the same GameObject.

b. This `Awake()` method searches for the BoundsCheck script component attached to this same GameObject. If there is not one, `bndCheck` will be set to `null`. Code like this that searches for components and caches references is often placed in the `Awake()` method so that the references are ready immediately when the GameObject is instantiated.

c. First checks to make sure `bndCheck` is not `null`. If you attached the Enemy script to a GameObject without attaching a BoundsCheck script as well, this could be the case. Only if `bndCheck != null` does the script check to see whether the GameObject is not on screen (according to BoundsCheck).

d. If `isOnScreen` is `false`, this line checks to see whether it is off screen because it has a `pos.y` that is too negative (i.e., it has gone off the bottom of the screen). If this is the case, the GameObject is destroyed.

This works and does what we want, but it seems a bit messy to be doing the same comparison of `pos.y` versus the `camHeight` and `radius` both here and in BoundsCheck.

It is generally considered good programming style to let each C# class (or component) handle the job it is meant to do and not have crossover like this. As such, let's alter BoundsCheck to be able to tell you in which direction the GameObject has gone off screen.

3. Modify the BoundsCheck script by adding the bolded code that follows:

```
public class BoundsCheck : MonoBehaviour {
    …
    public float     camHeight;
    [HideInInspector]
    public bool      offRight, offLeft, offUp, offDown;              // a

    void Start() { … }

    void LateUpdate () {
        Vector3 pos = transform.position;
        isOnScreen = true;
        offRight = offLeft = offUp = offDown = false;                // b

        if ( pos.x > camWidth - radius ) {
            pos.x  = camWidth - radius;
            offRight = true;                                          // c
        }
        if ( pos.x < -camWidth + radius ) {
            pos.x  = -camWidth + radius;
            offLeft = true;                                           // c
        }

        if ( pos.y > camHeight - radius ) {
            pos.y  = camHeight - radius;
            offUp = true;                                             // c
        }
```

```
        if ( pos.y < -camHeight + radius ) {
            pos.y = -camHeight + radius;
            offDown = true;                                              // c
        }

        isOnScreen = !(offRight || offLeft || offUp || offDown);         // d
        if ( keepOnScreen && !isOnScreen ) {
            transform.position = pos;
            isOnScreen = true;
            offRight = offLeft = offUp = offDown = false;                // e
        }
    }

    ...
}
```

a. Here you declare four variables, one for each direction in which the GameObject could go off screen. As bools, they all will default to `false`. The `[HideInInspector]` line preceding this causes these four public fields to not appear in the Inspector, though they are still public variables and can still be read (or set) by other classes. `[HideInInspector]` applies to all four `off__` bools (i.e., `offRight`, `offLeft`, and so on) because they are all declared on the line beneath it. If the `off__` bools were declared on four separate lines, a `[HideInInspector]` line would need to precede each line individually to achieve the same effect.

b. At the beginning of each `LateUpdate()` you set all four `off__` bools to `false`. In this line, `offDown` is first set to `false`, then `offUp` is set to the value of `offDown` (i.e., `false`), and so on until all `off__` bools hold the value `false`. This takes the place of the old line that set `isOnScreen` to `true`.

c. Each instance of `isOnScreen = false;` has now been replaced with an `off__ = true;` so that you know in which direction the GameObject has exited the screen. The possibility exists for two of these `off__` bools to both be true; for example, when the GameObject has exited the bottom-right corner of the screen.

d. Here, you set `isOnScreen` based on the values of all the `off__` bools. First, inside the parentheses, you take the logical OR (`||`) of all the `off__` bools. If one or more of them are `true`, this evaluates to `true`. You then take the NOT (`!`) of that and assign it to `isOnScreen`. So, if one or more of the `off__` bools are `true`, `isOnScreen` will be `false`, otherwise `isOnScreen` is set to `true`.

e. If `keepOnScreen` is true, and this GameObject is forced back on screen, `isOnScreen` is set to true, and all the `off__` bools are set to false.

4. Now, make the following bolded changes to the Enemy script to take advantage of the improvements to BoundsCheck.

```
public class Enemy : MonoBehaviour {
    ...

    void Update() {
        Move();
```

```
    if ( bndCheck != null && bndCheck.offDown ) {                         // a
        // We're off the bottom, so destroy this GameObject               // b
        Destroy( gameObject );                                            // b
    }
}

    ...

}
```

   a. Now, you just need to check against `bndCheck.offDown` to determine whether the Enemy instance has gone off the bottom of the screen.

   b. These two lines have lost one tab of indentation because there is now only one `if` clause instead of two.

This is a much simpler implementation from the viewpoint of the Enemy class, and it makes good use of the BoundsCheck component, allowing it to do its job without needlessly duplicating its functionality in the Enemy class.

Now, when you play the scene, you should see that the Enemy_0 ship moves down the screen and is destroyed as soon as it exits the bottom of the screen.

Spawning Enemies at Random

With all of this in place, instantiating a number of Enemy_0s randomly is now possible.

   1. Attach a *BoundsCheck* script to *_MainCamera* and set its `keepOnScreen` field to false.

   2. Create a new C# script called *Main* inside the __Scripts folder. Attach it to _MainCamera, and then enter the following code:

```
using System.Collections;              // Required for Arrays & other Collections
using System.Collections.Generic;      // Required to use Lists or Dictionaries
using UnityEngine;                     // Required for Unity
using UnityEngine.SceneManagement;     // For loading & reloading of scenes

public class Main : MonoBehaviour {
    static public Main S;                                   // A singleton for Main

    [Header("Set in Inspector")]
    public GameObject[]    prefabEnemies;                   // Array of Enemy prefabs
    public float           enemySpawnPerSecond = 0.5f;      // # Enemies/second
    public float           enemyDefaultPadding = 1.5f;      // Padding for position

    private BoundsCheck    bndCheck;

    void Awake() {
        S = this;
        // Set bndCheck to reference the BoundsCheck component on this GameObject
        bndCheck = GetComponent<BoundsCheck>();
```

```
    // Invoke SpawnEnemy() once (in 2 seconds, based on default values)
    Invoke( "SpawnEnemy", 1f/enemySpawnPerSecond );                    // a
}

public void SpawnEnemy() {
    // Pick a random Enemy prefab to instantiate
    int ndx = Random.Range(0, prefabEnemies.Length);                   // b
    GameObject go = Instantiate<GameObject>( prefabEnemies[ ndx ] );   // c

    // Position the Enemy above the screen with a random x position
    float enemyPadding = enemyDefaultPadding;                          // d
    if (go.GetComponent<BoundsCheck>() != null) {                      // e
        enemyPadding = Mathf.Abs( go.GetComponent<BoundsCheck>().radius );
    }

    // Set the initial position for the spawned Enemy                  // f
    Vector3 pos = Vector3.zero;
    float xMin = -bndCheck.camWidth + enemyPadding;
    float xMax =  bndCheck.camWidth - enemyPadding;
    pos.x = Random.Range( xMin, xMax );
    pos.y = bndCheck.camHeight + enemyPadding;
    go.transform.position = pos;

    // Invoke SpawnEnemy() again
    Invoke( "SpawnEnemy", 1f/enemySpawnPerSecond );                    // g
}
}
```

a. This `Invoke()` function calls the `SpawnEnemy()` method in 1/0.5 seconds (i.e., 2 seconds) based on the default values.

b. Based on the length of the array `prefabEnemies`, this chooses a random number between 0 and one less than `prefabEnemies.Length`, so if four prefabs are in the `prefabEnemies` array, it will return 0, 1, 2, or 3. The `int` version of `Random.Range()` will never return a number as high as the max (i.e., second) integer passed in. The float version is able to return the max number.

c. The random `ndx` generated is used to select a GameObject prefab from `prefabEnemies`.

d. The enemyPadding is initially set to the enemyDefaultPadding set in the Inspector.

e. However, if the selected enemy prefab has a BoundsCheck component, you instead read the `radius` from that. The absolute value of the `radius` is taken because sometimes the `radius` is set to a negative value so that the GameObject must be entirely off screen before registering as isOnScreen = false, as is the case for Enemy_0.

> **f.** This section of the code sets an initial position for the enemy that was instantiated. It uses the BoundsCheck on this _MainCamera GameObject to get the camWidth and camHeight and chooses an X position where the spawned enemy is entirely on screen horizontally. It then chooses a Y position where the enemy is just above the screen.
>
> **g.** Invoke is called again. The reason that `Invoke()` is used instead of `InvokeRepeating()` is that you want to be able to dynamically adjust the amount of time between each enemy spawn. After `InvokeRepeating()` is called, the invoked function is always called at the rate specified. Adding an `Invoke()` call at the end of `SpawnEnemy()` allows the game to adjust `enemySpawnPerSecond` on the fly and have it affect how frequently `SpawnEnemy()` is called.

3. After you've typed this code and saved the file, switch back to Unity and follow these instructions:

   a. Delete the instance of *Enemy_0* from the Hierarchy (leaving the prefab in the Project pane alone, of course).

   b. Select *_MainCamera* in the Hierarchy.

   c. Open the disclosure triangle next to `prefabEnemies` in the *Main (Script)* component of _MainCamera and set the *Size* of `prefabEnemies` to *1*.

   d. Drag *Enemy_0* from the Project pane into *Element 0* of the `prefabEnemies` array.

   e. *Save your scene!* Have you been remembering?

If you didn't save your scene after creating all of those enemies, you really should have. All sorts of things beyond your control could cause Unity to crash, and you don't want to have to redo work. Getting into a habit of saving your scene frequently can save you a ton of wasted time and sorrow as a developer.

4. Play your scene. You should now see an Enemy_0 spawn about once every 2 seconds, travel down to the bottom of the screen, and then disappear after it exits the bottom of the screen.

However, right now, when the _Hero collides with an enemy, nothing happens. This needs to be fixed, and to do so, you have to look at layers.

Setting Tags, Layers, and Physics

As was presented in Chapter 28, "Prototype 1: *Apple Picker*," one of the things that layers control in Unity is which objects may or may not collide with each other. First, let's think about the Space SHMUP prototype. In this game, several different types of GameObjects could be placed on different layers and interact with each other in different ways:

■ **Hero:** The _Hero ship should collide with enemies, enemy projectiles, and power-ups but should not collide with hero projectiles.

■ **ProjectileHero:** Projectiles fired by _Hero should only collide with enemies.

- **Enemy:** Enemies should collide with _Hero and hero projectiles but not with power-ups.
- **ProjectileEnemy:** Projectiles fired by enemies should only collide with _Hero.
- **PowerUp:** Power-ups should only collide with _Hero.

To create these layers as well as some tags that will be useful later, complete these steps:

1. Open the *Tags & Layers* manager in the Inspector pane (*Edit > Project Settings > Tags and Layers*). Tags and physics layers are different from each other, but both are set here.

2. Open the disclosure triangle next to Tags. Click the + below the Tags list and enter the tag name for each of the tags shown in the left image of Figure 30.7.

   In case it's difficult to see, the Tag names are: Hero, Enemy, ProjectileHero, ProjectileEnemy, PowerUp, and PowerUpBox.

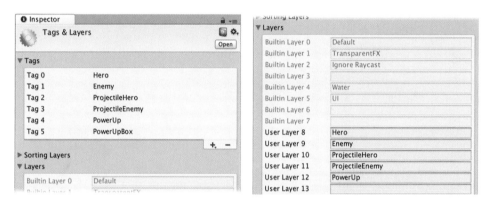

Figure 30.7 TagManager showing tags and layer names for this prototype

3. Open the disclosure triangle next to *Layers*. Starting with *User Layer 8*, enter the layer names shown in the right image of Figure 30.7. Builtin Layers 0–7 are reserved by Unity, but you can set the names of User Layers 8–31.

   The Layer names are: Hero, Enemy, ProjectileHero, ProjectileEnemy, and PowerUp.

4. Open the PhysicsManager (*Edit > Project Settings > Physics*) and set the *Layer Collision Matrix* as shown in Figure 30.8.

> **note**
>
> Unity has settings for both Physics and Physics2D. In this chapter, you should be setting Physics (the standard 3D PhysX physics library), not Physics2D.

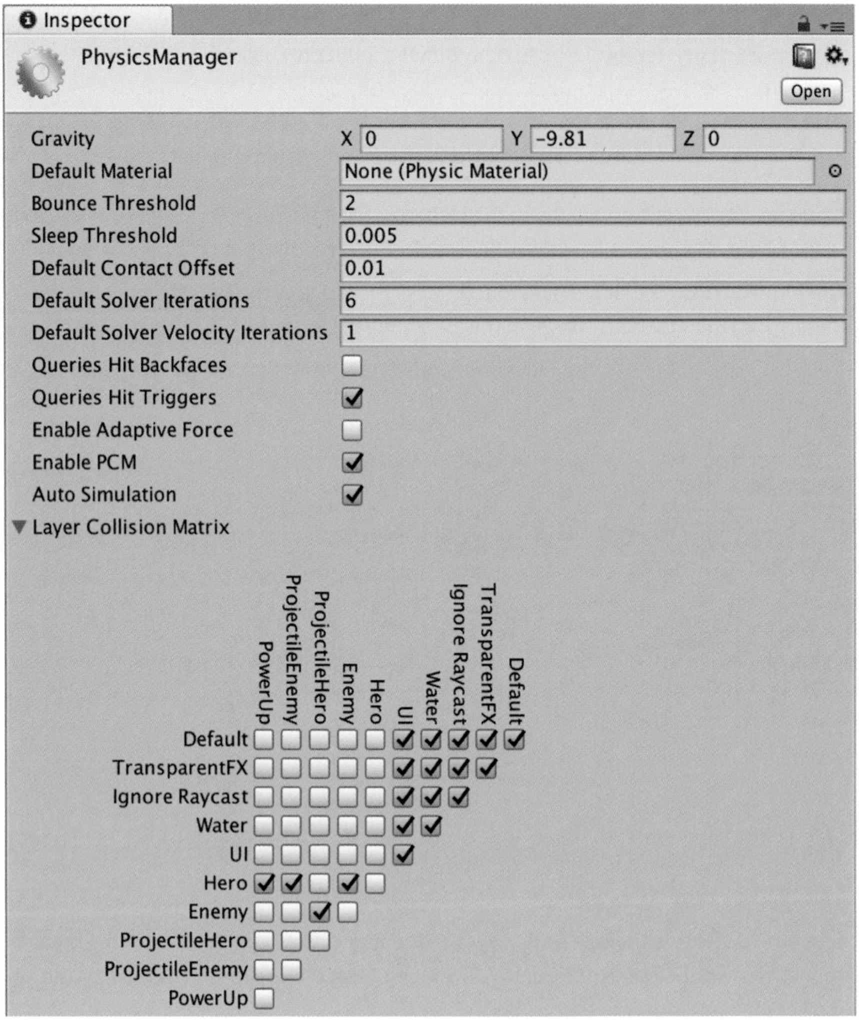

Figure 30.8 PhysicsManager with proper settings for this prototype

As you experienced in Chapter 28, the grid at the bottom of the PhysicsManager sets which layers collide with each other. If there is a check, objects in the two layers are able to collide, if there is no check, they won't. Removing checks can speed the execution of your game because it will test fewer objects versus each other for collision. As you can see in Figure 30.8, the Layer Collision Matrix that is selected achieves the collision behavior we specified earlier.

Assigning the Proper Layers to GameObjects

Now that the layers have been defined, you must assign the GameObjects you've created to the correct layer, as follows:

1. Select _Hero in the Hierarchy and choose *Hero* from the *Layer* pop-up menu in the Inspector. When Unity asks whether you want to also assign the children of _Hero to this new layer, choose *Yes, change children*.

2. Set the tag of _Hero to *Hero* using the *Tag* pop-up menu in the Inspector. You do not need to change the tags of the children of _Hero.

3. Select all five of the Enemy prefabs in the Project pane and set them to the *Enemy* layer. When asked, elect to change the layer of their children as well.

4. Also set the tags of all Enemy prefabs to *Enemy*. You do not need to set the tags of the children of each enemy.

Making the Enemies Damage the Player

Now that the enemies and hero have colliding layers, you need to make them react to collisions with each other.

1. Open the disclosure triangle next to _Hero in the Hierarchy and select its child *Shield*. In the Inspector, set the *Sphere Collider* of Shield to be a trigger (check the box next to *Is Trigger*). You don't need things to bounce off of Shield; you just need to know when they've hit.

2. Add the following bolded method to the end of the Hero C# script:

```
public class Hero : MonoBehaviour {
    …
    void Update() {
        …
    }

    void OnTriggerEnter(Collider other) {
        print("Triggered: "+other.gameObject.name);
    }
}
```

3. Play the scene and try running into some enemies. You can see that you get a separate trigger event for each of the child GameObjects of the enemy (e.g., Cockpit and Wing) but not for the enemy itself. You need to be able to get the Enemy_0 GameObject that is the parent of Cockpit and Wing, and if you had even more deeply nested child GameObjects, you would need to still find this topmost or *root* parent.

Luckily, this is a pretty common thing to need to do, so it's part of the Transform component of any GameObject. Calling `transform.root` on any GameObject gives you the transform of the root GameObject, from which it is easy to get the GameObject itself.

4. Replace the `OnTriggerEnter()` code of the Hero C# script with these bolded lines:

```
public class Hero : MonoBehaviour {
    ...
    void OnTriggerEnter(Collider other) {
        Transform rootT = other.gameObject.transform.root;
        GameObject go = rootT.gameObject;
        print("Triggered: "+go.name);
    }
}
```

Now when you play the scene and run the ship into enemies, you should see that `OnTriggerEnter()` announces it has hit *Enemy_0(Clone)*, an instance of Enemy_0.

> ## tip
>
> **ITERATIVE CODE DEVELOPMENT**   When prototyping on your own, this kind of *console announcement test* is something that you will do often to test whether the code you've written is working properly. I find that doing small tests along the way like this is much better than working on code for hours only to find at the end that something is causing a bug. Testing incrementally makes things *a lot* easier to debug because you know that you've only made slight changes since the last test that worked, so finding the place where you added a bug is easier.
>
> Another key element of this approach is using the debugger. Throughout the authoring of this book, any time I ran into something that worked a little differently than I expected, I used the debugger to understand what was happening. If you don't remember how to use the MonoDevelop debugger, I highly recommend rereading Chapter 25, "Debugging."
>
> Using the debugger effectively is often the difference between solving your code problems and just staring at pages of code blankly for several hours. Try putting a debug breakpoint into the `OnTriggerEnter()` method you just modified and watching how code is called and variables change.
>
> Iterative code development also has the same strengths as the iterative process of design, and it is the key to the agile development methodology discussed in Chapter 14, "The Agile Mentality."

5. Modify the `OnTriggerEnter()` method of the Hero class to make a collision with an enemy decrease the player's shield by 1 and destroy the enemy that was hit. It is also important to make sure that the same parent GameObject doesn't trigger the collider twice (which can happen with very fast-moving objects where two child colliders of one object hit the Shield trigger in the same frame).

```
public class Hero : MonoBehaviour {
    ...
    public float          shieldLevel = 1;
```

```
// This variable holds a reference to the last triggering GameObject
private GameObject        lastTriggerGo = null;                    // a

...

void OnTriggerEnter(Collider other) {
    Transform rootT = other.gameObject.transform.root;
    GameObject go = rootT.gameObject;
    //print("Triggered: "+go.name);                                // b

    // Make sure it's not the same triggering go as last time
    if (go == lastTriggerGo) {                                     // c
        return;
    }
    lastTriggerGo = go;                                            // d

    if (go.tag == "Enemy") {  // If the shield was triggered by an enemy
        shieldLevel--;          // Decrease the level of the shield by 1
        Destroy(go);            // ... and Destroy the enemy          // e
    } else {
        print("Triggered by non-Enemy: "+go.name);                 // f
    }
}
}
```

a. This private field will hold a reference to the last GameObject that triggered _Hero's collider. It is initially set to `null`.

b. Comment out this line here.

c. If `lastTriggerGo` is the same as `go` (the current triggering GameObject), this collision is ignored as a duplicate, and the function returns (i.e., exits). This can happen if two child GameObjects of the same Enemy both trigger the hero collider in the same single frame.

d. Assign `go` to `lastTriggerGo` so that it is updated before the next time `OnTriggerEnter()` is called.

e. `go`, the enemy GameObject, is destroyed by hitting the shield. Because the actual GameObject `go` that you're testing is the Enemy GameObject found by `transform.root`, this will delete the entire enemy (and by extension, all of its children), and not just one of the enemy's child GameObjects.

f. If _Hero collides with something that is not tagged "Enemy", then this will print to the Console and let you know what it is.

6. Play the scene and try running into some ships. After running into more than a few, you might notice a strange shield behavior. The shield will loop back around to full strength after being completely drained. What do you think is causing this? Try selecting _Hero in the Hierarchy while playing the scene to see what's happening to the `shieldLevel` field.

Because there is no bottom limit to `shieldLevel`, it continues past 0 into negative territory. The Shield C# script then translates this into negative X offset values for Mat_Shield, and because the material's texture is set to loop, it looks like the shield is returning to full strength.

To fix this, you must convert `shieldLevel` to a property that protects and limits a new private field named `_shieldLevel`. The `shieldLevel` property watches the value of the `_shieldLevel` field and makes sure that `_shieldLevel` never gets above 4 and that the ship is destroyed if `_shieldLevel` ever drops below 0. You should set a protected field like `_shieldLevel` to private because it does not need to be accessed by other classes; however, in Unity, private fields are not normally viewable in the Inspector. The remedy is to add the line `[SerializeField]` above the private declaration of `_shieldLevel` to instruct Unity to show it in the Inspector even though it is a private field. Properties are never visible in the Inspector, even if they're public.

7. In the Hero class, change the name of the public variable shieldLevel to _shieldLevel near the top of the class, set it to private, and add the `[SerializeField]` line:

```
public class Hero : MonoBehaviour {
    ...
    [Header("Set Dynamically")]
    [SerializeField]
    private float        _shieldLevel = 1; // Remember the underscore
    // This variable holds a reference to the last triggering GameObject
    ...
}
```

8. Add the `shieldLevel` property to the end of the Hero class.

```
public class Hero : MonoBehaviour {
    ...

    void OnTriggerEnter(Collider other) {
        ...
    }

    public float shieldLevel {
        get {
            return( _shieldLevel );                          // a
        }
        set {
            _shieldLevel = Mathf.Min( value, 4 );            // b
            // If the shield is going to be set to less than zero
            if (value < 0) {                                 // c
                Destroy(this.gameObject);
            }
        }
    }
}
```

a. The get clause just returns the value of _shieldLevel.

b. Mathf.Min() ensures that _shieldLevel is never set to a number higher than 4.

c. If the value passed into the set clause is less than 0, _Hero is destroyed.

The shieldLevel--; line in OnTriggerEnter() uses both the get and set clauses of the shieldLevel property. First, it uses the get clause to determine the current value of shieldLevel, and then it subtracts 1 from that value and calls the set clause to assign that value back.

Restarting the Game

From your testing, you can see that the game gets exceedingly boring after _Hero has been destroyed. You'll now modify both the Hero and Main classes to call a method when _Hero is destroyed that waits for 2 seconds and then restarts the game.

1. Add a gameRestartDelay field near the top of the Hero class:

```
public class Hero : MonoBehaviour {
    static public Hero     S; // Singleton                          // a

    [Header("Set in Inspector")]
    ...
    public float            pitchMult = 30;
    public float            gameRestartDelay = 2f;

    [Header("Set Dynamically")]
    ...
}
```

2. Add the following lines to the shieldLevel property definition in the Hero class:

```
public class Hero : MonoBehaviour {
    ...
    public float shieldLevel {
        get { ... }
        set {
            ...
            if (value < 0) {
                Destroy(this.gameObject);
                // Tell Main.S to restart the game after a delay
                Main.S.DelayedRestart( gameRestartDelay );        // a
            }
        }
    }
}
```

a. When you initially type DelayedRestart() into MonoDevelop, it appears red because the DelayedRestart() function does not yet exist in the Main class.

3. Add the following methods to the Main class to make the delayed restart work.

```
public class Main : MonoBehaviour {
    …

    public void SpawnEnemy() { … }

    public void DelayedRestart( float delay ) {
        // Invoke the Restart() method in delay seconds
        Invoke( "Restart", delay );
    }

    public void Restart() {
        // Reload _Scene_0 to restart the game
        SceneManager.LoadScene( "_Scene_0" );
    }
}
```

4. Click *Play* to test the game. Now, after the player ship has been destroyed, the game waits a couple of seconds and then restarts by reloading the scene.

> ### note
>
> If your lighting looks strange after you've reloaded the scene (e.g., your ship and enemy ships look a bit darker), then you might be experiencing a known bug with Unity's lighting system (as I also mentioned in Chapter 28). Hopefully, Unity has now resolved this, but if you are seeing issues, an interim fix is available. Follow these directions to resolve it for this project:
>
> 1. From the menu bar, choose *Window > Lighting > Settings*.
>
> 2. Click the *Scene* button at the top of the Lighting pane.
>
> 3. Uncheck the *Auto Generate* selection at the bottom of the Lighting pane (next to the *Generate Lighting* button). This stops Unity from constantly recalculating the global illumination settings.
>
> 4. To make sure the lighting is built properly, click the *Generate Lighting* button at the bottom of the Lighting pane to manually calculate the global illumination.
>
> 5. Wait a few seconds for this to finish, and then click *Play* to test. You should see that the lighting is consistent even after reloading the scene. You should not have to recalculate the lighting again in this chapter, but if you do change lighting in the game, be sure to come back and manually recalculate.

Shooting (Finally)

Now that the enemy ships can hurt the player, it's time to give _Hero a way to fight back. This chapter only includes a single type and level of projectile. In the next chapter, you will do much more interesting things with the weapons in the game.

ProjectileHero, the Hero's Bullet

Follow these steps to create the Hero's bullet:

1. Create a cube named *ProjectileHero* in the Hierarchy with the following transform values:

   ProjectileHero (Cube)   P:[10, 0, 0]   R:[0, 0, 0]   S:[0.25, 1, 0.5]

2. Set both the Tag and Layer of ProjectileHero to *ProjectileHero*.

3. Create a new material named *Mat_Projectile*, place it in the _Materials folder of the Project pane, give it the *ProtoTools > UnlitAlpha* shader, and assign it to the ProjectileHero GameObject.

4. Add a *Rigidbody* component to the ProjectileHero GameObject with these settings:

   - *Use Gravity* to false (unchecked)
   - *isKinematic* to false (unchecked)
   - *Collision Detection* to Continuous
   - *Constraints*: freeze Z position and X, Y, and Z rotation (by checking them)

5. In the *Box Collider* component of the ProjectileHero GameObject, set *Size.Z* to 10. This ensures that the projectile is able to hit anything that is slightly off of the XY (i.e., Z=0) plane.

6. Create a new C# script named *Projectile* and attach it to ProjectileHero. You'll edit the script later.

When you're finished with these steps, your settings should match those shown in Figure 30.9 (though you won't see the *BoundsCheck (Script)* component until you add it in step 8).

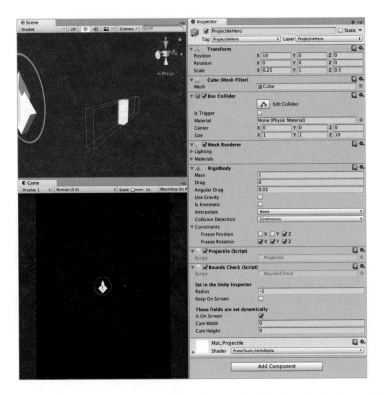

Figure 30.9 ProjectileHero with the proper settings showing the large Size.Z of the Box Collider

7. Save your scene.

8. Attach a *BoundsCheck* script component to ProjectileHero as well. Set `keepOnScreen` to `false` and `radius` to –1. The BoundsCheck `radius` will not affect collisions with other GameObjects; it only affects when the ProjectileHero thinks it has gone off screen.

9. Make ProjectileHero into a prefab by dragging it from the Hierarchy into the *_Prefabs folder* in the Project pane. Then delete the instance remaining in the Hierarchy.

10. Save your scene—yes, save it again. As I've said, you want to save as often as you can.

Giving _Hero the Ability to Shoot

Now you add the capability for the Hero to shoot the bullet.

1. Open the Hero C# script and make the following bolded changes:

```
public class Hero : MonoBehaviour {
    …
    public float          gameRestartDelay = 2f;
    public GameObject     projectilePrefab;
    public float          projectileSpeed = 40;

    …
```

```
void Update () {
    …
    transform.rotation = Quaternion.Euler(yAxis*pitchMult, xAxis*rollMult,0);

    // Allow the ship to fire
    if ( Input.GetKeyDown( KeyCode.Space ) ) {                    // a
        TempFire();
    }
}

void TempFire() {                                                 // b
    GameObject projGO = Instantiate<GameObject>( projectilePrefab );
    projGO.transform.position = transform.position;
    Rigidbody rigidB = projGO.GetComponent<Rigidbody>();
    rigidB.velocity = Vector3.up * projectileSpeed;
}

void OnTriggerEnter(Collider other) { … }
…
}
```

    a. This causes the ship to fire every time the space bar is pressed.

    b. This method is named `TempFire()` because you will be replacing it in the next chapter.

2. In Unity, select _Hero_ in the Hierarchy and assign _ProjectileHero_ from the Project pane to the `projectilePrefab` of the Hero script.

3. Save and click _Play_. Now, you can fire projectiles by pressing the space bar, but they don't yet destroy enemy ships, and they continue forever when they go off screen.

Scripting the Projectile

To script the projectile, follow these steps:

1. Open the _Projectile_ C# script and make the following bolded changes. All you need the Projectile to do is destroy itself when it goes off screen. You'll add more in the next chapter.

```
using System.Collections;
using System.Collections.Generic;
using UnityEngine;

public class Projectile : MonoBehaviour {

    private BoundsCheck      bndCheck;

    void Awake () {
        bndCheck = GetComponent<BoundsCheck>();
    }
```

```
    void Update () {
        if (bndCheck.offUp) {                                    // a
            Destroy( gameObject );
        }
    }
}
```

a. If the Projectile goes off the top of the screen, destroy it.

2. Of course, remember to save.

Allowing Projectiles to Destroy Enemies

You also need the capability of destroying enemies with the bullets.

1. Open the Enemy C# script and add the following method to the end of the script:

```
public class Enemy : MonoBehaviour {
    …
    public virtual void Move() { … }

    void OnCollisionEnter( Collision coll ) {
        GameObject otherGO = coll.gameObject;                       // a
        if ( otherGO.tag == "ProjectileHero" ) {                    // b
            Destroy( otherGO );       // Destroy the Projectile
            Destroy( gameObject );    // Destroy this Enemy GameObject
        } else {
            print( "Enemy hit by non-ProjectileHero: " + otherGO.name );   // c
        }
    }
}
```

a. Get the GameObject of the Collider that was hit in the Collision.

b. If otherGO has the ProjectileHero tag, then destroy it and this Enemy instance.

c. If otherGO doesn't have the ProjectileHero tag, print the name of what was hit to the Console for debugging purposes. If you want to test this, you can temporarily remove the ProjectileHero tag from the ProjectileHero prefab and shoot an Enemy.[4]

Now, when you click *Play*, Enemy_0s will come down the screen, and you can shoot them with projectiles. That's it for this chapter—you have a nice, simple prototype—but the next chapter, expands on it considerably by showing you how to add additional enemies, three kinds of power-ups, and two additional kinds of guns. It also offers some more interesting coding tricks.

---

4. You can't test this by running the _Hero into an Enemy because the collider on the Shield child of _Hero is a trigger, and triggers will not invoke a call to OnCollisionEnter().

Summary

In most chapters, I include a *next steps* section here to give you ideas of what you can do to extend the project and push yourself. However, for the *Space SHMUP* prototype, you're going to do some of those things in the next chapter and see some new coding concepts in the process. Take a break now so you can approach the next chapter fresh and congratulate yourself on a prototype well done.

CHAPTER 31

PROTOTYPE 3.5: *SPACE SHMUP PLUS*

Most of these prototype chapters end with a "Next Steps" section that suggests things you might want to add to the game. This chapter shows you the steps to do just that for the *Space SHMUP* game that you built in the previous chapter.

In this chapter, you add power-ups, multiple enemies, and different weapon types to the *Space SHMUP* game. In doing so, you learn more about class inheritance, enums, function delegates, and several other important topics. As an added bonus, you also make the game a lot more fun!

Getting Started: Prototype 3.5

At the end of the previous chapter, you had a pretty basic version of a space shooter. In this chapter, you'll make it more fun and expansive. In case you had any issues with the game as built in the previous chapter, you can download it from the website for the book.

SET UP THE PROJECT FOR THIS CHAPTER

Rather than following the standard project setup procedure, you have two options for this chapter:

1. Make a duplicate of your project folder from the previous chapter.

2. Download a finished version of the last chapter from the website for the book. To do so, find Chapter 31 at http://book.prototools.net.

After you've acquired a project folder, open _Scene_0 in Unity to get started.

Programming Other Enemies

Let's start by expanding the kinds of enemies that the hero will face. Later, you'll give your hero the chance to fight back against these more dire enemies.

1. Create new C# scripts named *Enemy_1*, *Enemy_2*, *Enemy_3*, and *Enemy_4*.
2. Place these scripts into the __Scripts folder in the Project pane.
3. Assign each of these scripts to their respective Enemy_# prefab in _Prefabs folder of the Project pane.

We'll work on the script for each enemy in turn.

Enemy_1

Enemy_1 moves down the screen in a sine wave. It extends the Enemy class, which means that it inherits all the fields, functions, and properties of Enemy (as long as they are public or protected; private elements are not inherited). For more information on classes and class inheritance (including method overriding), check out Chapter 26, "Classes."

1. Open the Enemy_1 script in MonoDevelop and enter the following bolded code:

```
using System.Collections;
using System.Collections.Generic;
using UnityEngine;

// Enemy_1 extends the Enemy class
public class Enemy_1 : Enemy {                                    // a
```

```csharp
[Header("Set in Inspector: Enemy_1")]
// # seconds for a full sine wave
public float    waveFrequency = 2;
// sine wave width in meters
public float    waveWidth = 4;
public float    waveRotY = 45;

private float    x0; // The initial x value of pos
private float    birthTime;

// Start works well because it's not used by the Enemy superclass
void Start() {
    // Set x0 to the initial x position of Enemy_1
    x0 = pos.x;                                                  // b

    birthTime = Time.time;
}

// Override the Move function on Enemy
public override void Move() {                                    // c
    // Because pos is a property, you can't directly set pos.x
    //    so get the pos as an editable Vector3
    Vector3 tempPos = pos;
    // theta adjusts based on time
    float age = Time.time - birthTime;
    float theta = Mathf.PI * 2 * age / waveFrequency;
    float sin = Mathf.Sin(theta);
    tempPos.x = x0 + waveWidth * sin;
    pos = tempPos;

    // rotate a bit about y
    Vector3 rot = new Vector3(0, sin*waveRotY, 0);
    this.transform.rotation = Quaternion.Euler(rot);

    // base.Move() still handles the movement down in y
    base.Move();                                                 // d

    // print( bndCheck.isOnScreen );
}
}
```

a. As an extension of the Enemy class, Enemy_1 inherits the public `speed`, `fireRate`, `health`, and `score` fields as well as the public `pos` property and the public `Move()` method. However, it does not inherit the private `bndCheck` field, which I discuss more in the next step.

b. Setting `x0` to the initial X position of this Enemy_1 works fine here in `Start()` because the position will have already been set by the time `Start()` is called. Had this line been put in an `Awake()` method, it would have been incorrect because `Awake()` is called in the instant that a GameObject is instantiated (i.e., before the position is set by the `Main:SpawnEnemy()` method (in Main.cs)).

Another reason to avoid adding an `Awake()` method to Enemy_1 is that it would override the `Awake()` method on Enemy. `Awake()`, `Start()`, `Update()`, and other built-in MonoBehaviour methods are scripted in a special manner so that—unlike standard methods in C# class inheritance—you don't need to use the `virtual` or `override` keywords to allow them to be overridden by subclasses (see Chapter 26, "Classes").

c. For normal C# methods like the `Move()` method that you wrote in Enemy, you must declare the method `virtual` in the superclass and `override` in the subclass for the subclass version properly override the superclass version of the method. Because `Move()` is marked as a virtual method in the `Enemy` superclass, you can override it here and replace it with another method (also named `Move()`).

d. `base.Move()` calls the `Move()` method on the superclass Enemy. In this case, the `Move()` method in the Enemy_1 subclass is responsible for moving horizontally in a sine wave, while the `Move()` method in the Enemy superclass still handles vertical movement.

2. Back in Unity, select _MainCamera in the Hierarchy and change *Element 0* of `prefabEnemies` from Enemy_0 to Enemy_1 (i.e., the Enemy_1 prefab in the _Prefabs folder) in the *Main (Script)* component. This allows you to test with Enemy_1 instead of Enemy.

3. Click *Play*. The Enemy_1 ship now appears instead of Enemy_0, and it moves downward in a wave. However, notice in the Scene pane that Enemy_1 instances don't disappear when they go off the bottom of the screen. This is because Enemy_1 doesn't have a BoundsCheck component attached to it.

4. You want to attach BoundsCheck to the Enemy_1 prefab and keep all the same values that it has set on the Enemy_0 prefab. To do this, follow these steps to learn another way to attach a script to a GameObject:

a. Select *Enemy_0* in the _Prefabs folder of the Project pane.

b. In the Inspector for Enemy_0, click the gear icon in the top-right corner of the *Bounds-Check (Script)* component and choose *Copy Component*.

c. Select *Enemy_1* in the _Prefabs folder of the Project pane.

d. In the Inspector for Enemy_1, click the *gear icon* in the top-right corner of the *Transform* component and choose *Paste Component as New*. This attaches a new *BoundsCheck (Script)* component to the Enemy_1 prefab that comes with all the same settings as those on the BoundsCheck component you copied from the Enemy_0 prefab.

Making bndCheck Protected Instead of Private

A somewhat subtle yet important point is that the field declaration of `bndCheck` in the Enemy class is currently *private*.

```
private BoundsCheck bndCheck;
```

This means that it can be seen within the Enemy class but not in any other classes, including Enemy_1, even though Enemy_1 is a subclass of Enemy. This means that the `Awake()` and `Move()` methods on Enemy can see and interact with `bndCheck`, yet the `override Move()` method on Enemy_1 doesn't know it exists. To test this:

1. Open the Enemy_1 script and uncomment the bolded at the end of the `Move()` method:

```
public override void Move() {

    …

    base.Move();

    print( bndCheck.isOnScreen );
}
```

Because `bndCheck` is a private variable of the Enemy class, it appears red here in Enemy_1 and cannot be read. To fix this, you need to make `bndCheck` *protected* instead of private. Like private variables, protected variables can't be seen by other classes, but unlike private variables, protected variables can be seen by and inherited by subclasses:

Variable Type	Visible to Subclasses	Visible to Any Class
private	No	No
protected	Yes	No
public	Yes	Yes

2. Open the Enemy script, change `bndCheck` from `private` to `protected`, and save.

```
protected BoundsCheck bndCheck;
```

Now, if you check the Enemy_1 script, `bndCheck.isOnScreen` will no longer be red, and your code will compile properly.

3. Return to the Enemy_1 script and re-comment out the `print()` line.

```
// print( bndCheck.isOnScreen ); // This line is now commented out again.
```

4. Click *Play*, and you should see the Enemy_1s now disappear after they exit the bottom of the screen.

> **tip**
>
> **SPHERE COLLIDERS ONLY SCALE UNIFORMLY**　You might have noticed that the collision with Enemy_1 actually occurs slightly before the projectile (or _Hero) touches the wing. If you select Enemy_1 in the Project pane and drag an instance into the scene, you will see that the green collider sphere around Enemy_1 doesn't scale to match the flat ellipse of the wing. This isn't a huge problem, but it is something to be aware of. A Sphere Collider will scale with the largest single component of scale in the transform. (In this case, because wing has a Scale.X of 6, the Sphere Collider scales up to that.)
>
> If you want, you can try other types of colliders to see whether one of them will scale to match the wing more accurately. A Box Collider will scale non-uniformly. You can also approximate one direction being much longer than the others with a Capsule Collider. A Mesh Collider will match the scaling most exactly, but Mesh Colliders are much slower than other types. This shouldn't be a problem on a modern high-performance PC, but Mesh Colliders are often much too slow for mobile platforms like iOS or Android.
>
> If you choose to give Enemy_1 a Mesh Collider, then when it rotates about the y axis, it will move the edges of the wing out of the XY (i.e., z=0) plane. This is why the ProjectileHero prefab has a Box Collider Size.z of 10 (to make sure that it can hit the wingtips of Enemy_1 even if they are not in the XY plane).

Preparing for the Other Enemies

The remaining enemies make use of linear interpolation, an important development concept that is described in Appendix B. You saw a very simple interpolation as part of the FollowCam script in Mission Demolition, but these will be a bit more interesting. Take a moment to read the *Interpolation* section of Appendix B, "Useful Concepts," before tackling the remaining enemies.

Enemy_2

Enemy_2 moves via a linear interpolation that is heavily eased by a sine wave. It rushes in from the side of the screen, slows, reverses direction for a bit, slows, and then flies off the screen along its initial velocity. This interpolation uses only two points, but the u value will be drastically curved by a sine wave. The easing function for the u value of Enemy_2 will be along the lines of:

$$u = u + 0.6 * Sin(2\pi * u)$$

This is one of the easing functions explained in the *Interpolation* section of Appendix B.

1. Attach a BoundsCheck script to the Enemy_2 prefab in the _Prefabs folder of the Project pane. The BoundsCheck component will be used extensively for Enemy_2.

2. In the Enemy_2 prefab BoundsCheck Inspector, set the `radius` = 3 and `keepOnScreen` = false.

3. Open the Enemy_2 C# script and enter the following code. After you have the code working, you should adjust the easing curve `sinEccentricity` value to see how it affects the motion.

```csharp
using System.Collections;
using System.Collections.Generic;
using UnityEngine;

public class Enemy_2 : Enemy {                                          // a
    [Header("Set in Inspector: Enemy_2")]
    // Determines how much the Sine wave will affect movement
    public float          sinEccentricity = 0.6f;
    public float          lifeTime = 10;

    [Header("Set Dynamically: Enemy_2")]
    // Enemy_2 uses a Sin wave to modify a 2-point linear interpolation
    public Vector3        p0;
    public Vector3        p1;
    public float          birthTime;

    void Start () {
        // Pick any point on the left side of the screen
        p0 = Vector3.zero;                                             // b
        p0.x = -bndCheck.camWidth - bndCheck.radius;
        p0.y = Random.Range( -bndCheck.camHeight, bndCheck.camHeight );

        // Pick any point on the right side of the screen
        p1 = Vector3.zero;
        p1.x = bndCheck.camWidth + bndCheck.radius;
        p1.y = Random.Range( -bndCheck.camHeight, bndCheck.camHeight );

        // Possibly swap sides
        if (Random.value > 0.5f) {
            // Setting the .x of each point to its negative will move it to
            //   the other side of the screen
            p0.x *= -1;
            p1.x *= -1;
        }

        // Set the birthTime to the current time
        birthTime = Time.time;                                        // c
    }

    public override void Move() {
        // Bézier curves work based on a u value between 0 & 1
        float u = (Time.time - birthTime) / lifeTime;
```

```
        // If u>1, then it has been longer than lifeTime since birthTime
        if (u > 1) {
            // This Enemy_2 has finished its life
            Destroy( this.gameObject );                                      // d
            return;
        }

        // Adjust u by adding a U Curve based on a Sine wave
        u = u + sinEccentricity*(Mathf.Sin(u*Mathf.PI*2));

        // Interpolate the two linear interpolation points
        pos = (1-u)*p0 + u*p1;
    }
}
```

a. Enemy_2 also extends the Enemy superclass.

b. This section chooses a random point on the left side of the screen. It initially chooses an x position that is just off the left side of the screen: `-bndCheck.camWidth` is the left side of the screen, and `-bndCheck.radius` makes sure that the Enemy_2 is entirely off screen (by pushing the X position off screen an amount equal to the radius of this Enemy_2).

Then, a random Y position is chosen that is between the bottom of the screen (`-bndCheck.camHeight`) and the top of the screen (`bndCheck.camHeight`).

c. `birthTime` is used by the interpolation in the `Move()` function.

d. If it has been longer than `lifeTime` since the `birthTime`, then `u` will be greater than 1, and this Enemy_2 will be destroyed.

4. Swap the Enemy_2 prefab into the *Element 0* slot of `prefabEnemies` using the _MainCamera Inspector and click *Play*.

As you can see, the easing function causes each Enemy_2 to have very smooth movement that goes forth, back, and forth between the points it has selected on either side of the screen.

Enemy_3

Enemy_3 uses a Bézier curve to swoop down from above, slow, and fly back up off the top of the screen. For this example, you will use a simple version of the three-point Bézier curve function. In the *Recursive Functions* section of Appendix B you can find a recursive version of the Bézier curve function that can use any number of points (not just three).

1. Attach *BoundsCheck* to the Enemy_3 prefab in the _Prefabs folder of the Project pane.

2. In the Enemy_3 prefab BoundsCheck Inspector, set `radius` = 2.5 and `keepOnScreen` = false.

3. Open the Enemy_3 script and enter the following code:

```
using System.Collections;
using System.Collections.Generic;
using UnityEngine;

public class Enemy_3 : Enemy {  // Enemy_3 extends Enemy
    // Enemy_3 will move following a Bezier curve, which is a linear
    //   interpolation between more than two points.
    [Header("Set in Inspector: Enemy_3")]
    public float            lifeTime = 5;

    [Header("Set Dynamically: Enemy_3")]
    public Vector3[]        points;
    public float            birthTime;

    // Again, Start works well because it is not used by the Enemy superclass
    void Start () {
        points = new Vector3[3]; // Initialize points

        // The start position has already been set by Main.SpawnEnemy()
        points[0] = pos;

        // Set xMin and xMax the same way that Main.SpawnEnemy() does
        float xMin = -bndCheck.camWidth + bndCheck.radius;
        float xMax =  bndCheck.camWidth - bndCheck.radius;

        Vector3 v;
        // Pick a random middle position in the bottom half of the screen
        v = Vector3.zero;
        v.x = Random.Range( xMin, xMax );
        v.y = -bndCheck.camHeight * Random.Range( 2.75f, 2 );
        points[1] = v;

        // Pick a random final position above the top of the screen
        v = Vector3.zero;
        v.y = pos.y;
        v.x = Random.Range( xMin, xMax );
        points[2] = v;

        // Set the birthTime to the current time
        birthTime = Time.time;
    }

    public override void Move() {
        // Bezier curves work based on a u value between 0 & 1
        float u = (Time.time - birthTime) / lifeTime;

        if (u > 1) {
            // This Enemy_3 has finished its life
            Destroy( this.gameObject );
            return;
        }
```

```
        // Interpolate the three Bezier curve points
        Vector3 p01, p12;
        p01 = (1-u)*points[0] + u*points[1];
        p12 = (1-u)*points[1] + u*points[2];
        pos = (1-u)*p01 + u*p12;
    }
}
```

4. Now try swapping Enemy_3 into *Element 0* of `prefabEnemies` on _MainCamera.

5. Click *Play* to see the movement of these new enemies. After playing for a bit, you'll notice a couple of things about Bézier curves:

   a. Even though the midpoint is at or below the bottom of the screen, no Enemy_3 ever gets that far down. That is because a Bézier curve touches both the start and end points but is only influenced by the midpoint.

   b. Enemy_3 slows down a lot in the middle of the curve. This is also a feature of the math that makes Bézier curves work.

6. To improve the motion along the Bézier curve and reduce the slowdown at the bottom of the curve, add the following bold line to the Enemy_3 `Move()` method. This adds *easing*[1] to the Enemy_3 movement that will speed up the middle of the curve:

```
public override void Move() {
    …
    // Interpolate the three Bezier curve points
    Vector3 p01, p12;
    u = u - 0.2f*Mathf.Sin(u * Mathf.PI * 2);
    p01 = (1-u)*points[0] + u*points[1];
    p12 = (1-u)*points[1] + u*points[2];
    pos = (1-u)*p01 + u*p12;
}
```

Saving Enemy_4 for Later

Before implementing Enemy_4, you first need to make some changes to projectiles and how they work. At this point, players can destroy any enemy with a single shot. In the next section, you learn how to change that and add the ability to have different kinds of weapons on the ship.

Shooting Revisited

The way that you learned to manage firing Projectiles in the previous chapter was fine for a rough prototype, but you need to add additional capabilities to get this game to the next level. In this section, you will learn to build two different kinds of weapons with the ability to expand that in the future. To enable this, you'll create a WeaponDefinition class that allows you to define the behavior of each type of weapon.

---

1. Appendix B, "Useful Concepts" covers the easing of Bézier curves in detail.

The WeaponType Enum

As described in Chapter 29, "Prototype 2: Mission Demolition," an *enum*—short for enumeration—is a way to associate various options together into a new kind of variable. In this game, players have the ability to switch and improve weapons by collecting power-ups dropped by defeated enemies. This is also how players increase their shield power. To provide a single variable type to store all the possible kinds of power-ups, you will create an enum called WeaponType.

1. Right click on the *__Scripts* folder in the Project pane and choose *Create > C# Script*. This creates a *NewBehaviourScript* in the *__Scripts* folder.

2. Rename NewBehaviourScript to *Weapon*.

3. Open the *Weapon* script in MonoDevelop and enter the following code. The public enum WeaponType declaration should go between `using UnityEngine;` and `public class Weapon : MonoBehaviour {`.

```
using System.Collections;
using System.Collections.Generic;
using UnityEngine;


/// <summary>
/// This is an enum of the various possible weapon types.
/// It also includes a "shield" type to allow a shield power-up.
/// Items marked [NI] below are Not Implemented in the IGDPD book.
/// </summary>
public enum WeaponType {
    none,       // The default / no weapon
    blaster,    // A simple blaster
    spread,     // Two shots simultaneously
    phaser,     // [NI] Shots that move in waves
    missile,    // [NI] Homing missiles
    laser,      // [NI]Damage over time
    shield      // Raise shieldLevel
}

public class Weapon : MonoBehaviour {
    ...             // The Weapon class will be filled in later in the chapter.
}
```

As a public enum outside of the Weapon class, WeaponType can be seen by and used by any other script in the project. You'll make use of this extensively throughout the rest of this chapter, and actually define the weapons via WeaponType in the Main C# script rather than the Weapon script.

For more information on enums, look at the Appendix B, "Useful Concepts," subsection titled "Enum" under *C# and Unity Coding Concepts*.

The Serializable WeaponDefinition Class

You now need to create a class to define the details of the various types of weapons. Unlike most of the other classes that you've created in this book, this will not be a subclass of MonoBehaviour, and you won't attach it individually to a GameObject. Instead, it is a simple, separate, public class that you define within the Weapon C# script, just as the public enum WeaponType was.

Another important aspect of this class is that it is *serializable*, allowing you to both see and edit it within the Unity Inspector!

Open the Weapon script and enter the following bolded code between the `public enum` WeaponType definition and the `public class Weapon` definition.

```
public enum WeaponType {
    …
}


/// <summary>
/// The WeaponDefinition class allows you to set the properties
///    of a specific weapon in the Inspector. The Main class has
///    an array of WeaponDefinitions that makes this possible.
/// </summary>
[System.Serializable]                                              // a
public class WeaponDefinition {                                    // b
    public WeaponType   type = WeaponType.none;
    public string       letter;             // Letter to show on the power-up
    public Color        color = Color.white;    // Color of Collar & power-up
    public GameObject   projectilePrefab;       // Prefab for projectiles
    public Color        projectileColor = Color.white;
    public float        damageOnHit = 0;        // Amount of damage caused
    public float        continuousDamage = 0;   // Damage per second (Laser)
    public float        delayBetweenShots = 0;
    public float        velocity = 20;          // Speed of projectiles
}

public class Weapon : MonoBehaviour {
    …              // The Weapon class will be filled in later in the chapter.
}
```

a. The `[System.Serializable]` attribute causes the class defined immediately after it to be serializable and editable within the Unity Inspector. Some classes are too complex to be serializable, but WeaponDefinition is simple enough that it will work.

b. You can alter each of the fields of WeaponDefinition to change an aspect of the bullets fired by your ship. You won't use all of these in this chapter, which leaves some for you to use if you choose to extend this game further.

As described in the code comments, the enum `WeaponType` declares all the possible weapon types and power-up types. `WeaponDefinition` is a class that combines a `WeaponType` with several variables that are useful for defining each weapon.

Modifying Main to Use WeaponDefinition and WeaponType

Now you need to use the new WeaponType enum and WeaponDefinition class in Main. You do this in the Main class because it is responsible for spawning enemies and eventually power-ups.

1. Add the following `weaponDefinitions` array declaration to the Main class and save.

```
public class Main : MonoBehaviour {
    ...
    public float            enemySpawnPerSecond = 0.5f; // # Enemies/second
    public float            enemyDefaultPadding = 1.5f; // Padding for position
    public WeaponDefinition[]   weaponDefinitions;

    private BoundsCheck     bndCheck;

    void Awake() {…}
    ...
}
```

2. Select _MainCamera in the Hierarchy. You should now see a `weaponDefinitions` array in the *Main (Script)* component Inspector.

3. Click the disclosure triangle next to `weaponDefinitions` in the Inspector and set the *Size* of the array to *3*.

4. Enter settings for the three WeaponDefinitions as shown in Figure 31.1. You can see that the WeaponType enum appears in the Inspector as a pop-up menu (though like other things in the Inspector, the enum types have been capitalized). The colors you pick don't have to be exactly right, but it is important to set the alpha value of each color to a fully opaque value of 255, which appears as a white bar beneath the color swatch.

> ### warning
>
> **COLORS SOMETIMES DEFAULT TO AN INVISIBLE ALPHA**   When you create a serializable class like WeaponDefinition that includes color fields, the alpha values of those colors can default to 0 (zero, or invisible). To fix this, make sure that the white lines under each of your color definitions are actually white (and not black). If you click on the color itself, you are presented with four values to set (R, G, B, and A). Make sure that A is set to 255 (fully opaque) or the color may be invisible.
>
> If you are using macOS and have chosen to use the macOS color picker in Unity instead of the default one, you set the A value using the Opacity slider at the bottom of the color picker window (which should be set to 100% for these colors to have full opacity).

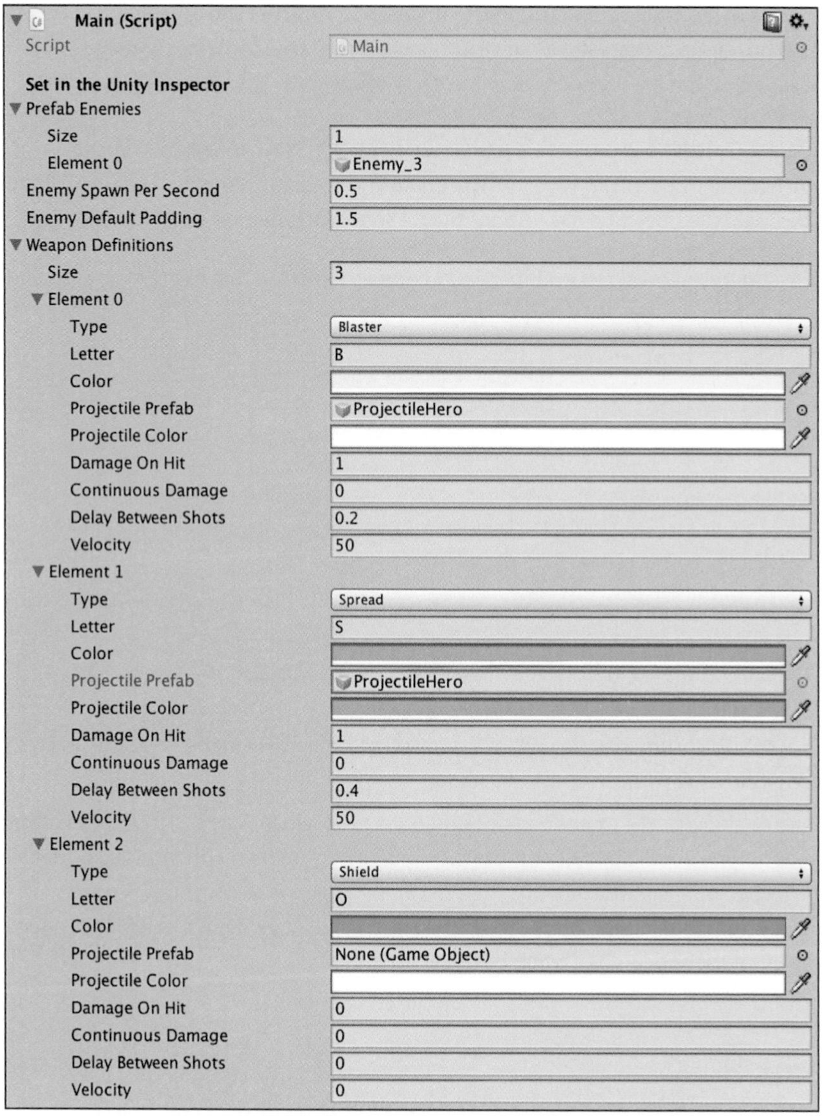

Figure 31.1 Settings for the WeaponDefinitions of blaster, spread, and shield on Main

A Generic Dictionary for WeaponDefinitions

To make accessing the WeaponDefinitions easier, you're going to copy them at runtime from the `weaponDefinitions` array to a private *Dictionary* field named `WEAP_DICT`. A Dictionary is a type of generic collection like List. However, where a List is an ordered (linear) collection, Dictionaries have a *key* type and *value* type, with the key used to retrieve the value. Dictionaries can be a good way to store a very large number of things because accessing any one of those things is a *constant time* operation, meaning that it takes the same small amount of time regardless of where that thing is in the data structure. Contrast this with a List or array; if you were searching through the `weaponDefinitions` array for the WeaponDefinition with the type `blaster`, you would encounter it immediately, whereas searching for the WeaponDefinition with the type `shield` would take three times as long. See Chapter 23, "Collections in C#" for more information.

Here, the `WEAP_DICT` Dictionary has the enum WeaponType as the key and the class WeaponDefinition as the value. Unfortunately, Dictionaries do not appear in the Unity Inspector, or you would have just used one from the start. Instead, the `WEAP_DICT` Dictionary is defined in the `Awake()` method of the Main class and then used by the static function `Main.GetWeaponDefinition()`.

   1. Open the Main script in MonoDevelop and enter the following bold code.

```
public class Main : MonoBehaviour {
    static public Main S;              // A singleton for Main
    static Dictionary<WeaponType, WeaponDefinition> WEAP_DICT;              // a
    …

    void Awake() {
        …
        Invoke( "SpawnEnemy", 1f/enemySpawnPerSecond );

        // A generic Dictionary with WeaponType as the key
        WEAP_DICT = new Dictionary<WeaponType, WeaponDefinition>();              // a
        foreach( WeaponDefinition def in weaponDefinitions ) {              // b
            WEAP_DICT[def.type] = def;
        }
    }
}
```

   a. Dictionaries are declared and defined with both a key type and value type. Making `WEAP_DICT` static but protected means that any instance of `Main` can access it and any static method of `Main` can access it, which you'll take advantage of later.

   b. This loop iterates through each element of the `weaponDefinitions` array and creates an entry in the `WEAP_DICT` dictionary that matches it.

Next, you need to create a static function to allow other classes to get access to the data in `WEAP_DICT`. Because `WEAP_DICT` is static as well, any static method of the Main class can access it (`WEAP_DICT` is not public, which means that only instances or static methods of Main can access `WEAP_DICT` directly[2]). Making the new `GetWeaponDefinition()` method public and static allows any other code within the project to call it as `Main.GetWeaponDefinition()`.

---

2. To be more exact, because `WEAP_DICT` is neither public nor private, it is automatically protected. Protected elements of a class can be seen by the class itself and any of its subclasses (subclasses are not able to see private elements of a class). As a result, instances and static methods of Main or any subclasses you made of Main could directly access `WEAP_DICT`.

2. Add the following bolded code to the end of the Main C# script:

```
public class Main : MonoBehaviour {
    …
    public void Restart() {
        // Reload _Scene_0 to restart the game
        SceneManager.LoadScene( "_Scene_0" );
    }


    /// <summary>
    /// Static function that gets a WeaponDefinition from the WEAP_DICT static
    ///    protected field of the Main class.
    /// </summary>
    /// <returns>The WeaponDefinition or, if there is no WeaponDefinition with
    ///    the WeaponType passed in, returns a new WeaponDefinition with a
    ///    WeaponType of none..</returns>
    /// <param name="wt">The WeaponType of the desired WeaponDefinition</param>
    static public WeaponDefinition GetWeaponDefinition( WeaponType wt ) {      // a
        // Check to make sure that the key exists in the Dictionary
        // Attempting to retrieve a key that didn't exist, would throw an error,
        //    so the following if statement is important.
        if (WEAP_DICT.ContainsKey(wt)) {                                       // b
            return( WEAP_DICT[wt] );
        }
        // This returns a new WeaponDefinition with a type of WeaponType.none,
        //    which means it has failed to find the right WeaponDefinition
        return( new WeaponDefinition() );                                      // c
    }
}
```

   a. The documentation in the code above this function now includes not only a summary but also descriptions of what is returned and the parameter passed in.

   b. This `if` statement checks to make sure that `WEAP_DICT` has an entry with the key that was passed in as `wt`. If you try to retrieve an entry that isn't there (e.g., if you try `WEAP_DICT[WeaponType.phaser]`), it will throw an error.

      In the expected case that there *is* an element with the proper WeaponType, that WeaponDefinition is returned.

   c. If there is no entry in `WEAP_DICT` with the proper `WeaponType` key, a new WeaponDefinition with a type of `WeaponType.none` is returned.

Modifying the Projectile Class to Use WeaponDefinitions

You must alter the Projectile class considerably to make it use your new WeaponDefinitions.

1. Open the Projectile class in MonoDevelop.

2. Make your code for the Projectile class match the following code listing.

```
using System.Collections;
using System.Collections.Generic;
using UnityEngine;
```

```
public class Projectile : MonoBehaviour {
    private BoundsCheck    bndCheck;
    private Renderer       rend;

    [Header("Set Dynamically")]
    public Rigidbody       rigid;
    [SerializeField]                                                    // a
    private WeaponType     _type;                                       // b

    // This public property masks the field _type and takes action when it is set
    public WeaponType      type {                                       // c
        get {
            return( _type );
        }
        set {
            SetType( value );                                          // c
        }
    }

    void Awake () {
        bndCheck = GetComponent<BoundsCheck>();
        rend = GetComponent<Renderer>();                               // d
        rigid = GetComponent<Rigidbody>();
    }

    void Update () {
        if (bndCheck.offUp) {
            Destroy( gameObject );
        }
    }

    /// <summary>
    /// Sets the _type private field and colors this projectile to match the
    ///    WeaponDefinition.
    /// </summary>
    /// <param name="eType">The WeaponType to use.</param>
    public void SetType( WeaponType eType ) {                           // e
        // Set the _type
        _type = eType;
        WeaponDefinition def = Main.GetWeaponDefinition( _type );
        rend.material.color = def.projectileColor;
    }
}
```

a. The [SerializeField] attribute above the _type declaration forces _type to
    be visible and settable in the Unity Inspector even though it is private. However, you
    should *not* set this field in the Inspector.

b. A common practice throughout this book is to name a private field accessed through a property with an underscore and the property name (e.g., the private field `_type` is accessed via the property `type`).

c. The get clause of the `type` property works like the other properties you've seen, but the set clause calls the `SetType()` method, allowing you to do more than just set `_type`.

d. You need to use the Renderer component attached to this GameObject in the `SetType()` method, so it is cached here.

e. `SetType()` not only sets the `_type` private field but also colors the projectile to match the color based on the `weaponDefinitions` in Main.

Using a Function Delegate to Fire

In this game prototype, the `Hero` class has a *function delegate* named `fireDelegate` that is called to fire all weapons, and each Weapon attached to it adds its individual `Fire()` target method to `fireDelegate`.

1. Before continuing, please read the *Function Delegates* section of Appendix B, "Useful Concepts." Function delegates are like nicknames for one or more functions that can all be called with a single call to the delegate.

2. Add the following bold code to the `Hero` class:

```
public class Hero : MonoBehaviour {
    ...
    private GameObject       lastTriggerGo = null;

    // Declare a new delegate type WeaponFireDelegate
    public delegate void WeaponFireDelegate();                     // a
    // Create a WeaponFireDelegate field named fireDelegate.
    public WeaponFireDelegate fireDelegate;


    void Awake() {
        if (S == null) {

            ...
        }
        fireDelegate += TempFire;                                  // b
    }


    void Update () {
        ...
        transform.rotation = Quaternion.Euler(yAxis*pitchMult,xAxis*rollMult,0);
```

```
          // Allow the ship to fire
//           if ( Input.GetKeyDown(KeyCode.Space) ) {                     // c
//               TempFire();                                              // c
//           }                                                            // c

          // Use the fireDelegate to fire Weapons
          // First, make sure the button is pressed: Axis("Jump")
          // Then ensure that fireDelegate isn't null to avoid an error
          if (Input.GetAxis("Jump") == 1 && fireDelegate != null) {       // d
              fireDelegate();                                             // e
          }
      }

   void TempFire() {                                                      // f
       GameObject projGO = Instantiate<GameObject>( projectilePrefab );
       projGO.transform.position = transform.position;
       Rigidbody rigidB = projGO.GetComponent<Rigidbody>();
//       rigidB.velocity = Vector3.up * projectileSpeed;                 // g

       Projectile proj = projGO.GetComponent<Projectile>();              // h
       proj.type = WeaponType.blaster;
       float tSpeed = Main.GetWeaponDefinition( proj.type ).velocity;
       rigidB.velocity = Vector3.up * tSpeed;
   }

   void OnTriggerEnter(Collider other) { … }
   …
}
```

a. Though both are public, neither the WeaponFireDelegate() delegate type nor the fireDelegate field will appear in the Unity Inspector.

b. Adding TempFire to the fireDelegate causes TempFire to be called any time fireDelegate is called like a function (see // e).

   Note that when you add TempFire to the fireDelegate, you don't follow the method name TempFire with parentheses. This is because you are adding the method itself rather than calling the method and adding the result it returns (which is what would happen if you put parentheses after the name of the method).

c. Be sure that you comment out (or delete) the entire section that was inside the if (Input.GetKeyDown(KeyCode.Space)) { … } statement.

d. Input.GetAxis("Jump") is equal to 1 when the space bar or jump button on a controller is pressed.

   If fireDelegate is called when it has no methods assigned to it, it will throw an error. To avoid this, fireDelegate != null is tested to see whether it is null before calling it.

e. `fireDelegate` is called here as if it were a function. This, in turn, calls all the functions that have been added to the `fireDelegate` delegate (at this point, this means that it will call `TempFire()`).

f. `TempFire()` is now used by the `fireDelegate` to fire a standard blaster shot. You'll replace `TempFire()` later when you make the Weapon class.

g. You need to either comment out or delete this line.

h. This new section pulls information from the WeaponType of the Projectile class and uses it to set the velocity of the `projGO` GameObject.

3. Click *Play* in Unity and try firing. You should fire a lot of blaster shots very rapidly. In the next section, you'll add a `Weapon` class that can better manage firing and replace `TempFire()` with the `Fire()` function on that `Weapon` class.

Creating a Weapon Object to Fire Projectiles

Let's start with the artwork for the new Weapon GameObject. The benefit of the Weapon is that you can attach as many as you want to _Hero, and each one can add itself to the `fireDelegate` on the Hero class and then be fired in concert when `fireDelegate` is called like a function.

1. In the Hierarchy, create an empty GameObject, name it *Weapon*, and give it the following structure and children:

Weapon (Empty)	P:[0, 2, 0]	R:[0, 0, 0]	S:[1, 1, 1]
Barrel (Cube)	P:[0, 0.5, 0]	R:[0, 0, 0]	S:[0.25, 1, 0.1]
Collar (Cube)	P:[0, 1, 0]	R:[0, 0, 0]	S:[0.375, 0.5, 0.2]

2. Remove the Collider component from both Barrel and Collar by selecting them individually and then right-clicking on the name of the Box Collider component and choosing *Remove Component* from the pop-up menu. You can also click the gear to the right of the Box Collider name to get the same menu.

3. Create a new material named *Mat_Collar* inside of the _Materials folder in the Project pane.

4. Drag this material on to Collar to assign it. In the Inspector, choose *ProtoTools > UnlitAlpha* from the Shader pop-up menu (see Figure 31.2).

5. Attach the *Weapon* C# script to the Weapon GameObject in the Hierarchy.

6. Drag the *Weapon* GameObject into the _Prefabs folder in the Project pane to make it a prefab.

7. Make the Weapon instance in the Hierarchy a child of _Hero and check that its position is [0, 2, 0]. This should place the Weapon on the nose of the _Hero ship, as is shown in Figure 31.2.

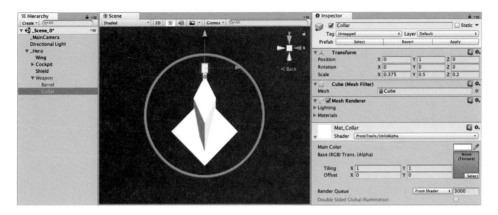

Figure 31.2 Weapon with the Collar selected and proper material and shader selected

8. Save your scene! Are you remembering to save constantly?

Adding Firing to the Weapon C# Script

To add firing to the weapon script, do the following:

1. Start by disabling the `fireDelegate` use of the `TempFire()` method in Hero. Open the Hero C# script in MonoDevelop and comment out the following bolded line:

```
public class Hero : MonoBehaviour {

    ...
    void Awake() {

        ...
//        fireDelegate += TempFire;
    }
    ...
}
```

Commenting out this line makes `fireDelegate` no longer call `TempFire()`. You may now delete the `TempFire()` method from the Hero class if you wish. If you click Play now and press the fire button, the Hero ship will not fire.

2. Open the *Weapon* C# script in MonoDevelop add the following bold code:

```
public class Weapon : MonoBehaviour {
    static public Transform    PROJECTILE_ANCHOR;

    [Header("Set Dynamically")]    [SerializeField]
    private WeaponType         _type = WeaponType.none;
    public WeaponDefinition    def;
    public GameObject          collar;
    public float               lastShotTime; // Time last shot was fired
```

```csharp
    private Renderer        collarRend;

    void Start() {
        collar = transform.Find("Collar").gameObject;
        collarRend = collar.GetComponent<Renderer>();

        // Call SetType() for the default _type of WeaponType.none
        SetType( _type );                                           // a

        // Dynamically create an anchor for all Projectiles
        if (PROJECTILE_ANCHOR == null) {                            // b
            GameObject go = new GameObject("_ProjectileAnchor");
            PROJECTILE_ANCHOR = go.transform;
        }
        // Find the fireDelegate of the root GameObject
        GameObject rootGO = transform.root.gameObject;              // c
        if ( rootGO.GetComponent<Hero>() != null ) {               // d
            rootGO.GetComponent<Hero>().fireDelegate += Fire;
        }
    }

    public WeaponType type {
        get {    return( _type );     }
        set {    SetType( value );    }
    }

    public void SetType( WeaponType wt ) {
        _type = wt;
        if (type == WeaponType.none) {                              // e
            this.gameObject.SetActive(false);
            return;
        } else {
            this.gameObject.SetActive(true);
        }
        def = Main.GetWeaponDefinition( _type );                   // f
        collarRend.material.color = def.color;
        lastShotTime = 0; // You can fire immediately after _type is set.    // g
    }

    public void Fire() {
        // If this.gameObject is inactive, return
        if (!gameObject.activeInHierarchy) return;                 // h
        // If it hasn't been enough time between shots, return
        if (Time.time - lastShotTime < def.delayBetweenShots) {    // i
            return;
        }
        Projectile p;
        Vector3 vel = Vector3.up * def.velocity;                   // j
        if (transform.up.y < 0) {
            vel.y = -vel.y;
        }
```

```
        switch (type) {                                          // k
            case WeaponType.blaster:
                p = MakeProjectile();
                p.rigid.velocity = vel;
                break;

            case WeaponType.spread:                              // l
                p = MakeProjectile();      // Make middle Projectile
                p.rigid.velocity = vel;
                p = MakeProjectile();      // Make right Projectile
                p.transform.rotation = Quaternion.AngleAxis( 10, Vector3.back );
                p.rigid.velocity = p.transform.rotation * vel;
                p = MakeProjectile();      // Make left Projectile
                p.transform.rotation = Quaternion.AngleAxis(-10, Vector3.back );
                p.rigid.velocity = p.transform.rotation * vel;
                break;

        }
    }

    public Projectile MakeProjectile() {                         // m
        GameObject go = Instantiate<GameObject>( def.projectilePrefab );
        if ( transform.parent.gameObject.tag == "Hero" ) {       // n
            go.tag = "ProjectileHero";
            go.layer = LayerMask.NameToLayer("ProjectileHero");
        } else {
            go.tag = "ProjectileEnemy";
            go.layer = LayerMask.NameToLayer("ProjectileEnemy");
        }
        go.transform.position = collar.transform.position;
        go.transform.SetParent( PROJECTILE_ANCHOR, true );       // o
        Projectile p = go.GetComponent<Projectile>();
        p.type = type;
        lastShotTime = Time.time;                                // p
        return( p );

    }
}
```

a. When the Weapon GameObject starts, it calls `SetType()` with whatever WeaponType
    `_type` is set to. This ensures that either the Weapon disappears (if `_type` is
    `WeaponType.none`) or shows the correct collar color (if `_type` is `WeaponType.`
    `blaster` or `WeaponType.spread`).

b. `PROJECTILE_ANCHOR` is a static Transform created to act as a parent in the Hierarchy
    to all the Projectiles created by Weapon scripts. If `PROJECTILE_ANCHOR` is null
    (because it has not yet been created), this script creates a new GameObject named
    ProjectileAnchor and assigns its transform to `PROJECTILE_ANCHOR`.

c. Weapons are always attached to other GameObjects (like _Hero). This finds the root GameObject of which this Weapon is a child.

d. If this root GameObject has a Hero script attached to it, then the `Fire()` method of this Weapon is added to the `fireDelegate` delegate of that Hero class instance. If you wanted to add Weapons to Enemies, you could add a similar `if` statement here to check for an attached Enemy script. Even if a subclass of Enemy (e.g., Enemy_1, Enemy_2, etc.) were attached to `rootGO`, it would still return when `rootGO` was asked for the Enemy script component because of class inheritance rules.

e. If `type` is `WeaponType.none`, this GameObject is disabled. When a GameObject is not active, it doesn't receive any MonoBehaviour method calls (e.g., `Update()`, `LateUp-date()`, `FixedUpdate()`, `OnCollisionEnter()`, and so on), it is not part of the physics simulation, and it visually disappears from the scene. However, calling functions and setting variables on the scripts attached to an inactive GameObject is still possible, so if something calls `SetType()` or sets the `type` property to `WeaponType.blaster` or `WeaponType.spread`, the `SetType()` method will be called, and it will reactivate the GameObject to which it is attached.

f. Not only does `SetType()` set whether or not the GameObject is active, it also pulls the proper WeaponDefinition from Main, sets the color of the Collar, and resets `lastShotTime`.

g. Resetting `lastShotTime` to 0 allows this Weapon to be fired immediately (see // i).

h. `gameObject.activeInHierarchy` will be `false` if either this Weapon is inactive or if the _Hero GameObject (the root parent of this Weapon) is inactive or destroyed. In any case where `gameObject.activeInHierarchy` is `false`, this function will return, and the Weapon will not fire.

i. If the difference between the current time and the last time this Weapon was fired is less than the `delayBetweenShots` defined in the WeaponDefinition, this Weapon will not fire.

j. An initial velocity in the up direction is set, but if `transform.up.y` is < 0 (which would be true for Enemy Weapons that are facing downward), the y component of `vel` is set to face downward as well.

k. This switch statement has options for each of the two WeaponTypes implemented in this chapter. The `WeaponType.blaster` generates a single Projectile by calling `MakeProjectile()` (which returns a reference to the `Projectile` class instance attached to the new projectile GameObject) and then assigns a velocity to its Rigidbody in the direction of `vel`.

l. If the `_type` is `WeaponType.spread`, then three different Projectiles are created. Two of them have their direction rotated 10 degrees around the `Vector3.back` axis (i.e., the -z axis that extends out of the screen toward you). Then, their Rigidbody.velocity is set to the multiplication of that rotation by `vel`. When a Quaternion is multiplied by a Vector3, it rotates that Vector3, causing the resultant velocity to point in the direction that the Projectile is angled.

   m. The `MakeProjectile()` method instantiates a clone of the prefab stored in the WeaponDefinition and returns a reference to the attached Projectile class instance.

   n. Based on whether this was fired by the _Hero or an Enemy, the Projectile is given the proper tag and physics layer.

   o. The Projectile GameObject's parent is set to be `PROJECTILE_ANCHOR`. This places it under _ProjectileAnchor in the Hierarchy pane, keeping the Hierarchy relatively clean to look at and avoiding the issue of having several Projectile clones cluttering the Hierarchy pane. The `true` argument passed in tells `go` to maintain its current world position through the transition.

   p. `lastShotTime` is set to the current time, preventing this Weapon from shooting for `def.delayBetweenShots` seconds.

3. Click *Play*, and the Weapon attached to _Hero disappears. This is because its WeaponType is `WeaponType.none`.

4. Select the Weapon attached to _Hero in the Hierarchy and set the `type` of its *Weapon (Script)* component to *Blaster*. Click *Play*; you can now hold the space bar to fire blaster shots every 0.2 seconds (as defined in the `weaponDefinitions` array of the *Main (Script)* component of _MainCamera).

5. Select the *Weapon* attached to _Hero in the Hierarchy and set the `type` of its *Weapon (Script)* component to *Spread*. Click *Play*; the Weapon Collar is now blue, and three shots are fired in a spread pattern every 0.4 seconds when you hold the space bar.

Revising the Enemy OnCollisionEnter Method

Now that your Weapons are firing shots that have the potential to do different amounts of damage (though they are currently set to do the same amount), you need to improve the `OnCollisionEnter()` method of the Enemy class.

1. Open the *Enemy* C# script in MonoDevelop and delete the `OnCollisionEnter()` method.

2. Replace the old `OnCollisionEnter()` method with this code.

```
public class Enemy : MonoBehaviour {
    ...
    public virtual void Move() { ... }

    void OnCollisionEnter( Collision coll ) {                       // a
        GameObject otherGO = coll.gameObject;
        switch (otherGO.tag) {
            case "ProjectileHero":                                 // b
                Projectile p = otherGO.GetComponent<Projectile>();
```

```
                    // If this Enemy is off screen, don't damage it.
                    if ( !bndCheck.isOnScreen ) {                              // c
                        Destroy( otherGO );
                        break;
                    }

                    // Hurt this Enemy
                    // Get the damage amount from the Main WEAP_DICT.
                    health -= Main.GetWeaponDefinition(p.type).damageOnHit;
                    if (health <= 0) {                                         // d
                        // Destroy this Enemy
                        Destroy(this.gameObject);
                    }
                    Destroy( otherGO );                                        // e
                    break;

            default:
                    print( "Enemy hit by non-ProjectileHero: " + otherGO.name ); // f
                    break;

        }
    }
}
```

a. Make sure you're replacing the old `OnCollisionEnter()` method entirely.

b. If the GameObject that hit this Enemy has the ProjectileHero tag, it should damage this Enemy. If it has any other tag, it will be handled by the `default` case (`// f`).

c. If this Enemy is not on screen, the Projectile GameObject that hit it is destroyed, and `break;` is called, which exits the switch statement without completing any of the remaining code in the `case "ProjectileHero"`.

d. If this Enemy's health is decreased to below 0, then this Enemy is destroyed. With a default Enemy health of 10 and blaster damageOnHit of 1, this will take 10 shots.

e. The Projectile GameObject is destroyed.

f. If somehow a GameObject tagged something other than a ProjectileHero hits this Enemy, a message about it posts to the Console pane.

3. Before clicking Play on the scene, you should switch from Enemy_3s being spawned back to spawning regular Enemies. Select *_MainCamera* in the Hierarchy and set *Element 0* of the `prefabEnemies` array of the *Main (Script)* component to be the Enemy_0 prefab.

Now when you play the scene, it is possible to destroy the enemies, but each enemy takes 10 shots to take down, and it's difficult to tell that they're being damaged.

Showing Enemy Damage

To show that an Enemy is being damaged, you will add code that makes the Enemy blink red for a couple of frames every time it is hit. However, to do so, you need to have access to all the materials of all the children of each enemy. This seems like something that might be useful in several different games, so let's make this part of a new *Utils* C# class that you will fill with reusable game code.

Creating the Reusable Utils Script

You will use the Utils class throughout the rest of this book. The Utils class is going to be almost entirely composed of static functions so that the functions can easily be called from anywhere in your code.

1. Create a new C# script named *Utils* and place it in the __Scripts folder. Open Utils in MonoDevelop and enter the following code:

```
using System.Collections;
using System.Collections.Generic;
using UnityEngine;

public class Utils : MonoBehaviour {

//============================= Materials Functions =============================\\

    // Returns a list of all Materials on this GameObject and its children
    static public Material[] GetAllMaterials( GameObject go ) {          // a
        Renderer[] rends = go.GetComponentsInChildren<Renderer>();       // b

        List<Material> mats = new List<Material>();
        foreach (Renderer rend in rends) {                               // c
            mats.Add( rend.material );
        }

        return( mats.ToArray() );                                        // d
    }
}
```

a. As a static public method, `GetAllMaterials()` can be called anywhere in this project via `Utils.GetAllMaterials()`.

b. `GetComponentsInChildren<>()` is a GameObject method that iterates over the GameObject itself and all of its children, and returns an array of whatever component type is passed into the generic `<>` parameter of the method (in this example, the component type Renderer).

c. This `foreach` loop iterates over the Renderer components in the `rends` array and extracts the `material` field from each. This Material is then added to the `mats` List.

d. Finally, the `mats` List is converted into an array and returned.

Using GetAllMaterials to Make the Enemy Blink Red

Now, modify Enemy to make use of the `GetAllMaterials()` static method of Utils:

1. Add the following bold code to the `Enemy` class:

```
public class Enemy : MonoBehaviour {
    ...
    public int        score = 100; // Points earned for destroying this
    public float      showDamageDuration = 0.1f; // # seconds to show damage // a

    [Header("Set Dynamically: Enemy")]
    public Color[]    originalColors;
    public Material[] materials;// All the Materials of this & its children
    public bool       showingDamage = false;
    public float      damageDoneTime; // Time to stop showing damage
    public bool       notifiedOfDestruction = false; // Will be used later


    protected BoundsCheck bndCheck;

    void Awake() {
        bndCheck = GetComponent<BoundsCheck>();
        // Get materials and colors for this GameObject and its children
        materials = Utils.GetAllMaterials( gameObject );                        // b
        originalColors = new Color[materials.Length];
        for (int i=0; i<materials.Length; i++) {
            originalColors[i] = materials[i].color;
        }
    }

    ...

    void Update() {
        Move();

        if ( showingDamage && Time.time > damageDoneTime ) {                     // c
            UnShowDamage();
        }

        if ( bndCheck != null && bndCheck.offDown ) {
            // We're off the bottom, so destroy this GameObject
            Destroy( gameObject );
        }
    }

    ...

    void OnCollisionEnter( Collision coll ) {
        GameObject otherGO = coll.gameObject;
```

```
        switch (otherGO.tag) {
            case "ProjectileHero":
                ...
                // Hurt this Enemy
                ShowDamage();                                    // d
                // Get the damage amount from the Main WEAP_DICT.
                ...
        }
    }

    void ShowDamage() {                                          // e
        foreach (Material m in materials) {
            m.color = Color.red;
        }
        showingDamage = true;
        damageDoneTime = Time.time + showDamageDuration;
    }

    void UnShowDamage() {                                        // f
        for ( int i=0; i<materials.Length; i++ ) {
            materials[i].color = originalColors[i];
        }
        showingDamage = false;
    }
}
```

a. Add all the new bolded fields at the top.

b. The materials array is filled using the new `Utils.GetAllMaterials()` method. Then, code here iterates through all the materials and stores their original color. Though all of the Enemy GameObjects are currently white, this method allows you to set whatever color you want on them, colors each one red when the Enemy is damaged, and then returns them to their original color.

   Importantly, this call to `Utils.GetAllMaterials()` is made in the `Awake()` method, and the result is cached in `materials`. This ensures that it only happens once for each Enemy. `Utils.GetAllMaterials()` makes use of `GetComponentsInChildren<>()`, which is a somewhat slow function that can take processing time and decrease performance. As such, it is generally better to call it once and cache the result rather than calling it every frame.

c. If the Enemy is currently showing damage (i.e., it's red) and the current time is later than `damageDoneTime`, `UnShowDamage()` is called.

d. A call to `ShowDamage()` is added to the section of `OnCollisionEnter()` that damages the Enemy.

e. `ShowDamage()` turns all materials in the `materials` array red, sets `showingDamage` to `true`, and sets the time at which it should stop showing damage.

f. `UnShowDamage()` turns all materials in the `materials` array back to their original color and sets `showingDamage` to `false`.

Now, when an Enemy is struck by a projectile from the hero, it will turn entirely red for `damageDoneTime` seconds by setting the color of all of its materials to red. After `damageDoneTime` seconds have passed, the Enemy script reverts itself and its child GameObjects to their original colors.

2. Click *Play* and test your game. It is now much easier to see that you're damaging the ship, but it still takes many hits before the enemy is destroyed. Let's make some power-ups to increase the power and number of the player's weapons.

3. Did you remember to save your project? Always save your project frequently.

Adding Power-Ups and Boosting Weapons

In this section, you will create three power-ups for the game:

■ **blaster [B]:** If the player weapon type is not blaster, this switches to blaster and resets the ship to have only a single gun. If the player weapon type is already blaster, it increases the number of guns.

■ **spread [S]:** If the player weapon type is not spread, this switches to spread and resets the ship to have only a single gun. If the player weapon type is already spread, it increases the number of guns.

■ **shield [O]:** This increases the player's shieldLevel by 1.

Artwork for Power-Ups

The power-ups are constructed of a letter rendered as 3D text with a spinning cube behind it. (You can see some of them in Figure 30.1 at the beginning of the previous chapter.) To make the power-ups, complete these steps:

1. Create a new 3D text (*GameObject > 3D Object > 3D Text* from the menu bar). Name it *PowerUp* and give it a *Cube* child and assign both the following settings:

PowerUp (3D Text)	P:[10, 0, 0]	R:[0, 0, 0]	S:[1, 1, 1]
Cube	P:[0, 0, 0]	R:[0, 0, 0]	S:[2, 2, 2]

2. Select the *PowerUp*.

3. Set the *Text Mesh* component properties of PowerUp to those shown in Figure 31.3.

4. Add a Rigidbody component to PowerUp (*Component > Physics > Rigidbody*) and set it as shown in the Figure 31.3.

5. Set both the *tag* and the *physics layer* of PowerUp to *PowerUp*. Respond *Yes, change children* to the question that appears.

6. Create a custom material for the PowerUp cube, as follows:

   a. Create a new Material named *Mat_PowerUp* inside the _Materials folder.

   b. Drag it onto the Cube that is a child of PowerUp.

   c. Select the Cube that is a child of PowerUp.

   d. Set the Shader of Mat PowerUp to *ProtoTools > UnlitAlpha*.

   e. Click the *Select* button at the bottom right of the texture box for Mat_PowerUp and choose the texture named *PowerUp* from the Assets tab. You will probably need to open the disclosure triangle in the bottom-left corner of the Mat_PowerUp component in the Inspector to see the texture for Mat_PowerUp.

   f. Set the *main color* of Mat_PowerUp to cyan (a light blue that is RGBA: [0, 255, 255, 255]), and you can see how the PowerUp will look when colored.

   g. Set the Box Collider of Cube to be a trigger (check the box next to *Is Trigger*).

Double-check that all the settings for PowerUp and its child Cube match those in Figure 31.3 and save your scene.

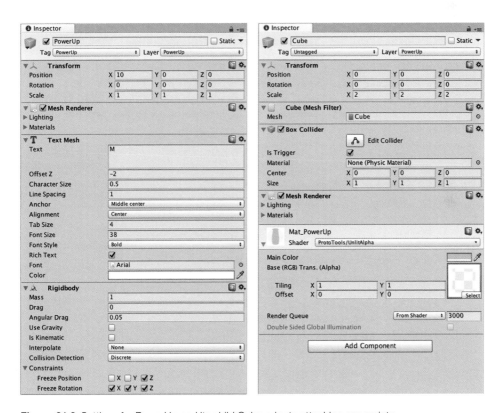

Figure 31.3 Settings for PowerUp and its child Cube prior to attaching any scripts

PowerUp Code

The power-up code is next:

1. Attach a BoundsCheck script to the PowerUp GameObject in the Hierarchy. Set `radius` to 1 and `keepOnScreen` to `false` (unchecked).

2. Create a new C# script named *PowerUp* in the __Scripts folder.

3. Attach the PowerUp script to the PowerUp GameObject in the Hierarchy.

4. Open the PowerUp script in MonoDevelop and enter the following code:

```csharp
using System.Collections;
using System.Collections.Generic;
using UnityEngine;

public class PowerUp : MonoBehaviour {
    [Header("Set in Inspector")]
    // This is an unusual but handy use of Vector2s. x holds a min value
    //   and y a max value for a Random.Range() that will be called later
    public Vector2          rotMinMax = new Vector2(15,90);
    public Vector2          driftMinMax = new Vector2(.25f,2);
    public float            lifeTime = 6f;   // Seconds the PowerUp exists
    public float            fadeTime = 4f;   // Seconds it will then fade

    [Header("Set Dynamically")]
    public WeaponType       type;          // The type of the PowerUp
    public GameObject       cube;          // Reference to the Cube child
    public TextMesh         letter;        // Reference to the TextMesh
    public Vector3          rotPerSecond;  // Euler rotation speed
    public float            birthTime;

    private Rigidbody       rigid;
    private BoundsCheck     bndCheck;
    private Renderer        cubeRend;

    void Awake() {
        // Find the Cube reference
        cube = transform.Find("Cube").gameObject;
        // Find the TextMesh and other components
        letter = GetComponent<TextMesh>();
        rigid = GetComponent<Rigidbody>();
        bndCheck = GetComponent<BoundsCheck>();
        cubeRend = cube.GetComponent<Renderer>();

        // Set a random velocity
        Vector3 vel = Random.onUnitSphere; // Get Random XYZ velocity
        // Random.onUnitSphere gives you a vector point that is somewhere on
        //   the surface of the sphere with a radius of 1m around the origin
        vel.z = 0;          // Flatten the vel to the XY plane
        vel.Normalize();    // Normalizing a Vector3 makes it length 1m
```

```
        vel *= Random.Range(driftMinMax.x, driftMinMax.y);                    // a
        rigid.velocity = vel;

        // Set the rotation of this GameObject to R:[ 0, 0, 0 ]
        transform.rotation = Quaternion.identity;
        // Quaternion.identity is equal to no rotation.

        // Set up the rotPerSecond for the Cube child using rotMinMax x & y
        rotPerSecond = new Vector3( Random.Range(rotMinMax.x,rotMinMax.y),
            Random.Range(rotMinMax.x,rotMinMax.y),
            Random.Range(rotMinMax.x,rotMinMax.y) );

        birthTime = Time.time;
    }

    void Update () {
        cube.transform.rotation = Quaternion.Euler( rotPerSecond*Time.time );// b

        // Fade out the PowerUp over time
        // Given the default values, a PowerUp will exist for 10 seconds
        //    and then fade out over 4 seconds.
        float u = (Time.time - (birthTime+lifeTime)) / fadeTime;
        // For lifeTime seconds, u will be <= 0. Then it will transition to
        //    1 over the course of fadeTime seconds.

        // If u >= 1, destroy this PowerUp
        if (u >= 1) {
            Destroy( this.gameObject );
            return;
        }

        // Use u to determine the alpha value of the Cube & Letter
        if (u>0) {
            Color c = cubeRend.material.color;
            c.a = 1f-u;
            cubeRend.material.color = c;
            // Fade the Letter too, just not as much
            c = letter.color;
            c.a = 1f - (u*0.5f);
            letter.color = c;
        }

        if (!bndCheck.isOnScreen) {
            // If the PowerUp has drifted entirely off screen, destroy it
            Destroy( gameObject );
        }
    }

    public void SetType( WeaponType wt ) {
        // Grab the WeaponDefinition from Main
        WeaponDefinition def = Main.GetWeaponDefinition( wt );
        // Set the color of the Cube child
```

```
        cubeRend.material.color = def.color;
        //letter.color = def.color; // We could colorize the letter too
        letter.text = def.letter; // Set the letter that is shown
        type = wt; // Finally actually set the type
    }

    public void AbsorbedBy( GameObject target ) {
        // This function is called by the Hero class when a PowerUp is collected
        // We could tween into the target and shrink in size,
        //   but for now, just destroy this.gameObject
        Destroy( this.gameObject );
    }

}
```

   a. Sets the velocity length to something between the x and y values of `driftMinMax`.

   b. Manually rotate the Cube child every `Update()`. Multiplying `rotPerSecond` by `Time.time` causes the rotation to be time-based.

5. Click *Play*, you should see the power-up drifting and rotating. If you fly the hero into the power-up, the console message "Triggered by non-Enemy: PowerUp" appears, letting you know that the Trigger Collider on the PowerUp cube is working properly.

6. Drag the *PowerUp* GameObject from the Hierarchy into the _Prefabs folder in the Project pane to make it into a prefab.

Enabling the Hero to Collect PowerUps

Next, you need to enable the Hero to collect PowerUps. First you'll just manage the collection, then you'll modify Hero to upgrade and change weapons in response to PowerUps.

1. Make the following changes to the Hero C# script to enable the hero to collide with and collect power-ups:

```
public class Hero : MonoBehaviour {
    …
    void OnTriggerEnter(Collider other) {
        …

        if (go.tag == "Enemy") {
            // If the shield was triggered by an enemy
            // Decrease the level of the shield by 1
            shieldLevel--;
            // Destroy the enemy
            Destroy(go);
        } else if (go.tag == "PowerUp") {
            // If the shield was triggered by a PowerUp
```

```
                AbsorbPowerUp(go);
        } else {
            print("Triggered by non-Enemy: "+go.name);
        }
    }

    public void AbsorbPowerUp( GameObject go ) {
        PowerUp pu = go.GetComponent<PowerUp>();
        switch (pu.type) {

            // Leave this switch block empty for now.

        }
        pu.AbsorbedBy( this.gameObject );
    }

    public float shieldLevel { … }
}
```

2. Now when you click Play, you can see that the Hero can run into the PowerUp and absorb it.

Before you can make absorbing a PowerUp actually do something, you need to do a little more Weapons set up.

3. Add the weapons array to the top of the Hero script as shown in bold code here.

```
public class Hero : MonoBehaviour {
    …
    public float           projectileSpeed = 40;
    public Weapon[]        weapons;                            // a

    [Header("Set Dynamically")]
    …
}
```

a. In the next section, you make five Weapon GameObjects as children of _Hero that will act as the guns for the ship. This `weapons` array will store a reference to each of them.

Expanding Weapon Options

Now that the code is set up, you need to make a couple of changes to _Hero in Unity.

1. Open the disclosure triangle next to the GameObject _Hero in the Hierarchy.

2. Select the *Weapon* child of _Hero. Press Command-D (or Ctrl+D on Windows) four times to make four duplicates of Weapon.[3] The duplicates should all still be children of _Hero.

---

3. If the keyboard command doesn't work, you can choose *Edit > Duplicate* from the menu bar or right-click the original Weapon in the Hierarchy and choose *Duplicate*.

3. Rename the four weapons *Weapon_0* through *Weapon_4* and configure their transforms as follows:

_Hero	P:[0, 0, 0]	R:[0, 0, 0]	S:[1, 1, 1]
Weapon_0	P:[0, 2, 0]	R:[0, 0, 0]	S:[1, 1, 1]
Weapon_1	P:[-2, -1, 0]	R:[0, 0, 0]	S:[1, 1, 1]
Weapon_2	P:[2, -1, 0]	R:[0, 0, 0]	S:[1, 1, 1]
Weapon_3	P:[-1.25, -0.25, 0]	R:[0, 0, 0]	S:[1, 1, 1]
Weapon_4	P:[1.25, -0.25, 0]	R:[0, 0, 0]	S:[1, 1, 1]

4. Select _*Hero* and open the disclosure triangle for the `weapons` field in the *Hero (Script)* component Inspector.

5. Set the *Size* of `weapons` to *5* and assign Weapon_0 through Weapon_4 to the five Weapon slots in order (either by dragging them in from the Hierarchy or by clicking the target to the right of the Weapon slot and selecting each Weapon_# from the Scene tab). Figure 31.4 shows the resultant setup.

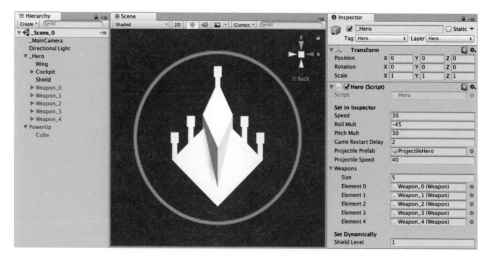

Figure 31.4 The _Hero ship showing five Weapons as children and assigned to the weapons field

Let's make absorbing a PowerUp actually do something. To do so, we'll need to make some changes to the Hero script.

6. Open the Hero script and add the following `GetEmptyWeaponSlot()` and `ClearWeapons()` methods to the bottom of the Hero class.

```
public class Hero : MonoBehaviour {
    …
    public float shieldLevel {

        …
    }
```

```
Weapon GetEmptyWeaponSlot() {
    for (int i=0; i<weapons.Length; i++) {
        if ( weapons[i].type == WeaponType.none ) {
            return( weapons[i] );
        }
    }
    return( null );
}

void ClearWeapons() {
    foreach (Weapon w in weapons) {
        w.SetType(WeaponType.none);
    }
}
}
```

7. Fill the switch block of the `AbsorbPowerUp()` method (that you previously left empty)
   with the following bold code.

```
public class Hero : MonoBehaviour {
    …
    public void AbsorbPowerUp( GameObject go ) {
        PowerUp pu = go.GetComponent<PowerUp>();
        switch (pu.type) {
            case WeaponType.shield:                              // a
                shieldLevel++;
                break;

            default:                                            // b
                if (pu.type == weapons[0].type) { // If it is the same type  // c
                    Weapon w = GetEmptyWeaponSlot();
                    if (w != null) {
                        // Set it to pu.type
                        w.SetType(pu.type);
                    }
                } else { // If this is a different weapon type  // d
                    ClearWeapons();
                    weapons[0].SetType(pu.type);
                }
                break;
        }
        pu.AbsorbedBy( this.gameObject );
    }
    …
}
```

a. If the PowerUp has the WeaponType shield, it increases the shield level by 1.

b. Any other PowerUp WeaponType will be a weapon, so that is the default state.

c. If the PowerUp is the same WeaponType as the existing weapons, a search occurs for an unused weapon slot and an attempt is made to set that empty slot to the same weapon type. If all five slots are already in use, nothing happens.

d. If the PowerUp is a different WeaponType, then all weapon slots are cleared, and Weapon_0 is set to the new WeaponType that was picked up.

8. To test this, select the PowerUp in the Hierarchy, and inside the *PowerUp (Script)* component of the Inspector, set the `type` (under the heading "Set Dynamically") to `Spread`. Normally, the type is set dynamically, but you can set it manually for testing.

9. Click *Play*, and you'll start with five blasters. When you run into the PowerUp, it will swap those blasters for a single spread gun. The PowerUp doesn't show the correct letter because you set the type manually. You can also try testing the PowerUp with a type of shield, and you can see that the shield level increases when you run over the PowerUp.

Managing Race Conditions

Now, we're going to break something to make a point. Bear with me; this is important, and you'll probably run into something like it in the future.

1. Add the following bolded lines to the `Awake()` method of the Hero script:

```
public class Hero : MonoBehaviour {
    ...
    void Awake() {
        S = this;  // Set the Singleton
//      fireDelegate += TempFire;

        // Reset the weapons to start _Hero with 1 blaster
        ClearWeapons();
        weapons[0].SetType(WeaponType.blaster);
    }
    ...
}
```

2. Click *Play*, and you should see something like the following error message:

> NullReferenceException: Object reference not set to an instance of an object
> Weapon.SetType (WeaponType wt) (at Assets/__Scripts/Weapon.cs:82)
> Hero.Awake () (at Assets/__Scripts/Hero.cs:36)

This tells you that something you are trying to use is null and that it encountered this error on the following line from the `SetType()` method of Weapon.cs (line 82 in my implementation, but your line number is probably different).

```
collarRend.material.color = def.color;
```

The error message also tells you that this line of Weapon.cs was reached via a function call on a specific line of the `Awake()` method of Hero.cs (line 36 for me, but yours might vary). That line is:

```
weapons[0].SetType(WeaponType.blaster);
```

So, tracing this back, it looks like the `Awake()` method of Hero is calling the `SetType()` method of the 0th Weapon in the weapons array. The `SetType()` method of Weapon is trying to set the color of `collarRend`, but `collarRend` is null, so this is throwing a null reference error.

Look at the `Start()` method in Weapon. That is where `collarRend` is set. However, the `Awake()` method of Hero is always called before the `Start()` method on Weapon, meaning that we are trying to read the value of `collarRend` before it has been set! Fixing this is going to involve some additional steps.

3. In the Hero script, change the name of the `Awake()` method to `Start()`.[4]

If you click Play, it might seem that this change has fixed everything, but that's not actually the case. What you've done is *possibly* fix things, because it's possible that `Weapon.Start()` will execute before `Hero.Start()`, but it's also still possible that `Hero.Start()` will execute first. You need to be sure.

4. Open the *Script Execution Order* Inspector by choosing *Edit > Project Settings > Script Execution Order* from the menu bar.

    a. Click the + button that is circled in image 1 of Figure 31.5 and choose the *Weapon* script from the pop-up menu. This creates a row in the table for Weapon with a value of 100. The 100 number represents the *execution order* of Weapon versus the other scripts, which all run at *Default Time*. If the number is higher (as it is now), all Weapon scripts will execute *after* other scripts, meaning that the `Weapon.Start()` method will execute after the `Hero.Start()` or any other script.

    b. Click the *Apply* button (this locks in the execution order) and click *Play*.

    c. You can see that you now definitely encounter a null reference exception. Instead of Weapon happening last, you need it to happen first.

    d. Open the Script Execution Order Inspector again, and use the two-bar thumb on the left side of the Weapon row (that the cursor is touching in image 2 of Figure 31.5) to drag the Weapon row *above* Default Time. This also changes the number on that row from 100 to -100 (as shown in image 2 of Figure 31.5). Now `Weapon.Start()` will execute *before* any other `Start()` methods.

    e. Click *Apply* and click *Play* again. This time, you should not get any errors.

---

4. Remember that `Awake()` is called the moment that a GameObject is instantiated, while `Start()` is called immediately before the first `Update()` on that GameObject. Two objects that are both part of a scene are both instantiated immediately when the game begins, so `Awake()` will be called on both before `Start()` is called on either; but there is no guarantee as to which GameObject will have its `Start()` method called first. Setting the Script Execution Order (as you do in step 4) fixes this uncertainty.

Race conditions and script execution order are subtle yet important things to keep in mind when you're working on your own projects.

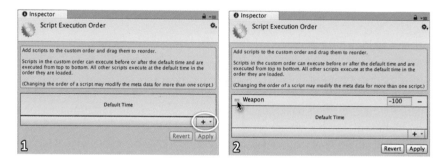

Figure 31.5 The Script Execution Order Inspector showing manipulation of the Weapon script's execution order.

Making Enemies Drop Power-Ups

Getting back to the power-ups. Let's make enemies have the potential to drop a random power-up when they are destroyed. This gives the player a lot more incentive to try to destroy enemies rather than just avoid them, and it gives the player a path to improving her ship.

When an Enemy is destroyed, it notifies the Main singleton, and then the Main singleton instantiates a new PowerUp. This might seem like a somewhat roundabout way to do this, but in general, it is best to limit the number of different classes that can instantiate new GameObjects into your scene. If fewer scripts are responsible an activity (like instantiation), then it'll be easier to debug if you see that something is going wrong with that activity.

1. Start by making the Main class able to instantiate new PowerUps. Add the following bolded code to the Main script.

```
public class Main : MonoBehaviour {
    ...
    public WeaponDefinition[]    weaponDefinitions;
    public GameObject            prefabPowerUp;                          // a
    public WeaponType[]          powerUpFrequency = new WeaponType[] {   // b
                                    WeaponType.blaster, WeaponType.blaster,
                                    WeaponType.spread,  WeaponType.shield };

    private BoundsCheck      bndCheck;

    public void ShipDestroyed( Enemy e ) {                               // c
        // Potentially generate a PowerUp
        if (Random.value <= e.powerUpDropChance) {                       // d
            // Choose which PowerUp to pick
            // Pick one from the possibilities in powerUpFrequency
            int ndx = Random.Range(0,powerUpFrequency.Length);           // e
            WeaponType puType = powerUpFrequency[ndx];
```

```
        // Spawn a PowerUp
        GameObject go = Instantiate( prefabPowerUp ) as GameObject;
        PowerUp pu = go.GetComponent<PowerUp>();
        // Set it to the proper WeaponType
        pu.SetType( puType );                                         // f

        // Set it to the position of the destroyed ship
        pu.transform.position = e.transform.position;
    }
}

void Awake() { … }
…
}
```

a. This will hold the prefab for all PowerUps.

b. This `powerUpFrequency` array of WeaponTypes determines how often each type of PowerUp will be created. By default, it has two blasters, one spread, and one shield, so the blaster power-up will be twice as common as the others.

c. The `ShipDestroyed()` method will be called by an Enemy ship whenever it is destroyed. It sometimes creates a power-up in place of the destroyed ship.

d. Each type of ship will have a `powerUpDropChance`, which is a number between 0 and 1. `Random.value` is a property that generates a random float between 0 (inclusive) and 1 (inclusive). (Because `Random.value` is inclusive of both 0 and 1, the number could potentially be either 0 or 1.) If that number is less than or equal to the `powerUp-DropChance`, a PowerUp is instantiated. The drop chance is part of the `Enemy` class so that various enemies can have higher or lower chances of dropping a PowerUp (e.g., Enemy_0 could rarely drop one, whereas Enemy_4 could always drop one). It appears red in the code listing because we have not yet added it to the Enemy class.

e. This line makes use of the `powerUpFrequency` array. When `Random.Range()` is called with two integer values, it chooses a number between the first number (inclusive) and the second number (exclusive); for example, `Random.Range(0,4)` would generate an int with a value of 0, 1, 2, or 3. This is very useful for choosing a random entry in an array, as you're doing on this line.

f. After a power-up type has been selected, the `SetType()` method is called on the instantiated PowerUp, and the PowerUp then handles coloring itself, setting its `_type`, and displaying the correct letter in its `letter` TextMesh.

2. Add the bolded code that follows to the Enemy script:

```
public class Enemy : MonoBehaviour {
    …
    public float      showDamageDuration = 0.1f; // # seconds to show damage
    public float      powerUpDropChance = 1f;  // Chance to drop a power-up  // a

    [Header("These fields are set dynamically")]
    …
```

```
void OnCollisionEnter( Collision coll ) {
    GameObject otherGO = coll.gameObject;
    switch (otherGO.tag) {
        case "ProjectileHero":
            …
            // Hurt this Enemy
            …
            if (health <= 0) {
                // Tell the Main singleton that this ship was destroyed  // b
                if (!notifiedOfDestruction){
                    Main.S.ShipDestroyed( this );
                }
                notifiedOfDestruction = true;
                // Destroy this Enemy
                Destroy(this.gameObject);
            }
            …
            break;
        …
    }
}
```

a. `powerUpDropChance` determines how likely this Enemy is to drop a PowerUp when it is destroyed. A value of 0 will never drop a PowerUp, and a 1 will always drop one.

b. Immediately before this Enemy is destroyed, it notifies the Main singleton by calling `ShipDestroyed()`. This only happens once for each ship, which is enforced by the `notifiedOfDestruction` bool.

3. Before this code can work, you need to select _ *MainCamera* in the Hierarchy and assign the PowerUp prefab from the _Prefabs folder in the Project pane to the `prefabPowerUp` field of the *Main (Script)* component of _MainCamera.

4. Select the PowerUp instance in the Hierarchy and delete it (you don't need it because you have a PowerUp prefab in the Project pane).

5. `powerUpFrequency` should already be set in the _MainCamera *Main (Script)* Inspector, but just in case, Figure 31.6 shows the correct settings.

Figure 31.6 `prefabPowerUp` and `powerUpFrequency` on the *Main (Script)* component of _MainCamera

6. Now play the scene and destroy some enemies. They should drop power-ups that improve your ship!

You should notice over time that the blaster [B] power-up is more common than spread [S] or shield [O]. This is because there are two occurrences of blaster in `powerUpFrequency` and only one each of spread and shield. By adjusting the relative numbers of occurrences of each of these in `powerUpFrequency`, you can determine the chance that each will be chosen relative to the others. You can also use this same trick to set the frequency of different types of enemies spawning by assigning some enemy types to the `prefabEnemies` array more times than other enemy types.

Enemy_4—A More Complex Enemy

As somewhat of a boss type, Enemy_4 has more health than other enemy types and has destructible parts (rather than all the parts being destroyed at the same time). It also stays on screen, moving from one position to another, until the player destroys it completely.

Collider Modifications

Before getting into code issues, you need to make a few adjustments to the colliders of Enemy_4.

1. Drag an instance of *Enemy_4* into the Hierarchy and make sure that it's positioned away from other GameObjects in the scene (it should default to the P:[20, 10, 0] that you set earlier).

2. Open the disclosure triangle next to Enemy_4 in the Hierarchy and select the *Fuselage* child.

3. Remove the Sphere Collider component from Fuselage by clicking the *gear* in the top-right corner of the Sphere Collider component in the Inspector and selecting *Remove Component*.

4. Add a Capsule Collider to the Fuselage by selecting *Component > Physics > Capsule Collider* from the menu bar. Set the Capsule Collider as follows in the Fuselage Inspector:

Center	[0, 0, 0]	**Height**	1
Radius	0.5	**Direction**	Y-Axis

Feel free to play with the values somewhat to see how they affect things. As you can see, the Capsule Collider is a much better approximation of Fuselage than the Sphere Collider was.

5. Select the *WingL* child of Enemy_4 in the Hierarchy and replace its Sphere Collider with a Capsule Collider as well. Set the *Direction* of this Capsule Collider to X-Axis.

Center	[0, 0, 0]	**Height**	1
Radius	0.5	**Direction**	X-Axis

The *Direction* setting of a Capsule Collider chooses which is the long axis of the capsule. This is determined in local coordinates, so the height of 1 along the X-axis is multiplied by the scale of 5 in the X dimension. The radius of 0.5 is multiplied by the maximum of either the Y or Z scales, so the actual radius of the capsule is 0.5 due to the Y scale of 1. You can see that the capsule does not perfectly match the wing, but again, it is a much better approximation than a sphere.

6. Select *WingR*, replace its collider with a Capsule Collider, and give that collider the same settings as used on WingL.

7. Select *Enemy_4* in the Hierarchy and add a *BoundsCheck (Script)* component to Enemy_4 by clicking the *Add Component* button in the Inspector and choosing *Add Component > Scripts > BoundsCheck*.

8. In the *BoundsCheck (Script)* component, set `radius` = 3.5 and `keepOnScreen` = `false`.

9. Click the *Apply* button to the right of the word *Prefab* at the top of the Inspector pane. This applies the changes make to this instance of Enemy_4 back to the Enemy_4 prefab in the Project pane.

10. To double-check that this worked successfully, drag a second instance of the Enemy_4 prefab into the Hierarchy pane and check to make sure that the colliders all look correct. When you first drag it in, the new instance should align exactly with the one you've been modifying.

11. Delete both instances of Enemy_4 from the Hierarchy pane.

12. Save your scene! Have you been remembering?

You could also apply this same Capsule Collider strategy to Enemy_3 if you want.

Movement of Enemy_4

Enemy_4 starts in the standard position off the top of the screen, picks a random point on screen, and moves to it over time using a linear interpolation. After it reaches the chosen point, it rests for a moment and then selects and moves to another point.

1. Open the *Enemy_4* script and input this code:

```
using System.Collections;
using System.Collections.Generic;
using UnityEngine;

/// <summary>
/// Enemy_4 will start offscreen and then pick a random point on screen to
///   move to. Once it has arrived, it will pick another random point and
///   continue until the player has shot it down.
/// </summary>
public class Enemy_4 : Enemy {

    private Vector3     p0, p1;      // The two points to interpolate
    private float       timeStart;   // Birth time for this Enemy_4
```

```
private float            duration = 4;  // Duration of movement

void Start () {
    // There is already an initial position chosen by Main.SpawnEnemy()
    //   so add it to points as the initial p0 & p1
    p0 = p1 = pos;                                              // a

    InitMovement();
}

void InitMovement() {                                          // b
    p0 = p1;   // Set p0 to the old p1
    // Assign a new on-screen location to p1
    float widMinRad = bndCheck.camWidth - bndCheck.radius;
    float hgtMinRad = bndCheck.camHeight - bndCheck.radius;
    p1.x = Random.Range( -widMinRad, widMinRad );
    p1.y = Random.Range( -hgtMinRad, hgtMinRad );

    // Reset the time
    timeStart = Time.time;
}

public override void Move () {                                 // c
    // This completely overrides Enemy.Move() with a linear interpolation
    float u = (Time.time-timeStart)/duration;

    if (u>=1) {
        InitMovement();
        u=0;
    }

    u = 1 - Mathf.Pow( 1-u, 2 );  // Apply Ease Out easing to u      // d
    pos = (1-u)*p0 + u*p1;        // Simple linear interpolation      // e
}
}
```

a. Enemy_4 interpolates from p0 to p1 (i.e., moves smoothly from p0 to p1). The Main. SpawnEnemy() script gives this instance a position just above the top of the screen, which is assigned here to both p0 and p1. InitMovement() is then called.

b. InitMovement() first stores the current p1 location in p0 (because Enemy_4 should be at location p1 any time InitMovement() is called). Next, a new p1 location is chosen that uses information from the BoundsCheck component to guarantee it is on screen.

c. This Move() method completely overrides the inherited Enemy.Move() method. It interpolates from p0 to p1 in duration seconds (4 seconds by default). The float u increases from 0 to 1 with time as this interpolation happens, and when u is >= 1, InitMovement() is called to set up a new interpolation.

d. This line applies easing to the u value, causing the ship to move in a non-linear fashion. With this "Ease Out" easing, the ship begins its movement quickly and then slows as it approaches p1.

e. This line performs a simple linear interpolation from p0 to p1.

To learn a lot more about both interpolation and easing, read the *interpolation* section in Appendix B, "Useful Concepts."

2. Select *_MainCamera* in the Hierarchy. Assign the Enemy_4 prefab in the _Prefabs folder of the Project pane to *Element 0* of the prefabEnemies array in the *Main (Script)* Inspector.

3. Click *Play*. You can see that the spawned Enemy_4s stay on screen until you destroy them. However, they're currently just as simple to take down as any of the other enemies.

Splitting Enemy_4 into Multiple Parts

Now you'll break the Enemy_4 ship into four different parts with the central Cockpit part protected by the others.

1. Open the *Enemy_4* C# script and add a new serializable class named Part to the top of Enemy_4.cs. Also be sure to add a Part[] array to the Enemy_4 class named parts. Add the bolded lines that follow to the Start() script of Enemy_4 to do so.

```
using System.Collections;
using System.Collections.Generic;
using UnityEngine;


/// <summary>
/// Part is another serializable data storage class just like WeaponDefinition
/// </summary>
[System.Serializable]
public class Part {
    // These three fields need to be defined in the Inspector pane
    public string      name;        // The name of this part
    public float       health;      // The amount of health this part has
    public string[]    protectedBy; // The other parts that protect this

    // These two fields are set automatically in Start().
    // Caching like this makes it faster and easier to find these later
    [HideInInspector]  // Makes field on the next line not appear in the Inspector
    public GameObject  go;          // The GameObject of this part
    [HideInInspector]
    public Material    mat;         // The Material to show damage
}

...
```

```
public class Enemy_4 : Enemy {
    [Header("Set in Inspector: Enemy_4")]                              // a
    public Part[]           parts;    // The array of ship Parts

    private Vector3         p0, p1;    // The two points to interpolate
    private float           timeStart; // Birth time for this Enemy_4
    private float           duration = 4;  // Duration of movement

    void Start () {
        // There is already an initial position chosen by Main.SpawnEnemy()
        //   so add it to points as the initial p0 & p1
        p0 = p1 = pos;

        InitMovement();

        // Cache GameObject & Material of each Part in parts
        Transform t;
        foreach (Part prt in parts) {
            t = transform.Find(prt.name);
            if (t != null) {
                prt.go = t.gameObject;
                prt.mat = prt.go.GetComponent<Renderer>().material;
            }
        }
    }
    ...
}
```

a. In the Inspector, all the public fields from Enemy are listed above those from Enemy_4. Adding the ": Enemy_4" to the end of the header here makes it more clear in the Inspector which script is tied to which field (see Figure 31.7).

The serializable[5] Part class stores individual information about the four parts of Enemy_4: Cockpit, Fuselage, WingL, and WingR.

2. Switch back to Unity and do the following:

    a. Select the *Enemy_4* prefab in the Project pane.

    b. Expand the disclosure triangle next to `parts` in the *Enemy_4 (Script)* Inspector.

    c. Enter the settings shown in Figure 31.7. Be careful to spell all the names correctly.

---

5. Remember that making a class *serializable* allows its fields to be seen and set in the Unity Inspector. Simple classes are more likely to be able to be seen in the Inspector. If a class is too complex, the Unity Inspector will not be able to show it.

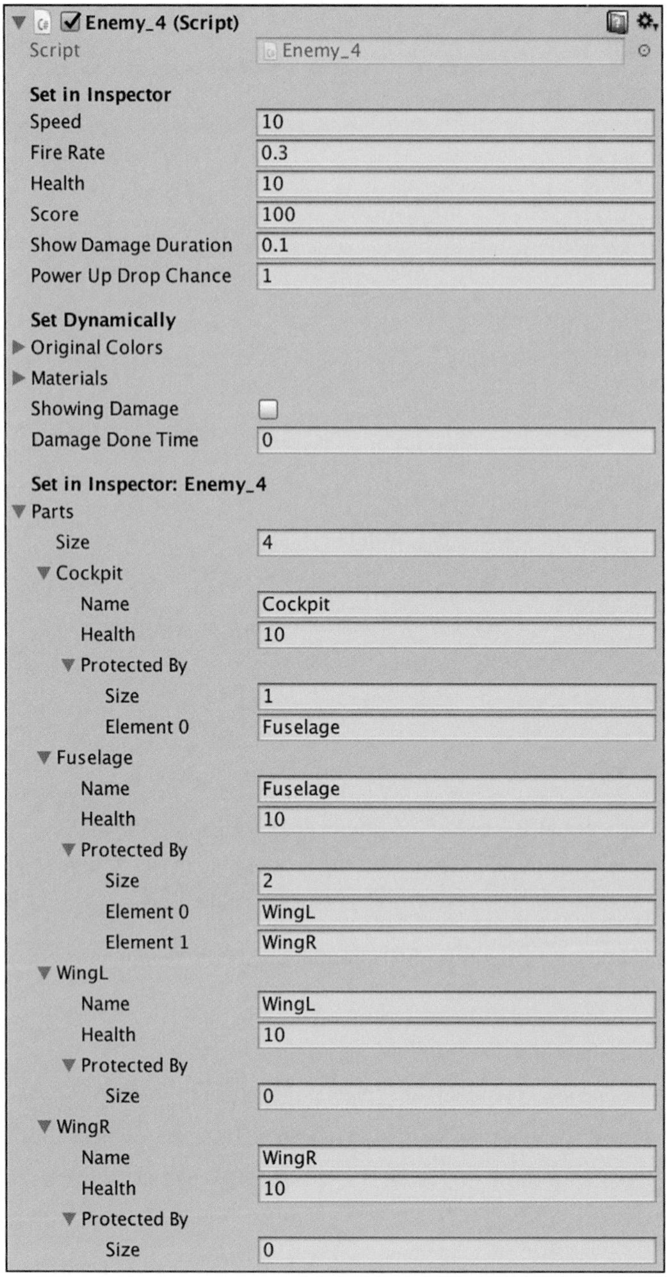

Figure 31.7 The settings for the `parts` array of Enemy_4

As you can see in Figure 31.7, each Part has 10 health, and there is a hierarchical tree of protection. Cockpit is protected by Fuselage, and Fuselage is protected by both WingL and WingR. Be sure to save your scene!

3. Switch back to MonoDevelop and add the following methods to the end of the Enemy_4 class to make this protection work:

```
public class Enemy_4 : Enemy {
    ...

    public override void Move () {
        ...
    }

    // These two functions find a Part in parts based on name or GameObject
    Part FindPart(string n) {                                        // a
        foreach( Part prt in parts ) {
            if (prt.name == n) {
                return( prt );
            }
        }
        return( null );
    }
    Part FindPart(GameObject go) {                                   // b
        foreach( Part prt in parts ) {
            if (prt.go == go) {
                return( prt );
            }
        }
        return( null );
    }

    // These functions return true if the Part has been destroyed
    bool Destroyed(GameObject go) {                                  // c
        return( Destroyed( FindPart(go) ) );
    }
    bool Destroyed(string n) {
        return( Destroyed( FindPart(n) ) );
    }
    bool Destroyed(Part prt) {
        if (prt == null) {  // If no real ph was passed in
            return(true);   // Return true (meaning yes, it was destroyed)
        }
        // Returns the result of the comparison: prt.health <= 0
        // If prt.health is 0 or less, returns true (yes, it was destroyed)
        return (prt.health <= 0);
    }

    // This changes the color of just one Part to red instead of the whole ship.
    void ShowLocalizedDamage(Material m) {                           // d
        m.color = Color.red;
        damageDoneTime = Time.time + showDamageDuration;
        showingDamage = true;
    }
```

```
// This will override the OnCollisionEnter that is part of Enemy.cs.
void OnCollisionEnter( Collision coll ) {                             // e
    GameObject other = coll.gameObject;
    switch (other.tag) {
        case "ProjectileHero":
            Projectile p = other.GetComponent<Projectile>();
            // If this Enemy is off screen, don't damage it.
            if ( !bndCheck.isOnScreen ) {
                Destroy( other );
                break;
            }

            // Hurt this Enemy
            GameObject goHit = coll.contacts[0].thisCollider.gameObject; // f
            Part prtHit = FindPart(goHit);
            if (prtHit == null) { // If prtHit wasn't found…               // g
                goHit = coll.contacts[0].otherCollider.gameObject;
                prtHit = FindPart(goHit);
            }
            // Check whether this part is still protected
            if (prtHit.protectedBy != null) {                            // h
                foreach( string s in prtHit.protectedBy ) {
                    // If one of the protecting parts hasn't been destroyed...
                    if (!Destroyed(s)) {
                        // ...then don't damage this part yet
                        Destroy(other);   // Destroy the ProjectileHero
                        return;           // return before damaging Enemy_4
                    }
                }
            }

            // It's not protected, so make it take damage
            // Get the damage amount from the Projectile.type and Main.W_DEFS
            prtHit.health -= Main.GetWeaponDefinition( p.type ).damageOnHit;
            // Show damage on the part
            ShowLocalizedDamage(prtHit.mat);
            if (prtHit.health <= 0) {                                    // i
                // Instead of destroying this enemy, disable the damaged part
                prtHit.go.SetActive(false);
            }
            // Check to see if the whole ship is destroyed
            bool allDestroyed = true; // Assume it is destroyed
            foreach( Part prt in parts ) {
                if (!Destroyed(prt)) {  // If a part still exists...
                    allDestroyed = false;  // ...change allDestroyed to false
                    break;                 // & break out of the foreach loop
                }
            }
            if (allDestroyed) { // If it IS completely destroyed...       // j
                // ...tell the Main singleton that this ship was destroyed
                Main.S.ShipDestroyed( this );
```

```
                        // Destroy this Enemy
                        Destroy(this.gameObject);
                    }
                    Destroy(other);   // Destroy the ProjectileHero
                    break;
                }
            }
        }
```

a. The `FindPart()` methods at `// a` and `// b` are *overloads* of each other, meaning that they are two methods with the same name but different parameters (one takes a string, and the other takes a GameObject). Based on what type of variable is passed in, the correct overload of the `FindPart()` function is executed. In either case, `FindPart()` searches through the `parts` array to find which part the string or GameObject is associated with.

b. A GameObject overload of `FindPart()`. Another overloaded function that you've used before is `Random.range()`, which has different behavior based on whether floats or ints are passed into it.

c. Three overloads of the `Destroyed()` method that checks to see whether a certain part has been destroyed or still has health.

d. `ShowLocalizedDamage()` is a more specialized version of the inherited `Enemy.ShowDamage()` method. This only turns one part red, not the whole ship.

e. This `OnCollisionEnter()` method completely overrides the inherited `Enemy.OnCollisionEnter()` method. Because of the way that MonoBehaviour declares common Unity functions like `OnCollisionEnter()`, the override keyword is not necessary.

f. This line finds the GameObject that was hit. The Collision `coll` includes a field `contacts[]`, which is an array of ContactPoints. Because there was a collision, you're guaranteed that at least one ContactPoint (i.e., `contacts[0]`) exists, and each ContactPoint has a field named `thisCollider`, which is the collider for the part of the Enemy_4 that was hit.

g. If the `prtHit` you searched for wasn't found (and therefore `prtHit == null`), then it's usually because—very rarely—`thisCollider` on `contacts[0]` will refer to the ProjectileHero that hit the ship instead of the ship part that was hit. In that case, just look at `contacts[0].otherCollider` instead.

h. If this part is still protected by another part that has not yet been destroyed, apply damage to the protecting part instead.

i. If a single part's health reaches 0, then set it to inactive, which makes it disappear and stop colliding with things.

j. If the whole ship has been destroyed, notify `Main.S.ShipDestroyed()` just like the Enemy script would have (if you hadn't overridden `OnCollisionEnter()`).

4. Play the scene. You should eventually be overwhelmed by many Enemy_4s, each of which has two wings that protect the fuselage and a fuselage that protects the cockpit. If you want more of a chance against these, you can change the value of the `enemySpawnPerSecond` field of *Main (Script)* on the _MainCamera to something lower, which gives you more time between Enemy_4 spawns (though it will also delay the initial spawn).

5. We're close to a playable game now! Next you'll set the `prefabEnemies` array on the *Main (Script)* of _MainCamera to spawn various enemies with reasonable frequency.

   a. Select _*MainCamera* in the Hierarchy.

   b. Set the *Size* of prefabEnemies on the *Main (Script)* Inspector to *10*.

   c. Set Elements 0, 1, and 2 to *Enemy_0* (from the _Prefabs folder of the Project pane).

   d. Set Elements 3 and 4 to *Enemy_1*.

   e. Set Elements 5 and 6 to *Enemy_2*.

   f. Set Elements 7 and 8 to *Enemy_3*.

   g. Set Element 9 to *Enemy_4*.

Doing all this should give you Enemy_0s pretty frequently and Enemy_4s rather rarely.

6. Set the `powerUpDropChance` of each enemy type.

   a. Select *Enemy_0* in the _Prefabs folder of the Project pane and set `powerUpDropChance` in the *Enemy (Script)* Inspector to 0.25 (meaning that an Enemy_0 will drop a PowerUp 25% of the time).

   b. Set the `powerUpDropChance` of Enemy_1 to *0.5*.

   c. Set the `powerUpDropChance` of Enemy_2 to *0.5*.

   d. Set the `powerUpDropChance` of Enemy_3 to *0.75*.

   e. Set the `powerUpDropChance` of Enemy_4 to *1*.

7. Save your scene and click *Play* to try out your game!

Adding a Scrolling Starfield Background

After all of that coding, here's something you can do just for fun to make the game look a little better: create a two-layer starfield background to make things look more like outer space.

1. Create a quad in the Hierarchy (*GameObject > 3D Object > Quad*). Name it *StarfieldBG*.

   StarfieldBG (Quad)   P:[0, 0, 10]   R:[0, 0, 0]   S:[80, 80, 1]

This places StarfieldBG in the center of the camera's view and fills the view entirely.

2. Create a new material named *Mat_Starfield* and set its shader to *ProtoTools > UnlitAlpha*. Set the texture of Mat_Starfield to the *Space* Texture2D that is in the _Materials folder you imported at the beginning of this tutorial.

3. Drag *Mat_Starfield* onto StarfieldBG, and you should see a starfield behind your _Hero ship.

4. Select *Mat Starfield* in the Project pane and duplicate it (Command-D on Mac or Ctrl+D on PC). Name the new material *Mat_Starfield_Transparent*. Select *Space_Transparent* (in the _Materials folder) as the texture for this new material.

5. Select *StarfieldBG* in the Hierarchy and duplicate it. Name the duplicate *StarfieldFG_0*. Drag the *Mat_Starfield_Transparent* material onto StarfieldFG_0 and set its transform to

   StarfieldFG_0   P:[0, 0, 5]   R:[0, 0, 0]   S:[160, 160, 1]

If you drag StarfieldFG_0 around a bit, you'll see that it moves some stars in the foreground past stars in the background, creating a nifty parallax effect.

6. Duplicate Starfield_FG_0 and name the duplicate *Starfield_FG_1*. You need two copies of the foreground for the scrolling trick that you are about to employ.

7. Create a new C# script named *Parallax* and edit it in MonoDevelop.

```csharp
using System.Collections;
using System.Collections.Generic;
using UnityEngine;

public class Parallax : MonoBehaviour {
    [Header("Set in Inspector")]
    public GameObject        poi; // The player ship
    public GameObject[]      panels; // The scrolling foregrounds
    public float             scrollSpeed = -30f;
    // motionMult controls how much panels react to player movement
    public float             motionMult = 0.25f;

    private float panelHt; // Height of each panel
    private float depth;   // Depth of panels (that is, pos.z)

    void Start () {
        panelHt = panels[0].transform.localScale.y;
        depth = panels[0].transform.position.z;

        // Set initial positions of panels
        panels[0].transform.position = new Vector3(0,0,depth);
        panels[1].transform.position = new Vector3(0,panelHt,depth);
    }

    void Update () {
        float tY, tX=0;
        tY= Time.time * scrollSpeed % panelHt + (panelHt*0.5f);

        if (poi != null) {
            tX = -poi.transform.position.x * motionMult;
        }
```

```
    // Position panels[0]
    panels[0].transform.position = new Vector3(tX, tY, depth);
    // Then position panels[1] where needed to make a continuous starfield
    if (tY >= 0) {
        panels[1].transform.position = new Vector3(tX, tY-panelHt, depth);
    } else {
        panels[1].transform.position = new Vector3(tX, tY+panelHt, depth);
    }
  }
}
```

8. Save the script, return to Unity, and attach the *Parallax* script to *StarfieldBG*. Select *StarfieldBG* in the Hierarchy and find the *Parallax (Script)* component in the Inspector. There, drag _Hero from the Hierarchy into the `poi` field and add StarfieldFG_0 and StarfieldFG_1 to the `panels` array.

9. Click *Play*, and you should see the starfield moving in response to the player.

10. Of course, remember to save your scene.

Summary

This was a long chapter, but it introduced a lot of important concepts that I hope will help you with your own game projects in the future. Over the years, I have made extensive use of linear interpolation and Bézier curves to make the motion in my games and other projects smooth and refined. Just a simple easing function can make the movement of an object look graceful, excited, or lethargic, which is powerful when you're trying to tune the feel of a game.

The next chapter moves on to a very different kind of game: a solitaire card game (actually, my favorite solitaire card game). It features reading information from an XML file to construct an entire deck of cards out of just a few art assets and also using XML to lay out the game itself. At the end, you'll have a fun digital card game to play.

Next Steps

From your experience in the previous tutorials, you already understand how to do many of the things listed in this section. These are just some recommendations for what you can do if you want to keep going with this prototype.

Tune Variables

As you have learned in both paper and digital games, tuning of numbers is critically important and has a significant effect on experience. The following is a list of variables you should consider tuning to change the feel of the game:

- **_Hero:** Change how movement feels
  - Adjust the `speed`.
  - Modify the gravity and sensitivity of the Horizontal and Vertical axes in the InputManager.

- **Weapons:** Differentiate weapons more
  - **Spread:** The spread gun could shoot five projectiles instead of just three but have a much longer `delayBetweenShots`.
  - **Blaster:** The blaster could fire more rapidly (smaller `delayBetweenShots`) but do less damage with each shot (reduced `damageOnHit`).

Add Additional Elements

Although this prototype has demonstrated five kinds of enemies and two kinds of weapons, infinite possibilities for either are open to you:

- **Weapons:** Add additional weapons
  - **Phaser:** Shoots two projectiles that move in a sine wave pattern (similar to the movement of Enemy_1).
  - **Laser:** Instead of doing all of its damage at once, the laser does continuous damage over time.
  - **Missiles:** Missiles could have a lock-on mechanic and have a very slow fire-rate but would track enemies and always hit. Perhaps missiles could be a different kind of weapon with limited ammunition that were fired using a different button (i.e., not the space bar).
  - **Swivel Gun:** Like the blaster but always shoots toward the nearest enemy. However, the damage would be very low.
- **Enemies:** Add additional enemies. You could create countless kinds of enemies for this game.
- Add additional enemy abilities
  - Allow some enemies to shoot.
  - Some enemies could track and follow the player, possibly acting like missiles homing in on the player.
- Add level progression
  - Make specific, timed waves instead of the randomized infinite attack in the existing prototype. You could accomplish this using a `[System.Serializable] Wave` class as defined here:

```
[System.Serializable]
public class Wave {
    float         delayBeforeWave=1; // secs to delay after the prev wave
    GameObject[] ships;              // array of ships in this wave
    // Delay the next wave until this wave is completely killed?
    bool          delayNextWaveUntilThisWaveIsDead=false;
}
```

- Add a Level class to contain the Wave[] array:

```
[System.Serializable]
public class Level {
    Wave[]        waves;  // Holder for waves
    float         timeLimit=-1; // If -1, there is no time limit
    string        name = ""; // The name of the level
}
```

However, this will cause issues because even if Level is serializable, the Wave[] array won't appear properly because the Unity Inspector won't allow nested serializable classes. This means that you should probably try something like an XML document to define levels and waves which can then be read into Level and Wave classes. XML is covered in the *XML* section of Appendix B, "Useful Concepts," and is used in the next prototype, Chapter 32, "Prototype 4: Prospector Solitaire."

- Add more game structure and GUI (graphical user interface) elements:

- Give the player a score and a specific number of lives (both of these were covered in the *Mission Demolition* prototype).

- Add difficulty settings.

- Track high scores (as covered in the *Apple Picker* and *Mission Demolition* prototypes).

- Create a title screen scene that welcomes players to the game and allows them to choose the difficulty setting. This could also show high scores.

CHAPTER 32

PROTOTYPE 4: *PROSPECTOR SOLITAIRE*

In this chapter, you make your first card game, a digital version of the popular *Tri-Peaks Solitaire* game. By the end of the chapter, you'll have not only a working card game but also a great framework for future card games you want to create.

This chapter includes several new techniques, including using XML configuration files and designing for mobile devices, and it offers your first look at Unity's 2D sprite tools.

Getting Started: Prototype 4

As with Prototype 3, this one starts with your being asked to download and import a Unity package of assets for this game. The art assets you'll be using are constructed from parts of the publicly available *Vectorized Playing Cards 1.3* by Chris Aguilar.[1]

SET UP THE PROJECT FOR THIS CHAPTER

Following the standard project setup procedure, create a new project in Unity. If you need a refresher on the standard project setup procedure, see Appendix A, "Standard Project Setup Procedure." When you create the project, you are asked whether you want to set up defaults for 2D or 3D. Choose 2D for this project.

- **Project name:** Prospector Solitaire.

- **Download and import package:** Go to Chapter 32 at http://book.prototools.net. Downloading this package should set up the scene and several folders.

- **Scene name:** (The scene __Prospector_Scene_0 will import with the starter package, so you don't need to create it.)

- **Project folders:** None (__Scripts, _Prefabs, _Sprites, and Resources should be part of the imported unitypackage.)

- **C# script names:** (none yet)

- **Rename:** Change Main Camera to _MainCamera.

Open __Prospector_Scene_0 and double-check the settings for _MainCamera.

> _MainCamera (Camera)   P:[0, 0, -40]   R:[0, 0, 0]   S:[1, 1, 1]
>
> > Projection: Orthographic
> >
> > Size: 10

Note that this unitypackage includes a version of the Utils script that has additional functions beyond what you wrote in the previous chapter.

Build Settings

This is the first project designed to be able to be compiled on mobile devices. As an example, I'll be using settings for the Apple iPad, but if you prefer using Android or even a WebGL or Stand-alone build instead, that is perfectly fine. The *Standalone* build option is automatically installed

---

1. The card images in this book and in the digital card games presented in the book are based on Vectorized Playing Cards 1.3, Copyright 2011, Chris Aguilar. Licensed under LGPL 3— http://www.gnu.org/copyleft/lesser.html, http://code.google.com/p/vectorized-playing-cards/.

with Unity, and you can use the Unity installer to add the capability to compile to iOS, Android, or WebGL. This project is designed for the 4:3 aspect ratio screen of an iPad in portrait mode, which is the same ratio as the *Standalone (1024x768)* aspect ratio that is part of the aspect ratio pop-up menu in the Game pane. For now, set the Aspect Ratio menu of the Game pane to *4:3*.

Though this project is designed to be able to be compiled for a mobile device, the actual build process for mobile devices is beyond the scope of this book (and would differ greatly based on which device you own), but you can find a lot of information about building for various platforms on Unity's website. Starter information for various platforms include:[2]

- **Android**—https://docs.unity3d.com/Manual/android-GettingStarted.html
- **iOS**—https://docs.unity3d.com/Manual/iphone-GettingStarted.html
- **WebGL**—https://docs.unity3d.com/Manual/webgl-gettingstarted.html

Now, let's get started with development. If you're going to try a non-Standalone platform:

1. Double-click the *__Prospector_Scene_0* scene in the Project pane to open it.
2. From the menu bar choose *File > Build Settings*, which opens the window shown in Figure 32.1.

Figure 32.1 The Build Settings window

---

2. All three of these links were last accessed January 31, 2017.

3. Click *Add Open Scenes* to add __Prospector_Scene_0 to the list of scenes for this build.

4. Select *iOS* (or whatever alternative platform you've chosen) from the list of platforms and click *Switch Platform*. Unity reimports all of your images to match the default iOS settings, and the *Switch Platform* button turns gray when the switch is complete. Once your Build Settings look like the image in Figure 32.1, you can close this window. (Don't click Build yet; that will happen after you actually finish coding the game.)

Importing Images as Sprites

Next, you need to properly import the images to use for the *sprites*. A sprite is a 2D image that can be moved around screen, scaled, and rotated. They are very common in 2D games:

1. Open the *_Sprites* folder in your Project pane and select all the images therein. (Click the top image and then Shift-click the bottom image in the _Sprites folder.) Looking at the Preview area at the bottom of the Inspector pane, you can see that all of them are currently imported with strange aspect ratios and no transparency. Let's change that and make them usable sprites.

2. In the *21 Texture 2Ds Import Settings* section of the Inspector pane, set the *Texture Type* to *Sprite (2D and UI)*. Click *Apply*, and Unity reimports all the images at their proper aspect ratio. Figure 32.2 shows the final import settings.

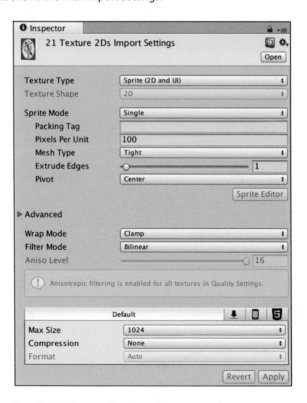

Figure 32.2 Import settings for the Texture 2Ds that will become sprites

Looking at the Project pane, you can see that each of the images now has a disclosure triangle next to it. If you open the disclosure triangle, you'll find a sprite with the same name under each image.

3. Select just the *Letters* image in the Project pane. For most of the images that were imported, a Sprite Mode of Single is appropriate because each image becomes a single sprite. However, the Letters image is actually a *sprite atlas* (a series of sprites saved as a single image), so it requires different settings.

4. In *Letters Import Settings* in the Inspector pane, change the Sprite Mode to *Multiple* and click *Apply*. This adds a new *Sprite Editor* button under the *Extrude Edges* field.

5. Click the *Sprite Editor* button to open the Sprite Editor. You'll see the Letters image there with a single blue box around it defining the bounds of the Letters sprite.

6. Click the small icon with either a rainbow or a letter *A* on it in the Sprite Editor (circled in Figure 32.3) to switch between viewing the actual image and the alpha channel of the image. Because Letters is an image of white letters over a transparent background, it may be easier to see what's happening if you look at the alpha channel.

7. Click the *Slice* pop-up menu in the top-left corner of the Sprite Editor and:

   a. Change the *Type* from Automatic to *Grid by Cell Size* (see Figure 32.3).

   b. Set the *Pixel size* to X:32 Y:32.

   c. Click the *Slice* button. This chops Letters horizontally into 16 sprites that are each 32x32 pixels in size.

   d. Click *Apply* (in the top-right corner of the Sprite Editor) to generate these sprites in the Project pane. Now instead of one Letters sprite under the Letters texture in the Project pane, there are 16 sprites named Letters_0 to Letters_15. This game uses Letters_1 to Letters_13 for each of the 13 ranks of cards (Ace through King). Now all the sprites are set up and ready to be used.

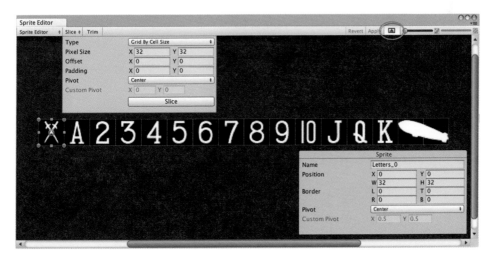

Figure 32.3 The Sprite Editor showing the correct settings for the grid slicing of Letters. The button circled in the top right switches between viewing the color channels and the alpha channel of Letters.

8. Save your scene. You haven't actually altered the scene yet, but saving your scene all the time is good practice. You should be in the habit of saving your scene any time you change anything.

Constructing Cards from Sprites

One of the most important aspects of this project is that you're going to procedurally construct an entire deck of cards from the 21 images that were imported. This makes the final build size smaller and gives you a chance to see how XML works.

The image in Figure 32.4 shows an example of how you will do this. The 10 of Spades in the image is constructed from the following sprites: *Card_Front*, 12 copies of *Spade*, and 2 copies of *Letters_10*.

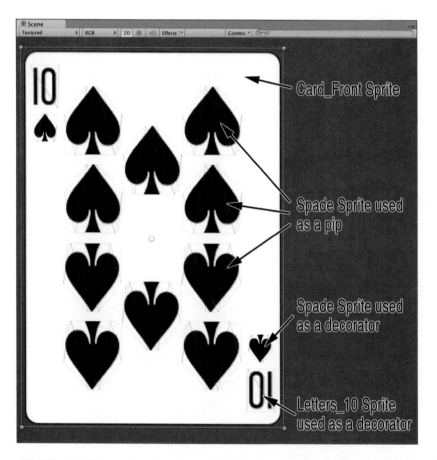

Figure 32.4 The 10 of Spades showing autogenerated borders around each of the sprites from which it is made. The visible part of this card is composed of 15 different sprites (12 *Spades*, 2 *Letter_10*s, and 1 *Card_Front*).

This is defined through the use of an XML file. Read the *XML* section of Appendix B, "Useful Concepts," now to learn more about XML and how it can be read using the PT_XMLReader script that was part of the imported unitypackage. The structure of the DeckXML.xml file used in this project is also covered in that section of Appendix B.

Making Use of XML Through Code

1. For the first part of this project, create three C# files named *Card*, *Deck*, and *Prospector*. Make sure that each one is inside the __Scripts folder.

   ■ **Card:** The class for each individual card in the deck. The Card script also contains the CardDefinition class (which holds information about where sprites are to be positioned on each rank of card) and the Decorator class (which holds information about the decorators and pips described in the XML document—Figure 32.4 shows the differences between decorators and pips).

   ■ **Deck:** The Deck class interprets the information in DeckXML.xml and uses that information to create an entire deck of cards.

   ■ **Prospector:** The Prospector class manages the overall game. Whereas Deck handles the creation of cards, Prospector turns those cards into a game. Prospector collects the cards into various piles (like the draw pile and discard pile) and manages game logic.

2. Start by opening the *Card* C# script and entering the following code. These small classes in Card.cs store the information created when Deck reads the XML file.

```csharp
using System.Collections;
using System.Collections.Generic;
using UnityEngine;

public class Card : MonoBehaviour {
    // This will be defined later
}


[System.Serializable] // A Serializable class is able to be edited in the
Inspector
public class Decorator {
    // This class stores information about each decorator or pip from DeckXML
    public string     type; // For card pips, type = "pip"
    public Vector3    loc;  // The location of the Sprite on the Card
    public bool       flip = false;  // Whether to flip the Sprite vertically
    public float      scale = 1f;    // The scale of the Sprite
}


[System.Serializable]
public class CardDefinition {
    // This class stores information for each rank of card
    public string              face; // Sprite to use for each face card
    public int                 rank; // The rank (1-13) of this card
    public List<Decorator>     pips = new List<Decorator>();  // Pips used    // a
}
```

a. `pips` are the Decorators used on non-face cards to show, for instance, the ten large spades on the 10 of spades in Figure 32.4. The Decorators in the corners of each card (e.g., the spades next to the number 10 in the corner of the Figure 32.4 card) don't need to be stored in a CardDefinition because they are in the same position on every card in the deck.

3. Open the *Deck* C# script in MonoDevelop and enter the following code:

```
using System.Collections;
using System.Collections.Generic;
using UnityEngine;

public class Deck : MonoBehaviour {

    [Header("Set Dynamically")]
    public PT_XMLReader                  xmlr;

    // InitDeck is called by Prospector when it is ready
    public void InitDeck(string deckXMLText) {
        ReadDeck(deckXMLText);
    }

    // ReadDeck parses the XML file passed to it into CardDefinitions
    public void ReadDeck(string deckXMLText) {
        xmlr = new PT_XMLReader();   // Create a new PT_XMLReader
        xmlr.Parse(deckXMLText);     // Use that PT_XMLReader to parse DeckXML

        // This prints a test line to show you how xmlr can be used.
        // For more information read about XML in the Useful Concepts Appendix
        string s = "xml[0] decorator[0] ";
        s += "type="+xmlr.xml["xml"][0]["decorator"][0].att("type");
        s += " x="+xmlr.xml["xml"][0]["decorator"][0].att("x");
        s += " y="+xmlr.xml["xml"][0]["decorator"][0].att("y");
        s += " scale="+xmlr.xml["xml"][0]["decorator"][0].att("scale");
        print(s);

    }
}
```

4. Now open the *Prospector* class and enter this code:

```
using System.Collections;
using System.Collections.Generic;
using UnityEngine;
using UnityEngine.SceneManagement;    // This will be used later in the project
using UnityEngine.UI;                 // This will be used later in the project
```

```
public class Prospector : MonoBehaviour {
    static public Prospector    S;

    [Header("Set in Inspector")]
    public TextAsset            deckXML;

    [Header("Set Dynamically")]
    public Deck                 deck;

    void Awake() {
        S = this; // Set up a Singleton for Prospector
    }

    void Start () {
        deck = GetComponent<Deck>(); // Get the Deck
        deck.InitDeck(deckXML.text); // Pass DeckXML to it
    }
}
```

5. Make sure that you have saved all of these script files before returning to Unity. Choose *File > Save All* from the MonoDevelop menu bar. If *Save All* is grayed out, then you have already saved them.

6. Now that the code is ready, go back to Unity and attach both the *Prospector* and *Deck* scripts to *_MainCamera*. (Drag each script from the Project pane onto _MainCamera in the Hierarchy pane.) Select _MainCamera in the Hierarchy. You should see both scripts attached as Script components.

7. Drag *DeckXML* from the Resources folder in the Project pane into the deckXML TextAsset variable in the Inspector for the *Prospector (Script)* component.

8. Save your scene and click *Play*. You should see the following output in the console:
   ```
   xml[0] decorator[0] type=letter x=-1.05 y=1.42 scale=1.25
   ```

This line comes from the test code in Deck:ReadDeck() and shows that ReadDeck() is properly reading the type, x, y, and scale attributes from the 0th decorator of the 0th xml in the XML file, as shown in the following lines from DeckXML.xml. (You can see the entire text of DeckXML.xml in the *XML* section of Appendix B or by opening the DeckXML.xml file in MonoDevelop.)

```
<xml>
    <!-- decorators are on every card as the suit and rank in the corners. -->
    <decorator type="letter" x="-1.05" y="1.42" z="0" flip="0" scale="1.25"/>
    ...
</xml>
```

Parsing Information from Deck XML

Now, let's actually do something with this information.

1. Make the following changes to the Deck class:

```
public class Deck : MonoBehaviour {

    [Header("Set Dynamically")]
    public PT_XMLReader            xmlr;
    public List<string>            cardNames;
    public List<Card>              cards;
    public List<Decorator>         decorators;
    public List<CardDefinition>    cardDefs;
    public Transform               deckAnchor;
    public Dictionary<string,Sprite>  dictSuits;

    // InitDeck is called by Prospector when it is ready
    public void InitDeck(string deckXMLText) {
        ReadDeck(deckXMLText);
    }

    // ReadDeck parses the XML file passed to it into CardDefinitions
    public void ReadDeck(string deckXMLText) {
        xmlr = new PT_XMLReader(); // Create a new PT_XMLReader
        xmlr.Parse(deckXMLText);   // Use that PT_XMLReader to parse DeckXML

        // The following prints a test line to show you how xmlr can be used.
        // For more information read about XML in the Useful Concepts Appendix
        string s = "xml[0] decorator[0] ";
        s += "type="+xmlr.xml["xml"][0]["decorator"][0].att("type");
        s += " x="+xmlr.xml["xml"][0]["decorator"][0].att("x");
        s += " y="+xmlr.xml["xml"][0]["decorator"][0].att("y");
        s += " scale="+xmlr.xml["xml"][0]["decorator"][0].att("scale");
        //print(s); // Comment out this line, since we're done with the test

        // Read decorators for all Cards
        decorators = new List<Decorator>(); // Init the List of Decorators
        // Grab an PT_XMLHashList of all <decorator>s in the XML file
        PT_XMLHashList xDecos = xmlr.xml["xml"][0]["decorator"];
        Decorator deco;
        for (int i=0; i<xDecos.Count; i++) {
            // For each <decorator> in the XML
            deco = new Decorator(); // Make a new Decorator
            // Copy the attributes of the <decorator> to the Decorator
            deco.type = xDecos[i].att("type");
            // bool deco.flip is true if the text of the flip attribute is "1"
            deco.flip = ( xDecos[i].att ("flip") == "1" );                    // a
            // floats need to be parsed from the attribute strings
            deco.scale = float.Parse( xDecos[i].att ("scale") );
            // Vector3 loc initializes to [0,0,0], so we just need to modify it
```

```
        deco.loc.x = float.Parse( xDecos[i].att ("x") );
        deco.loc.y = float.Parse( xDecos[i].att ("y") );
        deco.loc.z = float.Parse( xDecos[i].att ("z") );
        // Add the temporary deco to the List decorators
        decorators.Add (deco);
    }


    // Read pip locations for each card number
    cardDefs = new List<CardDefinition>(); // Init the List of Cards
    // Grab an PT_XMLHashList of all the <card>s in the XML file
    PT_XMLHashList xCardDefs = xmlr.xml["xml"][0]["card"];
    for (int i=0; i<xCardDefs.Count; i++) {
        // For each of the <card>s
        // Create a new CardDefinition
        CardDefinition cDef = new CardDefinition();
        // Parse the attribute values and add them to cDef
        cDef.rank = int.Parse( xCardDefs[i].att ("rank") );
        // Grab an PT_XMLHashList of all the <pip>s on this <card>
        PT_XMLHashList xPips = xCardDefs[i]["pip"];
        if (xPips != null) {
            for (int j=0; j<xPips.Count; j++) {
                // Iterate through all the <pip>s
                deco = new Decorator();
                // <pip>s on the <card> are handled via the Decorator Class
                deco.type = "pip";
                deco.flip = ( xPips[j].att ("flip") == "1" );        // a
                deco.loc.x = float.Parse( xPips[j].att ("x") );
                deco.loc.y = float.Parse( xPips[j].att ("y") );
                deco.loc.z = float.Parse( xPips[j].att ("z") );
                if ( xPips[j].HasAtt("scale") ) {
                    deco.scale = float.Parse( xPips[j].att ("scale") );
                }
                cDef.pips.Add(deco);
            }
        }
        // Face cards (Jack, Queen, & King) have a face attribute
        if (xCardDefs[i].HasAtt("face")) {
            cDef.face = xCardDefs[i].att ("face");                   // b
        }
        cardDefs.Add(cDef);
    }
    }
}
```

a. This is an atypical but perfectly fine use of the == comparison operator. It will return a true or false, which will be assigned to the bool `deco.flip`.

b. `cDef.face` is the *base name* of the face card Sprite. For example, *FaceCard_11* is the base name for the Jack face Sprites, the Jack of Clubs is FaceCard_11C, the Jack of Hearts is FaceCard_11H, and so on.

Now, the `ReadDeck()` method will parse the XML and turn it into a list of Decorators (the suit and rank in the corners of the card) and CardDefinitions (a class containing information about each of the ranks of card (Ace through King).

2. Switch back to Unity and click *Play*. Select the *_MainCamera* and look at the Inspector for the *Deck (Script)* component. Because both Decorator and CardDefinition were set to [System.Serializable], the `decorators` and `cardDefs` Lists appear properly in the Inspector for the *Deck (Script)* component of _MainCamera, as shown in Figure 32.5.

3. Stop playback and *save your scene*.

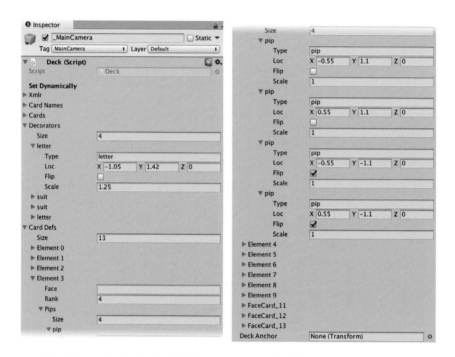

Figure 32.5 The Inspector for the *Deck (Script)* component of _MainCamera showing Decorators and CardDefs that have been read from the DeckXML.xml file

Assigning the Sprites That Become Cards

Now that the XML has been properly read and parsed into usable Lists, it's time to make some cards. The first step in doing so is to get references to all of those sprites that you made earlier in the chapter:

1. Add the following fields to the top of the Deck class to hold these sprites:

```
public class Deck : MonoBehaviour {
    [Header("Set in Inspector")]
    // Suits
    public Sprite                    suitClub;
```

```
public Sprite                suitDiamond;
public Sprite                suitHeart;
public Sprite                suitSpade;

public Sprite[]              faceSprites;
public Sprite[]              rankSprites;

public Sprite                cardBack;
public Sprite                cardBackGold;
public Sprite                cardFront;
public Sprite                cardFrontGold;

// Prefabs
public GameObject            prefabCard;
public GameObject            prefabSprite;

[Header("Set Dynamically")]
...
}
```

When you save and switch back to Unity, you can now see many new public variables that you need to define in the *Deck (Sprite)* Inspector on _MainCamera.

2. Drag the *Club*, *Diamond*, *Heart*, and *Spade* textures from the _Sprites folder in the Project pane into their respective variables under Deck (`suitClub`, `suitDiamond`, `suitHeart`, and `suitSpade`). Unity automatically assigns the sprite to the variable (as opposed to attempting to assign the Texture2D to a sprite variable).

3. The next bit is a touch trickier. Lock the Inspector on _MainCamera by selecting *_MainCamera* in the Hierarchy pane and then clicking the tiny *lock* icon at the top of the Inspector pane (surrounded by a red rectangle in Figure 32.6). Locking the Inspector pane ensures that it won't change which object is displayed when you select something new.

4. Assign each of the sprites starting with *FaceCard_* to an element of the array `faceSprites` in the Inspector for *Deck (Script)*:

   a. Select *FaceCard_11C* in the *_Sprites* folder of the Project pane and then Shift-click *FaceCard_13S*. This should select all 12 *FaceCard_* sprites.

   b. Drag this group from the Project pane over the name of the array `faceSprites` under *Deck (Script)* in the Inspector. You should see a plus icon and the word *<multiple>* appear next to your mouse cursor when hovering over the variable name `faceSprites` (on PC, you might only see the + icon).

   c. Release the mouse button, and if you did the steps correctly, this should expand the size of the `faceSprites` array to 12 and fill it with one copy of each of the *FaceCard_* sprites. If this doesn't work, you can also add them individually. The order doesn't matter as long as there is exactly one of each when you're done (see Figure 32.6).

5. Open the disclosure triangle next to the *Letters* Texture2D in the _Sprites folder of in the Project pane. Use the same process as in the previous step to select *Letters_0* through *Letters_15*. You should now have all 16 sprites under Letters selected. Drag this group of sprites onto the `rankSprites` variable in *Deck (Script)*. If you did the steps correctly, the `rankSprites` list should now be full of 16 *Letters_* sprites named *Letters_0* through *Letters_15*. Double-check to make sure that they're in the correct order with *Letters_0* in *Element 0* and *Letters_15* in *Element 15*; if not, you might have to add them one at a time.

6. Drag the sprites *Card_Back*, *Card_Back_Gold*, *Card_Front*, and *Card_Front_Gold* from the Project pane to their respective variable slots in the *Deck (Script)* Inspector.

Your Inspector for *Deck (Script)* should now look like what is shown in Figure 32.6.

7. Unlock the Inspector pane by clicking the tiny *lock* icon again (highlighted in red in Figure 32.6). Save your scene! You don't want to have to do all that work again.

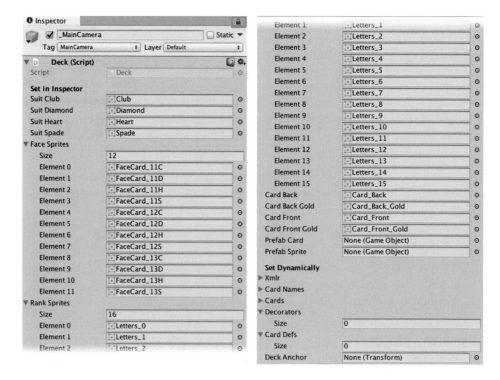

Figure 32.6 The Inspector for the *Deck (Script)* Component of _MainCamera showing the correct sprites assigned to each public sprite variable

Creating Prefab GameObjects for Sprites and Cards

Just like anything else on screen, sprites need to be enclosed in GameObjects. For this project, you need two prefabs: a generic *PrefabSprite* that you will use for all decorators and pips (which you imported as part of the starter asset package), and a *PrefabCard* that will form the basis of all the cards in the deck.

To create the PrefabCard GameObject, do the following:

1. From the menu bar, choose *GameObject > 2D Object > Sprite*. Name this GameObject *PrefabCard*.

2. Drag *Card_Front* from the Project pane into the *Sprite* variable of the *Sprite Renderer* in the PrefabCard Inspector. Now you should see the Card_Front sprite in the Scene pane.

3. Drag the *Card* script from the Project pane onto PrefabCard in the Hierarchy. This assigns the Card script to PrefabCard (and the *Card (Script)* component will now appear in the Inspector for PrefabCard).

4. In the Inspector for PrefabCard, click the *Add Component* button. Choose *Physics > Box Collider* from the menu that appears. (This is the same as choosing *Component > Physics > Box Collider* from the menu bar.) The *Size* of the Box Collider should automatically set itself to [2.56, 3.56, 0.2], but if not, set the *Size* to those values.

5. Drag *PrefabCard* from the Hierarchy into the *_Prefabs* folder to make a prefab from it.

6. Delete the remaining instance of PrefabCard from the Hierarchy, and save your scene.

Now, you need to assign the PrefabCard and PrefabSprite prefabs to their respective public variables in the Inspector for the *Deck (Script)* component on _MainCamera.

7. Select *_MainCamera* in the hierarchy, and drag *PrefabCard* and *PrefabSprite* from the Project pane into their respective variables in the *Deck (Script)* Inspector.

8. Save your scene.

Building the Cards in Code

Before actually adding the method to the Deck class to make the cards, you need to add variables to the Card class, as follows (this is a lot of code, but it's going to be awesome!):

1. Replace the comment `// This will be defined later` in the Card class with the following code.

```
public class Card : MonoBehaviour {
    [Header("Set Dynamically")]
    public string          suit; // Suit of the Card (C,D,H, or S)
    public int             rank; // Rank of the Card (1-14)
    public Color           color = Color.black; // Color to tint pips
```

```
    public string           colS = "Black"; // or "Red". Name of the Color

    // This List holds all of the Decorator GameObjects
    public List<GameObject> decoGOs = new List<GameObject>();
    // This List holds all of the Pip GameObjects
    public List<GameObject> pipGOs  = new List<GameObject>();

    public GameObject        back; // The GameObject of the back of the card

    public CardDefinition   def; // Parsed from DeckXML.xml
}
```

2. Now, add this code to Deck:

```
public class Deck : MonoBehaviour {
    …
    // InitDeck is called by Prospector when it is ready
    public void InitDeck(string deckXMLText) {
        // This creates an anchor for all the Card GameObjects in the Hierarchy
        if (GameObject.Find("_Deck") == null) {
            GameObject anchorGO = new GameObject("_Deck");
            deckAnchor = anchorGO.transform;
        }

        // Initialize the Dictionary of SuitSprites with necessary Sprites
        dictSuits = new Dictionary<string, Sprite>() {
            { "C", suitClub },
            { "D", suitDiamond },
            { "H", suitHeart },
            { "S", suitSpade }
        };

        ReadDeck(deckXMLText); // This is the preexisting line from earlier

        MakeCards();
    }

    // ReadDeck parses the XML file passed to it into CardDefinitions
    public void ReadDeck(string deckXMLText) { … }

    // Get the proper CardDefinition based on Rank (1 to 14 is Ace to King)
    public CardDefinition GetCardDefinitionByRank(int rnk) {
        // Search through all of the CardDefinitions
        foreach (CardDefinition cd in cardDefs) {
            // If the rank is correct, return this definition
            if (cd.rank == rnk) {
                return( cd );
            }
        }
        return( null );
    }
```

```csharp
// Make the Card GameObjects
public void MakeCards() {
    // cardNames will be the names of cards to build
    // Each suit goes from 1 to 14 (e.g., C1 to C14 for Clubs)
    cardNames = new List<string>();
    string[] letters = new string[] {"C","D","H","S"};
    foreach (string s in letters) {
        for (int i=0; i<13; i++) {
            cardNames.Add(s+(i+1));
        }
    }

    // Make a List to hold all the cards
    cards = new List<Card>();

    // Iterate through all of the card names that were just made
    for (int i=0; i<cardNames.Count; i++) {
        // Make the card and add it to the cards Deck
        cards.Add ( MakeCard(i) );
    }
}

private Card MakeCard(int cNum) {                             // a
    // Create a new Card GameObject
    GameObject cgo = Instantiate(prefabCard) as GameObject;
    // Set the transform.parent of the new card to the anchor.
    cgo.transform.parent = deckAnchor;
    Card card = cgo.GetComponent<Card>(); // Get the Card Component

    // This line stacks the cards so that they're all in nice rows
    cgo.transform.localPosition = new Vector3( (cNum%13)*3, cNum/13*4, 0 );

    // Assign basic values to the Card
    card.name = cardNames[cNum];
    card.suit = card.name[0].ToString();
    card.rank = int.Parse( card.name.Substring(1) );
    if (card.suit == "D" || card.suit == "H") {
        card.colS = "Red";
        card.color = Color.red;
    }
    // Pull the CardDefinition for this card
    card.def = GetCardDefinitionByRank(card.rank);

    AddDecorators(card);

    return card;
}
```

```
// These private variables will be reused several times in helper methods
private Sprite        _tSp = null;
private GameObject     _tGO = null;
private SpriteRenderer  _tSR = null;

private void AddDecorators(Card card) {                              // a
    // Add Decorators
    foreach( Decorator deco in decorators ) {
        if (deco.type == "suit") {
            // Instantiate a Sprite GameObject
            _tGO = Instantiate( prefabSprite ) as GameObject;
            // Get the SpriteRenderer Component
            _tSR = _tGO.GetComponent<SpriteRenderer>();
            // Set the Sprite to the proper suit
            _tSR.sprite = dictSuits[card.suit];
        } else {
            _tGO = Instantiate( prefabSprite ) as GameObject;
            _tSR = _tGO.GetComponent<SpriteRenderer>();
            // Get the proper Sprite to show this rank
            _tSp = rankSprites[ card.rank ];
            // Assign this rank Sprite to the SpriteRenderer
            _tSR.sprite = _tSp;
            // Set the color of the rank to match the suit
            _tSR.color = card.color;
        }
        // Make the deco Sprites render above the Card
        _tSR.sortingOrder = 1;
        // Make the decorator Sprite a child of the Card
        _tGO.transform.SetParent( card.transform );
        // Set the localPosition based on the location from DeckXML
        _tGO.transform.localPosition = deco.loc;
        // Flip the decorator if needed
        if (deco.flip) {
            // An Euler rotation of 180° around the Z-axis will flip it
            _tGO.transform.rotation = Quaternion.Euler(0,0,180);
        }
        // Set the scale to keep decos from being too big
        if (deco.scale != 1) {
            _tGO.transform.localScale = Vector3.one * deco.scale;
        }
        // Name this GameObject so it's easy to see
        _tGO.name = deco.type;
        // Add this deco GameObject to the List card.decoGOs
        card.decoGOs.Add( _tGO);
    }
}
```

a. MakeCard() and AddDecorator() are private helper methods for MakeCards(). This allows you to write a shorter MakeCards() method and, if you're working with multiple programmers, a different person could have written each of these three methods, as long as each does what is required of it. I've personally been moving toward shorter functions like these, as you'll see in Chapter 35, "Dungeon Delver."

3. Save all scripts, return to Unity, and click *Play*. You should see 52 cards lined up. They don't yet have pips, but they do appear, and the correct decorators and coloring are on them.

4. Now add the code for pips and faces via three more helper methods in the Deck class:

```
public class Deck : MonoBehaviour {
    …
    private Card MakeCard(int cNum) {
        …
        card.def = GetCardDefinitionByRank(card.rank);

        AddDecorators(card);
        AddPips(card);
        AddFace(card);

        return card;
    }

    private void AddDecorators(Card card) { … }

    private void AddPips(Card card) {
        // For each of the pips in the definition...
        foreach( Decorator pip in card.def.pips ) {
            // ...Instantiate a Sprite GameObject
            _tGO = Instantiate( prefabSprite ) as GameObject;
            // Set the parent to be the card GameObject
            _tGO.transform.SetParent( card.transform );
            // Set the position to that specified in the XML
            _tGO.transform.localPosition = pip.loc;
            // Flip it if necessary
            if (pip.flip) {
                _tGO.transform.rotation = Quaternion.Euler(0,0,180);
            }
            // Scale it if necessary (only for the Ace)
            if (pip.scale != 1) {
                _tGO.transform.localScale = Vector3.one * pip.scale;
            }
            // Give this GameObject a name
            _tGO.name = "pip";
            // Get the SpriteRenderer Component
            _tSR = _tGO.GetComponent<SpriteRenderer>();
            // Set the Sprite to the proper suit
```

```
            _tSR.sprite = dictSuits[card.suit];
            // Set sortingOrder so the pip is rendered above the Card_Front
            _tSR.sortingOrder = 1;
            // Add this to the Card's list of pips
            card.pipGOs.Add(_tGO);
        }
    }

    private void AddFace(Card card) {
        if (card.def.face == "") {
            return; // No need to run if this isn't a face card
        }

        _tGO = Instantiate( prefabSprite ) as GameObject;
        _tSR = _tGO.GetComponent<SpriteRenderer>();
        // Generate the right name and pass it to GetFace()
        _tSp = GetFace( card.def.face+card.suit );
        _tSR.sprite = _tSp;        // Assign this Sprite to _tSR
        _tSR.sortingOrder = 1;     // Set the sortingOrder
        _tGO.transform.SetParent( card.transform );
        _tGO.transform.localPosition = Vector3.zero;
        _tGO.name = "face";
    }

    // Find the proper face card Sprite
    private Sprite GetFace(string faceS) {
        foreach (Sprite _tSP in faceSprites) {
            // If this Sprite has the right name...
            if (_tSP.name == faceS) {
                // ...then return the Sprite
                return( _tSP );
            }
        }
        // If nothing can be found, return null
        return( null );
    }

}
```

5. Click *Play*, you should see all 52 cards laid out properly with pips and faces for face cards.

The next thing to do is add a back to the cards. The card won't actually flip over; instead the back will be a Sprite with a higher *sortingOrder* than anything else on the card, and it will be visible when the card is face down and invisible when the card is face up.

6. To accomplish this visibility toggle, add the following `faceUp` property to the end of the Card class. As a property, `faceUp` is actually two functions (a get and a set) masquerading as a single field:

```
public class Card : MonoBehaviour {
    ...
    public GameObject        back; // The GameObject of the back of the card

    public CardDefinition   def; // Parsed from DeckXML.xml

    public bool faceUp {
        get {
            return( !back.activeSelf );
        }
        set {
            back.SetActive(!value);
        }
    }
}
```

7. Now you can add a back to the cards in the Deck class. Add the following field and helper method to the Deck class:

```
public class Deck : MonoBehaviour {
    [Header("Set in Inspector")]
    public bool                 startFaceUp = false;
    // Suits
    public Sprite               suitClub;
    ...

    private Card MakeCard(int cNum) {
        ...
        AddPips(card);
        AddFace(card);
        AddBack(card);

        return card;
    }
    ...

    // Find the proper face card Sprite
    private Sprite GetFace(string faceS) { ... }

    private void AddBack(Card card) {
        // Add Card Back
        // The Card_Back will be able to cover everything else on the Card
        _tGO = Instantiate( prefabSprite ) as GameObject;
        _tSR = _tGO.GetComponent<SpriteRenderer>();
        _tSR.sprite = cardBack;
        _tGO.transform.SetParent( card.transform );
        _tGO.transform.localPosition = Vector3.zero;
        // This is a higher sortingOrder than anything else
        _tSR.sortingOrder = 2;
        _tGO.name = "back";
        card.back = _tGO;
```

```
        // Default to face-up
        card.faceUp = startFaceUp; // Use the property faceUp of Card
    }

}
```

8. Save all of your scripts in MonoDevelop, return to Unity, and click *Play*. All the cards now initially appear to be flipped face down.

9. Stop playback, change the `startFaceUp` field of the *Deck (Script)* Inspector on _MainCamera to true, and play again. Now all the cards will start face up.

10. Save your scene. Always save your scene.

Shuffling the Cards

Now that cards can be built and displayed on screen, the last thing that you need from the Deck class is the capability to shuffle cards.

1. Add the following public static `Shuffle()` method to the end of the Deck class:

```
public class Deck : MonoBehaviour {
    ...
    private void AddBack(Card card) { ... }

    // Shuffle the Cards in Deck.cards
    static public void Shuffle(ref List<Card> oCards) {                      // a
        // Create a temporary List to hold the new shuffle order
        List<Card> tCards = new List<Card>();

        int ndx; // This will hold the index of the card to be moved
        tCards = new List<Card>(); // Initialize the temporary List
        // Repeat as long as there are cards in the original List
        while (oCards.Count > 0) {
            // Pick the index of a random card
            ndx = Random.Range(0,oCards.Count);
            // Add that card to the temporary List
            tCards.Add (oCards[ndx]);
            // And remove that card from the original List
            oCards.RemoveAt(ndx);
        }
        // Replace the original List with the temporary List
        oCards = tCards;
        // Because oCards is a reference (ref) parameter, the original argument
        //   that was passed in is changed as well.
    }

}
```

a. The `ref` keyword is used to make sure that the `List<Card>` that is passed to `List<Card> oCards` is passed as a reference rather than copied into `oCards`. This means that anything that happens to `oCards` is actually happening to the variable that is passed in. In other words, if the cards of a `Deck` are passed in via reference, those cards will be shuffled without requiring a return variable.

2. Add the following lines to the `Prospector.Start()` method to see this work:

```
public class Prospector : MonoBehaviour {
    ...

    void Start () {
        deck = GetComponent<Deck>();        // Get the Deck
        deck.InitDeck(deckXML.text);        // Pass DeckXML to it
        Deck.Shuffle(ref deck.cards);       // This shuffles the deck by reference // a

        Card c;
        for (int cNum=0; cNum<deck.cards.Count; cNum++) {                          // b
            c = deck.cards[cNum];
            c.transform.localPosition = new Vector3( (cNum%13)*3, cNum/13*4, 0 );
        }
    }
}
```

    a. You must also use the `ref` keyword when calling the function.

    b. This `for` loop repositions the cards on screen in their new shuffled order.

3. If you save these scripts and play the scene now, you can select _MainCamera in the scene hierarchy and look at the `Deck.cards` variable to see a shuffled array of cards.

Now that the Deck class can shuffle any list of cards, you have the basic tools to create *any* card game. The game you will make in this prototype is called *Prospector*.

The *Prospector* Game

The code up till now has given you the basic tools to make any card game. Now let's talk about the specific game you're going to make.[3]

Prospector is based on the classic solitaire card game *Tri-Peaks*. The rules of both are the same, except for two things:

- The premise of *Prospector* is that the player is digging down for gold, whereas the premise of *Tri-Peaks* is that the player is trying to climb three mountains.

- The objective of *Tri-Peaks* is just to clear all the cards. The objective of *Prospector* is to earn points by having long chains of cards, and each gold card in the chain doubles the value of the whole chain.

---

3. *Prospector* was designed by Jeremy Gibson Bond, Ethan Burrow, and Mike Wabschall in 2001 for our company, Digital Mercenaries, Inc.

Prospector Rules

To try this out, grab a normal deck of playing cards (like a physical, real deck, not the virtual one you just made). Remove the Jokers and shuffle the remaining 52 cards:

1. Lay out 28 of the cards as shown in Figure 32.7. Make the bottom three rows of cards face-down, and the top row face-up. The card edges don't need to be touching, but the lower cards do need to be covered by the upper cards. This sets up the initial tableau of cards for the "mine" that your prospector will be excavating.

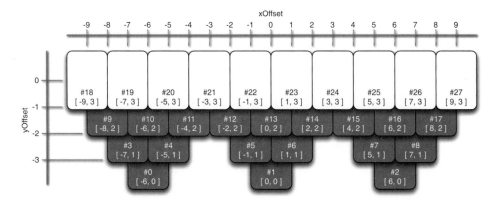

Figure 32.7 The initial tableau layout for the mine in Prospector

2. The rest of the deck forms a draw pile. Place it above the top row of cards face-down.

3. Draw the top card from the draw deck and place it face-up centered above the top row of cards. This is the target card. See Figure 32.8 for the full layout.

4. You may move any card that is either exactly one rank above or one rank below the target card from the tableau onto the target card, making it the new target card. Aces and Kings wrap around, so an Ace can be played on a King and vice versa.

5. If a face-down card is no longer covered by a card from a higher row, you can turn it face-up.

6. If none of the face-up cards can be played on the target card, draw a new target card from the draw pile.

7. If the tableau is emptied before the draw pile, you win! (I will save the discussion of scoring and gold cards for the digital version of the game.)

Example of Play

The image in Figure 32.8 shows an example starting layout for *Prospector*. In the situation shown, the player can initially play either the 9C (9 of Clubs) or the 7S (7 of Spades) onto the 8H.

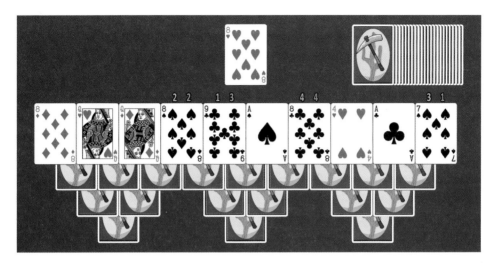

Figure 32.8 An example initial layout for *Prospector*

The amber and green numbers show two possible sequences of play. In the amber sequence, the 9C is played, becoming the new target card. This allows the play of 8S, 8D, or 8C. The player chooses 8S because it will then reveal the card that was hidden by 9C and 8S. Then the amber sequence continues with 7S and finally 8C. This results in the layout shown in Figure 32.9.

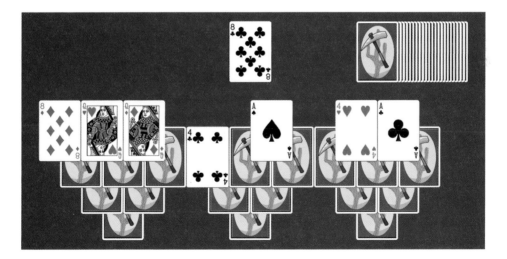

Figure 32.9 The *Prospector* example game after the first run

Now, because there are no more valid face-up cards to play from the tableau, the player must draw a card from the draw pile to become the next target card.

Again, I recommend that you try grabbing a real deck of cards and playing the game a few times to get a feel for it. Alternatively, you can play it on this book's website:

http://book.prototools.net — Look under Chapter 32

Implementing *Prospector* in Code

As you have seen from playing, *Prospector* is a pretty simple game, but it's also pretty fun. You can add to that fun later with some nice visuals and scoring tweaks, but for now, let's just get the basic game working.

Laying Out the Mine Tableau

You need to implement the same tableau layout for the mine cards in the digital version of *Prospector* as you did with the paper prototype you just played. To do this, you'll generate some XML code from the layout diagram in Figure 32.7.

1. In Unity, open the *LayoutXML.xml* file in the Resources folder to see this layout information. Note that comments in XML are bounded by `<!--` and `-->` (just like code bounded by `/*` and `*/` or following `//` in C#).

```xml
<xml>
    <!-- This file holds info for laying out the Prospector card game. -->

    <!-- The multiplier is multiplied by the x and y attributes below. -->
    <!-- This determines how loose or tight the layout is. -->
    <multiplier x="1.25" y="1.5" />

    <!-- In the XML below, id is the number of the card -->
    <!-- x and y set position -->
    <!-- faceup is 1 if the card is face-up -->
    <!-- layer sets the depth layer so cards overlap properly -->
    <!-- hiddenby is the ids of cards that keep a card face-down -->

    <!-- Layer0, the deepest cards. -->
    <slot id="0" x="-6" y="-5" faceup="0" layer="0" hiddenby="3,4" />
    <slot id="1" x="0"  y="-5" faceup="0" layer="0" hiddenby="5,6" />
    <slot id="2" x="6"  y="-5" faceup="0" layer="0" hiddenby="7,8" />

    <!-- Layer1, the next level. -->
    <slot id="3" x="-7" y="-4" faceup="0" layer="1" hiddenby="9,10" />
    <slot id="4" x="-5" y="-4" faceup="0" layer="1" hiddenby="10,11" />
    <slot id="5" x="-1" y="-4" faceup="0" layer="1" hiddenby="12,13" />
    <slot id="6" x="1"  y="-4" faceup="0" layer="1" hiddenby="13,14" />
    <slot id="7" x="5"  y="-4" faceup="0" layer="1" hiddenby="15,16" />
    <slot id="8" x="7"  y="-4" faceup="0" layer="1" hiddenby="16,17" />
```

```xml
<!-- Layer2, the next level. -->
<slot id="9"  x="-8" y="-3" faceup="0" layer="2" hiddenby="18,19" />
<slot id="10" x="-6" y="-3" faceup="0" layer="2" hiddenby="19,20" />
<slot id="11" x="-4" y="-3" faceup="0" layer="2" hiddenby="20,21" />
<slot id="12" x="-2" y="-3" faceup="0" layer="2" hiddenby="21,22" />
<slot id="13" x="0"  y="-3" faceup="0" layer="2" hiddenby="22,23" />
<slot id="14" x="2"  y="-3" faceup="0" layer="2" hiddenby="23,24" />
<slot id="15" x="4"  y="-3" faceup="0" layer="2" hiddenby="24,25" />
<slot id="16" x="6"  y="-3" faceup="0" layer="2" hiddenby="25,26" />
<slot id="17" x="8"  y="-3" faceup="0" layer="2" hiddenby="26,27" />


<!-- Layer3, the top level. -->
<slot id="18" x="-9" y="-2" faceup="1" layer="3" />
<slot id="19" x="-7" y="-2" faceup="1" layer="3" />
<slot id="20" x="-5" y="-2" faceup="1" layer="3" />
<slot id="21" x="-3" y="-2" faceup="1" layer="3" />
<slot id="22" x="-1" y="-2" faceup="1" layer="3" />
<slot id="23" x="1"  y="-2" faceup="1" layer="3" />
<slot id="24" x="3"  y="-2" faceup="1" layer="3" />
<slot id="25" x="5"  y="-2" faceup="1" layer="3" />
<slot id="26" x="7"  y="-2" faceup="1" layer="3" />
<slot id="27" x="9"  y="-2" faceup="1" layer="3" />

<!-- This positions the draw pile and staggers it -->
<slot type="drawpile" x="6" y="4" xstagger="0.15" layer="4"/>

<!-- This positions the discard pile and target card -->
<slot type="discardpile" x="0" y="1" layer="5"/>

</xml>
```

As you can see, this has layout information for each of the cards in the tableau (which is formed of <slot>s without a type attribute) as well as two special slots (that do have type attributes), the drawpile and discardpile types.

2. Let's write some code to parse this LayoutXML into useful information. Create a new script named *Layout* in the __Scripts folder and enter the following code:

```csharp
using System.Collections;
using System.Collections.Generic;
using UnityEngine;

// The SlotDef class is not a subclass of MonoBehaviour, so it doesn't need
//    a separate C# file.
[System.Serializable] // This makes SlotDefs visible in the Unity Inspector pane
public class SlotDef {
    public float      x;
    public float      y;
    public bool       faceUp = false;
    public string     layerName = "Default";
```

```
    public int          layerID = 0;
    public int          id;
    public List<int>    hiddenBy = new List<int>();
    public string       type = "slot";
    public Vector2      stagger;
}


public class Layout : MonoBehaviour {
    public PT_XMLReader     xmlr;  // Just like Deck, this has a PT_XMLReader
    public PT_XMLHashtable  xml;   // This variable is for faster xml access
    public Vector2          multiplier; // The offset of the tableau's center
    // SlotDef references
    public List<SlotDef>    slotDefs; // All the SlotDefs for Row0-Row3
    public SlotDef          drawPile;
    public SlotDef          discardPile;
    // This holds all of the possible names for the layers set by layerID
    public string[]         sortingLayerNames = new string[] { "Row0", "Row1",
                              "Row2", "Row3", "Discard", "Draw" };


    // This function is called to read in the LayoutXML.xml file
    public void ReadLayout(string xmlText) {
        xmlr = new PT_XMLReader();
        xmlr.Parse(xmlText);      // The XML is parsed
        xml = xmlr.xml["xml"][0]; // And xml is set as a shortcut to the XML

        // Read in the multiplier, which sets card spacing
        multiplier.x = float.Parse(xml["multiplier"][0].att("x"));
        multiplier.y = float.Parse(xml["multiplier"][0].att("y"));

        // Read in the slots
        SlotDef tSD;
        // slotsX is used as a shortcut to all the <slot>s
        PT_XMLHashList slotsX = xml["slot"];

        for (int i=0; i<slotsX.Count; i++) {
            tSD = new SlotDef();  // Create a new SlotDef instance
            if (slotsX[i].HasAtt("type")) {
                // If this <slot> has a type attribute parse it
                tSD.type = slotsX[i].att("type");
            } else {
                // If not, set its type to "slot"; it's a card in the rows
                tSD.type = "slot";
            }
            // Various attributes are parsed into numerical values
            tSD.x = float.Parse( slotsX[i].att("x") );
            tSD.y = float.Parse( slotsX[i].att("y") );
            tSD.layerID = int.Parse( slotsX[i].att("layer") );
            // This converts the number of the layerID into a text layerName
            tSD.layerName = sortingLayerNames[ tSD.layerID ];        // a
```

```
                switch (tSD.type) {
                    // pull additional attributes based on the type of this <slot>
                    case "slot":
                        tSD.faceUp = (slotsX[i].att("faceup") == "1");
                        tSD.id = int.Parse( slotsX[i].att("id") );
                        if (slotsX[i].HasAtt("hiddenby")) {
                            string[] hiding = slotsX[i].att("hiddenby").Split(',');
                            foreach( string s in hiding ) {
                                tSD.hiddenBy.Add ( int.Parse(s) );
                            }
                        }
                        slotDefs.Add(tSD);
                        break;

                    case "drawpile":
                        tSD.stagger.x = float.Parse( slotsX[i].att("xstagger") );
                        drawPile = tSD;
                        break;
                    case "discardpile":
                        discardPile = tSD;
                        break;
                }
            }
        }
    }
}
```

a. The `layerName` field of SlotDef is used to make sure that the correct cards are on top of the others. In Unity 2D, all of your assets are effectively at the same Z depth, so the layer is used to differentiate between them and determine which appears on top.

At this point, most of the preceding syntax should look familiar to you. The SlotDef class is created to store information read in from the XML `<slot>`s in a more accessible way. Then, the Layout class is defined, and the `ReadLayout()` method is created, which will take an XML-formatted string as input and turn it into a series of SlotDefs.

3. Open the Prospector class and add the following bolded lines:

```
public class Prospector : MonoBehaviour {
    static public Prospector     S;

    [Header("Set in Inspector")]
    public TextAsset             deckXML;
    public TextAsset             layoutXML;

    [Header("Set Dynamically")]
    public Deck                  deck;
    public Layout                layout;

    void Awake() {
        S = this; // Set up a Singleton for Prospector
    }
```

```
void Start () {
    deck = GetComponent<Deck>();        // Get the Deck
    deck.InitDeck(deckXML.text);        // Pass DeckXML to it
    Deck.Shuffle(ref deck.cards);       // This shuffles the deck

// This section can be commented out; we're working on real layout now
//      Card c;
//      for (int cNum=0; cNum<deck.cards.Count; cNum++) {
//          c = deck.cards[cNum];
//          c.transform.localPosition = new Vector3((cNum%13)*3,cNum/13*4,0);
//      }

    layout = GetComponent<Layout>();    // Get the Layout component
    layout.ReadLayout(layoutXML.text);  // Pass LayoutXML to it
}
}
```

4. Save all of your scripts in MonoDevelop and return to Unity.

5. In Unity, select *_MainCamera* in the Hierarchy. From the menu bar, choose *Component > Scripts > Layout* to attach a Layout script to _MainCamera (this is just another different way to attach a script to a GameObject). You should now be able to scroll down in the Inspector pane and see the *Layout (Script)* component at the bottom.

6. Find the *Prospector (Script)* component of _MainCamera. You'll see that the public fields `layout` and `layoutXML` have appeared there. Click the target next to `layoutXML` and choose *LayoutXML* from the Assets tab. (You might need to click the *Assets* tab at the top of the *Select TextAsset* window that appears.)

7. *Save your scene.*

8. Click *Play*. If you select _MainCamera in the Hierarchy and scroll down to the *Layout (Script)* component, you should be able to open the disclosure triangle next to `slotDefs` and see that all the `<slot>`s have been parsed from the XML.

Working with CardProspector—A Subclass of Card

Before you can position the cards in the tableau, you must add some features to the Card class that are specific to the *Prospector* game. Because Card and Deck are designed to be reused on other card games, you will create a CardProspector class as a subclass of Card rather than modifying Card directly.

1. Create a new C# script in the __Scripts folder named *CardProspector* and enter this code:

```
using System.Collections;
using System.Collections.Generic;
using UnityEngine;

// An enum defines a variable type with a few prenamed values        // a
public enum eCardState {
```

```
    drawpile,
    tableau,
    target,
    discard
}

public class CardProspector : Card { // Make sure CardProspector extends Card
    [Header("Set Dynamically: CardProspector")]
    // This is how you use the enum eCardState
    public eCardState          state = eCardState.drawpile;
    // The hiddenBy list stores which other cards will keep this one face down
    public List<CardProspector> hiddenBy = new List<CardProspector>();
    // The layoutID matches this card to the tableau XML if it's a tableau card
    public int                 layoutID;
    // The SlotDef class stores information pulled in from the LayoutXML <slot>
    public SlotDef             slotDef;
}
```

    a. This is an enum, which defines a type of variable that only has a few possible named values. The eCardState variable type has one of four values: drawpile, tableau, target, and discard, which help CardProspector instances track where they should be in the game. I like naming enums with a lowercase *e* at the beginning.

The extensions to Card in the new CardProspector class handle things like the four types of locations that the card can occupy in the game (drawpile, tableau [one of the initial 28 cards in the mine], discard, or target [the active card on top of the discard pile]), the storage of layout information (slotDef), and the information that determines when a card should be face-up or face-down (hiddenBy and layoutID).

Now that this subclass is available, you need to convert the cards in the deck from Cards to CardProspectors.

    2. To do this, add the following code to the Prospector class:

```
public class Prospector : MonoBehaviour {
    ...
    [Header("Set Dynamically")]
    public Deck                deck;
    public Layout              layout;
    public List<CardProspector> drawPile;

    void Awake() { ... }

    void Start () {
        ...
        layout = GetComponent<Layout>();   // Get the Layout component
        layout.ReadLayout(layoutXML.text); // Pass LayoutXML to it
```

```
        drawPile = ConvertListCardsToListCardProspectors( deck.cards );
    }

    List<CardProspector> ConvertListCardsToListCardProspectors(List<Card> lCD) {
        List<CardProspector> lCP = new List<CardProspector>();
        CardProspector tCP;
        foreach( Card tCD in lCD ) {
            tCP = tCD as CardProspector;                              // a
            lCP.Add( tCP );
        }
        return( lCP );
    }

}
```

    a. This `as` keyword will attempt to convert a Card to a CardProspector.

3. Save all your scripts in MonoDevelop and return to Unity.

4. Try playing the game and then look at the `drawPile` field of the *(Prospector Script)* component of _MainCamera in the Inspector pane.

You'll notice that all the cards in the `drawPile` are null. (You can also look at this happen by placing a break point on the line marked `// a` in the preceding code and running the debugger.) When you try to treat the Card `tCD` as a CardProspector, the `as` returns `null` instead of a converted Card. This is a result of how object-oriented coding works in C# (see the "On Superclasses and Subclasses" sidebar).

ON SUPERCLASSES AND SUBCLASSES

You're familiar, of course, with superclasses and subclasses from Chapter 26, "Classes." However, you might wonder why attempting to cast a superclass to a subclass doesn't work.

In *Prospector*, Card is the superclass, and the subclass is CardProspector. You could just as easily think of this as a superclass Animal and a subclass Scorpion. All Scorpions are Animals, but not all Animals are Scorpions. You can always refer to a Scorpion as "that Animal," but you can't refer to any Animal as "that Scorpion." Along the same lines, a Scorpion might have a `Sting()` function, but a Cow would not. This is why it's not possible to treat any Animal as a Scorpion, because trying to call `Sting()` on any other Animal might cause an error.

In *Prospector*, you want to use a bunch of Cards that are created by the Deck script as if they were CardProspectors. This is akin to having a bunch of Animals that you want to treat like Scorpions (but we've already decided this is impossible). However, referring to a Scorpion as an Animal *is* always possible. So the solution is this: If you just create

Scorpions from the beginning, and then treat them as Animals through several functions (which they can do because Scorpion is a subclass of Animal), when you choose to call `Scorpion s = Animal as Scorpion;` later, it will work perfectly because the Animal was always secretly a Scorpion.

To do the same in *Prospector*, instead of attaching a *Card (Script)* component to PrefabCard, you can attach a *CardProspector (Script)* component in its place. Then the CardProspector instance will be referred to as a Card by all the Deck functions, but will able to be referred to as a CardProspector when required.

As discussed in the sidebar, the solution in this case is to make sure that the `CardProspector` was always a `CardProspector` and was just masquerading as a `Card` for all the code in the `Deck` class.

5. To do this, select *PrefabCard* in the Project pane; it appears in the Inspector with a *Card (Script)* component.

6. Click the *Add Component* button and choose *Add Component > Scripts > CardProspector*. This adds a *CardProspector (Script)* component to the PrefabCard GameObject.

7. To delete the old *Card (Script)* component, click the gear icon in the top-right corner of the *Card (Script)* Inspector and choose *Remove Component* from the pop-up menu.

8. Select _*MainCamera* from the Hierarchy and play the scene now; you can see that all the entries in the Prospector `drawPile` are now full of CardProspectors instead of `null`.

When the Deck script instantiates PrefabCard and gets the Card component of it, this still works perfectly fine because a CardProspector can always be referred to as a Card. Then, when the `ConvertListCardsToListCardProspectors()` function attempts to call `tCP = tCD as CardProspector;`, it works just fine.

9. Save your scene. You know the drill.

Positioning Cards in the Tableau

Now that everything is ready, it's time to add some code to the Prospector class to actually lay out the game:

```
public class Prospector : MonoBehaviour {
    static public Prospector     S;

    [Header("Set in Inspector")]
    public TextAsset             deckXML;
    public TextAsset             layoutXML;
    public float                 xOffset = 3;
```

```csharp
public float                    yOffset = -2.5f;
public Vector3                  layoutCenter;


[Header("Set Dynamically")]
public Deck                     deck;
public Layout                   layout;
public List<CardProspector>     drawPile;
public Transform                layoutAnchor;
public CardProspector           target;
public List<CardProspector>     tableau;
public List<CardProspector>     discardPile;

void Awake() { … }

void Start () {
    …
    drawPile = ConvertListCardsToListCardProspectors( deck.cards );
    LayoutGame();
}

List<CardProspector> ConvertListCardsToListCardProspectors(List<Card> lCD) {
    …
}

// The Draw function will pull a single card from the drawPile and return it
CardProspector Draw() {
    CardProspector cd = drawPile[0]; // Pull the 0th CardProspector
    drawPile.RemoveAt(0);            // Then remove it from List<> drawPile
    return(cd);                      // And return it
}

// LayoutGame() positions the initial tableau of cards, a.k.a. the "mine"
void LayoutGame() {
    // Create an empty GameObject to serve as an anchor for the tableau  // a
    if (layoutAnchor == null) {
        GameObject tGO = new GameObject("_LayoutAnchor");
        // ^ Create an empty GameObject named _LayoutAnchor in the Hierarchy
        layoutAnchor = tGO.transform;                 // Grab its Transform
        layoutAnchor.transform.position = layoutCenter;   // Position it
    }

    CardProspector cp;
    // Follow the layout
    foreach (SlotDef tSD in layout.slotDefs) {
        // ^ Iterate through all the SlotDefs in the layout.slotDefs as tSD
        cp = Draw(); // Pull a card from the top (beginning) of the draw Pile
        cp.faceUp = tSD.faceUp;      // Set its faceUp to the value in SlotDef
```

```
            cp.transform.parent = layoutAnchor;   // Make its parent layoutAnchor
            // This replaces the previous parent: deck.deckAnchor, which
            //   appears as _Deck in the Hierarchy when the scene is playing.
            cp.transform.localPosition = new Vector3(
                layout.multiplier.x * tSD.x,
                layout.multiplier.y * tSD.y,
                -tSD.layerID );
            // ^ Set the localPosition of the card based on slotDef
            cp.layoutID = tSD.id;
            cp.slotDef = tSD;
            // CardProspectors in the tableau have the state CardState.tableau
            cp.state = eCardState.tableau;

            tableau.Add(cp); // Add this CardProspector to the List<> tableau
        }
    }

}
```

Save your script and return to Unity. When you play this, you will see that the cards are indeed laid out in the mine tableau layout described in LayoutXML.xml—and the right ones are face-up and face-down—but there are some serious issues with layering (see Figure 32.10).

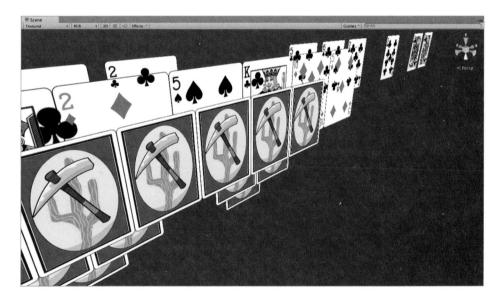

Figure 32.10 Cards are laid out, but there are several layering issues (and remaining cards from the initial grid layout that existed previously)

Hold the Option/Alt key down and use the left mouse button in the Scene window to look around. You can see that when you use Unity's 2D tools, the distance of the 2D object to the camera has nothing to do with the depth sorting of the objects (i.e., which objects are rendered on top of each other). Earlier, you actually got a little lucky with the construction of the cards because you built them from back to front so that all the pips and decorators showed up on top of the card face. However, here you have to be more careful about it for the layout of the game to avoid the problems shown in Figure 32.10.

Unity 2D has two methods of dealing with depth sorting:

- **Sorting Layers:** Sorting layers are used to group 2D objects. Everything in a lower sorting layer is rendered behind everything in a higher sorting layer. Each SpriteRenderer component has a `sortingLayerName` string variable that can be set to the name of a sorting layer.

- **Sorting order:** Each SpriteRenderer component also has a `sortingOrder` variable. This is used to position elements within each sorting layer relative to each other.

In the absence of sorting layers and sortingOrder, sprites are often rendered from back to front in the order that they were created, but this is not at all reliable. Stop playback before continuing.

Setting Up Sorting Layers

To set up sorting layer, follow these steps:

1. From the menu bar, choose *Edit > Project Settings > Tags and Layers*. You've used tags and layers for physics layers and tags before, but you haven't yet touched sorting layers.

2. Open the disclosure triangle next to *Sorting Layers*, and enter the layers as shown in Figure 32.11. You need to click the + button at the bottom-right of the list to add each of the new sorting layers. In this Inspector, the bottom row (Draw) is in front of all the other layers.

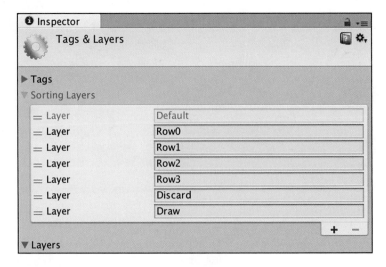

Figure 32.11 The sorting layers required for *Prospector*

Because SpriteRenderers and depth sorting are something that will be necessary for any card game built using this code base, you should add the code to deal with depth sorting to the Card class (as opposed to the CardProspector subclass, which is only used in this game).

3. Open the *Card* script and add the following code:

```
public class Card : MonoBehaviour {
    …
    public CardDefinition   def; // Parsed from DeckXML.xml

    // List of the SpriteRenderer Components of this GameObject and its children
    public SpriteRenderer[]        spriteRenderers;

    void Start() {
        SetSortOrder(0);  // Ensures that the card starts properly depth sorted
    }

    // If spriteRenderers is not yet defined, this function defines it
    public void PopulateSpriteRenderers() {
        // If spriteRenderers is null or empty
        if (spriteRenderers == null || spriteRenderers.Length == 0) {
            // Get SpriteRenderer Components of this GameObject and its children
            spriteRenderers = GetComponentsInChildren<SpriteRenderer>();
        }
    }

    // Sets the sortingLayerName on all SpriteRenderer Components
    public void SetSortingLayerName(string tSLN) {
        PopulateSpriteRenderers();

        foreach (SpriteRenderer tSR in spriteRenderers) {
            tSR.sortingLayerName = tSLN;
        }
    }

    // Sets the sortingOrder of all SpriteRenderer Components
    public void SetSortOrder(int sOrd) {                                    // a
        PopulateSpriteRenderers();

        // Iterate through all the spriteRenderers as tSR
        foreach (SpriteRenderer tSR in spriteRenderers) {
            if (tSR.gameObject == this.gameObject) {
                // If the gameObject is this.gameObject, it's the background
                tSR.sortingOrder = sOrd;  // Set it's order to sOrd
                continue;  // And continue to the next iteration of the loop
            }
```

```
                    // Each of the children of this GameObject are named
                    // switch based on the names
                    switch (tSR.gameObject.name) {
                        case "back": // if the name is "back"
                            // Set it to the highest layer to cover the other sprites
                            tSR.sortingOrder = sOrd+2;
                            break;

                        case "face": // if the name is "face"
                        default:     //  or if it's anything else
                            // Set it to the middle layer to be above the background
                            tSR.sortingOrder = sOrd+1;
                            break;
                    }
                }
            }
        }

        public bool faceUp { … }

    }
```

a. The white background of the card is on bottom (sOrd).

On top of that are all the pips, decorators, face, and so on (sOrd+1).

The back is on top so that, when it is visible, it covers the rest (sOrd+2).

4. *Prospector* needs one line added near the end of the `LayoutGame()` method to make sure that the cards in the initial mine layout are placed in the proper sorting layer:

```
public class Prospector : MonoBehaviour {
    …
    // LayoutGame() positions the initial tableau of cards, a.k.a. the "mine"
    void LayoutGame() {
        …
        foreach (SlotDef tSD in layout.slotDefs) {
            …
            cp.state = eCardState.tableau;
            // CardProspectors in the tableau have the state CardState.tableau
            cp.SetSortingLayerName(tSD.layerName); // Set the sorting layers

            tableau.Add(cp); // Add this CardProspector to the List<> tableau
        }
    }
}
```

5. Save all the scripts in MonoDevelop, return to Unity, and run the scene.

Now the cards stack properly on top of each other in the mine. You still have not yet collected the remaining cards into a draw pile, but that will come soon.

Implementing Game Logic

Before you move cards into place for the draw pile, let's start by delineating the possible actions that can happen in the game:

A. If the target card is replaced by any other card, the replaced target card then moves to the discard pile.

B. A card can move from the drawPile to become the target card.

C. A card that is one higher or one lower than the target card can move to become the target card.

D. If a face-down card has no more cards hiding it, it becomes face-up.

E. The game is over when either the mine is empty (win) or the draw pile is empty and there are no more possible plays (loss).

Letters B and C in the list are possible move actions, where a card is moved by the player, while letters A, D, and E are passive actions that happen as a result of either action B or C.

Making Cards Clickable

Because all of these actions are instigated by a click on one of the cards, the first task is to make the cards clickable.

1. Every card game needs cards to be clickable, so add the following method near the end of the Card class:

```
public class Card : MonoBehaviour {
    …

    public bool faceUp {
        get { … }
        set { … }
    }

    // Virtual methods can be overridden by subclass methods with the same name
    virtual public void OnMouseUpAsButton() {
        print (name);   // When clicked, this outputs the card name
    }

}
```

Now, when you click Play, you can click any card in the scene, and it will output its name.

2. However, in *Prospector*, card clicks need to do more than that, so add the following method to the end of the CardProspector class:

```
public class CardProspector : Card { // Make sure CardProspector extends Card
    …
    // The SlotDef class stores information pulled in from the LayoutXML <slot>
```

```
    public SlotDef                        slotDef;

    // This allows the card to react to being clicked
    override public void OnMouseUpAsButton() {
        // Call the CardClicked method on the Prospector singleton
        Prospector.S.CardClicked(this);
        // Also call the base class (Card.cs) version of this method
        base.OnMouseUpAsButton();                                    // a
    }
}
```

a. Because this line calls the base class (Card) version of `OnMouseUpAsButton()`, Card-Prospectors will still print their name to the Console pane when clicked (in addition to calling the new `Prospector.S.CardClicked()` method (see the next step).

3. You must still write the `CardClicked` method in the Prospector script (which is why it's currently red in the code you just typed), but first, you need a few helper functions. Add the `MoveToDiscard()`, `MoveToTarget()`, and `UpdateDrawPile()` methods to the end of the Prospector class.

```
public class Prospector : MonoBehaviour {
    …
    void LayoutGame() { … }

    // Moves the current target to the discardPile
    void MoveToDiscard(CardProspector cd) {
        // Set the state of the card to discard
        cd.state = eCardState.discard;
        discardPile.Add(cd);  // Add it to the discardPile List<>
        cd.transform.parent = layoutAnchor; // Update its transform parent

        // Position this card on the discardPile
        cd.transform.localPosition = new Vector3(
            layout.multiplier.x * layout.discardPile.x,
            layout.multiplier.y * layout.discardPile.y,
            -layout.discardPile.layerID+0.5f );
        cd.faceUp = true;
        // Place it on top of the pile for depth sorting
        cd.SetSortingLayerName(layout.discardPile.layerName);
        cd.SetSortOrder(-100+discardPile.Count);
    }

    // Make cd the new target card
    void MoveToTarget(CardProspector cd) {
        // If there is currently a target card, move it to discardPile
        if (target != null) MoveToDiscard(target);
        target = cd; // cd is the new target
        cd.state = eCardState.target;
        cd.transform.parent = layoutAnchor;
```

```
        // Move to the target position
        cd.transform.localPosition = new Vector3(
            layout.multiplier.x * layout.discardPile.x,
            layout.multiplier.y * layout.discardPile.y,
            -layout.discardPile.layerID );

        cd.faceUp = true; // Make it face-up
        // Set the depth sorting
        cd.SetSortingLayerName(layout.discardPile.layerName);
        cd.SetSortOrder(0);
    }

    // Arranges all the cards of the drawPile to show how many are left
    void UpdateDrawPile() {
        CardProspector cd;
        // Go through all the cards of the drawPile
        for (int i=0; i<drawPile.Count; i++) {
            cd = drawPile[i];
            cd.transform.parent = layoutAnchor;

            // Position it correctly with the layout.drawPile.stagger
            Vector2 dpStagger = layout.drawPile.stagger;
            cd.transform.localPosition = new Vector3(
                layout.multiplier.x * (layout.drawPile.x + i*dpStagger.x),
                layout.multiplier.y * (layout.drawPile.y + i*dpStagger.y),
                -layout.drawPile.layerID+0.1f*i );

            cd.faceUp = false; // Make them all face-down
            cd.state = eCardState.drawpile;
            // Set depth sorting
            cd.SetSortingLayerName(layout.drawPile.layerName);
            cd.SetSortOrder(-10*i);
        }
    }

}
```

4. Add the following code to the end of `Prospector.LayoutGame()` to draw the initial target card and arrange the drawPile. This code also adds an initial version of the `Card-Clicked()` method—to handle all clicks on CardProspectors—near the end of the Prospector class. For now, `CardClicked()` only handles moving a card from the drawPile to the target (letter B from the earlier list), but you'll expand this method more soon.

```
public class Prospector : MonoBehaviour {
    ...
    // LayoutGame() positions the initial tableau of cards, a.k.a. the "mine"
    void LayoutGame() {
        ...
        foreach (SlotDef tSD in layout.slotDefs) {
            ...
            tableau.Add(cpp); // Add this CardProspector to the List<> tableau
        }
```

```
        // Set up the initial target card
        MoveToTarget(Draw ());

        // Set up the Draw pile
        UpdateDrawPile();

    }


    // Moves the current target to the discardPile
    void MoveToDiscard(CardProspector cd) { … }

    void MoveToTarget(CardProspector cd) { … }
    …
    void UpdateDrawPile() { … }

    // CardClicked is called any time a card in the game is clicked
    public void CardClicked(CardProspector cd) {
        // The reaction is determined by the state of the clicked card
        switch (cd.state) {
            case eCardState.target:
                // Clicking the target card does nothing
                break;

            case eCardState.drawpile:
                // Clicking any card in the drawPile will draw the next card
                MoveToDiscard(target); // Moves the target to the discardPile
                MoveToTarget(Draw());  // Moves the next drawn card to the target
                UpdateDrawPile();      // Restacks the drawPile
                break;

            case eCardState.tableau:
                // Clicking a card in the tableau will check if it's a valid play
                break;
        }
    }

}
```

5. Save all scripts in MonoDevelop, return to Unity, and play the scene.

You can now click on the drawPile (in the top-right corner of the screen) to draw a new target card. You're getting close to having a game now!

Matching Cards from the Mine

To make the card in the mine work, you need to have a little code that checks to make sure that the clicked card is either one higher or one lower than the target card (and, of course, also handles Ace-to-King wraparound).

1. Add these bolded lines to the `CardClicked()` method of the Prospector script:

```
public class Prospector : MonoBehaviour {

    …

    // CardClicked is called any time a card in the game is clicked
    public void CardClicked(CardProspector cd) {
        // The reaction is determined by the state of the clicked card
        switch (cd.state) {

            …

            case eCardState.tableau:
                // Clicking a card in the tableau will check if it's a valid play
                bool validMatch = true;
                if (!cd.faceUp) {
                    // If the card is face-down, it's not valid
                    validMatch = false;
                }
                if (!AdjacentRank(cd, target)) {
                    // If it's not an adjacent rank, it's not valid
                    validMatch = false;
                }
                if (!validMatch) return; // return if not valid

                // If we got here, then: Yay! It's a valid card.
                tableau.Remove(cd); // Remove it from the tableau List
                MoveToTarget(cd);   // Make it the target card
                break;
        }
    }

    // Return true if the two cards are adjacent in rank (A & K wrap around)
    public bool AdjacentRank(CardProspector c0, CardProspector c1) {
        // If either card is face-down, it's not adjacent.
        if (!c0.faceUp || !c1.faceUp) return(false);

        // If they are 1 apart, they are adjacent
        if (Mathf.Abs(c0.rank - c1.rank) == 1) {
            return(true);
        }
        // If one is Ace and the other King, they are adjacent
        if (c0.rank ==  1 && c1.rank == 13) return(true);
        if (c0.rank == 13 && c1.rank ==  1) return(true);

        // Otherwise, return false
        return(false);
    }
}
```

2. Save your script in MonoDevelop and return to Unity.

Now you can play the game and actually play the top row correctly! However, as you play more, you'll notice that the face-down cards are never flipping to face-up. This is what the

List<CardProspector> CardProspector.hiddenBy field is for. The information about which cards hide others is in List<int> SlotDef.hiddenBy, but you need to be able to convert from the integer IDs in SlotDef.hiddenBy to the actual CardProspectors that have that ID.

3. Add this code to Prospector to do so:

```
public class Prospector : MonoBehaviour {
    …
    // LayoutGame() positions the initial tableau of cards, a.k.a. the "mine"
    void LayoutGame() {
        …
        CardProspector cp;
        // Follow the layout
        foreach (SlotDef tSD in layout.slotDefs) {
            …
            Tableau.Add(cpp); // Add this CardProspector to the List<> tableau
        }

        // Set which cards are hiding others
        foreach (CardProspector tCP in tableau) {
            foreach( int hid in tCP.slotDef.hiddenBy ) {
                cp = FindCardByLayoutID(hid);
                tCP.hiddenBy.Add(cp);
            }
        }

        // Set up the initial target card
        MoveToTarget(Draw ());

        // Set up the Draw pile
        UpdateDrawPile();

    }

    // Convert from the layoutID int to the CardProspector with that ID
    CardProspector FindCardByLayoutID(int layoutID) {
        foreach (CardProspector tCP in tableau) {
            // Search through all cards in the tableau List<>
            if (tCP.layoutID == layoutID) {
                // If the card has the same ID, return it
                return( tCP );
            }
        }
        // If it's not found, return null
        return( null );
    }

    // This turns cards in the Mine face-up or face-down
    void SetTableauFaces() {
        foreach( CardProspector cd in tableau ) {
```

```csharp
            bool faceUp = true; // Assume the card will be face-up
            foreach( CardProspector cover in cd.hiddenBy ) {
                // If either of the covering cards are in the tableau
                if (cover.state == eCardState.tableau) {
                    faceUp = false; // then this card is face-down
                }
            }
            cd.faceUp = faceUp; // Set the value on the card
        }
    }

    // Moves the current target to the discardPile
    void MoveToDiscard(CardProspector cd) { … }

    // Make cd the new target card
    void MoveToTarget(CardProspector cd) { … }

    // Arranges all the cards of the drawPile to show how many are left
    void UpdateDrawPile() { … }

    // CardClicked is called any time a card in the game is clicked
    public void CardClicked(CardProspector cd) {
        // The reaction is determined by the state of the clicked card
        switch (cd.state) {

            …
            case eCardState.tableau:

                …
                // If we got here, then: Yay! It's a valid card.
                tableau.Remove(cd); // Remove it from the tableau List
                MoveToTarget(cd);   // Make it the target card
                SetTableauFaces();  // Update tableau card face-ups
                break;

        }
    }

    // Return true if the two cards are adjacent in rank (A & K wrap around)
    public bool AdjacentRank(CardProspector c0, CardProspector c1) { … }

}
```

Now, after you save your scripts and return to Unity, an entire round of the game is playable!

4. Next up is making the game know when it's status only needs to be checked once after each time the player has clicked a card, so the check will be called from the end of Prospector.CardClicked(). Add the following to the Prospector class:

```csharp
public class Prospector : MonoBehaviour {
    …

    // CardClicked is called any time a card in the game is clicked
    public void CardClicked(CardProspector cd) {
        // The reaction is determined by the state of the clicked card
```

```csharp
        switch (cd.state) {
            …
            SetTableauFaces();   // Update tableau card face-ups
            break;
        }
        // Check to see whether the game is over or not
        CheckForGameOver();
    }


    // Test whether the game is over
    void CheckForGameOver() {
        // If the tableau is empty, the game is over
        if (tableau.Count==0) {
            // Call GameOver() with a win
            GameOver(true);
            return;
        }

        // If there are still cards in the draw pile, the game's not over
        if (drawPile.Count>0) {
            return;
        }

        // Check for remaining valid plays
        foreach ( CardProspector cd in tableau ) {
            if (AdjacentRank(cd, target)) {
                // If there is a valid play, the game's not over
                return;
            }
        }

        // Since there are no valid plays, the game is over
        // Call GameOver with a loss
        GameOver (false);
    }


    // Called when the game is over. Simple for now, but expandable
    void GameOver(bool won) {
        if (won) {
            print ("Game Over. You won! :)");
        } else {
            print ("Game Over. You Lost. :(");
        }
        // Reload the scene, resetting the game
        SceneManager.LoadScene("__Prospector_Scene_0");
    }


    // Return true if the two cards are adjacent in rank (A & K wrap around)
    public bool AdjacentRank(CardProspector c0, CardProspector c1) { … }


}
```

5. *Save All* scripts in MonoDevelop and return to Unity to test the game.

Now the game is playable and repeatable, and it knows when it has won or lost. To test losing the game, you can run the game and click on the draw pile until it's depleted; the scene should reload, and a new round will start. Testing whether winning the game works or not might take a few tries. ;-)

Next up, it's time to add some scoring.

Adding Scoring to *Prospector*

The original card game of *Prospector* (or *Tri-Peaks*, on which it was based) had no scoring mechanism beyond the player winning or losing. But as a digital game, keeping score and having a high score so that players have an impetus to keep playing (to beat their high score) is really helpful.

Ways to Earn Points in the Game

You will implement several ways to earn points in Prospector:

A. Moving a card from the mine to the target card earns 1 point.

B. Every subsequent card removed from the mine without drawing from the draw pile increases the points awarded per card by 1, so a *run* of five cards removed without a draw would be worth 1, 2, 3, 4, and 5 points each, for a total of 15 points for the run (1 + 2 + 3 + 4 + 5 = 15).

C. If the player wins the round, she carries her score on to the next round. Whenever a round is lost, her score for all rounds is totaled and checked against the high score list.

D. The number of points earned for a run will double for each special gold card in the run. If two of the cards in the example run from letter B were gold, then the run would be worth 60 points (15 x 2 x 2 = 60).

The Prospector class will handle the scoring because it is aware of all the conditions that could contribute to the score. You will also create a script named *Scoreboard* to handle all the visual elements of showing the score to the player.

You will implement letters A through C in this chapter, and I'll leave letter D for you to implement on your own later.

Making the Chain Scoring Work

To track the score in this game, you'll create a *ScoreManager* script to add to _MainCamera. Because you're enabling runs and the doubling of the value for the run, it makes sense to store the score for the run separately and then apply that to the total score for the round when the run has been ended (by drawing a card from the drawPile).

1. Create a new C# script in the __Scripts folder named *ScoreManager*.

2. Attach the *ScoreManager* script to _MainCamera.

3. Open *ScoreManager* in MonoDevelop and enter the following code:

```csharp
using System.Collections;
using System.Collections.Generic;
using UnityEngine;

// An enum to handle all the possible scoring events
public enum eScoreEvent {
    draw,
    mine,
    mineGold,
    gameWin,
    gameLoss
}

// ScoreManager handles all of the scoring
public class ScoreManager : MonoBehaviour {                          // a
    static private ScoreManager  S;                                  // b

    static public int     SCORE_FROM_PREV_ROUND = 0;
    static public int     HIGH_SCORE = 0;

    [Header("Set Dynamically")]
    // Fields to track score info
    public int          chain = 0;
    public int          scoreRun = 0;
    public int          score = 0;

    void Awake() {
        if (S == null) {                                            // c
            S = this;  // Set the private singleton
        } else {
            Debug.LogError("ERROR: ScoreManager.Awake(): S is already set!");
        }

        // Check for a high score in PlayerPrefs
        if (PlayerPrefs.HasKey ("ProspectorHighScore")) {
            HIGH_SCORE = PlayerPrefs.GetInt("ProspectorHighScore");
        }
        // Add the score from last round, which will be >0 if it was a win
        score += SCORE_FROM_PREV_ROUND;
        // And reset the SCORE_FROM_PREV_ROUND
        SCORE_FROM_PREV_ROUND = 0;
    }

    static public void EVENT(eScoreEvent evt) {                      // d
        try {  // try-catch stops an error from breaking your program
            S.Event(evt);
        } catch (System.NullReferenceException nre) {
```

```
                Debug.LogError( "ScoreManager:EVENT() called while S=null.\n"+nre );
        }
    }


    void Event(eScoreEvent evt) {
        switch (evt) {
            // Same things need to happen whether it's a draw, a win, or a loss
            case eScoreEvent.draw:       // Drawing a card
            case eScoreEvent.gameWin:    // Won the round
            case eScoreEvent.gameLoss:   // Lost the round
                chain = 0;               // resets the score chain
                score += scoreRun;       // add scoreRun to total score
                scoreRun = 0;            // reset scoreRun
                break;

            case eScoreEvent.mine:       // Remove a mine card
                chain++;                 // increase the score chain
                scoreRun += chain;       // add score for this card to run
                break;
        }

        // This second switch statement handles round wins and losses
        switch (evt) {
            case eScoreEvent.gameWin:
                // If it's a win, add the score to the next round
                // static fields are NOT reset by SceneManager.LoadScene()
                SCORE_FROM_PREV_ROUND = score;
                print ("You won this round! Round score: "+score);
                break;

            case eScoreEvent.gameLoss:
                // If it's a loss, check against the high score
                if (HIGH_SCORE <= score) {
                    print("You got the high score! High score: "+score);
                    HIGH_SCORE = score;
                    PlayerPrefs.SetInt("ProspectorHighScore", score);
                } else {
                    print ("Your final score for the game was: "+score);
                }
                break;

            default:
                print ("score: "+score+"  scoreRun:"+scoreRun+"  chain:"+chain);
                break;
        }
    }

    static public int CHAIN {  get { return S.chain; }  }            // e
    static public int SCORE {  get { return S.score; }  }
    static public int SCORE_RUN {  get { return S.scoreRun; }  }
}
```

a. In the first edition of the book, ScoreManager was a method of Prospector rather than a separate class, but since then, I've come to believe strongly in the *component pattern* of software design. In the component pattern, developers try to make small, reusable classes that are self-contained. By making ScoreManager a separate class, I've created something that I could use again in the future, and I've kept my code simpler. You can read more about component pattern design in Appendix B, "Useful Concepts," and you will use it extensively in Chapter 35, "Dungeon Delver."

b. The `static private ScoreManager S;` is a private version of the singleton pattern. While most of the singletons in this book have been public, this one is private to grant it more protection so that only the ScoreManager class can access it.

c. This more complex singleton assignment ensures that an error is thrown if two different ScoreManager instances try to assert themselves as the singleton `S`.

d. This static public version of the `EVENT()` method enables other classes (like Prospector) to send eScoreEvents to the ScoreManager class. When they do so, `EVENT()` calls the public, non-static `Event()` method on the ScoreManager private singleton `S`. The `try-catch` clause here will alert you if `EVENT()` is called while `S` is still null.

e. These static properties allow read-only access to the public fields of the private ScoreManager singleton `S`.

4. Add the following four bolded lines of code to the `CardClicked()` and `GameOver()` methods of Prospector to make use of the ScoreManager:

```
public class Prospector : MonoBehaviour {
    ...
    // CardClicked is called any time a card in the game is clicked
    public void CardClicked(CardProspector cd) {
        // The reaction is determined by the state of the clicked card
        switch (cd.state) {
            ...
            case eCardState.drawpile:
                // Clicking any card in the drawPile will draw the next card
                MoveToDiscard(target); // Moves the target to the discardPile
                MoveToTarget(Draw());  // Moves the next drawn card to the target
                UpdateDrawPile();      // Restacks the drawPile
                ScoreManager.EVENT(eScoreEvent.draw);
                break;

            case eCardState.tableau:
                ...
                // If we got here, then: Yay! It's a valid card.
                tableau.Remove(cd); // Remove it from the tableau List
                MoveToTarget(cd);   // Make it the target card
                SetTableauFaces();  // Update tableau card face-ups
                ScoreManager.EVENT(eScoreEvent.mine);
                break;
        }
```

```
            // Check to see whether the game is over or not
            CheckForGameOver();
        }

        // Test whether the game is over
        void CheckForGameOver() { … }

        // Called when the game is over. Simple for now, but expandable
        void GameOver(bool won) {
            if (won) {
                // print ("Game Over. You won! :)");   // Comment out this line
                ScoreManager.EVENT(eScoreEvent.gameWin);
            } else {
                // print ("Game Over. You Lost. :(");  // Comment out this line
                ScoreManager.EVENT(eScoreEvent.gameLoss);
            }
            // Reload the scene, resetting the game
            SceneManager.LoadScene("__Prospector_Scene_0");
        }
        …
}
```

5. Save the scripts in MonoDevelop, return to Unity, and click Play.

Now, as you play the game, you'll see little notes in the Console pane that tell you your score. Additionally, if you select _MainCamera in the Hierarchy and look at the *ScoreManager (Script)* Inspector, you will see that if you win a round, you keep your score when you move to the next round. This is great for us as developers, but now let's make things look a little better for our players.

Showing the Score to the Players

For this game, you'll also make a couple of reusable components that can show the score. One will be a *Scoreboard* class to handle manage all the score display. The other, *FloatingScore*, will be an on-screen number that can move itself around the screen. You'll also make use of Unity's `SendMessage()` feature, which can call a method by name with one parameter on any GameObject:

1. Create a new C# script in the __Scripts folder named *FloatingScore* and enter this code:

```
using System.Collections;
using System.Collections.Generic;
using UnityEngine;
using UnityEngine.UI;

// An enum to track the possible states of a FloatingScore
public enum eFSState {
    idle,
    pre,
    active,
```

```
        post
}

// FloatingScore can move itself on screen following a Bézier curve
public class FloatingScore : MonoBehaviour {
    [Header("Set Dynamically")]
    public eFSState          state = eFSState.idle;

    [SerializeField]
    protected int            _score = 0;
    public string            scoreString;

    // The score property sets both _score and scoreString
    public int score {
        get {
            return(_score);
        }
        set {
            _score = value;
            scoreString = _score.ToString("N0"); // "N0" adds commas to the num
            // Search "C# Standard Numeric Format Strings" for ToString formats
            GetComponent<Text>().text = scoreString;
        }
    }

    public List<Vector2>    bezierPts; // Bézier points for movement
    public List<float>      fontSizes; // Bézier points for font scaling
    public float            timeStart = -1f;
    public float            timeDuration = 1f;
    public string           easingCurve = Easing.InOut; // Uses Easing in Utils.cs

    // The GameObject that will receive the SendMessage when this is done moving
    public GameObject       reportFinishTo = null;

    private RectTransform   rectTrans;
    private Text            txt;


    // Set up the FloatingScore and movement
    // Note the use of parameter defaults for eTimeS & eTimeD
    public void Init(List<Vector2> ePts, float eTimeS = 0, float eTimeD = 1) {
        rectTrans = GetComponent<RectTransform>();
        rectTrans.anchoredPosition = Vector2.zero;

        txt = GetComponent<Text>();

        bezierPts = new List<Vector2>(ePts);

        if (ePts.Count == 1) { // If there's only one point
            // ...then just go there.
            transform.position = ePts[0];
```

```
            return;
    }

    // If eTimeS is the default, just start at the current time
    if (eTimeS == 0) eTimeS = Time.time;
    timeStart = eTimeS;
    timeDuration = eTimeD;

    state = eFSState.pre; // Set it to the pre state, ready to start moving
}

public void FSCallback(FloatingScore fs) {
    // When this callback is called by SendMessage,
    //   add the score from the calling FloatingScore
    score += fs.score;
}


// Update is called once per frame
void Update () {
    // If this is not moving, just return
    if (state == eFSState.idle) return;

    // Get u from the current time and duration
    // u ranges from 0 to 1 (usually)
    float u = (Time.time - timeStart)/timeDuration;
    // Use Easing class from Utils to curve the u value
    float uC = Easing.Ease (u, easingCurve);
    if (u<0) { // If u<0, then we shouldn't move yet.
        state = eFSState.pre;
        txt.enabled= false; // Hide the score initially
    } else {
        if (u>=1) { // If u>=1, we're done moving
            uC = 1; // Set uC=1 so we don't overshoot
            state = eFSState.post;
            if (reportFinishTo != null) { //If there's a callback GameObject
                // Use SendMessage to call the FSCallback method
                //   with this as the parameter.
                reportFinishTo.SendMessage("FSCallback", this);
                // Now that the message has been sent,
                //   Destroy this gameObject
                Destroy (gameObject);
            } else { // If there is nothing to callback
                // ...then don't destroy this. Just let it stay still.
                state = eFSState.idle;
            }
        } else {
            // 0<=u<1, which means that this is active and moving
            state = eFSState.active;
            txt.enabled = true; // Show the score once more
        }
```

```
        // Use Bézier curve to move this to the right point
        Vector2 pos = Utils.Bezier(uC, bezierPts);
        // RectTransform anchors can be used to position UI objects relative
        //   to total size of the screen
        rectTrans.anchorMin = rectTrans.anchorMax = pos;
        if (fontSizes != null && fontSizes.Count>0) {
            // If fontSizes has values in it
            // ...then adjust the fontSize of this GUIText
            int size = Mathf.RoundToInt( Utils.Bezier(uC, fontSizes) );
            GetComponent<Text>().fontSize = size;
        }
    }
  }
}
```

2. Create a new C# script in the __Scripts folder named *Scoreboard* and enter this code into it:

```
using System.Collections;
using System.Collections.Generic;
using UnityEngine;
using UnityEngine.UI;

// The Scoreboard class manages showing the score to the player
public class Scoreboard : MonoBehaviour {
    public static Scoreboard S; // The singleton for Scoreboard

    [Header("Set in Inspector")]
    public GameObject      prefabFloatingScore;

    [Header("Set Dynamically")]
    [SerializeField] private int     _score = 0;
    [SerializeField] private string _scoreString;

    private Transform      canvasTrans;

    // The score property also sets the scoreString
    public int score {
        get {
            return(_score);
        }
        set {
            _score = value;
            scoreString = _score.ToString("N0");
        }
    }

    // The scoreString property also sets the Text.text
    public string scoreString {
        get {
            return(_scoreString);
        }
        set {
            _scoreString = value;
```

```
            GetComponent<Text>().text = _scoreString;
        }
    }

    void Awake() {
        if (S == null) {
            S = this;  // Set the private singleton
        } else {
            Debug.LogError("ERROR: Scoreboard.Awake(): S is already set!");
        }
        canvasTrans = transform.parent;
    }

    // When called by SendMessage, this adds the fs.score to this.score
    public void FSCallback(FloatingScore fs) {
        score += fs.score;
    }

    // This will Instantiate a new FloatingScore GameObject and initialize it.
    // It also returns a pointer to the FloatingScore created so that the
    //  calling function can do more with it (like set fontSizes, and so on)
    public FloatingScore CreateFloatingScore(int amt, List<Vector2> pts) {
        GameObject go = Instantiate <GameObject> (prefabFloatingScore);
        go.transform.SetParent( canvasTrans );
        FloatingScore fs = go.GetComponent<FloatingScore>();
        fs.score = amt;
        fs.reportFinishTo = this.gameObject; // Set fs to call back to this
        fs.Init(pts);
        return(fs);
    }

}
```

3.　Save all scripts in MonoDevelop and return to Unity.

Now, you need to make the GameObjects for both the Scoreboard and the FloatingScore.

Making the FloatingScore GameObject Prefab

To create the FloatingScore GameObject:

1.　From Unity's menu bar, choose *GameObject > UI > Text*. Rename the *Text* GameObject to *PrefabFloatingScore*.

2.　Before changing any of the settings on PrefabFloatingScore, make sure that the aspect ratio of your Game pane is set to either *Standalone (1024x768)* or *iPad Wide (1024x768)*. This ensures that your settings and mine agree.

3.　Give PrefabFloatingScore the settings shown in Figure 32.12. Afterward, you should see a white zero floating in the middle of your Game pane.

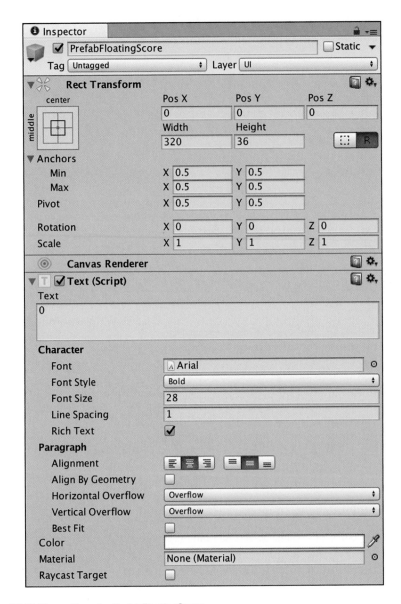

Figure 32.12 The settings for PrefabFloatingScore

4. Attach the script *FloatingScore* to the GameObject PrefabFloatingScore (by dragging the script onto *PrefabFloatingScore* in the Hierarchy).

5. Convert PrefabFloatingScore to a prefab by dragging it from the Hierarchy into the *_Prefabs* folder in the Project pane.

6. Delete the instance of PrefabFloatingScore that remains in the Hierarchy pane.

Making the Scoreboard GameObject

To make the Scoreboard GameObject:

1. Create another Text GameObject in the scene (*GameObject > UI > Text*).

2. Rename this Text GameObject to *Scoreboard*.

3. Attach the *Scoreboard* C# script to the Scoreboard GameObject and give the Scoreboard GameObject the settings shown in Figure 32.13. This includes dragging the prefab PrefabFloatingScore from the _Prefabs folder into the public `prefabFloatingScore` field of the *Scoreboard (Script)* component.

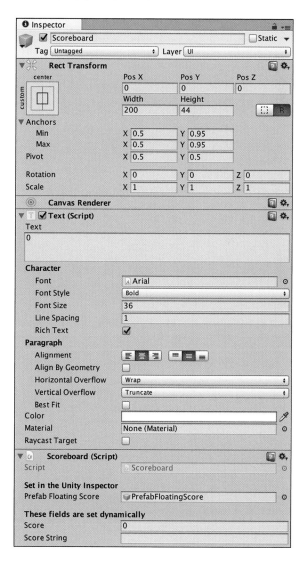

Figure 32.13 The settings for Scoreboard

4. Save your scene.

5. Now all you need to do is make a few changes to the Prospector class to incorporate the new code and GameObjects. Add the following bolded code to the Prospector class:

```csharp
public class Prospector : MonoBehaviour {
    …
    [Header("Set in Inspector")]
    …
    public Vector3              layoutCenter;
    public Vector2              fsPosMid  = new Vector2( 0.5f, 0.90f );
    public Vector2              fsPosRun  = new Vector2( 0.5f, 0.75f );
    public Vector2              fsPosMid2 = new Vector2( 0.4f, 1.0f  );
    public Vector2              fsPosEnd  = new Vector2( 0.5f, 0.95f );

    [Header("Set Dynamically")]
    …
    public List<CardProspector>  tableau;
    public List<CardProspector>  discardPile;
    public FloatingScore         fsRun;

    void Awake() { … }

    void Start () {
        Scoreboard.S.score = ScoreManager.SCORE;

        deck = GetComponent<Deck>(); // Get the Deck
        …
    }

    …

    // CardClicked is called any time a card in the game is clicked
    public void CardClicked(CardProspector cd) {
        // The reaction is determined by the state of the clicked card
        switch (cd.state) {
            …
            case eCardState.drawpile:
                …
                ScoreManager.EVENT(eScoreEvent.draw);
                FloatingScoreHandler(eScoreEvent.draw);
                break;

            case eCardState.tableau:
                …
                ScoreManager.EVENT(eScoreEvent.mine);
                FloatingScoreHandler(eScoreEvent.mine);
                break;
        }
        …
    }
```

```
// Test whether the game is over
void CheckForGameOver() { … }

// Called when the game is over. Simple for now, but expandable
void GameOver(bool won) {
    if (won) {
        // print ("Game Over. You won! :)");   // Comment out this line
        ScoreManager.EVENT(eScoreEvent.gameWin);
        FloatingScoreHandler(eScoreEvent.gameWin);
    } else {
        // print ("Game Over. You Lost. :(");   // Comment out this line
        ScoreManager.EVENT(eScoreEvent.gameLoss);
        FloatingScoreHandler(eScoreEvent.gameLoss);
    }
    // Reload the scene, resetting the game
    SceneManager.LoadScene("__Prospector_Scene_0");
}

…

// Return true if the two cards are adjacent in rank (A & K wrap around)
public bool AdjacentRank(CardProspector c0, CardProspector c1) { … }

// Handle FloatingScore movement
void FloatingScoreHandler(eScoreEvent evt) {
    List<Vector2> fsPts;
    switch (evt) {
        // Same things need to happen whether it's a draw, a win, or a loss
        case eScoreEvent.draw:      // Drawing a card
        case eScoreEvent.gameWin:   // Won the round
        case eScoreEvent.gameLoss:  // Lost the round
            // Add fsRun to the Scoreboard score
            if (fsRun != null) {
                // Create points for the Bézier curve
                fsPts = new List<Vector2>();
                fsPts.Add( fsPosRun );
                fsPts.Add( fsPosMid2 );
                fsPts.Add( fsPosEnd );
                fsRun.reportFinishTo = Scoreboard.S.gameObject;
                fsRun.Init(fsPts, 0, 1);
                // Also adjust the fontSize
                fsRun.fontSizes = new List<float>(new float[] {28,36,4});
                fsRun = null; // Clear fsRun so it's created again
            }
            break;
```

```
        case eScoreEvent.mine: // Remove a mine card
            // Create a FloatingScore for this score
            FloatingScore fs;
            // Move it from the mousePosition to fsPosRun
            Vector2 p0 = Input.mousePosition;
            p0.x /= Screen.width;
            p0.y /= Screen.height;
            fsPts = new List<Vector2>();
            fsPts.Add( p0 );
            fsPts.Add( fsPosMid );
            fsPts.Add( fsPosRun );
            fs = Scoreboard.S.CreateFloatingScore(ScoreManager.CHAIN, fsPts);
            fs.fontSizes = new List<float>(new float[] {4,50,28});
            if (fsRun == null) {
                fsRun = fs;
                fsRun.reportFinishTo = null;
            } else {
                fs.reportFinishTo = fsRun.gameObject;
            }
            break;
        }
    }

}
```

6. Save your scripts in MonoDevelop, and try playing the game in Unity.

Now when you play the game, you should see the score flying around. This is actually pretty important because it helps your players understand where the score is coming from and helps reveal the mechanics of the game to them through play (rather than requiring them to read instructions).

Adding Some Art to the Game

Let's add some theming to the game by giving it a background. In the Materials folder that you imported at the beginning of the project are a PNG named *ProspectorBackground* and a material named *ProspectorBackground Mat*. These are already set up for you, because you learned how to do so in previous chapters.

1. In Unity, add a quad to the scene (*GameObject > 3D Object > Quad*).

2. Drag the *ProspectorBackground Mat* from the Materials folder onto the quad.

3. Rename the quad *ProspectorBackground* and set its transform as follows:

    ProspectorBackground (Quad)   P:[0, 0, 0]   R:[0, 0, 0]   S:[26.667, 20, 1]

Because _MainCamera's orthographic size is 10, that means that it is 10 units between the center of the screen and the nearest edge (which in this case is the top and bottom), for a total height of 20 units visible on screen. The ProspectorBackground quad is 20 units high (Scale Y) because of this. Also, because the screen is at a 4:3 aspect ratio, 20 / 3 * 4 = 26.667 is the width (Scale X) that you need to set the background to.

4. Save your scene.

When you play the game now, it should look something like Figure 32.14.[4]

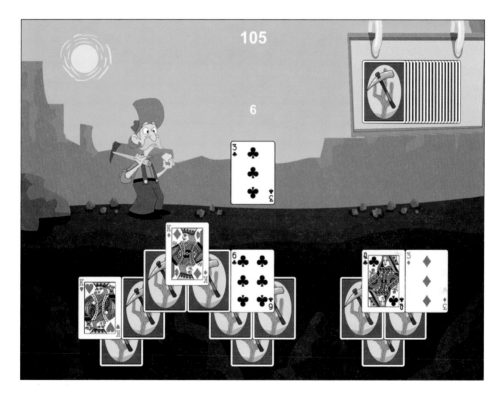

Figure 32.14 The *Prospector* game with a background

Announcing the Beginning and End of Rounds

I'm sure you've noticed that the rounds of the game end rather abruptly. Let's do something about that. First let's delay the actual reloading of the level using an `Invoke()` function. Add the following bolded code to Prospector:

---

4. This original art—including the character, background, and card backs—was created in 2001 for my company at the time, Digital Mercenaries, by the artist Jimmy Tovar (http://jimmytovar.com).

```
public class Prospector : MonoBehaviour {
    ...
    [Header("Set in Inspector")]
    ...
    public Vector2              fsPosEnd  = new Vector2( 0.5f, 0.95f );
    public float                reloadDelay = 2f;// 2 sec delay between rounds

    [Header("Set Dynamically")]

    ...

    // Called when the game is over. Simple for now, but expandable
    void GameOver(bool won) {
        if (won) {
            ...
        } else {
            ...
        }
        // Reload the scene, resetting the game
        // SceneManager.LoadScene("__Prospector_Scene_0"); // Now commented out!

        // Reload the scene in reloadDelay seconds
        // This will give the score a moment to travel
        Invoke ("ReloadLevel", reloadDelay);                        // a
    }

    void ReloadLevel() {
        // Reload the scene, resetting the game
        SceneManager.LoadScene("__Prospector_Scene_0");
    }

    // Return true if the two cards are adjacent in rank (A & K wrap around)
    public bool AdjacentRank(CardProspector c0, CardProspector c1) { ... }
    ...
}
```

a. The `Invoke()` command works by calling a function named `"ReloadLevel"` in `reloadDelay` seconds. This is similar to how `SendMessage()` works, but it does so with a delay. Now when you play the game, it waits for two seconds before the game reloads.

Giving the Player Feedback on Her Score

You also want to tell the player how she did at the end of each round.

1. Add a new UI Text to the scene: Select *Canvas* in the Hierarchy and from the menu bar choose *GameObject > UI > Text*.

2. Rename the *Text* to *GameOver* and give it the settings shown on the left side of Figure 32.15.

3. Add another UI Text to the scene: Right-click on *GameOver* in the Hierarchy and choose *Duplicate* from the pop-up menu.

4. Rename this *GameOver (1)* Text to *RoundResult* and give it the settings shown on the right side of Figure 32.15.

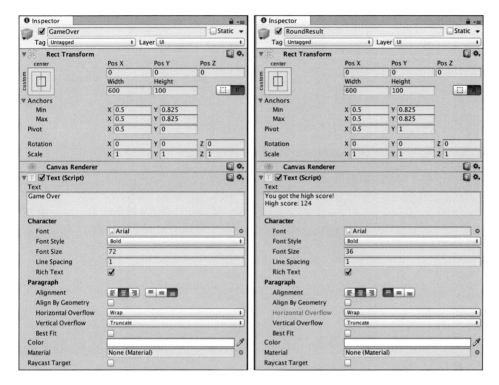

Figure 32.15 The settings for the GameOver and RoundResult UI Texts

5. Add the third UI Text as a child of Canvas and name it *HighScore*.

6. Give HighScore the settings shown in Figure 32.16.

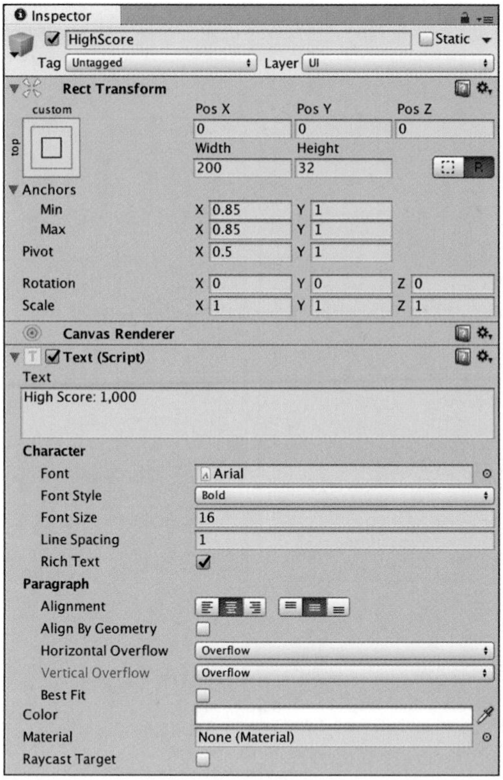

Figure 32.16 The settings for the HighScore UI Text

The numbers in these settings were determined by trial and error, and you should feel free to adjust them as you see fit. These settings should nestle the high score right above the sign on the right.

7. Save your scene.

8. To make these UI Texts functional, add the following bolded code to the Prospector class:

```
public class Prospector : MonoBehaviour {
    …
    [Header("Set in Inspector")]
    …
    public float              reloadDelay = 1f; // The delay between rounds
    public Text               gameOverText, roundResultText, highScoreText;

    [Header("Set Dynamically")]
    …
```

```csharp
void Awake() {
    S = this;
    SetUpUITexts();
}


void SetUpUITexts() {
    // Set up the HighScore UI Text
    GameObject go = GameObject.Find("HighScore");
    if (go != null) {
        highScoreText = go.GetComponent<Text>();
    }
    int highScore = ScoreManager.HIGH_SCORE;
    string hScore = "High Score: "+Utils.AddCommasToNumber(highScore);
    go.GetComponent<Text>().text = hScore;

    // Set up the UI Texts that show at the end of the round
    go = GameObject.Find ("GameOver");
    if (go != null) {
        gameOverText = go.GetComponent<Text>();
    }

    go = GameObject.Find ("RoundResult");
    if (go != null) {
        roundResultText = go.GetComponent<Text>();
    }

    // Make the end of round texts invisible
    ShowResultsUI( false );
}

void ShowResultsUI(bool show) {
    gameOverText.gameObject.SetActive(show);
    roundResultText.gameObject.SetActive(show);
}

...


// Called when the game is over. Simple for now, but expandable
void GameOver(bool won) {
    int score = ScoreManager.SCORE;
    if (fsRun != null) score += fsRun.score;
    if (won) {
        gameOverText.text = "Round Over";
        roundResultText.text ="You won this round!\nRound Score: "+score;
        ShowResultsUI( true );
        // print ("Game Over. You won! :)");   // Comment out this line
        ScoreManager.EVENT(eScoreEvent.gameWin);
        FloatingScoreHandler(eScoreEvent.gameWin);
```

```
    } else {
        gameOverText.text = "Game Over";
        if (ScoreManager.HIGH_SCORE <= score) {
            string str = "You got the high score!\nHigh score: "+score;
            roundResultText.text = str;
        } else {
            roundResultText.text = "Your final score was: "+score;
        }
        ShowResultsUI( true );
        // print ("Game Over. You Lost. :(");  // Comment out this line
        ScoreManager.EVENT(eScoreEvent.gameLoss);
        FloatingScoreHandler(eScoreEvent.gameLoss);
    }
    // Reload the scene in reloadDelay seconds
    // This will give the score a moment to travel
    Invoke ("ReloadLevel", reloadDelay);                        // a
    // SceneManager.LoadScene("__Prospector_Scene_0"); // Now commented out!
}

    ...

}
```

9. Save your scripts in MonoDevelop and try playing the game again in Unity.

Now, when you finish a round or game, you should see messages like those in Figure 32.17.

Figure 32.17 Example game over messages

Summary

In this chapter, you created a complete card game that constructs itself from XML files and that contains scoring, background images, and theming. One of the purposes of the tutorials in this book is to give you a framework on which to build additional games. The next chapter does just that. I'll guide you through building the *Bartok* game from the first chapter of the book based on the code that you created for this chapter.

Next Steps

The following are some possible directions in which you can take this game yourself.

Gold Cards

I mentioned gold cards as letter *D* in the list of ways to add scoring to the game, but you did not implement them in the chapter. Graphics are in the package you imported for gold cards (both *Card_Back_Gold* and *Card_Front_Gold*). The purpose of the gold cards is to double the value of any run that they are part of. Gold cards can only start in the mine, and any card in the mine has a 10% chance of being a gold card. Try implementing the gold cards on your own.

Compile This Game on a Mobile Device

Though the build settings in this game were designed for an iPad, instructing you on actual compilation for a mobile device is not within the scope of this book. Unity has several pages that document this process, however, and I recommend that you look at the proper one for the device that you own. To keep the information here as current as possible, my best recommendation for you is to do a web search for *Unity getting started* and the name of the mobile platform on which you want to develop (e.g., *Unity getting started iOS*). Right now, that could be *iOS* or *Android* for mobile platforms or *WebGL* for embedding in a website. The Unity documentation includes "getting started" pages for all of these platforms.

In my personal experience, I have found compilation on Android devices to be the easiest. Including the time to install and configure the additional software to do so, compiling this game for iOS took about two hours (most of which was spent setting up my Apple iOS developer account and provisioning profile), and compiling this game for Android took about 20 minutes.

I also highly recommend looking into some of the tools out there that can help you with mobile development. The *Test Flight* service that Apple acquired a few years ago helps you to distribute test builds of your game to iOS devices easily over the Internet (https://developer.apple.com/testflight/), and nearly everyone doing iOS development uses it. If you want a cross-platform approach that can distribute to Android as well (but is less convenient for iOS), check out *TestFairy* (http://testfairy.com).

I also highly recommend looking into *Unity Cloud Build*, which used to be the independent company, Tsugi (that was mentioned in the first edition of the book). *Unity Cloud Build* watches your *Unity Collaborate* (or other) code repository for changes in your code and automatically compiles new versions if it senses that anything has changed. If you're doing cross-platform mobile or WebGL development, *Unity Cloud Build* can save you a ton of time by offloading the heavy compiling tasks to a server instead of your personal machine.

CHAPTER 33

PROTOTYPE 5: *BARTOK*

This chapter differs somewhat from the other tutorials because instead of creating an entirely new project, this one shows you how you can build a different game on top of the kinds of tutorials that you've developed while reading this book.

Before starting this project, you should have first completed Prototype 4: *Prospector Solitaire* so that you understand the inner workings of the card game framework developed in that chapter.

Bartok is the game you first encountered in Chapter 1,"Thinking Like a Designer." Now you'll build it yourself.

Getting Started: Prototype 5

This time, instead of downloading a unitypackage as you did before, just make a duplicate of your entire project folder for the *Prospector* game from the previous chapter (or you can download it from http://book.prototools.net under Chapter 33). Again, the art assets you'll be using are constructed from parts of the Vectorized Playing Cards 1.3 by Chris Aguilar.[1]

Understanding *Bartok*

For a description of *Bartok* and how to play, see Chapter 1, where I use it extensively as an example. In short, *Bartok* is very similar to the commercial game *Uno*, except that it is played with a standard deck of cards, and in the traditional *Bartok* card game, the winner of each round is able to add a rule to the game. In the Chapter 1 example, I also included three variations of the rules, but you won't create those in this chapter; I'll leave that to you to accomplish later.

To play an online version of the *Bartok* game, you can visit http://book.prototools.net and look under Chapter 1.

Making a New Scene

As with much of this project, the scene is based on the scene you made for Prospector.

1. Select *__Prospector_Scene_0* in the Project pane and then choose *Edit > Duplicate* from the menu bar. This makes a new Scene named *__Prospector_Scene_1*.

2. Rename this new scene to *__Bartok_Scene_0* and double-click it to open it. You can tell that it has opened because the title bar of the Unity window changes to reflect the new scene name and __Bartok_Scene_0 appears at the top of the Hierarchy pane.

Let's get rid of some of the things you don't need for *Bartok*.

3. Select *_Scoreboard* and *HighScore* under the Canvas in the Hierarchy pane and delete them (*Edit > Delete* from the menu bar). This game won't be scored, so you don't need either of those.

4. Similarly, you should delete both the *GameOver* and *RoundResult* children of Canvas from this scene. You'll make use of them later but you can always grab copies from __Prospector_Scene_0 when you need them.

5. Select *_MainCamera* and remove the *Prospector (Script)*, *ScoreManager (Script)*, and *Layout (Script)* components (right-click the name of each [or click the gear to the right of the name of each] and choose *Remove Component*). You should be left with a _MainCamera that has all the proper settings for Transform and Camera and also still has a *Deck (Script)* component.

---

1. Vectorized Playing Cards 1.3 (http://code.google.com/p/vectorized-playing-cards/). ©2011 Chris Aguilar

6. Change the background. Select the *ProspectorBackground* GameObject in the Hierarchy pane (not the Texture2D in the Project Pane) and rename it *BartokBackground*.

7. Create a new Material in the Materials folder (*Assets > Create > Material* from the menu bar) and name it *BartokBackground Mat*. Drag this new material onto BartokBackground in the Hierarchy. Notice in the Game pane that this made things very dark. (This is because the new material has the Unity Standard shader whereas the previous material used the Unlit shader.)

8. To remedy this, add a directional light to the scene (*GameObject > Light > Directional Light*). The transform for the BartokBackground and directional light should be as follows:

BartokBackground (Quad)	P:[0, 0, 1]	R:[0, 0, 0]	S:[26.667, 20, 1]
Directional Light	P:[-100, -100, 0]	R:[50, -30, 0]	S:[1, 1, 1]

This should set the scene properly. Note that the position of the Directional Light doesn't matter at all to the scene (only rotation matters for directional lights), but it does get the light out of the way of what you need to do in the Scene pane. Save your scene.

The Importance of Adding Card Animation

This will be a game for a single human player, but the game of *Bartok* works best with four players, so three of the players will be AIs (artificial intelligences). Because *Bartok* is such a simple game, the AIs won't have to be good; they just need to act. When working with multiplayer turn-based games—particularly those that have AI opponents—you have to make it clear to the player whose turn it is and what the other players are doing. For this to work, you'll make the cards animate from place to place in this game. This wasn't necessary in *Prospector* because the player was taking all the actions herself, and it was obvious to her what the result should be. Because the player of *Bartok* is presented with three other hands that will be face-down to her, the animation can be used as an important way to communicate what actions the AI players are taking.

Much of the challenge in designing this tutorial was in creating good animations and making sure that the game waited properly for each animation to end before moving on to the next thing. Because of that, you will see use of `SendMessage()` and `Invoke()` in this project as well as the use of more specific callback objects than `SendMessage()` allows. Instead, you'll pass a C# class instance to an object and then call a *callback function* on the instance when the object is done moving, which is less flexible than `SendMessage()` but faster and more specific and can also be used for C# classes that don't extend the MonoBehaviour class.

Build Settings

Whereas the last project was designed as a mobile app, this is designed either as an online WebGL game or a standalone application for Mac or PC, so the build settings need to change.

1. From the menu bar, choose *File > Build Settings*, which opens the window shown in Figure 33.1.

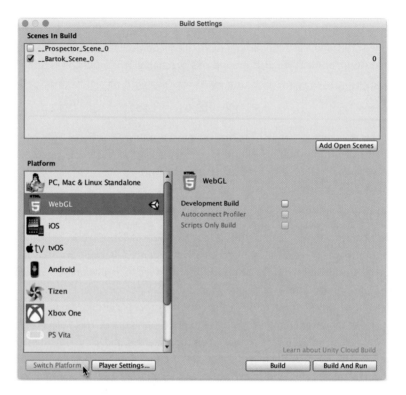

Figure 33.1 The Build Settings window

Under *Scenes In Build* on your machine, you will see that __Prospector_Scene_0 is currently in the list of *Scenes In Build*, but __Bartok_Scene_0 is not.

2. Click the *Add Open Scenes* button to add *__Bartok_Scene_0* to the list of scenes for this build.

3. Uncheck the box next to *__Prospector_Scene_0* to remove it from the list of scenes. Now your *Scenes In Build* section should match that in Figure 33.1.

4. If you have used the Unity installer to install the WebGL tools, select *WebGL* from the list of platforms; otherwise choose *PC, Mac & Linux Standalone*. Then click *Switch Platform*.

The *Switch Platform* button turns gray when the switch is complete. This might take a second or two, but it should be pretty fast. All the other settings should be fine as they are.

When your all of your build settings look like the image in Figure 33.1, you can close this window. (Don't click Build yet; you do that after actually making the game.)

5. Look at the pop-up menu under the title of the Game pane. From that list of aspect ratios, change it to *Standalone (1024x768)*. This ensures that your game aspect ratio looks the same as the examples that you'll see throughout this tutorial.

Coding Bartok

Just as you had a Prospector class to manage the game and a CardProspector:Card class to extend Card and add game-specific capabilities, this game will require both a Bartok and CardBartok:Card class.

1. Create both a *Bartok* and a *CardBartok* C# script in the ___Scripts folder of the Project pane (*Assets > Create > C# Script*).

2. Double-click the *CardBartok* script to open it in MonoDevelop and enter the following code. (If you want, you can copy some of this from the CardProspector script.)

```csharp
using System.Collections;
using System.Collections.Generic;
using UnityEngine;

// CBState includes both states for the game and to… states for movement    // a
public enum CBState {
    toDrawpile,
    drawpile,
    toHand,
    hand,
    toTarget,
    target,
    discard,
    to,
    idle
}

public class CardBartok : Card {                                            // b
    // Static variables are shared by all instances of CardBartok
    static public float     MOVE_DURATION = 0.5f;
    static public string    MOVE_EASING = Easing.InOut;
    static public float     CARD_HEIGHT = 3.5f;
    static public float     CARD_WIDTH = 2f;

    [Header("Set Dynamically: CardBartok")]
    public CBState          state = CBState.drawpile;
```

```
// Fields to store info the card will use to move and rotate
public List<Vector3>      bezierPts;
public List<Quaternion>   bezierRots;
public float              timeStart, timeDuration;

// When the card is done moving, it will call reportFinishTo.SendMessage()
public GameObject         reportFinishTo = null;

// MoveTo tells the card to interpolate to a new position and rotation
public void MoveTo(Vector3 ePos, Quaternion eRot) {
    // Make new interpolation lists for the card.
    // Position and Rotation will each have only two points.
    bezierPts = new List<Vector3>();
    bezierPts.Add ( transform.localPosition );  // Current position
    bezierPts.Add ( ePos );                      // Current rotation

    bezierRots = new List<Quaternion>();
    bezierRots.Add ( transform.rotation );      // New position
    bezierRots.Add ( eRot );                     // New rotation

    if (timeStart == 0) {                                            // c
        timeStart = Time.time;
    }
    // timeDuration always starts the same but can be overwritten later
    timeDuration = MOVE_DURATION;

    state = CBState.to;                                              // d
}

public void MoveTo(Vector3 ePos) {                                  // e
    MoveTo(ePos, Quaternion.identity);
}

void Update() {
    switch (state) {
        case CBState.toHand:                                        // f
        case CBState.toTarget:
        case CBState.toDrawpile:
        case CBState.to:
            float u = (Time.time - timeStart)/timeDuration;        // g
            float uC = Easing.Ease (u, MOVE_EASING);

            if (u<0) {                                              // h
                transform.localPosition = bezierPts[0];
                transform.rotation = bezierRots[0];
                return;
            } else if (u>=1) {                                      // i
                uC = 1;
                // Move from the to... state to the proper next state
```

```
            if (state == CBState.toHand)     state = CBState.hand;
            if (state == CBState.toTarget)   state = CBState.target;
            if (state == CBState.toDrawpile) state = CBState.drawpile;
            if (state == CBState.to)         state = CBState.idle;

            // Move to the final position
            transform.localPosition = bezierPts[bezierPts.Count-1];
            transform.rotation = bezierRots[bezierPts.Count-1];

            // Reset timeStart to 0 so it gets overwritten next time
            timeStart = 0;

            if (reportFinishTo != null) {                            // j
                reportFinishTo.SendMessage("CBCallback", this);
                reportFinishTo = null;
            } else { // If there is nothing to callback
                // Just let it stay still.
            }
        } else { // Normal interpolation behavior (0 <= u < 1)      // k
            Vector3 pos = Utils.Bezier(uC, bezierPts);
            transform.localPosition = pos;
            Quaternion rotQ = Utils.Bezier(uC, bezierRots);
            transform.rotation = rotQ;
        }
        break;
    }

  }

}
```

a. The enum CBState includes both the possible states that a CardBartok can have in this game and various to... states that represent a CardBartok as it animates toward one of those states.

b. CardBartok extends Card, just as CardProspector did.

c. If timeStart is 0, then it's set to the current time (causing movement to start immediately); otherwise, movement will begin at timeStart. This way, if timeStart has previously been set to something other than 0, it won't be overwritten. This will allow us to stagger the timing of various card animations.

d. Initially, state is set to just CBState.to. The calling method will later specify whether state should be CBState.toHand or CBState.toTarget.

e. This is an overload of MoveTo() that doesn't require a rotation to be passed in.

f. Because switch statements allow cases to "fall through" as long as there isn't any code between them, all the to... CBStates (i.e., toHand, toTarget, and so on)—where the card is interpolating from one place to another—can be handled together.

g. The float u interpolates from 0 to 1 across the course of this CardBartok's movement. u is derived from the current time since `timeStart` divided by the desired duration of the movement (e.g., if `timeStart` = 5, `timeDuration` = 10, and `Time.time` = 11, then u = (11-5) / 10 = 0.6). This u is then passed into the `Easing.Ease()` method of Utils.cs to curve the u value, resulting in a uC value that will make the card animation appear more natural. See *Easing for Linear Interpolations* in Appendix B for more info.

h. u usually ranges from 0 to 1. This handles the situation when u < 0, in which case you shouldn't move yet and should stay at the initial position. The u < 0 case can happen when you set `timeStart` to some future time to delay the beginning of movement.

i. In the case where u >= 1, you want to clamp u to 1 so that the card doesn't overshoot its movement target. This is also the time to stop movement by switching to another CBState.

j. If there's a callback GameObject, then use `SendMessage()` to call the `CBCallback` method with `this` as the parameter. After calling `SendMessage()`, `reportFinishTo` must be set to `null` so that it this CardBartok doesn't continue to report to the same GameObject every subsequent time it moves.

k. When 0 <= u < 1, just interpolate from the previous location to the next one. Use a Bézier curve function to move this to the right point. Position and rotation are handled separately by different overloads of the `Utils.Bezier()` method. See *Bézier Curves* in Appendix B for more information.

A lot of this is an adaptation and expansion of the code that you saw in the preceding chapter for the FloatingScore class. The CardBartok version of interpolation also interpolates Quaternions (a class that handles rotations), which will be important because you want the cards in *Bartok* to fan as if they were being held by a player.

3. Open the Bartok class and enter this code. The first thing you want to do in the Bartok class is to make sure that the Deck class is working properly to create all 52 cards:

```
using System.Collections;
using System.Collections.Generic;
using UnityEngine;
using UnityEngine.SceneManagement;

public class Bartok : MonoBehaviour {
    static public Bartok S;

    [Header("Set in Inspector")]
    public TextAsset         deckXML;
    public TextAsset         layoutXML;
    public Vector3           layoutCenter = Vector3.zero;
```

```
[Header("Set Dynamically")]
public Deck                deck;
public List<CardBartok>    drawPile;
public List<CardBartok>    discardPile;


void Awake() {
    S = this;

}

void Start () {
    deck = GetComponent<Deck>();          // Get the Deck
    deck.InitDeck(deckXML.text);          // Pass DeckXML to it
    Deck.Shuffle(ref deck.cards);         // This shuffles the deck           // a

}

}
```

    a. The `ref` keyword passes a reference to `deck.cards`, which allows `deck.cards` to be modified directly by `Deck.Shuffle()`.

As you can see, most of this is the same as what you saw in *Prospector*, except that you're now dealing with the CardBartok class for cards rather than the CardProspector class.

Setting Up PrefabCard in the Inspector

At this time, you should also adjust other aspects of PrefabCard in the Inspector.

1. Select *PrefabCard* in _Prefabs folder of the Project pane.

2. Set the Box Collider component's *Is Trigger* field to true.

3. Set the *Size.z* of the Box Collider component to 0.1.

4. Add a Rigidbody component to PrefabCard (*Component > Physics > Rigidbody*).

5. Set the Rigidbody's *Use Gravity* field to false.

6. Set the Rigidbody's *Is Kinematic* field to true.

The Box Collider and Rigidbody components on PrefabCard should now look like Figure 33.2.

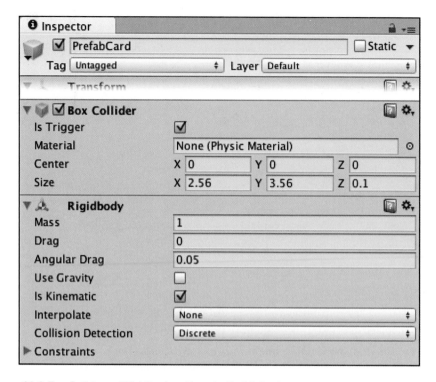

Figure 33.2 Box Collider and Rigidbody settings for PrefabCard

7. You need to swap a new *CardBartok (Script)* component for the existing *CardProspector (Script)* component.

    a. Click the gear icon to the right of the name of the *CardProspector (Script)* component and choose *Remove Component*.

    b. Attach a *CardBartok* script to PrefabCard.

Setting Up _MainCamera in the Inspector

Follow these steps to set up _MainCamera in the Inspector:

1. Attach the *Bartok* script to _MainCamera in the Hierarchy (assign it however you like; you should know what you're doing by now).

2. In the Hierarchy pane, select _*MainCamera*. The attached *Bartok (Script)* component is at the bottom of the Inspector. (If you want to move it up, you can click the gear next to its name and choose *Move Up*.)

3. Set the `DeckXML` field of *Bartok (Script)* to the *DeckXML* file that is in the Resources folder of the Project pane. (Because the deck remains unchanged [still 13 cards of 4 suits], this is the same file that was used by *Prospector*.)

4. Set the `startFaceUp` field of the *Deck (Script)* component to true (checked). This shows all the cards face-up when you click Play.

Now when you click *Play*, you should see a grid of cards just as you saw in the early stages of *Prospector*. In only a few pages, you're pretty far along.

The Game Layout

The layout for *Bartok* differs significantly from *Prospector*. *Bartok* has a draw pile and discard pile in the middle of the screen as well as four hands of cards distributed to the top, left, bottom, and right sides of the screen. The hands should be fanned as if they were being held by players (see Figure 33.3).

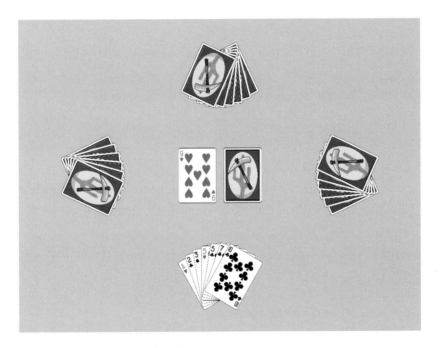

Figure 33.3 The eventual layout of *Bartok*

This requires a somewhat different layout XML document than you used for *Prospector*.

1. Select LayoutXML in the Resources folder of the Project pane and duplicate it (*Edit > Duplicate*).

2. Name the duplicate *BartokLayoutXML* and enter the following text. Bold text differs from the original LayoutXML text. Be sure to remove any text that you don't see here.

```xml
<xml>
    <!-- This file includes info for laying out the Bartok card game. -->

    <!-- The multiplier is multiplied by the x and y attributes below. -->
    <!-- This determines how loose or tight the layout is. -->
    <multiplier x="1" y="1" />

    <!-- This positions the draw pile and staggers it -->
    <slot type="drawpile" x="1.5" y="0" xstagger="0.05" layer="1"/>

    <!-- This positions the discard pile -->
    <slot type="discardpile" x="-1.5" y="0" layer="2"/>

    <!-- This positions the target card -->
    <slot type="target" x="-1.5" y="0" layer="4"/>

    <!-- These slots are for the four hands held by the four players -->
    <slot type="hand" x="0"   y="-8" rot="0"   player="1" layer="3"/>
    <slot type="hand" x="-10" y="0"  rot="270" player="2" layer="3"/>
    <slot type="hand" x="0"   y="8"  rot="180" player="3" layer="3"/>
    <slot type="hand" x="10"  y="0"  rot="90"  player="4" layer="3"/>

</xml>
```

The BartokLayout C# Script

Now you must also rewrite the class that does the layout to both fan the cards properly and to take advantage of the new ability to interpolate cards.

1.   Create a new C# script named *BartokLayout* in the Scripts folder and enter this code:

```csharp
using System.Collections;
using System.Collections.Generic;
using UnityEngine;

[System.Serializable]                                          // a
public class SlotDef {                                         // b
    public float      x;
    public float      y;
    public bool       faceUp = false;
    public string     layerName = "Default";
    public int        layerID = 0;
    public int        id;
    public List<int>  hiddenBy = new List<int>(); // Unused in Bartok
    public float      rot;          // rotation of hands
    public string     type = "slot";
    public Vector2    stagger;
```

```
    public int          player;    // player number of a hand
    public Vector3      pos;       // pos derived from x, y, & multiplier
}

public class BartokLayout : MonoBehaviour {
    // Leave this empty for now
}
```

    a. [System.Serializable] makes SlotDef able to be seen in the Unity Inspector.

    b. The SlotDef class is not based on MonoBehaviour, so it doesn't need its own file.

2. Save this code and return to Unity.

You'll notice that your change causes an error in the console:

    error CS0101: The namespace 'global::' already contains a definition for 'SlotDef'.

This is because the public class SlotDef in the Layout script (from *Prospector*) conflicts with the public class SlotDef in the new BartokLayout script.

3. Either delete the Layout script entirely or open the Layout script in MonoDevelop and comment out the section defining SlotDef.

    a. To comment out a large chunk of code, just place a /* before the code and a */ after the code you want to comment. You can also comment out a large section by selecting the lines of code in MonoDevelop and choosing *Edit > Format > Toggle Line Comment(s)* from the menu bar to place a single line comment (//) before each line you have selected.

    b. Regardless of which method you use to comment out SlotDef from the Layout script, make sure that you also comment out the [System.Serializable] line preceding the SlotDef definition there.

    c. After you have eliminated the SlotDef class from the Layout script, save the Layout script.

4. Return to the BartokLayout script and continue editing it by adding the bolded lines in the following code listing:

```
public class BartokLayout : MonoBehaviour {
    [Header("Set Dynamically")]
    public PT_XMLReader     xmlr;   // Just like Deck, this has a PT_XMLReader
    public PT_XMLHashtable  xml;    // This variable is for faster xml access
    public Vector2          multiplier;  // Sets the spacing of the tableau
    // SlotDef references
    public List<SlotDef>    slotDefs; // The SlotDefs hands
    public SlotDef          drawPile;
    public SlotDef          discardPile;
    public SlotDef          target;
```

```
// Bartok calls this method to read in the BartokLayoutXML.xml file
public void ReadLayout(string xmlText) {
    xmlr = new PT_XMLReader();
    xmlr.Parse(xmlText);        // The XML is parsed
    xml = xmlr.xml["xml"][0]; // And xml is set as a shortcut to the XML

    // Read in the multiplier, which sets card spacing
    multiplier.x = float.Parse(xml["multiplier"][0].att("x"));
    multiplier.y = float.Parse(xml["multiplier"][0].att("y"));

    // Read in the slots
    SlotDef tSD;
    // slotsX is used as a shortcut to all the <slot>s
    PT_XMLHashList slotsX = xml["slot"];

    for (int i=0; i<slotsX.Count; i++) {
        tSD = new SlotDef();   // Create a new SlotDef instance
        if (slotsX[i].HasAtt("type")) {
            // If this <slot> has a type attribute parse it
            tSD.type = slotsX[i].att("type");
        } else {
            // If not, set its type to "slot"; it's a card in the rows
            tSD.type = "slot";
        }

        // Various attributes are parsed into numerical values
        tSD.x = float.Parse( slotsX[i].att("x") );
        tSD.y = float.Parse( slotsX[i].att("y") );
        tSD.pos = new Vector3( tSD.x*multiplier.x, tSD.y*multiplier.y, 0 );

        // Sorting Layers
        tSD.layerID = int.Parse( slotsX[i].att("layer") );              // a
        tSD.layerName = tSD.layerID.ToString();                        // b

        // pull additional attributes based on the type of each <slot>
        switch (tSD.type) {
            case "slot":
                // ignore slots that are just of the "slot" type
                break;

            case "drawpile":                                          // c
                tSD.stagger.x = float.Parse( slotsX[i].att("xstagger") );
                drawPile = tSD;
                break;

            case "discardpile":
                discardPile = tSD;
                break;
```

```
                    case "target":
                        target = tSD;
                        break;

                    case "hand":                                    // d
                        tSD.player = int.Parse( slotsX[i].att("player") );
                        tSD.rot = float.Parse( slotsX[i].att("rot") );
                        slotDefs.Add (tSD);
                        break;


                }
            }
        }
}
```

a. In this game, the Sorting Layers are named 1, 2, 3, ... through 10. The layers are used to make sure that the correct cards are on top of the others. In Unity 2D, all of the assets are effectively treated as if they were at the same Z depth, so the sorting layers are used to differentiate between them.

b. This converts the number of the `layerID` to a text `layerName`.

c. The drawpile `xstagger` value is still read in, but this is not used in *Bartok* because the players don't actually need to know how many cards are in the draw pile.

d. This section reads in data particular to each player's hand, including the rotation of the hand and the number of the player who will have access to that hand.

5. Attach the *BartokLayout* script to _MainCamera. (Drag the BartokLayout script from the Project pane onto _MainCamera in the Hierarchy pane.)

6. In the *Bartok (Script)* component on _MainCamera, assign the *BartokLayoutXML* file in the Resources folder of the Project pane to the `layoutXML` field.

7. Open the Bartok script and add the following bolded code to have it make use of BartokLayout:

```
public class Bartok : MonoBehaviour {
    static public Bartok S;


    ...
    public List<CardBartok>      discardPile;

    private BartokLayout         layout;
    private Transform            layoutAnchor;

    void Awake() { ... }

    void Start () {
        deck = GetComponent<Deck>();          // Get the Deck
        deck.InitDeck(deckXML.text);          // Pass DeckXML to it
```

```
        Deck.Shuffle(ref deck.cards);    // This shuffles the deck

        layout = GetComponent<BartokLayout>();   // Get the Layout
        layout.ReadLayout(layoutXML.text); // Pass LayoutXML to it

        drawPile = UpgradeCardsList( deck.cards );
    }

    List<CardBartok> UpgradeCardsList(List<Card> lCD) {                // a
        List<CardBartok> lCB = new List<CardBartok>();
        foreach( Card tCD in lCD ) {
            lCB.Add ( tCD as CardBartok );
        }
        return( lCB );
    }

}
```

a. This method upgrades all the Cards in the `List<Card>` `lCD` to be CardBartoks
  and creates a new `List<CardBartok>` to hold them. This works just like it did in
  Prospector, so they were always CardBartoks, but this lets Unity know that.

8. Return to Unity and run the project.

When you run the project now, you should be able to select _MainCamera from the Hierarchy
pane and expand the variables in the *BartokLayout (Script)* component to see that they're being
populated with the correct values from BartokLayoutXML. You should also look at the `draw-Pile` field of *Bartok (Script)* to see that it is properly filled with 52 shuffled CardBartok instances.

The Player Class

Because this game has four players, I've chosen to create a class to represent players that can do
things like gather cards into a hand and eventually choose what to play using simple artificial intelligence. One thing that is unique about the Player class relative to others that you've
written is that the Player class does *not* extend MonoBehaviour (or any other class), yet it still
has its own separate C# script file. Because Player does not extend MonoBehaviour, it doesn't
receive calls from `Awake()`, `Start()`, or `Update()` and that you can't call some functions like
`print()` from within it or attach it to a GameObject as a component. However, none of that
is necessary for the Player class, so it is actually easier in this case to have Player not subclass
MonoBehaviour.

1. Create a new C# script in the __Scripts folder named *Player* and enter this code:

```
using System.Collections;
using System.Collections.Generic;
using UnityEngine;
using System.Linq; // Enables LINQ queries, which will be explained soon
```

```
// The player can either be human or an ai
public enum PlayerType {
    human,
    ai
}

[System.Serializable]                                                    // a
public class Player {                                                    // b
    public PlayerType          type = PlayerType.ai;
    public int                 playerNum;
    public SlotDef             handSlotDef;
    public List<CardBartok>    hand; // The cards in this player's hand

    // Add a card to the hand
    public CardBartok AddCard(CardBartok eCB) {
        if (hand == null) hand = new List<CardBartok>();

        // Add the card to the hand
        hand.Add (eCB);

        return( eCB );
    }

    // Remove a card from the hand
    public CardBartok RemoveCard(CardBartok cb) {
        // If hand is null or doesn't contain cb, return null
        if ( hand == null || !hand.Contains(cb) ) return null;
        hand.Remove(cb);
        return(cb);
    }
}
```

a. `[System.Serializable]` instructs Unity to serialize the Player class, enabling it to be viewed and edited within the Unity Inspector.

b. The Player class stores information that is important to each player. As mentioned before, it does not extend MonoBehaviour or any other class, so you must delete the ": MonoBehaviour" from this line.

2. Add the following code to Bartok to make use of the Player class:

```
public class Bartok : MonoBehaviour {
    ...
    [Header("Set in Inspector")]
    ...
    public Vector3             layoutCenter = Vector3.zero;
    public float               handFanDegrees = 10f;                     // a

    [Header("Set Dynamically")]
    ...
    public List<CardBartok>    discardPile;
    public List<Player>        players;                                  // b
```

```csharp
public CardBartok          targetCard;

private BartokLayout        layout;
private Transform           layoutAnchor;

void Awake() { … }

void Start () {
    …
    drawPile = UpgradeCardsList( deck.cards );
    LayoutGame();
}

List<CardBartok> UpgradeCardsList(List<Card> lCD) { … }

// Position all the cards in the drawPile properly
public void ArrangeDrawPile() {
    CardBartok tCB;

    for (int i=0; i<drawPile.Count; i++) {
        tCB = drawPile[i];
        tCB.transform.SetParent( layoutAnchor );
        tCB.transform.localPosition = layout.drawPile.pos;
        // Rotation should start at 0
        tCB.faceUp = false;
        tCB.SetSortingLayerName(layout.drawPile.layerName);
        tCB.SetSortOrder(-i*4); // Order them front-to-back
        tCB.state = CBState.drawpile;
    }
}

// Perform the initial game layout
void LayoutGame() {
    // Create an empty GameObject to serve as the tableau's anchor      // c
    if (layoutAnchor == null) {
        GameObject tGO = new GameObject("_LayoutAnchor");
        layoutAnchor = tGO.transform;
        layoutAnchor.transform.position = layoutCenter;
    }

    // Position the drawPile cards
    ArrangeDrawPile();

    // Set up the players
    Player pl;
    players = new List<Player>();
    foreach (SlotDef tSD in layout.slotDefs) {
        pl = new Player();
        pl.handSlotDef = tSD;
```

```
            players.Add(p1);
            p1.playerNum = tSD.player;
        }
        players[0].type = PlayerType.human; // Make only the 0th player human
    }

    // The Draw function will pull a single card from the drawPile and return it
    public CardBartok Draw() {
        CardBartok cd = drawPile[0];        // Pull the 0th CardProspector
        drawPile.RemoveAt(0);               // Then remove it from List<> drawPile
        return(cd);                         // And return it
    }

    // This Update() is temporarily used to test adding cards to players' hands
    void Update() {                                                         // d
        if (Input.GetKeyDown(KeyCode.Alpha1)) {
            players[0].AddCard(Draw ());
        }
        if (Input.GetKeyDown(KeyCode.Alpha2)) {
            players[1].AddCard(Draw ());
        }
        if (Input.GetKeyDown(KeyCode.Alpha3)) {
            players[2].AddCard(Draw ());
        }
        if (Input.GetKeyDown(KeyCode.Alpha4)) {
            players[3].AddCard(Draw ());
        }
    }
}
```

a. handFanDegrees determines how many degrees rotation there should be between each card in a fanned hand.

b. The List<Player> players holds a reference to the data for each player. Because the Player class is [System.Serializable], exploring the depths of the players List within the Unity Inspector is possible.

c. The layoutAnchor is a Transform created to be the parent in the Hierarchy over all the cards in the tableau. First, an empty GameObject is created named _LayoutAnchor. The Transform component of that GameObject is then assigned to the field layoutAnchor. Finally, the position of layoutAnchor is set to the location specified by layoutCenter.

d. This Update() function will be used to test the code you've written to add cards to each player's hand. It is only temporary and will be replaced by other code later in this chapter. The Keycode.Alpha1 through Keycode.Alpha4 refer to the number keys 1–4 on the main keyboard above the letters. When one of these keys is pressed, a Card is added to that player's hand.

3. Save the scripts, return to Unity, and run the game again.

4. Select _MainCamera in the Hierarchy and find the `players` field on the *Bartok (Script)* component. Open the disclosure triangle for `players`, and you'll see four elements, one for each player. Open those disclosure triangles, as well, and then open up the disclosure triangles for `hand` under each. Because of the new `Update()` method, if you click in the Game pane (which gives the game focus and allows it to react to keyboard input), you can press the number keys 1 to 4 on your keyboard (across the top of the keyboard, not the keypad) to add cards to the players' hands. The Inspector for the *Bartok (Script)* component should show cards being added to hands as shown in Figure 33.4.

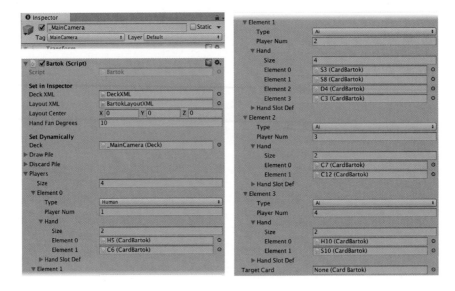

Figure 33.4 *Bartok (Script)* component showing players and their hands

This `Update()` method, of course, won't be used in the final version of the game, but building little functions like this that allow you to test features before other aspects of the game are ready is often useful. In this case, you needed a way to test whether the `Player.AddCard()` method worked properly, and this was a quick way to do so.

Fanning the Hands

Now that cards are logically being moved from the drawPile into players' hands, it's time to move them there graphically as well.

1. Add the following code to the Player class to make this happen:

```
public class Player {
    ...

    public CardBartok AddCard(CardBartok eCB) {
        if (hand == null) hand = new List<CardBartok>();

        // Add the card to the hand
```

```csharp
        hand.Add (eCB);
        FanHand();
        return( eCB );
    }


    // Remove a card from the hand
    public CardBartok RemoveCard(CardBartok cb) {
        // If hand is null or doesn't contain cb, return null
        if ( hand == null || !hand.Contains(cb) ) return null;
        hand.Remove(cb);
        FanHand();
        return(cb);
    }


    public void FanHand() {                                        // a
        // startRot is the rotation about Z of the first card      // b
        float startRot = 0;
        startRot = handSlotDef.rot;
        if (hand.Count > 1) {
            startRot += Bartok.S.handFanDegrees * (hand.Count-1) / 2;
        }


        // Move all the cards to their new positions
        Vector3 pos;
        float rot;
        Quaternion rotQ;
        for (int i=0; i<hand.Count; i++) {
            rot = startRot - Bartok.S.handFanDegrees*i;
            rotQ = Quaternion.Euler( 0, 0, rot );                  // c

            pos = Vector3.up * CardBartok.CARD_HEIGHT / 2f;        // d

            pos = rotQ * pos;                                      // e

            // Add the base position of the player's hand (which will be at the
            //   bottom-center of the fan of the cards)
            pos += handSlotDef.pos;                                // f
            pos.z = -0.5f*i;                                       // g

            // Set the localPosition and rotation of the ith card in the hand
            hand[i].transform.localPosition = pos;                 // h
            hand[i].transform.rotation = rotQ;
            hand[i].state = CBState.hand;

            hand[i].faceUp = (type == PlayerType.human);           // i

            // Set the SortOrder of the cards so that they overlap properly
            hand[i].SetSortOrder(i*4);                             // j
        }
    }
}
```

   a. `FanHand()` rotates the Cards to appear fanned in an arc as shown in Figure 33.1.

   b. `startRot` is the rotation about Z of the first card (the one rotated the most counterclockwise). It starts with the rotation of the entire hand as specified in BartokLayoutXML and then rotates counterclockwise so that the fanned cards will appear to be centered when rotated. After choosing `startRot`, each subsequent card is rotated `Bartok.S.handFanDegrees` clockwise from the previous card.

   c. `rotQ` holds the Quaternions representation of the `rot` about the Z axis.

   d. `pos` is then chosen, which is a Vector3 location one half Card height above the center (i.e., localPosition = [0, 0, 0]) of this hand, so `pos` is initially [0, 1.75, 0].

   e. The Quaternion `rotQ` is then multiplied by the Vector3 `pos`. When a Quaternion is multiplied by a Vector3, it rotates the Vector3, so now `pos` is rotated `rot` degrees around the Z axis of the local origin.

   f. The base position of the hand is added to `pos`.

   g. The `pos.z` of the various cards in the hand is staggered. While this isn't actually visible (because you're dealing with 2D sprites), it does keep the 3D Box Colliders you're using from overlapping.

   h. Apply the `pos` and `rotQ` you calculated to the ith Card in the hand.

   i. Only the human player's Cards should be face up.

   j. Setting the sort order of each card causes them to overlap properly within a single sorting layer.

  2. Save the Player script, return to Unity, and click *Play*.

Try pressing the numbers 1, 2, 3, and 4 on the top row of your keyboard; you should see cards jumping into the players' hands and being fanned correctly. However, you probably noticed that the cards aren't sorted by rank in the human player's hand, which looks kind of sloppy. Luckily, you can do something about that.[2]

A Tiny Introduction to LINQ

LINQ, which stands for *Language INtegrated Query*, is a fantastic extension to C# that has had many books written about it. Fully 24 pages of Joseph and Ben Albahari's fantastic *C# 5.0 Pocket Reference*[3] are devoted to LINQ (wherein they only devote four pages to arrays). Most of LINQ is far beyond the scope of this book, but I hope that this brief introduction will lead you to consider LINQ as a possible solution to problems you may encounter in later projects.

LINQ has the capability to do database-like queries within a single line of C#, allowing you to select and order specific elements in an array. This is how you will sort the cards in the human player's hand.

---

   2. You may have also noticed that if you draw all the cards out of the draw deck, it will throw an Argument Out Of Range Exception. Don't worry; we'll address this later.

   3. Joseph Albahari and Ben Albahari, *C# 5.0 Pocket Reference: Instant Help for C# 5.0 Programmers* (Beijing: O'Reilly Media, Inc., 2012).

1. Add the following bolded lines to `Player.AddCard()`:

```
public class Player {

    ...

    // Add a card to the hand
    public CardBartok AddCard(CardBartok eCB) {
        if (hand == null) hand = new List<CardBartok>();

        // Add the card to the hand
        hand.Add (eCB);

        // Sort the cards by rank using LINQ if this is a human
        if (type == PlayerType.human) {
            CardBartok[] cards = hand.ToArray();                      // a

            // This is the LINQ call
            cards = cards.OrderBy( cd => cd.rank ).ToArray();         // b

            hand = new List<CardBartok>(cards);                       // c
            // Note: LINQ operations can be a bit slow (like it could take a
            //   couple of milliseconds), but since we're only doing it once
            //   every round, it isn't a problem.
        }

        FanHand();
        return( eCB );
    }

    ...

}
```

a. LINQ works on arrays of values, so you create a `CardBartok[]` array `cards` from the `List<CardBartok>` hand.

b. This line is a LINQ call that works on the `cards` array of CardBartoks. It is similar to doing a `foreach(CardBartok cd in cards)` and sorting them by `rank` (which is what is meant by `cd => cd.rank`). It then returns a sorted array, which is assigned to `cards`, replacing the old, unsorted array. LINQ syntax is different from the normal C# you've seen, which is why this may look strange to you.

Note that LINQ operations can be a bit slow—a single call could take a couple of milliseconds—but because you're only making this LINQ call once every turn, it isn't a problem.

c. After the `cards` array is sorted, you create a new `List<CardBartok>` from it and assign that to `hand`, replacing the old unsorted List.

As you can see, with a single line of LINQ code, you were able to sort the list. LINQ has tremendous capabilities that are beyond the scope of this book, but I highly recommend you look them up if you need to do sorting or other query-like operations on elements in an array (e.g., if you had an array of people and needed to find all of them between the ages of 18 and 25 who had names that start with a "J").

2. Save the Player script, return to Unity, and play the scene. The cards in the human player's hand are now always in order by rank.

The cards are going to need to animate into position for the game to be intelligible to the player, so it's time to make the cards move.

Making Cards Move!

Now comes the fun part, where you make the cards actually interpolate from one position and rotation to the next. This makes the card game look much more like it's actually being played, and as you'll see, it makes it easier for the player to understand what is happening in the game.

A lot of the interpolation that occurs here is based on that which you did for FloatingScore in Prospector. Just like FloatingScore, you'll start an interpolation that the card itself will handle, and when the card is done moving, it will send a callback message to notify the game that it's done.

Let's start by moving the cards smoothly into the players' hands. CardBartok already has a lot of the movement code written, so let's take advantage of it.

1. Modify the following bolded code of the `Player.FanHand()` method:

```
public class Player {
    …

    public void FanHand() {
        …
        for (int i=0; i<hand.Count; i++) {
            …
            pos.z = -0.5f*i;

            // Set the localPosition and rotation of the ith card in the hand
            hand[i].MoveTo(pos, rotQ); // Tell CardBartok to interpolate
            hand[i].state = CBState.toHand;
            // After the move, CardBartok will set the state to CBState.hand

            /* <= This begins a multiline comment                        // a
            hand[i].transform.localPosition = pos;
            and[i].transform.rotation = rotQ;
            hand[i].state = CBState.hand;
            This ends the multiline comment => */                        // b

            hand[i].faceUp = (type == PlayerType.human);

            …
        }
    }
}
```

a. The /* begins a multiline comment, so all lines of code between it and the following */ are considered to be commented out (and are ignored by C#). This is the same way that you could have commented out the SlotDef class in the Layout script at the beginning of this chapter.

b. The */ ends the multiline comment.

2. Save the Player script, return to Unity, and play the scene.

Now when you play the scene and press the number keys (1, 2, 3, 4), you see the cards actually move into place! Because CardBartok does most of the heavy lifting, this took very little code to implement. This is one of the great advantages of object-oriented code. You trust that CardBartok knows how to move on its own so you can just call `MoveTo()` with a position and rotation, and CardBartok will do the rest.

Managing the Initial Card Deal

In the beginning of a round of *Bartok*, seven cards are dealt to each player, and then a single card is turned up from the drawPile to become the first target card.

1. Add the following code to Bartok to make this happen:

```
public class Bartok : MonoBehaviour {
    ...
    [Header("Set in Inspector")]
    ...
    public float            handFanDegrees = 10f;
    public int              numStartingCards = 7;
    public float            drawTimeStagger = 0.1f;

    ...
    void LayoutGame() {
        ...
        players[0].type = PlayerType.human; // Make the 0th player human

        CardBartok tCB;
        // Deal seven cards to each player
        for (int i=0; i<numStartingCards; i++) {
            for (int j=0; j<4; j++) {                              // a
                tCB = Draw (); // Draw a card
                // Stagger the draw time a bit.
                tCB.timeStart = Time.time + drawTimeStagger * ( i*4 + j );   // b

                players[ (j+1)%4 ].AddCard(tCB);                   // c
            }
        }

        Invoke("DrawFirstTarget", drawTimeStagger * (numStartingCards*4+4) );// d
    }
}
```

```
public void DrawFirstTarget() {
    // Flip up the first target card from the drawPile
    CardBartok tCB = MoveToTarget( Draw () );
}


// This makes a new card the target
public CardBartok MoveToTarget(CardBartok tCB) {
    tCB.timeStart = 0;
    tCB.MoveTo(layout.discardPile.pos+Vector3.back);
    tCB.state = CBState.toTarget;
    tCB.faceUp = true;

    targetCard = tCB;

    return(tCB);
}


// The Draw function will pull a single card from the drawPile and return it
public CardBartok Draw() { … }
    …

}
```

a. The `j` variable ranges from 0 to 3 because there are four players. If the game accommodated different numbers of players, this would need to be dynamic rather than using the integer literal `4` throughout this code. This would be a great place to use a const, but it wouldn't have fit within the width of the page.

b. Staggering the `timeStart` for each Card causes them to be dealt out one after the other. Remember the order of operations for math here: `drawTimeStagger * ( i*4 + j )` happens before adding `Time.time`. This will cause all cards after the 0th one to begin moving a little later in time, which will look like nice for your players.

c. Add the card to a Player's hand. The `(j+1)%4` causes the index of the `players` List loop through the numbers 1, 2, 3, 0 in succession, dealing cards sequentially to each Player, starting with `players[1]` (the Player clockwise after the human Player[0]).

d. After all the initial cards have been drawn, `DrawFirstTarget()` is called.

2. Save the Bartok script, return to Unity, and play the scene.

Upon playing the scene, you will see that the distribution of the seven cards and the draw of the first target happen properly on schedule; however, the human player's cards are overlapping each other in strange ways. Just as you did with *Prospector*, you need to very carefully manage both the `sortingLayerName` and the `sortingOrder` for each of the cards.

Managing 2D Depth-Sorting Order

In addition to the standard issue of depth-sorting 2D objects, you now have to deal with the fact that the cards are moving, and there will be some times that you want them in one sort order and layer at the beginning of the move and another when they arrive. To enable that, you need to add fields for an eventualSortLayer and eventualSortOrder to CardBartok. This way, when a card is moving, it will switch to the eventualSortLayer and eventualSortOrder partway through the move.

1. First, you need to rename all the sorting layers. Open the *Tags & Layers* settings by choosing *Edit > Project Settings > Tags & Layers* from the menu bar.

2. Set the names of Sorting Layers 1 through 10 to *1* through *10*, as shown in Figure 33.5. Add additional Sorting Layers as needed.

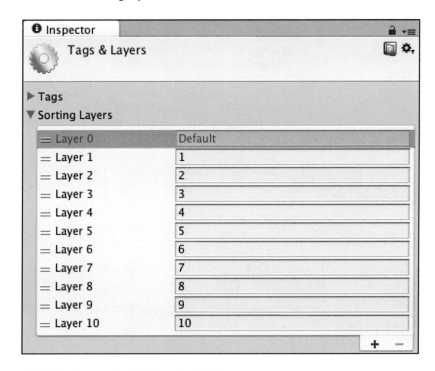

Figure 33.5 Simply named sorting layers for Bartok

3. Add the following bolded code to CardBartok:

```
public class CardBartok : Card {
    ...
    [Header("Set Dynamically")]
    ...
    public float            timeStart, timeDuration;
    public int              eventualSortOrder;
    public string           eventualSortLayer;

    ...

    void Update() {
        switch (state) {
            case CBState.toHand:
```

```
                        case CBState.toTarget:
                        case CBState.to:
                             ...
                          } else {
                              Vector3 pos = Utils.Bezier(uC, bezierPts);
                              transform.localPosition = pos;
                              Quaternion rotQ = Utils.Bezier(uC, bezierRots);
                              transform.rotation = rotQ;

                              if (u>0.5f) {                                    // a
                                  SpriteRenderer sRend = spriteRenderers[0];
                                  if (sRend.sortingOrder != eventualSortOrder) {
                                      // Jump to the proper sort order
                                      SetSortOrder(eventualSortOrder);
                                  }
                                  if (sRend.sortingLayerName != eventualSortLayer) {
                                      // Jump to the proper sort layer
                                      SetSortingLayerName(eventualSortLayer);
                                  }
                              }
                          }
                      }
                      break;
              }
          }
    }
```

a. When the move is halfway done (i.e., u>0.5f), the Card jumps to the eventualSor-
    tOrder and the eventualSortLayer.

Now that the eventualSortOrder and eventualSortLayer fields exist, you need to use
them throughout the code that has already been written.

4. Incorporate this into the MoveToTarget() method of the Bartok script and also add a
    MoveToDiscard() function that moves the target card into the discardPile:

```
public class Bartok : MonoBehaviour {
    ...

    public CardBartok MoveToTarget(CardBartok tCB) {
        tCB.timeStart = 0;
        tCB.MoveTo(layout.discardPile.pos+Vector3.back);
        tCB.state = CBState.toTarget;
        tCB.faceUp = true;

        tCB.SetSortingLayerName("10");
        tCB.eventualSortLayer = layout.target.layerName;
        if (targetCard != null) {
            MoveToDiscard(targetCard);
        }

        targetCard = tCB;
```

```
        return(tCB);
    }


    public CardBartok MoveToDiscard(CardBartok tCB) {
        tCB.state = CBState.discard;
        discardPile.Add ( tCB );
        tCB.SetSortingLayerName(layout.discardPile.layerName);
        tCB.SetSortOrder( discardPile.Count*4 );
        tCB.transform.localPosition = layout.discardPile.pos + Vector3.back/2;

        return(tCB);
    }

    // The Draw function will pull a single card from the drawPile and return it
    public CardBartok Draw() { … }
    …
}
```

5. You also need to make some changes to the AddCard() and FanHand() methods of Player:

```
public class Player {
    …
    public CardBartok AddCard(CardBartok eCB) {
        …
        // Sort the cards by rank using LINQ if this is a human
        if (type == PlayerType.human) {
            …
        }

        eCB.SetSortingLayerName("10"); // Sorts the moving card to the top    // a
        eCB.eventualSortLayer = handSlotDef.layerName;

        FanHand();
        return( eCB );
    }

    // Remove a card from the hand
    public CardBartok RemoveCard(CardBartok cb) { … }

    public void FanHand() {
        …
            hand[i].faceUp = (type == PlayerType.human);

            // Set the SortOrder of the cards so that they overlap properly
            hand[i].eventualSortOrder = i*4;                                    // b
            //hand[i].SetSortOrder(i*4);
        }
    }
}
```

    a. Setting the sorting layer of the moving card to `"10"` causes it to be above all other cards while it's moving. Based on the code you added to CardBartok in step 3 of this section, halfway through the move, the card will then jump to its `eventualSortLayer`.

    b. Comment out the line that was here (shown on the subsequent line now) and replace it with this one.

6. Make sure you've saved the changes to all of these scripts, return to Unity, and click *Play*. You should now see the cards layering much better.

Handling Turns

In this game, players need to take turns. Start by having the Bartok script track whose turn it is.

1. Open the Bartok script and add the bolded code shown here:

```
using System.Collections;
using System.Collections.Generic;
using UnityEngine;

// This enum contains the different phases of a game turn
public enum TurnPhase {
    idle,
    pre,
    waiting,
    post,
    gameOver
}

public class Bartok : MonoBehaviour {
    static public Bartok S;
    static public Player CURRENT_PLAYER;                             // a

        ...

    [Header("Set Dynamically")]
        ...
    public CardBartok          targetCard;
    public TurnPhase           phase = TurnPhase.idle;

    private BartokLayout        layout;

        ...

    public void DrawFirstTarget() {
        // Flip up the first target card from the drawPile
        CardBartok tCB = MoveToTarget( Draw() );
        // Set the CardBartok to call CBCallback on this Bartok when it is done
        tCB.reportFinishTo = this.gameObject;                       // b
    }
```

```
// This callback is used by the last card to be dealt at the beginning
public void CBCallback(CardBartok cb) {                                 // c
    // You sometimes want to have reporting of method calls like this
    Utils.tr("Bartok:CBCallback()",cb.name);                           // d
    StartGame(); // Start the Game
}


public void StartGame() {
    // Pick the player to the left of the human to go first.
    PassTurn(1);                                                        // e
}


public void PassTurn(int num=-1) {                                      // f
    // If no number was passed in, pick the next player
    if (num == -1) {
        int ndx = players.IndexOf(CURRENT_PLAYER);
        num = (ndx+1)%4;
    }
    int lastPlayerNum = -1;
    if (CURRENT_PLAYER != null) {
        lastPlayerNum = CURRENT_PLAYER.playerNum;
    }
    CURRENT_PLAYER = players[num];
    phase = TurnPhase.pre;

//      CURRENT_PLAYER.TakeTurn();                                      // g

    // Report the turn passing
    Utils.tr("Bartok:PassTurn()", "Old: "+lastPlayerNum,               // h
            ➥"New: "+CURRENT_PLAYER.playerNum);                        // h
}


// ValidPlay verifies that the card chosen can be played on the discard pile
public bool ValidPlay(CardBartok cb) {
    // It's a valid play if the rank is the same
    if (cb.rank == targetCard.rank) return(true);

    // It's a valid play if the suit is the same
    if (cb.suit == targetCard.suit) {
        return(true);
    }

    // Otherwise, return false
    return(false);
}


// This makes a new card the target
public CardBartok MoveToTarget(CardBartok tCB) { … }

…
```

```
/* Now is a good time to comment out this testing code              // i
// This Update method is used to test adding cards to players' hands
void Update() {
    if (Input.GetKeyDown(KeyCode.Alpha1)) {
        players[0].AddCard(Draw ());
    }
    if (Input.GetKeyDown(KeyCode.Alpha2)) {
        players[1].AddCard(Draw ());
    }
    if (Input.GetKeyDown(KeyCode.Alpha3)) {
        players[2].AddCard(Draw ());
    }
    if (Input.GetKeyDown(KeyCode.Alpha4)) {
        players[3].AddCard(Draw ());
    }
}
*/                                                                   // i
}
```

a. CURRENT_PLAYER is static and public here for two reasons: There should only ever be one current player in the game, and making this field static will allow the TurnLight that you'll set up in a subsequent section to access it easily.

b. reportFinishTo is a GameObject field that already exists on the CardBartok class. It gives the CardBartok a reference back to the gameObject of this Bartok instance (which is _MainCamera in this case). The existing CardBartok code will already call SendMessage("CBCallback",this) on the reportFinishTo GameObject if it is not null.

c. The CDCallback() method is called by the first target card when it is done moving into place (as just described in).

d. The call to Utils.tr() on this line reports to the Console that CBCallback() was called. This is the first use you've seen of the static public Utils.tr() method (tr being short for "trace"). This method takes any number of arguments (via the params keyword), concatenates them with tabs in between, and outputs them to the Console pane. It is one of the elements that was added to the Utils class in the unity-package that you imported into Prospector.

   tr() is called here with a string literal of the method name ("Bartok: CBCallback()") and the name of the GameObject that called CBCallback().

e. The game always starts with the player clockwise from the human player. Because the human is players[0], passing the turn to player 1 makes players[1] active.

f. The PassTurn() method has an optional parameter allowing you to specify which player to pass the turn to. Without any int passed in, num defaults to -1, and in the following four lines, num is then assigned the number for the next clockwise player.

g. This line is currently commented out because the Player class does not yet have a `TakeTurn()` method. You uncomment this line as part of the next section.

h. These two lines are actually a single line that was too long to fit in the book. You can type it as one line or as two. Because the first of these two lines does not have a semi-colon (;) at the end, Unity reads both lines as a single statement. Note that the `//` h at the end of the first line also does not break Unity's interpretation of it as a single line. In these cases, I use the ➡ code continuation symbol at the beginning of the second line. You **do not** need to type the ➡ symbol.

i. This `Update()` method was initially used for testing, but you no longer need it. You can comment out the whole thing by adding `/*` before it and `*/` after it.

2. Save the Bartok script, return to Unity, and click *Play*. You should see the initial hands deal out and then a console message that reads something like:

    Bartok:PassTurn()   Old: -1   New: 1

Shedding Some Light on the Situation

Although the `Bartok:PassTurn()` Console message from the preceding exercise lets you know whose turn it is while running Unity, your players won't have access to the Console. You need another way to show them whose turn it is. To accomplish you can highlight the background behind the current player with a light.

1. In Unity, choose *GameObject > Light > Point Light* from the menu bar to create a new Point Light.

2. Name the new light *TurnLight* and set its transform to the following:

    TurnLight (Point Light)   P:[0, 0, -3]   R:[0, 0, 0]   S:[1, 1, 1]

As you can see, this casts a nice, obvious light on the background. Now you need to add code to have it show who is the CURRENT_PLAYER.

3. Create a new script named *TurnLight* in the __Scripts folder of the Project pane.

4. Attach the *TurnLight* C# script to the GameObject *TurnLight* in the Hierarchy.

5. Open the TurnLight script and add the following code.

```
using UnityEngine;
using System.Collections;

public class TurnLight : MonoBehaviour {

    void Update () {
        transform.position = Vector3.back*3;                        // a
```

```
        if (Bartok.CURRENT_PLAYER == null) {                    // b
            return;
        }

        transform.position += Bartok.CURRENT_PLAYER.handSlotDef.pos;    // c
    }
}
```

a. This moves the light to its default position above the center of the board ([0, 0, -3]).

b. If `Bartok.CURRENT_PLAYER` is `null`, then you're done.

c. If `Bartok.CURRENT_PLAYER` is not `null`, then just add the position of the current Player to move the light above it.

In the previous edition of the book, the code to move TurnLight was part of the Bartok class, but in the time since I wrote that edition, I've been moving more toward *component-based* code, the core idea of which is to separate out your code into smaller chunks that have simpler purposes. There's no reason for the Bartok script to even know that a light exists, so in the second edition, I have the light manage itself.

6. Save the TurnLight script, return to Unity, and click *Play*.

Now when the cards are dealt, you should see the TurnLight move to hover over the left player, signifying that it is that player's turn.

A Simple Bartok AI
Now, let's make the AI players able to take turns.

1. Open the Bartok script and look for the line that was marked `// g` in the code listing under the heading "Handling Turns" a few pages back. Remove the comment slashes from the beginning of that line. After you do so, the line should read:

   ```
   CURRENT_PLAYER.TakeTurn();                                  // g
   ```

2. Save the Bartok script.

3. Open the Player script and add the following bolded code:

```
public class Player {
    …

    public void FanHand() {
        …
        Quaternion rotQ;
        for (int i=0; i<hand.Count; i++) {
            …
            pos += handSlotDef.pos;
            pos.z = -0.5f*i;
```

```
            // If  not the initial deal, start moving the card immediately.
            if (Bartok.S.phase != TurnPhase.idle) {                        // a
                hand[i].timeStart = 0;
            }

            // Set the localPosition and rotation of the ith card in the hand
            hand[i].MoveTo(pos, rotQ); // Tell CardBartok to interpolate
            …
        }

    }


    // The TakeTurn() function enables the AI of the computer Players
    public void TakeTurn() {
        Utils.tr ("Player.TakeTurn");

        // Don't need to do anything if this is the human player.
        if (type == PlayerType.human) return;

        Bartok.S.phase = TurnPhase.waiting;

        CardBartok cb;

        // If this is an AI player, need to make a choice about what to play
        // Find valid plays
        List<CardBartok> validCards = new List<CardBartok>();              // b
        foreach (CardBartok tCB in hand) {
            if (Bartok.S.ValidPlay(tCB)) {
                validCards.Add ( tCB );
            }
        }
        // If there are no valid cards
        if (validCards.Count == 0) {                                       // c
            // ...then draw a card
            cb = AddCard( Bartok.S.Draw () );
            cb.callbackPlayer = this;                                      // e
            return;
        }

        // So, there is a card or more to play, so pick one
        cb = validCards[ Random.Range (0,validCards.Count) ];             // d
        RemoveCard(cb);
        Bartok.S.MoveToTarget(cb);
        cb.callbackPlayer  = this;                                        // e

    }
```

```
    public void CBCallback(CardBartok tCB) {
        Utils.tr ("Player.CBCallback()",tCB.name,"Player "+playerNum);
        // The card is done moving, so pass the turn
        Bartok.S.PassTurn();
    }
}
```

a. Though you want cards to move in a staggered way during the initial deal at the start of the game, you don't want any delays later, so this makes sure the card gets moving.

b. Here, the AI looks for valid plays. It calls `ValidPlay()` on each card in its hand, and if the card is a valid play, it adds the card to a list `validCards`.

c. If the count of `validCards` is 0 (i.e., there are no valid plays), then the AI draws a card and returns.

d. If there are valid cards to pick from, the AI chooses one at random and makes it the new target card (i.e., it plays it to the discard pile).

e. `callbackPlayer` is red on these two lines because you have not yet added a public `callbackPlayer` field to CardBartok.

4. Save the Player script.

At the end of the Player script, you added a `CBCallback()` function that a CardBartok should call when it's done moving; however, because Player does not extend MonoBehaviour, you cannot use `SendMessage()` to call `CBCallback()`. Instead, you'll pass the CardBartok a reference to this Player, and then the CardBartok can call `CBCallback()` directly on the Player instance. This Player reference will be stored on CardBartok as the field `callbackPlayer`.

5. Open the CardBartok script and add this code:

```
public class CardBartok : Card {
    …
    [Header("Set Dynamically")]
    …
    public GameObject          reportFinishTo = null;
    [System.NonSerialized]                                         // a
    public Player              callbackPlayer = null;              // b

    // MoveTo tells the card to interpolate to a new position and rotation
    public void MoveTo(Vector3 ePos, Quaternion eRot) { … }
    …

    void Update() {
        switch (state) {
            case CBState.toHand:
            case CBState.toTarget:
            case CBState.to:
                …
```

```
        if (u<0) {
            …
        } else if (u>=1) {
            …
            if (reportFinishTo != null) {
                reportFinishTo.SendMessage("CBCallback", this);
                reportFinishTo = null;
            } else if (callbackPlayer != null) {                    // c
                // If there's a callback Player
                // Call CBCallback directly on the Player
                callbackPlayer.CBCallback(this);
                callbackPlayer = null;
            } else { // If there is nothing to callback
                // Just let it stay still.
            }
        } else {
            …
        }
        break;

    }
}
}
```

a. As with `[System.Serialized]`, `[System.NonSerialized]` affects the line below it. In this case, you are asking that the `callbackPlayer` field not be serialized, meaning two things: It will not appear in the Inspector, and the Inspector will not give it a value. The second one is most important in this case. See letter c that follows for why.

b. Now that you've defined `callbackPlayer`, it no longer appears in red in the Player script.

c. Here you only call `callbackPlayer.CBCallback()` if `callbackPlayer` is not null. This is why you needed `callbackPlayer` to be NonSerialized. If you allowed the Inspector to serialize `callbackPlayer`, it would have created a new Player instance for `callbackPlayer` so that it could be shown in the Inspector. To say that a different way, if `callbackPlayer` were serialized by the Inspector, it would be set to something other than `null` before the game even started. You make `callbackPlayer` NonSerialized to prevent this from happening. To test this, you can try commenting out the `[System.NonSerialized]` line and playing the game. You will get exceptions as a result because CardBartoks are trying to call `CBCallback()` on invalid Players that were created by the Inspector.

6. Save the CardBartok script and return to Unity.

Now, when you play the scene, the three AI players each play their turn.

Enabling the Human Player

It's time to make the human able to play as well. You do this by making the cards clickable.

1. Add the following bolded code to the end of the CardBartok class:

```
public class CardBartok : Card {

    …

    void Update() { … }

    // This allows the card to react to being clicked
    override public void OnMouseUpAsButton() {
        // Call the CardClicked method on the Bartok singleton
        Bartok.S.CardClicked(this);                            // a
        // Also call the base class (Card.cs) version of this method
        base.OnMouseUpAsButton();
    }

}
```

    a. CardClicked is red here because you have not yet added the `CardClicked()` method to the Bartok class.

2. Save the CardBartok script.

3. Add the `CardClicked()` method to the end of the Bartok script:

```
public class Bartok : MonoBehaviour {
    …
    public CardBartok Draw() { … }

    public void CardClicked(CardBartok tCB) {
        if (CURRENT_PLAYER.type != PlayerType.human) return;        // a
        if (phase == TurnPhase.waiting) return;                     // b

        switch (tCB.state) {                                        // c
            case CBState.drawpile:                                  // d
                // Draw the top card, not necessarily the one clicked.
                CardBartok cb = CURRENT_PLAYER.AddCard( Draw() );
                cb.callbackPlayer = CURRENT_PLAYER;
                Utils.tr ("Bartok:CardClicked()","Draw",cb.name);
                phase = TurnPhase.waiting;
                break;

            case CBState.hand:                                      // e
                // Check to see whether the card is valid
                if (ValidPlay(tCB)) {
                    CURRENT_PLAYER.RemoveCard(tCB);
                    MoveToTarget(tCB);
                    tCB.callbackPlayer = CURRENT_PLAYER;
                    Utils.tr("Bartok:CardClicked()","Play",tCB.name,
```

```
                                  ➥targetCard.name+" is target");              // f
                        phase = TurnPhase.waiting;
                    } else {
                        // Just ignore it but report what the player tried
                        Utils.tr("Bartok:CardClicked()","Attempted to Play",
                            ➥tCB.name,targetCard.name+" is target");           // f
                    }
                    break;
            }
        }
    }
}
```

a. If it's not the human's turn, don't respond to the click at all; just return.

b. If the game is waiting on a card to move, don't respond. This forces the player to wait until the game is still before playing.

c. This `switch` statement acts differently based on whether the clicked card was a card in the player's hand or on the `drawPile`.

d. If the card clicked was in the `drawPile`, draw the top card of the `drawPile`. Because the sprites of the `drawPile` are not sorted using a sort order or anything, the card drawn might not actually be the card that caught the mouse click.

e. If the card clicked was in the player's hand, check to see whether it is a valid play. If it is valid, play the card to the target (discard pile). If it is invalid, ignore the click, but report the attempt to the Console.

f. Remember that you do not need to type the ➥ line continuation character.

4. Save the *Bartok* script, return to Unity, and click *Play*.

Now you can play as well, and the game works! However, right now there is no logic to end the game when it's over. Just a few more additions, and this prototype will be done.

Handling an Empty Draw Pile

Now that you and the AIs can all play, you could empty the draw pile, which would currently crash the game. Let's add some code to Bartok to handle this case. Add the following code to the Bartok class to handle this:

```
public class Bartok : MonoBehaviour {
    …
    // The Draw function will pull a single card from the drawPile and return it
    public CardBartok Draw() {
        CardBartok cd = drawPile[0];      // Pull the 0th CardProspector

        if (drawPile.Count == 0) {        // If the drawPile is now empty
            // We need to shuffle the discards into the drawPile
            int ndx;
```

```
            while (discardPile.Count > 0) {
                // Pull a random card from the discard pile
                ndx = Random.Range(0, discardPile.Count);              // a
                drawPile.Add( discardPile[ndx] );
                discardPile.RemoveAt( ndx );
            }
            ArrangeDrawPile();
            // Show the cards moving to the drawPile
            float t = Time.time;
            foreach (CardBartok tCB in drawPile) {
                tCB.transform.localPosition = layout.discardPile.pos;
                tCB.callbackPlayer = null;
                tCB.MoveTo(layout.drawPile.pos);
                tCB.timeStart = t;
                t += 0.02f;
                tCB.state = CBState.toDrawpile;
                tCB.eventualSortLayer = "0";
            }
        }

        drawPile.RemoveAt(0);              // Then remove it from List<> drawPile
        return(cd);                        // And return it
    }
    ...
}
```

a. It's easier to use this `while` loop to pull random cards from the `discardPile` than to convert the `discardPile` from a `List<CardBartok>` to a `List<Card>` so you can call `Deck.Shuffle()` on it.

Adding Game UI

Just as with *Prospector*, you want to message the player when she finishes the game. To make it possible to do so, you need to create some uGUI Text fields.

1. From the menu bar, choose *GameObject > UI > Text* to add a new Text as a child of Canvas in the Hierarchy.

2. Rename this Text to *GameOver* and give it the settings shown on the left of Figure 33.6.

3. Duplicate *GameOver* by selecting it and choosing *Edit > Duplicate* from the menu bar.

4. Rename *GameOver (1)* to *RoundResult*, and give it the settings shown on the right of Figure 33.6. Often when you edit the Min and Max Anchors values, Unity changes the Pos X and Pos Y values as well. You can limit this by checking the *[R]* button in the RectTransform as I have, but Unity still messes with it a bit even after you do that.

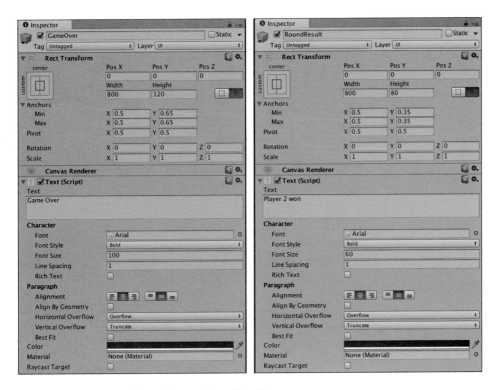

Figure 33.6 Settings for GameOver and RoundResult

Just like the TurnLight, you can give each of these Texts its own script so that Bartok doesn't have to worry about them.

5. Create a C# script named *GameOverUI* inside the __Scripts folder of the Project pane, attach it to the *GameOver* GameObject in the Hierarchy, and give it this code:

```
using System.Collections;
using System.Collections.Generic;
using UnityEngine;
using UnityEngine.UI;                     // Required for the uGUI classes like Text

public class GameOverUI : MonoBehaviour {
    private Text    txt;

    void Awake() {
        txt = GetComponent<Text>();
        txt.text = "";
    }

    void Update () {
        if (Bartok.S.phase != TurnPhase.gameOver) {
```

```
        txt.text = "";
        return;
    }
    // We only get here if the game is over
    if (Bartok.CURRENT_PLAYER == null) return;                       // a
    if (Bartok.CURRENT_PLAYER.type == PlayerType.human) {
        txt.text = "You won!";
    } else {
        txt.text = "Game Over";
    }
  }
}
```

    a. `Bartok.CURRENT_PLAYER` is `null` at the beginning of the game, so you need to accommodate that case.

6. Save the *GameOverUI* script.

7. Create a C# script named *RoundResultUI* inside the __Scripts folder of the Project pane, attach it to the *RoundResult* GameObject in the Hierarchy, and give it this code:

```
using System.Collections;
using System.Collections.Generic;
using UnityEngine;
using UnityEngine.UI;                        // Required for the uGUI classes like Text

public class RoundResultUI : MonoBehaviour {
    private Text    txt;

    void Awake() {
        txt = GetComponent<Text>();
        txt.text = "";
    }

    void Update () {
        if (Bartok.S.phase != TurnPhase.gameOver) {
            txt.text = "";
            return;
        }
        // We only get here if the game is over
        Player cP = Bartok.CURRENT_PLAYER;
        if (cP == null || cP.type == PlayerType.human) {                 // a
            txt.text = "";
        } else {
            txt.text = "Player "+(cP.playerNum)+" won";
        }
    }
}
```

a. Remember that || (logical OR) is a shorting function, so if cP is null, this line will never ask for cP.type and won't encounter a null reference exception.

8. Save the *RoundResultUI* script.

Game Over Logic

Now that you have the UI to show game over messages, let's actually allow the game to realize that it's over.

1. Open the Bartok script and add this bolded code to manage finishing the game.

```
public class Bartok : MonoBehaviour {
    ...

    public void PassTurn(int num=-1) {
        ...
        if (CURRENT_PLAYER != null) {
            lastPlayerNum = CURRENT_PLAYER.playerNum;
            // Check for Game Over and need to reshuffle discards
            if ( CheckGameOver() ) {
                return;                                            // a
            }
        }
        ...
    }

    public bool CheckGameOver() {
        // See if we need to reshuffle the discard pile into the draw pile
        if (drawPile.Count == 0) {
            List<Card> cards = new List<Card>();
            foreach (CardBartok cb in discardPile) {
                cards.Add (cb);
            }
            discardPile.Clear();
            Deck.Shuffle( ref cards );
            drawPile = UpgradeCardsList(cards);
            ArrangeDrawPile();
        }

        // Check to see if the current player has won
        if (CURRENT_PLAYER.hand.Count == 0) {
            // The player that just played has won!
            phase = TurnPhase.gameOver;
            Invoke("RestartGame", 1);                             // b
            return(true);
        }
```

```
            return(false);
        }

        public void RestartGame() {
            CURRENT_PLAYER = null;
            SceneManager.LoadScene("__Bartok_Scene_0");
        }


        // ValidPlay verifies that the card chosen can be played on the discard pile
        public bool ValidPlay(CardBartok cb) { … }
        …
    }
```

    a. If the game is over, you return before advancing the turn. This leaves CURRENT_ PLAYER set to the player who won, which allows GameOverUI and RoundResultUI to read from it.

    b. You invoke `RestartGame()` in 1 second, which shows the results for a second before restarting the game.

  2. Save the *Bartok* script, return to Unity, and click *Play*.

Now the game plays properly, it ends when it's over, and it restarts properly as well.

Building for WebGL

Now that you have a game, let's make a distributable version of it. These instructions are for WebGL, but building for Standalone is pretty similar. Building for iOS or Android involves several more steps.

  1. From the Unity menu bar, choose *File > Build Settings*. This is the window that you used at the beginning of the chapter.

  2. In the Build Settings window, click the *Player Settings* button. This opens PlayerSettings in the Inspector pane. If you're building for WebGL, the PlayerSettings should look like those shown in Figure 33.7.

  3. Click the *Resolution and Presentation* tab in PlayerSettings and set *Default Screen Width* to 1024 and *Default Screen Height* to 768 as shown in Figure 33.7.

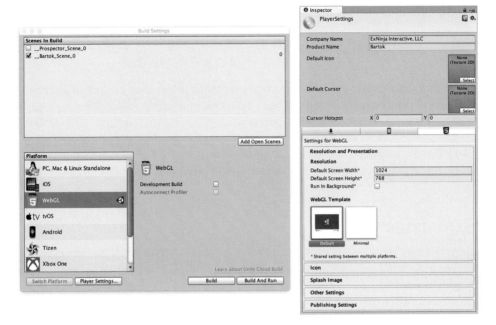

Figure 33.7 The Build Settings window and PlayerSettings in the Inspector pane

4. Feel free to set *Company Name* and *Product Name* to whatever you want. All the other PlayerSettings should be fine. Save your scene.

5. Return to the Build Settings window (if you closed it, use the *File > Build Settings* menu option to open it again) and click the *Build* button.

6. A standard file save dialog box appears, asking you to choose a folder name and place for the WebGL build. This will be a folder, and I recommend saving it on your Desktop so that you can find it easily (the default location is inside the project folder for this Unity project, which I don't think is ideal).

7. Type a folder name in the *Save As:* field. For a WebGL build, it's important that you **do not put any spaces in the folder name**; on some machines, JavaScript (WebGL) crashes if you try to run a file inside a folder with a space in the name (this is another reason that I don't recommend putting it in your Unity project folder; it or any folder above it could have a space in their name). Try the name *Bartok_WebGL*.

8. Click the *Save* button, and get ready to wait for a while. Sometimes, WebGL builds in a few minutes, in rare cases, it can take as many as 30 minutes or more. However, if the progress bar seems stuck for more than an hour, you should cancel it (sometimes the WebGL build process crashes). The build for *Bartok* took about 5 minutes on my i7 MacBook Pro.

9. Find and open the Bartok_WebGL folder on your Desktop. Open the folder and try double-clicking the index.html file.

You might get an error message that reads:

> It seems your browser does not support running Unity WebGL content from
> file:// urls. Please upload it to an http server, or try a different browser.

If so, that's because browsers like Google *Chrome* are trying to be security conscious and not run code like Unity's WebGL off of a local hard drive. I have found that *Firefox* opens the local Unity index.html files just fine (as of July 2017).

After you either get a browser that won't complain about running it off of your local drive or have uploaded it to space online, you should be able to play *Bartok* in a web browser.

Summary

The goal of this chapter was to demonstrate how possible it is to take the digital prototypes that you make in this book and adapt them to your own games. After you finish all the tutorial chapters, you will have the framework for a classic arcade game (*Apple Catcher*), a physics-based casual game (*Mission Demolition*), a space shooter (*Space SHMUP*), a card game (*Prospector* and *Bartok*), a word game (the next chapter), and a top-down adventure game (*Dungeon Delver*). As prototypes, none of these are finished games, but any of them could serve as a foundation on which to build your own games.

Next Steps

The classic paper version of the *Bartok* card game included the ability for the winner of any round to add additional rules to the game. Although allowing the player to just make up rules for this digital game is not possible, adding your own optional rules through code is certainly possible, just as I did for the version you played with in Chapter 1.

If you visit the http://book.prototools.net website, you can look under Chapter 33 for the Unity project of the expanded version of *Bartok* that includes all the optional rules you were able to play with in Chapter 1. That should be a good starting point for you to use to add your own rules to the game.

CHAPTER 34

PROTOTYPE 6: *WORD GAME*

In this chapter, you learn how to create a simple word game. This game uses several concepts that you have already learned, and it introduces the concept of *coroutines*, methods that can yield during execution to allow the processor to handle other methods.

By the end of this chapter, you'll have a fun word game that you can expand yourself.

Getting Started: Prototype 6

As usual, you'll import a unitypackage to start this chapter. This package contains a few art assets and some C# scripts that you created in previous chapters.

SET UP THE PROJECT FOR THIS CHAPTER

Following the standard project setup procedure, create a new project in Unity. If you need a refresher on how to do so, see Appendix A, "Standard Project Setup Procedure." When you create the project, you are asked whether you want to set up defaults for 2D or 3D. Choose 3D for this project.

For this project, you will import the main scene from the unitypackage, so you do not need to set up the _MainCamera.

- **Project name:** Word Game

- **Download and import package:** See Chapter 34 at http://book.prototools.net

- **Scene name:** _WordGame_Scene_0 (imported via the unitypackage)

- **Project folders:** _Scripts, _Prefabs, Materials & Textures, Resources

- **C# script names:** Just the imported scripts in the ProtoTools folder

---

Open the scene __WordGame_Scene_0, and you will find a _MainCamera that is already set up for an orthographic game. Additionally, some of the reusable C# scripts that you saw in previous chapters have been moved into the folder __Scripts/ProtoTools to keep them separate from the new scripts you'll create for this project. I find this is useful because it enables me to just place a copy of the ProtoTools folder into the __Scripts folder of any new project and have all that functionality ready to go.

In your Build Settings, I recommend setting this one is to *PC, Mac, & Linux Standalone*. Set the aspect ratio of the Game pane to *Standalone (1024 x 768)*. You could also compile this for WebGL or mobile if you like, but I won't cover any of that in this chapter.

About the Word Game

This game is a classic form of word game. Commercial examples of this game include *Word Whomp* by Pogo.com, *Jumbline 2* by Branium, *Pressed for Words* by Words and Maps, and many others. The player is presented with jumbled letters that can spell at least one word of a certain length (usually six letters), and she is tasked with finding all the words that can be created by rearranging the letters in that word. This chapter's version of the game includes some slick animations (using Bézier interpolations) and a scoring paradigm that encourages the player to find long words before short ones. Figure 34.1 shows an image of the game you'll create.

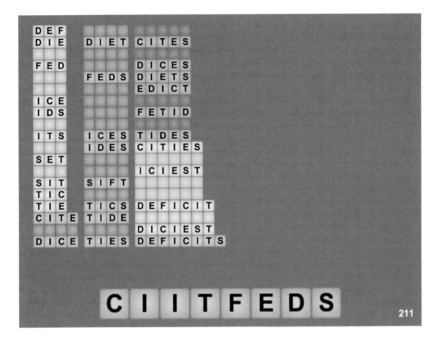

Figure 34.1 An image of the game created in this chapter using an eight-letter word as the base

In this image, you can see that each of the words are composed of individual letter tiles, and there are two sizes of these tiles: a large size for the letters at the bottom of the screen and a smaller size for all the words above that. For the sake of object orientation, you'll create a *Letter* class that handles each letter and a *Word* class to collect them into words. You'll also create a *WordList* class to read the large dictionary of possible words that you have and turn it into usable data for the game. The game will be managed by a *WordGame* class, and you'll use the *Scoreboard* and *FloatingScore* classes from previous prototypes to show the score to the player. In addition, you'll use the *Utils* class for interpolation and easing. The *PT_XMLReader* class is imported with this project, but is unused. I left this script in the unitypackage because I want to encourage you to start building your own collection of useful scripts that you can import into any project to help you get started (just as the ProtoTools folder is for the projects in this book). Feel free to add any useful scripts that you create to this collection, and think about importing it as the first thing you do for each new game prototype that you start.

Parsing the Word List

This game uses a modified form of the *2of12inf* word list created by Alan Beale.[1] I've removed some offensive words and attempted to correct others. You are more than welcome to use this word list however you want in the future, as long as you follow the copyright terms of both Alan Beale and Kevin Atkinson (as listed in footnote 1). I also modified the list by shifting all the letters to uppercase and by changing the line ending from \r\n (a carriage return and a line feed, which is the standard Windows text file format) to \n (just a line feed, the standard macOS text format). I did this to make it easier to split the file into individual words based on line feed, and for purposes of this chapter, it works on Windows just as well as macOS.

I have attempted to remove offensive words from the word list because of the kind of game this is. In a game like *Scrabble* or *Letterpress*, the player is given a series of letter tiles, and she is able to choose which words she wants to spell with those tiles. However, in this game, the player is forced to spell every word in the list that can be made from the collection of letters that she is given. This means that the game could force players to spell some terms that would be offensive to them. In this game, the decision of which words are chosen has shifted from the player to the computer, and I did not feel comfortable forcing players to spell potentially offensive words. However, in the more than 75,000 words in the list, I probably missed some, so if you find any words in the game that you feel I should omit (or ones I should add), please let me know by sending a message to me via the website http://book.prototools.net. Thanks.

To read the word list file, you need to pull its text into a single large string and split that string into an array of individual word strings (separated by \n in the original string). After this is done, you need to individually analyze each word and decide whether to add it to the dictionary for the game (based on its length). This one-by-one analysis of the words can take some time to execute; so rather than freeze the game on a single frame while waiting for this process to complete, you're going to create a *coroutine* to handle the process over multiple frames (see the following sidebar "Using Coroutines").

---

1. Alan Beale has released all of his word lists into the public domain apart from the aspects of the 2of12inf list that were based on the AGID word list, Copyright 2000 by Kevin Atkinson. Permission to use, copy, modify, distribute, and sell this [the AGID] database, the associated scripts, the output created from the scripts and its documentation for any purpose is hereby granted without fee, provided that the above copyright notice appears in all copies and that both that copyright notice and this permission notice appear in supporting documentation. Kevin Atkinson makes no representations about the suitability of this array for any purpose. It is provided "as is" without express or implied warranty.

> ## USING COROUTINES
>
> A *coroutine* is a function that can pause in its execution to allow other functions to update. It's a Unity C# feature that allows developers to have control over repeating tasks in code or to handle very large tasks. In this chapter, you learn to use it for the latter by having a coroutine parse all 75,000 words from the *2of12inf* word list.
>
> Coroutines are initiated with a call to `StartCoroutine()`, which can only be called within a class that extends MonoBehaviour. After it is initiated in this way, a coroutine executes until it encounters a `yield` statement. `yield` tells the coroutine to pause for a certain amount of time and allow other code to execute during the pause. After the designated time has passed, the coroutine continues on the next line after the `yield` statement. This means that you could have an infinite `while(true) {}` loop in a coroutine, and it wouldn't freeze your game as long as a `yield` statement existed somewhere within the `while` loop. In this game, the coroutine `ParseLines()` yields every 10,000 words that it parses.
>
> Look for how the coroutine is used in the first code listing of this chapter. Although the coroutine in this chapter probably isn't strictly necessary as long as you have a fast computer, this kind of thing becomes much more important when you're developing for mobile devices (or other devices with slower processors). Parsing this same word list on an older iPhone can take as much as 10 to 20 seconds, so including breaks in the parsing where the app can handle other tasks and not just look frozen is important.
>
> You can learn more about coroutines in the Unity documentation.

1. Create a new C# script named *WordList* in the __Scripts folder and enter the following code:

```
using System.Collections;
using System.Collections.Generic;
using UnityEngine;

public class WordList : MonoBehaviour {
    private static WordList    S;                                      // a

    [Header("Set in Inspector")]
    public TextAsset           wordListText;
    public int                 numToParseBeforeYield = 10000;
    public int                 wordLengthMin = 3;
    public int                 wordLengthMax = 7;

    [Header("Set Dynamically")]
    public int                 currLine = 0;
    public int                 totalLines;
    public int                 longWordCount;
    public int                 wordCount;
```

```csharp
// Private fields
private string[]      lines;                                          // b
private List<string>  longWords;
private List<string>  words;

void Awake() {
    S = this;  // Set up the WordList Singleton
}

void Start () {
    lines = wordListText.text.Split('\n');                           // c
    totalLines = lines.Length;

    StartCoroutine( ParseLines() );                                  // d
}

// All coroutines have IEnumerator as their return type.
public IEnumerator ParseLines() {                                    // e
    string word;
    // Init the Lists to hold the longest words and all valid words
    longWords = new List<string>();                                  // f
    words = new List<string>();

    for (currLine = 0; currLine < totalLines; currLine++) {          // g
        word = lines[currLine];

        // If the word is as long as wordLengthMax…
        if (word.Length == wordLengthMax) {
            longWords.Add(word);      // …then store it in longWords
        }

        // If it's between wordLengthMin and wordLengthMax in length…
        if ( word.Length>=wordLengthMin && word.Length<=wordLengthMax ) {
            words.Add(word);  // …then add it to the list of all valid words
        }

        // Determine whether the coroutine should yield
        if (currLine % numToParseBeforeYield == 0) {                 // h
            // Count the words in each list to show parsing progress
            longWordCount = longWords.Count;
            wordCount = words.Count;
            // This yields execution until the next frame
            yield return null;                                       // i

            // The yield will cause the execution of this method to wait
            //  here while other code executes and then continue from this
            //  point into the next iteration of the for loop.
        }
    }
```

```
        longWordCount = longWords.Count;
        wordCount = words.Count;
    }


    // These methods allow other classes to access the private List<string>s // j
    static public List<string> GET_WORDS() {
        return( S.words );
    }

    static public string GET_WORD(int ndx) {
        return( S.words[ndx] );
    }

    static public List<string> GET_LONG_WORDS() {
        return( S.longWords );
    }

    static public string GET_LONG_WORD(int ndx) {
        return( S.longWords[ndx] );
    }

    static public int WORD_COUNT {
        get { return S.wordCount; }
    }

    static public int LONG_WORD_COUNT {
        get { return S.longWordCount; }
    }

    static public int NUM_TO_PARSE_BEFORE_YIELD {
        get { return S.numToParseBeforeYield; }
    }

    static public int WORD_LENGTH_MIN {
        get { return S.wordLengthMin; }
    }

    static public int WORD_LENGTH_MAX {
        get { return S.wordLengthMax; }
    }
}
```

a. This is a private Singleton (because it's private, it is not exactly a Singleton any more). Making the singleton S private ensures that only instances of the WordList class can see it, protecting it from other code. This private Singleton is used by the accessors discussed in // j.

b. Because these fields are private, they do not appear in the Inspector. These variables will contain so much data that it would drastically slow playback if the Inspector were trying to display them, so you must make these private—restricting them to only be accessible by this instance of WordList—and make public accessor functions at the end of the class to allow code outside of this instance to access them.

c. Split the text of `wordListText` on line feeds (`\n`), which creates a large, populated string[] with an element for each word from the list.

d. This starts the coroutine `ParseLines()`. See the sidebar "Using Coroutines" for more info.

e. All coroutines must have the return type of `IEnumerator`. This enables them to yield their execution and allow other methods to run before returning to the coroutine, which is extremely important for processes like loading large files or like parsing a large amount of data (as you're doing in this case).

f. The string array `lines` will be sorted into two lists: `longWords` is for all the words that are composed of `wordLengthMax` characters, and `words` is for all the words that are between `wordLengthMin` and `wordLengthMax` (inclusive) characters. For example, if `wordLengthMin` were 3 characters and `wordLengthMax` were 6, the word DESIGN would be in `longWords`, while DIE, DICE, GAME, BOARD, and DESIGN would be in `words`.

You parse the whole list here so that the player only has to wait once and is then able to play many rounds in a row with many different words.

g. This `for` loop iterates over all 75,000 entries in `lines`. Every `numToParseBeforeYield` words, the yield statement pauses this `for` loop and allows other code to run. Then, on the next frame, execution returns to the `for` loop for another `numToParseBeforeYield` lines.

h. Determine whether the coroutine should yield. This uses a modulus (%) function to yield every 10,000[th] record (or whatever you have `numToParseBeforeYield` set to).

i. This yield statement yields execution of the coroutine until the next frame because it returns `null`. Yielding for a certain number of seconds is also possible with a statement like `yield return new WaitForSeconds(1);`, which would wait for at least 1 second before continuing coroutine execution (note that coroutine yield times are reasonably accurate but not exact). This also means that you can put timed repeating tasks in a coroutine rather than using the `InvokeRepeating()` method.

j. The four methods below the `// i` line are static public *accessors* for the private fields `words` and `longWords`. Code anywhere in the game can call `WordList.GET_WORD(10)` to get the tenth word in the private `words` array of this singleton instance of WordList. Additionally, the last several accessors are read-only static public properties, showing another way to access private variables of WordList. By convention, static variables and methods are often named with ALL_CAPS_SNAKE_CASE.

2. After writing and saving the code, switch back to Unity.

3. Attach the *WordList* C# script to _MainCamera.

4. Select *_MainCamera* in the Hierarchy and set the `wordListText` variable of the *WordList (Script)* component in the Inspector to be the file *2of12inf*, which you can find in the Resources folder of the Project pane.

5. Click *Play*.

You can see that the `currLine`, `longWordCount`, and `wordCount` count up progressively by 10,000s. This happens because the numbers are allowed to update every time the coroutine `ParseLines()` yields.

If you stop, use the Inspector to change `numToParseBeforeYield` to 100, and play again, you will see that these numbers build much more slowly because the coroutine is yielding every 100 words. However, if you change it to something like 100,000. these numbers will update only once because there are fewer than 100,000 words in the word list. If you're interested in seeing how much time each pass through the `ParseLines()` coroutine is taking, try using the profiler, as described in the sidebar titled The Unity Profiler.

THE UNITY PROFILER

The Unity profiler is one of the most powerful tools for optimizing the performance of your games, and it's one of the many tools available to you in the free version of Unity. For every frame of your game, the profiler maintains stats on the amount of time spent on each C# function, calls to the graphics engine, handling user input, and so on. You can see a great example of how this works by running the profiler on this project.

1. Make sure that the WordList code from the preceding pages is working properly.

2. Add a *Profiler* pane to the same group as the Scene pane. That ensures that you can see both the Game pane and the Profiler pane simultaneously. To add the Profiler pane, click the pop-up menu button at the top right of the current Scene pane and choose *Add Tab > Profiler* (as shown in Figure 34.2).

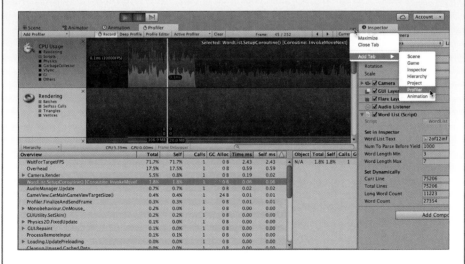

Figure 34.2 The Profiler pane

3. To see the profiler in action, click the Pause button at the top of the Unity window and then click *Play*. This causes Unity to prepare itself to run your game but to be paused before the first frame. If you click Pause again, a graph starts to appear in the profiler. Pause the game again when the graph is about an inch from the left side of the screen.

With the game paused, the profiler should stop graphing yet maintain the graph of the frames that have already passed. Each of the colors in the graph beside the heading *CPU Usage* covers a different aspect of things for which the CPU (the main processor in your computer) is used. In the later frames, if you're on a fast computer, you should see that most of the chart is yellow; the yellow represents the time Unity spends on VSync (that is, waiting for the screen to be ready to display another frame). This blocks your view of how much time is taken by the scripts (which are light blue), so you need to hide it from the graph.

4. The little colored boxes below *CPU Usage* on the left side of the profiler each represent a different kind of process that runs on the CPU. For now, turn off all of them off except for the *Scripts* box (which is blue). To do this, click the colored box next to everything except for Scripts. This should leave you with a blue graph like the one shown in Figure 34.2.

5. Click and drag the mouse along the blue graph in the *CPU Usage* section of the Profiler, and you should see a white line following the mouse. This white line represents a single frame in the graph. As you move, the text in the bottom half of the profiler updates to show how much processing time each function or background process took during that frame. The function you're interested in is the *WordList. SetupCoroutine() [Coroutine: InvokeMoveNext]* coroutine. This only runs in the first few frames, so you won't see it on the right side of the graph; however, you should see a spike of script activity at the beginning of the graph (as shown in Figure 34.2), which is the time taken by the coroutine `ParseLines()`.

6. There is a search field on the dividing bar between the top and bottom halves of the Profiler pane. (If you don't see the search field, try clicking in the top (*CPU Usage*) half of the graph.) Type "ParseLines" into this field to search for the WordList:ParseLines method. This method only runs in the first few frames, so you won't see it on the right side of the graph; however, you should see a spike of script activity at the beginning of the graph (as shown in Figure 34.2).

7. Move the white line to the part of the graph with the tall spike, and two *WordList. ParseLines()* rows will appear in the data area below the graph. Click *WordList. ParseLines() [Coroutine: MoveNext]* in the Search column below the graph. This highlights the graph contribution of that one routine and dims the others as shown in the figure. If you use the left and right arrow buttons at the top-right corner of the Profiler pane, you can step one frame back or forward (respectively) and see the CPU resources used by the coroutine in each frame. In my profiling shown in Figure 34.2,

> I set `numToParseBeforeYield` to 1,000 and found that for the first several frames, the coroutine took up about 6.7% of the CPU time spent on each frame (although your numbers might vary due to computer type and processing speed).
>
> In addition to profiling scripts, the profiler can also help you find what aspects of rendering or physics simulation are taking the most time in your game. If you ever run into frame rate issues in one of your games, try checking the profiler to see what's happening. (You'll want to be sure to turn all the other types of CPU profiling back on when you do [that is, re-check all the boxes that you unchecked earlier to isolate Scripts under CPU Usage].)
>
> To see a very different profiler graph, you can try running the profiler on the Hello World project from Chapter 19, "Hello World: Your First Program." You'll see that in Hello World, much more time is spent on physics than scripts. (You might need to turn the VSync element of the graph off again to see this clearly.)
>
> You can learn more about the profiler in the Unity documentation.
>
> After playing with the Profiler, be sure to set `numToParseBeforeYield` back to 10,000.

Setting Up the Game

You're going to create a WordGame class to manage the game, but before you do so, you need to make a couple of changes to WordList. First, you need to make it not start parsing the words on `Start()` but instead wait until an `Init()` method is called by another class. Second, you need to make WordList notify the upcoming WordGame script when the parsing is complete. To do this, you need to have the WordList send a message to the _MainCamera GameObject using the `SendMessage()` command. WordGame will interpret this message, as you'll soon see.

1. Change the name of the `void Start()` method in WordList to `public void Init()` and add the following bold code, including the `static public void INIT()` function and the lines at the end of the `ParseLines()` method in WordList:

```
public class WordList : MonoBehaviour {
    …
    void Awake() { … }

    public void Init () { // This line replaces "void Start()"
        lines = wordListText.text.Split('\n');
        totalLines = lines.Length;

        StartCoroutine( ParseLines() );
    }

    static public void INIT () {                                          // a
        S.Init();
    }
```

```
// All coroutines have IEnumerator as their return type.
public IEnumerator ParseLines() {
    …
    for (currLine = 0; currLine < totalLines; currLine++) {
        …
    }
    longWordCount = longWords.Count;
    wordCount = words.Count;

    // Send a message to this gameObject to let it know the parse is done
    gameObject.SendMessage("WordListParseComplete");                    // b
}

// These methods allow other classes to access the private List<string>s
static public List<string> GET_WORDS() { … }
    …
}
```

a. This `INIT()` method is static and public, meaning that the WordGame class can call it.

b. The `SendMessage()` command is executed on the GameObject _MainCamera (because WordList is a Script Component of _MainCamera). This command calls a `WordListParseComplete()` method on any script that is attached to the GameObject on which it is called (that is, _MainCamera).

2. Create a *WordGame* C# script in the __Scripts folder and attach it to _MainCamera. Enter the following code to take advantage of the changes just made to WordList:

```
using System.Collections;
using System.Collections.Generic;
using UnityEngine;
using System.Linq;                    // We'll be using LINQ

public enum GameMode {
    preGame,      // Before the game starts
    loading,      // The word list is loading and being parsed
    makeLevel,    // The individual WordLevel is being created
    levelPrep,    // The level visuals are Instantiated
    inLevel       // The level is in progress
}

public class WordGame : MonoBehaviour {
    static public WordGame      S; // Singleton

    [Header("Set Dynamically")]
    public GameMode             mode = GameMode.preGame;

    void Awake() {
        S = this; // Assign the singleton
    }

    void Start () {
        mode = GameMode.loading;
```

```
        // Call the static Init() method of WordList
        WordList.INIT();
    }

    // Called by the SendMessage() command from WordList
    public void WordListParseComplete() {
        mode = GameMode.makeLevel;
    }
}
```

3. Select _MainCamera in the Hierarchy pane, and look at the *WordGame (Script)* component in the Inspector. Click *Play*, and you will see the value of the mode field initially move from preGame to loading. Then, after all the words have been parsed, it changes from loading to makeLevel. This shows you that everything is working as hoped.

Building a Level with the WordLevel Class

Now, it's time to take the words in the WordList and make a level from them. The WordLevel class will include the following:

- The long word on which the level is based. (If maxWordLength is 6, this is the six-letter word whose letters will be reshuffled into the other words.)

- The index number of that word in the longWords array of WordList.

- The level number as int levelNum. In this chapter, every time the game starts, you'll choose a random word.[2]

- A Dictionary<,> of each character in the word and how many times it is used. Dictionaries are part of System.Collections.Generic along with Lists.

- A List<> of all the other words that can be formed from the characters in the Dictionary described in the preceding bullet.

A Dictionary<,> is a generic collection type that holds a series of key, value pairs that is covered in detail in Chapter 23, "Collections in C#." In each level, the Dictionary<,> uses char keys and int values to hold information about how many times each char is used in the long word. For example, this is how the long word MISSISSIPPI would look:

```
Dictionary<char,int> charDict = new Dictionary<char,int>();
charDict.Add('M',1); // MISSISSIPPI has 1 M
charDict.Add('I',4); // MISSISSIPPI has 4 Is
charDict.Add('S',4); // MISSISSIPPI has 4 Ss
charDict.Add('P',2); // MISSISSIPPI has 2 Ps
```
WordLevel also contains two useful static methods:

---

2. If you wanted, you could call Random.InitState(1); in the WordGame.Awake() method, which would set the initial random number seed of Random to 1 and ensure that the eighth level would always be the same word as long as you only ever used Random to choose the level. I describe another way to approach this in the "Next Steps" section at the end of the chapter.

- ■ MakeCharDict(): Populates charDict based on any string.
- ■ CheckWordInLevel(): Checks to see whether a word can be spelled using the chars in a WordLevel's charDict.

1. Create a new C# script named *WordLevel* in the __Scripts folder and enter the following code. Note that WordLevel *does not* extend MonoBehaviour, so it is not a class that can be attached to a GameObject as a Script component, and it cannot have StartCoroutine(), SendMessage(), or many other Unity-specific functions called within it.

```csharp
using System.Collections;
using System.Collections.Generic;
using UnityEngine;

[System.Serializable] // WordLevels can be viewed & edited in the Inspector
public class WordLevel { // WordLevel does NOT extend MonoBehaviour
    public int                      levelNum;
    public int                      longWordIndex;
    public string                   word;
    // A Dictionary<,> of all the letters in word
    public Dictionary<char,int>     charDict;
    // All the words that can be spelled with the letters in charDict
    public List<string>             subWords;

    // A static function that counts the instances of chars in a string and
    //  returns a Dictionary<char,int> that contains this information
    static public Dictionary<char,int> MakeCharDict(string w) {
        Dictionary<char,int> dict = new Dictionary<char, int>();
        char c;
        for (int i=0; i<w.Length; i++) {
            c = w[i];
            if (dict.ContainsKey(c)) {
                dict[c]++;
            } else {
                dict.Add (c,1);
            }
        }
        return(dict);
    }

    // This static method checks to see whether the word can be spelled with the
    //  chars in level.charDict
    public static bool CheckWordInLevel(string str, WordLevel level) {
        Dictionary<char,int> counts = new Dictionary<char, int>();
        for (int i=0; i<str.Length; i++) {
            char c = str[i];
            // If the charDict contains char c
            if (level.charDict.ContainsKey(c)) {
                // If counts doesn't already have char c as a key
                if (!counts.ContainsKey(c)) {
                    // ...then add a new key with a value of 1
```

```
                      counts.Add (c,1);
                 } else {
                      // Otherwise, add 1 to the current value
                      counts[c]++;
                 }

                 // If this means that there are more instances of char c in str
                 //  than are available in level.charDict
                 if (counts[c] > level.charDict[c]) {
                      //  ... then return false
                      return(false);
                 }
            } else {
                 // The char c isn't in level.word, so return false
                 return(false);
            }
        }
        return(true);
    }
}
```

2. To make use of the WordLevel class, make the following bolded changes to WordGame:

```
public class WordGame : MonoBehaviour {
    static public WordGame    S; // Singleton

    [Header("Set Dynamically")]
    public GameMode        mode = GameMode.preGame;
    public WordLevel        currLevel;

    …

    public void WordListParseComplete() {
        mode = GameMode.makeLevel;
        // Make a level and assign it to currLevel, the current WordLevel
        currLevel = MakeWordLevel();
    }

    public WordLevel MakeWordLevel(int levelNum = -1) {                     // a
        WordLevel level = new WordLevel();
        if (levelNum == -1) {
            // Pick a random level
            level.longWordIndex = Random.Range(0,WordList.LONG_WORD_COUNT);
        } else {
            // This will be added later in the chapter
        }
        level.levelNum = levelNum;
        level.word = WordList.GET_LONG_WORD(level.longWordIndex);
        level.charDict = WordLevel.MakeCharDict(level.word);

        StartCoroutine( FindSubWordsCoroutine(level) );                     // b
```

```
        return( level );                                        // c
    }

    // A coroutine that finds words that can be spelled in this level
    public IEnumerator FindSubWordsCoroutine(WordLevel level) {
        level.subWords = new List<string>();
        string str;

        List<string> words = WordList.GET_WORDS();              // d

        // Iterate through all the words in the WordList
        for (int i=0; i<WordList.WORD_COUNT; i++) {
            str = words[i];
            // Check whether each one can be spelled using level.charDict
            if (WordLevel.CheckWordInLevel(str, level)) {
                level.subWords.Add(str);
            }
            // Yield if we've parsed a lot of words this frame
            if (i%WordList.NUM_TO_PARSE_BEFORE_YIELD == 0) {
                // yield until the next frame
                yield return null;
            }
        }

        level.subWords.Sort ();                                 // e
        level.subWords = SortWordsByLength(level.subWords).ToList();

        // The coroutine is complete, so call SubWordSearchComplete()
        SubWordSearchComplete();
    }

    // Use LINQ to sort the array received and return a copy       // f
    public static IEnumerable<string> SortWordsByLength(IEnumerable<string> ws) {
        ws = ws.OrderBy(s => s.Length);
        return ws;
    }

    public void SubWordSearchComplete() {
        mode = GameMode.levelPrep;

    }
}
```

a. With the default value of -1, this method picks a random word from which to generate a WordLevel.

b. This starts a coroutine to check all the words in the WordList and see whether each word can be spelled by the chars in `level.charDict`.

   c. This returns the WordLevel `level` before the coroutine finishes. When the coroutine has completed, `SubWordSearchComplete()` is called.

   d. This is very fast because Lists are passed by reference. (So C# doesn't have to make a copy of WordList's `List<string> words`—it just returns a reference to it.)

   e. These two lines sort the words in the `WordLevel.subWords` List. `List<string>.Sort()` sorts the words alphabetically (because that is the default for List<String>). Then, the custom `SortWordsByLength()` method is called to sort the words by the number of characters in each word. This groups alphabetized words of the same length.

   f. This custom sorting function uses LINQ to sort the array received and return a copy. The LINQ syntax inside this method is different from regular C# and is beyond the scope of this book. You can learn more about it by searching for "C# LINQ" online.

   The Unity Gems website also offers a good explanation of LINQ. The following link is from the Internet Archive to ensure that it remains valid:

   https://web.archive.org/web/20140209060811/http://unitygems.com/linq-1-time-linq/

This code creates the level, chooses a goal word, and populates it with `subWords` that can be spelled using the characters in the goal word. Save all scripts, return to Unity, and click *Play*. You should now see the `currLevel` field populate in the _MainCamera *WordGame (Script)* component Inspector.

  3. Save your scene! If you haven't been saving your scene all along—and this served as a reminder to do so—you need to be reminding yourself to save more often.

Laying Out the Screen

Now that you've created the data representation of the level, it's time to generate on-screen visuals to represent both the big letters that can be used to spell words and the smaller letters of the words. To start, you need to create a PrefabLetter to be instantiated for each letter.

Making PrefabLetter

Follow these steps to make PrefabLetter:

  1. From the menu bar, choose *GameObject > 3D Object > Quad*. Rename the quad to *PrefabLetter*.

  2. From the menu bar, choose *Assets > Create > Material*. Name the material *LetterMat* and place it in the *Materials & Textures* folder.

  3. Drag *LetterMat* onto PrefabLetter in the Hierarchy to assign it. Click on *PrefabLetter*, and set the *shader* of LetterMat to *Unlit > Transparent*.

4. Select *Rounded Rect 256* as the texture for the LetterMat material (you might need to open the disclosure triangle in the LetterMat area of the PrefabLetter Inspector).

5. Double-click *PrefabLetter* in the Hierarchy, and you should now see a nice rounded rectangle there. If you can't see it, you might need to move the camera around to the other side. See the following "Backface Culling" sidebar for information about why quads are visible from one side and invisible from the other. Choose *ProtoTools > UnlitAlpha* as the shader for LetterMat to enable the quad to be seen from either side.

BACKFACE CULLING

Backface culling is a rendering optimization where polygons are only rendered if they are viewed from the correct side. This works well when rendering something like a sphere. When viewing a sphere, half of the polygons forming the surface of the sphere are facing the viewer, while the other half (those on the far side of the sphere) are facing away. Rather than render the whole sphere, computer scientists realized that they only needed to render the polygons facing toward the viewer. Those polygons on the far side of the sphere—facing away from the viewer—are never rendered. If the viewer is looking at the *back* of a *face* (i.e., polygon), it is *culled* from the rendering; hence the term "backface culling."

The quads in Unity are composed of only two triangular polygons that form a square, and both face in the same direction. When viewing a quad from behind in Unity, both of these polygons are usually culled, and the quad is not rendered.

There are some shaders in Unity that do not use backface culling, including the ProtoTools UnlitAlpha shader used in this chapter and Chapter 31, "Space SHMUP Plus."

---

6. Right-click *PrefabLetter* in the Hierarchy and choose *3D Object > 3D Text* from the pop-up menu. This creates a *New Text* GameObject as a child of PrefabLetter.

7. Change the name of the *New Text* child GameObject to *3D Text* (with a space after "3D").

8. Select *3D Text* in the Hierarchy and give it the settings in Figure 34.3. If the W doesn't line up in the center of the box, you might have accidentally typed a tab in the *Text* box after the W (as I did when writing this).

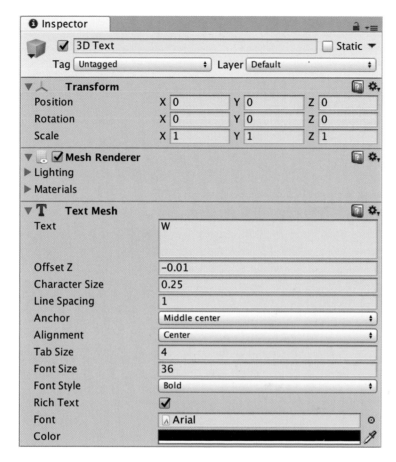

Figure 34.3 The Inspector settings for 3D Text, a child of PrefabLetter

9. Drag PrefabLetter from the Hierarchy into the _Prefabs folder in the Project pane and delete the remaining PrefabLetter instance from the Hierarchy. Save your scene.

The Letter C# Script

Now you will give PrefabLetter its own C# script to handle setting the character it shows, its color, and various other things.

1. Create a new C# script named *Letter*, place it in the __Scripts folder, and attach it to PrefabLetter.

2. Open the Letter script in MonoDevelop and enter the following code:

```
using System.Collections;
using System.Collections.Generic;
using UnityEngine;
```

```
public class Letter : MonoBehaviour {
    [Header("Set Dynamically")]
    public TextMesh        tMesh; // The TextMesh shows the char
    public Renderer        tRend; // The Renderer of 3D Text. This will
                                  //  determine whether the char is visible
    public bool            big = false; // Big letters act a little differently

    private char           _c;    // The char shown on this Letter
    private Renderer       rend;

    void Awake() {
        tMesh = GetComponentInChildren<TextMesh>();
        tRend = tMesh.GetComponent<Renderer>();
        rend = GetComponent<Renderer>();
        visible = false;
    }

    // Property to get or set _c and the letter shown by 3D Text
    public char c {
        get { return( _c ); }
        set {
            _c = value;
            tMesh.text = _c.ToString();
        }
    }

    // Gets or sets _c as a string
    public string str {
        get { return( _c.ToString() ); }
        set { c = value[0]; }
    }

    // Enables or disables the renderer for 3D Text, which causes the char to be
    // visible or invisible respectively.
    public bool visible {
        get { return( tRend.enabled ); }
        set { tRend.enabled = value; }
    }

    // Gets or sets the color of the rounded rectangle
    public Color color {
        get { return(rend.material.color); }
        set { rend.material.color = value; }
    }

    // Sets the position of the Letter's gameObject
    public Vector3 pos {
        set {
```

```
                transform.position = value;
                // More will be added her later
            }
        }
}
```

This class makes use of several properties (faux fields with get{} and set{} accessors) to perform various actions when variables are set. This enables, for instance, WordGame to set the char c of a Letter without worrying about how that gets converted to a string and then shown by *3D Text*. This kind of encapsulation of functionality within a class is central to object-oriented programming. You'll notice that if the get{} or set{} clause is just one statement, I'll often collapse it to a single line.

The Wyrd Class: A Collection of Letters

The Wyrd class will act as a collection of Letters, and its name is spelled with a *y* to differentiate it from the other instances of the word *word* throughout the code and the text of the book. Wyrd is another class that does not extend MonoBehaviour and cannot be attached to a GameObject, but it can still contain Lists of classes that are attached to GameObjects.

1. Create a new C# script named *Wyrd* inside the __Scripts folder.

2. Open *Wyrd* in MonoDevelop and enter the following code:

```
using System.Collections;
using System.Collections.Generic;
using UnityEngine;

public class Wyrd {                          // Wyrd does not extend MonoBehaviour
    public string        str; // A string representation of the word
    public List<Letter>  letters = new List<Letter>();
    public bool          found = false; // True if the player has found this word

    // A property to set visibility of the 3D Text of each Letter
    public bool visible {
        get {
            if (letters.Count == 0) return(false);
            return(letters[0].visible);
        }
        set {
            foreach( Letter l in letters) {
                l.visible = value;
            }
        }
    }

    // A property to set the rounded rectangle color of each Letter
    public Color color {
        get {
```

```
            if (letters.Count == 0) return(Color.black);
            return(letters[0].color);
        }
        set {
            foreach( Letter l in letters) {
                l.color = value;
            }
        }
    }

    // Adds a Letter to letters
    public void Add(Letter l) {
        letters.Add(l);
        str += l.c.ToString();
    }
}
```

The WordGame.Layout() Method

The `Layout()` method will generate Wyrds and Letters for the game as well as big Letters for the player to use to spell each of the words in the level (shown as large gray letters at the bottom of Figure 34.1). You'll start with the small letters, and for this phase of the prototype, you'll make the character of each Letter initially visible (rather than hiding it as you'll do in the final version).

1. Add the following bold code to WordGame:

```
public class WordGame : MonoBehaviour {
    static public WordGame    S; // Singleton

    [Header("Set in Inspector")]
    public GameObject        prefabLetter;
    public Rect              wordArea = new Rect( -24, 19, 48, 28 );
    public float             letterSize = 1.5f;
    public bool              showAllWyrds = true;

    [Header("Set Dynamically")]
    public GameMode          mode = GameMode.preGame;
    public WordLevel         currLevel;
    public List<Wyrd>        wyrds;

    private Transform        letterAnchor, bigLetterAnchor;

    void Awake() {
        S = this; // Assign the singleton
        letterAnchor = new GameObject("LetterAnchor").transform;
        bigLetterAnchor = new GameObject("BigLetterAnchor").transform;
    }

    ...
```

```csharp
public void SubWordSearchComplete() {
    mode = GameMode.levelPrep;
    Layout();  // Call the Layout() function once WordSearch is done
}


void Layout() {
    // Place the letters for each subword of currLevel on screen
    wyrds = new List<Wyrd>();

    // Declare a lot of local variables that will be used in this method
    GameObject  go;
    Letter      lett;
    string      word;
    Vector3     pos;
    float       left = 0;
    float       columnWidth = 3;
    char        c;
    Color       col;
    Wyrd        wyrd;

    // Determine how many rows of Letters will fit on screen
    int numRows = Mathf.RoundToInt(wordArea.height/letterSize);

    // Make a Wyrd of each level.subWord
    for (int i=0; i<currLevel.subWords.Count; i++) {
        wyrd = new Wyrd();
        word = currLevel.subWords[i];

        // if the word is longer than columnWidth, expand it
        columnWidth = Mathf.Max( columnWidth, word.Length );

        // Instantiate a PrefabLetter for each letter of the word
        for (int j=0; j<word.Length; j++) {
            c = word[j];  // Grab the jth char of the word
            go = Instantiate<GameObject>( prefabLetter );
            go.transform.SetParent( letterAnchor );
            lett = go.GetComponent<Letter>();
            lett.c = c;  // Set the c of the Letter

            // Position the Letter
            pos = new Vector3(wordArea.x+left+j*letterSize, wordArea.y, 0);

            // The % here makes multiple columns line up
            pos.y -= (i%numRows)*letterSize;

            lett.pos = pos;    // You'll add more code around this line later

            go.transform.localScale = Vector3.one*letterSize;

            wyrd.Add(lett);
        }
```

```
        if (showAllWyrds) wyrd.visible = true;

        wyrds.Add(wyrd);

        // If we've gotten to the numRows(th) row, start a new column
        if ( i%numRows == numRows-1 ) {
            left += ( columnWidth + 0.5f ) * letterSize;
        }
      }
    }
}
```

2. Before clicking *Play*, you need to assign the *PrefabLetter* prefab from the Project pane to the `prefabLetter` field of the *WordGame (Script)* component of _MainCamera. After doing so, click *Play*, and you should see a list of words pop up on screen, as shown in Figure 34.4.[3]

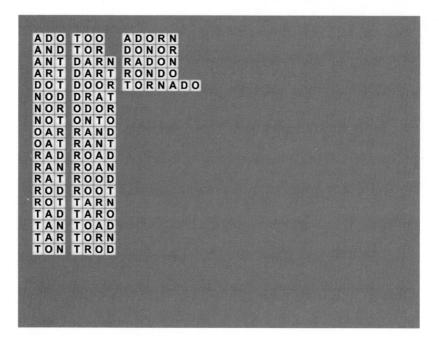

Figure 34.4 An example of the current state of the game: the level for the word *TORNADO*

Adding the Big Letters at the Bottom

The next step in `Layout()` is to place the large letters at the bottom of the screen.

1. Add the following code to do so:

```
public class WordGame : MonoBehaviour {
    static public WordGame    S; // Singleton
```

---

3. When you save these scripts and return to Unity, you will see two yellow warnings about unused variables (col and bigLetterAnchor) in your scripts. Don't worry about these; we'll use them soon.

```
[Header("Set in Inspector")]
…
public bool              showAllWyrds = true;
public float             bigLetterSize = 4f;
public Color             bigColorDim = new Color( 0.8f, 0.8f, 0.8f );
public Color             bigColorSelected = new Color( 1f, 0.9f, 0.7f );
public Vector3           bigLetterCenter = new Vector3( 0, -16, 0 );

[Header("Set Dynamically")]
…
public List<Wyrd>        wyrds;
public List<Letter>      bigLetters;
public List<Letter>      bigLettersActive;

…

void Layout() {
    …

    // Make a Wyrd of each level.subWord
    for (int i=0; i<currLevel.subWords.Count; i++) {

        …
    }

    // Place the big letters
    // Initialize the List<>s for big Letters
    bigLetters = new List<Letter>();
    bigLettersActive = new List<Letter>();

    // Create a big Letter for each letter in the target word
    for (int i=0; i<currLevel.word.Length; i++) {
        // This is similar to the process for a normal Letter
        c = currLevel.word[i];
        go = Instantiate<GameObject>( prefabLetter );
        go.transform.SetParent( bigLetterAnchor );
        lett = go.GetComponent<Letter>();
        lett.c = c;
        go.transform.localScale = Vector3.one*bigLetterSize;

        // Set the initial position of the big Letters below screen
        pos = new Vector3( 0, -100, 0 );
        lett.pos = pos;          // You'll add more code around this line later

        col = bigColorDim;
        lett.color = col;
        lett.visible = true; // This is always true for big letters
        lett.big = true;
        bigLetters.Add(lett);
    }
    // Shuffle the big letters
    bigLetters = ShuffleLetters(bigLetters);
```

```csharp
    // Arrange them on screen
    ArrangeBigLetters();

    // Set the mode to be in-game
    mode = GameMode.inLevel;
}

// This method shuffles a List<Letter> randomly and returns the result
List<Letter> ShuffleLetters(List<Letter> letts) {
    List<Letter> newL = new List<Letter>();
    int ndx;
    while(letts.Count > 0) {
        ndx = Random.Range(0,letts.Count);
        newL.Add(letts[ndx]);
        letts.RemoveAt(ndx);
    }
    return(newL);
}

// This method arranges the big Letters on screen
void ArrangeBigLetters() {
    // The halfWidth allows the big Letters to be centered
    float halfWidth = ( (float) bigLetters.Count )/2f - 0.5f;
    Vector3 pos;
    for (int i=0; i<bigLetters.Count; i++) {
        pos = bigLetterCenter;
        pos.x += (i-halfWidth)*bigLetterSize;
        bigLetters[i].pos = pos;
    }
    // bigLettersActive
    halfWidth = ( (float) bigLettersActive.Count )/2f - 0.5f;
    for (int i=0; i<bigLettersActive.Count; i++) {
        pos = bigLetterCenter;
        pos.x += (i-halfWidth)*bigLetterSize;
        pos.y += bigLetterSize*1.25f;
        bigLettersActive[i].pos = pos;
    }
}
}
```

2. Now, in addition to the Letters up top, you should also see big Letters below, the shuffled form of the goal word. It's time to add some interactivity.

Adding Interactivity

For this game, you want the player to be able to type words from the available big Letters on her keyboard and press Return/Enter to submit them. She can also press Backspace/Delete to remove a letter from the end of what she has typed and press the space bar to shuffle the remaining unselected letters.

When she presses Enter, the word she typed is compared with the possible words in the Word-Level. If the word she typed is in the WordLevel, she gets a point for each letter in the word. In addition, if the word she typed contains any smaller words that are also in the WordLevel, she also gets points for those plus a multiplier for each word. Looking at the TORNADO example earlier, if a player typed TORNADO as her first word and pressed Return, she would get 36 total points as follows:

TORNADO	7 x 1 points	1 point per letter x 1 for first word = 7 points
TORN	4 x 2 points	1 point per letter x 2 for second word = 8 points
TOR	3 x 3 points	1 point per letter x 3 for third word = 9 points
ADO	+ 3 x 4 points	1 point per letter x 4 for fourth word = 12 points
	36 total points	

All of this interactivity will be handled in WordGame by an `Update()` function and will be based on `Input.inputString`, a string of all the keyboard input that occurred this frame.

1. Add the following `Update()` method and supporting methods to WordGame:

```
public class WordGame : MonoBehaviour {
    …

    [Header("Set Dynamically")]
    …
    public List<Letter>        bigLettersActive;
    public string              testWord;
    private string             upperCase = "ABCDEFGHIJKLMNOPQRSTUVWXYZ";

    …

    void ArrangeBigLetters() { … }

    void Update() {
        // Declare a couple useful local variables
        Letter ltr;
        char c;

        switch (mode) {
            case GameMode.inLevel:
                // Iterate through each char input by the player this frame
                foreach (char cIt in Input.inputString) {
                    // Shift cIt to UPPERCASE
                    c = System.Char.ToUpperInvariant(cIt);

                    // Check to see if it's an uppercase letter
                    if (upperCase.Contains(c)) { // Any uppercase letter
                        // Find an available Letter in bigLetters with this char
                        ltr = FindNextLetterByChar(c);
```

```
                                // If a Letter was returned
                                if (ltr != null) {
                                    // ... then add this char to the testWord and move
                                    //  the returned big Letter to bigLettersActive
                                    testWord += c.ToString();
                                    // Move it from the inactive to the active List<>
                                    bigLettersActive.Add(ltr);
                                    bigLetters.Remove(ltr);
                                    ltr.color = bigColorSelected; // Make it look active
                                    ArrangeBigLetters();     // Rearrange the big Letters
                                }
                            }

                            if (c == '\b') { // Backspace
                                // Remove the last Letter in bigLettersActive
                                if (bigLettersActive.Count == 0) return;
                                if (testWord.Length > 1) {
                                    // Clear the last char of testWord
                                    testWord = testWord.Substring(0,testWord.Length-1);
                                } else {
                                    testWord = "";
                                }

                                ltr = bigLettersActive[bigLettersActive.Count-1];
                                // Move it from the active to the inactive List<>
                                bigLettersActive.Remove(ltr);
                                bigLetters.Add (ltr);
                                ltr.color = bigColorDim;    // Make it the inactive color
                                ArrangeBigLetters();        // Rearrange the big Letters
                            }

                            if (c == '\n' || c == '\r') { // Return/Enter macOS/Windows
                                // Test the testWord against the words in WordLevel
                                CheckWord();
                            }

                            if (c == ' ') { // Space
                                // Shuffle the bigLetters
                                bigLetters = ShuffleLetters(bigLetters);
                                ArrangeBigLetters();
                            }
                        }
                        break;
                }
            }

            // This finds an available Letter with the char c in bigLetters.
            // If there isn't one available, it returns null.
            Letter FindNextLetterByChar(char c) {
                // Search through each Letter in bigLetters
```

```csharp
    foreach (Letter ltr in bigLetters) {
        // If one has the same char as c
        if (ltr.c == c) {
            // ...then return it
            return(ltr);
        }
    }
    return( null );  // Otherwise, return null
}


public void CheckWord() {
    // Test testWord against the level.subWords
    string subWord;
    bool foundTestWord = false;

    // Create a List<int> to hold the indices of other subWords that are
    //  contained within testWord
    List<int> containedWords = new List<int>();

    // Iterate through each word in currLevel.subWords
    for (int i=0; i<currLevel.subWords.Count; i++) {

        // Check whether the Wyrd has already been found
        if (wyrds[i].found) {                                          // a
            continue;
        }

        subWord = currLevel.subWords[i];
        // Check whether this subWord is the testWord or is contained in it
        if (string.Equals(testWord, subWord)) {                        // b
            HighlightWyrd(i);
            foundTestWord = true;
        } else if (testWord.Contains(subWord)) {
            containedWords.Add(i);
        }
    }

    if (foundTestWord) { // If the test word was found in subWords
        // ...then highlight the other words contained in testWord
        int numContained = containedWords.Count;
        int ndx;
        // Highlight the words in reverse order
        for (int i=0; i<containedWords.Count; i++) {
            ndx = numContained-i-1;
            HighlightWyrd( containedWords[ndx] );
        }
    }
```

```
            // Clear the active big Letters regardless of whether testWord was valid
            ClearBigLettersActive();
        }


        // Highlight a Wyrd
        void HighlightWyrd(int ndx) {
            // Activate the subWord
            wyrds[ndx].found = true;    // Let it know it's been found
            // Lighten its color
            wyrds[ndx].color = (wyrds[ndx].color+Color.white)/2f;
            wyrds[ndx].visible = true; // Make its 3D Text visible
        }


        // Remove all the Letters from bigLettersActive
        void ClearBigLettersActive() {
            testWord = "";                  // Clear the testWord
            foreach (Letter ltr in bigLettersActive) {
                bigLetters.Add(ltr);      // Add each Letter to bigLetters
                ltr.color = bigColorDim; // Set it to the inactive color
            }
            bigLettersActive.Clear();  // Clear the List<>
            ArrangeBigLetters();       // Rearrange the Letters on screen
        }
    }
```

a. If the ith Wyrd on screen has already been found then continue and skip the rest of this iteration. This works because the Wyrds on screen and the words in the `subWords` List are in the same order.

b. Check whether this `subWord` is the `testWord`, and if so then highlight the `subWord`. If it's not the `testWord`, check to see whether `testWord` contains this `subWord` (e.g., SAND contains AND), and if so, then add it to the `containedWords` List.

2. Save the *WordGame* script and return to Unity.

3. Set `showAllWyrds` to false in the Inspector for the *WordGame (Script)* component of _MainCamera, and then click *Play*.

A working version of the game and a random level should appear. You can play the game using the keyboard as described earlier.

Adding Scoring

Because of the Scoreboard and FloatingScore classes that you wrote in previous chapters and imported into this project, adding scoring to this game should be very easy.

1. Create a Canvas for the UI Text fields to use by choosing *GameObject > UI > Canvas* from the menu bar.

2. Drag *Scoreboard* from the _Prefab folder in the Project pane onto Canvas in the Hierarchy pane, making Scoreboard a child of Canvas.

3. Double-check that the `prefabFloatingScore` field of the *Scoreboard (Script)* component of the Scoreboard GameObject is set to the PrefabFloatingScore prefab from the _Prefabs folder. (If you want to learn more about how the Scoreboard works, refer to Chapter 32, "Prototype 4: *Prospector Solitaire*.")

4. Create a new script named *ScoreManager* in the __Scripts folder and attach it to Scoreboard.

5. Open *ScoreManager* in MonoDevelop and enter the following code:

```
using System.Collections;
using System.Collections.Generic;
using UnityEngine;
using UnityEngine.UI;

public class ScoreManager : MonoBehaviour {
    static private ScoreManager S;  // Another private Singleton

    [Header("Set in Inspector")]
    public List<float>    scoreFontSizes = new List<float> { 36, 64, 64, 1 };
    public Vector3        scoreMidPoint = new Vector3( 1, 1, 0 );
    public float          scoreTravelTime = 3f;
    public float          scoreComboDelay = 0.5f;

    private RectTransform    rectTrans;

    void Awake() {
        S = this;
        rectTrans = GetComponent<RectTransform>();
    }

    // This method allows ScoreManager.SCORE() to be called from anywhere
    static public void SCORE(Wyrd wyrd, int combo) {
        S.Score(wyrd, combo);
    }

    // Add to the score for this word
    // int combo is the number of this word in a combo
    void Score(Wyrd wyrd, int combo) {
        // Create a List<> of Vector2 Bezier points for the FloatingScore.
        List<Vector2> pts = new List<Vector2>();

        // Get the position of the first Letter in the wyrd
        Vector3 pt = wyrd.letters[0].transform.position;         // a
        pt = Camera.main.WorldToViewportPoint(pt);

        pts.Add(pt); // Make pt the first Bezier point               // b
```

```
    // Add a second Bezier point
    pts.Add( scoreMidPoint );

    // Make the Scoreboard the last Bezier point
    pts.Add(rectTrans.anchorMax);

    // Set the value of the Floating Score
    int value = wyrd.letters.Count * combo;
    FloatingScore fs = Scoreboard.S.CreateFloatingScore(value, pts);

    fs.timeDuration = scoreTravelTime;
    fs.timeStart = Time.time + combo * scoreComboDelay;
    fs.fontSizes = scoreFontSizes;

    // Double the InOut Easing effect
    fs.easingCurve = Easing.InOut+Easing.InOut;

    // Make the text of the FloatingScore something like "3 x 2"
    string txt = wyrd.letters.Count.ToString();
    if (combo > 1) {
        txt += " x "+combo;
    }
    fs.GetComponent<Text>().text = txt;
    }

}
```

a. You want the starting position of the FloatingScore to be directly over the wyrd. First, you get the 3D, world coordinates location of the 0th letter of the wyrd. On the next line, you use the _MainCamera to convert it from 3D world coordinates to a *Viewport-Point*. ViewportPoints range from 0 to 1 in X and Y coordinates and indicate where the point is relative to the width and height of the screen and are used for UI coordinates.

b. When the Vector3 `pt` is added to the List<Vector2> `pts`, the Z coordinate is dropped.

6. Save the *ScoreManager* script.

7. Open the *WordGame* script and add scoring code to the `CheckWord()` by making the following bolded edits:

```
public class WordGame : MonoBehaviour {
    ...

    public void CheckWord() {
        ...
        for (int i=0; i<currLevel.subWords.Count; i++) {
            ...
            // Check whether this subWord is the testWord or is contained in it
            if (string.Equals(testWord, subWord)) {
                HighlightWyrd(i);
                ScoreManager.SCORE( wyrds[i], 1 ); // Score the testWord      // a
```

```
            foundTestWord = true;
        } else if (testWord.Contains(subWord)) {
            …
        }
    }

    if (foundTestWord) { // If the test word was found in subWords
        …
        for (int i=0; i<containedWords.Count; i++) {
            ndx = numContained-i-1;
            HighlightWyrd( containedWords[ndx] );
            ScoreManager.SCORE( wyrds[ containedWords[ndx] ], i+2 );      // b
        }
    }
    …
}

…
}
```

a. This line calls the `ScoreManager.SCORE()` static method to score the `testWord`
   that the player spelled.

b. Here, `ScoreManager.SCORE()` is called to score any smaller words contained within
   the `testWord`. The second parameter (`i+2`) is the number of this word in the combo.

8. Save the *WordGame* script, return to Unity, and click *Play*.

You should now get a score for each correct word you enter, and you get a multiplier for each
additional valid word contained in the word you type. However, the white scores are a bit difficult to see over the white Letter tiles. You'll fix this a little later when you add more color to the
game.

Adding Animation to Letters

In a similar manner to scoring, you can easily add smooth animation of Letters by taking advantage of the interpolation functions that you imported in the Utils script.

1. Add the following code to the *Letter* C# script:

```
public class Letter : MonoBehaviour {
    [Header("Set in Inspector")]
    public float              timeDuration = 0.5f;
    public string             easingCuve = Easing.InOut; // Easing from Utils.cs

    [Header("Set Dynamically")]
    public TextMesh       tMesh; // The TextMesh shows the char
    public Renderer       tRend; // The Renderer of 3D Text. This will
                               //   determine whether the char is visible
```

```
public bool              big = false; // Big letters act a little differently
// Linear interpolation fields
public List<Vector3>     pts = null;
public float             timeStart = -1;

private char             _c;      // The char shown on this Letter
...

// Sets the position of the Letter's gameObject
// Now sets up a Bezier curve to move to the new position
public Vector3 pos {
    set {
        // transform.position = value; // This line is now commented out

        // Find a midpoint that is a random distance from the actual
        //  midpoint between the current position and the value passed in
        Vector3 mid = (transform.position + value)/2f;

        // The random distance will be within 1/4 of the magnitude of the
        //  line from the actual midpoint
        float mag = (transform.position - value).magnitude;
        mid += Random.insideUnitSphere * mag*0.25f;

        // Create a List<Vector3> of Bezier points
        pts = new List<Vector3>() { transform.position, mid, value };

        // If timeStart is at the default -1, then set it
        if (timeStart == -1 ) timeStart = Time.time;
    }
}

// Moves immediately to the new position
public Vector3 posImmediate {                                           // a
    set {
        transform.position = value;
    }
}

// Interpolation code
void Update() {
    if (timeStart == -1) return;

    // Standard linear interpolation code
    float u = (Time.time-timeStart)/timeDuration;
    u = Mathf.Clamp01(u);
    float u1 = Easing.Ease(u,easingCuve);
    Vector3 v = Utils.Bezier(u1, pts);
    transform.position = v;
```

```
            // If the interpolation is done, set timeStart back to -1
            if (u == 1) timeStart = -1;
        }

    }
```

    a. Because setting `pos` now creates an interpolation to the new position, `posImmediate` was added to allow us to jump this Letter immediately to another position.

2. Save the Letter script, return to Unity, and click *Play*.

You'll now see the Letters all interpolate to their new positions. However, it looks a little strange for all the Letters to move at the same time and start from the center of the screen.

3. Let's add some small changes to the `WordGame.Layout()` method to improve this:

```
public class WordGame : MonoBehaviour {
    ...

    void Layout() {
        ...
        for (int i=0; i<currLevel.subWords.Count; i++) {
            ...
            // Instantiate a PrefabLetter for each letter of the word
            for (int j=0; j<word.Length; j++) {
                ...
                // The % here makes multiple columns line up
                pos.y -= (i%numRows)*letterSize;

                // Move the lett immediately to a position above the screen
                lett.posImmediate = pos+Vector3.up*(20+i%numRows);
                // Then set the pos for it to interpolate to
                lett.pos = pos;     // You'll add more code around this line later
                // Increment lett.timeStart to move wyrds at different times
                lett.timeStart = Time.time + i*0.05f;

                go.transform.localScale = Vector3.one*letterSize;
                wyrd.Add(lett);
            }
            ...
        }
        ...
        // Create a big Letter for each letter in the target word
        for (int i=0; i<currLevel.word.Length; i++) {
            ...
            // Set the initial position of the big Letters below screen
            pos = new Vector3( 0, -100, 0 );

            lett.posImmediate = pos;
            lett.pos = pos;         // You'll add more code around this line later
```

```
            // Increment lett.timeStart to have big Letters come in last
            lett.timeStart = Time.time + currLevel.subWords.Count*0.05f;
            lett.easingCuve = Easing.Sin+"-0.18"; // Bouncy easing

            col = bigColorDim;
            ...
        }
        ...
    }

    ...
}
```

4. Save the *WordGame* script, return to Unity, and click *Play*.

The game should now lay out with nice smooth, progressive motions.

Adding Color

Now that the game moves well, it's time to add a little color:

1. Add the following bold code to *WordGame* to color the Wyrds based on their length:

```
public class WordGame : MonoBehaviour {
    static public WordGame    S; // Singleton

    [Header("Set in Inspector")]
    ...
    public Vector3          bigLetterCenter = new Vector3( 0, -16, 0 );
    public Color[]          wyrdPalette;

    [Header("Set Dynamically")]
    ...

    void Layout() {
        ...
        // Make a Wyrd of each level.subWord
        for (int i=0; i<currLevel.subWords.Count; i++) {
            ...
            // Instantiate a PrefabLetter for each letter of the word
            for (int j=0; j<word.Length; j++) {
                ...
            }

            if (showAllWyrds) wyrd.visible = true;

            // Color the wyrd based on length
            wyrd.color = wyrdPalette[ word.Length - WordList.WORD_LENGTH_MIN ];
```

```
        wyrds.Add(wyrd);

        ...
    }
    ...
}
    ...
}
```

These last few code changes have been so simple because you already had supporting code in place (e.g., the `Wyrd.color` and `Letter.color` properties as well as the Easing code in the Utils class).

Now, you need to set about eight colors for `wyrdPalette`. To do this, use the *Color Palette* image included in the import at the beginning of the project. You're going use the eye dropper to set color, which might leave you wondering how to see both the Color Palette image and the _MainCamera Inspector at the same time. To do that, you'll take advantage of Unity's capability to have more than one Inspector window open at the same time.

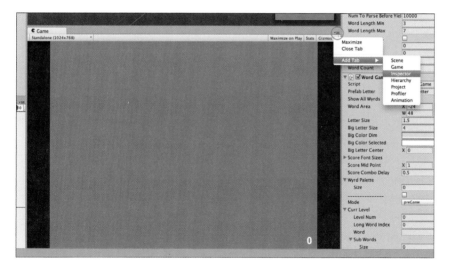

Figure 34.5 Using the pane options button to add an Inspector to the Game pane

2. As shown in Figure 34.5, click the pane options button (circled in red) and choose *Add Tab > Inspector* to add an Inspector to the Game tab.

3. Select the *Color Palette* image in the *Materials & Textures* folder of the Project pane. It now appears in both Inspectors. (You might need to drag up the edge of the image preview part of the Inspector to make it look like Figure 34.6.)

4. Click the lock icon on one inspector (circled in red in the Figure 34.6).

5. Select _*MainCamera* in the Hierarchy pane. Only the unlocked Inspector changes to _Main-Camera, while the locked one still shows the Color Palette image.

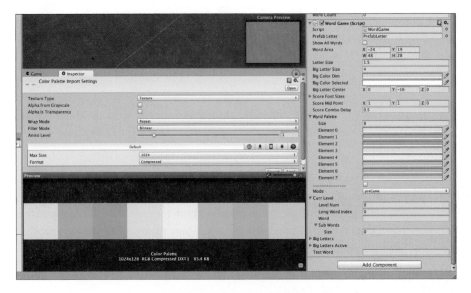

Figure 34.6 The lock icon on one Inspector (circled in red) and the eye dropper in the other Inspector (circled in light blue)

6. Expand the disclosure triangle next to `wyrdPalette` in the _MainCamera Inspector and set its *Size* to 8.

7. Click the *eye dropper* next to each `wyrdPalette` element (circled in light blue), and then click one of the colors in the Color Palette image. Doing this gives you the eight different colors of the Color Palette image, but they will all default to having an alpha of 0 (and therefore being invisible). You can tell the alpha is 0 by the black bar beneath each color in `wyrdPalette`.

8. Click each color bar in the `wyrdPalette` array and set each one's alpha (or A) to 255 to make it fully opaque. When you have done this, the bar beneath each color in the `wyrdPalette` will change from black to white.

9. As always, save your scene.

Now when you play the scene, you should see something that looks like the screenshot from the beginning of the chapter.

Summary

In this chapter, you created a simple word game and added a little flair to it with some nice interpolated movement. If you've been following these tutorials in order, you might have realized that the process of making them is getting a little bit easier. With the expanded understanding of Unity that you now have and the capabilities of readymade utility scripts like Scoreboard, FloatingScore, and Utils, you can focus more of the coding effort on the things that are new and different in each game and less on reinventing the wheel.

Next Steps

In the previous prototypes, you saw examples of how to set up a series of game states to handle the different phases of the game and transition from one level to the next. Right now, this prototype doesn't have any of that. On your own, you should add that kind of control structure to this game.

Here are some things to think about as you do so:

■ When should the player be able to move on to the next level? Must she guess every single word, or can she move on when she has either reached a specific point total or has guessed the target word?

■ How will you handle levels? Will you just pick a completely random word—as you are now—or will you modify the randomness to make sure that level 5 is always the same word (therefore making it fair for players to compare their scores on level 5)? Here's a hint if you decide to try for a modified randomness:

```
using UnityEngine;
using System.Collections;

public class LevelPicker : MonoBehaviour {
    static private System.Random   rng;

    [Header("Set in Inspector")]
    public int      randomSeed = 12345;

    void Awake() {
        rng = new System.Random(randomSeed);
    }

    static public int Next(int max=-1) {
        // Returns the next number from rng between 0 and max-1.
        // If -1 is passed in, max is ignored
        if (max == -1) {
            return rng.Next();
        } else {
            return rng.Next( max );
        }
    }

}
```

- How do you want to handle levels with too many or too few subWords? Some collections of seven letters have so many words that they extend off the screen to the right, whereas others have so few that there's only one column. Do you want to make the game skip the level in either case? If so, how do you then instruct something like the `PickNthRandom` function to skip certain numbers?

You should have enough knowledge of programming and prototyping now that you can take these questions and make this into a real game. You have the skills, now go for it!

CHAPTER 35

PROTOTYPE 7: *DUNGEON DELVER*

The *Dungeon Delver* game that you create in this chapter is a partial clone of the original *Legend of Zelda* game for the Nintendo Entertainment System. In my classes, I have found that recreating old games can really help designers to learn them, and *The Legend Of Zelda* has always been one of the best games to clone in this way.

This is the last prototype of the book and therefore the most complex. However, this prototype also uses stronger component-based design than many of the others, so individual scripts are going to be shorter. When you're done with this chapter, you'll have a nice skeleton for an action-adventure game that you can expand yourself.

Dungeon Delver—Game Overview

This chapter is considerably longer than most of the others, but it's also making a larger game. This is the only prototype that is completely new for the second edition of the book. It is an action-adventure game strongly based on *The Legend of Zelda* for the Nintendo Entertainment System. The game follows an adventurer named Dray as they explore a dungeon, fight Skeletos, and find a Grappler (grappling hook).[1]

Figure 35.1 shows what Dungeon Delver will look like at the end of this chapter. *Dungeon Delver* starts with a clone of the first dungeon encountered in *The Legend of Zelda* for the NES. Part way through the chapter, we will switch to a second dungeon (the one featured in Chapter 9, "Paper Prototyping"). After you're finished with the chapter, check Chapter 35 on the website for this book to find a level editor for this game and instructions on how to make your own dungeons.

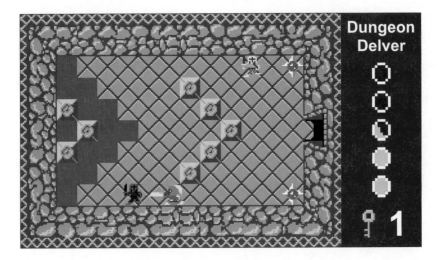

Figure 35.1 An example of what *Dungeon Delver* will look like

Component-Based Design

For this prototype, we'll attempt to work with *component-based design* as much as possible (see Chapter 27, "Object-Oriented Thinking"). To do this properly, you need to think ahead a bit about how you want the game to work. *The Legend of Zelda* and most other games of the time were tile-based, meaning that their maps were constructed of a limited number of tiles that were repeated several times throughout the stage. In Figure 35.2, you can see the set of tiles you'll use on the left and part of a map made from those tiles on the right.

---

1. Throughout this chapter, I'll use *they, them, their* pronouns to refer to Dray. Everyone deserves to be represented in game development and in this book.

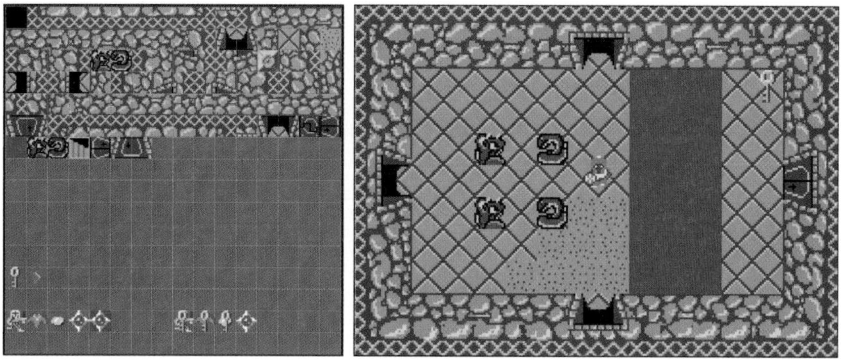

Figure 35.2 An atlas of tiles on the left and a room made from them on the right. A grid has been laid over the left image to help you see the edges of the tiles more clearly.

Unity does not have a built-in tile engine, so we'll have to make one. This means that we'll need both a prefab for the tiles and a script on the camera to arrange those tiles. Because we're trying to think in a more object-oriented way, we should have the script on each tile (Tile.cs) handle as much work as possible, with the camera script (TileCamera.cs) merely assigning a location to each tile. Here is the planned division of labor:

1. **TileCamera.cs**
   - **Position self**—The camera starts at the entrance to the dungeon and follows the player (Dray) into other rooms as they move into them.
   - **Read map data**—TileCamera reads the DelverData map file, the DelverCollisions collision information, and the DelverTiles Texture2D that contains all tiles Sprites.
   - **Assign locations to Tiles**—TileCamera instantiates Tile GameObjects and assigns them a position on the map.
2. **Tile.cs**—All of these require that TileCamera has assigned a location to this Tile.
   - **Position self**—The Tile should position itself at the location it has been assigned.
   - **Show proper tile sprite**—The Tile should look in the DelverData MAP data that the TileCamera manages to find which tile sprite it should display.
   - **Manage BoxCollider**—The Tile should look at the DelverCollisions data managed by TileCamera and set its BoxCollider appropriately.

Getting Started: Prototype 7

The unitypackage for this project includes a number of assets, materials, and scripts. Because you already have experience with building objects and slicing sprites in Unity, I do not ask you to do those things in this chapter. Instead, you import a series of prefabs to serve as the artwork in this game.

SET UP THE PROJECT FOR THIS CHAPTER

Following the standard project setup procedure, create a new project in Unity. If you need a refresher on the standard project setup procedure, see Appendix A, "Standard Project Setup Procedure." When you create the project, you are asked whether you want to set up defaults for 2D or 3D. Choose 2D for this project.

- **Project name:** Dungeon Delver

- **Download and import package:** Find Chapter 35 at http://book.prototools.net.

- **Scene name:** _Scene_Eagle (this scene will have a dungeon layout identical to that of the Eagle dungeon in *The Legend of Zelda*).

- **Project folders:** These are all imported from the unitypackage.

- **C# script names:** None other than the imported scripts.

The __Scripts folder in the unitypackage includes a Spiker.cs script with most of the code commented out. After you've finished the chapter, you can uncomment that code and attach the Spiker script to the Spiker prefab.

All images of characters, tiles, items, and so on in this chapter were created by my fantastic colleague and friend Andrew Dennis, who teaches art and animation at Michigan State University.[2]

Setting Up the Cameras

This is the first project where you will use more than one camera. The first, *Main Camera*, will show the actual gameplay, whereas the second, *GUI Camera*, will show the graphical user interface (GUI) for the game. This will allow you to manage each camera independently, which will make your GUI coding much simpler.

Game Pane

Before adjusting the cameras, you should prepare the Game Pane.

From the Aspect Ratio pop-up of the Game pane, choose *1080p (1920x1080)*. If you don't have that option in your Game pane aspect ratios, then do the following:

1. Click the Aspect Ratio pop-up menu at the top of the Game pane (the second pop-up menu from the left) and click the + at the bottom of that menu.

2. In the dialog box that appears, set:

---

2. Andrew's faculty page is http://gamedev.msu.edu/andrew-dennis/.

- Label to *1080p*
- Type to *Fixed Resolution*
- W to *1920*
- H to *1080*

3. Click *OK* to save this as a preset.

4. Choose *1080p (1920x1080)* from the Aspect Ratio pop-up.

Main Camera

Select *Main Camera* in the Hierarchy. In the Inspector, set the following:

- **Transform**—P:[23.5, 5, -10] R:[0, 0, 0] S:[1, 1, 1]
- **Camera**
  - **Clear Flags:** Solid Color
  - **Background:** Set this to black (RGBA:[0, 0, 0, 255])
  - **Projection:** Orthographic
  - **Size:** 5.5
  - **Viewport Rect:** X:0, Y:0, W:0.8, H:1

GUI Camera

Follow these steps to create a camera named GUI Camera.

1. Create a new camera by choosing *GameObject > Camera*.

2. Rename the Camera to *GUI Camera*.

3. Select GUI Camera in the Hierarchy and set the following in the Inspector:
   - **Tag: Untagged**—This ensures that `Camera.main` still refers to Main Camera.
   - **Transform**—P:[-100, 0, -10] R:[0, 0, 0] S:[1, 1, 1]
   - **Camera**
     - **Clear Flags:** Solid Color
     - **Background:** Set this to gray for now (RGBA:[128, 128, 128, 255])
     - **Projection:** Orthographic
     - **Size:** 5.5
     - **Viewport Rect:** X:0.8, Y:0, W:0.2, H:1
   - **Audio Listener**—You can only have one Audio Listener in a scene, and for this scene, that's Main Camera.
     - Click the gear icon on the right side of the Audio Listener component and select *Remove Component* from the pop-up menu.

These settings will split the Game pane into two smaller panes. The Main Camera will fill most of the screen, and the GUI Camera will fill the right 20%.

Understanding the Dungeon Data

Three files in the Resources folder of the Project pane hold all the information needed to display a dungeon in this game (the file extensions like .png do not appear in the Project pane):

- **DelverTiles.png**—A Texture2D image file that holds all the images that can be used to display a dungeon.

- **DelverCollisions.txt**—A text file that holds collision information for each of the tile sprites in DelverTiles.png. Later I will cover what each of the letters in this file mean.

- **DelverData.txt**—A text file containing the map information about which of the tile sprites from DelverTiles.png to place where.

Preparing DelverTiles

To prepare DelverTiles, follow these steps:

1. Select *DelverTiles* in the Resources folder of the Project pane.

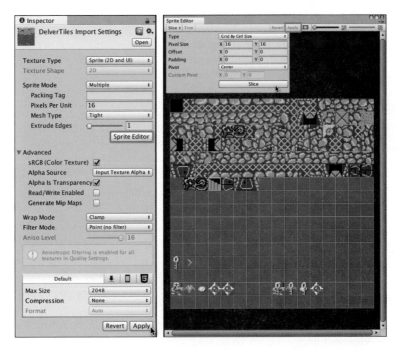

Figure 35.3 Import Settings and Sprite Editor for DelverTiles showing proper settings for both

2. Set the Import Settings in the Inspector to match those shown in Figure 35.3:
   - **Texture Type:** *Sprite (2D and UI)*
   - **Sprite Mode:** *Multiple*

- **Pixels Per Unit:** *16*. This means that in the scene, a sprite 16 pixels wide would appear 1m wide. Because each tile is 16x16, this makes each tile of the map take up 1 square meter (i.e., 1 square Unity unit).

- **Generate Mip Maps:** *False*. MIP maps are a way of speeding up rendering for things that are very far away by storing multiple versions of the image at different resolutions. They are not needed for this project.

- **Wrap Mode:** *Clamp*. If the texture coordinates for a polygon were set to less than 0 or greater than 1, the Clamp mode would cause this image to repeat the edge pixel (rather than tiling by repeating the entire image over and over).

- **Filter Mode:** *Point (no filter)*. This helps you keep the sharp, 8-bit look.

- **Compression** (in the Default tab of the box at the bottom): *None*. Although compression is great and often necessary for large images (and the png files you're importing do an excellent job of lossless compression), Unity's compression is very lossy, especially for small, 8-bit graphics like these.

- Each of the other tabs in this box at the bottom containing the *Compression* setting allow you to create import settings for specific platforms, including *PC, Mac & Linux Standalone*; *WebGL*; and any other platform you've installed (you can also see an *iOS* option in the image). Please check each of these to ensure that the **Override** checkbox under each is unchecked: *False.*

3. Click the *Apply* button (shown under the cursor in Figure 35.3).

4. Click the *Sprite Editor* button surrounded by red in Figure 35.3. This opens the Sprite Editor, which you can see on the right side of Figure 35.3.

5. Click the *Slice* pop-up menu in the top-left corner of the Sprite Editor, and use the following settings:

   - **Type**: *Grid by Cell Size*
   - **Pixel Size**: x:16 y:16

6. Click the *Slice* button (at the bottom of the Slice pop-up menu). This creates multiple sprites from the single image, all of them 16x16 pixels in size. They are numbered starting with 0 in the top-left, continuing to 15 in the top-right corner, and then on to the second row.

7. Click the *Apply* button at the top of the Sprite Editor window and then close the Sprite Editor. In all, 256 sprites will be created—DelverTiles_0 through DelverTiles_255—which you can now see in the Project pane by opening the disclosure triangle next to Resources/DelverTiles.

The DelverData Text File

DelverData stores hexadecimal information about which tile goes where in the dungeon.

In the Project pane, double-click *Resources/DelverData* to open it in MonoDevelop.

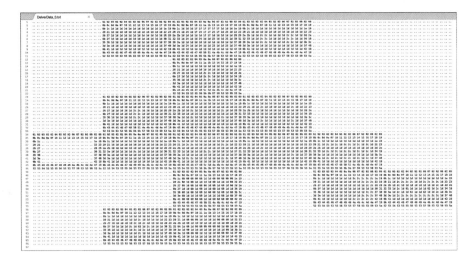

Figure 35.4 DelverData.txt

Figure 35.4 shows the contents of DelverData.txt. As you can see, it's an upside-down version of the Eagle dungeon from *The Legend of Zelda* that was described in Chapter 9, "Paper Prototyping."[3] The image is upside-down because text files are always read top-to-bottom, whereas the Y coordinate of your map will go from bottom-to-top.

This file includes several two-digit *hexadecimal* numbers (see sidebar), separated by spaces. To make it easier to see the dungeon pattern, I've replaced the hexadecimal value "00" with ". ." in this file.

HEXADECIMAL NUMBERS

If you've ever done any web development, you've seen an example of hexadecimal (or *hex*) numbers in the way that web colors are specified (e.g., FF0000 is bright red). The DelverData.txt file uses two-digit hex numbers that can count from 0 to 255 (in decimal).

Just as with your normal decimal numbers, hex numbers have digits in places (e.g., a ones place, a tens place, and so on). In regular decimal numbers, the digits can count from 0 to 9, whereas hexadecimal, the digits can count from 0 to 15. Hexadecimal uses the characters a through f to represent the numbers 10–15 as shown here:

---

3. This version of DelverData does not include any information about bombable walls because that is not necessary for this chapter. However, after this chapter, you could add them yourself. It also doesn't include enemy or item placement, though you'll see how to add those to another dungeon later in the chapter.

Decimal	0	1	2	3	4	5	6	7	8	9	10	11	12	13	14	15	16
Hexadecimal	**0**	**1**	**2**	**3**	**4**	**5**	**6**	**7**	**8**	**9**	**a**	**b**	**c**	**d**	**e**	**f**	**10**

The letters `a-f` can either be upper- or lowercase. I chose lowercase in the DelverData file because I thought it was slightly easier to read. In programming C#, you will see hex values preceded by `0x` to differentiate them from decimal numbers (for clarity in this sidebar, I list hex numbers with `0x` and in the `code font`, and I show decimal numbers in the regular text font).

Just as with decimal numbers, a number in a higher place means that number should be multiplied by 1 more than you can represent with digits. So, `0x10` in hex has a 1 in the *sixteens* place and represents 1*16 + 0*1 (just as 10 in decimal represents 1*10 + 0*1). So, `0x10` in hex is equal to 16 in decimal.

One of the nice things about using hex for tiles in the DelverTiles image is that there are exactly 256 possible tiles in that image and exactly 256 possible numbers in two-digit hex. This also means that the first hex digit is always the row, and the second hex digit is always the column when referencing that image. So, if I wanted to get the number in the map for the red statue facing right, I could count down the number of rows (starting with 0), put that in the *sixteens* place, and then count across the number of columns and put that in the ones place (see Figure 35.5).

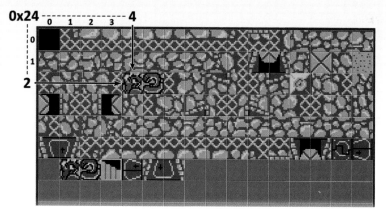

Figure 35.5 Demonstration of finding the number of a tile in DelverTiles

Generating a Map from Data

Now that you have both an image of the tiles and a text file that tells you which tile to put where, you can combine these into an actual map. You will create both the TileCamera and Tile classes, and they are interrelated, so I'll be taking you back and forth between them as you code.

Tile Class—Preparation

Let's start with the Tile class. At its core, the Tile class needs to be able to receive an int from TileCamera telling it which tile to show. This is all you need right now.

1. Create a new Sprite in the Hierarchy (*GameObject > 2D Object > Sprite*). Rename the New Sprite to *Tile*.

2. Create a new C# script in the __Scripts folder named *Tile*.

3. Attach the Tile script to the Tile GameObject in the Hierarchy.

4. Open the Tile script in MonoDevelop and enter this code:

```csharp
using System.Collections;
using System.Collections.Generic;
using UnityEngine;

public class Tile : MonoBehaviour {

    [Header("Set Dynamically")]
    public int              x;
    public int              y;
    public int              tileNum;

    public void SetTile(int eX, int eY, int eTileNum = -1) {          // a
        x = eX;
        y = eY;
        transform.localPosition = new Vector3(x, y, 0);
        gameObject.name = x.ToString("D3")+"x"+y.ToString("D3");      // b

        if (eTileNum == -1) {
            eTileNum = TileCamera.GET_MAP(x,y);                       // c
        }
        tileNum = eTileNum;
        GetComponent<SpriteRenderer>().sprite = TileCamera.SPRITES[tileNum]; // d
    }
}
```

a. This method declaration has a default (optional) parameter for `eTileNum`. If nothing (or a -1) is passed in for `eTileNum`, then the default tile number will be read from `TileCamera.GET_MAP()`.

b. The `ToString("D3")` method of the ints `x` and `y` output a string in a specific format. "D" causes the output to be in decimal (i.e., base-ten) numbers, and "3" forces it to use at least three characters (adding preceding zeroes as needed). So, if x=23 and y=5, then this line would output "023x005". For more information on the various formats, search online for "C# numeric format strings."

c. If -1 is passed into `eTileNum`, the tile number will be read from `TileCamera.MAP`. This text is colored red because you have not yet written the TileCamera class.

d. Once `TileCamera.SPRITES` exists, this will assign the proper sprite to this Tile.

5. Save the *Tile* script and return to Unity. You will see two red errors in the Console because you haven't yet written the TileCamera class.

6. Drag *Tile* from the Hierarchy to the _Prefabs folder in the Project pane to make it a prefab.

7. Delete the Tile instance from the Hierarchy.

That's all you need for now. This allows you to call `SetTile()` from TileCamera, and the Tile will automatically jump to the proper location and set its name.

TileCamera Class—Parsing Data and Sprite Files

The TileCamera class is responsible for parsing and storing all the sprites from the DelverTiles.png image and reading DelverData.txt to determine where to position those tiles. Let's start with reading the two files. It is important for this that both the DelverData and DelverTiles files are in the *Resources* folder of the Project pane. "Resources" is one of Unity's special project folder names. Any file in the Resources folder will be included in a compiled project by Unity, regardless of whether or not it is included in the scene, and files in the Resources folder can be loaded in code using the Resources class that is part of UnityEngine.

1. Create a new C# script named *TileCamera* in the __Scripts folder. You won't be able to attach it to a GameObject now because of the compiler errors that you see in the Console. If you look in Tile.cs now, you can see that `TileCamera` has turned blue, but the static field names after it are red because you have not defined them yet.

2. Open *TileCamera* in MonoDevelop and enter the following code:

```
using System.Collections;
using System.Collections.Generic;
using UnityEngine;

public class TileCamera : MonoBehaviour {
    static private int        W, H;
    static private int[,]     MAP;
    static public Sprite[]    SPRITES;
    static public Transform   TILE_ANCHOR;
    static public Tile[,]     TILES;

    [Header("Set in Inspector")]
    public TextAsset          mapData;
    public Texture2D          mapTiles;
    public TextAsset          mapCollisions; // This will be used later
    public Tile               tilePrefab;

    void Awake() {
        LoadMap();
    }

    public void LoadMap() {
        // Create the TILE_ANCHOR. All Tiles will have this as their parent.
        GameObject go = new GameObject("TILE_ANCHOR");
        TILE_ANCHOR = go.transform;
```

```
        // Load all of the Sprites from mapTiles
        SPRITES = Resources.LoadAll<Sprite>(mapTiles.name);              // a

        // Read in the map data
        string[] lines = mapData.text.Split('\n');                      // b
        H = lines.Length;
        string[] tileNums = lines[0].Split(' ');
        W = tileNums.Length;

        System.Globalization.NumberStyles hexNum;                       // c
        hexNum = System.Globalization.NumberStyles.HexNumber;
        // Place the map data into a 2D Array for faster access
        MAP = new int[W,H];
        for (int j=0; j<H; j++) {
            tileNums = lines[j].Split(' ');
            for (int i=0; i<W; i++) {
                if (tileNums[i] == "..") {
                    MAP[i,j] = 0;
                } else {
                    MAP[i,j] = int.Parse( tileNums[i], hexNum );        // d
                }
            }
        }
        print("Parsed "+SPRITES.Length+" sprites.");                    // e
        print("Map size: "+W+" wide by "+H+" high");
    }

    static public int GET_MAP( int x, int y ) {                         // f
        if ( x<0 || x>=W || y<0 || y>=H ) {
            return -1; // Do not allow IndexOutOfRangeExceptions
        }
        return MAP[x,y];
    }
    static public int GET_MAP( float x, float y ) { // A float GET_MAP() overload
        int tX = Mathf.RoundToInt(x);
        int tY = Mathf.RoundToInt(y - 0.25f);                           // g
        return GET_MAP(tX,tY);
    }

    static public void SET_MAP( int x, int y, int tNum ) {              // f
        // Additional security or a break point could be set here.
        if ( x<0 || x>=W || y<0 || y>=H ) {
            return; // Do not allow IndexOutOfRangeExceptions
        }
        MAP[x,y] = tNum;
    }
}
```

a. Because the `mapTiles` image (DelveTiles.png) is in the Resources folder, you can load all of its sprites using the `Resources.LoadAll<Sprite>()` method.

b. With DelverData.txt assigned to the TextAsset `mapData` field, you can access its text via `mapData.text`. This line splits it on carriage returns '\n', which puts each line of the map into an element of the `lines` string array. The total number of lines is assigned to `H`. Then, the first line is split on spaces ' ', which puts a two-digit hexadecimal code into each element of the `tileNums` array. The number of elements of tileNums is assigned to `W`.

c. To interpret the two-character hexadecimal strings in `tileNums` as hexadecimal numbers, you need the `System.Globalization.NumberStyles.HexNumber` constant to pass into the `int.Parse()` method. This constant requires so many characters to spell that I couldn't fit it on the `// d` line, so I placed it in the `hexNum` variable.

d. The `int.Parse()` method attempts to parse a string into an int. With the NumberStyles `hexNum` second parameter, it knows to look for a hexadecimal number. You can see in the `if` clause that each `tileNums` element is first checked to see whether it is `".."`, which is converted directly to the int `0`.

e. If you place a debug breakpoint on this line before running the game, you can see all the values that get stored in the static fields `MAP` and `SPRITES`.

f. The static public `GET_MAP()` and `SET_MAP()` methods provide protected access to get and set `MAP` while preventing things like IndexOutOfRangeExceptions.

g. The `y - 0.25f` here accounts for the forced perspective in this game where your player character can have the top half of their body outside of a tile and still be considered to be walking on that tile. This is important much later in this chapter when the Grappler needs to determine whether or not it has dropped Dray on an unsafe tile.

3. Save the *TileCamera* script, and switch back to Unity.

4. Now that there are no more compiler errors, attach the *TileCamera* script to Main Camera.

5. Assign the following fields of TileCamera in the Main Camera Inspector:

    ■ **mapData**: Assign *DelverData* from the Resources folder of the Project pane.

    ■ **mapTiles**: Assign *DelverTiles* from the Resources folder of the Project pane.

    ■ **mapCollisions**: Assign *DelverCollisions* from the Resources folder of the Project pane. You'll use mapCollisions later in the chapter.

    ■ **tilePrefab**: Assign Tile from the _Prefabs folder of the Project pane. Because this is of the type Tile instead of GameObject, you must drag it from the Project pane to the slot in the Inspector. Clicking the target next to tilePrefab in the Inspector will not work.

6. Save your scene.

7. Click *Play*, and you should see the following two lines output to the Console:

```
Parsed 256 sprites.
Map size: 96 wide by 66 high
```

Showing the Map

To show the map, you need to code another method.

TileCamera—ShowMap()

In the TileCamera class, we'll create a method that shows the entire map all at once. This is not the most efficient thing that we could do, but it will certainly run quickly enough for your prototype.

1. Add the following bolded code to TileCamera.

```
public class TileCamera : MonoBehaviour {
    …
    public void LoadMap() {
        …
        print("Parsed "+SPRITES.Length+" sprites.");
        print("Map size: "+W+" wide by "+H+" high");

        ShowMap();                                              // a
    }


    /// <summary>
    /// Generates Tiles for the entire map all at once.
    /// </summary>
    void ShowMap() {
        TILES = new Tile[W,H];

        // Run through the entire map and instantiate Tiles where necessary
        for (int j=0; j<H; j++) {
            for (int i=0; i<W; i++) {
                if (MAP[i,j] != 0) {
                    Tile ti = Instantiate<Tile>(tilePrefab);    // b
                    ti.transform.SetParent( TILE_ANCHOR );
                    ti.SetTile(i, j);                           // c
                    TILES[i,j] = ti;
                }
            }
        }
    }

    static public int GET_MAP( int x, int y ) { … }
    …
}
```

a. At the end of `LoadMap()`, `ShowMap()` is called to put the Tiles into the scene.

b. This is a different use of Instantiate than you have seen before. Because all you really need is the Tile instance and not the GameObject that it is attached to, you can instantiate the Tile `tilePrefab` as a Tile and pass that into the local variable `ti`. The containing GameObject is still instantiated in the scene; you just don't need to deal with it in code.

c. `SetTile()` is called on `ti` with just the location (omitting the optional `eTileNum` parameter and causing the tileNum from `TileCamera.MAP` to be used).

2. Save the script, return to Unity, and click *Play*.

In the Scene pane, you can see the entire map for the dungeon is built in a short amount of time. To get a good view of the whole thing, double-click TILE_ANCHOR in the Hierarchy.

The Main Camera should show a single room in the dungeon, as shown in Figure 35.6. (If you don't see this room, then double-check your Main Camera transform.position, which you set earlier in this chapter.)

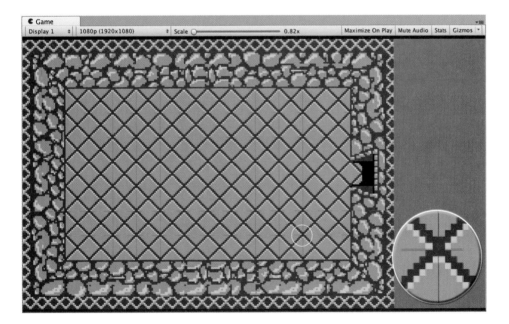

Figure 35.6 The results of adding the ShowMap code with a zoomed area showing anti-aliasing issues

Dealing with Anti-aliasing Issues

By default, Unity uses *anti-aliasing* when it wants to look good (which is nearly always), but this can cause problems when dealing with 8-bit style graphics like those in Dungeon Delver.

Anti-aliasing is a method of oversampled rendering where Unity creates a larger image of the screen in memory and then downsamples it to make graphics appear smoother, with the default setting being *2x Multi Sampling*. 2x Multi Sampling is a method of oversampling where Unity renders an image at double the size of the screen and then shrinks it down to regular size, blending the pixels in the process. This works very well for 3D graphics, but it can make 2D graphics look like the zoomed-in area of Figure 35.6 where the edges of the tiles overlap instead of being perfectly side-by-side. For Dungeon Delver, you should turn off anti-aliasing to get the look you want.

1. From the Unity menu bar, choose *Edit > Project Settings > Quality*. The QualitySettings inspector opens in the Inspector pane.

    By default, you should see that the *Ultra* row is highlighted (in darker gray). You should also see that under the Standalone column (the column for the Standalone build has a downward-pointing arrow atop it), the *Ultra* row has a green checkbox. This means that *Ultra* is the default quality setting for running a Standalone build (you can set the default quality for each build type by clicking the triangle in the Default row for each column).

2. Click the *Ultra* row to ensure that it is selected, and look for the *Anti Aliasing*[4] setting under the *Rendering* heading.

3. Set Anti Aliasing to *Disabled*.

4. Save your scene and try playing again.

You should now no longer see the overlapping tile borders. For more information on QualitySettings, click the box with a question mark in the top corner of the QualitySettings inspector.

Starting with Unity 2017, there is also a way to turn anti-aliasing on or off for individual cameras across all quality settings. Select both *Main Camera* and *GUI Camera* and set the *Allow MSAA* check box option to false. (MSAA stands for MultiSample Anti-Aliasing.)

Adding the Hero

The hero of this game will be Dray, a knight in armor. To mimic the 8-bit technology of the original *Legend of Zelda* game, this hero will be able to face in any of four directions and will have an animation play when they walk. Later, you will also add a lunging pose when they attack with their sword or other weapon.

This is the first time in the book that you will work with sprite animation in Unity. The Unity animation system is meant to allow you to create very complex, multi-layered, 3D animations. This is great, but is not really what you need for a simple game like *Dungeon Delver*. As such, you'll be using the Animator and Animations in slightly non-standard ways.

---

4. Most people spell anti-aliasing with a hyphen, but the Unity setting in the QualitySettings Inspector doesn't.

The Dray Sprite Naming Convention

The Dray sprites require a specific naming convention to allow them to be used in our code:

1. Open the disclosure triangle next to the _Images folder in the Project pane.

2. Open the disclosure triangle next to the *Dray* Texture2D image asset.

In here, you'll see that I have chosen specific sprite names on this image that you imported (I did so using the Sprite Editor in the Import Settings Inspector for the *Dray* image). Look at Figure 35.7 to see these names superimposed over the *Dray* image.

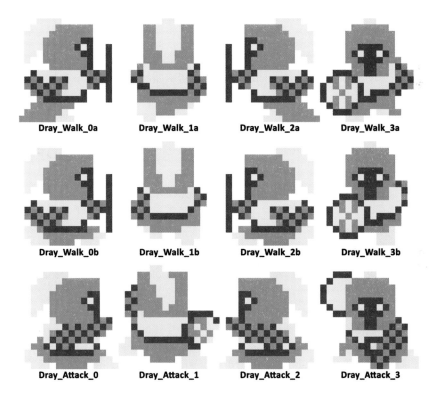

Figure 35.7 The named sprites of the Dray image.

One of the key aspects of how you'll create this game is the numbering convention specified in the sprite naming shown in Figure 35.7. Throughout this project, the number 0 refers to things facing to the right. 1 is up, 2 is left, and 3 is down. I chose this numbering because if you start with an arrow pointing to the right (along the positive X axis) and rotate it 90 degrees around the Z axis, it then points up. Rotating it 180 degrees (or 2 * 90°) points it left, and rotating it 270° (or 3 * 90°) points it down. As you'll see, this pairing of orientation and naming will be used to great effect throughout this game.

Your First Animation

To create your first animation, follow these steps:

1. Create a new folder in the Project pane named *_Animations* (*Assets > Create > Folder*).

2. Select *Dray_Walk_0a* and *Dray_Walk_0b* from the sprites under *Dray* in the *_Images* folder of the Project pane. (To do this, you can click one and then hold Shift and click the other.)

3. Drag them together from the Project pane to the Hierarchy pane and release. A dialog box appears asking you to name this animation.

4. Name it *Dray_Walk_0.anim* and save it into the *_Animations* folder.

    This creates several things:

    ▪ In the _Animations folder of the Project pane:

        ▪ Dray_Walk_0: The Animation that you saved as Dray_Walk_0.anim. This animation includes the two images of Dray walking to the right.

        ▪ Dray_Walk_0a: This is an *Animator*, which stores several different Animations and controls when to show each one.

    ▪ In the Hierarchy:

        ▪ A GameObject named Dray_Walk_0a that has the Dray_Walk_0a Animator attached. This is the main GameObject for your hero that the player will control.

Before anything else, you need to rename two of these things.

5. Select the *Dray_Walk_0a* GameObject in the Hierarchy and rename it *Dray*.

6. Select the *Dray_Walk_0a* Animator in the _Animations folder of the Project pane and rename it *Dray_Animator*.

7. Double-click *Dray_Animator* in the Project pane. The *Animator* pane opens in Unity (the Animator pane is shown on the upper image of Figure 35.8). If the Animator pane does not appear as a second tab in the same area of the screen as the Scene pane, then click the tab at the top of the Animator pane and drag and release it just to the right of the Scene pane tab.

8. If your Animator pane is too small to see what's going on (as mine is in Figure 35.8), click the open eye button (under the cursor in Figure 35.8) to hide a part of the Animator that you will not be using. You can hold Option/Alt on your keyboard while clicking and dragging on the background of the Animator to move the view around.

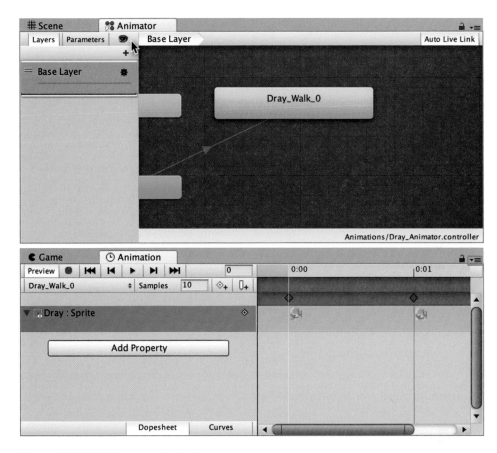

Figure 35.8 The Animator and Animation panes

9. Select *Dray* in the Hierarchy and set the transform position to P:[23.5, 5, 0]. This centers Dray in the Main Camera view of the Game pane.

10. Click the Unity *Play* button.

Unity switches to show you the Game pane, and you should see Dray running quickly in place in the middle of an open room.[5] Also, in the Animator view, you should see a blue progress bar repeatedly filling inside the orange Dray_Walk_0 rectangle. This shows you that Dray_Walk_0 is the Animation that is currently playing and that it is repeating.

11. Stop playback in Unity and **save your scene**.

---

5. Because we have not yet set the Sorting Layers of our sprites, it is possible that when you press Play, your Dray is hidden behind the map tiles. If that is the case, you can click TILE_ANCHOR in the Hierarchy and then click the checkbox next to TILE_ANCHOR's name in the Inspector. This will make TILE_ANCHOR and all of its children inactive and allow you to see Dray.

Sprite Layering

As Dray moved around the room, you might have noticed that they were sometimes in front of and sometimes behind the floor sprites. Based on the order in which you have created the various elements of the game, it is possible that you didn't encounter this in your Game pane, but you should still properly order the sprites to guarantee that you don't have sprite layering issues in the future.

1. Select *Dray* in the Hierarchy.
2. In Dray's *Sprite Renderer* component, click the pop-up menu next to *Sorting Layer* that currently reads *Default* and choose *Add Sorting Layer*. The *Tags & Layers* editor opens with *Sorting Layers* shown.
3. Click the + button on the bottom-right corner of the list of Sorting Layers, and name the new layer *Dray*.
4. Repeat this process to create three more layers: *Ground*, *Enemies*, and *Items*.
5. Arrange the four layers top-to-bottom: Ground, Default, Enemies, Dray, Items. This ensures that the Ground is always behind everything else, Enemies are between unspecified (Default) things and Dray, Dray is in front of everything but Items, and Items are in front of everything.
6. Select *Dray* in the Hierarchy and set the *Sorting Layer* of Dray's *Sprite Renderer* Inspector to *Dray*. (Don't try to change the Layer at the top of Dray's inspector; that's for physics layers.)
7. Select *Tile* in the _Prefabs folder of the Project pane and set the *Sorting Layer* of Tile's *Sprite Renderer* Inspector to *Ground*. This ensures that any Tile instance appears behind everything else in the game.
8. Save the scene.

As you add more things to the game, you will set their Sorting Layers as well.

Tweaking the Dray_Walk_0 Animation

Right now, Dray is running a little too quickly and is only able to run to the right. You'll fix both of these using the *Animation* pane.

1. Click the tiny three-bar menu on the right side of the Game pane (highlighted in red on the lower image of Figure 35.8). From that menu, choose *Add Tab > Animation* to open the Animation pane as a tab in the same pane as the Game pane (as shown in the lower image of Figure 35.8).
2. To make your Animation pane look like that shown in Figure 35.8, select *Dray* in the Hierarchy and open the disclosure triangle next to *Dray : Sprite* in the Animation pane.

There is a pop-up menu in the Animation pane that currently displays Dray_Walk_0 (it's just below the red *Animation Record* circle). I refer to this pop-up menu as the *Animation Selector* throughout the rest of this section. To the right of the Animation Selector is a field for entering number of *Samples*. Samples sets the rate at which the animation will play (as the number of frames that display every second).

3. Set the number of *Samples* to 10 and press Return/Enter. This causes Dray to take about 5 steps per second.

4. To see this movement from Dray:

   ▪ Switch to the *Scene* pane (click the Scene tab to display it instead of the Animator).

   ▪ Double-click *Dray* in the Hierarchy to focus on them in the Scene.

   ▪ Click the *Animation Play* button (within the Animation pane, just above the Animation Selector).

5. Click the *Animation Play* button again to stop playback.

If the timeline bar at the top of the Animation pane ever changes tint from blue to red, that means that you've shifted into *recording mode*. Prior to Unity 2017, this happened every time you clicked the Animation Play button, but that now seems to be fixed. However, if you do ever end up in recording mode, click the *Animation Record* button (the red circle to the left of the Animation Play button) to exit recording mode.

Adding Additional Dray Animation

You need to add additional Animations to Dray to allow them to animate in all four directions.

1. Click the Animation Selector menu and choose *Create New Clip*.

2. Name the new Animation clip *Dray_Walk_1.anim* and save it in the _Animations folder.

3. Set the *Samples* of the new Dray_Walk_1 Animation to 10 and press Return/Enter.

4. Select both *Dray_Walk_1a* and *Dray_Walk_1b* in the Projects pane and drag them into the timeline area of the Animation pane (where you can see the images of Dray in Figure 35.8).

This makes Dray_Walk_1 look like the Animation pane in Figure 35.8, except that Dray is now facing upward (the 1 direction) in the animation. It may also shift the Animation pane into recording mode. If so, click the red circle Animation Record button in the Animation pane to switch back out of recording mode.

5. Repeat steps 1 through 4 of this section for Dray_Walk_**2** and Dray_Walk_**3**, using the appropriate naming and sprites for each one.

6. Save your scene when you're done.

Animation States in the Animator

If you switch back to the Animator pane view (choose *Window > Animator* from the Unity menu bar), you can see four states are now listed for Dray here as well. This Animator is a component of the Dray GameObject in the Hierarchy, and it ties the Dray GameObject and the four Dray_Walk_# sprite animations together.

Moving Dray

Before moving Dray, you must add a Rigidbody to them.

1. Select the *Dray* GameObject in the Hierarchy.

2. Attach a Rigidbody component to Dray (*Component > Physics > Rigidbody*).

   - Set *Use Gravity* to false (unchecked).

   - Under Constraints:

     - Set *Freeze Position Z* to true.

     - Set *Freeze Rotation X, Y*, and *Z* to true.

3. Save your scene.

Now, add a script to Dray to get them moving.

4. Create a C# script named *Dray* in the __Scripts folder and attach it to the Dray GameObject in the Hierarchy.

5. Open the Dray script in MonoDevelop and enter this code:

```csharp
using System.Collections;
using System.Collections.Generic;
using UnityEngine;

public class Dray : MonoBehaviour {
    [Header("Set in Inspector")]
    public float          speed = 5;

    [Header("Set Dynamically")]
    public int            dirHeld = -1; // Direction of the held movement key

    private Rigidbody      rigid;

    void Awake () {
        rigid = GetComponent<Rigidbody>();
    }

    void Update () {
        dirHeld = -1;
        if ( Input.GetKey(KeyCode.RightArrow) ) dirHeld = 0;       // a
        if ( Input.GetKey(KeyCode.UpArrow   ) ) dirHeld = 1;
        if ( Input.GetKey(KeyCode.LeftArrow ) ) dirHeld = 2;
        if ( Input.GetKey(KeyCode.DownArrow ) ) dirHeld = 3;

        Vector3 vel = Vector3.zero;
        switch (dirHeld) {                                          // b
            case 0:
                vel = Vector3.right;
                break;
            case 1:
```

```
                vel = Vector3.up;
                break;
            case 2:
                vel = Vector3.left;
                break;
            case 3:
                vel = Vector3.down;
                break;
        }

        rigid.velocity = vel * speed;
    }
}
```

a. Due to the arrangement of the four single-line `if` clauses at the beginning of the
    `Update()` function, if multiple arrow keys are held at the same time, the last line that
    evaluates to true will override the rest (e.g., if the down and right keys are held, Dray will
    only move down). Because this game is so simple, I've chosen to make it work this way,
    though this might be something you would enjoy improving after finishing this chapter.

b. This entire `switch` clause is replaced by better code in the next section.

6. Save the Dray script, return to Unity, and click *Play*. Now using the arrow keys, you can
    move Dray around the stage in a very simplistic way.

A More Interesting Movement Approach

Because you are using a `dirHeld` integer value that ranges from 0 to 3, you can take advantage
of `dirHeld` in interesting ways. For instance, the switch case marked `// b` in the previous code
listing is very repetitive and uses the `dirHeld` value to choose one of four directions. Look at
the following code listing to see how can take advantage of the 0-3 value of `dirHeld`.

Open the Dray script in MonoDevelop again and update the code to match the following:

```
public class Dray : MonoBehaviour {
    ...
    private Rigidbody        rigid;

    private Vector3[]        directions = new Vector3[] {
        Vector3.right, Vector3.up, Vector3.left, Vector3.down };         // a

    void Awake () {
        rigid = GetComponent<Rigidbody>();
    }

    void Update () {
        dirHeld = -1;
        if ( Input.GetKey(KeyCode.RightArrow) ) dirHeld = 0;
        if ( Input.GetKey(KeyCode.UpArrow    ) ) dirHeld = 1;
        if ( Input.GetKey(KeyCode.LeftArrow ) ) dirHeld = 2;
        if ( Input.GetKey(KeyCode.DownArrow ) ) dirHeld = 3;
```

```
        Vector3 vel = Vector3.zero;
        // Delete the entire switch clause that used to be here
        if (dirHeld > -1) vel = directions[dirHeld];                    // b

        rigid.velocity = vel * speed;
    }
}
```

a. This `directions` Vector3 array allows you to reference each of the four directional vectors easily.

b. This one line has replaced the entire 14-line `switch` clause from the preceding code listing!

If you try playing the game in Unity again, you can see that you kept the same functionality with far fewer lines of code. You will continue to use `dirHeld` in this manner to simplify the code for this chapter.

A Better Way to Handle Input Keys

In a similar manner to the `directions` array, you can also store the keys that you want to use for movement in an array. Make the following code modifications to the `Dray` class.

```
public class Dray : MonoBehaviour {
    [Header("Set in Inspector")]
    public float          speed = 5;

    [Header("Set Dynamically")]
    public int            dirHeld = -1; // Direction of the held movement key

    private Rigidbody     rigid;

    private Vector3[]     directions = new Vector3[] {
        Vector3.right, Vector3.up, Vector3.left, Vector3.down };

    private KeyCode[]     keys = new KeyCode[] { KeyCode.RightArrow,
        KeyCode.UpArrow, KeyCode.LeftArrow, KeyCode.DownArrow };         // a

    void Awake () {
        rigid = GetComponent<Rigidbody>();
    }

    void Update () {
        dirHeld = -1;
        // Delete the four "if ( Input.GetKey..." lines that were here
        for (int i=0; i<4; i++) {
            if ( Input.GetKey(keys[i]) ) dirHeld = i;                    // b
        }
```

```
        Vector3 vel = Vector3.zero;
        if (dirHeld > -1) vel = directions[dirHeld];

        rigid.velocity = vel * speed;
    }
}
```

a. This array allows you to reference each of the four keys easily.

b. This `for` loop iterates over all the possible KeyCodes from the `keys` array and finds whether any are held.

With the new KeyCode array, you've again taken advantage of the 0-3 nature of `dirHeld` and maintained the ability to use the arrow keys via better code.

Animating Dray for Walking

Open Dray in MonoDevelop once more and make the following code additions:

```
public class Dray : MonoBehaviour {
    …
    private Rigidbody        rigid;
    private Animator         anim;                                  // a
    …
    void Awake () {
        rigid = GetComponent<Rigidbody>();
        anim = GetComponent<Animator>();                           // a
    }

    void Update () {
        …
        rigid.velocity = vel * speed;

        // Animation
        if (dirHeld == -1) {                                       // b
            anim.speed = 0;
        } else {
            anim.CrossFade( "Dray_Walk_"+dirHeld, 0 );             // c
            anim.speed = 1;
        }
    }
}
```

a. Cache a reference to the Animator component of Dray in the private field `anim`.

b. If no direction key is held (i.e., `dir` == -1) then the speed of the Animator is set to 0, freezing the current animation in place.

c. If Dray is moving in a direction, the `dirHeld` number is concatenated onto the end of "Dray_Walk_", which gives you the name of one of the Animations that you added to Dray![6]

The `anim.CrossFade()` function tells the Animator `anim` to switch to a new Animation by name and to take 0 seconds for the transition. If `anim` is already showing the named Animation, this has no effect.

Save the Dray script and return to Unity. You can play the game and see that Dray now animates when moved.

Giving Dray an Attack Animation

It's time to give Dray the ability to attack! To do so, you first need to give them an attack animation pose. (You'll implement the damage that Dray's attack does to enemies later in the chapter.)

Generating the Attack Pose Animations

Generate the attack poses by doing the following:

1. Select *Dray* in the Hierarchy and switch to the Animation pane (*Window > Animation* from the Unity menu bar).

2. Use the Animation Selector to choose *Create New Clip* and save the new clip as *Dray_Attack_0* inside the _Animations folder.

3. Choose *Dray_Attack_0* from the Animation Selector.

4. Set the *Samples* of Dray_Attack_0 to 10 and press Return/Enter.

5. Select the *Dray_Attack_0* sprite underneath the Dray image in the _Images folder of the Project pane.

6. Drag the *Dray_Attack_0* sprite from the Project pane into the timeline area of the Animation window.

7. Repeat steps 2 through 6 to create Animations named Dray_Attack_**1**, Dray_Attack_**2**, and Dray_Attack_**3** and assign the appropriate sprite for each.

If you check the Animator pane, you should see that the four new attack Animations now all appear in the Animator for Dray.

---

6. If your Dray animations aren't working, double-check that they are properly named: Dray_Walk_0, Dray_Walk_1, Dray_Walk_2, and Dray_Walk_3. You also need to check the animation names in the Animator pane because the names in the Animator can be different from the names of the .anim files that you saved.

Coding the Attack Pose Animations

To add another animation state to the Dray class, you need to make it a bit more complicated. As part of this, you need to differentiate between `dirHeld` (the direction of the currently held movement key) and a new field, `facing` (the direction that Dray is facing). When Dray is attacking, they will be temporarily frozen for the duration of the attack, and you need to ensure that they don't change direction during that time.

1. Open *Dray* in MonoDevelop and add the bolded enum and fields to the top of the script.

```
public class Dray : MonoBehaviour {
    public enum eMode { idle, move, attack, transition }               // a

    [Header("Set in Inspector")]
    public float          speed = 5;
    public float          attackDuration = 0.25f;// Number of seconds to attack
    public float          attackDelay = 0.5f;    // Delay between attacks

    [Header("Set Dynamically")]
    public int            dirHeld = -1; // Direction of the held movement key
    public int            facing = 1;   // Direction Dray is facing
    public eMode          mode = eMode.idle;                            // a

    private float         timeAtkDone = 0;                              // b
    private float         timeAtkNext = 0;                              // c

    private Rigidbody     rigid;
    private Animator      anim;
    ...
}
```

a. The `eMode` enum and `mode` field give you an expandable way to track and query Dray's state.

b. `timeAtkDone` is the time at which the attack animation should finish.

c. `timeAtkNext` is the time at which Dray will be able to attack again.

2. Because these new fields cause a major shift in how the `Update()` method works, the following code listing includes the entire listing of the `Update()` method of the `Dray` class. This includes all the same concepts presented in earlier code listings, just rearranged a bit. *Replace* the `Update()` method in your `Dray` class with the following (bold code is new):

```
void Update () {
    //——Handle Keyboard Input and manage eDrayModes——
    dirHeld = -1;
    for (int i=0; i<4; i++) {
        if ( Input.GetKey(keys[i]) ) dirHeld = i;
    }
```

```
    // Pressing the attack button(s)
    if (Input.GetKeyDown(KeyCode.Z) && Time.time >= timeAtkNext) {        // a
        mode = eMode.attack;
        timeAtkDone = Time.time + attackDuration;
        timeAtkNext = Time.time + attackDelay;
    }

    // Finishing the attack when it's over
    if (Time.time >= timeAtkDone) {                                       // b
        mode = eMode.idle;
    }

    // Choosing the proper mode if we're not attacking
    if (mode != eMode.attack) {                                           // c
        if (dirHeld == -1) {
            mode = eMode.idle;
        } else {
            facing = dirHeld;                                             // d
            mode = eMode.move;
        }
    }

    //——Act on the current mode——
    Vector3 vel = Vector3.zero;
    switch (mode) {                                                       // e
        case eMode.attack:
            anim.CrossFade( "Dray_Attack_"+facing, 0 );
            anim.speed = 0;
            break;

        case eMode.idle:
            anim.CrossFade( "Dray_Walk_"+facing, 0 );
            anim.speed = 0;
            break;

        case eMode.move:
            vel = directions[dirHeld];
            anim.CrossFade( "Dray_Walk_"+facing, 0 );
            anim.speed = 1;
            break;
    }

    rigid.velocity = vel * speed;
}
```

a. If the attack button (the Z key on the keyboard) is pressed and it has been long enough since the last attack, then mode is set to eMode.attack.

Additionally, the timeAtkDone and timeAtkNext fields are set, letting the Dray instance know when it should stop the attack animation and when it will be able to attack again.

b. After Dray switches into attack mode, they are stuck there until the attack completes (which happens after `attackDuration` seconds [0.25 seconds by default]). After this time has passed, `mode` returns to `eMode.idle`.

c. If Dray is not in attack mode, this code chooses between `idle` and `move` based on whether any movement key is held (i.e., `dirHeld > -1`).

d. `facing` is exclusively set here. The only time Dray changes `facing` is when moving in a direction. This ensures that Dray maintains a consistent facing when attacking or standing still.

e. After the proper `mode` for Dray has been determined, this `switch` statement manages what happens as part of that mode. Both `anim` and `vel` are handled here.

Now that Dray is facing in the proper direction and holding an attack pose, adding a weapon to the attack will be easy.

Dray's Sword

Dray's primary weapon is a sword, which they can stab in any direction. The Texture 2D and Sprites for this sword were imported with the starter unitypackage for this chapter.

1. Select *Dray* in the Hierarchy. Right-click on *Dray* in the Hierarchy and choose *Create Empty* from the pop-up menu. Rename the empty GameObject to *SwordController*

2. Set the Transform of SwordController to P:[0, 0, 0] R:[0, 0, 0] S:[1, 1, 1].

3. Open the disclosure triangle next to the *Swords* Texture 2D under the _Images folder.

4. Drag the *Swords_0* sprite from the Project pane to the Hierarchy pane. Make it a child of SwordController (and a grandchild of Dray).

  ▪ Rename the Swords_0 instance in the Hierarchy to *Sword*.

  ▪ Set the Transform of Sword to P:[0.75, 0, 0] R:[0, 0, 0] S:[1, 1, 1].

  ▪ Set the *Sorting Layer* of the Sword Sprite Renderer to Enemies (so it will be above Ground but beneath Dray).

5. Add a Box Collider to Sword (*Component > Physics > Box Collider*). It should assume a proper size, but if it did not, set the *Size* of the Box Collider to [1, 0.4375, 0.2].

  ▪ Set the *Is Trigger* of the Sword Box Collider to *true*.

6. Select *SwordController* in the Hierarchy.

  ▪ In the SwordController Inspector, click the *Add Component* button.

  ▪ Choose *New Script* from the pop-up menu that appears.

  ▪ Name the new script *SwordController*.

  ▪ In the Project pane, move the SwordController script into the __Scripts folder.

7. Open the SwordController script and enter the following code:

```
using System.Collections;
using System.Collections.Generic;
using UnityEngine;

public class SwordController : MonoBehaviour {
    private GameObject   sword;
    private Dray         dray;

    void Start () {
        sword = transform.Find("Sword").gameObject;               // a
        dray = transform.parent.GetComponent<Dray>();
        // Deactivate the sword
        sword.SetActive(false);                                   // b
    }

    void Update () {
        transform.rotation = Quaternion.Euler( 0, 0, 90*dray.facing );   // c
        sword.SetActive(dray.mode == Dray.eMode.attack);                 // d
    }
}
```

a. These two lines find references to the Sword child GameObject and the `Dray` class instance attached to the parent GameObject.

b. Calling `SetActive(false)` on a GameObject removes that GameObject from rendering, collision, running scripts, etc. When you deactivate Sword, it becomes invisible.

c. This line keeps the sword pointed in the direction that Dray is facing. Because Sword is a child of this SwordController GameObject that is offset 0.75 in the local X direction, the rotation of SwordController to match the `facing` of Dray makes the sword properly appear in Dray's hand regardless of the direction that Dray is facing.

d. Each Update, the sword will be made active if Dray is in `attack` mode.

8. *Save All* scripts in MonoDevelop,[7] return to Unity, and click *Play*. Now you can move Dray around the stage using the arrow keys and attack by pressing Z. The sword should only appear when Dray is attacking and always point in the right direction.

Enemy: Skeletos

The Skeletos will be Dray's basic enemy. Like the Stalfos in *The Legend of Zelda*, Skeletos randomly wander around the dungeon room that they're in. Skeletos can pass over each other and can damage Dray with a touch.

---

7. If the *File > Save All* option is grayed out, then you've already saved all of them. Yay!

Skeletos Art

To implement the art for Skeletos:

1. Select the two sprites named *Skeletos_0* and *Skeletos_1* (they are under *Project Pane > _Images > Skeletos*).

2. Drag these two sprites together into the Hierarchy. This creates a new Animation that you should name *Skeletos.anim* and save in the _Animations folder.

3. Rename the Skeletos_0 GameObject in the Hierarchy to *Skeletos*.

4. Set the Transform position of Skeletos to P:[19, 7, 0].

5. Attach a Rigidbody component to Skeletos (*Component > Physics > Rigidbody*).

   ▪ Set *Use Gravity* to false (unchecked).

   ▪ Under Constraints:

      ▪ Set *Freeze Position Z* to true.

      ▪ Set *Freeze Rotation X, Y*, and *Z* to true.

6. Add a Sphere Collider to *Skeletos* (*Component > Physics > Sphere Collider*).

7. In the *Sprite Renderer* component of the Skeletos Inspector, set *Sorting Layer* to *Enemies*.

8. Select *Skeletos* in the Hierarchy and switch to the Animation pane (*Window > Animation*).

9. Set the *Samples* of the Skeletos Animation to to 5 and press Return/Enter.

10. Save the scene.

Click *Play*, and you should see the Skeletos running in place in the same room with Dray.

The Enemy Base Class

All enemies in *Dungeon Delver* will inherit from a single base class named *Enemy*.

1. Create a new C# script named *Enemy* in the __Scripts folder of the Project pane.

2. Open the *Enemy* script in MonoDevelop and enter the following code:

```csharp
using System.Collections;
using System.Collections.Generic;
using UnityEngine;

public class Enemy : MonoBehaviour {
    protected static Vector3[]  directions = new Vector3[] {          // a
        Vector3.right, Vector3.up, Vector3.left, Vector3.down };

    [Header("Set in Inspector: Enemy")]                               // b
    public float               maxHealth = 1;                         // c

    [Header("Set Dynamically: Enemy")]
```

```
    public float                  health;                              // c

    protected Animator            anim;                                // c
    protected Rigidbody           rigid;                               // c
    protected SpriteRenderer      sRend;                               // c

    protected virtual void Awake() {                                   // d
        health = maxHealth;
        anim = GetComponent<Animator>();
        rigid = GetComponent<Rigidbody>();
        sRend = GetComponent<SpriteRenderer>();
    }
}
```

a. `directions` is used by enemies in a similar manner to how Dray uses it. Because its value is the same across all Enemy instances, you can make it `static`. It is declared `protected` so that it can be accessed by any subclasses of Enemy.

b. I've modified the standard `[Header(...)]`s that you use for the Inspector to show which fields are inherited from the Enemy base class and which are part of Skeletos and other Enemy subclasses.

c. The Enemy class also declares several fields that will commonly be used by the Enemy subclasses, including fields to track health and commonly referenced components.

d. The Enemy `Awake()` method sets default values for `health` and the common Component references `anim`, `rigid`, and `sRend`. Declaring this `protected virtual` allows it to be overridden in subclasses (as you'll see soon).

The Skeletos Subclass of Enemy

Follow these steps to create the Skeletos subclass:

1. Create a new C# script named *Skeletos* inside the __Scripts folder of the Project pane.

2. Attach the *Skeletos* script to the Skeletos GameObject in the Hierarchy.

3. Open the *Skeletos* script in MonoDevelop and enter the following code:

```
using System.Collections;
using System.Collections.Generic;
using UnityEngine;

public class Skeletos : Enemy {                                        // a
    [Header("Set in Inspector: Skeletos")]                            // b
    public int      speed = 2;
    public float    timeThinkMin = 1f;
    public float    timeThinkMax = 4f;
```

```
[Header("Set Dynamically: Skeletos")]
public int        facing = 0;
public float      timeNextDecision = 0;

void Update () {
    if (Time.time >= timeNextDecision) {                                // c
        DecideDirection();
    }
    // rigid is inherited from Enemy and is initialized in Enemy.Awake()
    rigid.velocity = directions[facing] * speed;
}

void DecideDirection() {                                                // d
    facing = Random.Range(0,4);
    timeNextDecision = Time.time + Random.Range(timeThinkMin,timeThinkMax);
}
}
```

a. Skeletos is a subclass of Enemy (not MonoBehaviour).

b. I've modified the standard [Header(…)]s here as well to show which fields are inherited from Enemy and which are part of Skeletos.

c. When it has been a sufficient amount of time since the Skeletos last changed direction, it will call DecideDirection() to decide again.

d. In DecideDirection() a random facing is chosen as well as a randomized amount of time before deciding again.

4. Save All scripts in MonoDevelop, switch to Unity, and click *Play*.

You should see the Skeletos wandering randomly across the floor and right out of the room! We need to make a script to keep the Skeletos and other enemies in the room.[8]

The InRoom Script

The dungeon is divided into several rooms, each of which is 16m wide by 11m tall. The InRoom script will provide several useful services. In order to know whether a Skeletos is attempting to walk out of the room, you need to know where it is in the room, and because all the rooms in the dungeon are the same size, this is pretty easy to do.

1. Create a new C# script named *InRoom* inside the __Scripts folder of the Project pane.

2. Open the *InRoom* script in MonoDevelop and enter the following code:

---

8. If your Skeletos is dancing in place for a long time, make sure that you did step 2 (attaching the script). However, standing still is a legitimate action for a Skeletos, so you might just need to wait a bit longer.

```
using System.Collections;
using System.Collections.Generic;
using UnityEngine;

public class InRoom : MonoBehaviour {
    static public float      ROOM_W = 16;                              // a
    static public float      ROOM_H = 11;
    static public float      WALL_T = 2;

    // Where is this character in local room coordinates?
    public Vector2          roomPos {                                  // b
        get {
            Vector2 tPos = transform.position;
            tPos.x %= ROOM_W;
            tPos.y %= ROOM_H;
            return tPos;
        }
        set {
            Vector2 rm = roomNum;
            rm.x *= ROOM_W;
            rm.y *= ROOM_H;
            rm += value;
            transform.position = rm;
        }
    }


    // Which room is this character in?
    public Vector2          roomNum {                                  // c
        get {
            Vector2 tPos = transform.position;
            tPos.x = Mathf.Floor( tPos.x / ROOM_W );
            tPos.y = Mathf.Floor( tPos.y / ROOM_H );
            return tPos;
        }
        set {
            Vector2 rPos = roomPos;
            Vector2 rm = value;
            rm.x *= ROOM_W;
            rm.y *= ROOM_H;
            transform.position = rm + rPos;
        }
    }

}
```

a. These static floats set the basic width and height of the room (measured in Unity units / meters / tiles, which are all the same). WALL_T is thickness of the walls.

b. The roomPos property allows you to get or set the location of the GameObject relative to the bottom-left corner of the room (which is X:0, Y:0).

    c. The `roomNum` property allows you to get or set the room in which the GameObject is located (with the bottom-left room of the dungeon being X:0, Y:0). If you set the GameObject to a different room, it maintains the same relative `roomPos` in the new room.

This basic version of InRoom can be attached to various GameObjects and to enable you to find out where that GameObject is in any room. InRoom also enables you to set the location of the GameObject in room-relative coordinates or to move the GameObject to another room.

Keeping GameObjects in the Room

As mentioned earlier, you want to keep the Skeletos inside the room. To do this, you need to add a `LateUpdate()` method that checks every frame to see whether the Skeletos has wandered outside the main area of the room. The `LateUpdate()` method is called every frame on every GameObject after the `Update()` method has been called on every GameObject.[9] `Late-Update()` is great for cleanup operations like returning wandering characters to the room they're supposed to be in.

1. Attach the *InRoom* script to the Skeletos in the Hierarchy.

2. Open *InRoom* in MonoDevelop and add the following bolded code:

```
public class InRoom : MonoBehaviour {
    static public float     ROOM_W = 16;
    static public float     ROOM_H = 11;
    static public float     WALL_T = 2;

    [Header("Set in Inspector")]
    public bool             keepInRoom = true;
    public float            gridMult = 1;                        // a


    void LateUpdate() {
        if (keepInRoom) {                                        // b
            Vector2 rPos = roomPos;
            rPos.x = Mathf.Clamp( rPos.x, WALL_T, ROOM_W-1-WALL_T );      // c
            rPos.y = Mathf.Clamp( rPos.y, WALL_T, ROOM_H-1-WALL_T );
            roomPos = rPos;                                      // d
        }
    }

    // Where is this character in local room coordinates?
    public Vector2          roomPos { … }
    …
}
```

---

9. For example, if five GameObjects have an `Update()` method, and two of them have a `LateUp-date()` method, `Update()` will be called on all five of them, and then `LateUpdate()` will be called on the two that have a `LateUpdate()` method.

    a. The `gridMult` field will be used later in the chapter.

    b. If `keepInRoom` is checked, then each frame, these lines check to see that the `roomPos` of this GameObject stays within the walls of the room.

    c. `Mathf.Clamp()` ensures that `rPos.x` is between a minimum value of `WALL_T` and a maximum value of `ROOM_W-1-WALL_T`, which keeps Skeletos from walking through the walls of the room.

    d. When the checks against the extents of the room are complete, `rPos` is assigned back to `roomPos`, which executes the `set` clause of the `roomPos` property and moves the GameObject (if it needs to be moved back into the room).

3. Save the InRoom script and return to Unity to test it. You should now see the Skeletos wandering all around the room but no longer walking through the walls as it did before.

The InRoom script is very useful for efficiently faking collision between enemies and the walls of the room, but you also need to have characters in the game collide directly with some tiles (e.g., the statues and obelisks in the middle of some rooms). For this, you need to implement collision on a per-tile basis.

Per-Tile Collision

The DelverData text file holds information about which tiles should be placed in each position of the dungeon, and the DelverTiles image provides the imagery for each tile. Another text file named *DelverCollisions* is responsible for storing the collision information for each type of tile, and it does so in a somewhat encoded way (see Figure 35.9).

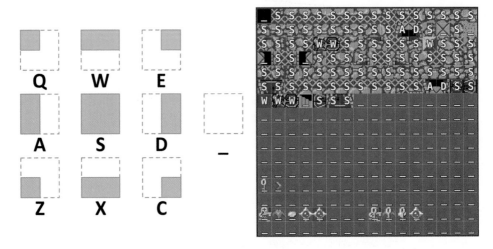

Figure 35.9 The encoding for the DelverCollisions text file (on the left) and an overlay of DelverCollisions text on top of DelverTiles (on the right)

On the left side of Figure 35.9, you can see the encoding of the DelverCollisions text file that matches correct Box Collider shapes with each tile in the DelverTiles image. Each letter on the left represents a specific collision. The gray dashed line represents the entire tile, and the green shaded box represents what the collider covers. For example, a tile with a W would only have a collider covering the top half of the tile, which is used for all pillars and statues that are placed in the middle of the room. *Dungeon Delver* uses only _ (no collision), S (full collision), A (left half collision), D (right half collision), and W (top half collision), but I provide the others (Q, E, Z, X, & C) for any further games you might want to develop.

On the right side of Figure 35.9, you can see the contents of the DelverCollisions text file super-imposed over the tiles in the DelverTiles image.

To make use of this DelverCollisions information, start by adding a collider to the Tile prefab.

1. Select the *Tile* GameObject in the _Prefabs folder of the Project pane.
2. Attach a *Box Collider* to the Tile (*Component > Physics > Box Collider*).[10]

Per-Tile Collision Scripts

Next, add some code to the TileCamera and Tile C# scripts to enable use of the DelverCollisions data.

1. Open the *TileCamera* script in MonoDevelop and add the bolded code:

```
public class TileCamera : MonoBehaviour {
    static public int        W, H;
    static private int[,]     MAP;
    static public Sprite[]    SPRITES;
    static public Transform   TILE_ANCHOR;
    static public Tile[,]     TILES;
    static public string      COLLISIONS;                          // a

    [Header("Set in Inspector")]
    …
    void Awake() {
        COLLISIONS = Utils.RemoveLineEndings( mapCollisions.text );   // b
        LoadMap();
    }
    …
}
```

---

10. Unlike most GameObjects that have colliders, the Tile prefab does not require a Rigidbody compo-
    nent because it will never be moved during the game. If you were to make something later like a
    sliding block, then you would want to also add a Rigidbody to the Tile prefab.

   a. The static public `COLLISIONS` string can be accessed by any other script. String is the perfect data type here because bracket access can be used to easily access individual chars in strings, enabling you to pull the collision char for any tileNum.

   b. Here, the text of the `mapCollisions` TextAsset is passed through a Utils method that strips away line endings (making the result a 256-char string with no line breaks), leaving an array of chars (in the form of a string) that aligns with the array of Sprites.

2. Save the *TileCamera* script.

3. Open the *Tile* script and make the following bolded additions:

```
public class Tile : MonoBehaviour {
    [Header("Set Dynamically")]
    public int             x;
    public int             y;
    public int             tileNum;

    private BoxCollider    bColl;                                    // a

    void Awake() {
        bColl = GetComponent<BoxCollider>();                        // a
    }

    public void SetTile(int eX, int eY, int eTileNum = -1) {
        …
        GetComponent<SpriteRenderer>().sprite = TileCamera.SPRITES[tileNum];

        SetCollider();                                              // b
    }

    // Arrange the collider for this tile
    void SetCollider() {
        // Collider info is pulled from DelverCollisions.txt
        bColl.enabled = true;
        char c = TileCamera.COLLISIONS[tileNum];                    // c
        switch (c) {
            case 'S': // Whole
                bColl.center = Vector3.zero;
                bColl.size = Vector3.one;
                break;
            case 'W': // Top
                bColl.center = new Vector3( 0, 0.25f, 0 );
                bColl.size =   new Vector3( 1, 0.5f, 1 );
                break;
            case 'A': // Left
                bColl.center = new Vector3( -0.25f, 0, 0 );
                bColl.size =   new Vector3( 0.5f, 1, 1 );
                break;
```

```
    case 'D': // Right
        bColl.center = new Vector3( 0.25f, 0, 0 );
        bColl.size =   new Vector3( 0.5f, 1, 1 );
        break;

    // vvvvvvvv-------- These are optional --------vvvvvvvv         // d
    case 'Q': // Top, Left
        bColl.center = new Vector3( -0.25f, 0.25f, 0 );
        bColl.size =   new Vector3( 0.5f, 0.5f, 1 );
        break;
    case 'E': // Top, Right
        bColl.center = new Vector3( 0.25f, 0.25f, 0 );
        bColl.size =   new Vector3( 0.5f, 0.5f, 1 );
        break;
    case 'Z': // Bottom, left
        bColl.center = new Vector3( -0.25f, -0.25f, 0 );
        bColl.size =   new Vector3( 0.5f, 0.5f, 1 );
        break;
    case 'X': // Bottom
        bColl.center = new Vector3( 0, -0.25f, 0 );
        bColl.size =   new Vector3( 1, 0.5f, 1 );
        break;
    case 'C': // Bottom, Right
        bColl.center = new Vector3( 0.25f, -0.25f, 0 );
        bColl.size =   new Vector3( 0.5f, 0.5f, 1 );
        break;
    // ^^^^^^^^-------- These are optional --------^^^^^^^^         // d

    default: // Anything else: _, |, etc.                          // e
        bColl.enabled = false;
        break;
    }
  }
}
```

a. `bColl` provides a reference to the Box Collider of this Tile.

b. At the end of the `SetTile()` method, `SetCollider()` is called.

c. Here, the `tileNum` is used to access the correct collision character from `TileCamera.COLLISIONS`.

d. The lines between the two `// d` lines (for the chars Q, E, Z, X, & C) are not necessary for *Dungeon Delver* but might be useful in your other projects.

e. The final `default` case is necessary to handle `'_'` collision chars.

4. Save the *Tile* script and return to Unity.

Adding a Collider to Dray

Finally, to see the results of the per-tile collision, you must add a collider to Dray.

1. Select *Dray* in the Hierarchy.

2. Add a *Sphere Collider* to Dray (*Component > Physics > Sphere Collider*).

   ■ Set the *Radius* of the Sphere Collider to *0.4*.

Try saving and playing your scene. Move around and see what happens when you run into walls. While the Skeletos is trapped in the room, you are able to walk into the doorway. However, you might notice two problems:

   ■ Lining up perfectly with the door is somewhat difficult.

   ■ You can't actually move to another room.

You'll tackle each one of these in turn.

Aligning to the Grid

The original *Legend of Zelda* game had an ingenious system that aligned players to a grid yet still made them feel like they were able to roam freely. A player had largely free-roaming movement, but the further she moved in the same direction, the more she would be subtly aligned to a 0.5-unit grid. To help with this in *Dungeon Delver*, we can take advantage of the InRoom script that you wrote earlier with a bit of an expansion to get information about the nearest location in the room that is on this grid.

1. Attach the *InRoom* script to the *Dray* GameObject in the Hierarchy.

   ■ Set `keepInRoom` to false for Dray.

2. Open the *InRoom* script in MonoDevelop and add the following method to the end of the class definition. `GetRoomPosOnGrid()` will find the nearest location to the GameObject that is in the room and on a grid (with the default grid size being 1m).

```
public class InRoom : MonoBehaviour {
    …
    // Which room is this character in?
    public Vector2          roomNum { … }

    // What is the closest grid location to this character?
    public Vector2 GetRoomPosOnGrid(float mult = -1) {
        if (mult == -1) {
            mult = gridMult;
        }
        Vector2 rPos = roomPos;
        rPos /= mult;
        rPos.x = Mathf.Round( rPos.x );
```

```
        rPos.y = Mathf.Round( rPos.y );
        rPos *= mult;
        return rPos;
    }

}
```

3. Save the *InRoom* script and return to Unity.

The IFacingMover Interface

In addition to Dray, you'll actually want all creatures in *Dungeon Delver* to align to the grid as they move, and you will eventually apply the upcoming *GridMove* script to all of them. Dray and the Skeletos have some of the same traits (e.g., a facing of 0-3, behavior where they sometimes move or stand still, etc.), but the only common ancestor class that Dray and Skeletos share is MonoBehaviour. This is exactly the kind of time when you should consider using a C# *interface*. If you would like a deeper introduction to interfaces than the one here, please read the *Interfaces* section of Appendix B, "Useful Concepts."

Briefly, an interface is a guarantee that declares specific methods or properties that will be included in a class. Any class that *implements* the interface can then be referred to in code as the interface type rather than as the specific class type. This differs from subclassing in several ways, the two most important of which are:

■ A class may implement several different interfaces simultaneously, whereas a class can only extend a single superclass.

■ Any class—regardless of superclass ancestry—can still implement the same interface.

You can think of an interface as a promise: Any class that implements the interface promises to have specific methods or properties that can be called safely.

The *IFacingMover* interface that you'll implement here is very simple, and you can easily apply it to both Skeletos and Dray.

1. Create a new C# script in the __Scripts folder named *IFacingMover* (interface names often start with an *I*).

2. Open *IFacingMover* in MonoDevelop and enter the following code. Note that IFacingMover *does not* extend MonoBehaviour and *is not* a class.

```
using System.Collections;
using System.Collections.Generic;
using UnityEngine;

public interface IFacingMover {                              // a
    int GetFacing();                                         // b
    bool moving { get; }                                     // c
```

```
    float GetSpeed();
    float gridMult { get; }                                              // d
    Vector2 roomPos { get; set; }                                        // e
    Vector2 roomNum { get; set; }
    Vector2 GetRoomPosOnGrid( float mult = -1 );                         // f
}
```

a. This is the public declaration of the IFacingMover interface.

b. Interfaces include methods and properties that must be publicly accessible on any class that implements this interface. This line declares that there will be a public `int` `GetFacing()` method on any class that implements IFacingMover.

c. In addition to methods, it is also possible to promise the implementation of properties with an interface. This line declares that a read-only `bool moving` property will be implemented on any class that implements IFacingMover.

d. The `gridMult` read-only property will allow IFacingMovers to pass the `gridMult` field of InRoom to scripts like GridMove without GridMove requiring direct access to InRoom.

e. The `gridMult` and `roomPos` properties and the `GetRoomPosOnGrid()` method will require you to implement access to InRoom on both Dray and Skeletos. However, although this requires Dray and Skeletos to have access to InRoom, it allows anything treating Dray or Skeletos as an IFacingMover to not require access to InRoom.

f. This interface method includes a default value for its `mult` parameter. If either no value or a value of -1 is passed into `GetRoomPosOnGrid()`, it will look to the `gridMult` property. Interestingly, if the default value for `mult` here disagrees with the default value for `mult` in any script that implements IFacingMover, the value here will override the default value in those implementing classes.

Implementing the IFacingMover Interface in the Dray Class

Next, follow these steps to implement the IFacingMover interface in the Dray class:

1. Open the *Dray* class and add the following code to make it properly implement the IFacingMover interface.

```
public class Dray : MonoBehaviour, IFacingMover {                        // a
    ...
    private Rigidbody        rigid;
    private Animator         anim;
    private InRoom           inRm;                                       // b

    ...

    void Awake () {
        rigid = GetComponent<Rigidbody>();
        anim = GetComponent<Animator>();
        inRm = GetComponent<InRoom>();                                   // b
```

```
}

void Update () { … }

// Implementation of IFacingMover
public int GetFacing() {                                          // c
    return facing;
}

public bool moving {                                             // d
    get {
        return (mode == eMode.move);
    }
}

public float GetSpeed() {                                        // e
    return speed;
}

public float gridMult {
    get { return inRm.gridMult; }
}

public Vector2 roomPos {                                         // f
    get { return inRm.roomPos; }
    set { inRm.roomPos = value; }
}

public Vector2 roomNum {
    get { return inRm.roomNum; }
    set { inRm.roomNum = value; }
}

public Vector2 GetRoomPosOnGrid( float mult = -1 ) {
    return inRm.GetRoomPosOnGrid( mult );
}
}
```

a. The ", IFacingMover" declares that this class implements the IFacingMover interface.

b. inRm provides access to the attached InRoom class and is assigned in Awake().

c. The implementation of the public int GetFacing() method dictated by IFacingMover.

d. Implementation of the public bool moving { get; } read-only property from IFacingMover.

e. Implementation of float GetSpeed() from IFacingMover.

f. Implementation of roomPos works just like any other read-and-write property.

2. Save *Dray* and return to Unity to make sure that everything compiles without issue.

This might seem like a lot of extra work now, but watch what happens after you have implemented the same interface for Skeletos.

3. Open the *Skeletos* script and enter the following bolded code.

```
public class Skeletos : Enemy, IFacingMover {                          // a
    …
    public float     timeNextDecision = 0;

    private InRoom   inRm;                                             // b

    protected override void Awake () {                                // c
        base.Awake();
        inRm = GetComponent<InRoom>();
    }

    void Update () { … }

    void DecideDirection() { … }

    // Implementation of IFacingMover
    public int GetFacing() {
        return facing;
    }

    public bool moving {  get { return true; }  }                    // d

    public float GetSpeed() {
        return speed;
    }

    public float gridMult {
        get { return inRm.gridMult; }
    }

    public Vector2 roomPos {
        get { return inRm.roomPos; }
        set { inRm.roomPos = value; }
    }

    public Vector2 roomNum {
        get { return inRm.roomNum; }
        set { inRm.roomNum = value; }
    }

    public Vector2 GetRoomPosOnGrid( float mult = -1 ) {
        return inRm.GetRoomPosOnGrid( mult );
    }
}
```

a. Most of the implementation in Skeletos is the same.

b. `inRm` must also be declared and defined for Skeletos.

c. The `Awake()` in Skeletos must be declared `protected override` to work in concert with the `protected virtual Awake()` method on the superclass Enemy. The first line in this `Awake()` method calls the `Awake()` method on the base class (`Enemy:Awake()`). Then `Skeletos:Awake()` proceeds to assign the value of `inRm`.

d. Skeletos are always moving, so the implementation of `bool moving { get; }` here just returns true, unlike the Dray class.

3. Save all scripts in MonoDevelop and return to Unity.

Now, either Dray or Skeletos can both be handled by the same code as an IFacingMover rather than your having to write separate code for each class. Let's implement the GridMove script to test this.

The GridMove Script

You will be able to apply GridMove to any GameObject with a class that implements IFacingMover attached.

1. Create a new C# script named *GridMove* in the __Scripts folder and attach it to Dray.

2. Open the *GridMove* script in MonoDevelop and enter the following code.

```csharp
using System.Collections;
using System.Collections.Generic;
using UnityEngine;

public class GridMove : MonoBehaviour {
    private IFacingMover    mover;

    void Awake() {
        mover = GetComponent<IFacingMover>();                      // a
    }

    void FixedUpdate() {
        if ( !mover.moving ) return; // If not moving, nothing to do here
        int facing = mover.GetFacing();

        // If we are moving in a direction, align to the grid
        // First, get the grid location
        Vector2 rPos = mover.roomPos;
        Vector2 rPosGrid = mover.GetRoomPosOnGrid();
        // This relies on IFacingMover (which uses InRoom) to choose grid spacing

        // Then move towards the grid line
        float delta = 0;
```

```
        if (facing == 0 || facing == 2) {
            // Horizontal movement, align to y grid
            delta = rPosGrid.y - rPos.y;
        } else {
            // Vertical movement, align to x grid
            delta = rPosGrid.x - rPos.x;
        }
        if (delta == 0) return; // Already aligned to the grid

        float move = mover.GetSpeed() * Time.fixedDeltaTime;
        move = Mathf.Min( move, Mathf.Abs(delta) );
        if (delta < 0) move = -move;

        if (facing == 0 || facing == 2) {
            // Horizontal movement, align to y grid
            rPos.y += move;
        } else {
            // Vertical movement, align to x grid
            rPos.x += move;
        }

        mover.roomPos = rPos;
    }
}
```

    a. `GetComponent<IFacingMover>()` finds any component attached to this GameObject that implements the IFacingMover interface. This will return either a Dray or Skeletos reference and would work equally well for any future class that implements the IFacingMover interface.

GridMove is implemented as part of `FixedUpdate()` because that is when the physics engine is updating and actually moving various GameObjects.

  3. Save all scripts in MonoDevelop, return to Unity, and click *Play*.

As you move Dray around, you will see that they will progressively align themselves to a one-unit grid. This makes it much easier to line up with the door.

  4. Stop playback.

  5. Select *Dray* and set the `gridMult` of the *InRoom* Inspector to 0.5.

Test again, and you'll see that you can now move on a half-grid just like in *The Legend of Zelda*.

  6. Attach *GridMove* to the Skeletos GameObject in the Hierarchy.

  7. Save your scene, and click *Play* again.

If you watch carefully, you can see that the Skeletos now moves along a one-unit grid.

Moving from Room to Room

Now that Dray can line up well with doors, it's time for them to venture out into the rest of the dungeon. Because Dray is the only one who will move from room to room, we can attach most of this code to the `Dray` class; however, global room information like the location of the doors and the overall size of the map should still be managed by InRoom.

1. Open the *InRoom* script in MonoDevelop and enter this code:

```
public class InRoom : MonoBehaviour {
    static public float      ROOM_W = 16;
    static public float      ROOM_H = 11;
    static public float      WALL_T = 2;

    static public int        MAX_RM_X = 9;                       // a
    static public int        MAX_RM_Y = 9;

    static public Vector2[] DOORS = new Vector2[] {              // b
        new Vector2(14,   5),
        new Vector2(7.5f, 9),
        new Vector2(1,    5),
        new Vector2(7.5f, 1)
    };

    [Header("Set in Inspector")]
    public bool              keepInRoom = true;
    ...
}
```

   a. The static ints `MAX_RM_X` and `MAX_RM_Y` mark the maximum boundaries of the map. The setting of 9 will work with the current maximum size of the *Delver Level Editor* mentioned at the end of this chapter. If you need to make a larger map, you'll have to change this.

   b. The static `DOORS` Vector2 array stores room-relative positions of each possible door.

2. Save the *InRoom* script.

3. Open the *Dray* class in MonoDevelop and enter the following code:

```
public class Dray : MonoBehaviour, IFacingMover {
    ...
    [Header("Set in Inspector")]
    ...
    public float            attackDelay = 0.5f;    // Delay between attacks
    public float            transitionDelay = 0.5f;// Room transition delay  // a

    [Header("Set Dynamically")]
    ...
    private float           timeAtkDone = 0;
    private float           timeAtkNext = 0;
```

```
    private float        transitionDone = 0;                      // a
    private Vector2      transitionPos;

    private Rigidbody    rigid;
    …

    void Update () {
        if ( mode == eMode.transition ) {                         // b
            rigid.velocity = Vector3.zero;
            anim.speed = 0;
            roomPos = transitionPos;   // Keeps Dray in place
            if (Time.time < transitionDone) return;
            // The following line is only reached if Time.time >= transitionDone
            mode = eMode.idle;
        }

        //——Handle Keyboard Input and manage eDrayModes——
        dirHeld = -1
        …
    }

    void LateUpdate() {
        // Get the half-grid location of this GameObject
        Vector2 rPos = GetRoomPosOnGrid( 0.5f );  // Forces half-grid      // c

        // Check to see whether we're in a Door tile
        int doorNum;
        for (doorNum=0; doorNum<4; doorNum++) {
            if (rPos == InRoom.DOORS[doorNum]) {
                break;                                             // d
            }
        }

        if ( doorNum > 3 || doorNum != facing ) return;           // e

        // Move to the next room
        Vector2 rm = roomNum;
        switch (doorNum) {                                        // f
            case 0:
                rm.x += 1;
                break;
            case 1:
                rm.y += 1;
                break;
            case 2:
                rm.x -= 1;
                break;
```

```
            case 3:
                rm.y -= 1;
                break;
        }

        // Make sure that the rm we want to jump to is valid
        if (rm.x >= 0 && rm.x <= InRoom.MAX_RM_X) {                    // g
            if (rm.y >=0 && rm.y <= InRoom.MAX_RM_Y) {
                roomNum = rm;
                transitionPos = InRoom.DOORS[ (doorNum+2) % 4 ];      // h
                roomPos = transitionPos;
                mode = eMode.transition;                              // i
                transitionDone = Time.time + transitionDelay;
            }
        }
    }

    // Implementation of IFacingMover
    public int GetFacing() { … }
    …
}
```

a. Be sure that you don't miss these lines.

b. These lines hold Dray in place for a short time whenever they transition from one room to the next. This prevents the player from walking into a dangerous room until the camera has had time to transition to the new room.

c. A half-grid setting of 0.5 is forced here because the `InRoom.DOORS` are on a half-grid.

d. This loop iterates through each of the doors and breaks when it finds the one where the player is standing. If the player is not standing at any door location, `doorNum` finishes the `for` loop with a value of 4.

e. If either `doorNum > 3` (i.e., Dray is not standing in a doorway) or if Dray is not facing toward the doorway (i.e., `doorNum != facing`), then execution returns here.

f. Execution will only reach this point if Dray should move through a door. This `switch` statement changes the Vector2 `roomNum` based on which door Dray is passing through.

g. Here, validity is checked on the extents of the map. For instance, this keeps Dray from walking out the entrance to the dungeon (which would set their `roomNum.y` to -1).

h. The `(doorNum+2) % 4` code picks the opposite door in the room (e.g., if Dray exits `DOORS[3]`, they will enter `DOORS[1]`). The `transitionPos` is then set to that value, and on the next line, Dray's `roomPos` is set to the same location as well, placing them in the doorway of the next room.

i. Dray is put into `transition` mode, which keeps them from moving for a moment, giving the player time to see the new room before moving into it.

4. Save all scripts in MonoDevelop, switch back to Unity, and click *Play*.

The camera won't yet follow Dray into a new room, so you need to watch this in the Scene pane, but you can now see Dray move through the doorway into another room.

Making the Camera Follow Dray

Now that Dray can move from one room to the next, it's time to make the camera follow them.

1. Create a new C# script named *CamFollowDray* in the __Scripts folder.

2. Attach *CamFollowDray* to *Main Camera* in the Hierarchy.

3. Open *CamFollowDray* in MonoDevelop and enter the following code:

```csharp
using System.Collections;
using System.Collections.Generic;
using UnityEngine;

public class CamFollowDray : MonoBehaviour {
    static public bool TRANSITIONING = false;

    [Header("Set in Inspector")]
    public InRoom       drayInRm;                              // a
    public float        transTime = 0.5f;

    private Vector3     p0, p1;

    private InRoom      inRm;                                  // b
    private float       transStart;

    void Awake() {
        inRm = GetComponent<InRoom>();
    }

    void Update () {
        if (TRANSITIONING) {                                  // c
            float u = (Time.time - transStart) / transTime;
            if (u >= 1) {
                u = 1;
                TRANSITIONING = false;
            }
            transform.position = (1-u)*p0 + u*p1;
        } else {                                              // d
            if (drayInRm.roomNum != inRm.roomNum) {
                TransitionTo( drayInRm.roomNum );
            }
        }
    }
}
```

```
    void TransitionTo( Vector2 rm ) {                                    // e
        p0 = transform.position;
        inRm.roomNum = rm;
        p1 = transform.position + (Vector3.back * 10);
        transform.position = p0;

        transStart = Time.time;
        TRANSITIONING = true;
    }
}
```

a. You will need to assign the public field `drayInRm` in the Inspector.

b. CamFollowDray makes use of its own *InRoom* instance as well.

c. If CamFollowDray is transitioning, it moves the camera from the old room (`p0`) to the new (`p1`) over the course of 0.5 seconds (by default).

d. If CamFollowDray is not transitioning, it watches for `drayInRm` to be in a different room from this GameObject (the Main Camera).

e. When `TransitionTo()` is called, CamFollowDray caches its current position in `p0`, then temporarily moves to the new room and caches that position in `p1`. The code "`+ (Vector3.back * 10)`" is required because just setting the `roomNum` on InRoom would set the Z position of the GameObject to 0. CamFollowDray then jumps back to the original position, initializes the linear interpolation from `p0` to `p1`, and sets `TRANSITIONING` to true.

4. Save the *CamFollowDray* script and return to Unity.

5. Select *Main Camera* in the Hierarchy.

6. Attach an *InRoom* script to Main Camera.

   ▪ Set `keepInRoom` to false (unchecked).

7. Assign *Dray* to the `drayInRoom` field in the *CamFollowDray* Inspector of Main Camera. This gives CamFollowDray a reference to the InRoom component attached to Dray.

8. Save the scene, and click *Play*.

You should now be able to move anywhere within the bottom three rooms of the dungeon, but the locked door in the middle room is now an issue.

Unlocking Doors

To unlock doors in this dungeon, you need a key, and you're going to have to swap out the locked door tiles with open door tiles. The code will watch for a collision between Dray and a locked door tile. If Dray has a key when they run into a locked door, the key count will be decremented by one. This is made slightly more complicated by the up and down doors (facings 1 and 3) because they are each a pair of tiles, but we'll handle that as well.

The IKeyMaster

Though Dray will be the only person opening doors in this dungeon, I've chosen to implement an IKeyMaster interface to show you the implementation of multiple interfaces in a single class.

1. Create a new C# script named *IKeyMaster* inside the __Scripts folder.

2. Open *Keymaster* in MonoDevelop and enter the following code:

```csharp
using System.Collections;
using System.Collections.Generic;
using UnityEngine;

public interface IKeyMaster {
    int keyCount { get; set; }                                        // a
    int GetFacing();                                                  // b
}
```

    a. `keyCount` will allow you to get and set the number of keys.

    b. `GetFacing()` is already implemented in the Dray class (because of IFacingMover).

3. Save IKeyMaster and open the *Dray* script. Enter this bolded code into Dray.

```csharp
public class Dray : MonoBehaviour, IFacingMover, IKeyMaster {         // a
    …
    [Header("Set Dynamically")]
    public int          dirHeld = -1;// Direction of the held movement key
    public int          facing = 1;  // Direction Dray is facing
    public eMode        mode = eMode.idle;
    public int          numKeys = 0;                                  // b

    private float       timeAtkDone = 0;
    …
    // Implementation of IFacingMover
    public int GetFacing() {                                          // c
        return facing;
    }
    …
    public Vector2 GetRoomPosOnGrid( float mult = -1 ) {
        return inRm.GetRoomPosOnGrid( mult );
    }

    // Implementation of IKeyMaster
    public int keyCount {                                             // d
        get { return numKeys; }
        set { numKeys = value; }
    }
}
```

a. IKeyMaster is added to the list of interfaces implemented by the Dray class.

b. The `public int numKeys` field stores the number of keys in Dray's possession. This is public to allow you to easily modify it in the Unity Inspector. A private field with the attribute [SerializeField] would have been another good option.

c. `GetFacing()` is already implemented in the Dray class (because of IFacingMover).

d. `keyCount` is implemented as a simple public property.

4. Save the *Dray* script. Now, you're ready to implement the GateKeeper class.

The GateKeeper

The *GateKeeper* class unlocks doors by replacing locked door tiles with open door tiles on the TileCamera.MAP. The `Tile.SetTile()` method already has the ability to either take two parameters (the x and y location of the tile as `eX` and `eY`) or three (an added `eTileNum` parameter that allows a specific tile to be assigned in addition to the location). You'll make a slight modification to this method to not only display the sprite of the `eTileNum` that was passed in but also modify TileCamera.MAP to reflect the new tile.

Providing a Little Protection for TileCamera.MAP

This is a book on game prototyping, so in it I have been much more concerned about getting the games running than properly protecting my classes, but I would like to point out here that writing code that allows the Tile class to directly manipulate the static public MAP array of the TileCamera class is not very good style, which is why TileCamera.MAP is private and has two accessor methods, `GET_MAP()` and `SET_MAP()`, both of which have the security of not allowing `eX` or `eY` values that are out of range for MAP, thereby obviating any IndexOutOfRangeExceptions.

Another reason to have accessor methods like `SET_MAP()` is improved ability to track down bugs. If, in the future, you find that something is modifying MAP in strange ways, you can always place a debugger breakpoint in the `SET_MAP()` function and run the debugger. Then, any time `SET_MAP()` is called, execution will pause on that breakpoint, and you can look at the *Call Stack* pane in MonoDevelop to see what method is calling `SET_MAP()` and what arguments are being passed in. If you see a method or arguments that you didn't expect, you've found your culprit.

Using Tile.SetTile() to Modify TileCamera.MAP

Open the *Tile* script in MonoDevelop and make the following bolded modifications to the `SetTile()` method:

```
public class Tile : MonoBehaviour {
    …
    public void SetTile(int eX, int eY, int eTileNum = -1) {
        …
```

```
        if (eTileNum == -1) {
            eTileNum = TileCamera.MAP[x,y];
        } else {
            TileCamera.SET_MAP(x, y, eTileNum); // Replace if non-default tileNum
        }
        tileNum = eTileNum;
        …

    }
    …
}
```

Implementing the GateKeeper Script
Create the GateKeeper script by following these steps:

1. Create a C# script named *GateKeeper* in the __Scripts folder.

2. Attach *GateKeeper* to the *Dray* GameObject in the Hierarchy.

3. Open *GateKeeper* in MonoDevelop and enter this code:

```
using System.Collections;
using System.Collections.Generic;
using UnityEngine;

public class GateKeeper : MonoBehaviour {
    // These consts are based on the default DelverTiles image.
    // If you rearrange DelverTiles you may need to change it!
    //————————Locked Door tileNums                                       // a
    const int            lockedR  = 95;
    const int            lockedUR = 81;
    const int            lockedUL = 80;
    const int            lockedL  = 100;
    const int            lockedDL = 101;
    const int            lockedDR = 102;


    //————————Open Door tileNums
    const int          openR  = 48;
    const int          openUR = 93;
    const int          openUL = 92;
    const int          openL  = 51;
    const int          openDL = 26;
    const int          openDR = 27;


    private IKeyMaster       keys;

    void Awake() {
        keys = GetComponent<IKeyMaster>();
    }

    void OnCollisionStay( Collision coll ) {                              // b
```

```csharp
// No keys, no need to run
if (keys.keyCount < 1) return;

// Only worry about hitting tiles
Tile ti = coll.gameObject.GetComponent<Tile>();
if (ti == null) return;

// Only open if Dray is facing the door (avoid accidental key use)
int facing = keys.GetFacing();
// Check whether it's a door tile
Tile ti2;
switch (ti.tileNum) {                                            // c
    case lockedR:
        if (facing != 0) return;                                 // d
        ti.SetTile( ti.x, ti.y, openR );
        break;

    case lockedUR:
        if (facing != 1) return;
        ti.SetTile( ti.x, ti.y, openUR );
        ti2 = TileCamera.TILES[ti.x-1, ti.y];
        ti2.SetTile( ti2.x, ti2.y, openUL );
        break;

    case lockedUL:
        if (facing != 1) return;
        ti.SetTile( ti.x, ti.y, openUL );
        ti2 = TileCamera.TILES[ti.x+1, ti.y];
        ti2.SetTile( ti2.x, ti2.y, openUR );
        break;

    case lockedL:
        if (facing != 2) return;
        ti.SetTile( ti.x, ti.y, openL );
        break;

    case lockedDL:
        if (facing != 3) return;
        ti.SetTile( ti.x, ti.y, openDL );
        ti2 = TileCamera.TILES[ti.x+1, ti.y];
        ti2.SetTile( ti2.x, ti2.y, openDR );
        break;

    case lockedDR:
        if (facing != 3) return;
        ti.SetTile( ti.x, ti.y, openDR );
        ti2 = TileCamera.TILES[ti.x-1, ti.y];
        ti2.SetTile( ti2.x, ti2.y, openDL );
        break;
```

```
            default:
                return; // Return and avoid key decrement
        }

        keys.keyCount--;
    }
}
```

a. The const ints here are the tile numbers of the tiles for each possible locked door and open door (e.g., `lockedR` is 95, and the 95th sprite of the DelverTiles Texture2D shows the locked door heading to the right).

b. This `OnCollisionStay()` method will return (and avoid further execution) if Dray has no keys, if the object collided with is not a Tile, or if Dray is not facing the locked door. This keeps a key from getting decremented unless a door is actually unlocked, and it allows the player to walk past a door without opening it.

c. The cases in a `switch` statement cannot be variables, which is one of the reasons that all the ints were declared `const` at the top of the class.

d. If Dray is not facing toward the door the method returns.

4. *Save All* scripts in MonoDevelop and return to Unity.

5. Click *Play* in Unity and walk one room to the right. If you try to exit the locked door to the north, you won't be able to (yet).

6. With Unity still playing, select *Dray* in the Hierarchy and set the `numKeys` field of the *Dray (Script)* component to *6* (which should be enough keys to get through the whole dungeon). Now if you approach the door, you should be able to walk through it and explore the whole dungeon![11]

Adding GUI to Track Key Count and Health

Your players won't be able to track the number of keys by viewing the Unity Inspector, so you need to add some GUI elements.

1. Create a new Canvas by choosing *GameObject > UI > Canvas* from the Unity menu. This creates both a *Canvas* and an *Event System* at the root level of the Hierarchy.

2. Select *Canvas* in the Hierarchy.

3. In the Canvas Inspector on the Canvas GameObject:

---

11. You still cannot enter the left-most room in this dungeon. That is a different kind of door that cannot be opened by a key.

■ Set *Render Mode* to *Screen Space – Camera*.

■ Click the *target icon* to the right of *Render Camera* and choose *GUI Camera* from the Scene tab in the box that appears.

When you imported the starter unitypackage for this chapter, a UI Panel named *DelverPanel* was included in the _Prefabs folder of the Project pane.

4. Drag the *DelverPanel* from the _Prefabs folder onto *Canvas* in the Hierarchy, making DelverPanel a child of Canvas. You should now see the panel appear on the right side of the screen in the image of the GUI Camera. By default the GUI shows 0 keys and half health.

Let's write a script to get this UI working.

Adding Health to Dray

Right now, the Dray class tracks the number of keys but doesn't yet have health tracking or take damage. Let's fix the first part of that.

1. Open the *Dray* script in MonoDevelop and enter the following code:

```
public class Dray : MonoBehaviour, IFacingMover, IKeyMaster {
    public enum eMode { idle, move, attack, transition }

    [Header("Set in Inspector")]
    public float          speed = 5;
    public float          attackDuration = 0.25f;// Number of seconds to attack
    public float          attackDelay = 0.5f;    // Delay between attacks
    public float          transitionDelay = 0.5f;// Delay during transition
    public int            maxHealth = 10;                               // a

    [Header("Set Dynamically")]
    public int            dirHeld = -1; // Direction of the held movement key
    public int            facing = 1;   // Direction Dray is facing
    public eMode          mode = eMode.idle;
    public int            numKeys = 0;

    [SerializeField]                                                    // b
    private int           _health;

    public int health {                                                // c
        get { return _health; }
        set { _health = value; }
    }

    private float         timeAtkDone = 0;
    private float         timeAtkNext = 0;
    ...
```

```
void Awake () {
    rigid = GetComponent<Rigidbody>();
    anim = GetComponent<Animator>();
    inRm = GetComponent<InRoom>();
    health = maxHealth;                                    // d
}
}
```

a. The GUI shows five circles, and each circle represents 2 health points, so it can display 10 total health.

b. The [SerializeField] attribute allows Unity to show (and edit) the field _health in the Inspector even though it's private.

c. This health property allows read and write access to the private int _health from anywhere. This aids in debugging because you could put a breakpoint on the set clause if _health were changing, and you weren't sure why.

d. When Dray is instantiated, health is set to the maximum value.

2. Save all scripts in MonoDevelop and return to Unity.

Connecting the GUI to Dray

You need to write a script for the UI to reflect the health and numKeys values of Dray.

1. Create a new script named *GuiPanel* in the __Scripts folder of the Project pane.

2. Attach the *GuiPanel* script to the *DelverPanel* GameObject (under Canvas in the Hierarchy).

3. Open *GuiPanel* in MonoDevelop and enter the following code:

```
using System.Collections;
using System.Collections.Generic;
using UnityEngine;
using UnityEngine.UI;

public class GuiPanel : MonoBehaviour {
    [Header("Set in Inspector")]
    public Dray          dray;
    public Sprite        healthEmpty;
    public Sprite        healthHalf;
    public Sprite        healthFull;

    Text                 keyCountText;
    List<Image>          healthImages;

    void Start () {
        // Key Count
        Transform trans = transform.Find("Key Count");        // a
        keyCountText = trans.GetComponent<Text>();
```

```
        // Health Icons
        Transform healthPanel = transform.Find("Health Panel");
        healthImages = new List<Image>();
        if (healthPanel != null) {                                    // b
            for (int i=0; i<20; i++) {
                trans = healthPanel.Find("H_"+i);
                if (trans == null) break;
                healthImages.Add( trans.GetComponent<Image>() );
            }
        }
    }

    void Update () {
        // Show keys
        keyCountText.text = dray.numKeys.ToString();                  // c

        // Show health
        int health = dray.health;
        for (int i=0; i<healthImages.Count; i++) {                    // d
            if (health > 1) {
                healthImages[i].sprite = healthFull;
            } else if (health == 1) {
                healthImages[i].sprite = healthHalf;
            } else {
                healthImages[i].sprite = healthEmpty;
            }
            health -= 2;
        }
    }
}
```

a. This code relies entirely on the children of the DelverPanel transform being named
   properly. Here, you search for a child of DelverPanel named *Key Count*. The Text
   component of this child transform is then assigned to `keyCountText`. There is no
   double-checking here, so if the name of *Key Count* changes, the GetComponent line
   will throw a null reference exception.

b. First a child of DelverPanel named *Health Panel* is sought. If it is found, you sequentially
   search for children of *Health Panel* named *H_0* through *H_19*. As long as they are found,
   the Image component of each is added to the `healthImages` List. If a child transform
   is not found (e.g., when you search for *H_5* in the current panel), the `for` loop is exited.

c. The `numKeys` from `dray` is assigned to the `text` of `keyCountText`.

d. The health indicator is a bit more complex. The current health is read in from `dray`
   and stored in a local `int health`. You iterate through a `for` loop once for each
   `healthImage`, starting at the bottom (*H_0*). If `health` is greater than 1, then you
   show the `healthFull` sprite. If `health` is 1, you show `healthHalf`, and if `health` is

less than 1, you show `healthEmpty`. After each loop, the local `health` int is decremented by 2, and the next loop executes. This way, each `healthImage` displays up to 2 units of health.

4. Save the *GuiPanel* script and return to Unity.

5. Select *DelverPanel* in the Hierarchy and set the following in the *GuiPanel (Script)* Inspector:

   ▪ Assign *Dray* from the Hierarchy to the `dray` field.

   ▪ Assign the *Health_0* Sprite from the Health image in the _Images folder of the Project pane to `healthEmpty`.

   ▪ Assign *Health_1* from the Health image in the Project pane to `healthHalf`.

   ▪ Assign *Health_2* from the Health image in the Project pane to `healthFull`.

6. Click *Play*, and you should see the health indicator in the GUI jump to full.

7. Select *Dray* in the Hierarchy while Unity is playing and adjust their `numKeys` and `_health` to various values in the *Dray (Script)* Inspector. You should see these reflected in the GUI panel. Save your scene.

Enabling Enemies to Damage Dray

It's time to add some danger to the world by making enemies able to damage Dray on contact. This will also knock Dray back a bit and make Dray invincible for a brief time.

Implementing DamageEffect

The *DamageEffect* script will be used to track how much damage an enemy will do to Dray and whether contact with the enemy will cause knockback. Later, you'll apply this same script to Dray's weapons to define how those weapons affect enemies.

1. Create a new C# script named *DamageEffect* in the __Scripts folder.

2. Attach the *DamageEffect* script to the *Skeletos* GameObject in the Hierarchy.

3. Open *DamageEffect* in MonoDevelop and enter the following code:

```
using System.Collections;
using System.Collections.Generic;
using UnityEngine;

public class DamageEffect : MonoBehaviour {
    [Header("Set in Inspector")]
    public int      damage = 1;
    public bool     knockback = true;
}
```

4. Save *DamageEffect* in MonoDevelop and switch back to Unity. You can now see that the *DamageEffect (Script)* Inspector on Skeletos has two public fields.

By default, the amount of damage done is 1, which is equal to one-half of a health indicator in the GUI you just made. The default values are fine for Skeletos, so you don't need to change anything in the Inspector.

Modifying the Dray Class

You must also make changes to Dray to enable use of the DamageEffect script that you just attached to Skeletos.

1. Open the *Dray* script in MonoDevelop and make the following bolded code changes.

```
public class Dray : MonoBehaviour, IFacingMover, IKeyMaster {
    public enum eMode { idle, move, attack, transition, knockback }    // a

    [Header("Set in Inspector")]
    …
    public float          attackDelay = 0.5f;    // Delay between attacks
    public float          transitionDelay = 0.5f;// Delay during transition
    public int            maxHealth = 10;
    public float          knockbackSpeed = 10;                          // b
    public float          knockbackDuration = 0.25f;
    public float          invincibleDuration = 0.5f;

    [Header("Set Dynamically")]
    …
    public int            numKeys = 0;
    public bool           invincible = false;                           // c

    [SerializeField]
    private int           _health;
    …

    private float         transitionDone = 0;
    private Vector2       transitionPos;
    private float         knockbackDone = 0;                            // d
    private float         invincibleDone = 0;
    private Vector3       knockbackVel;

    private SpriteRenderer sRend;                                        // e
    private Rigidbody     rigid;
    …
    void Awake () {
        sRend = GetComponent<SpriteRenderer>();                         // e
        rigid = GetComponent<Rigidbody>();
        …
    }
```

```
void Update () {
    // Check knockback and invincibility
    if (invincible && Time.time > invincibleDone) invincible = false;      // f
    sRend.color = invincible ? Color.red : Color.white;
    if ( mode == eMode.knockback ) {
        rigid.velocity = knockbackVel;
        if (Time.time < knockbackDone) return;
    }

    if ( mode == eMode.transition ) { … }
    …
}

void LateUpdate() { … }

void OnCollisionEnter( Collision coll ) {
    if (invincible) return; // Return if Dray can't be damaged              // g
    DamageEffect dEf = coll.gameObject.GetComponent<DamageEffect>();
    if (dEf == null) return; // If no DamageEffect, exit this method

    health -= dEf.damage;// Subtract the damage amount from health           // h
    invincible = true; // Make Dray invincible
    invincibleDone = Time.time + invincibleDuration;

    if (dEf.knockback) { // Knockback Dray                                   // i
        // Determine the direction of knockback
        Vector3 delta = transform.position - coll.transform.position;
        if (Mathf.Abs(delta.x) >= Mathf.Abs(delta.y)) {
            // Knockback should be horizontal
            delta.x = (delta.x > 0) ? 1 : -1;
            delta.y = 0;
        } else {
            // Knockback should be vertical
            delta.x = 0;
            delta.y = (delta.y > 0) ? 1 : -1;
        }

        // Apply knockback speed to the Rigidbody
        knockbackVel = delta * knockbackSpeed;
        rigid.velocity = knockbackVel;

        // Set mode to knockback and set time to stop knockback
        mode = eMode.knockback;
        knockbackDone = Time.time + knockbackDuration;
    }
}
```

```
// Implementation of IFacingMover
public int GetFacing() { … }
    …
}
```

a. A new `eMode.knockback` has been added to the enum `eMode`.

b. `knockbackSpeed`, `knockbackDuration`, and `invincibleDuration` can all be set in the Inspector.

c. The `public bool invincible` is true when Dray is impervious to damage. It is a bool rather than an eMode state because Dray can be invincible at the same time as several different eModes (if Dray were only invincible when being knocked back, this would not be necessary).

d. Several new private fields have been added to implement knockback and invincibility.

e. To show the player both that Dray has been damaged and that they are invincible, Dray will be colored red throughout the invincible time. To do this, you need a reference to the *Sprite Renderer* component of Dray.

f. New code at the beginning of each `Update()` checks to see whether invincible or knockback times have expired. If Dray is invincible, `sRend` is colored red. If Dray is being knocked back, `knockbackVel` is assigned to `rigid.velocity`.

g. This `OnCollisionEnter()` method is called by Unity anytime Dray collides with the collider of another GameObject.

   This method will return before doing anything if Dray is invincible or if the thing that collided with Dray does not have a *DamageEffect* component (i.e., Dray collides with walls all the time, but walls don't cause damage). It would be fine to have `OnColli-sionEnter()` methods on several scripts on the same Dray GameObject; Unity would call `OnCollisionEnter()` on each of them.

h. The `damage` amount of the DamageEffect is subtracted from `health`, and Dray is made temporarily invincible.

i. If the DamageEffect that Dray collided with calls for a knockback, then the contents of this `if` statement execute. This finds the positional difference between Dray and the GameObject they collided with, locks the difference to either vertical or horizontal, and converts that into the `knockbackVelocity`. Then, Dray is put into knockback mode until Time.time is greater than `knockbackDone`.

2. Save all scripts in MonoDevelop, return to Unity, and click *Play*.

Now if you walk Dray into the Skeletos, you can see Dray take damage, be knocked back, and turn invincible. If you want to test the invincibility, you can use the *Dray (Script)* Inspector on the Dray GameObject to increase the `invincibleDuration` to ten seconds and then walk into the Skeletos multiple times.

The plan is to use `OnCollisionEnter()` for damage on Dray and `OnTriggerEnter()` for damage on the Skeletos and other enemies. This works because all of Dray's weapons will have *isTrigger* set to true, and this distinction between triggers and collisions enables you to use DamageEffects for both damage to Dray and enemies.

Making Dray's Attack Damage Enemies

Dray has been able to swing their sword for a while; now it's time to give that sword some bite.

1. Select *Sword* in the Hierarchy (it is the grandchild of Dray).

2. Attach a *DamageEffect* script to Sword.

   ▪ Set the `damage` of the *DamageEffect (Script)* to *2*. The sword should be reasonably powerful.

3. Save the scene.

Modifying Enemy to Take Damage

Given the extensive use of interfaces in this chapter, you might be considering creating an IDamageable interface that could work for both Dray and Enemies as well as a Damage script that could be attached to both (as you did with the GridMove script). You certainly could do that, but I have chosen not to do so for two main reasons:

▪ Dray collides with Enemies `OnCollisionEnter()`, whereas Enemies collide with Dray's sword `OnTriggerEnter()` (because the Sword's collider is a trigger).

▪ All the enemies are intended to be subclasses of Enemy, so adding code to Enemy will handle all of them.

1. Open the *Enemy* script in MonoDevelop and add the following code:

```
public class Enemy : MonoBehaviour {
    ...
    [Header("Set in Inspector: Enemy")]
    public float          maxHealth = 1;
    public float          knockbackSpeed = 10;              // a
    public float          knockbackDuration = 0.25f;
    public float          invincibleDuration = 0.5f;

    [Header("Set Dynamically: Enemy")]
    public float          health;
    public bool           invincible = false;               // a
    public bool           knockback = false;

    private float         invincibleDone = 0;               // a
    private float         knockbackDone = 0;
    private Vector3       knockbackVel;
```

…

```csharp
protected virtual void Awake() { … }

protected virtual void Update() {                                    // b
    // Check knockback and invincibility
    if (invincible && Time.time > invincibleDone) invincible = false;
    sRend.color = invincible ? Color.red : Color.white;
    if ( knockback ) {
        rigid.velocity = knockbackVel;
        if (Time.time < knockbackDone) return;
    }

    anim.speed = 1;                                                  // c
    knockback = false;
}

void OnTriggerEnter( Collider colld ) {                               // d
    if (invincible) return; // Return if this can't be damaged
    DamageEffect dEf = colld.gameObject.GetComponent<DamageEffect>();
    if (dEf == null) return; // If no DamageEffect, exit this method

    health -= dEf.damage; // Subtract the damage amount from health
    if (health <= 0) Die();                                          // e

    invincible = true; // Make this invincible
    invincibleDone = Time.time + invincibleDuration;

    if (dEf.knockback) { // Knockback this
        // Determine the direction of knockback
        Vector3 delta = transform.position - colld.transform.root.position;
        if (Mathf.Abs(delta.x) >= Mathf.Abs(delta.y)) {
            // Knockback should be horizontal
            delta.x = (delta.x > 0) ? 1 : -1;
            delta.y = 0;
        } else {
            // Knockback should be vertical
            delta.x = 0;
            delta.y = (delta.y > 0) ? 1 : -1;
        }

        // Apply knockback speed to the Rigidbody
        knockbackVel = delta * knockbackSpeed;
        rigid.velocity = knockbackVel;

        // Set mode to knockback and set time to stop knockback
        knockback = true;
        knockbackDone = Time.time + knockbackDuration;
        anim.speed = 0;
```

```
        }
    }

    void Die() {                                                      // f
        Destroy(gameObject);
    }
}
```

a. Most of the added fields are the same between Enemy and the changes you recently made to Dray. The only major difference is that `knockback` is a bool here, where it was a `Dray.eMode` in the Dray script.

b. This `Update()` method is declared `protected virtual` so that it can be overridden in subclasses like Skeletos. You'll do this in the next code listing.

c. These two lines only happen if the knockback has ended.

d. This `OnTriggerEnter()` method is used because Dray's sword has a trigger collider. Note that `OnTriggerEnter()` is passed a Collider rather than a Collision. Other than that, most of the script is very similar to what you wrote in the `Dray` class.

e. If this Enemy's `health` drops to or below 0, the new `Die()` method will be called.

f. `Die()` is not much right now, but later modifications will allow enemies to drop items when they are killed.

2. Save the *Enemy* script.

3. Open the *Skeletos* script in MonoDevelop and make the following small changes:

```
public class Skeletos : Enemy, IFacingMover {
    ...
    protected override void Awake () { ... }

    override protected void Update () {                               // a
        base.Update();
        if (knockback) return;

        if (Time.time >= timeNextDecision) {
            DecideDirection();
        }
        // rigid is inherited from Enemy, which defines it in Enemy.Awake()
        rigid.velocity = directions[facing] * speed;
    }
    ...
}
```

a. You must add `override protected` to the beginning of the `Update()` method declaration.

The first line of this `Update()` method calls the `Enemy.Update()` base class method. If this Skeletos is being knocked back, then the code returns after calling the `base.Update()` method, preventing the Skeletos from changing its direction or adjusting its velocity until the knockback is done.

4. Save all scripts in MonoDevelop and switch back to Unity.

5. Select the *Skeletos* in the Hierarchy and set `maxHealth` in the *Skeletos (Script)* Inspector to 4. This allows the Skeletos to take 2 hits from Dray's sword (which does 2 damage per hit) before being destroyed.

6. Save the scene and click *Play* in Unity.

Now Dray can attack the Skeletos, cause it damage, and knock it back.

Picking Up Items

Now that Dray can kill Enemies, you have somewhere that you can get both keys and health items. Let's start with the key.

1. Drag the *Key* from the _Images folder of the Project pane into the Hierarchy. This creates a GameObject with a *Sprite Renderer* that shows the Key sprite.

2. Set the following in the Key Inspector:
   - **Transform**: P:[28, 3, 0]
   - **Sprite Renderer**: Sorting Layer: *Items*

3. Add a *Box Collider* to the Key GameObject.
   - Set *Is Trigger* to true on the Box Collider.

4. Save the scene.

5. Create a new C# script named *PickUp* in the __Scripts folder.

6. Attach the *PickUp* script to the Key GameObject in the Hierarchy.

7. Open the *PickUp* script in MonoDevelop and enter this code:

```csharp
using System.Collections;
using System.Collections.Generic;
using UnityEngine;

public class PickUp : MonoBehaviour {
    public enum eType { key, health, grappler }

    public static float      COLLIDER_DELAY = 0.5f;

    [Header("Set in Inspector")]
    public eType            itemType;

    // Awake() and Activate() disable the PickUp's Collider for 0.5 secs
    void Awake() {
        GetComponent<Collider>().enabled = false;
        Invoke("Activate", COLLIDER_DELAY);
    }
```

```
    void Activate() {
        GetComponent<Collider>().enabled = true;
    }
}
```

8. Save the *PickUp* script.

9. Open the *Dray* script and add the following bolded code:

```
public class Dray : MonoBehaviour, IFacingMover, IKeyMaster {
    ...

    void OnCollisionEnter( Collision coll ) { ... }

    void OnTriggerEnter( Collider colld ) {
        PickUp pup = colld.GetComponent<PickUp>();              // a
        if (pup == null) return;

        switch (pup.itemType) {
            case PickUp.eType.health:
                health = Mathf.Min( health+2, maxHealth );
                break;

            case PickUp.eType.key:
                keyCount++;
                break;
        }

        Destroy( colld.gameObject );
    }

    // Implementation of IFacingMover
    public int GetFacing() { ... }
    ...
}
```

a. If the GameObject that collided with this trigger doesn't have a *PickUp* script attached to it, this method returns without doing anything.

10. Save all scripts in MonoDevelop and return to Unity.

11. Select the *Key* in the Hierarchy and set the `itemType` to *Key* in the *PickUp (Script)* component Inspector.

12. Save the scene and click *Play*.

You should now be able to pick up the key, see the key count increase in the GUI, and then use the key to open the first door.

Enemies Dropping Items on Death

You want some enemies to always drop a key. You want other enemies to drop a health item some of the time.

Dropping Keys

Follow these steps to make enemies drop keys:

1. Open the *Enemy* script in MonoDevelop and enter these code additions:

```
public class Enemy : MonoBehaviour {
    …
    [Header("Set in Inspector: Enemy")]
    …
    public float                invincibleDuration = 0.5f;
    public GameObject           guaranteedItemDrop = null;

    [Header("Set Dynamically: Enemy")]
    …
    void Die() {
        GameObject go;
        if ( guaranteedItemDrop != null ) {
            go = Instantiate<GameObject>( guaranteedItemDrop );
            go.transform.position = transform.position;
        }
        Destroy(gameObject);
    }
}
```

2. Save the *Enemy* script and return to Unity.
3. Make *Key* a prefab by dragging it from the Hierarchy into the _Prefab folder of the Project pane.
4. Select *Skeletos* in the Hierarchy, and assign the *Key* prefab (from the _Prefabs folder) to the `guaranteedItemDrop` field of the *Skeletos (Script)* Inspector on the Skeletos GameObject.
5. Save the scene and click *Play*.

Now if you kill the Skeletos, it should drop a key that you can pick up.

Dropping Randomized Items

You also want to implement the possibility of Enemies dropping a randomized item. If there is no `guaranteedItemDrop`,[12] then a random item will be selected from an array of possible items, and the list will include several null entries so that an item is not always guaranteed.

First, you'll need to do some item prep work.

---

12. Although some data types like Vector3 are not allowed to be `null` in the Inspector, the GameObject `guaranteedItemDrop` can be set to *None (GameObject)*, a value that Unity resolves to `null`.

Creating the Health PickUp Item

To create the Health item, follow these steps:

1. In the Project pane, select the *Health_2* and *Health_3* sprites under the Health Texture 2D in the _Images folder.

2. Drag them into the Hierarchy to create a new GameObject and Animation.

3. Name the Animation that is created *Health.anim* and save it in the _Animations folder.

4. Select the *Health_2 GameObject* in the Hierarchy and do the following:

    ▪ **Name**: Change the *name* of Health_2 to *Health*.

    ▪ **Transform**: Set the *position* of Health to P:[28, 7, 0].

    ▪ **Sprite Renderer**: Set the *Sorting Layer* to Items.

    ▪ Add a *Box Collider* to Health.

    ▪ **Box Collider**: Set *Is Trigger* to true.

    ▪ Add a *PickUp (Script)* component to Health.

    ▪ **PickUp (Script)**: Set `itemType` to *Health*.

5. With the Health GameObject in the Hierarchy still selected, open the Animation pane (*Window > Animation*) and set the *Samples* of the Health animation to 4 (which makes the Health item blink at a reasonable rate of four frames per second).

6. Drag the *Health* GameObject from the Hierarchy into the _*Prefabs* folder of the Project pane to make a Health prefab.

7. Save the scene and click *Play*.

8. Walk Dray into the Skeletos a couple of times to take some damage. Then walk over the Health item, and you should regain some health.

Implementing Code for Randomized Item Drops

Follow these steps to create the code for randomized item drops.

1. Open the *Enemy* script in MonoDevelop and make the bolded code changes:

```
public class Enemy : MonoBehaviour {
    …
    [Header("Set in Inspector: Enemy")]
    …
    public float                invincibleDuration = 0.5f;
    public GameObject[]         randomItemDrops;                    // a
    public GameObject           guaranteedItemDrop = null;
    …
    void OnTriggerEnter( Collider colld ) { … }

    void Die() {
        GameObject go;
```

```
        if ( guaranteedItemDrop != null ) {
            go = Instantiate<GameObject>( guaranteedItemDrop );
            go.transform.position = transform.position;
        } else if (randomItemDrops.Length > 0) {                      // b
            int n = Random.Range( 0, randomItemDrops.Length );
            GameObject prefab = randomItemDrops[n];
            if (prefab != null) {
                go = Instantiate<GameObject>( prefab );
                go.transform.position = transform.position;
            }
        }
        Destroy(gameObject);
    }
}
```

a. The `randomItemDrops` array can hold any number of possible items (and null *None (GameObject)* entries) to select from when the Enemy is killed.

b. If there is no `guaranteedItemDrop` and there are entries in the `randomItemDrops` array, one of these entries will be chosen and assigned to `prefab`. If `prefab` is not null, then an instance of `prefab` will be instantiated.

2. Save the *Enemy* script and return to Unity.

3. Select the *Skeletos* GameObject in the Hierarchy.

   ▪ Delete the Key from the `guaranteedItemDrop`, leaving *None (Game Object)* in its place.

   ▪ Open the disclosure triangle next to `randomItemDrops` in the *Skeletos (Script)* inspector.

   ▪ Set the *Size* of `randomItemDrops` to 1.

   ▪ Assign the *Health* prefab (from the _Prefabs folder) to *Element 0* of `randomItemDrops`.

4. Make *Skeletos* a prefab by dragging it from the Hierarchy into the _Prefabs folder of the Project pane.

5. Save the scene and click *Play* in Unity.

Now when Dray kills the Skeletos, it will drop a Health item.

6. Select the *Skeletos* prefab in the _Prefabs folder of the Project pane (not the Hierarchy).

   ▪ Set the *Size* of `randomItemDrops` in the *Skeletos (Script)* Inspector to 2.

   ▪ Delete the Health prefab from Element 1.

   ▪ Set the *Size* of `randomItemDrops` to 3. This gives you two total null (*None (Game Object)*) entries, which will make the Skeletos (without a `guaranteedItemDrop` set) drop Health 1/3 of the time.

These changes in the Skeletos prefab should automatically be reflected in the Skeletos instance in the Hierarchy.

Implementing a Grappler

The last item that you'll implement is a grappling hook that enables you to pass over previously impassable red tiles.

1. The unitypackage that you imported at the beginning of this chapter included a *Grappler* prefab in the _Prefabs folder. Select that Grappler prefab in the _Prefabs folder of the Project pane.

    ■ **Sprite Renderer**: Set the *Sorting Layer* of the Grappler to *Items*.

2. Drag *Grappler* onto the *Dray* GameObject in the Hierarchy, making it a child of Dray (and a sibling of SwordController).

3. Create a new C# script named *Grapple* in the __Scripts folder. (This script is named Grapple—after the action, not the item—to differentiate it from the Grappler item; the name difference is because the Grapple script will be attached to Dray, not to the Grappler.)

4. Attach the *Grapple* script to Dray.

5. Open the *Grapple* script in MonoDevelop and enter the following code. This script is a bit longer than the others in this chapter.

```csharp
using System.Collections;
using System.Collections.Generic;
using UnityEngine;

public class Grapple : MonoBehaviour {
    public enum eMode { none, gOut, gInMiss, gInHit }          // a

    [Header("Set in Inspector")]
    public float            grappleSpd = 10;
    public float            grappleLength = 7;
    public float            grappleInLength = 0.5f;
    public int              unsafeTileHealthPenalty = 2;
    public TextAsset        mapGrappleable;

    [Header("Set Dynamically")]
    public eMode            mode = eMode.none;
    // TileNums that can be grappled
    public List<int>        grappleTiles;                       // b
    public List<int>        unsafeTiles;

    private Dray            dray;
    private Rigidbody       rigid;
    private Animator        anim;
    private Collider        drayColld;

    private GameObject      grapHead;                           // c
    private LineRenderer    grapLine;
```

```csharp
private Vector3        p0, p1;
private int            facing;

private Vector3[]      directions = new Vector3[] {
    Vector3.right, Vector3.up, Vector3.left, Vector3.down };

void Awake() {
    string gTiles = mapGrappleable.text;                    // d
    gTiles = Utils.RemoveLineEndings( gTiles );
    grappleTiles = new List<int>();
    unsafeTiles = new List<int>();
    for (int i=0; i<gTiles.Length; i++) {
        switch (gTiles[i]) {
            case 'S':
                grappleTiles.Add(i);
                break;

            case 'X':
                unsafeTiles.Add(i);
                break;
        }
    }

    dray = GetComponent<Dray>();
    rigid = GetComponent<Rigidbody>();
    anim = GetComponent<Animator>();
    drayColld = GetComponent<Collider>();

    Transform trans = transform.Find("Grappler");
    grapHead = trans.gameObject;
    grapLine = grapHead.GetComponent<LineRenderer>();
    grapHead.SetActive(false);
}

void Update () {
    if (!dray.hasGrappler) return;                          // e

    switch (mode) {
        case eMode.none:
            // If the grapple button is pressed
            if ( Input.GetKeyDown(KeyCode.X) ) {
                StartGrapple();
            }
            break;
    }
}

void StartGrapple() {                                       // f
    facing = dray.GetFacing();
```

```
        dray.enabled = false;                                              // g
        anim.CrossFade( "Dray_Attack_"+facing, 0 );
        drayColld.enabled = false;
        rigid.velocity = Vector3.zero;

        grapHead.SetActive(true);

        p0 = transform.position + ( directions[facing] * 0.5f );
        p1 = p0;
        grapHead.transform.position = p1;
        grapHead.transform.rotation = Quaternion.Euler(0,0,90*facing);

        grapLine.positionCount = 2;                                        // h
        grapLine.SetPosition(0,p0);
        grapLine.SetPosition(1,p1);
        mode = eMode.gOut;
    }

    void FixedUpdate() {
        switch (mode) {
            case eMode.gOut: // Grappler shooting out                      // i
                p1 += directions[facing] * grappleSpd * Time.fixedDeltaTime;
                grapHead.transform.position = p1;
                grapLine.SetPosition(1,p1);

                // Check to see whether the grapple hit anything
                int tileNum = TileCamera.GET_MAP(p1.x,p1.y);
                if ( grappleTiles.IndexOf( tileNum ) != -1 ) {
                    // We've hit a grappleable tile!
                    mode = eMode.gInHit;
                    break;
                }
                if ( (p1-p0).magnitude >= grappleLength ) {
                    // The grapple reached its end and didn't hit anything
                    mode = eMode.gInMiss;
                }
                break;

            case eMode.gInMiss: // Grappler missed; return at double speed  // j
                p1 -= directions[facing] * 2 * grappleSpd * Time.fixedDeltaTime;
                if ( Vector3.Dot( (p1-p0), directions[facing] ) > 0 ) {
                    // The grapple is still in front of Dray
                    grapHead.transform.position = p1;
                    grapLine.SetPosition(1,p1);
                } else {
                    StopGrapple();
                }
                break;
```

```
            case eMode.gInHit: // Grappler hit, pulling Dray to wall        // k
                float dist = grappleInLength + grappleSpd * Time.fixedDeltaTime;
                if (dist > (p1-p0).magnitude) {
                    p0 = p1 - ( directions[facing] * grappleInLength );
                    transform.position = p0;
                    StopGrapple();
                    break;
                }
                p0 += directions[facing] * grappleSpd * Time.fixedDeltaTime;
                transform.position = p0;
                grapLine.SetPosition(0,p0);
                grapHead.transform.position = p1;
                break;
        }

    }

    void StopGrapple() {                                                    // l
        dray.enabled = true;
        drayColld.enabled = true;

        // Check for unsafe tile
        int tileNum = TileCamera.GET_MAP(p0.x,p0.y);
        if (mode == eMode.gInHit && unsafeTiles.IndexOf(tileNum) != -1) {
            // We landed on an unsafe tile
            dray.ResetInRoom( unsafeTileHealthPenalty );
        }

        grapHead.SetActive(false);

        mode = eMode.none;
    }

    void OnTriggerEnter( Collider colld ) {                                 // m
        Enemy e = colld.GetComponent<Enemy>();
        if (e == null) return;

        mode = eMode.gInMiss;
    }
}
```

a. The four grapple modes are:

- none: Inactive

- gOut: The Grappler is extending

- gInMiss: The Grappler didn't hit anything and is retracting; Dray doesn't move

- gInHit: The Grappler hit something and is now pulling Dray towards it

b. `grappleTiles` stores a List of tile types that the Grappler can collide with to score a `gInHit`. The List `unsafeTiles` stores the types of tiles that it is unsafe for Dray to land on after a `gInHit`; this is important in rooms where grapple movement could leave Dray over a red tile.

c. `grapHead` is a reference to the GameObject for the head of the Grappler. `grapLine` is a reference to the LineRenderer on the Grappler.

d. On `Awake()` the `mapGrappleable` text file is read to generate the `grappleTiles` and `unsafeTiles` Lists. `Awake()` also finds references to the sundry components that need to be cached.

e. If the grapple `mode` is `none`, and Dray has the Grappler, the `Update()` method watches for the grapple key (X) to be pressed. `dray.hasGrappler` is red because you still need to add code to Dray to make use of the Grappler.

f. `StartGrapple()` aligns the grappler to Dray's position and orientation and sets it up to launch.

g. `StartGrapple()` also disables the `dray` script on Dray, which prevents player interaction with Dray until the grapple has finished. The `anim` is set to a specific state, and Dray's collider is also disabled.

h. Here the `grapLine` LineRenderer is set up. The Grappler always flies in a straight line, so the LineRenderer only needs two points.

i. When the Grappler is shooting out, it moves away from Dray at a fixed speed on `FixedUpdate()`. The `grapHead` is moved, and p1 of the LineRenderer is moved along with it. Rather than using a collider, the position of the `grapHead` is checked directly against `TileCamera.MAP` to see whether it hits any `grappleTiles`. If it does hit a `grappleTile`, the Grapple class changes into `gInHit` mode; if the Grappler moves far enough without hitting anything, it changes into `gInMiss` mode.

j. In `gInMiss` mode, the Grappler retracts at double speed. A dot product test is used to see if p1 is still in front of Dray (see Appendix B, "Useful Concepts" for more information on using dot products in your coding).

k. In `gInHit` mode, Dray is brought toward the `grapHead`. Because Dray's collider is disabled, they will pass through anything on the way there (allowing Dray to pass over the normally impassable red floor tiles).

l. `StopGrapple()` will re-enable both the `dray` script and `drayColld`. Then, if the Grapple script was in `gInHit` mode, it checks Dray's position, and if they are over an unsafe tile, they will take some damage and their position in the room will be reset to the last door through which they entered. The `Dray.ResetInRoom()` method that does this has yet to be written.

> **m.** This `OnTriggerEnter()` method causes the Grappler to retract with a `gInMiss` if the `grapHead` comes into contact with an Enemy. You will shortly add a DamageEffect script to the Grappler in the Hierarchy, which will cause it to also damage the Enemy.

6. Save the *Grapple* script.

Modifying Dray to Enable Grappler

Follow these steps to enable Dray to use the Grappler:

1. Open the *Dray* script in MonoDevelop and make the following bolded changes:

```
public class Dray : MonoBehaviour, IFacingMover, IKeyMaster {
    …
    [Header("Set Dynamically")]
    …
    public bool            invincible = false;
    public bool            hasGrappler = false;
    public Vector3         lastSafeLoc;                              // a
    public int             lastSafeFacing;

    [SerializeField]
    private int            _health;
    …

    void Awake () {
        …
        health = maxHealth;
        lastSafeLoc = transform.position; // The start position is safe.
        lastSafeFacing = facing;
    }
    …

    void LateUpdate() {
        …
        // Make sure that the rm we want to jump to is valid
        if (rm.x >= 0 && rm.x <= InRoom.MAX_RM_X) {
            if (rm.y >=0 && rm.y <= InRoom.MAX_RM_Y) {
                roomNum = rm;
                transitionPos = InRoom.DOORS[ (doorNum+2) % 4 ];
                roomPos = transitionPos;
                lastSafeLoc = transform.position;                   // b
                lastSafeFacing = facing;
                mode = eMode.transition;
                transitionDone = Time.time + transitionDelay;
            }
        }
    }
    …
```

```
void OnTriggerEnter( Collider colld ) {
    …
    switch (pup.itemType) {
        …
        case PickUp.eType.key:
            keyCount++;
            break;

        case PickUp.eType.grappler:                          // c
            hasGrappler = true;
            break;
    }
    …
}

public void ResetInRoom(int healthLoss = 0) {               // d
    transform.position = lastSafeLoc;
    facing = lastSafeFacing;
    health -= healthLoss;

    invincible = true; // Make Dray invincible
    invincibleDone = Time.time + invincibleDuration;
}

// Implementation of IFacingMover
…
}
```

a. `hasGrappler` is true when Dray has acquired the Grappler. `lastSafeLoc` and `last-SafeFacing` store the location and facing Dray was at when they last entered a room. If the Grappler lands them on an unsafe tile, they can reset to this position and facing.

b. `lastSafeLocation` and `lastSafeFacing` are set any time Dray enters a new room.

c. When Dray touches a PickUp of the grappler type, `hasGrappler` is set to true.

d. When Called, `ResetInRoom()` moves Dray to the last safe location and facing in the current room. Health is also deducted.

You might have noticed that you didn't add anything to the `Update()` method in Dray to make the Grappler fire. That's because the `Update()` method in the Grapple script is handling this interaction. Whether this is good style or not is up for debate: on the one hand, having all of your interaction code in the same place is often good; on the other hand, making it part of Grapple means that you could later add other weapons and tools and map keyboard presses to them without having to modify the interaction code in the Dray script. This is the kind of thing that becomes an important consideration when you move from prototyping a project to developing it.

2. Save all scripts in MonoDevelop and return to Unity.

3. Select *Dray* in the Hierarchy.

   ■ **Grapple (Script)**: Assign the *DelverGrappleable* text file from the Resources folder of the Project pane to the `mapGrappleable` field. This text file is used to populate both the `grappleTiles` and `unsafeTiles` lists of the Grapple script.

4. Save the scene.

Adding Damage to the Grappler

Attaching a DamageEffect script to the Grappler GameObject will cause it to damage enemies. This will give Dray a weak ranged weapon that they can use.

1. Select *Grappler* in the Hierarchy (a child of Dray).

2. Attach a *DamageEffect (Script)* component to Grappler.

   ■ Set `damage` to 1.

   ■ Set `knockback` to false (unchecked).

3. Save your Scene.

Implementing a Grappler PickUp

Dray needs the ability to pick up the Grappler partway through a level. Luckily, a Grappler-PickUp prefab was part of the unitypakage that you imported at the beginning of the chapter, but you still need to add the PickUp script to it to make it work.

1. Drag *GrapplerPickUp* from the _Prefabs folder of the Project pane into the Hierarchy.

2. Give it a Transform of P:[19, 3, 0], R:[0, 0, 0], S:[2, 2, 2].

3. Add a *PickUp (Script)* component to GrapplerPickUp and set the `itemType` of the *PickUp (Script)* component to *Grappler*.

4. Click the *Apply* button at the top of the GrapplerPickUp Inspector. This applies the changes made to the GrapplerPickUp instance in the Hierarchy back to the GrapplerPickUp prefab in the _Prefabs folder of the Project pane.

5. Select the *GrapplerPickUp* prefab in the Project pane to ensure that these changes did get applied to it.

Testing the Grappler

To test the Grappler, follow these steps:

1. Click *Play*. Press the X key on your keyboard. Nothing happens at this point.

2. Move Dray over the Grappler pickup, which will set the `hasGrappler` field on Dray to true.

Now you can press X to use the Grappler. It should attach to walls and pull you toward them. The Grappler can also be used to pick up items like keys and health. Additionally, it can do a little damage to the Skeletos—half the amount of the sword—but does not cause knockback.

3. Pause the game (click the *Pause* button in the middle at the top of the screen), and set Dray's transform.position to P:[39.5, 40, 0]. This places Dray directly below a room with several red tiles next to the walls (in the neck of the Eagle dungeon from *The Legend of Zelda*).

4. Unpause the game (click *Pause* again) and move Dray up through the door and into the room with many red tiles (moving into the room sets `lastSafeLocation` and `lastSafeFacing`).

5. Try grappling to the walls in this room so that Dray ends up on a red tile when the grapple ends. You'll see that Dray loses some health and is reset back to the safe doorway.

6. Pause again, set Dray's transform.position to P:[40, 49.5, 0], and unpause.

7. Face to the right, and fire the Grappler into the wall.

The `y - 0.25f` code in the `GET_MAP(float, float)` method of TileCamera (marked `// g` in the TileCamera code listing much earlier in the chapter under the heading *TileCamera Class—Parsing Data and Sprite Files*) makes this a safe location for Dray (without subtracting `0.25f`, Dray's location would have been rounded up into the red tile).

8. Stop playback and save your scene.

When you're done testing the Grappler, it's time to move on to another dungeon layout.

Implementing a New Dungeon—The Hat

Now you're going to implement the dungeon that was the example prototype in Chapter 9, "Paper Prototyping." As part of this, you'll also implement a way of embedding enemies in the DelverData file.

Preparing the Scene

Follow these steps to prepare the scene:

1. From the menu, choose *File > Save Scene As* to save a new copy of your scene as *_Scene_Hat*.

2. When you *Save Scene As*, Unity sometimes keeps you in the old scene. Double-check that the window title displays *_Scene_Hat*. If not, double-click *_Scene_Hat* in the Project pane to open it.

3. Ensure that you have created prefabs of *Skeletos*, the *Key* pickup, and the *Health* pickup. You should see them all in the *_Prefabs* folder of the Project pane. If any are not there, drag them from the Hierarchy into the *_Prefabs* folder.

4. Delete the Skeletos, Key, Health, and GrapplerPickUp game objects from the Hierarchy. There should now be only six GameObjects at the top level of your Hierarchy: Main Camera,

Directional Light,[13] GUI Camera, Dray, Canvas, and Event System (and Dray and Canvas will each have children).

5. Select *Main Camera* in the Hierarchy.

   ▪ **Transform**: Set the position to P:[55.5, 5, -10].

   ▪ **TileCamera (Script)**: Assign the *DelverData_Hat* text file from the Resources folder of the Project pane to the `mapData` field of the *TileCamera (Script)* component.

6. Select *Dray* in the Hierarchy.

   ▪ **Transform**: Set position to P:[55.5, 1, 0].

   ▪ **Dray (Script)**: Ensure that `hasGrappler` is false (unchecked).

7. Save the scene and click *Play*.

You'll see that the game has loaded an entirely new dungeon for you to explore. In the first room, you can see an image of an unreachable key. If you move one room to the left, you see two images of Skeletos enemies, but they aren't moving. Right now, all of these are just special floor tiles that look like enemies and items. You need to write some code to swap these special tiles for the real thing, because you can't explore much of this dungeon without Keys or a Grappler, and it's not very challenging without Enemies.

Swapping Map Tiles for Enemies and Items

This addition to the TileCamera script will swap special tiles in the map for an Enemy or Item and a floor tile. If you look at the DelverTiles image in the Resources folder of the Project pane, you can see that the lower quarter of the image includes tiles that look like various items, enemies, and enemies with keys. These are the special tiles that will be replaced in the final map by a normal ground tile with an item or enemy spawned on top.

1. Open the *TileCamera* script in MonoDevelop and make the following bolded code changes:

```
using System.Collections;
using System.Collections.Generic;
using UnityEngine;

[System.Serializable]
public class TileSwap {                                    // a
    public int              tileNum;
    public GameObject       swapPrefab;
    public GameObject       guaranteedItemDrop;
    public int              overrideTileNum = -1;
}
```

---

13. Sometimes, when you create a new project in Unity, the initial scene doesn't have a Directional Light included. You can just add one here if you don't have it, though the presence or absence of a Directional Light has no effect on the Sprite Renderer shader in this project (as of Unity 2017).

```csharp
public class TileCamera : MonoBehaviour {
    …
    [Header("Set in Inspector")]
    …
    public Tile              tilePrefab;
    public int               defaultTileNum;                              // b
    public List<TileSwap>    tileSwaps;                                   // c

    private Dictionary<int,TileSwap> tileSwapDict;                        // c
    private Transform        enemyAnchor, itemAnchor;

    void Awake() {
        COLLISIONS = Utils.RemoveLineEndings( mapCollisions.text );
        PrepareTileSwapDict();                                           // d
        enemyAnchor = (new GameObject("Enemy Anchor")).transform;
        itemAnchor = (new GameObject("Item Anchor")).transform;
        LoadMap();
    }

    public void LoadMap() {
        …
        MAP = new int[W,H];
        for (int j=0; j<H; j++) {
            tileNums = lines[j].Split(' ');
            for (int i=0; i<W; i++) {
                if (tileNums[i] == "..") {
                    MAP[i,j] = 0;
                } else {
                    MAP[i,j] = int.Parse( tileNums[i], hexNum );
                }
                CheckTileSwaps(i,j);                                     // e
            }
        }
        …
    }


    void ShowMap() { … }

    void PrepareTileSwapDict() {                                          // d
        tileSwapDict = new Dictionary<int, TileSwap>();
        foreach (TileSwap ts in tileSwaps) {
            tileSwapDict.Add(ts.tileNum, ts);
        }
    }

    void CheckTileSwaps(int i, int j) {                                   // e
        int tNum = GET_MAP(i,j);
        if ( !tileSwapDict.ContainsKey(tNum) ) return;
```

```
    // We do need to swap a tile
    TileSwap ts = tileSwapDict[tNum];
    if (ts.swapPrefab != null) {                                    // f
        GameObject go = Instantiate(ts.swapPrefab);
        Enemy e = go.GetComponent<Enemy>();
        if (e != null) {
            go.transform.SetParent( enemyAnchor );
        } else {
            go.transform.SetParent( itemAnchor );
        }
        go.transform.position = new Vector3(i,j,0);
        if (ts.guaranteedItemDrop != null) {                        // g
            if (e != null) {
                e.guaranteedItemDrop = ts.guaranteedItemDrop;
            }
        }
    }

    // Replace with another tile
    if (ts.overrideTileNum == -1) {                                 // h
        SET_MAP( i, j, defaultTileNum );
    } else {
        SET_MAP( i, j, ts.overrideTileNum );
    }
}

...
}
```

a. The serializable TileSwap class includes all the information necessary to swap out spe-
    cial tiles in the map for a normal ground tile with an enemy or item on top of it.

    ■ `tileNum`: The tile number of the special tile to replace

    ■ `swapPrefab`: The prefab of the enemy or item to spawn on top of this special tile

    ■ `guaranteedItemDrop`: Some special tiles indicate that a specific enemy should be
      guaranteed to drop a key when killed. Anything placed in this `guaranteedItem-
      Drop` field will be placed in the `guaranteedItemDrop` field of the spawned Enemy.

    ■ `overrideTileNum`: Most special tiles should be replaced by the `defaultTileNum`
      tile (which is the normal ground tile). Assign an int to this field to replace the special tile
      with a specific other tile. You will implement this for the Spiker enemies in the top-right
      room of the dungeon; they should sit over a red floor rather than the standard floor tile.

b. `defaultTileNum` is the tile number of the floor tile that will usually be swapped
    in for any special tiles. In this game, the `defaultTileNum` is 29, which refers to the
    DelverTiles_29 sprite showing the yellow floor.

c. Lists are serializable, but Dictionaries are not. However, Dictionaries are easier to
    search (their keys are built on hash tables, which allow very fast searching). You will
    enter TileSwap information into the `tileSwaps` List, and then on `Awake()` the
    `PrepareTileSwapDict()` method will parse it into the `tileSwapDict`.

   d. `PrepareTileSwapDict()` iterates over all the entries in the `tileSwaps` List and adds
   them to `tileSwapDict`, keyed on the `tileNum` of the special tile to be swapped out.

   e. `CheckTileSwaps()` takes a map location as input. It looks at that location in the
   MAP and will swap the tile if it is included in `tileSwapDict`. `CheckTileSwaps()`
   makes use of `GET_MAP()` and `SET_MAP()` to make later debugging easier (putting a
   breakpoint in an accessor function like `SET_MAP()` is always easier than tracking down
   a method that is changing a field directly).

   f. If `tileSwapDict` contains an entry for the tileNum (`tNum`) at the specified location,
   `CheckTileSwaps()` gets the appropriate instance of the `TileSwap` class from
   `tileSwapDict`. Then, if there is a `swapPrefab`, it instantiates the enemy or item
   prefab and positions it at the current tile's location.

   g. If there is a `guaranteedItemDrop` and the `swapPrefab` has an Enemy component,
   the `guaranteedItemDrop` from the TileSwap is placed into the `guaranteedItem-
   Drop` field of the instantiated Enemy.

   h. Finally, `TileCamera.MAP` is modified, replacing the initial special tile number with the
   `defaultTileNum` (the yellow floor). If the TileSwap `ts` includes an `overrideTileNum`
   that is not -1, that tileNum will be assigned to the MAP location instead of the default.

2. Save the *TileCamera* script and return to Unity.

3. Select *Main Camera* in the Hierarchy and set the following:

   ▪ **TileCamera (Script)**: Set `defaultTileNum` to 29.

   ▪ **TileCamera (Script)**: Set the *Size* of `tileSwaps` to 6.

   ▪ **TileCamera (Script)**: Set the `tileSwaps` settings to those shown in Figure 35.10.

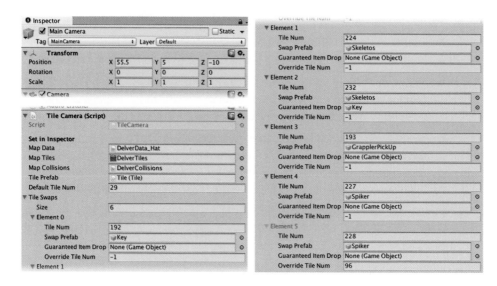

Figure 35.10 The settings for the `tileSwaps` List of the *TileCamera (Script)* component on Main
Camera

Elements 4 and 5 of the `tileSwaps` array use the *Spiker* prefab that was imported as part of the original unitypackage. Right now, the Spiker enemy doesn't do much, but these two entries do demonstrate the use of `overrideTileNum` to cause the special tile to be replaced with a non-default floor tile (in this case, the red tile). You can see this in the top-right room of the Hat dungeon.

4. Save the scene and click *Play*. Now you should be able to play through the entire level, including picking up all the Keys (many from defeated enemies) and the Grappler![14]

The Delver Level Editor

If you want to make your own *Dungeon Delver* levels, you can download the *Delver Level Editor* from the website for this book: http://book.prototools.net. Look in Chapter 35. The *Delver Level Editor* includes instructions for building your own levels and for importing them into the *Dungeon Delver* game prototype that you just wrote.

Summary

That's it for the final tutorial! This prototype introduced you to a lot of new concepts like interfaces and more extensive use of component-based thinking. This base can allow you to create all sorts of action-adventure games, and I encourage you to explore it further.

Next Steps

If you do continue with this project, here are some additional things you can add to make it a more interesting game:

1. Make your own levels! Try prototyping them as described in Chapter 9, "Paper Prototyping."

2. Implement the Spiker enemy. The prefab is already there, but it needs a little work. Instructions for implementing it are in a long comment at the top of the Spiker C# script that was included in the unitypackage you imported at the beginning of this chapter.

3. Make more enemies. Several more sprites for enemies are included in the unitypackage you imported at the beginning of the chapter than you implemented in this chapter. Try adding some new enemies with new behaviors.

4. Make the Grappler stun Enemies when it hits them. This would make it very similar in use to the boomerang in *The Legend of Zelda*.

---

14. If you don't have enough keys, make sure you've killed all the Skeletos enemies—some are holding keys. If your health gets too low, don't worry; you never implemented a lose condition for when Dray's health drops to 0. That's something you can definitely do on your own now.

5. Another element that could be borrowed from *The Legend of Zelda* is the magic sword that shoots out when Link is at full health. There is a second sword image in the Swords image file that could be used for this.

6. Design and implement a new weapon/item. You can look at many action-adventure games for inspiration. The Hookshot from *The Legend of Zelda* has always been one of my favorites, which is why I included it here as the Grappler.

7. Right now, if the Grappler is extending directly along the line between two tiles, it will only check collision against one of them. You could modify the `eMode.gOut` case in Grapple:FixedUpdate() so that it checked collision against either tile if it was on the line between two (remember to check both horizontal and vertical cases).

8. Make whatever you want! You've worked through the whole book and gotten here. The sky's the limit now!

Thank You!

Thank you again for reading this book. I sincerely hope that it helps you to achieve your dreams.

–Jeremy Gibson Bond

PART IV

APPENDICES

STANDARD PROJECT SETUP PROCEDURE

Many times throughout the book, you are asked to create a new project and then given code to try. This is the standard procedure that you should follow each time to create a new project, set up a scene, create a new C# script, and attach that script to the Main Camera of the scene. Instead of repeating these instructions throughout this book, they are collected here.

Setting Up a New Project

Follow these steps to set up a new project. The screenshots show the procedure on both OS X and Windows:

1. When you first launch Unity, you are presented with the start window shown in Figure A.1. Here, you can click the *New* button to create a new project. Alternatively, if you are already running Unity, you can choose *File > New Project…* from the menu bar.

Figure A.1 Creating a New project in the Unity start window

2. This opens the Unity *New Project Screen* shown in Figure A.2. After you have filled out the form in A.2, Unity will create a new project folder with the name you set in the *Project name** field at the location you set in the *Location** field. Clicking the ellipses on the right side of the *Location** field allows you to choose a location for your project using your standard system file dialog box. In general, for this book, you should choose the *3D* radio button and set Enable Unity Analytics to *Off*. For more information on the options, check out the New Project Options sidebar.

    As an example, with the settings in Figure A.2, Unity would create a project folder named *ProtoTools Project* on the Desktop of my Mac that was defaulted to a 3D layout.

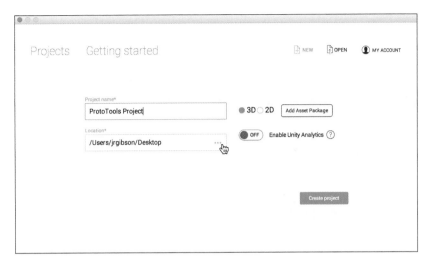

Figure A.2 The New Project Screen

NEW PROJECT OPTIONS

Unity gives you several options on the new project screen.

3D / 2D (Choose 3D)—The 3D / 2D radio button sets up a default camera in your project that is either perspective (3D) or orthographic (2D) and a default Scene view. That's it.

Enable Unity Analytics (Choose Off)—Unity Analytics is a way to get information on how many people are playing your game, what they're doing, etc. It's a fantastic tool, but it's not needed for the projects that you make in this book.

Add Asset Package (Don't)—Unity comes with a number of Asset Packages that provide things such as terrain tools, particle effects, etc. Many of them are pretty cool, but for this book, there's no reason to add them to your project during project creation. I generally avoid adding them for three reasons:

- **Project bloat:** If you import every possible package, the size of the project will bloat to 1,000 times its original size (from ≈300Kb to ≈300MB)!

- **Project pane clutter:** Importing all the packages will also add a huge number of items and folders to your Assets folder and Project pane.

- **You can always import them later:** At any time in the future, you can choose *Assets > Import Package* from the menu bar to import any of the packages available here.

3. On the New Project Screen, click the *Create project* button (shown in Figure A.2). Unity will then appear to close and relaunch, presenting you with the blank canvas of your new project. This relaunch might take a few seconds, so be patient.

Getting the Scene Ready for Development

The new project you just created comes with a default scene. To get ready for coding, follow these instructions:

1. **Save the scene.** The first thing you do in a project should *always* be to save the scene. Choose *File > Save Scene As…* from the Unity menu bar and choose a name. (Unity will automatically save the scene in the correct folder.) I tend to choose a name like *_Scene_0*, which is easily enumerable as I create more scenes in the future. The underscore at the beginning of the name sorts the scene to the top of the Project pane (on macOS).

2. **Create a new C# script (optional).** Some chapters ask you to create one or more C# scripts before beginning the project. To do so, click the *Create* button in the Project pane and choose *Create > C# Script*. A new script is then added to the Project pane, and its name highlighted for you to change. Do this for each script specified at the beginning of the chapter, and pay careful attention to capitalization when naming the scripts. When you have entered the name of the script into this field, press the Return or Enter key to save the name. The example script in Figure A.3 is named *HelloWorld*.

Figure A.3 Creating a new C# script and viewing that script in MonoDevelop

> ### warning
>
> **CHANGING A SCRIPT NAME AFTER IT HAS BEEN CREATED CAN CAUSE PROBLEMS** When you set the name of a script as part of the creation process, Unity automatically sets the name of the class in the class declaration as well (on line 4 in Figure A.3). However, if you choose to change the name of your C# script after that initial process, you need to change its name not only in the Project pane but also in the class declaration line of the script itself. In Figure A.3, this class declaration is on line 4, where *HelloWorld* would need to be changed to the new script name.

3. **Attach the C# script to the scene's Main Camera (optional).** Some chapters request that you *attach* one or more of the new scripts to the Main Camera. Attaching a script to a GameObject like Main Camera makes that script a *component* of the GameObject. All scenes start with a Main Camera already included, so that's a fantastic place to attach any basic script that you want to run. Generally, if a C# script is not attached to a GameObject in the scene, it will not run.

   Attaching a script to a GameObject is a bit tricky, but you'll soon be used to it because it is so frequently done in Unity. Click down on the name of the new script (in the Project pane), drag it over on top of the Main Camera in Hierarchy pane, and release the mouse button. It should look like what is shown in Figure A.4.

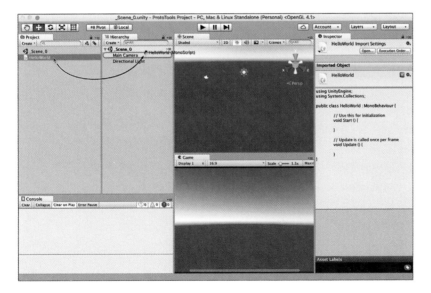

Figure A.4 Dragging the C# script from the Project pane onto the Main Camera in the Hierarchy pane to attach the HelloWorld script to the Main Camera GameObject

The C# script is now attached to the Main Camera and will appear in the Inspector if the Main Camera is selected. You are now all set to start work on any of the projects in the book.

USEFUL CONCEPTS

This appendix is full of concepts that will help you be a better and more effective prototyper and programmer. Some of these are code concepts, and others are methodologies. These are collected here in an appendix to make them easier for you to reference later when you look back at this book in the coming years.

Topics Covered

This appendix covers several different topics, categorized into four distinct groups and sorted alphabetically (rather than attempting to sort them conceptually). Many of these include Unity code examples, and others point you to specific parts of the book where the concept is used.

C# and Unity Coding Concepts

This section covers elements of C# coding that you might want to look back at for a refresher after you've finished the book. There are also some concepts here that, though important, didn't fit well into one of the regular chapters.

Bitwise Boolean Operators and Layer Masks

As you learned in Chapter 21, "Boolean Operations and Conditionals," a single pipe (|) can be used as a non-shorting conditional OR operator, and a single ampersand (&) can be used as a non-shorting conditional AND operator. However, | and & can also be used to perform *bitwise operations* on unsigned ints (uints), and are therefore sometimes referred to as *bitwise OR* and *bitwise AND*.

In a bitwise operation, the individual bits of an integer are compared using using one of the six different bitwise operators included in C#. The following list of them includes the effect that they would have on an 8-bit byte (a simple integral type of data that can hold numbers from 0 to 255). The operations work the same way on a 32-bit unit, but 32-bits wouldn't have fit on this page.

&	AND	`00000101 & 01000100` returns `00000100`
|	OR	`00000101 | 01000100` returns `01000101`
^	Exclusive OR	`00000101 ^ 01000100` returns `01000001`
~	Complement (bitwise NOT)	`~00000101` returns `11111010`
<<	Shift Left	`00000101 << 1` returns `00001010`
>>	Shift Right	`01000100 >> 2` returns `00010001`

In Unity, bitwise operations are most often used to manage LayerMasks. Unity allows developers to define up to 32 different layers, and a LayerMask is a 32-bit unsigned integer representation of which layers to consider in any physics engine or raycast operation. In Unity, the variable type LayerMask is used for LayerMasks, but it is just a wrapper for a 32-bit uint with a little additional functionality. When using a LayerMask, any bit that is a 1 represents a layer that is seen, and any bit that is a 0 represents a layer that is ignored (that is, masked). This can be very useful if you want to check collision against only a specific layer of objects or if you want to specify a layer to ignore. (E.g., the built-in layer 2, named *Ignore Raycast*, is automatically masked out for all raycast tests.)

Unity has eight reserved "built-in" layers, and all GameObjects are initially placed in the zeroth (0th) layer, which is named *Default*. The remaining layers, numbered 8 through 31, are referred to as *user layers*, and giving one of these a name places it in any pop-up menu of layers (e.g., the Layer pop-up menu at the top of each GameObject Inspector).

Because the layer numbers start at zero, the bitwise LayerMask representation of not masking the zeroth layer is a 1 in the farthest-right position of the LayerMask. (See the variable lmZero in the following code listing.) This can be a bit confusing (because the integer value of this representation is 1, not 0), so many Unity developers use the bitwise shift left operator (<<) to assign LayerMask values. (E.g., 1<<0 generates the value 1, which is the zeroth layer, and 1<<4 generates a 1 in the proper place to mask all but the fourth physics layer.) The following code listing includes more examples:

```
LayerMask lmNone = 0;     // 00000000000000000000000000000000 bitwise          // a
LayerMask lmAll = ~0;     // 11111111111111111111111111111111 bitwise          // b
LayerMask lmZero = 1;     // 00000000000000000000000000000001 bitwise
LayerMask lmOne = 2;      // 00000000000000000000000000000010 bitwise          // c
LayerMask lmTwo = 1<<2;   // 00000000000000000000000000000100 bitwise          // d
LayerMask lmThree = 1<<3; // 00000000000000000000000000001000 bitwise

LayerMask lmZeroOrTwo = lmZero | lmTwo;                                         // e
                    // Results in 00000000000000000000000000000101 bitwise

LayerMask lmZeroThroughThree = lmZero | lmOne | lmTwo | lmThree;
                    // Results in 00000000000000000000000000001111 bitwise

lmZero = 1 << LayerMask.NameToLayer("Default");                                 // f
                    // Results in 00000000000000000000000000000001 bitwise

LayerMask lmZeroOrOne = LayerMask.GetMask("Default", "TransparentFX");          // g
                    // Results in 00000000000000000000000000000011 bitwise
```

a. When all bits are set to 0, the LayerMask will *ignore* all layers.

b. When all bits are set to 1, the LayerMask will *interact* with all layers.

c. 2 is the integer value of the LayerMask for layer one, which demonstrates how it can get confusing to assign LayerMask values using integers. Layer one is the predefined "TransparentFX" layer in Unity.

d. Using the shift left operator (<<) makes more sense in this case because the 1 is shifted two places to the left to create a LayerMask for the second layer.

e. A bitwise OR is used to create a LayerMask that will interact with layers 0 and 2.

f. The static method LayerMask.NameToLayer() returns a layer number—an int number, not a LayerMask—when it is passed a layer name. For example, LayerMask.NameToLayer("TransparentFX") returns the int 1.

g. You can also go directly from a list of layer names to a LayerMask using GetMask().

Coroutines

A coroutine is a feature of C# that enables a method to pause execution in the middle of the method, allow other processes to execute, and then return to execution of the paused method from exactly where it left off. In Unity, coroutines are often used when the execution of a single function could take a very long time (and make the game look like it had frozen). One example of this is the *Dice Probability* section later in this appendix; the function to calculate all the possible outcomes of rolling many dice could take minutes or even hours to run, so pausing in the middle to let the screen update is very helpful. You can also use coroutines as timers for tasks that you want to happen on a repeating schedule (as an alternative to using an `InvokeRepeating` call).

Unity Example

This example coroutine prints the time once every second. A call to print the time in the `Update()` method would print it dozens of times per second, which is far too many.

Create a new Unity Project, create a C# script named *Clock* that is attached to Main Camera, and then enter this code:

```csharp
using UnityEngine;
using System.Collections;

public class Clock : MonoBehaviour {

    // Use this for initialization
    void Start () {
        StartCoroutine(Tick());
    }

    // All coroutines have a return type of IEnumerator
    IEnumerator Tick() {
        // This infinite while loop will keep the print happening until the
        //  coroutine is halted or the program is stopped
        while (true) {
            print(System.DateTime.Now.ToString());
            // This yield statement tells the coroutine to wait about 1 second
            //  before continuing. Coroutine timing is not perfectly exact.
            yield return new WaitForSeconds(1);
        }
    }

}
```

Unlike a normal function, it is okay to use the `while(true)` infinite loop within a coroutine as long as there is also a `yield` within the `while` loop.

There are a few different kinds of `yield` statements:

```
yield return null;     // Continue as soon as possible, usually on the next frame

yield return new WaitForSeconds(10);    // Wait 10 seconds

yield return new WaitForEndOfFrame();   // Wait until the next frame

yield return new WaitForFixedUpdate(); // Wait until the next fixed update
```

Another example of using a coroutine is the parsing of the very large dictionary text file in Chapter 34, "*Word Game*."

Enums

An enum is a simple way to declare a type of variable that only has a few specific options, and it is used throughout the book. Enums in this book are usually declared outside of class definitions. Enum names often begin with an e.

```
public enum ePetType {
    none,
    dog,
    cat,
    bird,
    fish,
    other
}

public enum eLifeStage {
    baby,
    teen,
    adult,
    senior,
    deceased
}
```

Later, a variable can be declared using the enum's type (e.g., public ePetType). The various options for an enum are referred to by the enum type, a dot, and the enum value (for example, ePetType.dog):

```
public class Pet {
    public string       name = "Flash";
    public ePetType     pType = ePetType.dog;
    public eLifeStage   age = eLifeStage.baby;
}
```

Enums are actually integers masquerading as other values, so they can be cast to or from int (as shown on lines 7 and 8 in the following code listing). This also means that an enum defaults to the 0th option if not explicitly set. For example, using the preceding definition of the enum eLifeStage, declaring a new variable eLifeStage age (as on line 4 in the following code) would automatically assign age the default value of eLifeStage.baby.

```
 1 public class Pet {
 2     public string      name = "Flash";
 3     public ePetType     pType = ePetType.dog;
 4     public eLifeStage   age;       // By default, age is eLifeStage.baby   // a
 5
 6     void Awake() {
 7         int i = (int) ePetType.cat;  // i is now 2                         // b
 8         ePetType pt = (ePetType) 4;  // pt is now ePetType.fish            // c
 9     }
10 }
```

a. `age` receives the default value of `eLifeStage.baby`.

b. The code `(int)` shown on line 7 is an explicit typecast that forces `ePetType.cat` to be interpreted as an int.

c. Here, the int literal `4` is explicitly typecast to a ePetType by the code `(ePetType)`.

Enums are often used in `switch` statements (as you've seen throughout this book).

Function Delegates

A function delegate is most simply thought of as a container for similar functions (or methods) that can all be called at once. You can see delegates used in Chapter 31, "*Space SHMUP Plus,*" to enable a single call to the `fireDelegate()` delegate to fire all weapons attached to a player's ship. Delegates are frequently used to implement *Strategy Pattern* for use in game AIs. You can learn more about Strategy Pattern in the *Software Design Patterns* section of this appendix.

The first step of using a function delegate is to define the delegate type (`FloatOpDelegate` in the example that follows). This definition sets the parameters and return type for any instance of this delegate type (e.g., the delegate field `fod` further down in this section). This also dictates the parameters and return type required for any function to be assigned to an instance of this delegate type.

```
public delegate float FloatOpDelegate( float f0, float f1 );
```

The preceding line creates a `FloatOpDelegate` (short for Float Operation Delegate) delegate definition that requires two floats as input and a single float as the return type. After the definition is set, you can define target methods that fit this delegate definition (e.g., `FloatAdd()` and `FloatMultiply()` that follow):

```
using UnityEngine;
using System.Collections;

public class DelegateExample : MonoBehaviour {
    // Create a delegate definition named FloatOpDelegate
    // This defines the parameter and return types for target functions
    public delegate float FloatOpDelegate( float f0, float f1 );
```

```csharp
    // FloatAdd must have the same parameter and return types as FloatOpDelegate
    public float FloatAdd( float f0, float f1 ) {
        float result = f0+f1;
        print("The sum of "+f0+" & "+f1+" is "+result+".");
        return( result );
    }

    // FloatMultiply must have the same parameter and return types as well
    public float FloatMultiply( float f0, float f1 ) {
        float result = f0 * f1;
        print("The product of "+f0+" & "+f1+" is "+result+".");
        return( result );
    }
    …
}
```

Now, a variable of the type `FloatOpDelegate` can be created, and either of the target functions can be assigned to it. Then, this delegate variable can be called just like a function (see the delegate field `fod` in the following syntax).

```csharp
using UnityEngine;
using System.Collections;

public class DelegateExample : MonoBehaviour {
    // Create a delegate definition named FloatOpDelegate
    // This defines the parameter and return types for target functions
    public delegate float FloatOpDelegate( float f0, float f1 );

    // FloatAdd must have the same parameter and return types as FloatOpDelegate
    public float FloatAdd( float f0, float f1 ) { … }

    // FloatMultiply must have the same parameter and return types as well
    public float FloatMultiply( float f0, float f1 ) { … }

    // Declare a field "fod" of the type FloatOpDelegate
    public FloatOpDelegate fod; // A delegate field

    void Awake() {
        // Assign the method FloatAdd to fod
        fod = FloatAdd;

        // Call fod as if it were a method; fod then calls FloatAdd()
        fod( 2, 3 ); // Prints: The sum of 2 & 3 is 5.

        // Assign the method FloatMultiply to fod, replacing FloatAdd
        fod = FloatMultiply;

        // Call fod(2,3); it calls FloatMultiply(2,3), returning 6
        fod( 2, 3 ); // Prints: The product of 2 & 3 is 6
    }
    …
}
```

Delegates can also be *multicast*, which means that more than one target method can be assigned to the delegate at the same time. This is the ability that allows a single call to one function delegate to fire all five Weapons in the Chapter 31, "*Space SHMUP Plus*," prototype. There, a single call to the `fireDelegate()` delegate in turn calls all of the `Fire()` methods of the various Weapons on the player's ship. If the multicast delegate has a return type that is not void (as in the FloatOpDelegate example), the return value of the final target method called will be returned by the call to the delegate. Beware that if a delegate is called without having any functions attached, it will throw an error. Prevent this by first checking to see whether it is null.

```
// This Start() method should be added to the DelegateExample class
void Start() {
    // Assign the method FloatAdd() to fod
    fod = FloatAdd;

    // Add the method FloatMultiply(), now BOTH are called by fod
    fod += FloatMultiply;

    // Check to see whether fod is null before calling
    if (fod != null) {
        // Call fod(3,4); it calls FloatAdd(3,4) & then FloatMultiply(3,4)
        float result = fod( 3, 4 );
        // Prints: The sum of 3 & 4 is 7.
        // Then Prints: The product of 3 & 4 is 12.

        print( result );
        // Prints: 12
        // The result is 12 because the last target method to be called
        //   is the one that returns a value via the delegate.
    }
}
```

Interfaces

An interface declares methods and properties that will then be implemented by a class. Any class that implements the interface can be referred to in code as that interface type rather than as the specific class. This differs from subclassing in several ways, one of the most interesting of which is that a class may implement several different interfaces simultaneously, whereas a class can only extend a single superclass. Interface names often begin with a capital I to distinguish them from class names. Interfaces are demonstrated in Chapter 35, "Dungeon Delver."

Unity Example—Interfaces

Create a new project in Unity. In that project, create a C# script named *Menagerie* and enter the code that follows:

```
using System.Collections;
using System.Collections.Generic;
using UnityEngine;
```

```
// Two enums to set specific options for fields in classes
public enum ePetType {
    none,
    dog,
    cat,
    bird,
    fish,
    other
}

public enum eLifeStage {
    baby,
    teen,
    adult,
    senior,
    deceased
}

// The IAnimal interface declares three public properties and two public methods
//   that all IAnimals must have.
public interface IAnimal {
    // Public Properties
    ePetType    pType { get; set; }
    eLifeStage  age { get; set; }
    string      name { get; set; }

    // Public Methods
    void        Move();
    string      Speak();
}

// Fish implements the interface IAnimal
public class Fish : IAnimal {
    private ePetType        _pType = ePetType.fish;                     // a
    public ePetType pType {
        get { return( _pType ); }
        set { _pType = value; }
    }

    public eLifeStage       age { get; set; }                          // b
    public string           name { get; set; }                         // c

    public void Move() {
        Debug.Log("The fish swims around.");
    }

    public string Speak() {
        return("...!");
    }
}
```

```csharp
// Mammal is a superclass that will be extended by Dog and Cat subclasses    // d
public class Mammal {
    protected eLifeStage        _age;
    public eLifeStage age {
        get { return( _age ); }
        set { _age = value; }
    }

    public string                name { get; set; }                          // c
}


// Dog is a subclass of Mammal AND implements IAnimal
public class Dog : Mammal, IAnimal {                                         // e
    private ePetType        _pType = ePetType.dog;

    public ePetType pType {
        get { return( _pType ); }
        set { _pType = value; }
    }

    public void Move() {
        Debug.Log("The dog walks around.");
    }

    public string Speak() {
        return("Bark!");
    }
}


// Cat is a subclass of Mammal AND implements IAnimal
public class Cat : Mammal, IAnimal {
    private ePetType        _pType = ePetType.cat;

    public ePetType pType {
        get { return( _pType ); }
        set { _pType = value; }
    }

    public void Move() {
        Debug.Log("The cat stalks around.");
    }

    public string Speak() {
        return("Meow!");
    }
}
```

```
// Menagerie is a subclass of MonoBehaviour
public class Menagerie : MonoBehaviour {
// This list can take instances of ANY class that implements IAnimal
public List<IAnimal>    animals;

void Awake () {
    animals = new List<IAnimal>();

    Dog d = new Dog();
    d.age = eLifeStage.adult;
    // When d is added to IAnimal, it is added as an IAnimal, not a Dog
    animals.Add( d );
    animals.Add( new Cat() );
    animals.Add( new Fish() );

    animals[0].name = "Wendy";
    animals[1].name = "Caramel";
    animals[2].name = "Nemo";

    string[] types = new string[] {"none", "dog", "cat", "bird",
        ➥ "fish", "other"};                                       // f
    string[] ages = new string[] {"baby", "teen", "adult", "senior",
        ➥ "deceased"};
    // In this loop, all IAnimals are treated the same way, even though they
    //   are actually different classes with differing superclasses
    string aName;
    IAnimal animal;
    for (int i=0; i<animals.Count; i++) {
        animal = animals[i];                                      // g
        aName = animal.name;
        print("Animal #" + i + " is a " + types[ (int) animal.pType ]
            ➥ + " named " + aName + ".");                         // h
        animal.Move();
        print(aName + " says: "+animal.Speak());

        switch (animal.age) {
            case eLifeStage.baby:
            case eLifeStage.teen:
            case eLifeStage.senior:
                print(aName + " is a " + ages[(int) animal.age] + ".");
                break;
            case eLifeStage.adult:
                print(aName + " is an adult.");
                break;
            case eLifeStage.deceased:
                print(aName + " is deceased.");
                break;
        }
    }
}
}
```

a. `_pType` is a private, hidden field with the `pType` property as its visible, public accessor.

b. This is an *automatic property*. When a property like `age` here has just `get; set;` between its braces, the compiler automatically creates a private variable to be accessed by the property.

c. `name` here is another automatic property.

d. Note that Mammal does *not* implement IAnimal. It certainly could do so, but I wanted to show that subclasses can implement an interface even when their superclass does not.

e. Dog is a subclass of Mammal *and* implements IAnimal. Because Dog is a subclass of Mammal, it inherits the protected field `_age` and the public properties `age` and `name`. If `_age` were private, Dog would not inherit `_age` from Mammal and could not access it directly. Because Dog can access the public property `age`, and `age` is defined in Mammal (not Dog), `age` can be used to set and retrieve `_age`. This inheritance of `age` fulfills the requirement that IAnimals have a public `age` property. For more information on protected fields and class inheritance, see the *Variable Scope*.

f. Remember that ➡ is the *code completion character*, so `"fish", "other" };` is a continuation of the previous line. You should not type the ➡ character.

g. Regardless of its initial type, the `i`th element of `animals` is assigned to the local variable `IAnimal animal` and treated as an IAnimal.

h. `animal.pType` returns the type of the IAnimal as an ePetType. `(int)` then casts that ePetType to an int, which is then used to access an element of the `types` string array.

As you can see in the code, having the `IAnimal` interface allows the `Cat`, `Dog`, and `Fish` classes to all be treated in the same way and stored in the same `List<IAnimal>` and assigned to the same local variable `IAnimal animal`.

Naming Conventions

I initially covered naming conventions in Chapter 20, "Variables and Components," but they're important enough to repeat here. The code in this book follows a number of rules governing the naming of variables, functions, classes, and so on. Although none of these rules are mandatory, following them makes your code more readable not only to others who try to decipher it but also to yourself if you ever need to return to it months later and hope to understand what you wrote. Every coder follows slightly different rules—my personal rules have even changed over the years—but the rules I present here have worked well for both me and my students, and they are consistent with most C# code that I've encountered in Unity:

1. Use *camelCase* for pretty much everything. In a variable name that is composed of multiple words, camelCase capitalizes the initial letter of each word (except for the first word, in the case of variable names).

2. Variable names should start with a lowercase letter (e.g., `someVariableName`).

3. Function names should start with an uppercase letter (e.g., `Start()`, `FunctionName()`).

4. Class names should start with an uppercase letter (e.g., `GameObject`, `ScopeExample`).

5. Interface names often start with a capital I (e.g., `IAnimal`).

6. Private variable names often start with an underscore (e.g., `_hiddenVariable`).

7. Static variable names are often all caps with *snake_case* (e.g., `NUM_INSTANCES`). As you can see, snake_case combines multiple words with an underscore in between them.

8. Enum type names often start with a lowercase e (e.g., `ePetType`, `eLifeStage`).

Operator Precedence and Order of Operations

Just as in algebra, some operators in C# take precedence over others. One example that you are probably familiar with is the precedence of * over + (e.g., 1 + 2 * 3 = 7 because the 2 and 3 are multiplied before the 1 is added to them). Here is a list of common operators and their precedence. An operator that is higher in this list will happen before one that is lower.

`( )`	Operations grouped by parentheses always take precedence
`F()`	The calling of a function
`a[]`	The access of an array
`i++`	Post-increment
`i--`	Post-decrement
`!`	NOT
`~`	Bitwise NOT (complement)
`++i`	Pre-increment
`--i`	Pre-decrement
`*`	Multiply
`/`	Divide
`%`	Modulus
`+`	Add
`-`	Subtract
`<<`	Bit shift left
`>>`	Bit shift right
`<`	Less than
`>`	Greater than
`<=`	Less than or equal to
`>=`	Greater than or equal to
`==`	Equal to (the comparison operator)
`!=`	Not equal to

&	Bitwise AND
^	Bitwise exclusive OR (XOR)
|	Bitwise OR
&&	Conditional, shorting AND
||	Conditional, shorting OR
=	Assignment

Race Conditions

Unlike many of the other topics in this section, a race condition is something that you definitely *don't* want in your code. A race condition occurs when it is necessary in your code for one thing to happen before another, but it's possible that the two things could happen out of order and cause unexpected behavior or even a crash. Race conditions are a serious consideration when designing any code that is intended for multiprocessor computers, multithreaded operating systems, or networked applications (where different computers around the world could possible end up in a race condition with each other), but it is also an issue for Unity games because they involve so many different GameObjects, each receiving `Awake()`, `Start()`, and `Update()` calls at roughly the same time as all the others. Race conditions are also explored in Chapter 31, "Space SHMUP Plus."

Let's create an example.

Unity Example—Race Conditions

Follow these steps:

1. Create a new Unity project named *Unity-RaceCondition*.

2. Create a C# script named *SetValues* and enter this code:

```csharp
using UnityEngine;
using System.Collections;

public class SetValues : MonoBehaviour {
    static public int[]          VALUES;

    void Start() {
        VALUES = new int[] { 0, 1, 2, 3, 4, 5 };
    }
}
```

3. Create a second script named *ReadValues* and enter this code:

```csharp
using UnityEngine;
using System.Collections;

public class ReadValues : MonoBehaviour {
```

```
void Start() {
    print( SetValues.VALUES[2] );
}

}
```

4. Be sure that you have saved both scripts before returning to Unity.

5. Attach both scripts to Main Camera and click *Play*. When you do so, you'll receive one of two possible outputs in the Console:

   ■ 2

   ■ **NullReferenceException**: Object reference not set to an instance of an object

The difference between these two outcomes is which of the two Start() functions happens to be called first. If SetValues.Start() is called before ReadValues.Start(), everything works great. However, if ReadValues.Start() is called before SetValues.Start(), you get a null reference exception because ReadValues.Start() is trying to access SetValues. VALUES[2] while SetValues.VALUES is still null.

Before Unity 5, it was extremely difficult to know which of these Start() methods would be called first. Happily, one of the improvements in recent versions of Unity allows you to choose the order in which scripts execute.

6. From the Unity menu bar, choose *Edit > Project Settings > Script Execution Order*. The Script Execution Order (SEO) Inspector opens, as shown in Figure B.1.

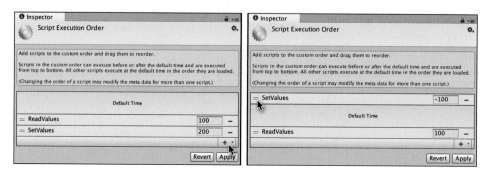

Figure B.1 The Script Execution Order Inspector

7. Add the *ReadValues* class to the SEO Inspector by clicking the + button that the cursor is pointing to in the left image of Figure B.1.

8. Do the same to also add *SetValues* class to the SEO Inspector.

By default, ReadValues and SetValues will get the execution order values 100 and 200 as shown in the left image of Figure B.1.

9. Click the *Apply* button in the SEO Inspector, and click *Play* in Unity. This execution order will guarantee that a NullReferenceException appears in the Console.

10. Stop Unity playback.

11. Use the double-line handle on the *SetValues* bar in the SEO Inspector (pointed at by the arrow on the right image of Figure B.1) to drag SetValues up above Default Time. Now your Inspector should look like the right image of Figure B.1.

12. Click *Apply* in the SEO Inspector and click *Play* in Unity.

Now that `SetValues.Start()` is guaranteed to be called before `ReadValues.Start()`, the "2" result is guaranteed to appear in the Console.

When dealing with two scripts that both use `Start()`, `Awake()`, or any other MonoBehaviour call that is managed by Unity, the Script Execution Order Inspector is the only way to guarantee that one will run before the other. All unspecified scripts run at Default Time, so you would have gotten the same results if you never explicitly added ReadValues to the SEO.

Recursive Functions

Sometimes a function is designed to call itself, this is known as a *recursive function*. One simple example of this could be a function to calculate the factorial of a number.

In math, 5! (5 factorial) is the multiplication of five and every other natural number below it:

$$5! = 5 * 4 * 3 * 2 * 1 = 120$$

It is a special case that 0! = 1, and for our purposes, the factorial of a negative number will be 0:

$$0! = 1$$

$$-123! = 0$$

Knowing this, you can write a recursive function to calculate the factorial of any integer:

```
1  using UnityEngine;
2  using System.Collections;
3
4  public class Factorial : MonoBehaviour {
5
6      void Awake() {
7          print( fac (-1) );    // Prints 0
8          print( fac (0)  );    // Prints 1
9          print( fac (5)  );    // Prints 120
10     }
11
12     int fac( int n ) {
13         if (n < 0) {          // This keeps it from breaking if n<0
```

```
14                return( 0 );
15            }
16            if (n == 0) {        // This is the "terminal case"
17                return( 1 );
18            }
19            int result = n * fac( n-1 ); // Here is the recursion
20            return( result );
21        }
22
23  }
```

When `fac(5)` is called in the preceding code, and the code reaches line 19, `fac(n-1)` is called, which results in the call `fac(4)`. This process continues with `fac(n-1)` called four more times until it reaches the case where `fac(0)` is called. On line 16 of the `fac(0)` recursion, `n == 0` is true, so a 1 is returned. This is the *terminal* case of the recursion, the case where the function starts returning values. This 1 is returned to line 19 of the `fac(1)` recursion, and `fac(1)` can then return 1 (the result of n * 1) on line 20. Each recursive call is then able to return up the chain and unwind the recursions. The chain of recursion resolves like this:

```
fac(5)
fac(5) * fac(4)
fac(5) * fac(4) * fac(3)
fac(5) * fac(4) * fac(3) * fac(2)
fac(5) * fac(4) * fac(3) * fac(2) * fac(1)
fac(5) * fac(4) * fac(3) * fac(2) * fac(1) * fac(0)
fac(5) * fac(4) * fac(3) * fac(2) * fac(1) * 1
fac(5) * fac(4) * fac(3) * fac(2) * 1
fac(5) * fac(4) * fac(3) * 2
fac(5) * fac(4) * 6
fac(5) * 24
120
```

The best way to really understand what's happening in this recursive function is to place a breakpoint at line 19, connect the MonoDevelop debugger to the Unity Process, and use *Step In* to watch the recursion happen step by step. If you need a refresher on the debugger, read Chapter 25, "Debugging."

A Recursive Function for Bézier Curves

Another fantastic example of a recursive function is the Bézier curve interpolation static method (named `Bezier`) that is included in the ProtoTools Utils class as part of the unitypackage imported at the beginning of Chapters 32 and beyond. This function can interpolate the position of a point along a Bézier curve composed of any number of points. The code for the `Bezier` function is listed at the end of the *Interpolation* section of this appendix.

Software Design Patterns

In 1994, the "Gang of Four" (Erich Gamma, Richard Helm, Ralph Johnson, and John Vissides) released the book *Design Patterns: Elements of Reusable Object-Oriented Software*,[1] which described various patterns that could be used in software development to create effective, reusable code. This book uses two of those patterns and refers to a third.

Singleton Pattern

The Singleton Pattern is the most commonly used in this book and can be found in several chapters. If you know that there will only ever be a single instance of a given class in the game, you can create a *singleton* for that class, which is a static variable of that class type that can be used to reference it from anywhere in code. The following code listing shows an example:

```
public class Hero : MonoBehaviour {
    static public Hero S;                                           // a

    void Awake() {
        if (S == null) {                                           // c
            S = this;                                              // b
        } else {
            Debug.LogError("The singleton S of Hero has already been set!");
        }
    }
}


public class Enemy : MonoBehaviour {
    void Update() {
        public Vector3 heroLoc = Hero.S.transform.position;        // d
    }
}
```

a. The static public field S is the singleton for hero. I usually name all of my singletons S.

b. Because there will only ever be one instance of the Hero class, it is assigned to S on Awake(), when the instance is created.

c. The if (S == null) statement protects you from accidentally having a second Hero instance somewhere in the code. If a second instance of Hero exists and tries to assign itself to S, then the error message will be thrown.

d. Because S is both public and static, it can be referenced anywhere in code via the class name as Hero.S.

---

1. Erich Gamma, Richard Helm, Ralph Johnson, and John Vissides, *Design Patterns: Elements of Reusable Object-Oriented Software* (Reading, MA: Addison-Wesley, 1994). The Factory Pattern is one of many described in the book. Others include the Singleton Pattern, which is used in many of the tutorials in this book.

If you search online, you're likely to find a lot of hate out there for the Singleton Pattern. This is largely because of two things:

- **Singletons are unsafe in a production environment**: Singletons are static and public, meaning that ANY class or function in your codebase could potentially access them. The danger here is that some random class written by someone else could change a public field of your singleton class instance, and you would have no idea who did it!

Luckily, you can avoid this danger in several ways. One that I like is making the singleton static and *private*, so that only class instances (and there will only be one because it's a singleton) can access it. You then write static *public* accessor properties through which other classes and functions can alter singleton fields. If you find that something unknown in your code is changing a property, then you can place a debugger breakpoint in the setter of the property and use the Call Stack in the debugger to see what method is setting the property.

- **Singleton Pattern is very simple to implement and therefore often overused**: As the simplest design pattern to implement, singleton was quickly used by a lot of people, and soon caused problems due to the preceding point. This meant that a lot of people used it in places where it wasn't really appropriate.

When you write prototypes, development speed is often more important than safety, so my recommendation is that you should feel free to use singletons when you need them while prototyping, but you should generally avoid using them in production code.

Component Pattern

Component Pattern is first covered in Chapter 27, "Object-Oriented Thinking," and it is used throughout Unity. The core idea of the Component Pattern is to group closely related functions and data into a single class while at the same time keeping each class as small and focused as possible.[2]

The *components* that are attached to GameObjects in Unity are all based on this pattern. Each GameObject in Unity is a very small class that can act as a container for several components that each do a specific—and isolated—job. For example:

- *Transform* handles position, rotation, scale, and hierarchy
- *Rigidbody* handles motion and physics
- *Colliders* handle actual collision and the shape of the collision volume

Although each of these jobs are related, they are separate enough to warrant their own component. Making each a separate component also enables easy expansion in the future: separating Colliders from the Rigidbody means that you could easily add a new kind of Collider—a

---

2. The full description of the Component Pattern is far more complex, but this definition serves our needs.

ConeCollider for instance—and Rigidbody would be able to use it without any changes to the Rigidbody code.

This is certainly important for game engine developers, but what does it mean to game designers and prototypers? The most important thing that thinking in a component-oriented way gives you is smaller, shorter classes. When your scripts are shorter, they are easier to code, easier to share with other people, easier to reuse, and easier to debug—all of which are very noble goals.

The only real negative of component-oriented design is that implementing it well takes a decent amount of forethought, which somewhat flies in the face of the prototyper's philosophy of getting things working as quickly as possible. As a result of this dilemma, Part III of this book covers both a more traditional prototyping style of just writing what works in the first several chapters and a more component-oriented approach in the last chapters. The best use of components in this book is Chapter 35, "Dungeon Delver," a brand new chapter written from scratch for the second edition of the book.

Strategy Pattern

As mentioned in the *Function Delegates* section of this appendix, the Strategy Pattern is often used in AI and other areas where you might want to change behavior based on conditions yet still only call a single function delegate. In Strategy Pattern, a function delegate is created for a type of action that the class can perform (e.g., taking an action in combat), and an instance of that delegate is given different functions to call based on the situation. This avoids complicated switch statements in the code, because the delegate can be called in a single line:

```
using UnityEngine;
using System.Collections;

public class Strategy : MonoBehaviour {
    public delegate void ActionDelegate();          // a

    public ActionDelegate act;                       // b

    public void Attack() {                           // c
        // Attack code would go here
    }

    public void Wait() { … } // These two methods would be defined too
    public void Flee() { … } // The ellipses ( … ) are placeholders

    void Awake() {
        act = Wait;                                  // d
    }

    void Update() {
        Vector3 hPos = Hero.S.transform.position;
```

```
    if ( (hPos - transform.position).magnitude < 100 ) {          // e
        act = Attack;
    }

    if (act != null) act();                                        // f
    }
}
```

a.   The `ActionDelegate` delegate type is defined. It has no parameters and a return type of void.

b.   `act` is created as an instance of `ActionDelegate`.

c.   The `Attack()`, `Wait()`, and `Flee()` functions here are placeholders that are meant to show that various actions would be defined matching the parameters and return type of the `ActionDelegate` delegate type.

d.   The initial strategy for this agent is to `Wait`, so `Wait` is assigned as the target method of `act`.

e.   If the Hero singleton comes within 100 meters of this agent, it will switch its strategy to `Attack` by replacing the target method of `act`.

f.   Regardless of which strategy is selected, `act()` is called to execute it. Checking that `act != null` before calling it is useful because calling a null function delegate (that is, one that has not yet had a target function assigned to it) will cause a runtime error.

More Information on Software Design Patterns

Game Programming Patterns[3] by Robert Nystrom is a fantastic book that covers the most common software design patterns used in games. You can purchase a print or electronic copy of it from most online retailers, or you can just read the web version for free on his website: http://gameprogrammingpatterns.com. It's a great resource for improving your coding.

Variable Scope

The *scope* of variables is an important concept in any programming language. A variable's scope refers to how much of the code is aware of the variable's existence. *Global* scope would mean that any code anywhere could see and reference the variable, whereas *local* scope means that the variable's scope is limited in some way, and it can not be seen by everything else in the code. If a variable is local to a class, then only other things within the class can see it. If a variable is local to a function, then it only exists within that function and is destroyed when the function has completed.

The following code demonstrates several different levels of scope for different variables within a single class. Lettered comments after the code explain what is happening on important lines. A variable that is red in the code indicates that it is *out of scope* in that section of the code.

---

3. Robert Nystrom, *Game Programming Patterns* (Genever Benning, 2014). ©2014 by Robert Nystrom.

This is the code for the class ScopeExample, which extends MonoBehaviour:

```csharp
using UnityEngine;
using System.Collections;

public class ScopeExample : MonoBehaviour {

    // public fields (public class variables)
    public bool              trueOrFalse = false;              // a
    public int               graduationAge = 18;
    public float             goldenRatio = 1.618f;

    // private fields (private class variables)
    private bool             _hiddenVariable = true;           // b
    private float            _anotherHiddenVariable = 0.5f;

    // protected fields (protected class variables)
    protected int            partiallyHiddenInt = 1;           // c
    float                    anotherProtectedVariable = 1.0f;

    // static fields (static class variables)
    static public int        NUM_INSTANCES = 0;                // d
    static private int       NUM_TOO = 0;                      // e

    public bool hiddenVariableAccessor {                       // f
        get { return _hiddenVariable; }
    }

    void Awake() {
        trueOrFalse = true; // Works: assigns "true" to trueOrFalse    // g
        print( "tOF: "+trueOrFalse ); // Works: prints "tOF: True"

        int ageAtTenthReunion = graduationAge + 10; // Works          // h
        print( "_aHV: "+_anotherHiddenVariable ); // Works: prints "_aHV: 0.5" // i
        NUM_INSTANCES += 1; // Works                                  // j
        NUM_TOO++; // Works                                           // k
    }

    void Update() {
        print( ageAtTenthReunion ); // ERROR                          // l
        float ratioed = 1f; // Works
        for (int i=0; i<10; i++) { // Works                           // m
            ratioed *= goldenRatio; // Works
        }
        print( "ratioed: "+ratioed ); // Works: prints "ratioed: 122.9661"
        print( i ); // ERROR                                          // n
    }
}
```

This is the code for the class `ScopeExampleChild`, which extends ScopeExample:

```
using UnityEngine;
using System.Collections;

public class ScopeExampleChild : ScopeExample {                          // o
    void Start() {
        print( "tOF: "+trueOrFalse );              // Works: prints "tOF: True" // p
        print( "pHI: "+partiallyHiddenInt );       // Works: prints "pHI: 1"    // q
        print( "_hV: "+_hiddenVariable );          // ERROR                     // r
        print( "NI: " +NUM_INSTANCES );            // Works: prints "NI: 1"     // s
        print( "NT: " +NUM_TOO );                  // ERROR                     // t
        print( "hVA: "+hiddenVariableAccessor );   // Works: prints "hVA: True" // u
    }
}
```

a. Public fields: The variables `trueOrFalse`, `graduationAge`, and `goldenRatio` are all **public** *fields*. *Fields* are class instance variables, meaning that they are declared as part of the class and are visible to all functions within any instance of that class. Because these fields are *public*, they are inherited by the subclass ScopeExampleChild, which means that ScopeExampleChild also has a bool `trueOrFalse`. Public variables can also be seen by any other code that has a reference to an instance of the class. This would allow a function with the variable `ScopeExample se` to see and set the field `se.trueOrFalse`.

b. Private fields: These two variables are **private** fields. *Private* fields can only be seen by this instance of ScopeExample (meaning that an instance of ScopeExample can access and modify its own private fields, but no other instance can see them). Subclasses do not inherit private fields, so the subclass ScopeExampleChild does not have a bool `_hidden-Variable`. A function with the variable `ScopeExample se` would not be able to see or access the private field `se._hiddenVariable`.

c. Protected fields: A field marked **protected** is between public and private. Subclasses *do* inherit protected fields, so the ScopeExampleChild subclass does inherit the int `partially-HiddenInt` that is declared in ScopeExample. However, protected fields are not accessible outside the class or its subclasses, so a function with a variable `ScopeExample se` would not be able to see or access the protected field `se.partiallyHiddenVariable`. Fields not explicitly marked private or public are protected by default.

d. Static fields: A **static** field is a field of the class itself, not the instances of the class. This means that NUM_INSTANCES is accessed as `ScopeExample.NUM_INSTANCES`. Public static fields are the closest thing to global scope that I use in C#. Any script in the codebase can access the **public static** field `ScopeExample.NUM_INSTANCES`, and NUM_IN-STANCES is the same for all instances of ScopeExample. A function with the variable `ScopeExample se` could not access `se.NUM_INSTANCES` (because it doesn't exist), but it could access `ScopeExample.NUM_INSTANCES`. The ScopeExampleChild subclass of ScopeExample can also access NUM_INSTANCES. Within an instance of ScopeExample, NUM_INSTANCES can be accessed directly (without the `ScopeExample.` prefix).

e. NUM_TOO is a `private static` field, which means that all instances of ScopeExample share the same value of NUM_TOO, but no other class can see it or access it. The ScopeExampleChild subclass cannot access NUM_TOO.

f. hiddenVariableAccessor is a read-only `public` property that allows other classes access to _hiddenVariable. Because there is no set clause, it is read-only.

g. The `// Works` comment means that this line executes without any errors. trueOrFalse is a public field of ScopeExample, so this method of ScopeExample can access it.

h. This line declares and defines a variable named ageAtTenthReunion that is locally scoped to the method ScopeExample.Awake(). This means that when the ScopeExample.Awake() function has finished executing, the variable ageAtTenthReunion will cease to exist. Also, nothing outside of this function can access or modify ageAtTenthReunion.

i. As a private field _anotherHiddenVariable can only be seen by methods within instances of this class.

j. Within a class, static public fields can be referred to by their name, meaning that the ScopeExample.Awake() method can reference NUM_INSTANCES without needing the class name before it.

k. NUM_TOO can also be accessed anywhere within the ScopeExample class.

l. The `// ERROR` comment means that this line will not run properly. This line throws an error because ageAtTenthReunion was a local variable of the method ScopeExample.Awake() so it has no meaning in the ScopeExample.Update() method.

m. The variable int i is declared and defined in this `for` loop and is locally scoped to the `for` loop. This means that i ceases to have meaning when the `for` loop has completed.

n. This line throws an error because i has no meaning outside of the preceding `for` loop.

o. This line declares and defines ScopeExampleChild as a subclass of ScopeExample. As a subclass, ScopeExampleChild has access to the *public* and *protected* fields and methods of ScopeExample but not to the *private* fields or methods. Because the Awake() and Update() methods of ScopeExample were not declared public or private, they are by default *protected* and therefore inherited by ScopeExampleChild. Because ScopeExampleChild does not have its own Awake() or Update() functions defined, it will run the versions defined in its base class, ScopeExample.

p. trueOrFalse is public, so ScopeExampleChild has inherited a trueOrFalse field. Additionally, because the base class (ScopeExample) version of Awake() has already run by the time Start() is called on ScopeExampleChild, trueOrFalse has already been set to true by the Awake() method of the base class (ScopeExample).

q. ScopeExampleChild also has a protected partiallyHiddenInt field that it inherited from ScopeExample.

r. _hiddenVariable is not inherited from ScopeExample because it is private.

s. NUM_INSTANCES is accessible by ScopeExampleChild because as a public variable, it is inherited from the base class ScopeExample. The two classes share the same value for NUM_INSTANCES, so if one instance of each class were instantiated, NUM_INSTANCES would be 2 regardless of whether it was accessed from ScopeExample or ScopeExampleChild.

t. As a *private static* variable, NUM_TOO is not inherited by ScopeExampleChild. However, it's worth noting that even though NUM_TOO is not inherited, when ScopeExampleChild is instantiated and calls the base class version of Awake() —that is, the Awake() method that is defined in the ScopeExample base class—that call to the Awake() method can access NUM_TOO without errors, because the base class version is running within the scope of the ScopeExample base class even though it's actually running on an instance of ScopeExampleChild.

u. In our most esoteric example, ScopeExampleChild can read the public property hiddenVariableAccessor, which easily makes sense until you look a bit deeper. Inside of the get clause of hiddenVariableAccessor, it reads the private field _hiddenVariable. This is a subtle but important aspect of variable scope. Because ScopeExampleChild extends ScopeExample, all the private fields of ScopeExample are created for a ScopeExampleChild instance, even though the ScopeExampleChild instance can't access them directly. The ScopeExampleChild instance can use public accessors like hiddenVariableAccessor—which is scoped to the ScopeExample base class—to access private fields—like _hiddenVariable—that are also scoped to the ScopeExample base class. Inherited methods like the Awake() that ScopeExampleChild inherited from ScopeExample can also access private fields of the base class.

These many notes have included both very simple and very complex examples of variable scope. If some if it didn't make sense to you, that's okay. You can come back and read it later after you've used C# some more and have more specific scope questions.

XML

XML (eXtensible Markup Language) is a file format that is designed to be both flexible and human-readable. Here is an example of some XML from Chapter 32, " Prototype 4: *Prospector Solitaire*." Additional spaces have been added to make it a little more readable, but that is okay because XML generally treats any number of spaces or line breaks as a single space.

```xml
<xml>
    <!-- decorators are the suit and rank in the corners of each card. -->
    <decorator type="letter" x="-1.05" y="1.42"  z="0" flip="0" scale="1.25"/>
    <decorator type="suit"   x="-1.05" y="1.03"  z="0" flip="0" scale="0.4" />
    <decorator type="suit"   x="1.05"  y="-1.03" z="0" flip="1" scale="0.4" />
    <decorator type="letter" x="1.05"  y="-1.42" z="0" flip="1" scale="1.25"/>
    <!-- A list of all cards that defines where pips are placed. -->
    <card rank="1">
        <pip x="0" y="0" z="0" flip="0" scale="2"/>
    </card>
```

```
    <card rank="2">
        <pip x="0" y="1.1"  z="0" flip="0"/>
        <pip x="0" y="-1.1" z="0" flip="1"/>
    </card>
</xml>
```

Even without knowing much at all about XML, you should be able to read this somewhat. XML is based on *tags* (also known as the *markup* of the document), which are the words between the two angle brackets (e.g., `<xml>`, `<card rank="2">`). Most XML *elements* have an *opening tag* (e.g., `<card rank="2">`) and a *closing tag* that contains a forward slash immediately after the opening angle bracket (e.g., `</card>`). Anything between the opening and closing tags of an element (e.g., the `<pip .../>` tags between the `<card>` and `</card>` in the XML listing) is said to be the *content* of that element. There are also *empty-element tags*, which are tags that serve as both the opening and closing tag with no content between them. For example, in the XML listing, the tag `<pip x="0" y="1.1" z="0" flip="0" />` is an empty-element tag that requires no matching `</pip>` tag because it ends in `/>`. In general, XML files should start with `<xml>` and end with `</xml>`, so everything in the XML document is content of the `<xml>` element.

XML tags can have *attributes*, which are like fields in C#. The empty-element `<pip x="0" y="1.1" z="0" flip="0"/>` that is seen in the XML listing includes x, y, z, and `flip` attributes.

In an XML file, anything between `<!--` and `-->` is a *comment* and is therefore ignored by any program that is reading the XML file. In the preceding XML listing, you can see that I use them the same way that I use comments in C# code.

A robust XML reader is included in C# .NET, but I have found it to be very large (it adds about 1 MB to the size of your compiled application, which is a lot if you're making something for mobile) and unwieldy (using it is not simple). So, I've included a much smaller (though not at all as robust) XML interpreter called PT_XMLReader in the ProtoTools scripts that are part of the unitypackage imported at the beginning of the later prototyping chapters. For an example of its use, take a look at the Chapter 32, "Prototype 4: *Prospector Solitaire*."

Math Concepts

A lot of people cringe when they hear the word *math,* but that really doesn't need to be the case. As you'll see throughout this book, it can do some really cool things for you. Below I cover just a few cool math concepts that can help you in game development.

Cosine and Sine (Cos and Sin)

Sine and cosine are functions that convert an angle value Θ (theta) into a point along a wave shape that ranges from -1 to 1. They are shown in Figure B.2.

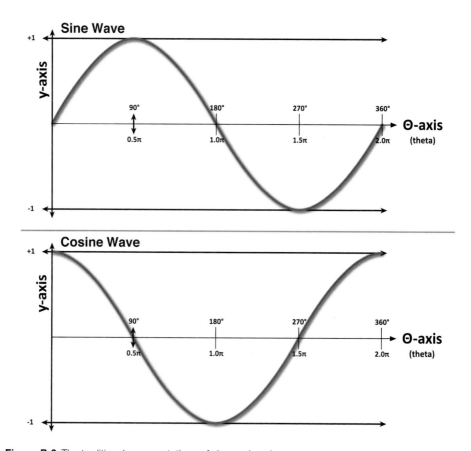

Figure B.2 The traditional representations of sine and cosine

However, sine and cosine are much more than just waves; they're descriptions of the relationship of X and Y when going around a circle. I'll demonstrate what I mean with some code.

Unity Example—Sine and Cosine

Follow these steps:

1. Open Unity and create a new scene. At the top of the Scene pane, look for a button that looks like a sine wave mountain in a box (it's to the right of the speaker icon). Click that mountain button; the background of the Scene pane changes from a skybox to a dark gray, making the elements in the Scene pane easier to see (you may need to click it more than once).

2. Create a new sphere in the scene (*GameObject > 3D Object > Sphere*). Set Sphere's transform to P:[0, 0, 0], R:[0, 0, 0], S:[0.1, 0.1, 0.1].

3. Add a *TrailRenderer* to Sphere. (Select *Sphere* in the Hierarchy and choose *Component > Effects > Trail Renderer* from the menu bar.) Open the disclosure triangle next to *Materials* in the Sphere's TrailRenderer Inspector and click the circle to the right of *Element 0* to select *Default-Particle* as the texture for the TrailRenderer. Set Time = *1* and Width = *0.1*.

4. Create a new C# script named *Cyclic*. Attach it to Sphere in the Hierarchy. Open the Cyclic script in MonoDevelop, and enter this code:

```csharp
using UnityEngine;
using System.Collections;

public class Cyclic : MonoBehaviour {
    [Header("Set in Inspector")]
    public float          theta = 0;
    public bool           showCosX = false;
    public bool           showSinY = false;

    [Header("Set Dynamically")]
    public Vector3        pos;

    void Update () {
        // Calculate radians based on time
        float radians = Time.time * Mathf.PI;
        // Convert radians to degrees to show in the Inspector
        // The "% 360" limits the value to the range from 0-359.9999
        theta = Mathf.Round( radians * Mathf.Rad2Deg ) % 360;
        // Reset pos
        pos = Vector3.zero;
        // Calculate x & y based on cos and sin respectively
        pos.x = Mathf.Cos(radians);
        pos.y = Mathf.Sin(radians);

        // Use sin and cos if they are checked in the Inspector
        Vector3 tPos = Vector3.zero;
        if (showCosX) tPos.x = pos.x;
        if (showSinY) tPos.y = pos.y;
        // Position this.gameObject (the Sphere)
        transform.position = tPos;
    }

    void OnDrawGizmos() {
        if (!Application.isPlaying) return; // Only show when Playing

        // Draw wavy colored lines (you can leave this for loop out if you like)
        int inc = 10;
```

```
for (int i=0; i<360; i+=inc) {
    int i2 = i+inc;
    float c0 = Mathf.Cos(i*Mathf.Deg2Rad);
    float c1 = Mathf.Cos(i2*Mathf.Deg2Rad);
    float s0 = Mathf.Sin(i*Mathf.Deg2Rad);
    float s1 = Mathf.Sin(i2*Mathf.Deg2Rad);
    Vector3 vC0 = new Vector3( c0, -1f-(i/360f), 0 );
    Vector3 vC1 = new Vector3( c1, -1f-(i2/360f), 0 );
    Vector3 vS0 = new Vector3( 1f+(i/360f), s0, 0 );
    Vector3 vS1 = new Vector3( 1f+(i2/360f), s1, 0 );

    Gizmos.color = Color.HSVToRGB( i/360f, 1, 1 );
    Gizmos.DrawLine(vC0, vC1);
    Gizmos.DrawLine(vS0, vS1);
}

// Draw the lines and circles relative to the Sphere GameObject
Gizmos.color = Color.HSVToRGB( theta/360f, 1, 1 );
// Show individual Sin and Cos aspects using Gizmos
Vector3 cosPos = new Vector3( pos.x, -1f-(theta/360f), 0 );
Gizmos.DrawSphere(cosPos, 0.05f);
if (showCosX) Gizmos.DrawLine(cosPos, transform.position);

Vector3 sinPos = new Vector3( 1f+(theta/360f), pos.y, 0 );
Gizmos.DrawSphere(sinPos, 0.05f);
if (showSinY) Gizmos.DrawLine(sinPos, transform.position);
    }
}
```

5. Before clicking Play, set the Scene view to 2D by clicking the *2D* button at the top of the Scene pane. Click *Play*.

You can see that the sphere doesn't initially move, but colored dots move along paths below and to the right of the sphere. (You might need to zoom out or in to see them.) The dot on the right follows the wave defined by `Mathf.Sin(theta)`, and the dot below follows the `Mathf.Cos(theta)` wave.

If you check `showCosX` in the *Sphere:Cyclic (Script)* Inspector, Sphere will start moving in the X direction following a cosine wave. You can see how the X motion of Sphere is connected directly to the cosine motion of the bottom wave. Uncheck `showCosX` and check `showSinY`. Now you can see how the Y motion of Sphere is connected to the sine wave. If you check both `showCosX` and `showSinY`, Sphere will move in the circle defined by combining X = cos(theta) and Y = sin(theta). A full circle is 360°, or 2π radians (that is, 2 * Mathf.PI).

This connection is also shown in Figure B.3, which uses similar colors to those in the Unity example.

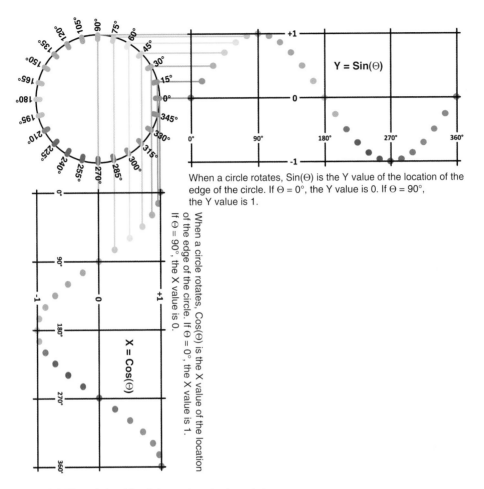

Figure B.3 The relationship of sine and cosine to a circle

This means that you can use sine and cosine for all sorts of circular or cyclic behavior!

These properties of sine and cosine are used in the Chapter 31, "Prototype 3.5: *Space SHMUP Plus*," prototype to define wavy movement for the Enemy_1 enemy type and to adjust the linear interpolation easing of the Enemy_2 type (see the *Interpolation* section in this appendix for information about linear interpolation and easing).

Dice Probability

Chapter 11, "Math and Game Balance," covered Jesse Schell's Rule 4 of probability: Enumeration can solve difficult math problems. Here is a quick Unity program that can enumerate all the possibilities for any number of dice with any number of sides. However, beware that each die you add drastically increases the number of calculations that must be done (e.g., 5d6 [five six-sided dice] take six times longer to calculate than 4d6 and 36 times longer to calculate than 3d6.)

Unity Example—Dice Probability

Follow these steps to create a program that will enumerate all possibilities for any number of dice with any number of sides. The default for this code is 2d6 (two six-sided dice). With these default values, the program will run through all possible rolls of the two dice (e.g., 1|1, 1|2, 1|3, 1|4, 1|5, 1|6, 2|1, 2|2, … 6|5, 6|6) and track the sum of the dice for each possibility.

1. Start a new Unity project. Create a new C# script named *DiceProbability* and attach it to the Main Camera in the Scene pane. Open *DiceProbability* in MonoDevelop and enter this code:

```csharp
using UnityEngine;
using System.Collections;

public class DiceProbability : MonoBehaviour {
    [Header("Set in Inspector")]
    public int      numDice = 2;
    public int      numSides = 6;
    public bool     checkToCalculate = false;
    // ^ When you set checkToCalculate to true, this will start calculating
    public int      maxIterations = 10000;
    // ^ The maximum number of iterations to perform in a single cycle of the
    //    CalculateRolls() coroutine
    public float    width = 16;
    public float    height = 9;

    [Header("Set Dynamically")]
    public int[]    dice;  // An array of the values of each die
    public int[]    rolls; // An array storing how many times a roll has come up
    // rolls for 2d6 would be [ 0, 0, 1, 2, 3, 4, 5, 6, 5, 4, 3, 2, 1 ].
    // The 1 in the second element of the array means that a 2 was rolled 1 time.
    // The 6 in the 7th element of the array means that a 7 was rolled 6 times.

    void Awake() {
        // Set up the main camera to properly display the graph
        Camera cam = Camera.main;
        cam.backgroundColor = Color.black;
        cam.orthographic = true;
        cam.orthographicSize = 5;
        cam.transform.position = new Vector3(8, 4.5f, -10);
    }

    void Update() {
        if (checkToCalculate) {
            StartCoroutine( CalculateRolls() );
            checkToCalculate = false;
        }
    }
}
```

```
void OnDrawGizmos() {
    float minVal = numDice;
    float maxVal = numDice*numSides;

    // If the rolls array is not ready, return
    if (rolls == null || rolls.Length == 0 || rolls.Length != maxVal+1) {
        return;
    }

    // Draw the rolls array
    float maxRolls = Mathf.Max(rolls);
    float heightMult = 1f/maxRolls;
    float widthMult = 1f/(maxVal-minVal);

    Gizmos.color = Color.white;
    Vector3 v0, v1 = Vector3.zero;
    for (int i=numDice; i<=maxVal; i++) {
        v0 = v1;
        v1.x = ( (float) i - numDice ) * width * widthMult;
        v1.y = ( (float) rolls[i] ) * height * heightMult;
        if (i != numDice) {
            Gizmos.DrawLine(v0,v1);
        }
    }
}

public IEnumerator CalculateRolls() {
    // Calculate max value (the maximum possible value that could be
    //  rolled on the dice (for example, for 2d6 maxValue = 12)
    int maxValue = numDice*numSides;
    // Make the array large enough to hold all possible values
    rolls = new int[maxValue+1];

    // Make an array with an element for each die. All are preset to a
    //  value of 1 except for the zeroth die which is set to 0 (to make the
    //  method RecursivelyAddOne() work properly)
    dice = new int[numDice];
    for (int i=0; i<numDice; i++) {
        dice[i] = (i==0) ? 0 : 1;
    }

    // Iterate on the dice.
    int iterations = 0;
    int sum = 0;

    // Usually, I avoid while loops because they can lead to infinite
    //  loops,but because this is a coroutine with a yield in the while
    //  loop, it's not as big of a problem.
```

```
while (sum != maxValue) {
    // ^ the sum will == maxValue when all dice are at their max value

    // Increment the 0th die in the dice Array
    RecursivelyAddOne(0);

    // Sum all the dice together
    sum = SumDice();
    // and add 1 to that position in the rolls array
    rolls[sum]++;

    // add to iterations and yield
    iterations++;
    if (iterations % maxIterations == 0) {
        yield return null;
    }
}
print("Calculation Done");

string s = "";
for (int i=numDice; i<=maxValue; i++) {
    s += i.ToString()+" "+rolls[i].ToString("N0")+"\n";          // a
}

int totalRolls = 0;
foreach (int i in rolls) {
    totalRolls += i;
}
s += "\nTotal Rolls: "+totalRolls.ToString("N0")+"\n";          // a

print(s);
}


// This is a recursive method, meaning that it calls itself. You can read
//   about recursive functions elsewhere in this appendix.
public void RecursivelyAddOne(int ndx) {
    if (ndx == dice.Length) return; // We've exceeded the length of dice
    //   Array, so just return

    // Increment the die at position ndx
    dice[ndx]++;
    // If this exceeds the capacity of the die...
    if (dice[ndx] > numSides) {
        dice[ndx] = 1;               // then set this die to 1...
        RecursivelyAddOne(ndx+1);    //   and increment the next die
    }
    return;
}
```

```
    public int SumDice() {
        // Sum the values of all the dice in the dice array
        int sum = 0;
        for (int i=0; i<dice.Length; i++) {
            sum += dice[i];
        }
        return(sum);
    }
}
```

a. The .ToString("N0") that you see here is an example of ToString() using one of the *Standard Numeric Format Strings* in C#. The N tells ToString() to add a separator every three digits (e.g., the commas in 123,456,789), and the 0 means that there should be zero digits after the decimal point. Search the Internet for "C# Standard Numeric Format Strings" to learn more.

2. To use the DiceProbability enumerator, click *Play* and then select *Main Camera* in the Hierarchy pane.

3. In the *Main Camera:Dice Probability (Script)* Inspector, you can set numDice (the number of dice) and numSides (the number of sides for each die) and then click checkToCalculate to calculate the probability of any specific number coming up on those dice.

Unity enumerates all the possible results and then outputs the results to the Console pane as well as a graph in the Scene pane. To better see the graph, you might need to click the mountain button at the top of the Scene pane (to turn off the skybox view), switch to the 2D view, and zoom out.

Try it first with the default setting of 2 dice of 6 sides each (2d6) and you'll get these results in the console (you will have to click the message in the console to see more than the first two lines):

```
2        1
3        2
4        3
5        4
6        5
7        6
8        5
9        4
10       3
11       2
12       1

Total Rolls: 36

UnityEngine.MonoBehaviour:print(Object)
<CalculateRolls>c__Iterator0:MoveNext() (at Assets/DiceProbability.cs:110)
UnityEngine.MonoBehaviour:StartCoroutine(IEnumerator)
DiceProbability:Update() (at Assets/DiceProbability.cs:34)
```

4. In the Inspector, try setting `numDice`=8 and `numSides`=6. Then check `checkToCalculate`.

You'll see that this takes a lot longer to calculate and that the results (and the curve graph) progressively update each time the coroutine yields (see the *Coroutines* section in this appendix). To speed this up, try setting `maxIterations`=100,000. `maxIterations` is the number of die rolls that the code will calculate before the coroutine yields and allows Unity to show you the results. The more `maxIterations` you allow, the faster the overall calculation will complete because the code will calculate more rolls in between showing you results. Choosing fewer `maxIterations` will show you results more frequently, but that will drastically slow down the overall time to calculate.

Now any time you want to know the probability of something like rolling a 13 on 8d6, you can figure it out through enumeration. Some salient lines from the console output are:

```
8       1
9       8
...
12      330
13      792
14      1,708
...
47      8
48      1


Total Rolls: 1,679,616
```

This means that the probability of rolling a 13 on 8D6 is 792 / 1,679,616 = 11 / 23,328 ≈ 0.00047 ≈ 0.05%.

You could also modify this code to roll the dice a specified number of times and choose random rolls each time. With a high number of rolls, this would give you a practical probability instead of the theoretical probability that is currently produced (see Jesse Schell's Rule 9 of probability in Chapter 11, "Math and Game Balance").

Dot Product

Another extremely useful math concept is the dot product. A dot product of two vectors is the result of multiplying the respective X, Y, and Z components of each vector together and adding the results, as shown in the following code listing:

```
1 Vector3 a = new Vector3( 1, 2, 3 );
2 Vector3 b = new Vector3( 4, 5, 6 );
3 float dotProduct = a.x*b.x + a.y*b.y + a.z*b.z;          // a
4 // dotProduct = 1*4 + 2*5 + 3*6
5 // dotProduct = 4 + 10 + 18
```

```
6 // dotProduct = 32
7 dotProduct = Vector3.Dot(a,b); // This is the real way to do it in C#    // b
```

a. Line 3 shows a manual calculation of the dot product of Vector3s a and b.

b. Line 7 shows the same calculation performed using the built-in static method `Vector3.Dot()`.

At first, this might not seem very important, but dot products have an *extremely* useful property: The float that the dot product[4] *a•b* returns is equivalent to *a*.magnitude * *b*.magnitude * Cos(Θ) where Θ is the angle between the two vectors, as shown in Figure B.4.

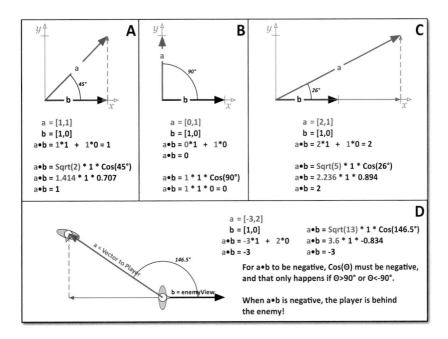

Figure B.4 Dot product examples (decimal numbers are approximate values)

Figure B.4.A shows a standard example of a dot product. In this example, the unit vector[5] *b* is pointing along the X axis. *b* has the coordinates [1, 0], and vector *a* has the coordinates [1, 1]. The *a* vector can be thought of as two parts: the part parallel to *b* (the X coordinate of *a*, shown with the thin green line on top of *b*) and the part perpendicular to *b* (the Y coordinate of *a*,

---

4. The • symbol is used here (and commonly in math) to represent the dot product, as opposed to the * that represents standard multiplication of floats and the × that represents a cross product of two vectors.

5. A *unit vector* is a vector with a magnitude of 1 (i.e., a length of 1).

shown with the dashed green line). The length of the part of *a* that is parallel to *b* is known as the *projection* of *a* onto *b* and is the result of the dot product *a•b*. The dot product takes the whole of *a* [1, 1], which has a length equal to the square root of 2 (≈1.414) and tells us how much of that vector is parallel to *b*. As mentioned previously, there are two different ways to calculate a dot product, both of which are shown in B.4.A and both of which give us the result of 1. This means that the length of vector *a* when projected onto unit vector *b* is 1.

Figure B.4.B shows that when two vectors are completely perpendicular, their dot product is zero. So here the projection of *a* onto *b* is zero.

Figure B.4.C shows the projection of a longer vector *a* onto *b*. Here again, both versions of the dot product calculation give us the same correct result.

As you see in Figure B.4.D, a dot product can also be used to tell whether an enemy is facing the player character (which can be useful in stealth games). Here, vector *a* is [-3, 2] and *b* is [1, 0]. The dot product *a•b* is -3. If the enemy is looking in the *b* direction, and the dot product of projecting the vector to the player *a* onto unit vector *b* is negative, then that means the player is behind the enemy. Although all the examples in Figure B.4 show *b* pointing along the X axis, the dot product still works perfectly regardless of the direction in which *b* is pointing, as long as *b* is a unit vector.

You can use dot products in several other places as well, and it's very common in computer graphics programming (for instance, dot products are used to determine whether a surface is facing toward a light).

Interpolation

An interpolation refers to any mathematical blending between two values. When I was working as a contract programmer after college, I feel that one of the major reasons I got a lot of job offers was because the motion of elements in my graphics code looked smooth and *juicy* (to use Kyle Gabler's term[6]). This was accomplished through the use of various forms of interpolation, easing, and Bézier curves, all of which I present in this section of the appendix.

Linear Interpolation

A *linear interpolation* is a way of mathematically defining a new value or position by stating that it is in between two existing values. All linear interpolations follow the same formula:

p01 = (1-u) * p0 + u * p1

---

6. "Juice It or Lose It" is a great 2012 talk by Martin Jonasson and Petri Purho about adding juiciness to games. You can try the link https://www.youtube.com/watch?v=Fy0aCDmgnxg or just search for "juice it or lose it."

In code, this would look something like this:

```
1 Vector3 p0 = new Vector3( 0, 0, 0 );
2 Vector3 p1 = new Vector3( 1, 1, 0 );
3 float   u  = 0.5f;
4 Vector3 p01 = (1-u) * p0  +  u * p1;
5 print(p01); // prints: ( 0.5, 0.5, 0 ) the point half-way between p0 & p1
```

In the preceding code listing, a new point p01 is created by interpolating between the points p0 and p1. The value u ranges in value between 0 and 1. This can happen with any number of dimensions, though you usually interpolate Vector3s in Unity.

Time-Based Linear Interpolations

In a time-based linear interpolation, you are guaranteed that the interpolation will complete in a specific amount of time because the u value is based on the amount of time that has passed divided by the total desired duration of the interpolation.

Unity Example—Time-Based Linear Interpolation

To create a Unity example, do the following:

1. Create a new Unity project named *Interpolation Project*. Save the scene as *_Scene_Interp*.

2. Create a cube in the hierarchy (*GameObject > 3D Object > Cube*).

    a. Select *Cube* in the Hierarchy pane and attach a TrailRenderer to it (*Components > Effects > Trail Renderer*).

    b. Open the Materials array of the TrailRenderer and set Element 0 to the built-in material *Default-Particle*. (Click the circle to the right of Element 0 to see *Default-Particle* in the list of available materials.)

3. Create a new C# script in the Project pane named *Interpolator*. Attach it to *Cube* and then open it in MonoDevelop to enter this code:

```
using UnityEngine;
using System.Collections;

public class Interpolator : MonoBehaviour {
    [Header("Set in Inspector")]
    public Vector3       p0 = new Vector3(0,0,0);
    public Vector3       p1 = new Vector3(3,4,5);
    public float         timeDuration = 1;
    // Click the checkToStart checkbox to start moving
    public bool          checkToStart = false;

    [Header("Set Dynamically")]
    public Vector3       p01;
```

```
public bool        moving = false;
public float       timeStart;

// Update is called once per frame
void Update () {
    if (checkToStart) {
        checkToStart = false;

        moving = true;
        timeStart = Time.time;
    }

    if (moving) {
        float u = (Time.time-timeStart)/timeDuration;
        if (u>=1) {
            u=1;
            moving = false;
        }

        // This is the standard linear interpolation function
        p01 = (1-u)*p0 + u*p1;

        transform.position = p01;
    }
}
}
```

4. Switch back to Unity and click *Play*. In the *Cube:Interpolator (Script)* component, check the box next to `checkToStart`, and Cube will move from `p0` to `p1` in 1 second. If you adjust `timeDuration` to another value and then check `checkToStart` again, you can see that Cube always moves from `p0` to `p1` in `timeDuration` seconds. You can also change the location of `p0` or `p1` while Cube is moving, and it will update accordingly.

Linear Interpolations Using Zeno's Paradox

Zeno of Elea (ca. 490–430 BCE) was a Greek philosopher who proposed a set of paradoxes having to do with the philosophical impossibility of everyday, commonsense motion.

In Zeno's Dichotomy Paradox, the question is posed of whether a moving object can ever reach a stationary point. Imagine that a frog is hopping toward a wall. Every hop, he covers half of the remaining distance to the wall. No matter how many times the frog hops, it will still have covered only half of the distance remaining to the wall after its last hop, so it will never reach the wall.

Ignoring the philosophical implications (and the complete lack of rationality) of this, you can actually use a similar concept along with linear interpolation to create a smooth motion that eases toward a certain point. This is used throughout this book to make cameras that smoothly follow various points of interest.

Unity Example—Zeno's Paradox Interpolation

Continuing the same *Interpolation Project* from before:

1. Add a sphere to the scene (*GameObject > 3D Object > Sphere*) and move it somewhere away from Cube.

2. Create a new C# script in the Project pane named *ZenosFollower* and attach it to Sphere.

3. Open *ZenosFollower* in MonoDevelop and enter this code:

```
using UnityEngine;
using System.Collections;

public class ZenosFollower : MonoBehaviour {
    [Header("Set in Inspector")]
    public GameObject           poi; // Point Of Interest
    public float                u = 0.1f;
    public Vector3              p0, p1, p01;

    // Update is called once per frame
    void FixedUpdate () {
        // Get the position of this and the poi
        p0 = this.transform.position;
        p1 = poi.transform.position;

        // Interpolate between the two
        p01 = (1-u)*p0 + u*p1;

        // Move this to the new position
        this.transform.position = p01;
    }
}
```

4. Save the code and return to Unity.

5. Set the `poi` of Sphere:ZenosFollower to be the cube (by dragging Cube from the Hierarchy pane into the `poi` slot of the *Sphere:ZenosFollower (Script)* Inspector).

6. Save your scene!

Now, when you click *Play*, the sphere moves toward the cube. If you select the cube and check the `checkToStart` box, the sphere will continue to follow the cube through its motions. You can also move the cube around in the Scene window manually and watch the sphere follow.

Try changing the value of `u` in the *Sphere:ZenosFollower* Inspector. Lower values will make it follow more slowly whereas higher values will make it follow more rapidly. A value of *0.5* would make the sphere cover half of the distance to the cube every frame, which would exactly mimic Zeno's Dichotomy Paradox (but in practice, this follows far too closely). It is true that with this specific code, the sphere will never get to exactly the same location as the cube, and the movement is not very controllable, but this is meant to just be a very quick, simple following script.

`FixedUpdate()` is used instead of `Update()` in ZenosFollower to make the behavior consistent across all computers. If `Update()` had been used, then depending on the processor load on your computer at any given time, the Sphere would follow closer or further away because more or fewer `Update()` calls would happen each second as the frame rate experienced natural variations. Using `Update()` would also cause the sphere to follow much closer on fast machines than on slow ones for the same reason. `FixedUpdate()` makes behavior consistent across all machines at all times because it is *always* called 50 times per second.[7]

Interpolating More Than Just Position

You can interpolate almost any kind of numeric value. In Unity, this means that you can very easily interpolate values like scale, rotation, and color among others.

Unity Example—Interpolating Various Attributes

You can either do this in the same scene as the previous interpolation examples or in a new project:

1. Create a new scene named *_Scene_Interp2* and create two new cubes in its Hierarchy named *c0* and *c1*.

2. Make a new material for each cube (*Assets > Create > Material*) named *Mat_c0* and *Mat_c1*.

3. Drag each material onto its respective cube to apply the material.

4. Select *c0* and set its *position*, *rotation*, and *scale* to anything you want (as long as it's visible on screen and the *scale X, Y,* and *Z* are positive). Under the *c0:Mat_c0* section of the Inspector, you should also set the *color* to whatever you want.

5. Do the same for the transform of *c1* and the color of Mat_c1, making sure that c1 and c0 have different positions, rotations, scales, and colors from each other.

6. Add a third cube to the scene, set its position to P:[0, 0, 0], and name it *Cube01*.

7. Create a new C# script named *Interpolator2* and attach it to Cube01. Enter this code into Interpolator2:

```
using UnityEngine;
using System.Collections;
```

---

7. `FixedUpdate()` is called 50 times per second because the default value for `Time.fixedDeltaTime` is 0.02 (one 50th of a second), but you can change the frequency at which `FixedUpdate()` is called by adjusting `Time.fixedDeltaTime`. This is especially useful if you've changed `Time.timeScale` to something like 0.1 (slowing down Unity to one 10th regular speed). At a `Time.timeScale` of 0.1, `FixedUpdate()` would only be called every 0.2 seconds in real time, leading to visibly stuttering physics movement. Any time you alter `Time.timeScale`, you should also alter `Time.fixedDeltaTime` by the same amount; so for a `Time.timeScale` of 0.1, you want a `Time.fixedDeltaTime` of 0.002 to still experience fifty `FixedUpdate()`s every real time second.

```csharp
public class Interpolator2 : MonoBehaviour {
    [Header("Set in Inspector")]
    public Transform    c0;
    public Transform    c1;
    public float        timeDuration = 1;
    // Click the checkToStart checkbox to start moving
    public bool         checkToStart = false;

    [Header("Set Dynamically")]
    public Vector3      p01;
    public Color        c01;
    public Quaternion   r01;
    public Vector3      s01;
    public bool         moving = false;
    public float        timeStart;

    private Material mat, matC0, matC1;

    void Awake() {
        mat = GetComponent<Renderer>().material;
        matC1 = c1.GetComponent<Renderer>().material;
        matC0 = c0.GetComponent<Renderer>().material;
    }

    // Update is called once per frame
    void Update () {
        if (checkToStart) {
            checkToStart = false;

            moving = true;
            timeStart = Time.time;
        }

        if (moving) {
            float u = (Time.time-timeStart)/timeDuration;
            if (u>=1) {
                u=1;
                moving = false;
            }

            // This is the standard linear interpolation function
            p01 = (1-u)*c0.position + u*c1.position;
            c01 = (1-u)*matC0.color + u*matC1.color;
            s01 = (1-u)*c0.localScale + u*c1.localScale;
            // Rotations are treated differently because Quaternions are tricky
            r01 = Quaternion.Slerp(c0.rotation, c1.rotation, u);
```

```
            // Apply these to this Cube01
            transform.position = p01;
            mat.color = c01;
            transform.localScale = s01;
            transform.rotation = r01;
        }
    }
}
```

8. Save the script and return to Unity.

9. Drag *c0* from the Hierarchy pane into the `c0` field of the *Cube01:Interpolator2 (Script)* Inspector. Also drag *c1* from the Hierarchy into the `c1` field of the *Interpolator2* script.

10. Click *Play* and then click the `checkToStart` check box in the *Cube01:Interpolator2* Inspector. You'll see that Cube01 now interpolates much more than just position.

Linear Extrapolation

All the interpolations so far have had u values that ranged from 0 to 1. If you allow the u value to go beyond this range, you get *extrapolation* (so named because instead of interpolating between two values, it now extrapolates data outside of the original two points).

Given the initial two points on a number line of 10 and 20, an extrapolation of u=2 would work as shown in Figure B.5.

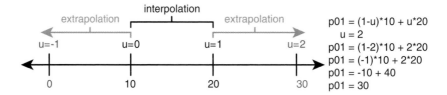

Figure B.5 An example of extrapolation

Unity Example—Linear Extrapolation

To see this in code, make the following bolded code additions to Interpolator2. In addition to extrapolation, this additional code also allows the movement to loop.

```
public class Interpolator2 : MonoBehaviour {
    [Header("Set in Inspector")]
    public Transform    c0;
    public Transform    c1;
    public float        uMin = 0;
    public float        uMax = 1;
    public float        timeDuration = 1;
    public bool         loopMove = true; // Causes the move to repeat
    ...
```

```
void Update () {
    ...
    if (moving) {
        float u = (Time.time-timeStart)/timeDuration;
        if (u>=1) {
            u=1;
            if (loopMove) {
                timeStart = Time.time;
            } else {
                moving = false; // This line is now within the else clause
            }
        }

        // Adjust u to the range from uMin to uMax
        u = (1-u)*uMin + u*uMax;
        // ^ Look familiar? We're using a linear interpolation here too!

        // This is the standard linear interpolation function
        p01 = (1-u)*c0.position + u*c1.position;
        ...
    }
}
}
```

Now, if you click *Play* in Unity and then click the `checkToStart` box on Cube01, you'll get the same behavior as before. Try changing `uMin` to -1 and `uMax` to 2 in the *Cube01:Interpolator2 (Script)* Inspector. Click `checkToStart`, and you'll see that the color, position, and scale all extrapolate and go beyond the original range that you set.[8] You can now also check `loopMove` to repeat the interpolation endlessly.

Rotation will not extrapolate beyond the rotation of c0 or c1 due to a limitation of the `Quaternion.Slerp()` method (which is short for the *Spherical Linear intERPolation* that is used for rotations in Unity). Rather than independently interpolate each of the X, Y, and Z rotation values, a Slerp attempts to choose the most direct path from one rotation to another. However, if `Slerp()` is passed any number below 0 as its u value, it treats it as 0 (and any number above 1 is treated as 1).

If you look at the documentation for Vector3, it also has a `Lerp()` (short for Linear intERPolation) method that can interpolate between Vector3s, but I never use that function because it also clamps the values of u to the range from 0 to 1 and doesn't allow extrapolation. In Unity 5, a `Vector3.LerpUnclamped()` method was added that does not clamp to the 0 to 1 range. I do use the unclamped version, but I still think it's important for you to learn how to Lerp

---

8. You might receive a warning in the console telling you that "BoxColliders does[sic] not support negative scale or size." Don't worry about this. The extrapolation of scale could cause negative scaling here, but we're not worried about collision detection in this example.

on your own, which is why you didn't use `Vector3.LerpUnclamped()` in the code for this section.

Easing for Linear Interpolations

The interpolations you've been doing so far are pretty nice, but they also have a very mechanical feel to them because they start abruptly, move at a constant rate, and then stop abruptly. Happily, several different *easing* functions can be used to make this movement more interesting. This is most easily explained with a Unity example.

Unity Example—Interpolation Easing

To create the example, follow these steps.

1. Create a new C# script named *Easing* and open it in MonoDevelop to add the following code. As you do so, note that Easing *does not* extend MonoDevelop.

```csharp
using UnityEngine;

public class Easing {

    public enum Type {                                          // a
        linear,
        easeIn,
        easeOut,
        easeInOut,
        sin,
        sinIn,
        sinOut
    }

    static public float Ease (float u, Type eType, float eMod = 2) {     // c
        float u2 = u;

        switch (eType) {                                        // b

            case Type.linear:
                u2 = u;
                break;

            case Type.easeIn:
                u2 = Mathf.Pow(u, eMod);
                break;

            case Type.easeOut:
                u2 = 1 - Mathf.Pow( 1-u, eMod );
                break;
```

```
case Type.easeInOut:
    if ( u <= 0.5f ) {
        u2 = 0.5f * Mathf.Pow( u*2, eMod );
    } else {
        u2 = 0.5f + 0.5f*(  1 - Mathf.Pow( 1-(2*(u-0.5f)), eMod )  );
    }
    break;

case Type.sin:
    // Try eMod values of 0.15f and -0.2f for Easing.Type.sin    // c
    u2 = u + eMod * Mathf.Sin( 2*Mathf.PI*u );
    break;

case Type.sinIn:
    // eMod is ignored for SinIn
    u2 = 1 - Mathf.Cos( u * Mathf.PI * 0.5f );
    break;

case Type.sinOut:
    // eMod is ignored for SinOut
    u2 = Mathf.Sin( u * Mathf.PI * 0.5f );
    break;
    }

    return( u2 );
    }
}
```

a. This enum is defined within the Easing type, so variables of this enum type outside of this class would be declared as Easing.Type. Within the `Easing` class, Type can be used instead.

b. This switch statement contains cases for each type of easing.

c. eMod is an optional float parameter of the static `Ease()` function. It is used in various ways as a modifier for many easing types. For example, for `easeIn`, it is used as the power to which u is raised; e.g., if eMod is 2, then $u2 = u^2$; if eMod is 3, then $u2 = u^3$. For `sin` easing, eMod is the multiplier for the amplitude of the sine curve that is added to the line (see Figure B.6 for some examples).

This `Easing` class holds all the easing functions for u, making it easy to import them into any of your projects. The various easing curves are shown and described in Figure B.6, except for `sinIn` and `sinOut`, which are sine-based, less flexible versions of `easeIn` and `easeOut`.

2. Save the *Easing* script, open the Interpolator2 script, and make the following modifications.

```
public class Interpolator2 : MonoBehaviour {
    [Header("Set in Inspector")]
    ...
```

```
public bool          loopMove = true; // Causes the move to repeat
public Easing.Type   easingType = Easing.Type.linear;
public float         easingMod = 2;

// Click the checkToStart checkbox to start moving
public bool          checkToStart = false;
...
void Update () {
    ...
    if (moving) {
        ...
        // Adjust u to the range from uMin to uMax
        u = (1-u)*uMin + u*uMax;
        // ^ Look familiar? We're using a linear interpolation here too!

        // The Easing.Ease function modifies u to change tweak movement
        u = Easing.Ease(u, easingType, easingMod);

        // This is the standard linear interpolation function
        p01 = (1-u)*c0.position + u*c1.position;
        ...
    }
}
}
```

3. Save the Interpolator2 script in MonoDevelop and switch back to Unity.

4. In the *Cube01:Interpolator2 (Script)* Inspector, set uMin = 0 and uMax = 1. Also check `loop-Move` to set it to true.

5. Save your scene!

6. Click *Play* and click `checkToStart`. Now, because `loopMove` is checked as well, Cube01 continuously interpolates between c0 and c1.

Try playing around with the different settings for `easingType`. `easingMod` only affects the `easeIn`, `easeOut`, `easeInOut`, and `sin` easing types. For the `sin` type, try an `easingMod` of *0.15* as well as one of *-0.3* to see the flexibility of this sine-based easing type.

In Figure B.6 you can see a graphical representation of various easing curves. In this figure, the horizontal dimension represents the initial u value, while the vertical dimension represents the eased u value (u2). You can see that in every example when u=0, u2 also equals 0 and when u=1, u2 also equals 1. Because of this, if the linear interpolation is time based, the value will always move completely from p0 to p1 in the same amount of time regardless of the easing settings.

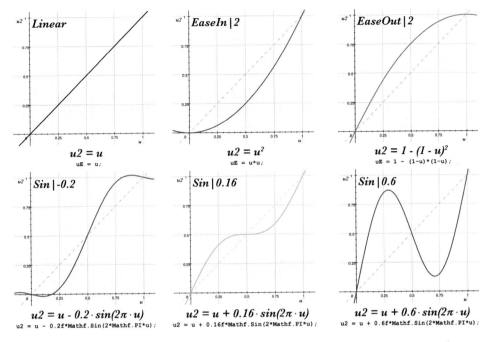

Figure B.6 Various easing curves and their formulae. In each case, the number after the pipe (|) represents the eMod (i.e., `easingMod`) value.

The *Linear* curve shows no easing (u2 = u). In each of the other curves shown, the u2 = u line remains as a dashed diagonal line to show normal, linear behavior. If the vertical component of a curve is ever below the dashed diagonal, the movement is lagging behind a linear curve. Conversely, if the vertical component of the curve is ever above the dashed diagonal, the eased curve is ahead of where the linear movement would have been. The slope of the curve represents the speed of the interpolation at that point: A 45° slope is the same speed as the linear interpolation, whereas a shallower slope is slower and a more steep slope is faster.

The *EaseIn* curve starts slowly and then moves faster toward the end (u2 = u*u). This is called "easing in" because the first part of the motion is "easy" and slow before it then speeds up.

The *EaseOut* curve is the opposite of the *EaseIn* curve. With this curve, the movement starts quickly and then slows at the end. This is commonly known as "easing out."

The three *Sin* curves on the bottom of the diagram all follow the same formula (u2 = u + eMod * sin(u*2π)), where eMod is a floating-point number (the variable eMod or `easingMod` in the code). The multiplication of u * 2π inside of the `sin()` ensures that as u moves from 0 to 1, it passes through a full sine wave (moving center, up, center, down, and back to center). If eMod=0, the sine curve has no effect on the curve (that is, the curve remains linear). As eMod gets further from 0 (either positively or negatively), it has more of an effect.

The curve *Sin|-0.2* is an ease-in-out with a bounce. The eMod value of *-0.2* adds a negative sine wave to the linear progression, causing a moving object to back up a bit from p0, move quickly toward p1, overshoot a bit, and then settle at p1. An eMod value closer to zero of *Sin|-0.1* would cause the object to ease-in to full speed at the center point and then slow as it approached p1 without the extrapolation bounce at either end.

In the curve *Sin|0.16,* a slight sine curve is added to the linear u progression, causing the curve to get ahead of linear, stop briefly in the middle, and then hurry to catch up at the end. If you're moving an object, this brings it to the center point, slows it in the middle to "feature" it for a while, and then moves it out.

The curve *Sin|0.6* is the easing curve that is used by Enemy_2 in Chapter 31, "Space SHMUP Plus." In this case, enough positive sine wave has been added to cause the object to shoot past the center point to a point about 80% of the way to p1, then move back to a point 20% of the way to p1, and then finally move to p1.

Bézier Curves

A Bézier curve is a linear interpolation between more than two points. Just as with a normal linear interpolation, the base formula is p01 = (1-u) * p0 + u * p1. The Bézier curve just adds more points and more calculations.

Given three points: p0, p1, and p2

$$p01 = (1-u) * p0 + u * p1$$

$$p12 = (1-u) * p1 + u * p2$$

$$p012 = (1-u) * p01 + u * p12$$

As is demonstrated in the preceding equations, for the three points p0, p1, and p2, the location of the point of the Bézier curve is calculated by first performing a linear interpolation between p0 and p1 (the resulting point is called p01), then performing a linear interpolation between p1 and p2 (called p12), and finally performing a linear interpolation between p01 and p12 to obtain the final point, p012. A graphical representation of this is shown in Figure B.7.

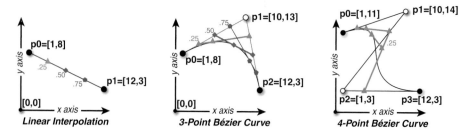

Figure B.7 A linear interpolation and three-point and four-point Bézier curves

A four-point curve requires more calculations to accommodate all four points:

$$p01 = (1-u) * p0 + u * p1$$

$$p12 = (1-u) * p1 + u * p2$$

$$p23 = (1-u) * p2 + u * p3$$

$$p012 = (1-u) * p01 + u * p12$$

$$p123 = (1-u) * p12 + u * p23$$

$$p0123 = (1-u) * p012 + u * p123$$

Four-point Bézier curves are used in many drawing programs as a way of defining very control-lable curves, including: Adobe *Flash*, *Illustrator*, and *Photoshop*; The Omni Groups' *OmniGraffle*; and many others. In fact, the curve editor used in Unity for animation and TrailRenderer thickness uses a form of four-point Bézier curves.

Unity Example—Bézier Curves

Follow these steps to create a Bézier curve example in Unity. When writing code, I don't use the accented *é* in Bézier because code tends to be written without any accented characters.

1. Create a new scene in your Unity project and save it as *_Scene_Bezier*.

2. Add four cubes to the Hierarchy named *c0, c1, c2,* and *c3*.

   a. Set the *transform.scale* of all cubes to S:[0.5, 0.5, 0.5].

   b. Position the cubes in various positions around the scene and adjust your Scene view so that you can see all of them.

3. Add a sphere to the scene.

   a. Attach a *TrailRenderer* to the sphere.

   b. Open the `Materials` array of the TrailRenderer and set `Element 0` to the built-in material *Default-Particle*.

4. Create a new C# script named *Bezier* and attach it to Sphere. Open *Bezier* in MonoDevelop and enter the following code to demonstrate a four-point Bézier curve in Unity:

```csharp
using UnityEngine;
using System.Collections;

public class Bezier : MonoBehaviour {
    [Header("Set in Inspector")]
    public float        timeDuration = 1;
    public Transform    c0, c1, c2, c3;
    // Set checkToStart to true to start moving
    public bool         checkToStart = false;

    [Header("Set Dynamically")]
    public float        u;
    public Vector3      p0123;
```

```
public bool        moving = false;
public float       timeStart;

void Update () {
    if (checkToStart) {
        checkToStart = false;
        moving = true;
        timeStart = Time.time;
    }

    if (moving) {
        u = (Time.time-timeStart)/timeDuration;
        if (u>=1) {
            u=1;
            moving = false;
        }

        // 4-point Bezier curve calculation
        Vector3 p01, p12, p23, p012, p123;

        p01 = (1-u)*c0.position + u*c1.position;
        p12 = (1-u)*c1.position + u*c2.position;
        p23 = (1-u)*c2.position + u*c3.position;

        p012 = (1-u)*p01 + u*p12;
        p123 = (1-u)*p12 + u*p23;

        p0123 = (1-u)*p012 + u*p123;

        transform.position = p0123;
    }
}
}
```

5. Save the Bezier script and return to Unity.

6. Assign each of the four cubes to their respective fields in the *Sphere:Bezier (Script)* Inspector.

7. Click *Play* and then click the `checkToStart` check box in the Inspector.

Sphere will trace a Bézier curve between the four cubes. It's important to note here that Sphere only ever touches c0 and c3. It is influenced by but does not touch c1 and c2. This is true of all Bézier curves. The ends of the curve always touch the first and last points, but no points in-between are ever touched. If you're interested in looking into a kind of curve where the midpoints are touched, look up "Hermite spline" online (as well as other kinds of splines).

A Recursive Bézier Curve Function

As you saw in the previous section, the additional calculations for adding more control points to a Bézier curve are pretty straightforward conceptually, but it takes a while to type all the additional lines of code. The upcoming code listing uses a recursive function to handle any number of points without any additional code. It's a little conceptually complex, so let's start by considering how it should work.

To interpolate a standard three-point Bézier curve, you start with three points: [p0, p1, p2]. However, in order to interpolate them, you need to first break it down into two smaller interpolations [p0, p1] and [p1, p2]. You interpolate each of these and return the interpolated points p01 and p12. Finally, you interpolate between p01 and p12 to get the final point p012.

The `Bezier()` function does the same thing, recursively breaking the problem down to smaller and smaller lists of points until each branch gets to a list of just one point, and then returning those points up the recursion chain, interpolating on the way up.

In the first edition of this book, the recursive `Bezier()` function created a new List<Vector3> with each recursion, but that was very inefficient because it wasted both memory and processing power with each creation of a new List. In fact, interpolating a four-point Bézier curve with the first-edition version of `Bezier()` would create *fourteen* additional lists.

Rather than make a ton of new lists, the second edition version of `Bezier()` just passes a reference to the same List into each of its recursions along with two integers—`iL` and `iR`—as you can see in the `Bezier()` function declaration.

```
static public Vector3 Bezier(float u, List<Vector3> pts, int iL=0, int iR=-1) {…}
```

The integers `iL` and `iR` are each an *index* into the List `pts`, meaning that `iL` and `iR` are references to elements of `pts`. If `iL` is 0, then it's pointing to the 0th element of `pts`. If `iR` is 3, then it's pointing to the third element of `pts`. `iL` and `iR` are optional parameters. If neither are passed in (i.e., `Bezier()` is called with just u and pts arguments), then `iL` will be 0, and `iR` will start as -1 but will thereafter be given the index of the last element of `pts`.

`iL` represents the leftmost element of `pts` that is being considered by any recursion of `Bezier()`, and `iR` represents the rightmost element. So, for a four-point List `pts`, the initial value of `iL` will be 0, and `iR` will start at 3 (the index of the last point in `pts`). Each time the `Bezier()` function recurs, it branches and sends fewer points to the next level. Rather than create new Lists, the new version of `Bezier()` adjusts iL and iR to look at a smaller section of the overall List `pts`. Eventually, terminal cases will be reached in each branch where `iL` and `iR` both point to the same element of `pts`, and then the value of that element is returned up the chain as a Vector3, and the series of actual interpolations takes place as the chain of recursion unwinds.

Figure B.8 shows the series of recursive calls that are made by a single four-point call to the `Bezier()` function. The green arrows trace the calls, and the red dashed arrows show the returns. You can see that either `iL` or `iR` is respectively incremented or decremented with each call, and the elements of `pts` that are black in the diagram are those that are in the range from `iL` to `iR` for each call to `Bezier()`.

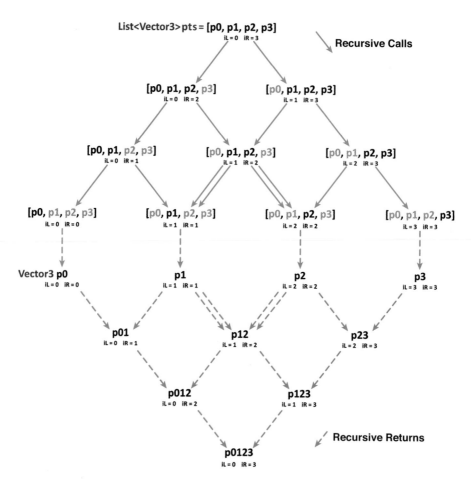

Figure B.8 The path of calls (solid green arrow) and returns (dashed red arrow) when recursively interpolating a four-point Bezier curve.

The way that this `Bezier()` function works does make two separate calls to determine the value of p12 (it has two green arrows pointing to it and two red arrows returning from it). This is somewhat inefficient, but eliminating that overlap would have required a lot more complex code.

The following code listing implements this recursive function to calculate a Bézier curve for any number of points. A version of this is included in the ProtoTools `Utils` class that is part of the initial unitypackage for Chapters 31 through 35:

```
static public Vector3 Bezier(float u, List<Vector3> pts, int iL=0, int iR=-1) { // a
    if (iR == -1) {                                                              // b
        iR = pts.Count-1;
    }
```

```
    if (iL == iR) {  // This is the terminal case                        // c
        return( pts [iL] );
    }

    // Two recursive calls to Bezier, each using one fewer of the points in l
    Vector3 lV3 = Bezier(u, pts, iL,   iR-1);                            // d
    Vector3 rV3 = Bezier(u, pts, iL+1, iR );                            // e

    // Interpolate the results from the Bezier recursions at lines d & e
    Vector3 res = Vector3.LerpUnclamped( lV3, rV3, u );                  // f
    return( res );
}
```

a. The `Bezier()` function takes as input a float `u` and a List<Vector3> `pts` of points to interpolate. It also has two optional parameters, `iL` and `iR`, which represent the indices in `pts` of the leftmost (`iL`) and rightmost (`iR`) element being considered by this recursion of `Bezier()`. See Figure B.8 for more information.

b. If `iR` does come in as -1, `iR` is set to the index of the last element in `pts`.

c. The terminal case of the recursive function is reached when `iL == iR`. If `iL == iR`, then both the left and right indices into the List `pts` are pointing at the same Vector3 element. When this occurs, the Vector3 to which they both point is returned.

d. This is one of the two recursive calls to `Bezier()`. Here, the `iR` index into `pts` is decremented by 1, and the full list `pts` is passed into the recursion with `iL` and `iR` as arguments. This has the same effect as creating a new List containing all but the last element of `pts`, but it is much more efficient.

e. This is the other recursive call to `Bezier()`. Here `iL` index into `pts` is incremented by 1. This has the effect of passing all but the first element of `pts` into the next recursion.

f. The results of the recursive calls on lines *d* and *e* have been stored in two Vector3s: `lV3` and `rV3`. These two Vector3s are interpolated by `Vector3.LerpUnclamped()`, and the result is returned up the recursion chain.

The Utils C# script includes several overloads of the `Bezier()` function for different point types (e.g., Vector3, Vector2, float, and Quaternion). It also includes overloads that use the `params` keyword to allow any number of points to be passed in as arguments to the `Bezier()` function rather than a List.

```
// This overload of Bezier() allows an Array or a series of Vector3s as input
static public Vector3 Bezier( float u, params Vector3[] vecs ) {          // g
    return( Bezier( u, new List<Vector3>(vecs) ) ); // Calls Bezier() on line a
}
```

g. As covered in Chapter 24, "Functions and Parameters," the `params` keyword allows the `vecs` array parameter to accept either a Vector3 array or a series of individual Vector3 parameters separated by commas (after the first float argument).

So, two possible valid calls to this overload of `Bezier()` for a five-point Bézier curve could be

```
float u = 0.1f;
Vector3 p0, p1, p2, p3, p4;

Vector3[] points = new Vector3[] { p0, p1, p2, p3, p4 };

Utils.Bezier( u, points );                              // h
Utils.Bezier( u, p0, p1, p2, p3, p4 );                  // i
```

h. Here, the array `points` is passed into the array `vecs`, which is nothing unexpected.

i. On this line, the `params` keyword allows the series of Vector3s parameters (i.e., `p0`, `p1`, `p2`, `p3`, `p4`) to automatically be converted into a Vector3 array and assigned to `vecs`.

Lines *h* and *i* will both call the overload of `Bezier()` with the `vecs` array (declared on line *g*). Then on the single line of that overload, the `vecs` array is converted to a List<Vector3>, and when `Bezier()` is called with a List<Vector3> as the second argument, it calls the original version of `Bezier()` declared on line *a* of the preceding code listing.

Role-Playing Games

Many good role-playing games (RPGs) are out there. The most popular is still probably *Dungeons & Dragons* by Wizards of the Coast (D&D), which is now in its fifth edition. Since the third edition, D&D has been based on the d20 system, which uses a single twenty-sided die in place of the many complex die rolls that were common in prior systems. I like D&D for a lot of things, but I have found that my students often get bogged down in combat when attempting to run D&D as their first system; it has a lot of very specific combat rules, especially in the fourth edition.

My personal recommendation for a first RPG system is *FATE* by Evil Hat Productions, especially the streamlined *FATE Accelerated* (FAE) system. *FAE* is a simple system that allows players to contribute directly to the narrative much more than other systems allow. (Other systems give all power over events to the *game master* running the game.) You can learn about the core version of *FATE* at the website http://faterpg.com, and you can read the free *FATE* system reference document (SRD) at http://fate-srd.com. For info on *FATE* Accelerated, and to get a free 50-page eBook with all the info you need to get started, check out http://www.evilhat.com/home/fae/.

Tips for Running a Good Role-Playing Campaign

Running a role-playing campaign can do wonders for your abilities as both a game designer and storyteller. Here are some tips that I've found to be very useful when my students start running campaigns:

- **Start simple:** A lot of different role-playing systems are out there, and they vary greatly in the complexity of their rules. As described in the preceding section, I recommend starting with a simple system like the *FATE Accelerated* system by Evil Hat Productions. After you've played a few games with that system, you can move on to more complex systems like D&D. The fifth edition of D&D has a relatively straightforward core rulebook with many supplemental rulebooks to add as you get deeper into the system.

- **Start short:** Rather than starting with the first episode of a campaign that you expect to take a full year of play to complete, try starting with a simple mission that can be wrapped up in a single night of play. This gives your group a chance to try out their characters and the system and see if they like both. If not, it's easy to change to something else, and it's much more important that the players enjoy their first experience role-playing than that you kick off an epic campaign.

- **Help the players get started:** If the players in your campaign have little or no prior experience role-playing, creating their characters for them is a very good idea. This gives you the chance to make sure that the characters have complementary abilities and stats so that they'll combine into a good team. A standard role-playing party is composed of the following characters:

  - A warrior to absorb enemy damage and fight up close (a.k.a., a tank)

  - A wizard to do long-range damage and detect magic (a.k.a., a glass cannon)

  - A thief to disarm traps and make powerful sneak attacks (a.k.a., a blaster)

  - A cleric to detect evil and heal the other party members (a.k.a., a controller)

  If you're going to create characters for your players, you should get early buy-in from them by asking them to tell you about the kind of play experience they would like and the kind of abilities that they want their character to have. Early buy-in and interest is one of the keys to getting your players past the rough patches that can happen at the beginning of a campaign.

- **Plan for improvisation:** Your players will frequently do things that you don't expect. The only way to plan for this is to prepare yourself for flexibility and improvisation. Be ready with things like maps of generic spaces, a list of names that could be used for NPCs (non-player characters) that the party may or may not encounter, and a few generic enemies or monsters of various difficulties that you can conjure at will. The more you have ready beforehand, the less time you'll have to spend looking through your rulebook in the middle of the game.

- **Be willing to make rulings:** If you can't find the answer to a question in the rules after 5 minutes of looking, just make a ruling using your best judgment and agree with the players that you'll look it up after the game session is over. This keeps the game from bogging down due to esoteric rules.

- **It's also the players' story:** Remember to allow the players to go off the beaten path. If you've prepared too narrow a scenario, you might be tempted to not let them do so, but that would run the risk of killing their enjoyment of the game.

- **Remember that constant optimal challenge isn't fun:** In the discussion of *flow* in Chapter 8, "Design Goals," you read that if players are always optimally challenged, they get exhausted quickly. This is also true in RPGs. Boss fights should always optimally challenge your players, but you should also have fights where the players win easily (this helps demonstrate to them that their characters are actually getting stronger as they level up) and sometimes even fights that the players need to flee from to survive (this is usually not expected by players, and can be really dramatic for them). Unlike most systems, FAE has a really intriguing game mechanic that makes giving up and fleeing a much better choice than fighting to lose, which is another reason I really like it.

If you keep these tips in mind, it should help your role-playing campaigns be a lot more fun for both you and your players.

User Interface Concepts

This section covers button mapping, which allows you to use Microsoft gamepad controllers on your Windows, macOS, or Linux machine and information about how to enable right-click on macOS computers.

Axis and Button Mapping for Microsoft Controllers

Although most of the games included in this book use a mouse or keyboard interface, I'm guessing you might want to eventually hook up a gamepad controller to your games. Generally, the easiest controller to get working on a PC, macOS, or Linux is the Microsoft Xbox 360 Controller for Windows, though I've also seen people have a lot of luck with a PS4 or Xbox One controller.

However, it is unfortunately true that each platform (PC, macOS, and Linux) interprets the controllers differently, so you'll need to set up a Unity InputManager that adapts to how the controller works on each platform.

Alternatively, you could save yourself a lot of trouble and choose an input manager from the Unity Asset Store. Several of my students have used *InControl* by Gallant Games, which maps input from Microsoft, Sony, Logitech, and Ouya controllers to the same input code in Unity. Just search in the Unity Asset Store for "InControl" or go to:

> http://www.gallantgames.com/pages/incontrol-introduction

If you do want to configure the Unity InputManager yourself, Figure B.9 contains information from the Unify community's page about the Xbox 360 controller.[9] The numbers in the figure indicate the joystick button number that can be accessed by the *InputManager Axes* window. The axes are designated with the letter *a* before them (for example, aX, a5). If working with multiple joysticks on the same machine, you can designate a specific joystick in the InputManager Axes by using *joystick # button #* (e.g., "joystick 1 button 3"). The same Unify page also includes a downloadable InputManager setup for four simultaneous Microsoft controllers.

---

9. The Unify community's page for this is http://wiki.unity3d.com/index.php?title=Xbox360Controller.

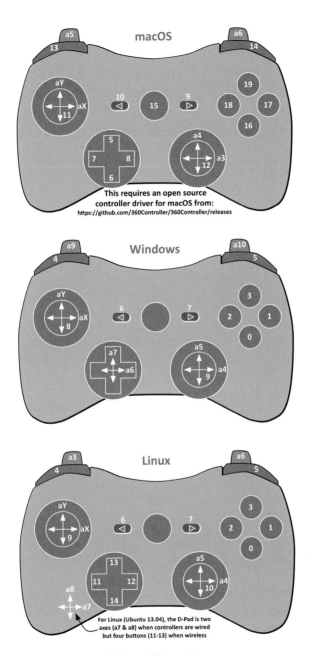

Figure B.9 Xbox controller mapping for PC, macOS, and Linux

On a PC, the driver for the controller should install automatically. On Linux (Ubuntu 13.04 and later), it should be included as well. For macOS, you need to download the driver from the GitHub open source project at https://github.com/360Controller/360Controller/releases.

Right-Clicking on macOS

Throughout this book, I sometimes ask you to right-click on something. However, many people don't know how to right-click on a Macintosh because it's not the default setting for macOS trackpads and mice. There are actually several ways to right-click, and the one you use depends on how new your Mac is and how you prefer to interact with your machine.

Control-Click = Right-Click

Near the bottom-left corner of all modern macOS keyboards is a *control* key. If you hold down the *control* key and then left-click (your normal click) on anything, macOS treats it as a right-click.

Use Any PC Mouse

You can use almost any PC mouse that has two or three buttons on macOS. I personally use a Logitech *MX Anywhere 2* or a Razer *Orochi*.

Set Your macOS Mouse to Right-Click

If you have a macOS mouse made in 2005 or later (the Apple Mighty Mouse or Apple Magic Mouse), you can enable right-click by

1. Open *System Preferences > Mouse* from the apple menu in the top left corner of your screen.

2. Select the *Point & Click* tab at the top of the screen.

3. Check the box next to *Secondary click*.

4. Choose *Click on right side* from the pop-up menu directly below *Secondary Click*.

This makes a click on the left side of the mouse left-click and a click on the right side right-click.

Set Your macOS Trackpad to Right-Click

As with the Apple Mouse, you can configure any Apple laptop trackpad (or the Bluetooth Magic Trackpad) to right-click.

1. Open *System Preferences > Trackpad* from the apple menu in the top-left corner of your screen.

2. Choose the *Point & Click* tab at the top of the window.

3. Check the box next to *Secondary Click*.

4. If you choose *Click or tap with two fingers* from the pop-up menu directly below *Secondary Click*, it will make tapping with one finger the standard left-click and tapping with two fingers the right-click. Other right-click trackpad options are also available.

ONLINE REFERENCE

Whereas many online references just give you a list of websites to check out, I thought using this appendix to show you where and how I tend to look for answers online when I need them would be more useful. Appropriately, this includes a few basic links, but it also includes strategies for tracking down information and answers to problems that you might encounter.

I recommend reading this straight through once (it's very short) and then returning to it when you encounter an issue.

Unity Tutorials

Unity has created a series of tutorials over the years that can be very useful to check out. This book focused on short gameplay tutorials to help you understand how to program game mechanics, whereas the tutorials created by Unity tend to spend an equal amount of time on art assets, animation, building scenes, and visual effects in addition to scripting. This book is about you learning how to design and prototype games; their tutorials are about learning all the different features of the Unity engine.

Be aware when looking at these that many were made with older versions of Unity, and they sometimes don't update the tutorials to match the new version of the engine (meaning that sometimes the elements of the Unity interface that the tutorial describes or some code libraries that they use might have changed). In addition, some of the very old tutorials were written in JavaScript rather than C#. This should be fine for you—especially after you've read and understood the code in this book—but in general, I recommend looking for tutorials written in C# to make sure you're finding more recent ones.

Unity's website offers a *Learn* section that is meant to introduce you to Unity through several different tutorials. This link takes you to that page. Choose a topic that you want to learn about, and you can view video tutorials to help you do so:

- **Learn section—Tutorials:** http://unity3d.com/learn/tutorials

Unite Conference Archive

After you have some experience with Unity under your belt, you might want to look at some more advanced resources. A great place to do this is to look at videos of various talks from the Unite conference over the years. Unity holds versions of Unite all over the world every year and records many of the talks. You can find them all here:

- https://unite.unity.com/archive

Programming Help

As you delve further into programming Unity, you'll find that the documentation for programming Unity with C# is primarily located in two places: Unity's scripting documentation and the Microsoft C# reference. The Unity scripting reference does a fantastic job of documenting Unity-specific features, classes, and components, but it doesn't cover any of the core C# classes (such as List<>, Dictionary<>, and so on). For these, turn to Microsoft's C# documentation. I recommend first looking for something in the Unity documentation available on your computer, and if it's not there, then look in the Microsoft docs.

Unity Scripting Reference

Unity scripting references include the following:

- **Online:** http://docs.unity3d.com/Documentation/ScriptReference/
- **Local:** From within Unity, choose *Help > Scripting Reference* from the menu bar. This brings up a version of the reference that is stored locally on your computer. Even if you don't have an Internet connection, this reference is available. (I use it while traveling all the time.)

Microsoft C# Reference

Search Bing.com for *Microsoft C# Reference*. The first hit should be what you're looking for. As of the time of writing this book, the direct URL is:

- http://msdn.microsoft.com/en-us/library/618ayhy6.aspx

Stack Overflow

Stack Overflow is an online community of developers helping developers. People post questions, and other members of the site answer them. In a bit of gamification, those who give the best answers (as voted by other members) earn experience points and prestige on the site:

- http://stackoverflow.com

Often, when I'm trying to figure out how to do something new or unusual, I'll end up finding a good answer on Stack Overflow. For instance, if I want to know how to sort a List<> using LINQ, I enter "C# LINQ sort list of objects" into Google, and as I write this, the top eight hits are Stack Overflow questions. I usually find myself there via a Google search rather than starting on the Stack Overflow website itself, but when a search result is on stackoverflow.com, it's my first choice for finding good answers.

Learning More C#

I highly recommend two additional books for learning more about C#:

- **For beginners:** Rob Miles's *C# Programming Yellow Book*,
  http://www.csharpcourse.com

  Rob Miles, a lecturer at the University of Hull, has written a fantastic book on C# programming that he updates often. You can find the current version on his website. It is witty, clear, and comprehensive.

- **For reference:** *C# 4.0 Pocket Reference, 3rd Edition*,
  http://shop.oreilly.com/product/0636920013365.do

  Although there is now a C# 5.0 version of this reference, Unity is still using the C# 4.0 standard (well, it's most of C# 4.0; there are actually a few bits missing), so this is the reference for you. Any time I have a C# question, this is the first place I turn. It is a truncated version of the information in O'Reilly's *C# in a Nutshell* book, but I actually find the pocket reference more useful. It also includes a ton of LINQ information.

Search Tips

Any time you want to search for something having to do with C#, make *C#* the first term in your search. If you just search for *list,* the first thing to come up has nothing to do with coding. Searching for *C# list* gets you to the right place immediately.

Similarly, if you want to find anything related to Unity, be sure to make *Unity* your first search term.

Finding Assets

The following sections provide advice on finding various art and audio assets.

The Unity Asset Store

You can access the Asset Store by opening the Asset Store window in Unity (choose *Window > Asset Store* from the menu bar) or by going to the website in a standard browser. The Asset Store has a huge collection of models, animations, sounds, code, and even complete Unity projects that you can download. Most of the assets are available for a small fee, and some of the assets on the site are free. Some assets are very pricey, but they are often worth it and can save you hundreds of hours of development:

- https://www.assetstore.unity3d.com/

Models and Animations

These sites are some places to look for 3D models. Some are free, but many are paid. Also, be aware that many of the free ones are for noncommercial use only:

- **TurboSquid:** http://www.turbosquid.com/
- **Google 3D Warehouse:** http://3dwarehouse.sketchup.com/

  Be aware that nearly all the assets on the Google 3D Warehouse site are in the SketchUp or Collada formats. Unity has an importer for SketchUp files, but as I am writing this, the importer only works with SketchUp 2015 files. You might need to open the SketchUp or Collada file in SketchUp and then save it as a SketchUp 2015 file for Unity to import it correctly.

Fonts

Nearly all the fonts on these sites are free for noncommercial use, but you will often need to pay to use them on commercial projects:

- http://www.1001fonts.com/
- http://www.1001freefonts.com/

- http://www.dafont.com/
- http://www.fontsquirrel.com/
- http://www.fontspace.com/

Other Tools and Educational Discounts

If you are a student or faculty member of a university, you qualify for many discounts on software.

- **Adobe:** Adobe offers the entire Creative Cloud suite of their tools to students at a discounted monthly rate, good for one year. This includes Photoshop, Illustrator, Premier, and others.

  http://www.adobe.com/creativecloud/buy/students.html

- **Affinity:** Affinity makes Designer (an Illustrator competitor) and Photo (a Photoshop competitor), which seem to be very good programs and only cost about $40 each to own forever (as opposed to paying Adobe every month). No student discount, but relatively cheap and high quality.

  http://affinity.serif.com/

- **AutoDesk:** AutoDesk gives students and educators a free 36-month license for almost any of their tools, including 3ds Max, Maya, Motionbuilder, Mudbox, and more.

  http://www.autodesk.com/education/free-software/featured

- **Blender:** Blender is a free, open source tool for modeling and animation. It includes many of the capabilities of software like Maya and 3ds Max but is entirely free and can be used for commercial purposes. However, its interface is quite different from what you might be used to from other modeling and animation software.

  http://www.blender.org/

- **SketchUp:** SketchUp is another tool for modeling. It has very intuitive modeling controls and is updated frequently. The basic version, *SketchUp Make*, is completely free (though not for commercial use), and *SketchUp Pro* is available at a discounted price for students and educators. In newer versions of SketchUp, exporting obj and fbx format files is possible, which Unity can import easily, though the best format for import into Unity is probably to save your model as a SketchUp 2015 file. If you're making your own models in SketchUp and exporting to obj or fbx, consider checking the *Triangulate all faces*, *Export two-sided faces*, and *Swap YZ coordinates* options and setting your Units to *Meters* when exporting files (these settings are not necessary if you save the model as a SketchUp 2015 file).

  http://www.sketchup.com/

INDEX

Symbols

& (bitwise AND) operator, 334, 889
&& (AND) operator, 332
// comment notation, 302, 314, 719
/* */ comment notation, 719
== (equality) operator, 336–338
> (greater than) operator, 338
>= (greater than or equal to) operator, 339
!= (inequality) operator, 338
< (less than) operator, 338
<= (less than or equal to) operator, 339
% (modulus operator), 357
! (NOT) operator, 332
|| (OR) operator, 332
. (period), 293
| (pipe / bitwise OR) operator, 334, 889
; (semicolon), 277, 292, 299, 405–407
<< (shift left operator), 890
_ (underscore), 296
2D depth-sorting order *(Bartok)*, 732–736
2of12inf word list, 756
2x Multi Sampling setting, 808
3-act structure, 52–54
3D / 2D button (New Project screen), 883
3D cameras, 467
3D printing, 48
3x5 note cards, 133
5-act structure, 50–52

A

AAA development, costs of, 241–242
absolute spreadsheet references, 165
AbsorbPowerUp(), 619–620
accessibility, color blindness and, 75
accessors, 424
achievers (player type), 68
acquaintances as playtesters, 147–148
action puzzles, 214
actions
    Apple Picker game, 263–264

    discernible, 65
    integrated, 65
acts
    five-act structure, 50–52
    three-act structure, 52–54
Add(), 361, 367, 370
AddBack(), 659–660
AddCard(), 729, 735–736
AddDecorators(), 655–657
AddFaces(), 657–658
AddPips(), 657–658
Adkison, Peter, 99
ADL (automated data logging) and
  playtesting, 155
Adobe
    educational discounts, 951
    Photoshop, 547–548
aesthetics
    cultural aesthetics (Layered Tetrad), 35,
      82–83
    dynamic aesthetics (Layered Tetrad), 34,
      70–75
    Elemental Tetrad framework, 28
    inscribed aesthetics (Layered Tetrad),
      33, 47–49
    MDA (mechanics, dynamics, and aesthetics)
      framework, 21
Affinity
    educational discounts, 951
    Photo, 547–548
Agile development
    Agile Alliance, 224
    manifesto for, 224–225
    Scrum
      BDCs (burndown charts), 227–238
      development of, 225
      meetings, 227
      product backlog, 226
      releases, 226–227
      sprints, 226–227
      teams, 226